Classics

From the Renaissance to the nineteenth century, Latin and Greek were compulsory subjects in almost all European universities, and most early modern scholars published their research and conducted international correspondence in Latin. Latin had continued in use in Western Europe long after the fall of the Roman empire as the lingua franca of the educated classes and of law, diplomacy, religion and university teaching. The flight of Greek scholars to the West after the fall of Constantinople in 1453 gave impetus to the study of ancient Greek literature and the Greek New Testament. Eventually, just as nineteenth-century reforms of university curricula were beginning to erode this ascendancy, developments in textual criticism and linguistic analysis, and new ways of studying ancient societies, especially archaeology, led to renewed enthusiasm for the Classics. This collection offers works of criticism, interpretation and synthesis by the outstanding scholars of the nineteenth century.

Pausanias's Description of Greece

Sir James Frazer (1854–1941) is best remembered today for *The Golden Bough*, widely considered to be one of the most important early texts in the fields of psychology and anthropology. Originally a classical scholar, whose entire working life was spent at Trinity College, Cambridge, Frazer also produced this translation of and commentary on the works of Pausanias, the second-century CE traveller and antiquarian whose many references to myths and legends provided Frazer with material for his great study of religion. The six-volume work was published in 1898, after the first edition of *The Golden Bough* (also reissued in this series), and while Frazer was working on material for the second. Volume 5 is a detailed commentary on Pausanias' Books IX–X, on Boeotia and Phocis, using both the experience of Frazer's own travels in Greece and the reports of other antiquarians and archaeologists.

Cambridge University Press has long been a pioneer in the reissuing of out-of-print titles from its own backlist, producing digital reprints of books that are still sought after by scholars and students but could not be reprinted economically using traditional technology. The Cambridge Library Collection extends this activity to a wider range of books which are still of importance to researchers and professionals, either for the source material they contain, or as landmarks in the history of their academic discipline.

Drawing from the world-renowned collections in the Cambridge University Library and other partner libraries, and guided by the advice of experts in each subject area, Cambridge University Press is using state-of-the-art scanning machines in its own Printing House to capture the content of each book selected for inclusion. The files are processed to give a consistently clear, crisp image, and the books finished to the high quality standard for which the Press is recognised around the world. The latest print-on-demand technology ensures that the books will remain available indefinitely, and that orders for single or multiple copies can quickly be supplied.

The Cambridge Library Collection brings back to life books of enduring scholarly value (including out-of-copyright works originally issued by other publishers) across a wide range of disciplines in the humanities and social sciences and in science and technology.

Pausanias's
Description of Greece

VOLUME 5:
COMMENTARY ON BOOKS IX, X. ADDENDA

EDITED AND TRANSLATED
BY J.G. FRAZER

CAMBRIDGE
UNIVERSITY PRESS

CAMBRIDGE UNIVERSITY PRESS

Cambridge, New York, Melbourne, Madrid, Cape Town,
Singapore, São Paolo, Delhi, Mexico City

Published in the United States of America by Cambridge University Press, New York

www.cambridge.org
Information on this title: www.cambridge.org/9781108047272

© in this compilation Cambridge University Press 2012

This edition first published 1898
This digitally printed version 2012

ISBN 978-1-108-04727-2 Paperback

PAUSANIAS'S
DESCRIPTION OF GREECE

PAUSANIAS'S

DESCRIPTION OF GREECE

TRANSLATED WITH A COMMENTARY

BY

J. G. FRAZER

M.A., LL.D. GLASGOW; FELLOW OF TRINITY COLLEGE, CAMBRIDGE;
OF THE MIDDLE TEMPLE, BARRISTER-AT-LAW

IN SIX VOLUMES

VOL. V

COMMENTARY ON BOOKS IX., X. ADDENDA

London

MACMILLAN AND CO., LIMITED

NEW YORK: THE MACMILLAN COMPANY

1898

CONTENTS

ILLUSTRATIONS

PLATES

BOOK NINTH

BOEOTIA

SPECIAL works on Boeotia were written in antiquity (1) by Hellanicus (Schol. on Homer, *Il.* ii. 494); (2) by a certain Boeotian named Aristophanes, to whom Plutarch refers (*De Herodoti malignitate*, 31); his work was in two books at least (Stephanus Byzantius, *s.v.* Χαιρώνεια); (3) by Crates an Athenian; (4) by a certain Ctesiphon in three books at least; Plutarch refers to him (*Parallela*, 12); (5) and by one Paxamus in two books (Suidas, *s.v.* Πάξαμος). See *Fragm. histor. Graecorum*, ed. Müller, 1. p. 46 *sqq.*; *id.*, 4. pp. 337 *sqq.*, 370, 375, 472.

1. 1. Boeotus —— a son of Itonus and the nymph Melanippe. The father of Boeotus was generally said to have been Poseidon (Diodorus, iv. 67, xix. 53; Schol. on Homer, *Il.* ii. 494; Nicocrates and Euphorion, cited by Stephanus Byzantius, *s.v.* Βοιωτία; Hyginus, *Fab.* 157 and 186). According to some his mother was not Melanippe but Arne (Diodorus, iv. 67; Schol. on Homer, *Il.* ii. 494; Nicocrates and Euphorion, *l.c.*).

1. 1. the greater part of them are called after women. This may perhaps be a trace of the prevalence among the early Boeotians of the system of female kinship, *i.e.* the system which counts kindred through the mother rather than through the father. See J. F. M'Lennan, 'Kinship in ancient Greece,' in his *Studies in ancient history* (London, 1886), especially p. 228 *sq.* Among the Pelew Islanders, who have female kinship, each tribe traces its descent from a common mother. See Kubary, *Die sozialen Einrichtungen der Pelauer*, pp. 35, 40; *id.*, 'Die Religion der Pelauer,' in A. Bastian's *Allerlei aus Volks- und Menschenkunde*, 1. p. 22 *sqq.*

1. 2. everywhere in Greece kingdoms —— were established. On the ancient kings of Greece, see Thucydides, i. 13. 1; Aristotle, *Politics*, iii. 14. 11 *sqq.*; G. Gilbert, *Griechische Staatsalterthümer*, 2. p. 265 *sqq.*

1. 3. they took part in the combat at Marathon. See Herodotus, vi. 108.

1. 3. they dared to help the Athenians to man the ships. See Herodotus, viii. 1.

1. 8. **The second capture of Plataea took place** etc. The city
was captured by the Thebans in 373 B.C. Cp. Diodorus, xv. 46, who
however places the capture of Plataea in 374 B.C., in the archonship of
Socratides. The archonship of Astius has been mentioned by Pausanias
already (vii. 25. 4).

1. 8. **the restoration of the Plataeans.** Cp. iv. 27. 10.

2. 1. **On Mount Cithaeron** etc. Pausanias has previously
described the route from Athens to Boeotia as far as Eleutherae, a
small fortified town on the southern skirts of Mt. Cithaeron, just on the
right of what is still the highroad from Athens to Thebes (see i. 38.
8 *sq.*) He now resumes the route in question and follows it into
Boeotia. From Eleutherae the road winds up a narrow pass among
the fir-clad slopes of Mt. Cithaeron, the highest peak of which (4620
feet) is visible from time to time on our left (west). The mountain
takes its modern name of *Elatiás* (Fir-mountain) from the forests of fir
which cover it ; these forests are the haunts of wild boars, wolves, foxes,
and deer. In about an hour from Eleutherae we reach the summit of
the pass. In antiquity the Boeotians called this pass the Pass of the
Three Heads ; the Athenians called it the pass of the Oak's Heads.
At the entrance to the pass on the Boeotian side the Persian cavalry
cut off a train of provisions which was on its way from Peloponnese to
the Greek camp (Herodotus, ix. 39). And from the road to Thebes
the escaped Plataeans, looking back through the darkness and the
falling snow, could see by the moving lights behind them that their
pursuers were making their way towards this pass over Cithaeron, in
the belief that the fugitives would take the nearest road to Athens
(Thucydides, iii. 24). The view from the summit of the pass has been
already described (vol. 2. p. 516 *sq.*) The highroad to Thebes keeps
on to the right ; but a path to the left (westward) descends the northern
declivities of Cithaeron to Plataea. The time from the summit of the
pass to Plataea is about an hour and a quarter.

See Dodwell, *Tour*, 1. p. 282 ; Mure, *Journal*, 2. p. 1 ; L. Ross, *Wanderungen*, 1. p. 16 ; Vischer, *Erinnerungen*, pp. 533, 540 ; Bursian, *Geogr.* 1. p.
249 ; Baedeker,[3] p. 179 *sq.* ; *Guide-Joanne*, 2. p. 8.

The lower slopes of Mt. Cithaeron, on its northern side, consist
"partly of steep swelling banks, covered with green turf of a richness
and smoothness such as I scarcely recollect having observed in any
other district of rugged Greece, or with dense masses of pine forest ;
partly of rocky dells, fringed with brushwood or stunted oaks. Towards
its summit the mountain, which was covered [12th March 1838] to
about one-half of its whole height with snow, becomes bare and stony"
(Mure, *Journal*, 1. p. 264). Mure points out how well the scenery of
Mt. Cithaeron still answers to the descriptions of it in Euripides's play
of the *Bacchae* (*v.* 1043 *sqq.*).

2. 1. **Hysiae and Erythrae.** The sites of these two towns have
not been identified with certainty. Pausanias, proceeding from
Eleutherae over Mt. Cithaeron to Plataea, says that Hysiae and
Erythrae lay a little to the right of the road. The present highroad to

Thebes crosses Mt. Cithaeron by the pass of Eleutherae and descends into Boeotia a little to the east of the large and seemingly prosperous village of *Kriekouki*, which stands on the lower slope of the mountain. In recent years a branch road has been made to the westward; it quits the old highroad on the side of the mountain above *Kriekouki*, passes through that village, and rejoins the old road about $1\frac{1}{2}$ miles below the village. It thus forms a loop to the old highroad, and though it is more circuitous it seems, if I may judge from the signs of traffic on it, to be preferred by drivers. The ancient highroad over Cithaeron to Thebes must have coincided very closely with the line of the present road in the actual pass; while in descending the northern slope of the mountain it may have followed the line either of the present branch road through *Kriekouki* or, more probably, of the old and more direct road a little farther to the east. The route to Plataea diverges to the left (westward) from the highroad to Thebes at a point close to Eleutherae, and crosses over Mt. Cithaeron by another pass which debouches about a mile to the west of the main pass and about 2 miles to the east of Plataea.[1]

The sites of Hysiae and Erythrae must accordingly be sought somewhere to the right of this route. That Erythrae lay to the east of Hysiae we learn from Herodotus, who tells us (ix. 15, 19, and 25) that the Persian camp extended along the Asopus from Erythrae past Hysiae to the land of Plataea, and that the Greeks, who had encamped opposite Mardonius at Erythrae, afterwards marched thence through the skirts of Mt. Cithaeron past Hysiae to the territory of Plataea. Erythrae must further have been on the slope of Mt. Cithaeron, not in the plain; for Herodotus says that when the Greek army was at Erythrae it did not go down into the plain (ix. 19 *sq.*); and he speaks of its subsequent change of position as a descent to Plataea (ix. 25). Though he describes the Persian camp as extending from Erythrae past Hysiae to Plataean territory he probably means no more than that it lay in the plain over against these towns. Thucydides says (iii. 24) that the men who escaped from Plataea when it was besieged by the Peloponnesians first followed the road to Thebes for 6 or 7 furlongs, then turning back took " the road which leads towards the mountains to Erythrae and Hysiae." That Erythrae and Hysiae were near each other and at the foot of Cithaeron is further shown by references made to them by Euripides (*Bacchae,* 751 *sq.*) and Strabo

---

[1] In this account of the route from Eleutherae to Plataea I follow Mr. G. B. Grundy (*Topography of the battle of Plataea,* pp. 6 and 10), who has made a survey of the battlefield, but I do so with some misgivings. For (1) Mr. Grundy has admittedly not traversed the path in question (Pass No. 2, as he calls it). (2) He says (p. 45) that the pass is clearly marked on the Austrian map. But on that map, as well as on the French survey map, the route to Plataea diverges not, as Mr. Grundy says, close to Eleutherae, on the southern side of the pass, but a considerable way to the north of Eleutherae, apparently on the northern side of the pass; in fact it seems to leave the highroad only at the point where the present loop road to *Kriekouki* (described above) leaves it, and to coincide with the loop road for some distance. (3) My own recollection of the main pass, which I have traversed twice is that between Eleutherae and the top of the pass the mountains on either hand are steep and unbroken by any other pass leading westward in the direction of Plataea.

(ix. p. 404). Leake believed that he had found the site of Erythrae near *Katzoula*, a village at the northern foot of Cithaeron, about 3 miles east of *Kriekouki*. The range is not very high at this point, and there is verdure among the rocks, where goats and sheep feed. At the foot of the rocks, to the eastward of the village, Leake saw some foundations of ancient Greek walls, together with a church containing a Doric column and its capital. These remains he believed to mark the site of Erythrae. To this identification it is objected by Mr. Grundy that Pausanias would not have described as "a little to the right" of the road a place which lay about 3½ miles from it, and that the Greeks would not be likely to take up a position so far to the east of the pass, thus leaving the pass open to the enemy and having their own backs to a part of the range through which there was no retreat. Accordingly Mr. Grundy would place Erythrae immediately to the east of *Kriekouki*, on the ridge round which the modern highroad to Thebes, descending from the pass, makes a loop, the older branch of the road skirting the ridge on the east and the new branch skirting it on the west. This is, according to Mr. Grundy, the traditional site of Erythrae, and there are "signs of remains of ancient buildings" on the spot. The signs he mentions are an ancient well and a heap of stones, in which two stones were found bearing inscriptions which relate to the worship of Demeter (see below). On a height above the site there is, he tells us, an ancient fort, but he does not describe it nor attempt to determine its date, only saying that "though we may possibly infer that it did not exist at the time of the battle, it is very likely to have been constructed by the inhabitants of Erythrae at a later date as a defence for their end of the pass." Against this identification of Erythrae it must be observed that one of the reasons why the Greeks quitted Erythrae was the want of a good supply of water (Herodotus, ix. 25); yet at *Kriekouki*, close to the supposed site of Erythrae, there are plentiful and permanent springs, which according to Leake are in fact the principal source of the Asopus. As to Hysiae, Leake would place it to the east of *Kriekouki*, a little beyond the highroad to Thebes, and hence apparently to the east of the site which Mr. Grundy identifies as that of Erythrae. Here at the foot of the mountain Leake observed "a great quantity of loose stones in the fields, together with some ancient walls, and the mouth of a well or cistern, of Hellenic construction, now filled up." These he supposed to be the remains of Hysiae. If he is right the ancient well which he observed may have been the sacred well mentioned by Pausanias whose water was drunk as a means of divination. Mr. Grundy conjectures that Hysiae was a little above *Kriekouki*, where there is a mound "with a more or less circular enclosure on the top, quite close to the great bend of the loop road above the village." This more or less circular enclosure, he thinks, may mark the site of the foundations of an ancient fort built to command the pass. If Mr Grundy is right in his identifications, Hysiae was situated within a mile of Erythrae, which seems improbable, though it might be paralleled by the case of Abae and Hyampolis in Phocis.

Beside a well a little to the east of *Kriekouki* there have been found, as we have seen, two stones bearing inscriptions which relate to the worship of Demeter. Both inscriptions seem to date from the early part of the fifth century B.C. One of them records a dedication to Demeter; the other is a metrical inscription from the base of an image of the goddess dedicated, according to Prof. Dittenberger, by a certain Kydadas (not Tisamenus, as the inscription is generally read), perhaps as a first-fruit offering (for references, see below). These inscriptions may perhaps have come from the sanctuary of Eleusinian Demeter beside which, at the battle of Plataea, the Spartan division under king Pausanias took up their final position; it was about 10 furlongs from the Gargaphian spring, at a place Argiopius, beside a river called Molois (Herodotus, ix. 57). Here they were attacked by the Persians, and a long and desperate fight took place just beside the sanctuary (*id.*, ix. 62); but though the Persians were defeated and many of them fell outside of the holy ground, we are told that not a man of them entered or died in the sacred grove (*id.*, ix. 65). The sanctuary was on the slope of Mt. Cithaeron, above Plataea; for when the Greeks who were posted at the sanctuary of Hera near Plataea heard of the Spartan success, a body of them marched "along the skirts of the mountain and over the low hills by the way that led straight up to the sanctuary of Demeter" (*id.*, ix. 69). This sanctuary is mentioned also by Plutarch in his description of the battle of Plataea; he says it was a very ancient sanctuary of Eleusinian Demeter and the Maid situated at the foot of Mt. Cithaeron near Hysiae, on ground very favourable for infantry, because it was too rugged to allow cavalry to manœuvre on it (*Aristides*, 11). It is possible that the sanctuary stood where the inscriptions were found, namely beside the ancient well close to the direct road to Thebes, a little to the east of *Kriekouki*. But inscribed stones are so easily and so commonly transported from their original place that the occurrence of the inscriptions here hardly proves more than that the sanctuary was somewhere in the neighbourhood. An American archaeologist who spent some time at Plataea, Mr. W. I. Hunt, supposes that the site of the sanctuary of Demeter is marked by the foundations of a large Byzantine church situated on high ground to the south-east of Plataea, and five or six minutes' walk east of the spring called *Vergoutiani*. Here have been found some ancient Greek tombstones, inscriptions, and many fragments of marble. Behind the church rises a wall of rock which is visible for miles in the valley, and which Mr. Hunt conjectures to be the place called Argiopius ('bright look') by Herodotus. These identifications are accepted by Mr. Hauvette. Against them it might be urged that according to Plutarch (*l.c.*) the sanctuary of Demeter was near the shrine of the hero Androcrates, which we know from Thucydides (iii. 24) to have been in quite a different situation, namely to the right of the road which led from Plataea to Thebes, and not more than 6 or 7 furlongs from the former town. But no weight can be attached to this statement of Plutarch, since it would lead us to place the sanctuary of Demeter somewhere below and to the north of Plataea, whereas we know from Herodotus that it was on high ground above that city. Mr. Grundy conjectures that the site of the sanctuary of Demeter is now occupied by the church of St. Demetrius or Demetrion, which stands rather more than a mile to the north of *Kriekouki*. He thinks that in the name of the saint to whom the church is dedicated we have a reminiscence of the name of the goddess, and that the brook which flows beside the church on the east may be the ancient Molois.

See Leake, *Travels in Northern Greece*, 2. pp. 326-329, 333; Bursian, *Geogr.* 1. p. 248; W. I. Hunt, in *American Journal of Archaeology*, 6 (1890), p. 467 *sqq.*; A. Hauvette, 'Rapport sur une mission scientifique en Grèce,' *Nouvelles Archives des Missions scientifiques et littéraires*, 2 (1892), p. 365; G. B. Grundy, *The topography of the battle of Plataea* (London, 1894), pp. 5 *sqq.*, 15 *sq.*, 32 *sqq.*, 45. As to the two inscriptions found near *Kriekouki*, see *C. I. G. G. S.* Nos. 1670, 1671; *Bulletin de Corresp. hellénique*, 3 (1879), p. 134 *sqq.*; Roehl, *I. G. A.* Nos. 143, 144; Loewy, *Inschriften griech. Bildhauer*, No. 44; Collitz, *G. D. I.* 1. Nos. 860, 861; E. S. Roberts, *Greek Epigraphy*, No. 223; E. Hoffmann, *Sylloge epigrammatum Graecorum*, No. 313.

2. 1. **people divined by drinking of the well.** So the priest of the Clarian Apollo at Colophon drank of a secret spring in a cave before he uttered oracles in verse; the priest, who was always chosen from certain families, generally of Miletus, was supposed to shorten his life by drinking of this water. Germanicus and Agrippina both consulted the oracle of the Clarian Apollo. See Tacitus, *Annals*, ii. 54, xii. 22; Pliny, *Nat. hist.* ii. 232. Cp. Paus. vii. 3. 1 note. The oracular spring at Colophon was said to have originated in the tears which the prophetess Manto wept over the destruction of Thebes, her native city (Schol. on Apollonius Rhodius, *Argonaut.* i. 308). It would indeed appear that at every oracle of Apollo the priest or priestess who acted as his mouthpiece drank of a sacred spring before uttering the prophetic words (Lucian, *Bis accusatus*, 1). At Delphi the priestess drank of the spring Cassotis (Paus. x. 24. 7).

2. 2. **the corpse of Mardonius disappeared** etc. See Herodotus, ix. 84.

2. 3. **On the road from Megara.** This implies that the road from Megara to Plataea was different from the road which led over Cithaeron by Eleutherae. The same distinction is made by Xenophon, who says that king Cleombrotus, marching with a Lacedaemonian army from Peloponnese, avoided the pass of Eleutherae, which was guarded by a force of Athenian targeteers under Chabrias, and mounted by the road which led to Plataea (*Hellenica*, v. 4. 14). The road from Megara probably descended the face of Cithaeron obliquely at a considerable height, and would pass near the fountain *Vergoutiani* (Leake, *Northern Greece*, 2. p. 334; as to the fountain *Vergoutiani*, see the next note). It seems to have crossed the mountain by a pass which debouches somewhat less than a mile to the east of Plataea. The pass is hardly used at the present day. It must have been always difficult, if not quite impracticable, for wheeled vehicles, but quite practicable for infantry. The spring *Vergoutiani* is near the mouth of the pass. See G. B. Grundy, *The topography of the battle of Plataea*, p. 7, with his plan.

2. 3. **a spring on the right** etc.   On the rocky slope of Mt. Cithaeron, about twenty-five minutes to the south-east of Plataea, there is a copious fountain called *Vergoutiani*, gushing from three mouths in an ancient wall. Five minutes farther on and higher up is a jutting rock which now serves as a shelter for cattle, in the midst of a natural theatre of rocks at the head of a green slope above the fountain. The place is at the end of the pass over which goes the footpath to Megara. Hence the fountain may be the one in which Actaeon was said to have seen Artemis bathing ; and the rock may be the one under or on which he slept when wearied with the chase. Bursian, however, would identify Actaeon's bed with a small cave in the rock, about 30 feet deep, farther west, above the village of *Kokla*. See Leake, *Northern Greece*, 2. pp. 326, 333 ; Bursian, *Geogr.* 1. p. 247 note 5 ; Vischer, *Erinnerungen*, p. 549 ; *Guide-Joanne*, 2. p. 25 ; G. B. Grundy, *The topography of the battle of Plataea*, p. 7.

2. 3. **the goddess threw a deer-skin round Actaeon** etc.   On a metope of one of the temples at Selinus the death of Actaeon is represented ; the hounds are leaping upon him, and over his back is thrown a deer-skin, the feet hang down before and behind him, and the deer's head and antlers are seen behind and above his head. See Müller-Wieseler, *Denkmäler*, 2. pl. xvii. 184 ; Roscher's *Lexikon*, 1. p. 215 ; Lucy M. Mitchell, *Hist. of Ancient Sculpture*, p. 423. The common story was that Artemis turned Actaeon into a stag (Apollodorus, iii. 4. 4 ; Hyginus, *Fab.* 181 ; Ovid, *Metam.* iii. 193 *sqq.* ; Nonnus, *Dionys.* v. 316 *sqq.*) Hence in a small marble group in the British Museum and in a painting at Pompeii the transformation is indicated by deer's horns growing from Actaeon's head. See Müller-Wieseler, *Denkmäler*, 2. pl. xvii. 183 a, 186 ; Daremberg et Saglio, *Dict. des Antiquités*, 1. p. 53. However, it seems that in the marble group the horns are modern, and the head, though ancient, does not belong to the body (Friederichs-Wolters, *Gipsabgüsse*, No. 457 ; cp. Baumeister's *Denkmäler*, 1. p. 35 *sq.*) Stesichorus, if Pausanias has reported him aright, would seem to have mixed up two distinct legends, one ascribing Actaeon's death to the wrath of Zeus at him for presuming to woo Semele, the other referring it to Artemis's displeasure at being seen bathing by him. The two legends are treated as distinct by Apollodorus (iii. 4. 4). The names of Actaeon's dogs are given in some verses quoted in the MSS. of Apollodorus (at the end of bk. iii. ch. 4). Bergk has tried to show that these are a fragment of Stesichorus's poem. See Westermann's *Mythographi Graeci*, p. 83 ; Apollodorus, ed. R. Wagner, p. 115 ; Bergk, in *Zeitschrift für Alterthumswissenschaft*, 8 (1850), pp. 401-408.

2. 4. **On what part of Cithaeron Pentheus ―― met his doom.** According to a legend mentioned by Strabo (ix. p. 408) Pentheus was caught by the Bacchanals at Scolus, as to which see below ix. 4. 4. Mr. A. G. Bather argues that the legend of the death of Pentheus at the hands of the infuriated Bacchanals is a reminiscence of a custom of annually slaying the human representative of Dionysus with the intention of regenerating, in the person of a new representative, the decaying

vitality of the god of vegetation.   See A. G. Bather, 'The problem of the Bacchae,' *Journal of Hellenic Studies*, 14 (1894), pp. 244-263.

2. 5. **Plataea.** The ruins of Plataea occupy a triangular or fan-shaped plateau which projects northward into the Boeotian plain from the foot of Mt. Cithaeron.   The base of the triangle is turned towards the plain and the north, while the apex almost touches the declivity of Mt. Cithaeron, from which it is divided by a shallow ravine some 150 yards wide at the narrowest point and about 16 feet deep.   The plateau, which is nearly a mile long from north to south by rather less than three-quarters of a mile wide at the widest, rises little above the level of the surrounding plain.   It is highest at its southern extremity, from which it slopes at first rather sharply and then gently to the north, where it terminates in a steep but short descent to the plain.   On its eastern and western sides it is bounded by the beds of watercourses. The sides of the plateau are rocky and precipitous only at a few points, as at the south-western end, where the wall runs along the edge of a rough and jagged cliff nearly vertical though only a few yards high, and again about the middle of the west side, where the wall overhangs a steep rocky cliff from 10 to 26 feet high.   But as a rule the sides slope gently down to the plain below ; and although the slope has been diminished since the classical age by the washing down of soil from the surface of the plateau, it was probably never high or steep enough to constitute a sufficient natural defence without the aid of walls.   The general surface of the plateau is not broken by any notable depression except in the north-east corner, where it is split by two small ravines or hollows, formed by a couple of tiny brooks running north.   The higher part of the plateau, towards the south, presents for the most part a rocky uneven surface, which does not admit of cultivation ; but the lower part, towards the north, which is also the larger, is covered with soil to a considerable depth (about 10 feet in places) and is cultivated throughout, except where the foundations of ancient or mediaeval buildings prevent the passage of the plough.   In many places, however, the soil is very thin and the rock crops up, especially towards the west and south.   The rock of the plateau as well as of the ridge of Mt. Cithaeron to the south is a coarse grey marble, which corrodes into deep holes and channels when it is exposed to the weather.   Of this rock all the existing walls of the ancient city are built.   The soil is a clayey lime earth, very loose when dry, but exceedingly clinging and sticky when wet ; indeed in rainy weather the mud makes the surrounding plain almost impassable, sticking to the traveller's boots in great clotted masses and driving him to walk in the beds of running streams as the only tolerable pathways through the slough.

The ancient walls may be traced all round the edge of the plateau ; in some places they are standing to a considerable height.   The length of the circuit is about 2½ miles.   Inside of the circuit-wall are two cross walls, an upper and a lower.   The upper cross-wall extends, roughly speaking, from east to west, and cuts off the apex of the triangle. The lower cross-wall cuts off the north-west corner of the site, and appears to have formed, at some date, an acropolis.

Five different styles of masonry may be distinguished in the existing walls, pointing to as many different periods of construction. (1) The earliest part of the walls is built of well-jointed polygonal masonry, the blocks being of fairly uniform size, often pentagonal and occasionally hexagonal in shape. The pieces of wall built in this style are the worst preserved of all, the stones being much corroded and weatherworn. (2) The walls of the second period are built in an intermediate style,

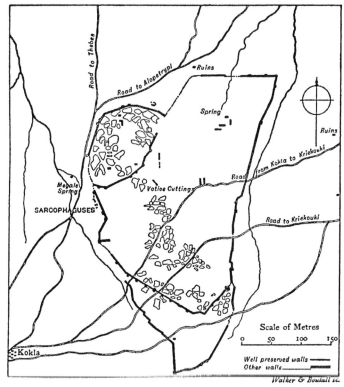

FIG. 1.—GROUND-PLAN OF PLATAEA.

better than the walls of the first period but not so well built as the walls of the third period; polygonal blocks hardly occur in them at all. (3) The walls of the third period are the best built and best preserved. To this period belong the upper cross-wall and the wall at the north-east corner. The blocks are large, measuring from 3 to 10 feet in length by 3 feet in height and 2 feet in thickness. They are four-sided and are laid in horizontal courses, with the edges neatly and accurately fitted. The vertical joints are commonly slanting, not perpendicular. The outer surface of the blocks is somewhat rounded or bulging ('bull-nosed'), and is cut vertically into wide and rather deep grooves. Altogether the workmanship is careful and excellent. (4) The fourth period is represented by the lower cross-wall alone. It is carelessly built of materials taken from earlier buildings, including architectural fragments and blocks of the walls of the second and third period. The joints are loose, and little trouble has been taken to fit the stones into their new positions; blocks taken from walls of the third period, for example, have their grooved side turned in just as often as out. At some time mortar and tiles were employed to fill up the chinks; but whether this was done when the wall was built or subsequently, does not appear. (5) Latest and worst of all are some fragments and stretches of Roman or, more probably, Byzantine wall, built of rubble and tiles laid in mortar. They may be seen here and there on the north and west sides.

The walls of the first four periods are very uniformly about 11 feet thick. The outer face is built of larger blocks and in a rather better style than the inner, but the difference is not great. In all the walls the space between the outer and the inner face was filled up with smaller rough stones and earth. Their height and the way in which they were finished at the top cannot be determined. In many places, especially at the north-west and south-west, the wall has wholly disappeared, and its line can only be traced by the smoothing of the natural rock as a bed in which to lay the first course of masonry. All the walls were defended at intervals by projecting towers, of which there are many remains. Four of these towers are round; all the rest are square.

The walls at the southern end of the site, beyond the upper cross-wall, belong to the earliest period. From the greater age of these walls and the height of this part of the site above the rest of the plateau it has been conjectured that the southern end of the site, forming the apex of the triangle, was the original acropolis or even the original city, which may have been a good deal smaller than the later city. No trace, however, has been found of an old wall enclosing this part of the site on the north. Such a wall may very well have extended east and west nearly on the line of the existing upper cross-wall and may have been taken down when that cross-wall was built. After the construction of the cross-wall the part of the site to the south, enclosed by the oldest walls, would seem to have been left outside of the city walls. For the cross-wall, strengthened by projecting towers, has all the appearance of being an outer wall; and of the older walls to the south of it not much is left, little more indeed than a single course. At the extreme southern point of the circuit there are the remains of a square tower, measuring 18 feet on the sides. From this point there is a fine view over the whole site and the plain of the Asopus away north to the line of low hills beyond which, hidden from sight, lies Thebes.

By far the best preserved or well or best built portion of the whole circuit is the upper cross-wall. Starting from the west wall it runs south-east for 445 yards in a nearly straight line, then bends round at an angle and runs north-east to join the eastern circuit-wall. It is everywhere 11 feet thick; both faces are carefully finished, and the intermediate space is filled with earth and rubble. The height of the existing wall varies greatly; in some places it barely appears above ground, while in one place (the third tower from the west) it is standing to a height of 12 ft. 6 in. Along the outer or southern side of the wall are remains of eight quadrangular towers projecting from the curtain at intervals of about 140 feet from each other. Each tower measures about 22 feet on the face by 16½ feet on the sides, and appears to have been built solid, the interior having been filled up with earth and rubble. A peculiarity of this cross-wall is that on its inner side there are several platforms or thickenings, each about 33 feet long and 3 feet thick. These were probably buttresses to strengthen the wall, but too little of them is left to allow us to be positive on this head. Both wall and towers are constructed on their outer and inner faces of very massive blocks, three courses of which make a height of about 7 feet. At one point in the wall I counted eight courses standing. The towers form an integral part of the wall; they were obviously built at the same time and continuously with it, not added at a later time.

The lower cross-wall, which cut off the north-western corner of the site so as to form an inner fortification, has seven quadrangular towers projecting from its outer side. They measure about 20 feet on the face by 18 feet on the sides. The third tower from the west is standing to a height of about 12 ft. 6 in. Leake and Vischer regarded this north-western enclosure as an acropolis or citadel. Mr. Grundy holds that the city which was besieged and taken by the Peloponnesian army in 429-427 B.C. was confined to this north-western corner of the site. He argues that this corner is strategically the strongest part of the whole site and must always have been surrounded by a fortification-wall. The slopes on the north and west are still steep, in places precipitous, and may have been much steeper in antiquity; and the foundation of a wall placed upon their edge would be from 60 to 90 feet above the plain at their base. The total circumference of the enclosure is 1430 yards; and a circuit-wall of this extent, aided by the natural strength of the ground, might very well (Mr. Grundy thinks) have been defended by 480 men, which we know to have been the strength of the garrison (Thucydides, ii. 78), whereas it is difficult or impossible to believe that so small a garrison could have successfully defended a circuit-wall of 2¼ miles in length, which is approximately the length of the existing circuit-wall of Plataea. We may agree with Mr. Grundy in thinking that the city which the 400 Plataeans and 80 Athenians defended for two years against the enormously superior numbers of the Peloponnesian army was much smaller than the later city of which the remains cover the plateau; but his theory that this earlier city coincided with the fortified enclosure at the north-western corner of the site is not borne out by architectural evidence. For, as we have seen, the cross-wall which cuts off this corner is of later date than almost all the rest of the walls. It may even belong to the Byzantine period, and would seem to have been constructed at a late time when the town had shrunk to these narrow limits.

The original city which was besieged and taken by the Peloponnesians may have occupied, as has already been suggested, the southern part of the site, the walls of which are the earliest of all. To this view, however, it is objected by Mr. Grundy that a town of this area, measuring perhaps from three-quarters of a mile to a mile in circumference and unaided, except to a small extent on the west side, by natural defences, could not have been held by 480 men against a large army. However that may be, it would seem that at some time subsequent to the Peloponnesian war the city was enlarged. This may have been done either when the Plataeans were restored after the peace of Antalcidas in 387 B.C. (Paus. ix. 1. 4) or at the time of their second restoration by Philip of Macedon in 338 B.C. (Paus. ix. 1. 8). That the ancient Plataea did not comprise the whole of the area afterwards occupied by the city is moreover made probable by the fact that in 479 B.C., at the time of the battle of Plataea, the temple of Hera was in front of the city (Herodotus, ix. 52), whereas when Pausanias visited Plataea the temple appears to have been within the city. It is true that the old temple which existed at the time of the Persian war was destroyed some time after 427 B.C. by the Thebans, who built a new temple in its place (Thucydides, iii. 68); but probably the new temple occupied the site of the old one. The remains of a large temple, which was probably that of Hera, were discovered a few years ago by the Americans within the area of the later city (see below, p. 17 *sq.*).

Inside of the walls of Plataea, or rather of the northern portion of it which is cut off by the upper cross-wall, lies a mass of ruins, including the remains of a number of Byzantine churches, some of which were excavated by members of the American School of Archaeology in 1889 and 1890. The number of these churches (there were at least eight of them within the walls) proves that in Byzantine times a populous town must have existed on the site. Some of the churches contain ancient architectural fragments of both the Greek and Roman periods, including some blocks of white marble with the 'egg and dart' pattern executed in good style. Most of these fragments (architraves, capitals, and bases) belong to the Roman age. Two springs, one immediately to the west of the walls where the women of the neighbouring village of *Kokla* wash their clothes, the other some 250 yards to the east of the plateau, have walls made of ancient fragments of white marble. The marble of all the architectural pieces found on the site resembles Pentelic, but probably came from a nearer quarry. Within the northern portion of the site, a little to the east of the lower cross-wall, are seven or eight small rectangular holes or niches cut in the rock, probably for the reception of votive or other tablets. Just outside of the west wall, and close to the spring, are some half-dozen sarcophaguses perched on the rocks ; each of them is hewn out of a single piece of the common coarse grey marble of which the rock consists. To the south of the sarcophaguses are some graves in the shape of rectangular pits hewn in the rock. Amongst the inscriptions found by the American archaeologists on the site were a long fragment of the Latin preamble to Diocletian's edict *On prices*, a fragment of the Greek text of the same edict, and a list of names of women who had dedicated various offerings (cups, earrings, rings, torches, cowheads, a girdle, etc.) to some deity not specified. This last inscription seems to belong to the second century B.C.

A little to the south-west of Plataea, on the lower slope of Mt. Cithaeron, stands the modern village of *Kokla*.

See Dodwell, *Tour*, I. p. 474 *sqq.* ; Leake, *Northern Greece*, 2. pp. 323 *sqq.*, 363 *sqq.* ; Mure, *Journal*, I. p. 266 *sqq.* ; Welcker, *Tagebuch*, 2. p. 24 *sqq.* ; L. Ross, *Wanderungen*, I. p. 16 *sq.* ; Vischer, *Erinnerungen*, p. 540 *sqq.* ; Bursian, *Geogr.* I. p. 243 *sqq.* ; Baedeker,[3] p. 176 *sqq.* ; *Guide-Joanne*, 2. p. 25 ; *American Journal of Archaeology*, 5 (1889), pp. 428-442 ; *id.*, 6 (1890), pp. 108-111, 215, 445-462 ; *id.*, 7 (1891), pp. 54-64, 404-421 ; G. B. Grundy, *The topography of the battle of Plataea*, pp. 53-72 ; P. Brandt, *Von Athen zum Tempethal* (Gütersloh, 1894), pp. 19-22. I visited Plataea in May 1890.

Plataea is chiefly memorable for the great and decisive defeat which the Greeks inflicted on the Persian army under Mardonius in the neighbourhood of the city in 479 B.C. (Herodotus, ix. 14-75 ; Diodorus, xi. 29-32 ; Plutarch, *Aristides*, 11-19). Herodotus's detailed account of the battle was probably derived from men who had themselves taken part in the fight ; but to reconcile his description with the natural features of the battlefield is not easy, and the attempts to do so have resulted in considerable divergences of opinion. The identification of some of the most important spots mentioned by Herodotus is still very uncertain. This is particularly the case with the sanctuary of Demeter (see above, p. 5 *sq.*), the Gargaphian spring (Herodotus, ix. 25, 49, 51, 52 ; Paus. ix. 4. 3), and the so-called Island (Herodotus, ix. 51). From Herodotus's description we gather that the Gargaphian spring, from which the whole Greek army drew their water, was situated among low hills at a distance of 20 Greek furlongs (2¼ miles) from the sanctuary of Hera which stood in front of Plataea. The spring is tradition-ally identified with a group of springs now called *Apotripi* which is situated about 1½ miles to the north-east of Plataea, beside the track which leads from *Kriekouki* to *Pyrgos* and Leuctra, about a quarter of a mile before it enters on the flat watershed which divides the basins of the Asopus and Oeroe. But Leake and Mr. Grundy identify it with another group of springs somewhat to the east of *Apotripi*, about 1⅔ miles to the north-east of Plataea. This group of springs apparently yields a more copious supply of water than *Apotripi*. It helps to form a stream which flows into the Asopus. As to the Island, to which the Greeks when hard pressed by the Persian cavalry had thoughts of retreating, we learn from Herodotus that it was formed by a stream called the Oeroe, the water of which, descending from Mt. Cithaeron, divided in two and then, after flowing round a tract of ground about 3 furlongs wide, reunited again in a single stream. The island so formed, Herodotus tell us, lay in front of Plataea at a distance of 10 Greek furlongs (a little over a mile) both from the Asopus and the Gargaphian spring. The advantages which the Greeks expected to reap from taking up a position on the Island were that they would be better supplied with water and be less exposed to the attacks of the formidable and enterprising cavalry of the enemy, who not only harassed them by continual charges but had choked up the Gargaphian spring on which the Greeks depended for their supply of water (Herodotus, ix. 49-51). At the present day there is no such island as Herodotus describes anywhere in the neighbourhood of Plataea. A number of streams flow down Cithaeron to the east of Plataea, and turn to the west, where they unite to form the Oeroe which flows into the Gulf of Corinth. Probably the Island was the strip of ground between two of these streams, above their junction. Leake and Vischer identified as the Island a level stretch of meadow-land intersected by several of the streams in question and situated about a mile to the north of Plataea. To this identification it is objected by Mr. Grundy (1) that even in winter after heavy rains the streams here contain very little water, and that in September, when the battle was fought, all of them would be almost certainly dry before they reached this part of the plain; (2) that the beds of the streams offer no serious obstacles to cavalry, which could indeed cross them in most places at full gallop; and (3) that in order to reach the supposed haven of refuge the Greek army, already shaken by the attacks of the Persian cavalry, would have had to cross a mile of open ground, where that cavalry would have had full play and might have turned the Greek march into a total rout. Hence Mr. Grundy would place the Island higher up the courses of the streams, where they contain more water and where their deep beds would afford an efficient protection against cavalry. Long ridges separate the deep watercourses which descend the slope of Cithaeron to the east of Plataea; and one of them, rendered conspicuous by a large hillock which rises on it and serves as a landmark, is identified by Mr. Grundy with the Island. It is distant somewhat less than a mile to the east of Plataea, and is enclosed on two sides by the deep beds of streams which rise near each other on the mountain and meet in the plain below. The more westerly of the streams is fed by numerous springs, of which two are large (one of them is the spring called *Vergoutiani*, see above, p. 7); and it is already swollen to a considerable size when it flows past the hillock on the ridge, but like the other streams which here descend to the plain its volume diminishes the farther it gets into the flat country. Here, then, the Greeks would have had a sufficient supply of water, while the rugged nature of the ground and the depth and steepness of the coombs on either side would have rendered them quite safe from the dreaded cavalry of the enemy. Mr. Grundy's theory has a good deal to recommend it; but on the other hand we must observe (1) that the streams which skirt the ridge in question meet, not immediately below it, but far away in the plain, so that the resemblance of the ridge to an island is not particularly striking; and (2) that the distance of the ridge from the Asopus is twice or thrice the distance (10 Greek furlongs, about a mile) of the Island from that river, as stated by Herodotus. To meet this last difficulty Mr. Grundy is driven to suppose that Herodotus was here speaking, not of the Asopus, but of one of its tributaries, which rises about 10 Greek furlongs from the ridge which Mr. Grundy would identify as the Island.

As to the topography of the battlefield see Leake, *Northern Greece*, 2. p. 335 *sqq.* ; J. Spencer Stanhope, *Topography illustrative of the battle of Plataea* (London, 1817); Vischer, *Erinnerungen*, p. 547 *sqq.* ; W. Irving Hunt, 'Notes on the battlefield of Plataia,' *American Journal of Archaeology*, 6 (1890), pp. 463-475 ; A. Hauvette, in *Nouvelles Archives des Missions scientifiques et littéraires*, 2 (1892), pp. 359-374 ; G. B. Grundy, *The topography of the battle of Plataea* (London, 1894); H. Awdry, in *Annual of the British School at Athens*, No. 1, Session 1894-5, pp. 90-98 ; P. Brandt, *Von Athen zum Tempethal*, p. 16 *sqq.* The credibility of Herodotus's narrative of the battle has been examined by H. Delbrück, *Die Perserkriege und die Burgunderkriege* (Berlin, 1887), p. 108 *sqq.* ; A. Hauvette, *Hérodote* (Paris, 1894), pp. 453-483 ; F. Rudolph, *Die Schlacht bei Platäa und deren Überlieferung* (Dresden, 1895).

2. 5. the graves of the men who fought against the Medes etc. A little to the south-east of Plataea, close to the line by which the road from Megara probably entered the city, there are many remains of tombs cut in the rock. These are believed by Mr. Grundy to be the graves of the men who fell in the battle with the Persians (*The topography of the battle of Plataea*, p. 7 *sq.*) The view is in itself highly improbable and is implicitly contradicted by the evidence both of Herodotus and Pausanias. It was the practice of the Greeks, as it is of the moderns, to bury the slain in one or more large trenches (*polyandria*) ; and it is very unlikely that on this occasion they so far departed from their usual practice as to hew a separate tomb in the living rock for each man that fell. Besides we have the positive testimony of Herodotus and Pausanias that the dead were buried in a few common graves. According to Pausanias there were three of these great graves, one for the Athenians, one for the Lacedaemonians, and one for the rest of the Greeks. According to Herodotus (ix. 85) the Athenians, Tegeans, Megarians, and Phliasians buried their dead in four separate graves, all the dead of each nation being laid together in one grave ; but the Lacedaemonians separated their dead into three groups—the young Spartans (*irenes*), the rest of the Spartans, and the Helots—and buried each group separately in one grave. Other Greek nations who had taken no part in the fighting and had consequently lost no men, nevertheless raised sepulchral mounds on the battlefield, but these were mere cenotaphs designed to impose upon posterity. The so-called grave of the Aeginetans, for example, was made ten years after the battle.

The Plataeans annually sacrificed to the Greeks who had fallen in the battle and were buried in Plataean earth. These sacrifices were still offered as late as the time of Plutarch, who has described them. They took place on the 16th day of the Attic month Maemacterion (November-December), which corresponded to the Boeotian month Alalcomenius. The procession started at dawn, headed by a trumpeter sounding the charge. After him came waggons laden with myrtle and garlands. A black bull was led in procession, and young men carried drink-offerings of wine and milk in pitchers, also jars of oil and perfume. The rear was brought up by the chief magistrate of Plataea, who carried a water-jar in procession from the Record Office all through the city to the graves. He was clad in purple and had a sword at his side, though at other times he might not touch iron nor wear any but a white garment.

He then filled his pitcher at the fountain, and with his own hands washed the tombstones and anointed them with perfume. Next he slaughtered the bull over a blazing pile, and after praying to Zeus and Hermes invited the brave men who had died for Greece to come and partake of the banquet and the blood. Then he filled a bowl with wine, poured it out, and said " I drink to the men who died for the freedom of Greece." See Plutarch, *Aristides*, 21. Amongst the offerings which were presented to the heroic dead at these annual sacrifices were clothes and the ripe fruits of the earth (Thucydides, iii. 58).

2. 5. an altar of Zeus of Freedom. After the battle of Plataea the Greeks were commanded by the Delphic oracle to set up an altar to Zeus the god of Freedom; but before sacrificing on it they were to extinguish all the fires in the land, because they had been polluted by the presence of the Persians, and to fetch a pure fire from 'the common hearth' at Delphi. So the Greek commanders went from place to place seeing that all the fires were put out; and Euchidas, a Plataean, quitting Plataea in the morning, ran to Delphi, took fire from the altar, and ran back with it to Plataea, which he reached before sunset. He had just strength to salute his fellow-townsmen and hand over the fire, when he dropped down and died. The distance which he had traversed in the day was (according to Plutarch) 1000 *stades*, or about 111 miles. (The distance between Plataea and Delphi in a straight line is about 46 miles. Allowing for the bends of the road, the distance is perhaps not less than the 500 *stades* or $55\frac{1}{2}$ miles at which Plutarch reckoned it.) Every year, on the anniversary of the great battle, the Plataeans sacrificed to Zeus god of Freedom in presence of deputies sent from every part of Greece. These deputies formed a representative Council or Assembly, and had the right of decreeing honorary statues to men who had deserved well of Greece. Such statues, as we learn from inscriptions, were decreed to the emperor Hadrian and to Tiberius Claudius Atticus Marathonius, the father of Herodes Atticus; the former statue was set up at Delphi. See Plutarch, *Aristides*, 19-21; Dittenberger, *Sylloge Inscr. Graec.* Nos. 282, 288; *C. I. G. G. S.* 1. No. 2509. Amongst the ruins of Plataea three semicircular bases have been found, which, as we learn from the inscriptions on them, supported tripods dedicated by the Boeotians to Zeus god of Freedom. The inscriptions date from the second half of the third century B.C. See *C. I. G. G. S.* 1. Nos. 1672-1674; *Bulletin de Corresp. hellénique*, 1 (1877), p. 208 *sq.*; *id.*, 13 (1889), p. 5 *sq.*, Nos. viii-x; Collitz, *G. D. I.* 1. No. 865. At Thebes there is the large blue marble base of the statue of a certain L. Egnatius Victor Lollianus, governor of Greece, which was dedicated to Zeus god of Freedom and to the Unanimity of the Greeks by the city of Plataea, apparently at the beginning of the third century A.D. (*C. I. G. G. S.* 1. No. 2510). The Plataeans seem to have dated public documents by the year of the priest of Zeus god of Freedom (*C. I. G. G. S.* 1. No. 1667).

2. 6. games called the Eleutheria. These games, as well as the annual meeting of the deputies at Plataea (see the preceding note), were instituted on the proposal of Aristides. The prizes were wreaths. See

Plutarch, *Aristides*, 21 ; Strabo, ix. p. 412.   The games are mentioned in inscriptions (*C. I. G. G. S.* 1. Nos. 49, 1856 ; Dittenberger, *Sylloge Inscr. Graec.* No. 398 ; *Bulletin de Corresp. hellénique*, 3 (1879), p. 443; Cavvadias, *Fouilles d'Épidaure*, 1. p. 78, No. 240).   Great crowds seem to have assembled to witness them ; for Dicaearchus, or the writer who commonly goes by his name, says that Plataea, ordinarily as solitary as the sea-shore, was indeed a city at the time of the Eleutheria (*Descriptio Graeciae*, i. 11).   When the Thebans razed the city to the ground, they built a large inn beside the temple of Hera, probably to accommodate the visitors who flocked to the games.   The inn seems to have been a square, 200 feet on the sides, enclosing a courtyard, round which the rooms were ranged in two stories (Thucydides, iii. 68).

2. 6. The trophy etc.   The Lacedaemonians and Athenians each set up a trophy of their own, according to Plutarch (*Aristides*, 20). Mr. W. I. Hunt thinks that the trophy (or trophies) may have stood near the ruined Byzantine church south-east of Plataea (see above, p. 5) ; the distance of that place from Plataea is about the 15 furlongs mentioned by Pausanias (*American Journal of Archaeology*, 6 (1890), p. 468 *sq.*)

2. 7. I have already mentioned etc.   See ix. 1. 3.

2. 7. a temple of Hera.   The foundations of what was probably the temple of Hera were discovered by the archaeologists of the American School in 1891.   They were situated on a small terrace about the middle of the northern division of Plataea, to the south-east of the later cross-wall which encloses the north-western corner of the plateau. The main axis of the building lies E. 10° S. (magnetic).   Its total exterior length is 49.90 metres ; its exterior width is 16.70 metres.   The outer wall (2.55 metres thick) is built of smoothly-cut blocks 2.55 m. long, 1.20 m. wide, and 0.40 high, laid without clamps or mortar, and fitting so closely that on the upper surface it is difficult to detect the joints. The lowest course rests on the rock, a very shallow trench having been cut for its reception.   The greatest number of courses in position is four, namely at the north-east angle.   Of the south wall only two courses are left, and of the north wall only one.   At the north-west corner was found, not in position, part of an upper course of the *crepidoma*, showing the face of one of the steps.

The inner walls are all 1.25 m. thick, except one cross-wall which is 1.30 m.   The blocks are laid in alternate courses of 'headers and stretchers,' *i.e.* transversely and longitudinally in alternate courses, and are closely fitted without clamps or mortar.   Fragments of roof-tiles are scattered about the terrace.   They are of baked clay, covered with a dull yellowish-grey glaze, and of a ⋀ shape, the angle being very obtuse. The temple was surrounded by a colonnade which was almost certainly of the Doric order.   From the style of the architecture and the clamps (which are of the ⊢⊣ shape) the temple seems to belong to the fifth or perhaps the sixth century B.C.

It is probable that this was the temple of Hera.   The site can be reconciled with the descriptions both of Herodotus who says that the temple was in front of the city (ix. 52), and of Pausanias, who implies that it was in the city. For we have seen that at the time of the battle of Plataea and as late as the capture of the city by the Peloponnesians in 427 B.C., the town may have occupied only the upper (southern) part of the plateau, so that the temple, standing on the lower (northern) part of the plateau, would be in front of the town ; whereas in the second century A.D., when Pausanias visited Plataea, the temple was, and had for centuries been, enclosed within the newer city which had spread over the northern part of the plateau. Again, the importance of the recently-discovered temple is shown by its size, which is larger than the temple at Bassae or the temple of Hera at Olympia. As Hera was the chief divinity of Plataea, it is natural to suppose that this large and important temple was sacred to her. We know from Thucydides (iii. 68) that some time, apparently about a year, after the capture of Plataea in 427 B.C., the Thebans razed the whole city to the ground and built a new stone temple of Hera one hundred feet long. Mr. Washington, who excavated the temple, concludes that the temple discovered by him is the one built by the Thebans soon after 427 B.C. The discovery of a layer of blackened earth under the temple seems to show that a former temple on this site had been destroyed by fire. See H. S. Washington, in *American Journal of Archaeology*, 7 (1891), pp. 390-405.

2. 7. **Rhea bringing to Cronus the stone** etc. In the existing monuments of ancient art this subject is rarely represented ; in fact only two such representations appear to be certainly known. One is a relief on a four-sided marble altar found at Albano, now on the Capitol at Rome. Cronus is seen seated on a chair, receiving in his right hand the pretended babe from Rhea, who stands in front of him. The style of composition is simple and dignified ; Overbeck even classed the relief with the greatest masterpieces of antiquity, and thought that, though of Roman date, it must be a copy of a very fine work of art. See Müller-Wieseler, *Denkmäler*, 2. pl. lxii. No. 804 ; Baumeister's *Denkmäler*, 2. p. 798, fig. 862 ; Overbeck, *Griech. Kunstmythologie*, 2. p. 326.

The other monument referred to is a red-figured vase of Sicilian workmanship. On it Cronus is depicted standing wrapt in an ample mantle, his left hand resting on a sceptre surmounted by a flower. Opposite him is Rhea, clad in a long robe, bringing him the stone. Behind this group, on the spectator's right, are two young girls, probably the nymphs Ida and Adrastia, to whose care, jointly with the Curetes, the infant Zeus was entrusted (Apollodorus, i. 1. 6). See J. De Witte, 'Cronos et Rhea,' *Gazette archéologique*, 1 (1875), pp. 30-33, with pl. 9. The same subject was perhaps represented on one of the metopes of the temple of Apollo at Bassae. See vol. 4. p. 402 *sq.*

2. 7. **They call Hera Full-grown.** Cp. viii. 22. 2 ; viii. 31. 9. She received this surname at Plataea because her marriage with Zeus was said to have been consummated on Mount Cithaeron (Plutarch, quoted by Eusebius, *Praep. Evang.* iii. 1. 3 *sq.*) It has been con-jectured that the noble colossal statue of Hera formerly known as the Barberini Juno, now in the Rotunda at the Vatican, is a copy of the Plataean statue of Full-grown Hera by Praxiteles. The statue

certainly appears to be a reproduction of some famous masterpiece, for
a number of statues of the same type, presumably copies of one original,
have come down to us. See Overbeck, *Griech. Kunstmythologie,* 3.
pp. 54-58, 111 *sq.* ; Müller-Wieseler, *Denkmäler,* 2. pl. iv. No. 56 ;
Baumeister's *Denkmäler,* 2. p. 647 *sq.* (fig. 715) ; Roscher's *Lexikon,*
1. p. 2115. Prof. W. Klein argues that the Praxiteles who made this
statue was not the great Praxiteles but an earlier and less famous
namesake (*Archaeolog. epigraph. Mittheil. aus Oesterreich,* 4 (1880),
p. 8 *sqq.*) Overbeck inclined to the same view (*Gesch. d. griech.
Plastik,*⁴ 1. p. 499), and so does Prof. Collignon (*Hist. de la Sculpture
grecque,* 2. p. 179). See note on i. 2. 4, vol. 2. p. 49 *sqq.*

2. 7. Callimachus. See i. 26. 6 note.

3. 1. Hera, enraged at Zeus etc. The following legend is told
also by Plutarch, quoted by Eusebius (*Praepar. Evang.* iii. 1 *sq.*)
According to Plutarch, the crafty person who suggested the stratagem
to Zeus was not Cithaeron but Alalcomenes ; by his advice a fine oak-
tree was cut down, shaped and dressed as a bride, and named Daedale.
The rest of the story follows as in Pausanias, except that Hera comes,
not from Euboea, but from Cithaeron, where she has been hiding.

3. 2. a festival called Daedala. This festival seems to have its
analogies in the spring and midsummer festivals of European peasantry
in modern times. See *The Golden Bough,* 1. p. 100 *sqq.*

3. 2. Daedalus, son of Palamaon. According to the oldest and
best-authenticated tradition the famous artist Daedalus was a son of
Metion (Pherecydes, quoted by the scholiast on Sophocles, *Oed. Col.*
472 ; Plato, *Ion,* p. 533 a ; Diodorus, iv. 76). According to another
tradition Daedalus was the son of Eupalamus, the son of Metion
(Apollodorus, iii. 15. 8 ; Schol. on Plato, *Repub.* p. 529 d ; Suidas, *s.v.*
Πέρδικος ἱερόν ; Servius on Virgil, *Aen.* vi. 14 ; Hyginus, *Fab.* 39, 244,
and 274). Metion the father or grandfather of Daedalus was a scion
of the royal house of Athens, being a son of Erechtheus, according to
Pherecydes (Schol. on Sophocles, *Oed. Col.* 472), or of Eupalamus the
son of Erechtheus (Diodorus, iv. 76). Pausanias notices elsewhere
(vii. 4. 5) the connexion of Daedalus with the royal house of the
Metionids. See J. Töpffer, *Attische Genealogie,* p. 165 *sqq.*

3. 5. the Great Daedala is held —— every fifty-ninth year etc.
That is, fifty-eight years elapsed between two successive celebrations of
the Great Daedala. We express this by saying that the festival was
held every fifty-ninth year ; the Greeks, adding to the intervening fifty-
eight years the two years in which the festival was celebrated, said that
it was held every sixtieth year. The first exile of the Plataeans lasted
forty years (427-387 B.C.) ; the second exile lasted thirty-five years
(373-338 B.C.) Hence the reason assigned by Pausanias for the interval between the celebrations of the Great Daedala cannot be the true
one. Doubtless, as K. O. Müller observed, the custom of celebrating
the festival at these intervals was much more ancient than the exile of
the Plataeans, and probably had its explanation in the calendar of the
early Boeotians and the cycle adopted by them in order to harmonise
the solar and lunar years. See K. O. Müller, *Orchomenos und die*

Minyer,[2] p. 216 *sqq.* The calendar of the Druids had a cycle of thirty years (Pliny, *Nat. hist.* xvi. 250).

3. 9. a cave of the nymphs of Cithaeron etc. Plutarch thus speaks of the cave: "On one peak of Cithaeron is the cave of the Sphragitidian nymphs, facing the north-west, in which, as they say, there was formerly an oracle, and many of the natives were possessed, whom they called *nympholepti* ('seized by the nymphs')" (*Aristides*, 11). As to the situation of the cave, Leake says: "Immediately opposite to the southern angle of the walls of Plataea on the steep rocky rise of the mountain, which is here separated only by a narrow level from the ancient site, is a cavern 30 feet in length, 10 feet wide, and 4 high. Before it there is a little verdant level, surrounded and overhung by rugged rocks. The beauty of the spot would tempt one to believe it to have been the cavern sacred to the Nymphs of Cithaeron, called the Spragitides, which once contained an oracle of the Nymphs, and was noted for Nympholepsy. But the testimony of Plutarch and Pausanias is positive in placing that cavern on the north-western side of one of the summits, and at a distance of only 15 stades [furlongs] below it, consequently much higher in the mountain, and having a different aspect." Leake adds that as there are two summits of Cithaeron equally conspicuous, it is not easy to determine on which we ought to look for the cavern, though the balance of probability inclines towards the one nearer to Plataea. See Leake, *Northern Greece*, 2. p. 335. Caves were dedicated to the nymphs, but especially to the Naiads, on account of the springs which bubbled up in them or the water which dripped from their roofs (Porphyry, *De antro nympharum*, 6 and 8). The ancients appear to have explained all extraordinary mental states, such as poetic rapture, prophetic frenzy, madness, idiocy, etc., by supposing that the person affected was possessed by a nymph; hence such persons were said to be 'seized by the nymphs' (νυμφόληπτοι). Cp. Plato, *Phaedrus*, p. 238 c d; Pollux, i. 19; Hesychius, *s.v.* νυμφόληπτοι. The same belief is still prevalent in Greece, and the same word νυμφόληπτος is sometimes used to express it. The Nereids (properly the sea-nymphs, but now extended so as to include all nymphs) are believed to be very mischievous at noon, especially a summer noon, and it is very dangerous at that hour to sleep or even to loiter beside a well, a spring, or a river, in the shadow of trees (especially plane-trees, poplars, fig-trees, nut-trees, and carob-trees), at mills, or at cross-roads, for these places are the mid-day haunts of the Nereids, and a man who lingers there may be struck by a nymph, the consequence of which would be some mental or bodily ailment, generally the loss of reason, but sometimes the crippling of a limb. See B. Schmidt, *Das Volksleben der Neugriechen*, p. 119 *sqq.* In the island of Siphnus Mr. Bent visited a cave, over which was the inscription ΝΥΜΦΩΝ ΙΕΡΟΝ, 'sanctuary of the nymphs.' Travellers who cross a certain stream near this cave, especially at midnight or mid-day, run the risk of being possessed by the nymphs, "and to cure such cases it is customary to prepare and place at a spot where three roads meet (τρίστρατα), or hang in the wells, some bread wrapped up in a clean napkin, and some honey, milk, and eggs, to appease these nymphs" (J. T. Bent, *The Cyclades*, p. 26 *sq.* ; cp. Lucy M. J. Garnett, *The Women of Turkey. The Christian Women*, p. 132 *sq.*) Cp. note on ii. 1. 8.

4. 1. a sanctuary of Athena surnamed Warlike. According to Plutarch (*Aristides*, 20) eighty talents were assigned to the Plataeans by the Greeks as their share in the booty taken at the battle of Plataea (not Marathon, as Pausanias says), and with these eighty talents the Plataeans built a sanctuary of Athena, set up an image, and adorned the temple with paintings which were in excellent preservation down to Plutarch's time. The circumstantiality of Plutarch's account of the dispute which ended in assigning eighty talents to the Plataeans makes it probable that he was better informed than Pausanias as to the origin of the sanctuary.

4. 1. the bronze image on the Acropolis. See i. 28. 2 with the note, vol. 2. p. 348 *sqq.*

4. 2. the other, by Onasias, depicts the former expedition of the Argives etc. Compare ix. 5. 11. The painter Onasias is otherwise unknown. Cp. Critical Note on this passage, vol. 1. p. 601.

4. 2. Arimnestus, who commanded the Plataeans. Cp. Herodotus, ix. 72 ; Plutarch, *Aristides*, 11.

4. 3. a sanctuary of Eleusinian Demeter. This can hardly have been the sanctuary beside which the Spartans were hotly engaged with the Persians at the battle of Plataea. See above, p. 5 *sq.*

4. 3. Leitus. He is mentioned as one of the Boeotian leaders by Homer, *Iliad*, ii. 494.

4. 3. The Gargaphian fountain. See above, p. 13. That the fountain was choked up by the Persian cavalry is mentioned by Herodotus (ix. 49).

4. 4. a river Oeroe. This is the small and sluggish stream, now the *Potami-Livadostro*, which, formed in the neighbourhood of Plataea by the union of several brooks descending from Mt. Cithaeron, flows due west, skirting the northern foot of Mt. Cithaeron, and falls into the bay of Creusis. See Bursian, *Geogr.* 1. p. 244 ; Vischer, *Erinnerungen*, p. 550 ; Baedeker,[3] pp. 176, 179 ; *Guide-Joanne*, 2. p. 26.

4. 4. Scolus. This place is mentioned by Homer (*Il.* ii. 497). It lay to the east of Plataea, for the Persian army under Mardonius ravaged the lands of Scolus on their march from Tanagra to Plataea (Herodotus, ix. 15). Strabo tells us that Scolus was a village in the Parasopia or valley of the Asopus, at the foot of Mt. Cithaeron, in a rugged situation ; there was a proverb "Go not to Scolus yourself nor follow another thither" (Strabo, ix. p. 408). On a little rocky table-height, at the foot of a spur of Mt. Cithaeron and overlooking the valley of the Asopus, stands a branch of the monastery of St. Meletius. Leake and H. N. Ulrichs thought that this position answers exactly to the descriptions of Strabo and Pausanias. It is a few minutes to the west of the large Albanian village of *Darimari*. Near the plateau is a spring, the source of a brook which flows north to join the Asopus about half a mile away. The Asopus dries up in summer, with the exception of a few deep pools, where fish abound. Its bed is overgrown with reeds, of which baskets are woven (cp. Paus. v. 14. 3). The district would seem to have been famed in antiquity for its grain-crops, for Demeter at Scolus went by the names of Megalartus ('she of the large wheaten loaf') and Megalomazus ('she of the large barley cake'). See Athenaeus, iii. p. 109 a b, x. p. 416 b c. The district still produces excellent wheat, which is much sought after on account of its fineness and white colour. As a frontier post in a narrow part of the valley between Mt. Cithaeron and the Asopus, Scolus was fortified by the Thebans with ditches and palisades; but the works were carried by Agesilaus in 377 B.C., who thus entered Boeotia from the east and ravaged the country up to the walls of Thebes (Xenophon, *Hellenica*, v. 4. 49 *sqq.*; *id.*, *Agesilaus*, ii. 22). See Leake, *Northern Greece*, 2. p. 330 *sq.*; H. N. Ulrichs, *Reisen und Forschungen in Griechenland*, 2. p. 73 *sq.*; Bursian, *Geogr.* 1. p. 248. Mr. Grundy was unable to find any remains of Scolus. He thinks that the site should be looked for on the Asopus from a mile to a mile and a half east of the bridge by which the road to Thebes crosses the river (*The topography of the battle of Plataea*, p. 13 *sq.*).

5. 1. **an epithet applied to Thebes —— is Ogygian.** See Aeschylus, *Persians*, 37 *sq.*; Sophocles, *Oed. Col.* 1769 *sq.*; Apollonius Rhodius, *Argonaut.* iii. 1178.

5. 3. **When Cadmus had gone away to dwell among —— the Encheleans.** The Illyrian tribe of Encheleans ('eel-men'), being hard pressed in war by the other Illyrians, were warned of God that they would overcome their enemies if they took Cadmus and Harmonia to be their leaders. They did so: the prophecy was fulfilled; and Cadmus reigned over the Illyrians till he and Harmonia were changed into snakes and transported by Zeus to the Elysian fields. The chiefs of the Encheleans traced their descent from the illustrious pair, whose graves were pointed out in Illyria long afterwards. See Apollodorus, iii. 5. 4; Strabo, vii. p. 326; *id.*, i. p. 46; Stephanus Byz., *s.v.* Δυρράχιον, cp. *id.*, *s.v.* Βουθόη; Athenaeus, xi. p. 462 b; Apollonius Rhodius, *Argonaut.* iv. 516 *sqq.* But Ovid and other writers seem to suppose that after their transformation into snakes Cadmus and Harmonia continued to lead a peaceful and happy life in Illyria, and this is the version of the legend followed by Matthew Arnold in the lines:

> Far, far from here,
> The Adriatic breaks in a warm bay
> Among the green Illyrian hills; and there
> The sunshine in the happy glens is fair, etc.

See Ovid, *Metam.* iv. 563-603; Hyginus, *Fab.* 6; Nicander, *Ther.* 607 *sqq.* In Illyria two rocks, called the rocks or stones of Cadmus and Harmonia, were shown; it was said that when misfortune was impending on the people, these two rocks shook and met (Dionysius, *Orbis ⟨illegible⟩, ⟨illegible⟩, ⟨illegible⟩, ⟨illegible⟩*). Perhaps these rocks were supposed to resemble serpents; for Nonnus says that Cadmus and Harmonia were turned into stone serpents (*Dionys.* xliv. 126-129; *id.*, xlvi. 367-369). The legends of the Phoenician descent of Cadmus and

his transformation into a serpent have led some writers, as Movers and
Baudissin, to regard him as a Phoenician serpent-god.   See Movers,
Die Phoenizier, 1. p. 513 *sqq.*; Baudissin, *Studien zur semitischen
Religionsgeschichte*, 1. pp. 272-275.

5. 5. The sequel of the story, how Nycteus died etc.   See ii.
6. 1 *sqq.*

5. 6. named it Thebes, because of their relationship to Thebe.
Thebe, daughter of the Asopus (Paus. ii. 5. 2, v. 22. 6), was the wife of
Zethus (Apollodorus, iii. 5. 6).

5. 7. attested by Homer in the Odyssey.   See *Od.* xi. 263 *sqq.*

5. 7. Amphion —— built the wall to the music of his lyre.
See Apollonius Rhodius, *Argonaut.* i. 736 *sqq.*; Apollodorus, iii. 5. 5;
Horace, *Odes*, iii. 11. 2 ; *id.*, *Ars poetica*, 394 *sqq.*; Propertius, i. 9. 10.
Cp. Paus. ix. 17. 7.

5. 7. he added three new strings to —— the lyre.   According
to another legend Amphion invented the lyre (Pliny, *Nat. hist.* vii. 204).

5. 8. The author of the poem on Europa.   This poem is ascribed
to Eumelus by a scholiast on Homer (*Iliad*, vi. 131, ed. Bekker).   But
Pausanias thought it was not by Eumelus.   See iv. 4. 1.   Clement of
Alexandria seems to have been of the same opinion, for in quoting a
couple of lines from the poem, he simply speaks of "the author of the
poem *Europia*" (*Strom.* i. 24, § 164, p. 419, ed. Potter).   Cp. *Epicorum Graecorum fragmenta*, ed. Kinkel, p. 192 *sq.*

5. 9. the son of Zethus.   His name was Neis (ix. 8. 4).

5. 10. While Laius sat on the throne etc.   The legend of Oedipus,
here told in outline by Pausanias, clearly resembles a popular tale
current in Finland.   The Finnish story is as follows : Two wise men
spent a night at a farmhouse.   Now it chanced that night at the farm that
a ewe dropt a lamb and the farmer's wife gave birth to a boy at the same
time.   The wise men foretold that the lamb would be devoured by a
wolf, and that the boy would kill his father and marry his mother.
The lamb was killed and was about to be served up at table, when a
wolf ate it all up.   Seeing how the first prophecy had been fulfilled, the
father proposed to kill his child ; however, at the mother's entreaty the
infant was tied to a board and flung into the sea, but not before he had
received a cut with a knife on his breast.   The board with the babe was
cast ashore and found by an abbot, who brought up the boy.   When he
grew up, the lad went out into the world and took service on a farm.
Here, being set to watch a field of turnips, he one night shot the farmer
himself, who had come to fetch an apronful of turnips.   Some time afterwards the widow married the servant-lad, but one day she discovered by
the scar on his breast that he was her son.   Despair seized the son, but
a monk told him that he and his mother would be forgiven if he could
bring water out of a rock and if a (black ?) sheep should turn white.
Both marvels came about, so his sin was forgiven.   See Gustave
Meyer's introduction to E. Schreck's *Finnische Märchen* (Weimar,
1887), p. xxv.   Some of the features of the Oedipus legend occur in a
Cyprian tale.   A certain lord has a daughter named Rose.   On the
night of her marriage a phantom appears to the bridegroom and warns

him to have nothing to do with Rose, as she is fated to have a son by her father and to marry her own son. So he divorces her. To escape her destiny Rose causes her father to be murdered ; but an apple-tree grows from his grave, Rose eats of the apples, and becomes pregnant. When her child is born, she stabs it in the breast, puts it in a box, and flings it into the sea. The child is picked up by a ship, and when he has grown to manhood, he comes to Rose's country and marries her. One day she recognises him by the scar on his breast, and in despair flings herself from a high place and dies. See L. Constans, *La légende d'Oedipe étudiée dans l'antiquité, au moyen-âge et dans les temps modernes* (Paris, 1881), p. 110 *sq.* An Albanian story combines features of the Oedipus and the Perseus legends. A certain king, who had two daughters, was warned that he would be killed by a grandson yet unborn. So he flung into the sea all his daughters' children as fast as they were born. However the third man-child was washed ashore alive and found by herdsmen who brought him up. When he was twelve years old it happened that in his father's kingdom there appeared a monster, who caused all the water to dry up, and it was foretold that the monster would not allow the water to flow till he had eaten up the king's daughter. Hence the princess was exposed to the monster, but rescued by the king's grandson, who killed it with his club. So the lad received the princess to wife, and at the marriage he accidentally killed the king by throwing his club. Thus the prophecy was fulfilled. (It is not said whether the princess whom the lad marries was his mother or his aunt.) See J. G. v. Hahn, *Griechische und albanesische Märchen*, 2. p. 114 *sq.* (No. 98). In the Middle Ages Judas Iscariot became the hero of a tale very like that of Oedipus. The story appears in 'The Golden Legend' ; it is doubtless the work of a monk or clerk who had read the Oedipus legend. See L. Constans, *op. cit.* p. 95 *sqq.* Cp. Comparetti, *Edipo e la mitologia comparata* (Pisa, 1867), p. 83 *sqq.* On the Oedipus legend in antiquity see (in addition to the works of Constans and Comparetti) F. W. Schneidewin, 'Die Sage von Ödipus,' *Abhandlungen d. könig. Gesell. d. Wissenschaften zu Göttingen*, 5 (1851 and 1852), pp. 159-206 ; E. Bethe, *Thebanische Heldenlieder* (Leipzig, 1891), pp. 1 *sqq.*, 158 *sqq.*

5. 10. **Homer —— says in the Odyssey** etc. See *Od.* xi. 271 *sqq.*

5. 11. **the mother of his children was Euryganea.** According to Pherecydes (quoted by a scholiast on Euripides, *Phoenissae*, 53) Oedipus had two sons, Phrastor and Laonytus, by his mother Jocasta (or Epicaste, as Homer calls her, *Od.* ix. 271) ; but he afterwards married Euryganea, daughter of Periphas, by whom he had two daughters Antigone and Ismene, and two sons Eteocles and Polynices. Pisander also stated that after Jocasta's death Oedipus married Eurygane (*sic*), by whom he had the four children (Schol. on Euripides, *Phoenissae*, 1760). The common legend, however, was that Antigone, Ismene, Eteocles and Polynices, were the offspring of Oedipus by his mother Jocasta (Euripides, *Phoenissae*, 55 *sqq.* ; Apollodorus, iii. 5. 8 ; Diodorus, iv. 64 ; Hyginus, *Fab.* 67).

5. 11. the poem they call the Oedipodia. This poem is said to have been composed by Cinaethon (see ii. 3. 9 note) in the third or fourth Olympiad. But the author's name and the date and place of the composition of the poem appear to be very uncertain. See L. Constans, *La légende d'Oedipe*, p 13 ;' E. Bethe, *Thebanische Heldenlieder*, pp. 1 *sqq.*, 191 *sqq.* ; *Epicorum Graecorum fragmenta*, ed. Kinkel, p. 8 *sq.*

5. 13. at Glisas —— Laodamas killed Aegialeus. See i. 44. 4 ; ix. 8. 6 ; ix. 9. 4 ; ix. 19. 2.

5. 13. Laodamas set out for Illyria etc. He settled among the Illyrian tribe of Encheleans, among whom Cadmus and Harmonia had settled before. See § 3 ; viii. 8. 6 ; Herodotus, v. 61.

5. 14. When the host of Agamemnon on its way to Troy etc. The epitome of Apollodorus, discovered a few years ago in the Vatican, thus describes these events : " Agamemnon was the leader of the whole host, and Achilles was the admiral at the age of fifteen. Not knowing the course to steer for Troy, they landed in Mysia and laid it waste, thinking it was Troy. Telephus, a son of Hercules, was king of the Mysians, and seeing the country laid waste he armed the Mysians, chased the Greeks to their ships, and slew many, and amongst them Thersander son of Polynices, who had stood his ground. But when Achilles rushed at him, Telephus did not wait for him but fled pursued by Achilles, and getting entangled in a vine-shoot he received a spear-thrust in the thigh. Departing from Mysia, the Greeks put to sea, and a furious storm coming on they were parted from each other and returned to their own countries. By reason of the return of the Greeks it is said that the war lasted twenty years ; for it was in the second year after the rape of Helen that the Greeks set out on their expedition ; and after their return from Mysia eight years elapsed before they again assembled at Argos and proceeded to Aulis " (*Epitoma Vaticana ex Apollodori Bibliotheca*, ed. R. Wagner (Leipsic, 1891), p. 63 ; Apollodorus, ed. R. Wagner, p. 193). Dictys Cretensis also says (ii. 9) that eight years elapsed between the first and the second expedition of the Greeks against Troy. He describes the Mysian campaign in detail (ii. 1-7). Cp. Philostratus, *Heroica*, ii. § 28 *sqq.* ; Schol. on Homer, *Il.* i. 59, ed. Bekker. The combat of Telephus with Achilles in the plain of Caicus was represented by Scopas in the eastern gable of the temple of Athena at Tegea (viii. 45. 7 note). Cp. i. 4. 6.

5. 14. His tomb —— consists of a stone etc. For other examples of tombs in market-places see note on i. 43. 3.

5. 15. Peneleus was killed by Eurypylus. This is mentioned also by Dictys Cretensis (iv. 17). Homer only says that he was slightly wounded by Pulydamas (*Iliad*, xvii. 597 *sqq.*)

5. 15. The Furies of Laius and Oedipus. There was a sanctuary of the Furies of Laius and Oedipus at Sparta. It was founded by the Aegid tribe in obedience to an oracle, because their children died young. The remedy was effectual, for the children who were afterwards born survived. See Herodotus, iv. 149. When the Furies are thus spoken of as attaching themselves to a particular person, they seem to be the avenging spirits who fulfil his curses. Cp. viii. 34. 4 ; Homer, *Iliad*,

xxi. 412 ; Sophocles, *Oedipus Colon.* 1299 ; and Stein's note on Herodotus, *l.c.*

6. 1. They were defeated by the Athenians etc.   See Herodotus, vi. 107.

6. 1. They sustained a second reverse etc.   This was at the great battle of Plataea in 479 B.C.   See Herodotus, ix. 67.

6. 3. a victory over the Athenians at Delium.   This battle was fought in 424 B.C.   See Thucydides, iv. 93-101.

6. 4. They were defeated at Corinth and Coronea.   These defeats took place in 394 B.C.   See iii. 9. 13 ; Xenophon, *Hellenica,* iv. 2. 9 *sqq.* ; *id.,* iv. 3. 10 *sqq.* ; Plutarch, *Agesilaus,* 18 *sq.*

6. 4. the Phocian, or —— Sacred War.   See x. 2 *sq.*

6. 5. I have already said etc.   See i. 25. 3.

6. 5. the Thebans contrived to overpower the garrison etc. Pausanias certainly seems to imply that the Thebans succeeded in capturing the Macedonian garrison who held the Cadmea.   Here, however, he is wrong, for we learn from the historians that the Thebans merely besieged the garrison in the Cadmea, surrounding it with palisades and ditches, and that when the Macedonian army stormed the city it was joined by the garrison.   See the references in the following note.

6. 5. God foreshadowed to them etc.   The prodigies which were said to have preceded and announced the destruction of Thebes by Alexander are described by Diodorus (xvii. 10) and Aelian (*Var. hist.* xii. 57).   They tell the story of the spiders' webs somewhat differently from Pausanias.   According to Aelian, a spider wove its web over the face of the image of Demeter.   According to Diodorus, the spider's web in the sanctuary of Demeter was as large as a cloak and resplendent in all the hues of the rainbow.   Thebes was destroyed by Alexander in 335 B.C. (Arrian, *Anabasis,* i. 7 *sq.* ; Diodorus, xvii. 8-14 ; Plutarch, *Alexander,* 11 ; Justin, xi. 2-4).

6. 6. Sulla engaged them in the war etc.   On the siege and sack of Athens by Sulla, see i. 20. 4-7 ; Plutarch, *Sulla,* 12-14 ; Appian, *Mithrid.* 30-39.

7. 1. The Thebans —— were afterwards restored by Cassander. Cp. iv. 27. 10 ; vii. 6. 9 ; ix. 3. 6.   Thebes was restored in the summer of 315 B.C., twenty years after its destruction by Alexander.   The greater part of the walls was built by the Athenians, who wore garlands on their heads in token of joy.   See Diodorus, xvii. 53 *sq.* ; Plutarch, *Praecept. gerend. reipub.* xvii. 9 ; Clinton, *Fasti Hellenici,* 2.³ p. 186.   Some years afterwards Thebes revolted from Demetrius, who besieged and captured it (Plutarch, *Demetrius,* 39, 40 ; Diodorus, frag. xxi. 14).   Diodorus says that Demetrius "having destroyed the walls by siege operations carried the city by storm " (πολιορκίᾳ τὰ τείχη καθελὼν τὴν πόλιν κατὰ κράτος εἷλε).   From this statement Prof. von Wilamowitz-Moellendorff appears to infer (*Hermes,* 26 (1891), p. 203 *sq.*) that Demetrius razed the whole circuit of the walls to the ground.   But as, in Diodorus's narrative, the destruction of the walls precedes the storming of the city, it would seem that Demetrius merely made a breach in the wall with siege-engines, then stormed the breach and captured the city. But no sure inference can be based on this passage of Diodorus, as it is not merely a fragment but an abridgment, and an ungrammatical abridgment to boot. Plutarch mentions the huge unwieldy battering-engine employed by Demetrius, but he does not say that Demetrius razed the walls to the ground.

7. 2. **he flung Olympias to the infuriated Macedonians** etc. Cp. Diodorus, xix. 51, and Justin, xiv. 6, who implies that she was not stoned but stabbed to death. Cp. Paus. i. 11. 4.

7. 3. **Alexander invoked the aid of Demetrius** etc. See Plutarch, *Demetrius*, 36 ; Diodorus, xxi. 7.

7. 4. **when Sulla invaded Boeotia** etc. The whole of Boeotia, with the exception of Thespiae, had declared for Mithridates. But as soon as Sulla entered the country, the Boeotians, with a few exceptions, shifted over to the side of the Romans. "Even the great city of Thebes," says Appian, "which had with great fickleness chosen to side with Mithridates instead of with Rome, went over to Sulla with even greater celerity and without striking a blow" (*Mithrid.* 29 *sq.*)

7. 5. **he took away half their territory** etc. Cp. Appian, *Mithrid.* 54 ; and for Sulla's mode of raising money by plundering the Greek temples, see also Plutarch, *Sulla*, 12. Sulla sent an agent to the Amphictyons at Delphi with a request that they would be so good as to let him have the treasures of the god, as he would either guard them better or make good what he spent. When the message was brought to the Amphictyons in council, some of them said they heard the twangling of a lyre in the sanctuary. This was reported to Sulla in the hope of working on his superstitious fears ; but the Roman general wrote in reply that the music was a clear proof how pleased the god was to give his treasures, so they might send them without scruple.

7. 6. **the lower city —— was all deserted** etc. Cp. viii. 33. 2. Even in Strabo's time, about a hundred and fifty years before Pausanias, Thebes was not so large as a respectable village (Strabo, ix. p. 403). The description of Thebes by Dio Chrysostom, who died about the time Pausanias was born, agrees with that of Pausanias. Dio says that the Cadmea was inhabited but the rest of the city deserted ; in the old market-place one solitary image stood among the ruins (*Or.* vii. vol. 1. p. 136, ed. Dindorf). It is interesting to compare an earlier description of Thebes contained in a geographical work which is commonly ascribed to Dicaearchus, the contemporary of Aristotle, but which seems to be the work of a later writer named Heraclides, the Critic, who wrote between 260 and 230 B.C. This writer says: "Thence (from Plataea) to Thebes the distance is 80 furlongs. The road is level and through a plain the whole way. The city stands in the middle of Boeotia with a circumference of 70 furlongs. It is altogether flat, its shape is round, the soil is a dark loam. In spite of its antiquity the streets are new, because, as the histories tell us, the city has been thrice razed to the ground on account of the overbearing and insolent character of the people. It is excellent for the breeding of horses, it is all well watered, green, and with a deep soil, and it has more gardens than any other

city in Greece. From the Cadmea water is brought down in underground channels, which were made of old, they say, by Cadmus. So much for the city. The inhabitants are high-spirited and wonderfully sanguine. They are bold, insolent, haughty, ready to give a blow, equally indifferent to a stranger and a fellow-countryman, despisers of all right. In disputes about bargains they resort not to arguments but to audacity and blows, transferring to legal pleadings the violence which is appropriate to the contests of athletes. Hence their lawsuits last thirty years at the least. For if a man mentions such a thing (*i.e.* complains of the law's delays) in public and does not immediately depart from Boeotia but remains the least time in the city, he is very soon waylaid and assassinated by the persons who have no wish that suits should be concluded. Murders are perpetrated among them on the most trivial pretexts. Such are the men as a whole, though among them are to be found scattered some worthy men, high-minded, deserving of all esteem. Their women, in respect of stature, gait, and proportion, are the comeliest and prettiest women in Greece. Sophocles attests it :

> You speak to me of seven-gated Thebes,
> Where alone mortal women give birth to gods.

On their heads they wear a hood which covers the whole face as with a mask, for only the eyes peep through, all the other parts of the face are hidden by the hood. They all wear white dresses. Their hair is yellow and is fastened up on the crown of the head. Their shoes are plain, not high, of a purple colour and low, but laced so that the feet are seen almost bare. The manners of the women in society are rather Sicyonian than Boeotian. Their voice is pleasing, but that of the men is harsh and deep. The city is one of the best places to pass the summer in, for it has plenty of cool water and gardens. Besides it is breezy and has a verdant aspect. It has fruit also and abounds in summer wares. But it lacks wood and is one of the worst of places to winter in, on account of the rivers and the winds ; for snow falls and there is much mud " ([Dicaearchus,] *Descriptio Graeciae*, i. 12-22, in *Geographi Graeci Minores*, ed. Müller, 1. p. 102 *sqq.* ; also in *Frag. Histor. Graec.* ed. Müller, 2. p. 258 *sq.*) That the work from which this passage is extracted was written by one Heraclides the Critic appears from a reference to it by Apollonius (*Histor. Mirab.* 19 ; cp. [Dicaearchus,] *op. cit.* ii. 5). Cp. Müller's remarks in *Geogr. Gr. Min.* I. p. li. *sqq.*, and in *Frag. Hist. Gr.* 2. p. 230 *sqq.* ; E. Fabricius, *Theben*, p. 13 ; von Wilamowitz-Moellendorff, in *Hermes*, 26 (1891), p. 206. To complete our picture of ancient Thebes, as it is painted for us by classical writers, it must be added that there was a dunghill at every door. At least so says the comic poet Eubulus, whose verses are preserved by Athenaeus (x. p. 417 d).

8. 1. **the ruins of Potniae.** Potniae would seem to have been near the site of *Tachi*, a modern village standing in an undulating district about a mile to the south of Thebes. The brook Dirce which flows past the western side of the Cadmea (the modern Thebes) takes its rise in several springs near *Tachi*. The main source is called *Kephalari ;*

it waters the surrounding gardens and maize-fields. A smaller spring named *Pegadaki* rises in a tract of marshy meadows and is easily distinguished by a tall willow that grows beside it. Many ancient blocks lie near this spring ; the large basin of the *Kephalari* spring and another water basin in *Tachi* are built of ancient blocks. A third spring flows from the roof of a small grotto and is thought to furnish the best water in the district. It is called the Cadi's Spring. The village of *Tachi* is not on the direct road from Plataea to Thebes, but is seen among fields a little to the left of the road as you approach Thebes.

See H. N. Ulrichs, *Reisen und Forschungen*, 2. p. 12 *sq.* ; Welcker, *Tagebuch*, 2. p. 31 *sq.* ; Bursian, *Geogr.* 1. p. 130 ; Baedeker,[3] p. 183 ; *Guide-Joanne*, 2. p. 11 *sq.*

8. 1. they throw sucking pigs into —— the halls. Compare Clement of Alexandria, *Protrept.* ii. § 17, p. 14 *sq.* ed. Potter ; Lobeck, *Aglaophamus*, p. 827 *sqq.* The ceremony is described in detail in a scholium on Lucian (*Dial. Meretr.* ii. 1), which was first published by Prof. E. Rohde (*Rheinisches Museum*, N. F. 25 (1870), p. 548 *sqq.*) From this scholium, taken in connexion with the present passage of Pausanias and the passage of Clement of Alexandria referred to above, we learn that at the festival of the Thesmophoria it was customary to throw pigs, cakes of dough, and branches of pine-trees into " the chasms of Demeter and Proserpine," which seem to have been sacred vaults or caverns. In these caverns or vaults there were said to be serpents, which guarded the caverns and consumed most of the flesh of the pigs and dough-cakes that were thrown in. Afterwards—apparently at the next annual festival—the decayed remains of the pigs, the cakes, and the pine-branches were fetched by women called ' drawers,' who after observing rules of ceremonial purity for three days, went down into the vaults, and frightening away the serpents by clapping their hands brought up the remains and placed them on the altar. Whoever got a piece of the decayed flesh and cakes, and sowed it with the seed-corn in his fields, was thought to be sure of a good crop. This curious rite was explained by the following tale. At the moment when Pluto carried off Proserpine, a swineherd named Eubuleus was herding his swine on the spot, and his herd was engulfed in the chasm down which Pluto had vanished with Proserpine. Accordingly at the Thesmophoria pigs were annually thrown into vaults to commemorate the disappearance of the swine of Eubuleus. Cp. C. Robert, in *Hermes*, 20 (1885), p. 367 *sqq.* ; Andrew Lang, in *Nineteenth Century*, April 1887 ; *id.*, *Myth, ritual, and religion*, 2. p. 268 *sq.* ; *The Golden Bough*, 2. p. 44 *sqq.* In the sanctuary of Demeter and the Infernal Deities at Cnidus Sir Charles Newton discovered a chamber which may have been one of the halls (*megara*) referred to by Pausanias and the scholiast on Lucian. It contained bones of pigs and marble effigies of pigs. See Sir C. T. Newton, *Discoveries at Halicarnassus*, etc., 2. p. 383 *sq.* ; *id.*, *Travels and discoveries in the Levant*, 2. p. 180 *sq.*

8. 1. next year those pigs <appear> at Dodona. If we accept an emendation which Lobeck proposed (*Aglaophamus*, p. 831) of a passage in Clement of Alexandria (*Protrept.* ii. 17, p. 14, ed. Potter, μεγάροις ζῶντας χοίρους ἐμβάλλουσι for μεγαρίζοντες χοίρους ἐκβάλλουσι), it would seem that the pigs were thrown alive into the halls or vaults (*megara*), and Pausanias apparently says that the pigs were supposed to reappear alive a year afterwards at Dodona. See, however, the Critical Note on this passage, vol. i. p. 602. In Yucatan human victims were thrown alive into wells in the belief that they would reappear on the third day (Diego de Landa, *Relation des choses de Yucatan* (Paris, 1864), p. 169).

8. 1. **Dionysus the Goat-shooter** etc.   On the goat in relation to Dionysus, see Fr. Lenormant, in *Gazette archéologique*, 2 (1876), p. 104 sq.; *The Golden Bough*, 1. p. 326 *sqq.*; *id.*, 2. p. 34 *sqq.*   With the tradition that a goat had been substituted for a boy in the sacrifices at this temple we may compare an Attic tradition that to stay a plague or a famine an oracle had commanded that a girl should be sacrificed by her father to the Munychian Artemis; accordingly a man volunteered to sacrifice his daughter, but instead he sacrificed a goat dressed up as a girl.   See Eustathius on Homer, *Iliad*, ii. 732 (p. 331); Apostolius, vii. 10; *Paroemiogr. Graeci*, ed. Leutsch et Schneidewin, 2. p. 402. On substitutes for human victims among the ancient Greeks and Italians, see Leist, *Graeco-Italische Rechtsgeschichte*, p. 268 *sqq.*   Mr. Bather suggests that in the local tradition at Potniae of the murder of the priest of Dionysus and the subsequent sacrifice of boys, we have a reminiscence of a custom of annually slaying the priest of Dionysus as a representative of the god (*Journal of Hellenic Studies*, 14 (1894), p. 260).

8. 2. **the mares —— that drink of this water go mad.** Aelian says that the horses which drank of the Potnian fountain became rabid, adding that Potniae was a place near Thebes; he attributes the same virtue to the water of the Cossinites river in Thrace (*Nat. anim.* xv. 25). It was said that Glaucus, driving in a four-horse car on his way to take part in a chariot-race, watered his mares at the spring; hence in the race they went mad, upset the chariot, and tore him to pieces with their teeth (Philargyrius, on Virgil, *Georg.* iii. 267).   According to another story it was through eating the grass at Potniae that the mares of Glaucus went mad and rent him in pieces (Schol. on Euripides, *Orestes*, 318; *Etymol. Magn. s.v.* Ποτνιάδες, p. 685, line 40 *sqq.*) Cp. Strabo, viii. p. 409. According to Pliny (*Nat. hist.* xxv. 94) the grass at Potniae had the same maleficent effect on asses as on horses. Ctesias says there was in Ethiopia a certain water, red as vermilion, of which all persons who drank went out of their mind (Antigonus, *Histor. Mirab.* 145 (160); Pliny, *Nat. hist.* ii. 9).

8. 3. **here the earth yawned for Amphiaraus.** According to others, the catastrophe happened at Harma (see ix. 19. 4; i. 34. 2). At this sanctuary of Amphiaraus near Thebes oracles were given in dreams to inquirers who slept within the precinct.   The oracle was consulted on behalf of Croesus king of Lydia, who dedicated to Amphiaraus a golden shield and a golden spear, which in the time of

Herodotus were preserved in the temple of Ismenian Apollo at Thebes. Mys, an agent of Mardonius, paid a man to consult the oracle of Amphiaraus at Thebes by sleeping within the sanctuary. No native Theban was allowed to consult the oracle. See Herodotus, i. chs. 47, 49, 52, viii. 134. The oràcle of Amphiaraus at Oropus, which was consulted in the same way (Paus. i. 34. 5), appears to have been transferred to that place from the neighbourhood of Thebes. For Strabo expressly says (viii. p. 404) that the oracle of Amphiaraus was brought to Oropus from Cnopia, in the territory of Thebes. Pausanias does not mention Cnopia, but it is probably the place described by him between Potniae and Thebes. The transference of the oracle to Oropus appears to have taken place between 431 B.C. and 414 B.C. For, in the first place, Herodotus, who wrote soon after 431 B.C., knew of only one oracle of Amphiaraus, and that was at Thebes, as appears plainly from his words (viii. 134). On the other hand, in his lost play *Amphiaraus*, exhibited in 414 B.C., Aristophanes appears to have ridiculed a superstitious man who consulted the oracle of Amphiaraus, and this must have been the oracle at Oropus, for no Athenian could have consulted an oracle at Thebes in 414 B.C., when the Peloponnesian war was raging. It would seem then, that between the time when Herodotus composed his eighth book and the time when Aristophanes wrote his *Amphiaraus, i.e.* some time between 431 and 414 B.C., the oracle was transferred from the neighbourhood of Thebes to Oropus. This is confirmed by the inscriptions found at the sanctuary of Amphiaraus near Oropus; for none of these inscriptions appears to be older than the beginning of the fourth century B.C. See Preller, in *Berichte über die Verhandl. d. kön. sächs. Gesell. d. Wissen. zu Leipzig*, Philolog. histor. Classe, 4 (1852), p. 166 *sqq.*; von Wilamowitz-Moellendorff, in *Hermes*, 21 (1886), p. 104 *sq.*; and especially W. Dittenberger, *Observationes de sacris Amphiarai Thebanis et Oropiis* (Halle, 1888).

8. 4. **Thebes.** Thebes stood on the north side of a range of low hills which extends from the foot of Mount Helicon, near Thespiae, on the west, to near Tanagra on the east, separating the northern from the southern plain of Boeotia. The line of hills, which is at its lowest in the neighbourhood of Thebes, is intersected by the channels of streams which flow toward the northern plain but mostly dry up in summer. By the deep beds of these streams the ridge is divided into a series of separate heights or plateaus. One such plateau is occupied by the modern town of Thebes (*Thivae*), which undoubtedly stands on the site of the Cadmea or acropolis of ancient Thebes. On its western side the plateau is bounded by the valley of the *Plakiotissa* stream, the ancient Dirce. On its eastern side it is bounded by a deep winding depression or gully (the 'hollow way' mentioned by Arrian, *Anabasis*, i. 8. 3), through which water flows northward after rain. The plateau slopes gently upward from north to south, reaching its highest point (208 feet above the level of the northern plain) near its southern extremity, where it is connected by a saddle with the somewhat higher heights to the south. Over this saddle the modern road from Athens now enters Thebes. The sloping sides of the Cadmea are

nowhere high and hardly anywhere precipitous, unless they can be said to be so at the south-western corner, above the Dragon's Cave (see note on ix. 10. 5). Some remains of the ancient walls of the Cadmea, consisting of a few blocks, were visible as late as 1890 at the northern end of the plateau, a little north of a conspicuous mediaeval tower; but on my last visit to Thebes in 1895 I sought for them in vain. The remains at this point were somewhat more extensive when Leake visited Thebes in 1805. He says : " The only undoubted relic which I can discover of the walls of Hellenic Thebes now forms the lowest part of the northern tower, just above the plain. [By 'the northern tower' Leake means the square mediaeval tower, which is a conspicuous feature at the north end of Thebes. The remaining blocks of the wall which I saw in 1890 were quite separate from, and a little to the north of, this tower.] About 30 yards of the ancient work are still traceable, and four or five courses are visible, if courses they can be called, the masonry of which, like that of Tiryns, is formed of very roughly-hewn masses of stone, originally fitted in the intervals with smaller stones, which have mostly fallen out. This wall is not straight, but forms a curve. Its masonry, its curved form, but above all its thickness, which is more than 28 feet, seem to prove that in antiquity it may vie with Mycenae, or even with that of the Τιρύνθιον πλίνθευμα ['Tirynthian brickwork'], which it most resembles " (*Northern Greece*, 2. p. 226). In 1895 I found at the opposite or southern end of the Cadmea a small piece of wall 3 feet high and 6 feet long which may have been part of the fortification-wall. It is on the edge of the rock, at the highest part of the hill, a little to the east of the point where the road from Athens enters Thebes. At present this fragment acts as a supporting wall to the superincumbent soil.

The Cadmea was supplied with water from Mt. Cithaeron by means of a tunnel. The mouth of the tunnel, a few feet wide, can be seen in the low hill immediately to the south of the Cadmea. From this point the water was conveyed, in Frankish times, across the intervening saddle to the Cadmea by means of an aqueduct, twenty arches of which are still standing immediately to the left of the high-road as you enter Thebes from Athens. Whether in antiquity the water was conveyed across the saddle in an aqueduct or in underground pipes, we cannot tell. The modern town of Thebes consists chiefly of two long streets running from north to south, intersected by shorter cross-streets. Viewed from any side the town presents a pleasing aspect owing to the trees with which it abounds ; some of the streets have rows of trees planted on each side. The distant views, too, from the town are superb ; the eye ranges over a magnificent circle of mountains of fine and varied outlines which bound the horizon on all sides. Conspicuous among them are Cithaeron on the south, Helicon on the west, the massive Parnassus far away on the north-west, the mountain of the Sphinx more to the north, Mount Ptous due north, and the bare rugged Mount Hypatus on the north-east.

But ancient Thebes seems not to have been confined to the low hill or plateau occupied by the modern town, but to have extended over the neighbouring hills or plateaus both to the east and to the west. Its

ANCIENT THEBES

according to E. Fabricius

Ancient names and line of ancient walls in red.
Modern names and modern town in black

500   0   500   1000   1500 SCALE FEET
100 50 0 100 200 300 400 500 METERS

eastern boundary might naturally be supposed to be the broad and deep bed of the Ismenus or river of *Hagios Joannes* (*St. John*), as it is now called ; but excavations made by Mr. Kalopais in 1892 appear to have revealed the remains of fortification-walls at a distance of from 300 to 350 metres to the east of the Ismenus. The remains are about 6 feet high and 10 feet thick, and are built of regularly-hewn blocks of a soft whitish conglomerate. They include the foundations of a semicircular tower measuring about 20 feet in diameter. On the other side of the present town, to the west of the Dirce, a sort of irregular plateau rises to a considerable height. It begins from the bed of the Dirce and slopes up westward till it attains at the south-west corner a height a good deal greater than that of the Cadmea. On the south and west it ends in high steep edges, being bounded on these sides by deep fissures. On the north it slopes much more gradually to the plain, and here too it is rent by deep fissures or depressions. This plateau would seem to have been included within the ancient city. The evidence for thinking so consists of (1) the ancient potsherds with which the plateau, especially at its edges, is strewn, and (2) some scanty remains of ancient walls at its western end.

(1) The first to call special attention to the potsherds as evidence of the extent of the ancient city was Mr. Fabricius. He was struck with the remains of what he regarded as fragments of roof-tiles of the good Greek period, well fired and with a black or red glaze on the outside. Tiles of this sort he traced along the southern edge of the plateau for a distance of nearly 1000 paces, above the little valley which joins the valley of the Dirce not far from the spring of Ares (*Paraporti*). The traces led him to the south-west corner of the plateau, where it is connected by a saddle with the hills lying to the west. From this point northward along the western edge of the plateau, which is here bounded by a small valley or deep fissure parallel to the bed of the Dirce, Mr. Fabricius traced the remains of the supposed roof-tiles for a distance of about 900 paces till they disappeared in the cultivated ground. The existence and position of these tiles he explains by supposing that the ancient city-walls ran along the southern and western edges of the plateau ; that they were built, like the walls of some other ancient cities (see vol. 4. p. 205) of sun-dried bricks and roofed with tiles of baked clay; and that when the walls had fallen the sun-dried bricks crumbled away, but the roof tiles, being of baked earthenware, remained where they fell. This explanation has been questioned by Prof. von Wilamowitz-Moellendorff, who examined the site in 1890 and found that in the north-west part of the site indicated in Mr. Fabricius's plan the tiles extended, not in a narrow line, as they must have done had they been merely the remains of the city-wall, but in a stripe over 300 yards broad. He also found tiles of the same sort 200 paces to the south of the Cadmea, on the way to *Tachi*. In 1895 I examined the western plateau for myself. On its southern and western edges I found a great many fragments of thick pottery, but none which I could identify as roof-tiles. Many of the potsherds were painted, and were therefore presumably *not* roof-tiles. Moreover I observed many potsherds, some

of them thick, quite away from the edge of the plateau, low down in its eastern part, towards the Dirce. Thus the existence of these potsherds, though it shows that the ancient city extended over the plateau to the west of the Dirce, does not enable us to trace with any certainty the line of the walls.

(2) The evidence of the potsherds is confirmed, as has been indicated, by some scanty remains of walls at the western edge of the plateau. Here Mr. Fabricius found many large squared blocks of limestone lying amongst the vineyards and fields for a distance of about 160 paces on both sides of the old road which led from Thebes to Thespiae and Lebadea. As the ground is here soft, a wall of unbaked clay would need a solid foundation or socle of stone. Further, at the south-western and highest point of the plateau some peasants, digging between 1885 and 1888, partially exposed a foundation constructed of massive blocks of yellowish limestone. Mr. Fabricius, who saw the foundation in 1888, conjectured that it belonged to a tower which may have flanked a gateway at this point. This foundation, of which, according to Mr. Kalopais, very little was left in 1892, seems now to have almost or wholly disappeared. At least in 1895 I observed on the edge of the plateau, just beyond the hollow in which Mr. Fabricius supposes the gate to have stood, nothing but a block or two (as it seemed) of a soft crumbling stone, the native stone of the plateau. On the other hand, I found in a dip on the western edge of the plateau, at some distance north of the supposed south-western gate, a single course of squared blocks of pebble conglomerate running north and south for 15 feet. This line of stones, which had apparently been exposed by a recent excavation, may be a remnant of the western wall of the city. Through the dip in which the remains lie a road may very well have come up from the deep earthy gully or valley which bounds the plateau on the west. It is here that Mr. Fabricius would place the Neistan gate (see below, p. 37). Some 30 yards north of this point another excavation had revealed what looked to me like a few hewn blocks of the soft crumbling stone in a line with the course of conglomerate blocks. A little farther to the north the plateau begins to descend in a gentle slope to the plain. From the point where the slope begins, the potsherds cease to occur with the same frequency as before, though some pieces may be found here and there.

Mr. Fabricius further holds that the line of the ancient walls on the opposite or eastern side of the city can be traced by the fragments of roof-tiles all along the western edge of the Ismenus ravine, from a point 150 paces north-east of the church of St. Luke as far as the depression through which the modern high-road goes to Chalcis. It is true that a large quantity of potsherds lies strewn about in the fields on the west bank of the Ismenus, but the fragments are by no means confined to the edge of the ravine. On the contrary, so far as my observation goes, the whole ground between the Ismenus and the 'hollow way' which bounds the present town on the east is thickly strewn with potsherds, more thickly indeed than the western plateau. Thus the evidence of the pottery goes to show that the ancient city certainly extended eastward as far as the Ismenus; but it does not prove that the city-wall on this side ran along the western edge of the Ismenus ravine. In point of fact, as we have seen, Mr. Kalopais seems to have discovered remains of the city-walls at some distance to the east of the Ismenus. As estimated by Mr. Fabricius, the circuit of ancient Thebes measured between 7000 and 8000 metres, or from 4½ to 5 miles, which agrees fairly with the statement of the geographer Dionysius that the circumference of the city was 43 Greek furlongs or about 5 miles (*Geographi Graeci Minores*, ed. Müller, 1. p. 241). On the other hand, Dicaearchus or the writer who passes under his name estimated the circumference of Thebes at 70 Greek furlongs or about 8 miles. See note on ix. 7. 6.

That the earliest city did not occupy the whole of the area indicated may be taken as certain. Probably it was at first confined to the Cadmea, from which it would naturally expand in course of time to the ravine of the Ismenus on the east and the opener valley of the Dirce on the west. At what time it extended its borders over the Dirce to the western plateau, one cannot say with certainty; but we may conjecture that the extension took place in 457 B.C., for it is recorded by Diodorus (xi. 81) that in that year the Lacedaemonians, having a large force in Boeotia, enlarged the circuit of Thebes, with the view of strengthening it and rendering it more of a counterpoise to the power of Athens. Certainly the extension would seem to have taken place before the time of Euripides, for in a recently-discovered fragment of Euripides's play *Antiope* Hermes is made to speak of the Dirce as flowing *through* the city (*Hermathena*, No. 17 (1891), p. 47).

See Wheler, *Journey*, p. 331 *sqq.*; Leake, *Northern Greece*, 2. p. 218 *sqq.*; Dodwell, *Tour*, 1. p. 262 *sq.*; Mure, *Journal*, 1. p. 252 *sqq.*; Welcker, *Tagebuch*, 2. p. 26 *sqq.*; Ulrichs, *Reisen und Forschungen*, 2. p. 3 *sqq.*; Forchhammer, *Topographia Thebarum Heptapylarum* (Kiel, 1854); Vischer, *Erinnerungen*, p. 562 *sqq.*; Bursian, *Geogr.* 1. p. 224 *sqq.*; Baedeker,[3] p. 180 *sqq.*; *Guide-Joanne*, 2. p. 9 *sqq.*; E. Fabricius, *Theben* (Friburg in Baden, 1890), p. 1 *sqq.*; von Wilamowitz - Moellendorff, 'Die sieben Thore Thebens,' *Hermes*, 26 (1891), p. 191 *sqq.*; Πρακτικὰ τῆς ἀρχαιολογικῆς Ἑταιρίας, 1892, pp. 41-46; P. Brandt, *Von Athen zum Tempethal* (Gütersloh, 1893), pp. 23-31.

In 1886-1888 an ancient graveyard was discovered and partly excavated about three-quarters of a mile (1200 metres) west of the present town of Thebes, on both sides of the old road to Lebadea. In the graves were found skeletons, vases of local Boeotian manufacture, vases with geometrical decorations in the 'Dipylum' style, numerous bronze clasps of various forms, bracelets, necklaces, and needles, iron knives and spear-points, gems and pastes. The vases of local Boeotian manufacture seem to belong to the seventh century B.C. See Boehlau, ' Böotische Vasen,' *Jahrbuch des archäolog. Instituts*, 3 (1888), pp. 325-364.

8. 4. seven gates. Lists of the famous seven gates of Thebes are given by Aeschylus (*Seven against Thebes*, 375 *sqq.*), Euripides (*Phoenissae*, 1104 *sqq.*), Statius (*Theb.* viii. 353 *sqq.*), and Apollodorus (iii. 6. 6.) Compare Nonnus, *Dionys.* v. 67 *sqq.*; Hyginus, *Fab.* 69.

There is some discrepancy as to the names of several gates, as will be
seen by the following table.

Pausanias	Aeschylus	Euripides	Apollodorus	Statius
Electran	Electran	Electran	Electran	Electran
Proetidian	Proetidian	Proetidian	Proetidian	Proetidian
Homoloidian	Homoloidian	Homoloidian	Homoloidian	Homoloidian
Ogygian	Seventh gate	Ogygian	Ogygian	Ogygian
Neistan	Neistan	Neistan	Oncaidian	Neitan
Hypsistan	Borraean	Seventh gate	Hypsistan	Hypsistan
Crenaean	Gate of Athena Onca	Crenaean	Crenidian	Dircaean

Nonnus (*l.c.*) names only two gates, the Electran and Oncaean.
Hyginus (*l.c.*) says that Amphion named the seven gates after his seven
daughters, who were Neaera, Cleodoxe, Astymone, Astycratia, Chias,
Ogygia, and Chloris. The only three gates of which the situations can
be approximately determined are the Electran, Proetidian, and Neistan
or Neitan.

(1) *The Electran gate.* Pausanias says (§ 7) that coming from
Plataea you entered Thebes by the Electran gate. Hence the Electran
gate must be the one which Arrian describes as leading to Eleutherae
and Attica (*Anabasis*, i. 7. 9). This is confirmed by Euripides; for
in his play the *Bacchae* (*v.* 780 *sqq.*) Pentheus king of Thebes, hearing
that the Bacchanals are at Hysiae and Erythrae on Mount Cithaeron,
orders his army to assemble at the Electran gate in order to march
against them. Again, in the *Suppliants* of the same poet (*v.* 651 *sqq.*)
the messenger watches the battle between the Thebans and Athenians
from a tower at the Electran gate; which seems to show that the road
from Athens, by which Euripides would naturally suppose the
Athenians to have approached the city, entered Thebes by the
Electran gate. Hence the Electran gate was probably at the
entrance to the 'hollow way' or gully at the south-eastern foot of the
Cadmea. The road from Athens used to enter the modern town at
this point; but the new road is carried higher up on an embankment
a little to the west of the old road. Leake, however, proposed to place
the Electran gate about a mile south of the modern town, at a place
where he observed some remains of ancient Greek walls and an oblong
quadrangular well or pit excavated in the rock.

(2) *The Proetidian gate.* The road from Thebes to Chalcis led
through the Proetidian gate (see ix. 18. 1). Hence the gate must have
been at the north-east side of the city, perhaps somewhere on the left
bank of the Ismenus. This is confirmed by Aeschylus, who says that
Tydeus took up his position over against the Proetidian gate, but that
the soothsayer would not suffer him to cross the Ismenus (*Seven against
Thebes*, 377 *sq.*) The gate was probably situated on some point of the
road which still leads to Chalcis. The road starts from the north-eastern
extremity of Thebes, and making a great bend to the south descends
into the gully or depression already referred to; it crosses this gully
on a bridge, then bending away round to the north again ascends the
eastern side of the gully, crosses the ridge and plunging into the valley

of the Ismenus, crosses it and then leads north-east past the suburb
of *Hagii Theodori*. Mr. Fabricius would place the Proetidian gate
at the point where the road crosses the ridge between the gully and the
valley of the Ismenus. Prof. von Wilamowitz-Moellendorff holds that
the great bend to the north which the road makes in order to ascend the
eastern side of the gully is modern, and that the old road, after crossing
the bridge, led straight east up the steep slope. Such a road, in fact,
still exists and can be used even by vehicles. This, Prof. von
Wilamowitz-Moellendorff holds, is the old road to Chalcis, and he
would place the Proetidian gate at the point where it crosses the ridge
before descending into the valley of the Ismenus.

(3) *The Neistan or Neitan gate.* Through this gate went the road
to the sanctuary of the Cabiri, to the temple of Cabirian Demeter,
and to Thespiae. See ix. 25. 4 *sq.* ; ix. 26. 6. The situation of
the sanctuary of the Cabiri is now known to have been due west
of Thebes in a small valley formed by two projecting spurs of the
long low chain which divides the southern from the northern plain of
Boeotia. The remains of the temple of Cabirian Demeter lie also
to the west of Thebes, on the old road which leads along the
northern foot of the ridge. This old road also goes to Thespiae.
It starts from the spring of *Paraporti* at the south-western foot of
the Cadmea, ascends the heights to the west of the Dirce, and then
descends into the earthy gully or fissure which Mr. Fabricius supposes to have bounded ancient Thebes on the west. Mr. Fabricius
would place the Neistan gate at the point where this old road cuts the
line of limestone blocks which he regards as remnants of the city-wall
(see above, p. 34). However, it would seem that the Neistan gate
must have been on the eastern, not, as Mr. Fabricius supposes, on the
western side of the Dirce. See note on ix. 25. 1. The modern high-
road to Thespiae and Lebadea starts from the northern end of Thebes
and descending into the northern plain leads westward through the
suburb of *Pyri*. That in antiquity the road took the direction of the
modern high-road is improbable, as the ground must have been swampy
in winter.

The situations of the remaining four gates cannot be identified with
any certainty. Prof. von Wilamowitz-Moellendorff has argued that they
never existed and were merely invented, to suit the exigencies of poetry,
by the author of the ancient epic known as the *Thebaid* (see ix. 9. 5).
His reasons are that (1) though Pausanias enumerates seven gates, in
his actual description of the city he mentions only three ; (2) it is unlikely
that an ancient city would have had so many gates, as every gate is a
source of weakness to the defenders ; (3) there are only three natural
exits from Thebes, namely the roads to Athens, Chalcis, and Lebadea.
It is on this last argument that Prof. von Wilamowitz-Moellendorff
seems chiefly to rely, but little weight can be attached to it, since we
do not know for certain the extent of ground covered by the ancient
city and cannot therefore say how many natural exits it had. And even
if we admit that, as seems probable, the original city was confined to the
Cadmea and its slopes, it might fairly be maintained that the city had

at least one more natural exit than Prof. von Wilamowitz-Moellendorff allows, namely by the valley of the Dirce to the south-west of the Cadmea. To me this exit appears as natural and easy as the one to Athens from the south-east of the Cadmea. Indeed, the professor himself confesses that a gate at this point is quite conceivable. If moreover we hold, as Prof. von Wilamowitz-Moellendorff seems to do, that in antiquity the road to Lebadea and Thespiae led westward from Thebes across the valley of the Dirce, we shall have to admit the possibility of at least five gates to the Cadmea, situated on the north, the north-east, the south-east, the south-west, and the west.

Pausanias asserts (§ 4) that the gates remained to his time. Prof. von Wilamowitz-Moellendorff argues that this could not have been the case, as the walls had been destroyed by Demetrius in 290 B.C. and had never been rebuilt. But whether the walls were actually destroyed by Demetrius or not is very doubtful. See note on ix. 7. 1. If the walls had been destroyed, as Prof. von Wilamowitz-Moellendorff supposes, they must have been restored before 396 A.D., for when Alaric marched through Boeotia in that year Thebes was the only place which escaped his ravages ; the city was so strong that it could only have been taken by a regular siege, and Alaric, impatient to capture Athens, made no attempt on Thebes (Zosimus, v. 5). However, even if the walls were standing when Pausanias visited Thebes, the gates could hardly have been the gates of the prehistoric city, since that city seems to have occupied a much smaller area than the later city. But we may suppose that, whether the walls were standing or not, the local guides and antiquaries would regularly point out to strangers what they regarded as the famous seven gates, or at least the sites of them. It is indeed neither impossible nor even improbable that the tradition of a city-gate should survive long after both gate and walls have disappeared. I suppose there is hardly an old city of any size in Europe which does not retain in the names of some of its streets or lanes the reminiscence of one or more of the gates. In Edinburgh, for example, there is the West Port ; in Glasgow there is the Gallowgate. And even if four out of the seven gates of Thebes had never existed, except in the imagination of poets, the sites where they might be supposed to have once stood would probably be fixed by local antiquaries and shown to the curious. Prof. von Wilamowitz-Moellendorff refers to the house of Desdemona at Venice and the sarcophagus of Julia at Verona. In Carlisle Sir Walter Scott was shown the cell in which Fergus MacIvor was said to have been confined, and the guide was very indignant when Sir Walter smiled.

It is not necessary to do more than mention the view broached by Nonnus (*Dionys.* v. 64 *sqq.*) and since revived by Movers and J. Brandis, that the seven gates of Thebes were connected with the worship of the stars, each gate being dedicated to a planet.

See Leake, *Northern Greece*, 2. p. 238 *sqq.* ; H. N. Ulrichs, *Reisen und Forschungen*, 2. p. 7 *sqq.* ; Bursian, *Geogr.* 2. p. 226 *sq.* ; Baedeker,[3] p. 183 ; *Guide-Joanne*, 2. p. 12 *sq.* ; E. Fabricius, *Theben*, p. 19 *sqq.* ; von Wilamowitz-Moellendorff, ‘Die sieben Thore Thebens,’ *Hermes*, 26 (1891), pp. 191-242 ;

Movers, *Die Phoenizier*, I. p. 642 *sq.* ; J. Brandis, 'Die Bedeutung der sieben Thore Thebens,' *Hermes*, 2 (1867), pp. 259-284 ; K. F. Meyer, 'Die Sieben vor Theben und die chaldäische Woche,' *Zeitschrift für Anthropologie, Ethnologie und Urgeschichte*, 7 (1875), pp. 105-137 ; *id.*, 8 (1876), pp. 1-45, 264-311 ; L. Constans, *La légende d'Oedipe*, p. 69 *sqq.*

8. 5. the Homoloidian. According to the historian Aristodemus the Homoloidian gate was so called "because it was near the Homoloian hero" (or mountain ?). See Schol. on Euripides, *Phoenissae* 1119 διὰ τὸ πλησίον εἶναι τοῦ Ὁμολώου ἥρωος, where we should perhaps read ὄρους for ἥρωος with P. Rabbow : see *Hermes*, 26 (1891), p. 215 *sq.*, and cp. Stephanus Byz. *s.v.* Ὁμόλη. C. Müller reads Ὁμολωοῦ, omitting ἥρωος (*Frag. Hist. Graec.* 3. p. 309). Zeus was worshipped under the title Homoloian in Thebes and other Boeotian cities, and also in Thessaly ; there was also a Homoloian Demeter at Thebes (Suidas and Photius, *Lexicon*, *s.v.* Ὁμολῷος Ζεύς). A small column has been found at Thebes on which is carved a dedication to Homoloian Zeus. The inscription is archaic ; it is anterior to the fourth century, and may belong to the sixth. See *C. I. G. G. S.* I. No. 2456 ; *Bulletin de Corresp. hellénique*, 3 (1879), p. 130 *sqq.* ; Roehl, *I. G. A.* No. 191 ; Roberts, *Greek Epigraphy*, No. 198 ; Collitz, *G. D. I.* I. No. 665. An inscription containing a dedication to Homoloian Zeus has also been found at Hyettus. Games called Homoloia were celebrated at Orchomenus (*C. I. G. G. S.* I. Nos. 3196, 3197); and in Oropus, Tanagra, Orchomenus and Chaeronea, as well as in several Thessalian cities, one of the months was called Homoloian. See *C. I. G. G. S.* I. Nos. 246, 308, 510, 517, 3172, 3301, 3307, 3309, 3312, 3314, 3322, 3353, 3356, 3367, 3374 ; Foucart, in *Bulletin de Corresp. hellénique*, 3 (1879), p. 132. The festival called Homoloia was described by the historian Aristodemus (Schol. on Theocritus, vii. 103).

8. 7. Capaneus —— was struck by a thunderbolt etc. See Euripides, *Phoenissae*, 1172 *sqq.* ; Apollodorus, iii. 6. 7.

9. 1. this war —— was the most memorable. The war of the Seven against Thebes, the subject of Aeschylus's tragedy of that name, is told in prose by Diodorus (iv. 65) and Apollodorus (iii. 6).

9. 1. the war of the Eleusinians etc. See i. 5. 2 ; i. 36. 4 ; i. 38. 3.

9. 1. the war of the Thebans against the Minyans. See ix. 37. 2.

9. 3. a Cadmean victory. The proverb is mentioned by Gregorius Cyprius (iii. 83), Apostolius (ix. 30), and in the lexicons of Suidas and Photius (*s.v.* Καδμεία νίκη).

9. 4. the Epigoni etc. The war of the Epigoni is told by Apollodorus (iii. 7. 2-4) and Diodorus (iv. 66). There was an epic poem on the subject called the *Epigoni* which some ascribed to Homer (Herodotus, iv. 32 ; *Biographi Graeci*, ed. Westermann, p. 42 *sq.*) A scholiast on Aristophanes (*Peace*, 1270) attributes the poem to a certain Antimachus. Mr. Bethe argues that the *Epigoni* was not a separate poem, but merely a part of the *Thebaid* (as to which see § 5). See Bethe, *Thebanische Heldenlieder*, p. 35 *sqq.* Cp. von Wilamowitz-Moellendorff, *Homerische Untersuchungen*, p. 345, note 26.

9. 5. the Thebaid. Callinus —— says etc. The elegiac poet Callinus seems to have flourished in the first half of the seventh century B.C., and as we here learn from Pausanias that the *Thebaid* was known to Callinus and attributed by him to Homer, its date can hardly be later than the eighth century B.C. Mr. Bethe holds that it was composed about the eighth century near Clarus, perhaps at Colophon. See Bethe, *Thebanische Heldenlieder*, p. 145 *sqq.* This early epic must not be confounded with the epic of the same name by Antimachus, a contemporary of Plato. The former was sometimes referred to as the Cyclic *Thebaid* to distinguish it from the latter. Cp. Athenaeus, xi. p. 465 e ; Schol. on Sophocles, *Oed. Col.* 1375. The fragments of both the *Thebaids* are collected by Kinkel, *Epicorum Graecorum fragmenta*, pp. 9 *sqq.*, 275 *sqq.*

10. 1. the dragon which he slew at the fountain. See § 5 note. Cadmus is said to have served Ares eight years as a serf by way of punishment for killing the dragon (Apollodorus, iii. 4. 2 ; Suidas and Photius, *Lexicon, s.v.* Καδμεία νίκη). The legend may be a trace of an old custom of exacting expiation and atonement for the slaughter of a sacred animal. See note on ii. 7. 7. It is remarkable that Apollodorus in relating the legend explains that eight of our years were in those days reckoned as one year. This, like the procession of the Laurel-bearing (see note on § 4), points to the use of a calendar based on an eight-years cycle.

10. 2. a hill —— called Ismenian. This is probably the low hill of *Hagios Loukas* (*St. Luke*), which rises to the south-east of the present town of Thebes, between the gully or 'hollow way' and the ravine of the Ismenus. The hill is seen a little way to the right (east) across a green valley as you enter Thebes by the high-road from Athens. A church of St. Luke, surrounded by a graveyard, stands on the top of the low hill, and probably occupies the site of the temple of Ismenian Apollo. Some large blocks and architectural fragments of white marble which lie near the church, as well as some large blocks of limestone which have been dug up in the graveyard, may be remains of the temple. Bursian, however, would identify the Ismenian hill with the hill farther south, at the eastern foot of which rises the spring of *Hagios Joannes* (*St. John*). See H. N. Ulrichs, *Reisen und Forschungen*, 2. p. 11 ; Bursian, *Geogr.* i. p. 229 ; Baedeker,[3] p. 184 ; *Guide-Joanne*, 2. p. 13 ; Fabricius, *Theben*, p. 22.

In the Berlin Museum there is a bronze statuette of a naked bearded man, with his right hand raised ; on his left thigh is the following inscription : Πτωῖων Μάστος ἀνέθεαν τοῖ Ἰσμηνίοι, "Ptoïon and Mastus dedicated (this statuette) to the Ismenian (god)." The statuette is said to have been found at Chalcis, but the inscription is Boeotian. Probably the statuette was a votive offering dedicated in the temple of the Ismenian Apollo at Thebes. See *C. I. G. G. S.* No. 2455 ; *Bulletin de Corresp. hellénique*, 3 (1879), p. 139 sq. ; Roehl, *I. G. A.* No. 129 ; Roberts, *Greek Epigraphy*, No. 202 ; Collitz, *G. D. I.* 1. No. 1132. The mode of divination practised at the temple of Ismenian Apollo was by observing the appearance of the flame and the ashes at the burnt-offerings. See Sophocles, *Oed. Rex*, 21 (with the scholiast); *id.*, *Antigone*, 1005-1011; Herodotus, viii. 134. The same mode of divination, Herodotus (*l.c.*) tells us, was practised at Olympia. As to this mode of divination by fire, see especially a scholiast on Euripides, *Phoenissae*, 1255-1257. Cp. Bouché-Leclerq, *Histoire de la divination*, i. p. 178 *sqq.*; *id.*, 3. p. 217 *sqq.*

10. 2. the river Ismenus. That the Ismenus was to the east of Thebes appears from a passage in Euripides (*Suppliants*, 383 *sq.*), in which Theseus directs his herald to proceed from Eleusis to Thebes, crossing first the Asopus and then the Ismenus on his way. There can be no doubt that the Ismenus is the stream now called the river of *Hagios Joannes* (*St. John*), which flows in a deep bed a little way to the east of the modern Thebes. Most of the water of the stream is at present diverted into a mill-race which runs on the eastern bank, above the bed of the stream.

10. 2. the Athena by Scopas. Several ancient statues exist which represent Athena as a young maiden, "a kind of Joan of Arc," with a mantle thrown over her in man's fashion, the left hand resting on her hip, the right grasping the lance, the head turned to the side and slightly upwards, in an attitude full of enthusiasm and fiery courage (Müller-Wieseler, *Denkmäler*, 2. pl. xxi. No. 233; *Königliche Museen zu Berlin: Beschreibung der antiken Skulpturen*, No. 73, p. 37 *sq.*) Prof. Furtwängler conjectures that these statues are copies of Scopas's statue of Athena (*Meisterwerke d. griech. Plastik*, p. 527 *sq.*)

10. 2. The image is of the same size as the one at Branchidae etc. See viii. 46. 3 note.

10. 3. Manto's seat. In an ancient vase-painting two women are depicted seated on a stone bench raised on two steps. One of them holds two olive twigs in her hand; the other stretches her hand towards a bearded man, clad in an embroidered robe and holding in his right hand a sceptre, who stands on the spectator's left. On the spectator's right stands a youth holding a bell-shaped helmet in his right hand and two darts in his left. Above this group are Hermes, Athena, and Apollo, the first standing, the two latter seated; all three are looking towards a tripod on the spectator's right. Panofka took the woman with the olive twigs to be Manto seated on her stone bench, with her sister Historis (see Paus. ix. 11. 3), who is pleading for her with Adrastus, the leader of the Epigoni, represented by the bearded man on the left; the young man on the right is Alcmaeon, Manto's lover (Apollodorus, iii. 7. 7); the Apollo is the Ismenian Apollo, with Hermes and Athena who shared his temple on the Ismenian hill. See Th. Panofka, 'Der Mantositz am Ismenion zu Theben,' *Archäologische Zeitung*, 1845, pp. 49-59, with pl. xxviii. As to Manto, see vii. 3. 1 *sq.*; ix. 33. 2.

10. 4. The following custom is still —— observed. The festival of the Laurel-bearing (*Daphnephoria*) is more fully described by Proclus (quoted by Photius, *Bibliotheca*, p. 321, ed. Bekker). He says: "They cover a staff of olive-wood with laurels and many-coloured flowers, and on the top of the staff is fitted a bronze globe, and from it they suspend

smaller globes.   To the middle of the staff they attach <a globe>
smaller than the one at the top, and purple fillets ; the lowest part of
the staff they swathe in a saffron pall.   The globe at the top is meant
to signify the Sun, with which they connect Apollo ; the globe beneath
it signifies the moon, and the small globes, which are fastened on,
signify the stars.   The fillets symbolise the course of the year, and they
make 365 of them.   The procession of the Laurel-bearing is headed by
a boy, whose parents are both alive.   His nearest kinsman bears the
wreathed staff, which they call *Kopo*.   The Laurel-bearer himself
follows grasping the laurel, his hair streaming down ; he wears a golden
crown and is clad in a bright-hued garment that reaches to his feet, and
he is shod with the shoes called *Iphicratides*.   A choir of virgins follows
him holding boughs in token of supplication and singing hymns.   The
procession of the Laurel-bearing is escorted to the sanctuary of the
Ismenian and Galaxian (Chalazian ?) Apollo."   Proclus describes the
Laurel-bearing (*Daphnephoria*) as a Boeotian festival, and from an inscription (*C. I. G.* No. 1595 ; *C. I. G. G. S.* 1. No. 3407) we learn that
at Chaeronea Apollo was worshipped under the title of Laurel-bearer (see
note on ix. 40. 5).   The festival, Proclus tells us, took place every
eighth or, as the Greeks expressed it, every ninth year ; in other words,
seven years elapsed between two successive celebrations.   Thus the
period of the festival was the same as that of the Delphic festival at
which a boy, whose parents were both alive, fetched the laurel from the
sacred laurel-tree at Tempe.   The two festivals may have been closely
alike.   The Delphic festival was explained as an imitation of the
slaughter of the Python by Apollo and the subsequent purification of
the god, the purification having apparently consisted in a year's servitude and the wearing of the laurel.   The resemblance between the two
festivals would be still greater if we supposed that the Laurel-bearing at
Thebes commemorated the slaughter of the dragon by Cadmus and the
subsequent purification of the slayer by servitude and the wearing of the
laurel.   But though Cadmus was said to have served Ares eight years
for slaying the dragon (see note on § 1), there seems to be no direct
evidence to connect that legend with the festival of the Laurel-bearing.
Still the eight years of Cadmus's servitude, compared with the octennial
period of the festival, seem to indicate a connexion between the legend
and the festival.   The traditional origin of the festival, according to
Proclus, was this.   The Aeolians of Arne abandoned that city at
the bidding of an oracle and laid siege to Thebes, which was held
by Pelasgians.   It happened that both sides desired to celebrate a
festival of Apollo ; so they made a truce and cut laurels, the Aeolians
on Mount Helicon and the Pelasgians at the Black River, and they
brought these laurels to Apollo.   But Polematas, the Boeotian leader,
dreamed that a young man gave him a suit of armour and commanded
that they should offer prayers to Apollo every ninth (eighth) year, wearing the laurel.   Two days afterwards Polematas attacked and conquered
the enemy ; so he performed in person the ceremony of the Laurel-
bearing, and the custom was observed from that time forth.   The
description and explanation which Proclus gives of the Laurel-bearing are

repeated verbally by a scholiast on Clement of Alexandria (*Protrept.* i. §
10, p. 9, ed. Potter).

As to the festival, see also Böckh's Pindar, *Explicationes*, p. 590; K. O.
Müller, *Orchomenos und die Minyer*,[2] p. 215 *sq.* ; *id.*, *Dorier*,[2] 1. pp. 236 *sq.*, 333 ;
Hermann, *Gottesdienstliche Alterthümer*,[2] § 63, 28 ; Schömann, *Griech. Alter-
thümer*,[3] 2. p. 463 *sq.* ; C. Bötticher, *Baumkultus der Hellenen*, p. 386 *sqq.* ;
Preller, *Griechische Mythologie*,[4] 1. p. 288, note 1.

The procession of the Laurel-bearing is the subject of a fine painting
by the late Lord Leighton.

10. 4. to dedicate a bronze tripod to the god. Pindar (*Pyth.* xi.
8 *sq.*) speaks of the temple of Ismenian Apollo as "a treasury of golden
tripods," and the scholiast on that passage explains the allusion by saying that there were many votive tripods in the temple. Herodotus saw
three tripods engraved with inscriptions in 'Cadmean letters' in the
sanctuary of the Ismenian Apollo at Thebes. One of them was the
tripod dedicated by Amphitryo, which Pausanias mentions ; the other
two were dedicated by Scaeus and Laodamus respectively. See Herodotus, v. 59-61.

**10. 5. the fountain —— sacred to Ares —— a dragon to guard
the spring.** Since Pausanias describes this fountain as situated
"higher up than the Ismenian sanctuary," it is clear that he identified
the dragon-guarded spring of Ares with the spring of the Ismenus.
This copious spring, now called the *Kephalari* of St. John, gushes from
the rock and fills a spacious basin, from which part of its water is drawn
off by an aqueduct to turn some mills. This spring seems to have
been called Melia by the ancients (Schol. on Pindar, *Pyth.* xi. 5).
Euripides, on the other hand, who certainly appears to speak of Thebes
from personal knowledge, identified the dragon-guarded spring of Ares
with what is now called the *Paraporti* spring at the south-west foot of
the Cadmea. The water of the spring flows from eight spouts into a
long tank partly constructed of marble and enclosed by low walls which
form a quadrangle round it. Thence the water finds its way into the
stream of the Dirce a few yards below. At this spring the Theban
women may be seen washing clothes at most hours of the day. A few
feet behind the spring is a precipitous rock of no great height at the
foot of the Cadmea, and in the face of this rock there is a shallow cave
about 7 feet high by 3 broad and 5 deep. Now Euripides makes
Menoeceus sacrifice himself for his country by cutting his throat on the
battlements and falling into the den of the dragon which had guarded
the water of the Dirce (*Phoenissae*, 931 *sqq.*, 1009 *sqq.*) Thus, according to Euripides, the shallow cave at the foot of the Cadmea must be
the dragon's cave, and the spring of *Paraporti* close by must be the
dragon-guarded spring of Ares. Other writers mention the cave or den
of the dragon (Philostratus, *Imagines*, i. 4 ; Ovid, *Metam.* iii. 26 *sqq.*)
A further proof that Euripides identified the spring of Ares with one of
the springs that form the Dirce is supplied by the recently-discovered
fragments of his play the *Antiope;* for in it Lycus is bidden by Hermes
to fling the charred bones of Dirce into the spring of Ares, in order that

the spring may henceforth be known as the Dirce. See *Hermathena*, No. 17 (1891), p. 47. Though the water of the *Paraporti* spring flows into the Dirce, it should be remembered that the real sources of the Dirce are about a mile away to the south. See above, p. 28 *sq.*

See H. N. Ulrichs, *Reisen und Forschungen*, 2. pp. 4, 13-15; Vischer, *Erinner-ungen*, p. 562; Bursian, *Geogr.* 1. p. 225 *sq.* note; Baedeker,[3] p. 183 *sq.*; *Guide-Joanne*, 2. p. 12; von Wilamowitz-Moellendorff, in *Hermes*, 26 (1891), pp. 198 *sq.*, 241 *sq.*

The notion that water, especially the water of a spring, is guarded by a dragon or serpent has been held by many peoples. We have seen that the water of Styx was supposed to be guarded by dragons or serpents and is still called the Dragon Water (note on viii. 17. 6). In Bechuanaland there is a species of large water-snake, which the Bechu-anas regard as sacred; they think that if one of these snakes be killed the fountain will dry up (J. Philip, *Researches in South Africa* (London, 1828), 2. p. 118). The Zulus believe in a fiery serpent which comes out of the water; it runs very fast. Some men once waylaid a serpent as it came out of its pool and killed it; so the pool dried up. See Callaway, *Nursery Tales, Traditions, and Histories of the Zulus*, p. 290. The Namaquas think that in every fountain there lives a snake, and that if the snake leave the fountain or be killed the fountain will dry up (Th. Hahn, *Tsuni-Goam, the supreme being of the Khoi-Khoi*, pp. 53, 77). The Budduma, who inhabit some islands in Lake Tchad, have the greatest veneration for a fabulous being who haunts the lake in the shape of a gigantic serpent; in great emergencies they implore his advice and help (G. Nactigal, *Sahârâ und Sûdân*, 2. p. 369). In a lagoon near Gimbo-amburi in West Africa, a prodigious serpent is be-lieved to reside, which has the power of curing mad people. A madman is bound hand and foot by his friends and flung into the lake; the serpent carries him off to the bottom of the lake, and after twenty-four hours releases him alive and in his right mind (Labat, *Relation historique de l'Éthiopie occidentale*, 1. p. 348). In a frightful ravine in Algeria there is a spring which was believed to have been once guarded by a serpent; the people fancied that the serpent was animated by the soul of one Sidi Mohammed and had the power of healing sore eyes (Certeux et Carnoy, *L'Algérie traditionnelle*, p. 129 *sq.*) The Australian blacks avoid a bubbling spring, because they think that the bubbling and gurgling of the water are caused by a serpent underground, which con-tinually spews up the water (A. Oldfield, 'The Aborigines of Australia,' *Transactions of the Ethnological Society of London*, N.S. 3 (1865), p. 239). The Arabs still regard medicinal waters as inhabited by *jinn*, usually of serpent form; the legend of a demon in serpent form is still told of the sacred fountain of Ephca in Palmyra (W. Robertson Smith, *Religion of the Semites*,[2] p. 168). The North American Indians are said to believe that waters are guarded by a serpent (J. G. Müller, *Geschichte der amerikanischen Urreligionen*, p. 131). They tell of a universal flood which was caused by the hero Menaboshu shooting the King of the Serpents, who dwelt in the water (Kohl, *Kitschi-Gami*, 1. p.

321 *sqq.*) In India serpents are especially worshipped at sacred pools and wells. A Hindoo legend relates that Bhîma, being thrown into the Ganges, fell into the kingdom of the serpents, who gave him the 'water of strength' to drink (M. Winternitz, 'Der Sarpabali, ein altindischer Schlangencult,' *Mittheilungen der anthropolog. Gesellschaft in Wien*, 18 (1888), p. 45 *sq.*) Annamite popular tales speak of spirits of the water who have the shape of serpents, but sometimes doff their serpent-skins and appear in human form among men. If meantime their serpent-skins are stolen, the water-spirits cannot return to their native element. See Landes, 'Contes et Légendes annamites,' Nos. 29, 31, 88, in *Cochinchine Française. Excursions et Reconnaissances*, ix. No. 22 (March-April 1885), pp. 384 *sqq.*, 387 *sq.*, xi. No. 25 (Jan.-Feb. 1886), p. 114 *sq.* In an Avar story a spring is guarded by a ten-headed dragon, who allows people to draw water one day in the year, and then only on condition that he receives a maiden to devour ; the hero of the tale kills the dragon by cutting off his ten heads (A. Schiefner, *Awarische Texte* (St. Petersburg, 1873), p. 21 *sq.*) A modern Greek tale describes how a spring was guarded by a twelve-headed serpent, who devoured a human being once a week and then kindly allowed the people to draw water at the spring (J. G. von Hahn, *Griechische und albanesische Märchen*, No. 70, vol. 2. p. 55 *sq.*)

10. 6. Tenerus. The plain which stretches to the north-west of Thebes towards the Copaic lake was called the Teneric plain after this Tenerus. See ix. 26. 1 ; Strabo, ix. p. 413 ; Schol. on Pindar, *Pyth.* xi. 5.

10. 6. it was called Ladon. Sostratus, quoted by the pseudo-Plutarch (*De fluviis*, ii. 1), says that the Ismenus was formerly called Cadmus's Foot for the following reason. After killing the dragon which guarded the spring, Cadmus found that the water was tainted by the monster's gore, so he went about the country looking for another spring. It fell out, by the providence of Athena, that at the Corycaean cave Cadmus plunged his right foot into the mud ; a river gurgled up through the mud, and the hero at once sacrificed an ox and named the river 'Cadmus's Foot.' Afterwards when Ismenus, son of Amphion and Niobe, was shot by Apollo, he flung himself, in his agony, into the river, which was henceforth called Ismenus.

11. 1. Anchasian Trophonius. The epithet Anchasian is perhaps derived from Anchoe, as to which see note on ix. 23. 7. But cp. Critical Note on this passage, vol. 1. p. 602.

11. 2. Panyasis. See x. 29. 9 note.

11. 2. the blow of the stone etc. Cp. Euripides, *Hercules Furens*, 1001 *sqq.*

11. 3. they kept Alcmena from bringing forth. According to Nicander (quoted by Antoninus Liberalis, *Transform.* 29), it was the Fates and Ilithyia who thus retarded Alcmena's delivery. According to Ovid (*Metam.* ix. 295 *sqq.*), it was Lucina (Ilithyia) alone ; and the mode in which she retarded the birth was by sitting with her right leg crossed over her left, and clasping her knees with her hands, the fingers of each hand being interlaced with those of the other. Pliny tells us that to sit with interlaced fingers beside a pregnant woman or beside a sick person while remedies were being applied, was equivalent to casting a harmful spell on the person, and he refers to the case of Alcmena. The spell, he says, was more baleful, first, if the hands, so clasped, were placed over one or both knees, and second, if one leg were crossed over the other. Such postures were supposed to impede whatever happened to be going on ; hence in ancient Rome at councils of war, at meetings of magistrates, at sacrifices and prayers, no one was permitted to sit with crossed legs or clasped hands. See Pliny, *Nat. hist.* xxviii. 59. A similar train of thought has given rise to a superstition, current both in Germany and among the Malays of Java, Sumatra, etc., that a woman's delivery is retarded if there is anything shut or locked in her neighbourhood. Hence at difficult births it is customary to unlock and open the doors, boxes, etc.   See Wuttke, *Der deutsche Volksaberglaube*,[2] § 574 ; *Tijdschrift vor indische Taal-, Land- en Volkenkunde*, 26 (1880), p. 310 ; Van Hasselt, *Volksbeschrijving van Midden-Sumatra*, p. 266 ; J. G. F. Riedel, *De sluik- en kroesharige Rassen tusschen Selebes en Papua*, pp. 135, 207, 325.   Cp. Panzer, *Beitrag zur deutschen Mythologie*, 2. p. 336 *sqq*.   In Oudh to sit with one leg over another is thought to bring bad luck (*Panjab Notes and Queries*, 2 (October 1884), p. 6, No. 34).   Cp. Brand, *Popular Antiquities of Great Britain*, 3. p. 257 *sq*. (Bohn's ed.)

11. 3. **Historis, daughter of Tiresias** etc. The stratagem which brought Alcmena relief is ascribed by Nicander (quoted by Antoninus Liberalis, *Transform*. 29) to Galinthias, daughter of Proetus, and by Ovid (*Metam.* ix. 306 *sqq*.) to Galanthis, one of Alcmena's handmaids. To punish her for having deceived the goddesses, Galinthias or Galanthis was turned into a weasel; but Hecate pitied her misfortune and made Galinthias, in weasel form, her minister. Hercules too, when he grew up, showed his gratitude for the service which Galinthias had rendered his mother by founding a shrine in her honour beside his house, and by offering sacrifices to her. These sacrifices were afterwards kept up by the Thebans who continued regularly to sacrifice to Galinthias before the festival of Hercules. See Nicander, *l.c.* Aelian says (*Nat. anim.* xii. 5) that the Thebans worshipped the weasel because a weasel had been the nurse of Hercules ; or because when Alcmena was in hard labour a weasel ran past and facilitated her delivery.

11. 3. **she set up a cry of joy.** This was probably a regular signal that a birth had taken place. In Abyssinia when a child is born "the women fill the air with cries of exultation ; repeating their cry twelve times if the infant be a male, and three times if a female" (Mansfield Parkyns, *Life in Abyssinia*,[2] p. 251 *sq*.) Among the Bogos, an Abyssinian tribe, when a man-child is born the women raise a cry of joy five times ; but when a female child is born, they are silent (Munziger, *Sitten und Recht der Bogos*, p. 37). Perhaps the same distinction was drawn by the ancient Greeks ; for Nicander tells us (*l.c.*) that the wily Galinthias rushed out and informed the Fates, much to their discomfiture, that Alcmena had just been delivered of a boy.

11. 4. **a sanctuary of Hercules.** That this sanctuary was outside

the walls, not far from the 'hollow way' or gully, appears from Arrian's description of Alexander's assault on Thebes (*Anabasis*, i. 8. 3-5). It may have occupied the site of the ruined church of St. Nicholas (*Hagios Nikolaos*), which stands a little to the south of modern Thebes, on the right of the high-road as you approach from Athens (H. N. Ulrichs, *Reisen und Forschungen*, 2. p. 12; E. Fabricius, *Theben*, p. 22). It is said that before the battle of Leuctra Epaminondas told the Thebans to pray in the sanctuary of Hercules. Instructions had been given to the priest of Hercules that he was to open the temple by night, take down and burnish the rusty old votive arms and set them beside the image, and then steal away with the sacristans, without saying a word to anybody. So when the soldiers with their officers came crowding to the temple and saw the doors open, no sacristans about, and the ancient weapons cleaned and shining in front of the image, they cheered lustily and were filled with confidence, thinking that Hercules himself was going to lead them to battle. See Polyaenus, ii. 3. 8. Cp. Xenophon, *Hellenica*, vi. 4. 7 ; Diodorus, xv. 73 ; Cicero, *De divinatione*, i. 34. § 74.

11. 4. **Xenocritus and Eubius.** These sculptors seem to be otherwise unknown.

11. 4. **This image —— Daedalus himself dedicated** etc. Apollodorus tells (ii. 6. 3) how Hercules found and buried the corpse of Icarus on the island of Doliche (afterwards Icaria), and how out of gratitude Daedalus made a statue of Hercules and set it up at Pisa. One night Hercules, mistaking the statue for a living man, threw a stone at it and hit it.

11. 4. **when he fled from Crete in small craft** etc. This is a dull rationalistic attempt to explain the legend that Daedalus and his son fled from Crete through the air on wings constructed by the former, and that as Icarus flew too near the sun, the heat melted the wax with which his wings were fastened on, so that he fell into the sea and was drowned. See Ovid, *Metam.* viii. 183 *sqq.* ; Hyginus, *Fab.* 40 ; Diodorus, iv. 77. Diodorus gives the rationalistic version of the story also, and so does Palaephatus (*De incredib.* 13, in Westermann's *Mythographi Graeci*, p. 280 *sq.*) The death of Icarus is the subject of a fine wall-painting at Pompeii. See Baumeister's *Denkmäler*, Tafel xxii., article 'Malerei.' A modern Greek tale narrates how a Captain Thirteen, being thrown into a deep hole by his enemies, found a dead bird, made himself wings out of its feathers, and flew away. But it came on to rain, the clay with which he had fastened his wings was wetted and softened, and the captain fell into the sea, where a sea-devil clawed him with a thirteen-pronged fork and turned him into a dolphin. See B. Schmidt, *Griechische Märchen, Sagen und Volkslieder*, p. 92. The story seems a reminiscence of the tale of Icarus.

11. 5. **an island, then nameless.** According to others the island was called Doliche ('long') before it was called Icaria (Apollodorus, ii. 6. 3 ; Pliny, *Nat. hist.* iv. 68). According to others its old name was Macris or Ichthyoessa (Pliny, *l.c.*)

11. 6. **by Praxiteles.** Prof. W. Klein supposes that this Praxiteles was an older namesake of the great Praxiteles (W. Klein, in *Archaeol. epigraph. Mittheil. aus Oesterreich*, 4 (1880), p. 15 *sq.*) Overbeck took the same view (*Gesch. d. griech. Plastik*,[4] 1. p. 500), and Prof. Collignon inclines to it (*Hist. de la Sculpture grecque*, 2. p. 179 note). As to this supposed earlier Praxiteles, see note on i. 2. 4.

11. 6. **the wrestling with Antaeus.** The wrestle of Hercules with Antaeus is the subject of a number of vase-paintings, in particular of one by Euphronius. See W. Klein, in *Archäologische Zeitung*, 36 (1878), p. 66 *sqq.*; *id., Euphronios*, p. 116 *sqq.*; Baumeister's *Denkmäler*, fig. 86, p. 82; *Catalogue of Greek and Etruscan Vases in the British Museum*, 2. Nos. B 196, B 122, B 322, B 596.

11. 6. **Thrasybulus —— set out from Thebes.** Cp. Xenophon, *Hellenica*, ii. 4. 2; Diodorus, xiv. 32; Plutarch, *Lysander*, 27; *id., Pelopidas*, 7.

11. 6. **Athena and Hercules —— works of Alcamenes.** Prof. Furtwängler holds that the Farnese Athena at Naples is a copy of a work of Alcamenes (*Meisterwerke d. griech. Plastik*, p. 104 *sqq.*)

11. 7. **an altar —— made of the ashes of the victims.** Cp. v. 13. 8 note; v. 14. 8; v. 14. 10; v. 15. 9.

11. 7. **divination by means of voices.** Cp. vii. 22. 2 *sq.*

12. 1. **departing from Delphi by the road which leads to Phocis.** The Lacedaemonians made Delphi independent of Phocis; hence Delphi had its own territory marked off from Phocis by definite boundaries. See Strabo, ix. p. 423. The Delphians did not like to be called Phocians (Paus. iv. 34. 11). But Pausanias is probably guilty of an anachronism in speaking of Delphi as if it were distinct from Phocis in the time of Cadmus. Cp. Critical Note, vol. 1. p. 602 *sq.*

12. 1. **he was guided on his journey by a cow** etc. The Delphic oracle which directed Cadmus to follow a cow and to build his city wherever the cow sank exhausted, is quoted at length by a scholiast on Euripides (*Phoenissae*, 638). Cp. Apollodorus, iii. 4. 1; Plutarch, *Sulla*, 17; Nonnus, *Dionys.* iv. 299 *sqq.* As to similar legends, see note on x. 6. 2. In the white moon-like marks on the cow (which are mentioned in the oracle quoted by the scholiast, *l.c.*) Prof. von Baudissin sees a symbol of the Phoenician moon-goddess (*Studien zur semit. Religionsgeschichte*, 1. p. 273).

12. 2. **Athena —— Onga.** From Aeschylus we learn that the image of Athena Onga (or Onca, as the name was generally spelt) stood outside, but near to one of the gates (*Seven against Thebes*, 149, 488 *sq.*, cp. 473 *sq.*, ed. Verrall). And from Hesychius (*s.v.* Ὄγκας Ἀθηνᾶς) it appears that the gate in question was the Ogygian gate. But as the situation of that gate (if it ever existed) is uncertain, the site of the altar and image of Athena Onga is equally so. There is said to have been a village Oncae on the spot (Schol. on Pindar, *Olymp.* ii. 48; Tzetzes, *Schol. on Lycophron*, 1225). Cadmus is said to have sacrificed to Athena Onga the cow which had guided him to Thebes (Schol. on Aeschylus, *Seven against Thebes*, 473 (486, ed. Dindorf); cp. Apollodorus, iii. 4. 1). A scholiast on Euripides (*Phoenissae*, 1062) says that Athena helped Cadmus against the Sparti, and that in grati-

tude he founded a sanctuary to her, under the Phoenician surname of Onca. Over the sanctuary, according to the scholiast, was carved the inscription : " This is the temple of Athena Onca, which Cadmus once founded and sacrificed a cow when he built the city of Thebes." On the left bank of the Dirce, about 200 paces south-west of the Cadmea, is a chapel of the Holy Trinity (*Hagia Trias*), which rests on ancient foundations built of squared blocks. It has been conjectured that these are the foundations of the sanctuary of Athena Onga. See H. N. Ulrichs, *Reisen und Forschungen*, 2. p. 15 ; Fabricius, *Theben*, p. 28 ; von Wilamowitz-Moellendorff, in *Hermes*, 26 (1891), p. 217. The ancient authorities (Pausanias ; Schol. on Pindar, *Olymp.* ii. 44 ; Schol. on Aeschylus, *l.c.* ; Schol. on Euripides, *l.c.* ; Stephanus Byz. *s.v.* Ὀγκαῖαι) are agreed that the name Onga or Onca is Phoenician. Relying on this statement of the ancients, Movers has constructed an elaborate theory of Athena Onca, which is not, I believe, accepted by modern Semitic scholars. See Movers, *Die Phoenizier*, 1. pp. 642-650. Cp. Selden, *De dis Syriis*, p. 294 *sqq.* ; Preller, *Griech. Mythologie*,[4] 1. p. 188. Onca is perhaps the feminine form corresponding to Oncius (masculine) and Onceum (neuter), which Pausanias has mentioned elsewhere (viii. 25. 4 *sqq.*) Prof. W. H. Roscher suggests that Onca may possibly be connected with ὀγκᾶσθαι, 'to bray, roar' (*Nektar und Ambrosia*, p. 97). A Greek vase-painting, which represents a man in a pointed cap preparing to sacrifice a bull or cow to a rude image, has been interpreted by Mr. Pervanoglu as a picture of Cadmus setting up the image of Athena Onca. The image stands on a heap of stones and is equipped with a plumed helmet, a large round shield, and two spears. See P. Pervanoglu, 'Götterdienst der Athena Onka zu Theben auf einer Vase aus Megara,' *Archäologische Zeitung*, 1865, pp. 68-70, with pl. cxcix. 3.

12. 2. **the Egyptian name of Sais.** Sais, in Egyptian *Sa* or *ha ent Net*, 'the city of Neith,' was the capital of the fifth district (*nome*) of Lower Egypt. The goddess Neith, who was worshipped here, appears on the monuments as a deity of the lower world, with the figure of a woman, green face and hands, and the crown of Lower Egypt on her head ; generally she carries a bow and arrows and also the flower-tipt sceptre. In mythology she is the mother of the gods, and sometimes she nourishes two crocodiles. The Greeks identified her with Athena (Herodotus, II. 59 ; Plato, *Timaeus*, p. 21 e ; Hesychius, *s.v.* Νηΐθ), partly perhaps on the ground of the resemblance between the names. On the coins of the Saitic district this identification is carried out by representing the goddess with an owl on her right hand and a spear in her left. See Wiedemann on Herodotus, ii. 62 ; *id.*, *Die Religion der alten Ägypter*, p. 77 *sq.* ; Brugsch, *Religion und Mythologie der alten Aegypter*, pp. 338-354 ; Tiele, *History of the Egyptian Religion*, p. 202 *sqq.*

12. 4. **Polydorus adorned this log with bronze** etc. It has been suggested that before the art of casting metal was discovered it may have been customary to cover wooden images with plates of hammered bronze, and that the image here described by Pausanias was perhaps

one of this class of images (A. S. Murray, *History of Greek Sculpture*,[2] 1. p. 75 *sq.*) See the Critical Note on this passage, vol. 1. p. 603.

12. 4. Dionysus Cadmus. With this title compare Hercules Manticlus (iv. 23. 10) and Hermes Aepytus (viii. 47. 4). Cp. Critical Note, vol. 1. p. 603.

12. 4. the sons of Praxiteles. Cp. i. 8. 4. Their names were Cephisodotus and Timarchus ([Plutarch,] *Vit. X. Orat.* vii. 39, p. 843 e). Two bases of statues inscribed with the joint names of these sculptors have been found. See Loewy, *Inschriften griech. Bildhauer,* Nos. 108, 109, and the note on i. 21. 1; Overbeck, *Schriftquellen,* §§ 1331-1341; A. S. Murray, *History of Greek Sculpture,* 2. p. 328. Cp. note on viii. 30. 10. They appear to have made some images for the sanctuary of Aesculapius in Cos (Herondas, *Mimiambi,* iv. 20 *sqq.*)

12. 5. Pronomus. Cp. Athenaeus, xiv. p. 631 e, who laments the degeneration of music caused by Pronomus's invention of a flute on which it was possible to play tunes of all three sorts, Dorian, Lydian, and Phrygian. Cp. Paus. iv. 27. 7.

12. 6. Epaminondas, son of Polymnis. See note on iv. 31. 10.

13. 2. Epaminondas was sent to Sparta on an embassy etc. Cp. Plutarch, *Agesilaus,* 27 *sq.* Pausanias is mistaken in assigning this embassy of Epaminondas to the period when the peace of Antalcidas was being negotiated (387 B.C.) Epaminondas represented Thebes at the congress held at Sparta in 371 B.C. for the purpose of concluding a general peace. It was on this occasion that he made his sharp retort to Agesilaus. Cp. Grote, *History of Greece,* 9. p. 387.

13. 3. took up a defensive position above the Cephisian Lake etc. Just before the battle of Leuctra in 371 B.C. there was a Lacedae-monian army under Cleombrotus in Phocis (Xenophon, *Hellenica,* vi. 4. 2 *sq.* ; Plutarch, *Agesilaus,* 28). Hence, in order to prevent the enemy from entering the Boeotian plain, Epaminondas marched westward and took up a position at Coronea in the defile between Mt. Helicon and the Copaic or Cephisian lake. Cp. Diodorus, xv. 52; Xenophon, *Hellenica,* vi. 4. 3. Cleombrotus, however, gave the Boeotians the slip. Instead of following the direct road which leads eastward from the Cleft Way by Lebadea to Coronea and the Boeotian plain, he struck southward through the mountains to Thisbe and thence to Creusis, a port on the Gulf of Corinth, captured it, and then marching north-eastward, probably up the valley of the Oeroe, he debouched on the Boeotian plain and encamped at Leuctra. See Xenophon, *Hellenica,* vi. 4. 3 *sq.* ; Diodorus, xv. 53. Leuctra was a small village belonging to Thespiae (Plutarch, *Amat. Narrat.* iii. 1) and stood on a hill, for Xenophon says (*Hellenica,* vi. 4. 4) that when Cleombrotus encamped at Leuctra the Boeotians encamped "on the opposite hill at no great distance from the Lacedaemonians."

The battlefield is a level alluvial plain, from half to three-quarters of a mile wide, bounded by a line of low hills on the north and south. Through the plain flows the head stream of the Asopus, which is here no more than a small brook. The plain is in fact merely a continuation westward of the great level plain or valley of the Asopus. At present it is treeless and covered chiefly with corn-fields. The hills on the north side of the plain, where the Theban army was posted, are low, rounded, gently-sloping hills which at the present day are ploughed to their summits. The hills on the opposite side of the plain, where the Spartan army took up its position, are higher and their slope to the plain is much steeper. The track to Thebes from the head of the Corinthian Gulf by which the Spartan army marched to Leuctra comes down the slope of these southern hills, crosses the plain, and ascends the northern line of hills through a small valley where there is a well, the sides of which are built of marble blocks. About 150 yards or so after passing the well the track to Thebes is cut nearly at right angles by the track from Thespiae to Plataea. On the upper edge of the southern hills there now stand three villages close together which collectively go by the name of *Parapoungia*. Leuctra must have been in this neighbourhood. It seems to have been an insignificant place, and probably was never surrounded by walls.

The ancient fragments (inscribed tombstones, shafts of columns, squared blocks, etc.) which are to be seen in the village churches of *Parapoungia* are perhaps vestiges of the ancient town. On the northern hill, where the Thebans were encamped, there are extensive foundations of massive polygonal walls above the copious spring of *Arkopodi* ('bear's foot'). These foundations run round the upper edge of the hill, forming a square of about 500 metres. The fields within this area are strewn with fragments of marble blocks, tiles, and vases. At the spring of *Arkopodi*, which rises at the southern foot of the hill, there are some large blocks, and drums of columns. These ruins, which lie exactly opposite the most easterly of the three villages of *Parapoungia*, have by some been supposed to be the remains of Leuctra, but they would seem rather to be those of Eutresis, a town mentioned by Homer (*Iliad*, ii. 502). For Eutresis lay beside the road leading from Thespiae to Plataea, and its walls were said to have been built by Amphion and Zethus, who dwelt there before they reigned at Thebes (Stephanus Byz. *s.v.* Εὔτρησις; Strabo, ix. p. 411). Now the ruins in question lie close to the track from Thespiae to Plataea, and the massive polygonal walls of which the foundations remain might well be regarded as the work of the mythical Amphion and Zethus.

Cicero tells us (*De inventione*, ii. 23) that the Thebans commemorated their victory by erecting a bronze trophy, contrary to Greek usage, which forbade the erection of a permanent trophy for a victory won by Greeks over Greeks (cp. Plutarch, *Quaest. Rom.* 37). At the foot of the hill on which the most westerly of the three villages *Parapoungia* stands, H. N. Ulrichs discovered in 1839 the remains of a large monument, which may have been the Theban trophy. The ruins consist of a square base supporting a portion of a round tower. The base is built of rough blocks of conglomerate. The remains of the tower consist of large blocks of a whitish limestone, very fine and hard. Six of the blocks are adorned with large shields over 3 feet in diameter, carved in relief. There are also triglyphs and metopes. In the centre is a large altar, of the ordinary cubical shape, with a round sinking in its upper surface. It is supposed that the monument, when entire, formed a round tower 3.46 metres in diameter, of the Doric style, with a dome-shaped roof; that the lower part of the roof was adorned with nine shields in relief; and that under the cornice of the roof twelve triglyphs were placed round the tower. The tower may have supported the bronze trophy of which Cicero speaks.

See Leake, *Northern Greece*, 2. p. 485 *sqq.* (who takes the ruins at the *Arkopodi* spring to be Leuctra, and supposes the battle to have been fought in the valley to the north of that place)·; L. Ross, *Wanderungen*, 1. p. 18 *sqq.*; H. N. Ulrichs, *Reisen und Forschungen*, 2.· pp. 102-113; Welcker, *Tagebuch*, 2. p. 32 *sq.*; Vischer, *Erinnerungen*, p. 550 *sqq.*; Bursian, *Geogr.* 1. p. 240; Baedeker,[3] p. 175 *sq*; *Guide-Joanne*, 2. p. 26; G. B. Grundy, *The topography of the battle of Plataea*, pp. 73-76. As to the battle of Leuctra, see Xenophon, *Hellenica*, vi. 4. 3-15; Diodorus, xv. 52-56; Plutarch, *Pelopidas*, 20-23.

Mr. Grundy is clearly wrong in supposing that the Spartan army reached Leuctra from Phocis by the route which leads from Lebadea along the ·northern slopes of Helicon to the valley of the Muses. No army, especially an army with cavalry, could make its way along this rugged and difficult track in face of an enemy encamped (as the Thebans were) in force at Coronea, which is close to the track. Even supposing that the Spartans had accomplished this almost impossible feat, why should they afterwards have turned out of their way to go by Thisbe to Creusis on the Gulf of Corinth and then returned on their steps to Leuctra? This marching backwards and forwards is unintelligible on the hypothesis that the Spartan army reached Leuctra from Phocis by the northern side of Helicon. The narratives of Xenophon, Diodorus, and Pausanias, harmonising with the natural features of the country, oblige us to suppose that Cleombrotus, finding the route along the north side of Helicon blocked by the Theban army at Coronea, made a complete circuit of Helicon, passed along the southern side of the mountain, and emerged on flat ground at Thisbe, not far from the Gulf of Corinth. Finding himself thus in the south of Boeotia, it was natural that he should wish to secure the port of Creusis before marching northward into the heart of the country. Having done so, he took the road to Thebes, but found it barred by the Theban army at Leuctra.

13. 4. **the Spartan kings —— used to be followed by sheep** etc. The sacrifices performed by a Spartan king in time of war are thus described by Xenophon or whoever wrote the treatise *The Constitution of Lacedaemon :* " First of all the king and his staff sacrifice at home to Zeus the Leader; and if the sacrificial omens are good, the Fire-bearer takes fire from the altar and leads the way to the frontier. Here again the king sacrifices to Zeus and Athena. Whenever the omens attending the sacrifices offered to these two deities are good, he crosses the frontier, and the fire taken from these sacrifices leads the way, being never allowed to go out, and victims of all sorts follow When the king sacrifices he sets about the work in the morning while it is still dark, as he wishes to secure God's favour before (the enemy can do so) " (*Constitution of Lacedaemon*, xiii. 2 *sq.*) On the field of battle,

when the troops were drawn up in array and the enemy was in sight, the king sacrificed a she-goat to the Huntress (*Agrotera*). Then he ordered the flutes to strike up Castor's tune, every man put a garland on his head, and the whole army advanced singing a marching song and stepping to the music of the flutes (Xenophon, *op. cit.* xiii. 8 ; *id.*, *Hellenica*, iv. 2. 20 ; Plutarch, *Lycurgus*, 22). But the first sacrifice offered by the king on the field of battle was to the Muses (Plutarch, *Lycurgus*, 21). The meaning of this sacrifice seems obvious. The stirring effects of martial music were probably explained by the early Greeks as due to the direct inspiration of the goddesses of music, the Muses. Hence sacrifices were offered to them and their favour entreated just before the flutes struck up the charge. As to the military music of the Greeks, see Plutarch, *De musica*, 26. Athenaeus says (xiii. p. 561) that the Lacedaemonians sacrificed to Love before an engagement, and that in Crete also sacrifices were regularly offered before a battle to Love by the handsomest men in the army dressed in gay attire.

13. 5. **the wrath of the daughters of Scedasus** etc. Cp. Xenophon, *Hellenica*, vi. 4. 7 ; Diodorus, xv. 54 ; Plutarch, *Pelopidas*, 20-22 ; *id.*, *Amat. Narrat.* iii.

13. 6. **Xenocrates.** Cp. iv. 32. 6 note.

13. 11. **The victory —— was the most famous** etc. The same estimate of the Theban victory at Leuctra is expressed by Plutarch (*Agesilaus*, 29).

13. 12. **The Thebans —— lost forty-seven men** etc. Xenophon says that the Lacedaemonians had nearly 1000 slain, of whom 400 were Spartans ; he does not mention the loss on the Theban side (*Hellenica*, vi. 4. 15). Diodorus says (xv. 56) that the Lacedaemonians lost not less than 4000, and the Boeotians about 300. Plutarch (*Agesilaus*, 28) puts the loss of the Lacedaemonians at 1000. According to Dionysius Halicarnassensis (*Antiquit. Rom.* ii. 17) the Spartans lost 1700. Pausanias's estimate of the loss on the Boeotian side is, as Grote remarks (*Hist. of Greece*, 9. p. 401), preposterously low. The Spartans, trained soldiers as they were, must have sold their lives more dearly.

14. 1. **Epaminondas ordered the rest of the Peloponnesians to depart** etc. Pausanias's statement that Epaminondas dismissed the allies of the Lacedaemonians but kept the Lacedaemonians themselves prisoners, seems inconsistent with the narrative of Xenophon, who says that the beaten army, including both the Lacedaemonians and their allies, retreated by a difficult road and met the fresh levies, which Archidamus was leading to their assistance, at Aegosthena in the territory of Megara (Xenophon, *Hellenica*, vi. 4. 26).

14. 2. **Ceressus.** The site of this place is uncertain. H. N. Ulrichs inclined to place it at *Eremokastro*, a modern village on an eminence close to Thespiae. On the slope towards Thespiae there are a few large stones, which Ulrichs thought might be remains of the walls of Ceressus. But the eminence on which *Eremokastro* stands can hardly be described as a 'stronghold.' It is low and nowhere, I think, in the least precipitous. Wheler thought that Ceressus may have been near *Palaeo-Panagia*, a village about 2 miles to the north-west

of *Eremokastro*. Here on a rocky hill, about a mile to the north-west of *Palaeo-Panagia*, stands a ruined mediaeval tower; lower down are some remains of churches and houses. This rocky hill Wheler took to be the site of Ceressus. It is nearer to Thespiae than the conspicuous conical hill of Ascra and is, like that hill, a spur of Helicon. See Wheler, *Journey*, p. 476; Leake, *Northern Greece*, 2. pp. 489 *sq.*, 499 *sq.*; H. N. Ulrichs, *Reisen und Forschungen*, 2. pp. 87, 92; Bursian, *Geogr.* I. p. 238; Baedeker,[3] pp. 162-164. Plutarch tells us (*Camillus*, 19) that more than two hundred years before the battle of Leuctra the Boeotians defeated the Thessalians under Lattamyas at Ceressus. This may have been the time when the Thespians took refuge in Ceressus.

14. 6. When his army had reached Lechaeum etc. According to Plutarch (*Pelopidas*, 24) the Athenians attacked Epaminondas not at Lechaeum, but at Cenchreae on the other side of the Isthmus. Xenophon blames Iphicrates for leaving the road by Cenchreae unguarded (*Hellenica*, vi. 5. 51).

14. 7. Epaminondas —— advanced to the Athenian capital. Neither Xenophon nor Plutarch, who describe the return of the Boeotian army from Peloponnese, makes any reference to this advance upon Athens. Grote thinks it unlikely that any such movement was made, and he attempts to interpret the statement of Pausanias as referring not to Athens but to Corinth. But the words of Pausanias can have no other meaning than that Epaminondas advanced against Athens itself. See Xenophon, *Hellenica*, vi. 5. 52; Plutarch, *Pelop.* 24; Grote, *Hist. of Greece*, 9. p. 456 *sqq.*; Thirlwall, *Hist. of Greece*, 5. p. 140 *sq.*; Curtius, *Griech. Gesch.*[6] 3. p. 323.

14. 7. He was tried for his life etc. Cp. Plutarch, *Pelopidas*, 25; Grote, *Hist. of Greece*, 9. p. 457 *sqq.*

15. 1. Pelopidas, paying a visit etc. On the imprisonment of Pelopidas by Alexander, tyrant of Pherae, and the expedition to release him, see Diodorus, xv. 71; Plutarch, *Pelopidas*, 27-29.

15. 3. the Thebans expelled the Orchomenians etc. According to Diodorus (xv. 79) the Thebans put the men to the sword and sold the women and children into slavery. There is a discrepancy between Pausanias and Diodorus as to the date of this foul deed. Diodorus places the imprisonment of Pelopidas by Alexander of Pherae in 368 B.C. and the destruction of Orchomenus in 364 B.C.; whereas Pausanias supposes that these two events were simultaneous. Grote (*Hist. of Greece*, 10. p. 72) follows Diodorus; Thirlwall (*Hist. of Greece*, 5. p. 158 *sq.*) follows Pausanias.

15. 4. defeated the Lacedaemonians at Lechaeum etc. See Xenophon, *Hellenica*, vii. 1. 15-17; Diodorus, xv. 68.

15. 4. Phoebia. This town is mentioned by Stephanus Byzantius (*s.v.*) The same geographer (*s.v.* Βουφία) mentions a village Buphia in the territory of Sicyon, which is probably identical with Phoebia. L. Ross identified Phoebia or Buphia with some ruins of an ancient Greek fortress situated on a height which projects into the valley of the Nemea river on the west, exactly opposite the table-mountain Apesas (*Phouka*). There are here some foundations of walls, built of unhewn blocks. Leake, however, preferred to identify these ruins with the fortress on Mt. Tricaranum mentioned by Xenophon (*Hellenica*, vii. 2. 1). See L. Ross, *Reisen*, p. 40; Leake, *Pelop.* p. 401; Schubart, *Methodologie*, p. 92.

15. 5. In the picture of the cavalry fight at Athens etc. See i. 3. 4; viii. 11. 5 *sq.*

15. 6. By my counsels Sparta was shorn of her glory. This line is translated by Cicero (*Tuscul. disput.* v. 17. § 49).

16. 1. Calamis. See note on v. 25. 5.

16. 1. the observatory of Tiresias. More literally "the place where Tiresias watched for omens" (οἰωνοσκοπεῖον Τειρεσίου). It seems to have been a seat on which the blind soothsayer sat and listened to the screams of birds and the whir of their wings in order to draw omens from these sounds. See Sophocles, *Antigone*, 999-1004.

16. 2. Xenophon, an Athenian. This sculptor was a contemporary of the elder Cephisodotus. See viii. 30. 10 note.

16. 2. the image of Peace with Wealth in her arms. See i. 8. 2 note.

16. 3. wooden images of Aphrodite etc. With these three images of Aphrodite compare the three at Megalopolis (viii. 32. 1). From a comparison of the two sets of images Mr. Berger infers that the nameless Aphrodite of Megalopolis must be the same with the Theban Aphrodite the Averter. He would also identify Aphrodite the Averter with the Marine Aphrodite (Aphrodite Pelagia) mentioned by Artemidorus (*Onir.* ii. 37); but his reasons seem inconclusive. Augustine speaks of three Aphrodites (*De civit. dei*, iv. 10), but hesitatingly and apparently with little or no authority. The legend that the three images of Aphrodite at Thebes were made out of the figure-heads of Cadmus's ships seems, in Mr. Berger's opinion, to show that these Aphrodites were Phoenician deities. We know from Herodotus (iii. 37) that the Phoenicians placed images called *Pataikoi* at the prows of their ships; and these images were probably the sailors' gods. Cp. Suidas and Hesychius, *s.v.* Πάταικοι. On Phoenician coins, supposed to be of Aradus, a galley is represented with an image, probably one of these *Pataikoi*, at the prow. See Perrot et Chipiez, *Histoire de l'art dans l'antiquité*, 3. p. 419, fig. 292. As to the supposed Oriental character of these Theban Aphrodites see Ph. Berger, in *Gazette archéologique*, 6 (1880), p. 25 *sqq.*; L. R. Farnell, *The Cults of the Greek States*, 2. p. 635.

16. 6. Beside the Proetidian gate —— a theatre. Through the Proetidian gate went the road to Chalcis (see ix. 18. 1). On the hill to the right of the present road to Chalcis there is a hollow, surrounded by a watercourse. It has been suggested that in this hollow may have been the seats of the ancient theatre (Baedeker's *Greece*,[1] Engl. Trans. p. 173 *sq.*) Excavations might decide the question.

16. 6. once a year —— they open the sanctuary. Cp. note on viii. 47. 5.

16. 7. Alcmena —— was turned into a stone. The early historian Pherecydes, who seems to have recorded many curious old legends, thus tells the story to which Pausanias briefly refers. "Meanwhile

Alcmena died of old age and the Heraclids carried her out to burial. They dwelt in the market-place beside the Electran gate, where Hercules had dwelt before them. But Zeus sent Hermes with orders to steal Alcmena and carry her away to the Islands of the Blest and there to give her to Rhadamanthys to wife. Hermes complied and stole away Alcmena, but he put a stone into the coffin in her stead. So the Heraclids, finding the coffin very heavy to carry, dumped it down and opened it, and there they found a stone instead of Alcmena. They took it out and set it in the grove where is the shrine of Alcmena at Thebes " (Pherecydes, quoted by Antoninus Liberalis, *Transform.* 33).

16. 7. that of the Megarians. See i. 41. 1.

16. 7. the tombs of the children of Amphion. Artstodemus, however, denied that the tombs of the children of Amphion and Niobe were at Thebes (Schol. on Euripides, *Phoen.* 159).

17. 1. a temple of Artemis of Good Fame. Cp. i. 14. 5 note. Her temple was in the market-place at Thebes (Sophocles, *Oed. Tyrann.* 161); indeed she had an altar and an image in every market-place in Boeotia and Locris, and men and women sacrificed to her before marriage (Plutarch, *Aristides*, 20). The runner who brought the sacred fire from Delphi to Plataea in a single day (see note on ix. 2. 5) was buried by his admiring townsmen in the sanctuary of Artemis of Good Fame (Plutarch, *l.c.*) On the goddess and her image by Scopas, see L. Ulrichs, *Skopas*, p. 77 *sqq.*

As the temple of Artemis of Good Fame at Thebes was near the Proetidian gate (see ix. 16. 6 *sq.*) and in the market-place, it follows that the market-place was in the north-eastern quarter of the city. There is only one place adapted for a market-place in this part of the site, namely the low ground to the north-east of the Cadmea, at the point where the gully, which bounds the Cadmea on the east, opens out into a tolerably wide and level stretch of ground. Here then we may place, with fair certainty, the ancient market-place of Thebes. Excavations here might prove fruitful. The market-place was surrounded by colonnades, the walls of which were covered with the arms taken from the Athenians at the battle of Delium. Indeed so great was the spoil taken by the Thebans on that occasion that out of it they built a large colonnade in the market-place and adorned it with bronze statues. See Diodorus, xii. 70. 5. The Theban senate was sitting in the great colonnade in the market-place on a hot summer noon, when the Spartans stole through the deserted streets and seized the Cadmea (Xenophon, *Hellenica*, v. 2. 29). Again it was in the market-place that the Theban patriots, who had resolved to expel the Spartan garrison from the Cadmea, mustered in driving snow and sleet, and armed themselves for the attempt with the weapons which lined the walls of the colonnades and with others which they procured from the shops of the sword-cutlers in the neighbourhood. See Xenophon, *Hellenica*, v. 4. 9; Plutarch, *De genio Socratis*, 30, 34. It is said that after the destruction of Thebes the only monument among all the ruins which the dejected Thebans cared to search out and restore was an image of Hermes bearing an inscription which attested the superiority of the Thebans to all the rest of the Greeks in playing on the flute ! In the days of Dio Chrysostom this image still stood solitary among the ruins of the market-place. See Dio Chrysostom, *Orat.* vii. vol. I. p. 136, ed. Dindorf. In Pausanias's time, as doubtless in Dio Chrysostom's, the new market-place was on the Cadmea. See ix. 12. 3.

17. 2. **Erginus.** Cp. ix. 37. I *sqq.* An ancient vase-painting, which has been variously interpreted, is explained by Mr. R. Engelmann to be a representation of Hercules's combat with Erginus. See *Archäologische Zeitung*, 33 (1876), pp. 20-23 ; *id.*, 37 (1879), pp. 186-196.

17. 3. **Athena surnamed Girder.** From an inscription (*C. I. G. G. S.* I. No. 548) we learn that Athena was worshipped under this title (Ζωστηρία) at Tanagra along with Zeus the Contriver (cp. Paus. ii. 22. 2). Both titles have probably reference to war.

17. 3. **Chalcodon.** See viii. 15. 6 ; ix. 19. 3. There was a shrine (ἡρῷον) of Chalcodon at Athens (Plutarch, *Theseus*, 27).

17. 3. **Homer, in comparing Agamemnon to Ares** etc. See *Iliad*, ii. 479.

17. 4. **The common tomb of Zethus and Amphion is a small mound of earth.** This tomb was on the north side of Thebes, near the gate which Aeschylus calls the North Gate (*Seven against Thebes*, 515 *sq.* ed. Verrall). It was outside the walls (Euripides, *Phoenissae*, 145 ; *id.*, *Suppliants*, 663). Ancient writers mention a place at Thebes called the Amphium ('Αμφεῖον or ″Αμφιον), which is perhaps to be distinguished from the tomb of Amphion and Zethus (Xenophon, *Hellenica*, v. 4. 8 ; Plutarch, *De genio Socratis*, 4 ; Arrian, *Anabasis*, i. 8. 6). H. N. Ulrichs and Prof. Fabricius incline to identify the Amphium with the hillock to the north of the Cadmea, just outside the present town, beyond the square mediaeval tower. See H. N. Ulrichs, *Reisen und Forschungen*, 2. p. 17 ; Fabricius, *Theben*, pp. 19, 31. The hillock is too large to answer to the "small mound of earth" of Pausanias ; otherwise I should have proposed to identify it with the tomb of Amphion and Zethus. Meerschaum is dug in the hillock. Cp. Fiedler, *Reise*, I. p. 93 *sqq.* ; Wheler, *Journey*, p. 332.

17. 4. **The people of Tithorea —— try to filch some of the earth** etc. One of the laws of the Twelve Tables at Rome forbade people to spirit away the crops from a neighbour's field by means of spells and incantations (Pliny, *Nat. hist.* xxviii. 17 *sq.* ; Servius on Virgil, *Ecl.* viii. 99 ; Augustine, *De civit. dei*, viii. 19 ; Apuleius, *De magia*, 47 ; Bruns, *Fontes juris Romani antiqui*,[5] p. 29). Cp. Tibullus, i. 8. 19 ; Virgil, *Ecl.* viii. 99. Once on a time a certain C. Furius Cresimus, whose small farm produced heavier crops than the largest farms in the neighbourhood, was shrewdly suspected of drawing away the corn from other people's fields by enchantment. Being brought before the public assembly at Rome to stand his trial on this charge, he produced in the sight of the people his ploughshares, his mattocks, his sturdy hinds, his sleek oxen, and pointing to them said, "These are my enchantments, gentlemen. I regret that it is not in my power to lay before you my toils and moils and sweatings." He was unanimously acquitted. See Pliny, *Nat. hist.* xviii. 41 *sqq.* The learned Betzius, a

Carmelite monk who lived about 1500, tells us how a certain witch walked round a field of ripe corn repeating the verse '*Super aspidem,*' etc. ; how she then went home and taking a pipe or tube repeated the same verse ; and how thereupon the whole of the corn came pouring through the tube, so that not a single grain was left on the field. See Delrius, *Disquisitiones Magicae*, p. 400 ; J. W. Wolf, *Niederländische Sagen*, p. 371. The sun enters Taurus on April 20th (Ovid, *Fasti*, iv. 715 *sqq.*) We may perhaps suppose that the Tithoreans chose this time for their depredations on the tomb of Amphion and Zethus because it was the season of the spring sowing. That the custom of stealing earth from the tomb originated in the oracle quoted by Pausanias is unlikely. More probably the oracle was fabricated to explain the custom.

17. 6. **The wife of Lycus —— suffered** etc. The legend that Dirce, the wife of Lycus, was bound by Amphion and Zethus to a bull which dragged her to death is familiar to every one through the group of 'the Farnese Bull,' executed by the sculptors Apollonius and Tauriscus (Pliny, *Nat. hist.* xxxvi. 34) and found in the sixteenth century in the baths of Caracalla at Rome. On the legend and the various representations of it in ancient art, see Otto Jahn, 'Antiope und Dirke,' *Archäologische Zeitung*, 11 (1853), pp. 65-105 ; K. Dilthey, 'Schleifung der Dirke,' *ib.* 36 (1878), pp. 43-54 ; Baumeister's *Denkmäler*, pp. 107 *sq.*, 455 *sqq.* A curious custom was observed at Thebes with regard to the grave of Dirce. The general of the cavalry was the only person at Thebes who knew where the grave was. When he was retiring from office, he took his successor alone and showed him the grave by night. They offered certain fireless sacrifices, and then, after carefully obliterating all traces of the rites which they had performed, they separated and went away in the darkness. See Plutarch, *De genio Socratis*, 5. Perhaps the grave was one of those talismans on which the safety of states was sometimes supposed to hang and the existence of which was accordingly kept a profound secret. See note on viii. 47. 5.

17. 6. **Antiope and Phocus share the same grave.** See x. 32. 11.

18. 1. **Melanippus.** The tyrant Clisthenes instituted a worship of Melanippus at Sicyon, assigning him a shrine or precinct in the Prytaneum and transferring to him the sacrifices and festivals which had previously been celebrated in honour of his foe, the Argive Adrastus (Herodotus, v. 67).

18. 2. **a line of the Iliad.** The line is *Il.* xiv. 114. But the ancient critics thought the line spurious. See Verrall's Introduction to Aeschylus, *Seven against Thebes*, p. xxv. *sq.*

18. 3. **the flame and the smoke —— part in two.** Other writers mention this marvel. See Hyginus, *Fab.* 68 and 71 ; Philostratus, *Imag.* ii. 29 ; Statius, *Theb.* xii. 429 *sqq.* ; Lucan, i. 550 *sqq.*

18. 4. **a smoke ascends of itself out of the grave.** On the hill of Vulcan in Sicily there were altars on which, when a sacrifice was to be offered, vine-twigs were heaped ; and if the god accepted the sacrifice, the twigs were said to catch fire of themselves without any light being put to them (Solinus, v. 23, p. 58, ed. Mommsen[1]). A great flame

was said to burst out of the cave of Zeus in Crete once a year (Antoninus Liberalis, *Transform.* 19). Cp. Lobeck, *Aglaophamus*, p. 123, n. ii., who refers to the annual new fire in the Church of the Holy Sepulchre at Jerusalem. The smoke which Pausanias saw curling up from the tomb of Pionis was doubtless a piece of priestly legerdemain of the same sort.

18. 5. the grave of Hector —— beside —— the fountain of Oedipus. According to Tzetzes (*Schol. on Lycophron*, 1194), Greece being afflicted with a plague, the oracle commanded the Greeks to fetch the bones of Hector from Ophrynum (Ophrynium) in the Troad and to deposit them honourably in a Greek city which had taken no part in the Trojan war. So Hector's remains were brought to Thebes and deposited near Oedipus's fountain. From Pausanias's description we infer that the fountain of Oedipus was near the gate through which the road to Chalcis ran. The fountain is doubtless the copious spring now called the spring of St. Theodore (*Hagios Theodoros*). Its clear cool water gushes out of twelve spouts under the hill on which the suburb of *Hagii Theodori* stands, a little to the right of the road to Chalcis. The water crosses the road and flows into the Ismenus a few paces lower down. Women wash clothes at it. H. N. Ulrichs thought that the grave of Hector might be one of the mounds a little farther on, to the left of the road. Sulla built an altar beside the spring of Oedipus and sacrificed on it for his victory over Archelaus, the general of Mithridates (Plutarch, *Sulla*, 19).

See H. N. Ulrichs, *Reisen und Forschungen*, 2. pp. 5, 19 *sq.*; Vischer, *Erinnerungen*, p. 562 *sq.*; Bursian, *Geogr.* 1. p. 230; Baedeker,[3] p. 184; *Guide-Joanne*, 2. p. 13; Fabricius, *Theben*, pp. 9, 23.

19. 1. Teumesus. Starting from the north-east corner of Thebes by the high-road which leads to Chalcis, we pass on the right the suburb of *Hagii Theodori*, and then descend into a wide dreary, treeless, ill-cultivated plain, which seems to have been known to the ancients as the Aonian Plain (Strabo, ix. p. 412; Moschus, iv. 36 *sq.*; Statius, *Theb.* xii. 192). On the south it is bounded by a chain of hills which divides it from the valley of the Asopus. The highest summit of the chain is now called Mt. *Soros*. About 5 miles from Thebes a low rocky hill, small but conspicuous from its isolated position in the middle of the plain, rises a few hundred yards to the left of the road. This isolated rocky hill is now called, from its position in the middle of the plain, *Mesovouni* ('middle hill'). It is the Teumesus of the ancients. The poet Antimachus described Teumesus as "a little windy hill" (Strabo, ix. p. 409; Aristotle, *Rhet.* iii. 6), and the description is apt; for the isolated situation of this little hill in the middle of a plain enclosed by mountains on the north and south must expose it to the full force of the winds both from the east and the west. Vestiges of ancient buildings have been observed at various points round the hill, especially on the eastern slope; here, therefore, may have stood the village or little town of Teumesus. The top of the hill is of some extent and fairly level, but so studded with rocks that we can hardly suppose that there was ever an ancient settlement of any size on it. However, towards its eastern end the top is somewhat smoother and here I picked up some sherds of red pottery decorated with bands of incised lines. On the south side of the hill, at the foot of the rocks, there is a conspicuous but shallow cave in which the Teumesian fox may be supposed to have had his lair. A broad stretch of level plain divides the hill on the north from the high rugged slopes of Mount Hypatus. The plain between Teumesus and Thebes is almost a dead flat and the high-road runs across it in a straight line. Some ancient writers speak of the grassy forest glades of Teumesus (Nonnus, *Dionys.* v. 59 *sq.*; Homer, *Hymn to Apollo*, 224 ; Statius, *Theb.* i. 485). From such expressions, which are quite inapplicable to the utterly bare rocky hill of *Mesovouni*, we may, perhaps, infer that the ancients extended the name Teumesus to the *Soros* hills on the south, where there are springs and grottoes, with here and there some patches of shrubs and trees.

See Leake, *Northern Greece*, 2. p. 245 *sq.*; H. N. Ulrichs, *Reisen und Forschungen*, 2. p. 23 *sq.* ; Vischer, *Erinnerungen*, p. 568 ; Bursian, *Geogr.* I. p. 224 ; Baedeker,[3] p. 188 ; *Guide-Joanne*, 2. p. 14.

19. 1. **the Teumesian fox.** This ravening beast was said to have infested the lands of Thebes, and the people paid him blackmail monthly in the shape of a boy. To rid the country of this pest, Amphitryo went to Athens and persuaded Cephalus, husband of Procris, to come and hunt the fox with his matchless hound. But Zeus turned both fox and hound into stones. See Apollodorus, iii. 4. 6 *sq.* ; Suidas and Photius, *Lexicon, s.v.* Τευμησία ; Apostolius, xvi. 42 ; *Frag. Hist. Graec.* ed. Müller, 3. p. 309 *sq.* ; cp. Hyginus, *Astronomica*, 35 ; W. Mannhardt, *Antike Wald- und Feldkulte*, p. 57 *sq.*

19. 1. **the Telchinians.** It has been argued by Mr. W. Prellwitz that the name Telchinians (Τελχῖνες) means 'copper-smiths,' being connected with the Greek χαλκός, the Lithuanian *geležis*, Old Prussian *gelso*, etc. See his article on the subject in Bezzenberger's *Beiträge zur Kunde der Indogermanischen Sprachen*, 15 (1889), pp. 148-154.

19. 2. **Glisas.** Glisas is mentioned by Homer (*Iliad*, ii. 504). It is described by Strabo (ix. p. 412) as situated on Mt. Hypatus, in the district of Thebes, near Teumesus. Pausanias found it in ruins, and these ruins may still be seen above the village of *Syrtzi* on a low rocky hill called Mt. *Tourleza* which projects from the foot of the high rugged Mt. Hypatus (the modern *Sagmatas*) into the Aonian plain. The town walls, rudely constructed of large polygonal blocks, run for a considerable distance along the slope of the hill above the village. Within their circuit and higher up the slope is a church of the Panagia built on ancient foundations and containing various fragments of antiquity, in particular a black stone inscribed with the word BYKATE in very archaic letters. On the summit of the hill of *Tourleza* are the remains of the acropolis, the wall of which seems to have been about 8 feet thick. The inner portion of the wall is built of small, beautifully-fitting polygonal blocks ; the outer side was probably constructed of larger blocks, but it is at present buried under the soil. Some foundations of buildings may also be seen on the acropolis. The general aspect of Glisas, perched on a rocky hill with a rugged ravine on the eastern side and dominated by the higher rocky slopes of Mt. Hypatus, is not unlike that of Mycenae.

See Leake, *Northern Greece*, 2. pp. 247, 250 (who seems to take the ruins now called *Kastri* for Glisas; see below § 4 note); Welcker, *Tagebuch*, 2. p. 27 *sq.*; H. N. Ulrichs, *Reisen und Forschungen*, 2. p. 27 *sq.*; L. Ross, *Wanderungen*, 1. p. 106; Bursian, *Geogr.* 1. p. 216; Vischer, *Erinnerungen*, p. 568.

19. 2. **a small mound shaded by a wild wood** etc. This is doubtless the tumulus in the plain in front of the village of *Syrtzi*. It is composed of earth and small stones and was enclosed by a wall of polygonal stones, of which many large blocks are still standing in their places. The tumulus is of considerable size, and rising as it does in the open plain strikes the eye from a distance. Pausanias calls it small, perhaps by comparison with the great tumulus at Marathon. But it certainly far surpasses in size the barrows commonly erected in Greece by private persons. See H. N. Ulrichs, *Reisen und Forschungen*, 2. p. 26; Welcker, *Tagebuch*, 2. p. 28; L. Ross, *Wanderungen*, 1. p. 106 *sq.*; Bursian, *Geogr.* 1. p. 216.

19. 2. **the tomb of Aegialeus is at Pagae.** See i. 44. 4.

19. 3. **Tiresias —— chopped off its head** etc. It was said that Tiresias, seeing two snakes coupling on Mt. Cithaeron or Mt. Cyllene, killed the female and was himself consequently transformed into a woman. Eight years afterwards he again saw two snakes coupling; this time he killed the male, and was changed back into a man. See Tzetzes, *Schol. on Lycophron*, 683; Eustathius, on Homer, *Odyssey*, p. 1665; Ovid, *Metam.* iii. 324 *sqq.*; Hyginus, *Fab.* 75; Apollodorus, iii. 6. 7. (These accounts partly differ from each other slightly, partly supplement each other. I have given above what would seem to be the original version of the story.) The idea that it is unlucky to see snakes coupling appears to be widespread. In the Himalayas certain religious ceremonies are prescribed when a person sees snakes coupling (*Journal of the Asiatic Society of Bengal*, 1884, pt. 1. p. 101; the nature of the ceremonies is not described). In Timorlaut, an island in the East Indies, it is deemed an omen of great misfortune to a man if he dreams that he sees snakes coupling (J. G. F. Riedel, *Sluik- en kroeshurige rassen tusschen Selebes en Papua*, p. 285).

19. 3. **a temple of Supreme Zeus.** Mount Hypatus is the conspicuous mountain now called *Mt. Sagmatas;* it is bold and rocky, and has a flat summit which is crowned with a monastery of the Transfiguration, founded by Alexis Comnenus. The church of the monastery contains fine mosaics, and stands on the foundations of the temple of Zeus. Both the church and the monastery, as well as two neighbouring chapels, contain many considerable fragments of antiquity built into the walls. The dome of the church is supported by two ancient monolithic columns, with their bases and capitals. From the summit the view is extensive and fine, embracing the great expanse of the Copaic plain (a lake no longer), the dark blue water of the deep lake of Hylica environed by

barren and rugged mountains, the Euboean sea, and on the horizon the peaks of Parnassus, Helicon, and Cithaeron.

See Leake, *Northern Greece*, 2. p. 219; H. N. Ulrichs, *Reisen und Forschungen*, 2. p. 28 *sq.*; L. Ross, *Wanderungen*, 1. p. 106; Bursian, *Geogr.* 1. p. 216; *Guide-Joanne*, 2. p. 14.

The lake of Hylica (*Likeri*), which Pausanias does not mention, is a large and beautiful sheet of blue water with winding bays and arms, dominated on the north by the grey precipitous crags of Mount Ptous. I was told that the lake has been much increased in depth and area since a portion of the water of the Copaic plain has been drained into it. From the lake the water passes by a tunnel into the sister lake of *Paralimni* on the north-east, from which again it passes into the sea near Anthedon. The path from Acraephnium (*Karditsa*) to Anthedon keeps along the slope of Mt. Ptous below the line of precipices but above the northern shore of the lake of Hylica. Thence it ascends steeply a rocky ridge and then descends to the shore of the lake *Paralimni*, a long straight sheet of water of uniform breadth and without bays or arms, bounded on the north along its whole length by an unbroken range of steep barren stony hills. The path runs along the southern bank of the lake where the ground is level or nearly so for more than half the length of the lake. But towards its eastern end the hills come close down to the water on this side also. It is strange that ancient history and mythology are almost wholly silent on the subject of these two lakes, one of which at least has good claims to beauty. In their secluded mountains they lay remote from the bustle and traffic of the world, from the caravans of commerce, and the march of armies.

As to lake Hylica, see Vischer, *Erinnerungen*, p. 568 *sq.*; Wheler, *Journey*, p. 468 *sq.*; Leake, *Northern Greece*, 2. p. 315; Fiedler, *Reise*, 1. p. 105. I followed the path beside the two lakes from *Karditsa* to Anthedon, 8th November 1895.

19. 3. the Thermodon. This stream was mentioned in an oracle of Bacis recorded by Herodotus (ix. 43), who tells us that it flowed between Tanagra and Glisas. It is probably the stream now called the *Calamites*, which rises west of Harma (see § 4 note), is fed chiefly by the rills from Mt. Hypatus, and flows westward through the Aonian plain to the lake of Hylica. See H. N. Ulrichs, *Reisen und Forschungen*, 2. p. 25.

19. 3. the tomb of Chalcodon. Near the hill of *Mesovouni* (Teumesus), on either side of the road to Chalcis, there are some sepulchral mounds or barrows. One of these may be the tomb of Chalcodon. See H. N. Ulrichs, *Reisen und Forschungen*, 2. p. 23.

19. 4. Harma. The high-road from Thebes to Chalcis, after running eastward through the plain for a distance of about 12 miles, makes a bend to the north and enters a pass among the hills which bound the plain on the north. Just where the road bends round, a hill of some height (perhaps 600 or 700 feet) rises on the right or east side of the road; its wooded or bushy summit is crowned with the remains of an ancient acropolis which seems to have been Harma. The walls are thin and built of rough polygonal blocks which are generally small. The north wall, however, is built of large hewn blocks, and so is an ancient foundation within the circuit of the walls. Another line of wall descends the hill into the pass, and ascends the hill on the opposite or western side of the road. This wall, crossing the pass and climbing the hills on each side, was doubtless a fortification built to defend the pass either against Chalcis or against Thebes. A khan now stands beside the high-road at the south-western foot of the hill of Harma. The ruins of Harma are now known as *Kastri*. About a mile or so to the west of it a good many graves have been excavated on the north side of the high-road. At this point I noticed also a few ancient squared blocks of fair size close together. The identification of the ruins on the hill as those of Harma is in harmony with the testimony both of Pausanias and Strabo; for Pausanias implies and Strabo directly states (ix. p. 404) that Harma was on the road which led from Thebes to Chalcis. Strabo further describes Harma as a deserted village in the district of Tanagra. The place, as Pausanias and Plutarch (*Parallela*, 6) tell us, was said to have received its name of Harma ('chariot') because Amphiaraus, fleeing from before the walls of Thebes, was here swallowed up by the earth in his chariot, or, according to others, because the chariot of Adrastus was here shivered (Strabo, *l.c.*) According to Philochorus (referred to by Strabo, *l.c.*), Adrastus himself was saved by the people of Harma, who were rewarded for this good deed by the grateful Argives with the citizenship of Argos. Harma sent its contingent of warriors to the siege of Troy (Homer, *Il.* ii. 499).

L. Ross, however, identified as Harma an ancient fortress of which some imposing remains are to be seen about 3 miles south-west of the acropolis which we have seen grounds for supposing to be Harma. The fortress in question is situated on a rocky plateau about ten minutes' walk to the west of the village of *Dritsa* (*Andritsa*). The path from Thebes to Tanagra runs at the southern foot of the plateau, close to the ruins. The plateau, which may average 50 or 60 feet high, is of some extent and its edges are steep and well defined, being formed for the most part of a line of rocks which on the west and south-west sides attain to the height of respectable cliffs. At the highest point of the plateau, close to its western end, there are the ruins of a square mediaeval tower, built, in the usual miserable style, of irregular blocks and bricks stuffed into the crevices. From the tower the plateau shelves away in a grassy slope to the edge of the cliffs. The view over the rolling plain in the direction of Thebes is closed by Parnassus on the west. Helicon is seen on the south-west, and Mt. Ptous appears beyond the nearer Mt. Hypatus on the north-west.

The ancient fortress did not occupy the whole of this plateau, but only its western portion. Hence it was necessary to defend it on the east, toward the rest of the plateau, by a massive wall, of which there are very imposing remains. The defence on this side was facilitated by a deep indentation or bay, with rocky edges, on the south side of the plateau at this point. The ancient fortification-wall, beginning at the head of this bay or indentation, extends northwards in a curve with the concave side turned to the east. Though of no great extent the wall is well preserved, and is one of the finest specimens of ancient masonry to be seen in Greece. At its southern end it begins with a very massive square tower, 23 feet broad and 8 feet 9 inches deep. The lower part of the tower, which alone is well preserved, is about 10

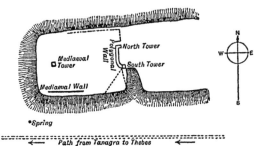

FIG. 2.—PLAN OF RUINS NEAR DRITSA (THE ANCIENT HELEON ?).

feet high and is beautifully constructed of quadrangular blocks, some of them of immense size. Two of the blocks measure 7 feet 6 inches long by nearly 5 feet high. The upper part of the tower was built of polygonal masonry; for a fragment of it, consisting of four large well-jointed polygonal blocks, is preserved. The total height of the tower as it stands is about 14 feet. On the north side of this massive tower the wall begins and runs in a long curve. It is magnificently built of very large, carefully-smoothed, and accurately-jointed polygonal blocks resting on a socle of squared blocks laid in horizontal courses. Some of the polygonal blocks are over 6 feet long and 5 feet high. Of the socle of quadrangular masonry one, two, and three courses are visible according to the slope of the ground, but probably more is concealed beneath the soil. The height of the wall above ground varies from 3 feet 6 inches to 10 feet. At one point, where there is only a single polygonal block resting on a single course of quadrangular masonry, the height of the wall is nevertheless 7 feet 8 inches, the polygonal block alone being fully 6 feet high. At its north end the wall makes a slight projection. Here there seems to have been a second square tower about 21 feet broad, corresponding to the tower at the south end of the wall and flanking a gateway. Beyond the gateway to the north there are some slight remains of a wall built of large rough stones in a style immeasurably inferior to that of the beautiful polygonal wall to the south. The northern face of the plateau is a steep grassy slope, and along its edge are more remains of a similar rough wall of grey stones, which however rise but little above the ground. Along the western face of the plateau there are no vestiges of fortification ; the cliffs here seem to have been thought a sufficient defence. The southern side of the plateau is also defended by a line of high and nearly perpendicular rocks, but they are not so high as the cliffs on the west, and here accordingly may be seen remains of a mediaeval fortification-wall, built of small stones and mortar, running along the very edge of the rocks. From the south side of the plateau a line of large rough stones running north-east in the direction of the great polygonal tower may be the remains of a fortification-wall completing the circuit. Thus the massive and beautiful wall of polygonal masonry exists on the eastern side of the fortress alone, and extends along only about a third of that side. There are no vestiges of a similar wall at any other point of the circuit. It seems as if the people of the little town had begun to replace their old rough walls by a magnificent new one, but were prevented by poverty or some other cause from carrying out the undertaking. The area enclosed by the walls and cliffs is not large, but this may have been merely the acropolis. It contains considerable vestiges of buildings in the form of rows of large rough stones. These buildings were probably mediaeval or modern, constructed out of the ruins of the ancient town. At the south-western foot of the plateau, where the cliffs are highest and steepest, there is a copious spring encased by masonry ; and near it, just under the cliffs, is a small chapel. The water of the spring forms a brook which flows northward to the foot of Mount Hypatus.

The ancient fortress which has just been described lies about 2 miles to the south of the high-road from Thebes to Chalcis. Hence it was probably not Harma, as L. Ross supposed, since Harma would seem to have been close to that road. Leake conjectured that the ruins might be those of Pharae, one of the four villages or petty towns which in the time of Strabo belonged to Tanagra. The other three were Heleon (or Eleon), Harma, and Mycalessus (Strabo, ix. p. 405). H. N. Ulrichs, however, has made it likely that the ruins in question are those of Heleon or Eleon. The spring at the south-western foot of the plateau is probably the ancient Acidusa ; the brook which it forms is probably the Glaucia ; and the stream to the east of *Dritsa* which flows in a broad and deep bed between low undulating hills to join the Asopus is probably the Scamander. See Plutarch, *Quaest. Graec.* 41. Heleon was said to have derived its name from a marsh (*helos*), which, however, in the days of Strabo had mostly or wholly disappeared (Strabo, ix. pp. 404, 406). There is no marsh now at *Dritsa*, but the stream which seems to have been the Glaucia disappears in the fields between *Dritsa* and Harma, and during the winter rains forms a marsh there. Pharae, the fourth of the small towns belonging to Tanagra, may very well be the ruined acropolis which crowns a rugged but not lofty hill about half-way between *Dritsa* and Tanagra, to the west of the village of *Vratsi*. The walls, over 7 feet thick, are built of well-jointed polygonal blocks and enclose a space about 70 paces square. Among the fir-trees on the lower slope of the hill are some large foundations, perhaps remains of the lower town.

See Leake, *Northern Greece*, 2. p. 466 *sqq.*; H. N. Ulrichs, *Reisen und Forschungen*, 2. pp. 77-80 ; L. Ross, *Wanderungen*, 1. p. 107 *sqq.*; Bursian, in *Berichte über die Verhandl. d. k. sächs. Gesell. d. Wissen. zu Leipzig*, Philolog. histor. Cl. 11 (1859), pp. 115-118. I visited the ruins at *Dritsa*, 14th November

1895, and have described them from personal observation.   The ruins of Harma I have seen only from a distance and below.

19. 4. where the Thebans say it vanished.   See ix. 8. 3.

19. 4. Mycalessus.   See i. 23. 3.   Between 2 and 3 miles beyond Harma on the road to Chalcis a broad low hill or sloping platform rises on the left.   On this hill there are ancient remains consisting of foundation-walls, tiles, blocks of stone, etc.   These are probably the ruins of Mycalessus.   The hill or platform is only about 100 feet above the plain; but behind rises a higher ridge, on which, according to H. N. Ulrichs, an acropolis may be clearly traced.   But according to Lieut. (afterwards Admiral) Spratt no acropolis or ruin is to be seen on this ridge.   The view to the east is cut off by the hills, and the Euripus is not visible.   A view of the Euripus is first obtained about an hour farther on in the direction of Chalcis; the road here ascends to a narrow pass, from which a beautiful prospect is obtained of the narrow strait with the town of Chalcis on the opposite shore and the mountains of Euboea in the background.   Thus Mycalessus was, as Pausanias says (i. 23. 3), an inland town, and the inhabitants little dreamed of being attacked by an enemy from the sea (Thucydides, vii. 29).   The statement of Strabo (ix. p. 404) that Mycalessus was a village belonging to Tanagra situated beside the road from Thebes to Chalcis accords perfectly with the situation of the ruins just described.   The district is now called *Rhitzona*, from a hamlet of that name lying in the valley about a mile and a half to the east of the ruins.   The valley is poorly cultivated, but some pine-trees, scattered singly and in clumps, serve to break the monotony of the landscape.   The pine-trees in the district of Mycalessus are mentioned by Statius (*Theb.* vii. 272).

The channel which separates Euboea from the mainland is narrowest at Chalcis, so narrow indeed that from antiquity it has been generally spanned at this point by a bridge.   This narrowest part of the channel was the Euripus proper (Strabo, ix. p. 403; Dionysius, *Descriptio Graeciae*, 91).   Immediately to the south of Chalcis the channel expands into the circular bay of *Vourko*, and then narrows again into a second strait, so that the bay of *Vourko* is nearly landlocked.   On the mainland a conspicuous hill called *Megalo Vouno* ('big hill') rises steeply from the southern shore of the bay to a height of perhaps 800 or 900 feet.[1]   Its sides are steep, rugged, and rocky, and its summit is encircled not far from the top by the considerable remains of an ancient acropolis.   The wall exists, though in ruins, almost all round the hill with hardly a break and in its full thickness, which is about 7 ft. 6 in.   In some places it is still more than 6 ft. high.   It consists of an outer and an inner face of rude irregular polygonal masonry with a core of small stones.   Even in the outer face of the wall the blocks are not large, and in the inner face they are as a rule a good deal smaller.   The wall is best preserved on the northern side of the hill, where it extends along pretty uniformly at a height of 4 and 5 feet.   Next to it the east wall is best

---

[1] I estimate the height partly by the eye and partly by the time I took (44 minutes) to ascend from the shore to the summit.

preserved. On the other hand the western and southern walls are mostly in ruins. But it was the south side that was most carefully fortified, as may be seen by the square towers which here project from the curtain at short intervals of 20 yards or so, whereas on the other sides towers hardly occur at all. The reason for this specially strong fortification on the south is that on this side the hill sends out a long ridge descending towards the bay of Aulis. This was therefore the most accessible and most easily assailable side of the fortress. For the same reason the two chief gates, each flanked with two square towers, are to be seen on the south side of the hill. One of these gateways, at the south-east corner, is 5 ft. 8 in. wide. The other principal gateway, a good deal to the west, is 6 ft. 6 in. wide. The tower which flanks it on the west is about 22 ft. broad on the face and projects 13 ft. from the curtain. The masonry of this tower is much more careful than that of the walls and approaches to the quadrangular or ashlar in style; the blocks are hewn and better fitted. On its western face it is standing to a height of from 4 to nearly 7 feet. The tower is set at a distance of about 9 feet to the west of the gateway. The tower on the eastern side of the gateway is more ruinous. Two of the other towers in the south wall have each a passage about 3 feet wide opening into them through the thickness of the wall. Another of them, about 20 feet broad and projecting 18 feet from the curtain, is built of large hewn blocks laid in roughly horizontal courses. In the eastern wall there is another gateway, 5 ft. 8 in. wide, facing north-east toward Chalcis, and beside a tower at the north-western corner of the fortress there is a postern 3 feet wide opening to the west. The number of towers of which there are undoubted remains is eight or nine. On the inner side of the eastern wall there are remains of a staircase leading down from the top of the wall.

Although the ground enclosed by the fortification-walls is rugged with rocks and at present overgrown with shrubs, there are vestiges of human habitation on it in the shape of broken stones and pottery; but these vestiges may be modern. Among the shrubs with which the ground is encumbered are holly-oaks and lentisks.

The top of the mountain commands grand views for long distances both up and down the Euripus as well as across it to Euboea. On the north-east, across the strait, the leaf-like promontory, on one branch of which Chalcis stands, is seen spread out below. Chalcis itself is in full view not much more than a mile away. To the south-east we descry the acropolis of Eretria. On the south is seen the Bay of Aulis, but the nearer little bay, the *Little Vathy*, is hidden by a protruding spur of the hill. Beyond Aulis to the south an undulating country stretches away in the direction of Tanagra; and beyond it again, on the southern horizon, rise the slopes of Mount Parnes in Attica. Low hills lie to the south-west in the direction of Thebes. On the west a high hill bars the view; while on the north-west soars the high pointed Mount Messapius.

From the south-east corner of the fortress a ruinous wall runs southward along a projecting spur or ridge of the hill. This wall makes several turns, but on the whole it keeps a southerly direction parallel to and at a considerable distance above the straits. Just above the narrowest part of the straits there are traces of a gateway blocked with fallen stones. Beyond it the wall is better preserved. In one place it is 3 ft. 6 in. high and 7 ft. 6 in. thick. The style of the masonry resembles that of the citadel. The wall comes to an abrupt stop on the side of the ridge not very far beyond the gateway. Its existence seems to show that the fortress on the top of the hill was only a citadel and that there was a lower town on the slope towards the straits.

It seems fairly certain that this ancient town on the *Megalo Vouno* must have been Hyria, a place coupled by Homer (*Il.* ii. 496) with Aulis. It had once belonged to Thebes but in the days of Strabo it was reckoned to Tanagra. Strabo tells us (ix. p. 404) that Hyria was near Aulis ; and Stephanus Byzantius says (*s.v.* 'Υρία) that it was on the Euripus. These statements accord perfectly with the position of the ruins in question, for the hill on which they stand rises from the shore of the Euripus, and at its south-eastern foot is Aulis. Yet Col. Leake held that the town on the *Megalo Vouno* was Mycalessus, and this view reappears in the guide-books of Baedeker and the *Joanne*. It is, however, not only in direct contradiction with the statements of Pausanias and Strabo, who say that Mycalessus was an inland town on the road from Thebes to Chalcis, but is wholly irreconcilable with Thucydides's account of the military operations in the Peloponnesian war, when Mycalessus was surprised and its population massacred by a corps of Thracian mercenaries. Thucydides's account of the affair is briefly this. The Athenians, not having money enough to pay these Thracian mercenaries, sent them home by sea under the charge of an Athenian officer Diitrephes. He was ordered to sail through the Euripus and to do the enemy as much harm as he conveniently could by the way. So he first landed in the territory of Tanagra and made a hasty foray ; then re-embarking he sailed along the Euripus to Chalcis in Euboea. But at evening he crossed the strait, landed his troops in Boeotian territory and led them against Mycalessus. During the night he bivouacked unseen at the Hermaeum, distant about 16 furlongs (nearly 2 miles) from Mycalessus, and at daybreak he stormed the city. The inhabitants were completely taken by surprise ; for, says Thucydides, " they kept no watch and never expected that any one would come so far up from the sea to attack them." The wall was weak, and in some places ruinous, and the gates stood open, for the people felt quite secure. Everything that breathed within the walls, including the very cattle and the school-children who had just assembled in a large school, was put to the sword by the Thracians. Word of this great disaster reached the Thebans, and they hastened to avenge it. Overtaking the Thracians before the latter had got far from the town, they recaptured the booty and pursued them down to the Euripus and the sea, where their transports were anchored. In the process of embarkation the Thebans slew most of the Thracians ; for the crews of the ships, seeing what was going on ashore, moored their vessels out of bowshot, and the Thracians fortunately could not swim. During the actual retreat the miscreants had lost few; for they kept in close order and from time to time halted and charged the Theban cavalry, who hung on their rear till the infantry could come up. This narrative implies that Mycalessus was at some distance (more than 2 miles) from the sea. For (1) the Thracians marching from the shore of the Euripus to attack Mycalessus halted for the night at the Hermaeum, which was still about 2 miles distant from the town. (2) The people were wholly unprepared for an attack from the side of the sea; they "never expected that any one would come so far up from the sea to attack them"; they kept no watch; their gates stood open. (3) The Thracians had to retreat some considerable distance from the town before they reached the sea, and they did so in good order, pressed by the Theban cavalry. Evidently, then, the ground between Mycalessus and the sea was level enough to allow cavalry to act on it.

Now if, with Col. Leake, we identify the town on *Megalo Vouno* with Mycalessus, we have to make the following extraordinary assumptions. We must suppose that the Mycalessians were fully aware of the proximity of the enemy; for the hill of *Megalo Vouno* rises abruptly from the shore of the Euripus and commands an uninterrupted view both up and down it. The inhabitants of this place may have seen the enemy landing in the territory of Tanagra and pillaging the country a few miles to the south; and they must certainly have seen his ships sailing past their town in broad daylight to Chalcis, which is in full view of the summit of the hill and not much more than a mile away. Is it credible that the inhabitants of Mycalessus, with the enemy's ships actually under their eyes about a mile off, should have so little dreamed of an attack that they posted no sentinels and left all their gates open, and that even the children were repeating their lessons as usual in the school? Such supine carelessness would almost have deserved the fearful fate which overtook Mycalessus. Again, if Mycalessus were the town on *Megalo Vouno*, the Thracians, in order to reach the sea and their ships after sacking the town, had nothing to do but to descend the steep side of the mountain to the shore, which they could have done easily in half an hour. Yet there was time for word of the massacre to be carried to Thebes (more than 16 miles distant as the crow flies) and for the Theban forces to hurry up and overtake the Thracians before the latter had got to the bottom of the hill! And we are to suppose that the Theban cavalry pursued the enemy down the steep, rugged, rocky mountain-side, while the Thracian infantry retreated before them in close military formation, occasionally halting and charging the cavalry who were riding down the break-neck declivity behind them!

On the other hand, if, with H. N. Ulrichs and Bursian, we identify Mycalessus with the ruins near *Rhitzona*, Thucydides's narrative is perfectly intelligible. The town was out of sight of the sea and distant fully 4 miles from the nearest salt water. From Chalcis the distance is about 6 miles. If we suppose that the Thracians landed opposite Chalcis, they would approach Mycalessus by the high-road which ran, and still runs, from Chalcis to Thebes. They landed in the evening, marched about 4 miles along the road, and halted for the night at the

Hermaeum, 2 miles from Mycalessus.   They attacked the town at daybreak; word reached Thebes (about 12 miles distant as the crow flies) a few hours later; the Theban cavalry came galloping to the scene of the massacre; overtook the retreating Thracians a mile or two along the road to Chalcis; and followed them all the way to the shore, but without making much impression on them, as the Thracians kept in close order.   It was only when the latter at last reached the shore and attempted to get on board their ships that they met the fate they so richly merited.

The site of the Hermaeum mentioned by Thucydides may have been at a point where the road to Chalcis leads through a natural pass (now called the pass of *Anephorites*) between two peaked heights. Here, on either side of the road, may be seen the remains of a thick wall of loose stones running at right angles to the road and ascending the heights both to the left and to the right of it.   On the right (east) the wall may be traced as far as the ruined town (probably Hyria) on the *Megalo Vouno*.   This wall, part of which was hastily repaired in the Greek War of Independence, seems to have been intended to defend the frontier of the Theban territory towards Chalcis; and as Hermes is associated with boundaries (cp. ii. 38. 7, viii. 34. 6, viii. 35. 2) he might very well have a sanctuary (Hermaeum) at the point on the road where the wall marked the Theban boundary.   The distance of this point from the ruins which, with H. N. Ulrichs and Bursian, I take to be those of Mycalessus, appears to correspond tolerably with the distance (16 furlongs) of the Hermaeum from Mycalessus.   The Hermaeum mentioned by Livy (xxv. 50) seems to have been a different place; it was on the shore of the Euripus and there was a regular ferry across from it to Euboea.   Leake appears to have involved himself in topographical difficulties from supposing that the Hermaeum of Thucydides and the Hermaeum of Livy were the same place.

Lieutenant (afterwards Admiral) Spratt was of opinion that the ancient road from Chalcis to Thebes did not, like the present road, go direct by the pass of *Anephorites*, but kept close to the coast, and made a circuit round the bay of *Vourko* to Aulis; for he found the ruts of chariot-wheels very distinct all round the bay of *Vourko*. But this only proves that there was, as we should expect, a coast road from Chalcis to Aulis, Delium, and Oropus.   It does not show that the high-road from Chalcis to Thebes did not follow the direct and natural route by the pass of *Anephorites*.

See Dodwell, *Tour*, 2. p. 249; Wordsworth, *Athens and Attica*, p. 4 *sqq.*; Leake, *Northern Greece*, 2. pp. 247 *sq.*, 251 *sqq.*, 264, 269 *sq.*; Welcker, *Tagebuch*, 2. p. 97 *sqq.* (Welcker took the ruins on *Megalo Vouno* to be those of Aulis); H. N. Ulrichs, *Reisen und Forschungen*, 2. p. 30 *sqq.*; Spratt, 'Remarks on Aulis, Mycalessus, and some parts of Euboea,' *Transactions of the Royal Society of Literature*, Second Series, 2 (1847), p. 238 *sqq.*; Bursian, *Geogr.* I. p. 217; Baedeker,[3] pp. 185, 189 *sq.*; *Guide-Joanne*, 2. p. 14.   I visited the ruins on *Megalo Vouno*, 12th November 1895, and have described them from personal observation.

19. 4. **because the cow that led Cadmus —— lowed —— here.** Cp. *Etymolog. Magnum*, s.v. Μυκαλησσός, p. 595.

19. 5. In the direction of the sea from Mycalessus etc. From
Mycalessus Pausanias appears to have pursued his way to the shore of
the Euripus, opposite Chalcis ; this we may infer from § 6, where he
appears to be speaking of the Euripus proper, *i.e.* of the narrowest part
of the channel which divides Euboea from the mainland. He therefore
continued to follow the line of the high-road from Thebes to Chalcis.
Beyond the ruins which we may consider to be those of Mycalessus, the
road rises steeply up a ridge of hills connected to the north with Mt.
Ktypa (the ancient Messapius), which now appears on the left. We
then enter the pass of *Anephorites* (see above, p. 70). From the summit
of the pass, now called *Tambouria* ('fortifications') *tou Krizioti* after
the Greek patriot Kriziotis who fortified the pass in 1829, we obtain a
beautiful view of the blue winding waters of the Euripus, the town of
Chalcis on the farther side of the strait, and the mountains of Euboea
rising behind. The road now descends rapidly into the maritime plain
and skirts the bay of *Vourko.* The plain consists of open corn land,
without trees, and is intersected by low rocks of white marble, covered
with wild thyme. The slopes of the lofty and conspicuous Mt. *Ktypa,*
which hem the plain in on the north-west, are also very rocky. Skirting the shore of the bay on the right, we pass on the left the low isolated
rocky hill of *Karababa* crowned with a fort. In the walls of this fort
there are some ancient blocks and pieces of marble, probably brought
from Chalcis ; and on the eastern and southern slopes of the hill there
are some rows of oblong sinkings cut in the rock, perhaps ancient
graves. The hill of *Karababa* has sometimes been wrongly identified
with the ancient Salganeus. It is probably the ancient Canethus,
which, in the time of Alexander, the people of Chalcis enclosed within
the fortifications of their city (Strabo, x. p. 447). Immediately after
passing this little hill we reach the strait and bridge of Chalcis. See
Leake, *Northern Greece,* 2. p. 247 *sq.* ; H. N. Ulrichs, *Reisen und
Forschungen,* 2. p. 33 *sq.* ; L. Ross, *Wanderungen,* 2. p. 110 *sq.* ; Bursian,
in *Berichte über die Verhandl. d. kön. sächs. Gesell. d. Wissen. zu
Leipzig,* Philolog. histor. Cl. 11 (1859), pp. 119-121 ; *Guide-Joanne,* 2.
p. 14 *sq.* When I visited Chalcis in 1895 there was no bridge across
the strait, the old bridge had been taken down and a new one was in
preparation.

It was no part of the plan of Pausanias to describe Euboea ;
hence, instead of passing the bridge to Chalcis, he turned south on his
way to Aulis. A little before he reached that port he came to the
sanctuary of Mycalessian Demeter, which was on the right (here the
south) of the strait. Hence that sanctuary probably stood somewhere
on the shore of the spacious circular bay of *Vourko.* That by 'the
right' of the Euripus Pausanias here meant 'the south' of the strait is
clear from ix. 22. 5, where 'the left' of the Euripus undoubtedly means
'north' of it.

H. N. Ulrichs supposed that after quitting Mycalessus, Pausanias,
instead of following the high-road north-east to Chalcis, turned off to the
right (east) by the valley of *Rhitzona* in the direction of Aulis. About
half an hour beyond *Rhitzona* there is a ruined church on the left of the

road, into which some ancient squared blocks have been built. Ulrichs thought that this might be the site of the sanctuary of Demeter. See his *Reisen und Forschungen,* 2. p. 38. This view, it appears to me, is decidedly wrong. Pausanias's words "at this point the Euripus separates Euboea from Boeotia" (§ 6) seem clearly to refer to the strait of Chalcis and to imply that he conceives himself standing at the strait and facing across it toward Chalcis. On his right (to the south) he then had the sanctuary of Demeter, and farther on in the same direction (still farther south) he came to Aulis. Pursuing his route southward he afterwards came to Delium and next to Tanagra. Thus the sanctuary of Mycalessian Demeter was north of Aulis, not south of it, as Ulrichs supposed.

19. 6. Aulis. If we follow for 3 or 4 miles the road which leads from the strait of Chalcis southward along the Boeotian coast, we come to a small winding nearly landlocked bay or creek at the southeastern foot of the rugged hill of *Megalo Vouno.* The bay is sheltered both on the north and on the south by rocky peninsulas, of which the southern is much the higher and attains the height of a small hill, though the ground which joins it to the mainland is flat. But in spite of the perfect shelter which it affords, the bay is not much used as a harbour, since its entrance is difficult. The rocky peninsula which protects the bay on the south divides it from a broader and straighter bay, which has a wide and open entrance on the east and a stretch of flat land and flat beach at its inner or western end. The smaller northern bay is now called the *Little Vathy;* the larger southern bay is called the *Great Vathy.* The latter is the famous Bay of Aulis from which the Greek fleet sailed for Troy. It was called by the ancients the Bathys Limen ('deep harbour') to distinguish it from the smaller bay on the north (Strabo, ix. p. 403 ; Diodorus, xix. 77), and the modern name of *Vathy* is doubtless only a slightly changed form of the ancient name, *b* being always pronounced as *v* by the modern Greeks. Strabo clearly distinguishes between the two bays (ix. p. 403) and says that the smaller would hold only fifty ships. The scenery of the Bay of Aulis is somewhat dull and tame. Vegetation is conspicuously absent, and the hills enclosing the bay and the small valley that runs up westward from its head are low, bare, and partly rocky. Through the mouth of the bay, however, there is a view eastward across the Euripus to the mountains of Euboea. The small town of Aulis would seem to have been situated on the peninsula which divides the Bay of Aulis (the *Great Vathy*) on the south from the *Little Vathy* on the north. For Strabo, who describes Aulis as "a rocky place and a village of the Tanagraeans," implies that it stood between the two bays (ix. p. 403) ; and Statius describes it as situated on a long rocky ridge jutting out into the sea (*Achill.* i. 447 *sqq.*) In point of fact H. N. Ulrichs observed the foundations of walls and of buildings on the low isthmus of the rocky peninsula which divides the two bays. These foundations may have been the remains of Aulis. They seem now to have disappeared ; at least in 1895 I looked for them in vain, and some shepherds on the spot informed me that there were no ancient ruins there. The epithet 'rocky' applied by Homer to Aulis (*Iliad*, ii. 496) is eminently suitable.

From the head of the Bay of Aulis a small valley, sloping gently upwards, runs inland between hills for something over a mile. It is watered by a brook which falls into the bay About a mile up the valley from the shore is a ruined Byzantine chapel of St. Nicholas (*Hagios Nikolaos*), which is supposed to occupy the site of the temple of Artemis, mentioned by Pausanias, where Iphigenia was led to the altar to be sacrificed. The scene, if it indeed be so, of this famous event in Greek legend was somewhat bleak and cheerless as I saw it under a leaden sky on a dull November afternoon. The ruined chapel, with its fallen dome and roofless walls, had a forlorn air, standing solitary in a bare stony ploughed field on the slope of the low hills that enclose the little valley on the south. Similar hills—low, stony and treeless—with higher hills rising above them on the north and west, shut in the valley on all sides except the east, where appeared, of a pale blue-green colour under the chill November sky, a bit of the bay of Aulis, beyond it the open channel of the Euripus, and still farther off, bathed in a gloomy purple, the coast and mountains of Euboea. Bare ploughed fields, with a small tree dotted here and there among them, occupied all the bottom of the valley, and formed the foreground of the melancholy scene. Yet bare fields, stony hills, leaden sky, cold steely sea, and purple mountains glooming in the distance, seemed a fitting framework for the ruined shrine, with its memories of departed glory. Almost the only patch of green to relieve the monotony of brown earth and grey rock was a verdant market garden some forty or fifty yards to the west of the chapel. The garden is watered by a well, not by a spring, and the gardener told my dragoman that the nearest spring was distant twenty minutes' walk to the west. Whether this spring, which I did not visit, is the one beside which the Greeks sacrificed "under a beauteous plane whence sparkling water flowed" (Homer, *Il.* ii. 305 *sqq.*), it might be hard to decide. In the chapel are some pieces of small columns, and built into the sides of the inner doorway are two blocks of white marble which seemed to me to be ancient. According to one account the temple of Artemis was built by Agamemnon (Dionysius, *Descriptio Graeciae*, 89 *sq.*); according to another it was much older than the Trojan war (Pliny, *Nat. hist.* xvi. 217). It was visited by L. Aemilius Paullus in 167 B.C., as we learn from Livy (xlv. 27), who describes Aulis as a harbour distant 3 miles from Chalcis. If Livy means to give the distance by sea, as he seems to do, he is nearly right; the distance by land, owing to the great sweep of the Bay of *Vourko*, is nearer 4 miles than 3. The inscribed pedestal of a statue of a lady named Olyppiche, daughter of Hagias, who had been priestess of Artemis of Aulis, is preserved in the museum at *Skimatari* near Tanagra (*C. I. G. G. S.* 1. No. 565).

See Wheler, *Journey into Greece*, p. 456 ; Dodwell, *Tour*, 2. p. 154 ; Leake, *Northern Greece*, 2. p. 262 *sq.* ; H. N. Ulrichs, *Reisen und Forschungen*, 2. p. 38 *sqq.* ; L. Ross, *Wanderungen*, 2. p. 106 *sqq.* ; Vischer, *Erinnerungen*, p. 677 *sq.* ; Bursian, *Geogr.* 1. p. 218 ; Baedeker,[3] p. 189 ; *Guide-Joanne*, 2. p. 3 *sq.* I visited Aulis 12th November 1895.

19. 6. one of the images carries torches. This image is represented on coins of Tanagra of the imperial age (Fig. 3). On these coins

Artemis is figured as a huntress in a tetrastyle temple,
with a spear in her raised right hand and a torch in
her left ; on each side of the temple is a palm-tree
(see § 8) ; and below is a ship with sailors. On one
of the coins the goddess holds a torch in each hand.
This may be the more correct copy of the image. Or
possibly Pausanias may have mistaken the spear in
the right hand of the goddess for a second torch.

FIG. 3.—ARTEMIS
(COIN OF TANAGRA).
See Imhoof-Blumer and Gardner, *Num. Comm. on
Paus.* p. 113, with pl. X iii.-v. As Aulis belonged to
Tanagra (see § 8), it was natural that the temple and image at Aulis
should appear on coins of Tanagra.

19. 6. to sacrifice Iphigenia. The sacrifice of Iphigenia is represented on a mosaic found at Ampurias (the ancient Emporiae) in Cata-
lonia. Heydemann held that this mosaic was a copy of the famous
picture of Timanthes, as to which see Pliny, *Nat. hist.* xxxv. 73 ;
Cicero, *Orator*, xxii. 74 ; Valerius Maximus, viii. 11. 6. On the mosaic
Iphigenia is being led to the altar by Ulysses ; beside Ulysses, on the
spectator's right, is Calchas with the knife in his hand, and next to him
is Menelaus ; on the other side of the altar Agamemnon is covering
his face with his right hand. Other figures appear in the background. On
a high column are images of Artemis and Apollo ; and in the top right-
hand corner Artemis appears holding by the antlers a stag, which is to
be substituted for Iphigenia. If this mosaic is a copy of the picture by
Timanthes, the artist has introduced an important variation into his copy
by representing Agamemnon with his head unmuffled. See H. Heydemann, 'Das Opfer der Iphigenia,' *Archäologische Zeitung*, 27 (1869),
pp. 7-10, with pl. 14. On representations of the sacrifice of Iphigenia
in ancient art, see O. Jahn, *Archäologische Beiträge*, p. 378 *sqq.* ; A. S.
Murray, *Handbook of Greek Archaeology*, p. 390.

19. 7. the plane-tree which Homer mentions. See *Iliad*, ii. 307.

19. 7. sacrificed —— male and female animals indiscriminately.
As to the sex of the victims in Greek sacrifices, see P. Stengel, in
Fleckeisen's Jahrbücher, 32 (1886), pp. 324-331 ; *id.*, *Griech. Sakral-
alterthümer*, § 81, p. 103 *sq.*

19. 7. the bronze threshold of Agamemnon's hut. Homer
speaks of a bronze threshold in the palace of Alcinous (*Od.* vii. 83 and
89) and in Tartarus (*Il.* viii. 15). Cp. Helbig, *Das homerische Epos,*[2]
p. 111.

19. 8. In front of the sanctuary grow palm-trees. The temple
with the palms growing in front of it is represented on coins of Tanagra.
See above, note on § 6. There was a grove of palm-trees in Chios,
beside a temple of Apollo (Strabo, xiv. p. 645). Coins of Tenos,
Carystus in Euboea, Siphnos, Ios, Delos, and the Cretan towns Priansus
and Hieropytna, seem to show that palms grew in these islands in
antiquity. Cp. note on viii. 48. 2. Theophrastus speaks of palms in
Greece, but says that the dates did not ripen (*Hist. plant.* ii. 2. 8, iii.

3. 5). Varro says that palms produced dates in Syria but not in Italy (*De re rust.* ii. 1. 27). Pliny tells us that the palms of Judaea were famous; that in Italy the tree grew but was barren; and that on the coasts of Spain the palm produced dates, which, however, did not ripen properly (*Nat. hist.* xiii. 26). At the present day tall palms grow in the gardens of Chalcis, a few miles from Aulis; and in various parts of Greece and the Greek islands the tree attains a height of 40 or 50 feet; but it is only in the hot, sub-tropical plain of *Kalamata* in Messenia that the date ripens, and even there it is of an inferior quality. Palms now grow in the open air in the king's garden at Athens, but nowhere else in Attica. See Fiedler, *Reise*, 1. p. 511 *sq.*; Hehn, *Kulturpflanzen und Hausthiere*,[4] p. 216 *sqq.*; Neumann und Partsch, *Physikalische Geographie von Griechenland*, pp. 410-412; Philippson, *Peloponnes*, pp. 362, 374 (who says that though the date-palm grows in sheltered spots on the coast of Messenia, the dates do not ripen).

19. 8. **Aulis, Mycalessus, and Harma, belong to Tanagra.** So too says Strabo (ix. pp. 403, 404).

20. 1. **Delium.** The site of Delium was probably near the abandoned village of *Dilisi*, situated on the southern side of a small maritime plain about half-way between Aulis and Oropus. The plain or valley is about a mile wide at the water-side and narrows from thence to *Dilisi*, which lies inland. Low hills, mostly overgrown with fir-woods, enclose the valley and separate it from the valley of the Asopus and the district of Oropus on the east. In the plain, close to the beach, is a well of good water, almost choked with large stones. Some large squared blocks lie near the well, and there are a few of them at the roofless chapel in the village. The way from the valley of *Dilisi* (Delium) to Oropus skirts the shore at the foot of the hills, which are overgrown with bushes and dwarf firs and rent by many deep beds of torrents. The road runs so close to the beach that when the surf is high the waves wash over it and render it impassable.

There was a sanctuary of Apollo at Delium which was said to have been founded from Delos (Strabo, ix. p. 403). The Athenians seized and fortified the sanctuary and temple in 424 B.C., and drew water from the neighbouring sacred well (Thucydides, iv. 90 and 97 *sq.*) The sacred well is probably the one near the shore, for there is no water at the village of *Dilisi*. The temple was probably near the well, and the squared blocks mentioned above may have been part of it. In a ruined chapel, hidden among bushes near the shore, H. N. Ulrichs saw a small Doric capital and other ancient fragments. Livy says (xxxv. 51) that Delium was 5 miles from Tanagra and less than 4 miles from the opposite coast of Euboea. These measurements agree very well with the situation of *Dilisi*. On the other hand, Strabo's statement (ix. p. 403) that Delium was 30 furlongs from Aulis does not apply to the situation of *Dilisi* at all, for *Dilisi* is about double that distance from Aulis. Hence some, following Strabo, have placed Delium at *Dramesi*, a village on the coast about 4 miles from Aulis. On the isolated hill beside this village there is a ruined mediaeval tower; and large stones strewn among the fields on the slope of the hill seem to show that there was an ancient settlement here. But the strait at *Dramesi* is only about a mile and a half broad, which does not answer to Livy's statement of the width of the channel at Delium. And in other respects *Dilisi* seems to answer better than *Dramesi* to the situation of Delium. The exact scene of the battle in which the Athenians were defeated by the Boeotians near Delium in 424 B.C. is uncertain. The Athenians had advanced 10 furlongs from Delium on their way homeward when they were attacked by the Boeotians (Thucydides, iv. 90 *sqq.*) Two roads lead from *Dilisi* to Athens. One goes eastward by the shore to Oropus, as already described. The other strikes inland (southward) up the little valley of *Dilisi* and joins the road from Chalcis and Aulis to Athens on the north bank of the Asopus, between the modern villages of *Staniates* and *Sykamino;* it then goes by the valley of *Kakosialesi* over the pass of Decelea (the modern *Tatoi*) to Athens. The former road is so hemmed in between the hills and the sea that there is not room for a pitched battle, such as Thucydides describes, between two armies drawn up in order of battle. Moreover it is more circuitous than the other road. Probably therefore the battle took place on the inland road, somewhat over a mile south of Delium. H. N. Ulrichs placed the scene of the battle in the narrow plain on the left (north) bank of the Asopus, east of the hill of *Staniates* with its high mediaeval tower. It was over this hill, Ulrichs thinks, that the Boeotians marched to attack the Athenians (Thucydides, iv. 93). The plain is now well cultivated and dotted with tall oak-trees. On the other (south) side of the river runs a range of low fir-clad hills. The road from *Dilisi* (Delium) to Athens passes over this plain, and after crossing the Asopus ascends the broad valley of *Kakosialesi*, and so on to Decelea and Athens. But the plain is about 3 miles from *Dilisi*, and therefore too far from Delium to be the scene of the battle. Moreover Thucydides says that both the wings of both the armies were prevented from engaging by the interposition of torrents or watercourses. But there seem to be no such obstacles in the plain where Ulrichs would place the battle; indeed he quite ignores the important statement of Thucydides as to the watercourses. On the whole it would seem that the battle was fought in the broken and hilly ground about a mile or so to the south of the modern *Dilisi*.

See Dodwell, *Tour*, 2. p. 155; Leake, *Northern Greece*, 2. p. 449 *sqq.*; H. N. Ulrichs, *Reisen und Forschungen*, 2. p. 47 *sqq.* ; Wordsworth, *Athens and Attica*, pp. 6-9; L. Ross, *Wanderungen*, 2. p. 105; Vischer, *Erinnerungen*, p. 678; Bursian, *Geogr.* 1. p. 218; Baedeker,[3] p. 186; *Guide-Joanne*, 2. p. 5 *sq.* As to the image of Apollo at Delium, see x. 28. 6 note.

20. 1. The people of Tanagra etc. The ruins of Tanagra are to be seen on and below an inconspicuous hill about 3 miles south of the village of *Shimatari*, where travellers find quarters for the night, for there is no village on the site of the ancient city. The hill of Tanagra is low and forms the last spur of the range of Mount Cerycius (*Soros*) on the east, being divided from that chain only by a slight hollow. To the east the hill descends towards the plain, at first as a narrow gently-sloping ridge, and afterwards in a steeper declivity. The slope of the ridge to the south is long and gradual ; the slope to the north is shorter and much steeper. Along the southern side of the hill, at no great distance, the Asopus flows eastward in a sharply-marked but not deep bed, and to the east of the hill is joined by a small stream, the *Lari*, which comes from the north. Thus the hill of Tanagra stands in the angle formed by the junction of the two streams. The view from the top of the hill westward is shut in by the near heights of Mount Cerycius ; on the other three sides it extends over rolling and rather bare plateaus to hills or mountains in the distance. Beyond the plateau on the north and north-east stretches the long line of the mountains of Euboea, affording a glimpse of the Euripus at their feet. To the east, in the direction of Oropus, are the low wooded hills through which the Asopus finds its way to the sea. In this direction appears the village of *Staniates*, and a little to the south of it a low hill crowned by a high conspicuous tower. The plain at the foot of these wooded hills is itself wooded—a contrast to the bareness of the rest of the plain nearer Tanagra. To the south-east rise the high slopes of Mount Parnes, wooded but presenting also some crags of grey rock. On the south, beyond the rolling and nearly treeless plateau of reddish earth on which the village of *Liatani* is in sight, appears a chain of lower hills, the western prolongation of Mount Parnes ; while to the south-west, above the hills from which the Asopus is seen to issue, Mount Cithaeron looms large.

The line of walls of the ancient city can be traced throughout their entire extent. Very little of them, indeed, is above the soil, but their position is clearly marked by a raised mound which runs round the site and which doubtless conceals portions of them, as well as by many separate blocks and by small pieces of wall occurring here and there, though seldom rising above the level of the ground. Scanty remains of a few square towers, flanking the line of wall, are also to be seen, and the sites of many more are indicated by the short mounds which project outwards at intervals from the long mound that represents the wall. The fortifications start from a tower which occupied the summit of the hill and of which there are some remains. From here one wall descended the steeper slope of the hill northwards into the plain ; the other wall ran eastward along the top of the ridge to its eastern end, where it descended north-eastward into the plain and met the first-mentioned wall, which after making a bend to the westward turned north and then east. Thus the city, so far as it lay within the walls, occupied the summit of the ridge and extended into the plain to the north and north-east, but not to the south of the hill. The existing walls are built partly of a dark hard stone, partly of a soft light-coloured sandstone. But the original walls would seem to have been built of the dark hard stone only ; for the remains which are built of this material are thoroughly ancient and Greek in style, whereas the sandstone portions of the wall, though constructed of well-hewn squared blocks, have thin bricks and small stones in the crevices. Yet the masonry of these sandstone walls seems much too good to be mediaeval. Hence we may conjecture that in late imperial times, when Greece began to be overrun with barbarians, the ancient walls, which may well have fallen into decay under the long Roman peace, were repaired and to a great extent rebuilt with the light sandstone. The best preserved pieces of wall exposed to view are on the crest of the ridge a few yards east of the summit, and on the steep northern slope of the hill a little below the summit. In the latter place the wall is preserved on both faces for a short way and for a varying height of several feet. It is 5 ft. 10 in. thick, and is 3 ft. 8 in. high in two places. But the blocks are in a loose tumbled condition ; they are little hewn and hardly fitted together ; in short the masonry is rough. The other piece of wall, on the crest of the ridge, is 6 ft. 8 in. thick and 4 ft. 9 in. high. Its two faces are built of squared blocks of sandstone, while the core is constructed of small stones. The blocks of the two faces are on the whole well cut, especially those of the outer or southern face of the wall. Higher up the ridge this sand-stone wall is three courses high ; bricks and small stones are inserted in the chinks. Of the towers the best preserved, or rather the least destroyed, stands facing south at the eastern end of the ridge, where the steeper slope begins. Its southern face is 17 ft. 6 in. broad, and one of its sides is at present 17 feet long, but may perhaps have been longer originally. The tower is built of squared blocks of the dark hard stone. One and two courses are standing to a height, at most, of 3 ft. 9 in. Some of the large squared blocks of the tower have fallen down beside it ; one of them is 6 feet long. Of the tower at the other and higher end of the ridge, on the top of the hill, nothing is visible in position except a single course of blocks of the dark hard stone forming an angle and hardly appearing above the ground. A tower in the north wall, down in the plain, measures about 25 feet on its northern face ; the remains consist of a single course and a block or two of a second course, all of the dark hard stone. Another tower at an angle of the west wall has one and two courses and a single block of a third course standing on its southern face ; its greatest height is 4 ft. 2 in. The distances between the towers are not uniform, but many of them are set at intervals of about 30 yards from each other. It is to be remembered that the sites of by far the most of the towers are marked only by mounds, so that their positions and number are to some extent matters of conjecture. In making the circuit of the walls I counted thirty-two more or less probable towers. According to Lolling (in Baedeker) the number is between forty and fifty. Of gateways I observed no certain or even very probable traces ; but in the west wall, some 60 paces south of its northern extremity, an unusually large mound projecting westward may possibly mark the site of a gateway flanked with towers. This is probably the north-west gateway noted by Lolling (in Baedeker), who further distinguished two other gateways, one on the north-east and one on the south-east.

On the top of the hill of Tanagra, a few yards to the east of and below the actual summit, are the remains of a large church about 130 feet long by 65 feet wide, which were excavated in 1890. They scarcely rise above the ground, but the eastern end of the church, including the apse, can be distinguished. The church is supposed to occupy the site of the temple of Dionysus mentioned by Pausanias, and within its area are ancient remains which are ascribed to that temple. These remains consist of (1) a row of foundation-stones running east and west in a line parallel with the fortification-wall for a length of about 9 paces or so ; the material is the same dark hard stone of which the original city-walls were built ; (2) four drums of small fluted columns and a base of a small column. Three of the drums are built into the later fortification-wall of sandstone on the ridge, within the precincts of the ruined church; the other drum and the base are close to the fortification-wall but not built into it. Both the base and the drums are made of the same soft light-coloured sandstone of which the later fortification-walls are built ; this sandstone is quite different in appearance and grit from the dark hard stone of which the foundations of the temple and the original walls of the city are built. If columns and foundations belonged to the same building, it would seem that while the foundations were constructed of the dark hard stone, the upper part of the edifice, or at all events the columns, were of the light sandstone. The entablature may perhaps have been of the dark stone, for outside of the church I saw a block of a cornice of that material with dentils cut in it. The columns were of the Ionic order ; for the flutes are blunt, and in the small museum at *Skimatari* I observed two Ionic capitals which corresponded in material and dimensions with the columns at Tanagra, and had doubtless been brought from it. The diameter of these two capitals, without the volutes, is 21 inches. This is the diameter of one of the three drums built into the fortification-wall at Tanagra, and also of the column which sprang from the existing base. The base itself is about 27 inches in diameter, and the diameter of the two other drums built into the fortification-wall is 18 inches. Within the area of the church on the hill of Tanagra are some remains of a plain mosaic pavement, but whether this pavement belonged to the temple or to the church which replaced it I could not say.

Not many yards to the north-east of the church is the site of the theatre—a great semicircular hollow scooped out of the northern side of the ridge and facing north-east. To judge from the size of the hollow, the theatre must have been large. A trench has been dug through the middle of the auditorium and continued through the orchestra ; but not a single stone of the theatre, so far as I observed, had been brought to light by it. When Leake visited Tanagra at the beginning of the century a part of the masonry which supported the two ends of the auditorium remained, but it seems to have since disappeared. Leake estimated the diameter of the theatre at between 300 and 400 feet. On a terrace below the temple, to the north-east of it, he saw " the well-constructed foundations of a public building, formed of marble of a very dark colour, with a green cast." Lastly, on the flat ground outside the north wall of the city there is a platform covered with broken pieces of the light-coloured sandstone and exhibiting on its northern edge the remains of a foundation-wall about 9 paces long built for the most part of squared blocks of the dark hard stone, but also in part of the light sandstone. These foundations run parallel to the city-wall, but their distance from it (about 20 yards or so) is too great to allow us to suppose that they belonged to a projecting tower. It may be conjectured that a temple, afterwards replaced by a chapel, occupied this platform, and that the foundations belonged to it.

The situation of Tanagra is advantageous and pleasing. A rich champaign country of fertile plains and low wooded hills stretches eastward to the Euboean strait, in agreeable contrast to the bare monotonous plains of north-eastern and central Boeotia. The valley of the Asopus between Tanagra and the sea is particularly charming. The road leads, now through fields of maize watered by runnels and dotted with olive-trees, now over gently-swelling heights shaded by oaks and firs. Between the villages of *Staniates* (or *Inia*, as it is also called) and *Sykamino* the valley contracts into a narrow dale, hemmed in on either side by hills thickly clothed with fir-woods. At *Sykamino*, a village with several mediaeval churches, picturesquely situated at the foot of a reddish hill, the valley expands into the level but still well-wooded plain of Oropus.

The aspect of the country seems to have changed very little since antiquity; for that lively traveller who passes under the name of Dicaearchus describes the route from Oropus to Tanagra as leading through a district planted with olives and wooded, adding that the whole road was perfectly safe from robbers. This last remark has certainly not always been true of the road in modern times. As late as the year 1890 I was offered a military escort at Oropus. The same traveller thus describes Tanagra, as it was in the third century B.C. "The city stands in a high and rugged situation, and has a white argillaceous appearance. The houses are handsomely adorned with porticoes and encaustic paintings. The country does not abound in corn, but its wine is the best in Boeotia. The people are blest with substance, but simple in their way of life; they are all farmers, not manufacturers. They are strict to observe justice, honour, and hospitality. They give freely of their goods to their needy fellow-townsmen and to tramps (τοῖς στειχοπλανήταις τῶν ἀποδημητικῶν), for they are utter strangers to meanness and cheeseparing. It is the safest city in all Boeotia for a stranger to dwell in; because the independent and industrious habits of the people beget a blunt, downright contempt for roguery. For in this city I observed none of those avaricious propensities which are generally the source of the greatest crimes. For where men have enough to live upon, there is no such thing as a craving after lucre. Among such men, therefore, roguery can hardly exist." See Dicaearchus [rather Heraclides], *Descriptio Graeciae*, i. 5 (*Frag. Hist. Graec.* ed. Müller, 2. p. 256; *Geogr. Graec. Min.* ed. Müller, 1. p. 101 *sq.*) In Strabo's time Tanagra and Thespiae were the only cities of any size in Boeotia; the rest, he says, were mere ruins and names (Strabo, ix. pp. 403, 410).

See Dodwell, *Tour*, 2. p. 156; Leake, *Northern Greece*, 2. p. 454 *sqq.*; Ch. Wordsworth, *Athens and Attica*, pp. 10-16; H. N. Ulrichs, *Reisen und Forschungen*, 2. p. 68 *sqq.*; Welcker, *Tagebuch*, 2. p. 99 *sqq.*; L. Ross, *Wanderungen*, 1. p. 109 *sq.*; Bursian, in *Berichte über die Verhandl. d. kön. sächs. Gesell.*

d. Wiss. zu Leipzig, Philolog. hist. Cl. 11 (1859), p. 114; *id., Geogr. v. Griech.*
1. p. 221 *sq.*; Baedeker,[3] p. 187 *sq.*; *Guide-Joanne*, 2. p. 5 *sq.*; Πρακτικὰ τῆς
Ἀρχαιολογικῆς Ἑταιρίας, 1890, p. 33 *sqq.* I visited Tanagra, 13th November
1895, and have described the situation and ruins almost wholly from personal
observation.

Of recent years great numbers of ancient graves have been excavated
in the neighbourhood of Tanagra. These graves line the various paths
leading from Tanagra for miles. To ride along one of these paths
nowadays with the open and empty graves gaping on either hand is
like an anticipation of the Resurrection Day. Two great cemeteries
have also been discovered. One of them is on the low ridge to the
east of Tanagra, just across the *Lari* stream. The other, called the
necropolis of *Bali*, is in the plain to the north-west of Tanagra. One
particularly fine tomb, which had been excavated not long before my
visit to Tanagra in November 1895, deserves a brief notice. It is
situated near the northern foot of Mount Cerycius, about half an hour's
ride to the west of Tanagra. A staircase leads down into the sepulchral
chamber which is about 11 feet square and is vaulted over with a
roof constructed on the true principle of the arch. The whole tomb,
including the walls and roof of the chamber and the walls of the
staircase, is finely constructed of the most regular masonry, the blocks
being large, squared, smoothed, and laid in horizontal courses. The
height of the courses is uniformly about 18 inches. A projecting
ledge runs all round under the spring of the vault. The stone door of
the tomb is preserved in the museum at *Skimatari*. It is a double
folding door, and across it are wrought in relief imitations of iron
bands studded with large nail-heads. In the tomb there are places
for three corpses, one at the back, and one at each of the sides.

Of the objects found in the graves at Tanagra the most famous are
the graceful and often extremely beautiful statuettes of painted terra-
cotta, which have been discovered in immense quantities and are now
scattered over the museums of Europe. It deserves to be noted that
these pretty statuettes are almost always found broken in a purposeful
manner, the head being generally torn off and lying by itself. And
they are as often found in the earth over and beside the grave as in the
grave itself. Hence it has been suggested that while the grave was
being filled in, the friends of the deceased stood beside it with these
figures in their hands, which they first broke and then threw down
into the hole; and this custom, it has been conjectured, may have
been a substitute for an older custom of sacrificing human victims at
the tomb, the breaking of the images taking the place of the earlier
slaughter.

See Ἀθηναῖον, 9 (1880), p. 458 *sqq.*; Πρακτικὰ τῆς Ἀρχαιολογικῆς Ἑταιρίας,
1881, p. 13 *sqq.*; *id.*, 1882, p. 63 *sq.*; *id.*, 1887, p. 64; Δελτίον ἀρχαιολογικὸν,
1888, pp. 34 *sq.*, 45 *sq.*, 56-62, 105-109, 125-131; Baedeker,[3] p. 188; *Guide-
Joanne*, 2. p. 6; A. S. Murray, *Handbook of Greek Archaeology*, p. 310 *sqq.*; P.
Gardner, *New chapters in Greek history*, p. 354 *sq.* For inscriptions found at
Tanagra, see *C. I. G. G. S.* 1. pp. 158 *sqq.*, 653 *sqq.*; C. Robert, in *Archäologische
Zeitung*, 33 (1876), pp. 148-160; Cauer, *Delectus Inscr. Graec.*[2] Nos. 357-373;
Collitz, *G. D. I.* 1. Nos. 869-1129; Ἐφημερὶς ἀρχαιολογική, 1883, p. 158 *sqq.* In

the museum at *Skimatari* in November 1895 I copied thirty small inscriptions (mostly names on tombstones) which the custodian told me had not yet been published. None of them was of any importance. One of them was ΘΙΩΝ ('of gods'); another was ΑΘ[Η]ΝΑ[Η]Σ ('of Athena'). The terra-cottas are noticed in the *Gazette archéologique* for the years 1876-1880, 1883; *Bulletino dell' Instituto*, 1874, pp. 120-127. Cp. also E. Curtius, 'Zwei Giebelgruppen aus Tanagra,' *Philolog. u. histor. Abhandl. d. k. Akad. d. Wissen. zu Berlin*, 1878, pp. 27-51; E. Fabricius, 'Ein bemaltes Grab aus Tanagra,' *Mittheil. d. arch. Inst. in Athen*, 10 (1885), pp. 158-164; Jamot, 'Terres cuites archaïques de Tanagra,' *Bulletin de Corr. hellén.* 14 (1890), pp. 204-223; Col. Lane Fox, in *Journal of the Anthropological Institute*, 6 (1877), pp. 310-316. On an archaic sepulchral relief found at Tanagra and now in the National Museum at Athens, which represents two beardless naked men, named Citylus and Dermis, standing side by side with their arms round each other, see *Mittheil. d. arch. Inst. in Athen*, 3 (1878), p. 311 *sqq.*; *Gazette archéologique*, 4 (1878), p. 160 *sqq.*; Friederichs-Wolters, *Gipsabgüsse*, No. 44; Cavvadias, Γλυπτὰ τοῦ Ἐθνικοῦ Μουσείου, No. 56; Collignon, *Hist. de la Sculpture grecque*, I. p. 193 *sqq.*

20. 1. **their founder was Poemander.** Before the time of Poemander, it is said, the people of the land lived in villages; he built the city and called it Poemandria, employing as his architect one Polycrithus. The old name of the district, we are told, was Poemandris, literally 'the pastoral land.' Tzetzes says that the oxen of Tanagra were very fine; but this may be merely an inference from the name. See Plutarch, *Quaest. Graec.* 37; Strabo, ix. p. 404; Tzetzes, *Schol. on Lycophron*, 326; Stephanus Byzantius, *s.v.* Τάναγρα; *Etymol. Magn.*, *s.v.* Γέφυρα, p. 228 *sq.* In two metrical epitaphs of Roman times, found at Tanagra, the land and people of Tanagra are spoken of poetically as the land and race of Poemander (*C. I. G. G. S.* I. Nos. 580, 581; Kaibel, *Epigrammata Graeca*, No. 495). Poemander's head appears on a coin of Tanagra (Imhoof-Blumer and Gardner, *Num. Comm. on Paus.* p. 113).

20. 2. **Graea.** In the line of Homer quoted by Pausanias (*Il.* ii. 498) Graea occurs as the name of a Boeotian city. Ancient writers differed as to its identification. The people of Tanagra, as we learn from Pausanias, identified Graea with their own city. Aristotle, cited by Stephanus Byzantius (*s.v.* Ὠρωπός) and by Eustathius (on Homer, *Il.* ii. 498) says that Graea was Oropus. According to others it was a seaside place in the district of Oropus, opposite Eretria (Stephanus Byzantius, *l.c.*) According to Strabo (ix. p. 404) Graea was the place near Oropus where was the famous sanctuary of Amphiaraus. Thucydides says (ii. 23) that in 431 B.C. the Peloponnesian invaders, retreating from Attica into Boeotia, marched past Oropus and in doing so laid waste "what is called the Peraean district (τὴν γῆν τὴν Περαϊκὴν καλουμένην) which is in the possession of the Oropians." In this passage of Thucydides some scholars would read Γραϊκήν for Περαϊκήν, which is the reading of the MSS. If this conjecture is correct, it follows that the Graean district was near Oropus. See H. N. Ulrichs, *Reisen und Forschungen*, II. p. 61 *sqq.*; H. von Wilamowitz-Möllendorff, 'Oropos und die Graer,' *Hermes*, 21 (1886), pp. 91-115.

20. 3. **Orion.** Orion seems to have been the Greek counterpart of the Wild Huntsman of northern mythology. See Grimm, *Deutsche Mythologie*,[4] 2. p. 766 *sqq.*; Simrock, *Deutsche Mythologie*,[5] p. 196

sqq. ; Kuhn, *Westfälische Sagen, Gebräuche und Märchen*, 2. p. 6 *sqq.* ;
Baring-Gould, *Iceland: its Scenes and Sagas*, p. 199 *sqq.*   He is very
seldom represented on existing monuments of ancient art.   In a
manuscript of the *Theriaca* of Nicander there is a painting of Orion
swinging the crooked staff called a *lagobolon* ('hare - hitter'), which
in appearance resembles a boomerang.   Under his feet is a large
scorpion, in reference to the story that Orion was killed by a scorpion's
bite (Nicander, *Ther.* 13 *sqq.* ; Lucan, *Phars.* ix. 833 *sqq.*)   See Fr.
Lenormant, in *Gazette archéologique*, 1 (1875), p. 125 *sq.*, with plate
32.

20. 3. **Mount Cerycius.**   If we take literally Pausanias's statement
that Mt. Cerycius was in Tanagra, the mountain can only be the summit
of the hill on which Tanagra was built.   But more probably we should
apply the name to the chain of hills which extends westward from
Tanagra and of which the hill of Tanagra is in fact the termination.
See Leake, *Northern Greece*, 2. p. 459 *sq.* ; H. N. Ulrichs, *Reisen und
Forschungen*, 2. p. 70 ; Bursian, *Geogr.* 1. p. 222.

20. 3. **a place called Polus.**   Polus (πόλος) in Greek often signifies the firmament or celestial sphere.   See note on vi. 19. 8.   In the
present passage Prof. E. Maass interprets it to mean 'a rounded hill-
top,' comparing Hesychius, *s.v.* πόλος, who says that the word sometimes meant 'a rounded top' (τόπος κορυφῆς κυκλοειδής).   On Prof.
Maass's view the story which connected Atlas with this place near
Tanagra arose from the mistake of understanding the name Polus
(πόλος) in its ordinary sense of 'the celestial sphere.'   See E. Maass,
Aratea (Berlin, 1892), p. 132 *sq.*

20. 3. **as Homer has said of him** etc.   See *Odyssey*, i. 52-54.

20. 4. **the image —— the Triton.**   On three coins of Tanagra
(Fig. 4) of the time of the Antonines and Commodus, the youthful
Dionysus is represented standing under a roof,
which is supported by two male statues (Atlantes)
on pillars; the god wears the fawn-skin and boots,
and he holds the *thyrsus* and a goblet (*kan-
tharos*) ; below is a Triton swimming to the left,
but looking back.   E. Curtius argued that the
Dionysus on these coins was a copy of the
image by Calamis, and that the Triton on the
coins was a copy of the Triton seen by Pausanias
in the same temple, which was, in Curtius's
opinion, a work of art separate from the image

FIG. 4.—DIONYSUS AND THE
TRITON (COIN OF TANAGRA).

of Dionysus.   See *Archäologische Zeitung*, 41 (1883), pp. 255-258.
But Mr. P. Wolters afterwards showed that the type of Dionysus
on the coins is certainly not earlier than the time of Phidias,
and cannot represent a work of Calamis, who was a predecessor of
Phidias, and whose style was more archaic than that of the Dionysus
on the coins (see note on v. 25. 5).   Further, as Mr. Wolters points
out, the manner in which Pausanias speaks of the Triton seems to prove
that it was not an image, but a real Triton or what was exhibited as
such.   For in the next chapter Pausanias says that he saw another

Triton at Rome, describes the appearance of the supposed creature, and then gives a list of other strange animals. That the Triton at Tanagra was professedly a real animal embalmed or stuffed, appears from a statement of Demostratus, reported by Aelian (*Nat. anim.* xiii. 21), that he had seen at Tanagra an embalmed or pickled Triton (τάριχον Τρίτωνα) ; the creature, according to Demostratus, resembled the pictures and images of Tritons except that the head was decayed with time and no longer distinct or recognisable ; and when he touched it, some hard rough scales fell off. A Roman senator, in the presence of Demostratus, took a piece of the beast's skin and burned it as an experiment ; it emitted a fetid odour ; but the spectators could not decide from the smell whether the creature was a sea or a land animal. From Demostratus's description and Pausanias's story (§ 5) it would seem that the Triton of Tanagra was headless. What was shown as a Triton may have been either a real sea-beast of some sort or an effigy made up by the priests. Had it been merely an effigy, it would prob- ably have been complete, since it is just as easy to make a false head as a false tail. The fact that the creature was headless seems to show that it was a real marine animal which the priests palmed off upon the credulous as a Triton. As the popular idea of a Triton was a fish with a man's head, it became necessary, before exhibiting a real fish as a Triton, to cut off its head or at least to mangle it past all recognition, and then to invent some story to account for the mutilation. This is what seems to have been done. It is not surprising, however, that on the coins of the city the creature should appear with its head complete. The people of Tanagra were doubtless proud of their Triton, which probably drew sightseers from afar ; and in putting him on their coins as a badge of their city they naturally represented him, not in the mauled and mangled condition which the exigencies of natural history unfortunately rendered necessary, but in all his glory, with a human head and a fish's tail.

Mr. Wernicke has suggested that the Triton may have been the old local god of Tanagra, who was afterwards ousted by Dionysus, and that the change of worship may have been embodied in the legend that the younger god had knocked his predecessor on the head. Amongst the terra-cotta statuettes of Tanagra there is one representing a very rude idol with two Tritons painted on its breast ; the Tritons are back to back, they have human heads and arms and the tails of fishes, and their attitude is not unlike that of the Triton on the coins. Mr. Wernicke sees in this statuette evidence of an ancient worship of Triton at Tanagra.

See E. C[urtius,] 'Dionysos von Kalamis,' *Archäologische Zeitung*, 41 (1883), pp. 255-258 ; P. Wolters, 'Der Triton von Tanagra,' *ib.* 43 (1885), pp. 263-268 ; Imhoof-Blumer and Gardner, *Num. Comm. on Paus.* p. 114, with pl. X vii. viii. ; Kalkmann, *Pausanias der Perieget* p. 29 *sq.* ; K. Wernicke, 'Der Triton von Tanagra,' *Jahrbuch des archäolog. Inst.* 2 (1887), pp. 114-118 ; J. Escher, *Triton und seine Bekämpfung durch Herakles*, p. 40 *sq.* ; F. R. Dressler, *Triton und die Tritonen*, p. 14 *sq.* The statuette with the two Tritons on its breast is represented in Heuzey's work, *Les figurines antiques de terre cuite du Musée du Louvre*, pl. 17. 1.

The Triton at Tanagra seems to have been monstrously fat and bloated. See Athenaeus, xii. p. 551 a (where Meineke wrongly printed Κητεῖ instead of κήτει; cp. Kaibel's edition); Hesychius, *s.v.* Ταναγραίων φυήν. From Hesychius (*l.c.*) it appears that Ephorus fell into the same mistake as Meineke, namely that of supposing the *ketos* of Tanagra to be a fat man of that name instead of a fat fish.

20. 4. went down to the sea to be purified. In ceremonial purifications a special cleansing virtue was attributed to sea-water. Persons who were being purified for homicide washed their garments in twice seven waves (Suidas, *s.v.* ἀπὸ δὶς ἕπτα κυμάτων). In Ceos on the day after a funeral the house was sprinkled with sea-water (Roehl, *I. G. A.* No. 395, l. 14 *sq.*; Dittenberger, *Sylloge Inscr. Graec.* No. 468; Cauer, *Delectus Inscr. Graec.*[2] No. 530 : the reading is, however, uncertain ; Koehler would supply θαλ[λοῖσ]ι instead of θαλ[λάση]ι). In Cos the priest purified himself with sea-water (Paton and Hicks, *The inscriptions of Cos*, No. 38 ; *Journal of Hellenic Studies*, 9 (1888), p. 329). The initiated at Eleusis perhaps bathed in the sea or in the salt pools called Rhiti. See Aug. Mommsen, *Heortologie*, p. 248. Instead of sea-water, a mixture of salt and water was sometimes used in ceremonial purifications (Theocritus, xxiv. 96 *sq.*) Cp. Tzetzes, *Schol. on Lycophron*, 135.

20. 4. the women prayed to Dionysus etc. There are various indications of a mythological connexion between Dionysus and the sea or water in general. At Smyrna in the month Anthesterion a ship was carried in procession to the market-place, the priest of Dionysus sitting in it and pretending to steer it (Philostratus, *Vit. Sophist.* i. 25. 1 ; Aristides, *Or.* xxii. vol. 1. p. 440, ed. Dindorf). The Argives summoned Dionysus from the water with the blast of trumpets. See ii. 37. 5 note. When his train of Bacchanals was attacked by Lycurgus, Dionysus is said to have plunged into the sea, where he was received by Thetis (Homer, *Il.* vi. 135 *sq.*) On a gold plate found in Syria the young Dionysus is represented walking on the waves (*Gazette archéologique*, 1 (1875), pl. 2, with De Witte's remarks, p. 5 *sqq.*)

21. 1. The appearance of the Tritons is this etc. In ancient works of art the Tritons are generally represented with the heads, arms, and upper bodies of men, but with the tails of fishes from the waist downward. See K. O. Müller, *Handbuch der Archaeologie der Kunst*,[3] § 402. Pausanias describes them with nothing human but the nose. The pretended specimens which he saw at Tanagra and Rome would seem to have differed considerably from the popular idea of a Triton. The conception of Triton as a deity half-fish half-man may have been borrowed by the Greeks from the Semites. The goddess Derceto was represented in Phoenicia as a woman to the waist, but as a fish from the waist downward (Lucian, *De dea Syria*, 14) ; and Dagon, the Philistine god, seems to have been similarly conceived as half-fish, half-man. See Movers, *Die Phoenizier*, 1. p. 589 *sqq.*; Winer, *Biblisches Realwörterbuch*, *s.v.* 'Dagon.' Cp. Escher, *Triton*, p. 110 *sqq.*; Dressler, *Triton und die Tritonen*, p. 15 *sqq.* Near Phigalia in Arcadia there was a curious image in the shape of a mermaid (Paus. viii. 41. 6).

21. 2. rhinoceroses. The rhinoceros was known to the Assyrians, for on the obelisk of Salmanasar, found at Nineveh, it is represented in company with the Indian elephant and the double-humped camel of Bactria. Its union on this monument with these Asiatic animals appears to show that the Assyrians derived their knowledge of the rhinoceros from Asia rather than from Africa. See Perrot et Chipiez, *Histoire de l'art dans l'Antiquité*, 2. pp. 564, 777, note 5. The rhinoceros seems first to have been exhibited in Rome by Pompey (Pliny, *Nat. hist.* viii. 71). From the name 'Ethiopic bull' which Pausanias applies to the animal it appears that he is describing the African rhinoceros, which has, as he says, two horns on its snout. The species known as the Indian rhinoceros, now found in Nepaul, Butan, and Assam, has only one horn. But two-horned species are also found in various parts of Eastern Asia (Assam, Burma, the Malay Peninsula, Sumatra, Java, etc.) See *Encyclopaedia Britannica*, 9th ed. article 'Rhinoceros,' vol. 20, pp. 521 *sqq.* Pliny and Aelian describe the one-horned Indian rhinoceros, and they distinguish it from the Ethiopic bull; their descriptions of this last animal are fabulous (Aelian, *Nat. anim.* xvii. 44 *sq.*; Pliny, *Nat. hist.* viii. 71 and 74).

21. 3. the elk. Cp. v. 12. 1. Caesar described the elk as one of the wild animals which roamed the great Hercynian forest of Germany. He says that it resembled a goat, but was somewhat larger; that its horns were short and that it had no joints in its legs; hence if it fell down, it could not get up again. So it slept leaning against a tree. The hunters noted the trees against which the elk was in the habit of leaning and undermined or cut them half through; so that when the beast leaned against one of these trees, the tree and the elk fell down together and the animal was captured! See Caesar, *Bell. Gall.* vi. 27. Pliny affirms (*Nat. hist.* viii. 39) that the elk was like a heifer, but with longer ears and a longer neck; and he says that in Scandinavia there was an animal like it called the *achlis*, about which he tells the same fable that Caesar tells about the elk. Erasmus Stella describes the elk as existing in Prussia in the early part of the sixteenth century ('De Borussiae antiquitatibus,' in *Novus Orbis regionum ac insularum veteribus incognitarum* (Paris, 1532), p. 507 [wrongly numbered 497] *sq.*) The elk or moose deer still ranges over the whole of Northern Europe and Asia as far south as East Prussia, the Caucasus, and North China. It was once common in the forests of Germany and France, and is still found in some parts of Norway and Sweden, where it is strictly protected. Pausanias's description of the appearance and habits of the animal is not so very wide of the mark. For the elk is the largest of all the deer tribe (*Cervidae*), and is "a shy and timorous creature fleeing at the sight of man." See *Encyclopaedia Britannica*, 9th ed. article 'Deer,' vol. 7. p. 24. The Irish elk was a huge creature, with enormous branching antlers. A fine skeleton of one of them is preserved in the Natural History Museum of Queen's College, Cork.

21. 4. Ctesias —— mentions a beast —— called martichoras. The word *martichoras* is the Persian *mard-khora*, 'man-eater' (Liddell and Scott, *Greek Lexicon, s.v.* μαρτιχόρας). Ctesias's description of this fabulous animal is reported more or less fully by Photius (*Biblio-*

theca, p. 45 b 31 *sqq.*, ed..Bekker), Aristotle (*Hist. anim.* ii. 1, p. 501 a 25 *sqq.*, ed. Bekker), Aelian (*Nat. anim.* iv. 21), Pliny (*Nat. hist.* viii. 75), and Philostratus (*Vit. Apollon.* iii. 45). All these writers treat Ctesias's statement with more or less incredulity. Aelian's account of the monster is the fullest. Cp. Ctesias, ed. Bähr, p. 280 *sqq.*

21. 6. winged snakes —— a scorpion that had wings. Megasthenes stated that there were winged snakes and winged scorpions in India (Strabo, xv. p. 703; Aelian, *Nat. anim.* xvi. 41). Herodotus mentions a story that every year in the spring winged snakes came flying from Arabia to Egypt, but were met in a certain pass by ibises, which destroyed them. The bones of the serpents were shown to Herodotus in the pass; the place was in Arabia, opposite the city of Buto. He describes the wings of these serpents as featherless and resembling the wings of bats. See Herodotus, ii. 75 *sq.*, with the notes in Rawlinson's translation and Wiedemann's edition. Pammenes stated that there were winged scorpions in Egypt (Aelian, *Nat. anim.* xvi. 41), and other writers speak of them as existing in other parts of Africa. See Strabo, xvii. p. 830; Pliny, *Nat. hist.* xi. 89; Lucian, *De dipsadibus*, 3.

22. 1. Hermes the Ram-bearer. On two coins of Tanagra (Fig. 5) Hermes is represented erect, facing the spectator and carrying a ram on his shoulders. "One arm of the god passes round the fore-feet and one round the hind-feet of the ram; on one coin the hands seem to meet on the breast as in the well-known Athenian statue of Hermes carrying a bull [see below], on the other coin one hand seems to be higher than the other. The pose of the god is stiff and his legs rigid: he is naked. He is also beardless, but whether his feet are winged, the scale of the coin makes it impossible to say" (Imhoof - Blumer and Gardner, *Num.*

FIG. 5.—HERMES WITH THE RAM (COIN OF TANAGRA).

Comm. on Paus. p. 116, with pl. X xi. xii.) See also Müller - Wieseler, *Denkmäler*, 2. pl. xxix. No. 324 a; Roscher's *Lexikon*, 1. p. 2396; Collignon, *Hist. de la Sculpture grecque*, 1. p. 399 *sq.* There can be little doubt that this Hermes on the coins reproduces the type of Calamis's statue of Hermes the Rambearer.

The archaic stiffness of the Hermes on the coins agrees very well with what we know of the style of this early master (see note on v. 25. 5). Other supposed copies of Calamis's statue are as follows :—

(1) Two terra-cotta statuettes of Tanagra which represent Hermes carrying a ram on his shoulders; he wears the conical Boeotian cap on his head and a garment (the *chlamys*) thrown over his shoulders and hanging down in front on each side. See *Gazette archéologique*, 4 (1878), p. 101. But the Hermes of the coins, which is doubtless the most faithful copy of the statue, wears neither the cap nor the garment.

(2) A terra-cotta statuette from Gela in Sicily, now in the British Museum. It resembles the Hermes of the coins, except that it has the *chlamys* hanging below the arms on each side. See *Guide to the Second Vase Room, British Museum*, pt. ii. (1878), p. 18, No. 144; *Gazette*

archéologique, 4 (1878), p. 163; A. S. Murray, *Hist. of Greek Sculpture*,[2] 1. p. 234.

(3) A small marble statue in the Pembroke Collection, at Wilton House, Salisbury. It represents Hermes standing with a ram on his shoulders ; he holds its fore-feet in his right hand, its hind-feet in his left. This statue differs from the coins in representing Hermes as bearded and wearing the *chlamys*. See Müller-Wieseler, *Denkmäler*, 2. pl. xxix. No. 324 ; Overbeck, *Gesch. d. griech. Plastik*,[4] 1. p. 278, fig. 75.

(4) A relief on a small altar in Athens. It represents Hermes in profile with a ram on his shoulders and holding its feet in his hands. It differs from the coins in representing the god as bearded and wearing the *chlamys* over his left arm. See *Annali dell' Instituto*, 41 (1869), pp. 253-262, with Tav. d' agg. I, K ; Overbeck, *Gesch. d. griech. Plastik*,[4] 1. p. 279, Fig. 76 a ; Lucy M. Mitchell, *Hist. of ancient Sculpture*, p. 289 ; Collignon, *Hist. de la Sculpture grecque*, 1. p. 400 *sq.*

It seems certain that Calamis did not create the type of the Ram-bearing Hermes ; for we find the idea of a god or man bearing an animal on his shoulders embodied in works of art which are probably older than the time of Calamis.

(1) The best known of these is the so-called Calf-bearing Hermes, which was found on the Acropolis of Athens. This is a statue of Hymettian marble representing a bearded man carrying a calf on his shoulders ; he wears a tight-fitting garment (apparently meant to resemble soft leather) which covers his upper arms and his sides. The style of the statue is stiff and archaic ; the inscription seems to show that it belongs to the first half of the sixth century B.C., hence that it is about a century older than the time of Calamis. See A. Conze, 'Kalbtragender Hermes,' *Archäologische Zeitung*, 1864, pp. 169-173, with pl. clxxxvii. ; Overbeck, *Gesch. d. griech. Plastik*,[4] 1. p. 187 *sq.* ; A. S. Murray, *Hist. of Greek Sculpture*,[2] 1. p. 164 *sq.* ; Collignon, *Hist. de la Sculpture grecque*, 1. p. 215 *sqq.*

(2) On a scarab, supposed to be of Phoenician manufacture, the god Bes is represented carrying on his shoulders a lion. See Perrot et Chipiez, *Histoire de l'art dans l'antiquité*, 3. p. 422, fig. 295.

(3) A Phoenician statuette made of calcareous stone represents a man in a long robe carrying an animal on his shoulders. The animal seems to be a ram or sheep, but the head is broken off. See Perrot et Chipiez, *op. cit.* 3. p. 433, fig. 307 ; cp. fig. 308 *ib.*

(4) A statue found in Cyprus represents a man carrying a ram on his shoulders ; he holds its feet in his hands. See Perrot et Chipiez, *op. cit.* 3. p. 589, fig. 402.

(5) An ancient statuette of Sardinia, of very primitive workmanship, represents a man holding an animal (a lamb ?) on his shoulders. See Perrot et Chipiez, *op. cit.* 4. p. 89, fig. 88.

(6) An archaic bronze statuette of Crete represents a man carrying a ram. See *Annali dell' Instituto*, 42 (1880), p. 213 *sq.*, Tav. d' agg. S.

(7) Another archaic bronze of Crete represents two men, of whom one carries an animal on his shoulders. Prof. Milchhoeffer thinks the

subject is the contest of Apollo and Hercules.   See *Annali dell'*
Instituto, l.c. Tav. d' agg. T. .

(8) On the so-called Island or Mycenaean gems human or semi-
human figures are not uncommonly represented carrying animals on
their shoulders.   See A. B. Cook, 'Animal-worship in the Mycenaean
age,' *Journal of Hellenic Studies*, 14 (1894), figs. 3, 9, 15, 19.

These examples show that the type of the god carrying an animal
on his shoulders was older than Calamis, and that it may have been
of Oriental, perhaps Phoenician, origin.   The custom of representing
a deity in such an attitude has probably its roots in that primitive
stage of religion when the gods were animals or at least were
conceived of as clothed in animal forms.   The advance of religious
thought turns the old beast gods into human gods ; but the change
is only gradually accomplished.   At first the god is represented as half-
beast, half-man ; then he appears as almost wholly human, retaining
only one or two bestial features such as a pair of horns.   Lastly
he is depicted in purely human form.   But the tradition of his old
animal nature, though obscured and misunderstood, still survives ; the
animal out of which he gradually emerged is now regarded as sacred
to him, and is represented in conjunction with him in works of art, in
which sometimes the animal stands beside the god, sometimes the god
carries the animal, sometimes the animal carries the god.   Hermes and
the ram, for example, are represented in all these various fashions in
ancient art.   See Müller-Wieseler, *Denkmäler*, 2. pl. xxix. Nos. 320, 322-
324.   The transition from the ram-god to the man-god with the ram is well
marked in a statuette of Baal-Ammon which portrays the god seated in
human form, but with the horns of a ram, and with a ram on each side
of him, on which his hands are placed.   See Perrot et Chipiez, *op. cit.*
3. p. 73, fig. 25.   As it appears to have been a widespread custom for
priests or worshippers to assume the garb and attributes of the god (cp.
notes on vii. 18. 12, viii. 13. 1), we cannot be sure whether the figures
which we have been discussing and other similar ones represent a god or
a man (priest or worshipper).   But if the explanation here given of the
origin of such representations is correct, the difference is not material ;
for even if these figures represent men, they represent them in the garb
and attitude of gods.   Thus at Tanagra, to go back to the point from
which we started, the youth who annually carried a ram on his shoulders
round the walls of the city, did so as a representative of Hermes, who
was traditionally said to have done the same.

It was not necessary that the Ram-bearing god should always carry
the ram on his shoulders.   In the statue at Olympia which Onatas
executed for the people of Pheneus the god was portrayed carrying
the ram under his arm.   See v. 27. 8.   We possess what seems to be
a loose copy of Onatas's statue in a terra-cotta statuette of Tanagra,
which represents Hermes wearing a conical cap and a cloak, and
carrying a lamb on his left arm.   See Conze, in *Annali dell' Instituto*,
30 (1858), pp. 347-351, Tav. d' agg. O ; Roscher's *Lexikon*, I. p. 2395.
On the vase of Sosias Hermes appears holding a ram in his arms.   See
Müller-Wieseler, *Denkmäler*, 1. pl. xlv. No. 210.   At the Carnasian

Grove in Messenia there was a statue of the Ram-bearing Hermes (iv. 33. 4) ; but whether the ram was on the shoulders or under the arm of the god, we do not know.

There can be little doubt that the Christian type of the Good Shepherd was copied from, or at least suggested by, the old type of the Ram-bearing god.

See E. de Chanot, ' Les divinités criophores,' *Gazette archéologique*, 4 (1878), pp. 100-104, 162 *sq.*, with Fr. Lenormant's remarks, *ib.* pp. 163-169 ; Veyries, *Les figures criophores dans l'art grec, l'art greco-romain et l'art chrétien* (Paris, 1884). In this last work lists are given of all the ram-bearing (or rather animal-bearing) figures in ancient art which were known at the time when the book was written. Cp. also Stephani, in *Compte-Rendu* (St. Petersburg) for 1869, pp. 96-100. At Rome there is a Greek inscription in verse referring to a statue of a man carrying a ram on his back (Kaibel, *Epigrammata Graeca*, No. 1102; Loewy, *Inschriften griech. Bildhauer*, No. 441). As to Hermes and the ram, see also ii. 3. 4 with the notes.

22. 2. Hermes the Champion. On a coin of Tanagra of Trajan's time Hermes is represented standing and holding in his right hand a scraper *(strigil)* and in his left a caduceus (?). He is nude, his hair is long, his left leg is advanced and bent. The type may represent a statue of the fifth century B.C. If the object in the god's right hand is a scraper (which is doubtful), the figure is probably a copy of the statue of Hermes the Champion. See Imhoof-Blumer and Gardner, *Num. Comm. on Paus.* p. 115 *sq.*, with pl. X xiii.

22. 2. the wild strawberry-tree etc. On coins of Tanagra of the age of the Antonines, Hermes appears standing naked, his feet winged, the caduceus in his left hand ; beside him is a tree on which sits an eagle ; his left hand rests on the tree. This tree is probably the wild strawberry-tree. At the foot of it is a carved object, perhaps a scraper. The figure of the god is youthful and he wears short hair, but his pose is rather stiff. See Imhoof-Blumer and Gardner, *Num. Comm. on Paus.* p. 115 *sq.*, with pl. X xiv.-xvi.

22. 2. at Tanagra the dwelling-houses are in one place, and the sanctuaries are in another place etc. The separation of the temples from the dwellings of men was recommended by Socrates (*Memorabilia*, iii. 8. 10). Compare Aristotle, *Politics*, vii. 12.

22. 3. the poetical victory which she gained over Pindar. According to Aelian (*Var. hist.* xiii. 25) and Suidas (*s.v.* Κόριννα) Corinna vanquished Pindar five times in poetical contests.

22. 4. There are two kinds of cocks at Tanagra etc. This passage is interesting to the ornithologist and the breeder as showing that in Pausanias's time there were two quite distinct breeds of poultry at Tanagra. One of the two breeds—the game-cocks—was famous in antiquity. See Suidas, *s.vv.* ἀλεκτρυόνα ἀθλητὴν Ταναγραῖον and Ταναγραῖοι ἀλεκτορίσκοι; Pliny, *Nat. hist.* x. 48 ; Babrius, v. 1 *sq.* ; Lucian, *Gallus*, 4. Varro says that the Tanagra cocks were handsome and good fighters, but somewhat sterile ; so he did not particularly advise the farmer to select them (*De re rustica*, iii. 9. 6). Columella says that they were tall birds and stubborn fighters, about the same size as the cocks of Rhodes and Media ; in habits they did not differ greatly from the Italian breed (*De re rustica*, viii. 2. 4 and 13). As to the representations of cock-fights in ancient art, see Jahn, *Archäologische Beiträge*, p. 437 *sqq.* The second breed of Tanagra cock described by Pausanias is not, so far as I know, mentioned by any other ancient writer. With its raven plumage and scarlet comb and wattles it must have been very like the breed now called Black Spanish ; so Prof. Alfred Newton tells me.

The domestic cock is a native of India, and seems to have been imported into Western Asia and Europe at a period much more recent than is commonly supposed. The bird does not appear on the Egyptian monuments and is not mentioned in the Old Testament or in Homer. In Greek literature it is first referred to by Theognis (*v.* 864), who wrote in the second half of the sixth century B.C. A cock is sculptured on the so-called Harpy Tomb from Lycia, which seems to date from the sixth century B.C. ; and on a frieze which was built into the wall of the acropolis of Xanthus in Lycia a number of cocks and hens are represented picking up food or fighting (A. H. Smith, *Catalogue of Sculpture in the British Museum*, 1. Nos. 82, 94, pp. 48, 56). See V. Hehn, *Kulturpflanzen und Hausthiere*,[4] p. 260 *sqq.* ; P. F. Perdrizet, ' Sur l'introduction en Grèce du coq et des combats de coqs, à propos d'un lécythe archaïque du Musée du Louvre,' *Revue archéologique*, 3me Série, 21 (1893), pp. 157-167.

22. 5. to the left of the Euripus, is Mount Messapius. Pausanias now returns to the Euripus, opposite to Chalcis, and pursues his way westward in the direction of Anthedon. The path at first runs for about 4 miles across an undulating plain which extends from the foot of Mount Messapius (the modern *Ktypa*) north-eastward into the sea in the form of a broad headland. The plain, though dry and treeless, is well cultivated, and is intersected by softly-swelling downs. Vineyards occupy a part of its surface, but most of it is in corn. A great deal of the land had been recently ploughed when I traversed it early in November 1895, and in some places the young corn had already begun to sprout, its fresh vivid green contrasting pleasantly with the bare brown earth of most of the plain. On the west the plain is bounded by round-topped hills of various heights, the southern spurs of Mount Messapius, which towers up grandly and conspicuously with high, steep, bushy, but not rocky slopes on the north-west. On the south a massive hill (the *Megalo Vouno*, crowned with the ruins of Hyria, see above, p. 66 *sqq.*) seems to bound the plain on this side, but between it and the plain lies the circular, nearly landlocked bay of *Vourko*. To the east of this hill the high-road to Thebes is seen ascending in several long zig-zags towards a dip in the hills. On reaching the western side of the plain, just at the point where Mount Messapius descends in one long steep unbroken slope from the summit to the shore, we come to an isolated flat-topped hillock rising abruptly like a redan with steep uniform sides from the level ground beside the sea. So regular indeed is the outline of the hillock on all sides that its slopes would seem to have been scarped and smoothed by art. Its flat top, which may be 90 yards long by 50 yards broad, is now a corn-field. On the western brow of the hillock, the sides of which measure about 50 yards on the slope, I found some traces of a wall consisting of four or five stones in a row, but whether the wall was ancient or modern seemed dubious.   Still fainter vestiges of a wall were visible on the south-western face of the hillock, where as well as on the southern slope a good many stones are strewn about.   There is hardly room to doubt that this place is the ancient Salganeus, which we know was situated on a height beside the shore, between Chalcis and Anthedon.   It was said to have been called after the Boeotian pilot Salganeus who steered the Persian fleet into the strait and was here put to death on a groundless suspicion of treachery.   See Strabo, ix. pp. 400, 403 ; Dicaearchus, *Descriptio Graeciae*, i. 26 ; Livy, xxxv. 50 *sq.* ; Diodorus, xix. 77.

Immediately beyond this point the plain comes abruptly to an end and the path runs along the steep bushy but not precipitous slope of Mount Messapius at some height above the sea, which on a bright sunshiny day is of a beautiful green colour, clear as crystal and dappled with patches of purple.   Thus proceeding along the steep mountain-side for about a mile we find ourselves opposite a pretty rocky island, wooded with pines, which lies a little way off the shore.   On the island is a ruin which, so far as I could judge by the eye from the shore, seemed to be mediaeval or modern.   Hereabouts, too, a row of large stones may be seen lying at the bottom of the clear water, but they appear to be boulders rather than hewn stones.   Farther on a high cliff, which seen from the east reminds one of the Lorelei Rock on the Rhine, rises close to the shore.   The path here descends and runs along the narrow beach at the foot of the cliff, from which a very copious spring of water rushes into the sea.   This high cliff is probably Glaucus's Leap (§ 6). On the morning when I passed it, the clear sunlit greenish-blue water at its foot looked very inviting ; one could fancy the sea-god taking his plunge into its cool delicious depths.   Beyond the cliff the path again runs along the foot of the long slope, covered with lentisk and holly-oak bushes, which descends from the high bold pointed summit of Mount Messapius in an unbroken sweep to the sea.   As we advance, however, the slope becomes more gradual.   At the head of it, just under the high steep summit of the mountain, is seen the village of *Loukisia*, and at the foot of it, on a little stretch of level ground beside the sea about a mile or more below the village, we come to the ruins of Anthedon.   The distance from Chalcis is about 8 miles.

See Leake, *Northern Greece*, 2. pp. 266-272 ; H. N. Ulrichs, *Reisen und Forschungen*, 2. pp. 34-36 ; L. Ross, *Wanderungen*, 2. pp. 126-131 ; Bursian, *Geogr.* 1. p. 215.   I traversed this route in the reverse direction, 8th November 1895, and have described it from my own observation.   My time from Anthedon to Chalcis was about three hours or a little more, but this included a stop at Salganeus.

88. 5 Anthedon   Anthedon was situated on nearly level ground at the foot of the long gradual slope which separates the high pointed summit of Mount Messapius from the sea.   Here there is a little semicircular harbour protected by the remains of two ancient moles ; and close to it on the south-east a flat-topped hillock, some 100 feet or so

high, rises just beside the shore.   This hillock would seem to have been
the acropolis of Anthedon ; for on its steep seaward brow, at a height
of 15 or 20 feet above the beach, the remains of an ancient fortification-
wall may be traced for some little way.   The wall is built of ashlar
masonry, the blocks being squared and laid in horizontal courses.   The
pieces of it are generally three or four courses high.   Above the seaward
brow of the hillock is a terrace some 20 or 30 yards wide, and above
this terrace another steep but short slope leads up to the flat top of the
hillock.   Here there are many broken stones and some blocks which,
though a good deal worn, seem to have been hewn.

But most of the ancient remains of Anthedon are to be seen at the
shallow harbour.   At its eastern side, about 50 yards to the west of the
acropolis, are the remains of an ancient wall running out northwards
into the water.   This was no doubt an ancient mole which enclosed the
harbour on this side.   At the opposite or north-western side of the
harbour are the more massive remains of another mole running out eastward into the water.   This northern mole, which defended the port
from the open sea, was built on a jutting ledge of rocks.   The masonry,
though ruinous, is obviously ancient in part ; a line of squared foundation stones may be seen under water, and there are many squared
ancient blocks above water.   This mole was probably surmounted in
antiquity by a fortification-wall forming a continuation of the city-wall.
The ends of the two moles probably approached each other closely,
leaving only a narrow passage between them, which may have been
barred in times of danger by a chain.   In addition to the ruined moles
there exist beside the harbour the well-preserved remains of an ancient
quay solidly built of large quadrangular blocks and extending along the
edge of the shallow water for a length of about 160 feet with an average
breadth of 9 or 10 feet.   The quay, which is still used by fishing boats,
is standing to a height of one and two courses.   On the inner edge of
this quay a considerable number of foundation-walls, in good preservation, were excavated by archaeologists of the American School in March
1889.   The foundations, which are well built of large squared blocks,
extend in lines parallel to and at right angles to each other, as if they
had supported quadrangular buildings, but the nature of these buildings
is uncertain.   The foundation-wall next the shore is about 30 paces
long.   Another, which makes a right angle with the first, is 7 paces
long ; and a third, which is parallel to the first, is 9 paces long.   I
measured the breadth of two of the foundation-walls ; one was 4 ft.
4 in. and the other 3 ft. 10 in. thick.   A few feet inland from the
foundations lies a piece of a curved base, and a few yards to the west
of the base is a mosaic pavement in black and white stones, which are
arranged in patterns.   Fragments of common red pottery are strewn
about the harbour.

Ancient foundations are further to be seen on the shore immediately
to the west of the harbour.   They begin some 20 yards or so to the
west of the northern mole and run along the shore for about 28 paces,
with a breadth of about 10 feet.   A few blocks of an upper course are
standing on them.   At their eastern end these foundations extend

under water. Beyond them to the west there are some very ruinous remains of a fortification-wall closely skirting the shore; two and three courses of the wall are standing. The vestiges of this fortification-wall extend westward as far as the remains of two solid foundation-walls, which meet each other at a right angle on the shore. The masonry of this angle is ashlar. One of the walls composing the angle is 9 paces, the other 8 paces long. This angle seems to have been the point at which the fortification-wall, after running westward beside the shore, turned south and struck inland. The place may be perhaps 120 yards west of the breakwater. I did not see any remains of fortification-walls inland, but Leake observed some, "built with well-squared stones, of the most regular kind of masonry"; and the American archaeologists were able to trace the course of the city-walls all round the site, which included within it the little acropolis hill. According to Leake, the entire circuit of the city seems not to have been more than 2000 yards.

On a hill just outside the city-walls to the south-east, between them and the dry bed of a stream, the Americans excavated the foundations of what they took to be a very small temple, with some irregularities of structure, built of well-cut blocks of the local stone. The foundations measure about 10.5 metres in length from east to west by 5 metres in breadth from north to south. Near them was found, at a depth of less than a foot below the surface, a collection of over twenty-five bronze implements and small ornaments, together with a great quantity of sheet bronze and bronze slag. The bronze implements include axe-heads, blades of knives, a drill, a chisel, etc. They may have belonged to the shop of a maker of bronze tools. A small Doric capital and a long unfluted drum of a column were also brought to light near the supposed temple, which Mr. Rolfe conjectures to have been the sanctuary of Dionysus mentioned by Pausanias. In this neighbourhood, about nineteen minutes' ride to the east of the harbour, I saw the ruins of a quadrangular building 6 paces long by 4 paces broad, constructed of large squared blocks set up on their narrow ends and very loosely fitted together, the chinks being filled with small stones. The blocks, which are about 3 ft. 6 in. high, may be ancient, but the building itself is not. It can hardly be the edifice which the Americans took for a temple.

The views from Anthedon across the beautiful Euripus are charming, especially at sunset when the opposite mountains of Euboea glow with delicate pink and lilac hues, and flakes of golden and rosy clouds are reflected in the mirror-like surface of the strait, which, apparently land-locked on all sides, resembles a calm lake. The effect is heightened if a fishing-boat happens to row along at the time, and a snatch of song is wafted from it across the water.

About a mile to the west of Anthedon, near the shore, is a villa built by the French Company which undertook to drain the Copaic Lake. The house suffered in the recent earthquakes and is now dismantled and deserted, but rough lodgings for the night can still be had in its bare empty rooms, where the cracks in the walls testify silently to the force of the earthquake. About a mile still farther to the west is the channel or canal by which the waters of the Copaic plain and the lakes of *Likeri* and *Paralimni* find their way into the sea. Not many yards beyond the mouth of the canal, and about 2 miles west of Anthedon, the hills project into the sea, forming a high bold cape, round the edge of which runs a line of rocks.

The writer who goes by the name of Dicaearchus thus describes Anthedon and its population as they were in the third century B.C. "The city is not large ; it is situated just on the shore of the Euboean sea. The market-place is all planted with trees and surrounded by double colonnades. It is well supplied with wine and fish ; but corn is scarce, for the district is rugged. The inhabitants are almost all fishermen, earning their livelihood by their hooks, by the purple-shell, and by sponges. They grow old on the beach, among the seaweed, and in their huts. They are all men of a ruddy countenance and spare figure ; their nails are worn away by reason of working constantly in the sea. They are mostly ferrymen and boat-builders. Far from tilling the land, they do not even own it, alleging that they are descendants of the marine Glaucus, who was confessedly a fisherman" (Dicaearchus, *Descriptio Graeciae*, i. 22 *sq.*, in *Geogr. Gr. Minores*, ed. Müller, 1. p. 104).

See Leake, *Northern Greece*, 2. pp. 272-275 ; H. N. Ulrichs, *Reisen und Forschungen*, 2. p. 36 *sq.* ; L. Ross, *Wanderungen*, 2. p. 131 *sq.* ; Bursian, *Geogr.* 1. p. 214 *sq.* ; C. D. Buck, F. B. Tarbell, and J. C. Rolfe, in *American Journal of Archaeology*, 5 (1889), pp. 78, 443-460 ; *id.*, 6 (1890), pp. 96-107 ; Δελτίον ἀρχαιολογικόν, 1889, p. 5. I visited Anthedon, 8th-9th November 1895, and have described its ruins mostly from personal observation.

22. 6. Homer and Pindar agree in saying etc. See Homer, *Od.* xi. 305-320 ; Pindar, *Pyth.* iv. 156 *sqq.*

22. 6. Glaucus' Leap. This was probably the high cliff beside the sea on the way from Anthedon to Chalcis (see above, p. 92). This seems to have been L. Ross's opinion (*Wanderungen*, 2. p. 131). Mr. Rolfe prefers to identify it with the steep cliff on the seaward side of the acropolis of Anthedon (*American Journal of Archaeology*, 6 (1890), p. 97). But that cliff is nowhere high or striking, and cannot vie in picturesque effect with the one on the way to Chalcis.

22. 7. by eating of a certain grass he was turned into a demon of the sea. One story ran that Glaucus was chasing a hare on Mt. Orla in Aetolia. The hare fainted, and Glaucus caught it and carried it to a spring. Here he plucked a wisp of grass which grew beside the spring and rubbed the hare with it. The animal at once revived ; Glaucus perceived the virtue of the grass, ate of it, became inspired, and, a storm coming on, flung himself into the sea. The taste of the grass was also said to have made him immortal. See Athenaeus, vii. p. 296 *sq.* The common story was that Glaucus discovered the marvellous properties of the grass by seeing that the fish which he had caught and laid on it came to life and sprang into the sea (Ovid, *Metam.* xiii. 924 *sqq.* ; Servius on Virgil, *Georg.* i. 437 ; Tzetzes, *Schol. on Lycophron*, 754 ; Schol. on Apollonius Rhodius, *Argonaut.* i. 1310). In yet another story Glaucus is associated with a life-giving herb in another way. As an infant, it is said, he was chasing a fly, and in doing so he fell into a jar of honey and was drowned. His father Minos insisted that the child must be restored to life, and the duty of doing so was laid upon a diviner named Polyidus. The poor man was at his wits' end till he saw a dead serpent brought to life by another serpent which had laid a certain herb on the body of its companion. Polyidus took the hint, applied the same herb to the body of the infant Glaucus, and so brought him back to life. See Apollodorus, iii. 3. 1 ; Hyginus, *Fab.* 136. The story of the discovery of a life-giving herb by somebody who observes how a serpent restores a dead serpent to life by means of it, is a common one. In antiquity Tylo was said to have been thus brought to life (Pliny, *Nat. hist.* xxv. 14) ; and similar incidents occur in modern popular tales. See Grimm, *Kinder- und Hausmärchen*, No. 16, 'Die drei Schlangenblätter,' with Grimm's note ; J. G. v. Hahn, *Griechische und albanesische Märchen*, 1. p. 56 ; *id.*, 2. pp. 204, 260, 274 ; Schleicher, *Litauische Märchen*, pp. 57, 59 ; E. Bédier, *Les Fabliaux* (Paris, 1893), p. 83. Cp. E. Rohde, *Der griechische Roman*, p. 125 *sq.*

22. 7. **Aeschylus made it the subject of a play.** It seems that Aeschylus wrote two plays on the subject of Glaucus, one a tragedy, the other a satyric drama. See G. Hermann, *Opuscula*, 2. pp. 59-75.

23. 1. **like the stadiums at Olympia and Epidaurus.** See vi. 20. 8 ; ii. 27. 5.

23. 1. **a shrine of the hero Iolaus.** Having described eastern and north-eastern Boeotia, our author now returns to Thebes and sets off from it in a northerly direction. In this and the following chapter he describes northern Boeotia, including Larymna, the eastern part of the Copaic Lake, and the mountains that bound it on the east. He quits the city by the Proetidian gate (the same through which he had passed on the way to Chalcis, ix. 18. 1), and the first place he comes to is a gymnasium of Iolaus. As to the worship of Iolaus, see note on x. 17. 5. Alexander the Great, approaching Thebes from Onchestus (hence from the north-west), encamped outside the city at the precinct of Iolaus. Next day he marched round the city and took up a position opposite the gate through which the road ran to Plataea and Attica. See Arrian, *Anabasis*, i. 7. 7 *sqq.* Hence it follows that the shrine of Iolaus was somewhere in the plain to the north of Thebes. From Pausanias it appears that the shrine was on the road which led from Thebes to Acraephnium (see § 5). The present road to Acraephnium branches off from the road to Chalcis at the fountain of Oedipus (see ix. 18. 5) and strikes off to the left through the plain in a northerly direction. If we assume that the ancient road coincided with the modern road, it will follow that the shrine of Iolaus was in the plain to the north of the fountain of Oedipus, on the road to *Karditsa* (Acraephnium) Cp. H. N. Ulrichs, *Reisen und Forschungen*, 2. p. 20 ; Fabricius, *Theben*, p. 23. The Proetidian gate, outside which was the shrine of Iolaus, was at the north-eastern end of the city. See note on ix. 8. 4. Games were celebrated at Thebes in honour of Iolaus ; the prize was a bronze tripod. See Schol. on Pindar, *Olymp.*

vii. 153 and 154, and xiii. 148; *id.* on *Pyth.* ix. 156; cp. *id.* on *Nem.* iv. 32. The Boeotians swore by Iolaus (Aristophanes, *Acharn.* 867).

23. 1. Iolaus met his end in Sardinia etc. Cp. i. 29. 5; vii. 2. 2 note; x. 17. 5 note. A scholiast on Pindar (*Nem.* iv. 32) also says that the tomb of Iolaus was in Sicily. But according to Diodorus (iv. 30. 3, v. 15. 6) Iolaus, after colonising Sardinia, returned to Greece, spending some time in Sicily on the way.

23. 2. the youthful Pindar was once journeying etc. Another version of this story was that as an infant Pindar had been exposed and that bees had fed him with honey (Aelian, *Var. hist.* xii. 45; Dio Chrysostom, *Or.* lxiv. vol. 2. p. 213, ed. Dindorf; Philostratus, *Imag.* ii. 12). Another story was that the incident of the bees happened to Pindar as he slept on Mt. Helicon, weary with the chase (Eustathius, in *Biographi Graeci*, ed. Westermann, p. 93, cp. *id.*, p. 97). Similar fables were told of Hesiod, Plato, Lucan, and others. See Robert-Tornow, *De apium mellisque apud veteres significatione*, pp. 100 *sq.*, 114 *sqq.*; cp. note on i. 32. 1, vol. 2. p. 425 *sq.*

23. 3. give to Pindar an equal share of all the first-fruits etc. It is said that at the sacrifices offered at Delphi the priest proclaimed aloud, " Let Pindar come to the banquet of the god "; or that when the sacristan was about to close the temple each day, he made a similar proclamation. See *Biographi Graeci*, ed. Westermann, pp. 92, 97, 99. The privilege was extended to Pindar's descendants; for in Plutarch's time at the Delphic festival of the Theoxenia a share was still set apart for the descendants of Pindar and they were invited by proclamation to partake of it (*De sera numinis vindicta*, 13).

23. 3. As he slept Proserpine stood by him etc. According to others it was Demeter who appeared to Pindar in a dream and complained that she alone had not been celebrated by him; Pindar accordingly composed a hymn in her honour and built an altar to Demeter and Proserpine in front of his house. See *Biographi Graeci*, ed. Westermann, pp. 92, 97. With the story which Pausanias here tells of Pindar's last hymn, we may compare the story (a true one) of the composition of Mozart's last work, the Requiem. Not long before the musician's death a stranger called upon him and asked him to compose a Requiem. Mozart agreed and set to work at the Requiem under a fixed impression that the stranger was a messenger come from the other world to warn him of his approaching death. He died before he had finished the work and it was afterwards completed by his friend Süssmayer. See W. Pole, *The Story of Mozart's Requiem* (London, 1879).

23. 5. Acraephnium. The ruins of Acraephnium are situated on a conspicuous hill on the eastern side of what was once the Copaic Lake. The hill is connected with Mount Ptous on the east by a long rocky ridge called *Kriaria*. At its northern foot the village of *Karditsa* lies in a trough among the hills, with narrow glens opening through them in several directions. One of these glens leads eastwards and upwards to Mount Ptous and the sanctuary of the Ptoan Apollo. Another track leads north-westward and downward through desolate glens with rocky and bushy sides to the great flat expanse of the Copaic plain, on which it debouches opposite the low isolated hill (once an island) of *Gla* or *Gha* with its mysterious prehistoric fortress and palace. The hill of Acraephnium is steep and rocky, but much less so on the northern side towards *Karditsa* than on the southern side, where it falls away to the Athamantine plain (ix. 24. 1), a branch which the great Copaic plain sends out eastward among the hills. The acropolis of Acraephnium occupied the summit of the steep hill, where some well-preserved remains of the fortification-wall may be seen. Ascending the hill from *Karditsa* we come in ten minutes to a ruined fortification-wall running straight up the slope of the hill in a direction from north to south. It is built of large squared blocks laid in horizontal courses. The number of courses preserved varies from one to five. In some places it is 7, 8, and 9 feet high. Thus the wall extends at varying heights but in an almost unbroken line to the top of the hill. There are no towers or gates in it, nor is it possible to estimate the original thickness of the wall, since nowhere are the two faces preserved together. At the summit, which is at the north-east end of the hill, the wall makes an angle and runs in a straight line south-westward along the top of the hill, which is broad and flat, but with a gentle inclination to the south-west and west. This wall on the top of the hill, though partly ruinous, is standing for the most part to a height varying from three to six courses. Where six courses are preserved, the height of the wall is about 10 feet. The masonry is on the whole quadrangular, like that of the wall on the northern slope, but some of the upright joints are aslant, not perpendicular, and the courses in some places are not quite regular. After running for about 100 yards south-westward from the highest point of the hill, the wall comes to a stop, but its line may be traced in the same direction for about 60 yards farther by means of a mound and broken stones. But beyond this I could find no certain trace of it in any direction. As there are no projecting towers, it is not quite easy to decide which was the outer and which the inner side of the walls. But apparently the wall on the northern slope of the hill faced west, and the wall on the top of the hill faced north-west. If this is so, it follows that a broad flat expanse on the summit lay outside the walls, which seems strange. Lolling (in Baedeker) speaks of polygonal walls on the side next the Copaic plain, but I did not observe them. The walls which I saw and have described belong evidently to one period, and that the best period of Greek masonry, probably the fourth century B.C. The stone of which they are built seemed to me to be a hard grey limestone.

From the summit of the hill we see to the south-west a great stretch of the Copaic plain with the new drainage canal crossing it in a straight line from Mount Helicon. The canal ends in the Athamantian plain, to the south of the hill of Acraephnium, where the water descends into a chasm (*katavothra*) to reappear in Lake *Likeri* (Hylica), which with all its blue winding bays lies stretched out below us on the south-east. Due eastward the eye ranges over hills beyond hills as far as the mountains of Attica. On the north-east Mount Ptous rises conspicuous over a nearer hill, and on its western slope, below a line of grey precipices, may be seen even at this distance the excavations which mark the site of the temple of Apollo. To the west the high mass of the omnipresent Parnassus appears on the horizon.

On the northern slope of the hill, towards *Karditsa*, Leake and H. N. Ulrichs observed many ancient foundations, extending down to the very foot of the hill. These probably indicated the site of the lower city. Here too, on the northern slope, a little above the village of *Karditsa*, stands a church of St. George which contains many ancient inscriptions as well as columns formed of pieces of ancient shafts with handsome Ionic capitals. These shafts and capitals perhaps belonged to the temple of Dionysus mentioned by Pausanias, which may have stood on the site now occupied by the church. Amongst the inscriptions found in the church is one (*C. I. G. G. S.* 1. No. 2713) containing the speech in which Nero proclaimed the independence of Greece. See vii. 17. 3 note.

To the west of Acraephnium a long rocky promontory runs out into the flat Copaic plain ; the natives call it *Vistrika ;* its extremity is called Cape *Phtelio* on the French map. At the foot of the cape an enormous cube of rock, which has perhaps fallen from the cliff, bears the following inscription (*C. I. G. G. S.* 1. No. 2792) :

$$\text{"Ορια Κ[ω]πήω[ν}$$
$$\text{ποτ' 'Ακρηφιεῖα[ς}$$
$$\text{ὀριττ[ά]ντων Βοιω[τῶν.}$$

"Boundary of the territory of Copae toward the territory of Acraephnium, as laid down by the Boeotians." This seems to show that Copae and Acraephnium had both claimed the Copaic Lake as part of their territory and that the Boeotian confederacy had decided in favour of Copae.

The name of the city is variously given by ancient writers as Acraephia (Herodotus, viii. 135 ; Stephanus Byzantius, *s.v.* 'Ακραιφία), Acraephiae (Strabo, ix. p. 410), Acraephium (*id.*, ix. p. 413), and Acraephnium (Pausanias). From inscriptions we learn that the true form was Acraephia (*C. I. G. G. S.* 1. Nos. 2871, 4135), or, in the Boeotian dialect, Acrephia (*C. I. G. G. S.* 1. No. 4136), both forms being the neuter plural.

See Dodwell, *Tour*, 2. p. 54 *sq.* ; Leake, *Northern Greece*, 2. pp. 295-305 ; H. N. Ulrichs, *Reisen und Forschungen*, 2. p. 242 *sqq.* ; L. Ross, *Wanderungen*, 1. p. 105 ; Bursian, *Geogr.* 1. p. 213 ; Baedeker,[3] p. 191 ; *Guide-Joanne*, 2. p. 18. I spent two nights at *Karditsa* (6th and 7th November 1895) and have described the ruins of the acropolis from personal observation. For inscriptions found at Acraephnium, see *C. I. G. G. S.* 1. pp. 469 *sqq.*, 704 ; *Bulletin de Corr. hellénique*, 2 (1878), p. 507 *sq.* ; *id.*, 12 (1888), pp. 305-315, 510-528 (Nero's speech) ; *id.*, 13 (1889), p. 407 *sq.* (boundary inscription) ; *Mittheil. d. arch. Inst. in Athen*, 3 (1878), p. 299 *sq.* ; *id.*, 9 (1884), pp. 5-14 ; Δελτίον ἀρχαιολογικόν, 1888, pp. 192-194 (Nero's speech) ; Cauer, *Delectus Inscr. Graec.*[2] No. 374 *sq.* ; Collitz, *G. D. I.* 1. No. 565 *sqq.* ; Roehl, *I. G. A.* Nos. 151, 162, 218, 298.

23. 6. **About fifteen furlongs to the right** —— **is the sanctuary of Ptoan Apollo.** Herodotus tells us that (viii. 135) that the sanctuary of

the Ptoan Apollo belonged to Thebes and was situated "above the Copaic Lake, beside a mountain, very near to the city of Acraephia." Strabo describes it (ix. p. 413) as situated "above the Teneric plain and the Copaic Lake, near Acraephium," adding that the oracle and the mountain had belonged to Thebes.   The remains of the sanctuary are to be seen in a little mountain valley high up on Mount Ptous.   They were excavated in 1885, 1886, and 1891, under the direction of Mr. Holleaux, of the French School of Archaeology at Athens.   In its wider sense Mount Ptous is the range or mass of mountains which bounds the Copaic plain on the east and extends thence north and east to the Euripus.   The range culminates in three peaks now called *Palagia* (3280 feet), *Tsoukourieli*, and *Megalo Vouno* ('big hill'), which enclose between them a small upland valley resembling a deep basin or trough. On three sides of the little valley the mountains rise like walls, but on the south side the basin, so to say, is broken and through the opening an uninterrupted view is obtained of the mountains from Parnassus round by Helicon to Cithaeron.   To the south-west is seen a piece of the Copaic plain with the modern canal running across it ; and on the south Lake *Likeri* lies like a Highland loch with all its winding bays spread out below us.   The slopes of the peaks which bound the little valley on the north and west are steep, stony, and bushy.   The peak which bounds it on the east is Mt. *Palagia*, the true summit of Mt. Ptous.   It is a high, sharp-pointed mountain, belted about half-way up with precipices of grey rock, below which a steep slope descends into the valley.   On this slope stood the sanctuary of Apollo, the buildings which composed it rising in terraces one above the other.

Six terraces, each supported by a wall of masonry, may be distinguished.   On the highest of them, not far below the grey crags which rise like a pinnacle above the sanctuary, a spring issues from a wall of modern masonry.   On the terrace next below stood the temple.   It was a small Doric temple, orientated north-west and south-east, and measuring 23.30 metres on the sides and 11.80 metres at the ends.   Mr. Holleaux states that the substructions, some steps, the lower course of some walls, and a small part of the pavement are still in their places. However, when I visited the sanctuary in November 1895, I observed nothing of the temple standing but the foundations, which are three and four courses or 6 feet high ; they are built of a very soft white crumbling limestone.   The supporting-wall of the terrace on which the temple stands is four and five courses (5 ft. 8 in.) high ; it is constructed of small squared stones laid in horizontal courses.   If we descend the hill by the ruined ramp at the western end of the temple we come to an artificial cavern hewn in the mountain-side.   This cavern communicates directly by an earthenware conduit with the spring on the highest terrace.   It is a plausible conjecture that the oracles were delivered in this cavern by the prophet, who had previously drunk the water of the spring, just as the prophet of the Clarian Apollo drank of the sacred spring in the cave as a means of procuring inspiration (see notes on vii. 3. 1 ; ix. 2. 1).

On the third terrace, below the temple to the south-west, are the foundations of a building 26 paces long by 6 paces broad, orientated in the same way as the temple. Its foundations are constructed of a hard grey stone. The upper walls, of which some parts exist, were seemingly built of the soft white limestone. Here there are two drums of unfluted columns, 30 inches in diameter, and a drum of a small fluted Doric column. The terrace is about 13 paces broad. The lower courses of the wall which supported it are built of the hard grey stone.

The fourth terrace is 6 paces broad. The lower courses of its supporting-wall are built of the hard grey stone; the upper courses (or at least the single existing upper course) of the soft white limestone.

The fifth terrace, on which lie two inscribed blocks, is supported by a wall in the shape of a crescent ; and on the sixth terrace, immediately in front of the crescent - shaped wall, is a curious edifice. It is a narrow building, 27 paces long by 3½ paces broad, and comprises seven quadrangular chambers, each 9 feet long by 6 feet wide. But the most remarkable feature of the edifice is that all these chambers are subterranean, being constructed of high walls of squared masonry, the top of which is flush with the surface of the terrace. These chambers have neither doors nor windows, and they seem to have been roofed over with large slabs, some of which are still in position. In the southernmost of the chambers the walls are nine courses high ; one of the blocks seems to show traces of red paint. Probably these chambers were cisterns ; they communicate with the spring on the highest terrace. The crescent-shaped wall at the back of the cisterns is standing to a height of three and four courses. Whether it is really the supporting-wall of the next terrace above (the fifth) seems doubtful. Beside the cisterns on the west lies a small drum of a fluted Doric column measuring 27 inches in diameter. Also there is a base 30 inches in diameter.

Below the sixth and lowest terrace is an ancient fountain now called *Perdiko-Vrysi* ('partridge-spring'), which gives its name to the little valley in which the sanctuary is situated. The water trickles through a stone channel into a small round stone basin. It originally issued from a wall of masonry, of which two blocks are standing, one of them serving also to form the basin into which the water flows. Other squared ancient blocks are lying about the little fountain. The water probably comes from the spring on the highest terrace ; for it can be traced flowing down the steep slope, making green with grass the bare hill-side over which it flows.

A short way, perhaps 100 yards or so, to the south-west of the sanctuary and lower down is the small chapel of *Hagia Paraskeve* (St. Friday), which has been lately rebuilt. The hill-side at the chapel is overgrown with bushes, and between it and the sanctuary is a grove of fine holly-oaks. The view from the chapel over the beautiful Lake *Likeri* and away to the mountains of southern Boeotia is charming. The lake, it should be said, is not visible from the sanctuary. Near the chapel a rocky glen descends to the south-west. Down this glen the path leads to *Karditsa* and Acraephnium. Descending it, we enjoy beautiful views over Lake *Likeri* framed between the rocky sides of the glen and backed by distant mountains. Soon, however, the path turns westward, the distant prospect of lake and mountain disappears, and we follow an opener and tamer glen, which leads us straight by a gradual and easy descent between low rounded bushy hills to *Karditsa*. The time from the sanctuary to *Karditsa* is about half an hour.[1]

In addition to the ruined buildings of the sanctuary, Mr. Holleaux's excavations brought to light a number of inscriptions, some archaic marble statues, bronze statuettes, small bronze animals of primitive style, bronze reliefs, and many fragments of early Corinthian pottery. Particularly interesting are the thin bronze plates adorned with reliefs, for they serve to illustrate the early history of decorative art in Greece. The decorations include linear and vegetable patterns, real and fantastic animals (sphinxes, griffins, human-headed birds) and human figures arranged in scenes, for example Zeus and Typhon, and Prometheus and the vulture. Mr. Holleaux thinks it likely that these bronze reliefs were imported from Corinth, since the style of their decoration resembles that of the early Corinthian pottery, and the reliefs were discovered in a layer where fragments of that pottery were found by hundreds. One of the marble statues brought to light by Mr. Holleaux belongs to the type of the so-called Apollo of Thera, Orchomenus, and Tenea (see note on ii. 5. 4). Another interesting discovery, made in 1891, is that of a socle and base of an offering which the inscription (ΗΙΠΠΑΡΧΟΣ ΑΝΕΘΕ[ΚΕΝ ΗΟ ΠΕΙΣΙΣ]ΤΡΑΤΟ, engraved in Attic letters of the sixth century B.C., proves to have been dedicated by the tyrant Hipparchus, son of Pisistratus. Mr. Holleaux conjectures that the tyrant's offering may have consisted of an image of Athena in the style of the archaic female statues found on the Acropolis at Athens (see vol. 2. p. 346), since the head of such a statue was found by him in the sanctuary.

Inscriptions show that games called Ptoia were celebrated at the sanctuary every fourth year. They appear to have consisted exclusively of musical and poetical contests, which were held in a theatre. The site of the theatre, however, has not been found. The contests were preceded or accompanied by sacrifices to Apollo and other gods, and by processions, national dances of the kind called *surtos*, and banquets. See *C. I. G. G. S.* 1. Nos. 2710, 2712, 4135, 4138, 4139, 4142, 4147, 4148; Holleaux, in *Bulletin de Corresp. hellénique*, 14 (1890), pp. 59-64. From one of these inscriptions (*C. I. G. G. S.* 1. No. 4135; *Bulletin de Corresp. hellénique*, 14 (1890), p. 19 *sqq.*) it appears that the games were instituted some time between 178 and 146 B.C. by a decree of the Amphictyonic Council, which enacted that the sanctuary of the Ptoan Apollo, within the limits marked by the boundary stones, should be an asylum, and that a sacred truce should begin on the 15th day of the Boeotian month Hippodromius or the Delpic month Apellaeus. From another of these inscriptions, found in the church of St. George at *Karditsa*, we learn that in the reign of Caligula or Nero these games,

---

[1] According to the writer of the *Guide-Joanne* the time is an hour and twenty minutes. On this I can only say that I left the sanctuary at 4.53 P.M. and riding leisurely was at *Karditsa* at 5.25 P.M. The distance is about 2 miles.

after having been in abeyance for thirty years, were revived by Epaminondas, the son of Epaminondas, and that out of gratitude for this and
other benefits the people of Acraephnium resolved to set up two
statues of Epaminondas, one in the sanctuary of the Ptoan Apollo and
one in the market-place of Acraephnium (*C. I. G. G. S.* 1. No. 2712;
C. I. G. No. 1625; Leake, *Northern Greece*, 2. pp. 297 *sq.*, 333).
Afterwards on the proposal of this same Epaminondas in his capacity of
high priest of the Augustuses and of Nero, the people of Acraephnium
testified their gratitude to Nero for his liberation of Greece by resolving
to dedicate an altar to him under the title of Zeus of Freedom beside
the altar of Saviour Zeus, and to set up images of him and Augusta
Messalina (?), as of a god and goddess, in the temple of the Ptoan
Apollo (*C. I. G. G. S.* 1. No. 2713; *Bulletin de Corresp. hellénique*, 12
(1888), p. 510 *sqq.*)

Pausanias seems to imply that the oracle of the Ptoan Apollo became
dumb after the destruction of Thebes by Alexander the Great in 335 B.C.
Inscriptions, however, prove that the oracle was again in use soon after
the restoration of Thebes by Cassander in 315 B.C. (see ix. 7. 1 note),
and that it continued to be consulted down to the middle of the first
century A.D. Thus an inscription, which can be dated with tolerable
certainty between 312 and 304 B.C., records that the Boeotians dedicated a tripod to the Ptoan Apollo in return for a good oracle which he
had delivered to them (*C. I. G. G. S.* 1. No. 2724; *Mittheil. d. arch.
Inst. in Athen*, 3 (1878), p. 86 *sqq.*; *Bulletin de Corresp. hellénique*,
13 (1889), p. 2, with Holleaux's comments, p. 7 *sqq.*; Collitz, *G. D. I.*
1. No. 571); and oracles of the god are expressly mentioned in
inscriptions which belong to the latter part of the third or the beginning
of the second century B.C. (*C. I. G. G. S.* 1. Nos. 2724 c, 2724 d, 4156,
4157; as to the dates, see Holleaux, in *Bulletin de Corresp. hellénique*,
13 (1889), pp. 14 *sq.*, 226 *sq.*; *id.*, in *Bulletin de Corresp. hellénique*,
14 (1890), p. 5). Further, it is mentioned as one of the many merits of
Epaminondas son of Epaminondas in the reign of Caligula or Nero, that
he worked the oracle (ἐπετέλει καὶ τὰ τοῦ θεοῦ μαντεῖα *C. I. G. G. S.*
1. No. 2712), which perhaps means that he acted as prophet or mouthpiece of the god. For we know from Herodotus (viii. 135) that the
oracles were delivered by the mouth of a prophet; and the prophet of
the god is mentioned in inscriptions which date variously from the
fourth century B.C. (*C. I. G. G. S.* 1. No. 4155), from between 178 and
146 B.C. (*C. I. G. G. S.* 1. Nos. 4135, 4138, 4142; see Holleaux, in
Bulletin de Corresp. hellénique, 14 (1890), p. 27 *sqq.*), and from the first
century B.C. (*C. I. G. G. S.* 1. No. 4147; see Holleaux, *ib.*, p. 190).
By the end of the first century of our era, however, the oracle would
seem to have fallen into disuse; for Plutarch tells us that in his time all
the oracles of Boeotia, except the oracle of Trophonius, were dumb or
deserted; on Mount Ptous, he says, you might search long without
finding even a shepherd tending his flock (*De defectu oraculorum*, 5 and
8). Even at the beginning of our era Strabo had spoken of the oracle
as if it were a thing of the past (ix. p. 413), which at least seems to
show that by his time it was no longer famous.

See Leake, *Northern Greece*, 2. p. 279; H. N. Ulrichs, *Reisen und Forschungen*,
I. p. 235 *sqq.*; Bursian, *Geogr.* I. p. 212 *sq.*; Baedeker,[3] p. 191; *Guide-Joanne*, 2.
p. 18 *sqq.*; *Mittheil. d. arch. Inst. in Athen*, 3 (1878), pp. 86-94; *Bulletin de
Corresp. hellénique*, 9 (1885), pp. 474-481; *id.*, 10 (1886), pp. 66-80, 98-101,
190-199, 269-275; *id.*, 11 (1887), pp. 1-5, 177-200, 275-287, 354-363; *id.*, 12
(1888), pp. 380-404; *id.*, 14 (1890), pp. 1-64 (inscriptions), 181-203 (inscriptions),
602 *sq.*; *id.*, 15 (1891), p. 661 *sq.*; *id.*, 16 (1892), pp. 347-369, 453-466; *Comptes
Rendus de l'Académie des Inscriptions*, 4me ·Série, 20 (1892), pp. 74 *sq.*, 91 *sq.*;
American Journal of Archaeology, 8 (1893), p. 259 *sq.*; Bouché-Leclercq, *Hist. de
la divination*, 3. pp. 214-217; Hertzberg, *Gesch. Griechenlands unter der Herrschaft der Römer*, 2. p. 64. I visited the sanctuary, 6th November 1895, and
have described the remains chiefly from my own observation.

**23. 6. a man of Europus named Mys was sent by Mar-
donius etc.** See Herodotus, viii. 135. There were two towns of the
name Europus, one in Emathia (Ptolemy, iii. 12. 36; Thucydides, ii.
100; Strabo, vii. p. 327; Stephanus Byz. *s.v.* Εὐρωπός), another in
Media (Strabo, xi. p. 524). There was a town of Caria named
Euromus (Strabo, xiv. p. 635; Stephanus Byzantius, *s.v.* Εὔρωμος);
and as Mys spoke Carian, it has been supposed that Euromus, not
Europus, was his native town. But Herodotus as well as Pausanias
calls him a man of Europus, though the reading Εὐρωμέα, instead of
Εὐρωπέα, has been introduced into the text of Herodotus by Holder.

23. 7. Having crossed Mount Ptous we come to —— Larymna.
To reach Larymna from the sanctuary of Apollo on Mount Ptous, we
quit the trough or little mountain-girdled valley in which the remains of
the sanctuary are to be seen and ascend the ridge which bounds it on
the north-west, forming a saddle between Mount *Tsoukourieli* and
Mount *Megalo Vouno*. From the summit of the ridge or saddle we
take a last look backwards at the vale of Apollo with its ruined sanctuary
and the beautiful Lake *Likeri* beyond and below it to the south; then
turning northwards we descend somewhat steeply a narrow glen with
high bushy sides, which leads us straight down to the north-eastern
corner of the great Copaic plain. Or, if we choose, after crossing the
saddle and descending through the glen a short way we may turn to the
left along the northern slope of the *Megalo Vouno*, a range of mountains
which, crested with a line of high grey cliffs, extends westward from the
vale of Apollo to the edge of the Copaic plain. High up on the
northern slope of the mountain stands the small village of *Kokkino*,
commanding distant prospects of the mountains of Euboea on the north
and Parnassus on the west. The village is reached in little more than
half an hour from the sanctuary. From *Kokkino* a stony but not very
steep path leads downwards between low hills with bushy and stony
slopes to the north-eastern extremity of the Copaic plain. Across this
corner of the plain, which until a few years ago was a marsh or even a
lake for many months of the year, but is now under cultivation, we ride
to the *Great Katavothra*, the largest of the natural chasms in the line
of cliffs through which the water of the Copaic lake found its way to the
sea. It is a great cave with a high-arched roof opening in the face of
a cliff of creamy white limestone. Unlike most of the other chasms
or emissories, it is still in use; the river Melas (the modern *Mavro-*

potamos or Black River), after traversing all the northern edge of the Copaic plain in a canal-like bed, pours its water in a steady stream into the cave and vanishes in the depths. A little way inward from the mouth of the cave there is an opening in the roof. When the sunshine streams down through it, lighting up the back of the gloomy cavern with its hanging rocky roof and hurrying river, the effect is very picturesque ; it is like a fairy grotto, and we could almost fancy that we stood

> "Where Alph, the sacred river, ran
> Through caverns measureless to man
> Down to a sunless sea."

But alas ! the women who may be seen any day washing their dirty linen at the mouth of the cave break the spell.

All this north-eastern part of the Copaic plain is bounded by a line of cliffs which till lately were washed by the waters of the lake. At the *Great Katavothra* we ascend the cliffs and follow a path which skirts the plain running not far from the edge of the cliffs, until we come to the dip in the hills over which the path goes to Larymna. Here the plain is bounded on the north only by a low ridge which rises little more than 150 feet above the level of the plain. At its foot, not many yards to the east of the point where the path to Larymna ascends the ridge, there are three more *katavothras* close together, all in the form of caverns in the face of red cliffs. They are called the *katavothras* of *Bynia*. The central one is the finest. It is a natural grotto overhung by the red cliff; we can walk into it a little way without stooping. None of these three chasms is now in use ; the two western are purposely blocked with stones, and tumbled masses of rocks lie at the sides of the third, which is a low opening at the foot of a semicircle of reddish rocks some 30 to 50 feet high. The path now turns away from the plain and ascends the ridge, which is thickly overgrown with lentisk bushes. A few yards from the edge of the plain we see among the bushes the mouth of a square perpendicular shaft hewn in the rock. It is the first of a series of sixteen similar shafts which exist near the path at intervals varying from 80 to 450 paces. The line in which the shafts occur is not straight, but follows exactly the pass or depression in the ridge. All the shafts are square, but their mouths vary, according to my measurements, from 4 ft. 6 in. to about 9 feet across.[1] Their depth is said to vary, according to the height of the ridge, from 59 feet to 207 feet. Some of the shafts have carefully-smoothed sides with foot-holes in them for descending. Heaps of red stones and earth, excavated when the shafts were sunk, mark their positions among the bushes. These shafts appear, as we shall see, to have been sunk in antiquity as a preliminary to making a tunnel through which to conduct the water of the Copaic Lake to the sea.

After reaching the summit of the ridge we begin to descend gradually to the north between the bush-clad slopes of low hills, still passing at short intervals the mouths of shafts hidden away in the dense shrubbery.

---

[1] According to Mr. Kambanis, however, the sides vary from 1.60 to 2 metres.

Thus we descend into an open valley enclosed by higher hills, with the high blue mountains of Euboea appearing at its northern end. The bottom of the valley is uncultivated but prettily wooded with tall lentisk bushes of a fresh green colour. This is the upper valley of *Larma* (a corruption of Larymna). In the valley, about ten minutes' walk to the right (east) of the path, and not far from the last shaft, a low cliff rises to a height of about 30 feet amid rocks and bushes. Its face is seamed and rent with many narrow fissures, through which the water of the Copaic Lake, after its subterranean passage from one or more of the *katavothras*, used to burst in a copious stream, forming first a deep pool and then a broad and rapid river, which the ancients called the Cephisus, because they supposed it to be a continuation of the river of that name which flowed into the Copaic Lake from the west (Strabo, ix. p. 406 *sq.*) The place where the water came to the surface again was named Anchoë by the ancients (Strabo, *l.c.*) It is now called *Kephalari* ('head springs'). In summer, however, when the lake was low, no water trickled through the rifted rock, and the bed of the stream was consequently dry. Now that the lake has been drained, the water has ceased to flow altogether; for the river which enters the *Great Kata-vothra* comes to the surface again not here but beside the bay of *Skroponeri*. About a mile farther on two rocky hills projecting from the mountains on either side close the valley and divide it from the lower valley or small maritime plain of Larymna. The two hills approach each other so closely that only a narrow gorge of grey rocks divides them. Through this gorge, which though picturesque is neither very deep nor very long, the river from the *Kephalari* springs used to find its way from the upper to the lower valley of Larymna. Now only its dry stony bed enters the ravine. But in the gorge a little lower down there rises a copious spring, forming at once a stream of fair size which, after issuing from the gorge, turns some mills in the valley below and flows into the sea a mile or so to the south of Lower Larymna. The spring itself is not visible, so far as I observed. But the water lies in pools and flows slowly from pool to pool, whereas the bed of the ravine higher up is totally dry; at least it was so in November 1895, when I passed that way. In the pools pretty green weeds grow thickly, and on the rocks tortoises may be seen sunning themselves in hot weather, ready to glide into the cool water at the approach of an intruder. The spring in the gorge is clearly inde-pendent of the Copaic Lake, since it continues to flow now that the lake has been drained. Even before the lake was drained, the natives denied that this spring was an emissory of the lake, asserting that changes in the level of the lake did not affect the volume of water of the spring.

The path to Larymna, after traversing the upper valley, crosses the dry bed of the stream and ascends the rocky slope of the hill on the right or east bank of the gorge. On the top of the hill, to the right, are the scanty ruins of Upper Larymna (see below). Below us to the left is the ravine; the path keeps along the slope of the hill at some distance above it. In front of us we soon see an olive-clad plain with a strip of blue sea, like a little lake, beyond it, the high mountains of Euboea closing the view on the north. This olive-clad plain is the lower valley or small maritime plain of Larymna. The spot where we descend into it from the rocky hill-side is a pretty one. A rushing stream bursts from the gorge beside which we have been journeying and flows seaward between banks thickly overgrown with reeds, myrtles, and tall oleanders. Its water is limpidly clear and water-plants grow in it. A church, much injured by the earthquakes of 1893, stands here, and farther on two mills are turned by the stream. Fine olive-trees and fig-trees rise among the fields which occupy the bottom of the valley. About a mile from the mills the river falls into the sea. Near its mouth we cross it on a bridge with five arches, and ride north-wards for a mile or more through an uncultivated plain, covered with rocks and bushes, close to the edge of the sea. On our way we pass a third mill driven by water which is brought to it in an artificial channel from the gorge at the head of the valley. Thus we reach *Kastri*, a small village beside the sea occupying part of the site of the ancient Larymna. The time from the sanctuary of Apollo to Larymna is about four hours or rather less.

Larymna stood in a little maritime plain on the western shore of a sheltered inlet which runs up into the land from the Euripus in a direction from north to south. Mountains rise around it in all directions. On the opposite or eastern side of the creek a high bushy hill descends to the water's edge, and hills rise beyond the little plain to the west and south; those on the south are partially wooded with pines. To the north, beyond the Euripus, are seen the high steep mountains of *Kandili* in Euboea towering like a great wall from the shore of the strait. The site of Larymna is perfectly level. A promon-tory or peninsula of some breadth sheltered a little semicircular bay at the north end of the town. This harbour appears to be disused at present, and there are no houses beside it. The village of *Kastri*, within the line of the ancient walls, is a little farther to the south, and vessels anchor off it. The walls and towers of the ancient city can be traced nearly all the way along the shore, but inland they have almost disappeared. They are built of a reddish stone in the most regular style of masonry, the blocks being accurately squared and laid in hori-zontal courses. Clearly they belong to the best period of Greek mili-tary architecture and may date from the fifth or perhaps rather the fourth century B.C. The number of courses preserved varies from one to seven; in the two places where seven courses are standing the height is about 10 feet 8 inches. Along the sea-shore beside the village, and again along the shore immediately to the north of the harbour, the wall is strengthened at intervals of about 10 feet by short cross-walls or buttresses, each 5 feet long, running inwards from it at right angles. The wall along the shore is a true sea-wall, its foundations being actually under water. The whole circuit of the walls was about a mile. Of the north and south walls, where they ran inland from the shore, there are some remains; the south wall, in particular, is preserved to a height of one and two courses, with a block or two of a third course, for a length

of 50 yards or so from the shore.   But the line of the greater part of
the north and the whole of the west wall, which defended the city on
the side of the plain, is traceable only by mounds and some blocks of
masonry.   The city can hardly have extended farther to the west, for
the native rock crops up in the plain outside the line of the west wall.
Remains of seven square towers, strengthening the wall, may be seen at
intervals along the shore.   Two of them defended the entrance to the
harbour.   Of these the tower on the eastern shore of the harbour-mouth
is preserved to a height of six and seven courses ; it measures 24 feet
on the face and projects 18 feet from the wall.   The other towers as a
rule are about 20 feet broad on the face and project 7 feet from the
wall.   Inside of the two towers which defended the mouth of the
harbour there are remains of two ancient moles projecting into the water
on either side and narrowing the entrance.   The western mole is the
better preserved.   It is 18 feet broad on its eastern face, and is standing to a height of two and three courses above water, while one or two
foundation-courses are submerged.   Beyond the end of this mole a line
of squared blocks, sunk at the level of the bottom, as well as many
tumbled blocks also under water, show that the mole formerly extended
much farther than at present.   The eastern mole measures only 8 feet
broad on its western face.   Both moles are solidly built of squared
blocks.   Between them, in the middle of the harbour-mouth, are the
remains of a pier or tower, built in the same style and rising a few feet
above the water.   The harbour is semicircular in shape and very small,
with a shelving beach of sand and gravel.   It is not more than 60 yards
long from north to south.   The breadth across the mouth, inclusive of
the moles, may be 80 yards or so.   Along the greater part of the east
side of the harbour, at a distance of 16 paces or so from the water, there
runs a wall about 8 feet high, built in a very rude style of polygonal
blocks almost unhewn and scarcely fitted together.   It certainly belongs
to a different period from the beautifully and regularly constructed walls
and towers which elsewhere line the shore.   Recently a German archaeologist, Mr. F. Noack, has pointed to this wall as evidence of a prehistoric settlement of the Minyans at Larymna ; he thinks that a people
who had drained the basin of the Copaic Lake must have constructed
fortresses on the coast to defend the outflow of the lake.   The wall,
according to him, is 4.50 metres (14 feet 8 inches) thick.   The stones
of which it is built, so far as my recollection goes, are small, certainly
not to be compared in size to the stones of which the walls of Tiryns
and Mycenae are constructed.   I took the wall to be more recent
than the rest of the fortifications, and thought that it belonged to a later
repair, of which there are traces at other points of the promontory which
defends the harbour on the east.   For example, on the eastern shore of
the promontory a square tower, built as usual of fine ashlar masonry, of
which there are considerable remains, has been replaced by a semicircular tower of polygonal masonry built of small stones with gaping
joints.   These polygonal walls, whatever their date, differ in material
as well as style from the rest of the fortifications, being built of a whitish
stone, whereas all the other walls and towers are built of a reddish

stone. A little to the south of the semicircular tower of polygonal masonry there are remains of an ancient quay or breakwater extending into the sea for a good many yards; it is built of squared blocks of the reddish stone. Within the circuit-wall of Larymna there are some remains of foundations of ancient buildings; these seem to have been more numerous and distinct in Leake's time than at present. According to him the promontory on the east side of the harbour was cut off by an inner cross-wall and served as an acropolis. Raikes, who travelled early in the nineteenth century, also observes that "across the neck of the peninsula a second wall has been built, but from the rude style of its construction, it is probably the work of a later time." Outside the walls to the south a salt spring called *Glyfonero* rises a few paces from the beach and forms a small deep pool. The natives regard it as a sacred water on account of its cathartic properties. The small village of *Kastri*, on the site of the ancient Larymna, suffered much from the earthquakes of 1893, and was partially deserted when I visited it in 1895.

Pausanias tells us that Larymna belonged of old to Locris, and Lycophron (*Cassandra*, 1146) mentions it among the Locrian cities which sent virgins annually to Troy to atone for the outrage of Cassandra by Ajax. The city still belonged to Locris at the time when the *Periplus* which is attributed to Scylax was written, namely about 338-335 B.C. (Scylax, *Periplus*, 6). But by 230 B.C. it was Boeotian (Polybius, xx. 5. 7); and to Boeotia it continued to belong in the times of Sulla (Plutarch, *Sulla*, 26), of Strabo (ix. pp. 405, 406), and of Pausanias.

On the other hand Upper Larymna belonged to Locris; but the Romans annexed it to Lower Larymna (Strabo, ix. p. 406). The scanty remains of the upper town, now called *Bazaraki* ('little bazaar'), are situated, as has been mentioned (p. 106), on one of the two rocky hills which divide the upper from the lower valley of Larymna. The path from Larymna to the Copaic plain runs along the lower slope of the hill, above the gorge that separates the two hills. In eight minutes we ascend from the path to the top of the hill. The distance from Larymna is about 2 miles. The hill commands the defile through which the route goes from the upper to the lower valley, and from its top there are good views north and south over both of them. On the east it is connected, without a break, with higher bushy and rocky hills, the slopes of which begin to ascend not many yards away. On the west the hill descends somewhat steeply to the gorge; but on the north and south it slopes gradually to the lower and upper valleys respectively. Among the lentisk bushes with which the hill is partly overgrown may be seen traces of former settlements on the gradual northern and southern slopes, especially on the latter. The traces consist of ruined walls and broken stones. Farther down, at the south-western foot of the hill, a small plateau, strewn with broken stones, irregular blocks, and pottery, seems also to have been included within the ancient town. It is a little above the gorge and is skirted by the path from the upper to the lower valley. Just below the path there are some remains of a

rough wall running parallel to the gorge.   On the eastern side of the
hill, at and near the top, a fortification-wall built of rather small stones
roughly squared may be traced for a good many yards.   It is standing
to a height of one, two, and three courses.   There are also some small
ruins of an ancient fortification-wall facing north, a little below the
summit.

I visited Larymna and Upper Larymna and traversed the route from Larymna
to the sanctuary of Apollo on Mount Ptous, 5th and 6th November 1895, and the
foregoing description is based mainly on personal observation.   See Raikes, in
Walpole's *Memoirs relating to Turkey* [2] (London, 1818), pp. 302-304 ; H. N.
Ulrichs, *Reisen und Forschungen*, I. pp. 222-231 ; L. Ross, *Wanderungen*, I.
p. 99 *sqq.* ; Bursian, *Geogr.* I. p. 192 ; Baedeker,[3] p. 194 *sq.* ; *Guide-Joanne*, 2.
p. 20 *sq.* ; M. L. Kambanis, in *Bulletin de Corresp. hellénique*, 17 (1893),
p. 322 *sqq.* (as to the shafts) ; F. Noack, in *Mittheilungen d. arch. Inst. in Athen*,
19 (1894), p. 449 *sq.* ; A. de Ridder, in *Bulletin de Corresp. hellénique*, 18
(1894), pp. 499-501 (inscriptions).

23. 7. **wild boars may be hunted in the mountains.**   In the first
half of this century there were still wild boars in the wooded mountains
which surround the bay of *Skroponeri*, a little to the south of Larymna
(H. N. Ulrichs, *Reisen und Forschungen*, I. p. 232).   The boars may
very well be there still.

24. 1. **the Cephisian or —— Copaic Lake.**   Within the last few
years the famous Copaic Lake has been completely drained, and its
place is now taken by a vast level plain, a great part of which is under
cultivation.   The area once covered by the swampy lake may be
described as a rectangle 8 miles broad from north to south by 15 miles
long from north-west to south-east, with bays running out from it among
the mountains by which the great basin is surrounded on all sides.
The total area of the Copaic basin has been estimated at 350 square
kilometres (about 140 square miles), of which, however, the lake at its
fullest occupied only 230 to 250 square kilometres (about 90 square
miles).   Strabo says (ix. p. 407) that the circumference of the lake was
380 Greek furlongs, or about 42 miles.   Like the basins of Pheneus
and Stymphalus in Arcadia, the Copaic basin is hemmed in so closely
by mountains that the water which pours down into it cannot escape
above ground and has been forced in the course of ages to hollow out
for itself subterranean passages through the limestone rock.   These
subterranean passages or *katavothras* exist at the foot of the mountains
on the north-eastern and eastern sides of the plain, which is here
bounded by a long line of precipitous limestone cliffs some 70 to 100
feet high, which, now advancing now retreating, form a series of capes
and bays once washed by the waters of the lake.   At the foot of these
cliffs are a vast number of fissures in the rock varying in size from tiny
rifts to caves of some size.   The largest of these fissures are the *katavothras*, of which twenty five are marked on the maps of the Copaic
lake, while sixteen of them have separate names.   In reality, however,
no hard-and-fast line can be drawn between the *katavothras* and the
smallest clefts, since the interval between the two is bridged by intermediate fissures of all sizes ; and the *katavothras* themselves have arisen

THE COPAIC LAKE DISTRICT

London : Macmillan & Co. Ltd.

Stanford's Geog.l Estab.t London.

SCALE OF KILOMETRES

SCALE OF MILES

only by the gradual widening of small rents. The surface of the plain, so far as it was formerly covered by the lake, is nearly level, but has a very slight general slope from west to east, and a very slight rise in the middle, which caused the water to flow towards the north, east, and south. The height of the plain above the sea averages about 95 metres (311 feet); the surface of the lake, when it was full, was about 97 metres (318 feet) above the sea. While the natural emissories by which the water of the lake escaped are situated on its northern and eastern banks, the streams which fed it flowed into it, without exception, from the west and south. Of these tributary streams the most important are the Lophis on the south, the Phalarus on the south-west, and the Hercyna, Cephisus, and Melas on the west. The last (the Melas) is the only one which, after the lake has been drained, continues to flow across the whole width of the plain in a deep bed of its own. Taking its rise in copious perennial springs in the bay of *Tzamali*, immediately to the north of Orchomenus it flows along the northern margin of the plain, skirting the foot of the hills till it comes opposite to *Stroviki*, which was till lately an island in the lake, about 2 miles south-west of Copae (the modern *Topolia*). Here a branch of the river turns to the left, and flowing through the strait between the island and the mainland vanishes into a small chasm, now half choked up, at the foot of the hill. The main stream, however, flows outside of the island, and crossing in a straight line the wide bay of *Topolia* falls into the *Great Katavothra* at the extreme north-eastern corner of the plain, to which even in the height of summer it brings a considerable body of water. None of the other rivers which poured their waters into the lake had, like the Melas, scooped out for itself in the bed of the lake a deep channel in which it flowed winter and summer. All the rest, even the Cephisus, merely lost themselves in the swamp. Yet the ancients, though they clearly distinguished the Melas at its origin from the Cephisus (see note on ix. 38. 6), appear to have given the name of Cephisus to the lower course of the Melas ; for Strabo says (ix. p. 405) that the stream which flowed into the sea at Larymna was the Cephisus, and the name Cephisian instead of Copaic which was sometimes applied to the lake (Homer, *Il.* ix. 709 ; Pindar, *Pyth.* xii. 46) seems to imply that the river which traversed it from end to end was the Cephisus and not the Melas. The mistake, however, was a natural and excusable one. For of all the streams which entered the lake the Cephisus had by far the longest course, whereas the Melas only rose on the margin of the swamp, and its course was for the greater part of the year concealed under the smooth surface of the mere.

Like other lakes which are drained not by rivers but by natural subterranean passages in the limestone mountains which surround them, the level of the Copaic lake varied greatly from time to time. Such variations depend upon two different sets of causes, first the varying capacity of the emissories, and second the varying amount of water poured into the lake.

In the first place, not only are the emissories subject to a gradual and regular process of change, their passages being slowly clogged and their mouths choked up by the alluvial deposits which in the course of ages raise the bed of the lake ; but they are also exposed to sudden and incalculable changes, wrought by earthquakes, landslips, floating logs and so on, which may in a few minutes either widen the passages or block them up altogether.   In the second place, while these changes, whether gradual or sudden, affect the outflow of the water, others not less marked influence its inflow.   For the rainfall, on which the inflow ultimately depends, varies not only with the year but with the season. In the subtropical climate of the Mediterranean rain hardly falls in summer, and as a consequence the streams in that season either flow with diminished volume or dry up entirely.   All these various causes combine to produce secular and periodic as well as irregular and unforeseen variations in the level of lakes like the Copaic mere.   In no lake, perhaps, have the annual changes been more regular and marked than in the Copaic ; for while in winter it was a reedy mere, the haunt of thousands of wild fowl, in summer it was a more or less marshy plain where cattle browsed and crops were sown and reaped.   So well recognised were these vicissitudes of the seasons that places on the bank of the lake such as Orchomenus, Lebadea, and Copae had summer roads and winter roads by which they communicated with each other, the winter roads following the sides of the hills, while the summer roads struck across the plain.   With the setting in of the heavy autumn rains in November the lake began to rise and reached its greatest depth in February or March, by which time the mouths of the emissories were completely submerged and betrayed their existence only by swirls on the surface of the mere. Yet even then the lake presented to the eye anything but an unbroken sheet of water.   Viewed from a height such as the acropolis of Orchomenus it appeared as an immense fen, of a vivid green colour, stretching away for miles and miles, overgrown with sedge, reeds, and canes, through which the river Cephisus or Melas might be seen sluggishly oozing, while here and there a gleam of sunlit water, especially towards the north-east corner of the mere, directed the eye to what looked like ponds in the vast green swamp.   Bare grey mountains rising on the north and east, and the beautiful wooded slopes of Helicon on the south, bounded the fen.   In spring the water began to sink.   Isolated brown patches, where no reeds grew, were the first to show as islands in the mere ; and as the season advanced they expanded more and more till they met.   By the middle of summer great stretches, especially in the middle and at the edges, were bare.   In the higher parts the fat alluvial soil left by the retiring waters was sown by the peasants and produced crops of corn, rice, and cotton ; while the lower parts, overgrown by rank grass and weeds, were grazed by herds of cattle and swine.   In the deepest places of all the water often stagnated the whole summer, though there were years when it retreated even from these, leaving behind it only a bog or perhaps a stretch of white clayey soil, perfectly dry, which the summer heat seamed with a network of minute cracks and fissures. By the end of August the greater part of the basin was generally dry, though the water did not reach its lowest point till October.   At that time what had lately been a fen was only a great brown expanse, broken here and there by a patch of green marsh, where reeds and other water-plants grew. In November the lake began to fill again fast.

Such was the ordinary annual cycle of changes in the Copaic Lake in modern times, and we have no reason to suppose that it was essentially different in antiquity. But at all times the water of the lake has been liable to be raised above or depressed below its customary level by unusually heavy or scanty rainfall in winter or by the accidental clogging or opening of the chasms. As we read in ancient authors of drowned cities on the margin of the lake (Strabo, ix. p. 407 ; Paus. ix. 24. 2), so a modern traveller tells of villagers forced to flee before the rising flood, and of vineyards and corn-fields seen under water.

Of the places at which the water of the lake, after vanishing into the chasms, comes or used to come to the surface again, three at least can be identified with tolerable certainty. One of them, as we have seen (p. 106), is the ancient Anchoë, the modern *Kephalari*, in the upper valley of Larymna. The spring which, before the lake was drained, used to issue from the rifted rock was the outflow of the water that fell into the chasms called *Bynia* (as to which see above, p. 105). Second, the river Melas, which still flows into the *Great Katavothra* at the north-eastern extremity of the Copaic plain, issues again some 4 miles away at the great springs beside the bay of *Skroponeri*. The way from the *katavothra* to the springs leads eastward over a ridge of the mountains, and then down a narrow glen to the head of the bay. High mountains clothed with low woods and dense shrubbery, where wild boars used to have their lair, rise on all sides from the shores of this deep, still, fjord-like inlet of the sea ; and at their foot, in the inmost corner of the bay, nine copious springs gush from the jagged limestone rocks and pour into the sea, which is so near that its waves wash over the springs and communicate a brackish taste to their water, or rather to all of them except the smallest and most northerly which rises among bushes somewhat farther from the shore. The largest of the springs issues from many rifts in the face of a perpendicular cliff and falls into a basin which used to be enclosed by a wall. The third natural outlet of the Copaic Lake was apparently through a subterranean channel communicating with the lakes *Likeri* and *Paralimni;* for the level of the water in these two lakes was observed to vary with the level of the water in the Copaic Lake. Before the Copaic Lake was drained, Lake *Likeri* stood generally at a height of 45 metres, and Lake *Paralimni* at a height of 35 metres above the level of the sea, or 52 and 62 metres respectively lower than the winter level of the Copaic Lake. Lastly, it has sometimes been held that the branch of the Melas which falls into a chasm at *Stroviki* (see above, p. 111) reappears in the copious salt springs called *Armyro* at Opus. Here, ten minutes to the south of the long south wall of the ancient city, a narrow pass runs between steep rocks and the sea. The springs issue from the rocks in such volume and with such force that they at once turn three mills. In support of the view that these springs are an outflow of the Copaic Lake, it has been observed that at the bottom of an old well in *Pavlo*, a village to the north of *Stroviki*, the water is seen to flow from south to north. The geologist Mr. Philippson, however, thinks that the stratification of the rocks through which, on this supposition, the water would have to pass is against the hypothesis.

The plan of draining the Copaic Lake, which has been successfully accomplished within the last few years, was conceived and apparently executed at a very remote time in antiquity. Strabo reports a tradition (ix. p. 415) that the whole basin of the lake had at one time been drained and cultivated by the people of Orchomenus, and this tradition has been strikingly confirmed by the recent discovery of a complete and very ancient system of drainage works in the bed of the lake. The discovery was made by the engineers charged with the execution of the modern drainage works. As described by them, the ancient works were composed of an ingenious combination of dykes and canals, which completely encircled the lake and, receiving the waters of the streams which flowed into it on the west and south, conducted them to the chasms on the east and north-east banks. Where the canal skirted closely the precipitous rocky shore of the lake a single dyke or embankment sufficed, the water being led between the dyke and the shore. But where the canal had to cross a bay, or where the bank of the lake was not high and steep enough to serve as one side of the canal, two parallel dykes were constructed and the water flowed between them. The remains of these ancient drainage works in the bed of the lake are of two sorts. In the first place we see them as low broad mounds, about 5 feet high and 50 to 60 yards wide, stretching for long distances across the plain, either in an unbroken line or with occasional gaps. Sometimes it is a single mound that we see, sometimes two parallel mounds at a short distance from each other. And between the two parallel mounds or beside the single one a long shallow depression marks the line of the ancient canal. These long low broad mounds are clearly the remains of the dykes which formerly enclosed the canals, and which have been gradually reduced to their present level by the ceaseless wash of the waters in the course of ages. In the second place, the line of the ancient canals may be traced by the walls built of great polygonal blocks which in many places support and case the inner side of the dykes. In some places these walls are well preserved, but in others nothing of them remains but a conspicuous line of white stones running for miles through the otherwise stoneless plain.

There were three of these ancient canals. One skirted the left or north bank of the lake, another skirted the right or south bank, and a third ran out into the middle of it.

(1) The first of these, the northern canal, began on the west bank of the lake, at the modern village of *Karya*, in the shape of a single dyke, which extending north-eastward dammed up the water of the Cephisus and conducted it to join the Melas at a point between *Pyrgo* and *Stroviki*. No attempt seems to have been made to drain the marsh in the bay of *Tsumali*, where the Melas rises. The water of the united rivers was then conducted along the north bank of the lake behind the island of *Stroviki* and the peninsula of Copae (*Topolia*), in a canal formed by the cliffs on one side and a strong dyke on the other. From Copae the canal, now enclosed by an artificial dyke on both sides, struck

north - eastward across the great bay of *Topolia* to the rocky cape at *Pyrgos H. Marina*, where it was joined by the southern canal. From this point the united waters were led eastward in a single canal for about 2 miles and then dispersed among several branches which conveyed them separately to the various chasms. Of these chasms at the north-eastern corner of the lake the most important are those which go by the name of *Spitia* (or *Varia*), *Bynia*, and the *Great Katavothra*. The branch canal which led into the *Spitia* chasm is especially well preserved. It is to be observed that the Melas river, which no doubt originally flowed in the great northern canal from near Orchomenus to the north-eastern corner of the lake, now parts company with the canal at the former island of *Stroviki* and thenceforward flows to the *Great Katavothra* in a deep bed of its own.

(2) The central canal received the waters of the Hercyna river, which were led to it by means of two dykes converging on the mouth of the canal like the sticks of a fan. For a length of $4\frac{1}{2}$ miles this canal, formed by two embankments without masonry, has been traced running out into the middle of the plain. But the embankments gradually diminish in height till they wholly disappear in an impenetrable jungle of reeds near a large barrow or tumulus surmounted by a block of marble. Beyond this point no vestige of the canal has been found. The French engineers who drained the lake think it likely that the canal was continued right across the plain and joined the southern canal on the eastern side of the lake near *Karditsa*. But to this it is objected by Mr. Philippson that it would have been a needless expenditure of labour to construct a canal for the waters of the Hercyna across the whole breadth of the plain, and that too the highest part of the plain, when it would have been easy to turn the water of that stream into the southern canal, thus making one canal do instead of two. He therefore plausibly suggests that the water of the central canal, after being conducted to the middle and highest part of the plain, was thence dispersed in a multitude of tiny rills and channels for the purpose of watering the fields.

(3) The southern canal was intended to collect the waters of the streams which flowed into the lake from the south, the chief of these streams being the Phalarus and Lophis. It begins at the mouth of the Phalarus, beside the village of *Mamoura*, and runs eastward till it is joined by a branch canal from the south. Both these canals, curiously enough, are embanked only on the right side. Soon after their junction the canal disappears in a deep natural depression which extends along the southern side of the plain and comprises the marsh of Haliartus. To the east of *Moulki* the canal begins again close to the bank, where it probably received the waters of the Lophis (river of *Moulki*). Mr. Kambanis, the French engineer, thinks that the canal was originally continuous all along the southern side of the plain, and that the missing central portion of it has been destroyed. Mr. Philippson, on the other hand, conjectures that the western portion of the canal ended in the marsh of Haliartus, where the water may have been either suffered to evaporate or dispersed in rills to irrigate the fields. However that may be, the portion of the canal which begins to the east of *Moulki* skirts the

eastern side of the plain, closely following the contour of the line of cliffs which once formed the shore of the lake, and which here acted as one bank of the canal. Where, however, the canal crossed a bay, as for example the bay of *Karditsa*, it was of course banked up artificially on both sides. In the cliffs on the eastern side of the plain there are many chasms (*katavothras*), and to most of the more important of these chasms a branch-canal led from the main canal, the intention of the ancient engineers clearly being to diminish as far as possible the volume of water which finally reached the great chasms in the north-eastern corner of the plain. The junction of the southern with the northern canal took place, as we have seen, at the rocky headland of *Pyrgos H. Marina*. A little before their junction the river Melas is crossed by a Turkish bridge with five arches, beyond which may be seen the ruins of a large ancient bridge.

When the system of drainage by canals which has just been described was in full operation the basin of the Copaic Lake must have been nearly dry. But as we have no ground to suppose that in the historical period of antiquity the lake was ever drained, it would seem that we must refer these ancient drainage works to the prehistoric ages. Now Strabo, as we have seen, has preserved a tradition that the bed of the lake was at one time drained and cultivated by the people of Orchomenus. We shall therefore hardly err in ascribing to the Minyans of Orchomenus—the Dutchmen of antiquity—the extensive system of dykes and canals by which the vast plain was reclaimed from the waters and converted into waving corn-fields and smiling vineyards, which poured wealth into the coffers of the burghers. This was the golden age of Orchomenus, when its riches vied with the treasures of Delphi and the wealth of Egyptian Thebes (Paus. i. 9. 3 ; viii. 33. 2 ; ix. 38. 8).

The principle adopted by the Minyans in draining the lake was to make use of the natural emissories, to which they led the water in canals. This plan appears to have been carefully thought out and completely executed. But we have evidence that another plan, based on a different principle, was conceived and attempted in antiquity but never carried to completion. This plan was to open artificial emissories for the water at the lowest points in the hills by which the basin of the lake is surrounded. Remains of works undertaken for the purpose of constructing these emissories are to be seen at two places : one is the low ridge at the north-eastern end of the plain over which the path goes to Larymna ; the other is the ridge at the head of the bay of *Karditsa* which divides the Copaic plain from Lake *Likeri*. The former works have been already partially described (p. 105). They consist of sixteen square shafts sunk in the rock to a depth varying from 18 to 63 metres (59 to 207 feet) according to the height of the ridge, the summit of which is only 147 metres (482 feet) above the sea. The distances between the shafts vary considerably, but the average distance between each pair is about 100 yards. Until lately two explanations were commonly given of the existence of these shafts. One was that they were meant to give access at various points to the *katavothras* or natural subterranean emissories of the lake, in order that when these became

choked workmen might descend and clear them.   The other explanation was that the shafts were sunk as a preliminary to the construction
of a tunnel which was to pierce the ridge and convey the waters of the
lake into the Upper Valley of Larymna, from which they would then
flow above ground into the sea.   That the latter explanation is the true
one has been conclusively proved by the investigations of the French
engineers in 1856 and again in 1882, who found short portions of the
tunnel between the shafts actually made.   The tunnel is carefully cut in
the rock and has an arched roof.   Its breadth varies from 1.45 to 1.60
metres, and its height from 1.65 to 1.75 metres.   The length to which
the various portions of the tunnel have been carried varies considerably.
Thus the piece which begins at the sixth shaft and extends in the direction of the seventh shaft is only 3 metres long ; whereas the corresponding section which begins at the seventh shaft and extends in the direction
of the sixth shaft is 32 metres long.   The first section of the tunnel,
from the Copaic Lake to the second shaft, seems to have been completed.   It has, indeed, been cleared only for a length of 36 metres,
the water which burst into the tunnel having prevented further exploration ; but the existence of water at the same level, as well as of shells
and remains of marsh plants, etc., in the first two shafts, seems to prove
that they communicate with each other and with the marsh.   The
mouth of this first section of the tunnel is in what used to be the bottom
of the lake, in front of the *katavothra* of *Bynia*, at a height of 92 metres
above the sea.   The whole tunnel, if completed, would have been 2400
metres (about 1½ miles) long ; and of this total length it is estimated
that about a third is made.   It is remarkable that in some of the shafts
there are remains of two tunnels at different levels, one above the other,
of which the upper tunnel is carried to a less distance in both directions
than the lower.   In the sixteenth shaft the upper tunnel is 3 metres
above the lower ; in the thirteenth shaft, on the other hand, the interval
between the two tunnels is only 2.15 metres, which shows that the
tunnels tend to converge.   Now if straight lines be drawn through the
various sections of the lower tunnel and prolonged, they will be found
to end at the mouth of the tunnel in the Copaic Lake.   From these
facts we conclude that after the tunnel had been begun the engineers
thought its slope insufficient, abandoned it, and began a second tunnel
which they intended to carry at a lower level and with a slightly steeper
slope than the first.   But the work was never finished, and the lower
tunnel consequently remained, like the upper, incomplete.   The slope
of the lower tunnel downwards from the Copaic Lake to the Upper
Valley of Larymna is 1.1 metres in every 100 metres.

   The other place at which remains exist of ancient works begun with
the intention of constructing an artificial emissory for the lake is the
ridge which divides the Copaic plain from Lake *Likeri*.   Here, at the
head of what used to be the Bay of *Karditsa* but is now a branch of the
Copaic plain, there are the beginnings of an ancient canal, 50 feet
broad, hewn in the rock, which if completed would have attained a
depth of 90 metres (295 feet) under the summit of the ridge which it
was designed to pierce.   Further, in a line with this rock-hewn canal,

there may be seen in the plain a row of shafts resembling those beside the path to Larymna except that their mouths are oblong instead of square and that they widen out below like cisterns. The position of some of these shafts is marked only by small hollows and surrounding mounds, at equal intervals; but a few of them are still open. Clearly this ancient canal, begun but never finished, was intended to convey the waters of the Copaic Lake or a part of them into Lake *Likeri* and thence into Lake *Paralimni* and so to the sea. Hence on the ridge which separates Lake *Likeri* from *Paralimni* and again on the ridge which divides Lake *Paralimni* from the sea there are vestiges of ancient works begun with the intention of cutting canals to facilitate the drainage of the lakes.

The attempts to open artificial emissories for the Copaic Lake to which the shafts, tunnels, and canals just described bear testimony are mentioned by no ancient writer; hence their authors and date must be matters of conjecture. Leake assigned them to the Minyans of Orchomenus; but the opinion more commonly held is that they were made by an engineer, Crates of Chalcis, in the age of Alexander the Great. Strabo tells us (ix. p. 407) that, the chasms having become clogged, Crates set about clearing them, but was obliged to desist in consequence of the quarrels of the Boeotians, although, as he informed Alexander in a letter, he had already recovered much land from the water. Further, Stephanus Byzantius mentions incidentally (*s.v.* 'Aθῆναι) that Crates dug trenches or canals through the lake. Thus it appears that in the time of Alexander an effort was made to drain the lake by clearing the chasms and conducting the water to them in canals, but that the attempt had to be abandoned. Nothing is said, however, of an attempt to provide artificial emissories in the shape of tunnels and canals for the escape of the water. Such an attempt, as has been already pointed out, proceeds upon a very different principle from that which guided the operations of the Minyans and, so far as we know, of Crates also. Hence Mr. Philippson inclines to attribute it to one of the Roman emperors, such as Nero or Hadrian, who meditated and partially executed large and costly schemes for the improvement of Greece by the construction of roads, aqueducts, and other public works. In the *Great Katavothra* there are two walls, one on each side, built of small irregular stones without mortar and extending up to the roof of the cave. These are sometimes ascribed to Crates, but they seemed to me modern, and this too is the opinion of Mr. Kambanis, who states that in none of the chasms are any certain traces to be discerned of the works executed by Crates.

In Roman times it would seem that, the ancient canals of the Minyans having long ceased to drain the water of the lake, their embankments served merely as dams to keep it from flooding the level ground in the neighbourhood. For we learn from an inscription, already mentioned (*C. I. G. G. S.* 1. No. 2712), that in the first century A.D. a wealthy citizen of Acraephnium, Epaminondas son of Epaminondas, repaired at a cost of 6000 *denarii* and for a length of 12 Greek furlongs (1⅓ miles) a great dam which protected the territory of Acraephnium but which had fallen into disrepair. The great dam referred to can hardly have been anything but the right bank of the Minyan canal (the canal of the right or southern bank) which crossed the mouth of the bay of Acraephnium (*Karditsa*) ; for so long as this embankment existed to its full height it probably protected the bay from the inroad of the water and converted it into a plain, which the people of Acraephnium doubtless turned to account as arable or pasture land. In modern times the embankments of the old Minyan canals have served as causeways through the swamp ; and for this purpose they seem to have been repaired by the Franks in the Middle Ages.

The work of draining the lake was begun by a French company in 1883 and taken over by an English company in 1889. By 1894 the work was practically finished. In 1890 I had seen the great green swamp from the slopes of Helicon, but when I visited the district again in November 1895 the place of the swamp was taken by a vast plain across which we rode freely. Some of it lay waste, and flocks of sheep browsed on the grass. But much of it was occupied by fields of cotton and maize, and a good deal of it had been recently ploughed. The plan of the modern drainage works is briefly this. Two canals, an inner and an outer, are carried along the western, southern, and south-eastern sides of the plain. The outer canal, which for a great part of its length lies outside the limits of the old lake, begins on the right bank of the Cephisus some 2 or 3 miles to the west of *Skripou* (Orchomenus), and receives the waters of all the considerable streams which formerly flowed into the lake except the Melas. The inner canal, which runs roughly parallel to the outer, is designed to collect the rain-water which falls in the basin once occupied by the lake. These canals convey the water to the bay or plain of *Karditsa* (Acraephnium), whence it is conducted by canals and tunnels first into Lake *Likeri*, then into Lake *Paralimni*, and thence into the sea about 2 miles or so to the west of Anthedon. Originally it was intended to construct a northern canal in the Copaic basin which should have received the water of the Melas and conducted it to meet the waters of the other two canals in the plain of *Karditsa*. This project, however, was wisely given up and the Melas allowed to flow, as before, in its natural bed to the *Great Katavothra* at the north-eastern corner of the Copaic plain. Only in its mid course through the plain the river was banked up ; in its lower course the bed is so deep that no embankment was needed.

The ancients believed that the waters of the lake rose higher than usual every eighth year ; and sometimes if the rains were very heavy the lake continued at this higher level for two years or more ; it stood high for several years before the battle of Chaeronea (Theophrastus, *Hist. plant.* iv. 11. 2 *sq.* ; Pliny, *Nat. hist.* xvi. 169). The Boeotian winters were thought to be less severe than usual when the lake was high (Theophrastus, *Caus. plant.* v. 12. 3). Reeds grew thickest in the marsh between the Cephisus and the Melas—a place which went by the name of Pelecania (Theophrastus, *Hist. plant.* iv. 11. 8) ; but the finest were those which grew at a place called Oxeia Kampe ('sharp turn') at the mouth of the Cephisus (Theophrastus, *l.c.*) There were

said to be floating islands in the lake (Theophrastus, *Hist. plant.* iv.
10. 2 ; Pliny, *Nat. hist.* xvi. 168).   The fable was probably told of the
islands in the bay of *Tzamali*, to the north of Orchomenus, whose banks
overhung and quaked under the tread, as do the banks of the river
Melas in some places.

See Wheler, *Journey*, p. 465 *sqq.* ; Walpole's *Memoirs relating to Turkey*[2]
(London, 1818), pp. 303-307 ; Dodwell, *Tour*, I. pp. 233-242 ; Leake, *Northern
Greece*, 2. pp. 158, 280 *sqq.*, 308-317 ; P. W. Forchhammer, *Hellenika* (Berlin,
1837), pp. 159-186 ; K. O. Müller, *Orchomenos und die Minyer*,[2] p. 45 *sqq.* ;
Mure, *Journal*, I. p. 226 *sq.* ; Fiedler, *Reise*, I. pp. 100-131 *y* H. N. Ulrichs,
Reisen und Forschungen, I. pp. 191-246 ; L. Ross, *Wanderungen*, I. pp. 25, 99-
103 ; Vischer, *Erinnerungen*, pp. 569-576 ; Bursian, *Geogr.* I. pp. 195-199 ;
Baedeker,[3] pp. 191 *sq.*, 193 *sq.* ; *Guide-Joanne*, 2. pp. 18, 20 ; Neumann und
Partsch, *Physikalische Geographie von Griechenland*, pp. 244-247 ; M. L. Kam-
banis, 'Le dessèchement du lac Copaïs par les anciens,' *Bulletin de Corresp.
hellénique*, 16 (1892), pp. 121-137 ; *id., ib.* 17 (1893), pp. 322-342 ; E. Curtius,
'Die Deichbauten der Minyer,' *Gesammelte Abhandlungen*, 2. pp. 266-280 ; A.
Philippson, 'Der Kopais-See in Griechenland und seine Umgebung,' *Zeitschrift
der Gesellschaft für Erdkunde zu Berlin*, 29 (1894), pp. 1-90.

Pausanias makes no mention of a very ancient and very remarkable
fortress of which the well-preserved remains are to be seen to this day
on a low rocky tableland of some extent which rises abruptly on all sides
from the dead flat of the Copaic plain.   The tableland, till lately an
island in the lake, is known variously as *Gha, Goulas*, and *Gla*.   It is
distant some 2 miles or so to the south-east of Copae *(Topolia)* and
something under a mile from the nearest point of the line of cliffs which
once formed the shore of the lake.   Seen from any point of the plain,
the low flat hill or plateau, with the long grey line of fortification-wall
stretching along its brow, is a conspicuous object.   Its shape roughly
resembles that of a pear with the point turned to the east ; its circumference is about 3 kilometres or 2 miles.   On all sides the edges of the
plateau fall away steeply, especially on the north, where it reaches its
highest point.   Here the plateau may be about 200 feet high, and here
it descends from its highest point at one drop to the plain.   Above
these imposing precipices and close to their edge is built the great
prehistoric palace of which the remains were excavated by a French
archaeologist, Mr. A. de Ridder, in June 1893.   From here the plateau
sinks gradually to half the height on the west and south.   On the east
it descends still lower, till at the north gate, to the east of the palace,
it is only about 40 feet above the plain.   A natural ramp leads up to
the most easterly point of the tableland.   All round the outer edge of
the plateau runs an immensely thick fortification-wall, which, though
ruinous, is nowhere interrupted and is still standing for long stretches
to a height of three and four courses (4 to 8 feet) on the outside.   In
places it is 10 feet high or more.   Its average thickness is 17 to 19
feet.   Viewed from the inside the wall generally presents the appearance only of a great heap of fallen stones following for hundreds of
yards the edge of the plateau.   It is built of solid masonry throughout,
and does not, like so many of the later fortification-walls of Greece,
consist merely of an outer and an inner face of masonry with a core of
rubble between.   But the style of masonry is rude.   The blocks are of

very varying sizes and are very roughly fitted together, the chinks being filled with small stones, not with mortar. Still the blocks are roughly squared, their outer surfaces are to some extent smoothed, and on the whole they are laid in horizontal courses, though the exceptions are so numerous that by some they might be thought to constitute the rule. Many of the stones are very large, some of them measuring 6 feet long by 3 feet deep and 3 feet thick. One stone which I measured at the southern gate was 7 ft. 8 in. long. The style of masonry of the walls is so thoroughly homogeneous that we cannot doubt that they were all built at the same period, probably within the space of a few

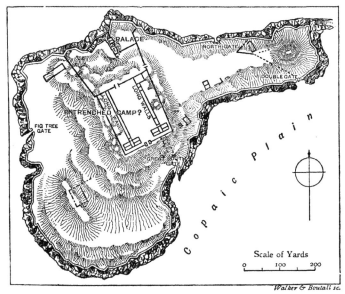

FIG. 6.—PLAN OF RUINS OF GLA (GHA, GOULAS) IN THE COPAIC PLAIN.

years. A remarkable feature of their construction is that they are built, not in a curved line, but in a series of retreating angles, these angles occurring at intervals which vary from about 20 to 40 feet, but which in general measure about 30 feet. The effect of this is to give to the outline of the walls, on the inner as well as on the outer side, an appearance resembling the edge of a saw or the steps of a staircase. The depth of these backsets of the wall varies from about 4 inches to about 2 feet; commonly they measure 10, 12, or 16 inches. And it is to be observed that the walls are built in this peculiar style not merely where the edge of the plateau is curved, but even where it is straight. This method of construction appears to have been characteristic of the Mycenaean age, for it occurs in the fortification-walls of the citadel of Troy (W. Dörpfeld, *Troja 1893*, p. 41 *sq.* ; *id.*, in *Mittheil. d. arch.*

Inst. in Athen, 19 (1894), p. 383 *sq.*), in portions of the walls of Tiryns and Mycenae, and in the walls of the Mycenaean fortress recently excavated by English archaeologists in Melos, as well as in the walls of Samia (Samicum) in Elis, which probably belong to a somewhat later period. The original intention of building walls in this manner was perhaps to compel an assailant to expose his flank to the defenders of the wall ; but since the backsets are often far too short to answer this purpose, and since moreover they occur on the inner as well as on the outer sides of fortification-walls, and even in the walls of ordinary buildings at Troy, it is clear that, whatever may have been its purpose originally, this mode of construction had become thoroughly conventional and had ceased to serve any practical end.

There are no towers on the walls except at the gates. Of these gates there are four, one on the north, one on the west, one on the south, and one on the south-east. The northern and the southern seem to have been the principal gates.

The northern gate, situated about 300 yards to the east of the palace at a point where the slope to the plain is low and gentle, is a simple opening in the wall, 18 feet wide, flanked on each side by two towers of solid masonry. These towers are about 19 feet broad on the face and about 23 feet deep from front to back ; they project only about 2 feet from the curtain. The tower on the east side is the better preserved ; seven courses are standing to a height of about 11 feet. The masonry of the towers is more massive and regular than that of the walls ; the blocks are larger, more carefully squared, smoothed on their outer surfaces, and laid in horizontal courses. Inside of the gateway there was a court about 20 feet deep by 28 feet broad, enclosed by slighter walls. On the inner side of the court, facing the outer gateway, was a second gateway about 13 feet wide.

The southern gate is flanked by towers which project obliquely (not, like those of the north gate, perpendicularly) from the line of wall. The opening of the gateway is 17 feet wide. The tower which flanks it on the west projects about 16 feet from the line of wall, while the tower on the east projects about 13 feet farther beyond the face of the western tower, thus forming a sort of bastion, which must have commanded the right or unshielded side of an enemy attacking the gate. The western tower is 18 feet broad on the face, and is standing to a height of six courses or 12 feet. The eastern tower is more ruinous. Both are built of rough but massive and solid masonry ; the blocks are rudely squared and smoothed on the outside, and the chinks are filled with small stones. The depth of the eastern tower from front to back is about 62 feet, and the depth of the western tower about 49 feet. These figures thus represent the respective lengths of the two sides of the passage which all who entered by this gate had to traverse. The southern gateway was naturally as well as artificially much stronger than the northern gateway. For whereas the latter is only about 40 feet above the plain, at the head of a gentle slope, the southern gateway stands on rocks at a height of about 130 feet above the plain, and can be reached from below only by a steep and narrow path.

The western gateway is much smaller than either of the preceding, its opening being only about 7 feet wide. On the north it is flanked by a tower which projects 5 ft. 5 in. from the curtain. The gateway seems to have led into a court about 17 feet square. The south-eastern gateway is double; that is, it consists of two openings, each about 16 feet wide, side by side in the wall. The flanking towers, about 23 feet deep, no longer rise above the line of the wall. From the length to which the lines of fallen stones run inward from the gate it may perhaps be inferred that this gate also, like the northern and western gates, opened into a court.

Such are in brief the remains of the prehistoric fortress of *Gha, Goulas*, or *Gla*. Although it is built on the whole of much less massive stones than Tiryns, and has not the grand situation of Mycenae, it far surpasses both of them together in size; and if we consider the immense length (about 2 miles) of the walls, their massiveness, and the excellence of their preservation, we shall be inclined to pronounce it the most imposing of all existing ancient fortresses in Greece.

Within the circuit of this great fortress the ruins of an ancient palace were laid bare by the excavations of Mr. A. de Ridder in 1893. As has already been indicated, the palace occupies the most northerly and highest ground of the whole tableland. Its north wall rests directly throughout its whole length on the fortification-wall, which here runs along the brow of high precipices. The inner walls, built of irregularly-shaped stones of various sizes, with small stones and mortar in the interstices, are everywhere standing to a height varying from 18 inches to 2 and 3 feet, so that the plan of the palace is completely revealed. It consisted of two long wings, one on the north and one on the east, which met each other at right angles. The northern wing ends on the west in a large tower of a roughly quadrangular shape; the eastern wing ended on the south in a much smaller quadrangular tower. Inclusive of these two towers, the north wing is 80.20 metres (about 263 feet) long with an average breadth of about 14.55 metres (about 48 feet); and the east wing is 72.65 metres (about 239 feet) with an average breadth of 12.25 metres (about 40 feet). Each wing comprises a series of chambers on its outer side, while its inner side is occupied for the greater part by two broad passages or corridors running beside and parallel to each other. But towards the western end of the north wing and the southern end of the east wing there is only one such corridor. Where two corridors exist, the chambers of course open off the inner corridor. Some of the chambers communicate with each other, forming suites. They are of very various sizes. The largest of all, towards the west end of the north wing, is about 11.75 metres long (39 feet) by 7 metres (23 feet) wide. Next to it in size is a room near the southern end of the east wing, which is 9.40 metres (30 ft. 10 in.) long by 6.55 metres (21 ft. 5 in.) wide.[1] Both these chambers or halls open through anterooms. The partition-walls, which, as has been

---

[1] These are Mr. de Ridder's measurements. My measurements were—largest chamber, length 36 feet, breadth 21 feet; second chamber, length 33 feet, breadth about 21 feet.

already mentioned, are built of irregularly-shaped stones of various sizes
with small stones and mortar in the crevices, average 3 ft. 3 in.
thick; but some of them are 4 ft. 5 in. thick.   They seem to have
been covered with a thick coating of stucco, which is preserved in many
places, especially in the eastern wing.   In one room and a vestibule
there are some remains of frescoes painted on the stucco.   Chambers
and corridors were alike paved with concrete, of which also there are
considerable remains, especially in the east wing.   The concrete is com-

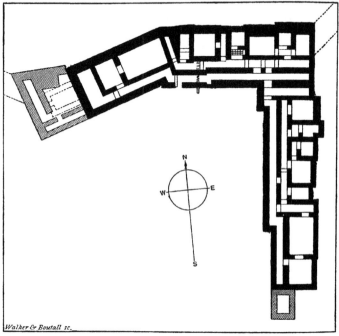

FIG. 7.—PLAN OF PALACE OF GLA (GHA, GOULAS) IN THE COPAIC PLAIN.

posed of lime-mortar mixed here and there with pebbles; it rests on a
bed of small stones.   Only in one room are there faint traces of a
painted decoration on the pavement; and only in one room, or rather
vestibule, in the north wing is there a stone pavement, which in this
case consists of eighteen large slabs of bluish limestone.   Many of the
thresholds of the chambers are preserved; they are formed of immense
slabs of stone carefully smoothed.   One of these slabs which I measured
was about 10 feet long by 6 feet wide; another was 9 feet long; another
8 ft. 6 in.   The threshold of the large hall in the north wing consists
of three great slabs, each about 7 feet long and 4 ft. 3 in. wide.
The long corridors which run along the whole length of both wings vary

in width from about 6 feet to about 6 ft. 7 in. What the object of the outer corridor may have been is not clear. The entrance to the palace is through this outer corridor, about the middle of the north wing.

With regard to the outer walls of the palace, the north wall rests, as has been said, on the circuit-wall of the fortress, from which it is indistinguishable. At the north-eastern corner of the palace the fortification-wall is preserved to a height of seven courses or about 12 feet; it forms a sort of bastion about 34 feet broad on the north face and projecting about 3 feet from the line of wall. The outer wall of the east wing of the palace, though it lies within the circuit-wall of the fortress, is itself a fortification-wall built of enormous blocks; one block is 2 ft. 6 in. high, 4 ft. 2 in. broad (deep), and over 7 feet long. The ground here falls away, so that this outer wall is much higher than the inner walls of the palace. At the south-east corner of the palace the outer wall is standing to a height of over 6 feet. The external walls of the palace on the inner side, that is the south wall of the north wing and the west wall of the east wing, are built in a style intermediate between that of the outer fortification-walls and the inner partition-walls. They are constructed of smaller blocks than the outer fortification-walls, bonded with mortar, and are from 5 to 7 feet thick.

Amongst the objects discovered by Mr. de Ridder in the palace are four bronze hinges. They were found near the stone thresholds of some of the doorways in the east wing. These are the only objects of bronze which have as yet come to light at *Gla*. Further, there were found in the palace a number of plates of lead, which would seem to have been used to fasten wooden doorposts to the walls; also fragments of stucco ornaments in the shape of small engaged columns, fluted, about 3 inches in diameter, which were attached to the walls of the rooms, three at least of them having been found so attached. The fragments of pottery discovered are few and insignificant. The vessels of which they formed part are of two sorts, cups and bowls. Though the forms are rude, they have all, with one exception, been made on the wheel. The quality of the ware is poor; the clay is not homogeneous and is mixed with splinters of stone. Only four fragments have been found coated with a glaze (*couverte*) on the outside; the colour of the glaze in one case is black, in the others yellow of various shades from orange to tawny. The inner side of one piece is coated with a dark brown glaze. Only two painted sherds, belonging to different vessels, have been found; the decoration consists of broad transverse bands of reddish brown or violet on a ground of creamy yellow.

But the palace is not the only ancient building of which there are ruins. Remains of walls may be traced which seem to have formed part of a great fortified enclosure or inner fortress stretching nearly across the middle of the plateau from north to south. Beginning at the northern edge of the plateau and including within it the palace, this inner fortress (if it was such) extended southward for a length of about 300 yards, with a breadth of about 140 yards. From the wall which closed this fortress on the south, two walls, each 83 yards long, ran southward to the great southern gateway, enclosing between them a passage about 21 feet wide. The effect of this was that the plateau was roughly divided in two by a fortified enclosure running right across it from north to south, so that no one could pass from its eastern to its western half without traversing this enclosure. We may suppose that within the enclosure lay the dwellings of the servants and retainers of the princely family who inhabited the palace. At all events there are remains of edifices within it. Of these the principal are two quadrangular buildings lying east and west of each other, close to the southern wall of the enclosure. Each of them is about 150 feet long by 60 feet broad, and is divided by an inner wall into two long rectangles. From each of these quadrangular buildings a pair of long walls extends northward for a distance of about 140 yards; the interval between the walls of each pair is about 26 feet, and the distance of the two pairs from each other is about 260 feet. Mr. de Ridder thinks that these four long walls, thus arranged in pairs, were ramparts. They ended on the north in a great cross-wall which traversed the enclosure from east to west, parallel to the south wall. Abutting on this cross-wall, between it and the northern end of the eastern pair of long walls, are the remains of a third quadrangular building divided by a partition-wall into two equal rectangles. A gateway, flanked with two pillars, gave access through the cross-wall to the northern part of the fortified enclosure.

All the walls which have just been described (except of course the partition-walls) are built in the same style as the outer walls of the palace, but in general of smaller and more irregular stones bonded simply with clay mortar and without any trace of a coating of stucco. Only in a few places, for example in parts of the walls of the rectangular buildings, are to be seen large blocks carefully fitted together in the style of the eastern outer wall of the palace. Within the fortified enclosure Mr. de Ridder found what he conjectures to have been a primitive cistern, constructed of great rough blocks arranged in a circle, of which the diameter is about 7 feet. But as he admits that even if thickly coated with clay (of which there is no trace) this rude structure could not have held water, we may doubt whether it was a cistern after all. Further, he discovered within the enclosure sherds of coarse pottery and some plates of lead and fragments of stucco ornaments like those found in the palace. The potsherds, though more numerous than those discovered in the palace, are still far from abundant. With very few exceptions they are unglazed; the colour varies, according to the clay, from whitish and greenish yellow to deep gamboge yellow and brick red. The glaze (*couverte*), where it exists, is of a rather deep yellow, sometimes almost brown. A single fragment is painted; it is the foot of a cup striped with bands of warm brown. Few as these objects are, their resemblance to those found in the palace goes, together with the similar structure of the walls, to prove that the fortified enclosure which has just been described is contemporary with the palace. But the fewness of the objects seems to indicate that the population of the place was small and that it was not resident for long.

Further, the extreme eastern corner of the plateau would seem to have been cut off from the rest of the plateau by a cross-wall so as to form a fortress by itself. The cross-wall, which is very ruinous, ends at the south-east gateway. Within the space which it encloses, to the east, are some traces of a long quadrangular edifice ending on the north in a semicircular apse. Lastly may be mentioned two ruins in the western part of the plateau, to the west of the great fortified enclosure. One of them, near the northern edge of the plateau, is a long narrow building, of which the western end is still standing to a height of two courses. The other, near the south-western corner of the plateau, seems to have been a large quadrangular enclosure.

When and by whom was this great fortress with its stately palace built? To these questions neither history nor legend supplies any answer. That the fortress belongs to the prehistoric ages is certain. Its massive walls differ wholly in the style of their masonry from the fortifications both of classical antiquity and of the Middle Ages, and on the other hand they resemble the prehistoric walls of Tiryns and Mycenae. In like manner the palace resembles in its technical construction, though not in its disposition, the palaces of Tiryns and Mycenae. In all three we see the same partition-walls meanly built of irregularly-shaped stones of various sizes bonded with mortar and coated on the outside with stucco ; the same floors of concrete ; the same stone thresholds. Burnt bricks seem to have been as little used at *Gla* as at Mycenae and Tiryns ; at least I observed none in the palace or on the plateau, and none are mentioned by Mr. de Ridder, who excavated the palace. Hence we may confidently assign the ruins of *Gla* to the Mycenaean period. Yet there are differences between them and the ruins of Tiryns and Mycenae which deserve to be noted. In the first place the gateways of the fortress are mere openings in the line of wall ; they are not, like the gateways of Tiryns and Mycenae, artfully placed in a recess of the walls so as to oblige all who approached the gates to traverse a narrow passage where, if they came with hostile intentions, they could easily be knocked over by the garrison. The idea of such an arrangement appears, indeed, but only in germ, in the great south gate of *Gla*, where one of the flanking towers projects considerably beyond the other. Hence military engineering would seem to have been at a less advanced stage in *Gla* than in Tiryns and Mycenae. Again, the palace at *Gla*, while it resembles the Tirynthian and Mycenaean palaces in its method of construction, differs widely not only from them but from all other known palaces of that period in its general plan, which is that of two long wings meeting at right angles. Moreover, the style of the scanty remains of pottery hitherto found at *Gla* is not distinctive enough to allow us to say positively that it is Mycenaean, though on the other hand there is nothing in it to contradict that view. On the whole, we may provisionally conclude that the fortress and palace of *Gla* were built in the Mycenaean period by a people akin in civilisation, if not in race, to the peoples of Tiryns and Mycenae. Such a people were the Minyans of the neighbouring Orchomenus, who appear, as we saw, to have constructed the great prehistoric works by which the Copaic Lake was drained. Probably, then, the fortress of *Gla* was a creation of the Minyans or of a branch of that people. It seems to have been erected at a blow and to have perished at a blow; for everything in it bears the imprint of a single period and of a single plan, there is not a trace on the plateau of an earlier or of a later settlement. The scantiness of the remains of pottery, and the seemingly total absence of all other objects of daily life, indicate that it was inhabited only for a short period; and the traces of fire in the palace point to the conclusion that its end was sudden and violent. From that day to this the island, now a plateau stranded in the great plain, seems never to have been inhabited again.

Not only the history but the very name of the ancient settlement on *Gla* is unknown. Various attempts have been made to identify it with ancient cities whose names have come down to us, but without success Forchhammer thought that it might be the Boeotian Midea (Homer, *Il.* ii. 507); Dodwell, H. N. Ulrichs, and Bursian suggested that it might be the original city of Copae, from which the inhabitants after-wards removed to the peninsula on the opposite side of the lake; Leake conjectured that it may have been a town or fortress named Athaman-tium. Recently Mr. F. Noack has argued that the place is the Boeotian Arne mentioned by Homer (*Il.* ii. 507) and Lycophron (*Cassandra*, 644). In historical times some people thought that the Homeric Arne was Acraephnium (Strabo, ix. p. 413) or Chaeronea (Paus. ix. 40. 5; Stephanus Byzantius, *s.v.* Χαιρώνεια); others said that it had been swallowed up by the lake (Strabo, *l.c.*) If this last tradition is correct, the ruins on *Gla* cannot be those of Arne, since they stand too high to have ever been flooded by the lake even when it was fullest.

Though Mr. Noack can hardly be held to have proved his case, he has done good service in calling attention to a number of smaller ancient fortresses which lie like outworks of *Gla* on the edge of the Copaic Lake or among the mountains which bound it on the east. A brief mention of some of them may not be out of place.

(1) We have seen that in the cliffs which bound the Copaic plain, a little to the west of the path that leads from it to Larymna, there is a chasm or *katavothra* called *Spitia* or *Varia* to which an ancient canal, still in preservation, used to conduct some of the water of the lake. Immediately to the west of this chasm two rocky hillocks, once pro-montories in the lake, jut out into the plain. The western hillock is the larger and higher; the eastern bears a ruined chapel of St. John. Both of them are surmounted by the remains of an ancient fortress, though the grey old walls, of which in general only a single course is preserved, are at first not easily distinguished from the grey rocks. The ruins on the eastern hillock are the more considerable; they are those of a fortress larger than Tiryns and apparently belonging to the same period, for the walls are built in the Mycenaean style and many remains of Mycenaean pottery are strown about, especially on the eastern side of the hillock. The walls, however, are much less massive than those of most fortresses of the Mycenaean age. At the point on the west side where they are best preserved they are 2.50 metres (8 ft. 6 in.) thick. Within the fortification-walls are some foundations of

buildings, the purpose of which is difficult to determine. The summit of the western hillock is surrounded by a short circuit-wall, from which another wall runs down the slope northward. The walls are of the same thickness as those on the eastern hillock and apparently belong to the same period. Within the circuit-walls are the tumbled and scattered ruins of a large building. No potsherds have been found on this hillock. The two sister fortresses just described may well have been built by the Minyans of Orchomenus or of *Gla* to command and protect the outflow of the lake at the neighbouring chasm.

(2) On the rocky hill called *Pyrgos H. Marina*, some 500 feet high, which projects like a promontory into the Copaic plain about 2 miles to the north-east of *Gla*, close to the meeting-place of the two ancient canals which drained the lake (see above, p. 116), are the remains of another fortress of the Mycenaean age. The walls are very ruinous, but on the south-east side portions are still standing to a height of about 7 feet. They appear to have consisted of two parts—an inner perpendicular wall built of moderately large and almost unhewn stones piled upon each other, and an outer sloping or battering wall built of smaller unwrought stones heaped up in front of the perpendicular wall. The use of sloping or battering walls in fortification seems to have been characteristic of the early Mycenaean period, since it occurs in those walls of the citadel of Troy which are assigned to the Mycenaean age (W. Dörpfeld, *Troja 1893*, p. 42 *sq.*) But it was by no means universally employed even then, since no such walls have been found at Tiryns, Mycenae, or *Gla*. In the historical age of Greece fortification-walls seem hardly ever to have been built in this manner, though part of the wall of the Acropolis at Athens, which is attributed to Cimon, batters slightly (see vol. 2. p. 355). Amongst the ruined walls at *Pyrgos H. Marina* lie many fragments of Mycenaean pottery, including pieces with brown or reddish stripes on a yellow lustrous glaze of fine quality. One fragment has circular lines painted in a dull pigment on a smooth polished ground of a yellowish-grey colour ; another shows red wave-lines and dots on a reddish ground.

(3) On the highest point of Mount Ptous, above the monastery of *H. Pelagia*, from which it can be reached in twenty minutes, are the scanty ruins of a semicircular fortification-wall built in a rough style. The two ends of the wall abut on the precipices which fall away towards the monastery. The opening of a gate which faced southward can be traced. Opposite this fort, on the rocky north-eastern summit of Mount *Tsikourieli*, stands the lowest part of a round tower, about 23 feet in diameter, built in the oldest style of polygonal masonry. These two forts were doubtless watch-towers belonging to one or other of the ancient cities which lay down in the valleys or on the edge of the great lake. From their lofty situation, commanding together views over the whole of northern and western Boeotia, together with the lakes of *Likeri* and *Paralimni*, they were well adapted to survey the country far and wide and to signal the approach of danger to watchers in the lowlands.

(4) At the east end of the long ridge of Mount *Megalo Vouno*, which extends westward from the vale of Apollo (*Perdiko-Vrysi*) to the Copaic

plain, are the remains of a small fort erected on the edge of the cliffs which here descend on the north.　The wall, built in a rough polygonal style and now almost completely destroyed, ran inward from and parallel to the edge of the cliffs, enclosing a space about 100 yards long by 20 yards wide.　Within the space thus enclosed, at its south-eastern end, are the ruins of a small round tower fairly built of polygonal masonry.　The place may be reached in about an hour from *Karditsa*.

(5) At the east end of Lake *Paralimni* rises a flat-topped hill crowned with a conspicuous mediaeval tower, which is partly built of ancient materials.　Round the edge of the hill are the remains of an ancient circuit-wall.　On the east side pieces of the wall, built of very regular polygonal masonry, are standing to a height of about 6 feet; and between them are traces of a still older wall which battered.

(6) At the western end of Lake *Paralimni* are the ruins of a small ancient fort standing at the east end of a line of hills which here advance from the south to the edge of the lake.　Nearly opposite it, on the northern bank of the lake, are the extensive ruins of a very ancient city, consisting of the remains of walls and the foundations of houses. Though partly obscured by the walls of modern sheep-folds which have been built on them, these ruins seem to belong to the Mycenaean age. The walls are built of great blocks, very little hewn, which are piled loosely on each other with small stones crammed into the interstices. The houses are mostly small and rectangular, with a narrow door in one of the long sides.　On a steep rocky spur of the mountain just above the ruins may be seen the remains of a very ancient fort, the dilapidated walls of which appear to have been originally about 23 feet thick.

See Dodwell, *Tour*, 2. p. 56; Leake, *Northern Greece*, 2. pp. 295, 306 *sq.*; P. W. Forchhammer, *Hellenika*, pp. 179-181; H. N. Ulrichs, *Reisen und Forschungen*, I. pp. 216-218; L. Ross, *Wanderungen*, I. p. 105; Vischer, *Erinnerungen*, pp. 581-583; Bursian, *Geogr.* I. p. 212; Baedeker,[3] p. 192 *sq.*; *Guide-Joanne*, 2. p. 20; F. Noack, 'Arne,' *Mittheilungen d. arch. Inst. in Athen*, 19 (1894), pp. 405-485; A. de Ridder, 'Fouilles de Gha,' *Bulletin de Corresp. hellénique*, 18 (1894), pp. 271-310; *id.*, 'Arne,' *ib.* pp. 446-452.　I visited the ruins of *Gla*, 7th November 1895, and have described them partly from personal observation.

24. 1. the Athamantian plain.　Pausanias tells us that the Athamantian plain lay on the straight road from Acraephnium to the Copaic Lake.　It is therefore probably the branch of the Copaic plain which lies immediately to the south of the hill of Acraephnium between it and the foot of the northern spurs of Mount *Phaga* (the Sphinx Mountain).　For in the first place the nearest road from Acraephnium to the Copaic Lake must, at least when the lake was full, have lain across this plain; and in the second place we know from an inscription which has already been referred to (*C. I. G. G. S.* 1. No. 2712) that in the later times of antiquity, about a century before Pausanias's day, this plain was indeed a plain, being protected from the encroachments of the lake by one of the great dykes of the Minyans which a patriotic citizen of Acraephnium had put in repair.　Leake, however, identified the Athamantian plain with that portion of the Copaic basin which lies to the north-west of Acraephnium and in which is situated the rocky plateau (lately an island) of *Gla*. This view has been accepted and defended by recent writers, including Messrs. Kambanis, de Ridder, and Noack, but it is open to two serious objections. First, this part of the Copaic basin is distant from Acraephnium half an hour's ride through a hilly country, whereas the part of it which we have seen reasons for identifying with the Athamantian plain lies immediately at the foot of the hill of Acraephnium. Second, the section of the Copaic basin about *Gla* was probably in antiquity, as it was till recently, not a plain at all but a part of the lake or marsh, at least for a great part of the year. Forchhammer says that *Gla* was surrounded by water even in the driest seasons ; and Dodwell, Leake himself, Ross, and Vischer all found it an island. Ulrichs says that it was an island in winter and in high floods. For these reasons it seems better to adhere to the opinion of Ulrichs and Bursian that the Athamantian plain was that branch of the Copaic basin which lies immediately to the south of Acraephnium.

See Leake, *Northern Greece*, 2. pp. 295, 306 *sq.* ; H. N. Ulrichs, *Reisen und Forschungen*, I. p. 244 *sq.* ; Bursian, *Geogr.* I. p. 213 ; Kambanis, in *Bulletin de Corresp. hellénique*, 16 (1892), p. 129 *sq.*, note ; de Ridder, *ib.* 18 (1894), p. 271 note ; F. Noack, in *Mittheil. d. arch. Inst. in Athen*, 19 (1894), p. 470 *sqq.*

24. 1. Copae. The site of Copae, now occupied by the village of *Topolia* or *Topolias*, is a low hill, which rises in perfect isolation, like an island, from the Copaic plain at a short distance from the line of cliffs that till lately formed the bank of the lake. Modern travellers, who visited the place before the lake was drained, describe it as a peninsula joined to the mainland only by a narrow isthmus. However, when I was at *Topolia* in 1895 I was told that till about five years before the little hill had been an island accessible only by boat. The hill may be a third of a mile long from east to west and 150 feet or so high above the plain. On the east, north-east, and north-west it is defended by lines of high rocks, which on the north-east attain the height of considerable cliffs. Elsewhere the slope of the hill, though abrupt, is not steep enough to be difficult. At its northern foot there stretches a strip of level ground some 50 to 100 yards wide which stands a few feet above the level of the plain and was protected on its northern edge, towards the lake, by a wall. The line of this wall can still be traced for some distance by a long row of blocks at the level of the ground as well as by many isolated stones ; in one place, immediately to the east of the causeway which used to connect the island with the shore, the wall, built of rough and rather small stones, is preserved to a height of two courses for a length of six paces. This stretch of level ground, now deserted (for the village of *Topolia* stands on the hill), was probably occupied by the lower city of Copae. It is joined to what used to be the shore by a causeway, some 100 yards or so long, roughly paved with large cobbles in the Turkish fashion and raised a few feet only above the level of the surrounding plain. Some large blocks, which may be ancient, support the causeway, and a few more such blocks lie about it. On the northern slope of the hill, a few yards to the west of the point where the line of cliffs begins, I found a piece of rough polygonal wall some 30 paces long and 7 feet high at most. The stones are rather small and but little hewn ; the masonry is bad ; one block is about 4 feet long.   Farther to the west, not many feet above the plain, some more blocks of the ancient wall are standing.   A good many ancient inscriptions are built into the walls of the numerous chapels of *Topolia ;* and on what was formerly the mainland, across the isthmus, ancient tombstones have been found, making it probable that the necropolis of Copae was here.   Strabo tells us (ix. p. 406) that Copae was once in danger of being swallowed up by the rising waters of the lake, when a chasm suddenly opened near the town into which the water ran away.   The chasm or *katavothra* may be seen at the foot of the line of cliffs to the west of the causeway ; a small branch of the Melas river still flows into it.

See Leake, *Northern Greece,* 2. p. 306 *sq.* ; Forchhammer, *Hellenika,* p. 179 ; H. N. Ulrichs, *Reisen und Forschungen,* 1. p. 198 *sqq.* ; Fiedler, *Reise,* 1. p. 127 ; Vischer, *Erinnerungen,* p. 580 ; Bursian, *Geogr.* 1. p. 212 ; Baedeker,[3] p. 196 *sq.* For the inscriptions of Copae, see *C. I. G. G. S.* 1. Nos. 2780-2807.   I visited Copae in November 1895 and have described the place and its remains from my own observation, except as regards the inscriptions, the tombstones, and the *katavothra.*   That a branch of the Melas still flows into the *katavothra* is mentioned by Mr. Philippson (*Zeitschrift der Gesellschaft für Erdkunde zu Berlin,* 29 (1894), pp. 40, 46 *sq.*)

24. 1. This town is mentioned by Homer.   See *Iliad,* ii. 502.

24. 1. sanctuaries of Demeter etc.   An inscription, built into a church of the Virgin (*Panagia*) at *Topolia* (Copae), mentions Demeter with the title of Tauropolus—a title commonly bestowed on Artemis rather than Demeter (*C. I. G. G. S.* 1. No. 2703, Δαμάτρα[ς] Ταυροπόλω).

24. 2. Athens and Eleusis.   The Boeotian towns of these names were situated beside the river Triton (Strabo, ix. p. 407).   Cp. Stephanus Byzantius, *s.v.* Ἀθῆναι.   K. O. Müller supposed that the Cecrops who had a shrine at Haliartus (ix. 33. 1) was the legendary founder of the Boeotian Athens, just as another Cecrops was commonly thought to have been the first king of Athens, and a third Cecrops to have founded the town of Athens in Euboea ; though the genealogical connexion of the founders of the Boeotian and Euboean Athens with the Athenian Cecrops was (according to K. O. Müller) an Athenian figment.   See K. O. Müller, *Orchomenos,*[2] p. 116 *sq.* ; and note on i. 5. 3.   As to the river Triton, see ix. 33. 7 note.

24. 2. the eels.   The eels of the Copaic Lake were famous in antiquity (Aristophanes, *Acharnians,* 880 *sqq.* ; cp. *id., Lysistrata,* 35 *sq.* ; Pollux, vi. 63).   The largest of the Copaic eels were sacrificed by the Boeotians to the gods, being crowned with garlands and sprinkled with meal like regular sacrificial victims (Agatharchides, referred to by Athenaeus, vii. p. 297 d, cp. Ael, p. 300 s).   In the nineteenth century, before the lake was drained, great numbers of eels were still caught in it, especially near the bridge over the Melas, beside the rocky promontory of *Pyrgos Hagia Marina.*   They were said to be large, white, of delicate flavour, and easily digested.   In the early part of the century they used to be salted, pickled, and sent as delicacies to various parts of Greece. The people of *Topolia* (Copae) caught large quantities of them, especially near the chasm (*katavothra*).

See Dodwell, *Tour*, 1. p. 237; Leake, *Northern Greece*, 2. pp. 157, 281; H. N. Ulrichs, *Reisen und Forschungen*, 1. p. 200; Fiedler, *Reise*, 1. p. 103; Vischer, *Erinnerungen*, p. 580; Baedeker,³ p. 193; *Guide-Joanne*, 2. p. 21.

24. 3. Hyettus. The site of Hyettus has been determined by inscriptions. The ruins are at a place now called *Dendra*, about 6 miles to the north-west of Copae (*Topolia*) and rather more than that to the west of the village of *Martini*. Excavations have laid bare the polygonal wall of the acropolis for a distance of 84 yards. At the foot of the acropolis a small chapel of St. Nicholas is built almost entirely of ancient materials. From two of the inscriptions found on the site (*C. I. G. G. S.* 1. Nos. 2833 and 2834) we learn that statues of the emperors Septimius Severus and Caracalla were set up by the city of Hyettus. From another inscription (*C. I. G. G. S.* 1. No. 2808) it appears that Aesculapius was worshipped here under the title of Saviour and that his worship was cared for by a Sacred Senate or Council of Elders.

See *Bulletin de Corresp. hellénique*, 2 (1878), pp. 492-507; Baedeker,³ p. 195; Cauer, *Delectus Inscr. Graec.*² Nos. 302-306; Collitz, *G. D. I.* 1. Nos. 527-551; *C. I. G. G. S.* 1. Nos. 2808-2847.

24. 3. The traditions —— about Hyettus —— and Olmus etc. See ix. 36. 6 *sqq.*

24. 3. he is represented —— by an unwrought stone. Cp. vii. 22. 4 note.

24. 4. Cyrtones —— on a lofty mountain. As the only high mountain in this part of Boeotia is Mt. *Chlomo* (3546 feet), to the north of the north-western extremity of the Copaic Lake, Leake conjectured that Cyrtones was near the summit of that mountain, on its eastern side (*Northern Greece*, 2. p. 184). To the south-east of the village of *Martini*, on a rocky hill about 60 feet high, there are extensive remains of a fortified town. L. Ross conjectured that this might be Cyrtones or Corsea (*Wanderungen*, 1. p. 98 *sq.*) Accordingly Koutorga (*Revue archéologique*, N. S. 2 (1860), p. 394 *sq.*) and Bursian (*Geogr.* 1. p. 212) identified the ruins with Cyrtones. But since they wrote, the site of Hyettus has been identified; and as Hyettus is more than 6 miles from *Martini*, either the ruins at *Martini* are not those of Cyrtones, or Pausanias is wrong in saying that Cyrtones was 20 furlongs from Hyettus.

24. 5. Corsea. Between *Martini* and *Proskyna*, not far from the latter village, are the remains of an ancient city, which Leake thought might be Corsea (*Northern Greece*, 2. p. 287; cp. Dodwell, *Tour*, 2. p. 57). Others place Corsea at *Mellenitsa*, a village a little to the south of Halae (see below) (Koutorga, in *Revue archéologique*, N. S. 2 (1860), p. 394 *sq.*; Bursian, *Geogr.* 1. p. 192 *sq.*); others at *Cheliadou*, 6 miles from Hyettus and 4½ miles from Halae (Baedeker,³ p. 195). Corsea is not to be confounded with the Corsiae mentioned by Demosthenes (*De falsa legatione*, p. 385), Scylax (*Periplus*, 38), Theopompus (referred to by Harpocration, *s.v.* Κορσιαί), and Diodorus (xvi. 58). Cp. Suidas, *s.v.* Κορσιαί. For Corsiae, the site of which has been determined by inscriptions (*C. I. G. G. S.* I. Nos. 2383, 2385, 2387, 2388) was in south-west Boeotia, near the bay of *Sarandi*. At the head of the bay is a small level, enclosed by lofty and luxuriantly-wooded mountains, the southern spurs of Mt. Helicon. In this beautiful retreat, just under the wooded steeps of Mt. *Palaeo-Vouna*, stands the large monastery of St. Taxiarches (the archangel Michael). On a projection of the mountain which advances into the plain about a quarter of an hour's walk below the monastery and a mile from the sea-shore, are the remains of Corsiae or Chorsiae, for the latter form of the name is supported by the inscriptions. A flat summit forms the acropolis, of which the walls can still be traced. The western side of the acropolis terminates in a precipice; on the eastern slope stood the lower town, of which the walls can also be traced. Within the enclosure are remains of terrace-walls; and to the south, towards the harbour, is a narrow ruined gate. The whole place is barely a mile round. It is about $5\frac{1}{2}$ miles to the west of Thisbe (ix. 32. 4 note). See Leake, *Northern Greece*, 2. p. 514 *sqq.* (who mistook the ruins of Corsiae for those of Tipha, see ix. 32. 4); Bursian, *Geogr.* I. p. 243; Baedeker,[3] p. 171; *Bulletin de Corresp. hellén.* 8 (1884), p. 408 *sq.*

24. 5. the Platanius. This is probably the large stream now called *Rheveniko* which enters the bay of *Hagios Joannes Theologos* a few miles to the west of the ruins of Halae. See Koutorga, in *Revue archéologique*, N.S. 2 (1860), p. 392 *sq.*; cp. Dodwell, *Tour*, 2. p. 57; Leake, *Northern Greece*, 2. p. 287; Bursian, *Geogr.* I. p. 192.

24. 5. Halae. Traces of the acropolis and harbour of this town are to be seen close to the sea, on the south-east side of a bay called the bay of *Hagios Joannes Theologos* from a church of that name which stands a little to the south-west of the ruins. These ruins are situated on a terrace a few feet high; they form an elongated parallelogram, of which the south-east side is washed by the sea. This terrace seems to have been the acropolis. The walls are well preserved on the south and west; there are two round towers and one square one. Two stone jetties project into the sea enclosing a small port. See especially Koutorga, in *Revue archéologique* N.S. 2 (1860), pp. 390-394; also Leake, *Northern Greece*, 2. p. 288; L. Ross, *Wanderungen*, I. p. 98; Bursian, *Geogr.* I. p. 192; Baedeker,[3] p. 195. Halae was destroyed by Sulla, but the remnant of the population afterwards returned to it (Plutarch, *Sulla*, 26). In the time of Strabo (ix. p. 425) as well as of Pausanias it was the frontier town of Boeotia in this direction.

25. 1. Close to the Neistan gate of Thebes etc. After describing the city of Thebes, Pausanias described the road which, starting from the Proetidian gate, led north-eastward to Chalcis, etc. (ix. 18. 1–ix. 22. 7). Then he returned to Thebes and described the road leading northward to Acraephnium, etc. (ix. 23. 1–ix. 24. 5). He now returns to Thebes and follows the road which leads from the Neistan gate westward to the sanctuary of the Cabiri, Onchestus, and Thespiae (ix. 25. 1-ix. 26. 8). As Pausanias, following this route, crossed the Dirce after he had quitted the Neistan gate (§ 3), it appears that the Neistan gate was on the eastern side of the Dirce, not on the western side as Mr. Fabricius supposes (see note on ix. 8. 4). Further, it is clear that Pindar's house (§ 3) must have been outside the walls, not inside them, as Mr. Fabricius supposes (*Theben*, p. 25 *sq.*) For after having completed his description of the city of Thebes in the seventeenth chapter of the book it is very unlikely that Pausanias would now return to the interior of the city to mention Pindar's house, etc. His method with regard to Thebes and the roads leading from it is exactly analogous to his method of describing Megalopolis and the roads leading from it. After he had described the city of Megalopolis he described separately each of the roads which led from it. See viii. 30-44.

25. 1. Menoeceus —— slew himself etc. According to Euripides (*Phoenissae*, 911 *sqq.*) and Apollodorus (iii. 6. 7) it was the soothsayer Tiresias, not the Delphic oracle, who declared that Thebes could only be saved by the voluntary death of Menoeceus.

25. 1. there grows a pomegranate-tree. See note on ii. 17. 4.

25. 2. Hera was beguiled etc. Cp. Diodorus, iv. 9.

25. 3. Pindar's house etc. Pindar's house would seem to have been outside the walls of Thebes, to the west of the Dirce. See note on § 1. In the life of Pindar by Thomas Magister it is said that the poet "dwelt in Thebes, having a house near the sanctuary of Rhea, the Mother of the Gods" (*Biographi Graeci*, ed. Westermann, p. 99). The scholiasts on Pindar, *Pyth.* iii. 137-139, mention that the poet dedicated a sanctuary of Rhea and Pan beside his house. It is said that when Alexander the Great destroyed Thebes, he spared Pindar's house. The poet's biographers tell a story of a similar forbearance exercised by the Lacedaemonians on an occasion when they are said to have burned the rest of Thebes. See *Biogr. Graeci*, ed. Westermann, pp. 93, 99, 102 ; Arrian, *Anabasis*, i. 9. 10 ; Dio Chrysostom, *Or.* ii. vol. 1. p. 27, ed. Dindorf; cp. Plutarch, *Alexander*, 11 ; H. N. Ulrichs, *Reisen und Forschungen*, 2. p. 21.

25. 4. Hercules —— cut off the noses of the heralds etc. The story, according to Apollodorus (ii. 4. 11), was this. In the precinct of Poseidon at Onchestus, Perieres the charioteer of Menoeceus had struck with a stone and mortally wounded Clymenus, king of the Minyans of Orchomenus. The dying Clymenus charged his son Erginus to avenge his death. So Erginus marched against Thebes and compelled the Thebans to agree that they would pay him a tribute of 100 oxen every twenty years. Meeting the heralds of Orchomenus on their way to demand the tribute, Hercules cut off their ears, noses, and hands, tied the severed members about the necks of the mutilated men, and mockingly bade them take back this tribute to their king.

25. 5. a grove of Cabirian Demeter. Pausanias is now following the road which led from Thebes westward to Onchestus. About 3 miles to the west of Thebes, at the northern foot of the line of low hills which, running east and west forms the southern boundary of the plain,

there is a conspicuous *eikonostasion* or oratory of St. Nicholas; it is
clearly the remnant of a Christian chapel and rests upon ancient foundations. This is supposed to be the site of the grove of Cabirian Demeter.
Its distances from Thebes and from the sanctuary of the Cabiri (the site
of which has been ascertained, see below) agree fairly with the distances
given by Pausanias. See *Mittheil. d. arch. Inst. in Athen*, 13 (1888),
p. 84 *sq.*

25. 5. the sanctuary of the Cabiri. The sanctuary of the Cabiri
was discovered and partially excavated by German archaeologists in
the winter of 1887-1888. It is situated about 4 miles to the west of
Thebes, in a small valley of the low range of hills which bounds the
Teneric plain on the south. The neighbourhood is now called *Dhara*.
To reach the spot from Thebes we take the carriage-road which goes to
Lebadea. The road descends northward into the plain, then turns to
the west, passes through the suburb of *Pyri*, and skirts the northern foot
of the low chain of hills which extends westward from Thebes all the way
to Mount Helicon. Across the treeless plain on the north-west rises a
group of bare low rounded hills, of which the somewhat higher summit
on the west (Mount *Phaga*) is the Mountain of the Sphinx. After about
half an hour's drive the road to Thespiae diverges to the left (southward)
from the road to Lebadea and enters a long valley which runs south-
westward through the hills that bound the plain on the south. In the
next valley to the west of that through which the carriage-road goes
to Thespiae is the sanctuary of the Cabiri. It is a small valley or hollow
in the hills opening northward on the Teneric plain and traversed by
the bed of a brook which is generally dry and choked with brown
thistles. The hills on either side are low, bare, and treeless. To the
north you look down the little valley and across the Teneric plain to the
group of low rounded hills already mentioned. The spot is quiet,
solitary, and sequestered.

The sanctuary lies on the right or east bank of the brook. It has
not been completely excavated; a number of trenches have been dug
exposing isolated pieces of wall. These walls are constructed of
squared blocks laid in horizontal courses, and are standing to a height
of from two to four courses (6 feet). The stone is a soft crumbling
sandstone which you can pull to pieces with your hands. The greatest
length of the sanctuary from north to south is 40 paces; its greatest
breadth from east to west is 23 paces. But beyond the sanctuary to
the south there is a quadrangular pit, the sides of which are lined with
masonry three courses high. A good many coarse thick potsherds lie
beside it as if they had been excavated here. I was unable to make
out the plan of the sanctuary, which appeared to me quite unlike that
of an ordinary Greek temple. Instead of a single large shrine there
seems to have been a number of small rooms. The German archaeologists, however, who excavated the sanctuary, succeeded in making out
the plan of the temple. Their account of it is as follows.

The remains of the temple date from three different periods—the
Greek period, the Macedonian period, and the Roman period.

(1) The remains of the Greek temple are very scanty : they consist

only of a polygonal wall forming a curve in what was afterwards the *cella*. This curved wall may have been part of the apse of the earliest temple; for the excavations at Samothrace have shown that an apse was not unknown in temples of the Cabiri. From the style of the wall it may date from the sixth or fifth century B.C.

(2) Of the second temple, built apparently in Macedonian times in the fourth century B.C., enough remains to enable us to recognise the plan. The temple stood east and west, and consisted of a small fore-temple (*pronaos*), a fore-*cella*, a *cella*, and a back-chamber (*opistho-domos*). This back-chamber was entered, not from the *cella*, but through two doors, one in each of the side walls. It appears never to have been roofed, and it contained two sacrificial pits lined with slabs of stone. These pits are side by side; each is about 2.10 metres long, 1.50 metre deep, and .90 metre wide. The plan of this temple is unique. Other temples have been found with a fore-*cella* as well as a *cella;* but no other temple is known to possess both a fore-*cella* and a special sacrificial chamber. From what Pausanias says below (§ 10) we may perhaps infer that the old temple was burnt during Alexander's invasion in 335 B.C. and rebuilt shortly afterwards.

(3) The temple was rebuilt in the Roman period, but the plan of the previous temple was retained, except that the fore-*cella* was now merged in the *cella*. Part of the pedestal which supported the statue of the god in the *cella* is still in its place. From the length of the pedestal it would seem that the god was represented reclining on a couch, as he is depicted on vases found in the sanctuary.

The temple was of the Doric order; it was *prostylos tetrastylos, i.e.* it had four columns on the east front, but no columns at the sides.

Thousands of painted potsherds and terra-cotta figures were found in the course of the excavations. Almost half of the potsherds are of local Boeotian manufacture. The figures on these Boeotian vases are painted dark on a light ground; they are mostly drawn in a style of broad humour or caricature. On one potsherd the Cabir (in the singular, ΚΑΒΙΡΟΣ) is represented reclining, with a goblet in his outstretched right hand; in front of him stands a boy (παῖς), his son, with a jug in his right hand, with which he is about to draw wine from a large vessel. The terra-cotta figures represent men, bulls, swine, rams, he-goats, and lions. Numerous votive offerings of bronze and lead were also found; hundreds of them represent bulls; a few represent he-goats. The bronze figures are of good workmanship and may date from the first half of the fifth century B.C. Many of them bear votive inscriptions; these dedications are generally to the Cabir (always in the singular) or to his son or to both together (τῷ Καβίρῳ καὶ τῷ παιδὶ τοῦ Καβίρου; see *Hermes*, 25 (1890), p. 4). There were also found a number of objects of a peculiar shape, some made of terra-cotta, others of bronze. They appear to be humming-tops (στρόβιλοι); for they are shaped like tops and an inscription found at the sanctuary (*C. I. G. G. S.* 1. No. 2420) mentions that a certain woman named Ocythoa dedicated four dice, a humming-top, a whip, and a torch, all of silver and weighing five drachms. Dice and a humming-top were among the playthings by which the Titans beguiled the youthful Dionysus (Clement of Alexandria, *Protrept.* 17 *sq.*, p. 15, ed. Potter).

See *Mittheil. d. arch. Inst. in Athen*, 12 (1887), pp. 269-271 ; *id.*, 13 (1888), pp. 81-99, 111 *sq.*, 412-428 ; Δελτίον ἀρχαιολογικόν, 1888, pp. 14-17, 62 *sq.* ; Baedeker,[3] p. 170 ; *Guide-Joanne*, 2. p. 15. I visited the sanctuary, 16th November 1895, and have described it partly from personal observation.

The Louvre possesses a small bronze figure of a bull bearing the inscription : Δαιτώνδ[ας] ἀνέθηκε τῶι ἱερῶι Καβείρωι. "Daetondas dedicated (this bull) to the sacred Cabir" (P. Girard, 'Un nouveau bronze du Kabirion,' *Revue archéologique*, 3me Série, 18 (1891), pp. 158-162, with pl. xx. ; *Classical Review*, 6 (1892), p. 185). This bronze bull, which was acquired only recently by the Louvre, no doubt came from the sanctuary of the Cabiri near Thebes, for in that sanctuary three other bronze bulls dedicated by Daetondas to the Cabir have been discovered (*C. I. G. G. S.* 1. Nos. 2457, 3575, 3576). As to the worship of the Cabiri in Boeotia, see O. Kern, 'Die boiotischen Kabiren,' *Hermes*, 25 (1890), pp. 1-16. Mr. Kern thinks that the Boeotian worship of the Cabiri was derived from Athens ; he relies partly on a statement of Pausanias (iv. 1. 7). Cp. H. B. Walters, in *Journal of Hellenic Studies*, 13 (1892-3), pp. 84-87.

26. 1. a plain called after a soothsayer Tenerus. Cp. note on ix. 10. 6. The plain is monotonous and destitute of trees and houses. It is bordered on the south by a line of gently-sloping heights, and on the north by the rugged sides of Mt. *Phaga.* The soil is fertile, and in summer the whole plain as far as Thebes, as well as the long slopes of the hills on the south, are for the most part one continuous corn-field, without a single fence. See Leake, *Northern Greece*, 2. p. 215 *sq.* ; Vischer, *Erinnerungen*, p. 561 *sq.*

26. 1. a great sanctuary of Hercules. Half an hour to the west of the sanctuary of the Cabiri, at the point where the southern chain of hills advances farthest into the plain, there are some foundations, built of squared blocks of limestone. Fragments of vases, tiles, and terra-cottas lie scattered round about in the fields. These may be the remains of the sanctuary of Hercules. See *Mittheil. d. arch. Inst. in Athen*, 13 (1888), p. 85 *sq.*

26. 2. the mountain from which they say the Sphinx etc. This is the rocky mountain now called *Phaga* (1860 feet high), which rises, bare, rugged, and grey, from the Teneric plain, at the south-eastern corner of what used to be the Copaic Lake. The Boeotian name of the mountain seems to have been Phicium (Φίκιον or Φίκειον), from Phix (Φίξ), the Boeotian form of Sphinx. See Apollodorus, iii. 5. 8 ; Hesiod, *Shield of Hercules*, 33 ; *id.*, *Theog.* 326 ; Tzetzes, *Schol. on Lycophron*, 1465 ; Stephanus Byzantius, *s.v.* Φίκειον ; Leake, *Northern Greece*, 2. p. 215 ; L. Ross, *Wanderungen*, 1. p. 25 ; Vischer, *Erinnerungen*, p. 561 ; Bursian, *Geogr.* 1. p. 231 ; *Mittheil. d. arch. Inst. in Athen*, 13 (1888), p. 86.

The riddle of the Sphinx was : What is that which on earth is two-footed, three-footed, and four-footed, and which is weakest when it has most feet? Answer—A man, for in infancy he crawls on all fours and in old age he supports his steps with a staff. This riddle, with the answer, is prefixed to the MSS. of Sophocles's *Oedipus Tyrannus*, and is quoted or referred to by ancient writers and scholiasts. See *Poetae Scenici Graeci*, ed. Dindorf, p. 33; Athenaeus, x. p. 456 b; Schol. on Euripides, *Phoenissae*, argum. (vol. I. p. 243 *sq*. ed. E. Schwartz) and on *v*. 50; Tzetzes, *Schol. on Lycophron*, 7; *Anthologia Palatina*, xiv. 64; Apollodorus, iii. 5. 8; Plutarch, *De amore*, iii. 5, vol. 5, p. 45, ed. Dübner. The riddle is said to be current, in a slightly different form, among the Mongols of the Selenga. "QUESTION—*Uglo durbo, edur dunda khoyir, udesi gurba?* Morning, four; noon, two; evening, three. ANSWER—A man" (Latham, *Descriptive Ethnology*, I. p. 325). A Gascon story tells how a great beast with a human head dwelt in a cave full of gold, of which it promised the half to him who could read three riddles. Those who could not read them were devoured by the monster. At last a poor young man, anxious to win the gold that he might marry his lady love, answers the questions, slays the monster, and carries off the gold. One of the riddles propounded by the monster was this: "At sunrise it creeps, like the serpents and worms. At noon it walks on two legs like the birds. At sunset it goes away on three legs." See Bladé, *Contes populaires de la Gascogne*, I. pp. 3-14.

26. 3. the oracle that had been given to Cadmus etc. See note on ix. 12. 1.

26. 3. the Delphic oracle referred only to Epicaste etc. See ix. 5. 10.

26. 5. the ruins of a city Onchestus. Two great plains of Boeotia—the Theban and the Copaic—are separated by a low ridge which connects the Sphinx Mountain (*Phaga*) with the roots of Helicon. On the summit of this ridge, and on the south side of the road, there is a small piece of ancient Greek wall, consisting of only two or three stones in their places. The direction of the foundation is oblique to the road. On the height on either side are many stones in the ploughed land, indications of an ancient site, which archaeologists are agreed is that of Onchestus. See Leake, *Northern Greece*, 2. p. 213 *sqq*.; L. Ross, *Wanderungen*, I. p. 25; Vischer, *Erinnerungen*, p. 561; Bursian, *Geogr.* I. p. 231 *sq*.; Baedeker,[3] p. 170; *Guide-Joanne*, 2. p. 15. Strabo tells us (ix. p. 412) that Onchestus stood in a bare situation on a height, beside the Copaic lake and the Teneric plain: he says that the Amphictyonic assembly used to meet there. In the Macedonian period the diet of the Boeotian confederacy appears to have assembled at Onchestus, probably in the sanctuary of Poseidon (see below); for inscriptions of Megara and Aegosthena, engraved at times when these towns belonged to the Boeotian confederacy, are dated by "the archon at Onchestus," by which is meant the federal archon of Boeotia (*C. I. G. G. S.* I. Nos. 27, 28, 209-212, 214-218, 220-222). See Foucart, in *Bulletin de. Corr. hellénique*, 4 (1880), p. 83 *sq*.; G. Gilbert, *Griech. Staatsalterthümer*, 2. p. 53; Dittenberger, on *C. I. G. G. S.* I. No. 27.

26. 5. a temple and image of Onchestian Poseidon etc. Homer speaks of "Sacred Onchestus, Poseidon's beauteous grove" (*Iliad*, ii.

506). The grove was bare and treeless at the beginning of our era
(Strabo, ix. p. 412). A mode of divination by means of horses and
chariots seems to have been practised at Onchestus. The horses were
left to their own guidance, and if they drew the chariot to the grove of
Poseidon, it was a good omen. See Homer, *Hymn to the Pythian
Apollo*, 52-60, with Baumeister's note ; Bouché-Leclercq, *Histoire de la
divination*, 2. p. 367 *sq.* A coin of Haliartus exhibits, on the
reverse, Poseidon advancing towards the right and striking with his
trident ; on the obverse is the Boeotian shield with a trident on it.
These types refer to the worship of Poseidon at Onchestus. See Head,
Coins of Boeotia, p. 46 ; *id., Historia numorum*, p. 293.

26. 6. **Thespiae.** The name of this city occurs in the singular form
Thespia (Homer, *Il.* ii. 498 ; Dionysius, *Descriptio Graeciae*, 100 ;
Stephanus Byzantius, *s.v.* Θέσπεια), but the plural form Thespiae is
much more commonly employed by ancient writers. Pausanias himself
is not consistent in this respect ; in the present passage he uses the
singular form (which in the translation, for the sake of uniformity, I
have turned into the plural), but below (ix. 27. 4) he employs the
plural. The city lay in a plain at the southern foot of the long
range of low hills which extends from Mount Helicon eastward to
Thebes and Tanagra. The site is distant about 3 miles from the
eastern foot of Mount Helicon. Overlooking it from the north are the two
villages of *Eremokastro* and *Kaskaveli*, situated on two twin summits of
the low range and separated from each other only by the bed of a stream
which flows to join the Thespius (now the *Kanavari*) in the plain
below. The Thespius, rising near Thespiae, flows for a short way in
the plain at the foot of the low chain of hills, then finds its way through
them in a long narrow valley to the Theban plain, which it crosses
north-eastward to fall into Lake Hylica (*Likeri*). The modern carriage-
road from Thebes to Thespiae, quitting the Teneric or Theban plain a
little to the east of the sanctuary of the Cabiri, follows the valley of
the Thespius through the hills. The hills which enclose the valley are
low, bare, and rounded ; the scenery is tame and monotonous. As we
approach Thespiae the valley opens out into a plain, and Helicon
appears towering up at no great distance to the south-west, with the
Valley of the Muses nestling among its northern slopes. To the right
of the Valley of the Muses, and forming a spur of Helicon, rises the
conical hill of Ascra crowned with its solitary tower. From Thebes to
Thespiae by the carriage-road is a drive of an hour and a half.

The ruins of Thespiae, situated in the plain on the right or southern
bank of the stream, are very insignificant. The only remains of military
architecture which survived to modern times was an oval enclosure,
scarcely half a mile in circumference, built of very solid masonry of a
regular kind. The masonry formed only a socle ; the upper part of the
wall was perhaps built of unburnt bricks. This fortified enclosure was
demolished in 1890 and 1891 by two French archaeologists, Messrs.
Jamot and de Ridder, for the sake of the inscriptions and other
remains of antiquity which were built into it. They found about 350
inscriptions together with some pieces of sculpture, and in the interior

of the enclosure the foundations of a temple which from an inscription found in its place appears to have been the temple of the Muses mentioned by Pausanias (ix. 27. 5). Down to the beginning of the nineteenth century all the adjacent ground to the south-east, like the interior of the fortress, was strewn with ancient foundations, squared stones, and other remains. The place used to be called *Leuka* (pronounced *Lefka*) from a village of that name, which no longer exists. Here Leake saw five or six ruined churches containing remains of ceilings, architraves, columns, and plain quadrangular blocks, all of white marble; and he reports that similar relics existed in all the surrounding villages and solitary churches. Archaeologists have made short work of most or all of these churches at Thespiae; but it is possible that in some of the more secluded districts a few may survive. When I revisited Thespiae in November 1895 I found a good many traces of recent excavations among the fields on the southern side of the high-road and distant from it perhaps 100 to 300 yards. Among these traces were hewn stones, large blocks of pedestals with marks of the attachment of statues on their tops, a small piece of an unfluted column, etc.

In 1882 the Greek archaeologist Mr. Stamatakes discovered remains of a large stone lion about 1200 yards to the east of Thespiae, on the right bank of the Thespius (*Kanavari*), beside the path which leads from *Eremokastro* to *Kokla* (Plataea). The lion resembles the one at Chaeronea, but is much smaller, measuring about 3 metres (10 feet) from the tail to the neck. Unlike the lion of Chaeronea, which is hollow, the lion of Thespiae is solid; the material is a soft whitish stone which is quarried on Mount *Karanta*, between Thespiae and Creusis. Only the body and the right hind-leg of the statue are preserved. The animal was seated looking to the north with his tail between his legs. Further excavations brought to light the scattered blocks of the pedestal and proved that the lion, raised on a pedestal, had occupied the middle of the north wall of an enclosure 32 metres (105 feet) long by 24 metres (79 feet) wide, within which were buried the ashes of many men. Only the northern and eastern walls of the enclosure were found; it is possible that they served to support a tumulus which may have been raised over the dead. Within the enclosure at a depth of about 2 feet below the surface was found a layer of broken pottery, terra-cotta statuettes, and scrapers, some of iron, some of bronze. Below this layer, which was about 18 inches thick, was found another layer, from 1 to 3 inches thick, composed of ashes and charcoal, together with bones, pottery, terra-cotta statuettes, bronze and iron scrapers, and iron nails, all broken and all showing marks of having been burnt. Further, there were found, about 8 feet to the north of the lion, nine tablets of dark limestone in a row, inscribed with the names of 101 men. There can be no doubt that these are the names of men who fell in some battle and whose remains were interred here, with the stone lion set over their grave as a symbol of valour. As the inscriptions appear to belong to the second half of the fifth century B.C., it is probable that we have here the remains of the men who fell in the battle of Tanagra (424 B.C.), for we know from Thucydides (iv. 96 and 133) that the

Thespian losses in that battle were very heavy.   Mr. Stamatakes
formerly conjectured that the grave contained the ashes of the Thespians
who fell at Plataea in 479 B.C.; but the character of the letters of the
inscription seems to exclude so early a date.   See P. Stamatakes, in
Πρακτικὰ τῆς Ἀρχαιολογικῆς Ἑταιρίας, 1882, pp. 67-74; *id.*, in
Ἐφημερὶς ἀρχαιολογική, 1883, p. 191 *sqq.*; A. Kirchhoff, *Studien zur
Geschichte des griechischen Alphabets,*[4] p. 140 *sq.*; *C. I. G. G. S.* 1. No.
1888; Collitz, *G. D. I.* 1. No. 791 *a-h.*

Among the deities whose worship at Thespiae is attested by
inscriptions though not mentioned by Pausanias are the Bull God, the
Dioscuri, Hermes, Artemis, Demeter, the Great Mother, Gracious Zeus,
the Good Demon, Themis, Aesculapius, and Isis (*C. I. G. G. S.* 1. Nos.
1787, 1792, 1793, 1809, 1810, 1811, 1812, 1814, 1815, 1816, 1824,
1867, 1869, 1871, 1872).   Further, the inscribed bases of many statues
of Roman emperors, from Julius Caesar to Valentinianus and Valens,
have been found at or near Thespiae (*C. I. G. G. S.* 1. Nos. 1835-1845,
1848, 1849).   This goes to show that down to late imperial times
Thespiae subsisted as a town of some size.   At the beginning of our
era Thespiae and Tanagra are said to have been the only considerable
cities left in Boeotia (Strabo, ix. p. 403).   At an earlier time the
Thespians had the reputation of being poor and proud.   They looked
down on men who got their living by handicraft or by farming; hence
most of them were needy and owed large sums to the Thebans (Heraclides Ponticus, *De rebus publicis*, 43).   They are said, too, to have
been contentious and quarrelsome (Dicaearchus, *Descriptio Graeciae*, i.
25, in *Geographi Graeci Minores*, ed. Müller, 1. p. 104).

On Thespiae and its remains see Wheler, *Journey*, p. 470 (who mistook the
ruins for those of Thisbe); Dodwell, *Tour*, 1. p. 252 *sqq.*; Leake, *Northern
Greece*, 2. p. 478 *sqq.*; Welcker, *Tagebuch*, 2. p. 33 *sq.*; Vischer, *Erinnerungen*,
p. 553 *sq.*; Bursian, *Geogr.* 1. p. 237 *sqq.*; Baedeker,[3] p. 173 *sq.*; *Guide-Joanne*,
2. p. 28 *sq.*; *Mittheil. d. arch. Inst. in Athen*, 3 (1878), pp. 311-313; *Bulletin de
Corresp. hellénique*, 8 (1884), pp. 409-416 (inscriptions); *id.*, 9 (1885), pp. 403-
423 (inscriptions); *id.*, 15 (1891), p. 659 *sq.* (excavations of Messrs. Jamot and
de Ridder); *id.*, 18 (1894), pp. 201-215 (sarcophagus of the Greek period with
reliefs representing some of the labours of Hercules); *id.*, 19 (1895), pp. 321-385
(inscriptions).   I visited Thespiae in 1890 and 1895.   On the latter occasion I
copied a few inscriptions which seemed to have been brought to light by recent
excavations and have not, so far as I know, been hitherto published.   Thus on
the site of a chapel, to the south of the high-road, I found a pedestal 3 ft. 5 in.
high and 23 inches wide, bearing the following inscription of the Roman age:

> Τ. Φλαούιον Φιλείνου
> υἱὸν Μόνδωνα Φλαου-
> ία Ἀρχέλα, ἢ καὶ Τειμο-
> ξένα, τὸν ἑαυτῆς ἄν-
> δρα.   Ψηφίσματι
> βουλῆς καὶ δήμου.

This Titus Flavius Mondon, son of Philinus, and his wife Archela or Timoxena,
are both known from other inscriptions found at Thespiae.   See *C. I. G. G. S.* 1.
Nos. 1830 (with Dittenberger's note), 1867, 2520, 2521.   On another stone at the
same place I copied the following inscription:

> ΕΠΙ
> ΑΡΣΙΝΟΗ.

A FOLK-TALE

26. 6. Thespius, a descendant of Erechtheus. Cp. Diodorus, iv. 29.
26. 7 once upon a time —— a dragon was ravaging the city
etc. The following story belongs to a widely-diffused group of folk-tales
which tell how a monster is appeased by the periodic sacrifice of a
human victim, till a champion appears, who slays the monster and
rescues the destined victim. The common form of the story is this.
A certain country is infested by a many-headed serpent, dragon, or other
monster, which would destroy the whole people if a human victim
(generally a virgin) were not delivered up to it annually, weekly, or
daily. Many victims have perished, and at last it has fallen to the lot
of the king's own daughter to be the victim. She is exposed to the
monster; but the hero of the tale, generally a young man of humble
birth, interposes in her behalf, slays the monster, and receives as his
reward the hand of the princess. This is the general scheme of the
story, but in the various versions of it there are many differences of
detail. To this group of stories belong the following tales :

(1) The story of Euthymus and the Hero. Paus. vi. 6. 7 *sqq.*

(2) The story of Cleostratus and Menestratus here told by Pausanias.

(3) The story of Perseus and Andromeda. Apollodorus, ii. 4. 3.
Ovid, *Metam.* iv. 669 *sqq.*

(4) The story of Hercules and Hesione. Apollodorus, ii. 5. 9.
Diodorus, iv. 42.

(5) The story of Sybaris. Antoninus Liberalis, 8. See note on
x. 8. 8.

All these five are ancient Greek versions of the tale.

(6) A modern Greek version. Hahn, *Griechische und albanesische
Märchen*, No. 70, vol. 2. p. 55 *sqq.*

(7) Another modern Greek version. Legrand, *Contes populaires
grecs*, p. 169 *sqq.*

(8) An Albanian version. Hahn, *op. cit.* No. 98, vol. 2. p. 114 *sq.*

(9) A Wallachian version. Schott, *Walachische Maerchen*, No. 10,
p. 140 *sqq.*

(10) An Italian version. Basile, *Pentamerone*, First day, Seventh
tale, vol. 1. p. 97 *sqq.* (Liebrecht's German trans.)

(11) A modern Italian version. Crane, *Popular Italian Tales*, No.
6, p. 31 *sqq*

(12) A Corsican version. Ortoli, *Contes populaires de la Corse*, No.
18, p. 123 *sqq.*

(13) A Sicilian version. Gonzenbach, *Sicilianische Märchen*, No.
40, vol. 1. p. 274 *sqq.*

(14) A Breton version. Sébillot, *Contes populaires de la Haute-
Bretagne*, No. 11, p. 79 *sqq.*

(15) A French version from Lorraine. Cosquin, *Contes populaires
de Lorraine*, No. 5, vol. 1. p. 61 *sqq.*

(16) A Gaelic version. J. F. Campbell, *Popular Tales of the West
Highlands*, No. 4, vol. 1. p. 77 *sqq.*

(17) A Norse version. Dasent, *Popular Tales from the Norse*,
' Shortshanks,' p. 131 *sqq.*

(18) A Swedish version. Cavallius und Stephens, *Schwedische Volks-sagen und Märchen*, No. 4, p. 62 *sqq.* (Oberleitner's German trans.)

(19) A Danish version. Grundtvig, *Dänische Volksmärchen*, First series (Leipzig, 1878), p. 285 *sqq.* (Leo's German trans.)

(20), (21), (22), (23) Four German versions. Grimm, *Household Tales*, No. 60 ; Kuhn und Schwartz, *Norddeutsche Sagen, Märchen und Gebräuche*, p. 340 *sqq.* ; J. W. Wolf, *Deutsche Hausmärchen*, p. 372 *sqq.* ; Philo vom Walde, *Schlesien in Sage und Brauch*, p. 81 *sqq.*

(24), (25) Two Tyrolese versions. Zingerle, *Kinder und Haus-märchen aus Tirol*, No. 24, p. 126 *sqq.* ; Schneller, *Märchen und Sagen aus Wälschtirol*, No. 39, p. 116 *sq.*

(26) A Transylvanian version. Haltrich, *Deutsche Volksmärchen aus dem Sachsenlande in Siebenbürgen*,[4] No. 25 (No. 24 of the first ed.), p. 103 *sqq.*

(27), (28), (29) Three Lithuanian versions. Schleicher, *Litauische Märchen, Sprichwörte, Rätsel und Lieder*, p. 57 *sqq.* ; Leskien und Brugman, *Litauische Volkslieder und Märchen*, Nos. 14, 16, pp. 404 *sqq.*, 407 *sqq.*

(30) An Avar version. Schiefner, *Awarische Texte*, No. 2, p. 21 *sqq.*

(31) A Kurdish version. Prym und Socin, *Kurdische Sammlung*, Erste Abtheilung, No. 10, p. 38 *sqq.* (German trans.)

(32) A Berber version. Basset, *Contes populaires Berbères*, No. 35, p. 73 *sq.* (cp. p. 178 *sqq.*)

(33) A Kabyl version. Rivière, *Contes populaires de la Kabylie*, p. 195 *sq.*

(34) A Senegambian version. Bérenger-Féraud, *Contes populaires de la Sénégambie*, p. 185 *sqq.* ; *id.*, *Les peuplades de la Sénégambie*, p. 169 *sqq.*

(35) A Burmese version. Ad. Bastian, *Die Völker des oestlichen Asien*, 1. p. 102 *sq.*

(36) An Annamite version. Landes, ' Contes et légendes annam-ites,' No. 4, in *Cochinchine Française. Excursions et Reconnaissances*, viii. No. 20 (Nov. Decemb. 1884), p. 302 *sq.*

(37) A Chinese version. Dennys, *The Folk-lore of China*, p. 110 *sq.* (In this version the dragon, after devouring nine maidens, one each year, is slain by the tenth.)

(38) A Japanese version. Brauns, *Japanische Märchen und Sagen*, p. 112 *sqq.*

(39), (40), (41) Three Basque versions. Webster, *Basque legends*, pp. 22-38.

In a considerable number of these tales (the Sicilian, Gaelic, Swedish, Kabyl, Senegambian, and the ancient Greek stories of Andromeda and Hesione) the monster, who is sometimes described as a serpent, lives in water, either the sea, a lake, or a fountain. In other versions (the two modern Greek, the Albanian, Avar, Kurdish, and Berber) the monster, who in these cases is generally a serpent, takes possession of the springs of water and only allows the water to flow or the people to make use of it on condition of receiving a human victim. This reminds us of the widespread belief that water, especially the water of a spring, is guarded by a serpent or dragon. See note on ix. 10. 5. It is possible that in these stories there is a reminiscence of a custom of periodically sacrificing human victims to water-spirits. Sacrifices are annually offered to the gods of the river Prah on the Gold Coast of Africa; formerly the victims were two human beings, a man and a woman (A. B. Ellis, *The Tshi-speaking Peoples of the Gold Coast*, p. 64 *sq.*) The princes of Kaepang, a state in the East Indian island of Timor, deemed themselves descended from crocodiles; and on the coronation of a new prince a solemn offering was presented to the crocodiles in presence of the people. The offerings consisted of a pig with red bristles and a young girl prettily dressed and decked with flowers. She was placed on the river-bank; and the crocodiles were invoked. One of the beasts soon appeared and dragged the damsel down into the water, where it was thought that he married her. But if she proved not to be a maid, he brought her back. See Wilken, ʻHet animisme,ʼ *De Indische Gids*, June 1884, p. 994; Ad. Bastian, *Indonesien*, 2. p. 8. In the same district girls were sometimes dedicated at birth to the crocodiles and then, with certain ceremonies, brought up to be married in time to priests (Bastian, *op. cit.* 2. p. 11). It is said that the coast of Buru, another East Indian island, was once ravaged by a holy crocodile, at whose request the king's daughter was tied to a post. The crocodile then dragged her down into the water, and from their union all crocodiles are descended (Bastian, *op. cit.* 1. p. 134). The type of folk-tale with which this note deals has been elaborately examined by Mr. E. S. Hartland (*The Legend of Perseus*, 3 vols. London, 1894-1896).

26. 8. The image of Dionysus. The worship of Dionysus at Thespiae is attested by inscriptions (*C. I. G. G. S.* 1. Nos. 1786, 1794, 1867, 1869; Collitz, *G. D. I.* 1. Nos. 797, 816; Roehl, *I. G. A.* No. 284; E. S. Roberts, *Greek Epigraphy*, No. 210 n; Kaibel, *Epigrammata Graeca*, No. 757 a, Praef. p. xvi.)

27. 1. the Thespians honour Love the most. To explain the Thespian worship of Love it was said that a youth Narcissus had slain himself in a love affair at Thespiae; that the flower of that name had sprung from his blood; and that ever after the Thespians had worshipped Love and sacrificed to him both publicly and privately (Conon, *Narrationes*, 24). The excavations of Messrs. Jamot and de Ridder at Thespiae in 1891 brought to light a series of marble statues of Love, of the Roman period, representing him as an infant, sometimes completely naked, sometimes with a mantle on his left arm, sometimes holding a goose, now standing, now seated, now crouching on his hams in an attitude of which Phoenician and Cypriote terra-cotta statuettes offer many examples (*Bulletin de Corresp. hellénique*, 15 (1891), p. 660). An inscription of Roman date, found at *Vaia*, near Thespiae, records that a certain Philinus, son of Mondon and Archela, "dedicated the image of Love and repaired the sanctuary and the doors of the fore-temple at his own expense" (*C. I. G. G. S.* 1. No. 1830; L. Stephani, *Reise durch einige Gegenden des nördlichen Griechenlandes*, p. 75). The emperor

Hadrian, having killed a she-bear with his own hand, commemorated his success by dedicating an offering to Love at Thespiae, accompanying the offering with some verses, apparently of his own composition, which have been found engraved on a block of white marble between the villages of *Dombrena* and *Eremokastro* (*C. I. G. G. S.* 1. No. 1828; Kaibel, *Epigrammata Graeca*, No. 811). As to the Greek worship of Love see E. Gerhard, in *Abhandlungen* of the Berlin Academy for 1848, Philolog. histor. Cl. pp. 261-298 (reprinted in his *Gesammelte Akademische Abhandlungen*, 2. pp. 58-93); cp. Jacob Grimm, in *id.* for 1851, pp. 141-156.

27. 1. **an unwrought stone.** See note on vii. 22. 4. Another primitive idol at Thespiae was a branch which was worshipped as an image of Hera in her capacity as goddess of marriage (Arnobius, *Adversus Nationes*, vi. 11 *coluisse . . . ramum pro Cinxia Thespios;* as to *Cinxia* see Festus, p. 63, ed. Müller).

27. 1. **His worship is equally observed by the people of Parium.** There was an image of Love by Praxiteles at Parium (Pliny, *Nat. hist.* xxxvi. 22). It is represented on the coins of that city from the time of Antoninus Pius downward, from which we learn that the god was por- trayed as a naked winged boy, with his right hand stretched out down- wards before him, his left hand planted on his side, and his head turned to the left. The Princess of Wales possesses a Greek statuette of Love, which Prof. Percy Gardner considers to be a copy of the statue by Praxiteles at Parium. See *Journal of Hellenic Studies*, 4 (1883), pp. 266-274; cp. Furtwängler, in Roscher's *Lexikon*, 1. p. 1358 *sqq.*; Overbeck, *Gesch. d. griech. Plastik,*[4] 2. p. 50; Head, *Historia Numorum*, p. 459.

27. 1. **a colony from Erythrae** etc. According to Strabo (xiii. p. 588) Parium was founded by the Milesians, Erythraeans, and Parians. Coins and inscriptions show that the town became a Roman colony in the time of Augustus (Smith's *Dict. of Greek and Rom. Geog., s.v.* 'Parium'; Head, *Historia Numorum*, p. 459).

27. 2. **Chaos first came into being** etc. See Hesiod, *Theogony*, 116 *sqq.*

27. 3. **Praxiteles —— made one of Pentelic marble.** As to this famous image of Love by Praxiteles, see i. 20. 1 *sq.* According to Strabo (ix. p. 410) it was not Phryne but Glycera who received the statue as a present from her lover Praxiteles and dedicated it at Thespiae. But the general voice of antiquity supported the claim of Phryne (Athenaeus, xiii. p. 591 a; *Anthol. Palat.* vi. 260, xvi. 203-206). The image was still at Thespiae in the time of Cicero, who says (*In Verr.* iv. 2 and 60) that it was the only thing which drew strangers to the town. In Pliny's time the statue stood in the Schools of Octavia at Rome (Pliny, *Nat. hist.* xxxvi. 22). The type of the image is not known; and among the numerous statues of Love (Eros) which have come down to us, none is recognised with any certainty as a copy of the Thespian statue. Prof. Furtwängler, however, conjectures that we have replicas of the image in seven life-sized statues and four statuettes of Love, all copies more or less exact of a common original, which seems

to have represented the winged god with down-turned head, his left hand grasping a large bow, the end of which rested on the ground, while his right hand hung at his side either empty or perhaps holding an arrow. Prof. Furtwängler thinks that the original was an early work of Praxiteles, executed about 370-360 B.C., and betraying the influence of Polyclitus.

See Brunn, *Gesch. d. griech. Künstler*, 1. p. 341 ; Overbeck, *Schriftquellen*, Nos. 1249-1261 ; *id.*, *Gesch. d. griech. Plastik*,[4] 2. p. 49 *sq.* ; Friederichs, *Praxiteles*, pp. 20-24 ; Stark, ' Ueber die Erosbildungen des Praxiteles,' *Berichte über die Verhandl. d. kön sächs. Gesell. d. Wissen. zu Leipzig*, Philolog. histor. Cl. 18 (1866), pp. 155-172 ; P. Wolters, 'Die Eroten des Praxiteles,' *Archäologische Zeitung*, 43 (1885), pp. 81-98 ; P. Gardner, 'A statuette of Eros,' *Journal of Hellenic Studies*, 4 (1883), pp. 266-274 ; C. Robert, *Archaeologische Maerchen*, pp. 160-178 ; Baumeister's *Denkmäler*, p. 1401 *sq.* ; Furtwängler, in Roscher's *Lexikon*, 1. p. 1360 *sq.* ; *id.*, *Meisterwerke d. griech. Plastik*, pp. 540-546.

The inscribed base of a statue of a certain Thrasymachus by Praxiteles was found at *Lefka* on the site of Thespiae, and is now in the museum at *Eremokastro*. See *C. I. G. G. S.* 1. No. 1831 ; Dodwell, *Tour*, 2. p. 513 ; Leake, *Northern Greece*, 2. pl. xvii. No. 77 ; Cauer, *Delectus Inscr. Graec.*[2] No. 345 ; Collitz, *G. D. I.* 1. No. 855 ; Loewy, *Inschriften griech. Bildhauer*, No. 76.

27. 4. Caius —— was despatched etc. As to Caligula's death, see Suetonius, *Caligula*, 56 and 58.

27. 4. a copy, by the Athenian Menodorus. Pliny (*Nat. hist.* xxxiv. 91) mentions a Menodorus in a list of sculptors who made figures of athletes, armed men, hunters, and sacrificers. " But as Pliny's list of artists seems to break off in the Augustan age, the Menodorus of Pausanias could be the same with the Menodorus of Pliny only on the supposition that in Caligula's time the Thespians had replaced the lost statue by a previously-existing copy " (Brunn, *Gesch. d. griech. Künstler*, 1. p. 556).

27. 5. an Aphrodite. Prof. Furtwängler conjectures that the statue of Aphrodite known as the Venus of Arles, now in the Louvre, may be a copy of Praxiteles's statue of Aphrodite at Thespiae. The right arm and the left hand of the statue are restored ; but the goddess seems to have been represented looking at herself in a mirror which she held in her left hand, while with her right hand she arranged her hair. The lower half of the body only is draped. A replica of the statue, though only a torso, was found near the choregic monument of Lysicrates at Athens. See Müller-Wieseler, *Denkmäler*, 2. pl. xxv. No. 271 ; Bernoulli, *Aphrodite*, p. 180 *sqq.* ; Friederichs-Wolters, *Gipsabgüsse*, No. 1456 ; Furtwängler, *Meisterwerke d. griech. Plastik*, pp. 546-549.

27. 5. an Aphrodite and a statue of Phryne. If we may trust Alciphron, the statue of Phryne stood between the images of Aphrodite and Love (*Epistolae*, Fragm. 3. p. 157 *sq.*, ed. Seiler). Cp. Plutarch, *Amatorius*, ix. 10.

27. 5. a small temple of the Muses. We have seen (p. 140 *sq.*) that in 1890 Mr. Jamot discovered the foundations of this temple in the middle of the old fortified enclosure at Thespiae. The temple is identified by an inscribed base found in its original position. See *Bulletin de Corresp. hellénique*, 15 (1891), p. 659.

27. 6. a sanctuary of Hercules. Near Leuctra an altar was found with an inscription setting forth that it had been dedicated to Hercules by a certain Philinus in consequence of a dream (*C. I. G. G. S.* 1. No. 1829).

27. 6. A virgin acts as his priestess till her death. Chastity seems to have been often required of the ministers of Hercules. Cp. vii. 24. 4 note. In Phocis there was a sanctuary of Hercules the Woman-hater. The man who acted as his priest had to remain chaste during his year of office; hence elderly men were generally appointed. See Plutarch, *De Pythiae oraculis*, 20.

27. 6. the fifty daughters of Thestius. Cp. iii. 19. 5. The father of these damsels is called Thestius also by Herodorus, cited by Athenaeus (xiii. p. 556 f); but he is called Thespius by Diodorus (iv. 29). Apollodorus in one passage (ii. 4. 9) calls him Thestius, but elsewhere (ii. 7. 6 and 8) Thespius. According to Apollodorus (ii. 4. 10) Hercules's intercourse with the daughters of Thestius took place in fifty nights; according to Herodorus (*l.c.*) in seven. The names of Hercules's sons by the daughters of Thestius are given by Apollodorus (ii. 7. 8). There were statues of the Thespiades or daughters of Thespius (Thestius) at Rome near the temple of Felicitas (Pliny, *Nat. hist.* xxxvi. 39). On two statuettes, which it has been proposed to refer to the story of Hercules and the daughters of Thestius, see *Gazette archéologique*, 3 (1877), pp. 168-171, with pl. 26; *id.*, 4 (1878), p. 14 *sq.* The first of the two stories here told by Pausanias implies that Hercules's sons by the daughters of Thestius were 49 in number; the second story (§ 7) implies that they were 52. On the other hand Diodorus (iv. 29) and Apollodorus (ii. 7. 6) give the number as 50.

27. 8. sanctuaries at Erythrae —— and at Tyre etc. As to the sanctuary of Hercules at Erythrae, see vii. 5. 5 *sqq.* As to the sanctuaries of Hercules (Melcart) at Tyre, see Herodotus, ii. 44 with Wiedemann's notes. Cp. Movers, *Die Phoenizier*, 1. p. 385 *sqq.*; Preller, *Griech. Mythologie*,³ 2. p. 167 *sqq.*

27. 8. the sanctuary of Mycalessian Demeter etc. See ix. 19. 5.

28. 1. Helicon. Mt. Helicon, in the wider sense, comprised the group of mountains which stretches from the Copaic plain on the north to the Corinthian gulf on the south, and from the neighbourhood of Thespiae on the east to the neighbourhood of Parnassus on the west. In its narrower sense the name Helicon seems to have designated the peak now called *Zagara* (5019 feet). The highest peak of the group is *Palaeo-Vouna* (5738 feet), to the south-west of *Zagara*, but not visible from Thespiae. The outlines of Helicon are beautiful and the mountain is still well wooded, at least on its northern slopes. Between Carmon and Ascra I passed through a considerable extent of thick oak coppice. The higher slopes are wooded with firs. See H. N. Ulrichs, *Reisen und Forschungen*, 2. p. 83; Vischer, *Erinnerungen*, p. 555; Bursian, *Geogr.* 1. p. 194 *sq.*; Baedeker,³ p. 170 *sq.* The woods of Helicon, to which

Pausanias refers, seem to have been famous in antiquity.   Cp. Horace, *Odes*, i. 12. 5; *id.*, *Epist.* ii. 1. 218; Solinus, vii. 22; Ovid, *Metam.* v. 265.

28. 1. the wild strawberry bushes.   Clarke observed the strawberry bush at the monastery of St. Nicholas on Helicon (*Travels*, 4. p. 98), and Leake found it growing on a southern spur of Mt. Helicon, to the west of the monastery of St. Taxiarches.   As to the fruit he says : "At the best, however, they may be compared to a very insipid strawberry, and are admissible only to the table at a season when no other fruit is to be had" (*Northern Greece*, 2. p. 516 *sq.*)   The arbutus or strawberry bush is common in Greece and grows to some height.   The fruit, which ripens in autumn, resembles in appearance a small strawberry.   I found it not unpalatable.

28. 1. the herbs and roots that grow on the mountain etc. Helicon was famous for its herbs, especially for its black hellebore (Pliny, *Nat. hist.* xxv. 49).   Hellebore, called by the modern Greeks *skarphē*, still grows commonly on *Palaeo-Vouna*, the highest mountain of the Helicon group.   The peasants of *Palaeo-Vouna* apply it externally to sores and ulcers.   See H. N. Ulrichs, *Reisen und Forschungen*, 2. p. 100.

28. 1. a Libyan of the race of the Psyllians.   The Psyllians, a tribe of Northern Africa, on the shore of the Greater Syrtis, were supposed to possess the power of alleviating by their touch or by suction persons who had been bitten by serpents.   A similar power was claimed by, or ascribed to, the Marsians in Italy and the people called Ophiogenes ('serpent-born') in Cyprus and at Parium on the Hellespont.   See Pliny, *Nat. hist.* xxviii. 30; Strabo, xiii. p. 588.   It is said that Octavius made use of these Psyllians in an attempt to restore Cleopatra to life (Dio Cassius, li. 14).   The Psyllians are related to have exposed their new-born children to serpents to see whether the children were legitimate or not; if the children were legitimate, the serpents did them no harm (Varro, in Priscian, x. 32, vol. 1. p. 524, ed. Keil; Pliny, *Nat. hist.* vii. 14; Dio Cassius, *l.c.*)

28. 3. The balsam-trees.   As to the balsam, see Pliny, *Nat. hist.* xii. 111 *sqq.*   According to Pliny it was found only in Judaea.

29. 1. Hegesinus —— in his Atthis.   This poem is not mentioned by any other ancient writer.   Cp. Welcker, *Der epische Cyclus*, 1. p. 320.

29. 2. Callipus of Corinth.   This writer is mentioned again by Pausanias (ix. 38. 10).   Nothing more is known of him.

29. 2. Ascra.   The scanty ruins of Ascra occupy the summit of a high conical hill, forming part of Mt. Helicon, though separated from the main mass of that mountain on the south and west by the Valley of the Muses.   The hill is stony and rugged; its sides are here and there overgrown with low bushes.   Strabo has correctly described the situation of Ascra.   He says (ix. p. 409): "In the territory of Thespiae, towards Mt. Helicon, is Ascra, the fatherland of Hesiod; it is on the right of Helicon, situated on a high and rugged place, distant about 40 furlongs from Thespiae."   The solitary tower mentioned by Pausanias still crowns the summit of the hill. It is a large structure, about 11 paces square, built of squared blocks, well jointed and laid in horizontal courses, of which thirteen are preserved. The conical hill of Ascra, surmounted by its tower, is a very conspicuous object from a distance, and is in fact one of the landmarks of Central Boeotia. The whole hill is now known as *Pyrgaki* or ' turret.' There are some vestiges of the walls which enclosed the summit of the hill, forming a small acropolis. Hesiod described Ascra as "a wretched village, bad in winter, disagreeable in summer, good at no time" (*Works and Days,* 639 *sq.*) Cp. Plutarch, *Comment. in Hes.* 35. The disagreeableness of Ascra as a residence "may have been caused by the confined circuit of its walls, the abruptness of the hill, and the proximity of the great summits of Helicon, rendering the winter long and severe, and in summer excluding the refreshing breezes of the west. Ascra, however, is surrounded by beautiful scenery, with delightful summer-retreats, and with fertile plains, enjoying a mild climate during the winter ; and it was less, perhaps, upon its intrinsic defects, than upon a comparison of it with the delightful Asiatic Aeolis, from whence his family came, that Hesiod founded his condemnation of Ascra " (Leake, *Northern Greece,* 2. p. 491 *sq.*) However, the summit of the hill is exposed to every wind that blows, and in winter the whole neighbourhood as far as Thespiae and even farther is said to be often buried under deep snow for weeks together. See H. N. Ulrichs, *Reisen und Forschungen,* 2. p. 94 *sq.*; Welcker, *Tagebuch,* 2. pp. 34-37 ; Vischer, *Erinnerungen,* p. 555; Bursian, *Geogr.* 1. p. 237 ; A. Conze, in *Philologus,* 19 (1863), p. 181 ; Baedeker,[3] p. 171 *sq.* ; *Guide-Joanne,* 2. p. 130.

29. 2. **the Muses were three in number.** This was the view of Ephorus and Varro (Arnobius, *Adversus Nationes,* iii. 37 ; Servius, on Virgil, *Ecl.* vii. 21). Cp. Diodorus, iv. 7. 2 ; Cornutus, *De natura deorum* 14, p. 15, ed. C. Lang ; Kalkmann, *Pausanias der Perieget,* p. 258 ; E. Maass, *Aratea,* p. 211 *sqq.* On the Muses see Fr. Roediger, 'Die Musen, eine mythologische Abhandlung,' in *Fleckeisen's Jahrbücher,* Supplem. 8 (1875-1876), pp. 251-290. On the representation of the Muses in ancient art see Oscar Bie, *Die Musen in der antiken Kunst* (Berlin, 1887).

29. 4. **Mimnermus —— says that the elder Muses are daughters of Sky.** According to a scholiast on Pindar (*Nem.* iii. 16), Mimnermus, Alcman, and Aristarchus held that the Muse (singular) was a daughter of Sky. Mnaseas said that the Muses were daughters of Earth and Sky (Arnobius, *Adversus Nationes,* iii. 37). Cp. Diodorus, iv. 7. 1 ; Cornutus, *De natura deorum* 14, p. 18, ed. C. Lang ; Kalkmann, *Pausanias der Perieget,* p. 258 *sq.* ; E. Maass, *Aratea,* p. 212 *sq.*

29, 5. **the grove of the Muses.** The grove of the Muses lay at the northern foot of Mount Helicon in a valley which is traversed by a stream (probably the ancient Termesus) flowing from west to east. Towards its western end the valley contracts, being hemmed in between the steep lofty and wooded slopes of Helicon on the south and another rugged but less lofty mountain on the north. The saddle which joins

the two mountains bounds the Valley of the Muses on the west. A
fine view of the valley is to be had from a ruined mediaeval tower
which surmounts a rocky hill of no great height on the northern side
of the vale about midway between Ascra and the village of *Palaeo-
Panagia.* Across the valley to the south rise the steep slopes of
Helicon, rocky below and wooded with pines above. In a glen at the
foot of these great declivities are seen the trees that hide the secluded
monastery of St. Nicholas, below which dark myrtle-bushes extend far
down the slope. At the head of the valley in the west the serrated top
of Helicon (*Zagara*) is seen foreshortened, and a little on this side
of the highest point appears the monastery of *Zagara*, delightfully
situated on a woody slope that falls away into the sequestered valley
where stand the two villages also called *Zagara*. To the left of the
summit the snowy top of Parnassus just shows itself in the distance.
In the nearer foreground, on the hither side of the valley, the conical
hill of Ascra, crowned with its ruined tower, stands out boldly. Vineyards cover the gently-swelling hills on the northern side of the vale,
and down the middle of it the brook *Archontitza* (probably the ancient
Termesus or Permessus), fed by many springs, flows through fields of
maize and corn.

In this sheltered valley, hidden among fine trees, are or were till
lately the ruins of several churches containing remains of antiquity.
One of them — the church of the Holy Trinity (*Hagia Triada*) —
occupied the site of the temple of the Muses. The place is on the
south side of the Termesus, about an hour's walk to the west of the
village of *Palaeo-Panagia*. The platform (*crepidoma*) on which the
temple rested was excavated by Mr. Stamatakes for the Greek Archaeological Society in 1882. It is built of large and well-smoothed blocks
of stone. Further excavations were begun by Mr. P. Jamot of the
French School in October 1888 and were continued by him in 1889
and 1890. He has not yet (December 1896) published the full results
of his researches.

The temple occupied exactly the site of the ruined church, which had
to be entirely removed in the course of the excavations. It measured
12.50 metres in length by 6.50 metres in breadth, and had four Ionic
columns at each of the narrow ends, but no columns at the sides. Thus
it resembled the temple of Victory on the Acropolis at Athens. Apparently it lacked both a fore-temple (*pronaos*) and a back-chamber (*opisthodomos*). The entrance was from the west. The pavement consisted
of slabs of white marble. In Roman times the temple was rebuilt and
widened, so as to form a square of 12.50 metres on each side. Facing
the west end of the temple was an Ionic colonnade 100 metres long,
beside which many bronze objects were found. Amongst the numerous
inscriptions discovered on the site are two dedications of statues erected
by the Thespians to Sulla and Agrippa. Considerable remains have
also been found of a very large pedestal which had clearly supported
statues of the nine Muses dedicated by the people of Thespiae. The
name of each Muse was inscribed separately with an elegiac distich
in the Ionic dialect beneath it ; the verses were composed by a man

named Honestus. Remains, more or less complete, of eight of these inscriptions have been found. See *C. I. G. G. S.* 1. Nos. 1796-1805. Other inscriptions record the dedication of land to the Heliconian Muses by Philetaerus of Pergamus, son of Attalus I. (*C. I. G. G. S.* 1. Nos. 1788-1790).

About five (or fifteen) minutes higher up are the remains of a theatre, which were first observed by Mr. Stamatakes in 1882. The stage has since been excavated by Mr. Jamot. The theatre occupied a conspicuous situation, and the spectators must have enjoyed a splendid view over a great part of Boeotia. The orchestra is reported to have been circular. The stage was 18.10 metres wide, and was adorned with fourteen half-columns of the Doric order, which are still in their places. (According to another account, there were only thirteen of these half-columns, and only seven of them have been found.) The diameter of the columns is 0.30 metre (about 1 foot); their height (exclusive of the capital) is 2.06 metres (6 ft. 7 in.); the distance between them is 0.88 metre (about 2 ft. 8 in.)

Amphion of Thespiae wrote a work, in at least two books, on the sanctuary of the Muses on Mt. Helicon (Athenaeus, xiv. p. 629 a). The sanctuary is said to have been visited by Apollonius of Tyana (Philostratus, *Vit. Apollon.* iv. 24).

See Wheler, *Journey into Greece*, p. 476; E. D. Clarke, *Travels*, 4. pp. 91-106; Leake, *Northern Greece*, 2. pp. 488-500; H. N. Ulrichs, *Reisen und Forschungen*, 2. pp. 88-97; Welcker, *Tagebuch*, 2. p. 37 *sq.*; Vischer, *Erinnerungen*, p. 554 *sq.*; Conze and Michaelis, in *Annali dell' Instituto*, 33 (1861), p. 86 *sqq.*; Conze, in *Philologus*, 19 (1863), p. 180 *sqq.*; Stamatakes, in Πρακτικὰ τῆς Ἀρχαιολογικῆς Ἑταιρίας for 1882, p. 66 *sq.*; Δελτίον ἀρχαιολογικόν, 4 (1888), pp. 182 *sq.*, 204 *sq.*; *id.*, 5 (1889), p. 107; *Bulletin de Corresp. hellénique*, 3 (1879), pp. 442-448; *id.*, 14 (1890), pp. 546-551; *id.*, 15 (1891), pp. 381-403; *Journal of Hellenic Studies*, 10 (1889), p. 273; *American Journal of Archaeology*, 5 (1889), p. 106; *Revue archéologique*, 3rd series, 14 (1889), p. 109; *Mittheil. d. arch. Inst. in Athen*, 14 (1889), p. 328; *Berliner philologische Wochenschrift*, 9 (1889), p. 74; Baedeker,³ p. 172; *Guide-Joanne*, 2. p. 30; cp. H. N. Ulrichs, *Reisen und Forschungen*, 2. p. 96. It is to be regretted that in the eight years which have elapsed since his excavations Mr. Jamot has not found leisure to publish an account, however brief, of the temple and theatre. I did not visit the site, and the second-hand reports of the excavations which are alone accessible to me are exceedingly meagre and to some extent discrepant.

29. 5. **the spring Aganippe.** The middle of the Valley of the Muses between the village of *Palaeo-Panagia* and Ascra (*Pyrgaki*) is watered by a torrent now called the *Archontitza* which is probably the Termesus or Permessus of the ancients (see below). From the left bank of the torrent, midway between *Palaeo-Panagia* and *Pyrgaki*, there issues a fine perennial source of water; many squared blocks lie around it. Leake thought that this source might be Aganippe. More probably, however, Aganippe is to be identified with a very picturesque spring of clear water which bubbles from the rock under shady trees near the deserted monastery of St. Nicholas. The monastery, which is sometimes inhabited by a solitary monk, stands in a beautiful theatre-shaped dale, close under the towering heights of Helicon (Mt. *Zagara*). A grove of pine, walnut, plane, olive, and fig-trees, mixed with myrtle,

bay and oleander, surrounds the monastery; and a constant verdure is maintained here in summer by the abundant water of the spring, which flows down the valley northward to join the Termesus. The situation of the spring accords well with Pausanias's description, from which we gather that Aganippe was not on the direct road from Thespiae to the grove of the Muses, but at a little distance to the left, that is (in this case) to the south of the road. The spring is often mentioned by Roman writers (Virgil, *Ecl.* x. 12; Ovid, *Metam.* v. 311 *sq.*; Juvenal, vii. 6; Pliny, *Nat. hist.* iv. 25; Solinus, vii. 22).

See E. D. Clarke, *Travels*, 4. pp. 97 *sq.*, 105; Leake, *Northern Greece*, 2. p. 493 *sq.*; H. N. Ulrichs, *Reisen und Forschungen*, 2. p. 88 *sqq.*; Vischer, *Erinnerungen*, p. 554; Bursian, *Geogr.* 1. p. 239; Conze and Michaelis, in *Annali dell' Instituto*, 33 (1861), p. 88 *sq.*; Conze, in *Philologus*, 19 (1863), p. 182 *sqq.*; Baedeker,[3] p. 172; *Guide-Joanne*, 2. p. 30.

29. 5. the Termesus. The Termesus or Permessus, as it is called by Strabo and in some MSS. of Hesiod, is mentioned by Hesiod as a stream or river of Helicon (*Theog.* 5). Strabo tells us (ix. p. 407) that it flowed from Helicon into the Copaic Lake near Haliartus. Hence Leake and Bursian identified it with the considerable stream which flows from Helicon about half an hour to the east of Haliartus. But Callimachus (cited by Servius, on Virgil, *Ecl.* x. 12) says that the Permessus had its source in the spring Aganippe, from which it is natural to infer that the Permessus or Termesus is the stream *Archontitza* which flows eastward through the Valley of the Muses and receives the water of Aganippe (the spring of St. Nicholas) from the south. Farther to the east this stream passes the village of *Neochori* on the right (south), and flows for three miles in the direction of Plataea. Then it takes a sudden turn to the south-west, and dividing the roots of Mt. *Korombili* from those of Helicon follows a nearly westerly course till it is lost in the plain of Thisbe, near *Dombrena*. Thus the stream flows round three sides of Mount Helicon, the north, the east, and the south, which tallies well with Pausanias's statement that the Termesus flowed round Helicon. Moreover, the fable that Aganippe was a daughter of Termesus points to the Termesus being the stream into which Aganippe flowed rather than a stream with which the spring Aganippe has no connexion.

See Wheler, *Journey into Greece*, p. 476; E. D. Clarke, *Travels*, 4. p. 101; Leake, *Northern Greece*, 2. p. 496 *sqq.*; H. N. Ulrichs, *Reisen und Forschungen*, 2. p. 92 *sq.*; Bursian, *Geogr.* 1. p. 233; Conze and Michaelis, in *Annali dell' Instituto*, 33 (1861), p. 89; Conze, in *Philologus*, 19 (1863), p. 183.

29. 5. Eupheme —— the Muses' nurse. She is mentioned as the Muses' nurse also by Eratosthenes (*Catasterismi*, 28) and Hyginus (*Astronomica*, 27).

29. 7. Linus —— Maneros. See Brugsch, *Adonisklage und Linoslied;* Buchsenschutz, in *Philologus*, 8 (1853), pp. 577-589; W. Mannhardt, *Mythologische Forschungen*, p. 1 *sqq.*; *The Golden Bough*, I. p. 363 *sqq.*

29. 7. the song of Linus. See *Iliad*, xviii. 569 *sqq.*

29. 9. **Linus —— was a teacher of music.** In a vase-painting
Linus is represented teaching Iphicles, the half-brother of Hercules, to
play on the lyre, while behind Iphicles stands Hercules, with a somewhat disdainful expression, holding an arrow in his right hand.   Behind
Hercules stands a wizen-faced person with a lyre, whom Mr. Helbig
explains to be an eunuch instigating Hercules to murder Linus.   See W.
Helbig, ' Il mito di Lino su vaso Ceretano,' *Annali dell' Instituto*, 43
(1871), pp. 86-96, tav. d' agg. F.

30. I. **images of all the Muses.**   The bronze images of the
Muses were carried off from Helicon by Constantine and placed in his
palace at Constantinople (Sozomenus, *Hist. Eccles.* ii. 5 ; Eusebius,
Vit. Constantini, iii. 54 ; Nicephorus Callistus, *Eccles. Hist.* viii. 33).

30. I. **Cephisodotus.**   See note on viii. 30. 10.

30. I. **Strongylion.**   See note on i. 23. 8.

30. I. **a bronze Apollo fighting with Hermes for the lyre.**   In
the course of his excavations at the sanctuary of the Muses, Mr. Jamot
discovered a very fine bronze arm, a little larger than life-size, two
bronze feet, and other fragments of bronze.   Mr. Jamot argues that
these are fragments of the group described by Pausanias ; the arm,
according to him, is that of Apollo, whom he supposes to have been
represented sitting with a lyre on his knees.   But the fragments are
too scanty to enable us to decide the question.   See P. Jamot, in
Bulletin de Corresp. hellénique, 15 (1891), pp. 381-401.   The fight
between Apollo and Hermes for the possession of the lyre seems not
to be mentioned by any other ancient writer ; but in a vase-painting
Apollo is represented fleeing with the lyre, while Hermes holds him
by the arm.   See Panofka, in *Annali dell' Instituto*, 2 (1830), p. 191 ;
Jamot, *op. cit.* p. 400 ; Overbeck, *Griechische Kunstmythologie*, 4. p.
419 *sq.*

30. 2. **Pindar's poem on him.**   Plutarch also tells us (*De musica*,
8) that Pindar mentioned Sacadas.

30. 3. **Hesiod, too, is seated** etc.   On supposed portraits of Hesiod
in existing monuments of ancient art, see Panofka, in *Archäologische
Zeitung*, 8 (1856), p. 253 *sq.*   The poet is mentioned in a metrical
inscription found on the site of the Grove of the Muses (*Bulletin de
Corresp. hellénique*, 14 (1890), pp. 546-551 ; *C. I. G. G. S.* 1. No.
4240).   Another inscription, found at *Vaia*, near Thespiae, proves that
a society for the worship of the Muses of Hesiod owned land on or near
Mount Helicon (*C. I. G. G. S.* 1. No. 1785).

30. 3. **he sang with a laurel wand in his hand.**   See Hesiod,
Theog. 30.   Cp. Panofka, in *Archäologische Zeitung*, 8 (1856), p. 254 *sq.*

30. 4. **Orpheus, the Thracian.**   On the relation of Orpheus to
the Thracians, see A. Riese, ' Orpheus und die mythischen Thraker,'
Fleckeisen's Jahrbücher, 23 (1877), pp. 225-240.   On Orpheus generally, see Gerhard, ' Orpheus und die Orphiker,' *Abhandlungen* of the
Berlin Academy, 1861, Phil. hist. Abth., pp. 9-95 ; E. Maass, *Orpheus*
(München, 1895).   In the popular songs of the modern Bulgarians
there is said to figure a musician named Orfen, who sings and plays so
sweetly that the birds and ravenous beasts come from the mountains to

hear him.   Hence it has been conjectured that this Orfen is Orpheus, and it is held by some that the present Bulgarian inhabitants of the Rhodope mountains are descendants of the ancient Thracians, who, though they have been affected by Slavonic influence, have preserved the poetical traditions, mythology, and religious customs of their ancestors.   See Geitler, 'Die Sage von Orpheus-Orfen der Rhodope-Bulgaren,' *Mittheilungen der anthropolog. Gesell. in Wien*, 10 (1881), pp. 165-196.

30. 4. beasts —— listening to his song.   A list of the existing works of ancient art (marbles, gems, coins, mosaics, etc.), which have for their subject the beasts listening to Orpheus, is given by Stephani in the *Compte-Rendu* (St. Petersburg) for 1881, p. 98 *sqq.*   None of these works of art seems to date from before the beginning of our era.

30. 4. he went alive to hell to beg his wife from the nether gods etc.   A story like that of Orpheus and Eurydice was told by the Huron Indians of North America to one of the Jesuit fathers.   An Indian lost a beloved sister by death and went to the village of souls to seek for and bring her back.   He succeeded in securing her soul in one gourd and her brain in another, and was told that to bring his sister to life he must go to the graveyard, take up her body, and carry it to his hut ; here he was to assemble his friends for a festival and in their presence to carry his sister's body round the hut, holding in his hands the two gourds.   As soon as he had done this, his sister would come to life, provided that all the guests kept their eyes fixed on the ground and did not look at what he was doing.   The man did as he was bid ; he had almost carried the corpse round the hut and he already felt it beginning to move, when one of the guests, out of curiosity, looked up at him.   Immediately his sister's soul fled, and he had to carry back her mouldering body to the grave.   See *Relations des Jésuites*, 1636, p. 105 *sq.* (Canadian reprint) ; Lafitau, *Mœurs des sauvages amériquains*, 1. p. 402 *sqq.* ; H. de Charencey, *Le folklore dans les deux Mondes* (Paris, 1894), p. 286 *sqq.*   In various islands of the Pacific (the Pelew Islands, Hawaii, and Mangaia) stories are told of a husband who went to the land of the dead to fetch back his wife to the world of the living.   See A. Bastian, *Allerlei aus Volks- und Menschenkunde*, I. pp. 8, 111 *sq.* ; Gills, *Myths and Songs of the South Pacific*, p. 221 *sqq.*

30. 5. the Thracian women plotted his death etc.   The murder of Orpheus is the subject of vase-paintings.   See *Annali dell' Instituto*, I (1829), pp. 265-269 ; *id.*, 43 (1871), pp. 126-130.   The Thracian women are said to have been tattooed by their husbands for their cruelty to Orpheus (Phanocles, quoted by Stobaeus, *Florilegium*, vol. 2. p. 387, ed. Meineke) ; and in some vase-paintings of the death of Orpheus the Thracian women are represented with tattoo-marks on their arms (*Monumenti Inediti*, i. pl. 5 ; *Annali dell' Instituto*, 43 (1871), p. 127).   On tattooing among the ancients, see Bähr on Herodotus, v. 6 ; Martius, *Zur Ethnographie Amerika's*, p. 55 note ; Lafitau, *Mœurs des sauvages amériquains*, 2. p. 38 *sqq.*

30. 6. Aornum in Thesprotis —— an oracle of the dead.   See notes on i. 17. 5 (vol. 2. p. 161) and iii. 17. 9.

31. 1. **Arsinoe —— carried by a bronze ostrich.** Eight pairs of ostriches figured in the grand procession which Arsinoe's husband Ptolemy Philadelphus exhibited at Alexandria (Athenaeus, v. p. 200 f). Catullus (lxvi. 54) speaks of Arsinoe's "winged horse," which may perhaps be a poetical expression for an ostrich.

31. 2. **a deer suckling the infant Telephus.** See viii. 54. 6. The subject is represented on coins, gems, etc. (O. Jahn, *Archäologische Aufsätze*, p. 160 *sqq.* ; Baumeister's *Denkmäler*, p. 1724).

31. 3. **Of the tripods that stand on Helicon** etc. A mutilated inscription, found in the sanctuary of the Muses on Mount Helicon, seems to have recorded the dedication of a tripod to the Heliconian Muses by the Boeotians (*C. I. G. G. S.* 1. No. 1795).

31. 3. **which Hesiod is said to have received at Chalcis** etc. Hesiod himself tells how he won the tripod at Chalcis and dedicated it to the Muses of Helicon (*Works and Days*, 650-659). But the passage is thought by some to be spurious.

31. 3. **games, called the Musaea.** The games held on Mount Helicon in honour of the Muses are seldom mentioned by ancient writers. A certain Nicocrates wrote a work in at least two books on the subject (Schol. on Homer, *Il.* xiii. 21). Plutarch tells us that they were held every fourth year (*Amatorius*, 1) ; and a certain Amphion of Thespiae, who published a work in at least two books on the sanctuary of the Muses on Helicon, recorded that solemn dances used to be held in the sanctuary, perhaps as part of the games (Athenaeus, xiv. p. 629 a). On the other hand, inscriptions found on Mount Helicon and at Thespiae throw a good deal more light on the history and character of the games. From them we learn that about the middle of the third century B.C. the games were reorganised and placed on a new footing ; the date of their original institution is unknown. They were held (as Plutarch also tells us) every fourth year, and the prizes awarded were crowns, not money. The ceremonies began with a solemn sacrifice offered to the Muses by the Thespians and the delegates of the societies of artists. In the third century B.C., at the time of their reorganisation, the games were held in the name of the city of Thespiae and of the Boeotian confederacy jointly, and they consisted exclusively of musical and poetical contests. But about the middle of the second century B.C. a fresh reform of the games took place ; dramatic contests were added to the list of competitions, and the games were now held in the name of Thespiae alone, the Boeotian confederacy having ceased to exist. The old competitions had been in epic poetry, flute-playing, lyre-playing, and singing to the accompaniment of the lyre and flute, to which the recitation of poetry (rhapsody) had been subsequently added. The contests added in the second century B.C. comprised trumpet-playing ; heraldry ; the composition of processional hymns, satyric dramas, tragedies and comedies ; and the acting of plays, both tragic and comic, both old and new. The reform thus instituted appears to have lasted at least a century, that is, to the middle of the first century B.C. But from that date until the second half of the second century A.D. the inscriptions fail us. Whether this is merely an accident, or whether the games actually fell into abeyance for a time, we cannot say.   Certainly they seem to have been celebrated in Plutarch's lifetime, and inscriptions show that in the second half of the second century A.D., when Pausanias wrote, they were in a very flourishing condition.   Among the new competitions mentioned in inscriptions of that period are the composition of panegyrics and poems on the emperor and on the Muses, and flute-playing as an accompaniment of choirs or dances.   The games continued to be held as late certainly as the first half of the third century A.D., for an inscription of that date (*C. I. G. G. S.* 1. No. 1776; *C. I. G.* No. 1586) gives a list of the victors in the games, but the number of competitions by that time was woefully diminished.   The composition of poetry, in particular, whether epic, dramatic, or lyric, seems to have disappeared from the list.

See P. Jamot, in 'Les jeux en l'honneur des Muses,' *Bulletin de Corresp. hellénique,* 19 (1895), pp. 321-366.   Cp. Reisch, *De musicis Graecorum certaminibus,* pp. 57, 106, 120 *sq.*; *C. I. G. G. S.* 1. Nos. 1735, 1760, 1774, 1775, 1776, 1819.

31. 3. games in honour of Love.   These games were called Erotidia or Erotica and were held by the Thespians every fourth year. See Athenaeus, xiii. p. 561 e; Plutarch, *Amatorius,* i.   As Pausanias mentions them in connexion with the games in honour of the Muses which were held in the sanctuary of the Muses on Helicon, we might infer that the games in honour of Love were also celebrated in that sanctuary; but from Plutarch (*Amatorius,* ii. 1-4) we gather that they were held in Thespiae; for he tells how certain persons, who had come to Thespiae to be present at the festival, were bored by a musical competition and retreated from the city to the stillness and seclusion of the grove of the Muses on Helicon.   The games in honour of Love are mentioned in a few inscriptions (*C. I. G. G. S.* 1. Nos. 48, 1857, 2517, 2518), from one of which we gather that they included boxing.   This confirms the statement of Pausanias that the games included athletic as well as musical competitions.   Hence the inscriptions containing lists of victors in athletic and equestrian contests which have been found in or near Thespiae (*C. I. G. G. S.* 1. Nos. 1764, 1765, 1766, 1769, 1770, 1772; *Bulletin de Corresp. hellénique,* 19 (1895), p. 369 *sq.*) probably refer to the games in honour of Love, since the games in honour of the Muses did not include athletic and equestrian competitions.   The inscriptions in question mention the customary athletic contests—running, wrestling, boxing, the pancratium, the pentathlum, the torch-race, etc., as well as horse-races and chariot-races.   They are all, however, fragmentary, so that we cannot make up from them a complete list of the various contests in the Erotidia.   In only one of them (*C. I. G. G. S.* 1. No. 1772) is there mention of a poetical contest; but this certainly does not justify Mr. Jamot in endeavouring to explain away Pausanias's statement that the Erotidia included musical as well as athletic competitions, especially as Pausanias's statement is confirmed by the evidence of Plutarch (*Amatorius,* ii. 4).   See P. Jamot, 'Les jeux en l'honneur d'Eros,' *Bulletin de Corresp. hellénique,* 19 (1895), pp. 366-374.

31. 3. the Horse's Fount (Hippocrene). To reach the far-famed Hippocrene ('the Horse's Fount') from the sanctuary of the Muses we ascend the steep eastern side of Mt. Helicon (*Zagara*), over moss-grown rocks, through a thick forest of tall firs. After a toilsome ascent of about two hours we emerge from the wood upon a tiny open glade of circular shape, covered with loose stones and overgrown with grass and ferns. All around rises the dark fir-wood. Here, in the glade, is Hippocrene, now called *Kryopegadi* or 'cold spring.' It is a well with a triangular opening, enclosed by ancient masonry. The clear, ice-cold water stands at a depth of about 10 feet below the coping of the well. But it is possible to climb down to the water by means of foot-holes cut in the side, or by holding on to the sturdy ivy, which, growing from a rock in the water, mantles the sides of the well. The coldness and clearness of the water of this perennial spring are famous in the neighbourhood, especially among the herdsmen, who love to fill their skin-bottles at it.

A hundred paces or so higher up, to the east, is the summit of Mt. Helicon (*Zagara*). Exactly on the summit surrounded by fir-trees, which interrupt the wide prospect on all sides, is a little roofless chapel of St. Elias. The walls, constructed of small, well-jointed polygonal stones, probably enclosed the altar of Zeus mentioned by Hesiod (*Theog.* 4).

See H. N. Ulrichs, *Reisen und Forschungen*, 2. pp. 97-99 ; Welcker, *Tage-buch*, 2. p. 38 *sq.* ; Vischer, *Erinnerungen*, p. 556 *sq.* ; Bursian, *Geogr.* 1. p. 239 *sq.* ; Baedeker,[3] p. 172 *sq.* ; *Guide-Joanne*, 2. p. 30.

31. 4. a leaden tablet —— on which are engraved the Works. For another example of books written on sheets of metal, see iv. 26. 8. A good many inscribed rolls of lead have been found in tombs in Cyprus ; but for the most part they contain either monetary accounts or else curses levelled at some enemy. See J. H. Middleton, *Illuminated manuscripts in classical and mediaeval times*, p. 2 *sq.*

31. 5. the poem on women, the poem called the Great Eoeae. See i. 3. 1, ii. 2. 3, with the notes.

31. 5. the poem on the soothsayer Melampus. It was called *Melampodia* and consisted of at least three books. See Athenaeus, xi. p. 498 a, xiii. p. 608 e ; Tzetzes, *Schol. on Lycophron*, 682, 683 ; *Epicorum Graecorum fragmenta*, ed. Kinkel, p. 151 *sqq.*

31. 5. the Precepts of Chiron. A scholiast on Pindar (*Pyth.* vi. 19) quotes three lines from this poem, which he says was by some attributed to Hesiod. According to Quintilian (*Inst. Or.* i. 1. 15), the grammarian Aristophanes was the first to deny that *The Precepts* was by Hesiod. Cp. *Epicorum Graecorum fragmenta*, ed. Kinkel, pp. 148-150

31. 5. the descent of Theseus and Pirithous to hell. For a list of the ancient monuments on which this subject is represented see E. Petersen, in *Archäologische Zeitung*, 35 (1877), pp. 119-123. Cp. x. 29. 9.

31. 6. Opposite accounts are also given of Hesiod's death. The legends as to the death of Hesiod are examined by Mr. O. Friedel, 'Die Sage vom Tode Hesiods,' *Fleckeisen's Jahrbücher*, Supplem. 10 (1878-1879), pp. 235-278.

31. 7. a small river, the Olmius. This stream is mentioned by Hesiod (*Theog.* 6). Strabo says (ix. p. 407) that it was a tributary of the Permessus, which according to him flowed into the Copaic Lake (see ix. 29. 5 note). Leake, however, preferred to suppose that the Olmius is the stream now called the *Archontitza*, which rises in the Valley of the Muses, receives the water of Aganippe, and, skirting the eastern and southern foot of Helicon, flows to the plain of *Dombrena* (Thisbe). Pausanias was apparently ignorant of the situation of the Olmius, for in saying that it was on the very top of Mount Helicon he seems, as Leake pointed out, to have simply misunderstood the passage of Hesiod in which the stream is mentioned. See Leake, *Northern Greece*, 2. pp. 212 *sq.*, 496-499. Cp. H. N. Ulrichs, *Reisen und Forschungen*, 2. p. 93 ; Bursian, *Geogr.* 1. p. 233.

31. 7. Donacon —— and —— Narcissus' spring etc. In the valley which bounds Mt. Helicon on the south-east and separates it from Mt. *Korombili* is the hamlet of *Tateza*. On the opposite side of the rivulet which flows by the village stands a ruined church, built of ancient fragments. Five minutes higher up the stream an abundant spring of clear water gushes from the ground ; it is surrounded by a modern enclosure, of which the materials are ancient squared blocks. In the corn-fields above may be seen many remains of former dwellings. Leake thought that this might be the site of Donacon, and that the fountain might be Narcissus's spring. See Leake, *Northern Greece*, 2. p. 500 *sq.* ; Dodwell, *Tour*, 1. p. 257 ; Bursian, *Geogr.* 1. p. 242.

The story of Narcissus is told somewhat differently by Ovid (*Metam.* iii. 339-510) and Conon (*Narrationes*, 24), who, however, both agree that Narcissus fell in love with his own image reflected in the water of a spring. According to Ovid, the youth gradually faded away and was changed into the flower narcissus ; according to Conon, he slew himself, and the flower sprang from his blood. Of the three versions of the tale that of Ovid is probably nearest to the original, which seems to be based on the widespread superstition that the soul or life is in the reflection or shadow, and hence that it is dangerous for a man to see himself reflected in water, because his soul, being present in the reflection, may be carried off by the monsters or spirits of the water. This is perhaps the explanation of the Pythagorean maxim that a man should not look at his face in water (*Fragmenta Philosoph. Graec.* ed. Mullach, 1. p. 510), and of the Greek superstition that to dream of seeing oneself so reflected was an omen of death (Artemidorus, *Onirocr.* ii. 7). See *The Golden Bough*, 1. pp. 144-148.

In a metrical inscription, found at Thespiae, which records an offering presented to Love by the emperor Hadrian for success in killing a bear, Love is addressed as "the archer son of clear-voiced Cypris, dwelling in Heliconian Thespiae, beside Narcissus's flowery garden" (*C. I. G. G. S.* 1. No. 1828 ; Kaibel, *Epigrammata Graeca*,

No. 811 ; see above, p. 145 *sq.*)   The killing of the bear by Hadrian is mentioned by his biographer Spartianus (*Hadrianus*, 20).

31. 9. The flower narcissus etc.   On the banks of a stream on Mt. Helicon Wheler observed (April 1676) the narcissus in great profusion "and so proliferous, that I had not before seen any the like ; having seven, eight, nine, sometimes ten flowers upon the same stalk, and very fragrant" (*Journey*, p. 479).   Cp. Chandler, *Travels in Greece*, p. 258 *sq.* (who repeats Wheler's statement).

32. 1. Creusis.   Creusis stood on the shore of the deep bay of *Livadostro*, which is bounded on the west by the fine, but barren and rocky mountain chain of *Korombili* (2950 feet).   The ruins of Creusis are close to the foot of the mountains.   Walls and towers and a gate, 10 feet wide, but without flanking towers, may still be clearly traced. The Oeroe flows into the head of the bay.   See Baedeker,[3] p. 179 ; cp. Wheler, *Journey*, p. 472 *sq.* ; Leake, *Northern Greece*, 2. p. 502 *sqq.*; Bursian, *Geogr.* 1. p. 241.   When the Lacedaemonians twice retired from the territory of Thespiae to the Isthmus by Aegosthena, they marched by Creusis : on one of these occasions they experienced the force of the hurricanes of which Pausanias here speaks (Xenophon, *Hellenica*, v. 4. 17 *sq.*, vi. 4. 25 *sq.* : see note on i. 44. 5, 'Aegosthena'). The place is called Creusa (Κρέουσα) by Strabo (ix. p. 405), Ptolemy (iii. 14. 5), and Livy (xliv. 1. 4).

32. 2. Thisbe.   The ruins of Thisbe are to be seen partly on a plateau, partly on a low rocky hill, which rise from a wide open valley or plain on the southern side of Mount Helicon.   The village of *Kakosi* is surrounded by the ruins, lying as it does in the little hollow between the plateau and the hill ; and ten minutes' walk to the east of it is the village of *Dombrena*, which is connected with Thespiae and Thebes by a carriage-road.   If we approach Thisbe from Thespiae by this road, our route lies for some distance between low hills which shut out the view on either side.   Then the valley opens out and we enter on a long gradual descent which continues all the way to *Dombrena*, a distance of a good many miles.   The bottom of the valley, which is fairly wide, is mostly in corn, though in one place the road passes through groves of olives.   On the west rise the steep, high, rather bare slopes of Helicon, while at a greater distance to the east appears Mt. *Korombili*.   Afterwards the valley contracts again into a pass between stony mountains. When the pass ends we see stretched out before us the spacious basin-like valley of Thisbe surrounded by low bare rounded hills on all sides except on the north-west, where the rugged slopes of Mount Helicon tower to a great height.   Thisbe lay on the northern side of the valley, close under the great slopes of Helicon, from which the north wind sometimes sweeps down with great violence.   The bottom of the valley is for the most part a dead flat covered with corn-fields ; but towards the east and south-east there are olive-groves, and in its north-western part, to the south of Thisbe, there are both olive-groves and vineyards.

The most considerable ruins of Thisbe occupy the north-western corner of a plateau, of some extent but no great height, which is defended on the west, north, and east by a line of precipitous rocks but melts gradually away into the plain by a gentle slope on the south. The village of *Kakosi* lies at the northern foot of the plateau, in the hollow between it and the rocky hill on which other remains of the ancient city are to be seen. But that Thisbe comprised not only the hill and the corner of the plateau but also the intermediate hollow now occupied by *Kakosi*, is proved by the remains of finely-constructed fortification-walls which are to be seen in various parts of the village. The villagers distinguish the ruins on the hill from the ruins on the plateau, calling the former *Palaeo-Kastro* ('old castle') and the latter *Neo-Kastro* ('new castle'); and the distinction is well founded, for the fortifications on the hill are built in a wholly different style from those on the plateau and seem to be much more primitive. But as the ruins on the plateau are much more extensive and much better preserved, I will describe them first.

They consist, roughly speaking, of two fortification-walls, which, meeting each other at a right angle, defended the north-western corner of the plateau on the east and south, that is, on the sides where the fortress was not protected by the low cliffs that bound the plateau on the north and west. The greatest length of the fortress thus formed is from east to west, or rather from north-east to south-west. The eastern wall is about 50 yards, and the southern wall about 300 yards long. The southern wall is strengthened by seven towers, each about 21 feet square and projecting about 9 ft. 8 in. from the curtain at intervals which vary from 33 to 49 paces. Walls and towers are comparatively well preserved and afford an excellent example of a Greek fortification of the best period and the most regular masonry, being massively built of large blocks, well squared and fitted together, and laid in accurately horizontal courses. The walls are about 7 ft. 6 in. thick and are standing on both faces for long stretches to a height of three and four courses or from 6 to 8 feet. The tower at the south-eastern angle is standing to a much greater height, but only the five or six lower courses, to a height of about 12 feet, are ancient. One block in the eastern wall is 6 feet long. The southern wall, which between the two last towers on the west is traceable only in isolated pieces appearing just above the ground, stops a few feet short of the western edge of the plateau, above the line of rocks; and from this point a short wall, only about 18 feet long, ran north to the edge of the low precipices which bound the plateau on that side. The great difference in length between the western and the eastern walls of the fortress (the western measuring about 6 yards while the eastern measures about 50 yards) is explained by the trend of the northern rim of the plateau from north-east to south-west. Along this northern edge of the plateau I found no traces of a fortification-wall. The cliffs were probably deemed a sufficient defence here; and besides the ground at the foot of them, now occupied by the village of *Kakosi*, was included within the city-walls. For, as we have seen, isolated pieces of fortification-walls are to be found here and there in the village towards its eastern and western end; and we cannot doubt that these are remains of walls which united the fortress on the plateau to the fortress on the hill, thus completing the circuit. They are built of the same fine ashlar masonry as the walls on the plateau and clearly belong to the same period. One of these fragments of walls, two courses high and about 8 paces long, exists outside the village between the northern foot of the plateau and the eastern end of the hill. Lower down and farther to the west a larger piece of the wall may be seen among the houses of the village; it is standing to a height of 6 feet and runs for about 20 yards westward towards the eastern foot of the hill. Other fragments of walls are dispersed among the houses at the opposite or western end of the village between the plateau on the south and the hill on the north. One piece, running in a southerly direction, is 9 feet long and three courses high. Another piece, near a well the mouth of which is enclosed by ancient blocks, consists of two sides of a square tower, which are preserved to a height of two to four courses (8 ft. 4 in.) A little to the south of it another piece of wall, about 10 feet thick but not rising above the ground, runs in a southerly direction as if to connect the tower with the western end of the plateau.

The hill so often mentioned is a rocky height with steep but not lofty sides which rises immediately to the north of *Kakosi* and extends westward as a ridge for a little way till it ends in a rocky glen that runs up into the recesses of Mount Helicon. On the top of the hill, to the north-west of the village, there are considerable remains of fortifications built in a totally different style from the walls on the plateau. In contrast to the fine ashlar masonry of the latter, the walls on the hill are rudely built of smaller stones, sometimes polygonal in shape, which are not accurately fitted together. It is quite possible that, as the natives think, these walls are older than the ashlar walls on the plateau. Lower down the hill and nearer the village are some remains of mediaeval or Byzantine walls built of small stones and mortar. At the south-western foot of the hill may be seen many tombs cut like shallow caves in the rock, and there are many similar tombs with arched roofs at the foot of the low cliffs which bound the plateau on the west. Several of these tombs have niches for three corpses, and I noticed one that had five such niches.

In the plain some 50 to 80 yards south of the plateau there are ruins of an ancient building in a field. They consist of a row of square bases placed at intervals of about 6 feet. The row extends east and west and is 31 paces long. Another row, of which there are some remains, seems to have extended parallel to the first at a distance of a few feet to the north of it. These rows of bases may perhaps be the ruins of a colonnade.

Homer describes Thisbe as abounding in pigeons (*Iliad*, ii. 502), and the description is still applicable, for immense numbers of wild pigeons are said to build their nests in the neighbouring precipices. Strabo remarked (ix. p. 411) that the rocky harbour of Thisbe was full of pigeons. This harbour, distant about 3 miles from Thisbe, is now called *Vathy*. It is a beautiful little bay enclosed by wooded hills. Its shore is very rocky and abounds in wild pigeons, as in the days of Strabo. The same geographer has correctly described the situation of

Thisbe itself. He says: "It is situated a little above the sea, bordering on Thespiae and Coronea, and lying, like them, at the foot of Helicon, but on the southern side" (Strabo, ix. p. 411). Further, he tells us that in his time the town was called, not Thisbe, but Thisbae; and herein he is confirmed by Pliny (*Nat. hist.* iv. 25), Polybius (xxvii. 5. 3, where for Θήβας we must read Θίσβας), Livy (xlii. 46. 7 and xlii. 63. 12, in both of which passages we must read *Thisbas* for *Thebas*), and an inscription found near *Kakosi* (*C. I. G. G. S.* 1. No. 2225; Dittenberger, *Sylloge Inscr. Graec.* No. 226; Hicks, *Greek historical Inscr.* No. 195). Ptolemy, on the other hand, uses the form Thisbe (iii. 14. 19); and Stephanus Byzantius (*s.v.* Θίσβη) notices both forms.

A good many inscriptions have been found at Thisbe, chiefly in the village of *Kakosi* which occupies part of the ancient site. From some of them we learn that Artemis was worshipped at Thisbe under the titles of Ilithyia, Saviour, and Huntress (*Agrotera*). See *C. I. G. G. S.* 1. Nos. 2228, 2232, 2234, 3564; *Bulletin de Corresp. hellénique*, 8 (1884), pp. 401-404. Others testify to the worship of Athena, Aesculapius, Health, Dionysus, Hermes, Hercules, and Apollo (*C. I. G. G. S.* 1. Nos. 2230, 2231, 2233, 2235, 3564). Two are from the bases of statues of Trajan and Caracalla (*C. I. G. G. S.* 1. Nos. 2236, 2239); and two more, which are unfortunately mutilated, set forth the conditions on which public lands were let out for the planting of trees and vineyards (*C. I. G. G. S.* 1. Nos. 2226, 2227). From other inscriptions we infer that Thisbe was a free city with magistrates of its own and was not, as had been formerly supposed, dependent on Thespiae (*C. I. G. G. S.* 1. Nos. 2223, 2234; *Bulletin de Corresp. hellénique*, 8 (1884), p. 405 *sq.*) Another inscription contains a clumsy Greek translation of two decrees of the Roman Senate passed in the year 170 B.C. and relating to the affairs of Thisbe at the time of the war with Perseus. See *C. I. G. G. S.* 1. No. 2225; Dittenberger, *Sylloge Inscr. Graec.* No. 226; Hicks, *Greek histor. Inscr.* No. 195; *Mittheil. d. arch. Inst. in Athen*, 4 (1879), pp. 235-249; C. T. Newton, *Essays on Art and Archaeology*, p. 128 *sq.* Lastly, an inscription found at the village of *Hagios Demetrios*, an hour and a half distant from *Skripou* (Orchomenus), contains two letters of the emperor Antoninus Pius to the people of Thisbe and Coronea concerning a dispute between them as to certain lands. The emperor's letters are of the date 155 A.D. See *C. I. G. G. S.* 1. No. 2870; *Bulletin de Corresp. hellénique*, 5 (1881), pp. 452-461.

The plain of Thisbe is so completely surrounded by hills that there is no issue for the river which rises in the Valley of the Muses near Ascra and after skirting the southern base of Helicon ends here. Hence a part of the plain is marshy. The dyke or causeway described by Pausanias still exists. It runs southward over the plain in the direction of the harbour, and serves for a road across the marsh. The foundations, which are of solid masonry, may be traced nearly half-way across the plain on the side opposite to *Kakosi*. The river flows from east to west through two openings in the dyke, converting the western and lower part of the plain into a permanent marsh. If the openings in the dyke were closed in winter or spring the eastern part of the plain would be flooded and the lower western part would be left fit for cultivation in summer.

See Dodwell, *Tour*, 1. pp. 257-259 ; Leake, *Northern Greece*, 2. pp. 501-513 ; Bursian, *Geogr.* 1. p. 242 *sq.* ; Baedeker,[3] p. 170 *sq.* ; *Guide-Joanne*, 2. p. 27 ; *American Journal of Archaeology*, 6. p. 112 *sq.* I visited the ruins of Thisbe, 16th and 17th November 1895, and have described them entirely from my own notes. But the remains of the dyke or causeway, as well as the marshy state of part of the plain, are described on Leake's authority. I saw no marsh anywhere in the plain, nor any remains of a causeway, though the road striking across the plain southward from *Kakosi* certainly exists at the present day. But I was only on the northern side of the plain, and from Leake's description it would seem that the remains of the dyke and the marsh are on the opposite or southern side. For the inscriptions of Thisbe see *C. I. G. G. S.* 1. Nos. 2223-2368, 3563-3574 ; Collitz, *G. D. I.* 1. Nos. 743-764 ; *Bulletin de Corresp. hellénique*, 8 (1884), pp. 399-407 ; *id.* 18 (1894), p. 533 *sq.*

32. 4. Tipha. About 6 miles to the south-east of Thisbe is the port of *Aliki*, a well-sheltered bay opening to the west and facing the port of *Vathy*, which opens to the east. On the crest of a ridge on the northern side of the harbour are the remains of an ancient Greek fortress, including a tower, of which the upper part has fallen in. Further there are remains of a wall along the crest of a ledge of rock on the eastern side of the harbour. A space at the foot of the heights was also enclosed within the ancient walls, and on the shore is a marshy flat, containing pools from which salt is obtained by evaporation, whence the name *Aliki*. It is commonly supposed that this fortified port is the ancient Tipha. But there is a serious objection to this view. *Aliki* is on the coast between Creusis (to the east) and *Vathy*, the port of Thisbe (to the west). If then *Aliki* is Tipha, we must suppose that Pausanias first passed it on his way westward from Creusis to the port of Thisbe, and then, after describing Thisbe, retraced his course eastward to Tipha. This seems improbable. From Pausanias's description we should certainly expect Tipha to be to the west of the port of Thisbe (port *Vathy*). Leake saw this, and proposed to identify the ruins at the monastery of St. Taxiarches with Tipha. But the ruins at that monastery, as we saw above (ix. 24. 5 note), are those of Corsiae. See Leake, *Northern Greece*, 2. pp. 502-505, 514-516 ; Bursian, *Geogr.* 1. p. 241 ; Baedeker,[3] p. 171 ; *Guide-Joanne*, 2. p. 27. Thucydides (iv. 76), Scylax (*Periplus*, 38), Ptolemy (iii. 14. 5) and Stephanus Byzantius (*s.v.* Σίφαι) call the place Siphae ; and the last writer mentions also a form Siphe.

32. 4. Tiphys —— pilot of the Argo. Cp. Stephanus Byzantius, *s.v.* Ἀφόρμιον.

32. 5. Haliartus. Haliartus was situated on the southern shore of the Copaic Lake. Occupying the space between the lake and the northern spurs of Mt. Helicon, it barred the pass from western into central Boeotia. Hence the military importance of the place. The ruins lie on a low rocky hill, which rises gradually from the plain on the south till it terminates on the side of what used to be the lake in precipitous bluffs, about 50 feet high, which overhung the water, or rather the morass. The northern and highest end of the hill was the acropolis. It has the form of an irregular quadrangle, three of its sides being precipitous, jagged, and indented, while the remaining side slopes gently to the south. Considerable remains of the wall of the acropolis exist, especially on the edge above the old bed of the lake, where six or seven courses are standing in some places. The style of the masonry is partly quadrangular, but mostly polygonal. The lower town stood chiefly on the gentle slope of the hill to the south of the acropolis. Few fragments of the town-walls remain, except a considerable piece, constructed of carefully squared stones, on the brow of the hill near the south-eastern tower of the acropolis. Some foundation-walls may be traced in the interior, and the whole slope of the hill is covered more or less with ruins. The extent of the town is probably marked by two streams which flow into the lake, one on the eastern, the other on the western side of the hill. One of these streams is perhaps the Lophis (see ix. 29. 5 note). Or the Lophis may be the much larger stream which comes down from the valley of. *Zagara* in Helicon and flows a mile or so to the east of Haliartus. This larger stream has sometimes been identified with the Termesus or Permessus (see ix. 29. 5 note). The village of *Mazi* lies at the foot of a peaked hill, about a mile to the south of Haliartus, which is now known as *Mitilene* or *the Palaeo-Kastro of Mazi*. In the cliffs of the hill of Haliartus there are several sepulchral crypts ; and at the northern foot of the cliffs is a copious spring of water flowing into the marsh. This spring is probably the fountain of Cissusa, in which the infant Dionysus is said to have been washed by his nurses as soon as he was born (Plutarch, *Lysander*, 28). A few hundred paces to the west of Haliartus is a barrow, where there are several sarcophaguses and ancient foundations near some sources of water. The barrow may perhaps be the grave of Rhadamanthys or of Alcmena, both of which were shown near Haliartus (Plutarch, *l.c.*) It cannot be the tomb of Lysander, for Plutarch informs us that Lysander was buried in the territory of Panopeus in Phocis, and that his tomb was to be seen on the road from Chaeronea to Delphi (Plutarch, *Lysander*, 29). Pausanias, indeed, tells us (§ 5 and ix. 33. 1) that the tomb of Lysander was in Haliartus, and it is quite possible that a tomb may have been shown him in Haliartus as the grave of Lysander. But Plutarch, who lived at Chaeronea only a few miles from Panopeus, can hardly have been mistaken as to the fact that the grave of Lysander was pointed out near Panopeus. From Plutarch (*De genio Socratis*, 5-7) we learn that the so-called grave of Alcmena at Haliartus was excavated during the Spartan occupation of the Cadmea at Thebes (383-379 B.C.) In the grave were found a small bronze bracelet, two earthenware jars containing "petrified earth," and a bronze tablet inscribed with many curious characters, which were supposed to be Egyptian. A copy of the tablet was sent to the Egyptian prophet Chonouphis at Memphis, who, after studying the characters for three days with the help of his ancient books, declared that the characters were Egyptian writing of the age of King Proteus, which writing had been learned by Hercules ; and that the tablet contained the advice of Hercules to the Greeks that they should live at peace and settle their differences by argument rather than by arms. As Wiedemann observes (on Herodotus, ii. 43), the grave was probably a prehistoric one, and the interpretation of the characters as Egyptian a mere fancy or rather a hoax.

In the war of the Romans with Perseus king of Macedonia the Haliartians sided with Macedonia (Polybius, xxvii. 1 and 5). Hence their city was besieged by the Romans and, in spite of a valiant defence, was captured and razed to the ground, and their territory bestowed upon Athens in 171 B.C. (Polybius, xxx. 18 and 18 a, ed. Dindorf; Livy, lxii. 56 and 63; Strabo, ix. p. 411). Strabo asserts that in his time the city existed no longer, never having recovered after its destruction by the Romans. But in this he appears to have been mistaken; for an inscription of Haliartus which is certainly later than the annexation of the city to Athens (since it is dated by the Athenian archon) and earlier than the time of Strabo, records a testimonial voted by a Club of Huntsmen to their treasurer for the upright way in which he had discharged his duties (*C. I. G. G. S.* 1. No. 2850). This seems to show that the city had in some measure revived between the Macedonian war and the time of Strabo. From the same inscription we learn that Artemis was worshipped at Haliartus, since the vote of thanks to the treasurer was moved by the priest of Artemis.

See Dodwell, *Tour*, 1. p. 248 *sqq.*; Leake, *Northern Greece*, 2. p. 206 *sqq.*; Mure, *Journal*, 1. p. 251 *sq.*; Welcker, *Tagebuch*, 2. p. 40 *sqq.*; L. Ross, *Wanderungen*, 1. p. 26; Vischer, *Erinnerungen*, p. 558 *sqq.*; Bursian, *Geogr.* 1. p. 232 *sq.*; Baedeker,[3] p. 169; *Guide-Joanne*, 2. p. 15 *sq.*

In Haliartus our author saw some roofless temples, which he believed had been burnt by the Persians (ix. 33. 3; x. 35. 3); but it is more probable that they perished in the Roman sack. It is curious, on the one hand that Pausanias betrays no knowledge of the destruction of Haliartus by the Romans, and on the other hand that he is the only ancient author who records the destruction of the city by the Persians. Herodotus has given us a list of the Phocian and Boeotian cities which were sacked by the Persians for opposing them (Herodotus, viii. 33 and 50), but in that list Haliartus does not appear. Nor does the name of the Haliartians occur in the roll of the Greek army which fought the Persians at Plataea (see note on x. 13. 9 'a bronze serpent'), though we should have expected to find it there if the Haliartians really sided against the Persians as Pausanias says they did. On these grounds Mr. Monceaux holds that the city was not destroyed by the Persians at all, and that the statement that they did destroy it is due merely to a gross mistake of Pausanias, who having read somewhere that the city was burned in "the Persic war"—an expression which Polybius uses (iii. 3. 8; iii. 5. 4; iii. 32. 8) to designate the war of the Romans with Perseus king of Macedonia—supposed that this meant the war of the Greeks with the Persians. See M. Monceaux, 'Pausanias et la destruction d'Haliarte par les Perses,' *Journal de Philologie*, N. S. 19 (1895), pp. 109-115. Mr. Monceaux may be right; if he is so, Pausanias has here blundered most egregiously.

32. 8. Autolycus, the pancratiast etc. See i. 18. 3 ; Plutarch, *Lysander*, 15. Plutarch calls Autolycus's adversary Callibius, not Eteocles. It was in honour of Autolycus that Callias gave the banquet described by Xenophon in his *Convivium*.

32. 10. warned by an oracle that avarice alone etc. The oracle is quoted by Zenobius (ii. 24), Diogenianus (ii. 36), a scholiast on Aristophanes (*Peace*, 622), and Suidas (*s.v.* διειρωνόξενοι). Cp. Cicero, *De officiis*, ii. 22. 77. According to Plutarch (*Instit. Lacon.* 42) the oracle was given to the Spartan kings Alcamenes and Theopompus.

32. 10. judging by the Persian law. The Persian law or custom to which Pausanias refers would seem to have been one which forbade or discouraged the accumulation of wealth.

33. 1. a shrine of the hero Cecrops. See note on ix. 24. 2.

33. 1. Mount Tilphusius and the spring called Tilphusa. To the west of Haliartus stretches a plain some 4 miles long, bounded on the south by the steep wooded slopes of Helicon and melting on the north into the vast expanse of the Copaic plain. When the Copaic basin was occupied by a swampy lake, the plain to the west of Haliartus was bounded on the north by its waters and had a breadth of only about a mile. In the west the plain is terminated by a projecting spur of Mount Helicon which advances to within a few hundred paces of what used to be the margin of the lake. The spur ends in a very steep rocky slope and goes by the name of *Petra* ('rock'). It is the ancient Mount Tilphusius. At its foot issues a copious spring—the ancient Tilphusa—which formerly, by swelling the neighbouring marsh, caused it to encroach so far on this part of the plain that there was just room enough between the lake and the hill for the high-road from Thebes to Lebadea. The place was thus a pass of some strength, and used to be a favourite post for robbers. The top of Mount Tilphusius commands an extensive view of the great Copaic plain with the surrounding heights from near Thebes westward to Parnassus. On the summit, just above the spring, are remains of a small ancient tower or fortress, consisting of a wall of polygonal masonry, together with the foundations of a triangular castle of later date. L. Ross thought that the polygonal wall was a remnant of the sanctuary of Tilphusian Apollo mentioned by Strabo (ix. p. 411). But Strabo seems to say that the sanctuary was beside the spring at the foot of the mountain. He calls the spring Tilphossa and the mountain Tilphossius. Demosthenes, who calls the mountain Tilphosaeus, seems to imply that there was a fortress on it (*De falsa legatione*, pp. 385, 387). Cp. Diodorus, iv. 67, xix. 53.

See Leake, *Northern Greece*, 2. pp. 136 *sq.*, 142, 205 ; Mure, *Journal*, 1. p. 249 *sq.* ; Welcker, *Tagebuch*, 2. p. 42 ; L. Ross, *Wanderungen*, 1. pp. 29-31 ; Vischer, *Erinnerungen*, p. 560 ; Bursian, *Geogr.* 1. p. 234 ; Baedeker,[3] p. 169 ; *Guide-Joanne*, 2. p. 16. The identification of *Petra* with Mt. Tilphusius has been questioned by Messrs. Conze and Michaelis, but on insufficient grounds. They conjecture that Alalcomenae (see below, § 5) was situated at the foot of *Petra*. See *Annali dell' Instituto*, 33 (1861), pp. 84-86 ; *Philologus*, 19 (1863), p. 180.

In the Homeric hymn to Apollo there is a curious legend that when Apollo was going up and down the earth seeking for a place to found an oracle he came to the spring Tilphusa (Telphusa or Delphusa, as the name appears in the MSS.), and being pleased with the spot resolved to build a temple there.   But the wily Tilphusa, the nymph of the spring, unwilling to cede the place of honour to the god, dissuaded him from his purpose, telling him that he would be disturbed by the noise of the horses and by the mules being watered at the spring.   She told him that he had better go and build a temple at Crisa, in a glen of Parnassus, where he would not be troubled by the rattling of chariots and the trampling of galloping horses.   The god did as she told him, but afterwards finding she had deceived him, he pushed a crag on the top of the spring and hid the stream that flowed from it.   Also he made an altar for himself in a shady grove near the spring, and at this altar men prayed to the Tilphusian god, who had defiled the flowing water of Tilphusa.   See the *Hymn to Apollo*, 244-276, 375-387.   The crag which Apollo is said to have pushed on the top of the spring is no doubt Mount Tilphusius.

33. 2. **his daughter Manto** etc.   See vii. 3. 1 *sq.*

33. 2. **the number of the years which he is recorded to have lived.**   Tiresias was said to have lived either seven or nine generations (Tzetzes, *Schol. on Lycophron*, 682).

33. 2. **he was changed from a woman into a man.**   See note on ix. 19. 3.

33. 2. **Homer in the Odyssey represents him** etc.   See *Od.* x. 493 *sqq.*

33. 3. **the goddesses, whom they call Praxidicae.**   Cp. iii. 22. 2. Photius (*Lexicon, s.v.* Πραξιδίκη) and Suidas (*s.v.* Πραξιδίκη) say: "Praxidice is a goddess, whose image consisted of a head merely. Mnaseas in his work on Europe says that Soter ('saviour') and his sister Praxidice had a son Ctesius and two daughters Homonoea ('unanimity') and Arete ('virtue'), and that the daughters were called Praxidicae after their mother.   But Dionysius in his work on Foundations says that Ogyges had three daughters Alalcomenia, Thelxinoea, and Aulis, who were afterwards named Praxidicae."   Hesychius says (*s.v.* Πραξιδίκη): "They say she was a kind of demon who completed or put the finishing touch to what was said (τέλος ἐπιτιθεῖσαν τοῖς τε λεγομένοις).   Wherefore her images were heads, and so were her victims."   The *Argonautica* attributed to Orpheus mentions (*v.* 31) "orgies of Praxidice"; and in an Orphic hymn (xxix. 5) Proserpine is addressed as Praxidice.   In some verses of Panyasis (quoted by Stephanus Byzantius, *s.v.* Τρεμίλη) Praxidice is called an Ogygian nymph who was married to Tremilus "beside the silvery eddying river Sibrus, and she had baneful sons Tlous, Xanthus, Pinarus, and Cragus, who in his might plundered all the fields."   Cp. Müller, *Orchomenos*,[2] p. 122 *sq.*

33. 3. **temples —— without roofs.**   Pausanias supposed that they had been burnt by the Persians.   See x. 35. 2, and above, p. 166.

33. 4. **a river Lophis.**   See note on ix. 32. 5.

33. 5. **Alalcomenae —— a temple of Athena.**   Immediately to the west of *Petra* (Mount Tilphusius) the plain expands, and here we come to the ruins of a church built of ancient blocks, which may occupy the site of the temple of Athena. Leake identified as the ruins of the temple some polygonal foundations on a rocky end of the hill-slope farther to the west, between the ruined church and the village of *Soulinari*, which stands on the heights to the south of the high-road. See Leake, *Northern Greece*, 2. p. 135 *sq.*; Bursian, *Geogr.* 1. p. 234 *sq.* Athena of Alalcomenae is mentioned by Homer (*Il.* iv. 8). Strabo says (ix. p. 413) that Athena of Alalcomenae was so much revered that the town, though small and situated in a plain, was always respected in war and continued inviolate.

33. 6. after perpetrating these frantic outrages etc. Pausanias has here imitated a phrase of Herodotus (iii. 33 and 37).

33. 6. he was overtaken by the most loathsome of diseases. Cp. i. 20. 7.

33. 7. the Triton. Leake thought that this was the stream near the village of *Soulinari* (*Northern Greece*, 2. p. 135 *sq.*) The Boeotian towns of Athens and Eleusis were situated on the banks of the Triton (ix. 24. 2 note). As to the mythical relation of Athena to the Triton, see K. O. Müller, 'Pallas-Athene,' §§ 40, 41 (*Kleine deutsche Schriften*, 2. pp. 187-190); Escher, *Triton und seine Bekämpfung durch Herakles*, p. 36 *sqq.*; L. R. Farnell, *The Cults of the Greek States*, 1. pp. 265-270. Cp. Paus. viii. 26. 6.

34. 1. the sanctuary of Itonian Athena. Cp. iii. 9. 13. Strabo tells us (ix. p. 411) that when the Boeotians, expelled from Arne in Thessaly sixty years after the Trojan war (Thucydides i. 12), invaded Boeotia, they seized Coronea and founded the sanctuary of Itonian Athena in the plain before the city and called the river which flowed past it the Cuarius. Here, says Strabo, they held the Pan-Boeotian festival, and along with the image of Athena there was set up an image of Hades for a certain mystic reason, which Strabo does not explain. The temple of Itonian Athena seems to have been on the site of the modern village of *Mamoura*, which lies in the plain, about 2 miles to the north-east of Coronea; for at *Mamoura* have been found some inscriptions containing decrees of the Boeotian confederacy (*C. I. G. G. S.* 1. Nos. 2859-2869). One of the inscriptions found here gives a list of the victors in the games held at the Pan-Boeotian festival. See *C. I. G. G. S.* 1. No. 2871; Foucart, in *Bulletin de Corr. hellén.* 9 (1885), p. 427 *sqq.* From this inscription we learn that the horse-races started from an image of Ares. Hence Mr. Foucart proposes, rather unnecessarily, to alter the name of Hades into that of Ares in the passage of Strabo cited above. In the time of the Antonines the Boeotian confederacy nominated a high-priestess of Itonian Athena (*Bulletin de Corr. hellén.* 4 (1880), p. 15 note). The tombstone of a high-priestess of Itonian Athena was found near Chaeronea (*C. I. G. G. S.* 1. No. 3426). During the celebration of the Pan-Boeotian festival a truce of God was observed (Polybius, iv. 3, ix. 34; cp. Plutarch, *Amat. Narr.* 4). Mr. Latischew argues that the festival was held in the tenth month of the Boeotian year, nearly corresponding to our October; he thinks that the name of this month was Pan-Boeotian. See B. Latischew, 'Die Festzeit der Pamboiotien,' *Mittheil. d. arch. Inst. in Athen*, 7 (1882), pp. 31-39. In the first century A.D. the Boeotian confederacy decreed that a portrait of Epaminondas of Acraephnium (see above, pp. 102 *sq.*, 118 *sq.*) should be dedicated in the sanctuary of Itonian Athena (*C. I. G. G. S.* I. No. 2711 ; H. N. Ulrichs, *Reisen und Forschungen*, I. p. 251 *sq.*; Keil, *Sylloge Inscr. Boeot.* p. 118). There was a sanctuary of Itonian Athena at Itonus in Thessaly, between Pherae and Larissa (i. 13. 2 ; cp. x. 1. 10) ; as to the site, see N. I. Giannopoulos, in *Bulletin de Corr. hellénique*, 16 (1892), pp. 473-478. From the Thessalian sanctuary the Boeotian sanctuary was perhaps derived.

34. 2. a woman places fire every day on the altar etc. We may compare the way in which the perpetual fire was tended by the nuns of St. Bridget at Kildare in Ireland. There were nineteen nuns, and each of them had the care of the fire for a single night in turn ; but on the evening before the twentieth night, the last nun, after heaping wood on the fire, used to say, " Bridget, take charge of your own fire ; for this night belongs to you." She then left the fire, and in the morning it was still burning and the usual quantity of fuel had been used. See Giraldus Cambrensis, *Topography of Ireland*, xxxiv. *sq.* St. Bridget's church at Kildare is still standing ; it may be seen from the railway, with a well-preserved round tower beside it.

34. 3. Coronea. The inconsiderable ruins of Coronea are near the village of *St. George* (*Hagios Georgios*) in a valley on the northern side of Mount Helicon, about 7 miles south-east of Lebadea. A two-peaked height at the entrance of the valley formed the acropolis ; it is watered on either side by a rivulet, and stretches southward toward Helicon in a direction parallel to the adjacent mountains, thus dividing the valley into two branches. The summit of the acropolis is about 200 paces long by 150 broad. A fine piece of polygonal wall remains on the eastern, and another on the southern side. On the southern verge of the acropolis are the remains of a Roman edifice of brick, which the peasants suppose to have been a bath ; hence they call the place *Loutro* ('bath'). At the bottom of the hill, on the south-eastern side, is a piece of the town-wall. Potsherds may be seen in the fields on all sides, especially toward the south-east, where most of the town seems to have lain. There are several springs of water on this side of the hill, and many pieces of ancient squared stones in two ruined churches. Between the eastern side of the citadel and a ruined mediaeval tower of late Greek or Frankish construction there is a hollow depression about 150 paces wide, which may have been the site of the theatre. Strabo says (ix. p. 411) that Coronea was situated on a height near Helicon.

See Wheler, *Journey*, p. 477 ; Leake, *Northern Greece*, 2. p. 132 *sqq.* ; Walpole's *Memoirs relating to Turkey*,[2] p. 342 ; Welcker, *Tagebuch*, 2. p. 42 ; L. Ross, *Wanderungen*, 1. p. 32 *sq.* ; Bursian, *Geogr.* 1. p. 233 ; Baedeker,[7] p. 169 ; *Guide-Joanne*, 2. p. 31.

From inscriptions found near Coronea we gather that among the deities worshipped there were Serapis, Isis, Anubis, Hercules, Palaemon, the Dioscuri, and Lawgiver Demeter (*C. I. G. G. S.* I. Nos. 2872,

2874, 2875, 2876). As to the letters of Antoninus Pius to the peoples of Coronea and Thisbe, see above, p. 163.

34. 3. an altar of the Winds. Cp. ii. 12. 1 note.

34. 3. Sirens. On the Sirens in ancient mythology and art, see Stephani, in *Compte-Rendu* (St. Petersburg) for 1866, p. 9 *sqq.*; *id.* for 1870-71, p. 143 *sqq.*; J. F. Cerquand, 'Les Sirenes,' in *Revue archéologique*, N. S. 10 (1864), pp. 282-303; H. Schrader, *Die Sirenen* (Berlin, 1868); Miss J. E. Harrison, *Myths of the Odyssey*, p. 146 *sqq.*; Langbehn, *Flügelgestalten*, p. 57 *sqq.*; R. Unger, 'Zur Sirenensage,' *Philologus*, 46 (1888), pp. 770-775.

In an article in the *Indian Antiquary*, 10 (1881), p. 291 *sq.*, Mr. W. E. A. Axon points out "some hitherto unnoticed analogies to the classical myth which are to be found in the early art and literature of the Buddhists. Thus, in many of the paintings at Börö Boedoer, in Java, we have the figures of the bird-women. In plate civ. of the great work of Wilsen, Brumond, and Leemens we have what the authors style two of these 'celestial gandharvîs, beings half-women, half-birds,' whose music has attracted the attention of a princely traveller and his suite." Mr. Axon also refers to an Indian story, translated from Pâli into Chinese, about 500 merchants who were shipwrecked on a shore inhabited by Rakshasîs or demons, who lived on human flesh, but who changed themselves into lovely women that they might enjoy the company of the merchants for a time and then devour them. The merchants, however, discover the mangled remains of previous victims and make their escape, regardless of the plaintive and alluring cries of the Rakshasîs. But in this story there seems to be no mention of the song of the demon-women, nor of their half-bird shape; so the story is scarcely a parallel to the myth of the Sirens. There is a Slavonic story which offers some points of analogy to the myth in question. Three sisters set out, one after the other, to find the Water of Life. Nobody knows where the Water of Life is except a fiery bird that perches on a singing tree in a king's garden far, far away. The trees in that garden sing and play so sweetly that every one who hears them stops to listen and is at once turned into stone. In the quest after the Water of Life two out of three sisters are turned to stone; but the third sister, warned by their fate, stops her ears with dough or wax and so walks safe through the enchanted garden, and catches the bird. See Żmigrodzki, *Die Mutter bei den Völkern des arischen Stammes*, p. 14 *sqq.* On the Oxus there is a water-fairy, a lovely lady with many feet, who wields over the boatmen of the river the same fatal charm that the Lorelei wields over the boatmen of the Rhine. See H. Vambery, *Das Türkenvolk*, p. 368.

34. 4. Mount Libethrius. Pausanias's statement that Mt. Libethrius was 40 furlongs from Coronea is not enough to enable us to identify the mountain. Leake and the French surveyors, followed by Lolling (in Baedeker) and the writer of the *Guide-Joanne*, identify Libethrius with the ridge on which is situated the village of *Koutoumoula*, picturesquely nestling among fruit-trees. The ridge forms part of Helicon, from the main mass of which it is separated on the south

by an upland wooded valley. In this valley is the village of *Zagara*.
L. Ross identified Libethrius with Mt. *Palaeo-Vouna*, the highest peak
of the Helicon group ; Bursian identified it with Mt. *Megali Loutza* to
the north-west of Mt. *Palaeo-Vouna*. See Leake, *Northern Greece*, 2.
p. 141 ; L. Ross, *Wanderungen*, 1. p. 33 ; Bursian, *Geogr.* 1. p. 236;
Baedeker,[3] p. 171 ; *Guide-Joanne*, 2. p. 31. There was a cave of the
Libethrian nymphs, said to have been consecrated by Thracian settlers
in Boeotia (Strabo, ix. p. 410, xi. p. 471).

34. 5. Mount Laphystius. This is supposed to be the steep
mountain of *Granitsa* (2940 feet high), which is practically a western
continuation of Mt. Helicon, though separated from it by a pass that
leads from the village of *St. George* to *Livadia*. The mountain advances
north-eastward into the plain, to the west of Coronea, exactly opposite
(south-west of) the hill of Orchomenus. It is composed of a reddish
stone ; the summit has the appearance of a crater ; and at its northern
foot there are warm springs. Hence it has been supposed that the
mountain is of volcanic origin. See Leake, *Northern Greece*, 2. p. 140
sq. ; L. Ross, *Wanderungen*, 1. p. 33 ; Bursian, *Geogr.* 1. p. 235;
Baedeker,[3] p. 170 ; *Guide-Joanne*, 2. p. 16. On Mt. Laphystius the
murdered Laius and his herald are said to have been buried by Epicaste
(Nicolaus Damascenus, *Frag.* 15, in *Fragm. Histor. Graec.* ed. Müller,
3. p. 367).

34. 5. when Athamas was about to sacrifice Phrixus etc. The
legend of Athamas and Phrixus was localised also at Halus or Alus in
Thessaly, which was said to have been founded by Athamas (Strabo, ix.
p. 433), and where there was a sanctuary of Laphystian Zeus. Both at
Halus and on Mt. Laphystius in Boeotia human sacrifices seem to have
formed part of the worship of Laphystian Zeus, and the victims appear
to have been the eldest sons of the royal and priestly family which, in
both places, traced their descent from Athamas. At Halus down to the
time of Xerxes the eldest son of the family was forbidden to enter the
town-hall ; if he was found there, he was decked with garlands, led out
in procession and sacrificed. Hence many of the family, fearing to incur
this doom, fled into foreign lands. See Herodotus, vii. 197 (with Stein's
notes). Indeed the practice of sacrificing, at least occasionally, certain
members of the family seems to have lasted into the fourth century B.C.,
for the author of the *Minos* (commonly ascribed to Plato) speaks of it
(p. 315 b c) as if it were still observed in his time ; he compares it to
the Carthaginian custom of parents sacrificing their own children to Baal
(Cronus). Athamas himself, according to one form of the legend, was
about to be sacrificed as a scapegoat for the whole land, when he was
rescued. This legend was the theme of a tragedy by Sophocles. See
Herodotus, *l.c.* ; Schol. on Aristophanes, *Clouds*, 257. At a later time,
perhaps the custom was mitigated into a rule that a member of the royal
and priestly family should sacrifice a ram to Laphystian Zeus in the
town-hall. See Schol. on Apollonius Rhodius, *Argonaut.* ii. 653. But
the original custom would seem to have been that the priestly or divine
king was put to death after a set time, because his death was deemed
necessary for the welfare of his people. See Grote, *Hist. of Greece*, 1.

p. 123 *sqq.* ; K. O. Müller, *Orchomenos,*[2] p. 156 *sqq.* ; Preller, *Griechische Mythologie,*[3] 2. p. 310 *sq.* Cp. *The Golden Bough,* 1. p. 213 *sqq.*

34. 5. a river Phalarus. This was perhaps the river of *St. George,* which flows past the western side of Coronea. Plutarch calls the stream the Philarus, and tells us that it had a tributary called the Isomantus, which joined it near Coronea (*Lysander,* 29). Leake thought that the Isomantus might be the rivulet of *Steveniko* which joins that of *St. George* a little above the ancient site. See Leake, *Northern Greece,* 2. p. 140 *sq.* ; Baedeker,[3] p. 169 ; *Guide-Joanne,* 2. p. 16.

34. 6. Over against Mount Laphystius is Orchomenus. Orchomenus, as we have seen (note on § 5 ' Mount Laphystius '), lies north-east of and opposite to Mount Laphystius, the wide plain watered by the Cephisus lying between them. Pausanias supposes himself standing on Mt. Laphystius and looking across the plain to Orchomenus, which lies at the eastern end of the chain of hills that here bounds the plain on the north. The Greek word here translated ' over against ' is πέραν. Prof. Ad. Michaelis, who has carefully examined Pausanias's use of this preposition (*Mittheil. d. arch. Inst. in Athen,* 2 (1877), pp. 1-4), observes on the present passage that " in all such expressions Pausanias is extraordinarily exact and vivid, not indeed for the mere reader, but for those who have the scenes before their eyes."

34. 7. Coronus. An inscription found at the village of *Soulinari* records that a certain Heras Castricius, son of Aulus, dedicated a temple to Coronius, who is doubtless no other than Coronus, the supposed founder of Coronea (*C. I. G. G. S.* 1. No. 2873).

34. 10. Olmones. See ix. 24. 3.

35. 1. Eteocles was the first person who sacrificed to the Graces. Cp. Strabo, ix. p. 414 ; Schol. on Pindar, *Ol.* xiv. 1. Theocritus addresses the Graces as " Eteoclean goddesses who love Minyan Orchomenus " (xvi. 104 *sq.*) From inscriptions we learn that musical and poetical contests were held at Orchomenus in honour of the Graces ; the contests, which were called Charitesia, included trumpet-playing, flute-playing, lyre-playing, heraldry, recitation, epic poetry, tragedy, comedy, the satyric drama, acting, etc. See Clarke, *Travels,* 4. p. 156 *sqq.* ; Leake, *Northern Greece,* 2. p. 631 *sq.* ; *C. I. G.* Nos. 1583, 1584 ; Cauer, *Delectus Inscr. Graec.*[2] No. 301 ; Collitz, *G. D. I.* 1. No. 503 ; *C. I. G. G. S.* 1. Nos. 3195-3197. On the worship of the Graces at Orchomenus, see K. O. Müller, *Orchomenos,*[2] p. 172 *sqq.* According to Professor Max Müller, the Greek name of the Graces (*Charites*) is etymologically identical with the Sanscrit *Haritas,* the name applied by Vedic poets to the horses of the sun, and both the Greek and the Sanscrit names are derived from a root GHAR meaning ' bright.' See F. Max Müller, *Lectures on the Science of Language,*[6] 2. pp. 404-413, 418-420 ; *id., Selected Essays,* 1. p. 438 *sqq.* Cp. J. F. Cerquand, ' Les Charites,' *Revue archéologique,* N.S. 6 (1862), pp. 325-340 ; *id.,* 7 (1863), pp. 52-64 ; H. Usener, *Götternamen* (Bonn, 1896), p. 131 *sqq.*

35. 1. The Lacedaemonians —— say that there are two Graces. Cp. iii. 18. 6 and 10. Prof. Studniczka conjectures that the two Lacedaemonian Graces are represented on a vase of Melos, where two goddesses, along with a god (Apollo) playing the lyre, are depicted driving in a chariot drawn by four winged steeds. See Fr. Studniczka, *Kyrene*, pp. 34, 162, with fig. 26.

35. 2. the Athenians also have worshipped —— two Graces. Prof. C. Robert has argued that the Athenians always recognised three Graces ; that their names were Thallo, Auxo, and Carpo (cp. Pollux, viii. 106) ; that Hegemone, which Pausanias gives as the name of one of the Graces, was an epithet of Hecate, who was worshipped with the three Graces at the entrance to the Acropolis ; and that Pausanias was misled by Callipus of Corinth, whose book on the history of Orchomenus he had read (see ix. 29. 2 ; ix. 38. 10). See Prof. Robert's paper, ' De Gratiis Atticis,' in *Commentationes philologicae in honorem Th. Mommseni*, pp. 142-150. As to the worth or worthlessness of this paper see H. Usener, *Götternamen*, p. 131 note 24.

35. 2. the other Season is worshipped —— by the Athenians. Pausanias seems to imply that the Athenians worshipped only two Seasons. Only two were represented on the throne of Apollo at Amyclae (iii. 18. 10). Philochorus, cited by Athenaeus (xiv. p. 656 a), tells us that the Athenians sacrificed boiled, not roast, meat to the Seasons, begging them to avert torrid heats and droughts, but to foster vegetation by due warmth and seasonable rains. In front of one of the temples in Egypt there were two colossal statues ; the people called one of them Winter and the other Summer ; they worshipped and treated well the statue of Summer ; but they ill-treated the statue of Winter (Herodotus, ii. 121). The Canadian Indians personified the seasons as two living beings, one of whom brought back the spring and summer, while the other brought back winter (*Relations des Jésuites*, 1634, p. 13 *sq.*, of the Canadian reprint).

35. 3. Angelion and Tectaeus —— in making the image of Apollo for the Delians etc. Angelion and Tectaeus were early sculptors, pupils of the old masters Scyllis and Dipoenus. See ii. 32. 5. Their image of Apollo is described more fully by Plutarch (*De musica*, 14). He says that the god had a bow in his right hand and the Graces in his left ; one of the Graces held a lyre, another flutes, and the one in the middle held a shepherd's pipe to her lips. But from Macrobius (*Sat.*

i. 17. 13) and a scholiast on Pindar (*Ol.* xiv. 16) it would seem that the god held the Graces in his right hand and the bow in his left. This is confirmed by Athenian coins. For we know that there was an image of the Delian Apollo at Athens (Bekker's *Anecdota*, p. 299. 8 *sq.*; cp. Athenaeus, x. p. 424 f); and on Athenian coins Apollo appears holding the Graces in his right

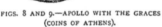

FIGS. 8 AND 9.—APOLLO WITH THE GRACES (COINS OF ATHENS).

hand and a bow in his left (Figs. 8 and 9). There can be little doubt that this Apollo on the coins is a copy of the image of the Delian

Apollo at Athens, and that the latter was a copy of the image by Angelion and Tectaeus at Delos. Thus the coins in question enable us to judge of the attitude and general style of the image at Delos. The god, it appears, was portrayed standing naked, with his feet close together, in a stiff archaic posture. On his head he wore a tall cap. In his right hand he held the three Graces on a sort of stand with a handle to it; in his left hand he grasped the bow. On some of the coins a griffin is represented rearing against the god on each side.

Among the inscriptions which were found by the French in the sanctuary of Apollo at Delos and which contain lists of the god's property, there is one that mentions a golden crown weighing 604 *staters*, with which 'the image' was crowned, and three other golden crowns, weighing 31 *staters*, with which the Graces were crowned; all four crowns were dedicated by queen Stratonice, daughter of Demetrius. Another inscription speaks of two bars or ingots of gold which were detached from the image of Apollo ($\chi \acute{v} \mu a \ \chi \rho v \sigma o \hat{v} v \ \mathring{a} \pi \grave{o} \ \mathring{A} \pi \acute{o} \lambda \lambda \omega v o s \ \tau o \hat{v}$ $\mathring{a} \gamma \acute{a} \lambda \mu a \tau o s$). Hence Mr. Homolle infers that the statue of Apollo by Angelion and Tectaeus was made either of gold and ivory or of wood plated with gold. See *Bulletin de Corresp. hellénique*, 6 (1882), p. 128 *sq.* Overbeck preferred, with justice, the view that this archaic Apollo was of wood plated with gold to the alternative view that it was of gold and ivory.

A scholiast on Pindar (*Ol.* xiv. 16) states that at Delphi there was an image of Apollo holding the Graces on his right hand. If this is true, the image may have been a copy of the one by Angelion and Tectaeus. Caligula used sometimes to dress himself up in the style of this famous Apollo, holding a bow and arrows in his left hand and the Graces on his outstretched right hand (Philo Judaeus, *De virtutibus et legatione ad Caium*, vol. 2. p. 559, ed. 1742). Apollo at Delos, as well as at Miletus, bore the surname of Ulius (Οὔλιος), which seems to have meant 'healing' (Strabo, xiv. p. 635; Curtius, *Griech. Etymologie,*[5] p. 371; Preller, *Griech. Mythol.*[4] 1. p. 278).

See K. O. Müller, *Archäologie der Kunst*, § 86; Beulé, *Monnaies d'Athènes*, p. 364 *sqq.* (Beulé, following De Witte, interprets the figure on the Athenian coins wrongly as the Colian Aphrodite with the Genetyllides; see Paus. i. 1. 5); Wieseler, *Der Apollo Stroganoff und der Apollo vom Belvedere*, p. 78 *sqq.*; O. Jahn, *De antiquissimis Minervae simulacris Atticis*, p. 9 note 27; Müller-Wieseler, *Denkmäler*, 2. pl. xi. No. 126; Imhoof-Blumer and Gardner, *Num. Comm. on Paus.* p. 144, with pl. CC xi.-xiv.; Overbeck, *Gesch. d. griech. Plastik,*[4] 1. p. 88 *sq.*; *id.*, *Griech. Kunstmythologie*, 4. pp. 17-21; Collignon, *Hist. de la Sculpture grecque*, 1. p. 224 *sq.*

35. 3. at Athens —— three Graces. See below, § 7 and i. 23. 8 note.

35. 4. Homer —— says that one was the wife of Hephaestus. See *Iliad*, xviii. 382 *sq.*

35. 4. He says, too, that <Sleep> was a lover etc. See *Iliad*, xiv. 270-276.

35. 5. Hesiod in the Theogony —— says that the Graces etc. See Hesiod, *Theog.* 907 *sqq.*

35. 6. **Who first represented the Graces naked** etc. The practice of representing the Graces naked appears not to be older than the third century B.C., but thenceforward it prevailed almost exclusively. We possess examples of the older type of the Graces in several reliefs and on some coins of Athens ; the goddesses are here represented in long robes which reach to their feet. See Furtwängler, in Roscher's *Lexikon*, i. p. 879 *sqq.* ; Baumeister's *Denkmäler*, p. 375 *sqq.* ; Müller-Wieseler, *Denkmäler*, i. pl. xi. No. 43. To the list which Pausanias here gives of the clothed Graces, may be added the images of them which he saw at Elis (vi. 24. 6).

35. 6. **at Smyrna, in the sanctuary of the Nemeses.** See vii. 5. 2 *sq.*, with the note.

35. 6. **Bupalus.** See iv. 30. 6 note.

35. 7. **Pythagoras of Paros.** Nothing more is known of this painter. Some have proposed to identify him with the sculptor Pythagoras of Samos, because Pythagoras of Samos is said to have begun as a painter (Pliny, *Nat. hist.* xxxiii. 60 ; Brunn, *Gesch. d. griech. Künstler*, i. p. 116). As to the sculptor Pythagoras of Samos, see note on vi. 6. 4.

35. 7. **Socrates ——— wrought images of the Graces** etc. See i. 22. 8 note.

36. 2. **made a raid on the sanctuary at Delphi.** Cp. x. 7. 1.

36. 3. **the lines in the Iliad.** See *Il.* xiii. 301 *sq.*

36. 3. **the Ephyrians of Thesprotis.** Ephyra in Thesprotis (Thucydides, i. 36) was in later times called Cichyrus (Strabo, vii. p. 324). See note on i. 17. 5, 'Cichyrus.'

36. 5. **the treasury of Minyas.** See below ix. 38. 2 note.

36. 6. **the village of Hyettus.** See ix. 24. 3 note.

36. 8. **Chloris, daughter of Amphion.** See Homer, *Od.* xi. 281 *sqq.* ; and cp. ii. 21. 9 note.

37. 2. **the Thebans were freed from the tribute** etc. Cp. ix. 17. 2 ; ix. 25. 4 with the note ; Diodorus, iv. 10 ; Apollodorus, ii. 4. 11 ; Strabo, ix. p. 414. Diodorus and Apollodorus say that Erginus was slain by Hercules.

37. 5. **Trophonius and Agamedes ——— built the temple at Delphi.** Cp. x. 5. 13 note.

37. 5. **Hyrieus.** Hyria, the town over which Hyrieus ruled, was near the Euripus and Aulis (Strabo, ix. p. 404 ; Stephanus Byzantius, *s.v.* Ὑρία).

37. 5. **In the treasury they contrived that one of the stones could be removed** etc. The story which follows is a folk-tale, of which there are many versions in many lands. A number of these versions have been collected and compared by various writers, especially by Dunlop and Liebrecht (*Geschichte der Prosadichtungen*, pp. 263-265), R. Köhler (*Orient und Occident*, 2 (1864), pp. 303-313), A. Schiefner (*Bulletin de l'Académie impériale des Sciences de Saint-Pétersbourg*, 14 (1870), pp. 299-316), and Mr. W. A. Clouston (*Popular Tales and Fictions*, 2. pp. 115-165).

(1) The best known version is the ancient Egyptian one told by

Herodotus (ii. 121), which runs thus. King Rhampsinitus had a treasury of stone built for himself; but the knavish builder contrived that a certain stone in the wall could be taken out at any time by one or two men. On his death-bed the builder tells the secret to his two sons, who soon avail themselves of the secret entry into the treasury to rob the king. Seeing his treasures steadily dwindling, the king sets traps about his coffers ; and on the next visit of the brothers to the treasury one of them is caught fast. To prevent recognition, the other thief cuts off his brother's head and escapes with it, taking care to replace the stone behind him. Next day the king is astonished to find the headless trunk of a thief caught in his treasury, but the walls apparently intact. Determined to discover the thief's accomplice, he causes the headless body to be hung up on the outside of his palace, guarded by soldiers who have orders to apprehend and take to the king any person whom they may see lamenting over the body. Meantime the mother of the two thieves is inconsolable for the death of one of her sons, and threatens the other that if he does not rescue his brother's body she will make a clean breast to the king. The brother accordingly contrives adroitly to intoxicate the guards, and after shaving the right cheeks of all the guards by way of mockery, he carries off the corpse. The king is now more anxious than ever to discover the clever thief. So he orders his daughter to grant her favours to any man who will first confess to her the most wicked and daring deed of his life. The thief visits the princess, having first provided himself with the severed hand of a fresh corpse. He confesses his crime to her, and she attempts to seize him, but he leaves the hand of the corpse in her grasp and makes his escape. The king, in an ecstasy of admiration at the daring and address of the thief, proclaims that if the thief will present himself and confess, he will receive a free pardon and a great reward. The thief accordingly presents himself to Rhampsinitus and receives the king's daughter in marriage.

(2) A Greek version of the story, differing from the one here related by Pausanias, was told by the historian Charax, quoted by a scholiast on Aristophanes (*Clouds*, 508). According to this version, Agamedes, prince of Stymphalus, had two sons, Trophonius and Cercyon, by his wife Epicaste. Trophonius was born out of wedlock, but Cercyon was legitimate. Now Agamedes and Trophonius were famed for their skill ; they built the temple of Apollo at Delphi, and they made a golden treasury for King Augeas at Elis. But they took care to leave a secret entrance into the treasury, by means of which they and Cercyon used to enter and rob the king. Augeas was at a loss what to make of it, but by the advice of Daedalus, who was staying with him, he set traps about his coffers. Agamedes was accordingly caught in one of them, but Trophonius, to prevent recognition, cut off his father's head and escaped with Cercyon to Orchomenus. Hither they were pursued by the messengers of Augeas ; so Cercyon fled to Athens and Trophonius to Lebadea, where he made for himself an underground chamber in which he lived.

Among the other versions of the story are—

(3) A modern Egyptian (Arabic) version. See Th. Nöldeke, 'Zu den ägyptischen Märchen,' *Zeitschrift d. deutsch. morgenländ. Gesell.* 42 (1888), pp. 68-72.

(4) A modern Greek version. See Legrand, *Contes populaires grecs,* 'Voleur par nature,' pp. 205-216.

(5) A version in *The Seven Wise Masters* (the third example of the empress). See also Köhler, *op. cit.* p. 311 *sq.* ; Clouston, *op. cit.* pp. 118-121.

(6) An Italian version in the *Novelle* of Ser Giovanni, written towards the end of the fourteenth century. See Dunlop-Liebrecht, *op. cit.* p. 263 *sq.* ; Köhler, *op. cit.* p. 307 *sq.* ; Clouston, *op. cit.* p. 121.

(7) A Sicilian version. See Pitré, *Fiabe, Novelle e Racconti popolari Siciliani,* No. 160 'Lu muraturi e sò figghiu' (vol. 3. pp. 210-219); Crane, *Italian popular tales,* 'The mason and his son,' pp. 163-167.

(8) An old French version, *L'histoire du Chevalier Berinus.* See Dunlop-Liebrecht, *op. cit.* p. 264 ; Köhler, *op. cit.* p. 310 *sq.* ; Clouston, *op. cit.* p. 126 *sqq.*

(9) A version in the French poem *Dolopathos.* See Köhler *op. cit.* p. 305 *sq.*

(10) A Breton version. See Clouston, p. 129 *sqq.*

(11) A Dutch version. See Köhler, p. 306 *sq.* ; Clouston, p. 137 *sq.*

(12) A Danish version. See Köhler, p. 312 ; Clouston, p. 139.

(13) A German version. See J. W. Wolf, *Deutsche Hausmärchen,* 'Vom Räuberhauptmann Hans Kühstock,' pp. 397-403.

(14) Another German version cited by Köhler, p. 312.

(15) A Tyrolese version. See Köhler, p. 309 *sq.* ; Clouston, p. 138 *sq.*

(16) A Gaelic version. See J. F. Campbell, *Popular tales of the West Highlands,* No. xvii. d 'The tale of the Shifty Lad' (vol. 1. pp. 330-349).

(17) A Russian version. See Schiefner, *op. cit.* p. 312 *sqq.*

(18) Another Russian version. See *Mélusine,* 1878, p. 136 *sq.*

(19) A Tibetan version. See Schiefner, *op. cit.* p. 301 *sqq.* ; *id.,* *Tibetan tales derived from Indian sources,* No. 4 'The Clever Thief,' pp. 37-43.

(20) A Tartar version. See W. Radloff, *Proben der Volkslitteratur der türkischen Stämme Süd-Sibiriens,* 4. pp. 193-201, 'Der Dieb.'

(21) A Cinghalese version. See Clouston, p. 157 *sq.*

(22) A Syrian version. See Prym und Socin, *Syrische Sagen und Maerchen,* No. 42, pp. 170-173.

(23) A Kabyl version. See J. Rivière, *Contes populaires de la Kabylie du Djurdjura,* No. 3 'Les deux frères,' pp. 13-19.

(24) A Georgian version. See M. Wardrop, *Georgian Folk Tales* (London, 1894), p. 88 *sqq.* 'The Two Thieves.'

The following tales have also been compared, with more or less justice, to the story we are considering :

(25) A story in the *Kathá Sarit Ságara,* a Sanscrit collection of tales. See E. B. Cowell, in *Journal of Philology,* 1 (1868), pp. 67-70; *The Kathá Sarit Ságara,* translated by C. H. Tawney, 2. p. 93 *sqq.*

'Story of the two thieves, Ghata and Karpara'; Schiefner, in *Bulletin de l'Académie, etc.* (cited above), p. 306 *sqq.*

(26) An Albanian story.   See Dozon, *Contes albanais*, No. 15 'Les trois frères et les trois sœurs,' pp. 121-126.

(27) A Bengalee story.   See Lál Behari Day, *Folk-tales of Bengal*, No. 11 'The adventures of two thieves and of their sons,' pp. 160-181.

(28) A Kalmuck story in the *Siddhi-Kûr* collection.   See Jülg, *Kalmückische Märchen*, No. 12, pp. 58-60.

Of these four last stories, the Sanscrit and the Albanian ones are almost certainly versions, much distorted, of the tale under consideration; but the Bengalee and Kalmuck stories appear to me to have little or nothing to do with it.   With regard to the other versions, though the variations between them are considerable, the general scheme of the story is the same, and even in details there are many striking coincidences.   The thieves are sometimes two brothers, sometimes father and son, sometimes uncle and nephew; sometimes they are not related to each other at all.   Generally they are simply thieves who break a way for themselves into the king's treasury; but in Nos. (6) and (7), and apparently also in No. (14) the thieves are the builder of the treasury and his son.   In No. (8) the thieves are father and son, and the father learns the secret of the movable stone from the son of the builder of the treasury.   The incident of the dead man's hand, which occurs in the ancient Egyptian version, seems to be found in only two of the other versions (I speak with hesitation, for in the works cited above some of the stories are given in a very abridged form), namely the modern Greek (No. 4) and the Tartar version (No. 20).   The same incident occurs in another Tartar story of a different type (Radloff, *op. cit.* 3. p. 338).   Again, in the modern Greek version, as in the ancient Egyptian one, the thief shaves off half the beard of each of the guards.   But in the Kabyl and Tartar versions it is the thief who is half shaved, either by the guards (in the Kabyl tale) or by the princess (in the Tartar tale) as a mark by which to recognise him.   In one of the Russian versions (No. 18) the thief is shaved by the guards and shaves them in return.   In most of the tales, as in the ancient Egyptian version of it, the surviving thief marries the princess.   But a comparison of all the versions shows that the old Egyptian story, as told by Herodotus, is not the original from which all the rest are derived.   On the contrary, it seems clear that Herodotus has given us a much abridged version, which we are able partly to fill up by a comparison with the other versions.   Thus in Herodotus it is said that King Rhampsinitus commanded his guards to observe and apprehend any person who should weep over the headless corpse of the robber.   Nothing comes of this command in Herodotus's version of the tale.   But in many of the other versions the mother of the thief is represented as weeping over her dead son and as only saved from detection by the cunning and presence of mind of her other son.   Here then, we may be pretty sure, there is a gap in the story as told by Herodotus.

37. 7. the pit of Agamedes.   See ix. 39. 6.

37. 7. Ascalaphus and Ialmenus.   See Homer, *Iliad*, ii. 511 *sqq.*

37. 8. shared with the sons of Codrus in the expedition etc. See vii. 2. 1 *sqq.*

37. 8. They were driven from their homes by the Thebans. See ix. 15. 3 note.

38. 1. Orchomenus. Orchomenus, one of the oldest and most famous cities in Greece, occupied the eastern extremity of a sharply-marked chain of hills, now known as *Dourdouvana*—the Mount Acontium ('javelin') of the ancients—which extends east and west for about 6 miles, bounding the broad level plain of the Cephisus on the north. Beginning nearly opposite to Chaeronea, which lies at the foot of the hills on the southern side of the plain, the ridge rises gradually to a considerable height, runs eastward at this level for some miles, and then slopes down into the Copaic plain. From beginning to end it is the stoniest, barest, barrenest, and most forbidding chain of hills that can well be conceived; looking up at it you wonder if the foot of man has ever trodden these rugged and pathless solitudes. Close to the southern base of these desolate hills the Cephisus—a fairly broad and deep stream of turbid whitish water—flows between low banks fringed with tall willows; ducks disport themselves on its surface, and pigs wallow in the mire on its banks. According as the weather has been dry or rainy, the current is sluggish or rapid. Riding beside it under the willows on a grey November day you might fancy yourself on the banks of an English Ouse or Avon, if the cotton fields by the river-side and the towering ridge of naked rock beyond did not remind you that you are in a foreign land.

At its eastern end the ridge descends in a long and gentle slope, expanding fan-like as it descends, to the Copaic plain. This long slope was the site of Orchomenus. The position is one of great natural strength. On the south and north it is protected by the steep and rugged sides of the ridge which form, as it were, a first line of defence. At the foot of these declivities the waters of the Cephisus on the south and of the Melas on the north constitute a second line of defence; while on the east, where the descent to the plain is gradual, the site was till lately rendered secure by the great Copaic swamp which advanced to within a few hundred yards of the end of the slope. The ancient walls, of which considerable remains exist, started from the broad eastern foot of the hill, and followed its northern and southern brows upwards, converging more and more as they rose till at the upper end of the slope they were within about 30 yards of each other. Here at the head of the slope the walls end at the foot of a cliff which rises like a wall to a considerable height. Its small summit, reached by a long, steep, and narrow staircase hewn out of the rock, was the ancient acropolis. Yet this cliff, which presents such an imposing appearance on the east, is separated on the west only by a shallow depression of a few feet from the long rugged ridge of the hills. This, therefore, was the weak point in the circuit; and art had to be called in to supply the want of a natural defence. Accordingly the little citadel, protected by precipices on the east and north, was fortified on the west and south by immense walls of massive masonry, the remains of which are amongst the finest specimens of ancient Greek fortification in existence.   The fortress thus formed is very small, measuring on the inside only about 30 paces from north to south by 22 paces from east to west.   In fact, with its walls, which are still standing to a height of more than 30 feet, it more resembles a castle than an acropolis of the ordinary Greek type. But the magnificent masonry of the walls leaves no room to doubt that it is a Greek fortress of the very best period, probably of the fourth century B.C.—the golden age of Greek military engineering.   The two walls meet at a right angle at the south-west corner of the citadel.   The southern wall is preserved almost throughout its whole length (about 22 or 23 paces), though not to its full height.   The western wall, on the other hand, runs only for about 12 paces, stopping considerably short of the northern edge of the cliff.   Probably it was continued originally to the edge of the cliff, for here in a line with it is a piece of wall from two to four courses high and about 14 feet long from east to west, which was perhaps the termination of the western wall in this direction. The western wall is standing on its inner or eastern face to a height of twenty-two courses.   The courses, so far as they can be measured by a person standing on the ground, are uniformly 18 inches high ; hence the present height of the wall may be fairly estimated at 33 feet.   It is beautifully built of squared blocks of fairly uniform size laid in horizontal courses.   On its eastern side, towards what may be called the courtyard of the castle, the faces of the blocks are not carefully smoothed but left rather rough.   On its other or western side the wall is so rough—the blocks protruding at different lengths from its face—that it is quite clear that the existing wall was in fact only one face of the original wall. There must have been another wall of the same thickness and height some feet to the west of the existing wall, and the space between them was no doubt either filled with rubble or occupied by chambers.   Thus the rough western face of the existing wall was not, as has been supposed, the outer but the inner face of the wall.   That this must have been so is manifest also from the dimensions of the wall.   Its average thickness at present is about 18 inches, for that is the average thickness of each block and there is only one block in the thickness of the wall.   But it is clear that 18 inches is far too little for the total thickness of a fortification-wall 33 feet high or more.

The south wall of the citadel, on the other hand, is preserved in its full thickness.   In other words, both its faces are standing.   Each of these faces is a wall built in the same style and in courses of the same dimensions as the western wall.   The space between them measures 6 feet across ; and as the thickness of each face, being equivalent to the thickness of a single block, is 18 inches, the total thickness of the wall is 9 feet.   The space between the faces is not filled with rubble, but is occupied by a series of quadrangular compartments separated from each other by little cross-walls.   These compartments measure about 19 feet long by 6 feet wide.   They seem not to have communicated with each other.   The southern wall is built, as I have said, in exactly the same style as the western wall.   Its two outer faces are smoothed to just the same extent as the eastern face of the western wall ; and its two inner faces, in the quadrangular compartments, are left quite rough, just like the western face of the western wall.   On its southern side the wall is standing to a height of nineteen courses (about 28 feet) ; on its northern side, where it stands on a higher level, the number of courses preserved varies from twelve to thirteen.

On the inner or northern side of this great hollow southern wall and parallel to it is another wall which may be called the inner south wall. The distance between the two walls is 6 feet.   At its eastern end only one and two courses of this inner south wall are standing ; but where it abuts on the western wall it is seventeen courses (about 25 feet) high. The purpose of this inner south wall is not clear.   Possibly it may have supported a staircase leading up to the ramparts.   The space between it and the outer south wall can hardly have been filled with masonry or even occupied by compartments like those in the thickness of the outer south wall ; for the northern face of the latter wall is sufficiently smoothed to indicate that it was meant to be seen, not to be hidden by a core of rubble or concealed in the thickness of a double wall.

So much for the fortifications, still standing, which enclose the castle courtyard on the south and west.   Whether there were also walls on the eastern and northern sides, along the edge of the precipices, is not clear ; but several blocks, apparently of a fortification-wall, are lying on the north side.

Outside of the existing western wall of the citadel the ground is at present a good many feet higher than in the castle courtyard.   At this higher level the ground continues for a few yards and then descends into the slight hollow which divides the acropolis from the long stony ridge of Mount Acontium.   Thus the highest point of the acropolis is outside of the existing fortification-walls.   But some slight remains of four walls starting from the western wall and running westward at right angles to it suffice to prove that this highest point of the whole ancient site was occupied by a massive fortification of some sort.   This is confirmed by the extreme roughness and inequality, already noticed, of the west face of the western wall—a roughness which is only explicable on the hypothesis that there was a similar wall to the west of it which concealed the roughness and inequality of the protuberant blocks.

On Mount Acontium, not many yards to the west of the acropolis, are vestiges of a wall running across the crest of the mountain from north to south.   The wall is about 5 ft. 6 in. thick, and is standing to a height of one course in some places ; in others its line is marked only by a heap of stones.   After extending north and south for some way it makes an angle and runs eastward, disappearing close to the edge of the rocks a little to the south-west of the acropolis.   This wall was clearly an outwork designed to protect the citadel against an attack from the west.

We now quit the citadel to examine the remains of the lower city, which, as we have seen, occupied the long eastern slope of the hill from the foot of the castle rock to the plain.   That slope expands as it descends, so that the shape of the city was that of a long narrow triangle with the acropolis at its apex and its base on the plain.   To reach the lower city from the acropolis we descend the staircase in the cliff. It is long and very steep. At first it goes down straight eastward between walls of rock on either hand. Many of the steps are ruinous and care has to be taken in descending. Some shrubs have rooted themselves among the rock-hewn steps. After a steep descent of fifty steps the staircase makes a sharp turn and then descends for forty-four steps more in a south-easterly direction.[1] In this part the staircase has the cliff on the right as you descend, but is open on the left. On reaching the bottom you find yourself within the ruined walls of the lower city. Of both these walls, which ran along the northern and southern edges of the hill respectively, there are very considerable remains, the northern wall standing for a length of 300 yards or so and the southern wall for a still greater distance. Starting from the foot of the acropolis rock, they at first run parallel to each other for some way at a distance of 30 yards or so, after which they diverge more and more as they follow the gentle slope of the hill downwards. The style of masonry is not quite the same in the two walls. In both it is rough and massive; but whereas in the north wall the blocks are polygonal and are not laid in courses, in the south wall they are approximately quadrangular and some attempt has been made to lay them in regular courses. In both it is only the outer face which is constructed of large blocks; on the inside both walls more nearly resemble stone dykes than fortification-walls, being built of small stones which are hardly hewn or fitted together. The northern wall is 6 feet thick and is preserved unbroken to a height of a good many feet for a considerable distance. Near its eastern end it runs for some yards at a height of 11 or 12 feet. Five square towers project at intervals from its outer side; they measure about 21 feet on the face and project about 4 ft. 6 in. from the curtain. The most easterly of these towers is partially preserved to a height of 9 feet. On the western side of the fourth tower, counting from the east, is a small gateway about 3 feet wide.

The southern wall varies in thickness from about 5 to about 6 feet. Two to six courses of it are standing; the height in many places is from 8 to 10 feet; in one place at least it is 11 or 12 feet. Like the northern wall it was strengthened with square projecting towers, of which seven are partly preserved, with some doubtful traces of an eighth. These towers are from 19 to 24 feet broad, and project from 4 ft. 5 in. to 8 feet from the curtain. Their height corresponds generally with that of the wall, the number of their courses varying from two to six, and their greatest heights from 7 ft. 6 in. to 10, 11, or 12 feet. They are built of large massive blocks, which are on the whole squared. In the wall a few yards below the acropolis is a gateway 5 ft. 9 in. wide; a block of the lintel is still in its place. A good deal lower down the hill, still in the south wall, there is another small gateway, only 3 ft. 9 in. wide. About 150 yards or so below the acropolis the wall makes an entering angle to the north and is then continued eastward on the new line for

---

[1] These numbers (fifty and forty-four) are given by Leake and repeated by Schliemann. According to Lolling (Baedeker) the numbers are forty-three and forty-five. I did not count the steps.

perhaps 100 yards.   But beyond the entering angle the wall is prolonged
on its original or outer line for 20 yards or so and ends in a tower, from
which a cross-wall ran obliquely to join the new inner line of wall.   The
effect of this is to form an irregular quadrilateral of this shape :—

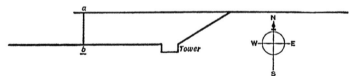

The space thus enclosed by walls would seem to have been an outwork
of some sort, but what the purpose of it may have been is not clear.   I
saw nothing in the conformation of the ground which called for it.
Apparently there was no gateway here, for the wall *a b* is closed.

Both the walls which have been described, the northern and the
southern, disappear entirely some way before they reach the foot of the hill,
though the southern is prolonged a good deal farther than the northern.
The long gently-sloping hill-side enclosed by the walls falls into two
sections, which may be approximately equal.   The upper section, which
begins at the citadel and has the shape of an elongated triangle, is a
good deal the steeper of the two and its surface is covered by rugged
rocks.   Clearly, therefore, it cannot have been inhabited.   The lower
section, of a quadrilateral shape, is much less steep ; its surface is mostly
a smooth and gentle slope of earth, though the rock also crops up here
and there.   The line between the two sections is a sharp one, being
marked both by the sudden cessation of the rocks which cover the upper
slope, and by the equally abrupt change in the inclination of the slope.
The two slopes, in fact, make a well-marked angle with each other.
The lower section, with its gentle slope and smooth surface of earth, was
no doubt the site of the ancient city.   Recent excavations have brought
to light ancient foundations on it, and probably many more remains are
hidden under the soil.   We can hardly doubt that on the east, just above
the plain, it was defended by a wall which united the northern and
southern walls at their eastern extremities.   But of this eastern wall I
could find no remains.   On the other hand, about 30 yards or so below
the line of rocks where the upper slope ends, I observed remains of a
wall running across the slope from north to south or rather from north-
west to south-east.   No piece of the wall is standing ; its line is traceable
merely by a row of rather large rugged blocks, and even these traces
extend across only a part of the slope.   Whether the wall originally
extended right across the slope, thus uniting the northern and southern
walls, does not appear.   Leake estimated the circumference of Orchomenus at about 2 miles.

On the lower slope of the hill, about 70 yards perhaps from the
point where the steeper rocky slope ends, a French archaeologist, Mr.
A. de Ridder, excavated in October 1893 the foundations of a building
which, from the inscriptions found near it, appears to have been a temple
of Aesculapius.   The temple apparently measured about 21 paces from

east to west by 12 paces from north to south ; at least the outer foundations of the building are preserved, with some gaps, to the extent
indicated. They are roughly built ; one and two courses of them are
visible. The temple seems to have been constructed of a dark grey
marble ; for some blocks of this stone, belonging to a higher course than
the foundations, are in position on the top of the northern and western
foundation-walls, and other squared blocks of the same marble are lying
about. Some pieces of the rough foundations are also standing in the
interior of the building. Part of one of the steps of the temple, built of
the dark marble, is in position at the western end, and on it lies a block
of the stylobate (?), which is also of the same material. Among the
inscriptions which enable us to identify the building as a temple of
Aesculapius is one which records a dedication to Aesculapius by a
certain Pythodorus, son of Theocydes. Two other inscriptions record
the dedication of slaves to Aesculapius ; one of them mentions an
offering dedicated "in the sanctuary of Aesculapius," while the other
makes mention of the priest of Aesculapius. This temple of Aesculapius,
discovered by Mr. de Ridder, is no doubt the one mentioned in two
inscriptions of Orchomenus which seem to date from about 250 B.C. and
contain the names of persons who contributed to the building or repair
of the temple (*C. I. G. G. S.* 1. Nos. 3191, 3192). This makes it
all the more curious that Mr. de Ridder should interpret the foundations
as those, not of a temple, but of two colonnades, an eastern and a
western, of which the eastern was built, according to him, about 600
B.C. and dedicated to some deity unknown. His reason for dating the
building, or rather the eastern half of it, so early is that all round about
it, and especially at the north-east corner, he found a great many archaic
objects of bronze which he would assign to the seventh or to the
beginning of the sixth century B.C. These objects include many diadems
engraved with spirals, volutes, dentils, and lozenges, or stamped with
rosettes and other patterns ; a spiral ring ; pear-shaped pendants ; and
a series of plates decorated with reliefs. The reliefs on these bronze
plates represent birds flying, sphinxes, a centaur, a griffin, a yoke of
horses, etc., arranged in horizontal bands which are broken up into compartments by vertical bands of spirals, maeanders, and other decorative
ornaments ; in some of the compartments there is a single animal, in
others a pair of animals facing each other. On the same site Mr. de
Ridder discovered potsherds of the various early types known to
archaeologists as Mycenaean, proto-Boeotian, and proto-Corinthian.
Among the Mycenaean potsherds is a fragment of a stirrup-vase (see
vol. 3. p. 112 *sq.*) In and about the temple Mr. de Ridder further laid
bare a number of later tombs hastily constructed of materials taken from
the temple.

About 50 yards farther up the hill than the temple of Aesculapius,
close to where the steeper slope and with it the rocks begin, I observed
two more foundation-walls which had apparently been laid bare by a
recent excavation. One of the walls is 15 paces long from east to west,
the other 7 paces long from north to south. The latter wall meets the
former at its west end, making a right angle. But the building clearly

measured originally about 12 paces from north to south. Part of the north foundation-wall is preserved.

At the eastern extremity of the long slope, outside the circuit of the ancient walls, is the great beehive tomb which Pausanias calls the Treasury of Minyas (see § 2 note). Not far from it, on the level ground at the foot of the hill, but a few feet above the village of *Skripou*, stands the monastery of 'the Falling asleep of the Mother of God' (*Koimesis tes Theotokou*). The church of the monastery, a domed building with three aisles, is very spacious and lofty. It is one of the oldest churches in Greece, having been built by Leo the *Protospatharius* in the year 872 A.D., as we learn from an inscription in the outer wall. Fragments of ancient buildings have been employed in the construction of the church and of part of the monastery. Many drums of columns, for example, are built into the walls of the church, and others are lying about. Hence it becomes probable that the monastery occupies the site of some ancient edifice, and this edifice would seem to have been the sanctuary of the Graces mentioned by Pausanias. For four inscriptions relating to the worship of the Graces have been found in the church. Three of these inscriptions contain lists of victors in the musical and poetical contests which were held in honour of the Graces (*C. I. G. G. S.* 1. Nos. 3195-3197). The fourth inscription records the dedication of a tripod to the Graces by the Boeotian confederacy (*C. I. G. G. S.* 1. No. 3207; *C. I. G.* No. 1593); it is engraved on one of two blocks of a round pedestal which no doubt supported the votive tripod. This pedestal still stands in the court of the monastery. The archaic statue known as the Apollo of Orchomenus was found at the monastery (see vol. 3. p. 40). From other inscriptions discovered at Orchomenus we learn that among the deities worshipped there were Gracious (*Meilichios*) Zeus, Full-grown (*Teleia*) Hera, Demeter, Artemis with the title of Ilithyia, the Mother of the Gods, Dionysus, Hermes, Serapis, Isis, and Anubis (*C. I. G. G. S.* 1. Nos. 3169, 3198-3204, 3210-3220). One fragmentary inscription, which seems to have contained a dedication, mentions together the names of Hermes and Minyas (*C. I. G. G. S.* 1. No. 3218); from which we may perhaps infer that Minyas received divine honours at Orchomenus. From coins and inscriptions it would seem that the forms Erchomenus and Erchomenian were more commonly employed than Orchomenus and Orchomenian. See Head, *Historia numorum*, p. 293 *sq.*; *C. I. G. G. S.* 1. Index, p. 764, *s.v.* Ἐρχομενός).

See Clarke, *Travels*, 4. p. 150 *sqq.*; Walpole's *Memoirs relating to Turkey* [2] (London, 1818), p. 341 *sq.*; Dodwell, *Tour*, 1. p. 226 *sqq.*; Leake, *Northern Greece*, 2. p. 144 *sqq.*; Mure, *Journal*, 1. p. 221 *sqq.*; H. N. Ulrichs, *Reisen und Forschungen*, 1. p. 178 *sqq.*; Fiedler, *Reise*, 1. p. 129; Welcker, *Tagebuch*, 1. p. 39 *sq.*; Vischer, *Erinnerungen*, p. 583 *sqq.*; Conze and Michaelis, in *Annali dell' Instituto*, 33 (1861), p. 79 *sqq.*; Bursian, *Geogr.* 1. p. 209 *sqq.*; H. Schliemann, *Orchomenos. Bericht über meine Ausgrabungen im böotischen Orchomenos* (Leipzig, 1881); *id.*, 'Exploration of the Boeotian Orchomenus,' *Journal of Hellenic Studies*, 2 (1881), pp. 122-163 (this article is a translation of the preceding work); J. P. Mahaffy, *Rambles and Studies*,[3] p. 221 *sqq.*; Baedeker,[3] p. 199 *sqq.*; *Guide-Joanne*, 2. p. 22 *sqq.*; P. Brandt, *Von Athen zum Tempethal*, p. 37 *sqq.*; A. de Ridder, 'Fouilles d'Orchomène,' *Bulletin de Corresp. hellénique*, 19 (1895), pp. 137-224. I was at Orchomenus, 1st and 2nd November 1895, and have described the situation and ruins from personal observation, except that I have borrowed from Leake the number of steps in the staircase leading up to the acropolis. Mr. de Ridder's account of the building which he excavated and which I have called the temple of Aesculapius appears to me partly so obscure and partly so improbable that I have put it aside and substituted for it my own imperfect notes, made on the spot.

With regard to the name of the range of hills at the end of which Orchomenus lies, the whole chain from Orchomenus westward to the defile of Parapotamii, where the Cephisus makes its way from Phocis into Boeotia, seems to have been called Acontium (Strabo, ix. p. 416) ; but the eastern extremity of it, on which Orchomenus stood, was known as Hyphanteum (Strabo, ix. p. 424). One part of the chain, probably the western, was distinguished from Acontium and called Hedylium or Hadylium (Plutarch, *Sulla*, 16 *sq.*), though the name Hedylium was sometimes applied to the whole range from Orchomenus to Parapotamii (Strabo, ix. p. 424). Cp. Leake, *Northern Greece*, 2. p. 99 *sq.* There is indeed a well-marked natural division between the two parts of the range. The eastern is the higher, more striking, and more desolate of the two.

38. 1. sanctuary —— of the Graces. This sanctuary, as we have seen (p. 186), probably occupied the site of the monastery of the *Koimesis tes Theotokou* at *Skripou* (Orchomenus). Cp. note on ix. 35. 1.

38. 1. They worship the natural stones most. That is, the most revered images of the Graces were unhewn stones. Cp. vii. 22. 4 note.

38. 1. a fountain at Orchomenus etc. This is probably the Acidalian fountain in which the Graces were said to bathe (Servius, on Virgil, *Aen.* i. 720; cp. Suidas, *s.v.* Ἀκιδαλία ; *Etymolog. Magnum*, *s.v.* Ἀκιδαλίη, p. 48). It may very well be the spring which rises at the northern foot of the hill of Orchomenus, at a point where the rocky slope is still low and gradual. There are traces of a flight of steps in the rock leading down to it. The water now issues from three spouts in a modern wall which bears the inscription :—

ΑΚΥΔΑΛΙΑ (*sic*)

ΚΡΗΝΗ

1843

The water of the spring forms a small pool, and immediately joins the little reedy marsh made at the northern foot of the hill by the Melas which here flows along eastward from sources farther to the west. The course of the stream is fringed with willows. Cp. H. N. Ulrichs, *Reisen und Forschungen*, 1. p. 183 ; Schliemann, in *Journal of Hellenic Studies*, 2 (1881), p. 156 ; Baedeker,[3] p. 200 ; *Guide-Joanne*, 2. p. 24. In the court of the monastery of the *Koimesis tes Theotokou* at Orchomenus there is an ancient well which has sometimes been taken for the Acidalian fountain (Clarke, *Travels*, 4. p. 155 ; Mahaffy, *Rambles and Studies*,[3] p. 223; *Guide-Joanne*, 2. p. 23). But the spring answers better to Pausanias's description than the well.

38. 2. The treasury of Minyas. This was a building of the same plan and nearly the same dimensions as the so-called Treasury of Atreus at Mycenae (see vol. 3. p. 124 *sqq.*) It was doubtless not a treasury (a treasury would never have been built outside the walls of the city), but the tomb of one or more of the old kings of Orchomenus. The ruins of it may be seen a little to the west of the monastery, imbedded in the short but steep declivity which forms the last step down to the plain of the long gently-sloping site of Orchomenus. Like the similar structures of which so many have been found in Greece, the so-called Treasury of Minyas comprised a spacious domed chamber of circular shape (the beehive tomb) approached by a broad straight passage (*dromos*) leading horizontally through the hill-side ; and, like the Treasury of Atreus at Mycenae, it had in addition a square inner chamber opening off the larger domed chamber. The entrance to the tomb was known to and described by travellers from the beginning of the nineteenth century onwards, but it was not till 1880 that the interior, which had long been blocked with fallen stones and rubbish, was excavated by Schliemann. In 1886 the same indefatigable explorer, accompanied by Dr. Dörpfeld, returned to the spot and made some fresh excavations. Before his time, in 1862, an enterprising mayor of the village, Mr. Gadakes, had pulled down the whole of the walls of the *dromos* in order to procure building materials for a new church, although, as Schliemann observes, the village already possessed two churches, each of them large enough to hold the whole population not only of *Skripou* but of the neighbouring village of *Petromagoula.*

Of the walls which had lined the passage (*dromos*) leading to the tomb a single stone had escaped the ravages of Mr. Gadakes, and from this it is inferred that the passage was 18 feet wide. The gateway with a block of the lintel is preserved. The walls on each side of it are standing to a height of twelve courses. The opening of the gateway, which is 18 ft. 4¾ in. high, narrows somewhat from bottom to top. On the level of the ground it is 9 ft. ⅖ in. wide ; at the top it is 8 ft. 2¾ in. wide. The length of the corridor from the doorway into the circular chamber is 17 ft. 8 in. A portion of the threshold remains, consisting of two superposed slabs, which are well polished and measure 9 ft. ⅖ in. in length by 3 ft. ⅜ in. in breadth. In the upper slab there are some curiously-shaped grooves and sockets which prove that there were double-folding doors. The block of the lintel which remains in its place over the inner part of the corridor leading from the doorway into the tomb is a huge block about 15 ft. long by 7 ft. 6 in. broad and 3 ft. 3 in. deep.[1] But as the outline of the block is irregular at the ends and sides it is not possible to give its dimensions exactly. On its inner side the stone is curved horizontally so as to follow the curve of the circular chamber, and vertically so as to follow the curve of the

---

[1] These are my measurements. According to Dodwell, the length of the lintel is 15 ft. 4 in. ; according to Leake, 16 feet ; according to H. N. Ulrichs, 18 feet ; and according to Baedeker, 6 metres or 18 ft. 8 in. If we could trust these measurements, the stone must have been steadily growing since the beginning of the century. Schliemann's measurements are as follows : length, 16 ft. 8 in. ; breadth, 7 ft. 5 in. ; depth, 3 ft. 2½ in.

dome. The tomb, including the lintel, is built of the same dark grey marble as the temple of Aesculapius (see above, p. 184 *sq.*) The colour inclines to a steely blue-black, but by exposure to the air this marble takes a creamy yellow colour, which is at present the general colour of the walls of the tomb. Hence Col. Leake described the marble as white. It is only indeed where the stones are broken that the dark grey colour appears. The roof of the inner chamber, however, was constructed of a totally different sort of stone (see below).

The diameter of the circular chamber is 46 ft. 10 in. from south-west to north-east and from west to east, but 46 ft. 1½ in. from north to south. The chamber is therefore smaller by 3 feet and some inches than the corresponding chamber in the Treasury of Atreus at Mycenae, which is 50 feet in diameter. The upper part of the dome of the circular chamber is gone, but the walls are still standing to a height, in general, of eight courses; at the doorway there are twelve courses standing. The masonry is quite regular; the blocks are quadrangular and laid in horizontal courses; they are smoothed on their outer surfaces and accurately fitted together. In appearance this most ancient wall is as fresh as if it had been built yesterday. The blocks of the two lowest courses are in general larger than the blocks of the upper courses; some of them are over 5 feet in length. From the fifth course upward almost every stone has a hole in it with the remains of a bronze nail. These nails appear to have been used to fasten circular bronze plates, probably shaped like rosettes, to the wall; for round the holes may be traced circular grooves cut in the stone, and some fragments of bronze plates were found in the tomb by Schliemann. The holes in each course of masonry are arranged so that a perpendicular line drawn through each hole would pass at equal distances between the two holes in the course above. Among the marble slabs found by Schliemann in the tomb is one which from its peculiarly-curved shape and general appearance he judged to be the keystone mentioned by Pausanias. It is pierced with a hole nearly 3 inches in diameter.

Nearly in the middle of the circular chamber, but somewhat nearer the north side, is a marble pedestal about 19 feet long with two short returns at each end, in this shape ⌐▭⌐. It supported several marble statues, of which some fragments have been found. The style both of the sculptures and of the mouldings of the pedestal proves that this monument is not earlier than the Macedonian period. In front of the base there seems to have been a table or sarcophagus. Schliemann conjectured that the monument was raised over the bones of Hesiod, which, as Pausanias tells us immediately, were brought back from Naupactus to Orchomenus. But Pausanias speaks as if the grave of Hesiod were quite distinct from this beehive tomb, which he calls the Treasury of Minyas; and we are expressly told that the poet's remains were deposited in the middle of the market-place (Proclus, *Vita Hesiodi*, 4, in *Biographi Graeci*, ed. Westermann, p. 49)—a spot which the Greeks often assigned as a last resting-place to the ashes of their most illustrious dead (see vol. 2. p. 533).

In the eastern side of the circular chamber a doorway 6 ft. 10 in.[1] high leads into the smaller quadrangular chamber. Like the great doorway of the circular chamber, this smaller doorway narrows somewhat from bottom to top. Below its width is 3 ft. 11 in. ; above its width is 3 ft. 8 in. In the wall of the circular chamber immediately above and on either side of this doorway is a triple row of holes, in most of which are the remains of bronze nails. This proves that the entrance to the side-chamber was even more elaborately adorned with bronze plates than the rest of the great domed chamber. The corridor leading from the doorway into the side-chamber is 9 ft. 4 in. long and 7 ft. 2 in. high. The threshold of the doorway is formed by a stone 1 ft. 3½ in. broad, on the upper surface of which are three quadrangular grooves on either side. The sides of the corridor are preserved to their full height ; the number of courses in the wall on each side is four. The side-chamber into which the corridor leads is hewn out of the native calcareous rock. It seems to have been sunk from above like a shaft, not excavated from the domed chamber ; for the hewn face of the rock rises vertically several feet above the line of the roof of the chamber. All four sides of the chamber thus hewn out of the rock were lined with walls built of small rough stones bonded with clay and averaging about 4 ft. 6 in. in thickness. Measured within these walls, the chamber was 12 ft. 7½ in. long from east to west and 9 ft. 3⅘ in. wide from north to south. The floor consists of the smoothed and levelled rock ; it is on the same level as the floor of the domed chamber. At a height of 8 feet above the floor the chamber was roofed with four slabs of pale greenish schist, which were laid across it in the direction from north to south. The lower sides of these slabs, forming the ceiling of the chamber, were delicately carved in low relief with a beautiful pattern composed of rosettes, spirals, and a sort of palmette. An outer border of rosettes enclosed rows of spirals intertwined with palmettes ; within these again there was a double border of spirals, which again enclosed rows of spirals intertwined with palmettes. It has been suggested that this elaborate design was copied from a carpet pattern. The walls of the chamber appear to have been lined with marble slabs carved with the same pattern ; above and below ran a border of rosettes, and the intermediate space was filled with spirals and palmettes. Schliemann found some remains of this marble lining of the walls still in position. But the magnificent roof had fallen in before he excavated the tomb. From the information given him by the villagers it would seem that the roof remained in its place till 1870, when it gave way with a loud crash, and the earth which it had supported having fallen in at the same time a deep hole in the ground was formed. When I visited the tomb in 1895 the side-chamber was choked with a mass of broken stones and some very large slabs. The walls which once lined the sides of the chamber had either fallen in or were buried under rubbish. Some of the slabs of the roof, exhibiting the pattern which has been described, lay in the beehive chamber. Altogether the place presented a neglected

---

[1] This is my measurement. According to Schliemann the height of the door is 6 ft. 3¾ in. high (*Journal of Hellenic Studies*, 2 (1881), p. 144.

and forlorn appearance. It was perfectly open; no precautions were taken to protect the tomb from the depredations of the villagers and of unscrupulous travellers.

The close resemblance of the great beehive tomb at Orchomenus to the beehive tombs at Mycenae, and especially to the so-called Treasury of Atreus, points to the conclusion that the ancient peoples who inhabited these cities and built these tombs were akin to each other in the type of their civilisation at least, if not in blood. This conclusion, drawn from the general plan and construction of the tombs, is confirmed by the decorative pattern carved on the roof and walls of the inner chamber in the Orchomenian tomb, since that pattern, in its combination of rosettes and spirals, is thoroughly Mycenaean in character. Additional confirmation is derived from the resemblance of the archaic pottery found at Orchomenus to that found at Mycenae as well as at other places where the Mycenaean type of civilisation prevailed. Of this Orchomenian pottery Schliemann says : " It is very remarkable that at Orchomenus painted pottery, with spirals and other Mycenian ornamentation, also cows with two long horns and the same variegated colours as at Mycenae, as well as goblets of the very same form and colour as at Mycenae, are generally only found down to a depth of about 6 feet below the surface of the ground, and that at a greater depth, monochrome, black, red, or yellow, hand-made or wheel-made pottery is found almost exclusively, analogous to some of that collected by me in the royal sepulchres at Mycenae. Very frequent here are the large hand-made black goblets or bowls, with a hollow foot and horizontal flutings in the middle, which I also found at Mycenae ; also fragments of vases having a perpendicular excrescence with a *vertical* perforation for suspension on either side ; also fragments of vases having on each side a horizontal excrescence with a *vertical* hole. But most fragments belong to vases having on each side excrescences with a *horizontal* tubular hole for suspension." Fragments of glazed or lustrous pottery, resembling the glazed Mycenaean ware, were also found by Schliemann in the tomb as well as in the lowest strata of the shafts and trenches which he dug somewhat higher up the hill to the north-west, not far from the Acidalian spring. Rude designs of curious form are painted on some of the glazed potsherds.

As to the beehive tomb of Orchomenus see (in addition to the works on Orchomenus referred to above, p. 186) *Verhandlungen der Berliner Gesellschaft für Anthropologie und Urgeschichte*, for 1886, pp. 376-379 (published with the Berlin *Zeitschrift für Ethnologie*) ; C. Schuchhardt, *Schliemann's Ausgrabungen*,[2] pp. 352-359 ; Ch. Belger, *Beiträge zur Kenntniss der griechischen Kuppelgräber*, pp. 34-37 ; Perrot et Chipiez, *Histoire de l'art dans l'antiquité*, 6. pp. 439-447. I visited the tomb, 2nd and 3rd November 1895, and have described it partly from personal observation.

38. 3. graves of Minyas and Hesiod. These are not to be looked for in the Treasury of Minyas (the great beehive tomb), though some writers have supposed that this is what Pausanias meant (see above, p. 189). Moreover, as we have seen (*ib.*), the bones of Hesiod are said to have been laid in the market-place of Orchomenus. This statement, if we accept it, seems fatal to the other identifications of the tomb of Hesiod which have been suggested ; for whereas the market-place must have been within the walls of the city, the suggested sites all lie outside of them. Thus H. N. Ulrichs found in the plain about five minutes to the north of the monastery, on the right of the path, the remains of what he conjectured to have been a *heroon* or chapel dedicated to the worship of Hesiod as a hero. The building had apparently been 22 feet long by 11 feet broad, but only about a third of it was standing ; amongst the blocks Ulrichs saw a piece of a cornice of bluish marble decorated with a simple Greek pattern. See H. N. Ulrichs, *Reisen und Forschungen*, 1. p. 193 *sq.* Two conical hillocks have also been pointed to as possibly marking the graves of Hesiod and Minyas. The natives call them *Magoula*. At present they are planted with vines and exactly resemble the so-called heroic tombs of the Troad. One of them is near *Skripou;* the other is farther to the west, near the village of *Rhomaiko.* See Schliemann, in *Journal of Hellenic Studies*, 2 (1881), pp. 130, 156; Dodwell, *Tour*, 1. p. 232 ; Clarke, *Travels*, 4. p. 150 *sq.*

38. 3. **they recovered the bones of Hesiod** etc. Cp. Aristotle, *Fragmenta*, ed. V. Rose (Leipzig, 1886), No. 565, p. 346 *sqq.*; *Biographi Graeci*, ed. Westermann, pp. 42, 49.

38. 3. **a crow would show them the spot** etc. Cp. Lucian, *De morte Peregrini*, 41.

38. 4. **Ascra with the many corn-fields.** The bottom of the pleasant valley of Ascra or Valley of the Muses is still mainly corn-land, though sheep may also be seen browsing in it.

38. 5. **a bronze likeness of the spectre** etc. On a coin of Orchomenus the chained image of the spectre (an ordinary human being in appearance) is represented on one side ; on the other side of the coin is Artemis kneeling, armed with a bow. See Daremberg et Saglio, *Dict. des Antiquités, s.v.* 'Actaeon,' vol. 1. p. 53.

38. 6. **a temple of Hercules —— the springs of the river Melas.** The river Melas, now known by the equivalent name of *Mavro-potamos* ('black river'), is formed by the union of several streams which take their rise in copious springs not far from Orchomenus. These springs issue at various points of that branch of the Copaic plain which lies immediately to the north of the hill of Orchomenus and which, when the Copaic Lake existed, was known as the Bay of *Tzamali.* At the present time, though the lake has been drained, this part of the plain remains still to a great extent a marsh overgrown with thickets of reeds and does not dry up even in summer ; for the springs which feed the marsh are not only abundant but perennial. One of these springs is the Acidalian fountain, already described (p. 187), which rises at the northern foot of the hill of Orchomenus, not far from the monastery. Another important spring, now called *Petakas,* rises farther north, in the direction of the village of *Tzamali ;* and a third, known as *Polygyra* or *Polyra*, comes to the surface under a rock at the north-west corner of the bay, near the site of the ancient Aspledon. The strong stream formed by this last spring is called, like the spring itself, *Polygyra* up to the point where it joins the other stream coming from the Acidalian and *Petakas* springs.

The river formed by the union of these streams has derived its name both in ancient and modern times from the dark colour of its deep clear water, in contrast to the light-coloured and muddy water of the neighbouring Cephisus.   This dark colour is said to be due to the absence of all solid particles which could reflect the light.   The river flows in a deep bed fringed with tall reeds.   Some of the ground about its sources is a reedy swamp.   The ancients, as we have seen (p. 111), confused the lower part of the course of the Melas with the Cephisus, though in reality the Cephisus used to lose itself in the swamp, whereas the Melas has from time immemorial flowed in a sharply-marked bed of its own from the western to the eastern end of the Copaic basin, disappearing finally into the great chasm or *katavothra* at the north-eastern corner of the plain.   This mistake was made even by Plutarch, the best informed of the ancient writers who have touched on the Melas.   It was to be expected that he should know it well, since he lived at Chaeronea, only a few miles from the river.   He says : "Of all the Boeotian plains the largest and fairest is that of Orchomenus.   It stretches away, flat and treeless, to the marshes in which the river Melas is swallowed up.   That river rises under the city of Orchomenus and is the only Greek river which is navigable at its sources.   It swells at the summer solstice, like the Nile, and bears plants like those of the Nile, only they are stunted and have no fruit.   The river, however, does not flow far.   Most of it immediately vanishes in stagnant and swampy meres ; but a small part of its water joins the Cephisus, and at the meeting of the rivers the reeds which are used for flutes grow most plentifully in the mere" (Plutarch, *Sulla*, 20).   Compare *id.*, *Pelopidas*, 16 ; Strabo, ix. pp. 407, 415 ; Theophrastus, *De causis plant.* v. 5. 2.   According to Theophrastus (*Hist. plant.* iv. 11. 8 *sq.*) the reeds used for making flutes grew most plentifully between the Melas and the Cephisus rivers, the best of all being those which grew in certain deep pools called Pots (*Chutroi*) in this part of the marsh ; whereas at the actual junction of the rivers, though the marsh was deep and the bottom rich and slimy, the reeds were scarce and of indifferent quality.

See Leake, *Northern Greece*, 2. pp. 154-157 ; Dodwell, *Tour*, 1. p. 234 ; Forchhammer, *Hellenika*, p. 174 *sq.* ; H. N. Ulrichs, *Reisen und Forschungen*, 1. pp. 183, 191 *sq.* ; A. Philippson, in *Zeitschrift d. Gesell. f. Erdkunde zu Berlin*, 29 (1894), pp. 39-42.

In 1893 Mr. de Ridder found what he believed to be the temple of Hercules which Pausanias tells us was situated at the source of the Melas.   The spot is at the northern foot of the hill of Orchomenus about three-quarters of a mile west of the Acidalian spring, between the hill on the south and a marsh on the north.   The marsh is formed by a spring which is the most westerly of the sources of the Melas.   Its water is enclosed by a wall which only allows it to escape in a north-easterly direction.   On the hill-side above the marsh are to be seen a number of steps, platforms, and pedestals, all hewn out of the rock at different levels.   In clearing away the soil to the level of the rock Mr. de Ridder discovered a few Mycenaean potsherds, including a piece of

a stirrup-vase of advanced style (see vol. 3. p. 112 *sq.*), also potsherds of
the styles known as proto-Boeotian, proto-Corinthian, and Corinthian,
bronze plates decorated with reliefs like those which he found at the
temple of Aesculapius in Orchomenus (above, p. 185), and a few archaic
terra-cottas.　No potsherds of the classical period were found, except
two fragments of black-figured vases.　These remains undoubtedly prove
that an ancient sanctuary existed here, but there is nothing to show that
it was a sanctuary of Hercules.　Certainly the temple of Hercules mentioned by Pausanias has not been found ; for the term *naos* ('temple')
employed by Pausanias could not possibly apply, as Mr. de Ridder supposes, to a collection of bases and votive offerings.　See A. de Ridder,
'Fouilles d'Orchomène,' *Bulletin de Corresp. hellénique*, 19 (1895),
pp. 150-155, 169 *sqq.*　Schliemann conjectured that the temple of
Hercules may have stood some 200 or 300 yards to the west of the
Acidalian spring near a vertical cavern about 60 feet deep, from the foot
of which bubbles forth one of the sources of the Melas.　The rocks
about the upper end of the cavern are artificially cut, apparently for the
foundations of a building.　But as the place is immediately below the
walls of Orchomenus it does not answer to Pausanias's description of
the situation of the temple.　See Schliemann, in *Journal of Hellenic
Studies*, 2 (1881), p. 132 *sq.* ; cp. A. de Ridder, *op. cit.* pp. 150, 154.

38. 7. **the river Cephisus was diverted by Hercules into the plain**
etc.　Polyaenus relates that Hercules in his war with the Minyans of
Orchomenus (see Paus. ix. 17. 2 ; ix. 24. 5 ; ix. 37. 2 *sq.*) blocked up
with huge stones the chasm through which the river flowed into the sea.
This he did in order to flood the plain and so render useless the cavalry
of the Minyans, in which their strength lay.　But after his victory he
cleared away the obstacles and the river returned to its old bed.　See
Polyaenus, i. 3. 5 ; cp. Diodorus, iv. 18. 7.　The legend seems to
show that at an early period the chasms on the north-east side of the
Copaic basin sufficed to receive and discharge all the water of the lake ;
but that afterwards they were blocked more or less completely and
consequently the adjoining plain became a marsh.　This blocking of
the chasms may have been brought about by natural causes such as
earthquakes or landslips ; for which the agency of Hercules may be only
a mythical expression.　Strabo tells us (ix. p. 406) that the chasms
(*katavothras*) were sometimes blocked and sometimes opened by earthquakes, and that according as they were shut or open the neighbouring
ground was a lake or a plain.　Cp. M. L. Kambanis, in *Bulletin de
Corresp. hellénique*, 16 (1892), p. 136 *sq.*　But it is also possible that
the obstruction of the chasms was the work of enemies, who took this
very effectual means of damaging their rivals.　The tradition which
attributed the blocking of the emissory to the Theban Hercules points
in fact, as D. Curtius held (*Gesammelte Abhandlungen*, i. p. 286), to
the view that the obstruction of the chasm and the consequent flooding
of the plain were the work of the Thebans in a war with their hated
rivals, the Minyans.　Now it is worth observing that one of the principal
katavothras or chasms by which the water of the lake escaped, the
katavothra of *Spitia* or *Varia*, a little to the west of the pass which

leads from the Copaic plain to Larymna on the Euripus, is blocked with great masses of fallen rocks, and that one of the most important of the ancient canals made by the Minyans is conducted directly to the mouth of this particular *katavothra*. See A. Philippson, in *Zeitschrift der Gesellschaft für Erdkunde zu Berlin*, 29 (1894), pp. 48, 57 *sq.* Cp. F. Noack, in *Mittheilungen d. arch. Inst. in Athen*, 19 (1894), p. 413 *sqq.* Two of the three chasms (*katavothras*) of *Bynia*, close to the point where the path to Larymna quits the Copaic plain, are also blocked artificially with stones, as I observed on my visit to them. But whether this obstruction is ancient or modern I could not say.

38. 7. Homer —— says. See *Iliad*, v. 709.

38. 8. This is proved by Homer etc. See *Iliad*, ix. 381.

38. 9. Aspledon. According to Strabo (ix. p. 415) Aspledon was 20 furlongs from Orchomenus, from which it was separated by the river Melas. He tells us that the place was sometimes called Spledon, and that the name of the town and district was afterwards changed to Eudielus, perhaps from its western exposure (Εὐδείελος — ἐκ τοῦ δειλινοῦ κλίματος). Leake thought that Aspledon may have been at *Tzamali*, a hamlet on the edge of what used to be the Copaic mere, to the north-west of Orchomenus. But *Tzamali* has an eastern exposure, and water is plentiful there, whereas Pausanias tells us that Aspledon was abandoned by its inhabitants on account of the want of water. Forchhammer and Lolling (Baedeker) were perhaps right in identifying with Aspledon the ruins now known as *Avriokastro* or 'Castle of the Hebrews,' which are to be seen on an isolated hill of whitish earth that rises conspicuously among darker heights on the northern edge of the great plain some 2 or 3 miles to the west of Tegyra (*Xeropyrgo*, see below). The ruins of the circuit-wall, about 600 paces in extent, may still be traced, and the foundations of houses appear above the soil. The spot has a southern aspect, is sheltered from the north by the lofty Mount *Chlomo*, and receives the evening sunshine long after the shadows have fallen on the places on the opposite or southern side of the plain. Dodwell conjectured that Aspledon might be at *Xeropyrgo* or *Pyrgo*, a village on an isolated round hill surmounted by a very tall square tower of the Middle Ages, 3 miles east-north-east of Orchomenus, from which it used to be divided by the Copaic Lake and is still divided by the deep waters of the Melas. However, *Xeropyrgo* answers better to Plutarch's description of Tegyra, which was near Orchomenus, but divided from it by the marsh caused by the Melas river, so that the one place could be reached from the other only by making a long circuit at the foot of the hills. At Tegyra, a little above the marshes, there was a temple of the Tegyraean Apollo with an oracle, which had been in high repute down to the Persian war but had come to an end not long before Plutarch's time. Apollo was said to have been born there; the neighbouring hill was called Delos; and behind the temple rose two copious springs of sweet and cold water. One of the springs was called Phoenix ('palm-tree') and the other Elaea ('olive-tree'), and Latona was said to have given birth to Apollo between them. See Plutarch, *Pelopidas*, 16; *id., De defect. Orac.* 5 and 8; Stephanus Byzantius, *s.v.* Τέγυρα. Into the tower at *Xeropyrgo* are built some large polygonal blocks. Remains of the ancient walls from which these blocks were probably taken may be seen between the tower and the marsh; one of the pieces of wall is 20 feet long by 7 or 8 feet thick.

See Dodwell, *Tour,* I. p. 233; Leake, *Northern Greece,* 2. pp. 159 *sq.,* 162 *sq.*; Forchhammer, *Hellenika,* p. 177; H. N. Ulrichs, *Reisen und Forschungen,* I. p. 196 *sq.* ; Bursian, *Geogr.* I. p. 211 ; Schliemann, in *Journal of Hellenic Studies,* 2 (1881), p. 161 ; Baedeker,[3] p. 197.

38. 9. the verses of Chersias. This poet seems to have been a contemporary and acquaintance of Periander, tyrant of Corinth. Plutarch introduces him into his *Banquet of the Seven Sages* (chapters 13, 14, and 21). Cp. *Epicorum Graecorum fragmenta,* ed. Kinkel, p. 207 *sq.*

39. 1. Lebadea. The modern town of Lebadea (*Livadia*) retains the ancient name slightly altered. It stands very picturesquely at the mouth of a wild gorge in the mountains, facing northward across the plain. The white houses with their red roofs and wooden balconies climb the hill-sides on both banks of the Hercyna, a clear and copious stream, which issues from the gorge and rushes noisily through the streets in a rocky bed, turning some mills and spanned by several bridges. At the back of the town a steep rocky hill, crowned with the ruins of a great mediaeval castle, descends in sheer and lofty precipices into the gorge on the left bank of the stream. The houses extend down into the plain, scattered among gardens and clumps of trees which give the town, as seen from below, an agreeable aspect. The mountains at the foot of which Lebadea lies are the northern spurs of Mount Helicon; the high conical summit to the east is the ancient Mount Laphystius, now the mountain of *Granitsa.* The plain that lies spread out below the town on the north melts eastward into the great Copaic plain; on the north it is divided by a chain of low hills from the parallel plain of Chaeronea.

The greater part of the water of the Hercyna rises in the profound gorge immediately behind the town. Here, at the foot of the great precipice which is surmounted by the ruins of the castle, a cold spring called *Kryo* ('cold') issues from the rocks and is conducted into a small well-house. Some niches for holding votive offerings are cut in the face of the cliff above it. The largest of these cuttings is a chamber about 12 feet square and 9 feet high, hewn out of the rock about 6 feet above the ground. The roof is slightly vaulted; just under it the remains of painted ornaments were still visible at the beginning of the nineteenth century. Right and left, in the sides of the chamber, are benches cut in the rock. In this cool retreat the Turkish governor of Lebadea used to smoke his pipe in the heat of the day. Below the chamber, a little to the left of it, a narrow opening leads 20 or 30 feet into the rock, ending in a hole at the bottom of which water lies. On the opposite side of the ravine, a few paces off, near some plane-trees, several springs of clear but lukewarm water rush turbulently from the ground, and, united with the water of the *Kryo,* form the Hercyna. They turn a cotton-mill close to the spot where they rise. That some

of these springs are the waters of Memory and Forgetfulness of which
all who would consult Trophonius had to drink before descending into
the oracular pit (§ 7 *sq.*), is highly probable ; but we have no means of
identifying these mystic waters.   An alteration in the flow of one of the
springs (the *Kryo*) is known to have occurred within the nineteenth
century ; and many such changes may have taken place since antiquity.
The general features of the spot, however, have probably changed but
little, and they are well fitted to impress the imagination.   The many
springs gurgling strongly from the ground, the verdant plane-trees, the
caverned rocks, the great precipices soaring on three sides of us and
overhung on the west by the ruins of the mediaeval castle, make up a
scene which once seen is not easily forgotten.   But the ravine of which
this is after all only the mouth does not end here.   Its deep, narrow,
stony bed, sometimes dry, sometimes traversed by a raging torrent,
winds far into the heart of the mountains, shut in on either hand like a
cañon by tremendous crags.   If you follow it upwards for some miles,
the country begins to open up and you find yourself in bleak and desolate
highlands.   A profound silence reigns, broken only by the cry of a
water-ouzel beside the torrent or the screaming of hawks far up the cliffs.

   In Turkish times *Livadia* was the capital of the province and a
place of considerable importance.   It is still a lively, cheerful town
with a busy bazaar and a population of 5000.   The extensive wool trade
of the Copaic basin and the valley of the Cephisus has its centre here.
As might have been expected, the materials of the ancient city have
long ago been employed to build or repair the modern town.   Some
large squared blocks, taken from an ancient edifice, are built into the
walls of the castle, which in its turn suffered severely from the great
earthquake of April 1894.   The old city probably stood on the eastern
bank of the Hercyna ; for Pausanias tells us that the river separated
the city from the grove of Trophonius (§ 2), and there is reason to
believe that the grove was on the western side of the river (see note on
§ 4 'a temple of King Zeus').   It would seem not to have occupied
the site of the modern town, but to have stood about ten minutes farther
to the north, on an isolated hill called *Trypaeolithari*, which rises from
the plain and round which the Hercyna flows in two branches.   On this
hill there are foundations and other traces of an ancient city.   The
French surveyors and L. Ross placed ancient Lebadea here, and this
situation certainly answers better to Pausanias's description of the city
as built on low ground.

   Amongst the deities who are known from inscriptions to have been
worshipped at Lebadea are Dionysus, Hermes, Artemis, Pan, and the
Nymphs (*C. I. G. G. S.* 1. Nos. 3092-3095, 3098, 3100).   One inscription
records a dedication to the Gentle Artemises (in the plural) (*C. I. G. G. S.*
1. No. 3101).   But the great deity of the place was Trophonius or Zeus
Trophonius, as he was also called (*C. I. G. G. S.* 1. Nos. 3077, 3090,
3098).

   See Wheler, *Journey*, p. 326 *sqq.* ; Clarke, *Travels*, 4. p. 117 *sqq.* ; Walpole's
Memoirs relating to Turkey [2] (London, 1818), p. 340 *sq.* ; Dodwell, *Tour*, 1. p. 211
sqq. ; Leake, *Northern Greece*, 2. p. 118 *sqq.* ; Mure, *Journal*, 1. p. 229 *sqq.* ;

Welcker, *Tagebuch*, 2. p. 42 *sqq.* ; H. N. Ulrichs, *Reisen und Forschungen*, 1.
p. 164 *sqq.* ; Fiedler, *Reise*, 1. p. 130 *sq.* ; L. Ross, *Wanderungen*, 1. p. 33 *sqq.* ;
Stephani, *Reise*, p. 66 *sqq.* ; Vischer, *Érinnerungen*, p. 588 *sqq.* ; Bursian, *Geogr.*
1. p. 206 *sqq.* ; Mahaffy, *Rambles and Studies*,[3] p. 215 *sqq.* ; H. Belle, *Trois
Années en Grèce*, pp. 143-165 ; Schliemann, in *Journal of Hellenic Studies*, 2
(1881), p. 128 *sq.* ; *id.*, *Orchomenos*, p. 9 *sqq.* ; Baedeker,[3] p. 167 *sq.* ; *Guide-
Joanne*, 2. p. 16 *sq.*; P. Brandt, *Von Athen zum Tempethal*, p. 36 *sq.* I visited
Lebadea in May 1890.

39. 1. This city —— was named Midea. Thus Pausanias
identifies Lebadea with the Homeric Midea (*Iliad*, ii. 507), which,
according to others, was engulfed by the Copaic Lake (Strabo, ix. p. 413).
Perhaps the identification rested on no better basis than the patriotic
pride of the burghers of Lebadea, who could not bear to think that
their native town was not mentioned by Homer. Cp. H. N. Ulrichs,
Reisen und Forschungen, 1. p. 171 *sq.* ; Bursian, *Geogr.* 1. p. 209.

39. 1. Lebadus. There was a tradition that Lebadus (or Lebeadus,
as Plutarch calls him) was one of the two sons of Lycaon who did not
share in their father's impious deed (see viii. 2. 3), but fled to Boeotia ;
hence the people of Lebadea enjoyed the rights of Arcadian citizenship.
See Plutarch, *Quaest. Graec.* 39.

39. 2. Hercyna —— had a goose in her arms. An ancient vase-
painting represents Hercyna or Proserpine playing with a goose in
presence of Zeus (Stephani, in *Compte Rendu* (St. Petersbury) for 1863,
p. 94). Cp. note on x. 32. 16. Welcker saw many geese in Lebadea ; he
observed them at one other place in Boeotia, but nowhere else in Greece
(*Tagebuch*, 2. p. 43).

39. 3. a temple of Hercyna on the bank of the river. According to a tradition mentioned by Tzetzes (*Schol. on Lycophron*, 153),
Hercyna was a daughter of Trophonius who founded a temple of
Demeter at Lebadea and called the goddess Hercyna after herself.
Livy tells us (xlv. 27) that when Aemilius Paulus visited Lebadea "he
sacrificed to Zeus and Hercyna, whose temple is there." There was a
festival of Demeter called Hercynia (Hesychius, *s.v.* Ἑρκύνια). The
maidens who carried the sacred baskets in the procession of King
Zeus at Lebadea had previously to bathe in the spring Hercyna, which
was no doubt one of the sources of the Hercyna river, in the deep gorge
at the back of the town (see note on § 1) (Plutarch, *Amator. Narrat.* 1).

39. 3. serpents are as sacred to Trophonius as to Aesculapius.
See note on § 11, 'barley-cakes.'

39. 3. Arcesilaus. He was said to be one of the captains who led
the Boeotians to Troy (Homer, *Iliad*, ii. 495).

39. 4. a temple and image of Trophonius. On the left bank of
the Hercyna at *Livadia*, near a high Turkish bridge over the river, there
is a church of the Virgin (*Panagia*). Partly built into the walls of the
church, partly lying around, Ulrichs found granite columns, squared
blocks, and architectural fragments. Here too were found two inscriptions, one a votive inscription in honour of Trophonius, the other a list
of moneys contributed by various people to the treasury of Trophonius.
Hence Ulrichs inferred that this was the site of the temple of Trophonius
(*Reisen und Forschungen*, 1. p. 167). For the inscriptions, see *C. I. G.*

G. S. I. Nos. 3055, 3087; *C. I. G.* Nos. 1571, 1588. Mr. J. Schmidt, however, suggests that the site of the temple of Trophonius is rather to be looked for at the chapel of St. Anna and St. Constantine, on the eastern slope of the castle-hill, not far below the walls of the fortress. Into the wall of this chapel, over one of the windows, is built one of the inscriptions containing a dedication to King Zeus and Trophonius (see below, note on 'a temple of King Zeus'). The chapel stands on an artificial terrace, large enough to support a considerable temple. The terrace is covered with masses of stones, among which are fragments of marble columns, Ionic capitals, etc. See *Mittheil. des arch. Inst. in Athen,* 5 (1880), pp. 138-140.

39. 4. an image of Rainy Zeus. Lebadea, lying at the foot of the massive Helicon, is a rainy place (Welcker, *Tagebuch,* 2. p. 50). Mure was detained here for four days and five nights, during which the rain poured incessantly "with the exception of about an hour on the afternoon of the third day, when the steady rain gave place to a sort of drizzle or Scotch mist" (Mure, *Journal,* 1. p. 237). When Fiedler was at Lebadea, the rain fell in sheets for three days (Fiedler, *Reise,* 1. p. 130).

39. 4. a temple of King Zeus. The remains of this temple were to be seen, down to nearly the middle of the present century, on Mt. *St. Elias,* about half an hour to the west of *Livadia.* The mountain is connected, on its eastern side, by a ridge with the castle-hill of *Livadia.* L. Ross found the remains of the floor and of the *cella* walls constructed of massive blocks. The ruins, like those of so many other temples in Greece, have since been mostly used to build a church on the same site. See L. Ross, *Wanderungen,* 1. p. 38; H. N. Ulrichs, *Reisen und Forschungen,* 1. p. 168; Welcker, *Tagebuch,* 2. p. 50; L. Stephani, *Reise,* p. 68; *Rheinisches Museum,* N. F. 42 (1887), p. 54; Baedeker,[3] p. 168; *Guide-Joanne,* 2. p. 17. A long inscription relating to the contract for the construction of the temple of King Zeus was discovered at Lebadea and published for the first time in 1876. See *C. I. G. G. S.* 1. No. 3073; Dittenberger, *Sylloge Inscr. Graec.* No. 353; Choisy, *Études épigraphiques sur l'architecture grecque,* p. 173 *sqq.* The Boeotians commemorated their victory over the Spartans at Leuctra by periodically celebrating games in honour of King Zeus at Lebadea (Diodorus, xv. 63). These games, called the Basileia or Royal Games, are mentioned in an inscription found at Lebadea (*C. I. G. G. S.* 1. No. 3091; Leake, *Northern Greece,* 2. p. 130; Keil, *Sylloge Inscript. Boeot.* p. 71, No. xi; Cauer, *Delectus Inscr. Graec.*[2] No. 323; Collitz, *G. D. I.* 1. No. 422), and in other Boeotian inscriptions (Kaibel, *Epigrammata Graeca,* No. 492; *C. I. G. G. S.* 1. Nos. 552, 1711, 2487, 2532, 4247). From another inscription containing a dedication to Queen Hera (*C. I. G. G. S.* 1. No. 3097; see below) we may gather that the games were held every fourth year (see Leake, *Northern Greece,* 2. p. 129 *sq.*). Another inscription found at Lebadea records a dedication to King Zeus and the city of Lebadea (*C. I. G. G. S.* 1. No. 3097; Keil, *Sylloge Inscr. Boeot.* p. 106, No. xxv. c). Several inscriptions have been found at Lebadea containing dedications of slaves to King Zeus and Trophonius (*C. I. G. G. S.* 1. Nos. 3080, 3081, 3083; *Bulletin de Corresp. hellénique,*

4 (1880), p. 96 *sq.* ; Cauer, *Delectus Inscr. Graec.*[2] Nos. 325, 328, 329; Collitz, *G. D. I.* 1. Nos. 425, 429, 430). In these inscriptions Zeus is distinguished from Trophonius, but in others the two divinities are confounded. Thus we hear of a dedication to Zeus Trophonius (*C. I. G. G. S.* 1. No. 3090; Cauer, *Delectus Inscr. Graec.*[2] No. 327 ; Collitz, *G. D. I.* 1. No. 423), the priest of Zeus Trophonius (*C. I. G. G. S.* 1. No. 3077), and an oracle of Zeus Trophonius (*C. I. G. G. S.* 1. No. 3098; L. Stephani, *Reise*, p. 71 ; Keil, *Sylloge Inscr. Boeot.* p. 79, No. xvi.) Strabo also speaks (ix. p. 414) of the oracle of Zeus Trophonius at Lebadea ; and the temple of Jupiter (Zeus) Trophonius at Lebadea is mentioned by Livy (xlv. 27). Hence it would seem that Trophonius, the old local god of Lebadea, was to some extent identified with Zeus ; but this identification was probably late. Games called Trophonia were held at Lebadea in honour of Trophonius (Schol. on Pindar, *Olymp.* vii. 154 ; Pollux, i. 37). They are mentioned in two inscriptions found at Megara (*C. I. G. G. S.* 1. Nos. 47, 49 ; *C. I. G.* No. 1068). It has been supposed that these Trophonia were the same as the Royal Games mentioned above ; but this seems doubtful. Queen Hera, as well as King Zeus, was worshipped at Lebadea, as we learn from an inscription found at Lebadea which contains a dedication to Queen Hera and the city of Lebadea (*C. I. G. G. S.* 1. No. 3097 ; Wheler, *Journey*, p. 327 ; Leake, *Northern Greece*, 2. p. 130 ; H. N. Ulrichs, *Reisen und Forschungen*, 1. p. 176 ; *C. I. G.* No. 1603).

39. 5. **As to the oracle, the procedure is as follows.** Dicaearchus wrote a work, in at least two books, on the manner of consulting the oracle of Trophonius (Athenaeus, xiii. p. 594 e f, xiv. p. 641 e f). Plutarch also wrote a book on the same subject, perhaps as a counterblast to the work of Dicaearchus, which, to judge from a specimen preserved by Athenaeus (xiii. p. 594 e f), would seem to have been of a sneering and sceptical tone. See K. O. Müller, *Orchomenos*,[2] p. 147. Of the extant accounts of the way of consulting the oracle, the one here given by Pausanias, from his own experience, is the fullest. It should be compared with the accounts given by Strabo (ix. p. 414), Plutarch (*De genio Socratis*, 21 *sq.*), Philostratus (*Vit. Apollon.* viii. 19), Lucian (*Dial. Mort.* iii. 2 ; cp. *Menippus*, 22), Maximus Tyrius (*Dissert.* xiv. 2), a scholiast on Aristophanes (*Clouds*, 508), and Suidas (*s.v.* Τροφωνίου κατὰ γῆς παίγνια). A mutilated inscription found at Lebadea records a decree of the people of Lebadea that whoever consulted the oracle should pay a silver coin into the treasury and offer ten cakes of the value of a drachm apiece (*C. I. G. G. S.* 1. No. 3055 ; Collitz, *G. D. I.* 1. No. 413, pp. 156 *sqq.*, 393). The same inscription gives a list of the persons who paid their money and inquired of the oracle ; among them was Amyntas, son of Perdiccas, king of Macedonia. On the oracle of Trophonius in general, see K. O. Müller, *Orchomenos*,[2] pp. 143-155 ; Bouché-Leclercq, *Histoire de la divination dans l'antiquité*, 3. pp. 321-332.

39. 5. **the Good Demon and Good Fortune.** On the Capitol at Rome there were statues of these two deities by Praxiteles (Pliny, *Nat. hist.* xxxvi. 23). According to Menander (quoted by Clement of Alexandria, *Strom.* v. 131, p. 727, ed. Potter) every man is attended

from birth by a demon who acts as his guide and good genius in life. We hear of a man being bidden by Apollo to honour and propitiate his own Good Demon (*Ancient Greek Inscriptions in the British Museum*, Part iv. No. 896). Similarly the Romans believed that each man has a guardian spirit or genius who accompanies him from the womb to the grave, never quitting him for an instant ; all through life a Roman sacrificed to his guardian spirit once a year (Censorinus, *De die natali*, 3). On the Good Demon, cp. Stephani, in *Compte Rendu* (St. Petersburg) for 1859, p. 110 *sqq.* ; E. Rohde, *Psyche*, p. 232 *sq.*, note 2.

39. 5. observes rules of purity. He had probably to eat certain foods, to abstain from others, to remain chaste, and (as Pausanias implies) to bathe regularly. Before entering the sanctuary of the Tyrant Men (a deity worshipped chiefly in Asia Minor) the worshipper had to abstain from garlic, pork, and women ; and he had to wash his head on the day when (but before) he entered the sanctuary. A woman might not enter the sanctuary for seven days after menstruation ; and on the day when (but before) she entered it she had to wash her head. A person who had been in contact with a corpse might not enter the sanctuary of the Tyrant Men for ten days afterwards. See Dittenberger, *Sylloge Inscr. Graec.* No. 379 ; Foucart, *Des associations religieuses chez les Grecs*, pp. 119 *sqq.*, 219 *sqq.* On similar rules, see Lobeck, *Aglaophamus*, p. 188 *sqq.* ; W. M. Ramsay, *The cities and bishoprics of Phrygia*, i. p. 136 *sq.*, with the inscriptions, p. 149 *sqq.*

39. 5. the children of Trophonius. The writer of the treatise *De facie in orbe lunae*, attributed to Plutarch, mentions (c. 30) "the Trophoniads at Udora in Boeotia" among the kindlier demons who busied themselves with oracles and orgiastic rites ; he classes them with the Idaean Dactyls of Crete and the Corybantes of Phrygia. These Trophoniads may be the children of Trophonius mentioned by Pausanias. Cp. K. O. Müller, *Orchomenos*,[2] p. 148.

39. 6. they sacrifice over a pit, calling upon Agamedes. The pit was no doubt the pit of Agamedes, down which Trophonius was said to have vanished (ix. 37. 7). As to the sacrifice of a black ram to the dead, see notes on iv. 32. 3 ; v. 13. 2. Whereas sacrifices were offered to Agamedes as to a dead man or hero (as we learn from this passage), Trophonius is said to have received the sacrifices usually offered to the gods (Schol. on Aristophanes, *Clouds*, 508). Lucian speaks of Trophonius as compounded of a man and a god (*Dial. Mort.* iii. 2). H. N. Ulrichs thought that the pit of Agamedes might be the hole which runs into the rock for a distance of 25 to 30 feet at the foot of the castle-hill, close to the springs of the Hercyna (see above, p. 196). The passage descends slightly, and is just wide enough to allow a man to creep along it (H. N. Ulrichs, *Reisen und Forschungen*, i. p. 167). Cp. Clarke, *Travels*, 4. p. 132 *sq.* ; L. Ross, *Wanderungen*, i. p. 37 ; Vischer, *Erinnerungen*, p. 589 *sq.* To this Bursian with justice objects that the sacrificial pit was probably a perpendicular hole or cleft in the ground, not a horizontal subterranean passage (*Geogr.* i. p. 208 n. 2). The view put forward by Ulrichs, that the square chamber cut in the rock close to this passage was the building sacred to the Good Demon and Good

Fortune, in which persons consulting the oracle resided for several days, is rightly rejected by Bursian.

39. 8. the Water of Forgetfulness —— the Water of Memory. These two springs are mentioned by Pliny (*Nat. hist.* xxxi. 15), who says that they were in the sanctuary of Trophonius, near the river Hercyna. In an Orphic poem inscribed on a gold tablet, which was found at Petelia in southern Italy, the soul of a deceased person is warned against drinking of a certain fountain beside a cypress-tree in the infernal world. This fountain is doubtless the Water of Forgetfulness, for the soul is directed to proceed till it finds another fountain of cold water flowing from Memory's lake. Guards stand before the fountain, but the soul is to accost them, saying : " I am a child of earth and of the starry sky ; but a heavenly stock is mine. Ye know it yourselves. But I am parched and perishing for thirst. Give me quickly the cold water that flows from Memory's lake." See *C. I. G.* No. 5772 ; Kaibel, *Epigrammata Graeca*, No. 1037 ; Comparetti, in *Journal of Hellenic Studies*, 3 (1882), pp. 110-118.

39. 8. the image which they say Daedalus made. This was an image of Trophonius. See ix. 40. 3. The sculptor Euthycrates, a son and pupil of Lysippus, made an image of Trophonius for the oracle ; his style was austere rather than graceful (Pliny, *Nat. hist.* xxxiv. 66).

39. 8. clad in a linen tunic girt with ribands. According to Philostratus (*Vit. Apollon.* viii. 19), persons who consulted the oracle of Trophonius were dressed in white. According to Maximus Tyrius (*Dissert.* xiv. 2), they were clothed in a garment of fine linen which reached to their feet, and over it they wore a red cloak. Lucian merely observes that they were arrayed in fine linen (*Dial. Mort.* iii. 2). A scholiast on Aristophanes (*Clouds*, 508) and Suidas (*s.v.* Τροφωνίου κατὰ γῆς παίγνια) say that they were dressed in a sacred costume or a costume meet for a god.

39. 8. shod with boots of the country. In the procession at the Andanian Mysteries (see iv. 1. 5 *sqq.*) the Sacred Women were not allowed to wear shoes, except shoes made of felt or of the skins of victims which had been sacrificed (Dittenberger, *Sylloge Inscr. Graec.* No. 388, line 23 *sq.*) At Rome the shoes of the Flaminica had to be made of the leather of a beast which had been killed or sacrificed ; it was sacrilege if her shoes were made from the hide of an animal that had died a natural death (Festus, *s.v.* ' Mortuae pecudis,' p. 191 A ed. Müller ; Servius, on Virgil, *Aen.* iv. 518). In certain late Syrian rites boys were initiated by a sacrifice in which their feet were shod in slippers made out of the hide of the victim (W. Robertson Smith, *Religion of the Semites*,[2] p. 438). No shoes at all were allowed to be carried into the sanctuary of Alectro at Ialysus in Rhodes (Dittenberger, *op. cit.* No. 357), and in Crete every one had to enter the temple of Britomartis barefoot (Solinus, xi. 8, ed. Mommsen). At the solemn annual ceremony of making the new fire, observed among the Creek Indians of the United States, the officiating priest, instead of going barefoot, wore a new pair of buckskin moccasins, made by himself and stitched with the sinews of the same animal ; these shoes he never wore except on this solemn occasion ; they were afterwards laid up in the holy place and left there (Adair, *History of the American Indians*, p. 82 *sq.*) Shoes and clothes become taboo by contact with the holy place and cannot afterwards be used in ordinary life. Hence, for the convenience of worshippers who cannot afford to keep a special suit for sacred occasions, a stock of old but holy clothes and shoes is kept at popular shrines and lent to pilgrims, who, arrayed in them, pay their devotions at the shrine and then return the borrowed costume to the priests. See the remarks of W. Robertson Smith on this subject, *op. cit.* p. 452 *sq.*

39. 9. The oracle is above the grove on the mountain etc. Philostratus describes the situation of the oracle much in the same way. He says : "The aperture at Lebadea is dedicated to Trophonius, son of Apollo, and is entered only by those who go for the sake of oracles. It is to be seen, not in the sanctuary, but a little above the sanctuary on a hill. It is enclosed all round by iron spikes." The narrowness of the hole through which the person had to squeeze himself into the oracular cave is vouched for also by Lucian (*Dial. Mort.* iii. 2 ; *id. Menippus*, 22), Maximus Tyrius (*Dissert.* xiv. 2), Suidas (*s.v.* Τροφωνίου κατὰ γῆς παίγνια) and a scholiast on Aristophanes (*Clouds*, 508). L. Stephani believed that he had discovered the actual shaft described by Pausanias down which the faithful descended by a ladder into the Holy of Holies. The spot is in a little ruined chapel within the mediaeval castle on the summit of the high rocky hill behind Lebadea. The chapel is on the brink of the precipice, perpendicularly above the rock cuttings at the bottom of the cliff (see above, p. 196). In the floor of the chapel Stephani found two square openings, down which he looked into a great hole hewn in the rock, regularly lined with masonry and pillars. This deep hole, Stephani thought, was the shaft described by Pausanias (*Reise*, p. 67 *sq.*) To me the hole, which appears to be opener than when Stephani saw it, seemed not to answer to Pausanias's description in the least. It is most probably a cistern. Stephani himself saw water in the bottom of it.

39. 9. a basement. The Greek word is κρηπίς. Pausanias uses it elsewhere (vi. 25. 1 ; viii. 4. 9 ; viii. 11. 4 ; viii. 16. 3).

39. 10. The shape of this structure is like that of a pot for baking bread in. "Pausanias probably means to liken it to those domical earthen ovens which are still used in the East for baking bread. Kilns of this sort were also used for firing pottery " (J. H. Middleton, in *Journal of Hellenic Studies*, 9 (1888), p. 313, who thought that the oracular chasm was a vaulted chamber shaped like the beehive tombs of Orchomenus, Mycenae, etc.) Ovens of this shape, resembling the half of an enormous egg, are often to be seen outside the cottages of the peasants in Greece.

39. 11. holding in his hands barley-cakes kneaded with honey. These honey-cakes were sops to be thrown to the serpents which were said to haunt the oracular cavern. There was a legend that the man who first descended into the cave found there two serpents, which he appeased with honey-cakes ; and that so the custom originated. It is even said that the oracles were delivered by the serpent or serpents in the cave.

See Schol. on Aristophanes, *Clouds*, 508 ; Suidas, *s.vv.* μελιτοῦντα and Τροφωνίου κατὰ γῆς παίγνια ; Philostratus, *Vit. Apollon.* viii. 19. Cp. Lucian, *Dial. Mort.* iii. 2 ; Hesychius, *s.v.* μαγίδες ; Pollux, vi. 76. Serpents, as we have seen (§ 3), were sacred to Trophonius. Cp. note on § 13 'the power of laughter' etc. Barley-cakes kneaded with honey were offered at Olympia to Sosipolis, who was also associated in legend with a serpent (Paus. vi. 20. 2 and 5) ; and honey-cakes were the food of the serpent which represented Erechtheus on the Acropolis at Athens (Herodotus, viii. 41 ; cp. above, vol. 2. p. 169).

39. 11. to one it is given to see, and to another to hear. Plutarch gives a long description of the wonderful sights and sounds said to have been seen and heard by Timarchus in the cave of Trophonius. His experiences began with a feeling that his head had split with a loud crack and that his soul had passed out through the sutures. See Plutarch, *De genio Socratis*, 21 *sq.*

39. 11. They return through the same aperture. Plutarch says that Timarchus, after spending a day and two nights in the oracular cave, found himself lying beside the entrance, where he had first laid himself down (*De genio Socratis*, 21 *sq.*) According to Suidas (*s.v.* Τροφωνίου κατὰ γῆς παίγνια) and a scholiast on Aristophanes (*Clouds*, 508), many persons, after consulting the oracle, were sent up through the same opening on the same day, but some were detained several days. Another scholiast on the same passage of Aristophanes says that after visiting the oracle they were cast up through a different opening. Philostratus absurdly relates that most of them came up about the frontiers of Boeotia, but that some reappeared beyond Locris and Phocis (*Vit. Apollon.* viii. 19).

39. 13. the power of laughter will come back to him. It was commonly said that persons who had visited the oracle of Trophonius never laughed again, the cause alleged being the fright which the serpents in the cave had given them. Hence of a glum and solemn person it used to be said, " He has been at the oracle of Trophonius." See Schol. on Aristophanes, *Clouds*, 508 ; Plutarch, *Proverb.* 51 ; Suidas, *s.v.* Εἰς Τροφωνίου μεμάντευται ; *Proverb. e. cod. Bodl.* 368 ; Zenobius, iii. 61 ; Diogenianus, i. 8 ; Gregorius Cyprius, ii. 24. Athenaeus tells a story of one Parmeniscus of Metapontum who lost the power of laughter by visiting the cave of Trophonius, and recovered it at the sight of the uncouth wooden image of Latona in her sanctuary at Delos. He had gone thither with highly-wrought expectations, and the sight of the reality proved too much even for his gravity. See Athenaeus, xiv. p. 614 a b.

39. 14. The shield of Aristomenes etc. See iv. 16. 5-7.

40. 2. saw a swarm of bees etc. Cp. Schol. on Aristophanes, *Clouds,* 508 ; and note on x, 5. 9.

40. 3. the image of Hercules at Thebes. See ix. 11. 4.

40. 3. the image of Trophonius at Lebadea. See ix. 39. 8.

40. 3. a Britomartis at Olus. " The Cretans worship Diana most religiously, calling her Britomartis, which in our tongue means Sweet Maid. No one may enter her temple save barefoot. Her temple boasts the handiwork of Daedalus" (Solinus, xi. 8, ed. Mommsen).

40. 3. At Cnosus there is also Ariadne's Dance etc. See Homer, *Iliad*, xviii. 590 *sqq.* Cp. Paus. viii. 16. 3 ; Overbeck, *Schriftquellen,* §§ 110-115. It has been suggested that the labyrinthine device which appears on coins of Cnosus (Head, *Historia Numorum,* pp. 389-399) reproduces the figure of Ariadne's Dance, the complex and involved lines of the device representing the mazy lines in which the dancers moved. At Delos there was danced a dance called the Crane Dance, in which the movements of the dancers were supposed to imitate the turnings and windings of the labyrinth ; it would seem to have been performed by two bands of dancers, each of which followed its leader in single file (Plutarch, *Theseus,* 21 ; Pollux, iv. 101). From a sketch incised on a vase found at Tragliatella it appears that in the Roman game called Troy, which consisted of certain evolutions performed by boys on horseback (Plutarch, *Cato,* 3 ; Dio Cassius, xliii. 23 ; Tacitus, *Ann.* xi. 11), the riders moved in lines which made up exactly the same figure. Further, the same figure is represented on the floor of old churches, where it is called ' the road of Jerusalem ' (*chemin de Jérusalem*), and processions move along it. Moreover, the same labyrinthine figure occurs commonly in the north of Europe, particularly Norway, Sweden, Denmark, Finnland, and the south coast of Russian Lappland ; in these countries it is marked out by raised lines of turf or rows of stones, and is used by children in certain games. See W. Meyer, in *Sitzungsberichte der philosoph. philolog. u. histor. Classe d. k. b. Akad. d. Wissenschaften zu München,* 1882, vol. 2. pp. 267-300 ; Otto Benndorf, ' Ueber das Alter der Trojaspieles,' in W. Reichel's *Ueber Homerische Waffen* (Wien, 1894), pp. 133-139.

40. 4. those which were brought from Omphace to Gela. See viii. 46. 2.

40. 5. Chaeronea. The ruins of Chaeronea lie between 4 and 5 miles to the north-west of *Livadia.* To reach them from the latter place we descend into the plain, cross it northward, and then ascend by a pass the low bare stony hills that divide the plain of Lebadea from that of Chaeronea. On reaching the plain of Chaeronea we hold on westward for about twenty minutes, skirting the northern foot of the hills till we reach *Kapraena,* the hamlet which occupies a part of the site of Chaeronea. It consists of only a few houses, but some trees growing about it give the tiny village a pleasing appearance. About five minutes before reaching *Kapraena* we pass the shattered remains of the colossal stone lion which marks the grave of the Thebans who fell in the battle of Chaeronea (see below, p. 209 *sq.*) The time from Lebadea to Chaeronea is about an hour and three-quarters.

The plain of Chaeronea—one of the largest plains in Greece— stretches in an unbroken sweep from the foot of Mount Parnassus east-ward to what used to be the Copaic Lake. Its length from east to west is about twelve miles, and its breadth from north to south about two. The plain is a dead flat, covered with fields of cotton and maize, and enclosed by bare stony barren hills both on the north and on the south.   Seen on a bright summer day, with the mountains beyond the Copaic plain appearing blue in the distance and Parnassus towering grandly on the west, the scene is beautiful enough; but on a grey November morning, with the mists down on the distant mountains, it wears a cheerless aspect that well becomes a battlefield where a nation's freedom was lost.

The city of Chaeronea lay on the southern side of the plain, at the foot of the hills which bound it on the south.   A sharp rocky summit, rising very steeply behind the town on the south, formed the acropolis. Its ancient name was Petrachus (ix. 41. 6).   The hill has two peaks, separated by a short dip or saddle; but as they lie north and south of each other, the southern peak, which is the higher, is not visible when you stand in the plain at the northern foot of the hill.   On the east the hill descends steeply and in places precipitously to a small valley or glen which here runs up into the hills.   At the northern end of this little valley are most of the houses of the village of *Kapraena*, and from it the two rocky peaks of the acropolis, with the saddle between them, are plainly visible.   To the west the hill slopes away in a long ridge towards Panopeus.   On the north it falls very steeply to the plain, its face on this side being composed of a broken mass of rugged grey rocks, to clamber up or down which requires some effort and attention.   Exactly at the foot of this rugged declivity is the small ancient theatre, hewn out of the rock (see below, p. 207).   The walls which enclosed the acropolis begin on a jutting rocky pinnacle above the theatre, but a good deal higher up.   From this point the wall runs very steeply up the hill in a south-westerly direction to the more northerly of the two peaks; then it makes a short bend to the west, and finally extends upward in a south-easterly direction to the southern and higher peak, where it ends in a square tower close to the glen. This was the western wall of the fortress.   The existing remains of it are very considerable, and form an admirable specimen of a Greek fortification of the best period.   The wall, from 6 feet to 6 ft. 5 in. thick, is solidly and strongly built throughout in the most regular style of masonry; the blocks are squared, fairly uniform in size, laid in horizontal courses, and closely fitted together without any admixture of small stones or mortar.   The material is the grey rock of which the hill is composed.   In general three to five courses are preserved, the height of the wall varying from 6 to 11 feet; but in some places eight to ten courses are standing for a good many yards together, particularly in the dip between the two peaks.   Near the northern peak, where ten courses are standing, the height is about 14 feet.   In the dip between the peaks the wall for a length of 50 yards or so batters, *i.e.* slopes inward, at a considerable angle, which, however, is not constant throughout.   The cause of this inward slope may simply be that the wall has fallen in; but if that is the case it is remarkable that all the courses and joints should remain (as they do remain) intact.   In some places, as on the pinnacle above the theatre and on the northern peak, the wall makes an angle, but the only tower is that on the southern peak.   This tower is quadrangular, measuring 31 feet by 23 feet on

the sides.   On the west, south, and east it is preserved to a height of
one, two, and three courses above the ground; but on the south side
an excavation has been made revealing six courses.   Near this tower the
wall shows traces of having been repaired in mediaeval times.

So much for the western wall of the acropolis, which towards its
southern end, at the summit of the hill, approaches very closely to the
precipitous slopes that descend eastward into the glen.   The eastern
wall of the fortress seems to have started a little below the northern
peak and to have gradually descended the steep hill-side above the glen
in a direction from north to south till it met another wall which came
down much more steeply from the southern peak.   But this eastern
wall is much less well preserved than the western.

The small theatre, hewn out of the rock at the northern foot of the
acropolis hill, faces northward across the plain.   The tiers of seats are
narrow, and rise steeply above each other.   They are divided horizontally
into three blocks or sets.   The lowest block contains only two tiers.
Above these a broad passage runs round the theatre, and above it
again rise ten tiers of seats without a break.   At the back of this
second block of seats the rock is scarped perpendicularly to a height
of 4 ft. 5 in., and above the scarp there are four more tiers of seats
extending all round the theatre, with a small part of a fifth tier at the
eastern end.   These upper seats are 15 inches high and 2 ft. 1 in.
broad.   There is no hollow such as we usually find in Greek theatres
at the back of each seat for the feet of the spectators sitting in the row
above.   Above the highest tier of seats a passage, 3 ft. 6 in. wide, has
been cut out of the rock all round the theatre.   In the face of the
perpendicular rock-cutting which forms the back of this passage a
few letters of an ancient inscription may be discerned.   They are at
the middle point of the passage and very large, measuring seven, ten
and eleven inches high, but so faint and worn that it is difficult to
determine what they are.   At the beginning of the nineteenth century
the inscription was still legible and ran as follows :—

'Απόλλωνος
Δαφναφορίω
'Αρτάμιδος
Σοωδῖνας

'Of Laurel-bearing Apollo, of Artemis who saves in travail' (*C. I. G. G. S.*
I. No. 3407), from which we infer that the theatre was dedicated to
these two deities.   There are no remains of a stage or of stage-
buildings.

Below the theatre is a spring, the water of which forms a small
brook flowing towards the Cephisus, though it only reaches that river
after heavy rain.   Near the spring is a fountain picturesquely built
of ancient blocks and architectural fragments.   The brook is the
ancient Haemon.   On its banks stood a sanctuary of Hercules, beside
which the Greek army encamped before the battle of Chaeronea (Plutarch, *Demosthenes*, 19).   In the church of the Panagia (the Virgin) in

the village there are preserved a good many remains of antiquity, including inscriptions built into the walls and a chair of white marble popularly known as Plutarch's Chair. A bust of Plutarch seems to have been set up by a certain Philinus at Chaeronea, for the stone pillar which was surmounted by a portrait head of the historian has been found bearing the following inscription : Φιλεῖνος Πλούταρχον τὸν εὐ[ε]ργέτην θεοῖς [ἀ]νέθηκεν. 'Philinus dedicated to the gods (this portrait of) Plutarch the benefactor' (C. I. G. G. S. 1. No. 3422). Other inscriptions attest the worship at Chaeronea of Dionysus, Hercules, and Artemis (C. I. G. G. S. 1. Nos. 3409, 3416, 3430). In later times the worship of Serapis would seem to have been very popular here, for we possess a large number of inscriptions, found at Chaeronea, which record the dedication of slaves to that deity (C. I. G. G. S. 1. Nos. 3301-3305, 3307, 3309, 3310, 3312-3315, 3317-3333, 3348-3367, 3371, 3374, 3376, 3377, 3387, 3399). Other inscriptions, much less numerous, record the dedication of slaves to Artemis Ilithyia (C. I. G. G. S. 1. Nos. 3386, 3391, 3412 ; cp. Nos. 3385, 3410) ; while two inscriptions attest similar dedications to the Mother of the Gods and to the Great Mother (C. I. G. G. S. 1. Nos. 3378, 3379). Isis and Anubis were also revered (C. I. G. G. S. 1. Nos. 3347, 3375, 3380) ; and near *Kapraena* was found the epitaph of a lady, Flavia Lanica, who had been priestess for life of Isis, of Itonian Athena, and of an abstraction called the Unanimity of the Greeks (C. I. G. G. S. 1. No. 3426). The epitaph seems to belong to the third century A.D.

See Clarke, *Travels*, 4. p. 138 *sqq.* ; Walpole's *Memoirs relating to Turkey*[2] (London, 1818), p. 342 ; Dodwell, *Tour*, 1. p. 219 *sqq.* ; Leake, *Northern Greece*, 2. pp. 112-117 ; H. N. Ulrichs, *Reisen und Forschungen*, 1. pp. 158-163 ; Mure, *Journal*, 1. pp. 212-221 ; Welcker, *Tagebuch*, 2. pp. 52-56 ; L. Ross, *Wanderungen*, 1. p. 40 *sq.* ; Vischer, *Erinnerungen*, p. 590 *sqq.* ; Bursian, *Geogr.* 1. p. 205 *sq.* ; Mahaffy, *Rambles and Studies*, pp. 227-235 ; Baedeker,[3] p. 165 *sq.* ; *Guide-Joanne*, 2. p. 32. I visited Chaeronea 17th May 1890 and again 1st and 2nd November 1895. I have described the theatre, and what I have called the western wall of the acropolis, from my own notes. But on both occasions I missed the eastern wall of the acropolis on the slope towards the glen, and I only learned of its existence from a photograph which I afterwards bought at Athens. In the photograph the line of wall is clearly seen descending the slope of the hill obliquely from the northern peak. The wall seems to be preserved to a height of a good many courses for some distance, and apparently there is a gateway in it above the village, at the head of what looks like an artificial passage made by clearing away the rocks which stud this part of the slope. The entrance to the acropolis was doubtless on this side. The photograph also shows, though less clearly, part of the line of wall descending from the southern peak to join the other wall low down on the hill-side.

For inscriptions of Chaeronea see *C. I. G.*, No. 1595 *sqq.* ; Preller, in *Berichte über die Verhandl. d. könig. sächs. Gesell. d. Wissen. zu Leipzig*, Philolog. histor. Cl., 6 (1854), pp. 195-202 ; Conze and Michaelis, in *Annali dell' Instituto*, 33 (1861), pp. 76-79 ; B. Latischew, in *Bulletin de Corresp. hellénique*, 8 (1884), pp. 52-67 ; Collitz, *G. D. I*, 1. Nos. 374-406. All the Chaeronean inscriptions hitherto published are now collected in the *C. I. G. G. S.* vol. 1., edited by W. Dittenberger.

40. 5. Arne. The Boeotian town of Arne is mentioned by Homer (*Iliad*, ii. 507). According to some, the Boeotian Arne had been swallowed up in the Copaic Lake (Strabo, ix. p. 413). Mr. F. Noack proposes to identify the Boeotian Arne with the great prehistoric fortress on the rocky plateau of *Gla* at the eastern end of the Copaic Lake (above, p. 128). The Thessalian Arne would seem to have been one of the original seats of the Boeotians, who, after their expulsion from Thessaly, settled in Boeotia and founded there a new Arne. There is probably little or no foundation for the identification of this latter Arne with Chaeronea. See Thucydides, i. 12 ; K. O. Müller, *Orchomenos*,[2] p. 384 *sqq.*

40. 5. Chaeron —— a son of Apollo by Thero. This genealogy was given by Hellanicus, in the second book of his work on the Priestesses of Hera, as we learn from Stephanus Byzantius (*s.v.* Χαιρώνεια). The name of Chaeron's mother was Thuro, according to Plutarch (*Sulla*, 17).

40. 6. he spoke of the river Egypt. See *Odyssey*, iv. 477, 581; xiv. 258.

40. 7. two trophies which the Romans under Sulla set up etc. Plutarch has described more exactly the situation of these trophies. One was in the plain, at the point where Archelaus, the general of the Asiatic army, was posted, and where his army broke and fled. On this trophy Sulla caused figures of Mars, Victory, and Venus to be carved. The other trophy was placed on the top of Mount Thurius, where a body of the enemy had been surprised. On this trophy Sulla carved in Greek letters the names of Homoloichus and Anaxidamus, who had acted as guides to the Romans. Mount Thurius appears to be the highest point of the range of hills behind Chaeronea, of which the acropolis of Chaeronea is a northern spur or projection. Sulla's victory over Archelaus was won in the spring of 86 B.C.

See Plutarch, *Sulla*, 17-19; Appian, *Mithrid.* 41-45; Leake, *Northern Greece*, 2. pp. 193-201 ; Mommsen, *History of Rome* (ed. 1868), 3. p. 318 *sq.* ; Hertzberg, *Geschichte Griechenlands unter der Herrschaft der Römer*, 1. p. 373 *sq.* ; Th. Reinach, *Mithridate Eupator*, p. 167 *sqq.*

40. 8. Caranus. He was said to have been a Heraclid who collected a force in Argos and Peloponnese, invaded Macedonia, carved out a kingdom for himself, and became the founder of the Macedonian dynasty. See Suidas, *s.v.* Κάρανος ; Diodorus, frag., vii. 16 ; Justin, vii. 1.

40. 10. a lion is placed on it. The fragments of this colossal lion are to be seen a few minutes' walk to the east of Chaeronea, close to the foot of the hills which bound the plain on the south. They were discovered by a party of English travellers (G. L. Taylor, Edward Cresy, etc.) on the 3rd of June 1818. At the time of the discovery they were almost wholly buried in the earth. The tomb was excavated by the Greek Archaeological Society in 1879. It consists of a large quadrangular space sunk in the ground to the depth of a few feet, and measuring about 26 paces from east to west by 16 paces from north to south. The sides of the enclosure are lined with masonry, several courses high, which banks up the soil so as to keep clear the enclosed space. Several buttresses project into the enclosure, and on the north side there is a sort of large quadrangular pedestal or platform, built of masonry, and measuring apparently 18 ft. by 12 ft., which also projects into the enclosure. In this enclosure 254 skeletons were found laid in seven rows; and it was ascertained by excavation that there was no deeper layer of bodies. This strongly confirms the statement of Pausanias that the tomb contained only the Theban dead. For the Greek loss in the battle amounted to far more than 254 ; the Athenians alone had not less than 1000 slain (Diodorus, xvi. 85 ; Paus. vii. 10. 5 ; Grote, *History of Greece*, 11. p. 306). The statement of Strabo (ix. p. 414) that the tomb contained 'the men who fell in the battle' is therefore misleading. With the skeletons in the tomb were found some iron scrapers, a good many bone buttons (the object of which is unknown), and some small earthenware pots. On my second visit to the tomb I learned that before the excavations it had been covered by a mound on which the lion lay, and that when the mound was cleared away the skeletons appeared packed 'like sardines' in the enclosure, with the marks of their wounds still visible on them. The fragments of the lion now lie outside of the enclosure on the south. The great head, 6 ft. long and 5 ft. high, lies looking up at the sky. It is well preserved, and so are two of the huge paws. One of the legs, I was told, is wanting. The lion was hollow, as may be seen by the existing fragments. The stone of which it is made is a grey marble.

See *Transactions of the Royal Society of Literature*, Second Series, 8 (1866), pp. 1-11 ; Mure, *Journal*, 1. p. 218 *sqq.* ; H. N. Ulrichs, *Reisen und Forschungen*, 1. p. 159 *sq.* ; Welcker, *Tagebuch*, 2. p. 55 *sq.* ; Vischer, *Erinnerungen*, p. 590; Bursian, *Geogr.* 1. p. 206 ; Baedeker,[3] p. 166; *Guide-Joanne*, 2. p. 32 ; Πρακτικὰ τῆς Ἀρχαιολογικῆς Ἑταιρίας for 1880, p. 16 *sqq.* ; P. Brandt, *Von Athen zum Tempethal*, p. 47 *sq.* I visited the spot in May 1890 and again in November 1895, and have described the lion and the tomb, as they exist at present, from my own notes. The full report of the excavation of the tomb is contained, I think, in the Ἀθήναιον, vol. 8 (1879), pp. 486-506, and vol. 9 (1880), p. 157 *sq.* I inspected this journal at Athens, but it is not accessible to me in Cambridge.

A colossal stone lion also surmounted the grave of the Thespians who fell at the battle of Tanagra (see above, p. 141 *sq.*) In the island of Ceos another colossal stone lion reposes on the hill-side "under the shadow of two olive-trees, looking down on one of the most magnificent views in Greece." See J. T. Bent, *The Cyclades*, p. 453 ; Πρακτικὰ τῆς Ἀρχαιολογικῆς Ἑταιρίας for 1880, p. 20. The custom of placing stone lions on tombs was by some people derived from Hercules, who, having lost one of his fingers by a bite of the Nemean lion, buried the finger at Lacedaemon and placed a stone lion over it (Ptolemaeus, *Nov. Hist.* ii., in *Mythographi Graeci*, ed. Westermann, p. 184).

40. 11. **the sceptre which Homer says** etc. See *Iliad*, ii. 101 *sqq.*

40, 11, **This sceptre they worship, naming it a spear.** Justin tells us (xliii. 3. 3) that in the time of Romulus "kings had, instead of a diadem, the spears which the Greeks call sceptres. For from the very beginning the ancients worshipped spears as immortal images, in memory whereof spears are still added to the images of the gods." Aeschylus says (*Seven against Thebes*, 516 *sq.*) that Parthenopaeus swore by his spear, which he trusted in and revered more than a god. Caeneus is related to have planted his spear in the middle of the market-place and forced people to treat it as a god. He himself sacrificed and prayed to it instead of to the gods, and he obliged passers-by to swear by it also. See Schol. on Homer, *Il.* i. 264 ; Schol. on Apollonius Rhodius, i. 57. Achilles swore by the herald's staff (Homer, *Iliad*, i. 234 *sqq.*) In concluding a treaty the Romans took a sceptre and a flint from the temple of Jupiter Feretrius ; they swore by the sceptre and 'struck (concluded) the treaty' with the flint (Festus, *s.v.* 'Feretrius Jupiter,' p. 92, ed. Müller ; cp. A. W. Verrall's note on Aeschylus, *l.c.*) The Romans worshipped a spear as the image of Mars and kept it in the Regia (Varro, cited by Clement of Alexandria, *Protrept.* iv. 46, p. 41, ed. Potter ; Plutarch, *Romulus*, 29 ; Arnobius, vi. 11). The Scythians revered an iron sword and offered annual sacrifices of sheep and horses to it (Herodotus, iv. 62), and a naked sword stuck in the ground is said to have been worshipped as an image of the war-god by the Alans (Ammianus Marcellinus, xxxi. 12. 23). Philo, quoted by Eusebius (*Praepar. Evang.* i. 9. 23 *sq.*), says that men used to worship the great benefactors of the race under the form of pillars and rods, which they consecrated and held festivals in their honour. See C. Bötticher, *Der Baumkultus der Hellenen*, pp. 232-240.

The Gonds of India worship an iron spear-head called Pharsa Pen, and a hero named Bhima, "represented by his mythical club, either in stone or wood" (*Journal of the Anthropological Institute*, 25 (1895), p. 170). In Samoa "the war-clubs of renowned warriors, *Anava*, were regarded with much superstitious veneration by the different members of their families. Before a battle, various rites and ceremonies were observed towards the war-clubs, which were considered essential to their owners' success in combat. I have often seen battered and blood-stained war-clubs treasured up and reverenced as articles of the highest value by natives who resisted for a long time all attempts to purchase them, even at a high price, as they considered that in parting with them all hopes of success in battle went with the club" (J. B. Stair, in *Journal of the Polynesian Society*, No. 17, March 1896, p. 40). A Samoan war-god named Tufi was represented by a coco-nut-tree spear 10 ft. long. When the people met for worship, the spear was set up and offerings were laid before it. It was also taken in the war-fleet as a sign that the god went with them. See G. Turner, *Samoa* (London, 1884), p. 61. In the Arorae or Hurd Islands, South Pacific, the people had sacred stocks or small pillars of wood, 4 or 5 ft. high, as the representatives of their household gods, and on these they poured oil, and laid before them offerings of coco-nuts and fish (*id.* p. 294 *sq.*) In Aneitum, New Hebrides, South Pacific, there used to be a sacred staff, made of iron-wood, rather longer and thicker than an ordinary walking-stick. It had been kept for ages in the family of medicine-men, and was regarded as the representative of the god. When the priest was sent for to see a sick person, he took the stick with him, and leaning on it harangued the patient, whose eyes always brightened at the sight of the stick (*id.* p. 327 *sq.*) In ancient Mexico when a merchant went on his travels he always took with him a smooth black stick, the image of the god Yacatecutli, which protected him from all perils by the way. The merchants generally travelled in companies, each man with his sacred stick. When they halted at a house for the night, they tied all their sticks together, worshipped them, and drawing blood from their ears, tongue, legs, or arms, offered it to the bundle of sticks. They also burned a sort of incense before the sticks. See Clavigero, *History of Mexico*, I. p. 388 *sq.* (trans. by Cullen) ; Sahagun, *Histoire générale des choses de la Nouvelle Espagne*, traduite par Jourdanet et Simeon, pp. 38 *sq.*, 296 *sq.*

41. 1. **Theodorus and Rhoecus.** See viii. 14. 8 note.

41. 2. **the chest which Eurypylus brought** etc. See vii. 19. 6 *sqq.*

41. 2. **The necklace was dedicated at Delphi** etc. See viii. 24. 8-10.

41. 2. **it was carried off by the Phocian tyrants.** According to Phylarchus, quoted by Parthenius (*Narr. Amat.* 25), the wife of Aristo, chief of the Oetaeans, conceived a great desire to possess the necklace of Eriphyle, which was preserved in the sanctuary of Forethought Athena (see Paus. x. 8. 6). Accordingly her lover Phayllus, one of the generals in the Sacred War, sacked Delphi and carried off the necklace, which he presented to his leman. She wore it for a time ; but one of her sons, in a fit of madness, set fire to the house, and she perished in the flames. The story is also told, with slight variations, by Diodorus (xvi. 64) and Plutarch (*De sera numinis vindicta*, 8). Ephorus or his son Demophilus, quoted by Athenaeus (vi. p. 232 *sq.*), says that the necklace was bestowed by one of the Phocian leaders (Onomarchus, Phayllus, or Phalaecus) upon his wife, a proud and sullen woman, who at last plotted her husband's death.

41. 3. **Homer —— says that the necklace —— was made of gold.** The line quoted by Pausanias is *Odyssey*, xi. 327. Hyginus (*Fab.* 73) describes the necklace as made of gold and precious stones. Mr. W. Schwartz has essayed to show that the necklace of Eriphyle or Harmonia was the rainbow ('Das Halsband der Harmonia und die Krone der Ariadne,' *Fleckeisen's Jahrbücher*, 29 (1883), pp. 115-127).

41. 4. **in the speech of Eumaeus —— he says.** See Homer, *Od.* xv. 459 *sq.*

41. 4. **he has represented Eurymachus** etc. See Homer, *Od.* xviii. 295 *sq.*

41. 6. **a crag called Petrachus.** This was the steep and rocky acropolis of Chaeronea. See above, p. 206. The name of the hill is mentioned also by Plutarch (*Sulla*, 17).

41. 6. **here Cronus was beguiled** etc. The people of Methydrium in Arcadia claimed that the scene of the famous trick played on Cronus by his wife was on Mount Thaumasius, near their town. See viii. 36. 3.

41. 7. **they distil unguents from —— the iris.** The unguent distilled from the Illyrian iris was very famous, ranking next after the unguent distilled from *malobathrum* (Pliny, *Nat. hist.* xiii. 14).

BOOK TENTH

PHOCIS

1. 1. Phocus, son of Ornytion. Cp. ii. 4. 3 ; ii. 29. 3.

1. 1. Phocus, son of Aeacus. Cp. ii. 29. 2 and 9 ; x. 33. 12.

1. 2. the Hypocnemidian Locrians. See the Critical Note on this passage, vol. i. p. 607. The commoner form of the adjective in classical writers is Epicnemidian.

1. 3. They took part in the Trojan war. See Homer, *Il.* ii. 517-526.

1. 3. they waged war with the Thessalians. The war seems to have taken place not very long before Xerxes's invasion. Our other authorities for these early wars of the Thessalians and Phocians are Herodotus (viii. 27 *sq.*), Plutarch (*De mulierum virtutibus*, ii.), and Polyaenus (vi. 18). As to the war, see H. Hitzig, ' Zu Herodotos und Pausanias,' *Fleckeisen's Jahrbücher*, 20 (1874), pp. 123-127.

1. 3. at Hyampolis —— they buried earthen water-pots etc. Cp. Herodotus, viii. 28 ; Polyaenus, vi. 18. 2. As to Hyampolis, see x. 35. 5 *sq.*

1. 6. they gathered together their women and children etc. The only other ancient writer who has recorded the desperate resolve of the Phocians and their decisive victory is Plutarch (*De mulierum virtutibus*, 2). According to him the Phocian commander who persuaded his countrymen to this step was Daiphantus, the son of Bathyllius (cp. below, § 8). Plutarch says that the Phocian women, and even the children, were consulted, and assented to the resolution. Cp. note on x. 35. 5.

1. 7. 'Phocian despair.' Cp. Plutarch, *l.c.* ; Stephanus Byzantius, *s.v.* Φωκίς.

1. 10. Itonian Athena. She had a sanctuary in Thessaly (i. 13. 2) as well as in Boeotia (ix. 34. 1).

1. 10. the Phocians sent votive offerings etc. In the ruined chapel of the Panagia at Elatea, Mr. P. Paris found a large inscribed marble pedestal which he conjectures may have supported some of the statues which the Phocians dedicated to the gods for the great deliverance here described by Pausanias. The inscription on the pedestal runs thus : " To Poseidon of the sea, lord of horses, son of Chronus (*sic*), the city vowed and dedicated these (statues of) saviour demigods on behalf of their forefathers and of themselves and of the land and of their children and of their wives." The style of the letters of the inscription, however, is not archaic ; Mr. Paris conjectures that the old dedication may have been re-engraved at a later time, as was certainly done sometimes. See P. Paris, in *Bulletin de Corresp. hellénique*, 10 (1886), p. 367 *sqq.* ; *id.*, *Élatée*, pp. 10 *sqq.*, 223.

1. 11. **five hundred picked Phocians** etc. Cp. Herodotus, viii. 27 ; Polyaenus, vi. 18. Herodotus says that the number of the Phocians was 600, that they slew 4000 Thessalians and took their shields, half of which they dedicated at Delphi and half at Abae ; while out of the tithe of the spoil they made the colossal statues that stood round about the tripod in front of the temple at Delphi, and they dedicated a number of similar statues at Abae. He also tells us that this defeat of the Thessalians was the last which they suffered at the hands of the Phocians before the invasion of Xerxes (480 B.C.), and that it took place not many years before that event.

2. 1. **the Phocians were compelled to side with the Persian king.** Cp. Herodotus, ix. 17. But before the Persians had actually entered Greece by the pass of Thermopylae, the Phocians refused to join them, and indeed guarded one of the passes against them. See Herodotus, vii. 203, 217 *sq.*, viii. 30. And even after the Persians were masters of a great part of central Greece, some of the Phocians remained loyal to the Greek cause, and took refuge among the heights of Mt. Parnassus, from which they made descents and harassed the Persian army (Herodotus, ix. 31).

2. 1. **it came to pass that they were fined by the Amphictyons.** According to Diodorus (xvi. 23) the fine was inflicted on the Phocians for having cultivated part of the sacred Cirrhaean land (cp. Paus. x. 15. 1) ; according to Justin (viii. 1) the Thebans accused the Phocians of having laid waste Boeotia ; and lastly, according to Duris, cited by Athenaeus (xiii. p. 560 b), the cause of the war was that the Phocians had carried off a Theban woman named Theano.

2. 2. **Philomelus, son of Theotimus** etc. With what follows, cp. Diodorus, xvi. 23 *sq.* According to Diodorus, the Sacred War began in the archonship of Callistratus at Athens, *i.e.* in 355 B.C. But according to Pausanias (§ 3) the seizure of Delphi by the Phocians, and with it the beginning of the war, took place in the archonship of Agathocles, *i.e.* in 357 B.C.

2. 3. **Prorus of Cyrene.** This Olympic victor is called Porus by Diodorus (xvi. 2) and Eusebius (*Chronic.* vol. i. p. 206, ed. Schöne), both of whom agree with Pausanias as to his native country and the date of his victory.

2. 4. **They fought for ten years.** Duris, cited by Athenaeus (xiii. p. 560), also says that the war lasted ten years. According to Pausanias, it began in 357 B.C. and ended in 348 B.C. (see § 3, and x. 3. 1). Diodorus states (xvi. 23 and 59) that the war began in 355 B.C. and

ended in 346 B.C. ; in two passages (xvi. 14 and 59) he says it lasted ten years ; in one passage (xvi. 23) he says it lasted nine years. If we reckon the first and the last years as complete years (though the war probably continued only during a portion of them), the war lasted ten years ; if we reckon the first and the last years as half-years, it lasted nine years. The Greeks reckoned by ordinal numbers in a way different from ours, for they included both terms of the series.

2. 4. **the Phocians were routed** etc. The defeat and death of Philomelus are similarly related by Diodorus (xvi. 31), according to whom the event took place in 354 B.C.

2. 5. **Onomarchus —— was shot down by his own men** etc. According to Diodorus (xvi. 35 and 61) Onomarchus was crucified by the victorious Philip in 353 B.C.

2. 6. **he was attacked by a wasting sickness.** Cp. Diodorus, xvi. 38 and 61.

2. 7. **his son Phalaecus —— being accused of embezzling** etc. According to Diodorus (xvi. 38) Phalaecus was the son of Onomarchus, not of Phaylus. As to the deposition and subsequent fortunes of Phalaecus, see Diodorus, xvi. 56, 59, 61-63. That historian tells us that some siege engines which Phalaecus was bringing against the walls of Cydonia were set on fire by lightning, and that Phalaecus, in attempting to extinguish the flames, was burnt to death with many of his men. The same writer mentions another tradition that Phalaecus was assassinated by a soldier whom he had offended.

3. 1. **in the ninth year —— Philip put an end to —— the Sacred War.** See note on x. 2. 4 ; and as to the conclusion of the Sacred War see Diodorus, xvi. 59 *sq.*

3. 1. **Polycles of Cyrene won the foot-race.** His victory fell in 348 B.C. Cp. Diodorus, xvi. 53 ; Eusebius, *Chronic.* vol. 1. p. 206, ed. Schöne.

3. 2. **Erochus, Charadra —— burned down by —— Xerxes.** Cp. Herodotus, viii. 33. The town of Erochus was apparently rebuilt after its second destruction at the close of the Sacred War; for it is mentioned in a Phocian inscription which seems posterior to the Sacred War. See *Bulletin. de Corresp. hellénique*, 11 (1887), p. 324 *sq.* ; P. Paris, *Élatée*, p. 248.

3. 2. **their inhabitants dispersed in villages.** Each village was to contain not more than fifty houses, and the villages were to be distant not less than a furlong from each other (Diodorus, xvi. 60).

3. 3. **the general assembly of Greece.** *i.e.* the Amphictyonic assembly or council. The Phocians had had two votes in that council, and these votes were now transferred to Macedonia (Diodorus, xvi. 60). See G. Gilbert, *Griechische Staatsalterthümer*, 2. p. 408 *sqq.* It would seem that the Macedonian members of the council were nominated by the king ; for in a list of members of the council, which has been found inscribed on a stone at Delphi, the Macedonian representatives are referred to as the members "sent by King Perseus." See *Bulletin de Corresp. hellénique*, 7 (1883), pp. 428, 432 *sq.*

4. 1. **It is twenty furlongs from Chaeronea to Panopeus.** This

estimate of the distance between Chaeronea and Panopeus is roughly correct. For 20 Greek furlongs are equal to about 2⅓ miles, and to ride at a foot pace from the one place to the other takes about three-quarters of an hour.

Panopeus is the first place in Phocis that you come to as you go westward from Chaeronea. The frontier between Boeotia and Phocis is not here marked by any natural boundary. The great plain of Chaeronea stretches westward into Phocis without a break, and Panopeus like Chaeronea stood on the edge of the range of low hills which bound the plain on the south. But while Chaeronea, with the exception of its acropolis, lay at the foot of the hills, Panopeus occupied the somewhat long and narrow summit of a hill which stands out from the range, with which, however, it is connected on the south, about its middle point, by a short neck or ridge. This ridge makes a bend westward so as to form a sort of elbow, within which, bounded by the hill of Panopeus on the north and the main mass of the hills on the south, is a shallow glen. This glen, which deepens from the ridge onward, makes in its turn a bend northward, and thus bounds the hill of Panopeus on the west. It is probably the ravine mentioned by Pausanias, where he saw the primaeval clay out of which mankind was moulded by Prometheus (see below, § 4 note). At its eastern end the hill of Panopeus descends into a narrow valley through which a path leads southward from the plain of Chaeronea to that of Lebadea. Thus the hill is nearly isolated on all sides except on the south, where it is joined to the other hills by the ridge already mentioned. Its greatest length is from east to west, and its height above the plain may be about 600 feet or so. The poor village of *Hagios Vlasis* lies at the northern foot of the hill, and it takes 10 minutes to ascend the steep hill-side from the village to the crest of rocks which runs along the brow of the hill. For the long narrow summit of the hill is nearly encircled by two lines of precipitous grey rocks, which, after extending along the northern and southern brows of the hill, meet in a sharp point at its eastern end. On the southern face of the hill the well-preserved walls and towers of the ancient city are built along the upper edge of this crest of rocks. On the northern face of the hill, on the other hand, the rocks are in general so high and precipitous that they served as a sufficient defence, and accordingly here we find remains of fortifications only in the gaps between the rocks. But on the west the two lines of rocks did not meet, and hence it was necessary to defend this open face of the hill by a fortification-wall. The remains of this western wall, like those of the southern wall, are very considerable, and are constructed in a better and more regular style. This completes the circuit. Its greatest length from east to west may be 400 yards or so. It is defended on the western and southern sides by quadrangular towers (six in all), which project at irregular intervals from the curtain.

The masonry of the greater part of the western wall and of the north wall, so far as it exists in the gaps between the rocks, is of the regular quadrangular sort, solid and good ; the blocks are squared and laid in horizontal courses. On the north side of the hill, towards its western end, the pieces of wall between the rocks are in some places from 6 to over 9 feet high ; the number of courses preserved varies from two to six.   Where it abuts on a line of high precipitous grey rocks, near the north-west corner of the circuit, this north wall is 8 ft. 6 in. thick.   Along the greater part of the northern brow of the hill, as I have said, the crest of rocks is so high and precipitous that fortifications were needless ; but at a point where this line of crags sends out a rocky spur down hill towards the village, there are some remains of a massive wall on the top of the rocks.

On the western face of the hill, the wall, which is but short, is well preserved.   It is here 10 feet thick.   Both faces are standing, though not to equal heights.   From five to nine courses are preserved, and the height varies from 10 to 12 or 13 feet, though there are a few gaps where the wall is ruinous.   About 23 paces from its northern end there is a gateway, 10 ft. 8 in. wide, and about 19 ft. 8 in. deep, flanked by two bastions.   The bastion on the north side of the gateway projects 16 ft. 6 in. from the curtain, and is 9 feet wide on its western face. Farther to the south is a square tower, partly ruinous, but 13 or 14 feet high at its south-west angle, where nine courses are preserved.   At the south-western angle, perched on the rocks which form the beginning of the rocky crest that runs along the southern brow of the hill, is another tower built of good ashlar masonry ; it measures about 19 feet by 24 feet on the sides ; three to five courses of masonry are standing.

In respect of preservation the south wall with its flanking towers deserves to rank with the best in Greece.   But the style of masonry on the whole is not good nor regular, certainly not so good and regular as that of the western wall.   The blocks of which it is built are not so uniform in size nor, as a rule, so large, though there are some very large blocks amongst them here and there.   Generally the blocks are not so high, thus making narrower (lower) courses, and these courses are not always horizontal.   But for long stretches together the wall is from 12 to 16 or 18 feet high, the number of courses preserved varying from four to eleven or even thirteen.   The average height in these places is about 14 feet, and the average number of courses about eight.   The thickness of the wall varies from 7 feet to 13 ft. 4 in.   Four square towers project from the curtain, without counting the tower at the south-west angle. Of these towers the third from the east is the best preserved.   It is 22 ft. 6 in. broad on the face, projects 11 feet from the curtain, and is preserved to its full original height (which I estimated at 30 feet), for a parapet runs almost all round its top.   The number of courses in this fine tower is twelve and thirteen.   The next tower to the east projects 11 feet from the curtain and is standing to a height of about 15 feet with seven courses of masonry.   The south wall ends on the east in another quadrangular tower, which measures 23 feet by 16 feet on the sides ; it has six and seven courses standing.   As usual, the towers are built in a more massive and careful style than the adjoining portions of the wall ; the blocks are better squared, and the courses more strictly horizontal.   This does not prove, as Dodwell fancied, that the towers are later than the wall ; for it was the regular practice of Greek military engineers (as the remains of Greek fortifications attest) to build the towers with an unusual degree of solidity, doubtless to compensate for their greater liability to suffer from the assaults of siege artillery.

In the southern wall, nearly above the ridge which connects the hill of Panopeus with the other hills to the south, there is a second gateway, 10 ft. 5 in. wide, undefended by flanking towers, though the wall makes a slight projection on the right (east) side as you enter. The gateway faces south-east. Remains of the two door-jambs are to be seen in it. It is here that the wall is 13 ft. 4 in. thick.

The space enclosed by these fortification-walls and by the rocky crests shows but few signs of habitation. On the highest point of the hill, among some holly-oaks, are the scanty tumble-down ruins of a mediaeval tower, built in the usual way of small stones with bricks and mortar in the chinks. A little lower down, and farther to the east, is a small chapel with remains of faded paintings on the walls. Scattered about the hill, especially round the chapel, is a good deal of broken pottery. A fine grove of beautiful holly-oaks now shades part of the summit, growing on a grassy slope amid low plants and shrubs. It is pleasant in the heat of the day to rest in the shade of these trees, to smell the wild thyme which grows abundantly on the hill, and to enjoy the distant prospects. To the north, across the broad Chaeronean plain, we look straight into the defile through which the Cephisus flows from Phocis into Boeotia ; at the northern end of the defile the low hill is visible on which are the scanty ruins of Parapotamii. To the west, Parnassus lifts his mighty head at no great distance from us, his middle slopes darkened by pine-forests that look like the shadows of clouds resting on the mountain-side.

On the northern side of the hill there are traces of two walls extending down the steep slope to the plain, in the direction of *Hagios Vlasis*. One of them, of which a few massive blocks are still in position, ran down the hill-side obliquely in a north-westerly direction, starting from near the eastern end of the summit. The other wall, of which there are more remains, started from the crest of rocks near the western end of the summit and ran straight down the hill in a due northerly direction. These two walls probably met at the foot of the hill so as to complete the fortified enclosure on the hill-side. At the beginning of the nineteenth century the two walls would seem to have been in much better preservation than at present, for Leake says that they "inclose the northern face of the hill, forming an angle, somewhat greater than a right angle, at the south-west [north-west?]. They included a small portion of the plain at the north-western end of the site. Here the walls are built in lines nearly straight, and were flanked with towers at the usual intervals." The proximity of the village of *Hagios Vlasis* has probably proved fatal to these walls, the villagers having used them as a quarry. As late as 1890, when I visited Panopeus for the first time, the long wall which descended the hill obliquely was, if I remember rightly, in much better preservation than when I returned to the spot in 1895. Even the fortifications of the summit, in spite of their greater distance from the village, would seem not to have escaped the hand of the spoiler, that is, of the village mason ; for Dodwell says of the towers that "some of them are extremely perfect, and contain doors and windows of the usual form, diminishing towards the top." At present there is only one tower in nearly perfect condition.

I visited Panopeus in May 1890 and again on 1st November 1895, and have described the present state of the ruins entirely from my own observation. See further, Dodwell, *Tour*, 1. pp. 207-210; Leake, *Northern Greece*, 2. pp. 106-112; H. N. Ulrichs, *Reisen und Forschungen*, 1. p. 151 *sqq.*; Mure, *Journal*, 1. p. 209 *sq.*; Welcker, *Tagebuch*, 2. p. 56 *sqq.*; L. Ross, *Wanderungen*, 1. p. 42; Vischer, *Erinnerungen*, p. 599; Bursian, *Geogr.* 1. p. 168; Baedeker,[3] p. 165; *Guide-Joanne*, 2. p. 33. The time from Chaeronea to Panopeus, according to Leake and Baedeker, is 35 minutes; according to the *Guide-Joanne* it is 45 minutes. I took 47 minutes.

4. 1. the Phocian parliament. See x. 5. 1 *sq.*

4. 1. Phlegyans who fled to Phocis. See ix. 36. 3.

4. 2. he speaks of the city of the Panopeans etc. See Homer, *Od.* xi. 581.

4. 2. he says that Schedius, son of Iphitus etc. See Homer, *Il.* xvii. 306 *sqq.*

4. 3. the women whom the Athenians call Thyiads. As to the Thyiads, see Panofka, 'Dionysos und die Thyiaden,' *Philog. histor. Abhandlungen* of the Berlin Academy, 1852, pp. 341-390; A. Rapp, 'Die Mänade im griechischen Cultus, in der Kunst und Poesie,' *Rheinisches Museum*, N. F. 27 (1872), pp. 1-22, 562-611. The road which the Thyiads took from Athens by Panopeus to Delphi was the same along which the Athenians periodically sent their offerings to Delphi. The offerings seem to have been conveyed by a sort of sacred caravan, called the Pythias. There was a tradition that Apollo followed the same road when he journeyed from Athens to Delphi, reclaiming mankind from savagery to civilisation. See Strabo, ix. p. 422 *sq.*; cp. Aug. Mommsen, *Delphica*, p. 315 *sq.* These facts seem to show that the road from Athens to Delphi by Panopeus was a sacred way. See K. O. Müller, *Dorier*,[2] 1. p. 241 *sqq.* (1. p. 267 *sqq.*, English trans.); E. Curtius, *Gesammelte Abhandlungen*, 1. p. 35 *sqq.*

4. 4. a small building of unburnt brick. See note on ii. 27. 6.

4. 4. At the edge of the ravine lie two stones etc. The ravine to which Pausanias refers is probably the shallow glen, with sloping, bushy and rocky sides, which bounds the hill of Panopeus on the west and partly on the south. When I visited it, the glen was absolutely dry. The soil in the bottom is a reddish crumbling earth. Probably it was out of this earth that Prometheus was said to have made mankind. But I could see no large detached lumps of it, and I could detect no odour emitted by the earth. But in the ravine on the eastern side of Panopeus, Col. Leake observed some large masses of stone which appeared to have fallen from the hill. He thought they might answer to the stones described by Pausanias, though he did not detect the smell of human flesh about them which Pausanias recognised (*Northern Greece*, 2. p. 111 *sq.*) Gell, however, quoted by Siebelis on this passage, says that in the brook here "is found a species of stone very different from the limestone of the country, and which on rubbing emits an odour."

**4. 4. the clay out of which the whole race of man was moulded
by Prometheus.** Prometheus was said to have fashioned men out of
earth kneaded with water (Apollodorus, i. 7. 1). One story ran that
when mankind had been destroyed by the great flood in the days of
Deucalion, Zeus ordered Prometheus and Athena to mould images out
of clay, to breathe the winds into them and make them live (*Etymolog.
Magnum*, *s.v.* Ἰκόνιον, p. 471, 1 *sqq.*) According to some, Prometheus
fashioned the animals as well as man, giving to each kind of beast its
own nature (Philemon, quoted by Stobaeus, *Florilegium*, ii. 27). Cp.
L. Preller, *Ausgewählte Aufsätze*, p. 211 *sqq.* The legend that the human
race was created by a god or hero who moulded the first men out of clay
or earth and breathed life into them, is found in many lands. The story
is obviously the creation of a savage philosophy. The best known form
of the myth is the Hebrew one, recorded in *Genesis*. A similar version
is told by the Australian blacks. They say that Pund-jel, the creator,
cut three large sheets of bark with his big knife. On one of these he
placed some clay, and worked it up with his knife into a proper con-
sistence. He then laid a portion of the clay on one of the other pieces
of bark, and shaped it into a human form ; first he made the feet, then
the legs, then the trunk, the arms, and the head. Thus he made a clay
man on each of the two pieces of bark ; and being well pleased with
them he danced round them for joy. Next he took stringy bark from the
Eucalyptus tree, made hair of it, and stuck it on the heads of his clay
men. Then he surveyed them critically, was pleased with his work,
and danced round them again for joy. He then lay down on them,
blew his breath hard into their mouths, their noses, and their navels ;
and presently they stirred, spoke, and got up. See Brough Smyth,
Aborigines of Victoria, 1. p. 424. The Maoris of New Zealand say that
Tiki made man after his own image. He took red clay, kneaded it
with his own blood, fashioned it into human form, and gave the image
breath (R. Taylor, *New Zealand*, p. 117 ; cp. Shortland, *Maori religion
and mythology*, p. 21 *sq.*) In Tahiti it was said that Taaroa, the
creator, made man out of red earth. One day he caused the man
to fall asleep, and while the man slept, the creator took out one of his
bones (*ivi*) and made a woman of it, whom he gave to the man as his
wife (Ellis, *Polynesian Researches*, 1. p. 110). The story of the creation
of woman out of a rib of the first man seems to have been current in
New Zealand also (J. L. Nicholas, *Narrative of a Voyage to New
Zealand*, p. 59). In Bowditch Island, South Pacific, the first man was
produced out of a stone. After a while he bethought him of making a
woman. So he collected some earth and moulded a woman out of it—
head, body, arms, and legs. Then he took a rib out of his left side,
thrust it into the earthen figure, and she started up a live woman. He
called her *Ivi* (*Eveve*) or ' rib,' and took her to wife, and the whole human
race sprang from this first pair. See G. Turner, *Samoa*, p. 267 *sq.* The
wide diffusion of this story in Polynesia makes it doubtful whether it
is merely a repetition of the Biblical story, learned from Europeans.
In Nui, or Netherland Island, South Pacific, the god Aulialia fashioned
earthen models of a man and woman, raised them up, and made them

live (Turner, *op. cit.* p. 300). In the Pelew Islands there is a legend that the first men were made out of clay kneaded with the blood of various animals, and that the characters of these first men and of their descendants were determined by the characters of the animals whose blood had been kneaded with the primordial clay (Kubary, ' Die Religion der Pelauer,' in Bastian's *Allerlei aus Volks- und Menschenkunde*, 1. pp. 3, 56). Among the Alfoers of Celebes a legend of the creation of man and woman out of earth is current, but it must be of Christian origin, since the name of the man was Adam and the name of the woman Ewa (Graafland, *De Minahassa*, 1. p. 97). Some of the wild tribes of Borneo tell how in the beginning two great birds tried to make man. For this purpose they first made trees ; but by this means they could not succeed. Then they tried to form him out of the rocks ; but they only succeeded in making statues. Then they took earth, mixed it with water, moulded it into the form of a man, infused into his veins the red gum of the kumpang-tree, and he lived. See *Transactions of the Ethnological Society of London*, N. S. 2 (1863), p. 27 ; H. Ling Roth, *The natives of Sarawak*, 1. p. 299. The Kumis of south-eastern India say that God made the world and the trees and the creeping things first, and then set about making man. He made a clay man and a clay woman ; but at night, while God slept, a great snake came and ate them up. This happened twice or thrice, and God was in despair, till at last he got up very early one morning and made a clay dog and put life into it ; then he made the clay man and the clay woman once more, and set the dog to watch over them, and that night when the snake came as usual to eat them up, the dog barked and frightened it away. See Lewin, *Wild Races of South-Eastern India*, p. 224 *sq.* The Kasyas of Assam tell the same story (A. Bastian, *Völkerstämme am Brahmaputra*, p. 8). The Innuit (Eskimo) of Point Barrow, Alaska, tell of a time when there was no man in the land, till a spirit named *á sĕ lu*, who resided at Point Barrow, made a clay man, set him up on the shore to dry, breathed into him and gave him life and sent him out into the world (*Report of the International Expedition to Point Barrow, Alaska* (Washington, 1885), p. 47). According to a Melanesian legend, told in Mota, one of the Banks Islands, the hero Qat made men of clay, the red clay from the marshy river-side at Vanua Lava. At first he made men and pigs just alike, but his brothers remonstrated with him, so he beat down the pigs to go on all fours and made men walk upright. Qat made the first woman out of supple twigs, and when she smiled he knew she was a living woman (R. H. Codrington, *The Melanesians*, p. 158). The myth of Prometheus has recently been discussed by Dr. K. Bapp (*Prometheus, Ein Beitrag zur griechischen Mythologie*, Oldenburg, 1896).

4. 5. the tomb of Tityus. Strabo mentions (ix. p. 422) that Tityus, a violent and lawless man, was put down by Apollo on his way from Athens to Delphi. Cp. Paus. iii. 18. 15 ; x. 11. 1. At the foot of the hills near Panopeus, on the south side of the road, Mure observed several large natural hillocks of a round form ; he thought one of them may have been the supposed tomb of Tityus (*Journal*, 1. p. 211).

4. 5. the verse of the Odyssey. See *Od.* xi. 577.

4. 6. he sailed away from the island with the rest of the multitude. The Phoenician city of Cadiz was built on the western end of the island, and at the eastern end of the island there was a very ancient, wealthy, and famous sanctuary of Hercules (Melcart). See Strabo, iii. p. 168 *sqq.* ; Mela, iii. 46, ed. Parthey ; Silius Italicus, iii. 13 *sqq.* ; Diodorus, v. 20 ; Philostratus, *Vit. Apollon.* v. 4 *sqq.* ; Appian, *Hispanica*, 65, ed. Mendelssohn. In the present passage Pausanias seems to refer to a custom which obliged all foreigners to quit the island of Cadiz at certain seasons, possibly during the festival of Hercules (Melcart). The monster whom Cleon declares he saw burning on the shore may perhaps have been an effigy of Hercules (Melcart), such as was periodically burned on a pyre at Tarsus in Cilicia, a city which recognised Hercules as its founder (Dio Chrysostom, *Or.* xxxiii. vol. 2. p. 16, ed. Dindorf). At the White Island in the Black Sea sailors were allowed to land and pay their devotions at the sanctuary of Achilles, to whom the island was sacred, but they had to embark before sunset, lest they should disturb Achilles and Helen at their nightly revels (Philostratus, *Heroica*, xx. 35).

4. 7. About seven furlongs from Panopeus is Daulis. This estimate of the distance of Daulis from Panopeus is much under the mark. The actual distance is about 4 miles (36 Greek furlongs). I took 1 hour 24 minutes to ride at a foot pace from *Davlia* (Daulis) to *Hagios Vlasis* (Panopeus).

The situation of ancient Daulis is exceedingly beautiful. It occupied the broad but somewhat uneven summit of a fine massive hill which rises abruptly from the glens at the eastern foot of Parnassus. Everywhere the sides of the hill—which in the grandeur of its outlines deserves almost to rank as a mountain—are high and steep, except at a single point on the west where a narrow ridge connects it with the main mass of Parnassus. On the south the hill falls away in sheer and lofty precipices of grey rock into a deep romantic glen, the sides of which, where they are not precipitous, are mantled with dark green shrubbery. Beyond the ridge to the west soar the immense grey precipitous slopes of Parnassus, mottled here and there with dark pines. High up on its side is seen a white monastery at the mouth of a dark gorge, through which a path ascends to the summit. In the hollow between the hill of Daulis and these great slopes, a mill nestles picturesquely among trees ; the water is led to it in a mill-race. Northward the ruined walls of Daulis, here thickly overgrown with ivy and holly-oak, look across a deep dell to the pretty village of *Davlia*, embowered among trees and gardens on the opposite hill-side. The descent to the valley on this side is steep and bushy, but not precipitous, except where a line of rocks runs obliquely up it on the north-west. Here and there in the valley the last slopes of the hill are terraced and planted with vines. At the eastern foot of the hill begins the great plain—the scene of so many famous battles—which stretches away for miles past the ruins of Panopeus and Chaeronea until at Orchomenus it melts into the still vaster expanse of the Copaic plain. To the south-east, beyond an intervening range of low hills, appears the sharp outline of Helicon. In this direction, at the southern end of the narrow valley which divides these low hills from the mighty steeps of Parnassus, is the famous Cleft Way, where Oedipus is said to have done the dark deed that was the beginning of all his woes. Altogether few places in Greece surpass Daulis in romantic beauty of situation and wealth of historical and legendary memories which the landscape, both near and far, is fitted to evoke. Standing on the brow of its precipices we feel that this mountain fastness, frowning on the rich champaign country below, was well fitted to be the hold of a wild wicked lord like Tereus, of whose bad deeds the peasants might tell tales of horror to their children's children. But now all is very peaceful and solitary in Daulis, for the tide of life has long rolled away from it. Parnassus still looks down on it as of old ; but ivy mantles the ruins, the wild thyme smells sweet on the hill, and the tinkle of goat-bells comes up sweetly from the glen. Only the shadow of ancient crime and sorrow rests on the fair landscape.

The only entrance to Daulis was on the west. Here the narrow ridge which connects the hill with Parnassus leads up to a gateway at the extreme north-western corner of the site. This gateway, about 10 ft. 7 in. wide, is flanked on the north by the remains of an ancient quadrangular tower built on a high precipitous rock. Both on the outer or northern and the inner or southern face of the tower several courses of masonry are preserved ; on its western front, above the high rock, the tower is 12 feet high. On the south the gateway is flanked by a ruined mediaeval tower built of small stones with bricks and mortar in the crevices. The tower is standing to a height of a good many feet ; one of its corners is rounded.

On passing through the gateway we find ourselves on the spacious summit of the hill. It is, on the whole, of a tabular form, though the surface is somewhat broken and uneven. The central and highest point is crowned by the ruins of a mediaeval tower, which seems to have been round and of no great size ; and at the north-eastern corner there are considerable remains of a mediaeval church meanly built of small stones, bricks, and mortar. Nearly all round the steep and sometimes precipitous edges of the summit may be traced the ancient fortification-walls, which in some places, especially on the western and eastern sides, are well preserved. They are flanked at irregular intervals by square towers, of which thirteen more or less ruinous can be made out. The style of masonry of the ancient walls, which evidently belong to the good Greek period, is partly polygonal and partly quadrangular. The towers on the whole are built in the quadrangular or ashlar style, the blocks being squared and laid in horizontal courses ; but in the walls pieces of quadrangular and of true polygonal, well-jointed masonry occur side by side. In a few places, especially at the north-west corner, the walls are mantled with ivy and holly-oak bushes which have rooted themselves in the crevices. The stone of which they are built is of a grey colour. Here and there the old walls have been repaired in the Middle Ages with the usual small stones, bricks, and mortar, which always look so poor beside the solid and beautiful masonry of ancient Greece.

On the western face of the hill the ancient wall, with its towers, is carried along the edge, partly of precipitous rocks, partly of a steep slope overgrown with bushes ; and on this side it is preserved in an almost unbroken line, though not to its full height. Three to seven courses of masonry are standing ; the average height of the wall is 8 or 9 feet, but where seven courses are preserved it is 12 feet high or more. The number of towers on the western face of the hill, exclusive of those which flank the gateway, is three. They measure about 21 feet on the face, project from 4 ft. 6 in. to 5 ft. 2 in. from the curtain, and are standing to a height of 7 to 9 feet, the number of courses varying from three to six.

On the southern side of the hill the wall is not nearly so well preserved. There are stretches where it is ruinous, and others again where it is from 5 to 8 feet high. At one point on this side the hill sends out a rocky, needle-like spur, overgrown with prickly holly-oak bushes, which falls away in high sheer precipices of grey rock into the deep glen below. This rocky spur lies outside the line of the fortifications, but immediately above it the wall is preserved to the height of 7 or 8 feet for many yards. Here the masonry partakes more of the ashlar and less of the polygonal style than in most of the rest of the wall ; three and four courses are standing. Only one tower can now be distinguished on the southern brow of the hill. It is about 120 yards to the east of the tower at the south-west corner, measures 20 ft. 3 in. on the face, and projects 4 ft. 5 in. from the curtain. Six to eight courses of masonry are preserved, giving the tower a height at most of 10 feet. The masonry is partly polygonal and partly quadrangular.

At its south-eastern corner the hill ends in an immense perpendicular cliff of grey rock, on the edge of which the fortification-wall naturally ceases. But farther to the north, on the eastern face of the hill, the wall reappears. Here there is a piece as much as 15 feet high, but the masonry is rough and irregular. On this eastern side of the hill the slope to the plain, though steep and high, is for the most part not precipitous except at its southern end ; and hence a fortification-wall was needed, the remains of which, more or less ruinous, may be traced along most of the eastern brow. In places the wall is still from 6 to over 10 feet high ; the number of courses preserved varies from one to seven. It is on this and the northern side of the hill that the wall has been repaired in mediaeval times. Remains of six quadrangular towers can still be made out on the eastern face of the hill. They are about 20 feet broad, and project about 9 feet from the curtain. With the exception of two which are very ruinous, they are standing in part to a height of 8 to 10 feet, with from five to seven courses of masonry preserved.

On the northern brow of the hill, which looks across to the village of *Daulia*, the wall is very ruinous, but at intervals there are short pieces from 6 to 10 feet high. Their style varies greatly : in one place the masonry is of the fine well-jointed polygonal sort ; in another it approaches the ashlar. At the western end, adjoining the tower which flanks the gateway, the wall seems to be about 10 or 12 feet high, with six to eight courses of masonry ; but it is here so thickly overgrown with ivy and holly-oak bushes that to examine it is not easy. Two towers can be discerned flanking the wall on the north side of the hill, without counting the one which flanks the gateway. They project about 5 feet from the curtain. One of them, built of very large blocks in a style which is almost ashlar, is standing to a height of 7 feet, with three courses of masonry. The other tower has been repaired in the Middle Ages, and little of the ancient masonry remains.

I visited Daulis, 31st October 1895, and have described the situation and ruins from my own observation. See also Pouqueville, *Voyage de la Grèce*, 4. p. 134 *sq.* ; Dodwell, *Tour*, 1. pp. 200-206 ; Leake, *Northern Greece*, 2. pp. 97-106 ; Mure, *Journal*, 1. p. 205 *sq.* ; H. N. Ulrichs, *Reisen und Forschungen*, 1. p. 148 *sqq.* ; Welcker, *Tagebuch*, 2. p. 58 *sqq.* ; L. Ross, *Wanderungen*, 1. p. 43 ; Vischer, *Erinnerungen*, p. 600 ; Bursian, *Geogr.* 1. p. 168 *sq.* ; Baedeker,[3] p. 164 *sq.* ; Guide-Joanne, 2. p. 33. For the inscriptions of Daulis, some of which serve to identify the site, see *C. I. G. G. S.* 3. Nos. 61-73.

Daulis was burnt by the Persians (Herodotus, viii. 35), and razed to the ground by Philip of Macedon after the Sacred War (Paus. x. 3. 1). It must have been afterwards rebuilt, for the walls defied all the attempts of the Romans under Flamininus to batter or escalade them. It was only by luring the garrison into a sally that the Romans were able to effect an entrance by the gate, no doubt the same gate which may still be seen at the north-western corner of the hill. See Livy, xxxii. 18. In the later times of antiquity the place was called Daulia (Strabo, ix. p. 423), which is still the name of the village close to the ancient site.

4. 7. they are still reputed the tallest and strongest in Phocis. The people of *Davlia* are still a fine race, distinguished by their vigour from the inhabitants of the fever-stricken plains in the neighbourhood of the Copaic marsh (L. Ross, *Wanderungen*, 1. p. 43).

4. 7. woody or shaggy places —— were called daula. Strabo (ix. p. 423) gives the same derivation of the name Daulis. The etymology seems to be correct. The Greek words *dasus* (δασύς) and *daulos* appear to be etymologically identical with each other and with the Latin *densus* (G. Curtius, *Griech. Etymologie*,[5] p. 233). Cp. *Etymol. Magnum*, *s.vv.* Δαυλός and Δαυλίς, p. 250 ; Suidas and Hesychius, *s.v.* δαυλόν (δαῦλον).

4. 7. Aeschylus called the beard of Glaucus etc. The verse of Aeschylus here referred to by Pausanias is preserved in the *Etymologicum Magnum*, *s.v.* Δαυλίς, p. 250. As to Aeschylus's play on Glaucus of Anthedon, see ix. 22. 7 note.

4. 8. the women —— dished up to Tereus his own boy etc. As to the legend of Tereus, Procne, and Philomela, see i. 41. 8 *sq.*

4. 8. The hoopoe into which —— Tereus was changed. Another legend was that Tereus had been transformed into a hawk (Hyginus, *Fab.* 45) ; and in an ingenious paper Mr. E. Oder has made it probable that this was the original version of the story. The first mention of the transformation of Tereus into a hoopoe occurs in a poetical fragment quoted by Aristotle (*Hist. anim.* ix. 49, p. 633 a, Berlin ed.), who refers it to Aeschylus. Probably, however, it is an extract from Sophocles's play of *Tereus* (Schol. on Aristophanes, *Birds*, 281). In this fragment the poet says that the bird changes from a hoopoe into a hawk; in spring it is a hawk, but in autumn a hoopoe. This belief, which was doubtless a popular superstition (cp. Aristotle *l.c.* and *Hist. anim.* ix. 15. p. 616, Berlin ed.), explains the change in the legend about Tereus. Originally the legend ran that he was transformed into a hawk. This appears from the verses of Aeschylus in which (*Suppl.* 60 *sqq.*) he speaks of "the unhappy spouse of Tereus, the hawk-chased nightingale." And this legend fits the nature of the birds better; for the hoopoe, in spite of its bellicose aspect, is not a fierce bird which chases the nightingale (Procne) and the swallow (Philomela). This is a calumny of the mythologists (Conon, *Narrat.* 31). In reality the hoopoe is a shy and timid bird which is scared even by a swallow flitting past. But the popular superstition which identified the hawk with the hoopoe, readily led to the substitution of the latter for the former in the legend of Tereus. This substitution must have been comparatively late, and may have been first made by Sophocles in his play of *Tereus*, if, as Mr. Oder tries to show, the hoopoe was a rare and unfamiliar bird in Greece in the fifth century B.C. See Eugen Oder, 'Der Wiedehopf in der griechischen Sage,' *Rheinisches Museum*, N. F. 43 (1888), pp. 540-556.

4. 9. in this country —— a swallow would not even build its nest on the roof of a house. Similarly, swallows were said not to fly under the roofs of houses in the Thracian town of Bizya on account of Tereus's crime. They were also said to avoid the houses of Thebes, because the city had been taken so often. See Pliny, *Nat. hist.* x. 70. At the present day in Greece, as the houses of the peasants are for the most part unceiled and have no glass in the windows, the swallows fly freely in and out the rooms, and even build their nests on the rafters over the heads of the occupants. They are not molested, as the people think it lucky to have swallows about the house. Cp. *Classical Review*, 5 (1891), p. 1 *sqq.*

4. 9. even in her bird-form Philomela has a dread of Tereus. This, taken in connexion with the preceding sentences, shows that Pausanias follows the legend which turned Philomela into a swallow (and Procne into a nightingale). This was the regular Greek tradition. See Aristotle, *Rhetoric*, iii. 3. 4; Conon, *Narrat.* 31; Apollodorus, iii. 14. 8; *Mythographi Graeci*, ed. Westermann, p. 383; Eustathius on Homer, *Od.* xix. 518, p. 1875. Eustathius says that the note of the swallow is harsh and unpleasing because Philomela's tongue was cut out by Tereus lest she should reveal his crime, whereas the nightingale begins her song with the name of Itys, the son whom his mother Procne had killed and served up at table to his father Tereus. The Latin writers, however, made Philomela the nightingale and Procne the swallow. See Virgil, *Georg.* iv. 15 and 511; Servius, on Virgil, *Ecl.* v. 78; Hyginus, *Fab.* 45. English poetry has followed the Latin tradition in making Philomela the nightingale, as in Milton's *Il Penseroso:*

> "'Less Philomel will deign a song,
> In her sweetest, saddest plight":

or in Sir H. Wotton's lines to Elizabeth of Bohemia :

> "What's your praise
> When Philomel her voice doth raise?"

The Greeks called the nightingale 'the bird of Daulis' (Thucydides, ii. 29) or 'the Daulian crow' (*Etymolog. Magnum, s.v.* Δαυλίς, p. 250). It seems that the nightingale can still be heard warbling in the thickets that clothe the banks of the *Platania* river not far from Daulis, and that in summer swallows dart about in the sunshine as if they feared Tereus no longer (H. N. Ulrichs, *Reisen und Forschungen*, 1. p. 148 *sq.*).

4. 9. a sanctuary of Athena. This sanctuary probably occupied the site of the ruined mediaeval church of St. Theodore which stands on the acropolis of Daulis, near its north-eastern corner (see above, p. 223); for built into a wall of this church was found a wordy inscription recording the liberation of slaves by dedicating them to Athena Polias (*C. I. G. G. S.* 3. No. 66). Another inscription found at Daulis proves that documents were sometimes dated by the priestess of Athena (*C. I. G. G. S.* 3. No. 65). Serapis and Saviour Artemis were also worshipped at Daulis (*C. I. G. G. S.* 3. Nos. 66, 67); the worship of Serapis was cared for by a priest, with whom copies of documents recording the manumission of slaves were, occasionally at least, deposited (*ib.* No. 66).

4. 10. a shrine of the hero-founder. A mile or so to the south of Daulis the road to the Cleft Way and Delphi passes near a large tumulus, flat at the top, with some fragments of tiles and pottery lying about it. Dodwell thought that this tumulus might be the shrine of the hero Xanthippus (*Tour*, 1. p. 201 *sq.*). An inscription found among the vineyards at the northern foot of the hill of Daulis provides that the road to the shrine of the founder-hero shall be two reeds broad, probably about 15 feet. See Leake, *Northern Greece*, 2. pp. 100-103; H. N. Ulrichs, *Reisen und Forschungen*, 1. pp. 150, 156; *C. I. G.* No. 1732; *C. I. G. G. S.* 3. No. 61.

4. 10. the Phocians bring victims, and the blood they pour through a hole into the grave etc. The custom of offering blood at the grave of the dead or of heroes is often referred to in ancient literature. Cp. iv. 31. 3; v. 13. 2. At the festival of the Eleutheria at Plataea the heroic dead were invited to partake of the banquet and the blood (Plutarch, *Aristides*, 21 ; see note on ix. 2. 5). Euripides refers to the custom repeatedly. Thus in the *Heraclidae* (v. 1040 *sq.*) he makes Eurystheus say : "But suffer them not to let libations or blood trickle into my grave." Cp. *id.*, *Troiades*, 381 *sq.* ; *Electra*, 90 *sqq.* Commonly a hole seems to have been dug, into which the libations of blood or of wine, etc., were poured (Lucian, *Charon*, 22 ; and for the many other passages in which this custom is mentioned, see Stephani in *Compte Rendu* (St. Petersburg) for 1865, pp. 6-8). But the present passage of Pausanias is the only one, so far as I know, in ancient literature which distinctly speaks of a hole carried right through into the grave, so that the libations poured down it could reach the bones or ashes of the dead. The hole, too, seems to have been, not a temporary one made for the occasion, but a permanent one. This is implied by the expres-

sion used by Pausanias (ὀπή, not βόθρος or ὄρυγμα); and it is what we should expect, since the offerings appear to have been made daily. Such a permanent opening into the grave, to be used for passing offerings in, has been found in the great barrow on the peninsula of Taman in the south of Russia. This large artificial mound or barrow is called by the peasants the Great Blisnitza, and is near the village of Steblejevka. It was the common burial-place of a rich and powerful Greek family settled here in the fourth century B.C. Excavations made in the barrow in 1864 brought to light two sepulchral chambers and a funnel-shaped aperture shut with a stone and leading down to a place enclosed with tiles, on which it appears that a meal had been offered to the dead. The funnel-shaped aperture is clearly such a hole as Pausanias here speaks of, made for the purpose of conveying libations into the tomb. See Stephani in *Compte Rendu* (St. Petersburg) for 1865, p. 5 *sq*. A very similar arrangement has recently been discovered in two Roman cemeteries near Carthage. The tombs, of which there are a great many, are built of masonry and are of a square shape, about 5 feet high by 2 or 3 feet broad. Each tomb encloses one or more urns containing calcined bones. Each urn is covered with a saucer (*patera*), in the middle of which there is a hole; and this hole communicates with the exterior of the tomb by means of an earthenware tube placed either upright so as to come out at the top of the tomb, or slanting so as to come out at one of the sides. Thus libations poured into the tube ran down into the urn, and after wetting the bones of the dead escaped by a hole into a lower cavity of the tomb. In this lower cavity (which, however, does not exist in all the tombs) are found coins, lamps, pottery, etc., deposited with the ashes and charred wood of the pyre. Thus each tomb was at the same time an altar on which sacrifices were offered to the dead. See A. L. Delattre, 'Fouilles d'un cimetière romain à Carthage en 1888,' *Revue archéologique*, 3me Série, 12 (1888), p. 151 *sqq*. At Mycenae the funnel-shaped aperture in the round altar which was found over one of the graves was probably used for the purpose of pouring blood down into the grave (Schuchhardt, *Schliemann's Ausgrabungen*,[2] p. 186; Tsountas, Μυκῆναι, pp. 107, 115; Perrot et Chipiez, *Histoire de l'art dans l'antiquité*, 6. p. 323; cp. note on ii. 16. 5, vol. 3. p. 107). These facts bring vividly before us the belief of the Greeks and Romans that the souls of the dead still lived and retained their bodily appetites in the tomb. The same primitive belief has led to similar practices in many parts of the world. The custom of laying food on or near the grave for the use of the dead is too familiar to call for illustration; but it may be worth while to give examples of the practice of actually conveying food into the grave through an opening or tube, as the people of Daulis poured the blood into the grave of their hero. On the funeral day of a king of Gingiro in Africa "they kill many cows close to the grave, so that the blood may run in and touch the dead body; and from that time forward, till the next king dies, they kill a cow there every day, and make the blood run in, the profit whereof belongs to their priests, or sorcerers, for they shed the blood, but eat the flesh " (*The Travels of the Jesuits in Ethiopia.*

Collected and historically digested by F. Balthazer Tellez, of the Society of Jesus; and now first translated into English (London, 1710), p. 198). This African custom is almost identical with the Greek one described by Pausanias. Again, in the Kingdom of Congo, when a king was buried, a tube was passed from the outside into the mouth of the corpse, and down this tube food and drink were poured every month (Labat, *Relation historique de l'Éthiopie Occidentale*, 1. p. 391). In Timannee, West Africa, the bodies of kings or chiefs are deposited in charnel-houses which are never opened; " but small apertures are left in the walls, through which cooked provisions and palm wine are occasionally introduced, the Timannese being impressed with an idea that they are actually necessary for, and consumed by, the dead" (A. G. Laing, *Travels in the Timannee, Kooranko, and Soolima countries in Western Africa*, p. 87). In Old Calabar, "when they buried their dead, the relatives, before the earth is filled into the grave, place a tube, formed of bamboo, or pithy wood with the pith extracted, and sufficiently long to protrude from the earth heaped up over the body, into the mouth of the deceased ; and down this they pour, from time to time, palm wine, water, palm oil, etc."; this is called 'feeding the dead' (A. B. Ellis, *The Land of Fetish*, p. 134 ; cp. T. J. Hutchinson, *Impressions of Western Africa*, p. 148 *sq*.). In Bonny the dead are buried in the house ; a funnel-like opening leads down to the grave ; and it is said that the negro never leaves his house without pouring a libation down the funnel (A. Bastian, *Der Mensch in der Geschichte*, 2. p. 335). Some of the ancient Peruvians buried their dead in tombs and placed vases round the corpses ; holes in the wall led from the outside into these vases, and through these holes the Indians poured liquor on the festivals held in honour of the dead (*The Travels of Cieza de Leon*, translated by C. R. Markham, p. 228 note 3). Another Spanish writer describes how the Peruvians poured a liquor called *chica* through a tube into the mouth of the dead man as he lay in the grave (Zarate, *Histoire de la Decouverte et de la Conquête du Perou* (Paris, 1716), 1. p. 66). The Indians of the West Indies left openings in the tombs through which they poured maize and wine for the consumption of the ghost (Hakluyt, *Historie of the West Indies*, Decade vii. ch. 10). In Java when an inhabitant of Teng'ger is buried and the grave is being filled in, a hollow bamboo is placed upright over the body ; and down this bamboo the relations, for seven successive days, pour daily a vessel of pure water ; they also lay beside the bamboo two dishes, which they daily replenish with food (Raffles, *History of Java*, 1. p. 331, ed. 1817). Among the Duphla of North-Eastern India the dead are buried near the house, and the relations daily supply them with food and drink through a bamboo which is let down into the grave (A. Bastian, *Völkerstämme am Brahmaputra*, p. 17 ; *id.*, in *Verhandlungen der Berliner Gesell. f. Anthropologie*, 1881, p. 160, appended to the *Zeitschrift für Ethnologie*). The Daores, a Tartar people, bury their dead in shallow graves and leave an opening at the head of the corpse ; and for some weeks after the burial the nearest relations come daily and pour food down this opening into the mouth of the corpse, using for the purpose a spoon which is only employed on these occasions (Ides, 'Voyage de Mouscou à la Chine,' in *Voyages au Nord*, 8. p. 102, Amsterdam, 1727). At the festival of Jubuich, in November, the Chuvash of Eastern Russia take a sacrificial meal at the graves of their relations. A hole is made at the head of the grave and a wooden pillar is set up in it. But before the pillar is set up, each person present throws a piece of flesh and pours some liquor into the hole. Then they consume the rest of the food and make merry. See Pallas, *Reise durch verschiedene Provinzen des russischen Reiches*, 1. p. 92. The natives of Fakaofu, or Bowditch Island (South Pacific) buried their dead under a heap of coral shingle, with a vertical slab of stone at the head. For five nights after the burial the relations came to the grave, removed the stone at the head, and poured in cocoanut oil (J. J. Lister, 'Notes on the natives of Fakaofu (Bowditch Island),' *Journal of the Anthropological Institute*, 21 (1891), p. 55).

5. 1. There is a way up through Daulis to the top of Parnassus. From the village of *Davlia* a path leads up wooded and not excessively steep slopes to the large monastery of Jerusalem, loftily and romantically situated on the edge of a torrent, in the midst of a grand forest of ancient firs. The monastery is reached in about two hours from *Davlia*. A steep and rocky path now winds up the bed of a deep gully, the lofty sides of which are crowned with woods. Looking back down the ravine we catch charming views over the plains of Lebadea and Chaeronea. We next ascend steep fir-clad slopes and reach the upper part of the mountain, which is barren and covered with blocks of stone. Through these we thread our way (path there is none) to the tableland which lies below the two highest peaks. Of these peaks the eastern (now called *Lykeri*) is the higher (8070 ft.). On the tableland are two wretched shelters, roughly built of stones. They are called respectively *Strounka tou Lazárou* and *Strounka Kaloghériki* ('monk's yard'). The latter is nearer the summit, from which it is distant an hour. The total time from *Davlia* to the summit of Parnassus may be about eight hours.

See Clarke, *Travels*, 4. p. 211 *sqq.* ; H. N. Ulrichs, *Reisen und Forschungen*, 1. p. 151 ; L. Ross, *Wanderungen*, 2. p. 193 *sq.* ; Baedeker,[3] p. 162 *sq.* ; *Guide-Joanne*, 2. p. 44 *sq.*

5. 1. the Phocicum. Pausanias now proceeds southward from Daulis, skirting the eastern foot of Mount Parnassus. The path leads along the left bank of the *Platania* river, which flows north to join the Cephisus in the plain of Chaeronea. Its banks are shaded by plane-trees, which give the stream its name. Near the ruined village of *Bardana* are some ancient foundations and fragments, half overgrown with bushes. These are supposed to mark the site of the Phocicum or Phocian parliament-house described by Pausanias. See Dodwell, *Tour*, 1. p. 201 ; H. N. Ulrichs, *Reisen und Forschungen*, 1. p. 148 ; Bursian, *Geogr.* 1. pp. 159, 169 ; Baedeker,[3] p. 165 ; *Guide-Joanne*, 2. p. 33. From Pausanias's description of the Phocian parliament-house we may conjecture that it closely resembled the Thersilium at Megalopolis (see vol. 4. p. 338 *sqq.*). His description further suggests that the part of Thersilium which corresponds to the stage of a theatre was occupied, at least in part, by images of gods.   As to the Phocian confederacy and its parliament, see G. Gilbert, *Griechische Staatsalterthümer*, 2. p. 33 *sq.*   Some details as to the officers etc. of the confederacy are ascertained from inscriptions found at Elatea.   Certain federal officials bore the title of *aristeres* (ἀριστῆρες).   See P. Paris, *Élatée*, pp. 61 *sqq.*, 212.

5. 3. **the Cleft Way.**   About 5 miles to the south-west of Daulis the road, after skirting the eastern foot of the mighty mass of Mount Parnassus, turns sharply to the west and begins to ascend through the long, narrow, and profound valley which leads to Delphi.   Just at the point where the road turns westward and before it begins the long ascent it is joined from the south-east by the direct road from Lebadea and Thebes.   The meeting of the three roads—the road from Daulis, the road from Delphi, and the road from Thebes—is the Cleft Way or Triple Road, the scene of the legendary murder of Laius by Oedipus. It is now known as the Cross Road of Megas (*Stavrodromi tou Mega*), after the gallant Johannes Megas, who met his death here in July 1856, while exterminating a band of brigands with a small troop of soldiers. His monument, on a rock at the meeting of the roads, bears a few verses in modern Greek.   Apart from any legendary associations the scene is one of the wildest and grandest in Greece, recalling in its general features, though on a vastly greater scale, the mouth of Glencoe.   On both sides of the valley the mountains tower abruptly in huge precipices ; the cliffs of Parnassus on the northern side of the valley are truly sublime.   Not a trace of human habitation is to be seen.   All is desolation and silence.   A more fitting spot could hardly be found for the scene of a memorable tragedy.

It has sometimes been supposed that the Cleft Way was not at the Cross Road of Megas, but several miles farther to the east.   In this direction the direct path from Delphi to Lebadea traverses a defile called the *Stene* or Narrow Way, enclosed by high rocky hills.   At the eastern end of the defile, where we pass out into an open valley, a road to Daulis and Panopeus diverges to the north.   Here then, where three roads meet—the road from Delphi, the road from Thebes, and the road from Daulis—the Cleft Way of the ancients has sometimes been placed. But the spot does not answer to Pausanias's description of it.   In the first place, it is not on the direct road from Daulis to Delphi ; a traveller from Daulis to Delphi who wished to go by the defile in question (the *Stene*) would have to make a detour of several miles to the east.   But Pausanias here implies and elsewhere (x. 35. 8) expressly asserts that the Cleft Way was on the direct road from Daulis to Delphi.   In the second place, Pausanias tells us that from the Cleft Way onward the road to Delphi began to ascend steeply (§ 5).   This is perfectly true if we place the Cleft Way at the Cross Road of Megas, but it is not true if we place it at the eastern end of the *Stene* pass ; for after traversing that pass we have still to cross a plain of some extent before we reach the Cross Road of Megas, where the real ascent to Delphi begins.   The scenery at the eastern end of the *Stene* defile is wild and picturesque ; the mountain on the south in

particular is high and rocky. But in grandeur it cannot compare with
the scenery at the Cross Road of Megas, the true Cleft Way of the
ancients.

Sophocles (*Oed. Tyr.* 733) and Euripides (*Phoen.* 38) call the spot
the Cleft Way. But Sophocles speaks of it also as the Triple Road
(*Oed. Tyr.* 730, 1398 *sq.*). When Oedipus and Laius met, Oedipus
was on his way from Delphi to Thebes, and Laius was on his way from
Thebes to Delphi. Cp. Apollodorus, iii. 5. 7.

See Wheler, *Journey*, p. 320 ; Chandler, *Travels in Greece*, p. 259 *sq.* ; Clarke,
Travels, 4. p. 173 *sq.* ; Dodwell, *Tour*, 1. p. 197 *sq.* ; Leake, *Northern Greece*,
2. p. 105 *sq.*, ; Mure, *Journal*, 1. p. 202 *sqq.* ; H. N. Ulrichs, *Reisen und Forschungen*, 1. p. 147 ; F. G. Welcker, *Tagebuch*, 2. p. 60 *sq.* ; L. Ross, *Wanderungen*, 1. p. 47 ; W. Vischer, *Erinnerungen*, p. 603 ; Bursian, *Geogr.* 1. p. 169 ;
Guide-Joanne, 2. p. 33 *sq.* ; Baedeker,[3] p. 154 (in the first edition Lolling seems
to have placed the Cleft Way in the *Stene*).

5. 4. unhewn stones are heaped upon them. See viii. 13. 3
note.

5. 4. Damasistratus, king of Plataea, found the bodies etc. This
is mentioned also by Apollodorus (iii. 5. 8). Cp. Bethe, *Thebanische
Heldenlieder*, p. 169.

5. 5. From this point the high road to Delphi grows steeper etc.
From the Cleft Way (*Stavrodromi tou Mega*) the road to Delphi ascends
westward through a deep valley enclosed both on the north and on the
south by the immensely high, steep, and rocky slopes of Mt. Parnassus
on the north and Mt. Cirphis (Strabo, ix. p. 418), now called *Xero-
Vouni* (' dry hill '), on the south. The slopes of the latter mountain are in
places covered with fir-woods. In an hour we reach the summit of the
pass, from which the valley, still enclosed by high precipitous slopes,
descends towards Delphi. This is the water-shed, and here are the
springs of one branch of the Plistus, which flows westward in a deep
ravine through the valley. A road leads down beside the bed of the river
and on to *Salona* (Amphissa). But instead of following it the traveller
to Delphi turns to the right and ascends for another hour by a steep
winding path to the modern village of *Arachova*, situated on the slope
of Parnassus, about 2000 feet above the sea. The steep sides of the
mountain are here planted with vineyards to a great height, terraces
being built in places to support the vines. At the point where the
road to *Arachova* crosses the bed of the Plistus there are considerable
remains of an ancient Greek fortress on a height or plateau to the right
and also beside the stream. The walls are partly built of polygonal
blocks, partly of roughly squared stones laid in horizontal courses.
Within the walls are a good many remains overgrown with bushes.
The ruins may be those of Aeolidae, a town which was burnt by the
Persians and appears to have been situated between Daulis and Delphi
(Herodotus, viii. 35). Or perhaps the place may be the Homeric
Cyparissus. See note on x. 36. 5. The situation of *Arachova*, a large
and prosperous village or rather town of over 3000 inhabitants, is
extremely picturesque. The houses, interspersed with trees, rise in
terraces above each other on the side of the hill, the top of which is

crowned with the church of St. George, the chief church of the village. Above the village soar the abrupt rocky slopes of Parnassus. The men of *Arachova* are tall, slim, and athletic; the women are famed for their beauty. The high bracing air makes them a healthy, long-lived race. They speak a comparatively pure dialect of Greek, and are noted for their independent spirit and the strength of their family ties. In summer they cultivate their vineyards on the declivities of Parnassus, or till their fields and herd their sheep in the upland dales. Their wines have a great reputation; and the women make party-coloured woollen rugs, which are sold far and wide. In winter the severity of the climate keeps them much indoors, and this is the season for many social gatherings and merry-makings, in which dancing and singing play a great part. The village perhaps occupies the site of the ancient Anemoria ('the windy town'), so called from the storms which came sweeping down from the outlying precipices of Parnassus. These precipices near the town were called 'the Look-out Place'; from the top of them Apollo is said to have spied and shot the dragon at Delphi. 'The Look-out Place' may be the cliffs now called *Petrites*, which rise at the back of *Arachova*. When Delphi was made independent of Phocis, Anemoria became the boundary between the territory of Delphi and that of Phocis. This would agree well with the site of *Arachova*, which, standing on the crest that forms the water-shed between the eastern and western slopes of the valley, is a natural frontier. As to Anemoria and the 'Look-out' see Strabo, ix. p. 423; Homer, *Il.* ii. 521 with the scholiast; Schol. on Euripides, *Phoen.* 233; Tzetzes, *Schol. on Lycophron*, 1073.

From *Arachova* the road descends gradually westward to Delphi, skirting the precipitous slopes of Mt. Parnassus on the right and keeping tolerably high above the deep glen of the Plistus on the left. The valley is clothed with olive-trees and the slopes with vineyards. In an hour and three-quarters from *Arachova* we reach Delphi, situated on the northern side of the valley at the foot of the great precipices of Mt. Parnassus, but yet high above the bed of the Plistus, which winds along far below in the depths of the valley. The time from the Cleft Way to Delphi is about four hours.

See Wheler, *Journey*, p. 399 *sq.*; E. D. Clarke, *Travels*, 4. p. 174 *sq.*; Dodwell, *Tour*, I. p. 195 *sqq.*; Thiersch, in *Abhandlungen der philos. philolog. Classe d. kön. bayer. Akad. d. Wissen.* (Munich), 3 (1840), p. 4 *sqq.*; H. N. Ulrichs, *Reisen und Forschungen*, I. pp. 129 *sqq.*, 145 *sqq.*; Mure, *Journal*, I. p. 199 *sqq.*; F. G. Welcker, *Tagebuch*, 2. p. 61 *sq.*; L. Ross, *Wanderungen*, I. p. 47 *sq.*; W. Vischer, *Erinnerungen*, p. 603 *sqq.*; Bursian, *Geogr.* I. p. 169 *sq.*; P. Foucart, *Mémoire sur les ruines et l'histoire de Delphes*, p. 1 *sq.*; J. P. Mahaffy, *Rambles and Studies*, p. 236 *sqq.*; Baedeker,[3] p. 163 *sq.*; *Guide-Joanne*, 2. p. 34 *sq.*

Mt. Cirphis, the bare precipitous mountain which bounds on the south the long valley that extends from the Cleft Way on the east to Delphi on the west, is not mentioned by Pausanias. We learn the name of the mountain from Strabo, who describes it accurately (ix. p. 418) as "a steep mountain lying in front of Delphi to the south, but separated from it by a glen through which flows the river Plistus." Cp. Antoninus Liberalis, *Transform.* 8.

The sacred precinct at Delphi, together with the theatre and stadium, have been fully excavated by French archaeologists at the expense of the French Government in the years 1892-1897. The excavations, begun in October 1892, have been directed by Mr. Th. Homolle, and he has been assisted by Messrs. Couve, Bourguet, Perdrizet, Millet, and Jouguet, members of the French school, Mr. Quellenec, engineer, Mr. Couvert, overseer of the works, Mr. Tournaire, architect, and Mr. Blot, draftsman (*Comptes Rendus de l'Académie des Inscriptions*, 22 (1894), p. 580 *sq.*). The work is not yet (November 1897) finished, for it is in contemplation to excavate also the ground on the eastern side of the Castalian gorge, where the gymnasium and the temple of Forethought Athena lay. Only preliminary reports of these important excavations have hitherto been published. On some points I have been able to supplement them, first, by notes of a visit which I paid to Delphi in October 1895, when I had the privilege of being conducted by Mr. Homolle himself over the scene of his labours and triumphs, and, second, by notes furnished to me by Mr. Cecil Smith, formerly Director of the British School at Athens, who was so good as to pay a visit to Delphi on my behalf in the summer of 1897. On that occasion he had the advantage of Mr. Perdrizet's courteous guidance and assistance.

5. 5. the oracle of Apollo. On the Delphic oracle see L. Preller's article 'Delphi' in Pauly's *Real-Encyclopädie d. class. Alterthumswiss.*; *id.*, 'Delphica,' *Aufsätze*, pp. 224-256; P. Foucart, *Mémoire sur les ruines et l'histoire de Delphes* (Paris, 1865); Aug. Mommsen, *Delphika* (Leipzig, 1878); A. Bouché-Leclercq, *Histoire de la divination dans l'antiquité*, 3. pp. 39-207. On the literature relating to Delphi published between 1880 and 1885, see Aug. Mommsen in *Bursian's Jahresbericht*, 48 (1886), pp. 315-325. A list of ancient and modern writers on Delphi is given by Mr. Bouché-Leclercq (*op. cit.* p. 39 *sqq.*). As to the authorities for the topography of Delphi, see note on x. 8. 6.

5. 5. in the most ancient times the oracle was an oracle of Earth. So Aeschylus (*Eumenides*, 1 *sq.*) speaks of Earth as the goddess who first gave oracles at Delphi. Cp. Plutarch, *De Pythiae oraculis*, 17. In one of the hymns to Apollo recently found by the French at Delphi allusion is made to Earth and Themis as having been peacefully dispossessed by Apollo when he came to Delphi from Tempe (*Bulletin de Corresp. hellénique*, 17 (1893), p. 566). Since the prophetic influence was supposed to emanate from a chasm in the ground (see note on § 7), it was natural to regard the Earth goddess as the source of it, as Diodorus remarks (xvi. 26). Cp. Plutarch, *De defectu oraculorum*, 43. According to a scholiast on Pindar (*Pyth.* Argum.) Night was the first to give oracles at Delphi. The author of the Homeric hymn to Apollo makes no mention of any oracle of Earth, Themis, or Poseidon at Delphi before Apollo made it the seat of his oracle. According to that poet Apollo built a temple at Delphi with the help of Trophonius and Agamedes; then he went to sea, and changing himself into a dolphin met a ship from Cnosus in Crete and led it to the Gulf of Crisa. (In the Mediterranean dolphins may still be seen playing for hours at the cut-water of steamers going at full speed.) Here the mariners landed and Apollo made them his priests in the temple of Delphi ; and they built an altar to him on the seashore and prayed to him as Dolphin Apollo, because they had first seen him rushing through the clear water in the form of a dolphin. See the *Hymn to Apollo*, 103 ; Tzetzes, *Schol. on Lycophron*, 208. Some good scholars, as K. O. Müller, L. Preller, and Mr. Bouché-Leclercq, have held that this tradition of the foundation of the Delphic oracle by Cretan settlers is historically correct. See K. O. Müller, *Dorians*, I. p. 238 *sqq.* ; L. Preller, *Ausgewählte Aufsätze*, p. 226 *sqq.* ; A. Bouché-Leclercq, *Histoire de la divination*, 3. p. 59 *sqq.* ; Th. Schreiber, *Apollon Pythoktonos*, p. 39 *sqq.* Their view receives some support from the circumstance that a sanctuary of the Delphinian Apollo existed at Cnosus in Crete, the city from which the Delphinian Apollo was said to have procured the priests for his temple at Delphi. See *C. I. G.* No. 2554, line 95 *sqq.*

   5. 5. **appointed Daphnis —— to be her prophetess.** Daphnis is only another form of Daphne ('laurel'). The legend ran that Daphne was a daughter of the Earth goddess by the river Ladon or Peneus ; that in order to escape the importunities of her lover Apollo she prayed to her mother Earth ; and that Earth received her daughter into a chasm, and caused a laurel to grow on the spot in her stead (Palaephatus, *De Incredib.* 50 ; Servius on Virgil, *Aen.* ii. 513 and iii. 91 ; Tzetzes, *Schol. on Lycophron*, 6). We may suppose that the chasm into which Daphne was said to have disappeared was no other than the oracular fissure at Delphi ; for we read that a laurel stood beside the prophetic cavern before Apollo took possession of it (Euripides, *Iphig. in Tauris*, 1245 *sqq.*) or stood beside the tripod and was shaken by the priestess when she delivered the oracles (Schol. on Aristophanes, *Plutus*, 213). This laurel was doubtless held to be the very tree which grew in place of Daphne. The legend which thus associates the laurel with the Delphic oracle even before Apollo became the god of the oracle, is interesting, since it shows how intimate was the connexion of the laurel with the oracle. It would seem that at all oracular seats of Apollo his priestess regularly chewed the laurel and drank of a sacred spring before she delivered her prophecies in the name of the god (Lucian, *Bis accusatus*, 1 ; Tzetzes, *Schol. on Lycophron*, 6). Further she fumigated herself with laurel before descending into the oracular cave (Plutarch, *De EI apud Delphos*, 2 ; *id.*, *De Pythiae oraculis*, 6). Perhaps the fumes of the burning laurel contributed to throw her into that convulsive and delirious agitation which the ancients regarded as a sign of divine inspiration. Among the tribes of the Hindoo Koosh, near Gilgit, the Dainyals or diviners, who are generally women, work themselves up into a prophetic frenzy by inhaling the pungent fumes of burning cedar-twigs, the cedar being the sacred tree of these people. The spirit of divination is supposed by them to lie dormant in winter and to be strong in proportion to the heat of the weather. The graphic description, given by an eye-witness, of the frantic behaviour of these women under the influence of the cedar-fumes

236 THE DELPHIC ORACLE BK. X. PHOCIS

may very well be compared with Lucan's description of the prophetic frenzy of the Delphic priestess (*Pharsalia*, v. 161 *sqq.*). See Major J. Biddulph's *Tribes of the Hindoo Koosh*, pp. 96-98. Pliny mentions, on the authority of Democritus, various plants which were used in potions to produce prophetic visions by the Magi and other Asiatics (*Nat. hist.* xxiv. 160, 164). Many examples of the use of drugs for similar purposes are cited by Dr. E. B. Tylor (*Primitive Culture*, 2. p. 416 *sqq.*).

5. 6. **a certain Greek poem called Eumolpia.** This is no doubt the poem which Suidas (*s.v.* Μουσαῖος) calls *Advice to his son Eumolpus* and attributes to Musaeus.

5. 6. **Pyrcon.** At Delphi there were priests called *pyrkooi* (πυρκόοι) who divined by means of omens drawn from burnt sacrifice (Hesychius, *s.v.* πυρκόοι). They may have been priests of Poseidon, who had an altar at Delphi (x. 24. 4), and may have traced their descent from the mythical Pyrcon.

5. 6. **Earth resigned her share to Themis.** Aeschylus also says that Themis succeeded her mother Earth in the control of the oracle (*Eumenides*, 2 *sqq.*). According to Euripides (*Iphig. in Taur.* 1259 *sqq.*) Apollo dismissed Themis and took her place at the oracle; but Earth, to avenge the wrong done her daughter, sent dreams which disturbed and confused the persons who consulted the oracle, till Zeus, at the entreaty of Apollo, compelled her to desist. Some thought that Apollo and Themis had founded the oracle jointly (Strabo, ix. p. 422). According to Aeschylus (*Eumenides*, 4 *sqq.*) Themis was succeeded by Phoebe, who presented the oracle, as a birthday gift, to Apollo.

5. 6. **Apollo gave Poseidon the island of Calauria** etc. Cp. ii. 33. 2.

5. 7. **shepherds feeding their flocks lit upon the oracle** etc. The story of the discovery of the Delphic oracle, as told by Diodorus (xvi. 26), is this. On the spot afterwards occupied by the inmost shrine (*adytum*) of the sanctuary there was a chasm in the ground. A flock of goats was browsing near the chasm, and each goat as it approached the chasm began to skip and utter unwonted sounds. The goatherd, observing this with surprise, went up to the hole, was affected in the same way as his goats, and began to prophesy. The fame of this was spread abroad, many people came to the chasm and fell into prophetic ecstasy. So the place was deemed an oracle of Earth. At last when many persons, in the height of their frenzy, had leaped into the hole and disappeared, the neighbours resolved to appoint one woman to the office of prophetess, and in order that she might receive the prophetic influence and give the oracles in safety, they devised a three-legged machine or tripod, which she mounted when she was about to prophesy. The oracular chasm is described by Strabo (ix. p. 419) as follows : " They say that the oracle is a perpendicular cavern, not very broad at the mouth, and that an inspiring air is wafted up from it, and that over the mouth of it stands a high tripod, which the Pythian priestess mounts and receiving the air

utters the oracles, some in verse and some in prose, and the prose
oracles are put into verse by poets employed in the service of the
sanctuary." Justin describes the situation of the oracular cavern as
follows (xxiv. 6. 6 *sqq.*) : "The temple of Apollo stands on a cliff which
overhangs on all sides. . . . The middle of the cliff recedes in the
shape of a theatre, . . . and in this recess, about half-way up the
mountain, is a small plateau. In this plateau there is a deep hole in
the ground, which emits the oracles (*quod in oracula patet*). From the
hole a cold air is forcibly expelled upwards, which turns the minds of
the prophetesses to madness and filling them with the god compels
them to give answers to enquirers." According to Plutarch (*De defectu
oraculorum*, 42 and 46) the name of the man who first discovered the
inspiring influence of the cavern by falling into it was Coretas. Some
have taken the name Coretas to be etymologically connected with
Curetes and *Crete* and hence have regarded it as a confirmation of the
legend that the Delphic oracle was of Cretan origin.

Before the priestess descended into the cavern, omens were taken
from goats. Cold water was poured on the goat's head, and if the
animal shivered and shook in all its limbs, the omen was good, the goat
was sacrificed, and the priestess descended into the cave. But if the
goat, when drenched with the water, stood motionless or only shook its
head, the omen was unfavourable, and the priestess did not go down.
The origin of this custom was explained by the story that the inspiring
influences which emanated from the cave had first been experienced by
goats. See Plutarch, *De defectu oraculorum*, 46, 49, and 51 ; Diodorus,
xvi. 26. Many peoples besides the Greeks have treated the shivering
of the victim as a token that the sacrifice is accepted by the deity. Thus
at harvest-time the Bawarias of India sacrifice a goat to their goddess.
They tether its hind legs to a peg, and pour water on its nose. If the
goat shivers, the goddess accepts it ; if it does not, the animal is rejected
and the operation is repeated on another. See *Panjab Notes and
Queries*, 3 (1886), No. 721. The Devil-worshippers of Southern India
sacrifice a black victim, generally a goat, to Kali. A pot of water is
dashed on its head ; if the creature shakes itself, it is acceptable to
Kali and is sacrificed (*Journal of the Anthropological Society of
Bombay*, 1 (1886), p. 103). When the Chuvash of Eastern Russia
offer a sacrifice, they pour a vessel of cold water over the victim. If
it shakes itself, they sacrifice it ; if it does not, they drench it a second
and a third time. Then, if it still stands motionless, they put it aside and
take another victim. See Pallas, *Reise durch verschiedene Provinzen
des russischen Reichs*, 1. p. 91 ; Vambery, *Das Türkenvolk*, p. 485.
When the heathen Harranians sacrificed a victim they poured wine on
it ; if it shook itself, they said : "This is a well-pleasing sacrifice" ; but
if it did not shake itself, they said, "God is angry, he does not accept
this vow" (Chwolsohn, *Die Ssabier und der Ssabismus*, 2. p. 37). For
more examples of the custom in Russia, the Hindoo Koosh, India, and
Tonquin, see Erman, *Archiv für wissenschaftliche Kunde von Russland*,
1. p. 377 ; J. Biddulph, *Tribes of the Hindoo Koosh*, p. 131 ; S. Mateer,
The Land of Charity, p. 216 ; *id., Native Life in Travancore*, p. 94 ;

Sir A. C. Lyall, *Asiatic Studies*, p. 14; *Lettres édifiantes et curieuses*, 16. p. 230 *sq.* The shivering of the victim was probably thought to indicate that the god had entered into it, just as convulsive shudderings of his prophets are regarded as a token of inspiration. When the Fijians were about to go to battle or engage in any other important enterprise, they desired the priest "to let the spirit enter into him forthwith, making him, at the same time, a present. The priest speedily begins to shake and shiver, and ere long communicates the will of the god, which always tallies with the wishes of the chief. It sometimes happens that the priest fails in exciting himself to convulsive action; but this, among a people so wrapt in superstition, can always be ingeniously accounted for: the most usual mode of excusing the failure is to say that Kalou is dissatisfied with the offering" (Wilkes, *Narrative of the United States Exploring Expedition*, 3. p. 89).

5. 7. **Phemonoe was the first prophetess of the god** etc. Cp. Strabo, ix. p. 419; Stobaeus, *Florilegium*, xxi. 26; Clement of Alexandria, *Strom.* i. 21. 107, p. 383 ed. Potter. According to some, Phemonoe was a daughter of Apollo (Pliny, *Nat. hist.* x. 7); according to others, she was a daughter of Delphus (Schol. on Euripides, *Orestes*, 1094). Lucan (*Pharsal.* v. 126 and 187) gives the name of Phemonoe to the Delphic priestess in the first century B.C.

5. 7. **first sang in hexameters.** The oracles were not always in hexameters; for example, Herodotus (i. 174) quotes an oracle of two lines in iambic metre. But though the metre of the verses varied, their quality did not; it was always vile. Hence it became a subject of anxious enquiry with the faithful how Apollo, the god of the Muses, could possibly have inspired such trash. Even in his best days he did not always rise to verse, and in Plutarch's time the god appears to have given up the attempt in despair and to have generally confined himself to plain, if not lucid, prose. "But even now," adds Plutarch, "people sometimes rush out of the sanctuary with an oracle in verse," and he quotes one of these poetical effusions. See Plutarch, *De Pythiae oraculis*, 5-7, 17-20.

5. 7. **who came from the land of the Hyperboreans.** In one of his poems Alcaeus described how, when Apollo was born, Zeus sent him in a chariot drawn by swans to Delphi, there to give laws to the Greeks. But Apollo, instead of going to Delphi, caused the swans to fly to the land of the Hyperboreans. The Delphians meantime composed a paean and ranging choruses of young men about the tripod called upon the god to come back from the far north. But Apollo staid a whole year among the Hyperboreans, giving them laws. Then he flew back on his swan-drawn chariot to Delphi, which he reached at midsummer. See Himerius, *Orat.* xiv. 10 *sq.*; and on the relation of Apollo and Delphi to the Hyperboreans, see K. O. Müller, *Dorians*, 1. p. 294 *sqq.*; L. Preller, *Griech. Mythologie*,⁴ 1. p. 242 *sqq.*; A. Bouché-Leclercq, *Histoire de la divination*, 3. p. 70 *sqq.*

5. 8. **only women as the mouth-pieces of the oracle.** According to Diodorus (xvi. 26) virgins were at first chosen to act as priestesses to Apollo at Delphi; but after the violation of one of them the Delphians

decreed that for the future the oracles should be pronounced, not by a virgin, but by a woman over fifty years of age, attired as a virgin.   In Plutarch's time, however, the Pythian priestess was always a maiden. See Plutarch, *De Pythiae oraculis*, 22 ; *id.*, *De· defectu oraculorum*, 46 and 51.   In the palmy days of Greece two Pythian priestesses were constantly employed, taking it in turns to deliver the oracles, and a third was always ready in case of accidents.   But in Plutarch's time so few people came to consult the oracle that one priestess sufficed. See Plutarch, *De defectu oraculorum*, 8.

5. 9. **the second temple was made by bees out of wax and feathers.**   Apollo "once inhabited a simple hut, and a small shanty was fashioned for him, to which bees are said to have contributed their wax and birds their feathers" (Philostratus, *Vit. Apoll.* vi. 10. 4).   The temple of feathers is mentioned also by Strabo (ix. p. 421) and Stobaeus (*Florilegium*, xxi. 26), and it is referred to in an ancient Delphic oracle quoted by Plutarch (*De Pythiae oraculis*, 17, "Bring together feathers, ye birds, and wax, ye bees").   In this connexion, it is to be remembered that the Delphic priestesses were called Bees.   See note on viii. 13. 1.   In the Homeric hymn to Hermes (*v.* 552 *sqq.*) mention is made of three prophetic nymphs called Thriae who dwelt on Parnassus and from whom Apollo in his youth had learned the art of soothsaying.   These nymphs fed on honeycomb.   After eating honey they spoke the truth ; but if deprived of it, they spoke lies.   (As to the divining pebbles called *thriae*, see note on vii. 25. 10.)   The oracle of Trophonius was said to have been discovered through a swarm of bees (see ix. 40. 2).   These facts seem to show that the Greeks associated prophetic powers with bees.   Cp. Lobeck, *Aglaophamus*, p. 815 *sqq.* ; W. Robert-Tornow, *De apium mellisque apud veteres significatione* (Berlin, 1893), p. 169 *sqq.* ; A. B. Cook, in *Journal of Hellenic Studies*, 15 (1895), p. 7.

5. 11. **the third temple —— made of bronze.**   The bronze temple is mentioned also by Stobaeus (*Florilegium*, xxi. 26).

5. 11. **Acrisius made a bronze chamber for his daughter.**   See ii. 23. 7 note.

5. 11. **Athena of the Bronze House.**   See iii. 17. 2.

5. 11. **the Forum at Rome** —— has a roof of bronze.   See v. 12. 6.

5. 12. **charmers all of gold.**   The exact nature of these golden charmers or songstresses is uncertain.   See Boeckh's Pindar, *Frag.* 25. Prof. Furtwängler has suggested that they may have been statues placed on the apexes of the gables.   See his article on such decorations (*akroteria*) in *Archäologische Zeitung*, 40 (1882), pp. 321-364.

5. 13. **The fourth temple was built by Trophonius and Agamedes.**   Cp. ix. 37. 5 ; Schol. on Aristophanes, *Clouds*, 508.   The author of the Homeric hymn to the Pythian Apollo (*v.* 116 *sqq.*) describes how Apollo himself laid the foundations broad and long, and how upon them Trophonius and Agamedes, the sons of Erginus, set a stone threshold, while countless tribes of men reared a temple of polished stone to be famous for ever.   It is said that after building the temple

Trophonius and Agamedes asked Apollo for a reward. The god promised to give them it in seven days, bidding them in the meantime to feast and make merry. They did so, and on the seventh night they fell asleep and woke no more (Plutarch, *Consol. ad Apoll.* 14). Cicero tells the same story, except that he says they died after three days (*Tuscul.* i. 47. 114).

5. 13. The present temple was built etc. As to the history and remains of this temple, see below, note on x. 19. 4.

6. 1. the Parnassian glen. Pindar (*Pyth.* vi. 9) speaks of Delphi as "Apollo's dell." Cp. Schol. on Pindar, *l.c.*; Schol. on Homer, *Il.* ii. 519.

6. 1. auguries from the flight of birds. A fragmentary inscription found at Ephesus gives some details as to the omens drawn from the flight of birds. The omens varied according as the bird was flying from right to left or from left to right, and as it raised or concealed one of its wings. See *C. I. G.* No. 2953; Roehl, *I. G. A.* No. 499; P. Cauer, *Delectus Inscr. Graec.*[2] 478; E. S. Roberts, *Greek Epigraphy*, No. 144. Cp. A. Bouché-Leclercq, *Histoire de la divination*, 1. p. 127 *sqq.* Auguries have been drawn from the flight and cries of birds by many peoples, by none perhaps more systematically than by the Dyaks. "The Dyak has his sacred birds, whose flight or calls are supposed to bring him direction from the unseen powers. The law and observance of omens occupy, probably, a greater share of his thoughts than any other part of his religion or superstition; and I cannot imagine that any tribe in any age ever lived in more absolute subservience to augury than do the Dyaks. The system, as carried out by them, is most elaborate and complicated, involving uncertainties innumerable to all who are not fully experienced in the science, and the younger men have constantly to ask the elder ones how to act in unexpected coincidences of various and apparently contradictory omens. . . . The birds thus 'used,' as Dyaks say, are not many. . . . Most are, I believe, beautiful in plumage; all are small, and, like most tropical birds, have nothing that can be called song; but their calls are sometimes shrill and piercing. . . . But in practice, the system goes beyond birds, and embraces" the deer, mouse-deer, gazelle, armadillo, various insects, the lizard, bat, python, and cobra. "All these may be omens in various ways and circumstances, and therefore, in this connexion, they are designated *burong* (birds), and to augur from any of them is *beburong*. But these other creatures are subordinate to the birds, which are the foundation upon which the superstructure of good luck is to be raised; and from which alone augury is sought at the beginning of any important undertaking" (J. Perham, 'Sea Dyak Religion,' *Journal of the Straits Branch of the Royal Asiatic Society*, No. 10 (December 1882), p. 228 *sq.*) Although Pausanias here says that the mythical hero Parnasus was believed to have discovered the art of divining by the flight of birds, there seems to be no evidence that this mode of divination was practised at Delphi. C. Boetticher, indeed, tried to show that it was so practised, but he failed to produce any adequate evidence, as his adversary F. Wieseler easily proved. See C. Boetticher, 'L' orneoscopia nella mantica di Delfo,' *Annali dell' Instituto*, 33 (1861), pp. 243-257 ; F. Wieseler, *ib.* pp. 356-365.

6. 2. Lycorea. Cp. Strabo, ix. p. 418. Pausanias derives the name from *lukos*, 'a wolf,' and *ōruesthai*, 'to howl.' The Delphians are said to have been sometimes called Lycoreans (Schol. on Apollonius, ii. 711). The highest peak of Parnassus is still named *Liakoura* or *Lykeri*, doubtless forms of the old name (Leake, *N. Greece*, 2. p. 579 ; Baedeker,[3] p. 162 ; *Guide-Joanne*, 2. p. 43). H. N. Ulrichs thought that Lycorea may have stood on a height to the west of the Corycian cave, where some remains of ancient Greek walls exist (*Reisen und Forschungen*, 1. p. 120 ; Bursian, *Geogr.* 1. p. 179 *sq.*). Leake (*l.c.*) held that ruins of the ancient city are to be seen at the village of *Liakouri*. Many stories have come down to us of animals that guided people to a new home. See iii. 22. 12 ; iii. 23. 7 ; iv. 34. 8 ; viii. 8. 4 ; ix. 12. 1 ; ix. 19. 4. We have seen (note on x. 5. 5) that Apollo in the form of a dolphin was traditionally said to have guided the Cretan mariners to the Crisaean Gulf. The site of Ephesus is said to have been indicated by a fish and a wild boar (Athenaeus, viii. p. 361 c d). Argilus in Thrace was founded, in obedience to an oracle, on the spot where a mouse had appeared, and the town was called Argilus, that being the Thracian word for a mouse (Heraclides Ponticus, *De rebus publicis*, 42, *Frag. Hist. Graec.* ed. Müller, 2. p. 224). Battus, the founder of Cyrene, was guided by a crow (Callimachus, *Hymn to Apollo*, 65 *sqq.*). Ilus founded Ilium on the spot where a speckled cow lay down (Apollodorus, iii. 12. 3). Lycia is said to have been named after the wolves which guided Latona to the country (Antoninus Liberalis, *Transform.* 25). The Muses in the form of bees led the Athenian colonists to Ionia (Philostratus, *Imagines*, ii. 8. 5). The sites of Cumae and Naples were indicated by doves (Velleius Paterculus, i. 4. 1 ; Statius, *Sylv.* iii. 5. 78 *sq.*). The Piceni were named after a woodpecker (*picus*) which had led their forefathers from the land of the Sabines to Picenum (Strabo, v. p. 240). A bull guided the Samnites to Samnium (Strabo, v. p. 250). The Irpini were led to their country by a wolf, and they took their name from the beast, *irpus* being the Samnite word for a wolf (Festus, *s.v.* 'Irpini,' p. 106 ed. Müller). In Germany stories are told of the sites of towns or churches having been pointed out by animals (F. Panzer, *Beitrag zu deutschen Mythologie*, 2. p. 405 *sqq.* ; K. Simrock, *Deutsche Mythologie*,[5] p. 533). The Aztecs seem to have had a legend that they were led to Mexico by a humming-bird. See J. G. Müller, *Gesch. der Amerikanischen Urreligionen*, p. 594 *sq.* ; H. H. Bancroft, *Native races of the Pacific States*, 3. p. 304 *sqq.* ; Andrew Lang, *Myth, Ritual and Religion*, 2. p. 69 *sqq.*

6. 3. Celaeno. A scholiast on Euripides (*Orestes*, 1094) calls her Melaenis.

6. 4. Castalius, an aboriginal. A scholiast on Euripides (*Orestes*, 1094) represents Castalius as a son of Delphus and Castalia. Another story ran that Castalius was a Cretan who set out to found a colony and was led to the Crisaean gulf by Apollo in the shape of or riding on a dolphin (Tzetzes, *Schol. on Lycophron*, 208 ; *Etymolog. Magn. s.v.*

Δελφίνιος). A similar story is told by Servius (on Virgil, *Aen.* iii. 332), except that he calls the Cretan colonist Icadius. See L. Preller, *Ausgewählte Aufsätze*, p. 229 *sq.*

6. 4. Thyia. She had a precinct at Delphi. At the approach of the Persian host under Xerxes the Delphians were bidden by the oracle to sacrifice to the winds. So they built an altar to the winds in the precinct of Thyia and sacrificed to them. Herodotus calls Thyia a daughter of Cephisus. See Herodotus, vii. 178.

6. 4. Thyiads. Cp. x. 4. 3 ; x. 32. 7. The worship of Dionysus had a great hold on Delphi ; indeed Plutarch says that Delphi belonged as much to Dionysus as to Apollo. During three winter months the Delphians invoked Dionysus instead of Apollo, and sang the dithyramb (the song of Dionysus) instead of the paean (the song of Apollo). See Plutarch, *De EI apud Delphos*, 9. On a Greek vase found at Kertsch in 1860 Apollo and Dionysus are depicted shaking hands in front of a palm-tree ; the scene is supposed to represent the meeting of the two gods at Delphi. See L. Stephani, in *Compte Rendu* (St. Petersburg) for 1861, p. 53 *sqq.* ; L. Weniger, 'Apollo und Dionysos zu Delphi,' *Archäologische Zeitung*, 24 (1866), pp. 185-195, with pl. ccxi. According to a scholiast on Pindar (*Pyth.* Argum. p. 297 ed. Boeckh) Dionysus was the first to give oracles from the tripod. As to the relations of Apollo and Dionysus at Delphi, see also E. Gerhard, ' Bacchischer Apollo,' *Archäologische Zeitung*, 23 (1865), pp. 97-110, with plates ccii., ccciii. ; F. Robiou, 'Apollon dans les mystères,' *Gazette archéologique*, 6 (1880), pp. 117-134 ; A. Bouché-Leclercq, *Histoire de la divination*, 3. p. 85 *sqq.* ; Aug. Mommsen, *Delphika*, p. 112 *sqq.*

6. 4. Delphus. According to Tzetzes (*Schol. on Lycophron*, 208) Delphus was a son of Poseidon by Melantho, daughter of Deucalion. Aeschylus represents Delphus as reigning at Delphi when Apollo first came thither from Delos (*Eumenides*, 16).

6. 5. as Homer has done in the list of the Phocians. See Homer, *Il.* ii. 519. Pausanias himself regularly uses the name Pytho instead of Delphi when he refers to the Pythian games held at Delphi. See Index, *s.v.* Pytho.

6. 5. he whom Apollo shot with his arrows. The slaughter of the Python by Apollo is celebrated in two of the hymns to Apollo which were recently discovered by the French at Delphi : in one of them the monster is described as a son of Earth, in the other as a dragon or serpent that guarded the prophetic tripod. See *Bulletin de Corresp. hellénique*, 17 (1893), p. 574 ; *id.*, 18 (1894), p. 352.

6. 5. Homer represented the island of the Sirens etc. See Homer, *Od.* xii. 45 *sq.* The story of Ulysses and the Sirens is the subject of a Pompeian wall-painting, now in the British Museum, and of paintings on at least two ancient vases, of which one is in the British Museum and the other in the National Museum at Athens. See Miss J. E. Harrison, *Myths of the Odyssey*, p. 146 *sqq.* ; Miss E. Sellers, in *Journal of Hellenic Studies*, 13 (1892-3), pp. 2-6.

6. 6. a dragon set by Earth to guard the oracle. On the Python as the guardian of the oracle before the advent of Apollo, compare

Apollodorus, i. 4. 1 ; Euripides, *Iphig. in Taur.* 1245 *sqq.* ; Schol. on Homer, *Il.* ii. 519 ; Schol. on Pindar, *Pyth.* Argum. ; Aelian, *Var. hist.* iii. 1 ; Hyginus, *Fab.* 140. As to the legend of Apollo and the dragon, of which no satisfactory explanation has yet been given, see the monograph of Mr. Th. Schreiber, *Apollon Pythoktonos* (Leipzig, 1879).

7. 1. it was attempted by the Phlegyan race. See ix. 36. 2 ; x. 34. 2.

7. 1. Pyrrhus, son of Achilles. Various explanations were given of the motives which brought Neoptolemus (Pyrrhus) to Delphi. One was that he came to plunder the oracle in order to provide himself with funds for an attack on Peloponnese ; another was that he intended to take vengeance on Apollo for the death of his father Achilles. See Schol. on Pindar, *Nem.* vii. 58 ; Schol. on Euripides, *Orestes,* 1655, and *Andromache,* 51 and 53 ; Apollodorus, ed. R. Wagner, p. 218.

7. 1. by a division of the army of Xerxes. The attack of the Persians on Delphi is described by Herodotus (viii. 35-39). On the approach of the enemy up the long defile from the Cleft Way, the Delphians sent their women and children away across the Gulf of Corinth, and abandoning the city betook themselves to the heights of Parnassus or to Amphissa in Locris. Only sixty men and the prophet remained in the town. But when the Persians approached Delphi and had reached the sanctuary of Fore-temple Athena (see note on x. 8. 6), the thunder rolled, lightning flashed and struck them, and two cliffs broke away from Parnassus and came crashing into their midst, laying many of them low. War-cries too were heard from the sanctuary of Athena. At these sights and sounds fear fell upon the barbarians, they turned and fled, and the Delphians descending from the heights of Parnassus smote them with the edge of the sword. The great stones which had fallen from Parnassus were still to be seen lying in the sanctuary of Athena in Herodotus's time. Compare Diodorus, xi. 14 ; Justin, ii. 12. 8 *sq.* Plutarch says (*Numa,* 9) that the Persians burnt the temple of Apollo. Ctesias mentions two expeditions of the Persians against Delphi (in Photius, *Bibliotheca,* p. 39 ed. Bekker). Mr. Wecklein has attempted to show that the whole story of the Persian attack on Delphi was a fiction of the Delphian priests. He makes much of a supposed contradiction between Herodotus's narrative (in viii. 35-39) and the declaration of Mardonius (Herodotus, ix. 42) that the Persians would not attack Delphi, because an oracle had predicted that if they plundered the sanctuary they would all perish. The supposed contradiction does not exist. The failure of their attempt on Delphi may very well have excited the superstitious fears of the Persians and have induced them to disseminate a prediction of this kind as an excuse for not repeating the attempt. They had not actually plundered the sanctuary, though they had made a very fair attempt to do so. Their consciences were therefore clear : they did not need to dread the penalty denounced in the oracle, and therefore had nothing to lose by bruiting it abroad. See Wecklein, in *Sitzungsberichte d. philos. philolog. u. histor. Cl. d. k. b. Akad. d. Wissen.* (Munich), 1876, pp. 263-269 ; H. Pomtow, 'Die Perserexpedition nach Delphoi,' *Fleckeisen's Jahr-*

bücher, 30 (1884), pp. 227-263; G. Busolt, *Griechische Geschichte*, 2.² p. 688 *sqq.*; A. Hauvette, *Hérodote* (Paris, 1894), p. 384 *sqq.*

7. 1. Nero —— robbed Apollo of five hundred bronze statues. Cp. x. 19. 2; Dio Chrysostom, *Or.* xxxi. vol. 1. p. 394 ed. Dindorf. The emperor also tried to stop up the prophetic chasm, into which he threw the bodies of some men whom he had caused to be murdered (Dio Cassius, lxiii. 14; Lucian, *Nero*, 10). But even after his spoliation a vast number of works of art remained at Delphi, including not less than 73,000 statues, if we may trust our texts of Pliny (*Nat. hist.* xxxiv. 36). The number is, however, probably a mistake of the author or his copyists.

7. 2. the most ancient contest —— was the singing of a hymn etc. The common legend seems to have been that the Pythian games were instituted by Apollo as a funeral celebration for the Python which he had slain. See Clement of Alexandria, *Protrept.* i. 1. p. 2, and ii. 34, p. 29 ed. Potter; Aristotle, *Peplos*, Frag. (*Frag. Hist. Graec.* 2. p. 189, No. 282 ed. Müller); John of Antioch, Frag. i. 20 (*Frag. Hist. Graec.* 4. p. 539 ed. Müller); Iamblichus, *De Pythagor. vit.* x. 52; Schol. on Pindar, *Pyth.* Argum.; Hyginus, *Fab.* 140; Ovid, *Met.* i. 445 *sqq.* Augustine tells a different story. He says (*De civ. dei*, xviii. 12) that Danaus had invaded the land of Delphi and burnt Apollo's temple. Apollo, angry with the Delphians for not defending his temple, afflicted the country with barrenness; and to appease him musical games were instituted in his honour. According to Ovid (*l.c.*), the games from their institution included boxing, running, and chariot-races; but herein he differs from Strabo, Pausanias, and the scholiast on Pindar, whose united testimony is to be preferred. At first the only contest was the singing of a hymn to Apollo to the accompaniment of the lyre. This is stated by Strabo (ix. p. 421), and is confirmed by Pausanias who mentions the hymn to Apollo and says (§ 3) that Hesiod was excluded from the competition because he could not play on the lyre. Cp. Schol. on Pindar, *Pyth.* Argum. In early times the management of the games was in the hands of the Delphians (Strabo, *l.c.*). But in Ol. 48. 3 (586 B.C.), at the conclusion of the Crisaean war, the conduct of the games was undertaken by the Amphictyonic Council, who added to the number of the musical contests and introduced athletic competitions for the first time (Strabo, *l.c.*; Pausanias, below § 4 *sq.*; Schol. on Pindar, *Pyth.* Argum. p. 298 ed. Boeckh). In the second Pythiad (Ol. 49. 3 = 582 B.C.) prizes consisting of wreaths were substituted for the old prizes in money or valuables (Pausanias, below § 5; *Marmor Parium*, l. 53 *sq.*) Hence some ancient authorities dated the series of Pythiads from the second Pythiad in 582 B.C. But this was a mistake. The succession of the Pythiads should be reckoned from the celebration in 586 B.C. See Boeckh, *Explicationes ad Pindarum*, p. 207 *sq.*; Clinton, *Fasti Hellenici*, p. 228. In the earliest times the Pythian festival was celebrated every eighth year (Schol. on Pindar, *l.c.*; Censorinus, *De die natali*, 18; A. Mommsen, *Delphika*, p. 153 *sq.*). But from 586 B.C. onwards the festival was held every fourth year, the year in which it fell being the third year of each

Olympiad. An annual Pythian festival seems also to have been held (*C. I. G.* No. 1688. 44; A. Mommsen, *Delphika*, p. 151 *sq.*); but it was doubtless of minor importance. Inscriptions prove that the great Pythian festival, held every fourth year, was celebrated in *Boukatios*, the second month of the Delphic year, corresponding to the Attic month *Metageitnion*. The day of the month on which the festival began is not mentioned by ancient writers or in inscriptions; but we may infer that it began on the seventh day of the month, because that was the day on which Apollo was said to have celebrated it (Schol. on Pindar, *Pyth.* Argum. p. 297 ed. Boeckh). This is confirmed by the fact that the number seven was sacred to Apollo (Plutarch, *De EI apud Delphos*, 17; *id., Quaest. Conviv.* ix. 3. 1); the seventh day of the month was holy because Apollo had been born on it (Hesiod, *Works and Days*, 771 *sq.*). Cp. A. Mommsen, *Delphika*, p. 176 *sq.* Hence, as the Delphic year began at the summer solstice, and the Pythian festival began on the seventh day of the second month, the time of its celebration must have been about the middle of August. See Kirchhoff, 'Ueber die Zeit der pythischen Festfeier,' *Monatsberichte der könig. preuss. Akad. d. Wissen. zu Berlin*, 1864, pp. 129-135; A. Mommsen, *Delphika*, p. 154 *sqq.* For the inscriptions which show that the Pythian games were celebrated in the month *Boukatios*, see *C. I. G.* No. 1688; W. Froehner, *Inscriptions grecques du Louvre*, No. 32; Wescher et Foucart, *Inscriptions recueillies à Delphes*, No. 410. On the Pythian festival in general see A. Mommsen, *Delphika*, pp. 149-214. Fragments of three of the hymns composed in honour of Apollo and intended to be sung at his festival have been found in recent years by the French at Delphi; all three are engraved on stone, and two of them are accompanied by musical notation. The poetical merit of these compositions is not great. Two of them allude to the Gallic invasion and were therefore written not earlier than 279 B.C., the year of the inroad; indeed one of these two belongs to the Roman period, for it winds up with a prayer for the prosperity of the Roman empire. See *Bulletin de Corresp. hellénique*, 17 (1893), pp. 561-610; *id.*, 18 (1894), pp. 345-389; O. Crusius, *Die delphischen Hymnen*, supplement to *Philologus*, vol. 53 (1894).

7. 2. **Chrysothemis of Crete sang.** "Chrysothemis the Cretan was the first who, attired in a splendid garb and with the lyre in his hands to imitate Apollo, sang the (Pythian) air. He won applause and hence the manner of the contest is still kept up" (Proclus, in Photius, *Bibliotheca*, p. 320 ed. Bekker).

7. 2. **Carmanor who is said to have purified Apollo.** See ii. 7. 7 note.

7. 4. **Sacadas.** He was said to have been the first who played the 'Pythian tune' on the flute at Delphi. See ii. 22. 8. This tune is described by Pollux (iv. 84) and Strabo (ix. p. 421 *sq.*). The melody, intended to represent musically Apollo's combat with the dragon, was a solo on the flute, but now and then the trumpets and fifes struck in. First Apollo was heard preparing for the fight and choosing his ground. Then followed the challenge to the dragon, then the battle, indicated by an iambic measure. Here probably the music imitated the twanging of

the silver bow and the swish of the arrows as they sped to their mark. It is expressly said that the gnashing of the monster's teeth was heard, as he ground them together in his agony. Here the trumpets came in, not in long-drawn winding bouts, but in short single blasts, one perhaps for each arrow-shot, every flourish marking a hit. The shrill wailing notes of the fifes mimicked the dragon's dying screams. Then the flute broke into a light, lilting air, beating time to the triumphal measure trodden by the victorious god. Cp. Boeckh, *De metris Pindari*, p. 182 n. 16; A. Mommsen, *Delphika*, p. 193 *sq.*; Th. Schreiber, *Apollon Pythoktonos*, pp. 17-32; H. Guhrauer, 'Der pythische Nomos,' *Fleckeisen's Jahrbücher*, Supplem. 8 (1875-1876), pp. 309-351; K. v. Jan, 'Der pythische Nomos und die Syrinx,' *Philologus*, 38 (1879), pp. 378-384. Mr. v. Jan argues that the imitation of the dragon's screams was produced, not by a separate accompaniment on the fifes, but by an instrument or mechanical contrivance of some sort attached to the flute itself. He refers especially to Plutarch, *De musica*, 21 : "Telephanes the Megarian was such a foe to the fifes that he never even allowed the flute-players to place them on the flutes ; and for this reason especially he abstained from the Pythian contest." As to the musician Sacadas and the Pythian tune, see E. Hiller, 'Sakadas der Aulet,' *Rheinisches Museum*, N. F. 31 (1876), pp. 76-88.

7. 5. **foot-races for boys.** The order of the contests at Delphi differed from that at Olympia. At Delphi the contests of boys alternated with the contests of men ; thus the wrestling - matches of the boys were followed by the wrestling-matches of the men ; the boxing-matches of the boys were followed by the boxing-matches of the men ; and so on with the other kinds of contests. But at Olympia all the contests of the boys took place first, and were then followed by all the contests of the men. See Plutarch, *Quaest. Conviv.* ii. 5. 1. The Delphic order seems the better. For the same boys or men often competed in more than one kind of contest ; and the Delphic plan allowed them a rest between each contest.

7. 7. **the victory of Damaretus of Heraea.** Cp. v. 8. 10, vi. 10. 4, viii. 26. 2.

7. 8. **in the sixty-ninth Pythiad —— the winner was Ptolemy, the Macedonian.** As the sixty-ninth Pythiad fell in 310 B.C., this Ptolemy was Ptolemy I., the son of Lagus. He called himself a Macedonian in an inscription on a statue at Olympia (vi. 3. 1).

7. 8. **the prize for a Pythian victory is a laurel wreath.** Cp. viii. 48. 2. The laurel boughs which furnished the victors' wreaths were brought from the sacred laurel in Tempe by a boy who personated Apollo. See Schol. on Pindar, *Pyth.* Argum. p. 298 ed. Boeckh ; and note on ii. 7. 7. Aelian also says (*Var. hist.* iii. 1) that the prize wreaths in the Pythian games were made from the laurel-tree at Tempe.

8. 1. **the council of the Greeks** etc. On the constitution and history of the Amphictyonic Council, on which fresh light has been thrown by inscriptions, see Aeschines, *De falsa legatione*, 116 ; Harpocration, *s.v.* Ἀμφικτύονες ; Strabo, ix. p. 420 ; Wescher et Foucart,

Mémoire sur les ruines et l'histoire de Delphes, p. 157 *sqq.*; P. Foucart, 'Décrets des Amphictions de Delphes,' *Bulletin de Corresp. hellénique*, 7 (1883), pp. 409-439; A. Bouché-Leclercq, *Histoire de la divination*, 3. p. 104 *sqq.*; G. Gilbert, *Griechische Staatsalterthümer*, 2. p. 407 *sqq.* For inscriptions containing decrees of the Amphictyonic Council, see Curtius, *Anecdota Delphica*, pp. 75-79 (Nos. 40-45); Wescher-Foucart, *Inscriptions grecques recueillies à Delphes*, Nos. 1-6; P. Foucart, in *Bulletin de Corresp. hellénique, l.c.*; W. Froehner, *Inscriptions grecques du Louvre*, No. 32.

8. 2. the following Greek tribes. According to Aeschines (*De falsa legatione*, 116) and Theopompus (cited by Harpocration, *s.v.* Ἀμφικτύονες) the peoples who had a share in the Amphictyonic Council were twelve. As enumerated by Aeschines they were the Thessalians, Boeotians, Dorians, Ionians, Perraebians, Magnesians, Locrians, Oetaeans, Phthiotians, Maliensians, and Phocians (eleven only — the name of the Dolopians has perhaps dropped out). As enumerated by Theopompus the peoples were the Ionians, Dorians, Perraebians, Boeotians, Magnesians, Achaeans, Phthiotians, Melians, Dolopians, Aenianians, Delphians, and Phocians. Strabo (ix. p. 420) also says that the peoples were twelve in number. According to Aeschines (*l.c.*) each people had two votes in the Council. An inscription found in recent years by the French at Delphi and dating from some time between 346 and 336 B.C., gives a complete list—the earliest authentic list we possess—of the Amphictyons (*Bulletin de Corresp. hellénique*, 17 (1893), p. 617). Unfortunately this important document has not yet been published. Another inscription found by the French at Delphi, but not yet published by them, records an answer of Hadrian's to a question of the Delphians touching the Amphictyonic Council. The emperor decrees that the votes which the Thessalians possess above the other peoples of the League shall be divided "among the Athenians, the Lacedaemonians, and the other cities, in order that the Council may be common to all the Greeks." See *Comptes Rendus de l'Académie des Inscriptions et de Belles-lettres*, 24 (1896), p. 88.

8. 2. the Macedonians contrived to join the League, whereas the Phocian nation —— were struck out etc. Cp. x. 3. 3 note. Inscriptions found by the French at Delphi show that at the conclusion of the Sacred War in 346 B.C. the Phocians were further excluded from the commission charged with the restoration of the temple of Apollo, and that their place was taken by representatives of Macedonia, one of whom was no less than King Philip himself. Further, the inscriptions prove that the statues of the Phocian generals Philomelus and Onomarchus were ejected from the sanctuary and their pedestals thrown down, and they mention the payment of instalments of the fine which had been inflicted on the Phocians for their sacrilege. See *Bulletin de Corresp. hellénique*, 17 (1893), p. 617; *id.*, 18 (1894), p. 181. Cp. note on x. 15. 7.

8. 3. the will of the emperor Augustus that Nicopolis etc. Cp. G. F. Hertzberg, *Geschichte Griechenlands unter der Herrschaft der Römer*, 1. p. 510 *sqq.*; Th. Mommsen, *Römische Geschichte*, 5. p. 232.

8. 6. On entering the city etc. The situation of Delphi is accurately described by Strabo (ix. p. 418). He says : " On the south side of Parnassus is Delphi, a rocky place in the form of a theatre, with the oracle and the city at the top. The circumference of the city is 16 furlongs. Higher up than the city is situated Lycorea, the place where the Delphians were formerly settled, above the sanctuary ; but now they dwell about the Castalian spring. In front of the city, to the south, lies Mount Cirphis, a precipitous mountain, separated from Delphi by a dale through which flows the Plistus river." For Justin's description, see note on x. 5. 7. The site of Delphi, till lately occupied by the modern village of *Kastri*, is in the highest degree striking and impressive. The city lay at the southern foot of the tremendous cliffs of Parnassus, which form a sheer wall of rock, about 800 feet high, running from north-west to south-east, and then bending round at an obtuse angle towards the south. These cliffs were known in antiquity as the Phaedriades or ' shining ' rocks. Over these frightful precipices Philomelus drove some of the defeated Locrians (Diodorus, xvi. 28 ; cp. Suidas, *s.v.* Αἴσωπος). Just at the angle where this vast wall of rock bends round towards the south it is rent from top to bottom by a deep and gloomy gorge, some 20 feet wide, in which there is a fine echo. Facing each other across this narrow chasm rise two stupendous cliffs, whose peaked summits tower considerably above the rest of the line of cliffs. They are nearly perpendicular in front, and perfectly so where they fall sheer down into the gorge. The eastern of the two cliffs was called Hyampia in antiquity ; from its top Aesop is said to have been hurled by the Delphians (Herodotus, viii. 39 ; Plutarch, *De sera numinis vindicta*, 12 ; cp. Suidas, *s.v.* Αἴσωπός). The eastern cliff is now called *Phlemboukos*, the western *Rhodini*. It has been suggested, though perhaps without sufficient reason, that when the later writers of antiquity, especially the Roman poets, speak of the two summits of Parnassus, they are really referring to these two cliffs. In point of fact the cliffs are far indeed from being near the summit of Parnassus ; but seen from Delphi they completely hide the higher slopes of the mountain. Cp. Lucian, *Charon*, 5 ; Lucan, v. 72 ; Ovid, *Met.* i. 316 *sq.*, ii. 221 ; Statius, *Theb.* vii. 346 ; Nonnus, *Dionys.* xiii. 131. In winter or wet weather a torrent comes foaming down the gorge in a cascade about 200 feet high, bringing down the water from the higher slopes of the mountain. At the mouth of the gorge, under the eastern cliff, is the rock-cut basin of the perennial Castalian spring (see § 9 note), a few paces above the highroad. The water from the spring joins the stream from the gorge, which, after passing over the highroad, plunges, in a fall about 100 feet high, into a deep rocky lyn or glen, which it has scooped out for itself in the steep side of the mountain. Down this glen the stream descends to join the Plistus, which flows along the bottom of the Delphic valley from east to west, at a great depth below the town. From the cliffs at the back of Delphi the ground slopes away so steeply to the bed of the Plistus that it is only by means of a succession of artificial terraces, rising in tiers above each other, that the soil can be cultivated and made fit for habitation. There are about thirty of these

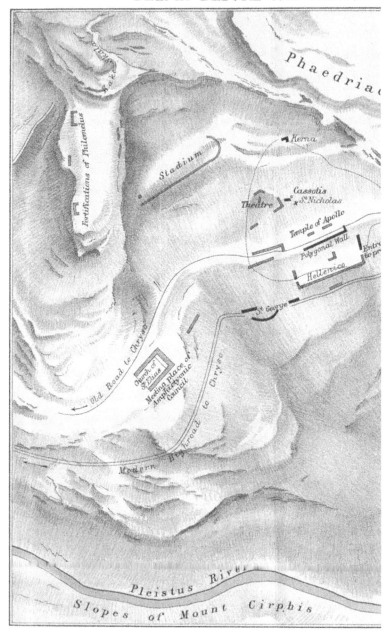

Phaedriad

Lake

Fortifications of Philomelus

Stadium

Kerna

Cassotis
St Nicholas

Theatre

Temple of Apollo

Polygonal Wall

Entr
to pr

Hellenico

St George

Old Road to Chryso

Church of
St Elias

Meeting Place of
Amphictyonic
Council

Highroad to Chryso

Modern Highroad to Chryso

Pleistus River

Slopes of Mount Cirphis

London : Macmillan &.C° L.ᵈ

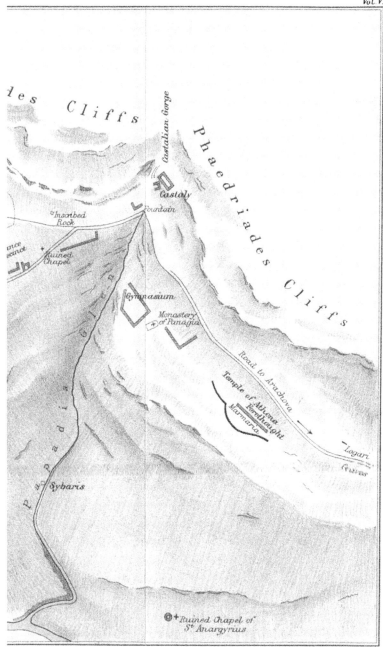

...des Cliffs

Castalian Gorge

Phaedriades

Castaly

Fountain

Inscribed Rock

...red...ce ...cinct

Ruined Chapel

Gymnasium

Monastery of Panagia

Green Glen

Road to Arachova

Temple of Athena Forethought Marmaria

Logari Tower

P. Pappadia

Sybaris

Ruined Chapel of S.t Anargyrus

terraces, supported by stone walls, mostly of polygonal masonry. The sanctuary of Apollo occupies only the five or six highest terraces at the foot of the cliffs, on the western side of the Castalian gorge. So high does it stand above the bottom of the valley that twenty minutes are needed to descend the steep terraced slope to the bed of the Plistus. Corn is grown on the terraces below the sanctuary; and the slopes on the eastern side of the Castalian gorge are wooded with fine olive and mulberry trees. Across the valley, on the southern side of the Plistus, rise the bare precipitous cliffs of Mount Cirphis, capped with fir-woods. From the western end of the precipices which rise at the back of Delphi a high rocky ridge projects southward toward the bed of the Plistus. This ridge closes the valley of Delphi on the west, shutting out all view of the Crisaean plain and the gulf of Corinth, though a glimpse of the waters of the gulf is obtained from the stadium, the highest part of Delphi (see x. 32. 1 note). Thus, enclosed by a rocky ridge on the west, by the tremendous precipices of the Phaedriades on the north and east, and faced on the south, across the valley of the Plistus by the lower but still precipitous sides of Mount Cirphis, Delphi lay in a secluded mountain valley; and rising on terraces in a semicircular shape, it resembled an immense theatre, to which it has justly been compared by ancient and modern writers. The whole scene is one of stern and awful majesty, well fitted to be the seat of a great religious capital. In respect of natural scenery no contrast could well be more striking than that between the two great religious capitals of ancient Greece, Delphi and Olympia—Delphi clinging to the rugged side of barren mountains, with frowning precipices above and a profound glen below; Olympia stretched out on the level margin of a river that winds in stately curves among the cornfields and vineyards of a smiling valley set between soft wooded hills.

See Wheler, *Journey*, p. 313 *sqq.* ; R. Chandler, p. 260 *sqq.* ; E. D. Clarke, *Travels*, 4. p. 177 *sqq.* ; Dodwell, *Tour*, 1. p. 162 *sqq.* ; Leake, *N. Greece*, 2. p. 551 *sqq.* ; Mure, *Journal*, 1. p. 185 *sqq.* ; H. N. Ulrichs, *Reisen und Forschungen*, 1. p. 25 *sqq.* ; Thiersch, ' Ueber die Topographie von Delphi,' *Abhandlungen der philosoph. philolog. Classe d. kön. bayer. Akad. d. Wissen.* (Munich), 3 (1840), p. 3 *sqq.* ; F. G. Welcker, *Tagebuch*, 2. p. 62 *sqq.* ; L. Ross, *Wanderungen*, 1. p. 64 *sqq.* ; W. Vischer, *Erinnerungen*, p. 606 *sqq.* ; C. Bursian, *Geogr.* 1. p. 170 *sqq.* ; P. Foucart, *Mémoire sur les ruines et l'histoire de Delphes*, p. 1. *sqq.* ; J. P. Mahaffy, *Rambles and Studies*, p. 244 *sqq.* ; H. Belle, *Trois Années en Grèce*, p. 182 *sqq.* ; Baedeker,[3] p. 156 *sqq.* ; *Guide-Joanne*, 2. p. 35 *sqq.* ; H. Pomtow, *Beiträge zur Topographie von Delphi*, p. 67 *sqq.* ; Th. Homolle, in *Comptes Rendus de l'Académie des Inscriptions*, 22 (1894), p. 582 *sq.* ; Ch. Belger, in *Berliner philolog. Wochenschrift*, 14 (1894), p. 860 *sq.* ; P. G. Kastriotes, Οἱ Δελφοί (Athens, 1894), p. 13 *sqq.*

Pausanias entered Delphi from the east, and by comparing his description with the existing remains we see that the ancient road, at least in its last part, must have been nearly or quite the same with the present road from *Arachova* to Delphi. See note on x. 5. 5. About a mile and a half from the Delphic sanctuary, on the left side of the road as you come from *Arachova*, there is a square structure called by the natives *Pyrgo* ('tower'). It is about 7 paces square, and is built of large squared

blocks laid in horizontal courses without mortar. The walls are standing
to a height of 9 or 10 feet. On the south side there is a doorway about
6 feet high and 2 ft. 6 in. wide, but narrowing somewhat towards the
top. The holes for the door are still visible. The lintel is formed by
a single stone, between 6 and 7 feet long. Leake, Bursian, and Mr.
Foucart regarded this square building as a watch-tower; on the other
hand, Thiersch, Mr. Haussoullier, and Mr. Pomtow have held it to be
a tomb; and this is the more probable view. A few paces from the
building is a broken sarcophagus of stone, which may once have stood
within the tomb.

Beyond this tomb or tower the road passes through one of the
ancient cemeteries of Delphi. The Greek statesman and patriot Capo
d'Istria caused excavations to be made here in the early part of the
nineteenth century. Some sepulchral chambers were found, two or
three of them of considerable size. The sloping ground to the left of
the road is strewn with ancient remains, consisting of sarcophaguses and
their lids, sepulchres hewn in the rock with steps leading down to
them, fragments of sepulchral reliefs and statues, etc. Of the sarcophaguses the best known is one of white marble adorned with fine reliefs
of Roman date; on the front Meleager is represented handing the head
of the Calydonian boar to Atalante. A tombstone inscribed with the
name of Apellius, son of Demon, a Massiliot, was found near the high-
road, between the *Pyrgo* and the *Logari* (see below) in 1894. The
inscription, carved in archaic letters on a block of limestone, seems to
date from the second half of the sixth century B.C. See P. Perdrizet,
'Delphes et Marseille,' *Revue des Universités du Midi*, vol. 3. No. 2
(Avril-Juin, 1897), pp. 129-132. The cemetery extended far down the
slope to the steep banks of the Plistus. Excavations here might prove
fruitful. In the rocks which overhang the road on the right there are
many sepulchral niches. From the square tomb, described above, the
cemetery extends for about three-quarters of a mile to what is now called
the *Logari*. This is the likeness of a great double door, barred and
studded with nails, chiselled in the smooth face of a rock which has
fallen from the cliffs above. The rock is split down the middle, and a
wild fig-tree grows out of the fissure. H. N. Ulrichs conjectured that
the door represented the Gate of Hell, and this conjecture has been
adopted by later travellers. It may have marked the entrance to the
necropolis. The rock stands close to the road, on the upper or right-
hand side as you approach Delphi. At this point two roads from Delphi
diverge. The higher road leads to *Arachova*, running along the foot of
the cliffs of Parnassus. This is the road by which Pausanias appears
to have entered Delphi. The lower road descends south-east through
the terraced slopes, once the cemetery of Delphi, now planted with
corn and olive trees, to the mills and vineyards of *Kastri*. This is the
ancient road to Ambrosus, by the pass of *Dhesphina* over Mount Cirphis.
In the foot of the cliffs, near the *Logari*, many small niches are carved
for the reception of votive-offerings.

See Leake, *N. Greece*, 2. p. 552 *sq.*; Thiersch, *op. cit.* p. 7; H. N. Ulrichs,
Reisen und Forschungen, 1. pp. 41, 44 *sq.*; Mure, *Journal*, 1. p. 192 *sq.*; F. G.

Welcker, *Tagebuch*, 2. p. 64 *sqq.*; Bursian, *Geogr.* 1. p. 171; P. Foucart, *Mémoire*, pp. 3, 9 *sq.*; Baedeker,[3] p. 158; H. Pomtow, *Beiträge zur Topographie von Delphi*, p. 70 *sq.*; *Guide-Joanne*, 2. p. 35; P. G. Kastriotes, Οἱ Δελφοί, p. 45 *sq.* A drawing of the *Logari* is given by Le Bas (*Voyage archéologique, Itinéraire*, pl. 40), and a photograph of it by Mr. H. Pomtow (*Beiträge zur Topographie von Delphi*, pl. x. No. 27).

8. 6. a row of temples etc. On its eastern side the city of Delphi appears to have begun about the point where the *Logari* now stands (see preceding note). Entering the city here Pausanias saw a row of four temples. They stood on a terrace to the left of the road. Considerable remains of the long wall which supported the terrace may be seen among the corn-land and olive-woods which slope away on the left side of the road. The place is now called *Marmaria*. The masonry is polygonal and of fine style. Some excavations were made on the terrace in 1838 by the German architect Laurent. He discovered the foundations of all the four temples mentioned by Pausanias. They stood in the following order (beginning at the east or towards *Arachova*): (1) foundations of a small temple, without any architectural fragments; (2) foundations of a large temple, also without architectural fragments; (3) foundations and architectural remains of a smaller Doric temple; (4) foundations and remains of a round Doric temple, with fragments of columns, architraves, and triglyphs of very fine work. Laurent thought that this round building was the temple of Forethought Athena. A colossal marble foot came to light, which, to judge from the sandal and the fragment of drapery, appeared to have belonged to a standing image of Athena, perhaps the image of the goddess which stood in the temple; for the larger image in the fore-temple, an offering of the people of Massilia, was of bronze (§ 7). All these foundations, together with the pieces of columns and other architectural fragments noticed by travellers in the first half of this century, have now disappeared, buried perhaps beneath the soil of the corn-fields and olive-woods. On either side of the east door of the monastery of the Panagia are still to be seen two fine Doric triglyphs built into the wall. They may have been brought from the neighbouring temple of Forethought Athena.

See Thiersch, *op. cit.* pp. 8, 10 *sqq.*; H. N. Ullrichs, *Reisen und Forschungen*, pp. 41, 45, 263 *sq.*; F. G. Welcker, *Tagebuch*, 2. p. 64; C. Bursian, *Geogr.* 1. p. 171; P. Foucart, *Mémoire*, p. 10 *sqq.*; Baedeker,[3] p. 158; *Guide-Joanne*, 2. p. 37; H. Pomtow, *Beiträge zur Topographie von Delphi*, p. 71 *sq.*

The temple of Forethought Athena is described by Demosthenes or a writer who passes under his name (*Or.* xxv. p. 780) as very large and beautiful and situated just at the entrance of the sanctuary. Instead of Forethought Athena (Athena *Pronoia*) the goddess of the sanctuary was sometimes called Fore-temple Athena (Athena *Pronaia*) by ancient writers, as by Herodotus (i. 92, viii. 37 and 39), Plutarch (*Praecept. gerend. reipub.* xxxii. 16), and Aristonous of Corinth in one of his hymns to Apollo which has been found by the French at Delphi (*Bulletin de Corresp. hellénique*, 17 (1893), p. 566). The surname *Pronaia* ('in the fore-temple') was explained by the position of the

temple not far from the entrance to the great temple of Apollo. See
Photius, *Lexicon, s.v.* Προναία 'Αθηνᾶ; Harpocration, *s.v.* Προναία;
Suidas, *s.v.* Πρόνοια 'Αθηνᾶ; *Etymol. Magnum*, p. 700. 1 *sqq.*;
Bekker's *Anecdota Graeca*, pp. 293 and 299. Aeschylus (*Eumenides*,
21) calls the goddess Fore-temple Pallas (Pallas *Pronaia*). Bursian
is perhaps right in supposing that *Pronaia* ('fore-temple') was the
original epithet of the goddess, which, by an ethical interpretation, was
afterwards changed into *Pronoia* ('forethought'). But the copyists
seem sometimes to have confused the two adjectives. The form
Pronoia ('forethought') is used by Aeschines (*Contra Ctesiph.* 108,
110, 111, and 121 ed. Franke), Aristides (*Orat. in Minerv.* vol. 1.
p. 21 ed. Dindorf), and Julian (*Or.* iv. p. 149 ed. Spanheim, p. 193 ed.
Hertlein). Cornutus says generally, "Temples of Forethought Athena
(Athena *Pronoia*) are founded" (*De nat. deor.* 18). Macrobius mentions
one such temple in the island of Delos (*Saturn.* i. 17. 55); and there
was another at Prasiae in Attica, said to have been founded by Diomede
(Bekker's *Anecdota Graeca*, p. 299). On the other hand the epithet
Pronaioi (plural) was applied to Athena and Hermes at Thebes, because
their images stood at the entrance into the sanctuary of the Ismenian
Apollo (Paus. ix. 10. 2). And that *Pronaia* ('fore-temple'), not *Pronoia*
('forethought'), was the official title of the goddess at Delphi is proved
by inscriptions found there. See E. Curtius, *Anecdota Delphica*, Inscr.
43 and 45, p. 77 *sq.*; W. Dittenberger, *Sylloge Inscr. Graec.* No. 186;
Bulletin de Corresp. hellénique, 6 (1882), p. 459. Cp. K. O. Müller,
'Pallas-Athene,' § 44, *Kleine Schriften*, 2. p. 195 *sqq.*; F. G. Welcker,
Griechische Götterlehre, 2. p. 306; L. Preller, *Griech. Mythologie,*[4]
1. p. 195 ; A. Mommsen, *Delphika*, p. 143 *sqq.*
     The necklace of Eriphyle or of Helen is said to have been pre-
served in this sanctuary. See note on viii. 24. 10. As to the repulse
of the Persians at the sanctuary, see note on x. 7. 1. We learn from
Vitruvius (vii. praef. 12) that Theodorus the Phocaean wrote a work
on 'the Round Building at Delphi' (*De Tholo qui est Delphis*). The
round building discovered by Laurent may have been the subject of
Theodorus's book, whether it was the temple of Athena or not.
     8. 6. Massilia is a colony of Phocaea. See Aristotle, quoted by
Athenaeus, xiii. p. 576 a; Strabo, iv. p. 179; Justin, xliii. 3. 4 *sqq.*
The story of the emigration of the Phocaeans from their old Asiatic
home is told by Herodotus (i. 162 *sqq.*), but he does not mention their
settlement at Massilia. As to the naval victory over the Carthaginians,
see Thucydides, i. 13, from whom we gather that the victory was gained
not, as Pausanias supposed, by the main body of the Phocaeans who
fled from Harpagus, but by the Phocaean emigrants who founded
Massilia in 600 B.C., many years before the conquest of Phocaea by the
Persians (Harpocration, *s.v.* Μασσαλία, citing the authority of Aristotle;
Scymnius Chius, *Orbis descriptio, v.* 206 *sqq.*, citing the authority of
Timaeus).
     8. 7. The golden shield given by Croesus etc. Herodotus tells us
(i. 92) that the shield, which was of large size, still existed in his time
in the temple of Athena at Delphi.

8. 7. a precinct of the hero Phylacus. The precinct was beside the road, above the sanctuary of Fore-temple (Forethought) Athena (Herodotus, viii. 39). Cp. Thiersch, *op. cit.* p. 13 *sq.* It is said that the two heroes Phylacus and Autonous appeared in bodily form, but taller than mortal men, during the attack of the Persians on Delphi, and were seen pursuing the terrified foe, smiting and slaying. Autonous had a precinct not far from that of his brother hero, near the Castalian spring, at the foot of the cliff called Hyampia (now *Phlemboukos*). See Herodotus, viii. 38 *sq.* ; cp. Paus. x. 23. 2. Inscriptions found by the French prove that the number of heroes worshipped at Delphi was unusually large.

8. 8. the gymnasium. On the left of the highroad as you approach the sanctuary of Apollo from *Arachova*, a little before you come to the Castalian gorge, is the monastery of the Panagia, a branch or farm (*metoche*) of the large monastery of Jerusalem near Daulis (see note on x. 5. 1). It stands in a shady garden, surrounded by olive and mulberry-trees. The ground slopes away to the deep glen down which the torrent from the Castalian gorge finds its way to the Plistus. A massive wall of very fine Greek masonry supports the terrace upon which the monastery stands. It probably formed part of the gymnasium. A well-preserved angle of the wall may be seen a little to the south of the chapel. Each of the walls that form the angle is about 12 paces long ; one of them has ten and the other five courses standing. The masonry is of the most regular sort, the blocks being squared and laid in horizontal courses. Still farther to the south I observed another piece of wall about 10 paces long built in the same style, with two and three courses standing. The stone of which these remains are built is of a reddish colour. On the opposite side of the monastery, towards the Castalian glen, are the ruins of a large structure of pentagonal form. One wall is standing to a height of about 6 feet above the ground ; it is built in regular courses of good masonry. Another of the walls is partly concealed by the buildings of the monastery and is not so well preserved. The other three walls were merely supporting walls, and are not so carefully built. The platform which they support is now covered with olive-trees. Mr. Foucart believes that this was the bath-room of the gymnasium. In the court of the chapel and in some of the surrounding buildings there are traces of a mosaic pavement, showing the level of the ancient floor. The chapel contains some triglyphs, unfluted columns with Doric capitals, two broken reliefs of fine workmanship, etc. A great festival is held at the monastery on the 15th of August.

See Dodwell, *Tour*, 1. p. 183; Leake, *N. Greece*, 2. pp. 553, 562 ; Thiersch, *op. cit.* pp. 8, 11 *sqq.* ; H. N. Ulrichs, *Reisen und Forschungen*, 1. pp. 41, 46 ; F. G. Welcker, *Tagebuch*, 2. p. 63 *sq.* ; Bursian, *Geogr.* 1. p. 172 ; P. Foucart, *Mémoire*, p. 16 *sqq.* ; H. Pomtow, *Beiträge zur Topographie von Delphi*, p. 72 ; P. G. Kastriotes, Οἱ Δελφοί, p. 44.

In regard to the gymnasium I have received from Mr. Cecil Smith the following note (July 1897) :—"This is to be excavated shortly. At present there is visible a strong supporting wall of rectangular well-faced

local stone ; and resting on this an open space at the back of which is a
water conduit, consisting of a long face of the same kind of masonry, in
which are a series of circular smooth depressions, sunk at regular
intervals to a number which amounted perhaps originally to nine.
Each depression is .19 m. in diameter, and has evidently been intended
for the attachment of a lion's head or other ornamental spout ; in the
upper part is the hole through which the pipe carrying water, probably
from Castalia, has passed.   From centre to centre the distance between
these depressions is 1.75 m.   It seems in fact to have been a kind of
Enneacrunus."

8. 8. when Ulysses —— was hunting etc.   The boar-hunt on
Mt. Parnassus and the wounding of Ulysses by the boar are described
by Homer (*Od.* xix. 428-466).

8. 8. descending not more —— than three furlongs, you come
to a river etc.   To reach the bed of the Plistus from the point of the
road which Pausanias has reached, we turn aside to left from the
gymnasium (now the monastery of the Panagia) and descend the deep
glen down which the water from the Castalian spring flows to join the
Plistus.   The direct distance is somewhat over four furlongs, but the
descent is so steep and fatiguing that it occupies about twenty minutes.
Among the olive-trees in the glen, a little below the monastery, lie some
large masses of the reddish-grey rock of which the neighbouring cliffs
are composed.   It is possible that these are the rocks which came
hurtling down from Parnassus on the Persians and were still to be seen
in Herodotus's time in the sanctuary of Fore-temple Athena (Herodotus,
viii. 37 and 39).   In the bottom of the glen, not far from the point
where the stream joins the Plistus, there is a deep well-like hole in the
rock, full of water.   It is the exit of an underground channel by which
the waters that form a lake on the high tableland above Delphi find an
exit.   In winter the water rushes with great violence from this hole,
which is called by the natives *Zaleska*.   Mr. Foucart thought this
might be the ancient spring of Sybaris.   The cave of Sybaris or Lamia
is a large cavern hidden away in a wild and deep ravine on the side
of Mt. Cirphis, beyond the Plistus.   A narrow path, not easily found,
leads up to it.   The cavern is now called *Krypsana*, or sometimes
Asketario ('hermitage') from a hermit who is said to have lived in it.
Many families from *Kastri* took refuge in the cave during the War of
Independence.   The old legend ran that a huge female monster called
Lamia or Sybaris dwelt in the cave and ravaged the country all round.
To appease her the Delphians, at the bidding of the oracle, resolved
to expose a boy at the cavern.   But a champion named Eurybatus
appeared who rushed into the monster's den, caught her up in his arms,
and staggering to the mouth of the cave, heaved her over the brink.
Down she rolled, bumping over the stones, and where she knocked her
head against the rock a spring of water gushed out and the natives
called it Sybaris.   From this Sybaris the famous city founded in
Southern Italy by the Locrians is said to have received its name.   See
Nicander, quoted by Antoninus Liberalis, *Transform.* 8.   The large
cave of Sybaris (now *Krypsana*) is not to be confounded with the much

smaller cave which may be seen from Delphi in the steep side of Mt. Cirphis across the valley to the south. This latter cave is only about 40 feet deep; it is now called the cave of Jerusalem and contains a rustic Greek chapel. A rough and difficult path leads up to it over rocks and through bushes.

See Dodwell, *Tour*, I. p. 184 *sqq.*; Thiersch, *op. cit.* p. 12 *sq.*; H. N. Ulrichs, *Reisen und Forschungen*, I. pp. 26 *sq.*, 34, 47; P. Foucart *Mémoire*, p. 19 *sq.*

8. 9. the water of Castaly. Proceeding onwards from the monastery of the Panagia, the site of the ancient gymnasium, we come in a few minutes to the immense gorge or fissure in the cliffs already described (see note on § 3). It is on the right-hand side of the road. Here, at the mouth of the gorge and just at the side of the road, the water of the Castalian spring gushes by several mouths out of a wall, probably built by the Turks. Near the fountain stand two plane-trees of moderate size. They are not gigantic, as a well-known guide-book affirms, nor are they fifty years old; for when Vischer visited Delphi in 1853 they did not exist, an older plane-tree, which used to grow here, having been cut down some time before his visit. Ascending from the fountain a few paces towards the gorge we come to a large quadrangular water-basin, deeply hewn in the rock at the foot of the eastern cliff, the ancient Hyampia, which rises in a perpendicular wall above it. The basin is 36 feet long by about 10 feet wide. Five steps hewn in the rock and extending along the whole length of its longer side, lead down into it. This pool of clear, cold water, lying deep in its rock-cut basin at the foot of the sheer cliff, is the true Castaly. It is constantly fed by subterranean sources and a small stream flows out of the basin into the bed of the adjoining torrent. The water, as Pausanias says, is sweet to drink; the natives of the village consider it lighter, more agreeable and wholesome than the water of Cassotis (see x. 24. 7 note). Just above the pool a tiny chapel of St. John has been hewn out of the face of the rock; it contains a drum of an ancient column and two holy pictures with a lamp burning before each of them. To the left of the little chapel are three semicircular niches, also cut in the face of the cliff, one of them large with a smaller niche on either side. They probably contained images. Higher up in the rock are some small square cuttings. Just below the niches an open channel, about 4 feet deep and 2 wide, has been hewn in the rock; it runs along the whole length of the pool on the side opposite the steps, and is tunnelled into the rock at either end. The channel probably served to carry off the superfluous water, when the water in the pool rose above a certain level. But it no longer serves its original purpose; for the villagers, who use the basin chiefly for washing clothes, have cut an opening through the upper steps, so that the depth of water in the basin can never be so great as it used to be. The water of the spring is conveyed to the Turkish fountain beside the road. Leake thought that the little chapel of St. John hewn in the rock above the pool might be the precinct of the hero Autonous, which was near the Castalian spring, at the foot of the cliff Hyampia (Herodotus, viii. 39). M. Foucart prefers to suppose that the precinct stood on a small platform between the pool and the road. Bursian thought he recognised a piece of the wall which had enclosed the precinct. The situation of the Castalian pool at the mouth of the tremendous gorge and overhung by prodigious cliffs is highly striking and romantic. Seen by moonlight it is still more weird and impressive.

See Wheler, *Journey*, pp. 314, 315 ; R. Chandler, *Travels in Greece*, p. 268 ; E. D. Clarke, *Travels*, 4. p. 184 *sqq.* ; Dodwell, *Tour*, 1. p. 171 *sqq.* ; Leake, *N. Greece*, 2. p. 555 *sqq.* ; Thiersch, *op. cit.* p. 9 *sq.* ; H. N. Ulrichs, *Reisen und Forschungen*, 1. pp. 40, 47 *sqq.* ; Mure, *Journal*, 1. p. 186 *sq.* ; F. G. Welcker, *Tagebuch*, 2. p. 63 ; W. Vischer, *Erinnerungen*, p. 610 ; Bursian, *Geogr.* 1. p. 172 ; P. Foucart, *Mémoire*, p. 20 *sqq.* ; J. P. Mahaffy, *Rambles and Studies*, p. 249 *sq.* ; *Guide-Joanne*, 2. p. 37 *sq.* ; P. G. Kastriotes, Οἱ Δελφοί, p. 40 *sqq.* A good drawing of the Castalian pool is given by Le Bas (*Voyage archéologique*, Itinéraire, pl. 37) and a very bad one by Clarke (*l.c.*).

Baedeker, strangely enough, makes no mention of the pool, re-marking that "in our time earthquakes have rendered the whole neighbourhood of Castaly quite unrecognisable." The pool certainly existed as I have described it in May 1890, after Baedeker's guide was written. I did not perceive the huge block of rock which Prof. Mahaffy saw lying in the pool and "covering the old work, as well as several votive niches cut into the rocky wall." But when I revisited the spot in October 1895 I found the sacred pool nearly dry and choked with stones and gravel which had been swept down by the torrent from the gorge. Mr. Cecil Smith informs me that the French archaeologists intend to examine the site thoroughly before long.

It would seem that the attendants of Apollo bathed or at least washed their hair in the water of the Castalian spring before they entered the temple (Euripides, *Ion*, 94 *sqq.* ; *id.*, *Phoen.* 222 *sq.*). Visitors, too, perhaps sprinkled themselves with the Castalian water before they approached the temple (Heliodorus, *Aethiopica*, ii. 26). The water of Castaly was also used to wash the temple of Apollo (Euripides, *Ion*, 144 *sqq.*). Chandler suggested that the Pythian priestess bathed in the Castalian pool, and the idea has been taken up by some later travellers, but it is not supported by any ancient authority. The idea that the water of the spring conferred prophetic power appears only in late classical writers. See Ovid, *Amores*, i. 15. 35 *sq.* ; Lucian, *Jupiter Tragoedus*, 30 ; Nonnus, *Dionys.* iv. 309 *sq.* ; Suidas, *s.v.* Κασταλία ; H. N. Ulrichs, *Reisen und Forschungen*, p. 58. Hadrian is said to have choked up the spring with a mass of rock, because he had learned his imperial destiny from its prophetic water and feared that others might consult it for a similar purpose : Julian intended to clear away the obstruction (Ammianus Marcellinus, xxii. 12. 8).

8. 9. **Panyasis.** He is said to have been a cousin or a maternal uncle of the historian Herodotus. His epic *Heraclea* on the exploits of Hercules was in fourteen books. See Suidas, *s.v.* Πανύασις ; W. Christ, *Gesch. d. griech. Litteratur*, p. 82 *sq.* The fragments of his

poetry are collected by G. Kinkel (*Epicorum Graecorum fragmenta*, p. 254 *sqq.*), F. P. Funcke (*De Panyasidis Halicarnassensis vita ac poesi*, Bonn, 1837), and Fr. Dübner (in the Didot edition of Hesiod, etc.).

8. 10. the Lilaeans —— throw cakes —— into the spring of the Cephisus etc. With this we may compare the custom of throwing cakes into the sea at Aegium in order to transmit them to the spring of Arethusa at Syracuse (vii. 24. 3). Cp. note on v. 7. 2. As to the source of the Cephisus at Lilaea, see x. 33. 5 note. The idea that cakes thrown into the springs of the Cephisus could reappear in the Castalian spring is absurd, since, as Leake observes (*Northern Greece*, 2. p. 85 note 2), the Castalian spring is in a much higher situation than the source of the Cephisus.

9. 1. The city of Delphi stands wholly on a slope etc. Leaving the Castalian spring already described and the great gorge on his right, Pausanias now proceeds westward towards the sacred close of Apollo. It would seem that the city proper of Delphi was situated wholly on the western side of the Castalian ravine, and that the part of Delphi to the east of the ravine (described by Pausanias ch. 8, §§ 6-10) was a suburb which included only temples and the gymnasium. This is inferred from the nature of the ground; for on the left side of the road the ground slopes so rapidly to the glen that there could hardly have been room for more than the row of temples described by him; and on the right side of the road the very narrow strip of ground rises steeply to the foot of the cliffs. The ancient road must have crossed the Castalian ravine at the point where the highroad from *Arachova* still crosses it, between the great gorge or fissure in the cliffs on the right and the deep glen on the left. The ravine is here filled up by a mass of rocks and earth brought down by the earthquake of 1870, so that the water from the gorge or upper part of the ravine flows over the road into the glen or lower part of the ravine on the left of the road. There used to be a bridge here.

Of the city of Delphi, situated on the western side of the Castalian ravine, the upper terraces were occupied by the sacred close of Apollo, the theatre, and, highest of all, the stadium : the lower terraces, where the ground slopes more steeply, supported the houses. The line between the upper and lower, or the sacred and profane, quarters of the city is roughly marked by the modern highroad to *Chryso*. Our author's attention is given wholly to the upper or sacred quarter of the city; he mentions not a single building in the lower quarter. However, in this lower quarter the terraces may still be seen on which rested, as on a great staircase, the streets and dwellings of the ancient city. On one terrace, below the chapel of St. George, the rock has been cut vertically and levelled to support houses. In modern times the upper or sacred quarter of the city was occupied by the village of *Kastri* down to 1892 when it was cleared away in order to allow the site to be excavated by the French. To this upper portion of the site, which has now been completely excavated, our attention will be exclusively directed.

About 350 yards west of the Castalian gorge there begins an ancient Greek wall which in modern times has been known as the *Hellenico*. It extends roughly east and west, parallel to and a little above the modern highroad from Delphi to *Chryso*. This was the southern enclosing wall of the sacred precinct of Apollo. It is built of large squared blocks, and towards its eastern end is preserved to a height of about 10 feet for a distance of about 100 yards. About 90 yards west of the point where this continuous stretch of wall terminates, another piece of it extends in nearly the same direction for about 25 yards more. These remains were visible before the French excavations ; and Mr. Homolle and his colleagues have proved that the enclosing wall exists almost in its full extent, constructed in some places of squared blocks laid in neat horizontal courses, in others of polygonal blocks put together in the Cyclopean style (*Comptes Rendus de l'Académie des Inscriptions*, 22 (1894), p. 583). But whereas the southern wall or *Hellenico* extends in a somewhat irregular or broken line, the walls which bound the precinct on the east and west run up the steep hillside in nearly straight lines. The main entrance to the precinct was in the east wall, about 13 yards from its southern extremity. The discovery of this entrance, together with the proof that Pausanias began his tour here, is due to Mr. H. Pomtow, who has made a patient and exact study of the topography and history of Delphi. Excavations directed by him in 1887 at the point indicated brought to light some well-preserved remains of an ancient stone staircase leading up to an opening in the eastern wall of the precinct. On these steps Mr. Pomtow found the inscribed base of the Tegean offering which Pausanias mentions immediately after entering the sacred close (see § 5 note). This discovery furnished the clue to Pausanias's tour through the sanctuary and taken in connexion with the order in which he mentions those buildings of which the positions were ascertained, such as the Colonnade of the Athenians (x. 11. 6), the temple of Apollo (x. 19. 4), the theatre (x. 32. 1), and the stadium (*ib.*), gave reason to believe that at Delphi he followed his usual plan of describing the various monuments in strictly topographical order. This belief has been amply confirmed by the French excavations, which have laid bare monument after monument on either side of the road in the exact succession in which Pausanias mentions them. Amongst these may be mentioned particularly the offerings of the Lacedaemonians (x. 9. 7), the statues of the Epigoni (x. 10. 4), the statues of the Argive kings (x. 10. 5), and the treasuries of the Sicyonians (x. 11. 1), the Siphnians (x. 11. 2), the Thebans (x. 11. 5), and the Athenians (*ib.*). The road which he followed has also been excavated in its full extent from the entrance at the south-eastern corner of the precinct up to the temple of Apollo. This road, which for the sake of convenience we may, with modern writers, call the Sacred Way, although there seems to be no ancient authority for such a designation, was paved throughout with stone, and a great part of the pavement is preserved. Grooves are cut in the pavement to prevent the feet from slipping. The direction in which the Sacred Way runs from the entrance up to the temple of Apollo has

The material originally positioned here is too large for reproduction in this reissue. A PDF can be downloaded from the web address given on page iv of this book, by clicking on 'Resources Available'.

been compared, not inaptly, to a great S reversed. First it ran westward, bordered on the right or north by the offerings of the Lacedaemonians (x. 9. 7) and the statues of the Argive kings (x. 10. 5), on
the left or south by the statues of the Epigoni (x. 10. 4) and the
treasuries of the Sicyonians and Siphnians (x. 11. 1, 2). Then ascending and making a great bend first to the north and then to the east it
passed on the left the treasuries of the Thebans and Athenians (x. 11. 5)
and reached a comparatively level and open space which Mr. Homolle
believes to have been the so-called Threshing-floor (ἅλως) where the
drama of the slaughter of the Python by Apollo was solemnly enacted
once every eight years (Plutarch, *De defectu oraculorum*, 15 ; see note
on ii. 7. 7, vol. 3. p. 53 *sq.*). The stone benches and seats by which
the space is surrounded confirm the view that a spectacle of some sort
was here exhibited ; and its circular form might very well suggest the
comparison with a threshing-floor of the sort which may still be seen
everywhere in Greece. This open space is bounded on the north by
the Colonnade of the Athenians (x. 11. 6 note), at the back of which
rises the long inscription-covered wall of polygonal masonry which has
been so long familiar to visitors to Delphi. The Sacred Way runs eastward past the front of the Athenian Colonnade. At the eastern end of
the polygonal wall it makes its second lap, first ascending the short
steep slope northward and then curving round westward to the eastern
front of the temple of Apollo, which stood on the terrace supported by
the polygonal wall. A staircase, however, furnishing a more direct
access from the lower part of the precinct to the temple of Apollo,
enabled people to avoid the detours of the Sacred Way. Along the
north side of the temple and close to it the Sacred Way then led westward, making a complete circuit of the northern and western sides of
the temple. We see then how accurately Plutarch has expressed
himself in saying : "We went round the temple and sat down on its
southern steps" (*De Pythiae oraculis*, 17). From the eastern end of
the temple a fine staircase, in good preservation, leads up to the spring
Cassotis, the Lesche or Club-room, and the theatre. It was by this
staircase doubtless that Pausanias himself ascended after quitting the
temple of Apollo (x. 24. 6). Finally, leaving the theatre he mounted
to the stadium (x. 32. 1), which occupies in fact, as we should expect
from his description, the highest point of Delphi. Above it rise the
imposing cliffs of Parnassus, and, true to the topographical order, our
author next ascends them on his way to the lonely Corycian cave,
situated high on the upper pine-clad slopes of the mountain (x. 32. 2).

But in addition to the Sacred Way which wound up through the
precinct in a general direction from south to north, the French excavations have laid bare several passages or roads running horizontally
through the precinct from east to west. These passages, of the
existence of which I was informed by Mr. Homolle on the spot, are no
doubt "the passages at short intervals through the precinct" to which
Pausanias refers (x. 9. 1). From Mr. Cecil Smith I learn that besides
the main entrance near the south-east corner two gates have been
discovered in the western wall and two posterns in the eastern wall

of the precinct; the posterns are higher up the slope than the main entrance.

See Leake, *Northern Greece*, 2. p. 558 *sqq.*; H. N. Ulrichs, *Reisen und Forschungen*, 1. pp. 38 *sq.*, 59 *sqq.*; P. Foucart, *Mémoire sur les ruines et l'histoire de Delphes*, p. 23 *sqq.*; H. Pomtow, *Beiträge zur Topographie von Delphi*, p. 50 *sqq.*; *id.*, in *Archäologischer Anzeiger*, 1894, pp. 5, 10 *sq.*; Th. Homolle, in *Bulletin de Corresp. hellénique*, 17 (1893), pp. 613, 619 *sq.*; *id.*, *Bull. de Corr. hellén.* 18 (1894), p. 183 *sqq.*; *id.*, in *Comptes Rendus de l'Académie des Inscriptions*, 22 (1894), pp. 304 *sq.*, 583 *sqq.*; Ch. Belger, in *Berliner philologische Wochenschrift*, 30th June 1894, p. 861 *sq.*; P. Kastriotes, Οἱ Δελφοί, p. 46 *sqq.*

9. 2. the athletes and musical competitors. A score or more of inscriptions relating to these men, whose statues Pausanias passes by so disdainfully, have been found at Delphi. Some record the offerings which they dedicated for their success; but most register decrees passed in their honour by the admiring Delphians, who voted them laurel wreaths, seats of honour at the games, and other privileges. See Wescher - Foucart, *Inscriptions recueillies à Delphes*, No. 469; *Bulletin de Corresp. hellénique*, 6 (1882), p. 217 *sq.*; L. Couve, 'Inscriptions de Delphes,' *Bulletin de Corresp. hellénique*, 18 (1894), pp. 70-100. One of the bards whom the Delphians honoured was Aristonous of Corinth, author of the hymn to Apollo which the French found at Delphi (*Bulletin de Corresp. hellénique*, 17 (1893), p. 565). In some cases the native cities of the victorious musicians erected statues at Delphi in their honour (*C. I. G.* Nos. 1719, 1720). From one inscription we learn that a Samian flute-player, Satyrus the son of Eumenes, having gained the prize for flute-playing without a contest, testified his gratitude by performing a choral hymn called *Dionysus* in the stadium, and playing an air for the lyre from the *Bacchae* of Euripides (*Bulletin de Corresp. hellénique*, 17 (1893), p. 84 *sq.*). The statues of the Pythian victors seem to have stood outside of the sacred precinct; for it is only after mentioning them that Pausanias enters the close (§ 3). At Olympia, on the other hand, the statues of the athletes stood within the Altis or sacred close. See vi. 1 *sqq.* Amongst the inscriptions found by the French at Delphi is one that contains the rules to be observed by runners in training. They were not allowed to drink new wine, and if any one broke the rule he had to pour libations of that wine to the god and to pay a fine, half of which went to the god and half to the informer (*Berliner philolog. Wochenschrift*, 27th June 1896, p. 831; *Journal of Hellenic Studies*, 16 (1896), p. 343; *Chronique des Arts*, 1896, p. 194).

9. 3. a bronze bull —— dedicated by the Corcyraeans. Cp. n. on 9 *sq.* The inscribed pedestal which supported this bull was found by the French near the great altar to the east of the temple of Apollo, more than 100 yards distant from its original position (Th. Homolle, in *Bulletin de Corresp. hellénique*, 18 (1894), p. 186; *id.*, in *Comptes Rendus de l'Académie des Inscriptions*, 22 (1894), p. 204; Ch. Belger, in *Berliner philolog. Wochenschrift*, 30th June 1894, p. 861;

H. Pomtow, in *Archäologischer Anzeiger*, 1895, p. 8). The inscription on the pedestal, Mr. Cecil Smith informs me, is in letters of the beginning of the fifth century B.C. It includes the name of the sculptor Theopropus. No other signature of this artist is known to be extant. With regard to the form of the Corcyraean offering it may be remarked that on coins of Corcyra a cow is represented suckling a calf. See P. Gardner, *Types of Greek Coins*, p. 39 *sq.*

9. 3. a countless shoal of tunnies. It was a custom with Greek fishermen, when they had a great haul of tunnies, to sacrifice to Poseidon the first tunny caught (Antigonus of Carystus, cited by Athenaeus, vii. pp. 297 e, 302 b). On the tunny fishery in antiquity, see P. Rhode, *Thynnorum captura quanti fuerit apud veteres momenti* (Leipsic, 1890). Cp. W. Ridgeway, *The origin of metallic currency and weight standards*, p. 315 *sqq.*

9. 5. offerings of the Tegeans etc. On the steps at the south-east entrance into the sacred close Mr. Pomtow discovered in May 1887 one of the bases that supported the statues which Pausanias calls the offerings of the Tegeans. The base is of black limestone and measures about 1 ft. high, 4 ft. 3 in. long, and 3 ft. broad. In addition to two inscriptions which have been carved on it at a later date, the base bears a metrical inscription in five couplets recording the dedication of the statues mentioned by Pausanias. The inscription is in good Greek letters of the fourth century B.C. It is slightly mutilated. Restoring a few missing words, we may translate it as follows : " Lord Pythian Apollo, the aboriginal people of sacred Arcadia gave to thee these images as first-fruits, to wit Victory, and Callisto daughter of Lycaon, with whom Zeus once had intercourse and begot Arcas, a youth of sacred lineage. And from Arcas sprang Elatus and Aphidas and Azan, all of whom the nymph Erato brought forth in Arcadia. But Laodamia, daughter of Amyclas, gave birth to Triphylus, and Erasus was a son of Amilo daughter of Gongylus. The Arcadians, descended from these ancestors, after laying waste Lacedaemon, set up in thy honour a monument to posterity." It seems clear from this inscription that the statues were dedicated, not by the Tegeans, but by the Arcadians in general. The success which it commemorated was probably the devastation of Laconia by the Arcadians either separately or in company with the Thebans under Epaminondas in the winter of 370-369 B.C. or the spring of 369 B.C. Mr. Pomtow thinks that the event commemorated was probably the defeat of the Lacedaemonians under Ischolaus at Oeum in the district of Sciris, which took place in 369 B.C. See Xenophon, *Hellenica*, vi. 5. 25 ; Diodorus, xv. 64. 3 *sq.* ; and note on viii. 45. 1. Hence Pausanias is wrong in describing the statues as votive offerings of the Tegeans, and in supposing (§ 6) that the event commemorated was the defeat and capture of the Lacedaemonians by the Tegeans in Tegean territory (see viii. 48. 5 note). The expression in the inscription "after laying waste Lacedaemon" could hardly be used to describe a Tegean victory in a purely defensive war. Besides two of the sculptors who made the statues in question are known to have been at work at the end of the fifth or in the early part of the fourth century B.C. (see notes on § 6), whereas the Tegean victory to which Pausanias refers took place long before, though its exact date is not known.   Hence, as Pausanias's only authority for the account he gives of the statues appears to have been the inscription on the base, it follows that he seriously misinterpreted it.   That he misunderstood the inscription is clear from his making Erasus a son of Triphylus ; whereas the meaning of the inscription is that Erasus was a son of Arcas by Amilo daughter of Gongylus.   See H. Pomtow, *Beiträge zur Topographie von Delphi*, p. 54 *sq.*, with pl. xiv. No. 39 ; *id.*, 'Ein arkadisches Weihgeschenk zu Delphi,' *Mittheilungen des arch. Inst. in Athen*, 14 (1889), pp. 15-40.   K. O. Müller pointed out (*Kleine Schriften*, 2. p. 372 note 2) that the offering was probably made at a time when Triphylia belonged to Arcadia, since one of the statues represented Triphylus, the eponymous hero of Triphylia. Now Triphylia belonged to Elis down to 399 B.C., when the Eleans were compelled by the Lacedaemonians to set it free (Xenophon, *Hellenica*, iii. 2. 30 ; cp. Diodorus, xiv. 34 ; Paus. iii. 8. 5) ; and from Diodorus (xv. 77) we learn that in 365 B.C. Triphylia belonged to Arcadia, but how long this connexion had lasted we do not know ; perhaps it may have been established in 399 B.C. as soon as the tie which bound Triphylia to Elis was severed.   In any case the appearance of the statue of Triphylus among those of the Arcadian heroes points to the offering having been made at some time between 399 and 365 B.C., and this indication tallies perfectly with the supposition that the statues were dedicated as a trophy of the success achieved by the Arcadians in 369 B.C.   See H. Brunn, *Geschichte der griech. Künstler*, I. p. 283 *sq.*

Most of the other inscribed bases of these Arcadian offerings have been found by the French at Delphi, but have not yet (November 1897) been published.   They were, however, shown to me by Mr. Homolle, who pointed out the names of the two sculptors Samolas and Antiphanes mentioned by Pausanias (§ 6), and the name of Azan, one of the heroes whose statue was made by Samolas.   From the character of the letters the inscriptions seem to belong to the beginning of the fourth century B.C.   An article on the so-called Tegean offerings at Delphi by G. Rathgeber ('Ueber das Weihgeschenk der Tegeater zu Delphoi,' *Archäologische Zeitung*, 14 (1856), pp. 244-252) has been superseded by the discovery of the bases with their inscriptions.

9. 6. Daedalus of Sicyon.   This sculptor is known to have been at work about 400-397 B.C.   See note on vi. 2. 8.   The discovery of the inscribed base of the Arcadian statues proves that he must have been at work as late as 369 B.C.   See the preceding note.

9. 6. Antiphanes of Argos.   He was a pupil of Periclytus, who studied under the elder Polyclitus of Argos (Paus. v. 17. 4).   His name has been found carved on the base of the Arcadian offerings here described by Pausanias (see above, note on § 5).   As these offerings are proved by the inscription to have been made not earlier than 369 B.C., Antiphanes must have been at work in or after that year.   With this date it agrees very well that Antiphanes is known from an inscription recently found at Delphi to have made one or more of the statues which the Argives set up to commemorate the share they took in founding Messene in 369 B.C. (Paus. x. 10. 5 note). On the other hand the sculptor would seem to have been at work a good deal earlier than 369 B.C., since he made the statues of the Dioscuri which formed part of the great trophy dedicated by the Lacedaemonians for the victory of Aegospotami in 405 B.C. (below, § 8). He also made the bronze statue of the Wooden Horse which the Argives set up at Delphi, probably for a victory won in 414 B.C. (below, § 12 note). Thus the artistic career of Antiphanes apparently extended over a period of not much less than fifty years, from about 414 B.C. to about 369 or 368 B.C. See H. Brunn, *Gesch. d. griech. Künstler*, I. pp. 283-285 ; J. Overbeck, *Gesch. d. griech. Plastik*,[4] I. p. 530 *sq.* ; M. Collignon, *Histoire de la Sculpture grecque*, 2. p. 164 *sq.* An inscription found on the Acropolis at Athens and dating from 407 B.C. proves that a certain Antiphanes carved some of the figures (a chariot and horses and a young man) in the frieze of the Erechtheum. See *C. I. A.* I. Nos. 323, 324 ; H. Brunn, *Gesch. d. griech. Künstler*, I. p. 248 *sq.* ; Loewy, *Inschriften griechischer Bildhauer*, Nos. 526, 527. But as this Antiphanes is expressly said in the inscription to have belonged to the Attic township of Ceramicus, he is most probably to be distinguished from the Argive sculptor of the same name.

9. 7. **offerings of the Lacedaemonians.** These offerings most probably occupied, as Mr. Homolle supposes, a spacious quadrangular chamber some 25 metres long, which stood on the right-hand or north side of the Sacred Way close to the main entrance. The remains of this chamber, excavated by the French, comprise the lower parts of the long back wall and the two short side walls, built of blocks of conglomerate laid in regular courses. The back wall was faced with stucco which was probably painted. Towards the Sacred Way the chamber was open, and here a socle or pedestal, which seems to have been built in several steps or tiers, skirts the road and partially fills the chamber. We may suppose that the many statues of gods, admirals, and generals which formed the proud trophy of the Lacedaemonians stood like soldiers in stiff formal rows at different heights on the steps of the pedestal, scowling at the Athenian trophy (x. 10. 1) which probably faced them on the opposite side of the road. Many fragments of the pedestals of these statues, with some of the dedicatory inscriptions, have been found by the French. On one of the pedestals is carved an epigram in which Lysander boasts that he has destroyed the power of the people of Cecrops (Κεκροπίδα δύναμιν). It has not yet been published but is said to be one of the finest Greek epigrams that have come down to us. The side wall of the monument on the east reaches almost to the boundary wall of the sacred precinct. Hence we must suppose that the other monuments mentioned by Pausanias on entering the sanctuary (the Corcyraean bull, the offerings of the Tegeans, the Wooden Horse, and the Athenian trophy of the battle of Marathon) were on the opposite or southern side of the Sacred Way, between the boundary wall of the precinct and the semicircular

monument which contained the statues of the Epigoni (x. 10. 4 note). See Th. Homolle, in *Bulletin de Corresp. hellénique*, 18 (1894), p. 186; H. Pomtow, in *Archäologischer Anzeiger*, 1894, p. 7.

The Lacedaemonian trophy at Delphi is repeatedly referred to by Plutarch. He says (*Lysander*, 18) that from the spoils of the battle Lysander set up bronze statues of himself and of all the admirals, together with golden stars of the Dioscuri ; and elsewhere (*De Pythiae oraculis*, 2) he tells us that in his time these old bronze statues of the admirals were covered with a beautiful blue patina, the growth of ages, so that people spoke of them as being true blue salts. Cicero specially mentions the statue of Lysander at Delphi (*De divinatione*, i. 34. 75). The reason for dedicating golden stars of the Dioscuri would seem to have been that Castor and Pollux were said to have appeared on the side of the Lacedaemonians at the battle of Aegospotami (Cicero, *l.c.*), just as they appeared on the Roman side at the battle of Lake Regillus (Cicero, *De natura deorum*, ii. 1. 3 ; Dionysius Halicarnassensis, *Antiquit. Rom.* vi. 13 ; Plutarch, *Aemilius Paulus*, 25). It is related that after the battle of Leuctra, which gave the death-blow to Spartan prestige and power, the golden stars disappeared from Delphi and were never seen again, as if in token that the star of Sparta's fortunes had set (Plutarch, *Lysander*, 18 ; Cicero, *De divinatione*, i. 34. 75). The dedication of the stars in memory of the appearance of the Dioscuri is an interesting confirmation of the view that the twins Castor and Pollux were the Morning and Evening Star, the equivalents of the Sanscrit Aśvins. See H. Oldenberg, *Die Religion des Veda* (Berlin, 1894), pp. 50, 207 *sqq.* ; A. A. Macdonell, *Vedic Mythology* (Strasburg, 1897), p. 49 *sqq.* It is notable that in Roman history the appearances of the Dioscuri as messengers of victory seem always to have taken place in the same season of the year, namely at the summer solstice or the first full moon after it. See A. Mommsen, ' Die Dioskuren,' *Philologus*, 11 (1856), pp. 706-744 ; L. Preller, *Römische Mythologie*,[3] 2. p. 302. The date of the battle of Aegospotami is uncertain, but it seems to have fallen in summer (Clinton, *Fasti Hellenici*, 2.[3] p. 327 *sqq.*).

9. 7. **Agias.** See iii. 11. 5 and Critical Note on this passage, vol. I. p. 608.

9. 8. **Theocosmus the Megarian.** He was a contemporary of Phidias (i. 40. 4). His son Callicles made the statue of Diagoras at Olympia (vi. 7. 2).

9. 8. **Pison, a native of Calauria.** See vi. 3. 5 note.

9. 8. **Dameas and Athenodorus.** They were pupils of Polyclitus (Pliny, *Nat. hist.* xxxiv. 50). An inscription found at Olympia bears the name of an Achaean sculptor Athenodorus ; but this Athenodorus must have been considerably older than the Athenodorus here mentioned by Pausanias. See Dittenberger und Purgold, *Die Inschriften von Olympia*, No. 630 ; Loewy, *Inschriften griech. Bildhauer*, No. 30 ; cp. W. Klein, in *Archaeolog. epigraph. Mittheilungen aus Oesterreich*, 7 (1883), p. 63.

9. 10. **Alypus of Sicyon.** Cp. vi. 1. 3 note ; vi. 8. 5.

9. 10. **Patrocles.** He was the father of the sculptor Daedalus of

Sicyon.   See vi. 3. 4; and the note on vi. 2. 8.   Pliny (*Nat. hist.*
xxxiv. 50 and 90) ranks him among the sculptors who flourished in Ol.
95 (400-397 B.C.), and also among those who distinguished themselves
by their statues of athletes, armed men, hunters, and sacrificers.   As the
son of Patrocles was a Sicyonian, we may infer that Patrocles himself
was so too.   Hence he is probably a different person from the Patrocles
of Crotona who made a box-wood image of Apollo with a gilt head in the
treasury of the Sicyonians at Olympia (Paus. vi. 19. 6).   Cp. H. Brunn,
Gesch. d. griech. Künstler, 1. p. 277 *sq.*

   9. 10. **Canachus.**   See note on vi. 13. 7.

   9. 11. **they were betrayed by their generals** etc.   Cp. iv. 17. 3.
Suspicion fell especially on Adimantus because he was the only Athenian
prisoner whose life Lysander spared (Xenophon, *Hellenica*, ii. 1. 32 ;
Lysias, *Or.* xiv. 38).   He was afterwards impeached by his colleague
Conon (Demosthenes, *Or.* xix. 191, p. 401), but on what grounds
we do not know.   Thirlwall has shown good grounds for questioning
the alleged treason of Adimantus (*History of Greece*, ch. 30, vol. 4.
p. 142 *sq.*).

   9. 12. **The combat —— for —— Thyrea.**   Pausanias clearly
supposed that the battle with the Lacedaemonians which the Argives
commemorated by dedicating a statue of the Wooden Horse was no
other than the famous one of 548 B.C.   See ii. 38. 5, and the note on
ii. 20. 7.   But Antiphanes, the artist who made the statue, lived
probably at the end of the fifth and certainly in the first half of the
fourth century B.C. (see note on § 6 of this chapter) ; and it seems very
unlikely that the Argives should have commemorated a victory some
hundred and fifty years or more after it had been won.   Now we know
from Thucydides (vi. 95) that in 414 B.C. the Argives made a raid into
Thyreatis and carried off booty from the Lacedaemonians to the value
of not less than five-and-twenty talents.   Most probably, therefore, as
H. Brunn pointed out (*Gesch. d. griech. Künstler*, 1. p. 283), the
Wooden Horse at Delphi was made out of the proceeds of the booty
carried off in the raid of 414 B.C.

   10. 1. **on the pedestal —— is an inscription** etc.   This express
mention of the pedestal and inscription seems to indicate that at the
time of Pausanias's visit the statues themselves were gone.   The
pedestal has not been found by the French excavators, but there can be
little doubt that it stood on the south side of the Sacred Way, near the
main entrance of the sanctuary.   See H. Pomtow, in *Archäologischer
Anzeiger*, 1895, p. 8.   However, in the place where the trophy of
Marathon probably stood the French discovered a large base of a tripod
with an inscription dating apparently from the middle of the fourth
century B.C. and stating that the tripod was dedicated by ten Athenian
deputies who had been sent to celebrate the Delphic worship.   Among
the names of the deputies are those of some well-known orators.   This
votive tripod no doubt stood beside the Athenian trophy of Marathon
mentioned by Pausanias.

   10. 1. **These gave names to tribes at Athens.**   See i. 5.   It is
remarkable that according to Pausanias only seven out of the ten heroes

who gave their names to the Athenian tribes were represented in this national Athenian trophy at Delphi. Why were there no statues of the remaining heroes, Ajax, Hippothoon, and Oeneus? Their omission becomes all the more remarkable when we observe that, as Pausanias tells us, the statues of Antigonus, Demetrius, and Ptolemy were subsequently added to the trophy; for these three men gave their names to three Athenian tribes which were instituted in later times (i. 5. 5 note). The intention plainly seems to have been to represent in this, national trophy all the eponymous heroes of the Athenian tribes. If this was so, we must conclude, with E. Curtius, that statues of Ajax, Hippothoon, and Oeneus formed part of the trophy originally, and that either they had been carried off before the time of Pausanias, or the mention of them has dropped out of his text. See E. Curtius, *Gesammelte Abhandlungen*, 2. p. 365 *sq.* As there is some ground for thinking that all the statues had disappeared, while the pedestal with its inscription certainly remained in the time of Pausanias (see the preceding note), the more probable view would seem to be that the mention of the statues of Ajax, Hippothoon, and Oeneus has been omitted through the carelessness of a scribe.

10. 1. Phyleus. Nothing is known of this Phyleus. E. Curtius plausibly conjectured (*Gesammelte Abhandlungen*, 2. p. 366) that the statue in question was really that of Philaeus, who first put the Athenians in possession of Salamis and gave his name to an Attic township (Paus. i. 35. 2; Plutarch, *Solon*, 10). A statue of Philaeus would be peculiarly appropriate in a monument which commemorated the victory won by Miltiades, since Miltiades was a descendant of Philaeus (Herodotus, vi. 35), and a portrait statue of him formed part of the trophy. Cp. Critical Note, vol. 1. p. 608.

10. 2. The statues —— were made by Phidias. Pausanias tells us that these statues by Phidias were made from a tithe of the spoils taken at the battle of Marathon. But at the date of the battle of Marathon (490 B.C.) Phidias could hardly have been more than ten years old, if so much, and it seems unlikely that the dedication of votive offerings from the spoils should have been deferred for many years after the battle. The number, too, of votive offerings which are said to have been dedicated out of the tithe of the spoils taken at the battle of Marathon is suspiciously large. See i. 14. 5; i. 28. 2; ix. 4. 1; x. 11. 5; x. 19. 3. It would seem that the Greeks, especially the Athenians, sometimes spoke of Marathon when they really referred to the Persian wars in general; hence, as the statues in question are ascribed to Phidias, who was born about 500 B.C., it has been conjectured that they were dedicated out of the spoils taken at the battle of Plataea (479 B.C.) or the Eurymedon (465 B.C.). See K. O. Müller, 'De Phidiae vita et operibus,' *Kunstarchaeologische Werke*, 2. p. 14 *sqq.*; H. Brunn, *Gesch. der griech. Künstler*, 1. p. 162 *sqq.*; M. Collignon, *Histoire de la Sculpture grecque*, 1. p. 520 *sq.* But the definite statement of the inscription on the pedestal that the statues were made out of the spoils taken at Marathon is not to be lightly set aside. Prof. Furtwängler, therefore, prefers to believe that the trophy actually commemorated the battle of Marathon and was dedicated not long after it, but that Pausanias is mistaken in ascribing the work to Phidias (*Meisterwerke d. griech. Plastik*, pp. 55-57).

10. 2. Ptolemy the Egyptian. This was Ptolemy II., Philadelphus, who aided the Athenians in their war with Antigonus. See i. I. I ; i. 7. 3 ; iii. 6. 4 *sqq.* In the chapel of St. Elias at Delphi an inscription has been found which may perhaps have been engraved on the base of a statue of the Ptolemy here mentioned by Pausanias. But the statue to which the inscription refers seems to have been set up by the Phocians and Locrians in gratitude to Ptolemy for helping to free their country from Cassander's garrisons. See H. N. Ulrichs, *Reisen und Forschungen*, I. pp. 36, 43 ; G. Kaibel, *Epigrammata Graeca*, No. 849.

10. 3. the descendants of Proetus. From Pausanias ii. 18. 4 *sq.* and a scholiast on Euripides, *Phoenissae*, 180 we learn that the relationship of Capaneus and Eteoclus to Proetus was as follows :—

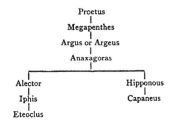

```
              Proetus
                |
          Megapenthes
                |
         Argus or Argeus
                |
           Anaxagoras
                |
      ┌─────────┴─────────┐
   Alector             Hipponous
      |                    |
    Iphis               Capaneus
      |
   Eteoclus
```

According to this table Capaneus was the cousin, though Pausanias speaks of him (ii. 18. 5) as the brother, of Iphis. Hence in that passage Clavier has proposed to alter ἀδελφοῦ ('brother') into ἀνεψιοῦ ('cousin').

10. 3. Adrastus' sister. Her name was Mythidice, according to Hyginus (*Fab.* 70).

10. 3. Baton, the charioteer and kinsman of Amphiaraus. Cp. ii. 23. 2 ; v. 17. 8.

10. 3. Alitherses. This may be the Alitherses, son of Ancaeus and Samia, whom Pausanias mentions elsewhere (vii. 4. 1).

10. 4. works of Hypatodorus and Aristogiton —— from the spoils of the victory —— at Oenoe. The victory of the Argives and Athenians over the Lacedaemonians was commemorated also by one of the pictures in the Painted Colonnade at Athens (i. 15. 1). The battle seems to have been fought and the monuments commemorative of it to have been set up between 463 and 458 B.C. See vol. I. p. 137 *sq.* From the inscription there referred to (*C. I. G.* No. 25 ; Roehl, *I. G. A.* No. 165 ; Loewy, *Inschriften griech. Bildhauer*, No. 101 ; etc.) we learn that Hypatodorus and Aristogiton were Thebans. Hypatodorus made the image of Athena at Aliphera (viii. 26. 7 note). If the Sostratus who helped him in making the image (Polybius, iv. 78) was the nephew of Pythagoras of Rhegium mentioned by Pliny (*Nat. hist.*

xxxiv. 60), this would be a confirmation of the date which, following Prof. C. Robert, I have assigned to the battle of Oenoe and hence to the sculptors Hypatodorus and Aristogiton ; for Pythagoras of Rhegium appears to have lived and worked in the early part of the fifth century B.C. See note on vi. 6. 4, vol. 4. p. 22. Other writers, however, whose opinion is entitled to respect, would assign a much later date to the battle and hence to the sculptors. See H. Brunn, *Gesch. d. griechische Künstler*, 1. p. 293 *sqq.* ; J. Overbeck, *Gesch. d. griech. Plastik,*[4] 2. p. 179 *sq.* ; M. Collignon, *Histoire de la Sculpture grecque,* 2. p. 355 *sq.*

10. 4. the statues of the Epigoni. These statues occupied a semicircular monument on the southern side of the Sacred Way. This monument, measuring about 9 metres (29 ft. 6 in.) in diameter and built of squared blocks of grey limestone, was discovered and partially excavated by Mr. Pomtow. Its remains, so far as they exist, have since been fully laid bare by the French. Though it bears no inscription, the monument can be identified with certainty by means of Pausanias's statement that the statues of the Epigoni were opposite the statues of the Argive kings ; for these statues of the kings are known from inscriptions (see note on § 5) to have occupied another semicircular monument which stands on the opposite side of the Sacred Way, exactly facing the monument in question. See Th. Homolle, in *Bulletin de Corresp. hellénique*, 18 (1894), p. 186 ; H. Pomtow, *Beiträge zur Topographie von Delphi*, p. 56 *sq.* ; *id.*, in *Archäologischer Anzeiger*, 1895, pp. 7, 8. Statues of the Epigoni—the chiefs who captured Thebes—were also set up at Argos (ii. 20. 5).

10. 4. Alcmaeon —— was preferred to Amphilochus on the ground of his age. Alcmaeon and Amphilochus were brothers, sons of Amphiaraus (Homer, *Od.* xv. 248). From Pausanias's statement we gather that of the two brothers only Alcmaeon, the elder, was represented among the Epigoni at Delphi. Both brothers were represented in the corresponding group of statues at Argos (ii. 20. 5), from which, on the other hand, Euryalus apparently was absent. In the list of the Epigoni given by Apollodorus (iii. 7. 2) both Amphilochus and Euryalus are included. A scholiast on Homer (*Il.* iv. 404) gives a list of nine Epigoni ; it includes Amphilochus but excludes Euryalus. Neither Amphilochus nor Euryalus appears in Hyginus's list of the Epigoni (*Fab.* 71), which is, however, imperfect.

10. 5. other statues, dedicated by the Argives. The structure which supported these statues was discovered and excavated by the French in May 1894. It is a semicircular edifice situated on the north side of the Sacred Way, not differing much in size from the corresponding semicircular monument on the opposite side of the road (see note on § 4). The substructure on which it rests rises to a height of more than a metre (3 ft. 3. in.) above the level of the Sacred Way. At the back, towards the upper slope of the hill, it is enclosed by a high semicircular wall built of regular masonry. At the foot of this wall, on the inner side, runs a low step, which supports a course of slabs cut in the shape of arcs of a circle. On these slabs are cut the names of the

Argive kings and heroes, Abas, Acrisius, Lynceus, Perseus, and Hercules. Each inscription occupied two slabs. In the middle of the semicircle, occupying a second line, is the signature of the sculptor, Antiphanes of Argos ('Ἀντιφάνης ἐποίησεν Ἄργειος). Curiously enough, while the name of the sculptor reads in the usual way from left to right, all the names of the kings and heroes read in the ancient fashion from right to left. This was probably done to give a more venerable air of antiquity to the statues of these ancient personages. The discovery of this monument furnishes a clue to the topography of the sacred precinct. Adjoining the monument on the east is the long chamber in which stood the offerings of the Lacedaemonians (x. 9. 7). See Th. Homolle, in *Bulletin de Corresp. hellénique*, 18 (1894), p. 186; H. Pomtow, in *Archäologischer Anzeiger*, 1895, p. 6 *sq.*

10. 6. offerings of the Tarentines. On the right hand or north side of the Sacred Way, opposite the Treasury of the Sicyonians (see x. 11. 1 note), there is a great supporting-wall built of polygonal masonry and bearing in large letters the inscription ΔΕΚΑΤΑΝ ('tithe'). Mr. Homolle conjectures that it may have formed part of the Tarentine monument (*Bulletin de Corresp. hellénique*, 18 (1894), p. 187; *Comptes Rendus de l'Académie des Inscriptions*, 22 (1894), p. 584). On the other hand Mr. Pomtow prefers to suppose that the Tarentine offerings stood on the southern side of the Sacred Way, close to the Treasury of the Sicyonians (*Archäologischer Anzeiger*, 1895, p. 9). His ground for thinking so is that Pausanias describes the Sicyonian treasury as near the offering of the Tarentines (x. 11. 1), which he would hardly have done if they had been on opposite sides of the road. Mr. Cecil Smith informs me that on the left or southern side of the Sacred Way a large slab has been found bearing some letters (ΣΔΕΚ) of what may very well have been part of the dedicatory inscription of the Tarentine offering. The letters of the inscription are simple and large (about .14 metre high), closely resembling the Melian letters of the fifth century B.C.

10. 6. Agelades. See note on iv. 33. 2.

10. 6. Tarentum is a Lacedaemonian colony etc. Tarentum was founded in 704 B.C. by a body of Spartans called Partheniae ('sons of virgins'), because they were born out of wedlock; their leader was Phalanthus (Jerome, on Ol. 18, in Eusebius, *Chronic.* vol. 2. p. 85 ed. Schoene; Antiochus and Ephorus, in Strabo, vi. pp. 278-280; Servius, on Virgil, *Aen.* iii. 551; Justin, iii. 4; Scymnus Chius, *Orbis descriptio*, 330 *sqq.*). The tradition as to the foundation of Tarentum has been discussed by Mr. J. Geffcken ('Die Gründung von Tarentum,' *Fleckeisen's Jahrbücher*, 39 (1893), pp. 177-192).

10. 7. and loused him. This is a service which savages very commonly render each other. See Pallas, *Reise durch verschiedene Provinzen des Russischen Reichs*, 3. p. 45; Marsden, *History of Sumatra*, p. 298; Raffles, *History of Java*, 1. p. 354 (ed. 1817); O. C. Stone, *A Few Months in New Guinea*, p. 106 *sq.*; Lewin, *Wild Tribes of South-Eastern India*, p. 140; J. G. Bourke, *Snake Dance of the Moquis of Arizona*, p. 29; G. M. Sproat, *Scenes and Studies of Savage*

Life, p. 97 note ; L. Lloyd, *Peasant Life in Sweden*, p. 94. In fairy tales the same operation is performed by princesses on the heads of kings, ogres, etc. See Dozon, *Contes Albanais*, p. 27 ; Gonzenbach, *Sicilianische Märchen*, I. p. 145 ; Hahn, *Griechische und Albanesische Märchen*, 2. p. 55 ; Radloff, *Proben der Volkslitteratur der türkischen Stämme Süd-Sibiriens*, I. p. 425 ; Landes, 'Contes et Légendes anna-mites,' No. 53 ii, No. 59 i, No. 111, *Cochinchine Française: Excursions et Reconnaissances*, x. No. 23, pp. 46, 52, xi. No. 25, p. 154.

11. 1. a treasury of the Sicyonians. On the left or south side of the Sacred Way, opposite the wall which Mr. Homolle supposes to have supported the offerings of the Tarentines (see x. 10. 6 note) the French excavations laid bare the remains of what was apparently the Sicyonian treasury. It was built of Sicyonian tufa in the form of a Doric temple *in antis*, with the entrance on the east side. The number of columns between the *antae* of the façade was two ; in other words, the building was distyle. The style of the architecture is very early Doric. Apparently the original treasury was circular, for the existing foundations, which are deep and go down to the virgin soil, comprise pieces of a circular architrave, fluted Doric columns, and other remains of an earlier building, with the initials of the stone-masons. The blocks of the architrave have the same loop-formed groove for convenience in raising them to their places that has been observed in the corresponding blocks of the temple in Aegina. From the style of these remains it would seem that the first treasury dated from the seventh century B.C. Probably its destruction was brought about by the agency of the spring which filters through from above : to this day the wall above is very damp from the same cause. The second treasury seems not to have been very much later in date than its predecessor ; Mr. Homolle would assign it to the first half of the sixth century B.C. (see below).

In and about the treasury were found a number of sculptured slabs of tufa, which doubtless adorned the treasury in the form either of metopes, as Mr. Homolle supposes, or of a frieze, as Prof. Furtwängler prefers to think. Whether they belonged to the first or to the second treasury is uncertain, but there are some grounds for believing that they belonged to the first. For they were found at a greater depth than most of the remains of the later treasury ; and they are too well preserved to allow us to suppose that they were long exposed to the weather, as they must have been if they had belonged to the second treasury. It is, however, to the second treasury apparently that Mr. Homolle would assign them.

Inscriptions slightly scratched on the stones and painted in black enable us to identify the scenes represented in relief on the slabs. These inscriptions seem to have been repeated twice over, being painted both on the background of the reliefs and on the moulding above them. As indicated by the inscriptions the scenes represented are : (1) the bull carrying off Europa ; (2) the ram carrying Helle ; (3) the Calydonian boar ; (4) the cattle-lifting raid of Castor, Pollux, and Idas in Arcadia (Apollodorus, iii. 11. 2 ; Tzetzes, *Schol. on Lycophron*, 511) ; (5) the Argo with its crew of warriors, in the midst of whom Orpheus is singing, while to the right and left of the ship appear Castor and Pollux on horseback. The figures, painted in red, brown, and black, stand out from the yellow background of the stone, which is left unpainted, like the figures on a Corinthian vase. Of the scenes the best rendered is the raid of the Dioscuri and Idas. We see the three sturdy youths, with long locks hanging down their breast and back, marching in single file; each carries a couple of spears on his left shoulder, while in his right hand, which hangs by his side, he grasps a curious object which has been interpreted as a spear or pole held horizontally. Between the men and in front of the foremost of them stalk, three by three, the cattle which are being driven off. The object which each of the raiders holds in his right hand seems to be intended as a barrier to keep the cattle in their places; of the nine animals the three next the spectator are butting with lowered heads against the object, whatever it is. The heads of the kine are truthfully rendered, but the figures of the men are somewhat heavy and thick-set, and the drapery is stiff. In the other scenes the archaic clumsiness and lifelessness of the figures are still more obvious; this is especially true of the figures of Orpheus and another minstrel who are represented playing on lyres to the Argonauts. Mr. Homolle compares these archaic sculptures with the well-known metopes of Selinus and assigns them to the first half of the sixth century B.C. He conjectures that the treasury may have been begun in the last years of the reign of Clisthenes at Sicyon (580-570 B.C.); it cannot, he thinks, be later than 560 B.C.

See Th. Homolle, in *Bulletin de Corresp. hellénique*, 18 (1894), p. 187 *sq.*; *id.*, in *Comptes Rendus de l'Académie des Inscriptions*, 22 (1894), pp. 339 *sq.*, 355 *sq.*; *id.*, in *Gazette des Beaux Arts*, Décembre 1894, p. 446 *sq.*, and Avril 1895, p. 324 *sq.*, with the illustration on p. 323; M. Collignon, in *Comptes Rendus de l'Académie des Inscriptions*, 22 (1894), p. 307 *sq.*; A. Furtwängler, in *Berliner philolog. Wochenschrift*, 29th September 1894, p. 1275 *sq.*; H. Pomtow, in *Archäologischer Anzeiger*, 1895, p. 9.

In the Treasury of the Sicyonians was preserved a "golden book" dedicated by an Erythraean poetess named Aristomache, who had won a prize for poetry at the Isthmian games. This fact was recorded by the antiquary Polemo, who wrote a work *On the treasures (or treasuries) of Delphi* (Plutarch, *Quaest. Conviv.* v. 2. 9 *sq.*). This "golden book" was perhaps a copy of Aristomache's poems written in letters of gold. Similarly a copy of Pindar's seventh Olympian ode was written in golden letters and dedicated in the sanctuary of Athena at Lindus in Rhodes (Schol. on Pindar, *Ol.* viii. Introd.). Cp. Polemo, ed. Preller, p. 55 *sq.*

11. 1. **an image of Triopas, founder of Cnidus.** He was said to be a son of the Sun and to have been driven from Thessaly for cutting down a sacred grove of Demeter and using the timber to build himself a palace with. He fled to Caria and there occupied a cape which took the name of Triopium from him. See Diodorus, v. 57 and 61. The cape was included within the city of Cnidus (Herodotus, i. 174). Cp. C. T. Newton, *History of discoveries at Halicarnassus, Cnidus, and Branchidae*, 2. p. 423 *sqq.* According to Herodotus (*l.c.*), Cnidus was

a Lacedaemonian colony. No trace of the images dedicated by the Cnidians has been found. They may have stood, as Mr. Homolle conjectures, between the treasury of the Sicyonians and the treasury of the Siphnians; at least this position would agree very well with the order of Pausanias's description.

11. 1. Apollo and Artemis shooting arrows at Tityus. Cp. iii. 18. 15 note.

11. 2. The Siphnians also made a treasury. On the south side of the Sacred Way, a few paces to the west of the Sicyonian treasury, there rises, like a bastion, a high quadrangular structure which rests towards the south on the *Hellenico* or boundary wall of the sacred precinct and towards the north on the Sacred Way. It is built of tufa cut in blocks of which some are quadrangular and some polygonal. The lower courses of the masonry are unwrought, showing that they were originally hidden either by the ground, which here slopes upward rapidly, or by steps. On this tower-like foundation, which rises above the level both of the Sacred Way and of the boundary wall, rested an edifice in the shape of an Ionic temple *in antis* with its front to the west. The number of columns between the *antae* of the front was two; in other words, the building was distyle. It is constructed of marble of various sorts, chiefly Parian or Naxian, and seems to date from the latter part of the sixth century B.C. From its shape we may safely infer that the building was a treasury. Its length from east to west was 8.90 metres; its breadth from north to south 6.35 metres. Access to it from the west was afforded by a platform supported on a wall of polygonal masonry and reached from the Sacred Way by steps. As this treasury adjoins that of the Sicyonians, and Pausanias mentions the Siphnian treasury immediately after the Sicyonian, archaeologists are generally agreed in regarding the edifice in question as the Siphnian treasury. The identification is further supported by the remark of Herodotus (iii. 57) that the Siphnian treasury was amongst the wealthiest at Delphi; for the delicacy and richness of its architectural and sculptural decoration give evidence of an unstinted expenditure of money. The building is indeed more lavishly decorated than any other found at Delphi. Remains of the architectural ornaments have been discovered on all sides in the sacred precinct, but entire pieces only about the treasury itself, distributed round its four sides just as they fell. Their exquisite finish is remarkable, and was heightened by a wealth of bright colours (red, blue, and green), of which vivid traces exist. "All the decorative details of this building," says Prof. E. A. Gardner, "the carved mouldings, cornices, etc., are cut with a depth, clearness, and delicacy that can be matched nowhere, except perhaps in the Erechtheum. It is simply a revelation of what decorative carving aan attain to." A characteristic feature is the gigantic ovolo moulding, forming half of a sphere of which the diameter is .56 metre. The general style is the old Ionic. The whole of the entablature was of Parian marble. Round the four outer sides of the building ran a sculptured frieze of Parian marble, .64 metre high, which has been discovered almost entire; and one of the gables, doubtless the western, was adorned with figures carved partly in relief and partly in the round, which have also come to light. The discovery of this beautiful treasury with its remarkable sculptures has been one of the chief results of the French excavations at Delphi. Inscriptions slightly scratched beside the figures and originally rendered conspicuous by red paint, which has now almost disappeared, enable us to identify the scenes represented on the frieze.

(1) On the west side is figured the apotheosis of Hercules. Athena, about to lead the hero to heaven, is mounting her car, which is drawn by winged horses. The heads of the fiery steeds are held by Hermes, recognisable by his herald's staff and his winged sandals. Behind the goddess stands Hercules, his earthly labours over, ready to mount the car that will bear him to his heavenly rest. Behind him Hebe appears descending from another car, the horses of which are held by a figure who corresponds to Hermes at the other end. Hermes, the winged horse Pegasus, Athena, Hercules, Hebe, and a bird as emblem of Victory have their names inscribed beside them.

(2) On the south side the scene is the chariot-race of Pelops and Oenomaus. In the chariot with Pelops is Hippodamia. The piece of the frieze which represents the chariot of Oenomaus and the altar of Zeus had been found before the French excavations. It is described and figured by Conze and Michaelis (*Annali dell' Instituto*, 33 (1861), p. 64 with Tav. d' agg. B), and a photograph of it is given by Mr. Pomtow (*Beiträge zur Topographie von Delphi*, pl. xii. No. 32). Horses and horsemen also form parts of the southern frieze. The inscribed names, so far as they exist, are Myrtilus, Pelops, Hippodamia, and Oenomaus. The altar bears the inscription: Ζανὸς Ὀλυμπίου ('of Olympian Zeus').

(3) On the east side the scene is the combat over the body of Sarpedon (Homer, *Il.* xvi. 530 *sqq.*) and an assembly of the gods watching the fight. The dead chief lies on the ground, and four warriors, armed with shields, helmets, and breastplates, are fighting over him, two on each side. This central group is flanked on either hand by a chariot drawn by four horses, which are held by a groom. One of the combatants is Patroclus clad in the armour of Achilles, whose name may be read on the shield. The others are Menelaus, Hector, and Aeneas, all identified by inscriptions. To the left of this scene of combat are represented the deities seated and gazing at the fight. All are identified by inscriptions. The gods of the Greeks sit together on the right; they are Nemesis, Hera, Athena, Thetis and Zeus. The gods of the Trojans (θεῖν τᾶς Τροέων πόλωος) sit together on the left; they are Apollo, Artemis, Aphrodite, and Ares. Thetis is laying her hand on the knee of Zeus with a gesture of supplication. Artemis is touching the chin of her brother Apollo to attract his attention. Ares, who sits apart, wears his armour and seems ready to rush into the fray.

(4) The scene on the north side is the battle between the gods and the giants. So far as they have been deciphered, the names inscribed, taken from right to left, are as follows: Aeolus, Hercules, Cybele the

Great Mother, Alcyoneus, Apollo, Artemis, Dionysus, Ephialtes, Palleneus, Hera, Athena, Enceladus, Hephaestus, and Ares. This is artistically the finest and happily also the best preserved of all the scenes of the frieze. Among the groups in it the following may be noted. At the extreme right is Aeolus, the god of the winds, with flowing locks and pointed beard; he holds one hand open over a large jar, while with the other he seems to be shutting up a half empty wind-bag. According to another interpretation, Aeolus is bending over two wind-bags, squeezing one of them with his left hand and opening the mouth of the bag with his right. Further to the left is Hercules, with the lion's skin knotted round his neck and stretched out like a buckler on his right arm; he is drawing his bow to shoot a giant who threatens him with a spear. In front of this latter group and partly concealing it is Cybele mounted on a car drawn by galloping lions, one of which has fastened its claws and teeth in a giant. Still further to the left are seen Apollo and Artemis, side by side, shooting arrows at a pair of giants. Beside them marches Dionysus, armed with sword and shield and wearing a helmet of which the crest has the form of a wine goblet. Further to the left is Hera vigorously spearing a prostrate giant, who seeks in vain to protect himself from the deadly thrust by holding up his shield. Close to Hera is seen Athena marching calmly forward and appearing to overthrow her adversaries, whom she meets shield to shield, without an effort; one of her foes has sunk on his knee, the other still stands. Still further to the left Hephaestus, recognisable by his pointed cap as well as by the inscription, is fighting a pair of giants, one of whom wields a spear while the other brandishes a huge stone. In the extreme left-hand corner Ares is also engaged with two giants. All the giants are represented in purely human form as armed men. Their helmets are adorned with various animals or parts of animals, such as the horns of oxen and goats, a horse's head with wings, and a serpent.

Like the architectural ornaments of the treasury the sculptured frieze was painted in bright colours, red, blue, and green, which were sometimes laid on whole surfaces, as in the case of hair and drapery, and sometimes employed to bring out details, such as the harness of horses, the hem of robes, and the straps of shields, or again to supply the want of carving, as in the reins of horses. Further, the effects of carving and painting were heightened and completed by bronze spear-heads and arrow-heads, bronze wheels and railings of chariots, and bronze harnesses, which were fastened to the marble.

The sculptures in the gable represented the contest between Hercules and Apollo for possession of the tripod. In the middle of the gable stands Athena, laying her hands on both adversaries or if to part them. Behind Apollo is Latona, who seeks to pacify her son; and behind her again is another female figure, perhaps Artemis. Behind Hercules are also two female figures, and beyond them are two horses, representing probably the chariot in which Hercules has come. The horses are matched by another pair of horses at the other end of the gable. A remarkable feature of these sculptures

2

Héliog. Prieux-Drouin

Imp. A. Clément - Paris

in the gable is that while the lower parts of the figures are carved in relief, the upper parts are carved in the round and stand clean out from the background, which is hollowed deeply away so that the figures appear sharply outlined against a black shadow.

The style and composition of these sculptures in the gable are very defective, far inferior to those of the frieze. The figures are squat, the outlines hard and angular, the modelling flat, the muscles exaggerated, and the attitudes stiff and awkward; the composition, tolerable in the centre, falls off lamentably towards the two ends, where the figures decrease successively in size with the regularity of organ-pipes. The artist was clearly a different person from the sculptor or sculptors who made the frieze. But in the frieze itself marked differences both of composition and of style point to the conclusion that it was executed by two artists of different degrees of ability. In the scenes on the western and southern sides (the apotheosis of Hercules and the chariot-race of Pelops and Oenomaus) the figures are merely placed side by side; in the scenes on the eastern and northern sides (the combat for the body of Sarpedon and the battle of the gods and giants) they are dramatically grouped together. In the sculptures on the western and southern sides, again, the figures share, though in a less degree, some of the defects which characterise the sculptures in the gable; we note a similar heaviness and squatness in the figures, a similar hardness of outline, lack of modelling, flatness of relief, and rudeness in the rendering of the muscles. In the eastern and northern sculptures, on the other hand, the surfaces and outlines are more rounded, the flesh and muscles more supple, the drapery more flowing, the movements freer. Yet with all this the differences are not so great as to indicate that the artist who made the western and southern friezes belonged to a different school from the artist who made the eastern and northern friezes or that he lived at a different time. With regard to the date of the sculptures, archaeologists are agreed in referring them to the latter part of the sixth century B.C., but they differ as to the school to which the sculptors belonged, Mr. Th. Homolle advocating the claims of the Argive, Prof. Collignon of the Ionian, and Prof. Furtwängler of the Parian school. In favour of his view Mr. Homolle appeals to an inscription, unfortunately mutilated and in part nearly illegible, on the shield of one of the giants in the northern frieze. The inscription, which recorded the name of the artist, is restored by Mr. Homolle as follows :

$$\text{'A}[ργεῖ]ο[ς \ Θρασυμή]δης \ Καλιορίσο \ (?) \ ἐμ' \ ἐποίει.}$$

"Thrasymedes, son of Caliorisus (?), an Argive, made me." But this restoration, as Mr. Homolle recognises, is very doubtful. The proof to which he chiefly pins his faith is the letter l, which has the characteristic Argive shape (Ͱ).

More recently the discovery of the figure of a lion among the sculptured decoration of the building has suggested to Mr. Homolle the theory that the treasury is that of the Cnidians mentioned by Pausanias below (x. 11. 5), and not that of the Siphnians, since a lion was an emblem of Cnidus, as we see by the coins of that city (B. V. Head, *Historia numorum*, p. 524 *sq.*). This theory, Mr. Homolle thinks, harmonises better with the Ionic style of the architecture, the presence of the Argive lambda (Ⱶ) in the artist's signature, and the subjects of the sculptured decorations. On the other hand it is to be observed that Pausanias does not mention the Cnidian treasury until after the Theban and the Athenian treasuries, both of which are known to be further up the Sacred Way than the treasury in question. If Mr. Homolle is right, we must suppose that Pausanias departed entirely from the topographical order in mentioning the Cnidian immediately after the Sicyonian treasury and before the treasuries of the Thebans and Athenians. Considering the constantly accumulating evidence that Pausanias in general adhered strictly to the topographical order in his descriptions, we are hardly justified by the facts shown in assuming that he here departed from it.

See Th. Homolle, in *Bulletin de Corresp. hellénique*, 18 (1894), pp. 188-194, and *ib.* 19 (1895), pp. 534-537; *id.*, in *Comptes Rendus de l'Académie des Inscriptions*, 22 (1894), pp. 208-210, 339 *sq.*, 355-358, 589-591, and *ib.*, 23 (1895), p. 392 *sq.* ; *id.*, in *Gazette des Beaux Arts*, Décembre 1894, p. 448, and *ib.* Avril 1895, pp. 325-331 ; M. Collignon, in *Comptes Rendus de l'Académie des Inscriptions*, 22 (1894), pp. 308-312 ; Ch. Belger, in *Berliner philolog. Wochenschrift*, 30th June 1894, p. 862 *sq.* ; A. Furtwängler, in *Berliner philolog. Wochenschrift*, 30th September 1894, pp. 1276-1278 ; H. Pomtow, in *Archäologischer Anzeiger*, 1895, p. 9 *sq.* ; E. A. Gardner, in *Journal of Hellenic Studies*, 14 (1894), p. 228, and *ib.* 15 (1895), p. 207 *sq.* ; P. Hartwig, 'Sur un Canthare de l'Acropole d'Athènes,' *Bulletin de Corresp. hellénique*, 20 (1896), pp. 364-373. In this last article Mr. Hartwig points out some resemblances between the battle of the gods and giants on the frieze and a similar scene on the fragments of a black-figured vase found on the Acropolis of Athens. On one of the fragments of the vase are seen two wind-bags, one full, the other half empty, with the remains of a man, who is doubtless Aeolus, standing beside them. Mr. Hartwig would date the vase about 560 B.C.

Herodotus, like Pausanias, says that the Siphnians dedicated the treasury at Delphi with a tithe of the produce of their mines, but he mentions silver as well as gold mines, and he says nothing as to the destruction of either by the sea, which may have taken place after his time (Herodotus, iii. 57). Some of the ancient mines of Siphnus are still to be seen near the little red-roofed chapel of St. Saviour (*Hagia Sosti*) which stands on a bare rocky headland jutting out into the sea at the north-eastern end of the island. See K. G. Fiedler, *Reise*, 2. p. 136 *sqq.* One of these mines is a great labyrinth of passages, the sides of which sparkle as with silver. Many tools, including pointed and cone-shaped axes, have been found in it, and there are many niches in the walls where the miners probably set their lamps. In the sea-cliff outside of the mine certain hollows exist which the people call furnaces, and in there it would seem that the ore was smelted by the admixture of other substances, such as iron and volcanic stones. Heaps of slag lie about the hollows, and traces of slag may be seen also in calm weather at the bottom of the sea a little way off the shore. "This," wrote the late J. T. Bent, "proves beyond a doubt that either the land must have subsided, or the sea encroached, since the time when the furnaces were

used, and corroborates the substance of the legend as told by Pausanias."
See J. T. Bent, 'On the gold and silver mines of Siphnos,' *Journal of
Hellenic Studies*, 6 (1885), pp. 195-198.

Beside the Siphnian treasury have been found the remains of four
figures of Caryatids. They are of colossal size and represent young and
graceful women each clad in a long tunic and robe and wearing a head-
dress of the sort called *polos*, in which a tiny column was fastened.
Apparently they supported a stand of some sort. From their archaic
style they seem to date from the end of the sixth century B.C., and hence
to be contemporary with the Siphnian treasury near which their remains
were found. Whether they belonged to the treasury or not, is uncertain.
Mr. Homolle inclines to believe that they did not. They recall the
archaic female statues found on the Acropolis at Athens (vol. 2. p. 346),
and might have served as the prototype of the Caryatids of the Erechtheum. See Th. Homolle, in *Bulletin de Corresp. hellénique*, 18 (1894),
p. 194 *sq.* ; *id.*, in *Comptes Rendus de l'Académie des Inscriptions*, 22
(1894), pp. 206-208, 585.

11. 3. The Liparaeans also dedicated statues for a naval victory
etc. Cp. x. 16. 7. Diodorus tells us (v. 9) that the inhabitants of the
small *Lipari* islands, to the north of Sicily, being harassed by Etruscan
pirates, built a fleet, and while some of them tilled the islands, the rest
scoured the sea in search of the rovers, whom they defeated in many
actions, and from the spoils they often sent tithe-offerings to Delphi.
Cp. Strabo, vi. p. 275. On some antiquities from the island of Lipara,
see Mr. A. S. Murray, in *Journal of Hellenic Studies*, 7 (1886),
pp. 51-56.

11. 3. These Liparaeans were colonists from Cnidus etc. That
the Liparaeans were colonists from Cnidus is mentioned also by Thucydides (iii. 88) and Strabo (vi. p. 275). Cp. Scymnus Chius, *Orbis
descriptio*, 262 *sq.* Diodorus tells us (v. 9) that the emigrants set out
from Cnidus with Pentathlus for their leader in Ol. 50 (580 B.C.), but
that Pentathlus fell in battle in Sicily, and that the settlement in Lipara
was made under the leadership of three kinsmen of his, Gorgus, Thestor,
and Epithersides.

11. 3. Antiochus the Syracusan. He was the oldest of the Greek
historians of Sicily. His history, divided into nine books, began with
the reign of Cocalus, king of the Sicanians, and ended with the year
424 B.C. See Diodorus, xii. 71. It is thought that Thucydides, in
his account of Sicily, drew upon Antiochus's work. The fragments of
Antiochus are collected by C. Müller in his *Fragmenta historicorum
Graecorum*, vol. 1. pp. 181-184, cp. *ib.* p. xlv. Cp. G. Busolt,
Griechische Geschichte, 1.² p. 366 *sq.* ; Th. Reinach, in *Revue des
Études grecques*, 3 (1890), p. 90 *sqq.*

11. 3. the Islands of Aeolus. The Homeric isle of Aeolus was a
fabulous floating island, with a wall of brass running all round the edge
of the sheer cliffs. See Homer, *Od.* x. 1 *sqq.*, on which passage
Mr. Merry has suggested that the description may be based on
the stories of some Phoenician sailors who, sailing northward in
the Atlantic, had fallen in with an iceberg and seen its tall sides

glittering like burnished brass in the sun.   Homer (*Od.* x. 19 *sqq.*)
makes Aeolus, as King of the Winds, give Ulysses the winds shut up in
a leather bag.   In Virgil (*Aen.* i. 52 *sqq.*) we read that Aeolus keeps
the winds chained up in a vast cave.   It is said that in Lithuanian
mythology Perdoytus the wind-god keeps the winds in a leather sack;
when they escape he catches them, beats them, and shuts them up
again.   See E. Veckenstedt, *Die Mythen, Sagen, und Legenden der
Zamaiten (Litauer)*, 1. p. 153.   (But the statements made in this book
are to be received with great caution : see *Folklore*, 2 (1891), pp.
100 *sqq.*, 483 *sq.*).   On the Slave Coast of Africa Wuo, the spirit of
the Harmattan wind, "is believed to be shut up in a cave under the
charge of a keeper named Wuo-hunto, who at certain seasons opens the
door and lets out Wuo to annoy mankind" (A. B. Ellis, *The Ewe-speak-
ing Peoples of the Slave Coast*, p. 76).   In the temple of the Winds at
Pekin there is the image of a man with a sack on his back in which are
the winds (A. Bastian, *Die Völker des oestlichen Asien*, 6. p. 33).   The
Maoris think that Mawe holds the winds in his hands or keeps them
shut up in caves.   The only wind he cannot catch is the West wind,
which blows almost constantly.   When any of the other winds is
blowing, the Maoris think that Mawe's enemies have rolled away the
stone from the mouth of the cave, or that Mawe has let them loose to
punish mankind or to ride on their wings in chase of the West wind.
See W. Yate, *Account of New Zealand*, p. 144.   The Motumotu in New
Guinea think that a sorcerer keeps each of the winds shut up in a
bamboo, which he opens at pleasure (J. Chalmers, *Pioneering in New
Guinea*, p. 177).   In the island of Huapine, in the Pacific, the people
used to believe that the winds were confined in two caves, one where
the sun rises, and the other where he sets, and that according to the
season the East wind or the West wind was let loose to blow over sea
and land (Tyermann and Bennet, *Voyages and Travels in the South Sea
Islands*, etc., p. 291).   The people of Mangaia, South Pacific, suppose
that the god Raka received the winds hidden in a great basket.   Raka's
children are the winds and storms which distress the world.   To each
child is allotted a hole on the verge of the horizon, through which he
blows at pleasure.   See W. W. Gill, *Myths and Songs of the South
Pacific*, p. 5.   In the Maldive Islands there are places sacred to the
King of the Winds, where those who have escaped shipwreck offer little
ships filled with perfumes, gums, and flowers.   The perfumes are set on
fire and the boats set sailing over the sea.   See Pyrard, *Voyages to the
East Indies*, etc., translated by Albert Gray (Hakluyt Society, 1887), 1.
p. 175 *sqq.*

   11. 4. the islands —— they till.   Here Pausanias may have
drawn on Thucydides (iii. 88), who says the same thing in words not
very different.   Diodorus tells us (v. 9) that at first all the lands in the
Aeolian (*Lipari*) Islands were held in common, and the people lived in
public messes.   Afterwards the lands in the island of Lipara, which
contained the capital, were divided amongst individuals, while the other
islands were cultivated in common.   Lastly the people adopted the
system of distributing the lands in all the islands by lot among private

owners, who held them for twenty years, after which a fresh distribution by lot took place. This is probably one of the earliest recorded examples of the periodic redistribution of all the lands of a state among the citizens. For examples of similar customs see Laveleye, *De la propriété et de ses formes primitives*, ed. 3. He says (p. 100) that among the Yoloffs of Africa "the land belongs to the villages in common. Every year the chief of the village, assisted by a council of elders, makes a redistribution of the lands to be tilled, calculating the lots according to the needs of each family. This is exactly the same custom as in Java and Russia." Diodorus's account of the Liparaean islands was almost certainly borrowed from Timaeus, who in turn seems to have copied from Antiochus the Syracusan (see § 3 note). There is therefore nothing to show that the land system described by Diodorus lasted later than the time of Timaeus, whose history stopped at Ol. 129 (164-161 B.C.). See Polybius, i. 5. 1. Mr. Théodore Reinach has made it highly probable that in the days of their independence the Liparaean islanders were an organised community of pirates, one half the men tilling the fields while the other half scoured the seas. The system would certainly be put down by the Romans when they conquered the islands in 251 B.C. See Th. Reinach, 'Le collectivisme des Grecs de Lipari,' *Revue des Études grecques*, 3 (1890), pp. 86-96 ; J. Geffcken, *Timaios' Geographie des Westens* (Berlin, 1892), p. 62 *sqq.* For evidence of Liparaean piracy, Mr. Reinach refers to Livy (v. 28), who, after mentioning the capture of Roman envoys by Liparaean corsairs, adds : "It was the custom of that state to divide the booty which had been earned by public piracy."

11. 4. **In Strongyle fire may be seen rising up out of the earth.** Strongyle and Hiera were active volcanoes in the time of Strabo (vi. p. 275 *sq.*) and Diodorus (v. 7). Cp. Thucydides, iii. 88 ; Scymnus Chius, *Orbis descriptio*, 257 *sqq.*; Pliny, *Nat. hist.* iii. 93 *sq.*; Mela, ii. 120. The volcanic fires of Strongyle (now called *Stromboli*) are not yet extinct. I have passed the island several times and twice saw a light cloud of smoke hanging over the summit.

11. 4. **baths beside the sea** etc. The hot springs of Lipara were famous ; they possessed a medicinal virtue. Hence patients from Sicily resorted to them in large numbers, and marvellous cures are said to have been effected. See Diodorus, v. 10 ; cp. Pliny, *Nat. hist.* xxxi. 61.

11. 5. **the treasury of the Athenians.** The remains of this treasury were excavated by the French in 1893 and 1894. The building, about 10 metres (32 ft. 10 in.) long from east to west by 6 metres (19 ft. 8 in.) broad from north to south, occupied a terrace higher up than the Sicyonian and Siphnian treasuries, on the north side of the Sacred Way, which at this point has already taken its first upward bend and is now running eastward and northward towards the eastern front of the temple of Apollo. Apparently the edifice was overthrown by an earthquake and crushed by the weight of materials which rolled down on it from the temple above ; drums of huge columns still encumber its ruins. But the foundations exist, and the architectural members and sculptured decorations have been found almost entire. Some of the

architectural pieces retain vivid traces of colour. The plan of the treasury was that of a small Doric temple *in antis* opening from the east ; the number of columns between the *antae* was two. With the exception of a single step, which is made of reddish limestone, the whole edifice is constructed of Pentelic or Parian marble[1] in the most exact and exquisite style of architecture. In shape the capitals resemble those of the temple of Athena in Aegina and the temple of Zeus at Olympia. On the north the treasury is protected by a supporting-wall built of polygonal and quadrangular blocks in alternate courses. In front there is a small court with inscriptions cut on its supporting-walls. Of the identity of the building there can be no doubt, for engraved on the walls are Athenian decrees in which mention is made of the 'treasury of the city' and 'house of the Athenians.' Moreover, remains of the dedicatory inscription can still be read on one of the steps, including the words AΘENAI . . . MAPA⊙ ('Athenians . . . . Marathon'). This inscription, mutilated as it is, suffices to confirm Pausanias's statement that the treasury was built out of the spoils of the battle of Marathon. Moreover, the walls of the building as high up as the architraves were covered with inscriptions, mostly Attic or relating to Athenians. By comparing the inscriptions it has been found possible to determine the order of the courses of masonry ; in this way the *antae* have been restored from top to bottom and will give the height of the edifice. Among the inscriptions engraved on the walls are decrees in honour of Athenians and others, passed by the Athenian people, by the Tetrapolis of Marathon (see vol. 2. p. 431), and by the Delphians ; a record of a law-suit between the Athenian Society of Dramatic Artists (τεχνῖται) and the corporation of Thebes ; lists of Athenians sent in various official capacities to the celebration of the Pythian games ; and one of the hymns to Apollo with musical notation (see note on x. 7. 2). Further, the supporting-wall at the back of the treasury is also covered with inscriptions recording decrees of public friendship and the liberation of slaves. Lastly, tall slabs of white marble have been found on the terrace bearing inscriptions on their four faces. The two remaining hymns to Apollo are engraved on two of these slabs.

A frieze of triglyphs and sculptured metopes extended round all four sides of the building. The metopes, thirty in number, have been found almost entire. They are made of fine white Parian marble, while the triglyphs are made of an inferior bluish variety of the same marble. Six metopes adorned each of the narrow ends of the treasury, and nine metopes each of the long sides. Inscriptions slightly scratched on the background of the reliefs enable us to determine the scenes represented. These comprise the battle of the gods and giants and the exploits of Hercules and Theseus. The battle of the gods and giants occupied the six metopes of the east front ; the deeds of Hercules filled the six western and the nine northern metopes ; while the nine southern metopes appear to have illustrated the exploits of Theseus. From the inscriptions we learn that among the gods and their adversaries who

---

[1] Mr. Homolle says Pentelic, Prof. Furtwängler says Parian.

figure in the six eastern metopes are Hercules and Alcyoneus, Athena and Enceladus, Hera and Porphyrion, Apollo and Ephialtes. The deeds of Theseus represented in the southern metopes comprise his combats with Periphetes, Sciron, Cercyon, the Amazons, the Minotaur, the bull of Marathon, and perhaps the robber Sinis. In one metope we see the meeting of Theseus and Athena. The two stand facing each other : Theseus, clad very lightly, holds up his right hand with a gesture of supplication or respect. Among the deeds of Hercules which the sculptor has chosen to illustrate are the hero's adventures with the Nemean lion, Pholus, Cycnus, Hippolyte (?), Antaeus, and Geryon. The affair of Geryon filled no less than five metopes, in which we see three groups of kine, the dog Orthrus on his back between the legs of Hercules, and Geryon himself represented as a triple-bodied monster, one of whose bodies succumbs while the other two continue the· fight. In regard to the style of these sculptures Mr. Homolle tells us that they combine something of archaic austerity with Attic grace and elegance, presenting many analogies to the later black-figured vases and still more to the fine red-figured vases of the severe style, especially to works of Euphronius. Of the treasury as a whole, with its sculptured decoration, he says : " I hope that I do not exaggerate in describing it as a masterpiece of archaic art. I know no monument, among the works of the beginning of the fifth century, of which the execution is more sharp, delicate and elegant. The sculptures have the same qualities of grace and precision. Their archaic severity is tempered by a softness of modelling rare in works of this date, and by a certain richness that both surprises and charms us." He would date the treasury between 490 and 480 B.C.

See Th. Homolle, in *Bulletin de Corresp. hellénique*, 17 (1893), pp. 217 *sq.*, 612 *sq.*, and *ib.* 18 (1894), pp. 169-172, 182 *sq.* ; *id.*, in *Comptes Rendus de l'Académie des Inscriptions*, 22 (1894), pp. 339, 357 *sq.*, 587-589 ; *id.*, in *Gazette des Beaux-Arts*, Décembre 1894, p. 449 *sq.*, and *ib.* Avril 1895, pp. 208-216 ; *id.*, in *American Journal of Archaeology*, 9 (1894), p. 121 ; M. Collignon, in *Comptes Rendus de l'Académie des Inscriptions*, 22 (1894), pp. 305-307, 313 ; A. Furtwängler, in *Berliner philolog. Wochenschrift*, 29th September 1894, pp. 1278-1280 ; H. Pomtow, in *Archäologischer Anzeiger*, 1894, pp. 183-185, and *ib.* 1895, p. 10 *sq.*

From Mr. Cecil Smith 1 learn that on a terrace immediately adjoining the Athenian treasury the following inscription is carved in large letters : Ἀθηναῖοι τἀπόλλονι ἀκροτίνια (*sic*) τῆς Μαρα-θῶνος. 'The Athenians (dedicated) first-fruits of Marathon to Apollo.' The inscription is cut in would-be archaic style, but seems really to date from the third century B.C. "The problem," adds Mr. Smith, " is unsolved."

11. 5. **The Theban treasury.** The remains of this building, identified by inscriptions engraved on its walls, were excavated by the French in 1893. It stood on the western side of the Sacred Way at the point where that road, after running westward from the main entrance, turns at a right angle northward and begins to ascend the slope. The treasury, which is considerably smaller than that of the

Athenians, is built of fine blue limestone in the shape of a Doric temple. The foundations are constructed of blocks of tufa which have been taken from an earlier edifice, apparently the same building which furnished the foundations of the Sicyonian treasury (see above, note on § 1). Inscribed on the walls are decrees in favour of various Boeotian and especially Theban persons ; the longest inscription refers to the regulation of boundaries between two Boeotian cities. See Th. Homolle, in *Bulletin de Corresp. hellénique*, 18 (1894), p. 184 ; *id.*, in *Comptes Rendus de l'Académie des Inscriptions*, 22 (1894), p. 203 *sq.* ; H. Pomtow, in *Archäologischer Anzeiger*, 1895, p. 10.

11. 5. the Cnidians built their treasury. On the eastern side of the Sacred Way, exactly opposite the Theban treasury, the remains of a quadrangular building of some size were laid bare by the French excavations. The building stands at the point where the Sacred Way, after running from east to west, makes a sharp turn northward. Thus the road skirts the building on two sides, namely its long southern and its short western side. Mr. H. Pomtow conjectures that this building may have been the Cnidian treasury. Mr. Homolle, who does not attempt to identify the edifice in question, now believes that the building which has been described as the Siphnian treasury is really the treasury of the Cnidians (see above, note on § 2). See Th. Homolle, in *Bulletin de Corresp. hellénique*, 18 (1894), p. 183 *sq.* ; *id.*, in *Comptes Rendus de l'Académie des Inscriptions*, 23 (1895), p. 392 *sq.* ; H. Pomtow, in *Archäologischer Anzeiger*, 1895, p. 11.

11. 5. they sent a bronze he-goat to Apollo. On the relation of Apollo to goats, see L. Stephani, in *Compte Rendu* (St. Petersburg) for 1869, p. 100 *sq.* Goats were sometimes sacrificed to Apollo (Homer, *Il.* i. 315 *sq.*). At Delos the god had an altar composed entirely of goats' horns (Callimachus, *Hymn to Apollo*, 60 *sqq.* ; Plutarch, *Theseus*, 21 ; *id.*, *De sollertia animalium*, 35). In Naxos he was worshipped under the title of Apollo Tragius, that is, 'Apollo of the he-goats' (Stephanus Byzantius, *s.v.* Τραγαία).

11. 5. The Potidaeans —— and the Syracusans have also treasuries. Remains of these buildings have been identified on the western side of the Sacred Way, between the Theban and Athenian treasuries, the treasury of the Syracusans being next to the Sacred Way and the treasury of the Potidaeans behind it (Th. Homolle, in *Comptes Rendus de l'Académie des Inscriptions*, 22 (1894), p. 584). Mr. Cecil Smith writes to me that the Syracusan treasury perhaps stood at the back of the Athenian, for here in 1895 was found a large block of tufa inscribed with some letters (ΡΑΚΩΣΙΩ) which may have been part of the name Syracusans.

11. 6. The Athenians also built a colonnade etc. Considerable remains of this colonnade were discovered and excavated by Mr. B Haussoullier in 1880. The building stands on the north side of the Sacred Way, higher up than the Treasury of the Athenians, immediately in front of the eastern part of the long polygonal wall that supports the terrace of the temple of Apollo. It is parallel to the polygonal wall which seems to have formed the back-wall of the colonnade. The depth of the colonnade, measuréd from the polygonal wall to the outer edge of the stylobate, is about 3.70 metres (12 ft. 1½ in.). Its length, so far as it was excavated by Mr. Haussoullier, is 24.07 metres (78 ft. 11¼ in.); but Mr. Haussoullier was unable to disengage the eastern end of the building. The base of the most westerly column was found in its original position. It is 0.225 metre high, 0.59 metre in diameter below, and 0.432 in diameter above. Two other bases and two shafts of columns have been found and have been set up, the original positions of the columns being clearly indicated by circular marks on the stylobate. The columns are of the Ionic order with sixteen blunt flutings of the usual sort. The shafts are monoliths measuring 2.85 metres (about 9 ft. 4 in.) in height. One of them was found broken in two, but the pieces have been clamped together. The distance between the columns, measured from centre to centre, is 3.57 metres (about 11 ft. 8½ in.). Seven columns stood originally in front of the excavated portion of the colonnade, and there was probably one more at the eastern end. Thus the colonnade seems to have had eight columns in front and to have been about 100 feet long. It stood on a three-stepped base. These three steps begin about the second column, counted from the west, and extend to the seventh column. Beyond this point eastward the two lower steps appear not to have reached ; for here the pavement of the Sacred Way skirts the colonnade at such a level that only the highest step of the colonnade rises above it. Of the capitals of the columns, the epistyle, and the roof nothing has been found. From the position and size of the columns it has been inferred that the roof was of wood. With regard to the materials of the existing remains, the stylobate and steps are of grey limestone ; the bases of the columns are of Parian marble ; and the shafts of the columns are of Pentelic marble. On the perpendicular face of the highest step is cut in large letters the inscription :

'Αθηναῖοι ἀνέθεσαν τὲν στοὰν καὶ τὰ
Hόπλ[α κ]αὶ τἀκροτέρια Hελόντες τὸν πο[λεμιό]ν.

" The Athenians dedicated the colonnade and the arms and the figureheads which they took from their enemies."

The floor of the colonnade is paved at the back by a row of blocks of stone which runs at the foot of the polygonal wall along the whole length of the colonnade on a level with the stylobate. The breadth of the stones, measured from the polygonal wall to their outer edge, is 1.34 metres (about 4 ft. 4½ in.). Mr. Haussoullier regarded this row of stones as part of the original pavement of the colonnade, and supposed that there had been a second row of slabs between the existing row and the stylobate. Mr. Koldewey with greater probability argues that this row of blocks formed the foundation of a base or pedestal which ran along the whole length of the colonnade, abutting on the back wall. In proof of this he points out, first, that the blocks are about a foot thick, which is too thick for a mere pavement, and, second, that on the back wall at the height of 90 centimetres (about 3 feet) above the stylobate there are traces which seem to show that a structure of some sort abutted on it. For at this height the wall has been smoothed in a horizontal line, as if to facilitate the exact joining of a row of stones; whereas below this line there are irregularities in the surface of the wall, which would have been concealed by a long pedestal such as Mr. Koldewey supposes to have extended along the back of the colonnade. On this pedestal probably stood, as Mr. Koldewey suggests, the shields and figure-heads of ships mentioned in the inscription and by Pausanias. It is no objection to Mr. Koldewey's view that a number of inscriptions, all much later than the colonnade, are carved on the polygonal wall at the back of the colonnade. For the lowest of the inscriptions is 93 centimetres above the level of the stylobate ; hence it is higher than the supposed pedestal and could have been carved on the wall even though the pedestal abutted on the wall below. Pausanias tells us that the inscription enumerated the states from the spoils of which the colonnade was set up. The inscription he refers to, which was clearly not the one that has been found carved on the step of the colonnade, may have been cut on the front of the pedestal.

As to the date and occasion of dedicating the colonnade, Pausanias tells us that it was erected with the produce of spoils taken by the Athenians in the Peloponnesian war (431-404 B.C.), and he connects it specially with the naval victory won in the year 429 B.C. by the Athenian fleet under Phormio over the Peloponnesians in the Gulf of Corinth (Thucydides, ii. 83 *sq.*). This opinion he apparently based on the inscription which enumerated the peoples from whom the spoils were taken, and we need not doubt that he saw the inscription and has given us the list of peoples correctly, though the inscription is now lost and we consequently cannot verify his statement. Now, since all the peoples mentioned in the list were ranged against Athens in the Peloponnesian war, and since moreover the inscription mentioned the name of Phormio and the sacrifice of thanksgiving offered at Cape Rhium, on which we know from Thucydides that the Athenians erected a trophy after the victory of 429 B.C., it becomes highly probable that Pausanias was right in inferring that the trophies to which the inscription referred were a first-fruit of Phormio's naval victory. But was he equally right in affirming that the colonnade itself, as well as these trophies, was dedicated from the spoils of the Peloponnesian war? This has been doubted or denied, and on good grounds. For the existing inscription which records the dedication of the colonnade appears to be considerably older than 429 B.C. This is inferred from the shape of the letters, particularly from the occurrence of the three-stroke *sigma* (ϟ) and the crossed *theta* (⊕) instead of the four-stroke *sigma* (Ϻ) and the dotted *theta* (⊙), for the three-stroke *sigma* seems to have fallen into disuse about the middle of the fifth century B.C. and the crossed *theta* somewhat earlier. Hence Mr. Haussoullier conjectured that the colonnade was erected to commemorate the naval victories won by the Athenians over the Corinthians, Epidaurians, and Aeginetans in or about the years 460-458 B.C. See Thucydides, i. 105 ; Diodorus, xi. 78. His view is shared by Mr. E. L. Hicks and Prof. W. Dittenberger. Prof. U.

Köhler, on epigraphical grounds, would date the inscription and consequently the colonnade still earlier. He thinks that the success commemorated by the colonnade was the naval victory won by the Athenians over the Aeginetans shortly before or after the battle of Marathon (490 B.C.). See Herodotus, vi. 92. Mr. Roehl would date the inscription still earlier, namely in the time of Pisistratus in the sixth century B.C.

If with Messrs. Haussoullier, Hicks, Dittenberger, and Köhler, we assume that the inscription in question and consequently the colonnade belong to the first half of the fifth century B.C., it will follow that the colonnade contained naval trophies of at least two separate wars, namely, (1) the war with the Aeginetans about 490 B.C. or the war with the Corinthians, Epidaurians, and Aeginetans about 459 B.C., and (2) the Peloponnesian war, particularly the victory of Phormio in 429 B.C. The trophies referred to in the dedicatory inscription, which is still to be seen on the upper step of the colonnade, were the first of these trophies; the trophies referred to in the inscription which was seen by Pausanias but is now lost, were the second trophies. Pausanias must certainly have seen the existing, as well as the lost, inscription; but he failed to notice the discrepancy in the style of the two inscriptions, and as both recorded the dedication of naval trophies, he not unnaturally inferred that the success commemorated by both was the same, namely Phormio's victory of 429 B.C. This led him into dating the erection of the colonnade in or soon after that year (429 B.C.), which, on the hypothesis of the scholars mentioned above, is too late by about thirty or sixty years, or even more.

Against this hypothesis the following considerations may be urged: (1) Arguments based on the style of the letters of an inscription are after all uncertain and are liable to be upset by the discovery of new inscriptions. Various circumstances may have caused an old-fashioned style of letter to be kept up by certain masons or in certain places after it had been generally abandoned. (2) The architectural style of the colonnade belongs, as I was informed by my friend the late J. H. Middleton, rather to the second than to the first half of the fifth century B.C. (3) Though possible, it is not very probable that the colonnade contained two duplicate sets of naval trophies (figure-heads and shields) won in totally different wars.

If the argument from the architectural style of the colonnade is allowed to outweigh the argument from the style of the inscription, it will follow that Pausanias was right in dating the erection of the colonnade in 429 B.C. or soon after it, and in referring all the trophies to the Peloponnesian war. But whether the epigraphical or the architectural evidence is more to be trusted, I am not competent to decide.

See B. Haussoullier, 'Fouilles à Delphes,' *Bulletin de Corresp. hellénique*, 5 (1881), pp. 1-25; R. Koldewey, 'Die Halle der Athener zu Delphi,' *Mittheilungen des archäologischen Instituts in Athen*, 9 (1884), pp. 264-270; *id.*, 14 (1889), pp. 205-208; H. Pomtow, *Beiträge zur Topographie von Delphi*, pp. 42-45, 56-63; *Guide-Joanne*, 2. p. 39 *sq.*; U. Köhler, 'Die Halle der Athener in Delphi,' *Rheinisches Museum*, N. F. 46 (1891), pp. 1-8; E. L. Hicks, *Greek Historical*

Inscriptions, No. 20; W. Dittenberger, *Sylloge Inscr. Graec.* No. 4; Roehl, *I. G. A.* No. 3a, p. 169; H. Pomtow, 'Zur Datirung der Halle der Athener zu Delphi,' *Rheinisches Museum*, N. F. 49 (1894), pp. 627-629.

12. 1. **a rock rising above the ground** etc. Plutarch mentions the rock at Delphi on which the first Sibyl was said to have sat and he tells us that it was opposite the Council House (*De Pythiae oraculis*, 9). If Pausanias here follows a strictly topographical order, we should expect to find the Sibyl's rock and the remains of the Council House near the eastern end of the polygonal wall which supported the temple of Apollo, since the Colonnade of the Athenians, which he has just mentioned, ran along in front of the eastern part of that wall. But the whole of the ground here has been cleared, and the monuments with which it is crowded leave no room for such a rock as Pausanias describes. Accordingly the rock and the Council House must be looked for elsewhere. Now between the Treasury of the Athenians and the Colonnade of the Athenians, to the north of the Sacred Way, there is a patch of ground encumbered by rocks, of which the highest rises in a conspicuous mass just beside the road. Clearly these rocks have not fallen from the cliffs above in recent times; they have been there from antiquity. Their surface has been worked with tools, and they seem to have stood in a sort of precinct enclosed by a wall of which vestiges have been found. The high conspicuous rock already mentioned is rent by a rather deep fissure, and its top is accessible by steps hewn in the rock itself. This was probably the rock on which the oldest Sibyl sat and prophesied. It is referred to as 'the rock' (ἁ πέτρα) in an inscription found in the neighbourhood. We may suppose that this patch of rocky ground was the sanctuary of Earth and the Muses mentioned by Plutarch (*De Pythiae oraculis*, 17). Its situation answers perfectly to his description, since it lies immediately to the south of the temple of Apollo. Plutarch says that he and his friends went round the temple of Apollo and "sat down on the southern steps looking towards the sanctuary of Earth and the water." He proceeds to explain "the water" by saying that a spring here came to the surface and that its water used to furnish libations in a sanctuary of the Muses situated beside the spring. Now just here there is a hole in the polygonal wall communicating with a conduit which passed under the temple. This, we may assume, was "the water" mentioned by Plutarch. The oracles of Earth (Paus. x. 5. 5) were no doubt believed to have been delivered in the sanctuary of the goddess, perhaps to have been pronounced by the goddess or her priestess on the Sibyl's Rock. The view that the sanctuary and oracle of Earth lay between the polygonal wall and the Sacred Way is confirmed, as Mr. Homolle points out, by the presence of a colossal figure of a sphinx which occupied the summit of a tall column in this neighbourhood, for the sphinx was a creature associated with prophecy. The shattered remains of the column and sphinx were seen and described by Mr. Foucart more than thirty years ago (*Mémoire sur les ruines et l'histoire de Delphes*, pp. 90-93; cp. J. H. Middleton, in *Journal of Hellenic Studies*, 9 (1888), p. 321 *sq.*), but it was reserved for Mr. Foucart's compatriots a few years ago to put together the fragments and prove that the image of the sphinx, made of white marble and represented sitting with extended wings, smiling a grave mysterious smile, occupied an enormous Ionic capital on the top of a column 7 or 8 metres (23 or 26 feet) high, the image itself being more than 2 metres (6 ft. 6 in.) high. Curiously enough this column, crowned with an Ionic capital, has no less than forty-four sharp-edged flutes of the Doric sort. On it is an inscription recording certain privileges of consulting the oracle accorded to the Naxians by the Delphians (P. Foucart, *Mémoire*, p. 90 ; Wescher-Foucart, *Inscriptions recueillies à Delphes*, No. 466 ; Dittenberger, *Sylloge Inscr. Graec.* No. 328 ; Ch. Michel, *Recueil d'Inscriptions grecques*, No. 257), from which it has been commonly inferred that the sphinx and the column were dedicated by the Naxians. But this inference, though probable, is by no means necessary; for the inscription is much later than the sphinx, being not earlier than the end of the fourth century B.C., while the image of the sphinx is archaic.

See Th. Homolle, in *Bulletin de Corresp. hellénique*, 17 (1893), pp. 613, 619; *id.*, in *Comptes Rendus de l'Académie des Inscriptions*, 22 (1894), pp. 585, 586 ; *id.*, in *Gazette des Beaux-Arts*, Décembre 1894, p. 447 ; H. Pomtow, in *Archäologischer Anzeiger*, 1894, p. 185.

In this neighbourhood above the Treasury of the Athenians are the remains of a building constructed of tufa which Mr. Homolle conjectures to have been the Council House mentioned by Plutarch (*De Pythiae oraculis*, 9). The building, Mr. Cecil Smith tells me, appears to have had no columns. See Th. Homolle, in *Bulletin de Corresp. hellénique*, 18 (1894), p. 184.

Above the sanctuary of Earth, on the left of the Sacred Way, two triangular blocks of marble were found with an inscription referring to the Messenians. It would seem that these and similar blocks of marble discovered at Delphi formed part of a tall triangular pedestal dedicated by the Messenians and Naupactians. The pedestal may have supported a colossal statue of Victory like the one which the same peoples set up on a similar pedestal at Olympia (Paus. v. 26. 1 note). See Th. Homolle, in *Comptes Rendus de l'Académie des Inscriptions*, 22 (1894), p. 585 *sq.* ; H. Pomtow, 'Die dreiseitige Basis der Messenier und Naupaktier zu Delphi,' *Fleckeisen's Jahrbücher*, 42 (1896), pp. 505-536, 577-639, 754-769.

The oracle of Earth was said to have been guarded by the dragon Python, whom Apollo slew (Paus. x. 6. 6). Hence Mr. Homolle conjectures that the dragon had his den in the rifted rock, which formed the Sibyl's seat, and that the sacred drama of the dragon's slaughter was periodically enacted in the adjoining open space in front of the Colonnade of the Athenians (*Bulletin de Corresp. hellénique*, 17 (1893), p. 619 *sq.* ; *Comptes Rendus de l'Académie des Inscriptions*, 22 (1894), p. 585). This conjecture, as we have seen (above, p. 259), is confirmed by the circular shape of the space, resembling a threshing-floor, and by the stone benches by which it is surrounded. Some of these benches were excavated and described by Mr. Haussoullier in 1880 (*Bulletin de Corresp. hellénique*, 5 (1881), pp. 3-5).

12. 1. Herophile, surnamed Sibyl etc.   In the following passage
Pausanias enumerates four Sibyls : (1) the oldest Sibyl, who seems,
according to him, to have been the Libyan Sibyl, but the passage is
defective ; (2) Herophile of Marpessus or Erythrae ; (3) the Cumaean
Sibyl ; (4) the Judaean Sibyl.   Elsewhere, when he has occasion to
refer to the Sibylline oracles, he speaks as if there had been only one
Sibyl.   See ii. 7. 1 ; vii. 8. 8 ; x. 9. 11 *sq.*   Hence it seems not
improbable that the whole of his present disquisition on the Sibyls was
copied by him from some other author.   Prof. E. Maass has argued
ingeniously that Pausanias's authority was Alexander Polyhistor ; but as
Polyhistor is not positively known to have written a work on the Sibyls,
the professor's view is hardly more than a plausible conjecture.   See E.
Maass, *De Sibyllarum Indicibus* (Berlin, 1879).   At first the Greeks
seem to have known of only one Sibyl (Heraclitus, cited by Plutarch,
De Pythiae oraculis, 6 ; Aristophanes, *Peace,* 1095, 1116 ; Plato,
Phaedrus, p. 244 b).   The first writer who is known to have dis-
tinguished several Sibyls is Heraclides Ponticus in his book *On oracles,*
in which he appears to have enumerated at least three, namely the
Phrygian, the Erythraean, and the Hellespontine.   See Clement of
Alexandria, *Strom.* i. 21. 108, p. 384 ed. Potter ; Schol. on Plato,
Phaedrus, p. 244 b ; Lactantius, *Divin. Inst.* i. 6.   Later writers dis-
tinguished many more ; Varro for example gave a list of ten.   See
Lactantius, *l.c.* ; *Oracula Sibyllina,* Prologue ; Isidore, *Origin.* viii. 8 ;
Suidas, *s.v.* Σίβυλλα ; Aelian, *Var. hist.* xii. 12 ; Schol. on Plato,
Phaedrus, p. 244 b.   Prof. Maass (*op. cit.* p. 56 *sqq.*) holds that two
only of the Greek Sibyls were historical, namely Herophile of Erythrae,
and Phyto of Samos ; the former, he thinks, lived in the eighth century
B.C., the latter somewhat later.   As to Phyto the Samian Sibyl, whom
Eratosthenes is said to have found mentioned in the ancient annals of
Samos, see Lactantius *l.c.* ; *Oracula Sibyllina,* Prologue ; Schol. on
Plato, *Phaedrus,* p. 244 b ; Aelian, *Var. hist.* xii. 35 ; Suidas, *s.v.*
Σίβυλλα ; Augustine, *De civ. dei,* xviii. 24 ; Isidore, *Orig.* viii. 8.   As
to the Sibyls, see also R. H. Klausen, *Aeneas und die Penaten,* I. pp.
203-312 ; A. Bouché-Leclercq, *Histoire de la divination,* 2. pp. 133-
214.   On the Sibylline books, see Ewald, 'Ueber die Entstehung,
Inhalt und Werth der sibyllinischen Bücher,' *Abhandlungen d. k.
Gesell. d. Wissen. zu Göttingen,* Histor. phil. Cl. 8 (1858-1859), pp.
43-152.

12. 1. The earlier Sibyl etc.   The mention of the nationality of
this earlier Sibyl seems to have dropped out of Pausanias's text.   See
Critical Note, vol. I. p. 608.   She was probably the Libyan Sibyl.   For
(1) Pausanias says that she was called Sibyl by the Libyans ; and (2)
her mother's name, according to Pausanias, was Lamia.   Now Lamia
was a mythical queen of Libya (Diodorus, xx. 41); and Euripides
mentioned the Libyan Sibyl in the prologue to his play *Lamia.*   See
Lactantius, *Divin. Inst.* i. 6 ; *Oracula Sibyllina,* Prologue ; Schol. on
Plato, *Phaedrus,* p. 244 b ; E. Maass, *De Sibyllarum Indicibus,* p. 6
sqq. ; R. H. Klausen, *Aeneas und die Penaten,* I. p. 207 ; A. Bouché-
Leclercq, *Histoire de la divination,* 2. p. 190 *sqq.*

12. 2. she calls herself —— Artemis. Cp. Suidas, *s.v.* Σίβυλλα.
12. 2. his daughter. According to some, the Sibyl was a daughter of Apollo and Lamia (Suidas, *s.v.* Σίβυλλα).

12. 3. my fatherland was red Marpessus. The lists of the Sibyls mention a Hellespontine Sibyl, a native of Marpessus. According to Heraclides Ponticus she was a contemporary of Solon and Cyrus. See Lactantius, *Divin. Inst.* i. 6; Suidas, *s.v.* Σίβυλλα; *Oracula Sibyllina*, Prologue; Schol. on Plato, *Phaedrus*, p. 244 b; Isidore, *Orig.* viii. 8. But the Hellespontine Sibyl was never so famous as the Erythraean Sibyl; and from the present passage of Pausanias it would seem that the people of Marpessus or their literary partisans endeavoured to appropriate the more famous Erythraean Sibyl by showing that her epithet 'Erythraean' was derived, not from the rival town of Erythrae, but from the red (*erythre*) soil of Marpessus. Prof. E. Maass has ingeniously suggested that the last of the four verses here quoted by Pausanias was forged in support of the claim of Marpessus against Erythrae by the unscrupulous writer Demetrius of Scepsis, who seems to have distorted more than one Greek tradition for the purpose of glorifying his native Troad. If we omit the last of the four verses, the statement as to the birth-place of the Sibyl will run thus :

" By my mother's side I am Ida-born, but my fatherland was Erythre,"

where Erythre is equivalent to Erythrae. And this was the way in which the people of Erythrae actually quoted the passage, omitting the last verse (see below §·7). If Prof. Maass's theory is correct (and it is certainly plausible) Polyhistor copied from Demetrius of Scepsis, and Pausanias copied from Polyhistor. See E. Maass, *De Sibyllarum Indicibus*, p. 22 *sqq.* As to Demetrius of Scepsis, see R. Gaede, *Demetrii Scepsii quae supersunt* (Greisswald, 1880); K. Tümpel, in *Philologus*, 49 (1890), p. 91 *sqq.* On the other hand Mr. Bouché-Leclercq thinks that the claim of Marpessus to be the home of the Sibyl was better founded than that of Erythrae (*Histoire de la divination*, 2. pp. 153 *sqq.*, 170 *sqq.*).

12. 5. the temple of Sminthian Apollo. As to the sanctuary of Sminthian Apollo, see Strabo, xiii. pp. 604 *sqq.*, 612. The remains of the temple were discovered by Captain (afterwards Admiral) Spratt in 1853, and the site was excavated by Mr. W. Pullan for the Dilettanti Society in 1866. The ruins are situated near the sea-shore, 12 geographical miles south of the ruins of Alexandria Troas, and 4 geographical miles north-east of Cape Lectum. The temple was of the Ionic order with eight columns at the ends and fourteen at the sides. It seems to have been built in a period of good, but not of the finest art. See *Antiquities of Ionia*, Part the Fourth (London, 1881), pp. 40-48, with plates xxvi.-xxx.; Captain Spratt, 'On the site of the temple of Apollo Smintheus,' *Transactions of the Royal Society of Literature*, Second Series, 5 (1856), pp. 236-242. Sminthian Apollo is equivalent to Mouse-Apollo, *sminthos* being one form of the Greek word for 'mouse.' Tame mice were kept and fed in the sanctuary of Sminthian Apollo; white mice lived under the altar. There was an image of a mouse beside the tripod; and the foot of the statue of the god rested on a mouse. See Strabo, xiii. pp. 604 *sq.*, 612 *sq.*; Aelian, *Nat. an.* xii. 5; Clement of Alexandria, *Protrept.* ii. 39, p. 34 ed. Potter; J. de Witte, 'Apollon Sminthien,' *Revue Numismatique*, N. S. 3 (1858), pp. 1-51. At a place called *Lisgyar* near Alexandria Troas a small bronze mouse has been found; it was probably a votive offering to the Sminthian Apollo (Sir C. Newton, *Travels and Discoveries in the Levant*, 1. p. 130). On a Carthaginian monument two mice are represented, one on each side of a human hand; Mr. Berger thought it might be a votive offering to Tanit (*Gazette archéologique*, 3 (1877), pp. 25, 75). Mr. Andrew Lang holds that the mouse in the worship of Sminthian Apollo is a survival of a mouse-totem (*Custom and Myth*, p. 103 *sqq.*). It is perhaps more probable that the worship of the mouse, or rather of a few selected mice, especially white mice, was intended to propitiate the mice in general and induce them not to ravage the corn-fields. This view is more in consonance with the classical traditions (Aelian, *Hist. an.* xii. 5; Polemo, cited by a scholiast on Homer, *Il.* i. 39; Eustathius on Homer, *l.c.* p. 34), and is supported by modern analogies (*The Golden Bough*, 2. p. 129 *sqq.*). As to the destructive ravages of mice, see Aristotle, *Hist. an.* vi. 37, p. 580 b 15 *sqq.*; Aelian, *Hist. an.* xvii. 41. In the spring of 1892 a plague of field mice threatened to destroy the whole harvest in Thessaly. See Mr. W. Warde Fowler, in *The Classical Review*, 6 (1892), p. 413, who takes the same view of Sminthian Apollo as the present writer. Compare note on v. 14. 1; H. Usener, *Götternamen*, pp. 260-263; A. Lang, *Modern Mythology* (London, 1897), p. 81 *sq.* Apollonius of Tyana is said to have rid Antioch of scorpions by making a bronze image of a scorpion and burying it under a small pillar in the middle of the city (Malala, *Chronographia*, p. 264 ed. Dindorf).

12. 5. Hecuba's dream. Hecuba, when she was pregnant with Paris, dreamed she had brought forth a fiery torch which burned the city. The soothsayers, being consulted, foretold that the child would prove the ruin of his country. See Apollodorus, iii. 12. 5; Schol. on Euripides, *Andromache*, 293; Cicero, *De divinatione*, i. 21. 42; Hyginus, *Fab.* 91.

12. 5. This Sibyl dwelt most of her life in Samos. Samos appears to have had a Sibyl of its own. See note on § 1.

12. 5. she also came —— to Delphi. Delphi, like Samos, is said to have had a Sibyl of its own. See E. Maass, *De Sibyllarum Indicibus*, p. 9 *sq.*; A. Bouché-Leclercq, *Histoire de la divination*, 2. p. 179 *sqq.*

12. 6. her tomb is in the grove of the Sminthian god. According to Stephanus Byzantius (*s.v.* Γέργις) the Sibyl's grave was in the sanctuary of the Gargithian Apollo, at Gergis or Gergithium, a city in the Troad near Marpessus, the Sibyl's birth-place. Compare *Oracula Sibyllina*, Prologue; Lactantius, *Divin. Inst.* i. 6; Schol. on Plato, *Phaedrus*, p. 244 b.

12. 7. The Erythraeans —— urge their claim to Herophile. Herophile the Sibyl is called an Erythraean by Plutarch (*De Pythiae* *oraculis*, 14) and Clement of Alexandria (*Strom.* i. 21. 108, p. 384 ed. Potter). The Erythraean Sibyl was the most famous of all the Sibyls ; hence when the temple of Jupiter on the Capitol at Rome was restored after its destruction by fire in 83 B.C., ambassadors were despatched to Erythrae, who brought back about a thousand Sibylline verses (Lactantius, *Divin. Inst.* i. 6).

12. 7. a cave in it. At *Lythri*, the wretched village which stands among the ruins of the ancient Erythrae, the cave of the Erythraean Sibyl was discovered in the summer of 1891. The place is at the eastern foot of the high mountain which formed the acropolis of Erythrae. The cave is close to the road, on the left-hand side as you approach the village from the south. An ancient aqueduct, now dry, leads from the back of the cavern. That this is really the Sibyl's cave appears from inscriptions found in it. Amongst them is one : Ἀγαθῆι τύχη (*sic*). [Σίβυλ]λα νύμφης καὶ Θεοδώρου [Ἐ]ρυθραία. "With good luck. The Erythraean Sibyl, daughter of a nymph and Theodorus." This confirms Pausanias's statement that the Erythraean Sibyl was said to be a daughter of a shepherd Theodorus by a nymph. The same genealogy is given in a metrical inscription found in the cave, of which the following is a translation : " I am the oracular Sibyl, the minister of Phoebus, eldest daughter of a Naiad nymph. My native land is Erythrae alone and no other, and Theodorus was my mortal sire. Cissotas was my birth-place, in which I uttered oracles to mankind as soon as I had issued from the womb. And seated on this rock I sang to mortal men prophecies of events which were yet to come. And living thrice three hundred years as an unwedded maid, I travelled over all the earth ; and here again beside this dear rock I now sit delighting in the kindly waters. And I rejoice that the time has now come true to me in which I said that Erythrae would flourish again, and would enjoy all good government and wealth and virtue, when a new Erythrus should have come to his dear native land." Here Cissotas seems to have been some place, perhaps a brook, in the territory of Erythrae. The emphasis laid on the statement that Erythrae alone was the birth-place of the Sibyl, clearly alludes to the rival claims set up by other places, such as Marpessus. The "new Erythrus " (*i.e.* the new founder of Erythrae, see vii. 3. 7) is probably the emperor Lucius Aurelius Verus, who seems to have visited Eleutherae. For an inscription found in the cave commemorates the dedication of the spring of water to Marcus Aurelius Antoninus and Lucius Aurelius Verus; and Verus is known to have visited the famous maritime cities of Asia Minor (Capitolinus, *Verus*, vi. 9). See K. Buresch, ' Die sibyllinische Quellgrotte in Erythrae,' *Mittheilungen des arch. Instituts in Athen*, 17 (1892), pp. 16-36 ; *Bulletin de Corresp. hellénique*, 15 (1891), p. 682 *sq.*

12. 8. the historian Hyperochus of Cumae. A history of Cumae passed under the name of Hyperochus, but some doubt was entertained as to its authorship (Athenaeus, xiii. p. 528 d). Cp. Festus, p. 266 ed. Müller ; *Frag. hist. Graec.* 4. p. 434 *sq.* ed. Müller.

12. 8. Demo. The name of the Sibyl of Cumae is variously given as

Amalthea, Demophile, Herophile, and Taraxandra. See Varro, cited by Lactantius, *Divin. Inst.* i. 6; *Oracula Sibyllina*, Prologue; Schol. on Plato, *Phaedrus*, p. 244 b. Virgil (*Aen.* vi. 36) calls her Deiphobe, daughter of Glaucus. She seems to have been commonly identified with Herophile, the Sibyl of Erythrae or Marpessus. See A. Bouché-Leclercq, *Histoire de la divination*, 2. p. 184.

12. 8. The Cumaeans have no oracle of hers to produce. After enumerating the ten Sibyls, Varro (cited by Lactantius, *Divin. Inst.* i. 6) says : " The verses of all these Sibyls are preserved and are handed about, except those of the Cumaean Sibyl ; for her books are concealed by the Romans and may not be inspected by any one except the Fifteen Men." The author of the *Exhortation to the Greeks*, which passes under the name of Justin Martyr, professes to have visited the Sibyl's cave at Cumae and to have been told by his guides that the oracles used to be taken down from the Sibyl's lips by uneducated persons and that this was the reason why some of the oracles were unmetrical. See Justin Martyr, *Cohort. ad Graecos*, 37. p. 34 c d (ed. 1742). Hence Prof. Maass has inferred that, in spite of the statements of Varro and Pausanias, oracles of the Sibyl must have been current (*De Sibyllarum Indicibus*, p. 11).

12. 8. a small stone urn in a sanctuary of Apollo etc. The author of the *Exhortation to the Greeks* was shown at Cumae a bronze bottle in which the remains of the Sibyl were said to be preserved (Justin Martyr, *Cohort. ad Graecos*, 37. p. 34 c, ed. 1742). Trimalchio in Petronius (*Sat.* 48) says : " At Cumae I saw with my own eyes the Sibyl hanging in a jar, and when the children said to her, ' Sibyl, what do you wish ?' she used to answer, ' I wish to die.'" Ampelius tells us (*Liber Memorialis*, viii. 16) that the Sibyl was said to be shut up in an iron cage which hung from a pillar in an ancient temple of Hercules at Argyrus. Cp. H. Diels, *Sibyllinische Blätter*, p. 57 note 1. It has been pointed out by Dr. M. R. James (*Classical Review*, 6 (1892), p. 74) that parallels to the story of the Sibyl's wish are to be found in German folk-tales. One of these tales runs as follows : " Once upon a time there was a girl in London who wished to live for ever, so they say :

> London, London is a fine town.
> A maiden prayed to live for ever.

And still she lives and hangs in a basket in a church, and every St. John's Day about noon she eats a roll of bread " (Kuhn und Schwartz, *Norddeutsche Sagen, Märchen und Gebräuche*, p. 70, No. 72. 1). Another story of the same collection (p. 70 *sq.*) tells of a lady who resided at Danzig and was so rich and so blest with all that life can give that she wished to live always. So when she came to her latter end, she did not really die but only looked like dead, and very soon they found her in a hollow of a pillar in the church, half standing and half sitting, motionless. She stirred never a limb, but they saw quite plainly that she was alive, and she sits there down to this blessed day. Every New Year's Day the sacristan comes and puts a morsel of the holy bread in her mouth, and that is all she has to live on. Long, long has she rued her fatal wish who set this transient life above the eternal joys of heaven. A third story in the same collection (p. 71) tells of a noble damsel who cherished the same foolish wish for immortality. So they put her in a basket and hung her up in a church, and there she hangs and never dies, though many, many a year has come and gone since they put her there. But every year on a certain day they give her a roll and she eats it and cries out "For ever! for ever! for ever!" And when she has so cried she falls silent again till the same time next year, and so it will go on for ever and for ever. A fourth story, taken down near Oldenburg in Holstein, tells of a jolly dame that ate and drank and lived right merrily and had all that heart could desire, and she wished to live always. For the first hundred years all went well, but after that she began to shrink and shrivel up till at last she could neither walk nor stand nor eat nor drink. But die she could not. At first they fed her as if she were a little child, but when she grew smaller and smaller they put her in a glass bottle and hung her up in the church. And there she still hangs, in the church of St. Mary at Lübeck. She is as small as a mouse, but once a year she stirs. See K. Müllenhoff, *Sagen, Märchen und Lieder*, p. 158 *sq.*, No. 217.

12. 9. **a prophetess —— Sabbe.** The name of the Judaean Sibyl is also given as Sambethe. Others regarded her as a Chaldaean or Persian Sibyl. It is said that she was the wife of one of the sons of Noah, entered with him into the ark, and predicted the building of the tower of Babel. She was mentioned by Nicanor, author of a life of Alexander. See Schol. on Plato, *Phaedrus*, p. 244 b; Suidas, *s.v.* Σίβυλλα; *Oracula Sibyllina*, Prologue. Her father, according to the author of the *Exhortation to the Greeks*, was Berosus, the Chaldaean historian (Justin Martyr, *Cohort. ad Graecos*, 37. p. 33 d, ed. 1742). See E. Maass, *De Sibyllarum Indicibus*, p. 13 *sqq.*; A. Bouché-Leclercq, *Histoire de la divination*, 2. p. 192 *sqq.*

12. 10. **Phaennis.** Cp. x. 15. 2; A. Bouché-Leclercq, *Histoire de la divination*, 2. p. 183. Pausanias here tells us that Phaennis was born when Antiochus Soter came to the throne after the capture of Demetrius Poliorcetes. Demetrius was captured by Seleucus in 286 B.C., and when Seleucus was murdered in 281 or 280 B.C., his son Antiochus succeeded him. See Plutarch, *Demetrius*, 49 *sq.*; Appian, *Syriac.* 62 *sq.*; Thirlwall, *Hist. of Greece*, 8. pp. 42, 51. Hence Phaennis would appear to have been born in 281 or 280 B.C. The capture of Demetrius by Seleucus has been mentioned by Pausanias before (i. 10. 2).

12. 10. **the Peleae ('doves') at Dodona.** See vii. 21. 2 note.

12. 10. **Phemonoe.** See x. 5. 7; x. 6. 7.

12. 10. **mother Earth.** The conception of Earth as the great Mother occurs in many mythologies. See E. B. Tylor, *Primitive Culture*,[2] 1. p. 326 *sqq.*

12. 11. **Euclus —— Musaeus —— Lycus —— Bacis.** See Index *s.vv.* and A. Bouché-Leclercq, *Histoire de la divination*, 2. p. 102 *sqq.*

13. 1. **a bison or Paeonian bull.** The bison (*Bison bonassus*) is

described by Oppian (*Cyneg.* ii. 159-175), who derives the name from Bistonis, a district in Thrace, where the animal was found. Pliny (*Nat. hist.* viii. 38) rightly distinguishes the bison from the *urus*, an extinct species of ox akin to the wild cattle which are still preserved at Chillingham in Northumberland. Caesar (*Bell. Gall.* vi. 28) describes the *urus* but not the bison. Formerly the bison ranged over Europe, as is proved by its fossil remains which have been found both on the Continent and in England along with bones of the extinct mammoth and rhinoceros. It is described by early writers in modern times. Erasmus Stella says that in his time the animal was very scarce in Prussia ('De Borussiae Antiquitatibus,' in *Novus Orbis regionum ac insularum veteribus incognitarum* (Paris, 1532), p. 507, wrongly numbered 497). Another early writer, Raphael Volaterranus, describes the mode of catching the bison practised by the Lithuanians. He says : "They hunt bears and bisons, which nearly resemble wild cattle. To avoid the danger of the chase they observe this method. They enclose a haunt of the bisons with a fence, leaving only one opening which leads to the bottom of a valley. This opening is purposely made greasy and slippery, and the beasts slip down it to the bottom of the valley. There, after being weakened and tamed by hunger for several days, they are easily caught" (*Commentarii Urbani* (ed. 1603), p. 250). Thus the method of catching the bisons described by Pausanias seems to have been practised in Lithuania as late as the sixteenth century (an edition of Volaterranus's work was published in 1559), unless we suppose that Volaterranus simply copied from Pausanias. On the *urus* and bison, see also Olaus Magnus, xviii. 35 *sq.* A few hundred bisons are still preserved in the forests of Lithuania, but they are gradually dying out. A good many years ago they numbered 1000, but in 1872 they had diminished to 528. They are protected by the Czar ; none of them may be killed without a written permission from him, signed with his own hand. See *Encyclopaedia Britannica*, 9th ed. *s.v.* 'Bison,' vol. 3. p. 792 ; Elton, *Origins of English History*, p. 58 *sqq.* (first ed.).

13. 1. **Dropion, king of the Paeonians, son of Leon.** Part of a pedestal which had supported a statue of this king was found in 1877 by the Germans to the north-east of the temple of Zeus at Olympia. The stone is a block of yellow sandstone and bears the following inscription in large letters :

[Δρω]πίωνα Λέοντος
[βα]σιλέα Παιόνων
[κ]αὶ κτίστην τὸ κοινὸν
τῶν Παιόνων ἀνέθηκε[ν]
ἀρετῆς ἕνεκεν
καὶ εὐνοίας τῆς εἰς αὐτούς.

" This statue of Dropion, son of Leon, king of the Paeonians, and their founder, was dedicated by the community of the Paeonians on account of his virtue and kindness to them." See Dittenberger und Purgold, *Die Inschriften von Olympia*, No. 303 ; *Archäologische Zeitung*, 35 (1877), p. 38, No. 37. Dropion is known only from this inscription and the present passage of Pausanias.

13. 4. offerings of the Phocians. The inscription on offerings which the Phocians dedicated out of spoil taken from the Thessalians is mentioned by Plutarch (*De Pythiae oraculis*, 15). Cp. below, § 6.

13. 4. whose territory marches with their own. The district of Malis, which intervened between Phocis and Thessaly proper, was reckoned to the latter. See Strabo, ix. p. 429.

13. 5. the statue of Apollo grasping the deer. On some ancient gems Apollo is represented standing with a bow in his left hand and grasping in his right the fore-feet of a stag which is rearing beside him. This may have been the pose of the statue here mentioned by Pausanias. See Müller-Wieseler, *Denkmäler*, i. pl. xv. No. 61; Cecil Smith, in *Proceedings of the Society of Antiquaries of London*, Second Series, 11 (1885-1887), pp. 251-255. But on five ancient vases Hercules is depicted carrying off a deer or stag, while Apollo seeks to hinder him by grasping the animal's hind feet. On two of these vases we see Hercules carrying off the deer or stag in his arms, and brandishing his club against Apollo, who has laid hold of the deer by its feet : Athena and Artemis are interposing to assist or separate the combatants. The combat between Apollo and Hercules for the stag is represented also in relief on a bronze Etruscan helmet found at Vulci ; but here the stag appears lying on the ground, while Apollo and Hercules are fighting over it, the former shooting an arrow, the latter brandishing his club. Perhaps these scenes refer to the story mentioned by Apollodorus (ii. 5. 3) that when Hercules was carrying the Cerynitian deer on his shoulders to Mycenae, he met Artemis and Apollo, the former of whom took the deer from him and reproached him for slaying her sacred animal. But from the resemblance of the scenes to those in which the struggle between Hercules and Apollo for the possession of the Delphic tripod is depicted (see below, § 7 note), it is perhaps more probable that they refer to a parallel Delphic legend of an attempt made by Hercules to carry off a stag or deer belonging to Apollo, although no such Delphic legend is mentioned in ancient books. See O. Jahn, *Archäologische Beiträge*, p. 224 *sqq.*; F. G. Welcker, *Alte Denkmäler*, 3. p. 269 *sqq.*, note 2 ; Overbeck, *Griechische Kunstmythologie*, Besonderer Theil, 3. pp. 415-418.

13. 5. The Greeks of Cyrene —— dedicated the chariot etc. At the head of the Sacred Way, to the east of the temple of Apollo, two life-size figures of horses have been found by the French. They are archaic in style, and the marks of harness prove that they were attached to a chariot. Mr. Homolle conjectures that they may have formed part of one of two Cyrenian offerings mentioned by Pausanias (here and x. 15. 6). In this neighbourhood, also, there have come to light a number of fragments of columns carved like stalks of silphium. They may, as Mr. Homolle suggests, have belonged to a treasury dedicated by the Cyrenians. See *Bulletin de Corresp. hellénique*, 18 (1894), p. 180 ; *Comptes Rendus de l'Académie des Beaux-Arts*, 22 (1894), p. 303 *sq.*

13. 5. The Dorians of Corinth also built a treasury. The remains of this treasury, Mr. Cecil Smith tells me, have been found on the right of the Sacred Way, to the north-east of the great altar (see x.

14. 7 note), near the bases which supported statues of the sons of Dinomenes (see below). The treasury was built by Cypselus, tyrant of
Corinth, but after the tyranny had been put down the Corinthians asked
and obtained leave to erase the name of Cypselus from the dedicatory
inscription and to substitute that of Corinth (Herodotus, i. 14; Plutarch,
Septem Sapient. Conviv. 21; *id., De Pythiae oraculis,* 13). In the
time of Herodotus the treasury contained the following votive offerings:
(1) six golden bowls weighing thirty talents, dedicated by Gyges,
king of Lydia (Herodotus, i. 14); (2) the royal chair of Midas,
king of Phrygia, in which he used to sit judging the people; it
was dedicated by king Midas himself (Herodotus, i. 14); (3) a
lion of fine gold, weighing six and a half talents, dedicated by
Croesus, king of Lydia; it stood originally in the temple of Apollo
and had weighed ten talents, but in the fire which destroyed the temple
the lion's weight was reduced by three and a half talents (Herodotus, i.
50); (4) four silver jars, also dedicated by Croesus (Herodotus, i. 51);
(5) a fine censer, dedicated by Euelthon, tyrant of Salamis (Herodotus,
iv. 162). The golden lion dedicated by Croesus may have been the
one which Phayllus melted down and minted to pay his troops
(Diodorus, xvi. 56). In Plutarch's time the solitary offering left in this
once resplendent treasury was a bronze palm-tree with frogs and water-
snakes worked in relief at the root (Plutarch, *De Pythiae oraculis,* 12).

Besides the treasuries mentioned by Pausanias we know from ancient
writers that others existed at Delphi. (1) There was a treasury of the
Acanthians which bore the inscription Βρασίδας καὶ ᾿Ακάνθιοι ἀπ᾿
᾿Αθηναίων "(Dedicated by) Brasidas and the Acanthians (out of
spoils taken) from the Athenians." Inside the treasury, beside the
door, stood a stone statue of Lysander, representing him with long hair
and flowing beard. Some people, misled by the inscription on the
building, mistook this statue for a portrait of Brasidas. See Plutarch,
Lysander, 1; *id., De Pythiae oraculis,* 14 and 15. This treasury must
have stood towards the east end of the temple of Apollo; for near it
the guide pointed out to Plutarch the place where the iron spits,
dedicated by the harlot Rhodopis as a tithe of her earnings, were
formerly to be seen (Plutarch, *De Pythiae oraculis,* 14), and we know
from Herodotus (ii. 135) that these spits were heaped up opposite the
temple, behind the altar of the Chians (see note on x. 14. 7). (2) The
Clazomenians had a treasury which in the time of Herodotus contained a golden bowl weighing eight and a half talents and twelve
minae. The bowl was an offering of Croesus and had stood originally
in the temple of Apollo, on the right-hand side as you entered, but
when the temple was burnt the bowl was removed to the Clazomenian
treasury. See Herodotus, i. 51. (3 and 4) Treasuries dedicated by
Gyges and Croesus and bearing their names inscribed on them are
mentioned by Strabo (ix. p. 421). (5) The Massiliots had a treasury
in which the Romans dedicated a golden bowl as a trophy of the
conquest of Veii (Diodorus, xiv. 93). (6) There was a treasury
dedicated by the people of Spina, a Greek city on the Adriatic (Strabo,
v. p. 214, ix. p. 421; Pliny, *Nat. hist.* iii. 120). The Delphic

offerings of the people of Spina are said to have been very splendid (Dionysius Halicarnassensis, *Antiquit. Rom.* i. 18). It seems that their treasury contained two stone statues of boys which were mentioned by the antiquary Polemo (Athenaeus, xiii. p. 606 a b, where the reading Σπινατῶν is a correction of Meineke's, the MSS. reading πινάκων; Polemo, ed. Preller, Frag. 28). (7) Lastly, the wealthy and luxurious Sybarites had, as might have been expected, a treasury at Delphi (Strabo, ix. p. 421).

It may be conjectured that some of the treasuries which Pausanias fails to mention may have stood in the western part of the sacred precinct, between the Treasury of the Athenians and the boundary-wall; for this part of the sanctuary would seem to have been left unvisited, or at least undescribed, by our author.

13. 6. **bronze images dedicated by the Phocians** etc. See x. 1. 10.

13. 6. **The Phliasians —— a bronze Zeus —— an image of Aegina.** Images of Zeus and Aegina were dedicated by the Phliasians also at Olympia (v. 22. 6). The offerings were appropriate, since Aegina was said to be a daughter of Asopus, the river which flowed beside Phlius, and to have been carried off from Phlius by Zeus. See ii. 5. 1 *sq.*, ii. 29. 2; Diodorus, iv. 72.

13. 7. **Hercules and Apollo, both grasping the tripod** etc. The same subject was represented in relief at Lycosura (viii. 37. 1) and in the gable of the Siphnian treasury at Delphi (above, p. 274 *sq.*). The attempt of Hercules to carry off the Delphic tripod is often mentioned by ancient writers and is the subject of many surviving works of ancient art, especially vase-paintings. The legend, according to Apollodorus, was this. Hercules in a fit of madness had murdered Iphitus by hurling him from the walls of Tiryns. As a punishment he was afflicted with a grievous illness and went to Delphi to enquire how he might be healed. The priestess refusing to answer him, Hercules attempted to rifle the temple, and carrying off the tripod he set up an oracle of his own. Apollo fought him, but Zeus parted the combatants by throwing a thunderbolt between them. Then Hercules was told by the oracle that if he would be healed, he must first be sold into slavery for three years and pay compensation to Eurytus, the father of the murdered Iphitus. See Apollodorus, ii. 6. 2. Cp. Schol. on Pindar, *Ol.* ix. 43; Hyginus, *Fab.* 32; Servius on Virgil, *Aen.* viii. 300; Cicero, *De nat. deor.* iii. 16. 42; Plutarch, *De EI apud Delphos*, 6; *id., De sera numinis vindicta,* 12. The myth has been variously interpreted. Panofka saw in it two solar deities quarrelling about the fire. E. Curtius explained it as a reminiscence of a conflict at Delphi between the Semitic religion (represented by Hercules) and the Greek religion (represented by Apollo). Stephani regarded it as a popular reminiscence of a refusal on the part of the Delphic oracle to give answers to the worshippers of Hercules. He enumerates no less than 89 existing works of ancient art on which the subject of the contest is depicted. They include 58 black-figured vases; 18 red-figured vases; 8 marble reliefs; 3 terra-cottas; and 2 engraved gems. Overbeck has added somewhat to the list. On most of these works Hercules is represented

carrying off the tripod and looking back at Apollo who hastens after him and seeks to wrest the tripod from him. But on some six or seven of the works enumerated, as in the group of statuary here described by Pausanias, Apollo and Hercules stand on either side of the tripod, each of them striving to pull it to himself. Further on many of the works enumerated, as in the two Delphic groups, Apollo and Hercules are associated with other deities; most commonly Hercules is accompanied by Athena and Apollo by Artemis.

See Panofka, 'L'enlèvement du trépied,' *Annali dell' Instituto,* 2 (1830), pp. 203-209; F. G. Welcker, *Alte Denkmäler,* 2. pp. 296-301, Taf. xiv. 27, 28, 29; *id.,* 3. pp. 268-285; *Archäologische Zeitung,* 16 (1858), Taf. cxi. ; E. Curtius, 'Herakles der Dreifussträger,' *Archäologische Zeitung,* 25 (1867), pp. 105-110, with Taf. ccxxvii. ; *id., Gesammelte Abhandlungen,* 2. pp. 215-234 ; Stephani, in *Compte Rendu* (St. Petersburg) for 1868, p. 31 *sqq.,* with Atlas, Taf. i. fig. 4; Klein, in *Annali dell' Instituto,* 53 (1881), p. 77 *sqq.* ; Müller-Wieseler, *Denkmäler,* i. pl. xi. No. 41; Baumeister's *Denkmäler,* 1. p. 463 *sq.* ; S. Reinach, *Peintures de Vases antiques,* Millingen, 30; Roscher's *Lexikon,* 1. p. 2232 *sq.* ; L. Preller, *Griechische Mythologie,*³ 2. pp. 162-164; Overbeck, *Griechische Kunstmythologie,* Besonderer Theil, 3. pp. 391-415.

The scenes in which Hercules appears striving to carry off the tripod while Apollo attempts forcibly to hinder him, are to be distinguished from the scenes in which Hercules appears carrying off the tripod peaceably without any opposition on the part of Apollo. See, *e.g.,* the relief figured in Welcker's *Alte Denkmäler,* 2. Taf. xv. 27, where Hercules bears away the tripod while Apollo sits calmly with his lyre on his knee looking after him. Curtius and Stephani (*ll.cc.*) think that such scenes refer to a custom of setting up a tripod in every town founded with the sanction of Delphi. See Paus. i. 43. 8; iii. 21. 8; and viii. 15. 5 compared with Plutarch, *De sera numinis vindicta,* 12.

13. 7. when Tellias the Elean led them etc. See x. 1. 8-11.

13. 7. Chionis. Vitruvius mentions (iii. Praef. 2) a Corinthian sculptor Chion, who is perhaps the same with the Chionis of Pausanias.

13. 8. So Hercules of Tiryns is a different person etc. The saying "This is a different Hercules" was proverbial and variously explained. See Zenobius, v. 48; Diogenianus, i. 63; Apostolius, ii. 40; Plutarch, *Theseus,* 29; Aelian, *Var. hist.* xii. 22; Schol. on Lucian, *Quomodo hist. conscrib.* 34; Ptolemaeus Hephaest., in Photius, *Bibliotheca,* p. 151 a 35 *sqq.,* ed. Bekker; Eustathius on Homer, *Iliad,* v. 638, p. 589. 41 *sqq.* ; [Aristotle,] *Ethic. Magn.* ii. 15, p. 1213 a 12 *sq.,* ed. Bekker; [*id.,*] *Ethic. Eudem.* vii. 12, p. 1245 a 30, ed. Bekker. Cp. note on x. 17. 2.

13. 8. the Egyptian Hercules. There was a sanctuary of Hercules at Heracleum, a town in the Delta of the Nile. It possessed the right of asylum; if a runaway slave took refuge in it and allowed himself to be tattooed or branded with certain sacred marks, he might not be touched. See Herodotus, ii. 113; Strabo, xvii. pp. 788, 801. The native Egyptian name of Heracleum was *Karba,* and the chief temple was dedicated to Ammon. But the Egyptian monuments seem to throw no light on the question who the god at Heracleum (*Karba*) was whom the Greeks identified with Hercules. Prof. Sayce thought he was the Tyrian Hercules, that is Melcart.   But this is positively denied by Prof. Wiedemann.   See the notes of Sayce and Wiedemann on Herodotus, *l.c.*   Cicero mentions an Egyptian Hercules, born of the Nile (*De natura deorum*, iii. 16. 42).   According to the *Etymol. Magnum* (*s.v.* Χῶνες, p. 816. 28 *sq.*) the native Egyptian name for Hercules was Chōn; according to Hesychius (*s.v.* Γιγνῶν) it was Gignōn or Gigōn.   See Parthey, in his edition of Plutarch's *Isis and Osiris*, p. 210 *sq.*   Diodorus (i. 74) relates a Libyan tradition that there were three heroes called Hercules, of whom the most ancient was the Egyptian : he conquered a great part of the world and set up the Pillar of Hercules on the African shore ; whereas the Pillar of Hercules on the Spanish shore (Gibraltar) was set up by the Greek Hercules (the son of Zeus and Alcmena), who was the youngest of the three.

13. 9. **a golden tripod resting on a bronze serpent** etc.   A base which is believed to have supported this famous trophy has been found by the French at the highest part of the Sacred Way, to the east of the temple of Apollo.   It is next above the pedestal of Gelo (see below, p. 310).   The bronze serpent on which the tripod rested is still to be seen in the *Almeidan*, the ancient Hippodrome, at Constantinople, whither it was transferred by Constantine.   The monument consists really, not of a single bronze serpent, but of three such serpents so skilfully intertwined that their bodies appear as a single spiral column, and a very attentive examination is necessary to convince an observer that there are actually three serpents, not one.   Hence ancient writers (Herodotus and Pausanias) and some modern travellers have fallen into the very natural mistake of speaking of it as a single serpent.   The history of the monument seems to have been as follows.

After the battle of Plataea and the capture of the Persian camp orders were issued by Pausanias, the general of the Greek army, that no man should presume to appropriate any part of the booty but that the whole of it should be brought together into one common heap.   So an immense quantity of gold and silver plate and ornaments was collected from the Persian camp and the bodies of the slain.   Out of this booty tithes were first of all set apart for the Delphic Apollo, the Olympic Zeus, and the Isthmian Poseidon.   Out of the tithe reserved for the Delphic Apollo was made what Herodotus describes as "the golden tripod that stands close to the altar, resting on the three-headed serpent."   Out of the tithe reserved for the Olympic Zeus was made a bronze statue of Zeus 12 ells high.   Out of the tithe reserved for the Isthmian Poseidon was made a bronze statue of Poseidon 7 ells high. The rest of the booty was divided as prize-money among the Greeks. See Herodotus, ix. 80 *sq.* ; and as to the bronze statue of Zeus at Olympia, see Paus. v. 23. 1 *sq.*   Thus it appears that both the golden tripod at Delphi and the bronze Zeus at Olympia were trophies, not of the Persian war in general, but of the battle of Plataea in particular, and Pausanias is perfectly right in so describing them.

On the golden tripod, or more probably on the stone pedestal which supported both it and the serpent-column, the Spartan general Pausanias caused an epigram to be inscribed to the following effect :

"Pausanias, as general of the Greeks, after he had destroyed the army of the Medes, dedicated this monument to Phoebus."

This arrogant inscription, composed by the poet Simonides, roused the indignation of the Greeks ; the Plataeans complained to the Amphictyonic Council, and the Lacedaemonians were compelled to erase the inscription. Instead of it they inscribed upon the serpent-column a list of the Greek states which had helped to vanquish the Persians. This inscription still exists on the serpent-column ; it is not a dedicatory inscription, but merely enumerates the names of the states which had fought either at Plataea or at Salamis. Thus with the new inscription the monument somewhat changed its character. Instead of being, as at first, a trophy of the battle of Plataea alone, it was now a trophy of the Persian war in general. The reasons for inscribing the list of states on the bronze serpents rather than on the stone pedestal may have been (1) that the pedestal was too low to receive the long inscription ; and (2) a wish to place the national character of the monument beyond the reach of any future tampering by making the inscription inseparable from the monument. But it was necessary that the monument should have a dedicatory inscription also. Hence in place of the erased inscription of Pausanias the Greeks engraved, probably upon the stone pedestal, a metrical inscription to the following effect :

> "The saviours of spacious Greece dedicated this (tripod),
> Having rescued the cities from hateful slavery."

See Thucydides, i. 132, iii. 57 ; Herodotus, viii. 82 ; [Demosthenes,] *Contra Neaer.* p. 1378 ; Diodorus, xi. 33 ; Cornelius Nepos, *Pausanias*, 1 ; Plutarch, *De Herodoti malignitate*, 42 ; Pausanias, iii. 8. 2 ; Aristides, *Or.* xlvi. vol. 2. p. 234 ed. Dindorf, with the scholiast (vol. 3. p. 569 ed. Dindorf) ; Suidas, *s.v.* Παυσανίας. Diodorus is the only writer who mentions the new dedicatory inscription ; but there is no reason to question his evidence. Nepos, indeed, says that on erasing Pausanias's dedicatory inscription the Lacedaemonians engraved in its stead the list of states and nothing more. But this latter statement is probably a mere inference from the silence of Thucydides, who mentions the list of states, but not the new dedicatory inscription. It is highly improbable that this important monument should have been allowed to stand without a dedicatory inscription at all. And that both the first and the second dedicatory inscriptions were engraved, not on the monument itself, but on the stone pedestal, is made almost certain by the nearly invariable practice of the Greeks in such matters.

In the Sacred War the Phocians, as Pausanias here informs us, carried off the golden tripod, leaving the serpent-column ; or, to give Pausanias's statement more exactly, they carried off all the golden part of the monument, but all the bronze part of it was still to be seen in his time, that is, in the second half of the second century A.D. This statement of Pausanias suggests that only a part of the tripod may have been of solid gold and the remainder of gilt bronze. The cauldron or basin was probably of solid gold ; the three legs which supported it may have been of gilt bronze. This view is borne out by the statements of later, especially Byzantine, writers, who continued to describe the trophy as a tripod long after the time of Pausanias. But this they could hardly have done if all that remained was the serpent-column which had once supported the tripod.

Constantine carried off the serpent-column and whatever remained of the tripod to Constantinople and placed the monument in the Hippodrome. See Schol. on Thucydides, i. 132; Eusebius, *Vit. Constantini*, iii. 54; Socrates, *Hist. Eccles.* i. 16; Zosimus, ii. 31; Sozomenus, *Hist. Eccles.* ii. 5; Nicephorus Callistus, *Eccles. Hist.* viii. 33. (The mention of "the famous statue of Pan" by Sozomenus and Nicephorus Callistus seems to be due to a false reading in the former writer. Instead of οἱ ἐν Δελφοῖς τρίποδες καὶ ὁ Πὰν ὁ βοώμενος ὃν Παυσανίας κτλ., we should probably read οἱ ἐν Δελφοῖς τρίποδες καὶ ὁ τὸ πᾶν βοώμενος [*scil.* τρίπους] ὃν Παυσανίας κτλ.).

From the year 1422 down to the present time the serpent-column at Constantinople has been seen and described by many writers. It is represented in an extant Turkish miniature painting of about 1520-1530, and we possess another drawing of it dating from 1578. Peter Gyllius, a French traveller of the sixteenth century, in his accurate work *De Constantinopoleos Topographia* (ii. 13), has described the serpent-column as composed of three serpents twined together, with their three heads projecting from the top of the column in three separate directions. He was acquainted with the true history of the monument. Not so the English traveller Wheler, who visited Constantinople in 1675. He saw and described the column as "cast in the form of three serpents wreathed together until the top, where their three heads part, and bend outwards, in a triangular form"; but of the history of the column he was ignorant. He gave a drawing of the column, showing the three heads of the serpents intact. See his *Journey into Greece* (London, 1682), p. 185. Not many years after Wheler's visit the three heads of the serpents seem to have been broken off. Tournefort, who was at Constantinople in 1701, says: "The bronze column of three serpents is not better known. It is about 15 feet high, formed by three serpents coiled together like a roll of tobacco; their contours lessen imperceptibly from the base up to the necks of the serpents; and their heads, diverging to the three sides like a tripod, formed a sort of capital. They say that Sultan Murat broke the head of one of these serpents. The column was thrown down and the heads of the two others were broken in 1700 after the peace of Karlowitz. What has become of them is not known; but the rest has been set up again and stands between the obelisks, at equal distances from them" (*Relation d'un Voyage du Levant*, Amsterdam, 1718, Lettre xii. vol. 2. p. 9). Similarly Chishull, writing 17th April 1701, says: "The second pillar is of wreathed brass, not above 12 feet high, lately terminated at the top with figures of three serpents rising from the pillar, and with their necks and heads forming a beautiful triangle. But this monument was rudely broken from the top of the pillar by some attendants of the late Polish ambassador, whose lodgings were appointed in this cirque, opposite to the said pillar" (*Travels in Turkey*, London, 1747, p. 40 *sq.*). However Lady Mary Montagu appears to have seen the column with the three serpent-heads intact as late as 1718, for writing from Constantinople on the 10th of April in that year she says : "This was the hippodrome in the reign of the Greek emperors. In the midst of it is a brazen column of three serpents twisted together with their mouths gaping. 'Tis impossible to learn why so odd a pillar was erected. The Greeks can tell nothing but fabulous legends, when they are asked the meaning of it, and there is no sign of its having ever had any inscription " (*Letters*, 3rd ed. 1861, vol. 1. p. 356).

Towards the end of 1855 Mr. (afterwards Sir) C. T. Newton excavated the base of the serpent-column. The soil had accumulated over it to the height of rather more than 6 feet. He found that the column rested on a rough-hewn stone plinth of the Byzantine period. A few feet from the plinth, at the depth of 8 feet below the surface, was an ancient aqueduct formed of cylindrical earthen pipes ; and close to the aqueduct was a foundation of tiles, apparently the remains of a small tank. Hence Sir C. T. Newton inferred that the column had been placed in the centre of the tank and had been used as a fountain. This conjecture was afterwards confirmed by the discovery of a piece of leaden pipe, bearing a Byzantine inscription, inside the hollow serpent-column. The plinth, too, on which the column stands, is hollow, doubtless to allow the passage of the water.

Since the excavations of Sir C. T. Newton in 1855 the column has been carefully examined and delineated. As it stands, the bodies of the serpents form twenty-nine coils, one above the other, and the total height of the column is 5.34 metres (about 17 ft. 6 in.). The heads and tails of the serpents are wanting. But in 1848 the architect Fossati, in the course of an excavation made near the mosque of St. Sophia, found the upper part of one of the heads, from which it appears that the mouth of the serpent must have been wide open. The serpent-column appears to have been cast in a single piece ; the most minute examination has failed to detect any joining in the metal. Nowhere on the surface of the bronze is there any trace of scales ; the bodies of the serpents are smooth.

Early in 1856 a German and an Austrian scholar, Dr. Otto Frick and Dr. Dethier, removed the thick earthy coating with which the lower part of the column was encrusted and discovered the inscription, which they published separately. It has since been re-examined by Prof. Ernst Fabricius. The dialect and alphabet of the inscription are Laconian. It does not run all round the column, but is confined to a narrow perpendicular strip on one side of the column, beginning on the third coil from the bottom and ending on the thirteenth. The lower part of the inscription, which was buried in the ground, is well preserved ; but the upper part, on the twelfth and thirteenth coils, is hardly legible. For here the surface of the bronze is not only worn and oxydised, but scarred and dinted with deep sabre-cuts. As deciphered and restored by Prof. Fabricius the inscription runs thus :

                              Μυκανῆς
[Τ]ο[ίδε τὸν]   20 Κεῖοι
πόλ[ε]μον [έ]   Μάλιοι
πολ[έ]μ[ε]ον   Τήνιοι

                              Νάξιοι
[Λ]ακ[εδ]α[ι]μόν[ιοι]   'Ερετριῆς
5 'Αθ[α]ν[α]ῖ[ο]ι   25 Χαλκιδῆς
Κορίνθιοι

                              Στυρῆς
                              Ϝαλεῖοι
    Τεγεᾶ[ται]   ϓιοτεῖοαῖαται
    Σικυώνιοι
    Αἰγινᾶται   Λευκάδιοι
                          30 Ϝανακτοριῆς
10 Μεγαρῆς   Κύθνιοι
    'Επιδαύριοι   Σίφνιοι
    'Ερχομένιοι

                          'Αμπρακιῶται
    Φλειάσιοι   Λεπρεᾶται
    Τροζάνιοι
15 'Ερμιονῆς

    Τιρύνθιοι
    Πλαταιῆς
    Θεσπιῆς

" The following fought in the war :

                            Mycenaeans
    Lacedaemonians   20 Ceans
5 Athenians   Melians
    Corinthians   Tenians

    Tegeans   Naxians
    Sicyonians   Eretrians
    Aeginetans   25 Chalcidians

10 Megarians   Styrians
    Epidaurians   Eleans
    Orchomenians   Potidaeans

    Phliasians   Leucadians
    Troezenians   30 Anactorians
15 Hermionians   Cythnians
                            Siphnians

    Tirynthians   Ambraciots
    Plataeans   Lepreans."
    Thespians

The names of the states occur in groups of three, one group of three on each coil, except that on the last coil there are only two names, and that on the fourth and the seventh coils from the ground there are four names. The fourth names on the two latter coils are those of the Siphnians and Tenians; they are much worse engraved than the other names in the list and were probably added at a later time. This, so far as the Tenians are concerned, is confirmed by the express statement of Herodotus (viii. 82) that the name of the Tenians was carved on the monument because, though the Tenians sided with the Persians, a Tenian ship had brought important tidings to the Greeks on the eve of the battle of Salamis. We may hence, perhaps, infer, that the name of the Tenians was at first excluded from the list because they had sided with the enemy, but was afterwards added as a special favour in consideration of the service rendered to the Greek cause by the single Tenian ship.

We may compare the list of states on the serpent-column with (1) the list carved on the corresponding trophy at Olympia, as reported by Pausanias (v. 23. 1 *sq.*); and (2) the list given by Herodotus (ix. 28-30 and 77) of the Greek states that fought at Plataea. In the following table (p. 305) the names printed in italics in the first column do not occur in the second column; the names printed in italics in the second column do not occur in the third column; and the names printed in italics in the third column occur in neither of the other columns.

The number (31) of names on the serpent-column is precisely the number of Greek states which, according to Plutarch (*Themistocles*, 20), fought against the Persians in the course of the war. The names in the third of the following columns are arranged in the order of battle in which the Greeks stood at Plataea, except that the Mantineans and Eleans arrived too late to take part in the engagement (Herodotus, ix. 77).

(1) If we compare the third column with the other two, we see that six peoples (Ceans, Melians, Tenians, Naxians, Cythnians, and Siphnians) who took no part in the battle of Plataea were nevertheless commemorated on one or other of the trophies, five out of the six being commemorated on both. Why was this? The answer doubtless is that all six peoples either fought on the Greek side at the battle of Salamis or at least rendered important service to the Greek cause on that occasion (Herodotus, viii. 46 and 82); and that the two trophies, though erected out of the booty taken at Plataea only, were afterwards treated as monuments of the Greek triumphs over the Persians both at Salamis and Plataea (cp. [Demosthenes,] *Contra Neaer.* p. 1378); hence states which had been represented by contingents at either of these battles were deemed entitled to have their names engraved on the trophies.

(2) If we compare the two first columns with each other, we see that the lists on the Delphic and Olympic trophies do not coincide. All the twenty-seven names on the Olympic trophy occur on the Delphic trophy, but the order is somewhat different, and on the Delphic trophy there are four names (Thespians, Eretrians, Leucadians, and Siphnians)

which, if Pausanias's list is correct, did not appear on the Olympic trophy.   How are these discrepancies to be explained ?   Some scholars

I. SERPENT-COLUMN.	II. STATUE OF ZEUS AT OLYMPIA (Pausanias, v. 23).	GREEKS WHO FOUGHT AT PLATAEA (Herodotus, ix. 28-30 and 77).
1 Lacedaemonians	Lacedaemonians	Lacedaemonians
2 Athenians	Athenians	Tegeans
3 Corinthians	Corinthians	Corinthians
4 Tegeans	Sicyonians	Potidaeans
5 Sicyonians	Aeginetans	Orchomenians
6 Aeginetans	Megarians	Sicyonians
7 Megarians	Epidaurians	Epidaurians
8 Epidaurians	Tegeans	Troezenians
9 Orchomenians	Orchomenians	Lepreans
10 Phliasians	Phliasians	Mycenaeans
11 Troezenians	Troezenians	Tirynthians
12 Hermionians	Hermionians	Phliasians
13 Tirynthians	Tirynthians	Hermionians
14 Plataeans	Plataeans	Eretrians
15 *Thespians*	Mycenaeans	Styrians
16 Mycenaeans	Ceans	Chalcidians
17 Ceans	*Melians*	Ambraciots
18 Melians	Ambraciots	Leucadians
19 Tenians	Tenians	Anactorians
20 Naxians	Lepreans	*Palaeans*
21 *Eretrians*	Naxians	Aeginetans
22 Chalcidians	Cythnians	Megarians
23 Styrians	Styrians	Plataeans
24 Eleans	Eleans	Athenians
25 Potidaeans	Potidaeans	Thespians
26 *Leucadians*	Anactorians	*Mantineans*
27 Anactorians	Chalcidians	Eleans
28 Cythnians		
29 *Siphnians*		
30 Ambraciots		
31 Lepreans		

have supposed that the lists on the two monuments must have been identical, and that the deficiencies and variations of order in the Olympic list, as reported by Pausanias, are simply due to the indolence or carelessness of the person who took down the Olympic inscription, whether that person was Pausanias himself or some other antiquary whom he may have copied.   This is the view of Prof. von Wilamowitz-Moellendorff and Mr. Kalkmann.   See *Hermes*, 12 (1877), p. 345, n. 29 ; A. Kalkmann, *Pausanias der Perieget*, p. 76 *sq.*   But it should be remembered that though the two trophies were made at the same time, the lists of states may have been engraved on them at different times and by different authorities.   We know as a fact that the list of states was not originally engraved on the Delphic trophy but was added at a later time in consequence of the accidental circumstance of the vanity and presumption of the Spartan general Pausanias.   If, then, the Delphic trophy was originally set up without any such list, the probability is that the Olympic trophy was so too. When and by whom the list was placed on the Olympic trophy, we do not know. It may have been added by the Lacedaemonians at the same time that they added the corresponding list to the Delphic trophy. But the writers who mention the latter addition say nothing about the former. Therefore knowing not when or by what authority the list of states was engraved on the Olympic trophy, we are not in a position to explain the discrepancies between that list and the list on the Delphic trophy.

Prof. Adolf Bauer has proposed to explain the discrepancies between the two lists by supposing that only those states are mentioned on either trophy which not only fought at Salamis or Plataea but contributed to defray the cost of the particular trophy. Thus he supposes that the reason why the names of the Thespians, Eretrians, Leucadians, and Siphnians occurred on the Delphic but not on the Olympic trophy was simply that these states had contributed to the former trophy but not to the latter. But Herodotus tells us that the cost of the two trophies was defrayed, not by subscriptions from the various states, but out of the booty taken at Plataea before that booty was divided among the states. There is absolutely no reason to question Herodotus's account. Prof. Bauer's view contradicts that account and must therefore be rejected.

It remains to say a few words as to the two rival theories of the way in which the serpent-column supported the golden tripod. (1) On the one hand it has been supposed that each of the three feet of the tripod rested on one of the three serpents' heads which projected from the top of the column. This is the view of Messrs. Dethier and Mordtmann. (2) On the other hand it has been argued that the legs of the tripod rested on the stone pedestal and that the serpent-column stood in the middle of them supporting, not the tripod as a whole, but only the cauldron or basin, in such a way that one of the serpent's heads projected between each pair of the tripod's legs. This is the view advocated by Wieseler, Dr. P. Wolters, and especially by Prof. Ernst Fabricius. That tripods sometimes had these central props in addition to their three legs, we know from the representations of them on vases and from small models of tripods found at Olympia. But there are serious objections to supposing that the serpent-column was nothing more than such a central prop under the middle of the cauldron. For on this view the golden tripod must have been of enormous size. Prof. Fabricius estimates that it was about 8 metres (26 ft. 3 in.) high and that the diameter of the cauldron was not quite 3 metres (3 ft. 3 in.). A tripod of solid gold of such dimensions is out of the question. This is practically admitted by Prof. Fabricius, who supposes that only parts of the tripod, such as the cauldron, the rings, and various ornaments, were of massive gold, while the rest, especially the legs, may have been of gilt bronze. But, quite apart from the question of the value of the material, a tripod of such an enormously exaggerated size seems little in keeping with the simple and austere character of Greek art in the early part of the fifth century B.C. It is true that in the description of the famous procession at Alexandria in the reign of Ptolemy Philadelphus we read of golden Delphic tripods

4, 6, and even 30 cubits high (Athenaeus, v. p. 202 b c); but the pomp and lavish display of an eastern court are no standards whereby to judge of the heroic age of Greece. Therefore unless it can be shown that the Greeks of the first half of the fifth century B.C. were accustomed to make votive tripods of a size even approximating to the supposed size of the tripod in question, it seems safer to adopt the first of the two theories as to the relation of the serpent-column to the golden tripod. On this hypothesis the tripod may have been some 6 or 7 feet high and from 2 to 3 feet across. Adopting this view of the size of the tripod, we are still at liberty to suppose that only parts of it (particularly the cauldron) were of solid gold, and that the rest of it was of gilt bronze. This would harmonise both with the language of Pausanias, who perhaps implies that more than the mere serpent-column survived to his day, and with the language of the Byzantine writers, who certainly speak as if the tripod, and not merely the serpent-column, had been transferred by Constantine to Constantinople.

See Gibbon, *Decline and Fall*, ch. xvii. ; C. T. Newton, *Travels and Discoveries in the Levant*, 2. pp. 25-35 ; Frick and Curtius, ' Ueber die Ausgrabung der Schlangensäule auf dem Hippodrom zu Constantinopel,' *Monatsberichte d. kön. preuss. Akad. d. Wissen. zu Berlin*, 13. März 1856, pp. 162-181 ; E. Curtius, ' Ueber die Weihgeschenke der Griechen nach den Perserkriegen und insbesondere über das platäische Weihgeschenk in Delphi,' *Nachrichten von der kön. Gesell. d. Wissen. zu Göttingen*, 23rd December 1861, No. 21. pp. 361-390; *id., Gesammelte Abhandlungen*, 2. pp. 369-374 ; L. Ross, ' Inschriften der dreiköpfigen ehernen Schlange aus Delphi in Konstantinopel,' *Fleckeisen's Jahrbücher*, 2 (1856), pp. 265-268 ; O. Frick, ' Das plataeische Weihgeschenk zu Konstantinopel,' *Fleckeisen's Jahrbücher*, Supplem. 3 (1857-1860), pp. 487-555 ; Schubart, in *Fleckeisen's Jahrbücher*, 7 (1861), pp. 474-481 ; Frick, ' Die Echtheit des platäischen Weihgeschenks zu Konstantinopel,' *ib.* 8 (1862), pp. 441-466 ; Fr. Wieseler, ' Zur sogenannten Schlangensäule in Konstantinopel,' *ib.* 10 (1864), pp. 242-259 ; Schubart, *ib.* 11 (1865), pp. 490-498 ; *id.*, ' Ueber das delphische Weihgeschenk zum platäischen Sieg,' *Archäologische Zeitung*, 20 (1862), pp. 245-248 ; Göttling, ' Ueber die Basis des platäischen Weihgeschenkes in Delphi,' *Gesammelte Abhandlungen*, 2. pp. 71-77 ; P. Foucart, *Mémoire sur les ruines et l'histoire de Delphes*, pp. 36-45 ; P. A. Dethier and A. D. Mordtmann, in *Denkschriften d. k. Akademie d. Wissenschaften*, Philosoph. histor. Classe, 13 (Wien, 1864), pp. 3-48 ; Rawlinson's *Herodotus*, 4. pp. 467-473 ; E. Fabricius, ' Das platäische Weihgeschenk in Delphi,' *Jahrbuch des archäol. Inst.* 1 (1886), pp. 176-191 ; Ad. Bauer, ' Die Inschriften auf der Schlangensäule und auf der Basis der Zeusstatue in Olympia,' *Wiener Studien*, 9 (1887), pp. 223-228 ; Röhl, *I. G. A.* No. 70; E. L. Hicks, *Greek Historical Inscriptions*, No. 12 ; W. Dittenberger, *Sylloge Inscr. Graec.* No. 1 ; E. S. Roberts, *Greek Epigraphy*, No. 259 ; A. Kirchhoff, *Studien zur Gesch. der griech. Alphabets*,[4] p. 153; Friederichs-Wolters, *Gipsabgüsse*, No. 227.

13. 10. **not far from Phalanthus is a dolphin** etc. On coins of Tarentum there commonly occurs the device of a man riding on a dolphin. See B. V. Head, *Coins of the Ancients*, Plate 7, Nos. 4-7, Plate 15, No. 4, Plate 24, Nos. 6-10, Plate 45, No. 15 *sq.* ; *id., Historia Numorum*, p. 44 *sqq.* According to Aristotle, cited by Pollux (ix. 80), the man so represented on the coins was Taras ; but from the present passage of Pausanias it would seem rather that he was Phalanthus. Modern numismatists have followed Aristotle, overlooking the present passage of Pausanias. The first, apparently, to correct this

mistake was Prof. Studniczka (*Kyrene* (Leipsic, 1890), p. 175 *sqq.*), who
further argues that Phalanthus, the supposed founder of Tarentum, was
not, as is generally supposed, an historical personage, but a form of
Poseidon worshipped in Achaia and Arcadia before the Dorian invasion.
Cp. x. 10. 6 *sqq.*

14. 1. The axes etc. According to Plutarch (*De Pythiae oraculis,*
12) the people of Tenedos dedicated an axe, because at a place
Asterium in Tenedos there were crabs, the shells of which bore a mark
like an axe. The Greek proverb about an axe of Tenedos, to which
Pausanias refers below (§ 3), was variously explained. According to
Aristotle, the proverb arose because a certain king of Tenedos had laid
down a law that adulterers should be slain with an axe ; the king's own
son, being convicted of adultery, was executed according to the law ;
hence on coins of Tenedos an axe was stamped on one side and a double
head (male and female) on the other. See Stephanus Byzantius, *s.v.*
Τένεδος ; Suidas and Photius, *Lexicon, s.vv.* Τενέδιος ἄνθρωπος and
Τενέδιος ξυνήγορος ; Conon, *Narrationes,* 28 ; Hesychius, *s.v.* Τενέδιον
βέλος ; Heraclides Ponticus, *De rebus publicis,* vii. (*Frag. Histor.
Graec.* ed. Müller, 2. p. 213 *sq.*) ; Diogenianus, iv. 94 and viii. 58 ;
Apostolius, xvi. 25 and 26 ; Zenobius, vi. 9 ; Eustathius, *Comment. in
Dionysii Perieg.* 537. The story of Tennes, as it is narrated here by
Pausanias, is told also, though without mention of the axe, by Diodorus
(v. 83), by Tzetzes (*Schol. on Lycophron,* 232-3), by Eustathius and a
Scholiast on Homer (*Il.* ii. 38), and by Apollodorus (p. 195 *sq.* ed. R.
Wagner, *Epitoma Vaticana ex Apollodori Bibliotheca,* ed. R. Wagner
(Leipsic, 1891), p. 64 *sq.*). As to coins of Tenedos with the double axe
on one side and the double head (male and female) on the other, see
B. V. Head, *Historia Numorum,* p. 476 *sq.* ; *id., Coins of the Ancients,*
plate 2 No. 19, plate 18 Nos. 20 *sq.*, plate 49 No. 13. My friend
Prof. Ridgeway holds that the reason why the double axe was put on the
coins of Tenedos may have been that axes were specially manufactured
in Tenedos and formed the unit of barter there before the introduction
of coined money, just as axes, or small models of them, still serve
as currency in some parts of Africa (W. Ridgeway, *The origin of
metallic currency and weight standards,* p. 317 *sq.*). In one of the
tombs on the citadel of Mycenae Dr. Schliemann found two small
double-headed axes of thin gold plate (Schliemann, *Mycenae,* p. 252).
In 1878 similar golden axes were found near *Aïdin* in Lydia (*Bulletin
de Corresp. hellénique,* 3 (1879), p. 129 *sq.*, with plates, iv. v.). On a
so-called Hittite relief at *Iasili-Kaia,* what appears to be a religious
procession is represented, and one figure, standing erect on a lion and
wearing a high conical cap, carries a double-headed axe (Perrot et
Chipiez, *Histoire de l'art dans l'antiquité,* 4. p. 637, fig. 313 ; *Revue
archéologique, 3rd Ser. 6 (1885), p. 300).* The Labrandean Zeus of
Caria is represented on coins carrying a double-headed axe (B. V. Head,
Coins of the Ancients, iii. A. 33-35). This deity seems to have taken
his surname from the axe, for *labrus* is said to be the Lydian word
for an axe (Plutarch, *Quaest. Graec.* 45 ; L. Preller, *Griechische Mythologie,*[4] 1. p. 141). On reliefs found at *Khodja-Tach,* on the borders of

Pisidia and Phrygia, the double-headed axe appears in the hand of the 'saviour god' (θεὸς σώζων), who is represented on horseback (*Bulletin de Corresp. hellénique*, 4 (1880), p. 294). According to L. Stephani, the double-headed axe appears very often on vase-paintings as the symbol of Dionysus or one of his train. He thinks that on coins of Tenedos the double-headed axe, which is generally accompanied by a cluster of grapes, is a symbol of the worship of Dionysus, and he explains the double head on the same coins as having originally represented the bearded and beardless Dionysus. See Stephani, in *Compte-Rendu* (St. Petersburg) for 1863, pp. 128-134. A double-headed axe of bronze has been found by the French at Delphi (*Berliner philolog. Wochenschrift*, 15th August 1896, p. 1086).

14. 2. **this Caletor was killed by Ajax** etc. See Homer, *Il.* ii. 419 *sqq.*

14. 4. **Tennes was slain by Achilles** etc. Tennes was worshipped at Tenedos, and because he had been slain by Achilles it was unlawful to mention the name of Achilles in his sanctuary. Flute-players were also forbidden to enter it, a prohibition which was explained by another legend. See Diodorus, v. 83; Plutarch, *Quaest. Graec.* 28.

14. 5. **a bronze Zeus at Olympia.** See v. 23. 1 *sq.*

14. 5. **an Apollo —— from the spoils of the sea-fights** etc. Herodotus tells us (viii. 121) that out of the spoils of the battle of Salamis the Greeks dedicated at Delphi a statue 12 ells high, holding in its hand the figure-head of a ship. This may have been the statue which Pausanias calls an Apollo. It stood near a golden statue of Alexander, king of Macedonia.

14. 6. **The expeditions of the barbarians —— foretold in the oracles of Bacis.** Oracles of Bacis referring to the Persian invasion of Greece are quoted or referred to by Herodotus (viii. 20, 77, 96, ix. 43).

14. 7. **the great altar.** Herodotus mentions (ii. 135) an altar of the Chians opposite the temple at Delphi. This altar of the Chians has been found by the French in the situation described by Herodotus. It is on the left-hand side of the Sacred Way, opposite to and on a level with the eastern front of the temple of Apollo. The base, a high tower-like structure of native limestone, is surmounted by a course faced with black marble. On this rested the altar proper, constructed of white, perhaps Parian, marble. A pavement, of which part has been removed and part has sunk into the ground, united the altar to the temple. The cornice, now lying on the ground, bears the inscription XIOI ΑΠΟΛΛΩΝI TON BΩMON 'The Chians (dedicated) the altar to Apollo.' On the side of the altar is carved another inscription :

ΔΕΛΦΟΙΕΔΩΚΑΝ
ΧΙΟΙΣΠΡΟΜΑΝΤ
ΕΙΗΝ

"The Delphians gave the Chians the right of consulting the oracle on behalf of others." (On the true meaning of προμαντεία, which is usually translated "the right of consulting the oracle before others," see Th. Homolle, in *Bulletin de Corresp. hellénique*, 19 (1895), p. 60 *sq.*) Thus there can be no doubt that the altar is the one mentioned by Herodotus. And from its position, size, and the order of Pausanias's description it would seem to have been also the great altar of the god. However, no ashes, bones, small votive offerings, or bronze utensils have been found in its neighbourhood. On the other hand at the western end of the temple a deposit of pottery and bronzes has been found in a layer of dark hard soil sometimes mingled with bones and ashes. Among the bronzes are pieces of tripods, bowls, and statuettes, a lion of the Assyrian type, two small horses, two birds with human faces, and three heads of griffins. The pottery, mostly broken, comprises sherds of the three styles known as geometrical, proto-Corinthian, and Corinthian; they were found in separate clearly-marked layers, one above the other. A few pieces of late Mycenaean ware have also come to light among them. This discovery proves either that an altar existed here or at all events that the refuse of an altar was systematically deposited here. See Th. Homolle, in *Bulletin de Corresp. hellénique*, 17 (1893), p. 614, and *ib.* 18 (1894), pp. 179, 180 *sq.*; *id.*, in *Comptes Rendus de l'Académie des Inscriptions*, 22 (1894), p. 204 *sq.*; *id.*, in *Gazette des Beaux-Arts*, Décembre 1894, p. 442 *sq.* The altar is mentioned without qualification in several Delphic inscriptions which declare that the ceremony of the dedication of slaves to Apollo took place "between the temple and the altar." See Wescher-Foucart, *Inscriptions recueillies à Delphes*, Nos. 345, 346, 376, 407. Cp. H. Pomtow, *Beiträge zur Topographie von Delphi*, p. 38 *sq.*; *id.*, in *Archäologischer Anzeiger*, 1894, p. 186 and *ib.* 1895, p. 5 *sq.*

The level space or esplanade to the east of the temple, near the great altar, was the most conspicuous in the whole precinct, and from the long list of votive offerings enumerated by Pausanias in this part of his tour we might infer that here the monuments stood thickest. This inference is confirmed by the excavations, which have revealed a continuous line of pedestals bordering this part of the Sacred Way. Here may be seen the base, inscribed with a fine Latin dedication, which supported the trophies of Aemilius Paulus. From Livy (xlv. 27) we know that the Roman conqueror, on his visit to Delphi, gave orders that these memorials of his victory should be set up on the very spot which his adversary Perseus had chosen as the site of a trophy he was never destined to erect. Just above the Sacred Way, at the point where it turns westward, stands a huge pedestal in the form of a column inscribed with a dedication by Gelo, son of Dinomenes, tyrant of Syracuse. His offering, which consisted of a golden tripod and a golden statue of Victory, was dedicated as a memorial of his great victory over the Carthaginians at Himera in 480 B.C. See Diodorus, xi. 26 ; Athenaeus, vi. p. 231 f. From the inscription we learn that the artist was Bion, son of Diodorus, a Milesian. This artist was mentioned by Polemo (Diogenes Laertius, iv. 7. 58), perhaps in his work on Delphi. To the right of the pedestal is another which from a fragmentary inscription carved on it appears to have supported another offering either of Gelo or of one of his brothers. A third pedestal, exactly alike, lies on the ground broken ; it bears no inscription. Lastly, a fourth pedestal of the same sort has been found below the Sacred Way. Hence it is believed that all the four sons of Dinomenes, namely Gelo, Hiero, Thrasybulus, and Polyzelus (Diodorus, xi. 48 and 67) dedicated offerings at Delphi to commemorate the victory of Himera. See Th. Homolle, in *Bulletin de Corresp. hellénique*, 18 (1894), p. 179 *sq.* ; *id.*, in *Comptes Rendus de l'Académie des Inscriptions*, 22 (1894), p. 586.

Next above the pedestal of Gelo is a base on which, as we have seen (p. 299), the Plataean trophy is believed to have rested. It would certainly be highly appropriate that the monuments of two great victories won in successive years over the barbarians of the West and of the East should stand side by side at the religious capital of Greece. Behind the pedestal of Gelo a long pedestal supported nine statues set up in honour of the Thessalian tyrant Daochus, his ancestors, and his sons. Seven of the inscriptions on the pedestal and most of the statues are preserved. Five of the inscriptions are in verse. They set forth the exploits and laud the merits of each of the personages represented, mentioning benefits conferred on Thessaly and athletic victories won at Olympia, the Isthmus, Nemea, and Delphi. The statues were found fallen at the foot of the pedestal. Most of the persons are represented wrapt in the heavy Thessalian mantle ; but one, an athlete, is nude. His spare hardy figure, small head, short hair, and upturned gaze are in the style of Lysippus. See Th. Homolle, in *Bulletin de Corresp. hellénique*, 19 (1895), p. 534 ; *id.*, in *Gazette des Beaux-Arts*, Décembre 1894, p. 452 ; *L'Illustration*, No. 2702 (8 Décembre 1894), p. 481. Daochus enjoys a less enviable immortality in the pages of Demosthenes (*Or.* xviii. p. 324), where he heads a long list of scoundrels who had truckled to Philip and betrayed and ruined their country. He was one of the envoys sent by Philip to Thebes immediately before the battle of Chaeronea to counteract the influence of the Athenian embassy headed by Demosthenes. But he was no match for the Athenian orator, whose resistless eloquence swept his hearers away as on a torrent. See Plutarch, *Demosthenes*, 18.

Several of the bases in this neighbourhood, as I am informed by Mr. Cecil Smith, supported chariots. An inscription on one of them mentions a bronze-gilt chariot dedicated by Rhodes. The boundary-wall of the sacred precinct on the east is here cut into by some extensive baths of the Roman period, above which is a large tank built of bricks with engaged brick columns. To the west of the baths is a large square building of Roman times, but its purpose is unknown.

14. 7. a bronze wolf etc. The story that the Delphians revered the wolf for having guided them to some stolen treasures of the god was told by Polemo (Aelian, *Nat. an.* xii. 40). Another reason assigned for the dedication of the bronze wolf was that Apollo delighted in wolves because his mother Latona had assumed the form of a she-wolf when she bore him (Aelian, *Nat. an.* x. 26). When the Lacedaemonians received from the Delphians the right of consulting the oracle on behalf of others as well as of themselves (προμαντεία, see above, p. 309 *sq.*), they engraved the decree on the forehead of this bronze wolf. Afterwards Pericles obtained from the Delphians a similar right for the Athenians and engraved the decree on the wolf's right side. See Plutarch, *Pericles*, 21. The dedication of a bronze wolf to Apollo points to that mythical connexion between the god and the animal of which we have many proofs. See notes on i. 19. 3 'The Lyceum' and ii. 9. 7 'Wolfish Apollo.'

15. 1. The gilded statue of Phryne etc. The statue stood on a lofty column of Pentelic marble between the statues of two kings, Archidamus, king of Sparta, and Philip, king of Macedonia. It bore the inscription "Phryne of Thespiae, daughter of Epicles." See Athenaeus, xiii. p. 591 b; Aelian, ix. 32; [Dio Chrysostom,] *Or.* xxxvii. vol. 2. p. 301 ed. Dindorf. Compare Plutarch, *De Pythiae oraculis*, 15; *id.*, *Amatorius*, ix. 10; *id.*, *De Alex. s. virt. s. fort.* Or. ii. 3; Tatian, *Or. ad Graecos*, 33. p. 132 ed. Otto. Most of the ancient writers who mention the statue speak of it as golden, not gilded. In one passage, however, Plutarch agrees with Pausanias in describing it as gilded (*Amatorius*, ix. 10). According to Pausanias the statue was dedicated by Phryne herself; but according to Aelian and Athenaeus it was dedicated by her admirers and neighbours (οἱ περικτίονες Athenaeus, *l.c.*). Phryne is said to have dedicated at Delphi a golden statue of Aphrodite (Diogenes Laertius, vi. 2. 60). But this is perhaps a mistaken reference to the gilt statue of Phryne herself, who may have been represented in the style and with the attributes of Aphrodite. Prof. Furtwängler conjectures that the statue known as the Aphrodite of Ostia, now in the British Museum, may be a copy of Praxiteles's statue of Phryne at Delphi. The whole of the left arm and the right arm from the elbow are restored; but the goddess or woman seems to have been represented as engaged at her toilet, probably holding a mirror in her right hand and some article of toilet in her raised left hand. The lower half only of the figure is draped. See Bernoulli, *Aphrodite*, pp. 178-180; Friederichs-Wolters, *Gipsabgüsse*, No. 1470; A. Furtwängler, *Meisterwerke d. griech. Plastik*, pp. 549-551. As to the statue of Phryne by Praxiteles at Thespiae, see ix. 27. 5.

15. 1. a victory which they won over the Athenians. In 445 B.C. the Megarians revolted from Athens and cut to pieces the Athenian garrison with the exception of some who made their escape to Nisaea (Thucydides, i. 114). This was the success commemorated by the statue of Apollo at Delphi; the god was represented holding a spear (Plutarch, *De Pythiae oraculis*, 16).

15. 1. when they imposed a fine on the Phocians etc. Cp. x. 2. 1 note, and note on x. 8. 2.

15. 2. an image of Artemis, one of Athena, and two of Apollo. Overbeck conjectured that the Artemis of Versailles, the Athena of the Capitol, and the Apollo Belvedere are copies of three of these statues. See note on x. 23. 1.

15. 2. the Celtic host would cross from Europe into Asia etc. See i. 4. 5 *sq.*, i. 8. 1, x. 23. 14.

15. 3. Attalus —— described in an oracle as bull-horned. The oracle is quoted by Suidas (*s.v.* Ἄτταλος). It predicts that Attalus and his children's children will attain to royal dignity.

15. 4. The bronze palm-tree and the gilt image of Athena etc. Plutarch describes the image of Athena as golden and as mounted on the bronze palm-tree (*Nicias*, 13). He agrees with Pausanias in saying that the image and palm-tree were dedicated out of the spoils of the Persian war, and that on the eve of the Sicilian disaster crows pecked off the golden fruit of the palm (*Nicias*, 13; *De Pythiae oraculis*, 8). Cp. Schubart, in *Archäologische Zeitung*, 20 (1862), pp. 233-235.

15. 5. Clitodemus. The fragments of his works are collected by C. Müller (*Fragm. hist. Graec.* 1. pp. 359-365). In the texts of classical writers his name often appears as Clidemus (C. Müller, *op. cit.* p. lxxxii.).

15. 6. The Cyrenians dedicated etc. Cp. x. 13. 5 note.

15. 6. it was Battus who led them —— to Libya. See Herodotus, iv. 155-158.

15. 7. Battus —— was cured of his stammer etc. A somewhat different version of the story is told by Justin (xiii. 7).

15. 7. the fine paid by the Phocians for their sacrilege. At the close of the Sacred War in 346 B.C. the Phocians were condemned to pay a fine of sixty talents yearly until they had restored the value of all the sacred treasures which they had carried off from the sanctuary (Diodorus, xvi. 60). Inscriptions have been found at the temple of Cranaean Athena near Elatea and at Delphi which prove that this sentence was in part at least carried out, for they record the payment of instalments of the fine by the Phocians. One instalment, apparently for half a year, is thirty talents; another, the eleventh, is ten talents. See P. Paris, in *Bulletin de Corresp. hellénique*, 11 (1887), p. 321 *sqq.* ; *C. I. G. G. S.* 3. Nos. 110-112; Th. Homolle, in *Bulletin de Corresp. hellénique*, 18 (1894), p. 181.

16. 1. the offerings sent by the kings of Lydia. These comprised treasuries dedicated by Gyges and Croesus (Strabo, ix. p. 421), six golden bowls and many silver objects dedicated by Gyges (Herodotus, i. 14), and a hundred and seventeen ingots of gold, a golden lion, two large bowls, one of gold and one of silver, four silver jars, two lustral vessels, one of gold and one of silver, a golden figure of a woman, many round vessels of silver, and his wife's necklace and girdles, all dedicated by Croesus (Herodotus, i. 50 *sq.*). To these must be added the golden shield dedicated by Croesus in the temple of Forethought Athena (Herodotus, i. 92; Paus. x. 8. 7) and the offerings of Alyattes (see next note).

16. 1. the iron stand of Alyattes' bowl etc. Alyattes king of Lydia dedicated at Delphi a large silver bowl on a stand of welded iron as a thank-offering for recovery from an illness. Herodotus (i. 25) describes it as "worth seeing above all the votive offerings at Delphi." Animals and plants were wrought in relief on the iron stand (Athenaeus, v. p. 210 c). Plutarch speaks of "the famous stand and base of the bowl" and says that it was made of iron softened in the fire and tempered with water (*De defectu oraculorum*, 47). Herodotus states (*l.c.*) that Glaucus the Chian, the maker of this bowl and stand, was the first man to invent the welding (κόλλησις) of iron. The statement was often repeated by later writers, some of whom speak of the 'artist as a Samian. See Hesychius, *s.v.* Γλαύκου τέχνη; Suidas, *s.v.* γλαῦξ ἵπταται; Stephanus Byzantius, *s.v.* Αἰθάλη; Schol. on Plato, *Phaedo*, p. 108 d; *Proverbia e Cod. Coislin.* 80 (*Paroemiographi Graeci*, ed. Gaisford, p. 128); Overbeck, *Schriftquellen*, §§ 263-272. As to Glaucus, see H. Brunn, *Gesch. d. griech. Künstler*, 1. p. 29 *sq.*, and as to the process which he is said to have invented, see E. Curtius, in *Archäologische Zeitung*, 34 (1876), p. 37 *sq.*; A. Michaelis, *ib.* p. 156 *sq.*; cp. G. Semper, *Der Stil*,[2] p. 489 *sq.*

There can be no doubt that the process said to have been invented by Glaucus was the welding and not the soldering of iron; for till a few years ago no method of soldering iron was known. Welding is the uniting of two separate pieces of metal into a single piece without the intervention of a third metal. In order to weld two pieces of metal together, it is necessary that the surfaces which are to be united should be heated white hot. But when iron is heated white hot, a process of oxidation takes place on its surface, and the oxide thus developed on the surfaces of two pieces of white-hot iron prevents them from uniting. This constitutes the difficulty of welding iron. To get rid of the oxide, sand is sprinkled on the two hot surfaces, which are then hammered together. The sand unites with the oxide and forms a fluid which in the process of hammering is expelled from between the two surfaces, leaving them free to unite. Soldering on the other hand is the joining of two pieces of metal by the interposition of a third metal of a different sort, which serves as a bond or link between them. The metal which is thus to act as a bond between two others must possess the property of melting at a lower temperature than either of them; hence an alloy of one or both metals (if the metals are of different sorts) is generally employed for the purpose, since the melting temperature of an alloy is usually lower than that of either of the metals of which it is composed. But no metal or alloy suitable for soldering iron was known till a few years ago; hence down to that time iron was never soldered. It is now found that two pieces of galvanised iron (iron coated with tin) can be soldered together, the tin on the surface of the two pieces of iron melting and acting as the bond between them. But galvanised iron was unknown to the ancients; hence the soldering of iron was equally unknown to them.—For the substance of this note on the processes of welding and soldering I am indebted to the kindness of my lamented friend, J. H. Middleton.

16. 3. What the Delphians call the Navel etc. It is said that Zeus, wishing to ascertain the exact centre of the earth, caused two eagles to fly simultaneously at equal speed from the eastern and western ends of the earth. The eagles met at Delphi, which was consequently regarded as the centre of the earth, and in memory of the way in which the supposed fact was said to have been ascertained, two golden eagles were set up beside the Navel (*omphalos*), which, as we learn from Pausanias, was a block of white marble believed to mark the exact

centre of the earth. Hence Pindar speaks of the Pythian priestess as
"seated beside the golden eagles of Zeus" (Pindar, *Pyth.* iv. 6). These
golden eagles were carried off by the Phocians in the Sacred War.
See Schol. on Pindar, *Pyth.* iv. 6; Strabo, ix. p. 419 *sq.*; Plutarch,
De defectu oraculorum, 1; Schol. on Sophocles, *Oedipus Rex*, 480;
Schol. on Euripides, *Orestes*, 331. According to some, the birds
employed by Zeus on this occasion were swans (Plutarch, *l.c.*) or crows
(Strabo, *l.c.*). It is said that a figure of the eagle was worked in mosaic
on the floor of the temple beside the Navel-stone. See Schol. on Lucian,
De saltatione, 38. (In this passage the reading of the MSS. is αἰετὸν
(*sic*) γέγραπται. The readings αἰτεούς or αἰετὼ γεγράφθαι are conjectures proposed by Ulrichs and Wieseler respectively.) It has been
supposed that this figure of an eagle in mosaic was made as a substitute
for the golden eagles carried off by the Phocians; but this is merely a
conjecture. Euripedes (*Ion*, 224) describes the Navel-stone as clothed
with fillets and with figures of Gorgons on either side of it. These
Gorgons are probably the figures which were more commonly described
as eagles; the figures were perhaps rude and archaic and might be
variously interpreted. Some people, as we have seen, thought that the
birds were swans or crows. After telling the legend of the two eagles
meeting at Delphi, Strabo says (*l.c.*): "And they show in the temple a
certain Navel, decked with fillets, and upon it the images of the myth."
From this we should infer that the eagles (or Gorgons) were still to be
seen beside the Navel-stone in Strabo's time. But we are expressly
told that the golden eagles had been carried off in the Sacred War, that
is, about three hundred years before Strabo's time. From this and the
silence of Pausanias as to the eagles, we may perhaps infer that the birds
were no longer to be seen in Strabo's time, and that his account of
the Navel-stone was based, not on personal observation, but on old
books which described the stone as it had been before the Sacred War.
Strabo's account of Greece is notoriously defective and erroneous; he
appears to have seen very little of the country and to describe it mostly
at second or third hand.

The Navel-stone (*omphalos*) is very frequently represented on
existing monuments of ancient art, especially on vases and coins, and
from these we can form a pretty accurate conception of its size and
appearance.

It appears especially often in vase-paintings of Orestes, pursued
by the Furies, taking sanctuary at the sacred stone. Generally it is
represented of a conical shape, like a half-egg, resting on a quadrangular
pedestal; but sometimes it is figured as nearly like a whole egg, with
one of the points cut off to enable it to stand upright on its pedestal.
Sometimes it is draped with fillets hanging straight down; sometimes
it is covered with a sort of net-work. In some cases the fillets are
ordinary ribbons; in others they are strings of what look like small
eggs. From these representations we should judge the Navel-stone to
have been from 2 to 5 feet in height and somewhat less across.

See S. Reinach, *Peintures de Vases Antiques*, Millin, ii. 68 ; Müller-Wieseler,
Denkmäler, ii. pl. xiii. No. 148; *Compte - Rendu* (St. Petersburg) for 1860,

Atlas, pl. ii. ; *id.*, for 1861, Atlas, pl. iv. ; *id.*, for 1863, Atlas, pl. vi. 5 ; *Archäologische Zeitung*, 18 (1862), pls. cxxxvii., cxxxviii. ; *id.*, 35 (1877), pl. 4, No. 1 ; Baumeister's *Denkmäler*, 2. pp. 1009, 1110, 1117, 1118 (fig. 1215, 1307, 1314, 1315) ; C. Bötticher, *Der Omphalos des Zeus zu Delphi*, pl. ; Th. Schreiber, *Bilderatlas*, pl. xii. 12 ; *Journal of Hellenic Studies*, 9 (1888), p. 296 *sqq.* ; *Annali del Instituto* 40 (1868), Tav. d' agg. E ; ed. Gerhard, *Gesammelte Abhandlungen*, Abbildungen, pl. lx. Nos. 1, 2.

The stone is represented in relief, together with a tripod and a lyre, on a monument found at Thespiae in 1891, which is inscribed with a

FIG. 10.—APOLLO ON THE OMPHALOS (COIN OF DELPHI).

decree in honour of some arbitrators who were sent from Delphi to Thespiae (*Bulletin de Corresp. hellénique*, 15 (1891), p. 659). On a coin struck by the Amphictyonic Council in the fourth century B.C., Apollo is represented seated on the Navel-stone, which is adorned with hanging strings of egg-like objects (Fig. 10). See Imhoof-Blumer and Gardner, *Num. Comm. on Pausanias*, p. 122, pl. Y vii. But the real shape and size of the Navel-stone are best given by two marble *omphaloi* recently found at Delphi (see below) and by another which was found at Athens some years ago. This last is shaped like a truncated cone, and on its flat top are traces of the feet of a statue. Its sides are ornamented in relief with strings of egg-like objects passing diagonally round the stone and linked together by short horizontal bands. See Conze, *Beiträge zur Geschichte der griech. Plastik*, pl. v. ; *Journal of Hellenic Studies*, 1 (1880), pl. v. ; *id.*, 9 (1888), p. 298 *sq.* Representations of the Navel-stone with the eagles on or beside it are very rare. On an electrum coin of Cyzicus the eagles appear clinging to the Navel-stone, one on each side of it. See *Numismatic Chronicle*, 3rd Series, 7 (1887), pl. I, No. 23. On a fine marble relief found at Sparta in 1885, the Navel-stone is represented resting on a step-base ; on either side of it is an eagle. Apollo stands by with a lyre, holding a bowl into which Artemis or Victory is pouring wine. See *Mittheilungen d. arch. Inst. in Athen*, 12 (1887), pl. xii. p. 378 *sqq.* A bronze coin of Megara, struck in the reign of Geta, represents Apollo with his lyre standing beside the Navel-stone, on the top of which are perched the two eagles. See Imhoof-Blumer and Gardner, *Num. Comm. on Paus.* p. 6, pl. A ix.

With regard to the position of the Navel-stone, it seems, originally at least, to have stood within the temple of Apollo. For in the *Eumenides* of Aeschylus (*v.* 39 *sqq.*) the Pythian priestess describes how, going to the inmost shrine of the temple, she saw Orestes seated on or at the Navel-stone. Again, in the *Ion* of Euripides (*v.* 223 *sqq.*), the Chorus of women, standing outside the temple, asks Ion if it is true that the temple occupies the " mid navel of the earth." Ion replies that it does, and he describes the Navel-stone (see above) ; the women answer that his description tallies with common report. Ion also tells them that they may not enter the temple except after offering sacrifice. So they decide not to enter it, but to satisfy their curiosity with what can be seen outside. This passage clearly implies that the Navel-stone stood within the temple and could not be seen from outside. Again, an inscription which refers to the restoration of the temple in the fourth century B.C. defines the façade of the *cella* as "the façade in front of the Navel-stone" (πρόστασις ἁ πρὸ τοῦ ὀμφάλου), making it nearly certain that in the fourth century the Navel-stone was still in the temple. This is confirmed by mention made in the same inscription (or in another relating to the same subject) of "work about the Navel-stone" (ἔργον τὸ περὶ τὸν ὄμφαλον), which was entrusted to a certain Sion ; for the name of this contractor occurs on stones which were found within the temple. See Th. Homolle, in *Comptes Rendus de l'Académie des Inscriptions*, 23 (1895), p. 335. Moreover, Strabo expressly says (ix. p. 420) that the Navel-stone was in the temple. Again, Varro (*De lingua Latina*, vii. 17) describes it as in the temple, at the side ; and a scholiast on Lucian (*De saltatione*, 38) says that it stood on the floor of the temple.

In opposition to these authorities Pausanias appears to describe the Navel-stone as outside the temple. For following, so far as we can judge, a strictly topographical order (see note on x. 9. 1), he does not begin his description of the temple till x. 19. 4, and he finishes it (after a long digression on the Gallic war) in x. 24. 6. He appears to place the Navel-stone somewhere outside the eastern end of the temple, not far from the great altar which he mentioned above (x. 14. 7). If he is right, the Navel-stone would seem to have been moved from the inside to the outside of the temple at some date between the first century B.C. (when Varro and Strabo wrote) and his own time. Dr. Verrall in his edition of the *Ion* of Euripides (p. xlvi. *sq.*) has suggested that the altar of Poseidon described by Pausanias in the fore-temple (see x. 24. 4) was really the Navel-stone, and that the two Fates which stood near it were in fact identical with the two eagles or Gorgons. He thinks that the figures were very archaic and rude, and that "little could really be decided, but that they were meant for creatures of some kind and seemed to have wings." To this view it may be objected that the original figures, whether eagles or Gorgons, were certainly carried off by the Phocians in the Sacred War, and that if they were afterwards replaced by new ones, these later substitutes would probably not be copies of the archaic originals, but would represent two unmistakeable eagles or Gorgons. But we are not told that the missing figures ever were replaced, unless the eagle inlaid in mosaic in the pavement is to be regarded as a substitute for them. And even if we grant that the original winged figures were afterwards replaced by accurate copies, these winged figures, however rude, could hardly have been mistaken for Fates, since the Fates were never, so far as I know, represented with wings. On the whole, considering the strictness with which Pausanias at Delphi as elsewhere adheres to the topographical order in his descriptions, it seems safer to conclude with Dissen (on Pindar, *Pyth.* iv. 6) and K. O. Müller (in his edition of the *Eumenides*, p. 101) that in the time of Pausanias the stone stood outside of the temple. Perhaps it was turned out of the temple by Nero, who wrought havoc at Delphi (see x. 7. 1 note and below, p. 332). In fact, a marble Navel-stone (*omphalos*), decorated with fillets, has been found by the French at Delphi just in the place where, from Pausanias's description, we should expect to find it, that is near the great altar (*Bulletin de Corresp. hellénique*, 18 (1894), p. 180). Whether it is really the famous *omphalos* or not, we cannot say. Another *omphalos*, not decorated with fillets, was found by the French at Delphi, as I learn from Mr. Cecil Smith.

Various attempts have been made to explain the Navel-stone in ancient and modern times. Some of the ancients thought that it was the grave of the Python or of Dionysus. See Varro, *De lingua Latina*, vii. 17 ; Hesychius, *s.v.* Τοξίου βουνός ; Tatian, *Or. adversus Graecos*, 8. Cp. Plutarch, *Isis et Osiris*, 35 ; Joannes Malala, *Chronogr.* ii. p. 45 ed. Dindorf. Modern scholars have suggested that the Navel-stone was a fetish of the Earth goddess (so H. N. Ulrichs), or a symbol of Hestia, goddess of the hearth (so Wieseler), or a symbol of the Pelasgic Zeus (so Mr. Bouché-Leclercq), etc.

See on the whole subject H. N. Ulrichs, *Reisen und Forschungen*, I. p. 77 *sqq.* ; P. Foucart, *Mémoire*, pp. 71-73 ; Fr. Wieseler, 'Intorno all' omfalo Delfico,' *Annali dell' Instituto*, 29 (1857), pp. 160-180 ; *id.*, *Göttingische gelehrte Anzeigen*, 1860, vol. I. Nos. 17-20, pp. 161-196 ; C. Boetticher, *Der Omphalos des Zeus zu Delphi* (Berlin, 1859) ; A. Bouché-Leclercq, *Hist. de la divination*, 3. p. 78 *sqq.* ; J. H. Middleton, in *Journal of Hellenic Studies*, 9 (1888), pp. 294-302.

Conical or pyramidal stones were revered in many other parts of the ancient world.

(1) At Megara there was a pyramidal stone known as Apollo Carinus (i. 44. 2).

(2) At Sicyon the image of Gracious Zeus had the shape of a pyramid (ii. 9. 6).

(3) Apollo as the Street God was commonly represented as a conical pillar (note on i. 31. 6).

(4) At Emesa in Phoenicia people revered a large black conical stone as an image of the Sun-god, who was called in the Phoenician tongue Eleagabalus. The stone was enshrined in a magnificent temple. On a coin of Emesa it is represented standing inside of the temple and enclosed by a balustrade, on which an eagle is perched right in front of the sacred stone. See Herodian, v. 3. 4 *sq.* ; Donaldson, *Architectura Numismatica*, No. xix. ; P. Gardner, *Types of Greek Coins*, pl. xv. No. 1. On another coin of Emesa the conical stone appears in the temple, but without the balustrade and eagle. See Ed. Gerhard, *Gesammelte Abhandlungen*, Abbildungen, lix. No. 5 ; Baumeister's *Denkmäler*, p. 603, No. 649.

(5) The image of Aphrodite in her temple at Paphos in Cyprus was a conical white stone (Tacitus, *Hist.* II. 3 ; Philostratus, *Vit. Apollon.* iii. 58 ; Servius, on Virgil, *Aen.* i. 720). This stone is represented on coins of Caracalla. See Donaldson, *op. cit.* No. xxxi. ; Gerhard, *op. cit.* Abbild. lix. No. 11.

(6) On a coin of Byblus in Phoenicia, struck in the reign of Macrinus, a temple is depicted containing a conical stone enclosed by a

balustrade. The temple may be that of Adonis, to whom the city was sacred (Strabo, xvi. p. 755). See Donaldson, *op. cit.* No. xxx. Conical stones, which seem to have been idols, have been found in Phoenician temples in Cyprus and Malta (Perrot et Chipiez, *Histoire de l'art dans l'antiquité*, 3. pp. 273, 298 *sq.*, 304 *sq.* ; cp. Cesnola, *Cyprus*, pp. 188 *sq.*, 213 *sq.*).

(7) In a vase-painting a conical stone, draped in a sort of net-work, like the Navel-stone at Delphi, seems to be represented as sacred to the Thymbraean Apollo. See Gerhard, *op. cit.* Abbild. lix. 1.

(8) The Artemis of Perge in Asia Minor (Strabo, xiv. p. 667) is represented on coins as a conical stone, but on some coins the cone approximates to a human image by the addition of a head etc. See Gerhard, *op. cit.* Abbild. lix. Nos. 2, 3, 4, and 20; Baumeister's *Denkmäler*, p. 603, figs. 645-648.

(9) The image of Ammon seems to have been a conical stone adorned with jewels (Curtius Rufus, iv. 7. 31).

(10) On a rock-cut relief at Pterium in Asia Minor a priest is represented standing on what seems to resemble the Navel-stone at Delphi, being a truncated cone covered with scales like those of a fir-cone. See Perrot et Chipiez, *Histoire de l'art dans l'antiquité*, 4. pl. viii. and p. 639 ; *Revue archéologique*, 3me Série, 6 (1885), p. 300.

(11) Some Babylonian cylinders exhibit a god seated on an object that closely resembles the Greek Navel-stone. See *Revue archéologique*, 3me Série, 26 (1895), pp. 300, 301, 302, 304, 306, figs. 3, 4, 5.

Conical stones have been revered by rude peoples in various parts of the world, as by the Natchez of Louisiana (Lafitau, *Mœurs des sauvages amériquains*, 1. p. 147 *sq.*), the Fijians (Th. Williams, *Fiji and the Fijians*, 1. p. 220 *sq.*), and the inhabitants of Tinian, one of the Ladrone Islands (W. W. Gill, *Myths and Songs of the South Pacific*, p. 32 *sq.*). As to the worship of stones see also vii. 25. 4 note.

Lastly, we may note other cases of stones or places which have borne the name of Navel. Thus in Rome there was a place called the Navel of Rome (*Umbilicus Romae*). It has been identified with a cylindrical structure of concrete, faced with brick and lined with thin slabs of marble, which exists near the Rostra in the Forum. See J. H. Middleton, 'The Rostra and Graecostasis, with the Umbilicus Romae and the Miliarium Aureum,' *Archaeologia*, vol. 19 ; *id.*, *The Remains of Ancient Rome*, 1. p. 263 *sq.* In the county of Meath in Ireland there was a stone called the Navel of Ireland ; it is said to have been a place of Pagan worship (Giraldus Cambrensis, *Topography of Ireland*, Distinct. iii. c. 4 ; J. Rhys, *Celtic Heathendom*, Hibbert Lectures for 1886, p. 192 *sq.*). At Phlius there was a spot called the Navel because it was thought to be the centre of Peloponnese (Paus. ii. 13. 7). In Crete a place bore the same name because here the Navel-string was said to have fallen from the infant Zeus (Diodorus, v. 70. 4). The Minahasa of Celebes tell of an old man who came to the Navel of the earth and found there a great stone (N. Graafland, *De Minahassa*, 1. p. 149). In the island of Ceram there is a sacred place called the Navel of the island ; curiously enough it is, as Delphi was, the seat of an oracle (Van Hoevell, *Ambon en de Oeliasers*, p. 155). Cuzco, the ancient capital of Peru, means in the Inca language Navel (Garcilasso de la Vega, *Royal Commentaries of the Yncas*, First Part, bk. i. ch. 18, vol. 1. p. 72 *sq.*, Markham's trans.).

16. 4. Hermione —— married Orestes etc. Cp. i. 33. 8.

16. 4. Eurydamus, an Aetolian general. Cp. vi. 16. 1.

16. 5. a city Elyrus. The site of this city, identified by means of inscriptions, is occupied by the village of *Rhodovani*, situated an hour and a half north-east of *Temenia* and two hours from the sea. In the village and on the neighbouring hill are some traces of the ancient city. See L. Thenon, in *Revue archéologique*, N. S. 14 (1866), pp. 396-403. On coins of Elyrus a wild goat is an almost constant type. Sometimes the animal is standing in front of a tree and raising his fore-foot against it; sometimes only its head appears. See Eckhel, *Doctrina Numorum*, 2. p. 312 ; B. V. Head, *Historia Numorum*, p. 393.

16. 5. Apollo —— in the house of Carmanor. See ii. 7. 7, ii. 30. 3.

16. 7. success achieved by the Liparaeans etc. See x. 11. 3 note.

17. 1. Ichnusa. As to this name for Sardinia see [Aristotle,] *De mirab. auscult.* 100 (104) ; Pliny, *Nat. hist.* iii. 85 ; Solinus, iv. 1 ; Isidore, *Origines*, xiv. 6. 39 ; Silius Italicus, xii. 356 *sqq.* ; Stephanus Byzantius, *s.v.* Σαρδώ.

17. 1. Its length is one thousand etc. According to Strabo (v. p. 224) Sardinia was 220 Roman miles long by 98 broad. According to Pliny (*Nat. hist.* iii. 84) the eastern coast of Sardinia measured 188 miles, its western coast 175, its southern coast 77 miles, and its northern coast 125. In point of fact the greatest length of the island is over 160 geographical miles and its greatest breadth is 77 miles (Smith's *Dict. of Greek and Roman Geog. s.v.* 'Sardinia').

17. 2. Libyans: their leader was Sardus etc. The African origin of the Sardinians is referred to by Cicero ; he calls Africa "the parent of Sardinia," and says that the Sardinians were settled in the island, or rather banished to it, by the Carthaginians. See Cicero, *pro Scauro*, xix. 42 and 45. That Sardus, son of Hercules, led a great host from Libya to Sardinia, occupied the island, and called it after his name, is stated also by Isidore (*Origines*, xiv. 6. 39). Cp. Silius Italicus, xii. 359 *sq.* ; Solinus, iv. 1. The head of Sardus with the inscription SARD PATER ('Father Sardus') occurs on Sardinian coins. See Perrot et Chipiez, *Histoire de l'art dans l'antiquité*, 4. p. 20 *sq.* ; Maltzan, *Reise auf der Insel Sardinien*, p. 114. There was a place called the Sanctuary of Father Sardus on the coast of Sardinia (Ptolemy, *Geogr.* iii. 3. p. 375 ed. Müller). Egyptian monuments inform us that from the time of Ramses II. onward the kings of Egypt retained in their pay a large body of foreign mercenaries called Shardana. These are said to have been originally prisoners taken by Ramses II., and in inscriptions they are often designated as "people of the sea." As depicted on the monuments they are easily distinguished by the type of their features and the style of their equipment: they carry round shields, long pointed swords, and a peculiar helmet adorned with a crescent and ball. In the reign of Merenptah (Minephtah), son of Ramses II., the Shardana and other "people of the sea" joined the Libyans in invading Egypt from the west, but the united host was defeated with great slaughter. It has been supposed by Mr. E. de Rougé and other scholars, including W. Max Müller, that the Shardana were the Sardinians. Professor Maspero's view is that the Shardana were originally settled in the west of Asia Minor, and that after the failure of the attack on Egypt in the reign of Merenptah (Minephtah) they moved westward and settled in Sardinia. Professor Wiedemann, on the other hand, holds that the Shardana were a Libyan tribe inhabiting the north coast of Africa not far from Egypt, and he denies their connexion with Sardinia. But that they were a sea-faring people, not merely coast-dwellers, is placed beyond doubt by an Egyptian wall-painting, which represents them sailing in ships with high curved prows and poops and attacking the Egyptians, who are in ships of a different type.

See E. de Rougé, 'Sur les attaques dirigées contre l'Égypte par les peuples de la Méditerranée, *Revue archéologique*, N. S. 16 (1867), pp. 35-45, 81-103; G. Ebers, in *Annali dell' Inst. di Corr. Arch.* 55 (1883), p. 121 *sqq.*; A. Wiedemann, *Ägyptische Geschichte*, pp. 473-476; Ed. Meyer, *Gesch. des Alterthums*, I. § 234; *id.*, *Gesch. des alten Aegyptens*, pp. 285 *sq.*, 304 *sqq.*; Brugsch, 'Troy and Egypt,' Appendix ix. to Schliemann's *Ilios*, pp. 745-751; Maspero, *Histoire ancienne*,[4] pp. 219, 253 *sqq.*, 270; F. Robiou, in *Gazette archéologique*, 7 (1881-1882), pp. 132-144; Perrot et Chipiez, *Histoire de l'art dans l'antiquité*, 4. p. 14 *sqq.*; W. Max Müller, *Asien und Europa nach altägyptischen Denkmälern* (Leipzig, 1893), p. 371 *sqq.*; U. Köhler, in *Sitzungsberichte d. k. preuss. Akad. d. Wissenschaften zu Berlin*, 11. März 1897, p. 269. As to the painting of the sea-fight between the "people of the sea" and the Egyptians, see P. Gardner, *New chapters in Greek history*, p. 74 *sq.*

Some light is thrown on the aboriginal tribes of Sardinia by the rude bronze statuettes which have been found in considerable numbers in Sardinia. These statuettes, according to Mr. G. Perrot, are of native workmanship executed under Phoenician influence. They represent warriors, shepherds, hunters, etc., in a great variety of costume and equipment. Mr. Perrot suggests that the Sardinians who had served abroad as mercenaries in the Carthaginian armies and had returned home, dedicated statuettes of themselves as thank-offerings in their native sanctuaries, and that the custom was imitated by their compatriots. He thinks that this native art may have lasted about three centuries, from the middle of the sixth century B.C. down to the Roman conquest. See G. Perrot, 'Trois figurines Sardes,' *Gazette archéologique*, 10 (1885), pp. 177-183, with pl. 24; Perrot et Chipiez, *Histoire de l'art dans l'antiquité*, 4. p. 64 *sqq.* On the legends as to the various early settlements in Sardinia, see Movers, *Die Phoenizier*, ii. 2. pp. 556-578.

17. 2. **Maceris whom the Egyptians and Libyans surname Hercules.** The name Maceris is etymologically equivalent to Melcarth ('king of the city'), the Tyrian god whom the Greeks identified with Hercules. The legend that Hercules led a motley host composed of many races into the west of Europe (Sallust, *Jugurtha*, 18; Diodorus,

iv. 18 *sqq.*) is believed by Movers to refer to the Tyrian colonies settled in the western basin of the Mediterranean, which were composed of men of various races and worshipped the old Tyrian god Melcarth (Hercules). In like manner he explains the legend which made Sardus a son of Maceris (Melcarth). See Movers, *Die Phoenizier*, 1. p. 417 *sqq.*, and ii. 2. pp. 109 *sqq.*, 556 *sqq.*; Olshausen, in *Rheinisches Museum*, N. F. 8 (1853), p. 328 *sqq.*; cp. E. Curtius, *Gesammelte Abhandlungen*, 2. p. 225.

17. 2. **they lived dispersed —— in huts and caves.** Strabo (v. p. 225) mentions four highland clans in Sardinia who dwelt in caves, namely the Parati, Sossinati, Balari, and Aconites; they scarcely tilled the ground but lived by rapine. According to Diodorus (iv. 30. 5, v. 15. 4) the Iolaean tribe, driven into the mountains by the Carthaginians, made for themselves underground abodes and bred cattle, living on the flesh, milk, and cheese.

17. 3. **Aristaeus and his company.** It is said that before the time of Aristaeus the African and Spanish settlers in Sardinia had formed two separate communities, but he united them and founded the city of Caralis (*Cagliari*) (Solinus, iv. 1 *sq.*). Aristaeus is reported to have been the first who planted and cultivated Sardinia; before his arrival the island was a savage wilderness (Diodorus, iv. 82. 4). The reason assigned by Pausanias for Aristaeus's emigration, namely, his sorrow at the death of Actaeon, is mentioned also by Silius Italicus (xii. 365 *sqq.*). Compare Servius on Virgil, *Georg.* i. 14 ; Sallust, *Hist. Frag.* ii. 7 ed. Kritz; and on the legend of Aristaeus's colonisation of Sardinia see Movers, *Die Phoenizier*, ii. 2. pp. 563-565.

17. 5. **Norax.** According to Solinus (iv. 1) Norax was a son of Mercury and migrated to Sardinia from Tartessus in Spain.

17. 5. **an army from Thespiae —— under —— Iolaus** etc. Compare vii. 2. 2 note. Amongst the colonists whom Iolaus is said to have led to Sardinia were forty of the sons whom Hercules had by the daughters of Thestius. See Apollodorus, ii. 7. 6 ; Diodorus, iv. 29 *sq.*, v. 15 ; Strabo, v. p. 225 ; cp. Silius Italicus, xii. 363 *sq.* ; Solinus, iv. 2 ; Paus. ix. 23. 1, ix. 27. 6 *sq.* According to Strabo (*l.c.*) the Iolaean tribe went also by the name of Diagesbians (Διαγησβεῖς). There is a statuette of Iolaus which is said to have been found at Olbia, the city founded by him. See Maltzan, *Reise auf der Insel Sardinien*, pp. 115, 388. But from the woodcut given by Maltzan I should judge the statuette to be a forgery. It represents Iolaus in Greek armour, with crested helmet, cuirass, and greaves, and holding a spear in rest. The genuine antiquities found in Sardinia are mostly Phoenician; traces of Greek influence are few. See below, note on § 9. That Olbia was founded by Iolaus is stated also by Solinus (i. 61, p. 18 *sq.* ed. Mommsen).

17. 5. **Ogryle, either in memory of one of their townships** etc. According to Stephanus Byzantius (*s.v.* ’Αγραυλή) this Sardinian town was called Agryle after the Attic township of the same name. Whatever may have been the name of the Sardinian town, the name of the Attic township was certainly Agryle (or Agraule), not Ogryle, as Pau-

sanias gives it. This township belonged to the Erechthean tribe and lay near the Panathenaic stadium.   See Stephanus Byzantius, *l.c.*; Harpocration, *s.vv.* Ἀγρυλή and Ἀρδηττος; Hesychius, *s.v.* Ἀγρυλή; Suidas, *s.v.* Ἀγρυλῆθεν; Bekker's *Anecdota Graeca*, p. 332. 30 *sq.*; Plutarch, *X. Orator. vit.* i. 27; *id.*, *Alcibiades*, 22; *id.*, *Themistocles*, 23; *C. I. G.* No. 160. 2, No. 293. 11-14; *C. I. A.* ii. No. 114. 4; Dittenberger, *Sylloge Inscr. Graec.* No. 333. 3 and 36; *id.*, No. 351. 147. Cp. Leake, *Topography of Athens*,[2] 1. p. 281 *sq.*; *id.*, 2. p. 183; A. Milchhoefer, *Karten von Attika, Erläuternder Text,* 2. p. 23; P. Kastromenos, *Die Demen von Attika*, p. 31 *sq.*

17. 5. Iolaus is worshipped by the inhabitants. Iolaus was said to be buried in Sardinia (see ix. 23. 1 note), and the Iolaeans "added a temple to his sepulchre," according to Solinus (i. 61, p. 19 ed. Mommsen). Those who sacrificed to Iolaus in Sardinia called him Father Iolaus (Diodorus, iv. 30). In Sicily also Iolaus had sacred precincts set apart for him and was worshipped with heroic honours. At Agyrium, in particular, he had a precinct in which sacrifices were annually offered to him down to the time of the historian Diodorus. The people of the city used to let their hair grow long in his honour until they had propitiated him with splendid sacrifices. It was believed that the children of persons who omitted to offer the customary sacrifices would be struck dumb but would recover their voices on fulfilling the religious obligation. See Diodorus, iv. 24 and 30. Iolaus was also worshipped at Athens and Thebes (Paus. i. 19. 3; ix. 23. 1). He appears among the gods jointly invoked by the Carthaginians and Macedonians in concluding a treaty (Polybius, vii. 9. 2). According to Fr. Lenormant he is properly a Carthaginian or Phoenician deity, his Semitic name being Iol. See Fr. Lenormant, in *Gazette archéologique*, 2 (1876), p. 126 *sqq.* Cp. Movers, *Die Phoenizier*, 1. pp. 536-538.

17. 6. When Ilium was taken etc. Cp. Silius Italicus, xii. 361 *sq.* The Ilians, who inhabited the rugged mountain-fastnesses of Sardinia (see § 7), are said by Mela (ii. 123 ed. Parthey) to have been the most ancient people in the island. Pliny reckons them amongst the most famous of the Sardinian tribes (*Nat. hist.* iii. 85). The legend which traced their origin to the settlement of Trojan (Ilian) fugitives in Sardinia, had probably no foundation but the similarity of the names. In 181 B.C. the Ilians rebelled against Rome, but were defeated in several engagements (Livy, xl. 19 and 34). In 178 B.C. they again took the field, aided by the Balari, and laid waste the open country. But the Romans under Tiberius Sempronius Gracchus worsted them with great slaughter in many battles and put down the insurrection. See Livy, xli. 7, 12, and 17.

17. 8. Corsicans. This tribe inhabited, as we should have expected, the most northerly part of Sardinia (Ptolemy, iii. 3. 6, p. 382 ed. Müller). They are mentioned by Pliny (*Nat. hist.* iii. 85).

17. 9. the Carthaginians —— subdued the whole population of Sardinia etc. Compare Polybius, i. 10. 5; Diodorus, iv. 29. 6, v. 15. 4 *sq.*, v. 35. 5. Many Phoenician tombs have been discovered in various parts of Sardinia, as at Caralis, Sulci, and Tharros. The necropolis at

Tharros in particular has furnished an immense quantity of Phoenician antiquities. The tombs are hewn in the rock and are reached either by staircases or perpendicular shafts. Among the common types of terra-cotta statuettes found in them are a naked goddess pressing her hands to her breasts, a draped goddess seated in a large chair, and a goddess or priestess standing and pressing the sacred dove to her breast. Hundreds of scarabs have also been found ; many of them are Egyptian in style, though of Phoenician manufacture. Some of these objects may have been imported by Phoenician and Carthaginian traders ; but there are good grounds for believing that many of them were manufactured in Sardinia by the Phoenician or Carthaginian settlers. The result of excavations made within the last half century in Sardinia is to show that the island, while scarcely affected at all by Greek civilisation, was thoroughly penetrated by Semitic influences : it became and remained more purely Phoenician than Cyprus itself.

See Maltzan, *Reise auf der Insel Sardinien*, pp. 207-240 ; C. M. Mansell, in *Gazette archéologique*, 3 (1877), pp. 74-76 ; *id.*, 4 (1878), pp. 50-53 ; G. Ebers, 'Antichità Sarde e loro provenienza,' *Annali dell' Inst. di Corr. Arch.* 55 (1883), pp. 76-132 ; Perrot et Chipiez, *Histoire de l'art dans l'antiquité*, 3. pp. 230-239, 449-453, 654-660; R. Tennant, *Sardinia*, p. 51 *sq.*

17. 9. Caralis and Sulci. These were the oldest cities in Sardinia, according to Mela (ii. § 123 ed. Parthey). Strabo singles them out (v. p. 224) as the most important in the island. Solinus says (iv. 2, p. 50 *sq.* ed. Mommsen) that Caralis was founded by Aristaeus. The ancient remains at Caralis (*Cagliari*) include a remarkable amphitheatre hewn in the rock and calculated to hold 20,000 spectators : there are also Carthaginian or Phoenician and Roman burying-grounds. See Maltzan, *Reise auf der Insel Sardinien*, p. 65 *sqq.* ; R. Tennant, *Sardinia*, p. 52 *sq.* As to Sulci, see Maltzan, *op. cit.* pp. 179-193.

17. 9. Balari. This tribe is mentioned also by Pliny (*Nat. hist.* iii. 85) and Strabo (v. p. 225). Cp. note on § 2 'they lived dispersed' etc.

17. 10. The northern side of the island etc. Cp. Silius Italicus, xii. 372 *sq.* Seen from the deck of a steamer passing through the straits of Bonifacio, the northern coast of Sardinia looks bleak, wild, and desolate. The sea is studded with ugly and jagged rocks, over which the waves break in foam.

17. 11. The air here is generally close and sickly etc. The unhealthiness of the Sardinian climate is often alluded to by ancient writers. See Strabo, v. p. 225 ; Cicero, *ad Quintum fratrem*, ii. 3. 7 ; Mela, ii. 123 ed. Parthey ; Martial, iv. 60. 6 ; Tacitus, *Ann.* ii. 85 ; Silius Italicus, xii. 371. The causes assigned by Pausanias for the unhealthiness of the climate appear to be the true ones. " There are a great many extensive lagoons, especially at the heads of the bays. Some of them are connected with the sea by openings ; others are fed by the infiltration of sea water. Moreover, salt marshes are found far from the sea and at a height above the sea of 76 metres (250 feet). In summer these marshes dry up, leaving the ground covered with a white crystalline crust; but in the rainy season they fill up again. Probably they once formed part of the sea, which has retired and left them; their saltness indicates their origin. Now experience shows that the evaporation of salt and brackish water, when stagnant and mixed with decaying sea-weed, breeds the most dangerous fever-germs; the Tuscans of the Maremma make it their first object to prevent the infusion of salt into fresh water. From these lagoons and morasses the mist rises so thick that it is impossible to see beyond the length of your arm, and this happens in the middle of summer as well as in the rainy season. If there happen to be many such mists at the time when the corn is sprouting, it is all over with the harvest. The wholesome north wind, which might have dispersed the noisome exhalations, is checked by the high mountains. . . . The wind from the sea drives the miasma over the treeless flats and the swampy river-valleys far into the land. The *intemperie*, as the pestilential air is here called, rises to a height unheard of in Italy and dominates coast-land and plains, including at least a fourth of the whole area, especially the fertile belts of cultivated land. In the mining district of the south-west the works are at a standstill from the middle of June to the end of October" (H. Nissen, *Italische Landeskunde*, p. 357 *sq.*). As to the sirocco, Mr. Tennant says that "the S.E. or 'scirocco' blows direct from the eastern coast of Africa, leaving its withering effects along its whole course. It is this wind which raises temperature to a suffocating heat, and at the same time carries with it a treacherous humidity, which it attracts in traversing the long marshy plains, and which is even more dreaded than its scorching aridity" (*Sardinia*, p. 33).

17. 12. Snakes —— will not live in the island, nor will wolves. The absence of serpents and wolves from Sardinia was remarked also by Isidore (*Origines*, xiv. 6. 40); the absence of serpents was noticed by Silius Italicus (xii. 370) and Solinus (iv. 3). The island is still free from both serpents and wolves (H. Nissen, *Italische Landeskunde*, p. 360). It is said that serpents did not exist in the island of Pharus, off Egypt (Aelian, *Nat. an.* ix. 21), and that the soil of Crete was fatal to them not only in the island itself but even when carried abroad (Aelian, *op. cit.* v. 2; cp. Pliny, *Nat. hist.* viii. 227 *sq.*, who says that there were no wolves, bears, nor any noxious animal in Crete). Similar fables were told of the soil of the Balearic islands, the islands of Ebusus, Thanet, etc. (Pliny, *Nat. hist.* iii. 78, xxxv. 202; Solinus, xxii. 8, xxiii. 11, xxix. 8; Mela, ii. 126; Vitruvius, viii. 4. 24), and of Ireland (Solinus, xxii. 3; Bede, *Hist. Eccles.* i. 1. 8); some Christian writers related how St. Patrick had cleared Ireland of all noxious creatures (Giraldus Cambrensis, *Topography of Ireland*, i. 23). Similarly it is said that hares died as soon as they landed in Ithaca (Pliny, *Nat. hist.* viii. 226), and that dogs did not enter the island of Sygaros or roamed about the shore till they perished (*ib.* vi. 155). To this day the soil of some of the Orkney and Shetland islands is popularly supposed to be fatal to mice; hence people take earth from these islands to distant places for the purpose of extirpating vermin (Ch. Rogers, *Social Life in Scotland*, 3. p. 222). We are told that cats cannot exist in the island of Vaila (Brand, ' Description

of Orkney, Zetland,' etc., in Pinkerton's *Voyages and Travels*, 3. p. 787).
It is said that in Quedam, one of the Hebrides, mice do not live, and
that if imported they soon die (Martin, 'Description of the Western
Islands of Scotland,' in Pinkerton's *Voyages and Travels*, 3. p. 591).

17. 12. The rams etc. This is the animal now known as the
moufflon (*Caprovis musimon*). It is confined to Sardinia, Corsica, and
the islands of the Greek archipelago. Strabo says (v. p. 225): "Here (in
Sardinia) live the rams with goats' hair instead of wool; they are called
mousmones, and cuirasses are made out of their hides." Cp. Aelian,
Nat. an. xvi. 34. According to Pliny (*Nat. hist.* viii. 199) the moufflon
was found chiefly in Corsica but also in Spain. The animal "has
more the appearance· of a wild sheep than of any other animal, though
it possesses many points of resemblance to the deer, and yet, in its
anatomical formation, it presents many points of difference from both.
The head, horns and body are like those of the sheep, but the head is
more broad and square, the horns are thicker, rougher, larger, and
more voluted, and, though standing higher than the sheep, the body is
thinner and longer. Its cry too closely resembles the bleating of a
sheep. On the other hand, the texture of its coat, instead of being
woolly, is like that of the deer, the hair being short and bristly, of a
dull brown colour, and white towards the lower parts of the body. The
tail, legs and hoof resemble those of the deer, but it has not the same
long black stripe down the back, nor does it shed its horns in the spring
like the deer tribe. For its size, the Moufflon is the strongest and most
active of animals" (R. Tennant, *Sardinia*, p. 194). Cp. Maltzan, *Reise
auf der Insel Sardinien*, p. 519 *sq.*, who says that the female moufflon
is almost always hornless.

17. 13. This fatal herb resembles celery etc. The Sardonic
smile is first mentioned by Homer (*Od.* xx. 300 *sq.*). Cp. Plato, *Rep.* i.
p. 337 a; Cicero, *ad Fam.* vii. 25. 1. The Sardinian plant which was
said to produce a convulsive laughter terminating in death is described
by Solinus (iv. 4) as growing plentifully in the water of springs. Other
writers, like Pausanias, compare it to celery (σέλινον). See Suidas,
s.v. σαρδάνιος γέλως; Hesychius, *s.v.* Σαρδόνιος γέλως; Eustathius
and a scholiast on Homer, *l.c.*; Isidore, *Origines*, xiv. 6. 40; Servius, on
Virgil, *Ecl.* vii. 41. The plant in question may perhaps have been a
kind of ranunculus, which the Greeks called *batrachion* or *selinon agrion*
('wild celery'). Dioscordides says (*De mat. med.* ii. 206) that a species
of this plant, with a more downy surface, a longer stalk, and more
serrated leaves than usual grew in great abundance in Sardinia, and he
describes it as excessively bitter. He says that a plaster composed of
the leaves, flowers, and stalks of the *batrachion* produced ulcers.
According to Conington (on Virgil, *Ecl.* vii. 41), the plant is known in
England as the celery leaved crowfoot. Various fanciful explanations of
the expression "a Sardonic laugh" are given by Suidas, Hesychius, and
Eustathius (*ll.cc.*).

**18. 1. dedicated by an Athenian, Callias, son of Lysimachides,
from spoils** etc. Callias the Torchbearer, an Athenian, gained great
riches in the Persian war and was nicknamed 'the pit of wealth.' See

Plutarch, *Aristides*, 5 and 25; *id.*, *De cupid. divit.* 8; Schol. on Aristophanes, *Clouds*, 64; Suidas and Photius, *Lexicon*, *s.v.* λακκόπλουτον; Hesychius, *s.v.* λακκόπλουτος; Apostolius, x. 43; and note on i. 23. 2. But Callias, 'the pit of wealth,' appears to have been Callias the son of Hipponicus, who was sent on an embassy to the Persian court (Herodotus, vii. 151). Hence he must be distinguished from Callias the son of Lysimachides, whose votive offering Pausanias saw at Delphi. See Aeschines Socraticus, *Dial.* ii. 9; Boeckh, *Die Staatsaushaltung der Athener*,[3] I. p. 566 *sq.*

18. 6. the hydra and Hercules are of iron. Pausanias has already mentioned (iv. 31. 10) an iron statue of Epaminondas at Messene. In the city of Rhodes there was an iron statue of Hercules, made by Alcon (Pliny, *Nat. hist.* xxxiii. 141).

18. 7. The Phocians of Elatea sent a bronze lion etc. Cp. i. 26. 3; x. 34. 3.

18. 7. the first-fruits of the sea-fight with the Carthaginians. Cp. x. 8. 6 note.

18. 7. an image of an armed woman, no doubt representing Aetolia. On federal coins of Aetolia, dating from after the repulse of the Gauls, Aetolia is represented as a woman armed with sword and spear, sitting on a pile of Gaulish and Macedonian shields, her feet resting on a Gaulish trumpet. This may be a copy of the trophy which the Aetolians set up at Delphi to commemorate their triumph over the Gauls. See P. Gardner, *Types of Greek Coins*, p. 202, with pl. xii. 40; B. V. Head, *Historia Numorum*, p. 283 *sq.* On personifications of countries and cities in ancient art, see P. Gardner, 'Countries and cities in ancient art,' *Journal of Hellenic Studies*, 9 (1888), pp. 47-81. Cp. note on i. 1. 3, vol. 2. p. 27 *sq.*

18. 7. chastised the Gauls for their cruelty etc. See x. 22. 3-7.

18. 7. a gilt statue —— of Gorgias. Cp. Hermippus, in Athenaeus, xi. p. 505 d; Cicero, *de Oratore*, iii. 32. 129; Pliny, *Nat. hist.* xxxiii. 83; Valerius Maximus, viii. 15. 12. Ext. 2; Philostratus, *Vit. Soph.* i. 9. 2; [Dio Chrysostom,] *Or.* xxxvii. vol. 2. p. 301 ed. Dindorf. All these writers differ from Pausanias in asserting that the statue was of gold, not merely gilt; Cicero expressly denies that it was gilt. On the other hand Hermippus and Pliny agree with Pausanias that the statue was dedicated by Gorgias himself, while Cicero and Valerius Maximus affirm that it was dedicated by all Greece. At Olympia there was a statue of Gorgias dedicated by a grand-nephew. The inscription of that statue has been discovered; it mentions the Delphic statue of Gorgias in terms which favour the view that the Delphic statue was dedicated by the orator himself. See vi. 17. 7 note. According to Pliny (*l.c.*), the statue of Gorgias at Delphi was dedicated about Ol. 70 (500-497 B.C.).

19. 1. Scyllis of Scione. See Herodotus viii. 8, who calls him Scyllias. The sea-god Glaucus fell in love with Hydne, daughter of Scyllis, according to Aeschrion the Samian (cited by Athenaeus, vii. p. 296 e). There is an epigram by Apollonidas on this famous diver (*Anthol. Palat.* ix. 296). Both Aeschrion and Apollonidas call him Scyllus.

19. 3. Some fishermen at Methymna etc. With what follows compare Eusebius, *Praepar. Evang.* v. 36, who quotes the oracle to which Pausanias refers. In an inscription found at Methymna in 1882, mention is made of a custom of " carrying round the image " at the festival of Dionysus (ἐν τοῖς Διονυσίοισι πρὸ τᾶς τῶ ἀγάλματος περιφορᾶς). See S. Reinach, ' Inscription de Méthymna,' *Bulletin de Corresp. hellénique,* 7 (1883), pp. 37-41. The image referred to in the inscription is probably the olive-wood image of Dionysus Phallen. As to the epithet Phallen, see Lobeck, *Aglaophamus,* pp. 1085-1088 ; L. Preller, *Griech. Mythologie,*[4] 1. p. 712, note 4.

19. 4. The sculptures in the gables etc. Pausanias, following up the Sacred Way from the main entrance of the precinct, has now reached the temple of Apollo. The scanty remains of the temple have been fully excavated by the French ; but before describing these remains it will be well to consider what light is thrown on the history of the building by ancient writers and inscriptions. Pausanias himself has sketched the history of the temple from the earliest times (x. 5. 9-13), but his sketch requires to be supplemented and perhaps corrected from other sources.

The old temple was burnt down in Ol. 57. 4 (549/8 B.C.) according to Jerome (in Eusebius, *Chronic.* vol. 2. p. 97 ed. Schöne), in Ol. 58. 1 (548/7 B.C.) according to Pausanias (x. 5. 13), or in Ol. 58. 2 (547/6 B.C.) according to the Armenian version of Eusebius (*Chronic.* vol. 2. p. 96 ed. Schöne). We may take it therefore as certain that the catastrophe happened in 548 or 547 B.C. Herodotus, without mentioning the date, tells us that the temple was accidentally destroyed by fire (i. 50, ii. 180). The Amphictyons contracted to have a new temple built for 300 talents, of which the people of Delphi were to contribute a fourth. To defray this expense emissaries went the round of the cities soliciting subscriptions. From the Greeks resident in Egypt they received twenty *minae*, and Amasis king of Egypt gave a thousand talents of alum. As Amasis died in 526 B.C., the envoys must have visited Egypt not later than that year. See Herodotus, ii. 180. The contract was undertaken by the noble Athenian family of the Alcmaeonids, then in exile and eager to secure their restoration to Athens together with the downfall of the tyrants, the sons of Pisistratus, by whom they had been banished. Hence to propitiate the god, or rather the priestly officials who worked the oracle, they rebuilt the temple in a more splendid style than had been stipulated in the contract, by constructing the façade of Parian marble instead of common stone. This they were able to do out of the wealth which they had inherited from a long line of distinguished ancestors. Such is the account which Herodotus gives (v. 62) of this transaction. Other writers, however, place the action of the Alcmaeonids in a less favourable light. They tell us that, far from expending their private fortune on rebuilding the temple, the Alcmaeonids as a last resort undertook the contract for the purpose of providing themselves with funds to be used in their machinations against the sons of Pisistratus (Aristotle, *Constitution of Athens,* 19 ; Philochorus, cited by a scholiast on Pindar, *Pyth.* vii. 9 ; Schol.

on Demosthenes, *Or.* xxi. p. 561. 16, vol. 9. p. 623 ed. Dindorf). The rhetorician Themistius (*Or.* iv. p. 53 a, p. 63 ed. Dindorf) merely says that the Alcmaeonids undertook the contract, without mentioning their motives or the means by which they executed it. Pausanias (x. 5. 13) and Strabo (ix. p. 421) do not refer to the Alcmaeonids at all in this connexion, simply stating that the temple of their day was built by the Amphictyons. To this Pausanias adds that the expenses were defrayed out of the sacred treasures and that the architect was Spintharus of Corinth. That the temple was built and in a style of some magnificence by the Alcmaeonids is expressly said by Pindar in an ode (*Pyth.* vii. 10 *sqq.*) of which the date has been a good deal discussed. The latest writer on the subject, Mr. H. Pomtow, concludes that the Pythian victory of Megacles which the ode commemorates was won in 486 B.C. (*Rheinisches Museum*, N. F. 51 (1896), pp. 577-588). The temple must have been finished, however, a good many years earlier, probably before 510 B.C., the date of the banishment of the tyrant Hippias and the restoration of the Alcmaeonids. From the description in the *Ion* of Euripides (*vv.* 184-218) we gather that the two façades of the temple, the eastern and western, were adorned with sculptures, and that among the scenes represented were the following : (1) Hercules slaying the Lernaean Hydra, while his comrade Iolaus stood beside him holding up a torch; (2) Bellerophon mounted on Pegasus and slaying the Chimaera; (3) Pallas Athena shaking her Gorgon shield against the giant Enceladus ; (4) Zeus hurling a thunderbolt at the giant Mimas ; and (5) Dionysus laying low another of the giant brood with an ivy-wand. Now none of these scenes answers to Pausanias's description of the sculptures in the gables. Hence it has been inferred that they occupied, not the gables, but the metopes under the gables at the eastern and western ends of the temple.

In the early part of the fourth century B.C. the temple seems to have been destroyed by earthquake or fire, and its reconstruction apparently was still proceeding in the second half of that century. A Delphic inscription, which from the character of the letters Professor Köhler would assign to the early part of the fourth century, mentions that a certain Agatho, son of Neoteles, and his brothers brought forward a proposal in favour of the Thurians at the time when the temple was thrown down or burnt (κατελύθη or κατεκαύθη, the reading is uncertain). See *Mittheilungen d. arch. Inst. in Athen*, 5 (1880), p. 202 *sqq.* ; *Rheinisches Museum*, N. F. 51 (1896), p. 351 *sqq.* The catastrophe would seem to have happened not later than 371 B.C., for at the peace congress held in that year at Sparta it was proposed by Prothous that the states should be invited " to contribute what they pleased to the temple of Apollo " (Xenophon, *Hellenica*, vi. 4. 2). That the object to which the contributions were to be applied was the rebuilding of the temple is made probable by an Attic inscription dating from 369/8 B.C., which mentions a letter sent by Dionysius, tyrant of Syracuse, to the Athenians about " the building of the temple and the peace " (*C. I. A.* ii. No. 51 ; Dittenberger, *Sylloge Inscr. Graec.* No. 72). The reference here to " the peace " is most probably to the negotiations for a general peace which were held at Delphi in 368 B.C. (Xenophon, *Hellenica*, vii. 1. 27 ; Diodorus, xv. 70), the very year in which Dionysius apparently wrote.   If that is so, the temple referred to can hardly be any other than the temple of Apollo at Delphi.   How the temple had been destroyed on this occasion is uncertain.   A scholiast on Aristides (p. 740 ed. Dindorf) asserts that the Phocians burnt it. They can hardly have done so at the time that they were in possession of the sanctuary during the Sacred War, for that war did not begin till 355 B.C., and the evidence just adduced goes to show that the destruction of the temple happened not later than 371 B.C.   More-over if to the sacrilege of plundering the temple they had added the further enormity of setting it on fire, this would hardly have been passed over in silence by the ancient writers who record the sacrilege.   Either, therefore, the scholiast on Aristides is wrong or he refers to some earlier misdeed of the Phocians about which we have no further infor-mation.   But whatever the cause and date of the destruction may have been, we possess in inscriptions lately found at Delphi abundant evi-dence as to the date and even the details of its restoration.   These inscriptions, dated by the archons of Delphi and extending over a period of about twenty years from 353 B.C. onward, contain the accounts of an international commission charged with the reconstruction of the temple and bearing the title of 'temple-makers' (ναοποιοί).   The commis-sioners, chosen from among the peoples who belonged to the Amphic-tyonic League, superintended the quarrying, transport, hewing, and placing of the stones in position, and acted besides as paymasters. Under their orders and paid by them were the workmen, contractors, and architect.   The stones came from Corinth and Sicyon, from which we may infer that the material was tufa, and were brought by sea to Cirrha, where they were slung in a crane and lowered on to the quay. The use to which the blocks thus brought were put gives us an idea of the nature and extent of the work.   They were distributed between the outer colonnade, the fore-temple (*prodomos*), the back-chamber (*opistho-domos*), and the *cella*.   We hear further of the great doorway, the doors, six architraves, fourteen triglyphs, gargoyles in the shape of lions' heads, and finally of roof-tiles of the Corinthian sort.   Even the cost of mending the crane and giving it a coat of pitch is set down in these minute accounts.   The name of the architect, who is repeatedly men-tioned, was Xenodorus.   The authority which disbursed the moneys to the commissioners is variously described in the inscriptions as "the city of the Delphians" and "the Council."   Clearly the works referred to in these inscriptions were no ordinary repairs.   They would seem to have amounted to something like rebuilding the temple from roof to pavement.   The period over which the accounts extend, beginning in 353/2 B.C. and continuing with one or more breaks to 328/7 B.C., shows that the work proceeded but slowly.   Indeed there is some ground for thinking that it dragged on for more than a century, since a Delphic inscription, which Mr. H. Pomtow would date about 230 B.C., makes mention of the care with which "Agatho, the architect of the temple, and after him his son Agasicrates, and now Agathocles, has superintended the works commanded by the god and by the Amphictyons" (Dittenberger, *Sylloge Inscr. Graec.* No. 206; H. Pomtow, in *Rheinisches Museum*, N. F. 51 (1896), p. 354 *sqq.*). As to the inscriptions which contain the accounts of the commission of 'temple-makers' see Th. Homolle, in *Bulletin de Corresp. hellénique*, 18 (1894), p. 181; *id.*, in *Comptes Rendus de l'Académie des Inscriptions*, 23 (1895), pp. 334-336; H. Weil, in *Bulletin de Corresp. hellénique*, 19 (1895), p. 394 *sq.*; P. Foucart, in *Comptes Rendus de l'Académie des Inscriptions*, 23 (1895), p. 193; E. Bourguet, 'Inscriptions de Delphes,' *Bulletin de Corresp. hellénique*, 20 (1896), pp. 197-241.

But though the last touches may not have been given to the temple for a century or more from the time when it was begun, the building must have been completed as far as the architrave by the year 340/339 B.C., for in that year the people of Amphissa proposed in the Amphictyonic Council that the Athenians should be fined fifty talents " for setting up golden shields on the new temple before its consecration," and for engraving on them an inscription which set forth that the shields had been taken by the Athenians from the Medes and Thebans when these peoples fought against the Greeks (Aeschines, *contra Ctesiph.* 115 *sq.*). The shields were no doubt hung on the architrave, where they remained down to the time of Pausanias, as he tells us in the present passage. Additional proof that the temple was still unfinished about this time is furnished by the paean to Dionysus which was found a few years ago at Delphi. For in this hymn, which seems to date from about 338 B.C., the poet, after telling us that "the god bids the Amphictyons complete the work with all speed," indulges in a beatific vision of the time when a happy generation shall behold the temple of Phoebus all glittering with gold, eternal and undefiled. See H. Weil, 'Un péan delphique à Dionysos,' *Bulletin de Corresp. hellénique*, 19 (1895), pp. 393-418.

The temple thus slowly brought to completion appears to have been destroyed or at least injured by fire during an irruption of northern barbarians in 84 or 83 B.C. Jerome says that in Ol. 174. 1 (84 B.C.) the temple at Delphi was burnt by Thracians for the third time (Eusebius, *Chronic.* vol. 2. p. 133 ed. Schöne). Appian tells us that in 88 B.C. the Illyrian tribes of the Scordiscians, Maedes, and Dardanians overran Greece and plundered the Delphic sanctuary (*Illyr.* 5, reading τριακοσιοστόν with H. Pomtow(*Rheinisches Museum*, N. F. 51 (1896), p. 370) for τριακοστόν). Again, Plutarch informs us that at the time of the Mithridatic and Social wars the temple at Delphi was burnt by the Maedes and that with the destruction of the altar the sacred and perpetual fire went out (*Numa*, 9, reading ὑπὸ Μαίδων περὶ τὰ ·Μιθριδιατικά κ.τ.λ. with H. Pomtow (*op. cit.* p. 365) instead of ὑπὸ Μήδων, περὶ δὲ τὰ Μιθριδιατικὰ κ.τ.λ.). Mr. H. Pomtow has shown grounds for rejecting the date (88 B.C.) assigned to this event by Appian and for holding that the inroad of the Maedes and the destruction of the temple took place in the first half of 83 B.C. Some attempt was probably soon made to repair or rebuild the burnt temple, but nearly a century, it would seem, elapsed before the edifice was once more completely rebuilt.   A scholiast on Aeschines (*contra Ctesiph.* 116, p. 335 ed. Schultz) tells us that the temple "remained for a long time unfinished, till Nero, the Roman emperor, completed it on his visit to Delphi." This scholiast, it is true, believed that the temple thus completed by Nero was the one which had been built or at least begun by the Amphictyons in the sixth century B.C.   Of the two subsequent catastrophes in the fourth and first centuries B.C. he appears to have been ignorant ; but this hardly invalidates his testimony as to the completion of the temple by Nero.   That testimony is confirmed by a scholiast on Aristides (vol. 3. p. 340 ed. Dindorf), who says that the seat of the oracle at Delphi was burnt by the Phocians, but that the emperor Nero on a visit to Delphi built it on a larger and more magnificent scale than before.   Afterwards, however, the scholiast goes on, the flighty emperor pulled it down again because his tender conscience took dire offence at an oracular response which seemed to reflect on his moral character. This story of the wilful destruction of the temple by the injured emperor is to some extent borne out by a fragmentary Latin inscription recently found at Delphi.   The inscription, which is cut in large fine letters and seems to have been set up at the head of the Sacred Way, mentions that the emperor Domitian repaired (*refecit*) the temple at his own expense in 84 A.D. (IMP. VII. COS. X.).   See *Comptes Rendus de l'Académie des Inscriptions*, 24 (1896), p. 87 ; *Bulletin de Corresp. hellénique*, 20 (1896), p. 717.

So much for the history of the temple, as far as it can be traced by the help of literature and inscriptions.   We have now to consider the existing remains of the building, and to see whether they tally with the literary and epigraphic evidence.

The temple rested on a great terrace which was and is supported on the west, south, and east by the remarkable wall of polygonal masonry to which reference has been repeatedly made.   This wall, one of the most beautiful specimens of Greek masonry in existence, is preserved on the long south side of the terrace in an unbroken stretch of about 250 feet.   Its height varies with the slope of the ground.   In part it is 10 ft. 6 in. high, without reckoning the coping, which consists of three courses of ashlar masonry, the stones in each course being about 18 inches high and from 4 to 5 feet long.   These top courses of rectangular blocks have been removed in many places.   The average height of the wall, when perfect, was nearly 15 feet.   Some of the polygonal blocks of which the wall, exclusive of the coping, is composed measure as much as 7 feet across, and the joints of all of them are worked and fitted with absolute accuracy without the use of mortar, while their exposed faces are dressed to a perfectly smooth surface.   "But the extraordinary point about the masonry is that many of the joints follow a curved instead of a straight line, involving a most exceptional amount both of skill and careful patience on the part of the Delphian masons, who have made the various curves fit each other with perfect accuracy. Some of the beds, which range in a horizontal direction, form very complex undulating lines.   The very smooth dressing of the face of the wall stops at the old ground line, and the part below this, which was hidden from sight, is left rough, in a way which shows that the wall-face was brought to its present smooth surface after the separate blocks were in their places. Possibly the extreme smoothness of the wall was not thought necessary till it began to be used for inscriptions, which now cover most of its surface" (J. H. Middleton). A small piece of the polygonal wall which supported the short eastern end of the terrace was laid bare by Mr. Wescher in 1862. The style of its masonry resembles that of the long southern wall just described and, like the latter, it is covered with inscriptions. Doubtless the remains of these remarkable terrace-walls have now been completely excavated on all three sides (east, south, and west) by the French, though no report of the excavation has, so far as I know, been published. The inscriptions, cut in small letters and closely packed together, with which the walls are covered, amount to more than seven hundred. A few of them record honours and privileges accorded by the city of Delphi to various persons, and one of them contains a long list of the honorary citizens or public friends (*proxenoi*) of Delphi (Wescher-Foucart, *Inscriptions recueillies à Delphes*, No. 18 ; W. Dittenberger, *Sylloge Inscr. Graec.* No. 198). But the vast majority of them merely register, with tiresome iteration of established legal phraseology, the emancipation of slaves under the form of a sale to the Pythian Apollo. A melancholy interest attaches to these inscriptions, for it was in copying them under a burning July sun that the great scholar K. O. Müller received the stroke which carried him off at the early age of forty-three (August 1st, 1840). It has been remarked as a curious coincidence that the scholar who denied Apollo to be the sun-god should have been killed by sun-stroke at Apollo's temple. The story of his last few days has been told by his companion and friend E. Curtius (*Alterthum und Gegenwart*, 2.[2] p. 247 *sqq.*).

Of the temple itself nothing is now standing except the foundations and some portions of the pavement at the eastern and western ends. It was an edifice about 60 metres (197 feet) long by 25 metres (72 feet) broad, lying nearly north-east and south-west, and raised on vast substructions at a height considerably above the coping of the polygonal retaining-wall. The foundations form two rectangles, enclosed one within the other. The outer rectangle supported the external colonnade ; the inner supported the walls of the *cella* and the columns of the fore-temple (*prodomos*) and back-chamber (*opisthodomos*). Two other foundations within the inner rectangle and parallel to its long sides, probably supported rows of columns on either side of the *cella*.

The outer foundation, on which rested the external colonnade of the temple, is well preserved on the eastern and southern sides. Here it is uniformly constructed of great blocks of the native conglomerate or breccia, roughly squared and dressed only on the beds. The workmanship is of the sixth century B.C. About 10 metres from the south-west angle, however, the material and workmanship of the foundations change completely. Here and along the whole of the west side it is only the two or three lowest courses that are built of the native breccia : above that the breccia is replaced by fine white marble cut in admirably worked quadrangular blocks, which retain traces of red paint. Amongst them are pieces of large mutules with some of the *guttae* still projecting from them. The dimensions of these mutules correspond with those of the temple. If put together, they would measure at least 20 metres (65 ft. 7 in.) in length.

The inner foundations are built of blocks of tufa, well worked. Like the outer foundations they are well preserved on the east and south, but on the west we find the same irregularity and a similar mixture of different materials, marble and tufa. Blocks of marble occur even in the lowest course, and amongst them is a sculptured triglyph which has been sawn and of which the dimensions correspond to those of the temple. On this triglyph a torso in high relief may be distinguished against a red background. Further it deserves to be noted that at the south-west corner the inner foundations are connected with and as it were buttressed against the outer foundations by a cross-wall which has obviously been added at some later time. This cross-wall, clearly built to support and strengthen the two sets of foundations which it bonds together, has been subsequently crushed between its two neighbours and cracked from top to bottom by an earthquake, the traces of which are manifest on the whole western half of the temple. Not only has the pavement, constructed of enormous square blocks of bluish limestone, been thrown down and its supports dislocated or broken, but the whole building has been shifted bodily backward so that the western line of foundations is twisted for a length of about 20 metres (65 ft. 7 in.).

From these facts we conclude that (1) a temple built in the sixth century B.C. was afterwards shaken by an earthquake which left some parts of the foundations standing, but overthrew other parts, especially at the south-west angle, down to the bed rock ; and (2) the marble portions of the temple were so much damaged that instead of being replaced in their old positions when the temple was rebuilt they were employed in repairing the ruined foundations. The temple thus overthrown can have been no other than the one constructed by the Alcmaeonids in the sixth century B.C., and the blocks of white marble built into the later foundations must have come from the façade of Parian marble with which, as Herodotus tells, these munificent nobles adorned the temple. To judge from the state of the foundations, the edifice suffered unequally in its different parts. At the eastern end it was only the upper structure that came down ; at the western end the whole building went, foundations and all.

Of the upper portions of the temple, above the foundations, there remain in position some of the steps and two pieces of the pavement, amounting to about 30 square metres, at the two ends of the building. Further there have been found, besides many drums of Doric columns lying in rows as they fell, some pieces of Doric capitals, a few fragments of triglyphs and metopes, many broken gargoyles of marble in the shape of lions' heads, and many pieces of marble Ionic columns, including drums, bases and capitals. These Ionic columns, of which the remains are dispersed all over the sanctuary, are smaller than the Doric columns and in their fully-developed type recall those of the Erechtheum or of the temple at Priene. The Doric columns and the triglyphs and metopes are made of tufa. Of the drums the late J. H. Middleton says : " In 1875 I was able to find and to measure thirty-two drums of Doric columns made of the rough siliceous limestone from the quarries of Mount Parnassus, and still in part retaining their coating of very hard fine stucco, made of lime and powdered white marble, which appears always to have been used by the Greeks to coat temples which were not built of real marble. This beautiful substance is quite unlike anything which we now call stucco. It was as hard and durable as real marble, and took by polishing the same delicate ivory-like surface as that of the best Pentelic marble. Moreover it had the advantage over real marble in affording a slightly absorbent ground for coloured decoration. These column-drums naturally varied in size owing to the diminution of the shaft ; the largest measured (including the stucco) close upon 5 ft. 9 in. in diameter, thus giving the size of the column at the bottom. The top diameter, 4 ft. 2$\frac{1}{2}$ in., is given by the neckings of the capitals, of which a few examples are still to be seen." The shafts of these columns are somewhat slender and diminish regularly upwards without exhibiting that swelling (*entasis*) in the middle which is a mark of antiquity. The *echinus* of the capitals is nearly straight, and the *abacus* has neither the thickness nor the prominence which we find in capitals of the sixth century B.C. The shape of the capitals and the triglyphs, the dimensions of the metopes, and the height of the architrave recall the corresponding details in the temple of Athena Alea at Tegea, which was built in the fourth century B.C., somewhere about 390 B.C. (vol. 4. p. 425). The date thus suggested for the temple is confirmed by the masons' marks carved on many blocks of tufa, for these marks consist of letters and names written in the alphabet of the fourth century B.C. Altogether the evidence both architectural and palaeographical points, in the opinion of Mr. Homolle, to the conclusion that the temple built by the Alcmaeonids in the sixth century was destroyed by an earthquake and rebuilt in the fourth century B.C. We have already seen that the evidence of ancient writers and inscriptions leads independently to the same conclusion, which may accordingly be regarded as established. A notable agreement between these two distinct lines of proof—the architectural and the epigraphical—has been justly emphasised by Mr. Homolle. Amongst the contractors mentioned in the accounts of the commission who were charged with the restoration of the temple there are three, to wit Daius, Pancrates, and Sion, whose names have been found engraved on blocks of tufa belonging to the temple. Amongst these Sion, as we learn from the accounts of the commissioners, was charged with the execution of some work about the Navel-stone (*omphalos*) which stood, as we have seen (p. 316 *sq*.), in the *cella* ; and it is precisely in the *cella* that the stones bearing the name of Sion have been found. As rebuilt in the fourth century B.C. the temple rested on a basement of three high steps and was surrounded by a Doric colonnade. It had a fore-temple (*prodomos*) and a back-chamber (*opisthodomos*) at its eastern and western ends respectively. The number of columns on each of the two façades was probably six. The number of the columns on the long sides is uncertain ; J. H. Middleton estimated it at fifteen. The interior of the *cella* seems to have been flanked on either hand by a row of those Ionic columns of which so many remains have been found. The *adytum* or oracular cavity in the temple has not been discovered. Perhaps it was destroyed by one of the many earthquakes which have visited Delphi. On the other hand beneath the floor of the temple there has been revealed a network of passages and cells, more than 6 feet high, their walls built of great stones from 4 feet to 6 feet long. But these subterranean corridors and chambers appear to have served no other purpose than the purely structural one of economising labour and materials. As it would have been impracticable, or at least exceedingly laborious and expensive, to construct a platform of solid masonry large enough to support an edifice which covered more than 1200 square metres, the architect contented himself with resting the temple on a series of piers linked to each other by stone walls. No vestige of a staircase leading down to these vaults has come to light, nor has any trace of human occupation been discovered in them. With the exception of some coarse pottery, the only objects found in them have been some insignificant bronze fragments and a couple of sherds of Mycenaean ware.

It remains to compare Pausanias's account of the temple with the existing remains of the building and with what we have learned of its history from other sources.

After giving the history of the temple down to its destruction by fire in 548 B.C., Pausanias proceeds thus (x. 5. 13): "The present temple" (more literally "the temple of our time") "was built for the god by the Amphictyons out of the sacred treasures : the architect was Spintharus of Corinth." Now we have seen that after its destruction in 548 B.C. the temple was rebuilt twice at least, perhaps four times, namely in the sixth and fourth centuries B.C., and perhaps by Nero and Domitian in the first century A.D. Clearly, therefore, Pausanias has omitted to mention one, two, or even three of the restorations which took place after 548 B.C. Which of the temples is he describing ? It is commonly supposed that he is describing the temple built by the Alcmaeonids in the sixth century B.C., but that this is so is by no means certain. For in the first place it is to be observed that he makes no mention of the Alcmaeonids and of the façade of Parian marble with which they enriched the temple—omissions all the more remarkable in a writer like Pausanias who knew Herodotus so well and followed him so closely. In the second place, his account in the present passage (x. 19. 4) of the sculptured decoration of the temple differs so entirely from the account which Euripides gives of it in the fifth century B.C. that it is quite plain the two writers are describing two totally distinct sets of sculpture. The difference may be explained by supposing, as is usually done, that the two sets of sculpture occupied different places in the same temple, but it may also be explained by supposing that they belonged to two different temples. In the third place, Pausanias mentions the golden shields on the architrave, which the Athenians dedicated from the spoils of Marathon, and also the Gallic shields dedicated by the Aetolians which hung at the back (west) and the left-hand side of the temple.   Now we have seen (p. 331) evidence that the golden shields commemorative of the victories in the Persian war were set up by the Athenians in the new temple which was built in the fourth century B.C. ; and that the shields taken by the Aetolians from the Gauls in 279 B.C. must have been hung in that temple is of course certain.   Moreover, Pausanias's statement as to the Gallic shields has been confirmed by the recent excavations, for on a metope found at the south-west angle of the temple there remains the mark of a long shield, more than 3 feet high, recalling the shape of the Gallic bucklers (*Bulletin de Corresp. hellénique*, 18 (1894), p. 176).

Thus far the evidence goes to show that the temple described by Pausanias was the one which was built in the fourth century B.C.   But there are difficulties in the way of accepting this view.   For in the first place the architect, according to Pausanias, was Spintharus of Corinth, whereas in the inscriptions relating to the restoration of the temple in the fourth century B.C. the architect named repeatedly is Xenodorus.   This difficulty, however, is not insuperable, for the first document in which the name of the architect Xenodorus occurs is dated in the archonship of Nicon (349/8 B.C.), and the destruction of the temple seems to have taken place not later than 371 B.C.   It is therefore quite possible that the temple may have been planned by Spintharus and partly constructed under his superintendence, and that dying before its completion he was succeeded in the work by Xenodorus.   We have seen that other architects were at work on the temple at a later time, the sons succeeding the father in the office ; and Pausanias himself tells us that the building of the temple lasted so long that the original sculptor died before it was finished, and his work had to be completed by another.   Of the date of the architect Spintharus nothing positive is known.   He seems to be mentioned by no other ancient writer except Pausanias.[1]

A more serious difficulty is created, at least, at first sight, by Pausanias's statement that the sculptures in the gables were begun by an Athenian artist Praxias, a pupil of Calamis.   Of this Praxias nothing more is known ; but since Calamis appears to have been at work in the first half of the fifth century B.C. (see note on v. 25. 5), it is natural to suppose that his pupil Praxias flourished in the second half of that century.   It is difficult to reconcile this date either with the view that the temple on which Praxias worked was the one built by the Alcmaeonids in the sixth century B.C. or with the view that the temple in question was the one repaired or rebuilt in the fourth century B.C.   If it was the temple built in the sixth century B.C., why were the gable sculptures begun so long afterwards ?   For observe that they were only begun by

---

[1] By an oversight Mr. H. Pomtow affirms that Spintharus is named by Herodotus as the architect of the temple built by the Alcmaeonids in the sixth century B.C. (*Rheinisches Museum*, N. F. 51 (1896), p. 333, cp. p. 345).   Herodotus neither mentions Spintharus nor alludes to any architect at all.

Praxias; the temple, if we may trust Pausanias, was not finished for some time afterwards. Yet Pindar writing in the early years of the fifth century B.C. speaks as if the temple had been finished, and that too in splendid style, by the Alcmaeonids some time before he wrote. It is difficult, therefore, to believe that the temple for which Praxias worked was the temple of the sixth century B.C.

Can it have been the temple of the fourth century B.C. ? Here we are reminded first, of the statement of Pausanias (i. 3. 5) that Calamis, the master of Praxias, made an image of Apollo at the close of the great plague which devastated Athens in the Peloponnesian war (427 B.C.), and, second, of the opinion of Prof. U. Köhler that the inscription which mentions the destruction of the Delphic temple dates from the early years of the fourth century B.C. If we can accept this statement of Pausanias and this opinion of Prof. Köhler, the difficulty created by the mention of Praxias as the sculptor of the temple vanishes at once. The destruction of the temple may have occurred at the beginning of the fourth century or even at the end of the fifth century B.C., for there is nothing whatever in the words of the inscription (ἐπεὶ ὁ ναὸς κατ[ελ]ύθη or κατ[εκα]λύθη) to prevent us from supposing that the catastrophe happened some years before the inscription was engraved. If then the temple was destroyed at the end of the fifth century or the beginning of the fourth century B.C., and its restoration was taken in hand soon afterwards, nobody need boggle at the statement that the sculptures were begun by an artist whose master had been at work in 427 B.C. On this view the temple described by Pausanias is the temple of the fourth century B.C., and his statement that its construction lasted some time is amply confirmed, not only by the poetical aspirations of the author of the paean to Dionysus, but by the more precise, if prosaic, accounts of the building commissioners, which prove that the work dragged on over many years and was not finished by about 330 B.C. or even later.

To this, however, it may be objected that the gable sculptures, at which Praxias worked, cannot have been made or at least placed in position until the temple was nearly finished ; and that the triglyphs, which must have been in position before the gables, were not all ready before 351/0 B.C., if even then (see *Bulletin de Corresp. hellénique*, 20 (1896), p. 199, cp. pp. 198, 237). Now a pupil of Calamis cannot possibly, it may be urged, have been at work after 350 B.C. Admitting the force of this objection, we are still free to suppose that the gable sculptures may have been begun long before they were placed in position. Or—another possibility—may Pausanias have simply erred in describing the Athenian Praxias as a pupil of Calamis ? From an inscription found at Oropus (*C. I. G. G. S.* 1. No. 430 ; Loewy, *Inschriften griech. Bildhauer*, No. 127a) we hear of an Athenian sculptor Praxias, son of Lysimachus, who made a statue of a certain Charias son of Neoptolemus shortly before 338 B.C.—precisely the time when the new temple is known to have been approaching completion, since the golden shields had been hung by the Athenians on the architrave not later than 339 B.C. (Aeschines, *contra Ctesiph.* 116). We are tempted, accord-

ingly, to conjecture that this Praxias, son of Lysimachus, who is known
also to have executed an image of Aphrodite at Athens (Loewy, *op. cit.*
No. 127), was no other than' the Praxias who about the same time made
some of the sculptures for the new temple of Apollo at Delphi, and that
Pausanias may have mistaken him for another sculptor of the same
name who was in fact a pupil of Calamis. Whatever may be thought
of this suggestion, the view that the temple described by Pausanias as
existing in his own time was the temple of the fourth century B.C. seems
open to fewer objections than the view that it was the temple built
by the Alcmaeonids in the sixth century B.C.

Of the subsequent destruction of the temple in 84 or 83 B.C. and its
restoration by Nero and perhaps Domitian, Pausanias says nothing.
It is possible that the destruction was only partial, and that the repairs
carried out by the emperors did not alter the essential character of
the building and were therefore not deemed worthy of notice by
Pausanias. The supposition is confirmed by the lack, apparently
total, among the existing ruins of any sign that the temple was ever
rebuilt in Roman times.

On the temple, its ruins and its history, see H. N. Ulrich's *Reisen und
Forschungen*, 1. p. 71 *sqq.*; L. Preller, in Pauly's *Real-Encyclopädie*,[1] *s.v.*
'Delphi,' 2. p. 916 *sqq.*; C. Wescher, in *Bulletino dell' Instituto di Corrisp.
Archeol.* 37 (1865), pp. 97-101 ; P. Foucart, *Mémoire sur les ruines et l'histoire
de Delphes*, p. 55 *sqq.*; *id.*, in *Comptes Rendus de l'Académie des Inscriptions*,
23 (1895), pp. 189-194; C. Bursian, *Geogr.* 1. p. 175 *sqq.*; J. H. Middleton, 'The
temple of Apollo at Delphi,' *Journal of Hellenic Studies*, 9 (1888), pp. 282-322;
Th. Homolle, in *Bulletin de Corresp. hellénique*, 18 (1894), pp. 175-178 ; *id.*, in
Comptes Rendus de l'Académie des Inscriptions, 22 (1894), p. 586 *sq.*, and *ib.* 23
(1895), pp. 328-341 ; M. Collignon, in *Comptes Rendus de l'Académie des
Inscriptions*, 22 (1894), p. 302 *sq.*; Penrose, in *Bulletin de Corresp. hellénique*,
20 (1896), pp. 383-385 (on the orientation of the temple); H. Pomtow, *Beiträge
zur Topographie von Delphi*, p. 24 *sqq.*; *id.*, in *Archäologischer Anzeiger*, 1895,
pp. 2-5; *id.*, 'Die drei Brände des Tempels zu Delphi,' *Rheinisches Museum*,
N. F. 51 (1896), pp. 329-380; *id.*, 'Die Thätigkeit der Alkmeoniden in Delphi,'
Rheinisches Museum, N. F. 52 (1897), pp. 105-125; *id.*, in *Berliner philolog.
Wochenschrift*, 16th January 1897, pp. 92-95. As to the inscriptions relating to the
restoration of the temple in the fourth century B.C. see above, p. 331. For the
inscriptions on the polygonal wall see C. Wescher et P. Foucart, *Inscriptions
recueillies à Delphes* (Paris, 1863); B. Haussoullier, ' Inscriptions de Delphes:
Inscriptions gravées sur le mur pélasgique,' *Bulletin de Corresp. hellénique*, 3
(1881), pp. 397-434 ; Couve et Bourguet, ' Inscriptions inédites du mur polygonal
de Delphes,' *Bulletin de Corresp. hellénique*, 17 (1893), pp. 343-396; Collitz's
G. D. I. vol. 2. Heft iii. Nos. 1684-2300. For other inscriptions of Delphi, see
E. Curtius, *Anecdota Delphica* (Berlin, 1843), p. 56 *sq.*; *Transactions of the Royal
Society of Literature*, Second Series, 2 (1847), pp. 4-12 ; B. Haussoullier,
' Inscriptions de Delphes,' *Bulletin de Corresp. hellénique*, 5 (1881), pp. 157-178,
372-390; *ib.* 6 (1882), pp. 213-240, 445-466 ; *ib.* 7 (1883), pp. 189-203, 409-439 ;
J. Schmidt, in *Hermes*, 15 (1880), pp. 275-288 ; 'Εφημερὶς ἀρχαιολογική, 1883,
pp. 161-166 ; L. Couve, ' Inscriptions de Delphes,' *Bulletin de Corresp. hellénique*,
18 (1894), pp. 70-100, 226-270 ; Th. Homolle, ' Inscriptions de Delphes.
Réglements de la phratrie des Λαβυάδαι,' *Bulletin de Corresp. hellénique*, 19 (1895),
pp. 5-69 ; P. Perdrizet, ' Inscriptions de Delphes,' *Bulletin de Corresp. hellénique*,
20 (1896), pp. 466-496.

The temple of Apollo is represented on the reverses of several
bronze coins of Hadrian and Faustina the Elder. On all of them the

subject is treated in the usual conventional style of the die-engraver: details are omitted to suit the exigencies of space or added out of regard to popular repute rather than to truth.   Thus on a coin of Hadrian the façade appears with only four columns instead of six, the two central

columns being sacrificed to make room for a large mystic E ; in the gable there seem to be several figures, but they are too small to be distinguished.   A coin of Faustina the Elder (Fig. 11) represents the façade with six columns, the correct number, and the mystic E in the central opening between them ; in the gable can perhaps be made out a standing figure with

FIG. II. — TEMPLE OF APOLLO WITH MYSTIC E (COIN OF DELPHI).

hand raised between two crouching animals.   Two coins present us with one of the flanks of the temple and the façade seen in perspective : on both of them the number of columns on the flank is six, and a figure

of Apollo appears standing between the columns of the façade.   In one of these representations (Fig. 12) Apollo is portrayed as naked with his left elbow resting on a pillar, his right hand advanced, and the Navel - stone (*omphalos*) or an altar at his feet.   See Imhoof-Blumer and Gardner, *Num. Comm. on Paus.* p. 119 *sq.*, with pl. X xxii.-xxv. ; J. H. Middleton, in *Journal of Hellenic Studies*, 9 (1888), p. 290.

In the time of Herodotus a great silver mixing-bowl, dedicated by Croesus, stood in a corner of the fore-temple.   It was wrought by Theodorus the Samian, and the Delphians mixed wine in it at the festival of the Theophany.   See Herodotus,

FIG. 12. — TEMPLE OF APOLLO (COIN OF DELPHI).

i. 51 ; and as to the festival of the Theophany, see A. Mommsen, *Delphika*, p. 280 *sqq.*   In the same corner of the fore-temple, close to the silver mixing-bowl, stood a bronze mast with three golden stars attached to it.   The Aeginetans had dedicated it as a thank-offering for the victory of Salamis.   See Herodotus, viii. 123.   Pliny tells us (*Nat. hist.* xxxv. 138) that the temple contained paintings by a certain Aristoclides ; but nothing more is known of the painter or his pictures.

With regard to the sculptures in the gables described by Pausanias, it seems probable that the figures of Artemis, Latona, Apollo, and the Muses occupied the front or eastern gable, while the figures of Dionysus and the Thyiads filled the back or western gable.   The Setting Sun is commonly supposed to have been in the eastern gable, but Welcker's view that it was in the western gable is perhaps to be preferred.   A Sunset would be more appropriate in the western than in the eastern gable.   In the representation of Apollo at one end of the temple and Dionysus at the other we see a fresh proof of the intimate relation in which these two gods stood to each other at Delphi.   See note on x. 6. 4.   Of the sculptures which occupied the gables not a fragment has been found by the French excavators (*Comptes Rendus de l'Académie des Inscriptions*, 23 (1895), p. 328).

See H. N. Ulrichs, *Reisen und Forschungen*, 1. p. 72 ; F. G. Welcker, 'Die Vorstellungen der Giebelfelder und Metopen an dem Tempel zu Delphi,' *Rheinisches Museum*, N. F. 1 (1842), pp. 1-28 ; *id.*, *Antike Denkmäler*, 1. pp. 151-178 ; P. Foucart, *Mémoire sur les ruines et l'histoire de Delphes*, p. 62 *sqq.* ; J. H. Middleton, in *Journal of Hellenic Studies*, 9 (1888), p. 288 *sq.*

19. 4. golden shields —— dedicated by the Athenians etc. See above, p. 331. The inscription on these shields or perhaps on the architrave ran thus : " The Athenians < dedicated these shields out of spoil taken > from the Medes and Thebans when they (the Medes and Thebans) fought against the Greeks " (Aeschines, *contra Ctesiph.* 116). There used to be a tradition at *Kastri*, the village which occupied the site of Delphi, that in the time of the Turks excavations were made near the ruins of the temple and that some ancient shields and helmets were found. These may possibly have been votive armour formerly dedicated in the temple. See P. Foucart, *Mémoire sur les ruines et l'histoire de Delphes*, p. 61.

19. 4. the Persian bucklers. These were made of wicker-work. See Herodotus, vii. 61, ix. 61.

19. 5. the invasion of Greece by the Gauls. The sight of the Gallic shields hung on the temple induces Pausanias to narrate the invasion of Greece by the Gauls in 279 B.C. This narrative, which runs to the end of chapter twenty-three, forms a long digression in the middle of his account of the temple. As he himself observes, he had already treated of the same subject, but more briefly, in his first book (i. 3. 5-i. 4. 4). The story of the inroad and final repulse of the Gauls is told at length also by Justin (xxiv. 4-8) and concisely in the fragments of Diodorus (xxii. 9). With regard to the historical sources on which these writers drew, it has been argued by Prof. C. Wachsmuth that all three — Pausanias, Justin or rather Trogus (whom Justin abridged), and Diodorus—derived their accounts from Timaeus, who, if we may trust his own assertion (reported by Polybius, xii. 28 a), had made such laborious inquiries into the manners and customs of the Celts as well as of the Ligurians and Iberians that if he were to tell of them all nobody would believe him. See C. Wachsmuth, 'Die Niederlage der Kelten vor Delphi,' in Sybel's *Historische Zeitschrift*, 10 (1863), pp. 1-18. On the other hand Droysen held that while Justin (Trogus) used Timaeus, the authority followed by Diodorus and Pausanias was Hieronymus of Cardia (J. G. Droysen, *Geschichte des Hellenismus*,[2] ii. 2. p. 342, note 4 ; as to Hieronymus of Cardia see Paus. i. 9. 8, i. 13. 9). Mr. Ch. Müller suggests that the authority used by all three writers may have been Menodotus of Perinthus or Agatharchides of Cnidus (*Frag. hist. Graec.* ed. Müller, 4. p. 640). Livy (xxxviii. 48. 2) represents Manlius as saying in 187 B.C. that the Gauls had spoiled Delphi, and Prof. Wachsmuth (*op. cit.* p. 5) maintains that in spite of the legend of their disastrous repulse the northern barbarians did sack and pillage the sanctuary. This, however, is disputed by Mr. L. Contzen (*Die Wanderungen der Kelten*, p. 204 *sq.*). A short memoir on the Gallic invasion has been written by General A. Jochmus, who served in Greece (*Journal of the Royal Geographical Society* (London), 27 (1857), pp. 12-16).

He observes (p. 15) that Pausanias "is as clear and precise in his narrative as can be desired."

The repulse of the Gauls is alluded to in two of the hymns to Apollo which have recently been discovered at Delphi (*Bulletin de Corresp. hellénique*, 17 (1893), p. 574 ; *id.*, 18 (1894), p. 355). The subject was wrought in relief on one of the ivory doors of the temple of Apollo on the Palatine (Propertius, iii. 23. 13). A curious bas-relief found near the temple of Apollo at Delphi represents a battle between Greek cavalry and barbarians whose long shields prove them to be Gauls. See H. N. Ulrichs, *Reisen und Forschungen*, 1. p. 38 ; E. Curtius, *Anecdota Delphica*, p. 97, with pl. iii. 5 and 6 ; Conze e Michaelis, in *Annali dell' Instituto di Corr. Archeol.* 33 (1861), p. 65 *sq.* ; Th. Homolle, in *Gazette des Beaux-arts*, Décembre 1894, p. 452.

19. 7. Brennus and Acichorius. Diodorus (xxii. 9. 2 *sq.*) calls the latter Cichorius and says that on the death of Brennus he succeeded to the command of the Gallic army. Mr. L. Contzen holds that Brennus and Acichorius were one and the same person, Brennus being merely a Celtic title and Acichorius being the chief's real name. The name Brennus has sometimes been explained as a Celtic word meaning 'king'; cp. Cymric *brennin* 'king.' However the derivation of Brennus from *brennin* is denied by Mr. Contzen. See L. Contzen, *Die Wanderungen der Kelten*, p. 110 note 1, p. 190 note 2.

19. 7. Bolgius. He is called Belgius by Justin (xxiv. 5. 1 ; *ib.* 6. 1).

19. 7. engaged in conflict with Ptolemy. Cp. i. 16. 2 note.

19. 9. one hundred and fifty-two thousand foot etc. According to Justin (xxiv. 6. 1), when the army of Brennus entered Macedonia it numbered 150,000 foot and 15,000 horse. Diodorus says (xxii. 9. 1) that Brennus entered Macedonia at the head of 150,000 infantry, 10,000 cavalry, a crowd of sutlers, and a baggage-train of 2000 waggons.

19. 10. the servants. These are spoken of as slaves lower down. Caesar says (*Bellum Gallicum*, vi. 15) that the Gallic knights had large numbers of dependants called *ambacti*. Diodorus tells us (v. 29) that the Gauls were attended by poor freemen who served their masters as charioteers and comrades in war. Posidonius, quoted by Athenaeus (v. p. 246 c d) says : "The Celts even in war carry about with them comrades whom they call parasites." But it does not appear that these 'parasites' were fighting men ; their business was to praise their masters to all and sundry.

19. 11. the Persian corps —— known as the Immortals. See vi. 5. 7 note.

19. 11. This organisation they called trimarcisia etc. The word *trimarcisia* is compounded of the Celtic *tri* (Welsh *tri*, Irish *tri*) 'three' and *marcisia* derived from *marc* (Irish, Gaelic, Breton *marc*, Welsh *march*) 'a horse.' In Welsh we still find *trimarch* 'of three horses,' and *trimarchwys* 'men driving three horses.' *Marc* or *march* seems to occur in all Celtic languages in the sense of 'a horse,' especially 'a war-horse.' In Gaelic we have *marc* 'a steed,' *marcaiche* 'a cavalier,' *Glen-*

mark or *Glen-markie* 'a glen where horses were sent to pasture in summer.' The Old High German *marah*, whence *marah-scalc* ('horse-servant'), *maréchal*, *marshal*, is thought to be borrowed from Celtic. No doubt the word often occurs in names of men and places; *e.g.* *Marquardt* is *mark-ward* ('horse-keeper'). See L. Contzen, *Die Wanderungen der Kelten*, p. 80 note 4, and the note on the present passage in Schubart and Walz's edition of Pausanias. These editors quote passages from old German poetry in which the word *marc* or *march* occurs in the sense of a war-horse. Mr. R. A. Neil of Pembroke College has kindly furnished me with some of the facts mentioned in this note.

20. 1. **the numbers that mustered at Thermopylae to meet King Xerxes.** The numbers which follow are taken from Herodotus (vii. 202).

20. 2. **The numbers of the Locrians** etc. See Herodotus, vii. 203.

20. 2. **the number of Athenians who marched to Marathon** etc. Elsewhere (iv. 25. 5) Pausanias had said that the Athenian force at Marathon numbered under 10,000. According to Cornelius Nepos (*Miltiades*, 5), the Athenian army at Marathon mustered 9000 and they were aided by 1000 Plataeans. Plutarch also (*Parallela*, 1) puts the Athenians at 9000. Justin says (ii. 9. 9) that there were 10,000 Athenians and 1000 Plataeans. Rawlinson argues that the 9000 Athenians included only the heavy-armed infantry and that there must have been besides a considerable force of light infantry, which he would put at 8000. But this contradicts the express statement of Pausanias in the present passage that the Athenian force, inclusive of boys, old men, and slaves, did not number more than 9000. See Rawlinson's *Herodotus*, 3. p. 518 *sq.*

20. 4. **The Aetolians were led by Polyarchus** etc. Another of the Aetolian generals was named Eurydamus; a statue of him stood at Delphi. See vi. 16. 1; x. 16. 4.

20. 5. **Callippus.** Cp. i. 3. 5; i. 4. 2.

21. 1. **if indeed the Celts possess an art of divination.** The Celts practised divination by means of human sacrifices; the victim was stabbed in the back and omens were drawn from his convulsions (Strabo, iv. p. 198). Cp. Aelian, *Var. hist.* i. 31; L. Contzen, *Die Wanderungen der Kelten*, pp. 87, 89. Justin mentions (xxvi. 2. 2) that, before engaging in battle with Antigonus, king of Macedonia, the Gauls slew victims and drew omens from their entrails.

21. 6. **the colonnade of Zeus of Freedom.** See i. 3. 2 *sq.* The shield of Olympiodorus was also dedicated to Zeus of Freedom and probably hung in the same colonnade. See i. 26. 2.

22. 3. **Callium.** This is the modern *Carpenitsa*, according to General Jochmus, who remarks that the place "was always regarded as a first-rate strategical point in the Turkish and Venetian wars" (*Journal of the Royal Geographical Society* (London), 27 (1857), p. 13).

22. 6. **the Patreans —— came to the aid of the Aetolians.** See vii. 18. 6.

22. 7. **Homer's account of —— the Cyclops.** The story of

Ulysses and the Cyclops (Homer, *Od.* ix. 166-542) is a folk-tale, of which versions are current in many lands. Grimm has collected Servian, Roumanian, Esthonian, Finnish, Russian, German, and other versions of the story. See W. Grimm, 'Die Sage von Polyphem,' *Philolog. und histor. Abhandlungen d. kön. Akad. d. Wissen. zu Berlin,* 1857, pp. 1-30. A summary of Grimm's memoir is given by Mr. W. W. Merry in Appendix II. to his larger edition of the *Odyssey,* bks. i.-xii. To the versions collected by Grimm may be added a Basque version (Webster, *Basque Legends,* p. 4 *sq.*), two Lapp versions (Poestion, *Lappländische Märchen,* Nos. 29, 35, pp. 122 *sqq.* 152 *sqq.*), a Lithuanian version (*Zeitschrift für Volkskunde,* 1 (1889), pp. 87-89), a Gascon version (Bladé, *Contes populaires de la Gascogne,* 1. pp. 32-42), a Syrian version (Prym und Socin, *Syrische Sagen und Maerchen,* No. 32, p. 115), and a Celtic version (J. F. Campbell, *Popular Tales of the West Highlands,* No. v. vol. 1. p. 111 *sqq.*; J. Jacobs, *Celtic Fairy Tales,* p. 41 *sqq.*). The Servian story, cited by Grimm from Karadschitsch's *Volksmärchen der Serben* (No. 38), is also given in F. S. Krauss's *Sagen und Märchen der Südslaven* (vol. 1. No. 35, pp. 170-173).

The adventure of Ulysses with the Cyclops is illustrated by some vase-paintings and other monuments of ancient art. As a rule the artists who executed these works have endued the Cyclops with the usual number of eyes, not, like Homer, with one only. However, the British Museum possesses a bronze head of the monster with a single eye set in the middle of his forehead (see the frontispiece to Butcher and Lang's translation of the *Odyssey*); and he is similarly depicted on the wall of a tomb at Corneto in Etruria. Occasionally an artist has given the Cyclops three eyes, one in the middle of his brow, and two in the usual places. It is thus that he figures in a marble group on the Capitol at Rome (W. Helbig, *Führer durch die öffentlichen Sammlungen klassischer Alterthümer in Rom,* 1. No. 406), and there is a marble head of him with three eyes in the Museum at Lyons. See E. Saglio, 'Polypheme,' *Gazette Archéologique,* 12 (1887), pp. 1-7, with pl. 1; Miss J. E. Harrison, *Myths of the Odyssey,* p. 1 *sqq.*; A. Schneider, *Der troische Sagenkreis,* pp. 53-65.

22. 8. **by this latter path —— Hydarnes, the Mede** etc. See Herodotus, vii. 213-218, who describes the path. Cp. Leake, *Northern Greece,* 2. p. 53 *sqq.*

22. 9. **Pindar —— says that every man** etc. See Pindar, *Nem.* i. 82 *sqq.*

22. 10. **a detachment of forty thousand men.** According to Justin (xxiv. 7. 9) the force with which Brennus attacked Delphi numbered 65,000 men, while the Delphians and their allies had only 4000.

23. 1. **the god bade them have no fear** etc. So when the Persians were advancing against Delphi, and the inhabitants in great fear inquired of the god whether they should bury the sacred treasures or carry them away to another land, Apollo bade them move nothing, because he was able to guard his own (Herodotus, viii. 36). The oracle vouchsafed to the Delphians by Apollo on the approach of the Gauls is said to have been this: "I and the white maidens will care for

these matters." The "white maidens" were generally supposed to be Artemis and Athena, who were said to have appeared in person along with Apollo fighting on the side of the Greeks. Why the goddesses were called "white" is doubtful; Cicero seems to refer the epithet to the snow-storm which contributed to the overthrow of the Gauls. See Diodorus, xxii. 9. 5; Suidas, *s.v.* ἐμοὶ μελήσει ταῦτα καὶ λευκαῖς κόραις; *Paroemiogr. Graeci*, ed. Leutsch et Schneidewin, Appendix, ii. 55; Cicero, *De divinatione*, i. 37. 81; Justin, xxiv. 8. 5 *sq.*

It has been suggested that the famous statue in the Vatican known as the Apollo Belvedere represents the god in the act of repelling the Gauls from Delphi by shaking the aegis at them. The left hand was missing when the statue was found near the Grotta Ferrata (not, as commonly said, at Antium, *Porto d' Anzo*) about the end of the fifteenth century; and the artist who restored it, Giovanni Montorsoli, a pupil of Michael Angelo, placed the stump of a bow in the god's left hand. But in 1860 L. Stephani published a small bronze statue of Apollo known as the Stroganoff Apollo, which resembles the Apollo Belvedere so exactly that the two statues must be regarded as copies of the same original. (The Apollo Belvedere is not an original, but a copy executed in Roman times and apparently, though this has been disputed, in Carrara marble.) The left hand of the Stroganoff Apollo is preserved and is grasping a fragment of what some authorities maintain to have been an aegis. If they are right, and if the Stroganoff Apollo is a genuine antique, it becomes probable that the missing left hand of the Apollo Belvedere also held the aegis. The conception of the statue may, in that case, have been suggested by a passage in Homer (*Il.* xv. 229 *sqq.*, 306 *sqq.*) where Apollo is said to have turned the Greeks to flight by shaking the aegis at them. But if, as other authorities assert with equal confidence, the Stroganoff Apollo does not hold the aegis, or if Prof. Furtwängler is right in declaring the Stroganoff Apollo to be a modern forgery, the Apollo Belvedere might perhaps more naturally and appropriately be restored with a bow in his left hand, his attitude being that of an archer who has just shot an arrow and is watching it in its flight. In whichever way restored, whether with the aegis or with the bow, the attitude of the god and his stern, intent gaze would harmonise excellently with the view that he is portrayed in the act of repelling the Gauls from Delphi. The style of the statue would also agree with the supposition that it was made in 279 B.C. (the date of the Gallic inroad) or soon after. For, on the one hand, it lacks the austere simplicity of Greek art of the fifth century B.C.; and, on the other hand, the passion conveyed by the look and attitude, the refined elegance rather than grandeur of form, and the general picturesque, not to say theatrical pose of the statue are all characteristics hardly to be found in Greek statuary before the days of Praxiteles, Scopas, and Lysippus. Hence the view, first propounded by Preller and afterwards accepted by many archaeologists (Welcker, Otto Jahn, Overbeck, etc.), that the original of the Apollo Belvedere was made to commemorate the repulse of the Gauls from Delphi is ingenious and plausible, but from the nature of the case can hardly amount to more than a conjecture. We know from Pausanias

(x. 15. 2) that the Aetolians dedicated at Delphi two statues of Apollo, together with statues of Artemis and Athena, in memory of their triumph over the Gauls.   Overbeck conjectured that the original of the Apollo Belvedere was actually one of these two statues, and that it formed a group with the statues of Artemis and Athena, the three deities being represented as they were supposed to have appeared in the act of driving back the Gauls from Delphi.   He thinks that we possess copies of these statues of Artemis and Athena in the Artemis of Versailles and the Athena of the Capitol Museum at Rome.   On the other hand Mr. Fr. Winter considers that on grounds of style the original of the Apollo Belvedere must be dated somewhat earlier than 279 B.C., and he assigns it to Leochares, a younger contemporary of Praxiteles and Scopas in the fourth century B.C. (see i. 1. 3 note).   Professors Furtwängler and Collignon agree with Mr. Winter in ascribing the original to Leochares. The former even traces the conception of the statue back to a supposed statue of the supposed elder Praxiteles, which again he identifies with the real statue of Locust Apollo on the Acropolis at Athens (i. 24. 8). One of the links in his chain of argument is furnished by a head of Apollo on coins of Amphipolis which Prof. Furtwängler believes to resemble the head of the Apollo Belvedere (P. Gardner, *Types of Greek Coins*, pl. vii. 11 ; B. V. Head, *Coins of the Ancients*, pl. 21, Nos. 7, 8). The resemblance, if it exists, is not striking.   Dr. H. Freericks thinks that the original of the Apollo Belvedere may have been the statue of Apollo by Leochares at Athens (i. 3. 4 note).   The view that the original of the Apollo Belvedere was a work of Leochares is rejected by Overbeck and Prof. E. A. Gardner.

See L. Stephani, *Apollon Boëdromios* (St. Petersburg, 1860); *id.*, in *Bulletin de l'Académie Impériale des Sciences de St. Pétersbourg*, 4 (1862), pp. 55-62; *id.*, in *Compte Rendu* (St. Petersburg) for 1863, pp. 86-88; Fr. Wieseler, *Der Apollon Stroganoff und der Apollon vom Belvedere* (Göttingen, 1861); *id.*, ' Epilog über den Apollon Stroganoff und den Apollon vom Belvedere,' *Philologus*, 21 (1864), pp. 246-283; C. Wachsmuth, in Sybel's *Historische Zeitschrift*, 10 (1863), p. 11 *sqq.*; E. Gerhard, 'Zum belvederischen Apoll,' *Archäologische Zeitung*, 19 (1861), Anzeiger, pp. 209*-213*; R. Kekulé, *ib.* pp. 213*-220*; Welcker, 'Der vaticanische Apoll,' *Archäologische Zeitung*, 20 (1862), pp. 331-333; Th. Pyl, 'Zum Vaticanischen Apoll,' *ib.* Anzeiger, pp. 351*-357*; Otto Jahn, 'Der Apollo von Belvedere,' *Archäologische Zeitung*, 21 (1863), pp. 66-69; R. K[ekulé], 'Sovra due scoperte archeologiche risguardanti l' Apollo di Belvedere,' *Annali dell' Inst. di Corr. Archeol.* 39 (1867), pp. 124-140; Overbeck, in *Berichte über die Verhandl. d. k. sächs. Gesell. d. Wissen.*, Philolog. histor. Classe, 19 (1867), pp. 121-150; *id.*, in *Berichte über die Verhandl. d. k. sächs. Gesell. d. Leipzig*, Philolog. hist. Cl. 45 (1893), pp. 34-40; *id.*, *Gesch. d. griech. Plastik*,[4] 2. pp. 368-382; *id.*, *Griechische Kunstmythologie*, Besonderer Theil, 3. p. 248 *sqq.* ; A. Furtwängler, 'Zum Apollo vom Belvedere,' *Archäologische Zeitung*, 40 (1882), pp. 247-254; G. Kieritzky, 'Der Apollo Stroganoff,' *Archäologische Zeitung*, 41 (1883), pp. 27-38; Friederichs-Wolters, *Gipsabgüsse*, No. 1509; A. S Murray, *History of Greek Sculpture*, 2. p. 371 *sqq.* ; Mrs. Mitchell, *History of Ancient Sculpture*, pp. 621-627; A. Geicke, 'Apollon der Golliersieger,' *Jahrbuch d. archäol. Instituts*, 2 (1887), pp. 260-264; Fr. Winter, 'Der Apollo von Belvedere,' *ib.* 7 (1892), pp. 164-177; A. Furtwängler, *Meisterwerke d. griech. Plastik*, pp. 659-671; H. Freericks, *Der Apollo von Belvedere* (Paderborn, 1894); M. Collignon, *Histoire de la Sculpture grecque*, 2. p. 314 *sqq.*; E. A. Gardner, *Handbook of Greek Sculpture*, p. 477 *sq.*

23. 2. **Then, too, appeared to them the phantoms of the heroes** etc. Cp. i. 4. 4 ; x. 8. 7 note. Apollo, Artemis, and Athena are also said to have appeared in person fighting for the Greeks against the Gauls (see the preceding note). The heroes Theseus and Echetlus were seen fighting on the Greek side at the battle of Marathon (Plutarch, *Theseus*, 35 ; Paus. i. 32. 5). At the battle of Salamis phantoms of armed men were perceived stretching their hands out from Aegina to protect the Greek ships ; they were believed to be the Aeacids, who had been prayed to for help before the battle (Plutarch, *Themistocles*, 15). The spirit of Aristomenes was said to have fought on the Theban side at Leuctra (Paus. iv. 32. 4). The Mantineans fancied they saw Poseidon fighting on their side against the Lacedaemonians (viii. 10. 8). In a battle between the people of Crotona and the people of Locri, two unknown youths, of wondrous stature, in strange armour, clad in scarlet and riding white horses, were seen fighting on the wings of the Locrian army ; after the battle they disappeared (Justin, xx. 3. 8). These two youths were probably regarded as Castor and Pollux, whose reported appearance at the battle of the Lake Regillus, charging with lances in rest at the head of the Roman cavalry, is well known (Dionysius Halicarnassensis, *Antiquit. Rom.* vi. 13 ; Cicero, *De nat. deorum*, ii. 2, iii. 5). It is said that when Alaric approached Athens he beheld Athena in full armour patrolling the walls, and Achilles guarding them with the same fiery valour with which he had avenged the death of Patroclus ; terrified by the vision Alaric gave up all thought of attacking the city (Zosimus, v. 6). Similarly in the battles between the Spaniards and the Indians of Mexico it is affirmed by grave historians that St. James, the patron Saint of Spain, was seen charging on his milk-white steed at the head of the Christian chivalry. In one of these battles a lady robed in white, supposed to be the Virgin, was visible by the side of St. James, throwing dust in the eyes of the infidels. The stout old chronicler Bernal Diaz, who fought in these wars, confesses that for his sins he was not found worthy to behold the glorious Apostle. See Prescott, *History of the Conquest of Mexico*, bk. ii. ch. 4, bk. v. chs. 2 and 4 ; Bernal Diaz, *Histoire de la Conquête de la Nouvelle-Espagne*, ch. 34, vol. 1. p. 138 *sq.* (French translation). For these Spanish parallels I am indebted to my late friend W. Robertson Smith. Niebuhr had previously made exactly the same comparison (*Lectures on Ancient History*, 3. p. 243).

23. 12. **he put an end to himself by drinking neat wine.** According to Diodorus (xxii. 9. 2) Brennus despatched himself with his sword, after swilling a great quantity of neat wine. Justin says (xxiv. 8. 11) that unable to bear the pain of his wounds Brennus put an end to himself with a dagger. Prof. Hitzig thinks that Pausanias means to say that Brennus put an end to himself, not by, but after drinking neat wine ; and it is true that his words, taken literally, will bear this interpretation. But the parallels which Prof. Hitzig quotes (vii. 13. 8 ; vii. 16. 6) are strongly in favour of the view that Pausanias regarded the wine as the actual cause of death. See Hitzig, *Weitere Beiträge zur Texteskritik des Pausanias*, p. 5 ; and the Critical Note on this passage, vol. 1. p. 610.

23. 13. **not a man of them returned home.** The same statement is made by Diodorus (xxii. 8. 11) and Justin (xxiv. 8. 16). But it appears to be an exaggeration. Pausanias himself says elsewhere (i. 4. 5) that most of the defeated Gauls crossed over to Asia, and in other ancient writers we find mention repeatedly made of a remnant of the Gallic host who had marched under Brennus against Delphi. See Polybius, iv. 46 ; Athenaeus, vi. p. 234 b ; Justin, xxxii. 3. 6 ; C. Wachsmuth, in Sybel's *Historische Zeitschrift*, 10 (1863), p. 5 *sqq.* ; L. Contzen, *Die Wanderungen der Kelten*, p. 203 *sqq.* ; Droysen, *Gesch. des Hellenismus*,[2] ii. 2. p. 351 *sq.* From inscriptions we learn that the Aetolians commemorated their victory over the Gauls by instituting games called Soteria in honour of Saviour (*Sōtēr*) Zeus and the Pythian Apollo. The games were held every fourth year and included musical, vocal, poetical, and dramatic, as well as athletic and equestrian contests. Four lists of victors in the games are preserved in inscriptions engraved on the great polygonal wall at Delphi. See Wescher-Foucart, *Inscriptions recueillies à Delphes*, Nos. 3, 4, 5, 6, 13 ; B. Haussoullier, ' Inscriptions de Delphes,' *Bulletin de Corresp. hellénique*, 5 (1881), pp. 300-316 ; E. L. Hicks, *Greek histor. Inscriptions*, No. 161 ; Dittenberger, *Sylloge Inscr. Graec.* Nos. 149, 150 ; C. Wachsmuth, in Sybel's *Historische Zeitschrift*, 10 (1863), p. 9 *sq.* From an inscription found at Tegea we learn that a player won prizes at the Soterian festival for acting in the *Hercules Furens* of Euripides and a play of Archestratus (*Bulletin de Corresp. hellénique*, 17 (1893), p. 15 ; cp. note on viii. 49. 1).

24. 1. **there are inscribed useful maxims for the conduct of life** etc. Plato says (*Protagoras*, p. 343 a b) that the Seven Sages met together and dedicated to Apollo in his temple at Delphi the sayings "Know thyself" and "Nothing in excess." Elsewhere (*Charmides*, p. 165 a) Plato mentions a third saying which was also to be seen in the temple at Delphi, "Go surety and ruin is at hand." All three sayings are attributed to Chilon alone by Diodorus (Fr. ix. 9) and Pliny (*Nat. hist.* vii. 119). The number of maxims inscribed in the temple is uncertain, but the three already mentioned were the most famous. According to Plutarch (*De garrulitate*, 17), these three sayings were engraved in the sanctuary by the authority of the Amphictyonic Council. Pliny says (*l.c.*) that they were written in letters of gold. The exact place which they occupied in the temple is uncertain. Pausanias here tells us that they were in the fore-temple. Macrobius says in one place (*Somn. Scip.* i. 9. 2) that the maxim "Know thyself" was engraved on the front of the temple ; in another place (*Sat.* i. 6. 6) that it was engraved on the door-post of the temple. According to Diodorus (Fr. ix. 9. 1 ed. Dindorf), the three maxims were carved on a pillar ; and Varro (*Sat. Menip.* 320 ed. Bücheler) says the same of one of them (" Nothing in excess "). A manuscript in the Laurentian library at Florence contains a collection of ninety-two proverbs headed " Maxims of the Seven Sages which were found carved on the pillar at Delphi" (ἐπὶ τοῦ ἐν Δελφοῖς κίονος). According to a scholiast on Plato (*Phaedrus*, 229 e), the maxim "Know thyself" was carved on the gateway of the Delphic sanctuary ; and Plato (*Charmides*, pp. 164 e-165 a) and Plutarch

(*De EI apud Delphos*, 17) speak of it as addressed by the god to all who entered or approached his temple. Porphyry seems to imply that a person entering the temple passed the saying " Know thyself " before he came to the vessels with holy water. See Porphyry, quoted by Stobaeus, *Florileg.* xxi. 26. Putting all these various indications together we may perhaps infer that the maxims were engraved on one of the two columns at the entrance into the fore-temple. On the whole subject of these maxims, see Göttling, ' Die delphischen Sprüche,' *Gesammelte Abhandlungen*, I. pp. 221-250 ; F. Schultz, ' Die Sprüche der delphischen Säule,' *Philologus*, 24 (1866), pp. 193-226. In the temple there were also to be seen a wooden letter E, said to have been dedicated by the Sages, a golden E dedicated by the Empress Livia, and a bronze E dedicated by the Athenians (Plutarch, *De EI apud Delphos*, 3). Plutarch wrote a treatise (*De EI apud Delphos*) to explain the mystic letter. The explanations he puts forward are more or less fanciful. On some coins of Roman date a large E appears between the central columns of the façade of the Delphic temple. See above, p. 340.

24. 1. These were —— Thales of Miletus etc. Cp. i. 23. 1. The ancients were not agreed as to the names of the Seven Sages. The list here given by Pausanias is identical with the one given by Demetrius Phalereus (Stobaeus, *Florileg.* iii. 79) and Plutarch (*De EI apud Delphos*, 3), though in the latter passage it is said that the tyrants Cleobulus and Periander had foisted themselves unfairly into the list. The list given by Clement of Alexandria (*Strom.* i. 14. 59, p. 350 ed. Potter) agrees with that of Pausanias, but he says that in place of Periander some people substituted Anacharsis the Scythian, and others Epimenides the Cretan. For other lists see Diogenes Laertius, i. 1. 41 *sq.* The only four Sages who appear in all the lists are Thales, Bias, Pittacus, and Solon. See Zeller, *Philosophie der Griechen*, I.[4] p. 97 *sqq.*

24. 1. the seventh place is assigned by Plato etc. See Plato, *Protagoras*, p. 343 a.

24. 1. Chenae. Opinions differed as to whether Chenae was on Mt. Oeta or in Laconia (Diogenes Laertius, i. 9. 10). Stephanus Byzantius, who calls it Chen, says (*s.v.* Χήν) that it was a town in Laconia.

24. 2. a likeness of Homer in bronze on a monument. A pedestal which supported a bronze statue of Homer has been found at Pergamus. On it are inscribed three sets of execrable verses which mention the various cities that claimed to be the poet's birth-place. See Fränkel, *Inschriften von Pergamon*, I. No. 203.

24. 2. the oracle which is said to have been given to him. The following oracle is quoted also by Stephanus Byzantius (*s.v.* Ἴος). Some of the lines of the oracle are quoted in the *Life of Homer* attributed to Plutarch (§ 4), in which, however, they are divided and assigned to two separate oracles.

24. 2. beware of the riddle of young children. It is said that, being in the island of Ios, Homer asked some boys returning from fishing whether they had caught anything. They gave him an

ambiguous answer, which he could not understand and he either died
of vexation or soon afterwards mortally injured himself by a fall.   See
[Plutarch,] *Life of Homer*, 4 ; Proclus, *Life of Homer* ; *Homeri et Hesiodi
certamen*, 19 ; cp. [Herodotus,] *Life of Homer*, 35 *sq*. (*Biographi
Graeci*, ed. Westermann, pp. 19, 23, 25 *sq*., 45).

24. 3. **wetted with the spray.**   The Greek is διερός.   But
according to Trendelenburg (on Aristotle, *De anima*, ii. 11. 6) διερὸς is
especially used of the liquid *air*.   He compares Aristophanes, *Clouds*,
336 (338).

24. 3. **express no views of my own as to the —— age of Homer.**
Cp. ix. 30. 3.

24. 4. **In the temple there is an altar of Poseidon.**   Pausanias
now describes the contents of the *cella* or central chamber of the temple.
It seems to have had an opening (*hypaethrum*) in the roof; for when
the Gauls were approaching Delphi, the priests, it is said, declared that
they had seen Apollo leaping down into the temple through the opening
in the roof (Justin, xxiv. 8. 4).   Dr. Verrall has suggested that what
Pausanias here calls the altar of Poseidon was really the Navel-stone
(*omphalos*).   See note on x. 16. 3, above, p. 317.   As to the old oracle
of Poseidon at Delphi, see x. 5. 6.

24. 4. **images of two Fates.**   It is odd that there should have
been images of only two Fates, since the Greeks universally believed
the Fates to be three in number.   Plutarch remarks on the anomaly
(*De EI apud Delphos*, 2).   Dr. Verrall would get over the difficulty by
supposing that the two so-called images of Fates were really the eagles
or Gorgons which stood beside the Navel-stone (*omphalos*).   See note
on x. 16. 3, above, p. 317.

24. 4. **Zeus, Guide of Fate.**   Cp. v. 15. 5 note.

24. 4. **the hearth on which the priest of Apollo slew Neoptolemus.**   As to the death of Neoptolemus or Pyrrhus see i. 13. 9, ii. 29.
9, iv. 17. 4 ; and as to his motives for coming to Delphi see x. 7. 1
note.   According to some he set the temple on fire and was slain by a
Delphian named Machaereus, son of Daetas, who may have been the
priest of Apollo mentioned by Pausanias (Apollodorus, ed. R. Wagner,
p. 218 ; *id., Epitoma Vaticana*, ed. R. Wagner, p. 72 ; Strabo, ix. p.
421 ; Schol. on Pindar, *Nem*. vii. 62 ; Eustathius, on Homer, *Od*. iv.
3, p. 1479. 13).   According to others, it was Orestes who killed him
out of revenge because Neoptolemus had robbed him of his bride
Hermione (Apollodorus, *l.c.* ; Virgil, *Aen*. iii. 330 *sqq*. ; Hyginus, *Fab*.
123 ; Velleius Paterculus, i. 1. 3 ; Heliodorus, ii. 34).   Euripides has
described at some length how Neoptolemus was slain at the altar by
the Delphians at the instigation of Orestes (*Andromache*, 1085-1165).
J. Töpffer suggested that in the legend of the death of Neoptolemus,
slain at Apollo's altar, we have a reminiscence of a human sacrifice such
as was offered at Apollo's festival of the Thargelia (J. Töpffer, *Beiträge
zur Altertumswissenschaft* (Berlin, 1897), p. 132).   The assassination of Neoptolemus at Delphi is the subject of a painting on a red-
figured vase found at Ruvo in Apulia.   The hero, wounded and
bleeding, half kneels on a bench beside the Navel-stone (*omphalos*), on

the other side of which Orestes flees with a drawn sword in his hand. Immediately beyond Orestes is a palm-tree, and above him sits Apollo, bow in hand, looking towards Neoptolemus. In the back-ground we see the temple, a Doric edifice with folding doors which stand open, and near it a large tripod on a pedestal. The figures of Neoptolemus, Orestes, and Apollo are identified by inscriptions. See G. F. Iatta, ' L' assassinio di Neottolemo,' *Annali dell' Inst. di Corrisp. Archeol.* 40 (1868), pp. 235-248, with tav. d' agg. E ; Baumeister's *Denkmäler*, 2. p. 1009, fig. 1215 ; J. Vogel, *Scenen Euripideischer Tragödien in griechischen Vasengemälden* (Leipzig, 1886), p. 36 *sqq.*

The hearth of Apollo at Delphi was famous and is often mentioned by ancient writers (Aeschylus, *Choeph.* 1038 ; *id., Eumenides,* 282 ; Sophocles, *Oedipus Rex,* 965 ; Euripides, *Ion,* 462 ; *id., Supplices,* 1200 ; *id., Andromache,* 1240 ; Diodorus, xvi. 56 ; Aelian, *Var. hist.* vi. 9). On this hearth probably burned the perpetual fire which was fed only with pine-wood and tended by women who had been married, and which, if it ever went out, had to be rekindled from the sun by means of burning-glasses (Plutarch, *De EI apud Delphos,* 2 ; *id., Numa,* 9). For Plutarch tells us that when the temple was burnt by the Maedes in the Mithridatic war the perpetual fire went out (*Numa,* 9 ; see above, p. 331), which seems to imply that the perpetual fire was in the temple, and if it was in the temple it could hardly have been anywhere but on the hearth. Again, Orestes, haunted by the Furies at Argos, declares that he will go as a suppliant to " that which is set at the mid-navel " (μεσόμφυλον ἵδρυμα) and to " the light of the fire that is called undying " (Aeschylus, *Choeph.* 1036 *sq.*). This is most naturally interpreted to mean that the perpetual fire was beside the Navel-stone (*omphalos*), which as we have seen (p. 316 *sq.*) stood in the temple at the time when Aeschylus wrote. Indeed from the *Eumenides* (*v.* 40 *sqq.* compared with *v.* 280 *sqq.*) it is clear that Aeschylus believed the Navel-stone to be beside the god's hearth. Elsewhere (note on viii. 53. 9) I have assumed that the fire of pinewood burned in the Prytaneum. And that a perpetual fire was in fact maintained in the Prytaneum at Delphi we have ground for believing, since pure fire was brought to Plataea from "the common hearth" at Delphi (Plutarch, *Aristides,* 20), and "the common hearth" is known from a Delphic inscription to have been in the Prytaneum (H. N. Ulrichs, *Reisen und Forschungen,* 1. p. 67 note 20 ; H. Pomtow, *Beiträge zur Topographie von Delphi,* p. 66). There may very well have been two perpetual fires at Delphi, one in the Prytaneum and one in the temple, just as at Athens there was one in the Prytaneum and another—the ever burning lamp—in the Erechtheum (see vol. 2. pp. 171, 341).

From Pausanias's description we infer that the hearth stood in the *cella* of the temple but not in the *adytum* or Holy of Holies ; for it is only after speaking of the hearth that our author proceeds to mention the inmost shrine in which stood the golden statue of Apollo. J. H. Middleton, however, preferred to suppose that both hearth and Navel-stone were in this inner shrine (*adytum*). His view is to some extent favoured by the statement that the sacrilegious Phocians dug for treasure in the temple "about the hearth and the tripod" (Diodorus, xvi. 56 ; Aelian, *Var. hist.* vi. 9) ; for this seems to imply that the hearth was beside the tripod, and the tripod was certainly in the inner shrine or *adytum.* See H. N. Ulrichs, *Reisen und Forschungen,* I. pp. 77 *sqq.*, 90 *sqq.* ; P. Foucart, *Mémoire sur les ruines et l'histoire de Delphes,* p. 70 *sqq.* ; J. H. Middleton, in *Journal of Hellenic Studies,* 9 (1888), p. 294 *sqq.*

24. 5. the inmost part of the temple. At the western end of the *cella* a door seems to have led into the inmost shrine or *adytum.* The golden statue of Apollo which stood, as Pausanias tells us, in this inner shrine, must have been set up after the Sacred War in the fourth century B.C., else the Phocians would probably have put it in the melting pot. Philochorus, who lived at the end of the fourth and beginning of the third century B.C., mentioned the golden statue (quoted by Joannes Malala, *Chronogr.* ii. p. 45 ed. Dindorf ; *Frag. hist. Graec.,* ed. Müller, I. p. 387), from which we may infer that it was made somewhere between 346 B.C. (the end of the Sacred War) and 261 B.C. (the date of Philochorus's death). Beside it, according to Philochorus, was the grave of Dionysus with this inscription : " Here lies Dionysus dead, the son of Semele." Cp. Plutarch, *Isis et Osiris,* 35 ; Tatian, *Or. ad Graecos,* 8. It is remarkable that the statue should have survived the sack of the temple by the barbarous Maedes in 83 B.C. (see above, p. 331). Perhaps they carried it off, and a new one was afterwards set up in its place. Delphic coins of Imperial date, from the reign of Hadrian onward, exhibit as a type a figure of Apollo which may be a copy of the golden statue in the inner shrine. Sometimes the statue appears by itself, sometimes it is represented standing between the columns of the façade of the temple ; in all cases the type seems to be a copy of one and the same original, though the details and attributes vary somewhat in the different copies. On three of the coins the god is portrayed standing naked, his left elbow resting on a pillar, his right hand advanced. On another coin, of the reign of Hadrian, Apollo stands naked, his left hand raised, his right hand lowered and grasping a branch : behind him is a tripod on a base : at his feet is a river-god, doubtless the Plistus, the stream that flows in its deep glen far below Apollo's temple. It has been suggested that the image of the god in the temple held a lyre, because when Sulla sent an emissary to 'borrow' some of the sacred treasures, the twangling of a lyre was reported to be heard in the inner shrine (Plutarch, *Sulla,* 12) ; and, again, the Athenians dedicated to Apollo a golden *plectrum,* with which the god of music might reasonably be supposed to play on his golden lyre (Plutarch, *De Pythiae oraculis,* 16). In fact a coin of Hadrian is reported to represent Apollo standing naked, his right foot supported on a square base, and holding a lyre in his right hand, which rests on his knee, while in his raised left hand he holds a branch of laurel. But it is doubtful whether the coin has been accurately described. See Imhoof-Blumer and Gardner, *Num. Comm. on Paus.* pp. 119-121, with pl. X xxii.-xxvi., Y i.

In or rather under the inmost shrine of the temple was the 'place of the oracle' (μαντεῖον or χρηστήριον). That the seat of the oracle was below the level of the temple seems proved by the passages in which the priestess is spoken of as "going down" to consult the oracle (Plutarch, *De Pythiae oraculis*, 6, 22, 28 ; *id.*, *De defectu oraculorum*, 51 ; Valerius Maximus, i. 8. 10 ; cp. Plutarch, *Timoleon*, 8). In the 'place of the oracle' there was a deep natural cleft or fissure in the ground, from which issued the exhalations that were believed to fill the priestess with the spirit of prophecy. In giving the oracular responses she sat on a tripod placed immediately over the mouth of the fissure. See Schol. on Aristophanes, *Plutus*, 39 ; and note on x. 5. 7. This oracular chasm was the *adytum* proper (Plutarch, *De Pythiae oraculis*, 6). We have already seen reason to believe that the inner shrine which the Greeks called an *adytum* (ἄδυτον), was generally if not always subterranean (vol. 3. p. 15). At Delphi it would seem to have been vaulted over with masonry, perhaps in the shape and style of the bee-hive tombs ; for Stephanus Byzantius (*s.v.* Δελφοί) says that the *adytum* was built of stone by Agamedes and Trophonius, the same mythical builders to whom the construction of the beehive tomb at Orchomenus was apparently attributed. See Paus. ix. 37. 5, compared with ix. 38. 2. How this subterranean chamber was reached from the temple, we do not know. A staircase may have led down to it ; or perhaps, as in the oracular pit of Trophonius at Lebadea, which was possibly also built in the style of the beehive tombs, the only mode of access may have been by a ladder placed when it was required. We have already seen (p. 336) that the recent French excavations have failed to discover any trace of the oracular chasm.

See H. N. Ulrichs, *Reisen und Forschungen*, I. pp. 79 *sqq.*, 94 *sqq.* ; P. Foucart, *Mémoire sur les ruines et l'histoire de Delphes*, p. 73 *sqq.* ; J. H. Middleton, in *Journal of Hellenic Studies*, 9 (1888), p. 293 *sqq.* As to the Delphic tripod, see K. O. Müller, ' De tripode Delphico,' *Kunstarchäologische Werke*, I. pp. 46-59 ; Fr. Wieseler, ' Ueber den delphischen Dreifuss,' *Abhandlungen der k. Gesell. d. Wissen. zu Göttingen*, 15 (1870), pp. 221-318.

24. 6. the grave of Neoptolemus etc. Cp. Strabo, ix. p. 421. According to a scholiast on Pindar (*Nem.* vii. 62), Neoptolemus was at first buried under the threshold of the temple, but Menelaus afterwards removed his remains to another part of the sacred precinct. If the account of the romance writer Heliodorus can be trusted, the Aenianes of Thessaly sent a grand procession and costly sacrifices to Delphi every fourth year in honour of Neoptolemus. The festival took place at the same time as the Pythian games. Heliodorus has described the procession and sacrifices. The victims included a hundred black oxen and a multitude of lambs and goats. Two bands of Thessalian maidens marched in the procession carrying baskets of flowers, fruits, cakes, and incense ; one of the bands sang, while the other danced to their singing. A troop of Thessalian cavalry, in showy uniforms, mounted on gallant steeds splendidly caparisoned, brought up the rear. Thrice the procession wound round the tomb. Then the victims were slaughtered and the customary parts laid on a huge altar which was heaped with faggots. Libations followed, and then fire was applied to the altar. The procession thereafter broke up, and the Thessalians betook themselves to feasting and revelry.   See Heliodorus, ii. 34-iii. 6. Cp. A. Mommsen, *Delphika*, p. 225 *sqq.* The tomb of Neoptolemus must have stood somewhat to the north of the temple, for Pausanias, quitting the temple by the eastern door, turned to the left to go to the tomb.   In this position, higher up the hill than the temple, and a little to the east of north, H. N. Ulrichs in 1838 found the remains of an ancient wall, adorned with mouldings.   This he supposed to have formed part of the wall which enclosed the tomb of Neoptolemus. It seems to have disappeared since Ulrichs's time.   See H. N. Ulrichs, *Reisen und Forschungen*, I. pp. 39, 104 ; P. Foucart, *Mémoire*, p. 98 *sq.* ; H. Pomtow, *Beiträge zur Topographie von Delphi*, p. 40.

24. 6. **On this stone they pour oil every day** etc.   In the *Characters* of Theophrastus, the Superstitious Man pours oil on the smooth stones at the cross-roads, and goes down on his knees and worships them.   Lucian (*Alexander*, 30) mentions a Roman named Rutillianus who, whenever he saw an anointed or crowned stone, used to fall on his knees before it, worship it, and remain standing beside it in prayer for a long time.   "If ever," says Arnobius (*adversus Nationes*, i. 39) "I spied an anointed stone, greasy with oil, I used to adore it as if there were some indwelling virtue in it."   The custom of anointing sacred stones is referred to by Apuleius (*Florida*, i. 1) and Minucius Felix (*Octavius*, 3).   It has prevailed in many parts of the world.   On the spot where Jacob had dreamed his dream, he set up a stone, poured oil on it, and called the place Bethel or 'the house of God' (Genesis, i. 39).   The Wárális, a tribe who inhabit the jungles of Northern Konkan, in the Bombay Presidency, worship Wághia, the lord of tigers, in the form of a shapeless stone smeared with red lead and clarified butter.   They give him chickens and goats, break cocoa-nuts on his head, and pour oil on him ; and he preserves them from tigers, gives them good crops, and keeps disease from them (*Journal of the Royal Asiatic Society of Great Britain and Ireland*, 7 (1843), p. 20). At Poona there is a sacred stone which is coloured red and oiled (*Asiatic Researches*, 7. p. 394 *sq.* 8vo ed.).   In the Key Islands, East Indies, every householder keeps a black stone at the head of his sleeping-place ; and when he goes out to war or on a voyage or on business, he anoints the stone with oil to secure success (J. G. F. Riedel, *De sluik- en kroesharige Rassen tusschen Selebes en Papua*, p. 223).   In Madagascar many stones are anointed with fat or oil by their worshippers, who sometimes sprinkle them with the blood of a victim.   Women in particular who desire to have children anoint certain stones, promising that if their prayers are answered they will come back and anoint the stone again (J. Sibree, *The Great African Island*, p. 305 ; *The Antananarivo Annual and Madagascar Magazine*, No. 2. p. 164 ; *id.*, No. 4. p. 404 *sq.*). At a certain spot which is particularly difficult for cattle in a mountain-pass in East Africa, every man of the Wakamba tribe stops and anoints a particular rock with butter or fat (*Zeitschrift für Ethnologie*, 10 (1878), p. 384).

The sacred stone at Delphi was not only anointed but also wrapt in wool at festivals.   The original intention of the wrapping was probably to keep the divine stone warm.   Similarly in one of the Samoan islands a smooth stone, regarded as the abode of a god named Turia, was covered with branches to keep it warm, and these branches were carefully renewed whenever special prayers were offered to the stone (G. Turner, *Samoa*, p. 62).   So in Bowditch Island, South Pacific, the chief god was embodied in a stone which was carefully wrapt in fine mats ; once a year the decayed mats were stript off and thrown away.   In sickness, offerings of fine mats were taken and rolled round the stone, till it became busked up to a prodigious size (Turner, *op. cit.* p. 268).

Perhaps the sacred stone at Delphi may have been meteoric. Among the ancient Greek objects found in the south of Russia and now preserved at St. Petersburg there is a rough, uncut, unpolished stone set in a gold ring ; the stone is said by an expert to have all the appearance of being meteoric, and was probably supposed to possess magic properties.   See *Compte Rendu* (St. Petersburg) for 1876, p. 111. With regard to superstitions as to 'thunder-stones,' see J. Grimm, *Deutsche Mythologie*,[4] 1. p. 149 ; E. T. Dalton, *Ethnology of Bengal*, p. 115.   As to the worship of stones, see note on vii. 22. 4.

24. 6. this stone was given to Cronus instead of the child etc. Cp. viii. 8. 2 ; viii. 36. 3 ; ix. 2. 7 note ; ix. 41. 6 ; Hesiod, *Theog.* 468 *sqq.*

24. 7. the spring Cassotis.   A little higher up the hill than the temple, and a few feet to the east of the theatre, a rivulet of clear cool water issues from a small underground channel lined with masonry.   It flows undiminished all through the summer.   This is doubtless Cassotis. The spot does not now, it is true, answer to Pausanias's description. But immediately above it there are remains of an ancient wall, and immediately above that again a rock projects from the soil.   Mr. Homolle was good enough to communicate to me his conjecture that the spring originally issued from under the rock, behind the wall, and that its course has been changed by one of the earthquakes which are so common at Delphi.   Against this, however, it has to be said that excavations made above the fountain in 1860 brought to light an ancient conduit, forming perhaps a part of the channel from which the water issues.   This tends to show that the water does not rise on the spot but is brought to it from higher up the hill.   Possibly it comes from the spring now called *Kerna*, a copious source which gushes from the foot of a high overhanging rock above the sacred precinct, a little to the east of the stadium.   Dodwell and Leake identified this upper spring with Cassotis, but in this they seem to have erred, for Cassotis was within, whereas *Kerna* is without, the sacred precinct.   *Kerna* may be, as H. N. Ulrichs thought, the fountain Delphusa mentioned by Stephanus Byzantius (*s.v.* Δελφοί).   That *Kerna* was outside of the sanctuary is proved by an ancient grave hewn in the rock from which the water issues ; for we may be sure that no burial was permitted within the sacred precinct.   The tomb of the hero Neoptolemus, of course, stood on a different footing.   Before the removal of the village of *Kastri* from its old site in 1892, a church of St. Nicholas used to stand in front of the fountain Cassotis, which watered the small garden attached to the church. Down to the middle of the nineteenth century a solitary laurel—the only one left in the valley of Delphi—grew in the garden; it was blighted in the winter of 1852-53. Perhaps the garden occupied part of the site of Apollo's grove, which may have extended down the hill to the temple. Cp. Pindar, *Nem.* vii. 65; Euripides, *Ion*, 76 and 116; Lucan, *Pharsalia*, v. 156. No other ancient writer besides Pausanias mentions Cassotis by name; but the author of the Homeric *Hymn to Apollo* (*v.* 300 *sq.*) perhaps refers to it as "the fair-flowing fountain" beside which Apollo slew the dragon. However there are grounds for thinking that the fountain beside which Apollo slew the dragon was lower down the hill, below the temple of Apollo (see above, pp. 286, 287).

See Dodwell, *Tour*, 1. p. 174; Leake, *Northern Greece*, 2. p. 555; Mure, *Journal*, 1. p. 195; Thiersch, 'Ueber die Topographie von Delphi,' *Abhandlungen d. philos. philolog. Classe d. kön. bayer. Akad. d. Wissen.* (Munich), 3 (1840), p. 18; E. Curtius, *Anecdota Delphica*, p. 3; H. N. Ulrichs, *Reisen und Forschungen*, 1. pp. 39, 105 *sqq.*, 109; W. Vischer, *Erinnerungen*, p. 610; P. Foucart, *Mémoire sur les ruines et l'histoire de Delphes*, p. 101 *sq.*; *Guide-Joanne*, 2. p. 41; Baedeker,³ p. 160 *sq.*; H. Pomtow, *Beiträge zur Topographie von Delphi*, p. 41 *sq.*

24. 7. the water —— inspires the women —— in the shrine of the god. The water of the Cassotis seems to have been conducted by a subterranean channel into the oracular chasm below the temple, where the prophetess drank of it before she uttered the oracles. In the course of the French excavations an aqueduct or conduit has been found extending under the foundations of the temple (*Bulletin de Corresp. hellénique*, 17 (1893), p. 614). Lucian tells us that at all the oracular seats of Apollo his priestess drank of the sacred stream and chewed the laurel before she prophesied (*Bis accusatus*, 1). Cp. ix. 2. 1 note.

25. 1. a building with paintings by Polygnotus. Plutarch has laid the scene of one of his dialogues (*De defectu oraculorum*) in this building. He says (ch. 6): "Advancing from the temple we reached the doors of the Cnidian club-house. So we entered and saw the friends of whom we were in search seated and awaiting us." Pliny mentions the paintings of Polygnotus at Delphi, but seems to suppose that they were in a temple (*Nat. hist.* xxxv. 59). Of the two series of paintings in the club-house, the one which represented Troy after its capture seems to have been especially famous: it is mentioned by Philostratus (*Vit. Apollon.* vi. 11. 64) and by a scholiast on Plato (Gorgias, p. 448 b). Lucian refers to the graceful eyebrows and rosy cheeks of Cassandra in this picture (*Imagines*, 7). In the time of Pausanias the pictures were already between four and five hundred years old, and they seem to have survived for at least two centuries more, for they are mentioned with admiration by the rhetorician Themistius, who lived in the fourth century of our era (*Or.* xxxiv. 11).

The scanty remains of the club-house (*Lesche*) which contained these famous paintings were excavated by the French in recent years. Although the building was completely excavated in 1895, when I visited it under Mr. Homolle's guidance, no account of it, so far as I know, has up to the present time (November 1897) been published by the French archaeologists. Little more than a bare mention of the discovery has appeared in the learned journals (*Athenaeum*, 7th December 1895, p. 800 ; *Archäologischer Anzeiger*, 1896, p. 73). To my great regret, therefore, I can offer the reader only a few jottings on this interesting monument. They are taken partly from my own journal, partly from the notes furnished to me by Mr. Cecil Smith.

The Lesche is situated, in accordance with the description of Pausanias, higher up the hill than the spring Cassotis, a few steps to the east of the theatre. It was built on a terrace, which is supported on the south by a high retaining-wall. A marble slab in this wall bears an inscription :

$$\text{ΚΝΙΔΙΩΝΟΔΑΜΟΣ}$$
$$\text{ΤΟΑΝΑΛΑΜΜΑ}$$
$$\text{ΑΠΟΛΛΩΝΙ}$$

" The Cnidian people (dedicated) the supporting-wall to Apollo." From the style of the letters the inscription seems to date from the third century B.C. On the terrace supported by this wall stood the Lesche, a building of no great size, with its long axis lying east and west. At the time of my last visit to Delphi (October 1895) Mr. Homolle explained to me that he believed the Lesche to have been a quadrangular and oblong building with a door in each of the two short sides. The paintings, in his opinion, probably occupied the two short walls as well as the long north and south walls. Now, however, as I learn from Mr. Cecil Smith, the building is believed to have been a colonnade open on three sides, with columns in front and the paintings of Polygnotus occupying only the long back wall. Considerable remains of this back wall exist ; and in my journal I find it noted that a small piece of the south wall and, to the best of my recollection (I was not allowed to make notes on the spot), a piece of the east wall also are preserved. But if the building was a colonnade open on three sides, it can hardly have had walls on the south and east. Towards the eastern end of the building, there are four foundations of columns placed so as to form a square (: :). This perhaps points to the existence of a double row of columns running along the whole length of the building. On the face of the back wall, close to the ground, are some remains of stucco painted with a bright blue pigment. This is all that remains of the paintings of Polygnotus. Behind the wall and separated from it by a channel about 18 inches wide rises a retaining-wall which supported an upper terrace. The interval between the back-wall of the Lesche and the terrace-wall behind it was no doubt left on purpose to prevent the damp from percolating through and injuring the pictures. Apparently the pavement of the Lesche was, like the lower part of the back wall, coloured blue.

For our knowledge of the paintings we are indebted to the minute account of them given by Pausanias (x. 25-31). So full and precise is his description that not a few attempts have been made in modern times to reconstruct the pictures from it. The first of these attempts was made by the Comte de Caylus in 1757, and the latest by Dr. Paul Weizsäcker in 1895. Amongst the others may be mentioned those by the brothers Riepenhausen in 1805 and again in 1826, of Mr. W. Watkiss Lloyd in 1851, of Prof. O. Benndorf in 1887, and of Prof. C. Robert in 1892 and 1893, who has accompanied his reconstructions with elaborate commentaries. Of these various restorations the most artistically beautiful are those which were drawn by Mr. Hermann Schenck for Prof. Robert. They are here reproduced (pl. vi. vii.). Some exceptions may be taken to them in detail, but on the whole they probably give a fairly correct idea of the composition and general effect of the pictures.

The arrangement of some of the figures above others, for which we have the authority of Pausanias, is probably to be explained, with Lessing (*Laokoon*, xix.) and Messrs. Weizsäcker and Schreiber, simply by the artist's ignorance of the laws of perspective rather than, with Prof. Robert, by supposing the figures to be placed one above the other on sloping ground. Some have held that the figures were disposed in regular horizontal bands, one above the other, but a better artistic effect is certainly produced by grouping them freely at various levels, as both Prof. Robert and Dr. Weizsäcker have done. This arrangement is supported by the analogy of many ancient vase-paintings, which taken along with Pausanias's description supply the most trustworthy materials for a reconstruction of the paintings in the Lesche. Probably many ancient vase-painters were influenced directly or indirectly by the pictures of Polygnotus, and it is quite possible that in some extant vase-paintings we possess imitations, more or less free, of certain masterpieces of the great painter. We have seen indubitable evidence that a famous work of art like the Chest of Cypselus at Olympia sometimes furnished subjects to the vase-painter (vol. 4. pp. 608 *sqq.*, 613); and if the Chest of Cypselus, why not the still more celebrated works of Polygnotus?

Much difference of opinion has prevailed as to the shape of the Lesche and the disposition of the paintings on its walls. From Pausanias we learn that the pictures fell into two great sets, one representing Troy after its capture, the other Ulysses in hell: the first was on the spectator's right as he entered the building, the second was on his left (Paus. x. 25. 2, x. 28. 1). Hence it may fairly be inferred either that the two sets of pictures were on opposite walls of a quadrangular building, or that they were on the same wall but divided from each other by a doorway. In the former case the paintings probably occupied the two long sides of the building, while the doorway was in one of the two short sides. In the latter case the building was probably in the form of a colonnade with one or three sides open and the doorway in the middle of the back wall. On the whole, archaeologists who have discussed the problem have declared themselves, with some minor differences of opinion as to details, in favour of one or other of these two solutions. The Riepenhausens, Letronne, Otto Jahn, Ch. Lenormant, and Prof. C. Robert decided for the quadrangular building with the pictures on the opposite walls: Ruhl, Schubart, Prof. Michaelis, Mr. P. Girard, Dr. Weizsäcker, and Dr. Th. Schreiber decided for the colonnade with both pictures on the back wall. The recent excavation of the ruined Lesche would seem to show that the latter were right. But pending an exact and authoritative description of the remains that have been found it might still be premature to award judgment in this long debate. We have seen that as late as 1895, after the excavation of the Lesche, Mr. Homolle was inclined to favour the quadrangular building.

When we learn the exact shape and dimensions of the Lesche, we shall be able by comparing them with Pausanias's description to estimate approximately the scale of the figures in the paintings and so to decide the question, which has lately been discussed by Prof. Robert and Dr. Schöne, whether they were life-size or not. That they were life-size is denied by Dr. Schöne and affirmed by Prof. Robert (*Die Marathon-schlacht in der Poikile*, p. 82 *sqq.*), who bases his opinion chiefly on an ambiguous passage of Aelian (*Var. hist.* iv. 3) which may perhaps be translated thus : " Polygnotus painted large figures and earned his prizes by life-size pictures " (ἔγραφε τὰ μεγάλα καὶ ἐν τοῖς τελείοις εἰργάζετο τὰ ἆθλα). This translation of the adjective τέλειος Prof. Robert defends by comparing the expression εἰκὼν γραπτὴ τελεία which occurs in two inscriptions (*C. I. G.* Nos. 3068, 3085) and the expression πίναξ τέλειος γεγραμμένος which occurs in the *Lives of the Ten Orators* (p. 843 e) attributed to Plutarch. However this verbal question may be settled, the scale of the pictures in the Lesche will be determined within certain limits as soon as the measurements of the building are made public. Speaking from impression (I was not allowed to take measurements) I should say that the building is too small to allow us to suppose that the figures were life-size.[1]

The further question discussed by Prof. Robert and Dr. Schöne whether Polygnotus painted directly on a marble wall or on stucco has been definitely decided in favour of Dr. Schöne and stucco by the remains of blue-painted stucco on the wall of the Lesche. It is due to Prof. Robert to add that in deference to the objections urged by his adversary he afterwards inclined with some hesitation to discard marble for stucco (*Die Marathonschlacht in der Poikile*, p. 104).

With regard to the date of the paintings it has been commonly supposed that they must have been executed before 467 B.C., since the couplet attached to the pictures (Paus. x. 27. 4 note) is ascribed to Simonides, who died in that year. This argument would have to be abandoned if with Prof. Robert and Prof. Hauvette (*De l'authenticité des épigrammes de Simonide* (Paris, 1896), p. 138) we believed the verses not to be by Simonides. But the reasons for this scepticism seem wholly insufficient to counterweigh the express testimony not only of Pausanias but of the compiler of the Palatine Anthology (ix. 700) as to the authorship of the epigram. It seems safer therefore to acquiesce in that testimony and to believe accordingly that one or both the pictures in the Lesche were painted in the lifetime of Simonides. Prof. Robert believes that a surer clue to the date of the paintings is

---

[1] Since writing as above I have obtained, through Mr. Homolle's courtesy, a copy of part of the *Bulletin de Corresp. hellénique* for 1896 in which (pp. 633-639) the remains of the Lesche are described and discussed. The description reached me too late to allow me to modify the text in accordance with it, the volume having been already set up in pages. But see below, p. 635 *sq.*

furnished by observing that of the four Theban ladies whom, according
to Homer (*Od.* xi. 260-280), Ulysses saw in hell, only one was depicted
in the lower world by Polygnotus (x. 29. 7). The omission of the
other three was intended, Prof. Robert thinks, as a deliberate slight to
the Thebans, and the picture must accordingly have been painted
between 458 and 447 B.C., when the Phocians, the bitter enemies of
Thebes, were in possession of Delphi. Without going so far as to
reverse the argument and affirm that the omission of the ladies from the
picture of hell may have been meant as a delicate compliment to
Thebes, I find Prof. Robert's reasoning in the highest degree improbable.
If three of the four women were left out for the reason supposed, why
was the fourth inserted? If the painter put her in before the Phocians
had time to stop him, surely it would have been easy for them to take
her out again with the help of a brush and a little paint or whitewash.
But to discuss such possibilities is futile.

See F. S. C. Koenig, *De Pausaniae fide et auctoritate* (Berlin, 1832), p. 46
sqq.; K. O. Müller, *Kleine deutsche Schriften*, 2. pp. 398-404; Otto Jahn,
'Die Gemälde des Polygnotus in der Lesche zu Delphi,' *Kieler philologische
Studien* (Kiel, 1841), pp. 81-154; F. G. Welcker, 'Die Composition der polygnotischen Gemälde in der Lesche zu Delphi,' *Philolog. und histor. Abhandlungen
d. kön. Akad. d. Wissen. zu Berlin*, 1847, pp. 81-151; J. Overbeck, 'Antepi-
critische Betrachtungen über die polygnotischen Gemälde in der Lesche zu
Delphi,' *Rheinisches Museum*, N. F. 7 (1850), pp. 419-454; W. Watkiss Lloyd,
'On the paintings by Polygnotus in the Lesche at Delphi,' *The Museum of
Classical Antiquities*, 1 (1851), pp. 44-77, 103-130; *ib.* 'On the plan and disposition of the Greek Lesche,' by the Editor, pp. 78-86; L. Ruhl und J. H. C.
Schubart, 'Glossen zur Beschreibung des Polygnotischen Gemäldes in der Lesche
zu Delphi bei Pausanias,' *Zeitschrift für die Alterthumswissenschaft*, 13 (1855),
Nos. 49-52; *ib.* 14 (1856), Nos. 38-42; C. Bursian, in *Fleckeisen's Jahrbücher*, 2
(1856), p. 517 *sqq.*; Ch. Lenormant, *Mémoire sur les peintures que Polygnote avait
executées dans la Lesche de Delphes* (Bruxelles, 1864); H. Blümner, 'Die Polygnotischen Gemälde in der Lesche zu Delphi,' *Rheinisches Museum*, N.F. 26
(1871), pp. 354-369; J. H. C. Schubart, in *Fleckeisen's Jahrbücher*, 18 (1872),
pp. 173-178; W. Gebhardt, 'Die polygnotischen Leschebilder,' *Fleckeisen's
Jahrbücher*, 19 (1873), pp. 815-820; Miss J. E. Harrison, *Myths of the Odyssey*,
pp. 118-134; *Wiener Vorlegeblätter für Kunstübungen*, 1888 (Wien, 1889),
Tafeln x., xi., xii.; A. S. Murray, *Handbook of Greek Archaeology*, p. 361 *sqq.*;
P. Girard, *La peinture antique*, pp. 157-165; C. Robert, *Die Nekyia des Polygnot*,
Hallisches Winckelmannsprogramm (Halle a/S, 1892); *id.*, *Die Iliupersis des
Polygnot*, Hallisches Winckelmannsprogramm (Halle a/S, 1893); *id.*, *Die
Marathonschlacht in der Poikile und Weiteres über Polygnot*, Hallisches Winckel-
mannsprogramm (Halle a/S, 1895); R. Schöne, 'Zu Polygnots delphischen
Bildern,' *Jahrbuch d. arch. Inst.* 8 (1893), pp. 187-217; Th. Schreiber, 'Die
Nekyia des Polygnot in Delphi,' *Festschrift für J. Overbeck* (Leipzig, 1893),
pp. 184-206; *id.*, 'Die Wandbilder des Polygnot in der Halle der Knidier zu
Delphi,' *Abhandlungen der philolog. histor. Classe der könig. sächs. Gesell. der
Wissenschaften*, 17 (1897), No. 6, pp. 1-178; P. Weizsäcker, *Polygnot's Gemälde
in der Lesche der Knidier in Delphi* (Stuttgart, 1895).

The restorations of the pictures by the Comte de Caylus, W. K. F. Siebelis,
the Riepenhausens, F. G. Welcker, W. Watkiss Lloyd, and W. Gebhardt are
republished in a convenient form in the *Wiener Vorlegeblätter für Kunstübungen*,
1888 (cited above), which also contains a reconstruction drawn by L. Michalek
for Prof. O. Benndorf.

25. 1. **the passage where Melantho rails at Ulysses.**   See
Homer, *Od.* xviii. 329 *sq.*

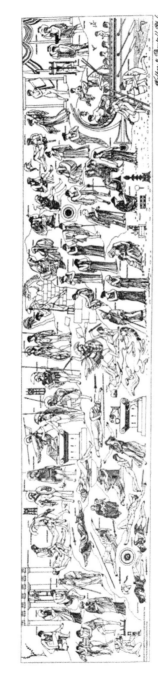

Polygnotus's picture of the Capture of Troy, restored by C. Robert.

Welker & Randell Ph.L

25. 2. **Ilium after its capture.**   As to representations of the sack of Troy in existing works of ancient art, especially vase-paintings, see H. Heydemann, *Iliupersis auf einer Trinkschale des Brygos* (Berlin, 1866); C. Robert, *Bild und Lied,* p. 59 *sqq.*; A. Schneider, *Der troische Sagenkreis in der ältesten griechischen Kunst,* p. 168 *sqq.*; W. Klein, *Euphronios,*[2] p. 159 *sqq.*; Baumeister's *Denkmäler, s.v.* 'Iliupersis.' Among the most notable of such representations is a fragmentary marble relief, known as the *Tabula Iliaca,* which is preserved in the Capitoline Museum at Rome.   It seems to date from about the first century A.D., and represents a great variety of scenes from the Trojan legends.   It professes to be based on the *Iliad* of Homer, the *Sack of Ilium* of Stesichorus, the *Aethiopis* of Arctinus, and the *Little Iliad* of Lesches.   From fragments of similar reliefs which have been discovered we may infer that tablets of this sort, illustrating the legends of the siege of Troy, were manufactured wholesale, probably for use in schools. These reliefs have been published with an elaborate commentary by Otto Jahn and Ad. Michaelis.   See their work *Griechische Bilderchroniken* (Bonn, 1873); Baumeister's *Denkmäler,* p. 716 *sqq.*; A. Brüning, ' Über die bildlichen Vorlagen der ilischen Tafeln,' *Jahrbuch d. archäolog. Instituts,* 9 (1894), pp. 136-165.   With regard to the poetical sources from which Polygnotus may be supposed to have drawn some at least of the scenes in his great tableau, Mr. F. Noack has argued at length that the painter borrowed everything except some names from the epic known as the *Little Iliad,* particularly from that part of it which Pausanias cites (x. 25. 5 note) under the title of *The Sack of Ilium* and attributes to Lesches.   See F. Noack, *Iliupersis : de Euripidis et Polygnoti quae ad Trojae excidium spectant fabulis* (Gissae, 1890), pp. 45-74.   Prof. C. Robert, while he admits that Polygnotus drew on this poem, holds that the painter's chief poetical authority was the epic poem of the same title (*The Sack of Ilium*) which Proclus ascribes to Arctinus (*Epicorum Graecorum fragmenta,* ed. Kinkel, p. 49).   See C. Robert, *Die Iliupersis des Polygnot,* pp. 74-80.

25. 2. **Homer represents Nestor —— saying —— that Phrontis** etc.   See *Od.* iii. 276 *sqq.*

25. 3. **Echoeax.**   His name means 'holding the tiller.'   Hence Prof. C. Robert conjectures that the name really applied to a figure seated at the helm in the ship, and not to the man going down the gangway (*Die Iliupersis des Polygnot,* p. 56 *sq.*).

25. 3. **Menelaus' hut.**   The Greek word here translated ' hut ' (σκηνή) may also mean ' tent ' ; and though the dwellings of the Homeric warriors were perhaps huts rather than tents, Polygnotus may have preferred to represent them, in accordance with the usage of his own time, as tents.   On red-figured vases and in Pompeian paintings the abodes of the Homeric heroes in the field are regularly represented as pavilions supported on round poles (C. Robert, *Die Iliupersis des Polygnot,* p. 39).

25. 3. **the only figure whose name Polygnotus has taken from the Odyssey.**   The name of Amphialus also occurs in the *Odyssey*

(viii. 114, 128), though not as the name of one of Menelaus's companions.

25. 4. Briseis —— Diomeda —— Iphis. These were female slaves of Achilles (Homer, *Il.* i. 184, ix. 664 *sqq.*). After his death they may have passed into the possession of his son Neoptolemus. Cp. C. Robert, *Die Iliupersis des Polygnot*, p. 57.

25. 4. Helen herself is seated etc. Prof. C. Robert compares a scene on a fine Attic vase now in the Hermitage Museum at St. Petersburg. It represents the wooing of Helen by Paris. The Grecian beauty appears seated among her maidens while Paris, in Phrygian costume, approaches and greets her. See *Compte Rendu* (St. Petersburg) for 1861, Atlas, pl. V 1, with Stephani's remarks, p. 115 *sqq.* The scene of course differs from that depicted in Polygnotus's picture but possibly there are traces of that picture in the attitude of Helen and her handmaids. Prof. Robert inclines, however, to think that the vase-painter stood directly under the influence of Zeuxis rather than of Polygnotus. See C. Robert, *Die Iliupersis des Polygnot*, pp. 34-36.

25. 4. Eurybates —— Ulysses' herald, though he had no beard. In the *Odyssey* (xix. 244 *sqq.*) Homer describes Eurybates, the herald of Ulysses, as older than his master and with a great shock of hair on his head. Hence the surprise of Pausanias that in the picture Eurybates appeared as youthful and beardless. Eurybates is mentioned as the herald of Ulysses in the *Iliad* also (ii. 184). But Agamemnon had a herald of the same name (*Il.* i. 320); and it is probable that he rather than the herald of Ulysses was represented by Polygnotus, since we know from Pausanias himself (below § 8) that Eurybates was sent by Agamemnon, not by Ulysses, to Helen.

25. 4. different from the names in the Iliad etc. See *Iliad*, iii. 143 *sq.*, where Helen's handmaidens are called Aethra and Clymene. As to Aethra, see § 8 note; as to Clymene see note on x. 26. 1.

25. 5. a man —— in an attitude of profound dejection etc. It is said that after Paris's death, the soothsayer Helenus and his brother Deiphobus quarrelled for the hand of Helen. Deiphobus was successful, and Helenus, mortified at his failure, withdrew from Troy to Mt. Ida. Here he was captured by the Greeks and was induced or compelled to reveal to them the means by which Troy could be taken. See Apollodorus, ed. R. Wagner, p. 206; Conon, *Narrationes*, 34; Servius on Virgil, *Aen.* ii. 166; Sophocles, *Philoctetes*, 604 *sqq.*; Quintus Smyrnaeus, *Posthomerica*, x. 344 *sqq.*; Dio Chrysostom, *Or.* lix. vol. 2. p. 187 ed. Dindorf. Hence Polygnotus appropriately depicted Helenus seated in the midst of the ruin of his native city overwhelmed with grief and remorse. The story of the capture and prophecy of Helenus was told by Lesches in the *Little Iliad*, from which Sophocles may have borrowed it (Ἐpῖλος και Cιασσιριου fragmenta, ed. Kinkel, p. 36).

25. 5. Lescheos of Pyrrha —— in his poem, The Sack of Ilium. This poem is repeatedly referred to by Pausanias in the sequel (§§ 6, 8, 9; x. 26. 1, 4, 8; x. 27. 1, 2). It is commonly supposed that the *Sack of Ilium* which Pausanias attributes to Lesches was not a separate poem but merely a part of the *Little Iliad* (D. B. Monro, in *Journal of*

Hellenic Studies, 4 (1883), p. 317 *sq.* ; Fr. Noack, *Iliupersis*, p. 45 *sq.* ;
as to the *Little Iliad* see note on x. 26. 2). That the *Little Iliad*
included a description of the sack of Troy is proved by the testimony of
Aristotle (*Poetics*, 23, p. 1459 b 4 *sqq.*), though Proclus in his summary
of the poem makes it end with the introduction of the Wooden Horse
into Troy (*Epicorum Graecorum fragmenta*, ed. Kinkel, p. 37). But
against the identification of the *Sack of Ilium* by Lesches with part of
the *Little Iliad* it must be observed that Pausanias certainly seems to
have regarded the two poems as distinct ; for whereas he assigns the
former poem to Lesches, he apparently considered that the author of
the *Little Iliad* was unknown (iii. 26. 9 ; x. 26. 2). That Pausanias
distinguished between the two poems has been recognised by Prof.
von Wilamowitz - Möllendorff (*Homerische Untersuchungen*, p. 342).
Prof. C. Robert's attempt to prove that Pausanias regarded the *Sack of
Ilium* by Lesches as part of the *Little Iliad* is unconvincing ('Homerische Becher,' 50*tes Programm zum Winckelmannsfeste*, Berlin 1890,
p. 64 *sqq.*). The name of the poet whom Pausanias always calls
Lescheos appears as Lesches on the *Tabula Iliaca* (Baumeister's
Denkmäler, pl. xiii.) and on an ancient vase (C. Robert, 'Homerische
Becher,' p. 33). The form Lesches is commonly regarded as the
correct one, but the form Lescheos is defended by Mr. O. Immisch
('Lescheos-Lesches,' *Rheinisches Museum*, N. F. 48 (1893), pp. 290-
298), whose view is, however, combatted by Mr. W. Schmid (*ib.*
pp. 626-628) and rejected by Prof. C. Robert (*Die Iliupersis des Polygnot*, p. 74 note 13).

25. 7. Demophon, one of the sons of Theseus. His mother was
Phaedra (Apollodorus, ed. R. Wagner, p. 179 *sq.*) or, according to
Pindar, Antiope (Plutarch, *Theseus*, 28).

25. 7. Theseus had also a son Melanippus etc. Pausanias implies,
though he does not say directly, that Melanippus was depicted along
with Demophon meditating the rescue of his grandmother Aethra. The
descendants of Melanippus, named Ioxids, are said to have revered
asparagus because their ancestress Periguna, daughter of Sinis, took
refuge in a bed of asparagus from the pursuit of Theseus (Plutarch,
Theseus, 8).

25. 8. As to Aethra, Lescheos says etc. It is said that Aethra,
the mother of Theseus, having been captured by the Dioscuri at Aphidna
(Paus. v. 19. 3 note), was given by them as a handmaid to Helen whom
she followed to Troy (Homer, *Il.* iii. 143 *sq.* ; Dio Chrysostom, *Or.* xi.
vol. 1. p. 184 ed. Dindorf). The story of her release from captivity after
the taking of Troy seems to have been told in somewhat different forms.
One version, here given by Pausanias on the authority of Lesches,
appears to have been followed by the poet Lysimachus (Schol. on Euripides, *Troades*, 31) and Dionysius, author of the prose *Cycle* (Schol. on
Euripides, *Hecuba*, 123 ; *Frag. Hist. Graec.* ed. Müller, 4. p. 653).
The other version was that during the sack of Troy her two grandsons
Demophon and Acamas, the sons of Theseus, found and rescued Aethra
without, apparently, having to beg for her release from Helen and the
Greek leaders. This latter version was seemingly followed by Arctinus

in his *Sack of Ilium* (*Epicorum Graecorum fragmenta*, ed. Kinkel, p. 50), Quintus Smyrnaeus (*Posthomerica*, xiii. 496-543), and Apollodorus (p. 211 ed. Wagner). It would appear to have been also adopted by Stesichorus ; at least in the *Tabula Iliaca* (see note on § 2), which in so far as it represents the capture of Troy is professedly based on Stesichorus's poem the *Sack of Ilium*, we see Aethra within the walls of Troy being hurried away by her two grandsons amid scenes of slaughter and flight. The same version of the story is depicted on red-figured vases, of which one is in the British Museum (*Catalogue of Greek and Etruscan Vases in the British Museum*, vol. 3, *Vases of the finest period*, by Cecil H. Smith, No. 458, p. 281). See H. Heydemann, *Iliupersis*, p. 21 *sq.* ; A. Michaelis, in *Annali dell' Inst. di Corrisp. Archeol.* 52 (1880), pp. 32-40 ; O. Jahn, *Griechische Bilderchroniken*, p. 34 ; Baumeister's *Denkmäler*, fig. 775, Tafel xiii., fig. 795, Tafel xiv., pp. 743, 748 ; Müller-Wieseler, *Denkmäler*, 1. pl. xliii. No. 202 ; C. Robert, *Bild und Lied*, pp. 72 *sq.*, 75 *sq.*

25. 9. this child, says Lescheos, was killed etc. The verses in which Lesches describes the murder of the infant Astyanax, son of Hector and Andromache, by Neoptolemus are preserved by Tzetzes (*Schol. on Lycophron*, 1263 ; *Epicorum Graecorum fragmenta*, ed. Kinkel, p. 46). Their substance is correctly given by Pausanias. According to another version of the legend the murderer of the child was not Neoptolemus but Ulysses. This latter is the version followed by Arctinus in his poem the *Sack of Troy* (*Epicorum Graecorum fragmenta*, ed. Kinkel, p. 50) by Tryphiodorus (*Excidium Ilii*, 644-646), and by Tzetzes (*Posthomerica*, 734). Euripides represents the death of Astyanax as resolved upon by the Greeks in solemn conclave, the chief advocate of the deed being Ulysses (*Troades*, 704 *sqq.*). According to Seneca (*Troades*, 1088 *sqq.*) Ulysses was deputed to execute the doom, but the child anticipated his fate by leaping from a tower. Quintus Smyrnaeus (*Posthomerica*, xiii. 251 *sq.*), Apollodorus (p. 212 ed. Wagner), and Hyginus (*Fab.* 109) merely say that the child was hurled from the walls by the Greeks ; they do not name the murderer. In the vase-paintings Neoptolemus is depicted seizing Astyanax by the leg and preparing to dash him to pieces against the altar at which the boy's grandfather, Priam, has taken refuge. See H. Heydemann, *Iliupersis*, pl. i. ; C. Robert, *Bild und Lied*, p. 59 ; Baumeister's *Denkmäler*, p. 745 ; *Catalogue of the Greek and Etruscan Vases in the British Museum*, vol. 2, *Black-figured Vases*, by H. B. Walters, p. 135, No. B 205. Cp. F. Noack, *Iliupersis : de Euripidis et Polygnoti quae ad Trojae excidium spectant fabulis*, pp. 29-36.

25. 9. Homer says that she left Troy etc. See *Iliad*, xiii. 170 *sqq.*

25. 10. her hair braided after the manner of maidens. See note on i. 19. 1.

25. 10. Poets tell how Polyxena was slain on Achilles' tomb. Among the poets who described the sacrifice of Polyxena at the grave of Achilles were Arctinus (*Epicorum Graecorum fragmenta*, ed. Kinkel, p. 50) and Euripides (*Hecuba*, 109-582).

25. 10. **at Athens —— I have seen pictures** etc. See i. 22. 6.

25. 11. **a horse —— about to roll on the ground.** Prof. C. Robert conjectures that we are to suppose this horse to have been ridden by Elasus and Astynous, two of the victims of Neoptolemus (see below x. 26. 4), and to have fallen under their weight, thus allowing their relentless pursuer to overtake and dispatch them. He thinks that the same subject is represented, at a somewhat earlier stage, on two of the northern metopes of the Parthenon. On one of the metopes (No. 29) we see two figures riding a horse which seems about to fall, while on the metope next to it (No. 28) appears a young warrior rushing along. If Prof. C. Robert is right, the scene on the former metope (No. 29) represents the flight of Elasus and Astynous, and the scene on the latter metope (No. 28) their pursuit by Neoptolemus. See C. Robert, *Die Iliupersis des Polygnot*, pp. 59-61 ; *id.*, *Die Marathonschlacht in der Poikile*, p. 124. Against this view of Prof. Robert's, which is accepted by Mr. P. Weizsäcker (*Polygnots Gemälde*, p. 26 *sq.*), it must be said that the horse in the picture, to judge by Pausanias's description, had not fallen but only seemed about to do so ; it is, therefore, a necessary part of Prof. Robert's theory that Pausanias mistook the attitude of the beast. A horse rolling on the ground is depicted on a black-figured vase (*Mittheil. d. arch. Inst. in Rom*, 4 (1889), pl. 7 ; the vase is B 364 in the British Museum) and is engraved on a number of ancient gems. See O. Rossbach, in *Aus der Anomia* (Berlin, 1890), pp. 195-200. The painter Pauson is said to have painted a horse in this posture (Lucian, *Demosthenis encomium*, 24 ; Aelian, *Var. hist.* xiv. 15 ; Plutarch, *De Pythiae oraculis*, 5).

26. 1. **Clymene.** In the *Iliad* (iii. 144) Clymene is one of the two handmaids of Helen, the other being Aethra. It is quite possible that in the picture she may have been represented as a Greek slave waiting on Helen, and that Pausanias made a mistake in classing her with the captive Trojan women. See F. Noack, *Iliupersis*, p. 56 *sq.* ; C. Robert, *Die Iliupersis des Polygnot*, p. 43 *sq.*

26. 1. **Stesichorus, in his Sack of Ilium.** The representation of the sack of Ilium on the *Tabula Iliaca* professes to be based on this poem of Stesichorus. See O. Jahn, *Griechische Bilderchroniken*, p. 32 *sqq.* Prof. Ad. Michaelis has argued that part of an abstract of this poem is contained in the fragments of Proclus's work in the Epic Cycle. See Michaelis, in Jahn's *Griech. Bilderchroniken*, p. 95 *sqq.* ; *id.*, in *Hermes*, 14 (1879), pp. 481-498.

26. 1. **in the Returns.** We must distinguish this poem of Stesichorus from the epic of the same name which was ascribed to Agias (or Hagias) of Troezen. See note on x. 28. 7. Cp. *Poetae Lyrici Graeci*, ed. Bergk,[3] 3. p. 983.

26. 1. **Touching Creusa, they say that the Mother of the Gods** etc. Virgil makes Creusa say (*Aen.* ii. 785 *sqq.*) that she will not be carried captive into Greece, because the Mother of the Gods detains her in Asia. Mr. D. B. Monro thinks that the story of Creusa was told in Arctinus's poem the *Sack of Ilium* (which is to be distinguished from the two poems of the same name by Stesichorus and Lesches). See *Journal of Hellenic Studies*, 5 (1884), p. 30 *sq.*

26. 1. the epic called the Cypria. The poem called the *Cypria* or *Cypriaca*, an epic in eleven books, was variously ascribed to Stasinus of Cyprus, Hegesinus of Salamis, Hegesias, and Homer (Photius, *Bibliotheca*, p. 319 ed. Bekker; Athenaeus, xvi. p. 682 d e). Herodotus explicitly denied (ii. 117) that the poem was by Homer; and Aristotle did so implicitly (*Poetics*, 23, p. 1459). The subject of the poem was the origin and progress of the Trojan war down to the point where the subject is taken up in the *Iliad*. See *Epicorum Graecorum fragmenta*, ed. Kinkel, p. 15 *sqq.*; F. G. Welcker, *Der epische Cyclus*, 1. p. 300 *sqq.*; *id.*, 2. p. 85 *sqq.*; D. B. Monro, in *Journal of Hellenic Studies*, 5 (1884), p. 2 *sqq.*; W. Christ, *Gesch. d. griech. Litteratur*, p. 59 *sq.* " The *Cypria* was considered one of the grandest epics of antiquity, scarcely inferior to the *Iliad* and the *Odyssey*. . . . It would appear that the poem of Stasinus [the *Cypria*] was more popular, had greater influence over the poets and painters of Greece, than the poems of Homer. At least, in the poems and plays which have come down to us the subject is oftener taken from the *Cypria* than the *Iliad*. In the case of Greek painted vases, whereas representations taken from the *Iliad* are rare, we find very frequent paintings of the incidents of the *Cypria*, such as the Judgment of Paris, the marriage of Peleus and Thetis, or the surprise of Troilus and Polyxena by Achilles at the well " (P. Gardner, *New Chapters in Greek History*, p. 160 *sq.*).

26. 2. the Little Iliad. Here and in iii. 26. 9 Pausanias refers to the *Little Iliad* in a way which seems to imply that he thought the author unknown. It was ascribed to Lesches by Proclus (*Epicorum Graecorum fragmenta*, ed. Kinkel, p. 36), a scholiast on Aristophanes (*Lysistrata*, 155), a vase painter (C. Robert, ' Homerische Becher,' 50*tes Programm zum Winckelmannsfeste*, Berlin, 1890, p. 30 *sqq.*), and the sculptor of the *Tabula Iliaca*. Proclus (*l.c.*) calls Lesches a native of Mytilene in Lesbos; but a scholiast on Aristophanes (*l.c.*) and the sculptor of the *Tabula Iliaca* agree with Pausanias (x. 25. 5) in calling Lesches a native of Pyrrha in Lesbos. Others attributed the *Little Iliad* to Thestorides of Phocaea; others, including the historian Hellanicus, to Cinaethon the Lacedaemonian (see ii. 3. 9 note); others to Diodorus of Erythrae. See Schol. on Euripides, *Troades*, 822. Prof. C. Robert has argued that the claim of Lesches to the authorship of the poem is invalidated by the evidence of Hellanicus, who, being himself a Lesbian, would have certainly attributed the poem to a fellow-country-man if there had been any plausible ground for doing so. Prof. Robert concludes that Lesches is a literary myth concocted in the fourth century B.C. by local Lesbian patriotism as a counterblast to the Ionic legend which claimed the poem for Thestorides of Phocaea. See C. Robert, *Bild und Lied*, p. 225 *sqq.*; cp. *id.*, ' Homerische Becher,' p. 64 *sqq.* Aristotle, like Pausanias, refers to " the author of the *Little Iliad*" in a way which seems to indicate that the author's name was unknown to him (*Poetics*, 23, p. 1459, Berlin ed.). According-ing to Proclus's abstract of the *Little Iliad*, the poem was in four books, and related the events of the Trojan war from the award of the arms of Achilles down to the introduction of the Wooden Horse into Troy. But in its original form the poem must have carried the history of the war down to the sack of Troy and the departure of the Greeks. See Aristotle, *l.c.* ; *Epicorum Graecorum fragmenta*, ed. Kinkel, p. 36 *sqq.* ; F. G. Welcker, *Der epische Cyclus*, 1. p. 267 *sqq.* ; *id.*, 2. p. 237 *sqq.* ; D. B. Monro, in *Journal of Hellenic Studies*, 4 (1883), p. 317 *sq.* ; *id.*, 5 (1884), p. 18 *sqq.* ; W. Christ, *Gesch. d. griech. Litteratur*, p. 61 *sq.*

26. 2. **Polypoetes, son of Pirithous.** He is repeatedly mentioned by Homer (*Il.* ii. 740, xii. 129, 182).

26. 3. **Ajax —— taking an oath with regard to the outrage on Cassandra.** Presumably he swore that he had not been guilty of the outrage. This explanation, however, is too simple for Prof. C. Robert, who conjectures (*Die Iliupersis des Polygnot*, p. 63 *sq.*) that Ajax was swearing to atone for his sacrilege by sending two maidens periodically to Athena at Troy. For we are told that in expiation of the guilt of the Locrian Ajax the cities of Locris used to send annually to Athena at Troy two maidens whom the Trojans slew, and burning their bodies on the wood of certain trees which bore no fruit threw the ashes into the sea. If the maidens managed to escape, however, they took refuge in the sanctuary of Athena, which they thenceforward swept and washed, never quitting it except at night, and always going barefooted, shorn, and clad in a single garment. Probably the custom of sacrificing the maidens was sooner or later mitigated by allowing them regularly to escape to the sanctuary, though for form's sake a show of pursuing them was kept up. The custom is said to have been observed for a thousand years down to the Phocian war in the fourth century B.C. See Strabo, xiii. p. 600 *sq.* ; Plutarch, *De sera numinis vindicta*, 12 ; and especially Lycophron, *Cassandra*, 1141 *sqq.*, with the scholia of Tzetzes, who refers to the historian Timaeus (*Frag. Hist. Graec.* ed. Müller, vol. 1. p. 297, No. 66) as his authority. The trial of Ajax before the Greek leaders for his outrage on Cassandra was depicted by Polygnotus also in the Painted Colonnade at Athens (Paus. i. 15. 2).

26. 3. **Cassandra herself is seated** etc. Lucian especially refers to the beauty of Cassandra's eyebrows and her rosy cheeks in this painting (*Imagines*, 7).

26. 3. **she overturned the wooden image** etc. This scene was described by Arctinus in his epic the *Sack of Ilium*, and was carved on the Chest of Cypselus at Olympia. See v. 19. 5 note.

26. 3. **the prodigy which appeared etc.** When the Greeks were sacrificing at Aulis before they set sail for Troy, a serpent issued from under the altar and devoured a sparrow and eight young ones which were perched on a neighbouring plane-tree. Having done so the serpent was turned to stone. The seer Calchas interpreted the prodigy to mean that the war would last nine years and that Troy would be captured in the tenth. See Homer, *Il.* ii. 303-330.

26. 4. **In a straight line with the horse** etc. This seems to mean that the following group (Neoptolemus slaying Elasus) was on

the same line with and next to the group of Nestor and the horse (see
x. 25. 11).   The groups which Pausanias has described in the intermediate passage (the captive Trojan women, Epeus throwing down the
walls of Troy, Polypoetes, Acamas, Ulysses, Ajax, etc.) were on the
upper line.   Nestor and the horse were on the lower line, and next to
them also on the lower line was Neoptolemus in the act of slaying
Elasus.   The Greek expression which I have translated " in a straight
line with" is κατ᾽ εὐθὺ τοῦ ἵππου.   The same expression is used by
Pausanias elsewhere.   Thus in v. 11. 3 τῷ μὲν δὴ κατ᾽ εὐθὺ τῆς
ἐσόδου κανόνι, "the bar which is in a straight line with (i.e. faces) the
entrance."   Again in vii. 23. 10 ἐν δὲ οἰκήματι κατευθὺ τῆς ἐσόδου
"in a chamber in a straight line with (i.e. facing) the entrance."   The
expression has been misunderstood in different ways by Welcker and
Prof. C. Robert.   See F. G. Welcker, 'Die Composition der polygnotischen Gemälde,' p. 101 ; O. Jahn, in *Kieler philologische Studien*
(Kiel, 1841), p. 93 *sq.* ; Overbeck, in *Rheinisches Museum*, N. F. 7
(1850), p. 444 ; Schubart, in *Zeitschrift für die Alterthumswissenschaft*,
13 (1855), p. 409 *sqq.* ; Ch. Lenormant, *Mémoire sur les peintures*, etc.,
p. 54 *sq.* ; C. Robert, *Die Iliupursis des Polygnot*, p. 49.

26. 4. Elasus —— Astynous.   In the *Iliad* (v. 144 and xvi. 696)
a Trojan named Elasus and another named Astynous are slain by
Patroclus and Diomede respectively.

**26. 4. The son of Achilles is always named Neoptolemus by
Homer.**   See *Iliad*, xix. 327, *Od.* xi. 506.

26. 4. because Achilles began to make war at an early age.
The name Neoptolemus ('young warrior') is explained more naturally
by Eustathius (on Homer, *Il.* xix. 327, p. 1187) as referring to the
martial youth of Neoptolemus himself.   A scholiast on Homer (*Il.* xix.
326) seems to take the same view.   See Critical Note on this passage,
vol. 1. p. 610.   However, Pausanias's view of the origin of the name
is supported by the parallel case of Gorgophone, who was so called
because her father Perseus had slain the Gorgon (ii. 21. 7).

26. 5. on the altar is a bronze corselet.   Prof. C. Robert suggests
that we are to suppose this corselet to have been brought by Laodice,
daughter of Priam (*Il.* vi. 252), to her father at the altar where he had
taken refuge, and that before Priam could put it on he was murdered by
Neoptolemus (*Die Iliupersis des Polygnot*, p. 64).   Virgil has described
the aged king arming his feeble body (*Aen.* ii. 509 *sqq.*).   In Polygnotus's picture Laodice was portrayed standing beside the altar
(below, § 7).   Prof. Robert's explanation of the corselet on the altar
is accepted by Mr. F. Noack (*Iliupersis*, p. 64 *sq.*).

26. 5. They consisted of two bronze pieces called guala.   See
Homer, *Iliad*, v. 99, 189, xiii. 507, 587, xv. 530, xvii. 314.   As to
coats of mail in the Homeric age, see Buchholz, *Die homerischen
Realien*, 2. i. p. 370 *sqq.* ; W. Leaf, in *Journal of Hellenic Studies*, 4
(1883), p. 73 *sqq.* ; W. Helbig, *Das homerische Epos aus den Denk-
mälern erläutert*,[2] p. 286 *sqq.* ; Baumeister's *Denkmäler*, p. 2018 *sq.* ;
A. Bauer, 'Die Kriegsaltertümer,' in Iwan Müller's *Handbuch der klass.
Altertumswissenschaft*, 4. p. 235 *sq.*   Mr. W. Reichel has adduced

arguments to prove that in the Homeric, as apparently in the Mycenaean age, coats of mail were unknown, the want of them being supplied by the large heavy shield which covered nearly the whole body of the warrior, and that wherever the mention of a cuirass or coat of mail occurs in Homer the verse is a late interpolation. See W. Reichel, *Ueber homerische Waffen*, pp. 79-111. His views are accepted by Dr. Walter Leaf (*Classical Review*, 9 (1895), p. 55 *sq.*).

26. 6. **Homer represents Phorcys** etc. See *Iliad*, xvii. 312 *sqq.*

26. 6. **a painting by Calliphon the Samian** etc. This was doubtless Calliphon's picture of the battle at the ships, which Pausanias has already mentioned (v. 19. 2). Cp. H. Brunn, *Gesch. d. griech. Künstler*, 2. p. 56.

26. 7. **I do not find Laodice —— in the list of captive Trojan women.** According to one story, Laodice was swallowed up by the earth at the sack of Troy (Quintus Smyrnaeus, *Posthomerica*, xiii. 544 *sqq.*; Tryphiodorus, *Excidium Ilii*, 660 *sqq.*; Tzetzes, *Posthomerica*, 736; *id.*, *Schol. on Lycophron*, 497; Apollodorus, ed. R. Wagner, p. 212; *Epitoma Vaticana ex Apollodori Bibliotheca*, ed. R. Wagner, pp. 69, 247 *sqq.*). Polygnotus depicted her also among the captive Trojan women in the Painted Colonnade at Athens. See note on i. 15. 2.

26. 7. **Homer in the Iliad describes** etc. See *Iliad*, iii. 205 *sqq.*

26. 7. **Laodice was the wife of —— Helicaon.** See Homer, *Il.* iii. 122 *sqq.*

26. 8. **The tale which Euphorion —— tells about Laodice.** The story was that Laodice fell in love with Acamas, son of Theseus, and bore him a son named Munitus, who was afterwards killed by a snake while he was out hunting. This tale is told by Tzetzes, who has preserved some of Euphorion's verses on the subject (*Schol. on Lycophron*, 495), and it is told in greater detail by Parthenius (*Narrat. Amat.* 16). According to a different version of the legend the name of the child was Munychus and his father was Demophon, another of the sons of Theseus (Plutarch, *Theseus*, 34).

26. 9. **a bronze wash-basin on a stone stand.** In Greece at the present day many fluted pedestals of stone, about 2 feet high, may be found, especially in or about the churches. They have sometimes Ionic, but more commonly Doric capitals, mouldings, and flutings. The common shape is illustrated by the annexed cut.

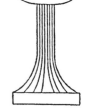

"The use of these pedestals," says Leake, "I conceive to have been, that of supporting large basins for holding lustral or sacrificial water, and many of them may have become baptismal fonts after the conversion of Greece. That the ancient basins are never entire is easily accounted for, their form being so much more liable to fracture than that of the pedestal, which has the solidity of the column increased by its shorter dimensions; it is probable also that the basin was often of metal, and therefore tempting to the plunderer. The pedestals thus deprived of their lustral vases now often serve to support the holy table or altar of the church." The reason why these pedestals are now so commonly found in Greek churches may be, as Leake suggested, that the ancient temples to which they belonged were converted into churches on the establishment of Christianity. In the Museum at Sparta I remarked a number of such stands with the top or capital complete. (In the similar pedestals at Athens the top is often wanting.) In these tops there is a square hole, obviously intended for fastening something, probably a water-basin, as Leake conjectured. Indeed one of the pedestals at Sparta actually supports a sort of ornamental font, which is clearly of the same workmanship as the pedestal. This confirms Leake's conjecture as to the use of these stands. Leake may be also right in suggesting that the stone stand supporting the washbasin in Polygnotus's picture may have been a pedestal of this sort. See Leake, *Morea*, 1. p. 498 *sq.*; *id.*, *Northern Greece*, 2. p. 302 *sq.* Pausanias calls the stand ὑποστατής and ὑπόστατον. The latter form of the name is the one given by Pollux (x. 10. 46; x. 22. 79). In an Attic inscription recording the sacred treasures of Athena and the other gods mention is made of a golden ὑπόστατον (*C. I. A.* ii. No. 652; Dittenberger, *Sylloge Inscr. Graec.* No. 366. 44); and in the double Sigean inscription the pedestal which supported the bowl is called ὑποκρητήριον (Ionic) and ἐπίστατον (Attic) (*C. I. G.* No. 8; Roehl, *I. G. A.* No. 492; Loewy, *Inschriften griech. Bildhauer*, No. 4; E. S. Roberts, *Greek Epigraphy*, No. 42).

26. 9. **Medusa.** This daughter of Priam is mentioned also by Apollodorus (iii. 12. 5) and Hyginus (*Fab.* 90). Mr. F. Noack conjectures that her name, as written by Polygnotus beside her figure, was not Medusa but Melusa (*Iliupersis*, p. 73). The conjecture, which seems to have nothing to recommend it, is rejected by Prof. C. Robert (*Die Iliupersis des Polygnot*, p. 65).

26. 9. **the ode of the Himeraean poet.** The Himeraean poet is Stesichorus. His 'ode' is probably the *Sack of Ilium*. See § 1.

26. 9. **an old woman.** Prof. C. Robert suggests that this may have been Hecuba (*Die Iliupersis des Polygnot*, p. 65 *sq.*), and the suggestion is approved by Mr. F. Noack (*Iliupersis*, p. 68 *sq.*).

27. 1. **Eioneus.** He is mentioned by Homer as the father of Rhesus (*Il.* x. 435).

27. 1. **Coroebus, son of Mygdon.** Coroebus is not mentioned by Homer, but Virgil tells how he came to Troy for love of Cassandra and how at the capture of the city he perished in the attempt to rescue her (*Aen.* ii. 341 *sqq.*, 407 *sq.*). Quintus Smyrnaeus says that Coroebus was slain by Diomede before he could enjoy the marriage for the sake of which he had come to Troy (*Posthomerica*, xiii. 168 *sqq.*). Mygdon, the father of Coroebus, is mentioned by Homer (*Il.* iii. 186).

27. 1. **Obestorium** The remains of Stectorium are near *Ille Mesjid* in the valley of *Sandykli*. Among the ruins is a small theatre. Professor W. M. Ramsay identified the site by means of an inscription in 1891. He had previously supposed the ruins to be those of Eucarpia. See W. M. Ramsay, in *Journal of Hellenic Studies*, 8 (1887), p. 476; *id.*, *Historical Geography of Asia Minor*, p. 139; *id.*, in *Athenaeum*,

15th August 1891, p. 234 ; *American Journal of Archaeology*, 7 (1891), p. 505.

27. 1. poets have been wont to give to the Phrygians the name of Mygdones. In a passage of the *Argonautica* of Apollonius Rhodius (ii. 787) the name of Mygdones was by some ancient authorities read in place of Phrygians, according to a scholiast on the passage. Moschus speaks of a Mygdonian flute (i. 97 *sq.*), meaning a Phrygian flute. On the borders of Phrygia there was a tribe called Mygdones· and a district Mygdonia or Mygdonis (Strabo, xii. pp. 550, 564, 575, 576 ; Pliny, *Nat. hist.* v. 145 ; Stephanus Byzantius, *s.v.* Μυγδονία).

27. 2. Priam —— was dragged from the altar etc. Another version of the legend was that Priam was actually slain on the altar by Neoptolemus. This was the version followed by Arctinus in the *Sack of Ilium*, if we may trust the brief abstract of the poem by Proclus (*Epicorum Graecorum fragmenta*, ed. Kinkel, p. 49). Stesichorus in his poem the *Sack of Ilium* seems to have adopted the same version ; for in the *Tabula Iliaca*, which in this part is professedly based on Stesichorus's poem, Priam is seen seated on an altar in the middle of the courtyard of his palace, while Neoptolemus seizes him by the head with his left hand and prepares to stab him. See O. Jahn, *Bilderchroniken*, pl. i. ; Baumeister's *Denkmäler*, pl. xiii. fig. 775. Later writers seem to have followed Arctinus and Stesichorus in representing Priam as slain at the altar. See Euripides, *Troades*, 16 *sq.*, 481 *sqq.* ; *id.*, *Hecuba*, 23 *sq.* ; Quintus Smyrnaeus, xiii. 220 *sqq.* ; Tryphiodorus, *Excidium Ilii*, 634 *sq.* ; Tzetzes, *Posthomerica*, 732 *sq.* ; Virgil, *Aen.* ii. 550 *sqq.* ; Dictys Cretensis, v. 12 ; Apollodorus, p. 211 ed. R. Wagner ; *Epitoma Vaticana ex Apollodori Bibliotheca*, ed. R. Wagner, pp. 69, 236 *sq.* ; Pausanias, iv. 17. 4 (cp. ii. 24. 3). The death of Priam is the subject of vase-paintings, and in all cases the painters appear to have followed Arctinus and Stesichorus rather than Lesches. See H. Heydemann, *Iliupersis*, pp. 15 *sq.*, 34 ; A. Michaelis, in *Annali dell' Inst. di Corr. Arch.* 52 (1880), p. 40 *sqq.* ; A. Schneider, *Der troische Sagenkreis*, p. 169 *sqq.* ; Baumeister's *Denkmäler*, p. 745 ; E. A. Gardner, in *Journal of Hellenic Studies*, 14 (1894), pp. 170-177, with pl. ix. ; *Catalogue of Greek and Etruscan Vases in the British Museum*, vol. 2 (London, 1893), Nos. B 205, B 241 ; *id.*, vol. 4 (London, 1896), No. F 278.

27. 2. Agenor —— was butchered by Neoptolemus. This is mentioned also by Quintus Smyrnaeus (*Posthomerica*, xiii. 216 *sq.*).

27. 3. Sinon, a comrade of Ulysses. He was a cousin of Ulysses, according to Tzetzes (*Schol. on Lycophron*, 344).

27. 3. The house of Antenor —— with a leopard's skin hung over the entrance etc. In his play of the *Locrian Ajax* Sophocles mentioned that at the sack of Troy a leopard's skin was hung up before Antenor's door as a sign that his house was to be respected. See Schol. on Aristophanes, *Birds*, 933 ; Pollux, vii. 70 ; Strabo, xiii. p. 608 ; Eustathius, on Homer, *Il.* iii. 207, p. 405 ; Sophocles, *Frag.* 16, ed. Dindorf. The same story is told by Tzetzes (*Posthomerica*, 741-743). Antenor and his sons are said to have escaped to Thrace and thence to Venetia (Strabo, *l.c.* ; Eustathius, *l.c.*). Hence Polygnotus painted the family preparing to set out on the journey.

27. 3. Theano. She was the wife of Antenor (Homer, *Il.* vi. 298 *sq.*).

27. 3. Glaucus —— Eurymachus. Apollodorus mentions (p. 211 ed. R. Wagner) that when Troy was sacked Glaucus son of Antenor took refuge in his father's house, where he was recognised and protected by Ulysses and Menelaus. According to Tzetzes (*Schol. on Lycophron,* 874) the two sons of Antenor, whom he calls Glaucus and Erymanthus, sailed from Troy with Menelaus, and being shipwrecked at Cyrene in Crete took up their abode there. Homer mentions three sons of Antenor, namely Polybus, Agenor, and Acamas (*Il.*. xi. 59 *sq.*). Virgil gives the names of the three as Glaucus, Medon, and Thersilochus (*Aen.* vi. 483 *sq.*), borrowing them from a passage of Homer (*Il.* xvii. 216), where, however, nothing is said to show that the three men so called were sons of Antenor.

27. 4. Servants are putting —— gear upon an ass. Hesychius in a gloss (*s.v.* Πολυγνώτου τοῦ ζωγράφου ὄνος) describes a picture by Polygnotus of an ass represented facing the spectator and bearing on his back a load of myrtle and a sutler. This picture, which would seem to have been famous, may very well have been the one at Delphi here described by Pausanias. It is true that at the end of the gloss Hesychius says, "It is preserved in the Anaceum"; but he seems to be here referring to Polygnotus's picture of the hare which was certainly in the Anaceum at Athens (see vol. 2. p. 166), and which Hesychius mentions in the present passage immediately before the words "It is preserved in the Anaceum," though the full description of it has fallen out. Prof. C. Robert ingeniously suggests that the myrtle boughs with which the ass was loaded pointed to Antenor's intention of going forth to seek a new home in a foreign land, myrtle boughs having been apparently carried by colonists (Aristophanes, *Birds,* 43, with the scholiast's note). See C. Robert, *Die Iliupersis des Polygnot,* p. 54 *sq.*

27. 4. a couplet of Simonides etc. This epigram occurs in the *Palatine Anthology* (ix. 700). It is quoted, but without mention of the author's name, by Plutarch (*De dejectu oraculorum,* 47) and a scholiast on Plato (*Gorgias,* p. 448 b), and it is clearly alluded to by Philostratus (*Vit. Apollon.* vi. 11). The words which contain the names of the artist and his father are cited, with the change of a word, by Photius (*Lexicon, s.v.* Θάσιος παῖς Ἀγλαοφῶντος) and Hesychius (*Lexicon, s.v.* Θάσιος πᾶϊς Ἀγλαοφῶντος). These numerous references show that the couplet was celebrated, though its poetical merit is of the slightest. That it was composed by Simonides is denied on insufficient grounds by Prof. C. Robert (*Die Nekyia des Polygnot,* p. 76 ; *id., Die Marathon-* *schlacht in der Poikile,* p. 70 *sq.*) and Prof. Hauvette (*De l'authenticité des épigrammes de Simonide* (Paris, 1896), p. 137 *sq.*). The genuineness of the verses is rightly maintained by Prof. Milchhöfer (*Jahrbuch des archäolog. Instituts,* 9 (1894), p. 72 note 36). Cp. Bergk's *Poetae Lyrici Graeci,* 3.³ p. 1178.

28. 1. The descent of Ulysses to hell etc. On the literary

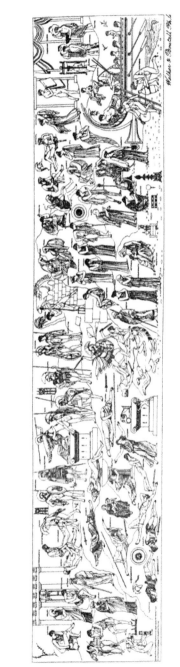

Polygnotus's picture of the Capture of Troy, restored by C. Robert.

authorities followed by Polygnotus in his delineation of the nether world, see F. Dümmler, ' Die Quellen zu Polygnot's Nekyia,' *Rheinisches Museum*, N. F. 45 (1890), pp. 178-202 ; C. Robert, *Die Nekyia des Polygnot*, p. 74 *sqq*. Prof. Dümmler holds that Polygnotus followed the epic poem called *The Returns* ; Prof. Robert holds that he did not. As the poem in question has perished, it is obvious that either opinion may be maintained with equal confidence and absence of conflicting evidence. A brief abstract of *The Returns* has been preserved by Proclus (*Epicorum Graecorum fragmenta*, ed. Kinkel, p. 52 *sq*.), but there is no mention in it of a descent to hell. On the other hand Prof. Robert accepts the view of Pausanias (below, § 2) that Polygnotus knew and used the *Minyad* in addition to the *Odyssey*. With regard to copies of Polygnotus's picture on existing vases, Prof. Robert tells us that none has yet been found, but he is of opinion that some of the particular groups of the famous painting have been freely adapted by vase-painters to form new scenes (*op. cit.* p. 53). Scenes of the under world are depicted on about a dozen existing vases of Lower Italy. See A. Winkler, *Die Darstellung der Unterwelt auf unteritalischen Vasen* (Breslau, 1888); E. Kuhnert, ' Unteritalische Nekyien,' *Jahrbuch d. archäolog. Instituts*, 8 (1893), pp. 104-113.

28. 2. the poem called the Minyad. This poem was attributed to Prodicus of Phocaea. See iv. 33. 7. F. G. Welcker conjectured that it was identical with the *Phocaeis*, a poem which Homer was said to have composed at Phocaea ([Herodotus,] *Vita Homeri*, 16, in *Biographi Graeci*, ed. Westermann, p. 8). See *Epicorum Graecorum fragmenta*, ed. Kinkel, p. 215 *sqq*. ; F. G. Welcker, *Der epische Cyclus*, I. p. 248 *sqq*. ; *id.*, 2. p. 422 *sqq*. ; W. Christ, *Gesch. d. griech. Litteratur*, p. 64.

28. 2. Ferryman, Charon. The belief in Charon still survives among the modern Greeks. They call him *Charos* and regard him as a personification of Death, who with his own hand snatches the souls of the dying from their bodies and conveys them to the nether world. But the conception of him as a ferryman who transports the souls of the departed across the river of Death is also occasionally to be met with. See B. Schmidt, *Das Volksleben der Neugriechen*, p. 222 *sqq*.

28. 3. Tellis —— Cleoboea. It has been supposed that these two personages were chosen by Polygnotus on account of their connexion with Thasos in order to indicate the Thasian origin of the painter himself (C. Robert, *Die Nekyia des Polygnot*, p. 81 ; R. Schöne, in *Jahrbuch d. arch. Inst.* 8 (1893), p. 200 note 23 ; P. Weizsäcker, *Polygnots Gemälde*, p. 15). The connexion of Cleoboea with Thasos is mentioned by Pausanias himself. But what had Tellis to do with Thasos ? Nothing whatever, so far as we know. His son Telesicles, the father of Archilochus, did indeed migrate from Paros to Thasos (Eusebius, *Praepar. Evang.* vi. 7. 6 ; Stephanus Byzantius, *s.v.* Θάσσος); but that can hardly be regarded as establishing a Thasian connexion for Tellis himself. Mr. Dieterich may be right in supposing that the identification of the Tellis of the picture with the grandfather of Archilochus may have been nothing but a guess of the ciceroni, and that the painter may have chosen the name merely with a punning reference to the mysteries (*telos*) which his companion in the infernal bark had brought to Thasos (A. Dieterich, *Nekyia: Beiträge zur Erklärung der neuentdeckten Petrusapokalypse*, Leipzig, 1893, p. 69).

28. 3. **a box such as they make for Demeter.** The 'box' was probably the mystic *cista*, which seems to have been a basket rather than a box. See viii. 25. 7 note.

28. 4. **the —— Pious Folk at Catana.** These Pious Folk were generally said to have been two brothers, Amphinomus and Anapias (or Anapius). The spot where the torrent of lava surrounded them and their parents without scathing them was called the Place (or Field) of the Pious, and stone statues of the brothers were erected there. See Conon, *Narrationes*, 43; Lycurgus, *contra Leocratem*, xxiii. 95 *sq.*; [Aristotle,] *De Mundo*, p. 400 Berlin ed.; [Aristotle,] *De mirab. Auscultat.* 154 (165), p. 56 ed. Westermann; Seneca, *De beneficiis*, iii. 37, vi. 36; Solinus, v. 15; Strabo, vi. p. 269; Valerius Maximus, v. 4. Ext. 4; Silius Italicus, xiv. 196 *sq.*; Philostratus, *Vit. Apollonii*, v. 17. The Syracusans claimed the pious brothers for Syracuse and called them Emantias and Crito (Solinus, *l.c.*). In his list of people distinguished for piety Hyginus says (*Fab.* 254) that at the first eruption of Etna Damon saved his mother from the fire and Phintias saved his father. In a Greek metrical inscription found at Catana, the city is called "the famous town of the Pious" (Εὐσεβέων κλυτὸν ἄστυ) (G. Kaibel, *Epigrammata Graeca*, No. 887).

28. 5. **The woman who is chastising him is skilled in drugs** etc. How was her skill in drugs indicated in the picture? Was she depicted administering a dose to the miscreant? And did the wry face he pulled betray his internal anguish? This is the view of Prof. E. Rohde (*Psyche*, p. 291), Mr. R. Schöne (*Jahrbuch d. arch. Instituts*, 8 (1893), p. 201 note 25), and Mr. A. Dieterich (*Nekyia*, p. 68 note 2). Prof. C. Robert, on the other hand, suggests (*Die Nekyia des Polygnot*, p. 60) that the woman was not an apothecary or poisoner at all but a goddess of vengeance who was represented belabouring the sinner with a club which Pausanias mistook for a pestle, remembering the figures of women with pestles on the chest of Cypselus (v. 18. 2). This seems improbable, and we shall do better to adhere to the more natural view that she was offering a poisoned cup to the sacrilegious man. Mr. Dieterich (*l.c.*) has well pointed out that such a punishment seems to have been regularly inflicted in hell by Tisiphone (Valerius Flaccus, ii. 194 *sq.*).

28. 6. **when they captured the sanctuary of Olympian Zeus at Syracuse.** It does not appear from Thucydides that the Athenians ever captured this sanctuary, which stood in a suburb of Syracuse. The Syracusans put a garrison into it to protect the treasures which it contained, but the Athenians did not approach it. See Thucydides, vi. 70 *sq.*, vii. 4 and 37. Plutarch says (*Nicias*, 16) that although the Athenians were eager to gain possession of the sanctuary on account of the many votive offerings of gold and silver which were stored in it, the pious general Nicias purposely hung back and allowed the enemy to throw a garrison

into it unmolested, for fear his soldiers might plunder the treasures and the blame of the sacrilege might rest on himself. On the other hand, Diodorus relates (xiii. 6) that the Athenians succeeded in seizing and fortifying the sanctuary and repelled an attack of the Syracusans.

28. 6. the words he spoke to the Delians. When the inhabitants of Delos fled at the approach of the Persian fleet, the Persian commander Datis sent a herald after them with a message inviting the "sacred men" to return and assuring them that no harm would be done to them or to their sacred island, the birthplace of Apollo and Artemis (Herodotus, vi. 97).

28. 6. finding an image of Apollo in a Phoenician ship etc. According to Herodotus (vi. 118), who is doubtless Pausanias's authority for the anecdote, Datis himself conveyed the image to Delos and charged the inhabitants to restore it to Delium. The Delians neglected to obey this injunction, but twenty years afterwards the Thebans, in compliance with an oracle, had the image brought back to its original home.

28. 7. Eurynomus. This demon appears to be mentioned by no other ancient writer. Prof. C. Robert regards him as a personification of death, pointing out that his name, which signifies 'wide-ruling,' would on this hypothesis be appropriate (*Die Nekyia des Polygnot*, p. 61 ; *Die Marathonschlacht in der Poikile*, pp. 117-119). Mr. A. Dieterich prefers to consider him as a personification of the grave in which the dead are laid and which, as it were, consumes their bodies, leaving only the bones (*Nekyia*, p. 47 *sq.*).

28. 7. The Returns —— speak of hell etc. In Proclus's abstract of the epic called *The Returns* there is no mention of a descent to hell. See *Epicorum Graecorum fragmenta*, ed. Kinkel, p. 52 *sq.* Hence Mr. D. B. Monro has conjectured (*Journal of Hellenic Studies*, 4 (1873), p. 319) that the editor or editors who redacted the Epic Cycle left out this episode, because a similar one had been already described in the eleventh book of the *Odyssey*.

28. 8. Auge went to the court of Teuthras in Mysia etc. Cp. viii. 47. 4, viii. 48. 7 ; and see the note on i. 4. 6 'the band which crossed to Asia with Telephus.' Prof. C. Robert conjectures that it was Leda and not Auge whom Polygnotus here painted in the under world, and that the mistake of Pausanias or of his authority originated in misreading the name attached to the figure, the name ΛΗΔΗ being easily confused with ΑΥΓΗ. He points out that in the *Odyssey*, which Polygnotus may have followed, Auge is not mentioned among the famous dames seen by Ulysses in the lower world, but that on the other hand Leda is so mentioned and is moreover coupled with Iphimedea (*Od.* xi. 208, 305), just as the figure in question in Polygnotus's picture is coupled. See C. Robert, *Die Nekyia des Polygnot*, p. 75. The conjecture is ingenious and not improbable. Even if it be accepted, however, it would involve no change in the text of Pausanias, as the mistake, if it be one, was obviously made by Pausanias himself and not by a copyist. As to Iphimedea cp. ix. 22. 6.

29. 1. the comrades of Ulysses, bringing sacrificial victims.

Dr. R. Schöne conjectures that they were really represented carrying away the carcasses of the slaughtered rams in order to skin and sacrifice them to Pluto and Proserpine, as they are ordered by Ulysses in the *Odyssey* (xi. 44 *sqq.*) to do. He points out that in Polygnotus's picture Ulysses was supposed to have already slaughtered the rams, since he was depicted holding his sword over the trench in which their blood had flowed (x. 29. 8). See R. Schöne, in *Jahrbuch d. arch. Inst.* 8 (1893), p. 200. To this Prof. C. Robert replies that in the *Odyssey* there is nothing said about carrying away the victims and that it is much more probable that they were to be offered to the infernal deities on the spot (*Die Marathonschlacht in der Poikile*, p. 120 *sq.*).

29. 1. **Indolence —— plaiting a rope** etc. This punishment of Indolence in hell seems to have been a familiar topic with the ancients and to have been often depicted in art. We know of two paintings of it by distinguished artists, the one by Polygnotus which Pausanias here describes, the other by Nicophanes, a pupil of the Sicyonian painter Pausias (Pliny, *Nat. hist.* xxxv. 137 ; H. Brunn, *Gesch. d. griech. Künstler*, 2. p. 155). Plutarch refers to "the picture of the rope-twister in hell who allows a browsing ass to consume what he is plaiting' (*De tranquillitate animi*, 14). Cratinus, in one of his comedies, also referred to "the man plaiting a rope in hell and the ass eating what he plaits" (Photius, *Lexicon*, *s.v.* ὄνου πόκαι ; Suidas, *s.v.* ὄνου πόκαι). Propertius speaks of the subject (v. 3. 21 *sq.*) as if it were proverbial. The story is illustrated by at least six existing monuments of ancient art, namely :

(1) A round marble well-head, sometimes described as an altar, formerly in the Museo Pio-Clementino, now in the Vatican. Here Indolence is represented in relief seated on a knoll and plaiting his rope, while at his back the other end of the rope is being eaten by an ass. Beside him the Danaids are also represented in relief pouring water into a great jar. See Visconti, *Musée Pie-Clementin*, vol. 4. pl. xxxvi. and pl. xxxvi.* (both plates illustrate the same monument, but the second gives a more careful and accurate rendering of Indolence and the ass), with Visconti's remarks, p. 264 *sqq.* ; *Berichte über die Verhandl. d. k. sächs. Gesell. d. Wissenschaften zu Leipzig*, Philolog. histor. Cl. 8 (1856), pl. iii. A ; J. J. Bachofen, *Versuch über die Gräbersymbolik der Alten* (Basel, 1859), pl. ii. ; Baumeister's *Denkmäler*, p. 1925, fig. 2041 ; W. Helbig, *Führer durch die öffentlichen Sammlungen klassischer Alterthümer in Rom*, 1. p. 278 *sq.*, No. 372 (179).

(2) A stucco relief in a Columbarium of the Vigna Campana near the Porta Latina at Rome. Here Indolence is represented as an old bearded man kneeling and plaiting his rope, while the ass quietly eats the other end of the rope full in front of him. See *Berichte* (*l.c.*), pl. iii. E ; J. J. Bachofen, *op. cit*, pl. i. ; Müller-Wieseler, *Denkmäler*, 2. pl. lxix. No. 867.

(3) A wall-painting in a Columbarium of the Villa Pamfili at Rome. Here Indolence appears sitting idly on a stone, holding in his right hand the end of a rope, which an ass, lying on the ground in front of him, is eating. The buildings and trees in the background prove

that the scene is not laid in the lower world.　See *Abhandlungen d. philosoph. philolog. Cl. d. k. bayer. Akad. d. Wissenschaften*, 8 (1858), pl. iii. 8, with the remarks of O. Jahn, pp. 245-249 ; J. J. Bachofen, *op. cit.* pl. ii.

(4) A painting found in a tomb at Ostia, now in the Lateran Museum at Rome.　Here Indolence is depicted sitting and plaiting his rope, while the ass is eating the other end of it behind his back.　The scene is laid in the lower world.　We see the figures of Pluto, Orpheus, and Eurydice, all with their names attached, and the gate of hell guarded by Cerberus and a doorkeeper.　The painting, executed in an exceedingly dull prosaic style, is believed to date from the first century of our era.　See *Monumenti Inediti*, 8 (1864-1868), pl. xxviii. 1 ; C. L. Visconti, in *Annali dell' Instituto*, 38 (1866), pp. 292-307 ; W. Helbig, *op. cit.* vol. 1. p. 540, No. 696 (1064).

(5) A painting on a vase (*lekythos*) found in a grave on Monte Saraceno near Ravanusa.　The picture treats the stories of the nether world in a spirit of caricature.　Male and female figures, representing probably the uninitiated (see below, x. 31. 9 note), are depicted carrying water in pitchers on their heads to pour it into a large jar, and Indolence is seated gazing before him at some lines which are supposed to stand for his rope.　Behind him is the ass falling on its nose, while one of the male water-carriers pulls it by the tail.　See *Archäologische Zeitung*, 28 (1871), pl. 31. 22, with the remarks of H. Heydemann, p. 42 *sq.*

(6) A drawing in the Codex Pighianus (fol. 47) preserved in Berlin. The drawing exhibits in five separate compartments five scenes of the lower world, namely, Ixion stretched on his wheel, Hercules fetching up Cerberus, the Danaids engaged in pouring water into a large broken jar, Sisyphus heaving his rock up hill, and Indolence and the ass.　In this last scene Indolence appears as a beardless man clad in a shirt and trousers, seated on a four-legged stool and plaiting a rope, of which the other end is being eaten by an ass.　The drawing may be, as O. Jahn supposed, a copy of reliefs on a Roman sarcophagus.　See *Berichte* (*l.c.*), pl. ii. with the remarks of O. Jahn, p. 267 *sqq.* ; *Abhandlungen* (*l.c.*), pl. vii. 21 ; Bachofen, *op. cit.* pl. iii. 2.

Diodorus reports (i. 97) that at Acanthus in Egypt certain ceremonies were observed which bore some resemblance to the stories of the Danaids and Indolence in hell.　Every day three hundred and sixty priests brought water from the Nile and poured it into a jar which had a hole in it ; and at a certain festival one man twisted an end of a long rope, while many men at his back untwisted it just as fast.　This latter ceremony Diodorus expressly compares to the Greek story of Indolence and his rope.

The story of Indolence further occurs, with a slight variation, in the Buddhist collection of stories known as the *Jatakas.*　" 'A man was weaving rope, sir, and as he wove, he threw it down at his feet.　Under his bench lay a hungry she-jackal, which kept eating the rope as he wove, but without the man knowing it.　This is what I saw.　This was my seventh dream.　What shall come of it ? '　' This dream too shall not have its fulfilment till the future. For in days to come, women shall lust after men and strong drink and finery and gadding abroad and after the joys of this world. In their wickedness and profligacy these women shall drink strong drink with their paramours; they shall flaunt in garlands and perfumes and unguents; and heedless of even the most pressing of their household duties, they shall keep watching for their paramours, even at crevices high up in the outer wall; aye, they shall pound up the very seed-corn that should be sown on the morrow so as to provide good cheer;—in all these ways shall they plunder the store won by the hard work of their husbands in field and byre, devouring the poor men's substance even as the hungry jackal ate up the rope of the rope-maker as he wove it'" (*The Jataka or stories of the Buddha's former births*, vol. i. translated by R. Chalmers (Cambridge, 1895), bk. i. No. 77, p. 189). The parallelism of this Indian tale to the Greek one was first pointed out, so far as I know, by Mr. A. Grünwedel (*Original-Mittheilungen aus der ethnologischen Abtheilung der königl. Museen zu Berlin*, I (1885), p. 42). It was afterwards indicated independently by Mr. W. H. D. Rouse (*Folklore*, I (1890), p. 409).

The fable of the rope-weaver and the ass or jackal seems a sufficiently obvious apologue of misdirected and therefore fruitless labour. This explanation, which lies to hand, is not however profound enough to satisfy most of the scholars who have touched upon the subject. They have accordingly propounded interpretations of varying degrees of improbability and even absurdity. The tale has been treated as a symbolical expression of the creative forces of primitive nature, as an allegory of the sea devouring the ships of the Phoenicians, as a folktale of a man who gathered sticks in a wood, as a high moral allegory of the weakness of the will, and as a veiled description of a bucket being let down into a well.

See J. J. Bachofen, *op. cit.* pp. 301-412; P. Cassel, *Aus Literatur und Symbolik* (Leipzig, 1884), pp. 290-309; E. Rohde, *Psyche*, p. 290 *sq.*; U. von Wilamowitz-Möllendorff, *Homerische Untersuchungen*, p. 202; C. Robert, *Die Nekyia des Polygnot*, p. 62 *sq.*; A. B. Cooke, in *Journal of Hellenic Studies*, 14 (1894), p. 96 *sqq.*

29. 2. The same name —— is also given to a certain bird etc. The species of heron which the Greeks nicknamed Indolence (*oknos*) is the bittern. Its ordinary Greek name was *asterias*. Aristotle distinguished three kinds of herons, of which the bittern (*asterias* or *oknos*) was one. He says that the ancestors of the bittern were fabled to have been slaves and that in accordance with its name (*oknos* 'indolence') the bird was the laziest of the heron tribe. See Aristotle, *Hist. anim.* ix. i. p. 609 b 21 *sqq.*, ix. 18. p. 617 a 5 *sqq.* Cp. Callimachus, quoted by a scholiast on Homer, *Il.* ii. 971, p. 706 ed. Bekker; Pliny, *Nat. hist.* x. 164. Aelian assures us that in Egypt, where the bittern (*asterias*) was tamed, the bird understood human speech and felt hurt if any one called it 'slave' or 'indolence' (*oknos*) (*Nat. anim.* v. 36). Antoninus Liberalis (*Transform.* 7) tells a fable of the transformation of a man named Antonous into a bittern (*oknos*). That the heron was a bird of

omen we learn from a passage in Homer (*Il.* x. 274 *sqq.*), where Athena
sends a heron to Ulysses and Diomede, as they are about to set forth on
their perilous adventure by night ; they hear the bird screaming on their
right in the darkness and greet it as a good omen.   Pliny tells us (*Nat.
hist.* xi. 140) that a species of heron called *leucon* (Greek λευκός,
English ' egret ') was of very good omen if seen flying south or north. The
heron is said to have been sacred to Hera (Hesychius, *s.v.* νυκταίετος).
See J. J. Bachofen, *Versuch über die Gräbersymbolik der Alten*, p.
354 *sqq.* ; L. Stephani, in *Compte-Rendu* (St. Petersburg) for 1865,
p. 125 *sqq.*

29. 3. **he appears as a dim and mangled spectre.**   The Greek
words are ἀμυδρὸν καὶ οὐδὲ ὁλόκληρον εἴδωλον.   Professors Benndorf
and C. Robert suppose this to mean merely that the figure of Tityus
was partially hidden by a line indicating a rise in the ground (O. Benndorf, in Ἐφημερὶς ἀρχαιολογική, 1887, p. 127 *sq.* ; C. Robert, *Die
Nekyia des Polygnot*, p. 63), and this view has been accepted by Mr.
P. Girard (*La peinture antique*, p. 175 *sq.*).   But the words of Pausanias
are more naturally interpreted to mean that the body of Tityus was
represented as partially consumed by the vultures that had been preying
on his vitals (Homer, *Od.* xi. 578 *sq.*).   And on this interpretation the
figure of the sinner has a tragic significance which is wholly wanting on
the other.

29. 3. **Phaedra who is in a swing** etc.   Otto Jahn conjectured that this euphemistic way of hinting at Phaedra's suicide may
have been suggested by the Swinging Festival, which was commonly
said to have been instituted as an expiation for the death of Erigone
who had hung herself from grief at the murder of her father Icarius
(Hyginus, *Fab.* 130).   See O. Jahn, *Archäologische Beiträge*, p. 324 *sqq.*

29. 4. **Dionysus —— first led an army against India.**   On the
warlike character and exploits of Dionysus, particularly his expedition
to India, and the works of ancient art illustrative of it, see L. Stephani,
in *Compte-Rendu* (St. Petersburg) for 1867, pp. 161 *sqq.*, 182 *sqq.* ;
Graef, *De Bacchi expeditione Indica monumentis expressa* (Berlin, 1886).

29. 5. **tales told of Dionysus —— by —— Egyptians.**   By
Dionysus is here meant Osiris, whom the Greeks identified with
Dionysus.   See Herodotus, ii. 42, 144 ; Plutarch, *Isis and Osiris*, 13,
34 *sq.* ; Diodorus, i. 13, 25, 96, iv. 1.

29. 5. **Thyia.**   See x. 6. 4.   There was a precinct dedicated to
her at Delphi, and here the Delphians set up an altar to the winds on
the eve of the Persian invasion (Herodotus, vii. 178).

29. 5. **Chloris was the wife of Neleus.**   Cp. ix. 36. 8.

29. 6. **Procris —— was slain by her husband.**   Cp. i. 37. 6.

29. 7. **Megara.**   Dr. Th. Schreiber conjectures that this Megara
was not, as Pausanias supposed, the wife of Hercules, but the mother
of Ixion (*Anthol. Palat.* iii. 12) (*Festschrift für Johannes Overbeck*,
p. 194).

29. 7. **the daughter of Salmoneus.**   Her name was Tyro.   See
Homer, *Od.* xi. 235 *sq.*

29. 7. **in the folds of the tunic she is grasping the famous**

necklace. As to the necklace of Eriphyle see v. 17. 7, v. 24, 8, ix. 41. 2 *sqq.*, with the notes.   The attitude in which the painter portrayed

Eriphyle is perhaps illustrated by a graceful bronze statuette found at Corinth which represents a woman standing and holding her hands on her breast concealed under a flap of her tunic; the fingers are pushing up the flap from underneath and touching the neck (Fig. 13). See J. Six, 'Die Eriphyle des Polygnot,' *Mittheilungen des archäolog. Instituts in Athen,* 19 (1894), pp. 335-339. As Mr. Six, who was the first to compare the attitude of the statuette with that of Eriphyle in the picture, has well observed, it is indifferent whether we suppose Eriphyle to have actually grasped the necklace under her robe or merely to have been unable to take away her hand from the place where the fatal bauble, which had cost her and hers so dear, had once rested. In the latter case the pathetic significance of the figure would be even deepened.

FIG. 13. — ERI-
PHYLE ? (BRONZE
STATUETTE).

However that may be, the indication of the whole tragic story by a mere gesture is worthy of a great artist and, as Mr. Six again remarks with justice, comes near the manner and spirit of Dante.   Prof. Robert has done well to accept Mr. Six's view and to abandon the rash conjecture by which he had corrupted the text of Pausanias (*Die Marathonschlacht in der Poikile,* p. 121 *sq.*).   For Prof. Robert's now abandoned conjecture see vol. i. p. 611.

29. 8. **Ulysses is crouching and holding his sword over the trench** etc.   The interview of Ulysses with Tiresias in the lower world (see Homer, *Od.* xi. 90 *sqq.*) is the subject of (1) a fine wall-painting in a Roman house on the Esquiline; (2) a marble relief now in the Louvre; (3) a vase-painting; (4) an engraving on an Etruscan mirror.   See Miss J. E. Harrison, *Myths of the Odyssey,* p. 99 *sqq.*; Baumeister's *Denkmäler,* figures 939, 1254, 1255.   The vase-painting in question (*Monumenti Inediti,* vol. 4 (1844-1848), pl. xix.) represents Ulysses, almost naked, seated on a heap of rough stones; in his right hand he holds his drawn sword, in the left the scabbard.   Under his feet is the slaughtered ram, and close to the ram's head appears the face of the aged Tiresias, emerging from the ground, which conceals the rest of his body.

29. 8. **a mat, such as is commonly worn by sailors.**   The fishermen in Theocritus (xxi. 13) sleep with "a small mat, their clothes, and their caps" under their heads; but it does not seem certain that this mat was a garment.

29. 9. **Theseus and Pirithous seated on chairs** etc.   In the recently-discovered Epitome of Apollodorus it is said that when Theseus arrived in hell with his friend Pirithous to carry off Proserpine, he was outwitted; for in the expectation of receiving friendly presents they sat down on the chair of Forgetfulness (Lethe), to which they grew and were held fast by coils of serpents.   See *Epitoma Vaticana ex Apollodori bibliotheca,* ed. R. Wagner, pp. 58, 155 *sq.*; Apollodorus, ed.

R. Wagner, p. 182.   The editor, Mr. Wagner, conjectures that Apollodorus's authority was Panyasis; for Panyasis, as we learn from Pausanias,
represented Theseus and Pirithous growing to the rock on which they
sat. Cp. Suidas, *s.v.* λίσποι. "The chair of Forgetfulness" is not
expressly mentioned by any other ancient writer, but there seems to be
an allusion to it in Horace, where he says (*Odes*, iv. 27 *sq.*) that Theseus
was not able to free his dear Pirithous from the "Lethaean bonds"
(*vincula Lethaea*). With the "chair of Forgetfulness" we may compare
the chair in which Hephaestus caused Hera to be held fast by invisible
bonds (see i. 20. 3), and the chair in which the smith in the folk-tale
holds fast Death or the Devil.   See note on ii. 5. 1.   The story of
Theseus and Pirithous in hell is the subject of a painting in an Etruscan
tomb at Tarquinii, and is illustrated by vase-paintings and other monuments of ancient art. See E. Petersen, 'Theseus und Peirithoos im
Hades,' *Archäologische Zeitung*, 35 (1877), pp. 119-123.

    29. 10. Ulysses is represented saying etc.   See Homer, *Odyssey*,
xi. 631 *sq.*   But the second of these lines, in which Theseus and
Pirithous are mentioned, was said by Hereas of Megara to have been
interpolated by Pisistratus to please the Athenians.   See Plutarch,
Theseus, 20.

    29. 10. For never saw I yet etc.   The lines are from *Iliad*,
i. 262 *sqq.*   But here again the line (265) in which Theseus is mentioned
is thought by some modern critics to have been interpolated by a patriotic
Athenian from the pseudo-Hesiodean *Shield of Hercules*, v. 182.   Other
scholars reverse this theory and suppose that the author of the *Shield
of Hercules* borrowed the line from the *Iliad*. This latter is the view
of Professor von Wilamowitz-Moellendorf (*Homerische Untersuchungen*,
p. 260) and J. Töpffer (*Aus der Anomia*, p. 31).

    30. 1. the daughters of Pandareos etc.   See Homer, *Od.* xx.
66-78.   According to an account preserved by Eustathius (on Homer,
Od. xix. 518, p. 1875) and a scholiast on Homer (*Od.* xx. 66, vol. 2.
p. 688 ed. Dindorf) the damsels were three in number and their names
Merope, Cleothera and Aedon.   The story of their father's guilt and of
their own tragic fate is told by Eustathius (*l.c.* and on *Od.* xx. 66, p.
1883), the scholiast on Homer (*l.c.*), a scholiast on Pindar (*Olymp.* i.
97), and, with some variations, by Antoninus Liberalis (*Transform.* 36).
It ran thus. Zeus had a golden dog which guarded his sanctuary in
Crete.   Pandareos of Miletus stole the dog, but fearing to take it home
with him entrusted it for safe keeping to Tantalus, who dwelt on Mount
Sipylus.   When Zeus sent Hermes to reclaim the stolen animal, Tantalus
swore a great oath he knew nothing about it.   But Hermes found the
dog in the house, and Zeus punished the perjured Tantalus by burying
him under Mount Sipylus.   Hearing of the fate of his accomplice,
Pandareos fled with his wife and maiden daughters to Athens, and
thence to Sicily.   But Zeus saw him and killed both him and his wife.
As for the orphan daughters, the angry god set the Harpies on them,
who snatched them up and delivered them over to the Furies to be
their slaves.   "Moreover," adds the scholiast on Homer, "Zeus inflicted on them a disease, which is called 'dog.'"   This 'dog' disease,

as Dr. W. H. Roscher has lately pointed out in a learned and instructive paper, was probably a form of insanity which seems to have prevailed among many races and the essence of which consists in the patient imagining himself to be an animal and behaving as such. This sort of madness was known to the ancients as the cynanthropic ('dog-man') or lycanthropic ('wolf-man') disease, and is thus described in the medical treatise *On Melancholy* which is printed among the works of Galen (vol. 19. p. 719 ed. Kühn). "Persons afflicted with the cynanthropic or lycanthropic disease go out by night in the month of February, imitating wolves or dogs in all respects, and till break of day they pass most of their time in grubbing among the graves." The writer then describes the symptoms of the disease—the pale face and hollow eyes, the dry tongue, parched mouth, and ulcered legs of the patients. A similar form of insanity occurs among the inhabitants of the Garrow Hills in Bengal. It has been described as follows by a writer of last century who was sent on a mission to the hills : "Among the Garrows, a madness exists, which they call transformation into a tiger, from a person who is afflicted with this malady walking about like that animal, shunning all society. It is said, that, on their being first seized with this complaint, they tear their hair, and rings from their ears, with such force as to break the lobe. It is supposed to be occasioned by a medicine applied to the forehead : but I endeavoured to procure some of the medicine thus used, without effect : I imagine it rather to be created by frequent intoxications, as the malady goes off in the course of a week or a fortnight : during the time the person is in this state, it is with the utmost difficulty he is made to eat or drink. I questioned a man, who had thus been afflicted, as to the manner of his being seized, and he told me he only felt a giddiness without any pain, and that afterwards he did not know what happened to him" (J. Eliot, in *Asiatick Researches*, vol. 3. p. 34 of the octavo edition). At the present day a type of madness of the same sort is very common in Japan. The patient is popularly believed to be possessed by an animal, most commonly by a fox, and behaves "as much like the animal itself—be it badger, fox, or what not—as it is possible for a human being to do." Sometimes the sufferer takes to the woods and hills, where he lives on berries and what he can find, all the while running or crawling about on all fours. So generally are foxes feared for their power of possessing human beings that shrines and temples in their honour exist in nearly every part of the country, and opposite their holes images of foxes in clay or stone are set up and receive propitiatory offerings of the food in which the creature is known to delight. This form of insanity, which is accompanied by "strange and apparently unaccountable swellings in different parts of the body, or various forms of nervous disease," attacks women chiefly, indeed almost exclusively. Exorcism of the fox-spirit is practised largely at celebrated shrines, and in some places there are hospitals devoted entirely to this purpose. See W. Weston, *Mountaineering and Exploration in the Japanese Alps* (London, 1896), pp. 308-316. From facts like these Dr. Roscher would explain other ancient legends and religious practices, such as the story of the madness of the daughters of Proetus who fancied they were cows and roamed the woods bellowing (Virgil, *Ecl.* vi. 48, with the note of Servius), and the behaviour of the Bacchanals, who clothed themselves in the skins of beasts, tore live animals to pieces and devoured the flesh raw as if they were themselves wild beasts, and fondled and suckled wolf-cubs, fawns, and young panthers as if they were their own offspring (see Roscher's *Lexikon*, 1. p. 1037 *sqq.*, 2. p. 2250 *sq.*). It would seem to have been especially women who were liable to such attacks of insanity in antiquity, just as at the present day it is women who are chiefly subject to the fox-madness in Japan. Dr. Roscher makes the pregnant suggestion that delusions of this sort are closely connected with the religious beliefs of the patients, who seem peculiarly liable to fancy themselves transformed into that particular animal which is especially associated with the deity they worship. Thus the cow-madness of the daughters of Proteus, who were Argives, may have taken its special form through the association of cows with the worship of the Argive Hera; and the dog-madness of the daughters of Pandareos would seem to have been in some way connected with a worship of the dog, if we may judge from the legend of the theft of the sacred dog by their father Pandareos. Dr. Roscher conjectures that the bear-dances of the young Attic maidens (see above, vol. 4. p. 224) may perhaps have originated in a similar epidemic of insanity among girls under puberty. For the girls who acted as bears might not be more than ten years old (Schol. on Aristophanes, *Lysistrata*, 645); and the symptoms of hysteria, of which such illusions are apparently a special form, often manifest themselves before puberty is reached. If he is right, the questions would still have to be asked, Why are certain animals specially associated with the worship of certain deities? and are the illusions we have been considering merely the effects of such religious associations? may they not have been in some cases the cause? The prosecution of these enquiries may possibly throw some light on the origin of totemism or the primitive system of belief that the men and women of a particular kin are the brothers and sisters of animals or plants of a particular sort. In any case Dr. Roscher can hardly fail to be right in connecting closely the belief in were-wolves and similar superstitions with the type of insanity under consideration. See his essay ' Das von der Kynanthropie handelnde Fragment des Marcellus von Side' in the *Abhandlungen der philolog. histor. Classe der k. sächs. Gesell. der Wissenschaften*, vol. 17 (1896), No. 3 (pp. 3-92).

30. 2. **Miletus in Crete.** This town is mentioned by Homer (*Il.* ii. 647). It is said to have been the mother-city of Miletus in Ionia (Strabo, xii. p. 573, xiv. p. 634).

30. 2. **he was an accomplice in Tantalus' theft** etc. The reference is to the theft of the golden dog, as to which see above, note on § 1 'the daughters of Pandareos.'

30. 3. **Antilochus, with —— his face and head resting on both his hands.** He had brought to Achilles the evil tidings of Patroclus's death and had wept as he delivered his message. See Homer, *Il.* xvii. 694 *sqq.*, xviii. 16 *sqq.* Prof. C. Robert thinks that Pausanias's description

(τὸ δὲ πρόσωπον καὶ τὴν κεφαλὴν ἐπὶ ταῖς χερσὶν ἀμφοτέραις ἔχων ἐστίν) means no more than that Antilochus rested his chin on one hand and supported that hand with the other (*Die Nekyia des Polygnot*, p. 65). This interpretation, which would empty the posture of Antilochus of meaning, can hardly be reconciled with the words of Pausanias. This is only one of several cases in which Professor Robert would strip the figures of all the character and pathos with which the genius of the great painter had invested them and thereby reduce them from the tragic to the commonplace. Compare his remarks on the figures of Tityus (x. 29. 3), Eriphyle (x. 29. 7), Hector (x. 31. 5), and Orpheus (x. 30. 6).

30. 4. Phocus —— crossed from Aegina etc. Cp. ii. 29. 2 *sq.*, 9, x. 1. 1.

30. 5. Maera. She is mentioned by Homer, *Od.* xi. 326. According to Eustathius (on *Od.* xi. 325) Maera was one of the maidens who attended on Artemis ; but she had an intrigue with Zeus and was therefore slain by Artemis. "But others," adds Eustathius, "say that Maera died a maid." From the present passage of Pausanias we learn that among the "others" who held the latter view was the author of the epic called *The Returns*.

30. 6. Orpheus seated as it were on a sort of hill . . . The aspect of Orpheus is Greek. On existing monuments of ancient art Orpheus is generally represented in full Thracian attire, or at all events clad in a gay minstrel's robe with a tiara on his head. He seldom appears in ordinary Greek costume. See O. Jahn, in *Kieler philologische Studien* (Kiel, 1841), p. 112 ; E. Gerhard, *Ueber Orpheus und die Orphiker* (Berlin, 1861), pp. 35 *sqq.*, 89 *sqq.* Philostratus Junior (*Imagines*, 7) describes a picture of Orpheus wearing a glittering tiara on his head, and Callistratus (*Descript.* 7) mentions a statue of Orpheus in the grove of the Muses on Mount Helicon which represented him with a spangled tiara on his head and girt with a golden belt under his breast. But on the other hand on all Attic vases of the first two-thirds of the fifth century B.C. the bard appears, as in the contemporary painting of Polygnotus, clad in Greek costume, without any indication of his Thracian descent (A. Furtwängler, in *Fünfzigstes Programm zum Winckelmannsfeste* (Berlin, 1890), p. 156 *sq.*). Thus on a fine vase found at Gela but now at Berlin he is depicted sitting on a knoll, singing and playing on the lyre ; his costume consists merely of a loose mantle which covers the lower part of his body, but the four men who stand listening wear the full Thracian attire, namely caps of foxskin and long-striped mantles hanging from the shoulders. See *Fünfzigstes Programm zum Winckelmannsfeste* (Berlin, 1890), Tafel ii., with the observations of Prof. A. Furtwängler, p. 154 *sqq.* Prof. C. Robert holds that in style and date this vase-painting comes nearest to Polygnotus's picture of Orpheus. He further compares a Neapolitan vase of somewhat later date on which Orpheus, similarly attired, is depicted playing on the lyre amid a group of listening Thracians (Raoul-Rochette, *Monuments inédits d'antiquité figurée* (Paris, 1833), pl. xiii.), and a red-figured Boeotian vase which presents us with a like scene except that both the minstrel and his listeners wear the Phrygian costume (Dumont et Chaplain, *Céramiques de la Grèce propre*, I. pl. xiv.). See C. Robert, *Die Nekyia des Polygnot*, pp. 53-55.

30. 6. he touches some willow-branches. Why Orpheus should be depicted touching the branches of a willow tree is not clear. Pausanias has himself rightly pointed out that willows grew in the grove of Proserpine, but that does not suffice to explain the gesture of Orpheus in the picture. Mr. J. Six ingeniously suggests (*Mittheilungen d. arch. Inst.* 19 (1894), p. 338 *sq.*) that when Orpheus went to hell to fetch the soul of his lost Eurydice he may have carried in his hand a willow-branch, just as Aeneas carried the Golden Bough, to serve as a passport or 'open Sesame' to unlock the gates of Death to a living man, and that in memory of this former deed the painter may have depicted the bard touching the willow. Virgil tells how at sight of the Golden Bough, "not seen for long," the surly Charon turned his crazy bark to shore and received Aeneas on board (*Aen.* vi. 406 *sqq.*). Mr. Six suggests that here the words "not seen for long" refer to the time when Orpheus, like Aeneas, had passed the ferry with the Golden Bough in his hand. If he is right, Polygnotus took a different view of the Golden Bough from Virgil, who certainly regarded it as a glorified mistletoe (*Aen.* vi. 201 *sqq.*). Prof. C. Robert accepts Mr. Six's explanation (*Die Marathonschlacht in der Poikile*, p. 122). Formerly he held that Pausanias had misinterpreted the gesture of Orpheus (*Die Nekyia des Polygnot*, p. 32). The bard, on Prof. Robert's earlier view, was depicted merely holding the lyre with one hand and playing on it with the other, and a branch of the willow under which he sat drooped down and touched the hand that held the *plectrum*. This view, which Prof. Robert has wisely abandoned, is open to several objections. It substitutes a commonplace gesture, which Pausanias could hardly have so grossly mistaken, for a remarkable one which, however it is to be explained, had clearly struck Pausanias as unusual and significant. Again, if Orpheus had been depicted playing, would not some one have been represented listening? But so far as appears from Pausanias's description not a soul was paying any heed to the magic strains of the great minstrel. It seems better, therefore, to suppose that, like Thamyris, he sat sad and silent, dreaming of life in the bright world, of love and music.

30. 6. the grove of Proserpine etc. See Homer, *Od.* x. 509 *sq.*

30. 8. Schedius, who led the Phocians to Troy. See x. 4. 2, x. 36. 10; Homer, *Il.* ii. 517, xvii. 306 *sqq.* The grass with which in the picture Schedius was crowned may have been the special kind which grew on Parnassus (Dioscorides, *De materia medica*, iv. 32; Pliny, *Nat. hist.* iv. 178 *sq.*). Such a crown would be very appropriate to the Phocian leader.

30. 8. Thamyris with his sightless eyes etc. Cp. iv. 33. 3, 7, ix. 30. 2.

30. 9. Marsyas seated on a rock etc. On a vase found in Crete and now at Athens Marsyas is depicted sitting under a tree and playing the double flute in presence of Artemis, Athena, and Apollo (Ἐφημερὶς ἀρχαιολογική, 1886, pl. 1). Prof. C. Robert holds that this vase-painting reflects the style of Polygnotus (*Die Nekyia des Polygnot*, p. 56).

31. 1. amusing themselves with dice. Prof. C. Robert conjectures (*Die Nekyia des Polygnot*, p. 57 note 37) that Euripides may have had this group in his mind in describing the two Ajaxes and Protesilaus playing at draughts (*Iphigenia in Aulis*, 192 *sqq.*). The subject of warriors playing at dice is depicted on vases, but apparently all such vase-paintings are older than the time of Polygnotus and cannot therefore be copies of the group here described by Pausanias (C. Robert, *l.c.*).

31. 1. The complexion of the latter Ajax is like that of a castaway etc. The Locrian Ajax was said to have been shipwrecked and drowned on his return from Troy (Homer, *Od.* iv. 499 *sqq.*). Hence every year the Locrians used to lade a ship with costly sacrifices, hoist a black sail on the mast, set the ship on fire, and then let the burning bark drift away across the sea, that it might convey the offerings to the ghost of the drowned hero (Tzetzes, *Scholia on Lycophron*, 365).

31. 2. Ulysses advised the Greeks to stone him etc. Arctinus in his poem the *Sack of Ilium* described how the indignant Greeks were eager to stone Ajax and how he escaped their fury by flying to the altar of Athena. See Proclus, in *Epicorum Graecorum fragmenta*, ed. Kinkel, p. 49 *sq.* As to stoning as a mode of execution, see note on iv. 22. 7.

31. 3. Homer says that the Fury hearkened to the curses of Althaea etc. See *Iliad*, ix. 565 *sqq.* Meleager's death is mentioned by Homer elsewhere (*Il.* ii. 642).

31. 4. The legend of the fire-brand etc. See Aeschylus, *Choeph.* 604 *sqq.*; Apollodorus, i. 8. 2 *sq.*; Hyginus, *Fab.* 171 and 174; Diodorus, iv. 34. 6; Antoninus Liberalis, *Transform.* 2; Ovid, *Met.* viii. 445 *sqq.* The legend of Meleager, including the story of his death, is illustrated by reliefs on Roman sarcophaguses and other monuments of ancient art. See R. Kekulé, *De fabula Meleagrea*, p. 35 *sqq.*; F. Matz, 'Sarcofaghi di Meleagro,' *Annali dell' Inst. di Corr. Archeol.* 41 (1869), pp. 76-103; G. Körte, *ib.* 53 (1881), pp. 168-181; Th. Hartmann, *Meleager in der griechisch-römischen Kunst* (Wohlau, 1889); Baumeister's *Denkmäler*, p. 914 *sqq.* According to another version of the story Meleager's life depended, not on a fire-brand, but on a twig of olive which his mother swallowed in her pregnancy and which afterwards she gave birth to along with the child, and it was the burning of this olive twig which caused Meleager's death. See Tzetzes, *Schol. on Lycophron*, 492; Malala, *Chronogr.* vi. p. 165 *sq.*, ed. Dindorf; G. Knaack, 'Zur Meleagersage,' *Rheinisches Museum*, N. F. 49 (1894), pp. 310-313, 476-478. For parallels to the story of Meleager see *The Golden Bough*, 2. p. 296 *sqq.*

31. 5. Hector seated : his hands are clasped round his left knee. In vase-paintings some figures are depicted in this attitude (Raoul-Rochette, *Monuments inédits d'antiquité figurée* (Paris, 1833), pl. xxxi. A; Baumeister's *Denkmäler*, p. 860, fig. 940; P. Girard, *La peinture antique*, p. 173, fig. 93, p. 174, fig. 94), and one of the seated gods, perhaps Ares, is so represented in the Parthenon frieze (E. Petersen, *Die Kunst des Pheidias*, p. 250 *sq.* ; A. H. Smith, *Catalogue of Greek Sculpture in the British Museum*, 1. p. 155 *sq.*). Prof. C. Robert holds that Pausanias was wrong in interpreting the attitude as indicative of sorrow (*Die Nekyia des Polygnot*, p. 68), and it may be admitted that to nurse one's leg is not necessarily a mark of deep grief. But the sorrow which Pausanias detected may have been expressed by Hector's face rather than by his legs. He had reason enough to be sad. Cp. R. Schöne, in *Jahrbuch d. arch. Inst.* 8 (1893), pp. 214-216.

31. 6. on certain days these birds go to Memnon's grave. Aelian describes the birds of Memnon as black in colour and like hawks in shape ; they were not carnivorous but fed on seeds only. They inhabited the districts of Parium and Cyzicus on the Propontis ; but every year, at the beginning of autumn, they flew in flocks to the tomb of Memnon in the Troad. Here they took sides and fought till half of them were killed ; whereupon the rest flew back to the place from which they had come. See Aelian, *Nat. anim.* v. 1. According to some authorities the birds came from Ethiopia to Memnon's tomb in the Troad ; and Cremutius affirmed that the birds fought in like manner at Memnon's palace in Ethiopia (Pliny, *Nat. hist.* x. 74). Some said that the birds were originally Memnon's comrades who had bewailed his death so bitterly that the gods in pity had turned them into birds (Servius on Virgil, *Aen.* i. 751). According to Ovid (*Met.* xiii. 600 *sqq.*) the volumes of black smoke rising from Memnon's pyre were changed, by the will of Jupiter, into birds, which afterwards behaved in the way described above. Near Memnon's grave in the Troad there was a village called Memnon's village. The river Aesepus was not far off (Strabo, xiii. p. 587). According to Simonides in his poem *Memnon* the grave of Memnon was at Paltus in Syria (Strabo, xv. p. 728). The name Memnon is said to be the Semitic *Naaman*, 'darling.' W. Robertson Smith identified Memnon with Adonis. He says : "The characteristic feature in the ritual of Adonis is that the god was worshipped first as dead and then as again alive, and accordingly his tomb was shown at various places of his worship in connexion with temples of Astarte. Adonis ('lord') is a mere title, and essentially the same worship is associated with other names, especially with that of the eastern Memnon, a figure quite indistinguishable from Adonis, whose tombs (Memnonia) were shown in various parts of the East." See W. Robertson Smith, 'Ctesias and the Semiramis legend,' *English Historical Review*, 2 (1887), p. 307.

31. 7. he came to Ilium —— from Susa in Persia. Cp. i. 42. 3 ; iv. 31. 5 note.

31. 7. The Phrygians still show the road etc. This was probably not the 'Royal Road' to Susa (Herodotus, v. 52 *sq.*), for that road was very circuitous, whereas Memnon's road, according to Pausanias, took short cuts. Prof. W. M. Ramsay, whom I consulted as to the present passage, wrote to me (20th September 1892) : " I have not a Pausanias by me ; but the sentence seems to imply a different road from the Royal Road, forking at Leonton Kephalai from it and going down the Rhyndacus. I had vainly sought for some evidence of this path having been in use in early time ; and I hope you have supplied it." In my letter to Prof. Ramsay I suggested that Memnon's road was possibly so called on account of certain sepulchral mounds by which it may have been lined at intervals and which might have been known as the graves of Memnon (see note on § 6). In his reply Prof. Ramsay says : "The Royal Road was certainly marked by a series of large tumuli, several of which to my knowledge retain traces of old religious feeling attaching to them." In a subsequent letter, Prof. Ramsay mentions that one of these large tumuli contains a 'Hittite' inscription, which he published in the *Mittheil. d. arch. Inst. in Athen* some years ago.

31. 8. Paris —— is clapping his hands. Prof. C. Robert (*Die Nekyia des Polygnot*, p. 56) compares a vase-painting in which a Bacchanal is represented dancing and clapping her hands (Dumont et Chaplain, *Les céramiques de la Grèce propre*, pl. xvii.).

31. 9. The women —— are carrying water in broken pitchers etc. These women, described by the legend as being of the number of the uninitiated, were most probably carrying the water to pour it into the wine-jar mentioned below. That jar, though Pausanias does not say so, may be supposed to have been represented as broken, so that the task of attempting to fill it with water would be endless. "To pour water into a broken jar" was an ancient proverb (Xenophon, *Oeconomicus*, vii. 40 ; Aristotle, *Oeconomicus*, i. 6 ; Lucretius, iii. 936 *sq.* ; Plautus, *Pseudolus*, Act i. Scene iii. 150). Plato refers to the uninitiated in hell carrying water in a sieve to a broken jar (*Gorgias*, p. 493 b). It has been suggested that the reason for assigning this peculiar punishment to the uninitiated in hell is illustrated by the ancient Greek custom of placing a pitcher of a special sort called ' bath-bearer' (*loutrophoros*) on the grave of an unmarried person (Demosthenes, xliv. 18 and 30, pp. 1086, 1089). Some of the ancient interpreters, who wrote after the custom had fallen into disuse, supposed that the 'bath-bearers' placed on the tombs of the unmarried were figures of boys or girls carrying such pitchers (Harpocration and Suidas, *s.v.* λουτροφόρος ; Pollux, viii. 66) ; but archaeological discoveries have confirmed the view of Eustathius (on Homer, *Il.* xxiii. 141, p. 1293) that it was the pitcher itself, or at all events a representation of it carved in relief, which was thus used to mark the graves of maids and bachelors. In shape these pitchers, of which some have been found, were tall and slender, with a high neck and high handles on either side. See A. Milchhöfer, in *Mittheilungen d. arch. Inst. in Athen*, 5 (1880), pp. 174-177 ; A. Herzog, 'Lutrophoros,' *Archäologische Zeitung*, 40 (1882), pp. 131-144 ; P. Wolters, 'Rotfigurige Lutrophoros,' *Mittheilungen d. arch. Inst. in Athen*, 16 (1891), pp. 371-405, and *ib* 18 (1893), p. 66 *sq.* The intention was, according to Eustathius (*l.c.*), to intimate that the person on whose grave one of these pitchers stood had never enjoyed the bath which a Greek bride and bridegroom took on their wedding day, and for which the water was fetched from a special spring by a boy who was a near kinsman (Harpocration and Suidas, *s.v.* λουτροφόρος; Photius, *Lexicon*, *s.v.* λουτρά; Pollux, iii. 43, who is probably wrong in saying that the water was fetched by a girl). Now since marriage was regarded and spoken of as an initiation (Pollux, iii. 38), it is possible that persons who died unmarried were believed to be subjected to the same penalty in the nether world as those who had never been initiated in the Eleusinian or other great religious mysteries, and that their penalty was to fetch water for ever for that bath which, having failed to take in the upper world, they could never more take in a world where there is neither marrying nor giving in marriage. Similarly we may suppose that candidates for initiation in the great mysteries had always to take a bath, as they had in the case of the Eleusinian mysteries (Hesychius, *s.v.* ἅλαδε μύσται; Polyaenus, iii. 11. 2 ; G. F. Schömann, *Griechische Alterthümer*,[3] 2. p. 387), and that their punishment in the lower world was in like manner a vain attempt, prolonged for ever, to enjoy the sacred privilege which they had missed in life. It is possible that the original reason why the Danaids were believed to be condemned to this punishment in hell was not so much that they murdered, as that they did not marry, the sons of Aegyptus. According to one tradition, indeed, they afterwards married other husbands (Paus. iii. 12. 2) ; but according to another legend they were murdered by Lynceus, apparently before marriage (Schol. on Euripides, *Hecuba*, 886). They may, therefore, have been chosen as types of unmarried women, and their punishment need not have been peculiar to them but may have been the one supposed to await all unmarried persons in the nether world. Further, if this explanation of their punishment is correct, it may very well be that some of the water-pouring figures in existing monuments of ancient art, which have been interpreted as the Danaids, really represent unmarried or uninitiated women in general, not the Danaids in particular. This view is confirmed by a vase-painting, already referred to (note on x. 29. 1), which represents male as well as female figures bringing water in pitchers and pouring it into a large jar (*Archäologische Zeitung*, 28 (1871), pl. 31. 22). This scene, which is proved to be laid in hell by the presence of Indolence and his ass, probably represents the punishment of the uninitiated or unmarried. The explanation here given of the punishment in question is substantially the one which has been put forward or accepted by Prof. E. Rohde (*Psyche*, p. 292 note 1), Mr. E. Kuhnert (*Jahrbuch des archäolog. Instituts*, 8 (1893), pp. 109-111), and Mr. A. Dieterich (*Nekyia : Beitrage zur Erklärung der neuentdeckten Petrusapokalypse* (Leipzig, 1893), p. 70 note 1). It may be suggested that originally the custom of placing a water-pitcher on the grave of unmarried persons had a more kindly significance than that of hinting at the weary task to which they were doomed to all eternity. It may have been meant to help them to obtain in another world the happiness they had missed in this. In fact, it may have been part of a ceremony designed to provide the dead maiden or bachelor with a spouse in the spirit land. Such ceremonies have been observed in various parts of the world by peoples who, like the Greeks, esteemed it a great misfortune to die unmarried. Thus Marco Polo reports that among the Tartars " if any man have a daughter who dies before marriage, and another man have had a son also die before marriage, the parents of the two arrange a grand wedding between the dead lad and lass. And marry them they do, making a regular contract! And when the contract papers are made out they put them in the fire, in order (as they will have it) that the parties in the other world may know the fact, and so look on each other as man and wife. And the parents thenceforward consider themselves sib to each other just as if their children had lived and married. Whatever may be agreed on between the parties as dowry, those who have to pay it cause to be painted on pieces of paper and then put these in the fire, saying that in that way the dead person will get all the real articles in the other world" (Marco Polo, translated by Col. H. Yule, 2nd ed., i. p. 259 *sq.*). The same custom is also vouched for the Tartars by Alexander Guagninus ('De religione Muscovitarum omniumque Ruthenorum,' printed in *De Russorum, Muscovitarum et Tartarorum religione, sacrificiis, nuptiarum, funerum ritu* (Spirae libera civitate, 1582), p. 253). Similarly in China at the present day the spirits of boys who died in infancy are, after a proper interval, formally married to the spirits of girls who have been cut off at a like early age ; the ceremony is performed over two paper effigies representing the bride and bridegroom, which are afterwards burned, together with a liberal supply of paper clothes, paper money, paper man-servants and maid-servants, etc., for the use of the newly-wedded couple in the spirit land (J. H. Gray, *China*, i. pp. 216-218 ; cp. S. Kidd, *China*, p. 179 *sq.*). Amongst the Ingush of the Caucasus when a man's son dies another man whose daughter is dead will go to him and say, "Your son may need a wife in the other world, I will give him my daughter. Pay me the price of the bride." Such an obliging offer is never refused, though the price of a bride is sometimes as much as thirty cows. See J. von Klaproth, *Reise in den Kaukasus und nach Georgien*, i. p. 616 *sq.* ; Potocki, *Voyage dans les steps d'Astrakhan et du Caucase* (Paris, 1829), i. p. 127 (who, however, merely copies Klaproth). The old Slavonians "so severely pitied the lot of the unmarried dead, that, before committing their bodies to the grave, they were in the habit of finding them partners for eternity. The fact that, among some Slavonian peoples, if a man died a bachelor a wife was allotted to him after his death, rests on the authority of several witnesses, and in a modified form the practice has been retained in some places up to the present day. In Little Russia, for instance, a dead maiden is dressed in nuptial attire, and friends come to her funeral as to a wedding, and a similar custom is observed on the death of a lad. In Podolia, also, a young girl's funeral is conducted after the fashion of a wedding, a youth being chosen as the bridegroom who attends her to the grave, with the nuptial kerchief twined around his arm. From that time her family consider him their relative, and the rest of the community look upon him as a widower. In some parts of Servia when a lad dies, a girl dressed as a bride follows him to the tomb, carrying two crowns ; one of these is thrown to the corpse, and the other she keeps, at least for a time" (W. R. S. Ralston, *Songs of the Russian People*, p. 309 *sq.*). Similar practices appear to have prevailed in Germany in the Middle Ages, for the Würzburg Synods of 1329 and 1330 forbade the priests to bless the survivor of a betrothed pair beside the dead body of the other (G. Lammert, *Volksmedizin und medizinischer Aberglaube in Bayern* (Würzburg, 1869), p. 153). This blessing of the living beside the dead may possibly have been the relic of a more barbarous and realistic marriage ceremony such as is still, or was till lately, celebrated between the living and the dead in the caste known as *namboury* in Travancore (J. A. Dubois, *Mœurs, Institutions, et Cérémonies des peuples de l'Inde*, 1. p. 4 *sq.*). Amongst the Romans it was customary, when a number of corpses were being burned together, to place one woman's body with every ten bodies of men (Plutarch, *Quaest. Conviv.* iii. 4. 2 ; Macrobius, *Saturn.* vii. 7. 5). It is possible that this custom originated in the feeling that it was necessary to provide dead men with female companions in the other world. The notion that it is highly improper to appear in the spirit-land without a wife or a female companion of some sort is deeply impressed on the Fijian mind. At a certain place on the road to the Fijian hell "there lies in wait a terrible god, called Nang-ganangga, who is utterly implacable towards the ghosts of the unmarried. He is especially ruthless towards bachelors, among whom he persists in classing all male ghosts who come to him unaccompanied by their wives. Turning a deaf ear to their protestations, he seizes them, lifts them above his head, and breaks them in two by dashing them down on a projecting rock. Hence it is absolutely necessary for a man to have at least one of his wives, or, at all events, a female ghost of some sort following him " (Lorimer Fison, in *Journal of the Anthropological Institute*, 10 (1881), p. 139). Hence in Fiji a woman was always killed and buried with a dead man, and the Roman custom just mentioned may have been originally similar. Women who died before their husbands in Fiji, on the other hand, were not obliged to produce their husbands' ghosts before being admitted to the spirit land ; it was enough if they showed a certificate of marriage in the shape of their husband's beard, which the widower was careful to place under his wife's left arm in committing her to the grave (Fison, *ib.*).

31. 10. **as the price of Pero's hand —— Neleus demanded** etc. See Homer, *Od.* xi. 287 *sqq.*

31. 10. **Callisto has a bearskin for a mat.** See note on viii. 3. 6.

31. 10. **the statement of the Arcadians that Nomia** etc. See viii. 38. 11.

31. 10. **The poets say that the nymphs live a great many years** etc. See the Homeric *Hymn to Aphrodite*, 257 *sqq.* ; Hesiod, quoted by Plutarch, *De defectu oraculorum*, 11. According to Hesiod, a crow lives nine times as long as a man, a deer four times as long as a crow, a raven three times as long as a deer, a phoenix nine times as long as a raven, and a nymph ten times as long as a phoenix.

31. 10. **Sisyphus —— struggling to shove the stone** etc. See Homer, *Od.* xi. 593 *sqq.* Sisyphus and his stone are depicted on vases and form the subject of a wall-painting found on the Esquiline hill at

Rome. See Müller-Wieseler, *Denkmäler*, 1. pl. lvi. No. 275 a; *id.*, 2. pl. lxviii. No. 861; *id.*, 2. pl. lxix. No. 866; Miss J. E. Harrison, *Myths of the Odyssey*, pp. 116 *sq.*, 135, pl. vii. and 33; Baumeister's *Denkmäler*, pp. 1923 *sq.*, 1928, 1929, 1930, figures 2040, 2042 A, 2042 B.

31. 12. Tantalus suffering all the torments that Homer has described. See *Od.* xi. 582 *sqq.*

31. 12. the stone hung over him etc. This punishment of Tantalus, which is not mentioned by Homer, was alluded to by the poets Alcaeus, Alcman, and Archilochus. The couple of lines in which Archilochus referred to the stone of Tantalus have been preserved. See Schol. on Pindar, *Olymp.* i. 97; Plutarch, *Praecept. gerend. reipub.* 6; *Poetae Lyrici Graeci*, ed. Bergk, 2.[3] p. 696. The author of the epic *The Return of the Atridae*, which was probably identical with the epic commonly known as *The Returns (Nostoi)*, also mentioned this punishment (Athenaeus, vii. p. 281 b c; *Epicorum Graecorum fragmenta*, ed. Kinkel, p. 56), and in the extant works of classical writers it is often referred to. See Pindar, *Olymp.* i. 89 *sqq.*, *Isthm.* vii. [viii.] 20 *sq.*; Euripides, *Orestes*, 5 *sq.*; Plato, *Cratylus*, p. 395 d; Hyperides, Frag. 176, p. 102 ed. Blass; Antipater, in *Anthologia Palatina*, *Appendix Planudea*, iv. No. 131; Apollodorus, ed. R. Wagner, p. 182; *Epitoma Vaticana ex Apollodori bibliotheca*, ed. R. Wagner, p. 58; Plutarch, *De superstitione*, 11; Philostratus, *Vit. Apollon.* iii. 25; Apostolius, *Cent.* vii. 60, xvi. 9; *Mythographi Graeci*, ed. Westermann, Appendix, p. 386, No. 73; Lucretius, iii. 980 *sq.*; Cicero, *Tuscul.* iv. 16. 36, *De Finibus*, i. 18. 60; Hyginus, *Fab.* 82. In the original version of the story it would seem that Tantalus endured this torment not in hell but in heaven, where he had been admitted to the table of the gods. Zeus promised to give him whatever he desired, and Tantalus asked to live for ever, like the gods. Angry at his presumption Zeus kept his promise by granting him the wished-for immortality, but hung a great stone, like the sword of Damocles, over his head, the fear of which prevented Tantalus from enjoying the heavenly banquet which was for ever spread out before his eyes. This was apparently the form which the story took in *The Return of the Atridae*, if we may judge from the abstract of it given by Athenaeus. See F. G. Welcker, 'Alcmanis fragmentum de Tantalo,' *Rheinisches Museum*, N. F. 10 (1856), pp. 242-254; D. Comparetti, 'Die Strafe des Tantalus bei Pindar,' *Philologus*, 32 (1873), pp. 227-251; J. E. Hylén, *De Tantalo* (Upsala, 1896), pp. 51 *sqq.*, 77 *sqq.* Cp. K. Schwenk, in *Rheinisches Museum*, N. F. 11 (1857), p. 451 *sq.*

32. 1. Abutting on the sacred close is a theatre. The statement of Pausanias that the theatre abutted on the sacred precinct is exact. It stood in fact outside of the precinct on the north-west, occupying an angle formed by the wall of the precinct which bounds the theatre on two sides, the south and east. When the early traveller Cyriacus of Ancona visited Delphi in the fifteenth century, he counted thirty-three rows of seats in the theatre, built of large stones. After his time, however, the building was gradually buried under the soil which slipped down from the steep ground above, so that towards the end of the nineteenth century very little of it appeared above ground. The south-east corner, however, together with pieces of the southern and eastern walls and a good piece of the north wall, supported by two buttresses, were visible. On the south wall, which was standing to a height of about 9 feet, inscriptions might be read like those on the polygonal terrace-wall of the temple, with which they are approximately contemporary; they record the manumission of slaves. Chandler saw these inscriptions in the eighteenth century (*Travels in Greece*, p. 267). Now, however, the whole theatre has been excavated by the French and turns out to be, contrary to expectation, one of the best preserved in Greece. The foundations of the stage, the orchestra with its stone pavement, and the seats of the spectators almost or quite to the top of the theatre, together with the supporting-walls of the auditorium at both sides, are all preserved. The material of which the edifice is constructed is the common stone of Parnassus. Thirty-three tiers of seats exist, divided into seven wedge-shaped blocks by staircases radiating from the orchestra. The *diazoma* or horizontal passage dividing the tiers of seats into an upper and a lower section, is paved with stone and is well pre-served. There are no chairs in the front row, next to the orchestra; the seats there are just like those in the rest of the theatre, except that they are covered with inscriptions recording the manumission of slaves. The passage (*parodos*) leading into the orchestra from the west is blocked with a large marble pedestal, on the north side of which an inscription, now upside down, mentions that the offering, whatever it was, had been dedicated by the Cnidians. We may conjecture that the offering was no other than the image of Dionysus mentioned by Pausanias. The front of the stage was adorned with sculptured reliefs in white marble about .80 metre (2 ft. 7½ in.) high, of which considerable remains have been found. They represent the labours of Hercules. We see the hero shooting arrows at the Stymphalian birds, rescuing Hesione from the sea-monster, fighting the Centaurs, and contending with the giant Antaeus and with King Diomede and his man-eating steeds. It is supposed that these sculptured decorations were added by Attalus, king of Pergamus, and that the subject of the reliefs was chosen with reference to the legendary connexion of Pergamus with Hercules through Telephus, the son of the hero by Auge. The remains of the stage-buildings, Mr. Homolle informed me, throw no fresh light on the vexed question of the use of a raised stage in Greek theatres. The earliest inscription which mentions the theatre dates from about 150 B.C., and to this period approximately the building may be assigned. It faces south-east across the deep glen of the Plistus : the view from it is fine.

See *Athenaeum*, 29th June 1897, p. 846 ; *Berliner philolog. Wochenschrift*, 13th July 1895, p. 928 ; *id.*, 27th February 1897, p. 287 ; *Archäologischer Anzeiger*, 1896, p. 73. For notices of the theatre before its complete excavation see H. N. Ulrichs, *Reisen und Forschungen*, 1. p. 108 ; F. G. Welcker, *Tagebuch*, 2. p. 67 *sq.* ; P. Foucart, *Mémoire sur les ruines et l'histoire de Delphes*, p. 103 *sq.* ; Baedeker,³ p. 160 ; *Guide-Joanne*, 2. p. 41 ; H. Pomtow, *Beiträge zur Topographie von Delphi*, p. 40 *sq.*

32. 1. a stadium in the highest part of the city. In accordance with this statement of Pausanias the stadium occupies a commanding situation in the very highest part of Delphi, to the north-west of the sacred precinct. Standing on its southern edge you look, as it seems, almost perpendicularly down on the ruins of the sanctuary and the deep glen of the Plistus, across which rise, in full view, the high rocky mountains that stretch thence southward to the sea. On the other three sides, west, north, and east, the stadium is bounded by steep ascending slopes of rugged rocks and the soaring precipices of Parnassus. A more striking scene for the celebration of national games could hardly be imagined.

The narrow shelf of flat ground which thus breaks the slope of the mountain and was chosen as the site of the stadium extends east and west or, to be more exact, north-east and south-west for a length of about 630 feet. In breadth as well as length the stadium includes every foot of flat ground that was to be had. On its southern or rather south-eastern side it is supported on the abrupt slope by a massive and well-preserved wall of ancient polygonal masonry, which is still in some places from 9 to 12 feet high with from five to seven courses of stones. Some of these stones are large : one of them measures 13 feet long. The antiquity of the wall is attested by an inscription, carved on it in letters of the sixth century B.C., which forbids the bringing of new wine into the sanctuary of Eudromus. The interior of the stadium was entirely excavated by the French in 1896, and was found to be in almost perfect preservation from end to end. Like the southern supporting-wall it is built of the reddish local stone. There are twelve tiers of seats, and at regular intervals of 14 metres a flight of twenty-four steps, forming a gangway, leads up through them. The seats resemble those in Greek theatres. The front of each is hollowed out somewhat below, and on the upper surface, towards the 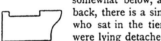 back, there is a sinking to receive the feet of the person who sat in the tier above. A good many of the seats were lying detached on the southern edge of the stadium before the French excavations. In the middle of the lowest tier of seats on the north side there is a seat of honour for the presidents of the games. It consists of a long bench with projecting ends. At the eastern end of the race-course a few seats are hewn in the side of a massive rock, which here bounds the stadium at the foot of the tall cliffs of Parnassus. From these seats we catch a glimpse of the Gulf of Crisa away to the south-west.

Of the Pentelic marble with which, according to Pausanias, Herodes Atticus refaced the stadium, not a scrap has been discovered by the French. There is no need, however, on that ground to question the accuracy of Pausanias's statement ; for his testimony is confirmed by that of his contemporary Philostratus, who in his well-informed life of Herodes Atticus tells us that the wealthy sophist dedicated the stadium at Pytho (Delphi) to the Pythian Apollo (*Vit. Sophist.* ii. 1. 9). Philostratus does not indeed mention the facing of Pentelic marble, but that a radical reconstruction was carried out may safely be inferred from the fact that Herodes Atticus dedicated the stadium afresh to Apollo. A man of his vast wealth and princely munificence would certainly not have had the effrontery to offer the old stadium to the god unless he had first beautified it in some such way as Pausanias indicates. He had similarly adorned the stadium at Athens (Paus. i. 19. 6). Moreover, the marble seats existed apparently in good preservation down to the middle of the fifteenth century, and some of them were still to be seen towards the end of the seventeenth century. In the fifteenth century Cyriacus of Ancona described·"the hippodrome 600 feet long, richly adorned with marble steps (*ornatissimum gradibus marmoreis*), in the high citadel of the city, at the foot of most lofty rocks" (quoted by P. Foucart, *Mémoire*, p. 105). In the seventeenth century Wheler, who describes the situation of the stadium correctly, says: "Some of the degrees yet remain of white marble" (*Journey*, p. 315). The accuracy and good faith of these two early travellers in Greece have never, I believe, been questioned. The fidelity of Cyriacus has been recently confirmed at Delphi itself by the excavation of the theatre, in which the number of tiers of seats discovered (thirty-three) tallies exactly with the description of Cyriacus. We may therefore safely conclude that the marble seats were to be seen for at least twelve centuries after the time of Pausanias. They have probably gone the way of so many other ancient marbles in Greece, into the lime-kiln.

See Wheler, *Journey into Greece*, p. 315; E. D. Clarke, *Travels*, 4. p. 190; Dodwell, *Tour*, I. p. 181 *sq.*; Leake, *Northern Greece*, 2. p. 577; H. N. Ulrichs, *Reisen und Forschungen*, I. p. 37; Mure, *Journal*, I. p. 187 *sq.*; Thiersch, 'Ueber die Topographie von Delphi,' *Abhandlungen d. philos. philolog. Classe d. kön. bayer. Akad. d. Wissen.* (Munich), 3 (1840), pp. 18 *sq.*, 51; F. G. Welcker, *Tagebuch*, 2. p. 68 *sq.*; C. Bursian, *Geogr.* I. p. 178; P. Foucart, *Mémoire sur les ruines et l'histoire de Delphes*, p. 104 *sq.*; *Guide-Joanne*, 2. p. 41; *Berliner philolog. Wochenschrift*, 15th August 1896, p. 1086 *sq.*; *Journal of Hellenic Studies*, 16 (1896), p. 343. For the account of the excavation of the stadium I am indebted to the notes of Mr. Cecil Smith.

Pausanias has now concluded his description of Delphi. Here may be the most convenient place to notice some ancient remains of which he says nothing.

To the south-west of Delphi, on the slope of the ridge which bounds the valley on the west, is the small chapel of St. Elias. It lies to the south of the stadium and a good deal lower down the hill. The chapel stands upon a quadrangular platform 51.2 metres (about 167 feet) long by 37 metres (about 123 feet) wide, the supporting-walls of which on the eastern and northern sides are partly composed of ancient masonry. On the west the platform is bounded by a terrace-wall of polygonal masonry about 58 paces long and 10 feet high, which supports the higher ground above, and with it the old road to *Chryso* (Crisa) and *Itaea*. The modern road is now carried a good deal lower down the hill than the chapel of St. Elias. Of the wall which supports the platform on the east a considerable piece, about 21 paces long, is ancient. It is built in a massive style and is strengthened by five buttresses which project 2 ft. 3 in. The stones on the whole are squared and laid in horizontal courses, but a tendency to the polygonal style may be observed in some places. For a short distance the wall is standing to a height of about 13 or 14 feet with nine courses of masonry. One of the buttresses has ten courses, but its top is flush with the top of the wall. This ancient wall also extends round the north-east corner and partly supports the platform on the north side. The material of which these walls are built is the reddish stone of the district. On the quadrangular platform supported by them, outside of the chapel, is a piece of an ancient mosaic pavement consisting of red, white, black, and blue stones set in an ornamental pattern. At the beginning of the nineteenth century Clarke found two very large architraves of Parian marble in the chapel of St. Elias, and many years afterwards Mr. Foucart found, a few feet below the platform, some fragments of Doric columns of Pentelic marble, which from the width (.25 metre) of their flutes may have measured about 5 metres (16 ft. 5 in.) in circumference.

These architectural remains have now disappeared, having been broken up to be used in repairing the chapel. It is supposed that the ancient building, to which they belonged and which doubtless occupied the quadrangular platform, was the Pylaea or place of assembly of the Amphictyonic Council. Commonly the name Pylaea designates one of the two annual meetings of the Amphictyonic Council, but that it also designated the place of assembly appears from one of the inscriptions engraved on the polygonal wall at Delphi, which speaks of the services rendered by a certain man Hermias "both at Pylaea and at Delphi." See *Bulletin de Corresp. hellénique*, 7 (1883), p. 417 *sqq.* Plutarch says (*De Pythiae oraculis*, 29) that in his time Pylaea renewed its youth along with Delphi and had been more adorned with "sanctuaries and places of assembly and waters" than it had been for a thousand years before. From this passage of Plutarch it has sometimes been inferred that a new suburb sprang up here in Hadrian's time ; but Plutarch makes no mention of houses ; he speaks only of public buildings, sacred and civil. That the place of assembly of the Amphictyonic Council at Delphi must have been situated near the chapel of St. Elias is shown by a passage of Aeschines (*contra Ctes.* 115-124), in which he says that the Cirrhaean plain lay spread beneath and in full view of the meeting-place of the Amphictyonic Council. The orator himself, he tells us, was one of the Athenian representatives at a meeting of the Council. Addressing it he pointed to the smiling and peaceful plain stretched at their feet, with its olive-groves and corn-fields, its cottages and potteries, and in the distance the shining waters of the gulf, with the port-town visible beside it. "You see," he cried, "yonder plain tilled by the men of Amphissa and the potteries and cottages they have built. You see with your eyes the fortifications of the cursed and execrated port. You know for yourselves that these men levy tolls and take money from the sacred harbour." He then reminded his hearers of the oath sworn by their ancestors that this fair plain should lie a wilderness for ever. His words were received with a tumult of applause, and next day at dawn the men of Delphi, armed with shovels and mattocks, marched down into the plain, razed the fortifications of the port to the ground, and gave the houses to the flames. It is refreshing to know that on their way back they were hotly pursued by the Amphissaeans in arms and had to run for their lives. This was the beginning of the chain of events which in a few months more brought Philip at the head of a Macedonian army into Greece and ended in the overthrow of Greek freedom at Chaeronea.

The view described by the orator, whose ill-omened eloquence brought all these miseries and disasters in its train, is to be obtained, not from the platform on which the chapel of St. Elias stands, but from a point a little way to the south-west of it, where the traveller coming from Delphi reaches the end of the high ridge that shuts in the valley of Delphi on the west. Here as he turns the corner the whole Crisaean plain, now covered with luxuriant olive-woods, comes suddenly into sight. The scene is again as rich and peaceful as it was before Aeschines raised his voice, like the scream of some foul bird snuffing the carrion afar off, and turned it into a desert. We may suppose either that in his time the Amphictyonic Council met at this point, or, what is far likelier, that the orator's description of that day's doings is more graphic than correct.

An interesting inscription on an upright hewn stone which may still be seen beside the chapel of St. Elias confirms the view that here the Amphictyonic Council met. The inscription, which was found within the enclosure in 1877, records that the Delphians and Chaeroneans, in compliance with a decree of the Amphictyonic Council, set up a portrait of Plutarch. From the style of the pedestal on which the inscription is cut we see that the portrait must have been a bust. As Plutarch was manager (ἐπιμελητής) of the Amphictyonic Council in the reign of Hadrian (see *C. I. G.* No. 1713 ; H. Pomtow, *Beiträge zur Topographie von Delphi*, p. 77 *sq.*), it is natural enough that a portrait of this excellent man and admirable writer, erected by order of the Council, should have been placed in or near the place where the Council held their meetings.

Between the chapel of St. Elias and the site of the old village of *Kastri*, now destroyed, is another platform supported by substructions. It is on the slope of the hill, lower down than the old road to *Chryso* but higher than the new road. The supporting-wall of the terrace, built of ashlar masonry, is 34.5 metres (113 feet) long and 4 to 5 metres (about 13 to 16 feet) high ; it is strengthened by twelve buttresses which project about 12 feet. Buttresses were not used in Greek architecture before the time of the Roman empire. Hence this platform may have supported one of the new sanctuaries with which this part of Delphi seems to have been adorned in Plutarch's age (Plutarch, *De Pythiae oraculis*, 29).

Between this platform and the chapel of St. Elias, just above the old road which leads to *Chryso*, is a large sepulchral chamber hewn in the rock, with a high doorway and arched roof. On the three sides of the chamber are three niches for sarcophaguses, also hewn in the rock. There were paintings on the walls above each grave ; above the middle grave a red and green parrot with a long tail could still be plainly made out in the first half of the nineteenth century. A few yards to the east of this sepulchral chamber a semicircular recess is hewn in the rock, with a rock-cut bench running all round it. The spot commands a wide prospect over the valley of Delphi and the course of the Plistus, away to the mountains beyond which lay the ancient Ambrosus.

See Wheler, *Journey*, p. 314 *sq.* ; Chandler, *Travels in Greece*, p. 266 *sq.* ; Clarke, *Travels*, 4. p. 191 *sq.* ; Dodwell, *Tour*, 1. p. 180 *sq.* ; Leake, *Northern Greece*, 2. p. 566 *sq.* ; H. N. Ulrichs, *Reisen und Forschungen*, 1. pp. 25, 36, 110; Fiedler, *Reise*, 1. p. 143; F. G. Welcker, *Tagebuch*, 2. p. 69 *sq.* ; W. Vischer, *Erinnerungen*, p. 610; C. Bursian, *Geogr.* 1. p. 178 *sq.* ; P. Foucart, *Mémoire sur les ruines et l'histoire de Delphes*, p. 107 *sqq.* ; Baedeker,[3] p. 161 ; Guide-Joanne, 2. p. 41 *sq.* ; H. Pomtow, *Beiträge zur Topographie von Delphi*, p. 73 *sqq.* A view, a plan, and a section of the sepulchral chamber are given by Le Bas, *Voyage archéologique*, Itinéraire, pl. 39. See also H. Pomtow, *op. cit.* pl. xi. No. 31.

On the ridge which shuts in the valley of Delphi on the west, foundations of well - built Greek walls, flanked with towers, may be traced at intervals along the crest of the ridge as far as the lofty preci-pices which rise to the north of Delphi and which were themselves a sufficient protection on that side. The wall and towers are standing in some places to a height of several courses. These were evidently the western walls of Delphi, and may have been built by Philomelus in 355 B.C. when he seized Delphi in the Sacred War, for we are told that he built a fortification-wall round the sanctuary (Diodorus, xvi. 25). Before his time Delphi seems to have been an open town, and the fortifications erected by him appear to have soon fallen into decay ; for Justin, describing the attack of the Gauls on Delphi in 278 B.C., expressly affirms (xxiv. 6. 7) that the town was defended not by walls but by precipices, not by art but by nature. Further, an expression used by Livy (xlii. 15. 5) in narrating the attempted assassination of King Eumenes near Delphi in 172 B.C. seems to imply that Delphi was then unwalled.

Outside these walls, on the western side, are many graves hewn in the rock ; and on the crest of the ridge, about midway between the old road to *Chryso* and the foot of the high cliffs at the back of Delphi, is a conspicuous tumulus which (if I am not mistaken) is popu-larly identified as the tomb of Philomelus.

The view from the crest of the ridge is magnificent. It embraces on the one side the profound valley of Delphi as far east as *Arachova*, on the other side the Crisaean plain with its olive-groves, bounded on the west by the lofty mountains of Locris, wooded with dark pines, and on the south by the Gulf of Corinth with the distant mountains of Pelo-ponnese rising beyond it.

See Leake, *Northern Greece*, 2. p. 565 *sqq.* ; H. N. Ulrichs, *Reisen und Forschungen*, 1. p. 117 ; P. Foucart, *Mémoire sur les ruines et l'histoire de Delphes*, p. 110; Baedeker,[3] p. 156 ; *Guide-Joanne*, 2. p. 41. On the western necropolis of Delphi, see H. Pomtow, *Beiträge zur Topographie von Delphi*, p. 72 *sqq.*

Lastly it may be mentioned that the French excavations have brought to light a beehive tomb cut in the rock and approached by a short passage (*dromos*). In the tomb were found a dagger, knife, razor, and brooch, all of bronze, and some Mycenaean pottery of the lustrous sort decorated in the usual fashion with lines and circles or complicated patterns that mark a transition towards the purely geometrical style of ornamentation. The finest of the vases found is a stirrup-vase (see vol. 3. p. 112) adorned with two large octopuses, splendidly drawn and accompanied by geometrical patterns. These discoveries, as Mr. Homolle says, remind us of the legend which connects the foundation of the Delphic sanctuary with Crete, the country where Mycenaean remains abound. See Th. Homolle, *Gazette des Beaux-Arts*, Décembre 1894, p. 442 ; *id.*, in *Bulletin de Corresp. hellénique*, 18 (1894), p. 195 *sq.* Mycenaean tombs, Mr. Cecil Smith informs me, have been discovered immediately below the middle point of the south wall of the sacred precinct, and two more on the site of the present Museum. All around the temple and altar the soil is reported to be full of Mycenaean remains, including pieces of amber.

32. 2. **The ascent to the Corycian cave** etc. Two, or rather three, paths lead from Delphi up the slopes of Parnassus to the Corycian cave, but they meet on the spacious table-land above the cliffs which rise at the back of the town. Two of the paths start from above the stadium. One of them, known as the Evil Staircase (κακὴ σκάλα), ascends steeply in a series of zigzags cut in the rock, often in the form of steps, of which there are over a thousand. This very steep and rugged path is obviously exceedingly ancient. The other of these two paths keeps more to the west and is somewhat longer. The third way (which I have not seen mentioned in any book) is to keep along the road to *Chryso* past the chapel of St. Elias, and, after rounding the foot of the ridge which is crowned with the fortifications of Philomelus, to turn off the road to the right by a path which strikes northwards up the face of the mountain. Gradually ascending we reach, in an hour or more, the summit of the range of heights which bounds Delphi on the north. This range of heights is, as it were, a gigantic step in the grand Parnassian staircase. On reaching the summit of the heights we see stretching before us northward and eastward an extensive tableland, more than 3000 ft. above the level of the sea ; at the farther end of it rise, massive and grand, the upper slopes of Parnassus. The first part of the tableland is broken with shallow ravines and wooded, sometimes sparsely, sometimes thickly, with firs. The farther or eastern half of the plateau (called *Livadi*) is more level ; it is treeless and, so far as I observed, uncultivated, being merely covered with rather scanty grass. Of the well-tilled fields of wheat, barley, and oats mentioned by some travellers I saw nothing ; but it was the middle of May when I was there, and the harvest on these high uplands is not till the middle of August. On the east this tableland is bounded by the upper slopes of Parnassus. On the north it is terminated by a line of lower hills. The most westerly of these hills are thickly wooded with firs. On the face of the most easterly of them (the hill next to the real slopes of Parnassus, but separated from them by a valley) is the Corycian cave situated about 500 feet or so above the plateau. The path up to it, if

path it can be called, is steep, rough, and fatiguing. Horses or mules can be brought from Delphi as far as the foot of this last slope, but there they must be left. Pausanias might well say that "the ascent to the Corycian cave is easier for a well-girt man than for mules and horses." It is in fact impossible for mules and horses. The bronze image of Dionysus, which Pausanias mentions, probably stood at the point where the path begins to ascend from the tableland to the cave; for the distance of 60 furlongs agrees fairly well with the distance from Delphi to the point in question.

The cave is called by the peasants *Sarantavli* or 'forty-chambered.' At the mouth of it, on the right as you enter, is a rough stone, on which is cut a dedication to Pan and the Nymphs by one Eustratus, an Ambrysian. (Ulrichs and Vischer are mistaken in saying that the inscription had disappeared. I copied it at the mouth of the cave, 15th May 1890.) On the upper surface of the same stone is an inscription, partly illegible, in which mention is made of the Nymphs, of Pan, and of the Thyiads. These inscriptions confirm Pausanias's statement (§ 7) that the cavern was sacred to Pan and the Nymphs. The natives of *Arachova* still think that the cave is a favourite haunt of the Nereids (B. Schmidt, *Das Volksleben der Neugriechen*, p. 103). The great chamber of the grotto is upwards of 200 feet in length and may be (as Leake thought) about 40 feet high in the middle, though the average height is probably about 20 feet. Water, dripping from the roof, has formed stalagmites rising from the floor (as Pausanias correctly observes, § 7), while stalactites hang from the roof and sides. The upper end of the cave is rugged, irregular, and very dark. Here on the right a narrow opening leads into a second chamber, which extends for about 100 feet inward and turns round nearly at a right angle to the direction of the outer cavern. The rocks in this inner cavern are smooth, clammy, and slippery. Caution is needed in clambering over them. It is also totally dark, and without a light it would be impossible to find one's way except by groping. The effect as you look out from the interior of the gloomy cavern through the grove of stalactites and stalagmites to the green grass and the sunlight at the mouth of the cave is highly picturesque; it is like a fairy grotto. From the mouth of the cave we look down on the tableland already described. In the distance, to the south-west, a long stretch of the Gulf of Corinth is visible with the Peloponnesian mountains beyond it. On the other side, to the east, rises the great cone of Parnassus, its lower spurs clothed with dark fir-woods, its upper slopes bare.

See Wheler, *Journey*, p. 316 *sqq.* ; Gell, *Itinerary of Greece* (London, 1819), pp. 190-192 ; Leake, *Northern Greece*, 2. p. 578 *sqq.* ; H. N. Ulrichs, *Reisen und Forschungen*, 1. p. 117 *sqq.* ; Welcker, *Tagebuch*, 2. p. 76 *sqq.* ; Vischer, *Erinnerungen*, p. 611 *sqq.* ; Bursian, *Geogr.* 1. p. 179 ; Foucart, *Mémoire sur les ruines et l'histoire de Delphes*, p. 112 *sqq.* ; Baedeker,³ p. 161 *sq.* ; Guide-Joanne, 2. p. 43 *sq.* ; P. G. Kastriotes, Οἱ Δελφοί, pp. 69-72. For the inscriptions at the mouth of the cave, see H. G. Lolling, in *Mittheil. d. arch. Inst. in Athen*, 3 (1878), p. 154 ; Collitz, *G. D. I.* 2. No. 1536. When the Persians advanced against Delphi, some of the inhabitants took refuge in the Corycian cave (Herodotus, viii. 36). There was another famous Corycian cave in Cilicia. See Pindar, *Pyth.* i. 32 ; Strabo, xiv. p. 670 *sq.* ; *American Journal of Archaeology*, 6 (1890), p. 354.

32. 2. **as I pointed out a little above.** See x. 6. 3.

32. 3. **The Phrygians who dwell by the river Pencalas** etc.　Cp.
viii. 4. 3.

32. 4. **Themisonium.** The site of Themisonium is at *Kara Eyuk
Bazar* in the valley now called *Kara Eyuk Ova.*　Coins show that
the chief deity of Themisonium was ΛΥΚαβας ΣΩΖΩΝ, 'the saving
Lycabas.'　See W. M. Ramsay, in *American Journal of Archaeology*, 3
(1887), p. 362 ; *id., Historical Geography of Asia Minor,* pp. 101, 135 ;
id., The Cities and Bishoprics of Phrygia, 1. p. 252 *sq.*

32. 6. **Men sacred to the god leap down precipices.**　Similarly
at the sanctuary and during the festival of Apollo in Leucadia a criminal
was made to leap from the top of a high cliff into the sea.　His fall was
lightened by bundles of feathers and even by birds attached to his person.
Small boats, too, were waiting below to pick him up as he rose to the
surface after his plunge and to convey him beyond the boundaries.　He
was regarded as a scapegoat who carried away the sins of the people.
See Strabo, x. p. 452.　According to one of our authorities, it was the
priests who thus cast themselves from the cliff into the sea (Photius,
Lexicon, s.v. Λευκάτης, where the MS. reading ἱερεῖς has been conjecturally altered into ἐρασταί).　The men sacred to Apollo of whom Pausanias
here speaks may very well have been scapegoats who, if they survived
the leap, might be regarded as consecrated to the god for the rest of
their lives.　This suggestion is due to the late J. Töpffer, who rightly
refers in this connexion to the Athenian custom of stoning to death two
human scapegoats at the Thargelian festival of Apollo (Harpocration,
s.v. φαρμακός).　See J. Töpffer, *Beiträge zur griechischen Altertumswissenschaft* (Berlin, 1897), pp. 130-133.

32. 6. **tear exceedingly lofty trees from their roots** etc.　C.
Bötticher conjectured that, as the men were inspired by Apollo, the trees
which they tore up may have been laurels (*Baum-
kultus der Hellenen,* p. 391).　Probably, however, the god was not a genuine Greek Apollo,
but a native Asiatic deity, and there is nothing
in Pausanias's words to limit the trees to laurels.
The custom described by Pausanias is represented
on some coins of Magnesia of imperial date, on
the reverse of which appears a man carrying
an uprooted tree (Fig. 14).　See F. B. Baker,
in *Numismatic Chronicle,* Third Series, 12
(1892), p. 89 *sqq.*　Mr. Baker asks whether
the custom may not be a relic of very ancient
tree-worship.

FIG. 14. — MAN CARRYING
TREE (COIN OF MAGNESIA).

32. 7. **it is sacred to the Corycian nymphs, and especially to
Pan.**　See note on § 2.　The nymphs of the Corycian cave are
mentioned also by Aeschylus (*Eumenides,* 22 *sq.*), Sophocles (*Antigone,*
1128), and Strabo (ix. p. 417).

32. 7. **to reach the peaks of Parnassus.**　The ascent of Mt.
Parnassus from Delphi takes about eight hours.　The route as far as the
Corycian cave has been already described (note on § 2).　To reach the

summit of the mountain from the Corycian cave we must descend the steep hill-side by the way we came, then cross the eastern part of the bare treeless tableland *Livadi* to the *Kalyvia* of *Arachova*. This is a collection of neat and trim cottages or chalets at the eastern end of the tableland, just at the foot of the upper slopes of Parnassus. The village is inhabited only in summer, when the people of *Arachova* come hither to tend the herds of cattle that browse on these upland pastures or to reap the harvest, which is two months later here than in the valleys below. Numerous flocks of sheep and goats roam the mountain-slopes; the tinkle of their bells may be heard far off. Passing the village we ascend a narrow wooded glen. All cultivation now ceases. The firs, though often tall, mostly grow crooked. Higher up they become scarce. The route now leads over sharp rocks and stones, varied here and there with small tracts of pasture and the hovels of cow-keepers rudely constructed of rough stones and fir-branches. Above us rise conspicuous the two peaks of Parnassus, known respectively as *Gerontovrachos* ('the old man's rock') on the west and *Lykeri* to the north-east. *Lykeri* (8070 feet) is the higher summit, but only by about 78 feet. On the northern and eastern sides of *Gerontovrachos* large patches of snow remain all through the summer. The somewhat deep valley which lies between the two peaks is covered with loose stones and boulders, and is known as the Devil's Threshing-floor. In this valley or plateau are two wretched shelters, roughly built of stone, in which travellers, who wish to see the sunrise from the summit, sometimes pass the night. In clear weather the view from the summit includes Euboea and the northern Sporades on the east, and extends from Mt. Athos and Mt. Olympus on the north to Mt. Cyllene (*Ziria*) and the Aroanian mountains (*Chelmos*) in Arcadia on the south. To the west the prospect is limited by the lofty mountains of Locris and Aetolia, the highest summits of which out-top Parnassus itself.

See Clarke, *Travels*, 4. p. 203 *sqq.*; H. N. Ulrichs, *Reisen und Forschungen*, I. p. 120 *sqq.*; L. Ross, *Wanderungen*, 1. p. 55 *sqq.*; *id.*, 2. p. 191 *sqq.*; W. Vischer, *Erinnerungen*, p. 613 *sqq.*; P. Foucart, *Mémoire sur les ruines et l'histoire de Delphes*, p. 116 *sqq.*; Baedeker,[3] p. 162 *sq.*; *Guide-Joanne*, 2. p. 44 *sq.* For the ascent from Daulis, see x. 5. 1 note.

32. 7. **the Thyiad women rave on them** etc. Cp. x. 4. 3 note; Catullus, lxiv. 390 *sq.* Plutarch mentions an occasion when the Thyiad women were caught in a snow-storm on Parnassus, and the clothes of the men who went to their rescue were frozen so hard that when stretched out they broke in pieces (*De primo frigore*, 18).

32. 8. **Tithorea.** The site of Tithorea, first identified by Clarke in 1801, is occupied by the modern village of *Velitsa*, which stands very picturesquely among trees on the north-eastern slopes of Parnassus, overlooking the broad valley of the Cephisus. About two-thirds of the village are enclosed within the ancient ivy-mantled walls, which rank with those of Messene and Eleutherae as among the finest existing specimens of Greek fortifications. At the back of the village to the south rises a huge mountainous cliff of grey rock, its ledges tufted with pines. Between

TITHOREA

the foot of this great cliff and the village there intervenes a very steep slope, mostly overgrown with holly-oak bushes. On the east the village as well as the site of the ancient city is bounded by a very deep rocky ravine, which winds southward into the heart of the mountains. At the bottom of the ravine a torrent flows from Parnassus over a broad gravelly bed to join the Cephisus in the plain below. This torrent, now called *Kakorevma* or Evil stream, is the ancient Cachales. In the time of Pausanias, the townspeople, he tells us, had to fetch their water in buckets from the depths of the lyn. Nowadays a portion of the water of the stream is diverted higher up the glen and brought in a conduit to the village, where it turns two mills and waters the gardens and orchards. As Tithorea was thus naturally defended on two sides, namely by the great cliff on the south and by the deep ravine on the east, it needed walls on two sides only, the west and the north. These walls, starting from the foot of the cliff, first descend the steep slope in a straight line above the village, then follow the gentler slope within the village, still in a direction due north, till they turn round at an obtuse angle and run eastward to the brink of the ravine. Here they stop. Along the edge of the ravine a number of ancient blocks may be observed, but whether they are the remains of an ancient fortification wall is not clear. Perhaps the deep precipitous side of the ravine may have been considered a sufficient defence by itself. The walls so far as they exist are finely and solidly built of regular ashlar masonry, and are flanked by massive square towers constructed in the same style. Walls and towers are best preserved in the lower ground among the houses and gardens of the village, but on the steep slope above the village the remains are also considerable. At the highest point of the site, just under the perpendicular cliff, which has possibly been here cut artificially so as to form a smooth wall of rock, a piece of the wall is standing to a height of perhaps 12 feet; eleven courses are preserved. It seems to have been part of a square tower, for it comprises two fragments of walls meeting at a right angle. From this point the line of the ancient wall may be traced running straight down the slope. For the most part it is ruinous, but in one place it is preserved to its full height for some 20 or 30 yards, with the coping-stones running along its top. It here descends the slope in a series of long slanting steps, thus:—

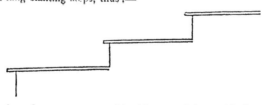

The number of courses preserved in this part of the wall is from seven to ten. Higher up the slope another piece of the wall is standing to a still greater height, the number of courses being about fourteen; and between these two pieces is a well-preserved rectangular tower resting on a high basement of natural rock. This tower, built of fine massive squared blocks laid in horizontal courses, of which eight are standing, measures in the inside 14 ft. 8 in. by 8 ft. 5 in.   The door leading into it from the top of the wall is preserved almost entire ; it is 5 ft. 7 in. high by 2 ft. 11 in. wide.   In the walls of the tower are two windows and a piece of a third.   Lower down the hill the wall is much more ruinous, but in one place it has still seven courses standing, and in another place it is about 7 ft. 8 in. thick, though whether this was its full original thickness is doubtful.   The investigation of the ruined fortifications on this slope, it may be observed, is a matter of some difficulty, for the slope is not only very steep but overgrown with prickly shrubs and cumbered with huge fallen blocks.   The antiquary who picks his way painfully among these obstacles is mortified by the contrast between his own slow progress and that of the village urchins who accompany him ; for they climb and skip like goats on the top of the walls, now appearing suddenly on the highest pinnacles and then again leaping from stone to stone with wonderful confidence and agility.

The remains of the walls in the village, on the other hand, can be examined without discomfort, and they better repay study.   Here on the north and north-west the wall, flanked by square towers, is standing in an unbroken line for a considerable distance.   It is from about 8 to about 20 feet high, with courses varying in number from four to eight. The towers, of which there are seven, measure from 20 to 22 feet on the face and project from 10 ft. 7 in. to 12 feet from the line of wall.   The blocks of which the towers are built are especially massive.   One fine tower, the best preserved of all, is standing to a height of perhaps 27 feet, with fourteen courses.   It is at the west end of the north wall, with which it makes an acute angle.   Two doors, each about 6 feet high and 3 feet wide, lead into it from the top of the wall, one on each side.   In the interior the tower is about 18 ft. 8 in. square.   Its walls are pierced at the top with windows, two on the north side, and one on the east ; one of the two northern windows is entire.   Three courses lower down than the windows there are loopholes in all the walls of the tower, one in the eastern and southern walls, two in the northern and western. Beyond the last tower to the south may be seen a gate about 9 feet wide in the wall, but whether it is ancient seems doubtful.   In the north wall there is a gap beside the most easterly of the towers, and the natives say that there was a gate here formerly.   As a whole, the masonry of the walls and towers is splendid, massive, and almost quite regular, without being absolutely so.   The beauty of these venerable walls is much enhanced by the thick green veil of ivy and other creepers which clothes their sides and droops in graceful festoons from their summits.   Such a mantle of clinging verdure is very rare in Greece, where the ancient temples and fortresses, unlike the ivy-clad abbeys and castles of England, remain for the most part to this day as bare as when they were built, without even a patch of moss to soften their hard outlines and to tell of the lapse of ages.

Distant views complete the charm of Tithorea.   From its ivied walls, rising among the gardens and houses of the village, we look up at the huge grey crag that hides the higher slopes of Parnassus, or down the long gradual declivity to the wide valley of the Cephisus and across it to the hills, somewhat low and tame, at whose foot lie the scanty ruins of Elatea.

The site of Tithorea is identified by inscriptions which are still to be seen at *Velitsa*. Thus a stone built into the apse of the church of the Panagia Theotokos ('the Most Holy Mother of God'), which stands in the highest part of the village, bears an inscription (*C. I. G.* No. 1733; *C. I. G. G. S.* 3. No. 200) recording that the city of Tithorea set up a statue of the emperor Nerva in his fourth consulship, *i.e.* in the year 98 A.D. Lower down in the village, opposite a small chapel of St. John and distant from it some 60 yards or so, there is a quadrangular base with mouldings, which serves to support the balcony of a house. The original inscription on this base records that a certain Gnosiphus and his wife Epixena dedicated a statue of their son Theonidas to Serapis, Isis, and Anubis ; but besides this original inscription there are carved on the pedestal a number of later inscriptions, most of them dated by the archon of Tithorea, which attest the sale of slaves to Serapis (*C. I. G. G. S.* 3. Nos. 187-194 ; Collitz, *G. D. I.* 2. Nos. 1554, 1555). The sale of a slave to a god was a form by which he recovered his freedom. Possessing no civil rights he could not legally purchase his own freedom ; but he paid the price and a god was made the nominal purchaser. From these inscriptions we infer that there was a sanctuary of Serapis at Tithorea and that the inscribed pedestal was set up in it. In the inscriptions the name of the city appears sometimes as Tithorea and sometimes as Tithora. The form Tithora is used by Plutarch (*Sulla*, 15 ; *Amatorius*, ii. 2). Herodotus (viii. 32), like Pausanias, uses the form Tithorea.

The other remains of antiquity at Tithorea are very scanty. Outside the church of the Panagia Theotokos lie a number of ancient blocks, some of them bearing a few letters of inscriptions. Some ancient blocks are also to be seen at the chapel of St. Elias which stands above the village, near the foot of the cliff. I also observed two pieces of small columns at the chapel of St. John and the house of the mayor.

See Clarke, *Travels*, 4. p. 215 *sqq.* ; Dodwell, *Tour*, 2. p. 137 *sqq.* ; Gell, *Itinerary of Greece* (London, 1819), p. 214 ; Leake, *Northern Greece*, 2. p. 76 *sqq.* ; H. N. Ulrichs, *Reisen und Forschungen*, 2. p. 114 *sqq.* ; W. Vischer, *Erinnerungen*, p. 624 *sqq.* ; Bursian, *Geogr.* I. p. 166 *sq.* ; Baedeker,[3] p. 202 ; *Guide-Joanne*, 2. p. 48. According to Ulrichs, the walls are about 19 feet thick with a core of rubble. I was at *Velitsa* (Tithorea), 26th and 27th October 1895, and have described the situation and ruins from my own observation.

As to the date of the existing walls of Tithorea, opinions have differed ; but their fine style leaves little room to doubt that they belong to the best period of Greek military architecture, namely to the fourth century B.C. Ulrichs may be right in thinking that they cannot be earlier than the second Sacred War (355-346 B.C.), since at the end of that war the cities of Phocis were razed to the ground (Paus. x. 3. 1). But his ground for dating them not earlier than the end of the third century B.C. does not hold good. It is that the towers contain loopholes, and that loopholes were invented by Archimedes at the siege of

Syracuse in 214 B.C. (Polybius, viii. 7. 6 ; Livy, xxiv. 34. 9). Ulrichs seems to have forgotten that there are loopholes in the towers of Messene, which were built about a century and a half before the supposed invention of loopholes by Archimedes. Moreover neither Polybius nor Livy, to whose evidence Ulrichs appeals, expressly asserts that Archimedes invented loopholes ; all they say is that he caused them to be made in the walls of Syracuse. Probably, then, the existing fortifications of Tithorea were built in the second half of the fourth century B.C., between the end of the Sacred War and the battle of Chaeronea, that is, between 346 B.C. and 338 B.C. See Pausanias, x. 3. 3. Leake's view that they were built in the early days of the Roman empire is preposterous. Under the *pax Romana* of that age, not yet disturbed by the rumours of barbarian invasions, a town of Phocis had as little reason to surround itself with massive walls and towers as an English town in Surrey or Hertfordshire at the present day ; and even if the burghers had been willing to lay out their money to so little purpose, it is in the last degree unlikely that they would have been suffered to do so by the Romans, who would certainly have regarded the rising fortifications as a menace to their authority and would have treated then accordingly. Would we allow a petty prince in India to fortify his capital and mount Krupp cannon on the walls ?

32. 8. Tithorea is distant —— eighty furlongs from Delphi etc. Pausanias has underestimated the distance, which, as the crow flies, is about 12 English miles. Leake suggested that the two roads from Tithorea to Delphi perhaps coincided as far as the upper end of the ravine of the Cachales, after which the carriage-road, diverging to the left, may have crossed the tableland of *Livadi* and then, below *Arachova*, joined the highroad which led from the Cleft Way to Delphi ; while the direct route from Tithorea, keeping on to the right, may have joined that from Lilaea just above the cliffs of Delphi, where the remains of the ancient way still exist. He thought it possible that the carriage-road might still be traced by the marks of the wheels in the rocks. In Leake's time there was no road in common use from *Velitsa* (Tithorea) across the mountain either to *Arachova* or Delphi ; the inhabitants of *Velitsa* penetrated no farther than a woody slope at a little distance where they cut firewood. See Leake, *Northern Greece*, 2. p. 81 *sq.*

32. 9. Herodotus' account of them is etc. Herodotus says (viii. 32) that when the Persians invaded Phocis, they did not catch the inhabitants, "for some of the Phocians ascended to the summits of Parnassus. Now there is a peak of Parnassus fitted to receive a multitude. It is over against the city of Neon and its name is Tithorea. To this the Phocians conveyed their property and ascended to it themselves." Some have supposed that this "peak of Parnassus," to which Herodotus gave the name of Tithorea, was the site which at a later time was occupied by the city of Tithorea (the modern *Velitsa*). This was Plutarch's view, for he expressly says that the city of Tithorea was the place in which the Phocians had taken refuge at the approach of Xerxes. If this view is correct, the city of Neon must have occupied a site different from and lower down than Tithorea (*Velitsa*). Now three or four miles to the north of *Velitsa*, in the plain on the right bank of the Cephisus, there exist the remains of an ancient city of considerable size. The walls formed an irregular quadrangle. In many places the foundation or socle of large squared blocks is to be seen, and the remains of towers, some square, some round, may also be recognised. Inside the circuit of the walls are many foundations of various sizes, and the ground is littered with potsherds. H. N. Ulrichs conjectured that these ruins, which are now called *Palaia Pheva* ('Old Thebes') by the natives, are the remains of Neon. That Neon was distinct from Tithorea and continued to subsist even after Tithorea was built seems to be indicated by the statement of Pausanias (x. 2. 4) that a battle was fought at Neon in the Sacred War of 355-346 B.C. Yet on the other hand it has sometimes been held, as by Pausanias himself, that Neon and Tithorea were identical, Neon being the earlier, Tithorea the later name of the town. On this view the peak to which Herodotus gave the name of Tithorea must have been one of the higher summits of Parnassus. See Leake, *Northern Greece*, 2. p. 79 *sq.* ; H. N. Ulrichs, *Reisen und Forschungen*, 2. p. 116 *sqq.* ; Bursian, *Geogr.* 1. p. 166.

32. 10. A generation before me the fortune of Tithorea declined. In Plutarch's time, about a generation before Pausanias, Tithorea was a considerable town, for he says that in the Mithridatic war it "was not so great a city as it is now, but merely a fortress surrounded by precipices" (*Sulla*, 15). Ancient foundations of considerable size are said to be seen outside the walls of Tithorea, proving that in the days of its prosperity the town had spread beyond the walls. Plutarch seems to allude to this in the passage just cited. See H. N. Ulrichs, *Reisen und Forschungen*, 2. p. 115 *sq.*

32. 10. the structure of a theatre. Outside the walls of Tithorea, towards the plain, Vischer observed many seats lying about, which he took to be those of the theatre (*Erinnerungen*, p. 625).

32. 10. a somewhat ancient market-place. Clarke thought that he had discovered this market-place. He describes it (*Travels*, 4. p. 220) as "a square structure, built in the Cyclopean style, with large masses of stone ; but laid together with great evenness and regularity, although without any cement ; the work being not so antient as the architecture of Argos, of Tiryns, or of Mycenae."

32. 10. In my account of Thebes I showed etc. See ix. 17. 5 *sq.*

32. 12. dwellings for the suppliants. Cp. ii. 11. 6 ; ii. 27. 2 note.

32. 12. to sacrifice to the god all animals except goats. Cp. ii. 26. 9 note. Goats were not sacrificed to Isis at her great shrine near Tithorea (below, § 16). An inscription on a votive-relief found in Thasos and now in the Louvre forbids the sacrifice of goats to the Graces (Roehl, *I. G. A.* No. 379 ; Roberts, *Greek Epigraphy*, No. 22).

32. 13. shrine of Isis. The worship of Isis, Serapis, and Anubis at Tithorea is attested by a dedicatory inscription found at *Velitsa* (the ancient Tithorea). See above, p. 405 ; H. N. Ulrichs, *Reisen und Forschungen*, 2. p. 121. Further evidence of the worship of Serapis at Tithorea is furnished by the inscriptions on the same stone recording the manumission of slaves under the form of a sale of them to Serapis (above, p. 405). On the worship of Isis outside of Egypt, see G. Lafaye, *Histoire du culte des divinités d'Alexandrie Sérapis, Isis, Harpocrate et Anubis hors de l'Égypte* (Paris, 1884).

32. 13. the nether gods in the cities on the Maeander etc. Strabo has described the procedure observed at a sanctuary of Pluto near the city of Acharaca, between Tralles and Nysa, in the valley of the Maeander. There was a sacred grove here, with a temple of Pluto and Proserpine; and above the grove was a certain cave called the Charonium or place of Charon. Sick people lodged in the village near the cave and were treated by the priests, who professed to be guided in their treatment by revelations vouchsafed to them in dreams while they slept in the cave. Sometimes the priests brought the patients to the cave and kept them there for several days without food. Sometimes the mode of cure was revealed to the patient himself in a dream, but he was always guided by the advice of the priests. No other persons were allowed to enter the cave. See Strabo, xiv. p. 649 *sq.*; Bouché-Leclercq, *Histoire de la divination dans l'antiquité*, 2. p. 372 *sqq.* As to Pausanias's use of the preposition ὑπὲρ in the present passage, see E. Reitz, *De praepositionis ὑπὲρ apud Pausaniam periegetam usu locali*, p. 36 *sqq.* Mr. Reitz understands it to refer to the situation of the cities perched on heights above the river. But it seems to mean no more than what we express by 'on,' *i.e.* near. A city beside a river is naturally also above it.

32. 14. festivals are held —— one in spring and one in autumn. Cp. Lafaye, *op. cit.* p. 129.

32. 16. The richer people sacrifice —— deer. The head and antlers of a stag are carved on what seems to have been an altar of Serapis at Chaeronea. See Preller, in *Berichte über die Verhandl. d. k. sächs. Gesell. d. Wissen. zu Leipzig*, 6 (1854), p. 197. Deer were sacrificed to Artemis at Patrae (Paus. vii. 18. 12), and in the month Elaphebolion, doubtless at the festival of the Elaphebolia, deer were sacrificed to her in her character of Deer-hitter (*Elaphebolos*) (Bekker's *Anecdota Graeca*, 1. p. 249). At the Elaphebolia cakes called 'deers' were made, probably in the shape of deer (Athenaeus, xiv. p. 646 e). In graphic representations of the Attic calendar, carved in relief on marble, Artemis is portrayed drawing a stag to herself; this no doubt stands for her festival of Elaphebolia ('deer-hitting') in the month Elaphebolion. See Le Bas, *Voyage archéologique*, Mon. fig., 21; Friederichs-Wolters, *Gipsabgüsse*, No. 1909; Daremberg et Saglio, *Dictionnaire des antiquités*, 1. p. 824.

32. 16. the poorer folk sacrifice geese. In an illustrated manuscript of the calendar of Philocalus, under the month November, Isis is depicted with a goose at her feet. The MS. is in the Imperial Library at Vienna. See Lafaye, *op. cit.* p. 267. Amongst the victims which it was lawful in general to sacrifice, the goose is mentioned (Suidas, *s.vv.* βοῦς ἕβδομος and θῦσον; Diogenianus, iii. 50). Martial speaks (ix. 31. 5 *sq.*) of the sacrifice of a goose to Mars. Sacred geese were sometimes bred in temples and to kill one of them seems to have been a heinous offence (Artemidorus, *Onirocr.* iv. 83; Petronius, *Sat.* 136 *sq.*;

Plutarch, *Camillus*, 27). One of the first duties of the Roman Censors when they entered on office was to give out a contract for supplying the food of the sacred geese (Pliny, *Nat. hist.* x. 51 ; Plutarch, *Quaest. Rom.* 98). The goose was used in divination (Schol. on Aristophanes, *Birds*, 521 ; Petronius, *Sat.* 137). On geese in ancient literature and art see Stephani in *Compte-Rendu* (St. Petersburg) for 1863, p. 17 *sqq.*; O. Keller, *Thiere des classischen Alterthums*, pp. 286-303.

32. 16. **wrap the victims in bandages of linen** etc. The Egyptian method of swathing mummies in linen bandages is described by Herodotus (ii. 86). As to the kind of fine linen (*bussos*) here mentioned by Pausanias, see v. 5. 2 note.

32. 17. **burn the booths —— and depart in haste.** Similarly at the Delphic festival of Crowning, certain persons set fire to a shed and fled away without looking behind them (Plutarch, *De defectu oraculorum*, 15 : see note on ii. 7. 7). As for the custom of erecting temporary huts or booths in a sacred precinct, see note on i. 18. 1, vol. 2. p. 165 *sq.*

32. 18. **she is mourning for Osiris** etc. The Egyptian legend of the death of Osiris is told by Plutarch (*Isis and Osiris*, 13 *sqq.*). Pausanias here says that the mourning of Isis for Osiris was supposed to take place when the Nile began to rise. But according to Plutarch (*op. cit.* 39) the ceremony of mourning for Osiris took place when the waters of the Nile were sinking and lasted four days, beginning on the 17th of the month Athyr. According to Brugsch the mourning for Osiris lasted from the 8th to the 12th of November. See Brugsch, *Religion und Mythologie der alten Aegypter*, p. 616 *sqq.* The annual lamentations for the dead Osiris are described by Firmicus Maternus (*De errore profanarum religionum*, ii. 3). Specimens of Egyptian hymns in which Isis is represented mourning for Osiris have been discovered. See Brugsch, *op. cit.* p. 631 *sqq.* ; *Records of the Past*, 2. p. 119 *sqq.*

32. 18. **it is the tears of Isis that cause the river to rise.** Similarly it was said by the Pythagoreans that the sea was the tear of Cronus (Plutarch, *Isis and Osiris*, 32).

32. 18. **a true saying of Homer's** etc. See *Iliad*, xx. 131.

32. 19. **The olive-oil of Tithorea** etc. According to Clarke (*Travels*, 4. p. 218) the olives of Tithorea still maintained their reputation at the beginning of the present century and were sent as acceptable presents to the Turkish Pashas and other grandees. Dodwell, however, who visited Tithorea a few years after Clarke, saw no olive-trees in the immediate neighbourhood of Tithorea (*Tour in Greece*, 2. p. 139). The cultivation of the olive is represented in ancient vase-paintings. See Baumeister's *Denkmäler*, p. 1046 *sq.* ; and on the ancient methods of manufacturing oil from the olives, see Blümner, *Technologie*, 1. p. 328 *sqq.*

32. 19. **the Iberian oil** etc. The olive-oil of Turdetania (the south-western part of Andalusia) was of very fine quality, and it was exported in large quantities (Strabo, iii. p. 144). According to Pliny (*Nat. hist.* xv. 8) the olive-oil of Baetica (Andalusia) and Histria ranked next after that of Italy, which, Pliny says, was the finest in the world. Martial speaks of the oil of Cordova as equal both to the oil of Istria and to the

best Italian oil (*Epigr.* xii. 63. 1 *sq.*).   Cp. V. Hehn, *Kulturpflanzen und Hausthiere*,[4] p. 94 *sq.*   Istria, which Pausanias calls an island, is a peninsula.

33. 1. **Ledon.**   Leake conjectured that this might be identical with the city of the Pedienses mentioned by Herodotus (viii. 33).   He thought the ruins now called Old Thebes (see note on x. 32. 9) may be those of Ledon or the city of the Pedienses.   See Leake, *Northern Greece*, 2. p. 89 *sq.*

33. 2. **the fickleness of Histiaeus** etc.   See Herodotus, v. 11, 23 *sq.*, 35.

33. 2. **the impiety of Philomelus** etc.   Philomelus was a native of Ledon.   See x. 2. 2.

33. 3. **Lilaea is a winter day's journey from Delphi** etc.   The well-preserved ruins of Lilaea are situated near the source of the Cephisus, at the north-western foot of Parnassus.   The route from Delphi leads across and down Parnassus, as Pausanias correctly says.   I followed this route, and my notes of it may supplement our author's too concise description.   We left the new village of Delphi, which stands a little to the south-west of the ancient sanctuary, shortly after eight o'clock, and at once struck up the mountain-side at the back of the village.   The path for a good way is the same as that to the Corycian cave.   It climbs the bare rocky face of the mountain in a series of zigzags, from which as we rose higher and higher a wide prospect opened up behind us to the Gulf of Corinth and the distant mountains of Peloponnese.   On reaching the top of this long and steep declivity we found ourselves on the edge of an expanse of comparatively level, though broken, ground, sparsely wooded with pines, beyond which rose the upper slopes of Parnassus, its summit lightly capped with snow.   The high plateau on which we now stood is bounded on the north by an outlying spur of Parnassus, clothed with pine-forest, in the southern face of which is the Corycian cave.   Instead of crossing the tableland in the direction of the cave, we skirted its south-western corner, keeping the wooded mountain on our right.   The path continued to wind for hours along grey rocky slopes where pines grew more or less thickly.   On either hand rose sombre mountains of the same general character—grey and rocky with patches of pine-forest on their sides.   Now and then a little moss relieved with its verdure the barrenness of the rocks, and a stony glade through which we passed was speckled with pale purple crocuses.   On these heights the air felt chilly, for the season was late October, and a little snow—the first of autumn—had fallen in the night, just touching with white the peaks of Parnassus and the high Locrian mountains in the west.   The morning had been bright when we left Delphi, but as the day wore on the sky became overcast, its cold and lowering aspect harmonising well with the wild and desolate scenery through which we rode.   The jingling of the mule-bells and the cries of the muleteers were almost the only sounds that broke the silence, though once in the forest to the right we heard the clapper-like note of a pelican, and once in an open glade we passed some woodmen hewing pine-logs.   In time, the path beginning to descend, the rocks gave place to earthy slopes; a little pale thin grass and some withered ferns grew in the glades ; the sun shone out between the clouds, and as we descended into the warmer lowlands it seemed as if we were pursuing the departing summer. In about four hours from Delphi high purple mountains, sunlit and flecked with cloud-shadows, appeared in the north through and above the pine-forest. Farther down the forest grew thin and then disappeared from the stony bottom of the valley, though the upper slopes of the mountains on either side were still wrapt in their dark mantle of pines. It was near one o'clock when we reached *Ano-Agoriani*, a village nestling among trees in a hollow of the mountains and traversed by a murmuring brook. After a halt of about an hour we quitted *Ano-Agoriani* and descended into the deep bed of the stream below the village ; then ascending steeply its western bank we pursued our way along the rocky mountain-side high above the glen. In three-quarters of an hour we came in sight of the broad valley of the Cephisus lying stretched below us and backed by mountains on the north. By steep rocky winding paths we now descended into the valley and at a quarter to four reached *Kato-Agoriani*. The village stands just at the foot of Parnassus. About a mile to the east the grey ruined walls and towers of Lilaea climb a steep and rugged hill-side—the last fall of Parnassus to the plain. The situation of the place at the northern foot of the mountain is such that it can receive very little sun at any time of the year, which, though an advantage in the torrid heat of a Greek summer, must render the winter climate severe. As we rode downwards to *Kato-Agoriani* the sun set behind the mountains at our back soon after three o'clock, but it was not till nearly two hours afterwards that his light faded from the hills on the opposite or northern side of the valley. This may illustrate the remarks of Pausanias as to the climate of Lilaea.

Little now remains of Lilaea except the fortifications of the acropolis, but these are well preserved (Fig. 15). Their situation is striking and peculiar. The last slope of Parnassus to the valley of the Cephisus here consists of a steep hill-side studded with rugged rocks, overgrown with prickly shrubs, and terminated on the east by a deep glen, into which the hill descends abruptly in sheer and lofty precipices. The walls, flanked with square towers, ascend the steep rocky bushy slope of the hill at a short distance to the west of these precipices, which they gradually approach, till only a narrow strip of shelving rocky ground is left between them and the brink of the cliffs. This strip may be from 20 to 50 yards wide in some places, but in others it is only broad enough to allow of a passage between the walls and the crags. Indeed at one place the precipitous slope (here not actually a precipice) begins at the very foot of the wall. Towards the summit the wall makes an angle westward for a few yards, thus leaving a somewhat wider, but still very small space between it and the precipices on the east. This narrow area, enclosed by massive walls on three sides and by precipices on the remaining side, was the citadel proper ; and the walls and towers on the hill-side below, which from their massiveness and height would seem to have been erected at an enormous expenditure of labour, if not of money, were apparently intended merely to connect the tiny citadel with the town in the plain; for the hill-side itself, hemmed in between the wall and the precipices, is too steep and rugged to allow us to suppose that any part of the town was built on it.

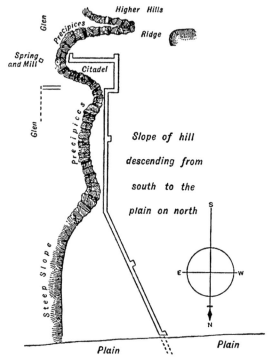

FIG. 15.—PLAN OF RUINS OF LILAEA.

Walls and towers are finely and solidly built of squared blocks laid in horizontal courses. The masonry is nearly but not quite regular; the blocks of the lower courses are especially massive. The fortifications begin at the foot of the hill with a well-preserved square tower which is standing to a height (as I estimated it) of 27 feet, with twelve courses of masonry. It is 20 feet broad on its western face and projects 12 feet from the curtain. In the top of the tower, on its western side, is a square window, and a little lower down is a loophole for arrows. Above the tower the wall ascends the steep bushy slope of the hill. In some places it is ruinous, consisting chiefly of a jumble of huge fallen blocks among the prickly holly-oak bushes. But to a great extent it still has from two to ten courses standing, and is preserved on both faces, its thickness being about 9 feet. Where four courses are standing the height is about 9 feet; where nine or ten courses are preserved, the height is about 18 or 19 feet. On the steepest part of the slope the wall rises in steps, and here it is preserved to its full height (about 18 feet, with nine or ten courses) ; for it is surmounted by a course of coping-stones composed of flat projecting slabs. Two square towers are standing on the slope of the hill. One of them is 22 ft. 8 in. broad and projects 10 ft. 8 in. from the curtain ; at its north-west angle it is still about 24 feet high with twelve courses of masonry. The other tower, lower down the hill, is only 14 feet broad and about 12 feet high, with eight courses. The little citadel on the summit of the hill measures about 100 yards long on its western and 70 yards on its southern side. Two to eight courses of the walls are standing. The masonry is splendid ; the blocks are huge and solid and laid in horizontal courses. Two square towers project from the southern wall, one at its western angle, the other at its eastern end, just above the precipices which bound the citadel on this side. The western tower is at least 40 feet high, but the upper part is mediaeval or modern, being miserably constructed of small stones and mortar. However about six courses of masonry on one side and nine or ten courses on another seem to be ancient. This tall and conspicuous tower is about 14 paces broad and projects 12 ft. 7 in. from the curtain. The eastern tower is square, like all the others ; it projects 13 ft. 8 in. from the curtain and has seven courses standing on one of its sides. Outside of the citadel to the south there is a piece of level ground between the wall and the precipices, which here curve westward. Why the engineer did not include this flat ground within the citadel and carry the fortifications (if fortifications were needed) along the brink of the precipices, is not evident. To the south the hill of Lilaea is dominated by much higher mountains, the outlying masses of Parnassus.

Down the eastern side of the broad and deep glen that bounds the hill on the east there flows a stream to join the Cephisus ; and on the western side of the glen, just at the foot of the immense perpendicular crag which is crowned by the fortifications of the citadel, a small spring rises amid luxuriant vegetation. Beside the spring is a mill, now disused, to which the water is led in a channel from higher up the glen.

The town of Lilaea seems to have stood on the flat ground at the foot of the steep hill which formed the acropolis, for scanty remains of its walls may be seen at various points in the plain and the glen. Thus, for example, from the tall well-preserved tower at the foot of the hill slight but indubitable traces of a wall may be discerned extending northward into the plain ; and in the glen about 100 yards down from the mill I saw remains of a wall coming down, in an easterly direction, from the acropolis. On the slope of the hill, below the precipitous rocks, the wall is preserved for several yards, with two and three courses of masonry, and there are some traces of it in the glen further to the north, at the foot of the hill. Lastly, in the flat ground at the mouth of the glen, about a quarter of a mile to the north-east of the hill, a few isolated remains of walls may be seen : two courses are standing, and other squared blocks are lying about.

I visited Lilaea from *Kato-Agoriani*, 23rd-25th October 1895, and have described its situation and ruins from my own observation. See also Dodwell,

Tour, 2. p. 133; Gell, *Itinerary of Greece* (London, 1819), p. 207; Leake, *Northern Greece*, 2. pp. 71 *sq.*, 84 *sqq.*, 581; Welcker, *Tagebuch*, 2. p. 79 *sqq.*; Bursian, *Geogr.* 1. p. 161; Lolling, in *Mittheil. d. arch. Inst. in Athen*, 9 (1884), p. 311 *sq.*; Baedeker,[3] p. 162; *Guide-Joanne*, 2. p. 44.

33. 5. The river has its source here etc. The copious springs which the ancients regarded as the source of the Cephisus rise at the northern base of Parnassus, about a mile or so to the east of Lilaea. Here at the foot of a rocky hill a terrace, about ten paces broad, is supported by a wall of polygonal masonry 6 to 9 feet high and 100 yards long or more. On the top of this polygonal wall, towards its eastern end, there rests a stretch of ashlar masonry, two courses high, which also served to support the terrace on this side. A small ancient building, probably a temple of the river Cephisus, must have stood on the terrace, near its eastern end; for here two fragments of small unfluted columns, and a small piece of wall, consisting of four or five blocks, are standing, and many large squared blocks are lying about. The diameter of the columns is 13 inches; their height is 5 ft. 3 in. and 4 ft. 5 in. respectively. Immediately below the terrace, a few feet from the polygonal wall, a very copious spring of clear water wells forth, forming a large pool at the foot of the wall not many yards to the west. Tall grass and other plants grow in abundance beside the stream just opposite the spring, and accompany its course through the plain, where some willows grow on its banks. Beside the spring, lower down than the polygonal wall, are some remains of other walls, and many ancient squared blocks lie tumbled about. One small hewn stone, with its top shaped like a gable or pediment, lying close to the water, bears the following inscription :

ΞΕΝΟΦΑΝΗΣ
ΞΕΝΟΔΩΡΑ
ΑΝΔΡΙΣΚΟΝ
Κ]ΑΦΙΣΩΙ

The stone is broken at the bottom left hand corner, and a letter has clearly been lost. The missing letter was no doubt K. Thus the inscription records a dedication to the river Cephisus by three persons, Xenophanes, Xenodora, and Andriscon, and proves that the spring is indeed the one which the ancients regarded as the source of the river. Further, it shows that the Cephisus was worshipped here, and it makes it probable that the building on the terrace above the spring was a temple of the river god. The inscription seems to have been entire when Lolling copied it (*C. I. G. G. S.* 3. No. 232).

About 150 yards or so to the east of the spring is a building which from the crosses carved over the doorways would seem to have been used as a chapel, though in plan it differs wholly from the common type of Greek church. There is no apse; the door is in the north wall instead of at the east end; and in the interior there is a cross-wall pierced with three doorways, each of which has a large stone lintel and stone doorposts. The masonry of the building is so good and so regular that at first I took it for ancient; but in the foundations there are some bits of bricks.

It was about half-past eight in the morning when I visited the spring, and the water then welled up with a gentle murmuring sound very unlike the bellowing of a bull, to which Pausanias compares the noise made by it at mid-day. It is true I heard a rushing roaring sound, but it was only the sough of wind in the willows.

Ancient writers from Homer onward seem to be unanimous in regarding as the source of the Cephisus this spring near Lilaea. See Homer, *Il.* ii. 523; *id., Hymn to Apollo,* 240 *sq.*; Strabo, ix. pp. 407, 424; Pliny, *Nat. hist.* iv. 8; Statius, *Theb.* vii. 348 *sq.*; Paus. ix. 24. 1. Yet it is not the highest source of the river. A considerable stream of turbid water comes down the valley from the west, flows through the middle of the plain in a broad gravelly bed, and is joined by the stream formed by the spring which has just been described. Moreover the stream which comes down the glen on the eastern side of Lilaea and joins the Cephisus must also take its rise much further up among the mountains than the supposed source of the river. It may also be mentioned that about a mile or less to the west of *Kato-Agoriani*, and hence about two miles to the west of Lilaea, another spring issues from the foot of the rocky hills which bound the flat valley of the Cephisus on the south. The water is clear and forms at once a fair-sized stream, which is directed in a long straight canal, edged with poplars, in a northerly or north-easterly direction across the plain, probably to join the Cephisus.

I visited the springs 24th and 25th October 1895, and have described them from personal observation. See also Dodwell, *Tour,* 2. p. 133; Leake, *Northern Greece,* 2. pp. 70 *sq.*, 84 *sq.*; Welcker, *Tagebuch,* 2. p. 81; Bursian, *Geogr.* 1. p. 161.

33. 5. owing to Mount Parnassus its winters are not correspondingly mild. See above, p. 411. The upper valley of the Cephisus, in which lay Lilaea, Tithorea, and Elatea, is bounded on the south by the great mountain-mass of Parnassus, and on the north by the mountains of Locris. The inhabitants "complain of the intensity and duration of the winter cold. These lofty summits continually attract and break the clouds by which they are assailed with long and violent showers of rain and snow" (Dodwell, *Tour,* 2. p. 137). *Velitsa* (the ancient Tithorea), lying right under the northern declivities of Parnassus, is in shadow in winter even before one o'clock (Leake, *Northern Greece,* 2. p. 119). Another proof of the absence of sunshine in this district is that the vintage is later here than in Peloponnese. When I was at Lilaea towards the end of October, the vines were still laden with purple clusters, which the peasants were engaged in gathering and crushing; whereas in Peloponnese, which I had quitted a few days before, the vintage was mostly over. The manner of pressing the grapes, it may be observed, differs in different parts of Greece. In some places, as at Phlius, the grapes are trodden with the feet; in other places, as at Clitor in Arcadia and Lilaea in Phocis, they are crushed with wooden clubs or beetles in tubs.

33. 6. Charadra, perched on a high crag. The ruins which may with some probability be identified as those of Charadra, occupy the slopes and summit of a steep rocky hill, perhaps 400 feet high, which projects slightly into the plain from the northern foot of Parnassus. On the west the hill slopes very steeply to a glen, down which a brook, coming from a gully in the mountains further to the south, flows northward to join the *Kanianitis* or *Kaienitza*, a tributary of the Cephisus. This brook is probably the Charadrus, mentioned by Pausanias; it was dry when I visited the place in October, which so far confirms Pausanias's remark as to the lack of water at Charadra. The very steep rocky slope of the hill towards the glen on the west would seem to be the "high crag" of which our author speaks. On the south the hill descends gradually to the glen, which here makes a sort of bend as if it would encircle the hill. In this bend lies the village of *Mariolates*. The high rugged mountains to the south and south-west, beyond the village of *Mariolates*, are wooded with pines on their upper slopes. On the east the hill of Charadra is connected with higher rocky hills by a short ridge or saddle. On the north it slopes steeply to the wide level expanse of the Cephisian plain, through which the *Kanianitis* flows eastward in a broad gravelly bed to join the Cephisus. The place is about 3 miles north-west of Lilaea, which is somewhat in excess of the distance (20 Greek furlongs, about $2\frac{1}{3}$ miles) which Pausanias mentions.

The fortification-walls of Charadra, of which there are considerable remains, seem to have been disposed as follows. On the northern side

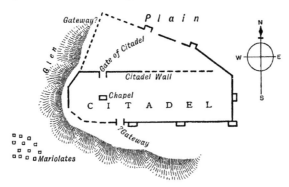

FIG. 16.—PLAN OF RUINS OF CHARADRA (?).

of the hill they ascended the slope obliquely from north-west to south-east, starting probably from the plain (though here they no longer exist) and reaching the highest point of the enclosure at the eastern summit of the hill. Here the wall, now preserved in an unbroken line though not to any great height, turns southward, and runs in a straight line for some 70 yards or so, till at the south-eastern angle it turns westward and, gradually descending, extends as far as the glen which bounds the hill on the west. On this southern side of the hill the wall with its flanking towers is better preserved than in any other part of the circuit. On the western side of the hill the wall ran along the edge of the glen, then descended the slope northward into the plain, where the last traces of it may be seen at a rocky pinnacle, partly overgrown with holly-oak bushes, at no great height above the glen. But of this western wall only a few isolated pieces are standing.

Such was apparently the circuit of Charadra, which thus embraced not only the summit but a great part of the northern slope of the hill. Within the circuit, however, a fortification-wall, which is partially preserved, ran along the northern brow of the hill, thus forming, with the other walls on the east, south, and west, an upper fortress or citadel of a roughly quadrangular shape. The whole fortified enclosure, however, is but small. The citadel may measure perhaps 150 yards from east to west by 70 yards from north to south.

The masonry of the walls and towers is on the whole of the regular ashlar sort; the blocks are large, squared, and laid in horizontal courses. From two to six courses are preserved; the height in many places is from 8 to 10 or 11 feet. For example the southern wall is preserved unbroken for a length of nearly 100 yards and a height of 8 or 10 feet, with six courses of massive ashlar masonry; and the eastern wall, built in the same style, is preserved throughout its whole length (about 70 yards) to a height of two and three courses. Four square towers project from these two walls, namely two towers from the south wall, one tower from the east wall, and one tower from the angle between the two walls. With the exception of the most westerly, which is ruinous, each of these towers is 21 or 22 feet broad, and projects about 11 feet from the curtain. One of the towers on the south wall is 11 or 12 feet high, with five courses of masonry. The tower at the angle is 4 ft. 5 in. high with two courses. The remains of the wall which ascends the northern slope obliquely from the north-west are not continuous, but there are isolated pieces about 10 feet high with from three to six courses of masonry. Remains of two square towers may be seen projecting from it. On this northern slope the rugged rocks which jut from the hill-side clearly formed part of the line of the fortifications, for the wall abuts against them in some places. The inner wall of the citadel, along the northern brow of the hill, is partly built on the top of rocks. It runs unbroken for a length of about 60 paces, except that about 14 paces from its western end there is a gateway 11 feet wide, undefended by towers. To the west of this gateway the citadel-wall is about 6 feet high; to the east of it the wall has five courses of masonry, and its height, inclusive of the rock on which it rests, is over 12 feet. The masonry of this eastern part of the citadel-wall is not so good as that of the circuit-wall; the blocks are smaller and rather irregular, and holly-oak bushes, growing out of it, have loosened the joints. In the circuit-wall there are some traces of gateways, one in the south wall beside the ruined tower, the other at the north-western corner beside the rocky pinnacle to which reference has already been made. This latter gateway seems to have opened westward to the glen, the descent to which at this point of the slope is neither high nor steep. On the summit of the hill a little chapel rudely built of small stones stands beside a holly-oak. It contains no ancient blocks, so far as I saw.

Leake was of opinion that the ruins which have been described were

not in Phocis but in Doris, and he would identify them as those of
Boeum, one of the small towns of the Dorian Tetrapolis (Thucydides, i.
107; Strabo, x. p. 476; Scymnus Chius, *Orbis descriptio*, 593; Diodorus, iv. 67, xi. 79; Ptolemy, iii. 14. 14, ed. Müller; Pliny, *Nat. hist.*
iv. 28). He argues that since Lilaea was sometimes regarded, for
example by Ptolemy (*l.c.*), as a Dorian town, though in general it was
held to belong to Phocis, it must have been on the frontier; and that
consequently the ruins at *Mariolates*, being about 3 miles to the north-
west of Lilaea, must certainly have been in Doris. He would place
Charadra at *Souvala*, a village at the head of a long slope, where he
remarked some remains of a small fortified town. There are two
villages of *Souvala*, an upper and a lower (*Ano Souvala* and *Kato
Souvala*). Leake seems to have referred to the upper village, which is
distant about $2\frac{1}{2}$ miles to the south-east of Lilaea. The lower village is
on the edge of the plain, in sight of Lilaea and distant from it only
about a mile to the north-east.

See Dodwell, *Tour*, 2. p. 132; Leake, *Northern Greece*, 2. pp. 70, 72, 85·94;
W. Vischer, *Erinnerungen*, p. 622; Bursian, *Geogr.* 1. p. 161 *sq.*; H. G. Lolling,
in *Mittheil. d. arch. Inst. in Athen*, 9 (1884), pp. 312 *sq.*, 317. I visited the ruins
at *Mariolates*, 24th October 1895, and have described them from personal observation.

**33. 7. The valley of the Cephisus is decidedly the best land in
Phocis** etc. The upper valley of the Cephisus, between the northern
slopes of Parnassus and the southern slopes of the Locrian mountains,
is still fertile and well tilled; in some places it is one continuous corn-
field, in which the ripe wheat stands as high as a man and yields a return
of eight to one. Numerous large villages lie at the foot of the mountains.
See Leake, *Northern Greece*, 2. pp. 73, 74; Vischer, *Erinnerungen*, p.
622. Theophrastus remarked on the quantity of flour yielded by the
wheat grown about Elatea (*Hist. plant.* viii. 8. 2). When I passed
through the valley of the Cephisus in Phocis at the end of October, the
wheat had long been reaped and the fields lay either in stubble or had
lately been ploughed. Even the Indian corn, which is an autumn crop,
had been got in; but the cotton was still in some of the fields. The
soil is so fertile that it yields two crops in the year, namely wheat in
early summer and maize or cotton in autumn. In the upper part of the
valley, near Lilaea, there are vineyards and some tobacco. In the lower
part of the valley, from *Dadi* (Amphiclea) eastward there are no vineyards and the peasants have to buy their wine. The bottom of the
valley is for the most part a dead flat, several miles wide. The Cephisus
traverses it in a shallow bed; its water is turbid and of a whitish colour.

33. 7. the verse etc. See Homer, *Il.* iii. 522.

33. 7. a city named Parapotamii. After flowing south-east for
more than 20 miles through a broad and spacious valley bounded by the
massive Parnassus on the south and a range of rather low, bushy,
uninteresting hills on the north, the Cephisus turns sharply to the south
and flows through a narrow valley or defile into the wide plain of
Chaeronea. The defile, which thus forms a pass from Phocis into
Boeotia, is now called the *Stena* ('Narrows'). It may be about a mile

and a half long and about a quarter of a mile wide at the narrowest point, which is at the northern end of the defile ; but south of this point it expands to a width of perhaps three-quarters of a mile. The flat and fertile land in the defile yields wheat in early summer and cotton in autumn. The Cephisus, turbid as usual, flows through it in a muddy bed which is neither wide nor deep. On both sides the defile is bounded by low rocky hills. The hills on the west, which are a good deal the higher, form the last spur sent out by Parnassus to the east. The hills on the eastern side of the defile are the termination of a low chain which extends eastward for some miles, bounding the plain of Chaeronea on the north and connected with the higher range of Mount Acontium (the modern *Dourdouvana*), which ends on the east at Orchomenus. Parapotamii occupied the flat summit of the low hill that overhangs the narrowest part of the defile of the Cephisus on the east. The hill, which is connected by a ridge with the similar low stony hills to the east, is probably not more than 150 or 200 feet high at the most. Yet it is well fitted to be the site of a city ; for the summit is level and of some extent, and the rocky sides, though nowhere very steep or high, afford a natural defence. The situation, too, is strategically important, commanding as it does one of the chief passes from Phocis into Boeotia and overlooking the two great plains of Elatea and Chaeronea. Nevertheless Parapotamii would seem always to have been an insignificant place. The want of a strong acropolis may partly account for this. The city had ceased to exist in the first century B.C. ; but Sulla, with the intuition of a general, occupied the deserted hill before he gave battle to the Mithridatic army in the neighbouring plain of Chaeronea (Plutarch, *Sulla*, 16). Two centuries later, if we may trust Pausanias, the very site of Parapotamii was forgotten. Yet the line of the ancient walls can still be traced nearly all round the edge of the summit, and considerable stretches of the wall are standing to the height of a few feet (5 or 6 feet at most), though for long distances together the line is marked only by broken stones. The wall, where it remains, is built of small rough polygonal stones in a very poor style ; indeed it is amongst the worst specimens of ancient masonry that I observed in Greece. I walked all round the site, but observed no traces of flanking towers. On the north-east side of the hill there are vestiges of a gateway opening to the north-west. The level top of the hill is now under cultivation. Pottery is strewn about it. On the slope at the north-western corner the rocks seem to have been cleared away in order to afford an easy access from the plain to the summit of the hill.

That the scanty ruins which have just been described are those of Parapotamii is quite certain, for their situation answers exactly to the description of Theopompus (quoted by Strabo, ix. p. 424), who says that Parapotamii stood on a hill of moderate height at a pass leading from Boeotia into Phocis, between Parnassus and Mount Hedylium, and that the Cephisus flowed through the pass, which was only 5 furlongs wide. Mount Hedylium is the chain of low hills which extends eastward from the defile. See above, p. 187.

About a mile or so to the east of Parapotamii is the village of *Belesi* lying at the northern foot of Mount Hedylium. Fair quarters for the night may be obtained in the village.

I visited Parapotamii from *Belesi*, 31st October 1895, and have described the ruins as I saw them. See also Gell, *Itinerary of Greece* (London, 1819), p. 219 *sq.* ; Leake, *Northern Greece*, 2. pp. 95 *sqq.*, 191, 195, 200 *sq.* ; Vischer, *Erinnerungen*, p. 626 *sq.* ; Bursian, *Geogr.* I. p. 164; Baedeker,[2] p. 202 ; *Guide-Joanne*, 2. p. 48.

33. 8. Likewise Herodotus, enumerating the cities etc. See Herodotus, viii. 33.

33. 9. The distance to Amphiclea from Lilaea is sixty furlongs. The path from Lilaea to Amphiclea follows the edge of the wide valley of the Cephisus, skirting the foot of the outlying slopes of Parnassus the whole way. At first it runs north-eastward for about 3 miles, and then, bending round a protruding spur of the hills, runs south-eastward for about $2\frac{1}{2}$ miles more. At the point where the route bends round, the Cephisus approaches it closely, flowing near the foot of the hills among trees and spanned by two stone bridges. One of the bridges is new ; the other is old, high-arched, and picturesquely shaded with trees. The modern carriage-road from Lamia to Athens crosses the river from north to south by the new bridge, and we follow it, as far as *Dadi*, still skirting the foot of the hills, beyond which to the south rise high pine-clad mountains. The hills on the opposite or northern side of the great valley are low, tame, and overgrown with bushes. Some way before *Dadi* we pass through the *Kalyvia* of *Dadi*, which in this case is not a village inhabited by the people of *Dadi* in winter, but merely a collection of granaries and storehouses, where the country produce is laid up before it is conveyed to *Dadi* to be consumed.

Dadi itself is a town of a thriving well-to-do appearance, built at the foot of the out-lying spurs of Parnassus, the higher slopes of which, however, are not visible. For the most part the houses rise above each other on the hill-side, but some of them are built on the plateau below, from which again the ground slopes away gradually to the valley of the Cephisus. Immediately to the west of the modern town rises a low hill or eminence on which are the scanty ruins of Amphiclea. The hill, or rather plateau, slopes away gradually to the valley of the Cephisus on the north ; on the east it descends, also gradually, to the lower plateau on which stand some of the houses of *Dadi;* on the south it is divided by a hollow from the hills which rise steeply on this side, their summits wooded with pines ; and on the west it is connected by a ridge with the higher eminences, which are themselves but the last spurs sent down by Parnassus to the valley of the Cephisus. The hill or plateau of Amphiclea reaches its highest point (which after all is but low) at the south-west, where stands a ruined mediaeval tower. On its northern and eastern sides the plateau ends in a gentle slope some 15 feet or so high. Nearly all round the plateau, which is of a roughly triangular shape with the base turned to the east, the line of the ancient walls may be traced. For the most part the remains are very scanty, consisting only of one or two courses of masonry. On the southern side, however, they are somewhat better preserved than elsewhere. Here the wall has from one to five courses of masonry standing for many yards together. One piece is 54 paces long and another is 27 paces long. Where three to five courses are preserved the wall is from 5 ft. 5 in. to 7 feet high. The masonry is on the whole ashlar, but not very good or regular. A square tower, 20 feet broad and built of large squared blocks laid in horizontal courses, projects 9 feet from the curtain. On its southern face the tower is 9 feet high, with five courses of masonry; on its eastern side four courses are standing. Further to the west there are some slight remains of another square tower; and an angle of a third tower, with one and two courses of masonry, may be seen on the eastern side of the plateau. The ruined mediaeval tower which stands within the circuit of the walls on the highest part of the plateau is built of stones and mortar in the usual indifferent style; but in the lower courses are some large blocks which were probably taken from the ancient walls. A few steps to the west of this tower is a small chapel; and to the east of the tower is a church standing in an area of some extent enclosed by walls. The southern wall of this enclosure is built upon the ancient fortification-wall. In the church there is an inscription (*C. I. G.* No. 1738; *C. I. G. G. S.* 3. No. 218) which serves to identify the ruins as those of Amphiclea. The inscription records that a statue of Marcus Ulpius Damasippus, high-priest of Dionysus, was set up by his wife, Quintilia Plutarcha, in the sacred precinct of the god. The name of Amphiclea does not indeed occur in the inscription; but we may conjecture that the church occupies the site of the shrine of Dionysus, and that Marcus Ulpius Damasippus was one of the inspired priests, mentioned by Pausanias (§ 11), who delivered oracles in the name of the god. From a comparison with an inscription of Anticyra in which the name of this Damasippus occurs (*C. I. G. G. S.* 3. No. 8) it appears that his statue at Amphiclea was set up in the reign of Septimius Severus or of Caracalla.

I visited the ruins of Amphiclea, 26th October 1895, and have described them from personal observation, except that I did not see the inscription referred to above. See also Clarke, *Travels*, 4. p. 227 *sq.*; Dodwell, *Tour*, 2. p. 134; Leake, *Northern Greece*, 2. p. 73 *sqq.*; Vischer, *Erinnerungen*, pp. 621, 625; Bursian, *Geogr.* 1. p. 162; Baedeker,⁹ p. 163.

33. 9. Herodotus ——called it Amphicaea. See Herodotus, viii. 33. The form Amphicaea is mentioned also by Stephanus Byzantius (*s.v.* ᾿Αμφίκαια).

33. 9. The natives tell the following tale etc. The following story is substantially identical with the legend told of Beth Gellert in Wales. Prince Llewellyn, it is said, had a favourite hound named Gellert. One day on coming home he went into the nursery where he had left his infant son. Here he met the hound dripping with blood and wagging his tail. But the cradle was overturned and no child was to be seen. Hastily concluding that the dog had devoured his son, he drew his sword and slew the dog. Then lifting up the cradle he found the child alive under it and the body of a dead wolf.

Then he perceived that his faithful dog had saved his child's life by killing the wolf. In great grief he buried the dog, and the place is still known as Beth Gellert or 'Gellert's Grave.' The Hon. W. R. Spencer, who put this story into verse in 1800, asserted that the tale was traditionary in a village at the foot of Snowdon. But Mr. Joseph Jacobs has shown that no trace of the tradition can be found in connexion with Beth Gellert before Spencer's time. The story occurs in the Sanscrit collection of tales called the *Panchatantra*, bk. v. Tale 2, where, however, the faithful animal is an ichneumon and the hostile animal a serpent. The *Panchatantra* is supposed to have been written not later than the fifth century A.D. Another version, in which the faithful animal is a mongoose and the noxious creature is a serpent, occurs in a Chinese Buddhist work called the *Vinaya Pitaka*, dating from 412 A.D. This Chinese book was translated from an Indian original, which was supposed to date from the time of Asoka's Council (say 230 B.C.). See Dr. S. Beal, in *Academy*, 4th November 1882, No. 548, p. 331. In the Middle Ages the story was diffused over Europe and the west of Asia in the collections of tales known as the *Fables of Bidpai*, the *Book of Sindibad*, *The Seven Sages*, and the *Gesta Romanorum*. In most or all of these European and West Asiatic versions the faithful animal is a dog and the hostile animal a serpent.

See Benfey, *Pantschatantra*, 1. p. 479 *sqq.*; *id.*, 2. p. 326 *sq.*; Dasent, *Popular Tales from the Norse*, p. xxvii. *sqq.*; Dunlop, *Geschichte der Prosadichtungen*, übertragen von F. Liebrecht, p. 198; Baring-Gould, *Curious Myths of the Middle Ages*, p. 134 *sqq.*; *The Gentleman's Magazine Library*, edited by G. L. Gomme, *English Traditional Lore*, p. 99; *Sindban oder die Sieben Weisen Meister*, syrisch und deutsch von F. Baethgen, p. 26; W. A. Clouston, *Popular Tales and Fictions*, 2. pp. 166-186; Joseph Jacobs, *Celtic Fairy Tales*, pp. 192 *sqq.*, 259 *sqq.*

The Greek version of the story, given in the present chapter by Pausanias, is older than the Chinese and Sanscrit versions by more than two centuries, and is in fact the oldest of all the extant versions. Yet it appears to have been overlooked by all the scholars who treated of the subject from Dunlop and Benfey down to Messrs. Clouston and Jacobs. The first to point to it in print was Mr. E. S. Hartland, in *Folklore*, 3 (1892), p. 127 *sqq.* To the versions already indicated I may add (1) a Malay version, in which the faithful animal is a tame bear and the hostile creature is a tiger; see *Journal of the Straits Branch of the Royal Asiatic Society*, No. 7 (June 1881), p. 23; and (2) a Sinhalese version, in which the faithful animal is a mongoose and the hostile animal is a cobra; see *Panjab Notes and Queries*, 3 (1886), p. 148, No. 619.

33. 11. **He communicates cures —— in dreams.** Cp. notes on ii. 27. 3; x. 32. 13. The *Sacred Speeches* (ἱεροὶ λόγοι) of the rhetorician Aristides contain many examples of remedies prescribed by the gods in dreams.

33. 12. **Tithronium.** In the plain, about an hour's ride to the north of *Dadi*, on the further side of the Cephisus, are the remains of an ancient city now known as *Moulki*. They are immediately below the ruined village of *Vertzana*, and occupy an oblong elevation beside

the river of *Dernitsa*, which, descending from a village of that name situated among the hills on the northern side of the valley of the Cephisus, runs in a clear and rapid stream at the foot of some low but precipitous rocks. The town was defended on three sides by the steep rocky banks of the river. The walls are much dilapidated, but seem to have been built in the quadrangular style. Here Dodwell found a fine circular foundation regularly constructed of large blocks, with some fragments of Doric columns 2 ft. 3 in. in diameter. The ruins were identified by Leake as those of Tithronium, and this identification has since been confirmed by the discovery at this place of two inscriptions. One of them records decrees of the citizens of Tithronium in honour of two men who had deserved well of the city (*C. I. G. G. S.* 3. Nos. 222, 223; Collitz, *G. D. I.* 2. No. 1552). This inscription, carved on a block of blue marble, is now built into a house at *Dadi*. The other inscription, carved on a block of limestone, records that the city of Tithronium set up a statue of the emperor Caracalla (*C. I. G. G. S.* 3. No. 224). Tithronium was burnt by the Persians, as we learn from Herodotus (viii. 33), who names it Tethronium. In the inscriptions the place is called "the city of the Teithronians" (ἡ πόλις τῶν Τειθρωνίων). See Dodwell, *Tour*, 2. p. 136; Gell, *Itinerary of Greece* (London, 1819), p. 211; Leake, *Northern Greece*, 2. pp. 76, 86 *sq.*; Bursian, *Geogr.* 1. p. 162; M. Beaudouin, in *Bulletin de Corresp. hellénique*, 5 (1881), pp. 440-444 (the inscriptions).

33. 12. **Drymaea.** The ruins of Drymaea lie on the southern face of a hill, neither high nor steep, which projects somewhat into the plain from the chain of hills that bounds the broad valley of the Cephisus on the north. The place is about a mile to the south-west of the village of *Glounista* and about 5 miles to the north-west of *Dadi* (Amphiclea). The fortification-wall, flanked with square towers, is remarkably well preserved. It ascends the western side of the hill, runs for a short distance along the summit on the north, and then descends to the plain on the east. In the whole of this circuit, with exceptions not worth noticing, the wall has from one to eight courses of masonry standing. But it is best preserved on the west, especially towards the foot of the hill, where it is often from 6 to 12 or 14 feet high, with from three to eight courses of masonry. The masonry is on the whole ashlar, the blocks being squared and laid in horizontal courses, though the style is not perfectly regular. Many of the blocks are very large. One in the eastern wall is 4 feet high and more than 10 feet long. Sixteen square towers project from the circuit-wall; some of them are ruinous, but three on the west side and one on the east are about 27 feet high, with from thirteen to fifteen courses of masonry. They are from 21 to 23 ft. 6 in. broad and project about 9 feet from the curtain. One of the towers in the north wall has been built or repaired in mediaeval or modern times; and at one point at least the north wall itself has obviously been repaired at a later time, the core consisting of small stones and mortar. The material of which the ancient fortifications are built is a pebble conglomerate (breccia), which by exposure to the air assumes

a grey uniform appearance like that of limestone, for which I at first mistook it.

So much for the remains of the circuit-wall on the hill. Whether the circuit was completed by a southern wall running along the foot of the hill and joining the eastern and western walls, may be doubted. There are at present few or no traces of such a wall, although towards the western end some blocks lie in a row at the foot of the hill, and many more squared blocks are lying about. It is possible, however, that no wall existed here, and that the eastern and western walls, after descending the hill, were prolonged into the plain and joined by a south wall there, not at the foot of the hill. Certainly the town seems to have extended into the plain, if we may judge from the mass of common red pottery strewn about the level ground as well as from some scattered hewn blocks. For example, on a sort of platform a little way from the southern foot of the hill I observed some blocks standing at intervals as if they had formed part of a building, possibly of a temple.

The upper part of the hill was cut off from the lower and converted into a citadel by an inner wall, flanked with towers, which extends across the slope from east to west, abutting on the circuit-wall at both ends. This inner wall, of which there are considerable remains, is clearly ancient, though it has been repaired in mediaeval or modern times. Some of the original masonry is very fine, the blocks being large and massive. Two, three, and four courses are standing, and in one place at least the wall is over 6 feet high. Three towers, more or less ruinous, project from the wall. Their dimensions seem to have corresponded to those of the towers in the circuit-wall. The best preserved of the three is 22 ft. 8 in. wide, projects about 9 feet from the curtain, and has four courses of masonry standing. Another has three courses standing and projects about 9 feet from the wall. Common red pottery lies strewn about the citadel as well as the ground at the foot of the hill.

That the ruins which have just been described are those of Drymaea is made nearly certain by an inscription built into the church of St. John in the neighbouring village of *Glounista* (*C. I. G. G. S.* 3. Nos. 226-230). The inscription, carved on a block of bluish marble, refers to money which the people of Drymaea borrowed from the Oetaeans and which they seem to have had some difficulty in repaying. By a comparison with Delphic inscriptions the document may be dated shortly after 170 B.C. Another inscription at the same church records a dedication to Aesculapius by a certain Damocrates, son of Calliteles (*C. I. G. G. S.* 3. No. 231).

Drymaea was one of the Phocian cities which were burnt by the Persians (Herodotus, viii. 33); it is called Drymus by Herodotus (*l.c.*).

See Dodwell, *Tour*, 2. p. 135 *sq.* ; Leake, *Northern Greece*, 2. pp. 73, 87 *sq.* ; Bursian, *Geogr.* 1. p. 162. I visited Drymaea, 25th October 1895, and have described the ruins from personal observation. But I did not see the inscription at *Glounista*. It is published by M. Beaudouin, in *Bulletin de Corresp. hellénique*, 5 (1881), pp. 137-145, and by Fr. Bechtel, in Collitz's *G. D. I.* 2. No. 1529.

33. 12. **eighty furlongs.** See Critical Note on this passage, vol. 1. p. 612.

33. 12. **Naubolenses.** This name (Ναυβολεῖς) seems not to be mentioned by any other ancient writer.

34. 1. **Elatea.** The scattered and insignificant ruins of Elatea lie about a mile and a half or two miles to the north-east of *Drachmani*, a large village near the foot of the hills which bound the valley of the Cephisus on the north. The site of Elatea, now a bare hill-side, is substantially the lower slope of these hills, which are low and naked, with a crest of rocks running along their brows. But towards its eastern end the highest part of the site is separated by a hollow, perhaps 100 feet deep, from the upper slope of the hills, so that it forms a little flat-topped hill or plateau by itself on the hill-side. This low flat-topped eminence (for it hardly deserves to be called a hill) seems to have been the ancient acropolis. It is defended on all sides by slopes, of which those to the north (down into the hollow already mentioned) and to the east are the steepest. The slope to the south is longer but more gradual. The line of the ancient fortification-wall may be traced, chiefly by isolated blocks, along the northern brow of the plateau, which faces across the hollow to the higher rock-crested hills on the north. On this brow, towards its western end, a piece of the wall is standing for a length of about 20 yards or so, with two courses of stones ; it is 6 feet high at the most. The masonry is of the rough polygonal sort, almost indeed Cyclopean. The blocks are hardly hewn, and some of them are large ; one which I measured is more than 6 feet long by 3 feet high. On the northern edge of the plateau a small knoll, partly perhaps artificial, forms the summit of the whole site. The remains of a quadrangular building, probably a tower, may be observed on this knoll ; the building seems to have measured about 8 paces from east to west by perhaps 20 paces from north to south. On the west side the foundations are visible, two courses high. The masonry, like the stone, is rough. Some blocks of the wall, not merely of the foundations, are in position on the eastern side. From this square tower, if tower it was, a line of wall may be traced running south for a few yards, then turning eastward so as to meet the steep slope of the plateau on that side. The small enclosure so formed may have been an inner fortress or keep within the acropolis. At its south-western corner there are some vestiges of a square projecting tower. On the south face of the plateau and a little way below its crest, outside of the keep, there are more remains of the fortification-wall built in the same rude almost Cyclopean style as on the northern brow of the plateau. The remains extend for some yards, and consist of one and two courses to the west, with some isolated blocks further to the east.

Below this insignificant acropolis the ground descends southwards to the plain in a long and gentle slope. This was the site of the lower city, a few scanty remains of which may be seen scattered at various points. Some of them have been brought to light by excavations. On the east the site is bounded by a glen, neither deep nor picturesque, up which the path goes to the temple of Cranaean Athena (see below, p. 431). Near the entrance to the glen, a little to the east of the acropolis, was the site of the village of *Lefta*. The village has long been deserted ;

all that remains of it are some trifling vestiges of houses and a quantity of broken stones and pottery littering the earthy slope of the hills. Part of the site was being ploughed and sown when I visited it. The plough was drawn by two slow-paced oxen, and behind it walked the sower scattering the seed broadcast from a bag. Later in the day, on my return from the temple, a flock of goats was dispersed about the site of the deserted village, seeking what nourishment they could find on the stony ground. Some slight remains of antiquity in this neighbourhood seem to show that Elatea extended thus far to the east. A chapel of St. George is still standing here, and built into its walls are some squared blocks, which may perhaps be ancient. Outside of the chapel lies a piece of a column, and a little higher up the hill-side I observed another piece of a small unfluted column, 17 inches in diameter. The chapel perhaps occupies the site of the temple of Aesculapius mentioned by Pausanias (§ 6), for built into one of the jambs of the doorway is a long inscription relating to the dedication of slaves to Aesculapius (*C. I. G. G. S.* 3. Nos. 120-127; Collitz, *G. D. I.* 2. No. 1532). A little lower down than the chapel there are some squared blocks on a knoll.

A good way to the south-west of the chapel of St. George another chapel, dedicated to St. Athanasius or to St. Theodore,[1] rises solitary from the bare hill-side. This chapel, distant thirty-five minutes' walk to the north-east of *Drachmani*, seems to occupy approximately the middle of the site of Elatea. Some remains of antiquity, including large hewn blocks, a piece of a column 6 ft. 7 in. long, and several fragments of small columns, lie outside of the chapel. Here, too, a head of a serpent made of red terra-cotta, was found by Mr. P. Paris ; it probably represented one of the sacred serpents of Aesculapius and was dedicated in his temple. On the hill-side for a great way round about the chapel isolated blocks may be seen protruding at irregular intervals from the soil ; and the ground is littered with broken stones. Here and there in the wide area some slight excavations have been made, perhaps by Mr. P. Paris, who spent some time here and has written a monograph on Elatea ; but the results of these excavations seem to have been exceedingly scanty. About 150 yards or so to the north-east of the chapel of St. Athanasius the diggings have laid bare a foundation-wall 27 paces long, running east and west ; one and two courses of the wall are standing. A few yards further up the hill some blocks of a wall are in position ; and still further up are traces of a foundation-wall extending, with gaps, for 26 paces from east to west. These may be the remains of a temple. Apparently a chapel of the Panagia stood formerly on or near this spot, and here Mr. Paris found a mutilated inscription which seems to have recorded a dedication to Aesculapius and Health (*C. I. G. G. S.* 3. No. 136). This, taken with the remains of the foundation-wall, raises a presumption that the temple of Aesculapius was here rather than on the site of the chapel of St. George at *Lefta*.

---

[1] According to Mr. P. Paris the chapel is dedicated to St. Theodore. But St. Athanasius was the name given to me on the spot in 1895. The chapel may perhaps have changed its patron saint between Mr. Paris's visit and mine.

A few hundred yards to the west of the chapel of St. Athanasius a number of ancient hewn blocks are scattered about, some of them in their original positions; amongst them is a worn capital of a column, 3 ft. 3 in. in diameter. From the curve of several of the blocks it would seem that a circular or semicircular building stood here. It was here perhaps that Mr. Paris excavated a large semicircular wall built of eight parallel courses of common stone, the blocks being large and accurately jointed. The convex side of the wall was turned to the hill, the concave side to the plain ; and in front of the wall were three drums of fluted columns laid end to end so as to form a chord of the semicircle. Mr. Paris conjectures that the semicircular building was one of a series of *exedras* or monumental seats which may have lined the road up to the acropolis. With the exception of the few blocks I have mentioned I did not see the building described by Mr. Paris ; its remains may now be usefully employed in the neighbouring village of *Drachmani*. About half a mile or so to the south-west of the chapel of St. Athanasius another excavation has laid bare a number of squared ancient blocks and some trifling vestiges of foundation-walls. A small quadrangular building may have stood here. A little to the west of these remains five or six massive blocks of a foundation-wall are exposed, forming a line which runs from south-east to north-west. Besides the chapel of St. Athanasius almost the only object which now breaks the monotony of the bleak hill-side is a group of large rocks, in which a fig-tree has rooted itself, about halfway between the chapel and the acropolis. The distance between the chapel and the acropolis may be about half a mile. Towards the south-eastern end of the site the path which leads from *Drachmani* to the temple of Cranaean Athena runs for some way along the edge of a plateau raised only a few feet above the plain. The slope is so regular that it must be artificial. The city-wall may have been built along its upper edge.

From the acropolis of Elatea there is a grand view across the broad valley to Parnassus and the still higher mountains of Locris extending in an unbroken line from the south far away into the west. On the south-east the outlying masses of Helicon are seen rising over the nearer hills. Here too is visible the gap in the hills through which the Cephisus flows from Phocis into Boeotia, and through which Philip of Macedon, after capturing Elatea, marched to meet the Greeks at Chaeronea. The battlefield is just beyond these low hills. It is a mistake, however, to suppose that the chief pass from Thermopylae and Northern Greece ends at Elatea. On the contrary the hills rise steeply behind the site of the ancient city ; a mere footpath leads up the small glen on the eastern side of Elatea, and the glen is far too narrow and rugged ever to have been a military highway. The real pass, by which the carriage-road now goes to *Atalanti* and Thermopylae, is through a natural opening in the hills about 4 miles to the east of Elatea. It was probably by this pass that Philip marched into Phocis. If so, after debouching on the valley of the Cephisus he must have made a detour of 4 miles to the west to seize Elatea, before pursuing his march southward into Boeotia. Strabo, indeed, says (ix. p. 418) that Elatea was strategically the most important city in Phocis "because it stands on the pass, and he who possesses Elatea commands the entrances into Phocis and Boeotia." But Strabo knew little or nothing of the interior of Greece at first hand. He probably had in his mind Demosthenes's famous picture of the consternation that spread like wildfire through Athens one evening when a courier came in with news that Philip had seized Elatea (*De corona*, p. 284 *sq.*). The alarm was fully justified, for the capture of Elatea meant that Philip had gained a footing in Greece and that no serious natural obstacle now barred his road to Athens. But Demosthenes does not say that Elatea was at the mouth of the pass ; and even if he had said so, it would not have been true.

See Dodwell, *Tour*, 2. p. 139 *sqq.* ; Gell, *Itinerary of Greece* (London, 1819), p. 216 *sq.* ; Leake, *Northern Greece*, 2. p. 82 *sq.* ; Pouqueville, *Voyage de la Grèce*, 4. p. 146 *sq.* ; L. Stephani, *Reise*, p. 61 *sq.* ; Vischer, *Erinnerungen*, p. 626 ; Bursian, *Geogr.* 1. p. 163 ; Baedeker,[3] p. 203 ; *Guide-Joanne*, 2. p. 48 *sq.* ; P. Paris, *Élatée* (Paris, 1892). The inscriptions of Élatea have been published by Mr. Paris in *Bulletin de Corresp. hellénique*, 10 (1886), pp. 356-385, as well as in his monograph. I was at *Drachmani* 27th-29th October 1895, and visited Elatea on the 28th. I have described the situation and ruins as I saw them, except that I did not see the inscription in the chapel of St. George at *Lefta*. Mr. Paris is mistaken in affirming (p. 46) that of the walls of the acropolis only two stones are left. By a curious inadvertence he has shifted round the points of the compass by 90°, so that in his plans as well as in the text the north is called the east, and the west figures as the north, and so *mutatis mutandis* all round the compass.

Inscriptions attest the worship of the Dioscuri, Poseidon, Zeus the Averter, and Apollo at Elatea (*C. I. G. G. S.* 3. Nos. 129, 130, 134, 135) ; and from the same source we learn that the Elateans set up a statue of Faustus Cornelius Sulla, son of the dictator, and statues of the emperors Hadrian and Caracalla (*C. I. G. G. S.* 3. Nos. 143, 144, 145). The necropolis of Elatea lies on the slope of the hills to the north-west, beyond the bed of a torrent which bounds the site on the west. The graves, consisting of rectangular holes cut in the rock, had been already opened and plundered by the peasants before Mr. Paris examined them. See his work, *Élatée*, p. 47 *sq.*

In the ruined chapel of the Panagia Mr. Paris found a large block of grey marble bearing a late Greek inscription to the following effect : " This is the stone from Cana of Galilee where our Lord Jesus Christ made the water into wine." This stone has been transferred to Athens, where it is preserved in the small Metropolitan church. See Ch. Diehl, ' La pierre de Cana,' *Bulletin de Corresp. hellénique*, 9 (1885), pp. 28-42 ; P. Paris, *Élatée*, pp. 299-312.

34. 1. next to Delphi, the largest city in Phocis. According to Strabo (ix. pp. 407, 417 *sq.*, 424) Elatea was the largest city in Phocis, larger than Delphi. The relative sizes of the two cities may have altered between the time of Strabo and the time of Pausanias. Harpocration, Suidas, and Stephanus Byzantius (*s.v.* Ἐλάτεια) also speak of Elatea as the largest city in Phocis.

34. 1. the distance by road is one hundred and eighty furlongs.

There seems to be a mistake here, for the direct distance between Elatea and the ruins of Amphiclea at *Dadi* is only about 11 miles. The journey occupies about three hours and forty minutes (Dodwell, *Tour*, 2. p. 140). Otherwise Pausanias's description of the situation of Elatea relatively to Amphiclea is quite correct. Amphiclea lies due west of Elatea at the foot of the mountains on the opposite side of the great Cephisian valley, and the ground between them is level, till it begins to slope gently up as you approach Elatea. Cp. Leake, *Northern Greece*, 2. p. 82.

34. 1. the birds that chiefly frequent its banks are the bustards. Leake observed immense numbers of bustards in the plains of Boeotia (*Northern Greece*, 2. p. 419).

34. 2. The Elateans succeeded in repulsing Cassander. Cp. i. 26. 3, x. 18. 7 ; Droysen, *Geschichte des Hellenismus*,[2] ii. 2. p. 241.

34. 2. contrived to baffle Taxilus. Cp. §§ 4 and 6, and i. 20. 6.

34. 2. they were Arcadians originally etc. Cp. vii. 15. 5 ; viii. 4. 4 ; viii. 48. 8. As to the expedition of the Phlegyans against Delphi, see also ix. 36. 2.

34. 3. Elatea —— burned by the Medes. Cp. Herodotus, viii. 33.

34. 3. Philip, son of Demetrius, terrified the populace etc. In 207 B.C., during his war with the Romans, Philip, king of Macedonia, occupied Elatea. See Livy, xxviii. 7.

34. 4. Titus, the Roman general etc. The siege and capture of Elatea in 198 B.C. by the Romans under Titus Quintius Flamininus is described by Livy (xxxii. 18, 19, and 24).

34. 5. The robber horde of the Costobocs, who overran Greece in my time etc. According to Ptolemy (iii. 8. 3) the Costobocs inhabited the north-western part of Dacia. But in another passage (iii. 5. 8) he reckons them among the tribes inhabiting Sarmatia to the east of the Vistula. There may have been two tribes of this name, or Ptolemy may have embodied two discrepant reports of one and the same tribe. Pliny (*Nat. hist.* vi. 19) includes the Costobocs among the Sarmatian tribes in the valley of the Tanais (the *Don*). The seat of the tribe is vaguely described by Ammianus Marcellinus (xxii. 8. 42). That their territory was outside the Roman province of Dacia is clear from a passage in Dio Cassius (lxxi. 12), who says that the Astingi attempted to settle in Dacia ; but failing in their intention they entrusted their wives and children to the safekeeping of Clement, the Roman governor of Dacia, and turned their arms against the Costobocs, purposing to take possession of their land ; they conquered the Costobocs, but even after the conquest they continued (says Dio) to molest Dacia as much as before. We may perhaps infer that the land of the Costobocs was to the north of Dacia, possibly in northern Hungary. Cp. K. Müllenhoff, *Deutsche Altertumskunde*, 2. p. 83 *sqq.* The raid of the Costobocs into Greece is recorded by no ancient writer except Pausanias, but it seems to be referred to in a Latin inscription found at Rome, which mentions that a certain Julianus had commanded a troop in Greece, Macedonia, and Spain against the Costobocs and the rebel Moors, and also in the time of the German and Sarmatian war. See *Archäolog. epigraph.*

Mittheilungen aus Oesterreich-Ungarn, 13 (1890), p. 189. (The invasion
of Spain by the Moors in the reign of Marcus Antoninus is mentioned
by Capitolinus, *Marcus Antoninus*, 21 ; cp. Spartianus, *Severus*, 2.)
The date of the inroad cannot be fixed precisely. It must have been
after 161 A.D., for in that year Mnesibulus, the Greek general who fell
in the battle with the barbarians, won an Olympic victory (see Pausanias
below). We learn from Capitolinus (*Marcus Antoninus*, 22) that the
Costobocs sided with the great confederacy of German and Sarmatian
tribes which made war on the Roman empire in the reign of Marcus
Antoninus. Hence we may suppose that the marauding expedition of the
Costobocs took place in the course of that war, that is, probably, somewhere between 166 and 180 A.D. (see note on viii. 43. 6). It has been
suggested with some probability that the immediate occasion of the
incursion was the attack of the Astingi (see above) ; the Costobocs, it
has been supposed, being worsted in battle and dispossessed of their
lands, invaded Greece in the hope of winning a new home for themselves
there. The attack of the Astingi, as we learn from Dio, took place
when a certain Clement was governor of Dacia ; and from an inscription
found at Iglitza (see *Archäolog. epigraph. Mittheilungen aus Oesterreich-
Ungarn*, 11 (1887), p. 30 *sq.*) and a passage in Capitolinus (*Pertinax*, 2) Mr.
Heberdey has argued that Clement was governor of Dacia 170-175 A.D.
He supposes that the incursion of the Costobocs into Greece took place
about 176 A.D. But his arguments are not convincing.

The name of the tribe is spelt differently by our authorities. In
Pausanias and Capitolinus (*Marcus Antoninus*, 22) the name appears as
Costobocs (Κοστώβωκοι or Κοστωβῶκοι, *Costoboci*) ; in Dio Cassius
(lxxi. 12) as Κοστούβωκοι or Κοστουβῶκοι ; in Ptolemy (iii. 5. 9 ; iii.
8. 3) as Κοιστοβῶκοι ; in Pliny (*Nat. hist.* vi. 19) as *Cotobacchi ;* in
Ammianus Marcellinus (xxii. 8. 42) as *Costobocae ;* in the inscription
found at Rome (see above) as *Castabocae ;* while in another Latin
inscription (quoted by Müller on Ptolemy, iii. 5. 9) the adjectival form
Coistobocensis occurs.

See Hertzberg, *Geschichte Griechenlands unter der Herrschaft der Römer*, 2. p.
372 ; H. Schiller, *Gesch. der römischen Kaiserzeit*, 1. pp. 631, 644 ; W. Gurlitt,
Ueber Pausanias, p. 61 *sq.* ; Bencker, in *Fleckeisen's Jahrbücher*, 36 (1890), p. 375 ;
P. Paris, in *Bulletin de Corresp. hellénique*, 11 (1887), p. 342 *sqq.* ; *id., Élatée*,
p. 20 *sq.* ; R. Heberdey, ' Der Einfall der Kostober in Griechenland,' *Archäolog.
epigraph. Mittheilungen aus Oesterreich-Ungarn*, 13 (1890), pp. 186-191.

34. 5. Mnesibulus. At the temple of Cranaean Athena near
Elatea Mr. P. Paris found a tablet of grey marble bearing a mutilated
inscription which may perhaps be thus restored :

> Μνασίβου[λον
> Μνασιβού[λου
> δὶς περιο[δονί
> κου ἀρίστ[ου Ἑλ-
> λ]ήνων, [υἱὸν ἡ βουλὴ καὶ ὁ δῆμος Ἐλατέων].

"‹The Council and People of Elatea dedicated this statue of›
Mnasibulus, son of the Mnasibulus who was twice victorious at all

the great games and was the bravest of the Greeks." The Mnasibulus
whose statue seems to be referred to in this inscription was most
probably a son of the Greek captain who fell in the battle with the
Costobocs.   See P. Paris, in *Bulletin de Corresp. hellénique*, 11 (1887),
p. 342 *sqq.* ; *id.*, *Élatée*, pp. 21, 241 *sq.* ; *C. I. G. G. S.* 3. No. 146.

   34. 5. **the double race with the shield.**   See note on vi. 10. 4.

   34. 6. **a temple of Aesculapius.**   Some remains of the foundations
of this temple have perhaps been found at Elatea, a little to the north of
the chapel of St. Athanasius.   Or the temple may have stood in or near
the site now occupied by the chapel of St. George at *Lefta.*   See above,
p. 426.   The inscription relating to the sale of slaves to Aesculapius,
which is built into the chapel of St. George, makes mention of the
priest of Aesculapius (P. Paris, *Élatée*, p. 226, Inscr. 31-34, line 21 ;
C. I. G. G. S. 3. Nos. 121, 125).

   34. 6. **Timocles and Timarchides.**   See note on vi. 4. 5.

   34. 7. **a sanctuary of Cranaean Athena.**   The remains of the
sanctuary and temple of Athena are situated on the summit of a rocky
hill about two miles north-east of Elatea in a straight line.   From
Drachmani they are distant about three and a half miles ; but on account
of the ruggedness and steepness of the route the time taken from the
village to the temple is about one hour and forty minutes.   Proceeding
in a north-easterly direction we cross the last slopes of the hills, skirting
the southern and eastern sides of the site of Elatea and passing the site of
the deserted village of *Lefta.*   We then enter the glen which penetrates
the hills to the north-east of Elatea.   The glen is, in its lowest reach at
least, neither deep nor particularly picturesque.   The hills on both sides
are clothed with the low dark green bushes which are so common on
Greek mountains.   Ascending the western side of the glen a little way,
we cross the bed of the stream and strike up a little side glen which
comes down from the east.   The crossing of the brook, at the meeting
of the glens, is a pretty spot enough, with its flowing water, its rocks,
and its planes growing as bushes in the bed of the stream.   Through
the opening of the glen, too, there is a distant prospect of Parnassus.
After crossing the stream and ascending the little side glen for a short
way we begin to ascend the hill-side to the left or north ; and a path,
rather steeper than Pausanias's description of it would lead us to expect,
winding up the bushy slope brings us to the small level summit of the
hill, which is occupied by the sanctuary of Athena.   As we rise above the
glen, distant views of the mountains of Boeotia on the south-east open up
behind us.

   The situation of the temple, like that of so many ancient temples in
Greece, is remarkably fine.   Immediately to the south, across the broad
valley of the Cephisus, rises the towering many-peaked Parnassus.   To
the south-east, beyond the Cephisus, the low hills of Boeotia are seen,
range behind range, backed by Helicon, blue and distant, on the south.
Tame hills, overgrown with bushes, rise in the neighbourhood of the
temple on the north and east, shutting out the views in these directions.
A deep glen, winding into them, skirts the temple-hill on the north and
west.   It is the glen that we ascended from Elatea till we quitted it to

follow the shallower glen into which the temple-hill slopes away on the south.   Into this deep glen the hill descends in very steep rocky declivities on the north and west.   In the latter direction the summit of the hill runs out into a sharp rocky point or ridge, overgrown with bushes, which overhangs the ravine.

The top of the hill was probably levelled artificially to furnish a site for the temple.   At all events a platform, natural or artificial, is supported by a wall of which there are considerable remains on the south and east and scantier remains towards the east end of the north side. On the south and east the wall is preserved for a good many yards, perhaps 20 yards in each direction ; the two sections of it meet at the south-east angle.   Here eight courses of masonry are standing, and the height of the wall is 10 or 11 feet.   The blocks are not large, and the masonry is rough ; in style it is intermediate between the ashlar and the polygonal.   Holly-oak bushes grow out of the crevices of the eastern wall.   On the north side of the platform, towards its eastern end, the supporting-wall is about 6 feet high, with five courses.

The temple was built close to the northern edge of the hill.   Its remains, which were seen by Dodwell in 1805, were excavated under the direction of Mr. P. Paris, of the French Archaeological School, in 1883 and 1884.   Though somewhat scanty they suffice to prove that the temple was orientated east and west and surrounded by a Doric colonnade.   The lowest course of a wall which bounded the temple on the north is preserved for a length of 25 paces.   The wall is 4 ft. 7 in. thick, and is built of squared blocks of grey limestone on each face, the core being formed of small stones.   On the outer or northern face this wall is 2 ft. 2 in. high and rests on a foundation-wall, of which two courses, mostly built of blocks of a yellowish stone, quite different from the grey limestone of the upper wall, are visible on the outside.   On its inner side this north wall is in contact along its whole length with the stylobate of the temple, above which it rises 1 ft. 4 in.   Eight broken drums of columns are standing in position on the stylobate within an inch or so of the north wall.   Only five of these drums were found by Mr. Paris in their original positions ; the other three were set up by him where they now stand.   Stylobate and columns are made of the same yellowish friable stone as the foundations.   The grey limestone of which the north wall is built is native to the hill, where it crops up all round the temple.   The columns are of the Doric order with twenty flutes.   Their diameter at the height to which they are standing is about 2 ft. 7 in. The interval between them, measured between the exteriors of the columns, is 4 ft. 5½ in.   Close to the drums are lying two broken Doric capitals of the same material, with four rings round the neck; their diameter is about 3 feet.   The platform of masonry on which the temple rested is preserved in its full breadth (about 14 paces) at the west end. Mr. Paris thinks it probable that the temple had six columns on the two façades and thirteen columns at the sides, the columns at the corners being counted twice ; and he calculates that it was 27.5 metres (90 ft. 2 in.) long by 11.5 metres (37 ft. 8 in.) broad.   Of the upper part of the temple the only architectural fragments found by Mr. Paris were several

Doric capitals, pieces of mutulés with *guttae*, and a piece of a triglyph. The capitals belong to two different types, in one of which the *echinus* is straight and in the other curved. The *geison* or projecting cornice seems to have been adorned both at the sides and at the gable-ends of the temple with bands of painted terra-cotta, from which heads of lions, also made of terra-cotta, projected at intervals as gargoyles. Fragments of these terra-cottas, as well as ante-fixes of terra-cotta adorned with palmettes, were discovered by Mr. Paris. The lion-heads are executed in good style. This use of painted plaques of terra-cotta to cover the outer cornices of a building occurs, as we have seen (vol. 4. p. 70 *sq*), in the Treasury of Gela at Olympia, and it seems to have been commonly employed in the temples of Sicily and Magna Graecia. The temple of Cranaean Athena must further have been roofed with tiles of terra-cotta, for fragments of such tiles were found by Mr. Paris in thousands. This extensive employment of terra-cotta is held to be a mark of antiquity; for the custom of casing cornices with plaques of terra-cotta seems to date from a time when buildings were constructed of wood, and when consequently it was necessary to protect their most exposed parts from the weather. In later times, when temples were built of stone, such a casing was superfluous and ceased to be employed, and roof-tiles were then made of marble instead of terra-cotta. In dimensions as well as in the number of its external columns the temple of Cranaean Athena closely resembles the so-called Theseum at Athens (vol. 2. p. 150 *sqq.*); but Mr. Paris thinks that its proportions were somewhat heavier than those of the Theseum, from which he infers that the temple of Athena is the older of the two. Many votive offerings, most of them broken, were discovered by Mr. Paris in the course of his excavations. They comprise terra-cotta statuettes of women and animals, potsherds, a small bronze horse, a small bronze dolphin, a bronze duck, a bronze swan, bronze pins and brooches, etc. Amongst the inscriptions found on the site are some which serve to identify the ruins. Thus one mutilated inscription records that Lyseas (?) and Prima dedicated to Cranaean Athena a statue of their son Onesiphorus, who had been priest of the goddes (*C. I. G. G. S.* 3. No. 139). Another inscription, relating to the liberation of a slave, contains a provision that the deed shall be recorded in the sanctuary of Cranaean Athena (*C. I. G. G. S.* 3. No. 109). A third inscription, recording a decree of the Phocian confederacy, mentions that three copies of the decree were to be engraved on stone or metal and set up, one "in the sanctuary of Athena at Cranae," another in the market-place of Elatea, and the third at Delphi (*C. I. G. G. S.* 3. No. 97). This last inscription seems to prove that the epithet Cranaean applied to Athena was derived from the name of the place where her sanctuary was situated. Further, the name of the place (Cranae) appears to mean no more than 'springs,' and may be derived from a clear and copious spring which rises near the summit of the hill. Another inscription found at the sanctuary contains a treaty of alliance between the Phocians and Boeotians which seems to have been entered into about the beginning of the second century B.C. (*C. I. G. G. S.* 3. No. 98). The representatives of either side were to swear by King Zeus, Queen

Hera, Poseidon, and Athena, and all gods and goddesses to observe the terms of the treaty.

The entrance to the sacred precinct seems, as we should have expected from the nature of the ground, to have been from the south-west. Here close to the levelled summit of the hill is a piece of well-jointed polygonal masonry, 5 feet high. It is probably part of a wall which once lined the approach to the sacred precinct from the south. Towards the west end of the summit, where the hill runs out into the rocky ridge already mentioned, there are some ruinous remains of walls and a quantity of broken stones. Fragments of thick red pottery are plentifully strewed about the site to the east, south, and west of the temple. Some of the potsherds bear traces of pigments, red, brown, and yellow ; and some of them clearly belonged to large round-mouthed jars (see below, note on § 8).

On the slope of the hill to the south of the temple and only some 20 feet or so lower than it there is a terrace, along the eastern face of which traces of a wall may be perceived. Many broken stones are strewn about here, and beside the path is a piece of wall two courses high. Much further down the slope of the hill stand the ruins of a small chapel.

See Dodwell, *Tour*, 2. p. 141 *sq.* ; Gell, *Itinerary of Greece* (London, 1819), p. 217 *sq.* ; Lolling, in *Mittheil. d. arch. Inst. in Athen*, 3 (1878), p. 19 ; Baedeker,[3] p. 203 ; *Guide-Joanne*, 2. p. 49 ; P. Paris, in *Bulletin de Corresp. hellénique*, 11 (1887), pp. 39-63, 318-346, 405-444 ; *id.*, *ib.* 12 (1888), pp. 37-63 ; *id.*, *Élatée*, p. 73 *sqq.* In describing the sanctuary Mr. Paris has again mistaken the points of the compass. What he calls north is west ; what he calls east is south ; and so with the rest. But he seems not quite consistent in his mistake. I visited the temple 28th October 1895, and have described the situation and remains mainly from my own observation.

34. 7. colonnades with dwellings opening off them. In the precinct of the temple Mr. Paris found a fragmentary inscription (*C.I.G.G.S.* 3. No. 137) relating to the repair of one of these colonnades. See P. Paris, *Élatée*, pp. 90, 240. Inside the wall of the precinct and abutting on it H. G. Lolling observed the remains of a series of chambers side by side, like the cells in the cloisters of a monastery. He thought that these were the ruins of the dwellings which, as we here learn from Pausanias, were set apart for the ministers of the goddess. But they seem to have been mediaeval. See H. G. Lolling, in *Mittheil. d. arch. Inst. in Athen*, 3 (1878), p. 19 ; P. Paris, *Élatée*, p. 81 *sq.*

34. 8. They choose the priest from among boys etc. Among the inscriptions found by Mr. Paris in the precinct of Cranaean Athena is one already referred to (*C. I. G. G. S.* 3. No. 139), which records that a statue of one of these boy-priests had been dedicated by his parents to the goddess. The inscription, which is of Roman date, is somewhat mutilated, but the priest's name seems to have been Onesiphorus, and those of his parents Lyseas and Prima. It is carved on a large block of grey limestone, 3 feet long by 2 ft. 6 in. high, which, set up on its narrow edge, still stands at the eastern end of the temple. See *Bulletin de Corresp. hellénique*, 11 (1887), p. 318 ; P. Paris, *Élatée*, pp. 180 *sq.*, 241. As to the rule that the priest must be under the age of puberty, see note on vii. 24. 4 ; and for another instance of a boy-priest of Athena, see viii. 47. 3.

34. 8. bathes in tubs after the ancient fashion.   In the precinct of Cranaean Athena Mr. Paris found a number of fragments of large earthenware jars or basins, which he conjectures may have been the baths used by the boy-priests.   On the handle of one of the fragments is the inscription ΑΘΑΝΑΣ ΙΕΡΟΣ 'sacred to Athena,' and pieces of the same inscription have been found on other fragments.   See P. Paris, in *Bulletin de Corresp. hellénique*, 12 (1888), p. 39 *sqq.* ; *id., Élatée*, p. 181 *sqq.* ; *C. I. G. G. S.* 3. Nos. 149-159.   In Homer (*Od.* iv. 128) we hear of silver bathing-tubs (ἀσάμινθοι, the word here used by Pausanias) ; and in another passage (*Od.* iv. 48) Homer speaks of "well polished bathing-tubs," from which we might infer that the tubs were of metal.   But Mr. Helbig thinks that they may have been of earthenware.   See W. Helbig, *Das homerische Epos aus den Denkmälern erläutert,*[2] p. 123 *sq.*   A piece of an earthenware bath-tub was found in the palace at Tiryns (see vol. 3. p. 225).

34. 8. The image is another work of the sons of Polycles etc. On coins of Elatea of the third or second century B.C. Athena is represented armed ; on one coin she is portrayed stand-ing, on another (Fig. 17) she is charging to the right with spear advanced and the shield on her left arm ; her skirt flutters behind her.   The latter may have been the attitude of the statue here described by Pausanias.   The coin is perhaps older than the statue (see note on vi. 4. 5, vol. 4. p. 12 *sqq.*) ; but if so, the sons of Polycles may have modelled the statue on a traditional type of Athena current at Elatea.   See Imhoof-Blumer and Gardner, *Num.*

FIG. 17.—ATHENA (COIN OF ELATEA).

Comm. on Paus. p. 124, pl. Y xv. xvi. ; Head, *Historia Numorum*, p. 290 ; Müller-Wieseler, *Denkmäler*, 2. pl. xx. No. 214 b.   Among the ruins of the sanctuary of Cranaean Athena Mr. Paris found a few fragments of a statue larger than life-size.   Three of them, being put together, represent the folds of a woman's skirt streaming backwards on the wind or in rapid motion.   The piece of the robe extends from below the knees to the ground and is about 3 feet high.   From the colossal size of the statue to which these fragments must have belonged, and from their agreement with the charging Athena on the coin, Mr. Paris is probably right in concluding that we have here a portion of the temple-statue described by Pausanias.   See P. Paris, *Élatée*, p. 121 *sqq.*   I observed some of the fragments of the marble drapery on my visit to the temple in October 1895.   One block, about 3 ft. 4 in. in diameter but split in two, represents the lowest part of the drapery, where it touches the ground.   The folds are deeply cut and undercut ; one of them is 13 inches deep.   In another block, measuring 23 inches in height by about 2 feet in breadth, there is a fold 9 inches deep.   The marble is white and of a large grain, resembling Parian rather than Pentelic.   The pieces are clearly being smashed, as appears from the number and the fresh and glistering appearance of the marble splinters lying about.

The sons of Polycles, the sculptors who made the statue, were

Timocles and Timarchides, the same artists who made the statue of Aesculapius for the neighbouring city of Elatea. At the sanctuary of Cranaean Athena Mr. Paris found a marble block (apparently part of the base of a statue) inscribed with the name of Polycles son of Tim<archides>. The Polycles of this inscription was probably a son of the Timarchides who, jointly with his brother Timocles, made the statue of Cranaean Athena. See P. Paris, *Élatée*, p. 125 *sqq.*; Loewy, *Inschriften griech. Bildhauer*, p. 393, No. 241a; *C. I. G. G. S.* 3. No. 141; and the note on vi. 4. 5 already referred to.

34. 8. the reliefs on the shield of the Virgin etc. See i. 17. 2 note.

35. 1. Abae. From Elatea Pausanias proceeds eastward to Abae, which stood in a side valley opening into the great valley of the Cephisus on the eastern side of the latter, a little way to the north of the narrow defile through which the Cephisus passes from Phocis into Boeotia. The distance from Elatea is about 9 miles in a bee-line ; but on account of the detour to the south which it is necessary to make, the journey between the two places occupies about three and a half hours. From *Drachmani* (near Elatea) the route goes south-eastward across the dead flat of the Cephisian plain. In about 1 hour and 20 minutes we cross the highroad to *Atalanti* and Thermopylae, which runs in a straight line northeastward, rising up to a dip in the hills. Beyond the line of this highroad to the east the plain contracts greatly ; low bare rounded hills rise on either hand, to the north and south, at no great interval. Here the route passes close to a village where there are some large threshing-floors, and almost immediately beyond the village it crosses a river [1] by a bridge from the right to the left bank. The water of the river is clear ; water-plants grow in it, and some of it is diverted to turn a mill, which we pass a few minutes after crossing the bridge. After this the path leads along a stony hillside in an easterly direction. A small ruined chapel is passed in about two and a half hours from *Drachmani*. We then enter on the tolerably wide and open valley of Hyampolis, up which our route leads in a north-easterly direction. The ruins of Abae occupy the summit of a sharp-pointed hill that rises on the eastern side of the valley, from which, however, it is divided by a lower hog-backed hill. The remains of Hyampolis lie in the valley at a distance of only about a mile to the north-west of Abae.

The hill of Abae is a nearly isolated rocky hill rising in a sharp point to a height of perhaps 800 feet above the valley. The top is small and rocky, and grey rugged rocks crop up all over the steep sides of the hill. So steep and in part precipitous is the hill on the east that fortifications seem to have been omitted on this side. On the other hand it is defended, not very far below its summit, by two fortification-walls, one above the other, on the western and southern sides. The

---

[1] At the time I took this river to be the Cephisus, but probably it was a tributary of that river, flowing into it from the north. Had it been the Cephisus, we must have previously crossed it from the left to the right bank, and I have no note or recollection of having done so. The river was probably the one called *Kineta* on the French map.

narrow northern face of the hill has no wall running along it, but a wall ascends the slope on this side meeting the lower of the two circuit-walls (if they may be called so) at the north-western corner of the hill. From the point where these two walls meet, the upper circuit-wall begins, rises up the hill in a southerly direction, runs along its western face a little way below the summit, then bends round at an angle and descends in a south-easterly direction to the south-east side of the hill, where it stops on the edge of precipices that render fortification needless. The lower circuit-wall, from the point where the upper circuit-wall diverges from it at the north-western corner of the hill, follows in general the same directions as the upper wall, running along first the western and then the southern face of the hill, and ending at the south-east corner, above the same line of precipices though a little lower down than the upper wall. The accompanying rough sketch-plan (Fig. 18) will explain the positions of the walls. But it should be understood that the summit of the hill enclosed by the walls is not a tableland. On the contrary it descends in unbroken slopes on all sides from the very small top, so that the fortification-walls are built along the slopes of the hill, not along the edges of a plateau. The walls are on the whole ruinous, but many isolated pieces are standing to heights varying from 5 to over 9 feet. The masonry is of the fine polygonal sort.

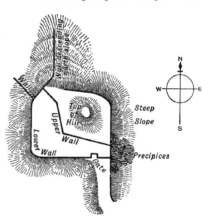

FIG. 18.—PLAN OF RUINS OF ABAE.

The blocks, many of which are of great size, are hewn into a great variety of shapes, fitted neatly together, and smoothed on their outer faces. So large are they that in some places two of them suffice to give the wall a height of 6 feet and more. On the whole the lower wall is built of larger blocks than the upper and is better preserved; for whereas the upper wall is nowhere (I think) more than 6 feet high, the lower is often from 7 to 9 feet high. Contrary to the usual practice, the walls seem not to have been flanked with towers except at the southern gateway. But on the other hand the outer wall makes several salient angles which project from 3 feet to 4 ft. 3 in. from the curtain. The wall which descends the northern slope of the hill towards a projecting rocky spur is very ruinous; great masses of tumbled blocks and broken stones lie along its face. In general it is standing to a height of only one or two blocks (the masonry being strictly polygonal we can hardly speak of courses); but in a good many places it is preserved for short stretches to a greater height. Still more ruinous is a wall which descends the hill from the lower circuit-wall in a north-westerly direction. It is traceable for a short way, but only in the form of a heap of broken stones, except just at the point where it starts from the circuit-wall. Here, though composed of only two blocks, it is 8 feet high ; one of the blocks is over 5 feet high.

The main approach to Abae was evidently from the south, for here the hill is connected by a saddle with lower hills, so that the ascent to it on this side was easiest and most gradual. Here, accordingly, in the outer circuit-wall, close to the south-eastern corner of the fortified enclosure, we find the principal gateway, which, though partly buried under the soil, is still in very good preservation. The gateway faces south, and only a short piece of wall intervenes between

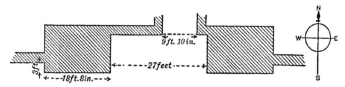

FIG. 19.—PLAN OF GATEWAY AT ABAE.

it and the precipices which here bound the hill on the east. The present width of the gateway at the level of the ground is 9 ft. 10 in., but the opening is narrowed towards the top by stones which project on each side. The lintel is still in its place over the gateway. It is a single block of stone 8 feet long, 3 ft. 8 in. wide, and about 1 ft. 7 in. high. Owing to the accumulation of soil the clear height of the gateway is only about 5 feet, but the wall at its side is about 9 feet high. The gateway is set back from the line of the circuit-wall and is flanked on each side by a tower. These towers, however, are not at equal distances from the gate, the eastern tower being much nearer to it than the western. The distance between the towers is about 27 feet. The western tower, which is much the better preserved of the two, is 18 ft. 8 in. broad on its face and 9 feet high. On its western side it projects 3 feet from the wall, which is here about 9 feet high. The blocks of which it is built are polygonal, of immense size, and well fitted together. There is also a small gateway about 5 feet wide, unflanked with towers, in the western outer wall, and nearly opposite to it is a doorway about 3 ft. 6 in. wide in the inner (upper) wall. Within the walls at the south-eastern corner of the hill there is some broken pottery.

The small rocky peak of the hill commands fine views of Parnassus on the west, Helicon on the south, and the more distant mountains of Boeotia to the east. To the north-west is seen the acropolis of Hyampolis lying low down in the valley, about a mile or so away.

At the northern foot of the neighbour hill of Abae on the west many tombs seem to have been excavated in recent times. Here then was the necropolis of Abae, or perhaps of Hyampolis.

I visited Abae from *Belesi* 30th October 1895, and have described the situation and remains from personal observation. See also Gell, *Itinerary of Greece*

(London, 1819), p. 225 *sq.* ; Leake, *Northern Greece*, 2. p. 163 *sqq.* ; Vischer, *Erinnerungen*, p. 627 *sq.* ; Bursian, *Geogr.* 1. p. 165 *sq.* ; Baedeker,[3] p. 201 *sq.* ; *Guide-Joanne*, 2. p. 48; V. W. Yorke, in *Journal of Hellenic Studies*, 16 (1896), pp. 294-296. According to Mr. Yorke the height of the hill is about 500 feet.

The route from Orchomenus to Abae, which Pausanias mentions, was traversed by Col. Leake, who thus describes it : "This forenoon, having quitted the monastery of *Skripou*, I cross the north-eastern angle of the ancient city, and at 10.58 begin to pass by a narrow paved road, between the foot of the upper cliffs which formed the northern boundary of the city and the summit of the lower, which immediately overhang the principal source of the Melas, or that which joins the Cephissus. . . . At 11.9, we quit the lower range of cliffs, the higher still overhanging the road, and soon afterwards begin to descend the rugged side of the mountain, by a most perilous path. At 11.33, having arrived at the foot of the hill, we enter a plain on the north-eastern side of Mount Acontium, bounded eastward by the marshes of the Melas, and pursue the borders of the marsh to *Tzamali*, a small collection of huts on the brink, where we arrive at 11.45. . . . At *Tzamali* we quit the *Topolia* road and turn to the left to the head of the plain ; at 11.55 leave to the right that which conducts to the places lying between the northern shore of the Cephissis [Copaic Lake] and the Euboic frith, and at 12.11, arriving at the western extremity of the plain of Aspledon, ascend some rugged hills which connect Mount Acontium with the peak now called *Chlomo*. At 12.35, at the head of the ascent, we enter upon a plain which, interrupted by some small heights, reaches to the northern side of Mount Acontium, and is connected in the opposite direction with a hollow which slopes to *Choubavo*, *Belissi*, and the *Stena* of the Cephissus. At 12.45 we halt till 1.24 at a fountain to dine ; and after a rugged descent, arrive at 1.40 at *Exarcho*, a village of thirty houses, in a spot where two narrow valleys meet, which rise from hence towards two summits of the ridge of *Chlomo*. The northern is the largest, and is in great part cultivated" (*Northern Greece*, 2. pp. 161-163). A little to the west of *Exarcho* and in full view of the village rises the hill of Abae. As to the route from Orchomenus to Abae, see also Baedeker,[3] p. 201 *sq.* ; *Guide-Joanne*, 2. p. 48. An inscription built into the outer wall of the church of St. George at *Exarcho* records that a certain Crinolaus, "having been priest, dedicated the portal, the colonnades, and the houses to Serapis, Isis, and Anubis as a thank-offering" (*Bulletin de Corresp. hellénique*, 5 (1881), p. 449 *sq.*; Collitz, *G. D. I.* 2. No. 1535 ; *C. I. G. G. S.* 3. No. 89). The inscription seems to have been brought from Hyampolis. Cp. below, p. 445.

35. 1. **they came to Phocis from Argos.** According to Aristotle, cited by Strabo (x. p. 445), Abae was at one time occupied by Thracians, who thence colonised Euboea.

35. 1. **an oracle of Apollo.** The oracle of Apollo at Abae, according to Stephanus Byzantius (*s.v.* "Αβαι), was older than that at Delphi. It was consulted by Croesus (Herodotus, i. 46), Mardonius (*id.* viii. 134), and by the Thebans before the battle of Leuctra (Paus. iv. 32. 5). It is mentioned by Sophocles (*Oedipus Rex*, 900).

35. 2. the army of Xerxes burned down the very sanctuary.
Herodotus tells us that when the sanctuary was burnt down by the
Persians it was wealthy and full of treasures and votive offerings, which
the Persians carried off. See Herodotus, viii. 33 ; Plutarch, *De malignitate Herodoti*, 35. Amongst the offerings were large statues dedicated
by the Phocians for a victory over the Thessalians (Herodotus, viii. 27 ;
cp. Paus. x. 1. 10).

**35. 2. The Greeks —— resolved not to restore the burnt
sanctuaries.** According to Lycurgus (*c. Leocr.* 31) and Diodorus (xi.
29) the Greeks before the battle of Plataea took a solemn oath that they
would not rebuild any of the temples which had been burnt or thrown
down by the Persians, but would leave them to be a perpetual memorial
of the impiety of the barbarians. Cicero also refers to this resolution
(*De re publica*, iii. 9). But Herodotus makes no mention of it ; and
Isocrates cannot have known of it or he would hardly have ignored it
in praising the Ionians for making a similar vow (*Or.* iv. 156). Moreover Pericles's proposal to restore all the temples burnt by the Persians
(Plutarch, *Pericles*, 17) seems inconsistent with the supposition of any
such oath or resolution. Probably therefore the story of the oath is a
figment of some rhetorician of the fourth century B.C. See F. Koepp,
' Die Herstellung der Tempel nach den Perserkriegen,' *Jahrbuch d.
archäolog. Institute*, 5 (1890), pp. 268-278.

35. 2. the temples in the land of Haliartus. See ix. 33. 3, with
the note on p. 166.

35. 2. the temple of Hera —— the temple of Demeter. See
i. 1. 4 and 5.

35. 3. in the Phocian war a band of defeated Phocians etc. In
347 B.C. during the Phocian or Sacred War the Phocians were fortifying
a post near Abae. But when the Boeotians marched against them
they dispersed among the neighbouring cities with the exception of
five hundred men who took refuge in the temple of Apollo. A great
quantity of straw was lying about the temple and some fire which the
fugitives had left in their huts caught the straw. It blazed up and consumed the temple and the fugitives in it. See Diodorus, xvi. 58.

**35. 3. the sanctuary —— stood down to my time the most
tumble-down building** etc. The very scanty ruins of the two temples of
Apollo mentioned by Pausanias are situated about a quarter of a mile
or so to the north-west of the hill of Abae. We have seen (p. 436)
that the sharp-peaked hill of Abae is divided from the valley of Hyampolis on the west by a lower hog-backed hill. From the northern foot
of this lower hill a hillock protrudes northward. The remains of
the two temples are to be seen on the top of the hillock. They were
excavated by Mr. Bather and Mr. Yorke, members of the British School
of Archaeology, in 1894. The excavations proved that the temples stood
within a small precinct enclosed by a wall of polygonal masonry which
runs round the upper slope of the hillock. The precinct thus formed
seems to have been roughly oval in shape, and to have measured at most
about 80 yards from north to south by about 60 yards from east to west.
From the primitive style of its masonry the polygonal wall is judged to

be the original one which enclosed the old temple. Its line is broken by gateways, one on the west and one at the south-east. A third gate was apparently constructed in later times a little to the south of the western gate. The remains of the old temple lie towards the southern end of the precinct. Foundations of three sides only are preserved : the western foundations have disappeared. The temple was turned nearly east and west. Its breadth is 18 feet : its length from east to west, so far as the foundations are preserved, is about 30 feet. Two courses of the foundation remain : the blocks of the upper course measure uniformly 3 ft. 7 in. by 1 ft. 5 in. Above these in the north wall the English archaeologists found one block of the first course of the temple proper ·in its original position : it measured 3 feet by 4 ft. 1 in. When I visited the temple in 1895 this block had seemingly been removed : at least I have no note or recollection of seeing anything but foundations in position. The insignificant ruins of the smaller temple lie about 18 yards north of the old temple. All that remains of it is one course of foundations forming three sides of a rectangle and composed of four blocks on the west side, two on the north side, and two on the south. This, we may suppose, was the temple dedicated by Hadrian.

Much more abundant are the remains of a colonnade which occupied a great part of the western side of the precinct, extending north and south for a length of about 110 feet with a depth of 24 feet. Of the external foundation-walls the western is visible to a height of three and four courses. It is built of long blocks laid in horizontal courses and ·is supported at intervals of about 20 feet by buttresses to prevent it from slipping down the side of the hillock. Where four courses of this wall are visible the height is about 6 feet. The northern wall is three courses high, and the southern wall four courses, but the latter wall is partly hidden under the soil. The eastern wall is also preserved throughout its entire length, but only its upper surface is visible. It consists for the most part, according to Mr. Yorke's report, of a single course. On the top of the western foundation-wall are standing considerable portions (12 blocks) of the first course of the upper wall, that is of the back-wall of the colonnade. Down the middle of the colonnade, throughout its whole length from north to south, there runs a row of quadrangular foundations or bases, which doubtless supported columns. These bases are at present eight in number, and apparently there never were more of them. The interval between each pair of them is 8 ft. 8 in. Some fragments of stone columns were found near the colonnade, and the points of a gabled roof of stone were discovered at each corner of the building. We may suppose that the colonnade opened eastward on the sacred precinct and that its roof rested on two rows of columns, one down the middle of the building and the other along its eastern front. Ante-fixes of terra-cotta and a lion's head, also of terra-cotta, which had served as a gargoyle, were found in and near the colonnade to which they seem to have belonged. From their fine style Mr. Yorke infers that the colonnade was built in the fourth century B.C. The stone of which it is constructed seemed to me to be a rough conglomerate of pebbles. According to Mr. Yorke, however, the temples and colonnade are all built of "a light coloured *poros* stone weathering almost white."

Within the precinct the English excavators found some pieces of bronze bowls ornamented with delicate *repoussé* work, "apparently Greek developments from Phoenician work," also fragments of thin bronze plates decorated with elaborate floral designs in the same style, and a few remains of Roman bronze work. All are sadly mutilated. The bowls and plates may have been votive offerings dating from a period before the destruction of the temple by the Persians. The inscriptions found in the precinct are few, fragmentary, and insignificant. One seems to refer to the restoration of an offering to a deity, either Apollo or Artemis ; another contains the name of the Athenian sculptor Eubulides, son of Euchir, whom Pausanias mentions (i. 2. 5 note).

See V. W. Yorke, in *Journal of Hellenic Studies*, 16 (1896), pp. 297-302, 304-308. I visited the sanctuary of Apollo 30th October 1895, and have described the remains partly from my notes. Some of the foundation-walls were visible above ground before the English excavations. See Leake, *Northern Greece*, 2. p. 165 ; W. Vischer, *Erinnerungen*, p. 628 ; Baedeker,[3] p. 202 ; *Guide-Joanne*, 2. p. 48.

A letter of Philip, king of Macedonia, was found inscribed on a block of white marble at the now deserted village of *Vogdani*, a little to the west of Abae. The people of Abae had sent envoys to King Philip begging that the sacred land of the sanctuary should remain free from imposts as formerly ; and in this letter Philip grants their petition. The Philip of this inscription seems to be Philip V., and his letter may have been written between 207 and 195 B.C. The inscription is now preserved in the church of St. George at *Kalapodi*, a village about 4 miles north-west of Abae. See *Bulletin de Corresp. hellénique*, 6 (1882), pp. 171-176 ; Dittenberger, *Sylloge Inscr. Graec.* No. 192 ; *C. I. G. G. S.* 3. No. 78 ; Ch. Michel, *Recueil d'Inscriptions grecques*, No. 42.

35. 5. Hyampolis. Hyampolis stood, as Pausanias tells us, on the direct route from Orchomenus to Opus. Between these two latter places is interposed a chain of hills, the highest summit of which— now called Mount *Chlomo*—is a mountain of imposing appearance. To avoid this natural barrier the ancient highroad appears to have made a considerable detour, following the easy valleys to the west of Mount *Chlomo* instead of taking a direct course over the mountain. Hence it traversed the site of the modern village of *Exarcho*, and leaving the hill of Abae and the temple of Apollo on the left turned northward up the valley of Hyampolis, into which the valley of *Exarcho* opens at right angles at its western end. The valley of Hyampolis extends north and south and is enclosed on both sides by bare rocky hills of no great height. A stream traverses it flowing from north to south. In the middle of the valley, about half a mile or so to the north-west of the temple of Apollo, rises a sort of natural redan or tableland, defended on all sides by slopes about 100 feet high. On the west side the slope is steep and rocky ; on the other sides it is neither rocky nor very steep. Ancient squared blocks, some fallen, some standing in position, dot the surface of the tableland, which is now overgrown with thin pale stubbly grass and the dry yellow-brown thistles so characteristic of Greece. Some excavations were made on the tableland by Messrs. A. G. Bather and V. W. Yorke, members of the British School at Athens, in 1894. The high pointed hill of Abae is in full view a little way to the south-east, and to the south-west Parnassus rises grandly in the distance.

This natural redan seems to have been the acropolis of Hyampolis; for considerable remains of fortification-walls, flanked with a few square towers, exist on its western and eastern sides, but the place seems too small to have contained the whole city. The fortifications are built of ashlar masonry in a very fine and regular style. The blocks, which are massive and of a fairly uniform though not excessive size, are squared and laid in horizontal courses; but here and there the joints in the courses are oblique. The stone seems to be a grey limestone. On the western face of the tableland the wall is preserved in an unbroken line nearly from end to end. It descends the steep rocky slope obliquely in a direction from south-east to north-west; its length is some 150 yards or so. From three to six courses of masonry are preserved; the height of the wall is from 5 to 9 feet. About the middle of the wall a square tower, 22 feet broad on the face, projects 9 feet from the curtain. It is standing to a height of about 11 feet, with six courses of masonry. In the wall a few feet to the south of this tower is a gateway about 6 ft. 6 in. wide; the side-wall of the passage, on the south, is 9 feet long. On the northern edge of the tableland only a few small isolated and insignificant remains of the fortification-wall exist. Among them are the ruins of a square tower; its northern face is preserved to a height of three and four courses, and a piece of its eastern side is standing. On the eastern face of the tableland, towards its northern end, the wall is again fairly preserved, though not so continuously as on the west. From two to six courses of masonry are standing, and the height of the wall in some places is from 6 to 9 feet. A square tower is preserved to a height of about 11 feet, with six courses of masonry. It is 21 ft. 9 in. broad, and projects 10 ft. 9 in. from the wall.

On the southern face of the tableland, a little below its edge, are some massive blocks of squared masonry. More remains of a building may be seen a little way further up; and still further to the north, on the summit of the tableland, some slight excavations have laid bare a rough foundation-wall and some large architectural blocks. One broken block of dark marble bears a few letters of an inscription which, from the ornamental shape of the letters, would seem to have been late. Another excavation has laid bare a tomb or cistern sunk in the rock. The tomb or cistern is 9 ft. 8 in. long by 3 ft. 7 in. wide and may be about 6 feet deep. Its upper edge is lined with masonry. Mr. V. W. Yorke, who is probably right in regarding the structure as a cistern rather than a tomb, suggests that it may be the one well of Hyampolis mentioned by Pausanias (§ 6). Two blocks of dark marble in this neighbourhood have clearly belonged to a circular or semicircular building. On the eastern side of the plateau, close to its edge, is a small ruined chapel containing some pieces of small columns and a broken block of a cornice (?) on which is engraved an inscription relating to the festival of Artemis (see below, note on § 7). Potsherds are strewn about the surface of the tableland.

To the south of the tableland which seems to have been the acropolis a lower plateau, strewn with stones, extends southward for about a mile. It ends in a ledge of rocks which here runs across the valley from east to west, forming a natural terrace-wall to the plateau. Part of this plateau may perhaps have been the site of the lower city of Hyampolis. On it I saw, a little to the south of the acropolis, an ancient tombstone which seemed to have been recently excavated. It was a slab of dark marble about 5 feet long and 1 ft. 11 in. broad at the broadest; the bottom was broken off. A finely-carved floral device, about 3 feet high, one of the finest I have ever seen, adorned the upper part of the stone, and below it was engraved the following inscription :

ΕΠΙΝΙΚΑΣΙΩΙ
ΦΙΛΟΜΗΛΙΔΑΙ
ΞΕΝΙΧΩΙ
ΠΟΛΥΞΕΝΩΙ,

from which we learn that the stone marked the grave of four men, Nicasius, Philomelidas, Xenichus, and Polyxenus.

From the ledge of rocks which bounds the plateau on the south, near a ruined chapel, a spring of beautifully clear water gushes forth. Some ancient blocks lie tumbled about the spring, and a tall poplar tree grows opposite it. The day was very hot when I passed it on my way to and from the ruins of Hyampolis ; but the leaves of the poplar rustled in the breeze, and the water flowed from under the rocks with a soothing murmur. Parnassus loomed dim in the distance through a haze of heat. On my return from the ruins I found a shepherd boy at the spring who offered to share his bread with me. This picturesque spot, on which a poet of the Anthology might have written an epigram, is perhaps the site of the temple of Artemis mentioned by Pausanias. It is now known as *Smixi*. See § 7 note.

The situation of Hyampolis, at the entrance of one of the main passes from Phocis to Locris and northern Greece, was strategically important. It was in this pass that the Phocians once met and defeated the invading Thessalian cavalry (x. 1. 3 ; Herodotus, viii. 28). Jason of Pherae captured a suburb of the city on his march from Phocis to Heraclea in 371 B.C. (Xenophon, *Hellenica*, vi. 4. 27). In the Sacred War the Boeotians defeated the Phocians at Hyampolis in 347 B.C. (Diodorus, xvi. 56). The city was captured by the Romans under Flamininus in 198 B.C. (Livy, xxxii. 18).

I visited Hyampolis from *Drachmani* 29th October 1895, and have described the ruins from personal observation. The inscription on the tombstone has not, so far as I know, been published before. See also Gell, *Itinerary of Greece* (London, 1819), p. 223 *sq.* ; Leake, *Northern Greece*, 2. p. 167 *sqq.* ; Vischer, *Erinnerungen*, p. 628 *sq.* ; Bursian, *Geogr.* 1. p. 164 *sq.* ; Baedeker,[3] p. 202 ; *Guide-Joanne*, 2. p. 48 ; V. W. Yorke, in *Journal of Hellenic Studies*, 16 (1896), pp. 291, 293 *sq.*, 303 *sq.*

35. 5. the Hyantians of Thebes, who fled thither etc. See

ix. 5. 1. As to the Hyantians, see K. O. Müller, *Orchomenos und die Minyer*,[2] p. 124.

35. 6. The city was burnt down by King Xerxes. Cp. Herodotus, viii. 33.

35. 6. The Emperor Hadrian built a colonnade. Outside of the acropolis of Hyampolis, on its southern side, Messrs. Bather and Yorke dug some trenches in 1894. They came upon the remains of a building, which they took to be a colonnade of the Roman period. As, however, the building seemed to be of considerable extent and lay at some depth beneath the surface, they did not clear it completely. It may be, as they conjecture, the colonnade built by Hadrian. In the neighbourhood of this building the English archaeologists observed on the slope of the acropolis some faint remains which they thought might possibly be those of the theatre mentioned by Pausanias. See V. W. Yorke, in *Journal of Hellenic Studies*, 16 (1896), p. 303 *sq.*

35. 7. They worship chiefly Artemis etc. The temple of Artemis perhaps stood at the picturesque spot called *Smixi* a short way to the south of the ruins of Hyampolis (see above, p. 444), for here two inscriptions relating to the worship of Artemis have been found. One of them records a dedication to Artemis by a certain Demetrius, son of Thraso (*C. I. G. G. S.* 3. No. 88; *Bulletin de Corresp. hellénique*, 5 (1881), p. 449): the other, found built into the wall of a ruined chapel, relates to sacred lands of Artemis and Apollo, but it is too mutilated to be fully intelligible (*C. I. G. G. S.* 3. No. 87; *Bulletin de Corresp. hellénique*, 18 (1894), p. 59 *sqq.*). A great festival of Artemis called the Elaphebolia was periodically celebrated at Hyampolis down to Plutarch's time. It was supposed to commemorate a victory won by the Phocians over the Thessalians. See Plutarch, *De mulierum virtutibus*, 2 ; *id.*, *Quaest. Conviv.* iv. 1. 1. The victory commemorated by the festival has been described by Pausanias (x. 1. 6 *sqq.*). An inscription which may be seen in a ruined chapel on the acropolis of Hyampolis, close to its eastern edge, mentions that a certain man, whose name is lost, had introduced, alone and unaided, the Great Caesarian games and the Great Elaphebolian and Laphrian games (*C. I. G. G. S.* 3. No. 90 ; *Journal of Hellenic Studies*, 16 (1896), p. 309). The Great Caesarian games were probably held in honour of Julius Caesar or Augustus, for had they been held in honour of a later emperor his name would probably have been added. Hence it would seem that the Elaphebolian festival was instituted in the reign either of Julius Caesar or of Augustus. The inscription, which I copied on the spot, is carved on a block of stone, apparently grey limestone, 3 ft. 2 in. long by 13 inches high, but broken off at the right hand side. Under the inscription is a moulding, which perhaps indicates that the block formed part of a cornice. Inscriptions further prove that the Egyptian deities Serapis, Isis, and Anubis were worshipped at Hyampolis (*C. I. G. G. S.* 3. Nos. 86, 89, 92). One of these documents (No. 89) records the dedication of a portal, colonnades, and chambers to the Egyptian deities by a certain Crinolaus who had been their priest. Another of them (No. 86) ranks the Emperor Trajan with the Egyptian divinities as a witness to a deed of manumission.

35. 7. whatever cattle they pronounce sacred to Artemis. As to the relation of Artemis to cattle, see Preller, *Griech. Mythologie,*[4] 1. p. 302; Schreiber, in Roscher's *Lexikon,* 1. p. 565 *sq.*; L. R. Farnell, *The Cults of the Greek States,* 2. p. 449 *sqq.*

35. 8. Stiris. The ruins of Stiris, identified by inscriptions, are situated on the summit of a rocky hill now called *Palea Chora,* about 2 miles south-east of the monastery of St. Luke. To reach Stiris from the Cleft Way on the highroad to Delphi (see x. 5. 3 note) we turn southward and follow a quiet open valley enclosed by the outlying masses of Parnassus on the west and of Helicon on the east. Leaving the village of *Distomo* (the ancient Ambrosus) on the right we turn to the south-east and continue to follow the valley, which is still open and planted with vines and afterwards with corn. We now see the village of *Stiri* on the right, standing on the northern slope of a bare rocky hill of oblong shape. Here the valley contracts into a somewhat narrow defile between the long hill of *Stiri* on the right and another considerably higher hill, also bare and rocky, on the left. Through the bottom of the defile runs a water-course which, when I saw it in May 1890, was quite dry. At the southern end of the defile the valley opens out again, and at this point there is a well with some plane-trees growing beside it. The track now ascends a little, and winding round the northern side of a hill prettily overgrown with bushes, brings us to the monastery of St. Luke, with its famous Byzantine churches The monastery is pleasantly situated on the south-eastern face of the bushy hill already mentioned. It looks eastward over a spacious circular valley or basin, beyond which rise the lofty rugged slopes of Mt. Helicon. The valley is not more than 2 or 3 miles across, but its surface is agreeably diversified with pastures, corn-fields olive-trees, and copses of holly-oak. Into this valley we descend and crossing it in a south-easterly direction we come in about half-an-hour more to the tabular hill of *Palea Chora,* rising from the valley and crowned with the ruins of Stiris. The time from the Cleft Way is about three hours. A torrent descending from near the village of *Zeriki,* flows westward along the northern foot of the hill of *Palea Chora* and is joined at the south-western end of the hill by another torrent which comes down from the village of *Kyriaki.* Both these streams are dry in summer. The sides of the hill are rocky and precipitous, especially on the north and east. The summit. which is a good deal lower than that of the hill on which the monastery of St. Luke stands, lies north-east and south-west; it is between 700 and 800 yards long, but not more than 100 yards broad at the widest. A wall of loose construction, approaching the Cyclopean in style, but built with much smaller stones, encircles it. No citadel can be traced, but the surface of the rock within the walls has been excavated in many places for dwellings, and there are two or three ancient cisterns near a ruined church of St. Nicholas, where some ancient remains, including pieces of columns and other architectural fragments, may also be seen. Here, too, some inscriptions have been found. Several record the enfranchisement of slaves by dedicating them to Aesculapius. One of them, dated in the fourth month of the year, when Philo son of Philocrates was archon at Stiris, mentions the dedication of the slaves "to Aesculapius at Stiris" (*C. I. G. G. S.* 3. No. 39); a second declares that the enfranchised slaves are placed under the safe-keeping of "the gods and Aesculapius and the citizens and the Phocians" (*C. I. G. G. S.* 3. No. 34); a third mentions Aesculapius and the Stirians repeatedly (*C. I. G. G. S.* 3. No. 35); and a fourth, which also speaks of Aesculapius again and again, is dated by the archon at Stiris (*C. I. G. G. S.* 3. No. 36). Hence we infer that the ruins on the hill are those of Stiris, and we may conjecture that the church of St. Nicholas occupies the site of a temple of Aesculapius.   All the inscriptions recording the manumission of slaves seem to date from the third century or the first half of the second century B.C.   Another inscription found among the ruins confirms the identification of the site as that of Stiris and throws some light on the history of the town (*C. I. G. G. S.* 3. No. 32).   It records a treaty of union between the city of Stiris and the city of Medeon on the basis of entire equality both in civil and religious affairs; Stiris was to be the seat of government and to give its name to the united state; but the old religious worships were to continue to be celebrated both at Medeon and at Stiris; a copy of the treaty of union was to be engraved on stone and set up in the sanctuary of Athena, and another copy was to be sealed and deposited with a private person   The date of this union of Stiris and Medeon must have been later than 181 B.C., for in two Delphic inscriptions of that year (Wescher-Foucart, *Inscriptions recueillies à Delphes*, Nos. 392, 436) mention is made of citizens of Medeon, which would not have been done after Medeon had been absorbed in Stiris.   Thus from the inscriptions it appears that Stiris existed at *Palea Chora* as late at least as the first half of the second century B.C.   This disposes of the theory, started by L. Ross and accepted by Vischer and Bursian, that after its destruction at the close of the Sacred War (Paus. x. 3. 2) the city was rebuilt, not on the old site, but about 2 miles away to the north-west, on the site of the monastery of St. Luke, where some foundations and remains of ancient walls, partly built in regular courses, are to be seen both on the summit of the hill above the monastery and on the slope of the hill a little below it.   An angle of an ancient wall is standing to the north-east of the monastery, which is itself in great part built of large old square blocks.   On Ross's hypothesis these are the remains of the Stiris which Pausanias saw and described.   But, as Leake pointed out, the site does not answer to his description.   For there is a copious fountain of beautiful water in the courtyard of the monastery; whereas according to Pausanias there was no drinking-water to be had at Stiris and the inhabitants were obliged to go down 4 furlongs to draw water at a spring.   The ancient remains at St. Luke's may possibly be those of Medeon; for since Stiris and Medeon united and formed a single state, the two cities were probably neighbours.   Into the wall of the church of St. Luke is built an inscription which records that Xenocrates and Eumaridas dedicated to the gods Augustuses (the Roman emperors) and to the city a fountain with steps, a covered building, and a conduit of water (*C. I. G. G. S.* 3. No. 47). Hence if, as I have conjectured, Medeon occupied the site of the monastery of St. Luke, it must have continued to exist as a town long after its political union with Stiris. In Pausanias's time it was in ruins (see below, x. 36. 6). But Medeon was perhaps on the bay of *Aspra Spitia.* See note on x. 36. 6. Other inscriptions at St. Luke's monastery record the manumission of slaves and dedications to Aesculapius (*C. I. G. G. S.* 3. Nos. 41, 42, 43) : one of them (No. 42) is dated by the archon at Stiris. Built into a wall of the monastery is the inscribed pedestal of a statue of Julia Domna, wife of Septimius Severus, which was set up by the city of Stiris (*C. I. G. G. S.* 3. No. 48).

The monastery of St. Luke was founded about 960 A.D. The great church of St. Luke, the finest Byzantine church in Greece, is built in the form of a Greek cross, with a vestibule and three doors at the western end, a dome in the centre, and galleries at the sides supported by columns. The roof and walls are still lined with many fine mosaics, though many have been destroyed. Under the church is a crypt which is used as a church of St. Barbara. Adjoining the church of St. Luke and entered from it is another much smaller church of the Mother of God (*Theotokos*) ; it has not, so far as I observed, any mosaics except on the floor. The monastery is rather cleaner and better kept than most Greek monasteries. From a balcony overlooking the abbot's garden there is a pleasant view across the valley to Mt. Helicon.

See Wheler, *Journey,* p. 320 *sqq.* ; Chandler, *Travels in Greece,* p. 247 *sqq.* ; Gell, *Itinerary of Greece* (London, 1819), p. 175 *sq.* ; Leake, *Northern Greece,* 2. p. 528 *sqq.* ; Pouqueville, *Voyage de la Grèce,* 4. p. 126 *sqq.* ; Bursian, *Geogr.* 1. p. 183 *sq.* ; Baedeker,[3] p. 164 ; *Guide-Joanne,* 2. p. 28. For the inscriptions found at Stiris (*Palea Chora*) and St. Luke's monastery see *C. I. G.* Nos. 1724b, 1730; *Bulletin de Corresp. hellénique,* 5 (1881), pp. 42-54, 446-449 ; Cauer, *Delectus Inscr. Graec.*[2] Nos. 221, 223, 224 ; Dittenberger, *Sylloge Inscr. Graec.* Nos. 294, 445 ; Collitz, *G. D. I.* 2. Nos. 1539-1551. They are now all collected by Prof. W. Dittenberger in *C. I. G. G. S.* 3. Nos. 32-57. I spent a night at the monastery of St. Luke (16th May 1890), but did not visit the ruins of Stiris. My friend Mr. R. W. Schultz, who spent some time at the monastery of St. Luke in 1890, has kindly furnished me with notes on the ancient remains there and at *Palea Chora.* They confirm Leake's evidence.

35. 8. Peteos, son of Orneus. Cp. ii. 25. 6. Peteos was the father of Menestheus, who led the Athenian contingent to Troy (Homer, *Il.* ii. 552, xiii. 690).

35. 8. the township of Stiria. Stiria was a township belonging to the Attic tribe of Pandionis (Stephanus Byzantius, *s.v.* Στείρια ; Hesychius, *s.v.* Στειριεῖς ; Harpocration, *s.v.* Στειριεύς). Strabo mentions Stiria (ix. p. 399) between Prasiae and Brauron. It was situated on · the northern part of the *Porto Raphti,* a bay on the custom coast of Attica, south of Marathon. See vol. 2. p. 404 ; Lolling, in *Mittheil. d. arch. Inst. in Athen,* 4 (1879), p. 360 ; Milch-höfer, *Karten von Attika, Erläuternder Text,* Heft iii.-vi. p. 9 ; Leake, *Topography of Athens,* 2. p. 71 ; Kastromenos, *Die Demen von Attika,* p. 56 *sq.* Some rock-cut tombs of the prehistoric period, containing Mycenaean pottery, clay idols, and perforated stone whorls or buttons,

have been excavated here recently by Mr. B. Staes ; they are situated
in the slope of the hill opposite the church of St. Spyridion ('Εφημερὶς
ἀρχαιολογική, 1895, pp. 199-202).

35. 9. **a spring about four furlongs down from the town.** To
the south-west of Stiris (*Palea Chora*) there is a spring, which according
to Leake is the only spring in the valley of Stiris, except the one within
the walls of St. Luke's monastery. It is not more than a furlong and a
half from the ancient site, and instead of being in a hollow among rocks
it rises to the surface of the cultivated part of the valley. So it does
not answer to Pausanias's description. See Leake, *Northern Greece*, 2.
p. 530 ; cp. Vischer, *Erinnerungen*, p. 602 ; Bursian, *Geogr.* 1. p. 184
note. But Mr. R. W. Schultz informs me that about half a mile or less
to the north of *Palea Chora* there is a spring in the valley, the water
of which turns an adjoining mill. This may be the spring to which
Pausanias refers.

35. 10. **made of unburnt brick.** Cp. note on x. 4. 4.

35. 10. **with ribbons tied to it.** Cp. viii. 31. 8, and vi. 20. 19
note.

36. 1. **Ambrosus.** The site of Ambrosus, identified by inscriptions, is at the large modern village of *Distomo*, about 3 miles south
of the Cleft Way. The distance from Stiris (*Palea Chora*) is about
8 miles, which agrees fairly with the 60 furlongs at which Pausanias
estimates it. His description of the scenery by the way (a plain planted
with vineyards and enclosed on either hand by mountains) is still
applicable to a good part of the route, particularly between the modern
village of *Stiri* and *Distomo*, though towards *Stiri* corn takes the place
of vines. *Distomo* is situated at the point where the valley, after
extending due south from the Cleft Way, bends away in a south-easterly
direction towards Stiris. The village stands at the eastern foot of Mt.
Cirphis, which is the southern continuation of the great Parnassian
group of mountains. The houses are partly built with fragments of
large blocks of dark stone, extracted from the ruins of the ancient
Ambrosus. The acropolis occupied a round hill a few hundred feet to
the north of the village. Here some scanty foundations of the wall may
be seen ; at one point Vischer made out traces of the double wall
described by Pausanias (§ 3). The church of St. Elias on the hill
probably occupies the site of a temple, as it is built almost wholly
of ancient blocks, with several architectural fragments of marble and
some mutilated inscriptions. The town stood in the plain ; Dodwell saw
a few remains of the ancient walls built of regular masonry. In the
cliffs which enclose the valley there are some large sepulchral chambers
hewn in the rock, with semicircular niches above them. Ambrosus, in
spite of its strong walls, was captured by the Romans under Flamininus
in 198 B.C. (Livy, xxxii. 18).

See Wheler, *Journey*, p. 321 ; Chandler, *Travels in Greece*, p. 246 *sq.* ;
Dodwell, *Tour*, 1. p. 198 *sq.* ; Pouqueville, *Voyage de la Grèce*, 4. p. 124 *sq.* ;
Vischer, *Erinnerungen*, p. 600 *sq.* ; Bursian, *Geogr.* 1. p. 183 ; Baedeker,[3]
p. 164 ; *Guide-Joanne*, 2. p. 34.

The name of the city is spelt differently both by ancient writers and in inscriptions. The MSS. of Pausanias here and elsewhere (iv. 31. 5, ix. 13. 3, x. 3. 2) do not agree in the spelling; but the best authenticated forms are Ambrōsus, Ambrōssus, Ambrŏsus, and Ambrŏssus ("Αμβρωσος, "Αμβρωσσος, "Αμβροσος, and "Αμβροσσος). See the note on this passage in Schubart and Walz's critical edition of Pausanias. At all events we may feel sure that Pausanias spelt the second syllable of the name with an *o*; and this form in *o* (Ambrŏssus or Ambrōssus) is supported by inscriptions of the second and third centuries A.D. (*C. I. G. G. S.* 3. Nos. 12, 17, 18). On the other hand Polybius (iv. 25. 2), Strabo (ix. p. 423), and Livy (xxxii. 18) spell it Ambrysus, and the kindred form Ambryssus is supported by inscriptions of the second century B.C. (*C. I. G. G. S.* 3. Nos. 1, 10, 11). These facts seem to show that sometime about the beginning of our era the name of the city was changed from Ambrysus or Ambryssus to Ambrosus or Ambrossus, and that therefore Pausanias in using the form Ambrosus or Ambrossus conformed to the custom of his day and was not copying from older writers who had employed the earlier form Ambrysus or Ambryssus. This observation has been made by Prof. Dittenberger (on *C. I. G. G. S.* 3. No. 18).

Some of the inscriptions found at *Distomo* prove that Apollo, Demeter, the Maid (Proserpine), and Athena were worshipped at Ambrosus (*C. I. G. G. S.* 3. Nos. 13, 14, 15; *C. I. G.* Nos. 1726, 1727; Collitz, *G. D. I.* 2. Nos. 1517, 1518). Another records the dedication of a colonnade and portal to Serapis, Isis, and Anubis (*C. I. G. G. S.* 3. No. 16; Collitz, *G. D. I.* 2. No. 1519). From another (*C. I. G. G. S.* 3. No. 12; *Bulletin de Corresp. hellénique,* 5 (1881), p. 439 *sq.*) we learn that a certain Aurelius Parmenides founded competitive games at Ambrosus which were held every third year and comprised foot-races and wrestling-matches for men and boys, chariot-races, contests in trumpet-playing and heraldry, etc. Other inscriptions show that statues of the emperors Trajan, Commodus, and Alexander Severus were set up at Ambrosus (*C. I. G. G. S.* 3. Nos. 17, 18, 19).

36. 1. **the shrub which the Ionians —— name kokkos.** The shrub described by Pausanias is the *Quercus coccifera,* a small species of the evergreen holly-oak. Sibthorp, travelling from *Distomo* (Ambrosus) to the monastery of St. Luke, observed that "the *Quercus coccifera* abounds throughout the whole of this tract of country; one of our guides brought me a *coccus* adhering to a small branch of the tree, which, squeezed between my fingers, gave out a most beautiful scarlet dye. The *coccus* generally deposits itself on the leaves and branches of the oak, seldom on its fruit, as Pausanias affirms" (R. Walpole, *Memoirs relating to Turkey,*[2] London, 1818, p. 69). Dioscorides, like Pausanias, calls the shrub *kokkos,* though he gives the same name *kokkos* to the so-called kermesberries which adhere to the shrub and from which the scarlet dye is expressed. He adds that the kermesberry, in shape like a small snail, is produced on oaks in Cilicia and that the women there gathered it, scraping off the berry with their nails. See Dioscorides, *De materia medica,* iv. 48. On the other hand Theophrastus (*Hist. Plant.* iii. 7. 3) calls the shrub by its generic name of *prinos* (holly-oak,

ilex); and so does Simonides in a line quoted by Plutarch (*Theseus*, 17). In modern Greek the holly-oak is called *prinari* or, more vulgarly, *pirnari* or *pournari*, and the kermesberries are called *prinokokkia*. The holly-oak is one of the commonest plants in Greece, and is found of all sizes from a stunted shrub up to a tree 30 feet high. The leaf is small, dark-green, and glossy, with fine, but hard and sharp prickles round the edge ; in short it closely resembles the leaf of the holly, except that it is much smaller. The plant is very hardy and thrives in chinks and crannies of the barest limestone mountains where no other green thing would grow. Hence, while it is found on rocky hillsides all over Greece and the Greek islands up to a height of about 3000 feet, it is especially characteristic of the barren mountains and stony declivities of eastern Peloponnese. Here you may travel for miles without seeing another tree or shrub. Nothing is more monotonous than the sight of these round stunted bushes with their dark-green foliage sprouting at long intervals from the rocky ground. So tough and matted are the boughs, so dense and stiff the leaves of these shrubs that you can stand on one of them, as on a hard cushion, without sinking into it. The ancients seem generally to have regarded the kermesberry as really a berry (cp. Simonides, cited above ; Pliny, *Nat. hist.* ix. 141). In point of fact it is an insect of the same kind as that which produces cochineal, gall, etc. Pausanias, as we see from the present passage, was aware that the dye was made from an insect ; but it is not clear whether he knew that the kermesberry was itself the insect. Dioscorides, by comparing the kermesberry to a snail and speaking of it as adhering to the shrub, appears to have been acquainted with its true character. Isidore expressly says that the kermesberry is an insect (*Origines*, xix. 28. 1). The name *kermes*berry and our English word *crimson* are derived from the Arabic name of the insect (*el kermes*). The insects are still collected for purposes of commerce on Mt. Parnassus and in the neighbourhood of Mantinea.

See Dodwell, *Tour*, 1. p. 201 ; Leake, *Morea*, 1. p. 249 *sqq.* ; *id.*, *Northern Greece*, 2. p. 534 *sq.* ; Fiedler, *Reise*, 1. p. 520 *sq.* ; H. Blümner, *Technologie*, 1. pp. 240-242 : Neumann und Partsch, *Physikalische Geographie von Griechenland*, p. 380 *sq.* ; A. Philippson, *Peloponnes*, p. 534.

36, 1. which the Galatians ――― call in their native tongue *hus*. The Galatians retained their native Celtic speech as late as the fourth century A.D., for Jerome says that in his day their language hardly differed from that of the Treveri, a Celtic tribe on the Moselle whose name is preserved in *Treves* (Jerome, *Commentar. in Epist. ad Galat.* bk. ii. praef.). I am informed that the word *hus* has left no trace in any Celtic language. Leake thought it identical with the French *houx* 'holly' (*Northern Greece*, 2. p. 535 note). But it appears that *houx* is of Teutonic origin. See Diez, *Etymologisches Wörterbuch der romanischen Sprachen*,[4] p. 617 ; Brachet, *Etymological Dictionary of the French Language*, *s.v.* 'houx.'

36. 3. a double wall etc. Pausanias has already mentioned the walls of Ambrosus as amongst the finest specimens of Greek fortification. See iv. 31. 5.

36. 5. a sanctuary of Dictynnaean Artemis. Built into a wall at the village of *Aspra Spitia*, near the site of Anticyra, is an inscription recording a decree of the Council and People of Anticyra in honour of a certain Euporia who had been priestess of Artemis Dictynna (*C. I. G. G. S.* 3. No. 5). We can hardly doubt that this Artemis Dictynna is the Dictynnaean Artemis of Pausanias, though from his account it would seem that the sanctuary belonged to Ambrosus rather than to Anticyra. Apparently the sanctuary lay about the border of the two territories and may, as Prof. Dittenberger in his comment on the inscription suggests, have belonged now to the one petty state and now to the other.

36. 5. Anticyra. From Ambrosus (*Distomo*) a narrow defile by the side of a water-course leads due south to the head of the spacious bay of *Aspra Spitia*, a distance of about 4 miles. The bay is surrounded by steep, barren ridges "which exhibit an appearance almost as dismal as any part of Dalmatia, or Albania." Proceeding southwestward along the shore of the bay for a mile and a half or so we enter a small cultivated plain and slope. On a hill to the right is the hamlet of *Aspra Spitia* ('The White Houses'). About a mile to the south of the hamlet a high, rocky, indeed mountainous, peninsula called *Kephali* projects eastward into the bay. It is about 3 miles in circumference and is connected with the mainland by a flat isthmus, which is planted with corn and olives. At the head of the bay, about half a mile north of the isthmus, Leake discovered, among olive plantations, foundations enough to indicate an ancient site ; and from inscriptions found at the village of *Aspra Spitia* (*C. I. G. G. S.* 3. Nos. 1, 2, 3, 5, 6, 7) it appears that the site is that of Anticyra. Two of the inscriptions (Nos. 6 and 7) prove that the people of Anticyra set up statues of Commodus and Julia Domna. In digging a well at *Palatia*, the site of Anticyra, a proprietor lately came on some remains of ancient Greek walls built of tufa and a tombstone bearing a metrical inscription of the third century B.C. in memory of a certain Aristarchus who had fallen in battle (*Bulletin de Corresp. hellénique*, 19 (1895), p. 391 *sq.* ; *C. I. G. G. S.* 3. No. 1064).

See Wheler, *Journey*, p. 480 *sq.* ; Chandler, *Travels in Greece*, p. 245 *sq.* ; Leake, *Northern Greece*, 2. pp. 524, 539 *sqq.* ; Gell, *Itinerary of Greece* (London, 1819), p. 174 ; Bursian, *Geogr.* 1. p. 182 ; Baedeker,[3] p. 164.

36. 5. Cyparissus etc. Cyparissus is mentioned by Homer in his list of the Phocian towns which sent contingents to the Trojan war (*Iliad*, ii. 519).

36. 5. Anticyreus. It is said that after his madness Hercules was dosed with hellebore by Anticyreus (Stephanus Byzantius, *s.v.* Ἀντικύρα).

36. 6. the ruins of Medeon. The site of Medeon is uncertain. That Medeon was near Stiris may be inferred from the treaty of union concluded between the two towns (see note on x. 35. 8). Hence I have suggested above that the ancient remains at St. Luke's monastery may be those of Medeon. On the other hand, Pausanias's statement that Anticyra was over against the ruins of Medeon would lead us to

look for the latter place on the shore of the bay of *Aspra Spitia* opposite to Anticyra. Now on the eastern shore of the bay, opposite to
Anticyra, there is a little valley watered by the stream which comes
down from Stiris (*Palea chora*); the valley opens out on a beach, and
at the northern end of this beach there is a rocky headland crowned
with some ruins of an ancient Greek fortress. The wall of the fortress
is well preserved on the north side of the hill, where in some places it is
still standing to more than half its original height. On the other sides
it has almost wholly disappeared; but within the enclosure there are
some terrace walls, especially one fine specimen of polygonal masonry.
On the roadside, at the foot of the headland, may be seen a heap of
ruins near the shore, consisting of some ancient blocks in their original
positions, covered with the remains of a church. The summit of the
headland commands a good view over the gulf of *Aspra Spitia* with the
cultivated lands fringing it and the bold rocky peninsula of *Kephali*
jutting out from the opposite shore of the bay. The headland with
its ruins, as well as an anchorage for boats within the cape, are called
Sidero-Kafchio. The ruins may perhaps be those of Medeon. See
Leake, *Northern Greece*, 2. p. 537 *sq.* The statement of Strabo
(ix. p. 410) that Medeon was on the Crisaean gulf, 160 furlongs from
Boeotia, seems irreconcilable with Pausanias's statement that the ruins
of Medeon were opposite Anticyra; and if Medeon had been so far
from Stiris, it is hardly likely that the two towns would have united as
we know they did. On the strength of Strabo's statement, however,
Leake conjectured that Medeon might be near *Desphina*, a village
situated on the western slope of a high rocky hill between the gulf
of Anticyra and the Crisaean gulf, but nearer the latter; it is about
6 miles east of Cirrha. There are many ancient catacombs hewn in the
rock near the village. See Leake, *Northern Greece*, 2. p. 546 *sqq.*

36. 6. I mentioned that . . . committed sacrilege. The Greek
text is defective, but the reference seems to be to x. 3. 2, where Medeon
is mentioned among the cities which were razed to the ground for the
sacrilegious seizure of Delphi.

36. 6. Otilius, the Roman. See vii. 7. 8 note.

36. 7. The mountains above Anticyra are very rocky. This
description is perfectly just; the mountains here are barren and rocky
(Leake, *Northern Greece*, 2. p. 545 *sq.*).

36. 7. hellebore grows in great abundance etc. According to
Dioscorides (*De materia medica*, iv. 148 and 149) the best hellebore,
both of the black and the white sort, grew at Anticyra. Cp. Alciphron,
iii. 2. Dioscorides agrees with Pausanias in saying that the white
hellebore acted as an emetic and the black as a purge. Theophrastus
states (*Hist. plant.* ix. 10) that the best black hellebore grew on Mt.
Helicon and the best white sort on Mt. Oeta. Cp. Pliny, *Nat. hist.*
xxv. 49. Hellebore is still common on *Palaeo Vouna*, one of the chief
peaks of Helicon (H. N. Ulrichs, *Reisen und Forschungen*, 2. p. 100).
According to some the only difference in the appearance of the two
sorts of hellebore was that the root of the one was white and the root
of the other black; but others said that the leaves also differed in shape.

Dioscorides and Pliny give long lists of the ailments, bodily and mental, which were supposed to be cured by hellebore. The black sort was sometimes called Melampodium, because the seer Melampus healed the daughters of Proetus of their madness by dosing them with it. It was also sprinkled on houses and cattle as a mode of purification, the sprinkling being accompanied by the recitation of a spell. Special precautions were used in gathering the black hellebore. The bold adventurer who proposed to cut it drew a circle round the plant with a sword, then faced eastward and prayed that the gods would favour the enterprise. He also watched the flight of an eagle ; for if the eagle flew near him or saw him cutting the hellebore, he would die within the year. Having observed all these necessary precautions he proceeded to cut the hellebore as fast as he possibly could, for the plant gave out an exhalation which produced a splitting headache. Hence before he addressed himself to the dangerous task he fortified himself by eating garlic and drinking wine. See on the whole subject Dioscorides and Theophrastus, *ll.cc.* ; Pliny, *Nat. hist.* xxv. 47-61. Strabo says (ix. p. 418) that sick people resorted to Anticyra for the hellebore cure, not because the best hellebore grew there, but because the medicine was best prepared by the druggists of Anticyra, who mixed the finest Oetaean hellebore with a sesame-like plant which grew in Phocis. Cp. Dioscorides, *De materia medica*, iv. 150 (152). We read of a Roman nobleman in the reign of Caligula who staid at Anticyra for the sake of his health (Suetonius, *Caligula*, 29). Black hellebore (*Helleborus orientalis*, Modern Greek *skarphē*) still grows to the south of Parnassus and in the neighbourhood of Anticyra, according to Fiedler (*Reise*, I. p. 780). Sibthorp, however, found no trace of the black or white helle-bore at *Aspra Spitia*, the ancient Anticyra. He says : " The immediate environs of *Asprospiti* present a dry sun-burnt soil. The hellebores were probably brought from the higher and colder regions of Parnassus, or cultivated by the physicians of Anticyra in gardens " (quoted in Walpole's *Memoirs relating to Turkey*,[2] London, 1818, p. 70).

In antiquity Greek women wore certain gold ornaments called 'hellebores.' See Aristophanes, *Frag.* 309 ; Pollux, v. 101, vii. 196 ; Hesychius, *s.v.* ἐλλέβορος. The exact nature of these ornaments was made plain some years ago by the discovery, in the south of Russia, of four small gold plates of ancient Greek manufacture. The blossom of the hellebore is represented on them, and there are holes in the plates for fastening them to the dress. See L. Stephani, in *Compte Rendu* (St. Petersburg) for 1874, pp. 90-92.

36. 9. **the only Olympiad which is omitted in the Elean register.** Pausanias has already told us that in the 8th, 34th, and 108th Olympiads the Olympic games had been celebrated, not by the Eleans themselves, but by intruders ; and that hence the Eleans regarded these Olympiads as invalid and did not enter them in the register. See vi. 4. 2 ; vi. 8. 3 ; vi. 22. 2. The case of the 211th Olympiad was different. It had been presumably celebrated by the Eleans themselves and its validity does not appear to have been contested ; but it was either not entered in the register at all, or after being entered it was struck out. The reason

for its omission is supplied by Julius Africanus, who tells us that the celebration of the 211th Olympiad, which should have fallen in 65 A.D., was deferred two years by Nero's desire to allow him to be present, and that when the festival was celebrated two years after its proper time (in 67 A.D. instead of in 65 A.D.), Nero was awarded prizes in no less than six competitions, including the ten-horse chariot-race, though he had fallen out of the chariot and did not finish the race (Suetonius, *Nero*, 24 ; Dio Cassius, lxiii. 14). Probably, therefore, the Eleans, ashamed of having truckled to the tyrant, struck the 211th Olympiad out of the register after Nero's death, which happened only about a year after the celebration of the Olympic games. For a similar reason the Eleans may have refused to allow the statues of victors in the 211th Olympiad to be set up at Olympia ; hence the statue of Xenodamus was erected in his native town of Anticyra. Pausanias saw it there with its inscription, and not finding the name of Xenodamus in the list of Olympic victors, he inferred that if the inscription were correct, the Olympic victory of Xenodamus must have been won at the only Olympiad which had been erased from the register. See Schubart, in *Fleckeisen's Jahrbücher*, 29 (1883), p. 472 *sq.*; H. Brunn, in *Fleckeisen's Jahrbücher*, 30 (1884), p. 24. Thus the objection taken by G. Hirschfeld (*Archäologische Zeitung*, 40 (1882), p. 110) to the present passage of Pausanias, as inconsistent with vi. 22. 3, falls to the ground.

36. 10. **the sons of Iphitus.** Schedius and Epistrophus, the sons of Iphitus, led the Phocian contingent in the Trojan war. Schedius was slain by Hector. See Homer, *Il.* ii. 517 *sq.*, xvii. 306 *sqq.* According to some, the grave of Schedius was at Daphnus in Locris (Strabo, ix. p. 425). As to Schedius, cp. x. 4. 2 ; x. 30. 8.

37. 1. **a sanctuary of Artemis.** Following Pausanias's directions H. G. Lolling discovered in 1888 what he believed to be the remains of the sanctuary of Artemis. They are situated at the northern foot of the high rocky peninsula of *Kephali*, five minutes distant from the innermost corner of the bay of *Aspra Spitia*, and five minutes from the level beach and the boundary of the ancient Anticyra. The remains are well known in the neighbourhood under the name of *Palatia*. The sanctuary stood at the foot of a high cliff, with one of its narrow ends abutting on the face of the rock. Here the face of the cliff is cut in the form of a gable, and beneath this rock-hewn gable are a few votive niches also cut in the rock, with a larger square one which probably contained an image of the goddess. From near the two ends of the gable the foundations of two walls extend outwards at right angles to the face of the cliff. Only a few blocks of these foundations remain. Farther out from the cliff and parallel to it are the remains of two other walls. The sanctuary was thus of quadrangular shape. The rock-cut gable is remarkable ; Lolling, who knew Greece so well, remembered no parallel to it in Greece, though similar rock-cuttings are common enough in Asia Minor. Hence he conjectured that the sanctuary was primarily intended for the use of foreign seamen. That it was the sanctuary of Artemis is made probable by a mutilated inscription (*C. I. G. G. S.* 3. No. 4) which Lolling found built into the steps of a house in *Aspra Spitia*. The

inscription, which seems to be of Roman date, contains the name of Artemis, and is cut on a piece of grey limestone brought from the ruined sanctuary. See H. G. Lolling, in *Mittheil. d. arch. Inst. in Athen*, 14 (1889), pp. 229-232.

37. 1. **a work of Praxiteles. She has a torch in her right hand** etc. On a bronze coin of Anticyra, of which only two specimens are known, Artemis is represented advancing towards the right, with a torch in her left hand, a bow in her right, and a dog at her feet (Fig. 20). This is probably a free copy of the statue by Praxiteles which Pausanias here describes. See Imhoof-Blumer and Gardner, *Num. Comm. on Paus.* p. 124 *sq.*, with pl. Y xvii. ; A. Michaelis, in *Archäologische Zeitung*, 34 (1876), p. 167 *sq.* ; and against him L. Stephani, in *Compte Rendu* (St. Petersburg) for 1875, pp. 140-142.

FIG. 20.—ARTEMIS (COIN OF ANTICYRA).

37. 2. **Bulis.** The remains of Bulis are to be seen at the port now called *Zalitza*, about 7 miles east of the bay of Anticyra (*Aspra Spitia*). The distances from Thisbe and Anticyra by land are about 10 miles and 12 miles respectively, which agree fairly with the 80 furlongs and 100 furlongs at which Pausanias estimates them. His description of the site of Bulis is also accurate. The ruins occupy the summit of a rocky height, which slopes on one side towards the small harbour. The slope is cultivated, and between the foot of it and the sea there is a level stretch of land about two-thirds of a mile broad. On the other side the hill of Bulis is defended by an immense cliff which descends into the bed of a torrent. Across this ravine rise the precipitous slopes of Mt. Helicon, consisting of perpendicular white cliffs broken here and there by narrow terraces on which pine-trees grow. The ancient name of the torrent, as we learn from Pausanias, was Heracleus. The ruins of Bulis include some handsome pieces of wall of the third order. See Wheler, *Journey*, p. 324 *sq.* ; Leake, *Northern Greece*, 2. p. 518 *sq.* ; Bursian, *Geogr.* 1. p. 185 *sq.* The port of Bulis is perhaps the harbour which Strabo (ix. p. 423) calls Mychus.

37. 2. **so impassable and rugged are the mountains between Anticyra and Bulis.** Colonel Leake journeyed westward from Bulis in the direction of Anticyra, following the side of the rocky mountain by a road which overhung the sea. He found the hills covered with wild olive, ilex, holly-oak, and juniper of a large growth. "As we proceed, the hills become very steep, and terminate precipitously in the sea, affording only an extremely rugged and difficult path along the side of them : it was no better in the time of the Roman empire, for Pausanias doubted whether there was any road at all from Anticyra to Bulis" (*Northern Greece*, 2. p. 523). However, as Leake pointed out, before the battle of Leuctra the Lacedaemonian army under Cleombrotus marched along this rugged and mountainous coast in order to evade the Theban army which had occupied the ordinary pass leading from Phocis into Boeotia. See Xenophon, *Hellenica*, vi. 4. 3 ; Diodorus, xv. 53 ; and the note on ix. 13. 3.

37. 3. fishers of the shell-fish which yields the purple dye. The murex still exists in the sea on this coast, though it is no longer fished for (Leake, *Northern Greece*, 2. p. 520). Cp. note on iii. 21. 6.

37. 4. Cirrha, the port of Delphi. Cirrha was situated beside the sea about a mile to the east of *Itea*, the modern port of Delphi. The site, now partly occupied by the miserable decaying village of *Magoula*, is desolate and forbidding. The shore, devoid of any natural harbour, is nothing but an open beach exposed to the full fury of the south wind. At the back of the village, beyond a great bare field strewn with pottery and some broken or weathered stones, rise high bleak mountains, with steep and absolutely naked sides. Indeed the hills all round the plain of Cirrha are exceedingly bare and dismal ; nothing green seems to grow on them. If any remains of Cirrha now exist above ground they are very few and insignificant. I sought for them without finding a single stone which I could recognise with certainty as ancient. In the desolate field at the back of the village I saw what looked like three square bases of columns in a row ; also a single course of a wall extending for about 28 yards, but so buried in the ground that only the worn edges of the stones were visible. But this wall appeared to me not to be ancient. In the village there is a tower beside the sea, 7 paces square and standing to a height of a good many feet. It seems to be solid. In its seaward face there are some large blocks, but I doubt if any of them is ancient. The tower itself is certainly mediaeval, as appears from the bad and irregular masonry and the bricks and mortar stuffed into the crevices. From Mr. Cecil Smith I learn that at *Hagios Nikolaos* there are still considerable traces of a mole in the sea.

The remains of Cirrha seem to have been much more extensive in 1837 when H. N. Ulrichs visited the site. In the midst of the scattered ruins the walls of an ancient fortress could still be traced in their entire circuit, for in most places they stood several feet above the ground. They formed a rectangle 575 feet long by 425 feet broad, and were built of carefully jointed polygonal blocks. Ulrichs at first supposed that this fortified enclosure was the citadel ; but afterwards he held, with more probability, that it was the emporium or mart ; for on the inside of it a colonnade ran all round the walls ; most of the squared stones on which the pillars had rested were still to be seen in their places. This colonnade probably contained the warehouses and shops of the merchants. From the south side of this mart two walls, each 300 paces long, ran down to the sea ; the westerly of the two walls ended in an ancient wharf or mole extending some distance into the water. On the mole, near a chapel, were the ruins of a mediaeval tower built of large quadrangular ancient blocks cemented with mortar. Beside the tower there is a small turbid spring. In the chapel Ulrichs found only a small Ionic capital of common stone.

The distance of Cirrha from Delphi is about five and a half miles, but the windings of the road between *Chryso* (Crisa) and Delphi add to the length of the route. From the time he took to go from Delphi to Cirrha, Leake estimated that the 60 furlongs at which Pausanias puts the distance must be very near the truth, certainly much more so than the 80 furlongs of Strabo (ix. p. 418), or the 30 furlongs of Harpocration (*s.v.* Κιρραῖον πεδίον).

See Leake, *Northern Greece*, 2. p. 584 *sq.*; H. N. Ulrichs, *Reisen und Forschungen*, 1. p. 7 *sq.*, and 2. p. 207 *sq.*; *id.*, in *Abhandl. d. philos. philolog. Cl. d. k. bayer. Akad. d. Wissen.* 3. i. (1840), p. 78 *sq.*; Welcker, *Tagebuch*, 2. p. 73 *sq.*; Bursian, *Geogr.* 1. p. 181 *sq.*; *Guide-Joanne*, 2. p. 42. I visited Cirrha from *Itea* 21st October 1895.

37. 4. a hippodrome. An inscription containing a decree of the Amphictyonic Council makes mention of 'the racecourse and the fountain in the plain' (*C. I. G.* No. 1688, line 36; Froehner, *Les Inscriptions grecques du Louvre*, No. 32; Cauer, *Delectus Inscr. Graec.*[2] No. 204). The fountain here mentioned is probably the spring of fine water which rises not far from the shore at *Itea* in a basin built of large ancient blocks. Hence the hippodrome would seem to have been near the site of *Itea*. The only other spring of sweet water in the whole plain as far north as *Chryso* (Crisa) is the scanty spring of turbid water at Cirrha (see preceding note). In Pindar's time the stadium (the course for the foot-races) seems also to have been in the Cirrhaean plain, probably near the hippodrome. See Pindar, *Pyth.* x. 23, xi. 20 *sqq.*, 73 *sqq.* Afterwards the stadium was removed to Delphi, where Pausanias saw it. See x. 32. 1 note. Pindar often refers to the athletic contests at Cirrha. See, besides the passages quoted above, Pindar, *Pyth.* iii. 132, vii. 14, viii. 26. Later classical writers, misunderstanding these references, use 'Cirrha' and 'Cirrhaean' as equivalent to 'Delphi' and 'Delphic' (Lucan, v. 95; Statius, *Sylv.* iii. 1. 141; *id.*, *Theb.* iii. 106, 611; Seneca, *Oedipus*, 269; Juvenal, vii. 64, xiii. 79; Nonnus, *Dionys.* iv. 318; Clement of Alexandria, *Protrept.* ii. 11. p. 10, ed. Potter). See H. N. Ulrichs, *Reisen und Forschungen*, 1. pp. 7, 10, 14; *id.*, in *Abhandl. d. philos. philolog. Cl. d. k. bayer. Akad. d. Wiss.* 3. i. (1840), pp. 79, 81, 89 *sq.* Leake thought that the hippodrome may have been situated in a small retired level called *Komara* immediately below *Chryso* and enclosed between two projections of its hill. The spot is just at the entrance to the glen of the Plistus. See Leake, *Northern Greece*, 2. p. 595.

37. 4. Taraxippus. See vi. 20. 15 note.

37. 5. The plain all the way from Cirrha is bare etc. From the head of the Crisaean gulf (now the bay of *Salona*) a level plain stretches northward into the heart of the mountains for a distance of about 11 miles. About a mile and a half from the sea the plain is narrowed by two projecting mountain-spurs which advance toward each other, one from the east and one from the west. The eastern spur is called *Myttikas*, the western *Goutas*. At the foot of the former lies the village of *Xeropegado*. Beyond these projecting spurs the plain again expands. Thus, although it is really continuous, the plain may conveniently be regarded as divided into two parts, a southern and a northern, the division between them being marked by the mountain-spurs which advance from either side into the plain. Of these two parts the southern is the Cirrhaean plain. It is much the smaller of the two and differs in character from the other. For whereas the northern plain is fertile and well wooded with luxuriant olive-groves, the Cirrhaean plain is still almost as treeless as it was in the days of Pausanias. Some corn, cotton, and vines grow on it; but it is mostly covered with grass and rushes, on which numerous herds of cattle browse. After the destruction of Cirrha in Solon's time the Cirrhaean plain was consecrated to Apollo and set apart to lie untilled and ungrazed for ever. See Demosthenes, *de Corona*, p. 277 *sqq.*; Aeschines, *contra Ctesiph.* 107 *sqq.*; Diodorus, xvi. 23; Polyaenus, iii. 5; Dio Cassius, lxiii. 14. By mistake Isocrates (*Or.* xiv. 31, p. 302) calls the plain the Crisaean plain. He implies that it was lawful to feed sheep on it; whereas in the decrees of the Amphictyonic Council, quoted by Demosthenes (*l.c.*), one of the articles of accusation against the Amphissaeans is that they had put cattle to graze on the sacred land. But the genuineness of these decrees is very dubious. In a genuine decree of the Amphictyonic Council about the sacred land (*C. I. G.* No. 1688, see note on § 4) no mention is made of a prohibition to graze cattle on it.

The northern and much larger part of the plain is the Crisaean plain proper, though the name Crisaean was perhaps sometimes extended so as to include the whole plain from the sea northwards to Amphissa (*Salona*). See Herodotus, viii. 32; Strabo, ix. pp. 418, 427; Callimachus, *Hymn to Delos*, 178. The Crisaean plain proper is a wide expanse of perfectly flat and very fertile land, covered with luxuriant olive-groves, vineyards, and corn-fields, and hemmed in by lofty mountains. The olive-woods in particular are among the finest in Greece as well for the stately growth of the trees as for the excellence and abundance of the olives. In early summer the greyish-green of their foliage sets off the red blossoms of the pomegranates and oleanders that grow in moist spots. The mountain-wall that bounds the Crisaean plain on the east is broken, at a point about $2\frac{1}{2}$ miles from the sea, by the profound glen of the Plistus river, which after flowing westward between Mt. Parnassus on the north and Mt. Cirphis on the south, enters the Crisaean plain, where it turns southward and traversing the plain falls into the sea a little to the west of the site of Cirrha.

At the mouth of the glen, where it opens on the Crisaean plain, are the remains of the very ancient city of Crisa, which gave its name to the plain. They occupy the extremity of a long rocky spur which projects southward from Parnassus and overhangs the northern bank of the Plistus in great precipices. The modern village of *Chryso*, which may derive its name from the ancient city, stands on the mountain-side at the point where the rocky spur begins to project from it. The surface of the spur is a sort of rocky uneven plateau. On two sides, the north and the west, it was enclosed by massive but rough walls of Cyclopean masonry, of which there are considerable remains. On the other two sides, the east and the south, the sheer and lofty precipices descending to the deep glen of the Plistus rendered all fortification needless, and it does not appear that walls were ever built along their brink. The north wall may be traced running across the whole neck of the spur from east to west. A fortification-wall was here absolutely necessary, since the ground, being nearly level, affords no natural defence; there is merely a slight dip between the ancient city and the site of the modern *Chryso*. In general only one course of the north wall is standing, but close to its eastern end two courses are preserved, giving the wall a height of over 6 feet. The masonry is of the true Cyclopean order; the blocks are all very rough, being almost unhewn, and some of them are very large. One stone is over 9 feet long by 5 feet high; another is 7 ft. 6 in. high. The western wall follows the edge of the plateau above a slope which, though steep, is not precipitous. It is traceable throughout and is much better preserved than the northern wall, the number of courses varying from two to six. In some places it is from 5 feet to 12 feet high. Both faces of the wall are preserved for a considerable distance; the thickness, where I measured it, was 13 or 14 feet. The size of the blocks varies; some are large, others comparatively small. In one place two blocks give a height of 5 ft. 7 in., and one of the two is more than 5 feet long. Near the southern extremity of the plateau is a chapel of the Forty Saints, which according to Bursian is built almost entirely of large ancient blocks. Within the area of the ancient city, to the north of the chapel of the Forty Saints, there formerly stood a very ancient altar with two round holes for burnt-sacrifices on its upper surface. It was a double altar consecrated to the service of two divinities, as we learn from an ancient *boustrophedon* inscription (see v. 17. 6 note) which is engraved on two of the sides and, being translated, runs as follows: "In order that he might have imperishable renown, Aristus set up this altar and sacrificed oxen to Hera and victims to Athena, goddess of property" (*C. I. G.* No. 1; H. N. Ulrichs, *Reisen und Forschungen*, i. pp. 21 *sqq.*, 31; Roehl, *I. G. A.* No. 314; Collitz, *G. D. I.* 2. No. 1537).

The bottom of the deep glen of the Plistus, below the ruins of Crisa, is covered with olive-groves, except in the gravelly bed of the stream. On the opposite or south side of the glen the mountains rise in very steep but not quite perpendicular rocky slopes. Ancient Delphi is not visible from Crisa, being hidden in a recess of the mountain to the east, but the modern village is in full view. To the west there is a fine prospect over the Crisaean plain covered with olive-groves; and to the north-west *Salona* (Amphissa) is clearly visible at the foot of the dark high mountains of Locris.

The situation of Crisa is accurately described in the Homeric hymn to Apollo, where it is said that it stands on a height looking westward, above a deep and rugged glen, at the foot of the steep rocks of the snowy Parnassus. See the *Hymn to Apollo*, 269, 282 *sqq.*, 438. If we took the evidence of this hymn literally we should have to suppose that Crisa was older than Delphi; for in narrating the origin of Delphi the writer speaks of Crisa as if it existed before the Cretan settlers founded the sanctuary at Delphi (*v.* 445 *sqq.*; cp. note on x. 5. 5). At all events Delphi was probably in its origin not a town at all but merely a sanctuary dependent on Crisa, which, situated at the mouth of the glen of the Plistus, completely commanded the approach to it from the sea. The road to Delphi from the modern port *Itea* still passes through the village of *Chryso*, from which it winds up the steep rocky slope in a north-easterly direction to the ancient sanctuary. Hence when the fame of

Delphi attracted crowds of worshippers, the Crisaeans, by commanding the road to it, were able to levy toll on the pilgrims, a practice which, by exciting the indignation of the Amphictyonic Council, was the occasion of the First Sacred War, which ended in the destruction of Crisa and its port Cirrha. See Strabo, ix. p. 418 *sq.* ; Schol. on Pindar, *Pyth.* i. Introd. Cirrha was afterwards rebuilt (Aeschines, *c. Ctes.* 113; Polybius, v. 27; Livy, xlii. 15; Dionysius, *Descriptio Graeciae*, 73), and still existed as the port of Delphi in Pausanias's time. But Crisa never rose from its ruins, and its very existence was sometimes forgotten. Thus Pausanias, as we see from the present passage, regarded Crisa merely as the Homeric name for Cirrha, and a scholiast on Pindar (*Pyth.* i. p. 300, ed. Boeckh) thought it was an old name for Delphi. See also *Etymol. Magn.*, *s.v.* Κρίσα, p. 515. Strabo knew that Crisa was a different place from Cirrha, but he wrongly placed Crisa on the coast between Cirrha and Anticyra (Strabo, ix. pp. 416, 418).

See especially H. N. Ulrichs, *Reisen und Forschungen*, 1. pp. 7-34; *id.*, 'Ueber die Städte Crissa und Cirrha,' *Abhandlungen der philos. philolog. Cl. d. k. bayer. Akad. d. Wissen.* 3. i. (1840), pp. 75-98. Compare Dodwell, *Tour*, 1. pp. 149 *sq.*, 158-161; Leake, *Northern Greece*, 2. pp. 583-587; Pouqueville, *Voyage de la Grèce*, 4. p. 105 *sqq.* ; Welcker, *Tagebuch*, 2. p. 70 *sqq.* ; L. Ross, *Wanderungen*, 1. pp. 68 *sqq.*, 71 *sq.* ; Vischer, *Erinnerungen*, p. 617 *sqq.* ; Bursian, *Geogr.* 1. p. 180 *sq.* ; Sandys, *An Easter Vacation in Greece*, p. 69 *sqq.* ; Baedeker,[3] p. 156; *Guide-Joanne*, 2. p. 42 *sq.* I have twice traversed the plains of Cirrha and Crisa, in 1890 and 1895. On the latter occasion (21st October) I visited the ruins of Crisa, and have described the situation and ruins from personal observation. Dodwell and Leake rightly distinguished Crisa from Cirrha, placing the latter on the coast and the former at *Chryso.* But other modern scholars confused the two, till the researches of Ulrichs finally settled the question. On the history of Crisa and Cirrha, see especially Preller, ' Krisa und sein Verhältniss zu Kirrha und Delphi,' *Berichte über die Verhandl. d. k. sächs. Gesell. d. Wissen. zu Leipzig*, 6 (1854), pp. 119-140 (reprinted in Preller's *Ausgewählte Aufsätze*, pp. 224-244).

37. 5. Homer —— calls the city by its original name of Crisa. Crisa is mentioned by Homer (*Il.* ii. 520; *Hymn to Apollo*, 269, 282, 431, 438, 445). But Pausanias is mistaken in supposing that Crisa was identical with Cirrha. See the preceding note.

37. 6. the Amphictyons resolved to make war on the Cirrhaeans etc. On the first Sacred War see the works of H. N. Ulrichs and Preller referred to in the note on § 5. The ancient authorities for the war are Aeschines, *c. Ctes.* 107-112; Schol. on Pindar, *Pyth.* Introd., and on *id.*, *Nem.* ix. 2; Athenaeus, xiii. p. 560 b c; Polyaenus, iii. 5, vi. 13; Fronto, *Strateg.* iii. 7. 6; Plutarch, *Solon*, 11; Suidas, *s.v.* Σόλων (Suidas copies Pausanias). The participation of Clisthenes in the war is mentioned by Polyaenus, Fronto, and the Schol. on Pindar, *Nem.* ix. 2. The participation of Solon in it is mentioned by Aeschines, Plutarch, and Suidas.

37. 6. Ye shall not take and cast down etc. This oracle is quoted by Aeschines (*c. Ctes.* 112) and Suidas (*s.v.* Σόλων), and the substance of it is given by Polyaenus (iii. 5).

37. 7. He devised yet another stratagem against the Cirrhaeans etc. The following stratagem is described also by Polyaenus (iii. 5), Fronto (*Strat.* iii. 7. 6), and Suidas (*s.v.* Σόλων). Fronto attributes it

to Clisthenes. Polyaenus in one passage (iii. 5) ascribes it to Clisthenes, in another (vi. 13) to Eurylochus. Suidas, who copies Pausanias almost literally, refers it to Solon.

About a quarter of an hour to the east of Cirrha a small but rapid stream of salt water flows into the sea. It rises at the foot of Mt. Cirphis, which here bounds the plain on the east. The salt-spring fills a large basin and formerly turned a mill. Near it is a small chapel of St. John. A draught of the water acts as a strong purge, and the water is so used by people in the neighbourhood. It is possible, as H. N. Ulrichs suggested, that at the siege of Cirrha the besiegers turned the water of this stream into the canal which flowed through the city, and that thus they may have produced the effects which the ancient writers ascribe to an infusion of hellebore. See H. N. Ulrichs, in *Abhandl. d. philos. philolog. Cl. d. k. bayer. Akad. d. Wissen.* 3. i. (1840), p. 79; *id., Reisen und Forschungen,* I. p. 9.

38. 1. the Ozolian Locrians. The Ozolian Locrians were also called the Hesperian (Western) Locrians, to distinguish them from the Opuntian and Epicnemidian or Hypocnemidian Locrians, and the crest engraved on their public seal was the Evening Star (Strabo, ix. p. 416). According to Aristotle the Western Locrians were of the stock of the Leleges. See Strabo, vii. p. 322; Dionysius, *Descriptio Graeciae,* 70 *sq.*; cp. Pliny, *Nat. hist.* iv. 27. Plutarch, like Pausanias, has collected various explanations of the epithet Ozolian, which he seems to take in the sense of 'stinking' or 'smelling' (from *ozein* 'to stink,' 'smell'). Some suppose, he says, that the Locrians were called Ozolian because the carcase of Nessus or of the dragon Python had been washed ashore in their country and had rotted there. Others thought it was because the Locrians stank through wearing sheep-skins and goat-skins and living among flocks of goats. Others said that the land was a land of many flowers and took its name from their perfume. This last was the explanation naturally adopted by a patriotic native poet, Archytas of Amphissa. See Plutarch, *Quaest. Graec.* 15. According to a scholiast on Homer (*Il.* ii. 527) the name Ozolian was derived either from the untanned and stinking goat-skins worn by the people, or from a river Ozon, which was so called because its water stank with the carcase of the centaur Nessus slain by Hercules. Cp. Eustathius on Homer, *Il.* ii. 529, p. 276. 9 *sqq.*; *Etymol. Magnum, s.v.* Βόδλος, p. 192; Servius, on Virgil, *Aen.* iii. 399. Dodwell thought that the name might have been given to the country on account of a kind of spurge or euphorbia with a yellow flower and a white caustic juice in its stem; the modern Greeks think that the plant causes bad air, and it certainly, says Dodwell, gives a peculiar sour smell to the whole country when it is in bloom. The modern Greek name of the plant is *galaxidi,* and this is now the name of a town in Locris, the ancient Oeanthea. Dodwell identified the plant with the *Tithymalus characias* of Dioscorides (*De mat. med.* iv. 162). See Dodwell, *Tour,* I. p. 131.

38. 1. When Orestheus, son of Deucalion, reigned in the land etc. The following story is told by Hecataeus in a fragment preserved by Athenaeus (ii. p. 35 b). Another story, which seems to be con-

nected with it, is related by Plutarch (*Quaest. Graec.* 15). He asks
"What is the wooden dog in the land of the Locrians?" and he answers
the question thus. "Physcius son of Amphictyon had a son Locrus,
who had a son Opus by Cabya. But Locrus quarrelled with his son
and taking many of the citizens with him he enquired of the god whether
he should found a colony. As the god bade him found a city wherever
he should chance to be bitten by a wooden dog, he crossed over to the
other sea and in doing so he trod on a dog-thorn. Being maimed by
the hurt he tarried there some days, in the course of which he perceived
that the place was indeed the promised land, and he built cities."

38. 4. **Amphissa.** The site of the ancient Amphissa is occupied
by the modern *Salona*, a thriving town of over 5000 inhabitants. It
lies very picturesquely at the north-western extremity of the Crisaean
plain, shaded by trees and straggling among gardens on the first gentle
slopes of the lofty Locrian mountains, about half an hour distant from
the western foot of Parnassus. The houses, though mostly built of
mud, are trim and of a fair size. Immediately above the town an abrupt
rocky hill rises grandly, crowned with the ruins of a mediaeval castle,
which was once the seat of the Frankish counts of *Salona*. The ruins are
very extensive. The castle was built on the remains of the walls of the
ancient acropolis, or perhaps of the ancient city itself; for it is doubtful
whether Amphissa extended into the plain. Colonel Leake thought
that the keep of the castle occupies the site of the ancient acropolis, and
that the extensive outer walls nearly follow the line of the ancient city-
walls. Below and among the Frankish walls may be seen large pieces
of old Greek masonry built partly in the quadrangular and partly in the
polygonal style. Remains of two ancient Greek towers are standing on
the northern slope of the hill, perched on the summit of a rocky brow
which here overhangs the houses of the modern town. In the castle-
walls two ancient gateways are still in perfect preservation. One of
them is constructed of three immense blocks of stone. There is also
a cistern, the lower part of which is ancient Greek masonry; the
upper part is mediaeval. At the foot of the castle-rock a fine Turkish
fountain may be seen; the water comes spouting out in clear rills from
many mouths under a horse-shoe arch, and forms one of the chief
sources of the river of *Salona*, which flows southward through luxuriant
vineyards and olive-groves to join the Plistus. But the water of the
river is diverted to irrigate the plain, and it is only after heavy rains
that any of it reaches the Plistus. That *Salona* occupies the site of
Amphissa is proved by two Greek inscriptions recording the sale of
slaves to Aesculapius at Amphissa (*C. I. G. G. S.* 3. Nos. 318, 1066;
Collitz, *G. D. I.* 2. No. 1474; *Bulletin de Corresp. hellénique*, 5 (1881),
p. 451 *sq.*; *id.*, 19 (1895), p. 385 *sq.*), and by a late Latin inscription,
discovered by Wheler, which can still be seen at the church of the
Transfiguration (*Metamorphosis*). This solitary church stands on the
mountain-side about a quarter of a mile above the town, and is reached
by a steep and stony path. The inscription (*C. I. L.* iii. 1. No. 568)
contains a letter of the proconsul Decimus Secundinus to the people
of Amphissa, in which he desires that the aqueduct be cleaned and the

water turned into the old cisterns. From the parapet in front of the church there is a good view over the plain of Amphissa with its olive-woods, traversed by white roads, and hemmed in on all sides by lofty mountains.

The smiling verdure of Amphissa and its neighbourhood forms a striking contrast to the stern, arid, and rocky scenery of Delphi, which is only ten miles off. (Pausanias puts the distance at 120 furlongs, but he is wrong. Aeschines, *c. Ctes.* 123, estimates the distance at 60 furlongs, which is equally wide of the mark but on the other side.) At Amphissa, indeed, we are on the borders of almost Swiss scenery. For the fir-clad and torrent-rent mountains of Locris and Doris which rise to the north-west are the loftiest in the present kingdom of Greece. Two of the peaks are over 8000 feet high. A fine specimen of this Alpine scenery may be obtained by following the mule-path which leads north from Amphissa over the mountains to the village of *Gravia* in the ancient canton of Doris. With the exception of the village of *Topolia*, which we leave on the right, and here and there a small farm far up on the mountain-side, not a human dwelling is to be seen. At first the path ascends the western declivities of Parnassus. Looking down to the left we see below us a narrow dale, where in early summer the course of the stream, now nearly dried up, is marked by the red oleander-blossoms. Beyond the dale Mt. *Kiona* rears its snowy head, the loftiest mountain in Greece; and behind it the long and almost equally lofty ridge of *Vardousia* is seen stretching north and south. The finest point on the route is at a clear spring which bubbles up at the top of the pass, just where the road surmounts the ridge that joins Parnassus to the mountains of Locris. Hitherto we have been ascending from the south; from this point the road begins to descend to the north. The valley now contracts. The snowy peaks in the west disappear, but their lower spurs form, with the western declivities of Parnassus, a narrow pass, down which a brook babbles over rocks and stones, its banks overhung with plane-trees. Pines and oaks of various kinds contrast pleasantly with the steep cliffs and bushy slopes; and now and then we come to a little grassy glade or a patch of corn. "It is," says the Swiss traveller Vischer, whose description of the road I have borrowed, "almost a Swiss region, and I might have fancied myself transported to my native land, if the holly-oaks and oriental plane-trees had not reminded me that I was in the south." Thus descending by a steep and rugged path we reach the village of *Gravia* at the northern end of the pass, in five or six hours from Amphissa.

See Wheler, *Journey*, p. 310 *sqq.* ; Dodwell, *Tour*, 1. p. 146 *sqq.* (with a view of *Salona*) ; Pouqueville, *Voyage de la Grèce*, 4. p. 99 *sqq.* (Pouqueville copies without acknowledgment from Dodwell) ; Leake, *Northern Greece*, 2. p. 588 *sqq.* ; L. Ross, *Wanderungen*, 1. p. 70 ; Vischer, *Erinnerungen*, p. 619 *sq.* ; Bursian, *Geogr.* 1. p. 150 *sq.*; H. Belle, *Trois années en Grèce*, p. 190 *sqq.*; Baedeker, p. 155 ; *Guide-Joanne*, 2. p. 45 *sq.* ; G. Deschamps, *La Grèce d'aujourd'hui*, p. 253 *sqq.* The worship of Aesculapius at Amphissa, which is not mentioned by Pausanias, is attested by an inscription found at Delphi (*Bulletin de Corresp. hellénique*, 17 (1893), p. 361) as well as by the inscriptions found at Amphissa itself to which reference has been made above.

38. 4. when the Roman Emperor turned the Aetolians etc. Cp. v. 23. 3; vii. 18. 8.

38. 5. tombs of Amphissa and Andraemon. According to Aristotle (quoted by Harpocration *s.v.* Ἄμφισσα) Andraemon was the founder of Amphissa.

38. 5. the image was brought by Thoas from Ilium. Thoas, son of Andraemon, was the captain of the Aetolian contingent at the Trojan war (Homer, *Il.* ii. 638).

38. 6. Rhoecus —— Theodorus. See viii. 14. 8 note.

38. 6. a stone wall above the altar. The Greek word here translated 'wall' is θριγκός. In all other passages of Pausanias the word appears to mean an enclosing wall, a breastwork, parapet, balustrade. See i. 42. 8; ii. 15. 3; ii. 35. 10; v. 13. 1; vi. 20. 7; vi. 25. 1; viii. 31. 5; viii. 37. 10. In three passages (v. 13. 1; viii. 31. 5; viii. 37. 10) the θριγκός encloses a grove or at all events a place planted with trees. Hence it would seem that in the present passage we must understand the word in the same sense. Sir Charles Newton interpreted it 'cornice,' a meaning which it often bears in classical writers (see Liddell and Scott's *Lexicon*; also Hesychius, Suidas, Photius (*Lexicon*), and *Etymol. Magnum*, *s.v.* θριγκός); and he conjectured that the fragments of a frieze found by Mr. Wood in the lowest stratum of his excavations at Ephesus were the remains of the very θριγκός here mentioned by Pausanias. But Mr. A. S. Murray believes that the fragments in question belonged to the cornice of the older temple. See Sir Ch. Newton, *Essays on Art and Archaeology*, p. 80 *sq.*; A. S. Murray, 'Remains of archaic temple of Artemis at Ephesus,' *Journal of Hellenic Studies*, 10 (1889), p. 1 *sqq.*

38. 6. the Ephesians call it Night. Sir Charles Newton suggested that this statue may have represented Latona (Leto), the mother of Artemis (*Essays on Art and Archaeology*, pp. 74, 81).

38. 7. mysteries of the Boy Lords etc. Cp. Lobeck, *Aglaophamus*, p. 1233 *sq.*

38. 8. Myonia. The slope of the hills which bound the plain of Amphissa on the west is crowned by a rocky brow. Above the line of rocks there is a plain of considerable extent reaching to the great steeps of the snowy fir-clad peak now commonly called Mt. *Elato*. In the middle of this high plain stands the village of *Hagia Efthymia* (or *Thymia*), near which are the well-preserved walls and towers of an ancient city, probably Myonia. The place is about three and a half miles south-west of Amphissa, which agrees fairly with the 30 furlongs of Pausanias. The circuit of the walls may be about a mile and a half. In style the masonry is nearly regular, and the blocks are ornamented with parallel perpendicular lines cut in them. The towers are square and are distributed all round the walls at equal intervals; the steps up to many of them remain. None of the gates is entire. Like Mantinea and Megalopolis, the town seems to have had no acropolis. There are hardly any vestiges within the walls, nothing but some heaps of small stones and tiles. From *Hagia Efthymia* a road leads south to *Galaxidi*

(Oeanthea) through a barren, treeless, rocky country, bounded by bare hills. The distance is about 7 miles.

See Dodwell, *Tour*, 1. p. 144 *sqq.*; Leake, *Northern Greece*, 2. p. 592 *sq.*; Pouqueville, *Voyage de la Grèce*, 4. p. 98; Bursian, *Geogr.* 1. p. 151 *sq.*; Deschamps, *La Grèce d'aujourd'hui*, p. 259 *sq.* Stephanus Byzantius (*s.v.* Μύων) calls the town Myon, though in another passage (*s.v.* Μυονία) he calls it Myonia. Cp. the Critical Note on vi. 19. 5, vol. 1. p. 589. The territory of Myonia marched with that of Amphissa. See Thucydides, iii. 101. Bursian thought (*Geogr.* 1. p. 149) that the ruins at *Hagia Efthymia* might be those of Phaestum (Pliny, *Nat. hist.* iv. 7) or Physcus (Stephanus Byz., *s.v.* Φύσκος; Plutarch, *Quaest. Graec.* 15).

38. 8. dedicated the shield to Zeus at Olympia. See vi. 19. 4 *sq.*

38. 8. the Gracious Gods. These would seem to have been nether gods, since the sacrifices to them were offered at night. Cp. E. Rohde, *Psyche*, p. 249 n. 1; Hermann, *Gottesdienstliche Alterthümer*,[2] § 23. 18.

38. 8. to consume the flesh on the spot before the sun rises. Cp. note on ii. 27. 1.

38. 9. Oeanthea. The site of Oeanthea is probably occupied by *Galaxidi*, a small town with some ship-building yards on the western shore of the Crisaean gulf. Polybius says (iv. 57) that Oeanthea was opposite to Aegira in Achaia. This exactly answers to the situation of *Galaxidi* which is due north of Aegira, on the opposite side of the gulf of Corinth. *Galaxidi* stands on a low rocky promontory forming two harbours, of which the southern is the deeper and snugger, being sheltered by a projecting cape and by two rocky islands off the coast. On the shore there are some remains of an ancient mole. Pieces of fortification-walls, built partly in the polygonal, partly in the quad-rangular style, may be seen here and there among the houses. A sepulchral inscription, of no importance, is built into one of the churches. But the chief part of the ancient city seems to have occu-pied the peninsula which runs out a few hundred yards to the east of the modern town. Here there are some large hewn blocks, and the rock has been cut and levelled for the foundations of houses. Across the Crisaean gulf Mt. Parnassus towers majestically. The eye can distinguish the lofty cliffs above Delphi and the great rent or fissure, at the foot of which is the Castalian spring.

See Chandler, *Travels in Greece*, p. 273; Dodwell, *Tour*, 1. p. 130 *sqq.*; Leake, *Northern Greece*, 2. p. 593 *sqq.*; H. N. Ulrichs, *Reisen und Forschungen*, 1. p. 5; Fiedler, *Reise*, 1. p. 146; L. Ross, *Wanderungen*, 1. p. 73 *sq.*; Bursian, *Geogr.* 1. p. 149; Baedeker,[3] p. 34; *Guide-Joanne*, 2. p. 63 *sq.*

Some interesting light is thrown on the barbarous condition of the Locrians by an inscription on a bronze tablet which was found at Oeanthea (Ὀάνθεια). The inscription contains a treaty between Oeanthea and Chaleum, another sea-port of Locris. By the terms of the treaty it is provided that neither of the petty states shall molest foreign merchants who visit the other's port; but the citizens of both states are free to commit piracy anywhere except within their own or their ally's harbours. The two towns would seem in fact to have been pirate communities, like the Aeolian islands in antiquity (see note on x. 11. 3) or Algiers in modern times. The date of the inscription is probably not earlier than 431 B.C. It confirms what we know from the historians that the western Greek states outside of Peloponnese lagged behind the rest of Greece in civilisation. In the days of Thucydides the Ozolian Locrians, Aetolians, and Acarnanians were all pirates and prided themselves on their profession ; and the men went about armed even in time of peace (Thucydides, i. 5).

See A. R. Rangabé, *Antiquités helléniques,* No. 356 b, vol. 2. pp. 2-9 ; A. Kirchhoff, in *Philologus,* 13 (1858), pp. 1-14 ; *id., Studien zur Gesch. des griech. Alphabets,*[4] p. 144 *sqq.* ; Roehl, *I. G. A.* No. 322 ; Cauer, *Delectus Inscr. Graec.*[2] No. 230 ; Hicks, *Greek Historical Inscriptions,* No. 31 ; Roberts, *Greek Epigraphy,* No. 232, with the commentary on p. 354 *sqq.* ; Collitz, *G. D. I.* 2. No. 1479 ; C. T. Newton, *Essays on Art and Archaeology,* p. 107 *sq.* ; Ed. Meyer, *Forschungen zur alten Geschichte,* 1. pp. 307-318 ; R. Meister, ' Rechtsvertrag zwischen Chaleion und Oianthea,' *Berichte über die Verhandlungen d. k. sächs. Gesell. d. Wissen.,* Philolog. histor. Classe, 1896, pp. 19-43 ; Ch. Michel, *Recueil d'Inscriptions grecques,* No. 3 ; *C. I. G. G. S.* 3. No. 333.

38. 10. **Naupactus.** The fortress and town of Naupactus (*Efpaktos* or *Epaktos,* in Italian *Lepanto*) occupy the south-eastern and southern slopes of a hill beside the sea. The hill is a spur of the lofty summit now called Mount *Rigani,* and reaches down in the shape of a steep pyramid almost to the sea-shore, separating two spacious maritime plains, one on the east, the other on the west of the town. Mount *Rigani* towers immediately at the back of the hill. The place was fortified in the manner generally adopted by the Greeks in similar situations ; that is to say, it occupies a triangular slope with a citadel at the apex and one or more cross-walls on the slope, dividing it into lesser enclosures. At Naupactus there are no fewer than five of these enclosures between the summit and the sea, with gates of communication from one to the other, and a side gate on the west, leading out of the fortress from the second enclosure on the descent. The walls are of Venetian construction, but it is not unlikely that they follow exactly the line of the ancient walls ; for in many places they stand upon ancient Greek foundations, and even retain large pieces of the old masonry amidst the modern work. The present town occupies only the lowest enclosure, the houses being clustered round the small circular port. It has a mean and decayed appearance ; the streets are encumbered with the ruins of mosques and Turkish houses. The port is sanded up and is too shallow to admit even the larger boats which ply on the gulf. Two turrets flank the narrow entrance into it. However, the general aspect of the place, with its old battlemented Venetian walls climbing the steep hill-side above the town, is highly picturesque. The plain to the east of the town is wooded and verdant, being watered by the river of *Morno* and some smaller brooks. In general it is well cultivated, but near the shore the marshes render it unhealthy. At the foot of the hills it wears a more desolate aspect, the ground here being strewn with boulders that have been swept down by the torrents. The plain on the western side of Naupactus is about a mile wide near the town ; olives and corn-fields, varied here and there with vineyards,

cover it. There was a sanctuary of Apollo at Naupactus close to the harbour (Thucydides, ii. 91). Inscriptions found at Naupactus show that Dionysus was worshipped here and that slaves were freed by being formally sold to him (*C. I. G. G. S.* 3. Nos. 372-378).

See Chandler, *Travels in Greece*, p. 274 *sq.* ; Dodwell, *Tour*, 1. p. 128 *sq.* ; Leake, *Northern Greece*, 2. p. 606 *sqq.* ; Bursian, *Geogr.* 1. p. 146 *sqq.* ; Baedeker,[3] p. 33 ; *Guide-Joanne*, 2. p. 65 ; R. Weil, in *Mittheil. d. arch. Inst. in Athen*, 4 (1879), p. 22 ; W. J. Woodhouse, *Aetolia* (Oxford, 1897), p. 309 *sqq.*

38. 10. the Dorians —— built here the vessels etc. The name Naupactus means 'ship-built,' which was explained by the legend here mentioned by Pausanias. Cp. Strabo, ix. p. 426 *sq.* ; *Etymolog. Magnum*, *s.v.* Ναύπακτος, p. 598.

38. 10. The history of Naupactus—how the Athenians etc. See iv. 24. 7 ; iv. 26. 1 *sq.*

38. 11. the Locrians assembled once more in Naupactus. On a bronze tablet found at Oeanthea (*Galaxidi*) there is an inscription relating to a colony of the Hypocnemidian (Epicnemidian) or Opuntian Locrians who had settled or were about to settle at Naupactus. W. Vischer and Mr. E. L. Hicks suppose that the occasion of the colony was the one here mentioned by Pausanias, and that accordingly the inscription dates from about 403 B.C. Mr. R. Meister seems to incline to the same view. But epigraphists in general (A. Kirchhoff, H. Roehl, E. Curtius, E. S. Roberts, F. Bechtel, W. Dittenberger, and the editors of the *Recueil des Inscriptions juridiques grecques*) judge from certain palaeographical peculiarities that the inscription dates from the early part of the fifth century B.C. E. Curtius suggested that the colony was planted at the instigation of Corinth at the time when Megara had formed an alliance with Athens. By this alliance Athens obtained a port (Pegae) on the Corinthian gulf, and the Corinthians, jealous of this encroachment of Athenian influence on waters which they regarded as a preserve of their own, induced the Locrians to settle a garrison-colony at Naupactus, which might act as a check on the Athenian naval power in these waters. Hence the Athenians attacked and captured Naupactus. See Thucydides, i. 103. Such is Curtius's theory. He dates the capture of Naupactus by the Athenians in 458 B.C. Whatever date we may assign to the inscription in question, it supplies some valuable information on the subject of Greek colonial law, for it details the precise legal relations which should exist between the colonists and the mother-country. Briefly the conditions are these : " the colonists shall not separate politically from the Hypocnemidian Locrians ; at Naupactus they shall pay taxes only as citizens of Western Locris ; if they return of their own accord to the mother-country they shall pay an entrance-fee for enrolment, the entrance-fee, however, not being required in the case of one who has left an adult son or a brother in his place at Naupactus. Persons who have remained in the mother-country may inherit the property of kinsmen who have died at Naupactus, and *vice-versa*" (Roberts).

See W. Vischer, 'Lokrische Inschrift von Naupaktos aus der Sammlung Woodhouse,' *Rheinisches Museum*, N.F. 26 (1871), pp. 39-96 ; E. L. Hicks, *Greek*

Historical Inscriptions, No. 63; P. Cauer, *Delectus Inscr. Graec.*[2] No. 229; Roehl, *I. G. A.* No. 321; E. S. Roberts, *Greek Epigraphy*, No. 231, with the commentary on pp. 241 *sq.*, 346 *sqq.*; A. Kirchhoff, *Studien zur Geschichte des griech. Alphabets,*[4] p. 146; E. Curtius, in *Hermes*, 10 (1876), p. 237 *sqq.*; *id.*, *Griech. Geschichte,*[6] 2. p. 172 *sq.*; Ed. Meyer, *Forschungen zur alten Geschichte*, 1. pp. 291-307; Collitz, *G. D. I.* 2. No. 1478; R. Dareste, B. Haussoullier, Th. Reinach, *Recueil des Inscriptions juridiques grecques*, No. xi. pp. 180-192; R. Meister, ' Das Colonialrecht von Naupaktos,' *Berichte über die Verhandl. d. kön. sächs. Gesell. d. Wissen. zu Leipzig*, Philolog. histor. Classe, 47 (1895), pp. 272-334; Ch. Michel, *Recueil d'Inscriptions grecques*, No. 285; *C. I. G. G. S.* 3. No. 334.

38. 11. **the Naupactia.** Cp. ii. 3. 9; iv. 2. 1.   Prof. Aug. Fick thinks that the Milesian to whom the authorship of the *Naupactia* was sometimes ascribed may have been Cercops of Miletus, the contemporary and rival of Hesiod.   See Athenaeus, xi. p. 503 d, xiii. p. 557 a; Diogenes Laertius, ii. 5. 46.   Prof. Fick suggests that Cercops may have revised and edited the *Naupactia*, just as, according to Prof. Fick's conjecture, he edited the poems of Hesiod after doing them into quasi-Ionic.   See Fick, *Hesiods Gedichte in ihrer ursprünglichen Fassung und Sprachform wiederhergestellt*, p. 85; *The Classical Review*, 2 (1888), p. 197.   The fragments of the *Naupactia* are collected in Kinkel's *Epicorum Graecorum Fragmenta*, p. 198 *sqq.*

38. 11. **Charon, son of Pythes.**   According to Suidas (*s.v.* Χάρων Λαμψακηνός) the name of this early Greek historian's father was Pythocles.   As to Charon's life and works see *Frag. Hist. Graec.* ed. Müller, 1. pp. xvi. *sqq.*, 32 *sqq.*

38. 12. **a temple of Poseidon beside the sea.**   There is no trace of this temple at Naupactus.   Mr. W. J. Woodhouse conjectures that it stood, not in Naupactus, but on the promontory of Antirrhium, which runs out into the gulf five or six miles to the south-west of the town. In confirmation of this view he points out that there was a sanctuary of Poseidon on Rhium, the cape on the opposite side of the narrows (see vol. 4. p. 157); that Scylax mentions a sanctuary in Aetolia at the entrance to the gulf of Corinth, westward from Naupactus (*Periplus*, 35); that a great festival, accompanied by sacrifice, was regularly held on the cape down to Plutarch's time (Plutarch, *Sept. Sapient. Conviv.* 19); and that the Athenians under Phormio, after defeating the Peloponnesian fleet in the straits, "sailed away to Molycreum, and, having set up a trophy on Rhium and dedicated a ship to Poseidon, returned to Naupactus" (Thucydides, ii. 84).   In this passage of Thucydides the mention of the Aetolian Molycreum seems to show that the Rhium referred to was the cape on the Aetolian, not the cape on the Achaean shore.   Plutarch, also, in the passage cited above, gives the name of Rhium to the Aetolian cape.   The evidence adduced by Mr. Woodhouse certainly makes it probable that a sanctuary of Poseidon existed on Cape Antirrhium; but it can hardly have been the temple here mentioned by Pausanias, which, to judge from his language, must surely have been at Naupactus itself.   At Antirrhium there are remains of a dismantled Turkish fort.   A lighthouse is built on the wall next the sea.   See W. J. Woodhouse, *Aetolia*, pp. 312, 323.

38. 12. **Artemis —— represented in the act of hurling a dart.**

Mr. Woodhouse regards this type of Artemis as a warrior-goddess armed
with the national Aetolian weapon, with regard to which he compares
Euripides, *Phoenissae*, 139 *sq.*, 1165 *sqq.*, Pollux, i. 149. He suggests
that the type may have been adopted as a national emblem after the
repulse of the Gauls, in which the Aetolians with their javelins played a
part (cp. Paus. x. 22. 6). See W. J. Woodhouse, *Aetolia*, pp. 320-322.
But I see no reason why Artemis hurling a dart should have been a
warrior rather than a huntress.

38. 12. a grotto. In the limestone hills to the north-east of
Naupactus there are many caverns and grottos; but the grotto of
Aphrodite has not yet been identified (*Mittheil. d. arch. Inst. in Athen*,
4 (1879), p. 23 note). Mr. Woodhouse thinks that a small rocky
eminence, to the east of the sanctuary of Aesculapius (as to which see
the next note) and separated from it only by a marshy pool, is well
adapted to be the site of Aphrodite's shrine. A modern church of St.
George stands on the hill, but no ancient remains are visible. The
suburb in the plain below goes by the name of Aphrodite, but the
appellation may very well be modern. Many remains of late date, such
as small columns, bases, and cisterns, are to be met with here. Mr.
Woodhouse conjectures that this was the unwalled suburb captured by
the united Peloponnesian and Aetolian army under Eurylochus in
426 B.C. (Thucydides, iii. 102). See W. J. Woodhouse, *Aetolia*, p. 316.

38. 13. The sanctuary of Aesculapius. About a quarter of an
hour to the east of Naupactus a rocky spur advances towards the road
from the chain of low hills which runs parallel to the road on the north.
At the foot of the rock a copious spring, overshadowed by three spreading plane-trees, gushes from a Turkish fountain. The water of this
spring is deemed the best and most abundant in the neighbourhood
and is still conducted to Naupactus, as it appears to have been conducted in antiquity. In the rock immediately over the spring, at a
height of about 40 feet above the road, but hidden from it by the thick
leafage of the plane-trees, is a terrace about 50 feet long and 30 feet
wide. The wall of rock at the back of the terrace is about 12 feet
high and was once covered from end to end, to a height of 2 feet,
with inscriptions, of which the time-worn and weathered remains suffice
to show that here was the sanctuary of Aesculapius. The sanctuary was
already in ruins when Pausanias saw it. Some inscriptions recording
the enfranchisement of slaves by means of a formal sale to Aesculapius
have been dug up on the terrace.

See R. Weil, 'Die Asklepieion von Naupaktos,' *Mittheil. d. arch. Inst. in
Athen*, 4 (1879), pp. 22-29; W. J. Woodhouse, 'Aetolian inscriptions,' *Journal of
Hellenic Studies*, 13 (1892-3), p. 338 *sqq.*; *id.*, *Aetolia*, pp. 313-316; *C. I. G. G. S.*
3. Nos. 357-371.

There was another sanctuary of Aesculapius in the ravine now called
Old Skala about two hours' walk to the north-east of Naupactus. It is
a wild secluded spot in the heart of the hills; few but the shepherds
ever penetrate to it. A very difficult path leads up the ravine to
a moderately level and open space on the mountain-side half-way up
the glen. The place is called *Longa*. From here by clambering down

into the ravine we reach the ruins of the temple, romantically situated on the very brink of the foaming torrent, on the farther side of which the lofty bank rises almost perpendicularly. A column which has been tumbled down by the peasants into the bed of the stream is inscribed with legal deeds recording the emancipation of slaves by means of a nominal sale to "Aesculapius in the springs" (τôι 'Ασκλαπιôι ἐν κρουνοῖς), from which we learn that "Aesculapius in the springs" was the god of the temple. Other fallen columns, also inscribed, are said to be buried under a landslip on the site of the temple. The title "in the springs" is appropriate, for the spot is not far from the head of the gorge, where the torrent takes its rise. Moreover, another spring rises on the level ground above the temple, and there is a tiny spring also in the steep bank on the opposite side of the torrent. See W. J. Woodhouse, *Aetolia*, p. 331 *sqq.* ; *id.*, in *Journal of Hellenic Studies*, 13 (1892-93), p. 341 *sqq.*; *C. I. G. G. S.* 3. Nos. 379-387.

38. 13. the poetess Anyte. She was the authoress of some graceful epigrams preserved in the Greek Anthology. Three of them are translated in Mr. Mackail's *Select Epigrams from the Greek Anthology* (Nos. ii. 36 ; vi. 14, 24). Tatian says (*Or. ad Graecos*, xxxiii. p. 130, ed. Otto) that her statue was made by Euthycrates and Cephisodotus. As Euthycrates was a son of Lysippus (Pliny, *Nat. hist.* xxxiv. 66), his colleague Cephisodotus must have been the younger sculptor of that name (see note on viii. 30. 10). The younger Cephisodotus flourished about 296 B.C. This, therefore, must be approximately the date of the poetess Anyte and hence of the foundation of the sanctuary of Aesculapius at Naupactus.

38. 13. two thousand golden staters. The golden stater weighed 130 grains and was worth about twenty-three shillings. See Prof. P. Gardner, in Smith's *Dict. of Gr. and Rom. Antiquities*,[3] article 'Stater.' Hence the sum paid to Anyte by Phalysius was equal to about £1900. Prof. Ridgeway has shown that the golden stater was the equivalent of the old unit of barter, the ox. See his work, *The Origin of Metallic Currency and Weight Standards* (Cambridge, 1892), pp. 1 *sqq.*, 304 *sqq.*

ADDENDA

VOL. I

P. 561. In Paus. i. 1. 5 we should probably insert εἰ before καθὰ λέγουσιν with SW, Dindorf, and R. Förster (*Rheinisches Museum*, N. F. 38 (1883), p. 423).

P. 562. In Paus. i. 2. 5 A. Milchhöfer proposes to read Ἀθηνᾶς ἄγαλμα Παιανίας instead of Ἀθηνᾶς ἄγαλμα Παιωνίας (*Archäologische Studien H. Brunn dargebracht*, Berlin, 1893, p. 45). In the same sentence he prefers the reading Ἀπόλλωνος to the reading Ἀπόλλων. G. Loeschcke has suggested that instead of Ἀπόλλων or Ἀπόλλωνος we should read Ἀπολλωνίδος (J. Töpffer, *Attische Genealogie*, p. 204 note 1).

P. 562 line 26 from foot, Καλάδης. For Καλάδης we should probably read Σακάδας with S. N. Dragoumes (*Mittheilungen d. arch. Inst. in Athen*, 21 (1896), p. 30. See below, p. 482.

P. 562. In Paus. i. 12. 4, χρείας is an emendation proposed by Emperius (*Opuscula*, p. 341). The MSS. read χεῖρας, which Hitzig now replaces in the text. Cp. Schubart, *Methodologie*, p. 92.

P. 563, note on i. 18. 6. C. Wachsmuth proposed to remove the words ἃς Ἀθηναῖοι καλοῦσιν ἀποίκους πόλεις from the position which they occupy in the MSS. and to place them two lines lower down after ἀπὸ γὰρ πόλεως ἑκάστης (*Die Stadt Athen im Alterthum*, 1. p. 690 note 3). This ingenious and convincing emendation, approved by W. Gurlitt (*Ueber Pausanias*, p. 327), is rightly accepted by Hitzig in his recension of the text.

P. 563 note on i. 18. 9. Read with Hitzig in his edition ἑκατόν εἰσι κίονες Φρυγίου λίθου. πεποίηνται δὲ καὶ ταῖς στοαῖς κατὰ τὰ αὐτὰ οἱ τοῖχοι. καὶ οἰκήματα ἐνταῦθά ἐστιν ὀρόφῳ τε ἐπιχρύσῳ—πρὸς δὲ ἀγάλμασι κεκοσμημένα καὶ γραφαῖς· κατάκειται δὲ καὶ ἐς αὐτὰ βιβλία. This is closer to the MSS. and altogether better. Schubart, while he corrected the passage in one place (εἰσὶ for εἴκοσι), corrupted it by his conjectures in many.

P. 563, note on i. 19. 1. Hitzig in his edition is probably right in accepting Dindorf's conjecture παρῆγε for παρῆν, and retaining the rest of the sentence as it stands in the MSS. The ὄροφος mentioned in the text may have been reeds for thatching the roof (Pollux, x. 170).

P. 569, note on ii. 1. 4 ἐν Ἐπιδαύρῳ τῇ ἱερᾷ. The adjective ἱερά here applied to Epidaurus is defended by inscriptions found in the Epidaurian sanctuary of Aesculapius. See P. Cavvadias, *Fouilles d'Épidaure*, vol. i. p. 68, Inscr. No. 106 line 9 ἐν Ἐπιδαύρῳ τῇ ἱερᾷ, Inscr. No. 106 line 12 τῇ ἱερᾷ Ἐπιδαύρῳ, line 16 ἐν Ἐπιδαύρῳ τῇ ἱερᾷ, and p. 106 Inscr. No. 260 line 3 ἡ ἱερὰ Ἐπιδαυρίων πόλις.

P. 573, note on ii. 32. 6. The emendation διαβάντος for διαβάς has been independently suggested by S. Wide (*De sacris Troezeniorum, Hermionensium, Epidauriorum*, p. 74).

P. 577. In Paus. iii. 22. 2, S. Wide would read Θέμιδος for Θέτιδος (*op. cit.* p. 37).

P. 585. In Paus. v. 15. 3 it has been proposed by Hitzig (*Zur Pausaniasfrage*, p. 72) to read τοῦ Λεωνιδαίου πέραν ⟨προιέναι⟩ μέλλοντι instead of τοῦ Λεωνιδαίου περᾶν μέλλοντι. The change would certainly be an improvement, for the phrase τοῦ Λεωνιδαίου περᾶν in the sense of "to pass beyond a place" seems inadmissible. It is not defended by Sophocles, *Oed. Tyr.* 673 *sq.* ὅταν θυμοῦ περάσῃς, as to which see Jebb's note.

P. 588. In Paus. vi. 4. 5 von Wilamowitz-Möllendorff proposed to read Ἐρέσιον for Ἐφέσιον (*Hermes*, 11 (1876), p. 294). The conjecture is approved by W. Gurlitt (*Ueber Pausanias*, pp. 361, 415).

P. 611. In Paus. x. 29. 7 C. Robert has now withdrawn his proposed alteration of the words διὰ μὲν τοῦ χιτῶνος κ.τ.λ. He would now leave the text as it stands except that with Buttmann he would insert ἐντός before the words ἐν τοῖς κοίλοις εἰκάσεις τῶν χειρῶν. See C. Robert, *Die Marathonschlacht in der Poikile* (Halle a. S., 1895), p. 121 *sq.* This insertion of ἐντός is a simple and easy emendation, and is to be preferred to the insertion of τῇ ἑτέρᾳ after τῶν χειρῶν, which I had provisionally adopted. The translation should accordingly run : "You may guess that within her tunic she is grasping the famous necklace in the hollows of her hands."

VOL. II

·P. 1 line 8 from foot, **Sunium.** A visit paid by me to Sunium (28th November 1895) gave me an opportunity of correcting and supplementing on some points the description given in the text. The remains of the fortifications are now but scanty. They exist in a very dilapidated state on the east and north sides of the cape ; they are best preserved on the north side. On the south and west sides hardly a trace of them is to be found. The material is mostly a light brown stone, which seemed to me to be sandstone ; but some pieces of the fortifications, especially the towers, are built of the native rock of the cape. This is a crystalline rock which takes a yellow coating by exposure to the weather. It is only where pieces are chipped off that its crystalline structure is exposed. No part of the existing fortification-walls is built of white marble as stated in the text. The number of courses of masonry preserved varies from one to six. The greatest height to which any piece of wall or tower is preserved is between 8 and 9 feet. The thickness of the wall, where both faces are standing, is 10 feet 2 inches, according to my measurement. Towards its eastern end the north wall is built regularly of squared blocks of the light brown stone laid in horizontal courses; but farther to the west the wall with its towers is constructed of the yellow-coated crystalline rock in a very irregular and miserable style, the stones being small and hardly hewn or fitted together. Still farther to the west there are some remains of the better built wall of light brown sandstone. These marked differences in style between portions of the north wall seem to indicate that at some later time the original fortifications were hastily and rudely repaired.

The terrace to the north of the temple is supported on the north and west by two walls, of which the northern is 40 paces long and the western 37 paces. Both these supporting walls are built of quadrangular blocks of white marble laid in horizontal courses; the blocks are unusually low in proportion to their length. At the north-west corner the wall is twelve courses or about 13 feet high. On the terrace there are remains of two walls meeting at a right angle; one of them runs along the western side of the terrace within a foot or so of the edge; the other, of which one and two courses are preserved, runs east and west at a distance of 10 paces from the northern edge of the terrace. Both walls are built of the light brown sandstone referred to above. They may be the remains of a sanctuary of Poseidon, who is known to have been worshipped at Sunium. How the terrace, situated as it is, could have supported a *propylaeum* or portal leading into the sacred precinct, as has sometimes been supposed, it is difficult to see.

Of the sculptured slabs of marble said to lie in front of the temple I found only one that bore undoubted remains of reliefs. The others have perhaps been removed.

After the battle of Salamis the Greeks dedicated a captured Phoenician ship at Sunium (Herodotus, viii. 121).

P. 4 line 26 from foot, **Laurium.** As to the working of the silver mines of Laurium in antiquity, see J. J. Binder, *Laurion: die attischen Bergwerke im Alterthum* (Laibach, 1895). The work is illustrated with plates and with a map of the district which shows the positions of the ancient mines.

P. 8 line 22 from foot, **the fortification-wall** etc. The fortification-wall which skirted the shore of Piraeus is especially well preserved at two places, one on the eastern and the other on the western side of the peninsula. On the eastern side, a little to the south of the harbour of Zea, the wall is preserved beside the road for a length of about 100 paces at a distance of about 40 yards from the sea. Its height varies from one to five courses of masonry, but the average is nearer five than one. In this stretch of wall there is a square projecting tower standing to a height of from two to five courses. It is

6.25 metres broad and projects 4.75 metres from the curtain. The masonry both of the wall and of the tower is of the regular ashlar sort. The other place where the wall is in good preservation is a little bay on the western side of the peninsula, near its southern extremity. The bay opens southwards, and the wall is preserved almost all round it to a height of from two to five courses. Two square towers project from it. The masonry is again of the fine ashlar sort. But the thickness of the wall does not appear, nor is it possible to say whether it was here built of solid masonry or had a core of rubble. However, at one point on the south side of the peninsula the wall seems to have consisted of an outer and inner facing of ashlar masonry with a core of rubble between; and from the quantity of small broken stones lying about the line of wall round the edge of the peninsula, I incline to think that the wall which skirted the shore had everywhere a core of rubble.

P. 10 line 18 *sq.* from top, **The principal gate** etc. The remains of the principal gateway of Piraeus, briefly described in the text, are to be seen about six minutes' walk to the east of the Piraeus railway-station. The gateway, which faces north, is about 20 paces wide, and is flanked by two square towers resting on oval bases. Of these towers the eastern is the better preserved. It is 8 paces broad and projects 9 paces from the curtain. The oval base on which it rests is exposed on one side to a height of four courses, and the tower itself is standing to a height of three courses. The height of the seven courses together is 3 metres (9 ft. 10 in.). The masonry is of the fine ashlar kind, the blocks being squared and laid in exactly horizontal courses. Adjoining this gateway on the west the wall, built in the same style, is preserved to a height of three and four courses for a length of about 18 paces. As it stands, the wall is 4.33 metres thick, but it may have been thicker originally.

Some 40 yards to the east of the gateway is another piece of the fortification-wall with a round tower built as before of fine ashlar masonry. This tower, which in shape is more than a semicircle, is 12 paces in diameter and is standing to a height of five courses. The wall adjoining the tower on the east has four courses standing for a length of 18 or 19 paces; it is 5.60 metres thick, and this seems to have been its full thickness at this point. It appears to be built of solid masonry without any core of rubble. About 44 paces east of the round tower is a second round tower, beyond which the wall is 5.30 metres thick, built of solid masonry without any core of rubble. Not more than two courses of it, however, are here preserved. From the last-mentioned tower the wall extends up hill eastward for 35 paces to a second gateway, through which the road between the Long Walls is believed to have gone. This gate, as stated in the text, is double. An outer gate, about 6 paces wide, led into a court 19 paces square, at the farther end of which there was an inner gate. The outer gate was probably flanked with a round tower on each side, but only the tower on the west side now exists or at least is visible; it has from one to three courses of masonry standing. The walls of the court are three courses high. On the west side of the court the wall is 7 metres (23 feet) thick; the masonry here is again solid, without any core of rubble. From the gateway the wall strikes up hill in a north-easterly direction, but is concealed almost immediately by modern walls.

P. 27 line 8 from top, **statues of Zeus and the People.** A statue representing the People of Elis was set up by the people of Lacedaemon, as we learn from an inscription found at Olympia. The inscription seems to date from the Imperial age. See Dittenberger und Purgold, *Die Inschriften von Olympia*, No. 316.

P. 32 line 25 *sq.* from foot, **two ancient theatres.** As to these two theatres, see W. Dörpfeld in *Das griechische Theater* (Athens and Leipsic, 1896), p. 97 *sqq.* Of the theatre on the hill of Munychia nothing is known but the situation; the remains are buried under the soil. Some of the walls were excavated in 1880, but afterwards covered up. The other theatre, which lies a little to the west of the harbour of Zea, closely resembles in its plan the Dionysiac theatre at Athens as built by Lycurgus. The form of the auditorium is that of a semicircle with the wings prolonged in straight lines. Fourteen staircases divided the seats into thirteen wedge-shaped blocks. A semicircular passage and open gutter separate the lowest row of seats from the orchestra. The orchestra forms a complete circle, the diameter of which, measured within the gutter, is 16.34 metres. Its floor is the native rock. From the foundations of the stage-buildings which remain we gather that the stage was about 18 metres long exclusive of two square wings which projected 2.61 metres from it, one at either end, and that its front was adorned with fourteen Doric columns. Between the two middle columns there would seem to have been a door; at least the space between these columns (2.12 metres) is wider than the space (1.39 metres) between the other columns. The depth of the stage, between the wings, was probably about 3 metres.[1] The fronts of the wings were adorned with five columns apiece. At the back of the stage extended a hall about 34 metres long by nearly 5 metres wide. This was no doubt the green-room. The stage-buildings show no sign of having been altered in Roman times.

P. 32 line 26 from foot, **Before we quit the peninsula of Piraeus** etc. Here may be mentioned the recent discovery of the Serangeum at Piraeus. The Serangeum is mentioned by Isaeus (*Or.* vi. 33) and Alciphron (*Epist.* iii. 43) as a place in which there was a bath, and from the Greek lexicographers (Harpocration, Photius, Suidas, *s.v.* Σηράγγιον) we learn that it was in Piraeus. Harpocration says it was mentioned by Lysias and Aristophanes; and Photius informs us that it was founded by a certain Serangus, and contained the shrine of a hero. The name, which signifies 'place of caverns,' recalls Strabo's description of the hill of Munychia (ix. p. 395) as "in great part hollow

---

[1] Its depth, as measured by me (16th December 1895) from the front of the stylobate, is 2.73 metres, but to this we must add something for the projection of the cornice. The distance of the stylobate from the back wall of the stage is, according to Dr. Dörpfeld, 2.17 metres, but in this measurement the breadth of the stylobate is naturally not included. The measurement of the projection of the wings (2.61 metres) which is given in the text is taken from my own notes.

and tunnelled, naturally adapted for dwellings, and entered by a narrow mouth." Following these indications Mr. J. Dragatsis lately discovered the Serangeum. The entrance is beside the sea, at the eastern foot of the hill of Munychia, near the modern sea-baths of Paraskeuas. Here Mr. Dragatsis found a subterranean chamber, which had clearly been used as a bath, with openings from it through the cliffs in several directions. On the right of the bath-room is an artificial cavity with a double row of niches. In the upper row of niches the bathers may have deposited their clothes, in the lower the vessels used in the bath. The floor of the bath-room is a mosaic of black and white stones arranged to represent several scenes. Most of these have been at some time or other demolished, but enough remains to allow us to make out a woman moving to the left followed by two dogs, also a beardless young man driving a four-horse car with a dolphin swimming below it. The driver of the car may be Serangus, the hero who gave his name to the place. The discovery of a stone bearing an inscription Ἡρῴου ὅρος 'boundary of the hero's shrine' confirms the statement of Photius that there was a shrine of the hero in the Serangeum; and the marble tablets adorned with snakes in relief which have been found on the site were probably dedicated to him, since we know that the supernatural beings whom the Greeks called heroes were commonly associated with snakes (Plutarch, *Cleomenes*, 39; Photius, *Lexicon*, *s.v.* ἥρως ποικίλος; E. Rohde, *Psyche*, p. 223 note 5). See the letter of Mr. S. P. Lambros, in *Athenaeum*, 20th March 1897, p. 385 *sq.*

P. 35 line 10 from foot, **Cape Colias.** The view, adopted in the text, that Cape Colias is the modern Cape *Cosmas*, has recently been again defended by Mr. P. Kastromenos (Ἐφημερὶς ἀρχαιολογική, 1897, pp. 93-96). In support of it he points out that fine pottery was made from Colian clay (Athenaeus, xi. p. 482 b), and that the clay at Cape *Cosmas* is of excellent quality, whereas at *Trispyrgi*, which some writers identify with Cape Colias, the soil is sandy and not adapted for the manufacture of pottery.

P. 44 line 24 from top, **Between the Dipylum** etc. The outer wall between the Dipylum and the Sacred Gate is 19 ft. 8 in. distant from the inner wall. Three courses of it are preserved on the outer face, and one and two courses on the inner face. The large blocks placed on the socle of the inner wall are squared and of different kinds of stone (conglomerate, etc.); they are not of the blue limestone of which the socle is built.

P. 45 line 7, **sixteen courses.** The highest part of this wall, so far as I could see, is only ten courses high (about 13 feet).

P. 49 line 18 *sq.* 'giant-pillars' or 'serpent-pillars.' As to these monuments see the monograph of Dr. G. A. Müller, *Die Reitergruppe auf den römisch germanischen Giganten-Säulen* (Strassburg i/E. und Bühl, 1894). They are found on both slopes of the Vosges mountains, in the districts of Saar and Meurthe as far as the Moselle in Luxemburg, the Palatine, and the lower valleys of the Neckar and Main. Some of them are inscribed with the date and a dedication to Jupiter or to Jupiter and Juno. One well-preserved specimen, found at Schierstein in

1889, is dated the 28th February of the year 221 A.D. Another, found at Heddernheim, bears the date 241 A.D. All of the monuments seem to belong to the third century A.D. Thus Mr. Körn's interpretation of them as copies of a statue of Caligula vanquishing the Ocean becomes improbable. Dr. G. A. Müller would explain them as memorials, erected on various occasions, of victories won by the Romans over the barbarians of Germany, the struggle being represented in the mythical form of a god trampling a giant under foot. The figure of the rider is believed by Dr. Müller to stand variously for Jupiter, Neptune, or a Roman emperor.

P. 52 line 21 from foot, **the sculptor Eubulides.** The inscribed base of another statue by this Athenian sculptor, Eubulides son of Euchir, was found by Messrs. Bather and Yorke at Hyampolis in 1894. See *Journal of Hellenic Studies*, 16 (1896), p. 307, No. 3. For the family tree of the artist, see Loewy, *Inschriften griech. Bildhauer*, p. 166.

P. 55 line 7 from top, **the Ceramicus.** Pausanias's description of the market-place of Athens is examined in a special dissertation by Mr. O. B. Fallis (*Pausanias auf der Agora von Athen*, München, 1895). He accepts Dr. Dörpfeld's conjecture that the Pnyx was "the old market-place" mentioned by Apollodorus (Harpocration, s.v. Πάνδημος Ἀφρο-δίτη), and he follows Dr. Dörpfeld also in his identification of the Enneacrunus.

P. 56, **the rest of the building is of common stone.** But on the inner side of the back wall of the colonnade there is a socle of grey marble built in two courses, a low one and a high one.

P. 57 line 17 from top, **the Royal Colonnade.** Excavations conducted by the German Archaeological Institute in 1895-97, laid bare some remains of a building which Dr. Dörpfeld thinks may have been the Royal Colonnade. The remains are situated on the west side of the modern Poseidon Street, at the eastern foot of the hill on which the so-called Theseum stands. This is, as I have pointed out in the text, exactly the place where we should expect to find the Royal Colonnade. However the building which has been brought to light has not the usual shape of a Greek colonnade. It was a chamber about 9 metres square with a façade opening to the east between six columns. There was one door in the middle of the façade and another in the north wall. Dr. Dörpfeld assigns the building to the beginning of the fifth century B.C. at latest. To the south of and in a line with it are the remains of a similar edifice of later date which appears to have occupied the site of an older building. See W. Dörpfeld, in *Mittheilungen d. arch. Inst. in Athen*, 21 (1896), pp. 107-109, and *ib.* 22 (1897), p. 225.

P. 63 line 22 *sqq.* from top, **the kings from Melanthus to Clidicus** etc. The list of the Athenian kings has been discussed, with characteristic insight and sobriety, by the late J. Töpffer ('Die Liste der athenische Könige,' *Hermes*, 31 (1896), pp. 105-123; reprinted in the writer's *Beiträge zur griech. Altertumswissenschaft* (Berlin, 1897), pp. 275-292), who refutes the objections raised by Professor von

Wilamowitz-Moellendorff (*Aristoteles und Athen*, 2. p. 134) to the authenticity of the list of the Medontid kings.

P. 66 line 3 from foot, **the regular ascent from the market-place to the Acropolis** etc. A passage in one of the letters ascribed to Diogenes (No. 30) shows that in antiquity, as at the present day, two separate roads led up to the Acropolis from the low ground at the northern foot of the Areopagus, "one of them short, steep, and difficult, the other long, smooth, and easy." The former no doubt coincided or nearly so with the steep footpath which still ascends on the east side of the Areopagus, near the cave of the Eumenides. The latter is the broad road enclosed by walls of polygonal masonry of which a considerable part has been laid bare by Dr. Dörpfeld's excavations. In the text I have assumed that this broad and easy road is the one of which Arrian was thinking when he spoke of the ascent to the Acropolis, and that consequently the Metroum and the statues of the tyrannicides stood on the western side of the Areopagus. But it is quite possible that Arrian was referring to the steep footpath, not to the broad road, and consequently that the statues of the tyrannicides and perhaps the Metroum too were on the eastern side of the Areopagus. This latter is the view preferred by Professor C. Wachsmuth on the ground that the statues of the tyrannicides were, according to Arrian (*Anabasis*, iii. 16. 8), not far from the altar of the Eudanemi, and that this altar, on account of the connexion of the Eudanemi with Eleusis (J. Töpffer, *Attische Genealogie*, p. 112), probably stood near the cave of the Eumenides (C. Wachsmuth, 'Neue Beiträge zur Topographie von Athen,' *Abhandlungen d. philolog. histor. Classe d. k. sächs. Gesell. d. Wissen*. 18 (1897), No. 1. p. 30 *sq.*).

P. 70 line 17 from top, **Counsellor Zeus.** Zeus was worshipped under the same title at Aegae, as we learn from an inscription (R. Bohn, *Altertümer von Aegae*, p. 34); and Counsellor Zeus appears as a legend on coins of Mytilene of imperial date (B. V. Head, *Historia numorum*, p. 488).

P. 71 line 12 from top, **the Clotted Sea.** Since this note was written I see that the explanation of the Clotted Sea to which I have given the preference is accepted also by Sir John Lubbock (*Prehistoric Times*,[5] p. 69). He says: "Round the island of Thule Pytheas saw a substance which was neither earth, air, nor water, but a substance resembling medusae or jelly-fishes (πνεύμονι θαλασσίᾳ ἐοικός), which could neither be passed on foot nor in ships. This passage, which has completely puzzled southern commentators, is justly regarded by Professor Nilsson as a striking evidence of Pytheas's veracity. For when the Northern Ocean freezes, this does not happen as in our ponds or lakes, but small, separate plates of ice are formed, and as soon as this process commences, the fisherman hurry to the shore, lest they should be caught in the ice, which for some time is too thick to permit the passage of a boat, yet too weak to support the weight of a man. A very similar description is given by Captain Lyon. 'We came,' he says, 'amongst young ice, in that state called sludge, which resembles in appearance and consistency a far better thing—lemon ice. From this we came to small round plates, of about a foot in diameter, which have the appearance of the scales of gigantic fishes.' Richardson also particularly mentions the 'circular plates of ice, six or eight inches in diameter.' These discs of ice tossed about by the waves suggested to Professor Nilsson himself, when he first saw them, the idea of a crowd of medusae, and if we imagine a southerner who had never before witnessed such a phenomenon, and who on his return home wished to describe it to his fellow-countrymen, it would have been difficult to find an apter or more ingenious simile."

P. 72 line 21 from top, Celts —— Gauls. Some modern writers have attempted to distinguish the Gauls from the Celts. Thus Mr. H. Schaaffhausen would confine the name Celts to the peaceful settled inhabitants of Southern Gaul, while he would give the name of Gauls to the warlike tribes of the north and to the roving bands who invaded Greece and finally settled in Asia Minor. He points out that the distinction has the support of Diodorus (v. 32), according to whom the Celts were the people inland from Marseilles, about the Alps, and on the hither side of the Pyrenees, while the Gauls inhabited the lands beyond that region towards the south,[1] beside the ocean and the Hercynian mountains as far as Scythia. See H. Schaaffhausen, ' Die Kelten,' in *Festschrift zum fünfzigjährigen Jubiläum des Vereins von Alterthumsfreunden im Rheinlande am* 1 October 1891, p. 65 *sqq.*

P. 73 line 9 from top, Pergamus —— Teuthrania. The distinction between Pergamus and Teuthrania is rightly maintained by Mr. E. Thrämer (*Pergamos*, p. 207 *sqq.*).

P. 75 line 8 *sqq.* from top. The Pergamene inscriptions recording the victories over the Gauls are published by Fränkel (*Inschriften von Pergamon*, 1. Nos. 20-24). As to these inscriptions and the history of the wars of the kings of Pergamus with the Gauls see also E. Thrämer, *Pergamos*, pp. 230-232, 246-263 ; H. Gäbler, *Erythrae* (Berlin, 1892), p. 39 *sqq.*; M. Fränkel, 'Das grosse Siegesdenkmal Attalos I.,' *Philologus*, 54 (1895), pp. 1-10 ; Köpp, in *Berliner philolog. Wochenschrift*, 24 August 1895, p. 1115 *sqq.*, and in *Archäologischer Anzeiger*, 1895, p. 123 *sqq.* Mr. Thrämer would place the great victory of Attalus I. over the Gauls at the beginning of the king's reign, namely in 240 B.C. or at latest in 239 B.C. Mr. Fränkel holds that the war with the Gauls was not victoriously concluded until 228 B.C.

P. 75 line 9 from foot, **two different stories of the coming of Telephus to Asia** etc. As to these two different legends see E. Thrämer, *Pergamos*, pp. 369-406. Perhaps, as Mr. Thrämer supposes, Euripides may have borrowed his version of the tale from Hecataeus ; for Pausanias (viii. 4. 9, cp. viii. 47. 4) cites Hecataeus as his authority in relating that form of the legend which we know from Strabo (xiii. p. 615) to have been adopted by Euripides. The smaller frieze found at Pergamus which illustrates the career of Telephus from his infancy upwards (*Die Ergebnisse der Ausgrabungen zu Pergamon*, Vorläufiger Bericht, Berlin 1880, pp. 65-69) has been carefully discussed and

---

[1] εἰς τὰ πρὸς νότον νεύοντα. For νότον we should perhaps read ἄρκτον here, as Diodorus seems to place the Gauls to the north, not to the south, of the Celts.

explained by Prof. C. Robert ('Beiträge zur Erklärung des pergame-nischen Telephos-frieses,' *Jahrbuch des archäolog. Instituts*, 2 (1887), pp. 244-259; *id.*, 3 (1888), pp. 45-65, 87-105). The scene on the frieze representing the making of the chest in which Auge is to be committed to the sea is well reproduced in Collignon's *Histoire de la Sculpture grecque*, vol. 2. p. 528, Fig. 274.

P. 75 line 13 from foot, **the Cabiri.** The worship of the Cabiri at Pergamus is referred to in an oracle of which a copy, engraved on stone, was found at Pergamus (*C.I.G.* No. 3538; Kaibel, *Epigrammata Graeca*, No. 1035). The inscription seems to date from the reign of Antoninus Pius and hence to be contemporary with Pausanias. Mr. Thrämer argues that the divinities at Pergamus whom Pausanias and Aristides call Cabiri were really Corybantes, attendants of the great Asiatic goddess, and that the identification of them with the Cabiri was a late fancy of the mythologists. See E. Thrämer, *Pergamos*, pp. 263-270.

P. 90 line 3 from top, **a statue of Demosthenes.** A pedestal found in the sanctuary of Aesculapius at Athens bears the name of Demo-sthenes (*C. I. A.* iii. 1. No. 944 a, p. 508). The inscription is of the Roman period, but the person represented was probably the great orator.

P. 92 line 14 from top, **Calades.** Mr. S. N. Dragoumes proposes to ubstitute the name of the famous musician Sacadas for that of the unknown Calades in the text of Pausanias. The change is easy (ΣΑΚΑΔΑΣ for ΚΑΛΑΔΗΣ) and the emendation probable. That a statue of Sacadas should be placed near statues of Apollo and Pindar would be eminently appropriate, since Sacadas was believed to have won the esteem of Apollo by his music (Paus. ii. 22. 8 *sq.*) and was celebrated in a poem by Pindar (Paus. ix. 30. 2; Plutarch, *De musica*, 8). See S. N. Dragoumes, in *Mittheilungen d. arch. Inst. in Athen*, 21 (1896), pp. 27-32.

P. 96 line 10 *sqq.* from top. As to the statues of Harmodius and Aristogiton, particularly the copy of them on the Scaramanga vase, see further Overbeck in *Berichte über die Verhandlungen d. k. sächs. Gesell. d. Wissen. zu Leipzig*, Philolog. histor. Cl., 44 (1892), pp. 34-38.

P. 100 line 4 from top, **Ptolemy, surnamed Philometor.** This was not Ptolemy VI., surnamed Philometor, but Ptolemy VIII., surnamed Soter II. and Philometor, who reigned, with a long break, from 117 B.C. to 81 B.C. See Justin, xxxix. 3-5. An inscription found at Athens (*C. I. A.* ii. 1. No. 464) records a decree for the erection of a bronze statue in his honour. The statue may have been the one seen by Pausanias. Compare W. Gurlitt, *Ueber Pausanias*, p. 257 *sq.* In the same chapter (i. 9. 4) Pausanias mentions a statue of Alexander the Great, and an inscription from the pedestal of a statue in Alexander's honour has been found at Athens (*C. I. A.* iii. 1. No. 945). The inscription belongs to the Roman period.

P. 104 line 13 from top, **Pergamus.** The story of Pergamus who was said to have given his name to the city is told somewhat differently by Servius (on Virgil, *Ecl.* vi. 72), according to whom Pergamus, a son of Neoptolemus and Andromache, came from Epirus to Asia at the invitation of Grynus, son of Eurypylus, to aid that prince in his wars with his neighbours. In gratitude for his help Grynus founded a new city and named it Pergamus after his defender. Mr. Thrämer shows grounds for thinking that the story of the coming of Pergamus from Epirus to Asia was a fiction posterior to the age of Alexander the Great. See E. Thrämer, *Pergamos*, p. 241 *sqq.*

P. 107 line 16 *sq.* from top, **dwarf tribes in various parts of Equatorial Africa.** The reports, ancient and modern, of the existence of dwarf tribes in Africa have been examined again in recent years by Professor O. Lenz of Prague ('Historisches über die sogenannten Zwergvölker,' *Verhandlungen der 42sten Versammlung deutscher Philologen* (Leipzig, 1894), pp. 525-535). He concludes that there are still remnants in Africa of a race of men totally different from the negroes of the Sudan, the Bantu tribes, and the Hottentots, living as hunters or fishers, and characterised by low stature, primitive manners, and the possession of a language different from that of their neighbours ; further that this dwarf race was formerly more widely diffused than at present, and that its existence, especially about the sources of the Nile, was known to the Mediterranean peoples in the remotest antiquity.

P. 112 line 15 from foot, **a fountain called Enneacrunus.** Since this note was written the excavations conducted by Dr. Dörpfeld between the Pnyx and the Areopagus with the view of discovering the Enneacrunus and other ancient structures mentioned by Pausanias have been continued, and detailed accounts of the work have been published by Dr. Dörpfeld and his colleagues (*Mittheilungen d. arch. Inst. in Athen*, 19 (1894), pp. 248-282, 496-509 ; *id.*, 20 (1895), pp. 161-206 ; *id.*, 21 (1896), pp. 103-107, 265-332). Dr. Dörpfeld believes, as we have seen, that he has discovered the Enneacrunus or Callirrhoe. What he identifies as such is a small square chamber hewn out of the rock at the eastern foot of the Pnyx hill and communicating with a smaller round basin, also cut out of the rock, a few feet lower down. In the back wall of the square chamber there is a niche from which water sometimes issues in winter. This, according to Dr. Dörpfeld, is the spring Callirrhoe. In early Roman times the square chamber seems to have been deepened by nearly 5 feet, and at a later time a large Roman house was built in front both of the square chamber and the round basin, blocking them up and cutting them off from the ancient road which ran at the foot of the hill. In the walls of this house were found some hewn blocks of stone which Dr. Dörpfeld conceives to have formed part of the casing of masonry with which Pisistratus or his sons enclosed the spring Callirrhoe. One of the blocks shows a channel for water with two mouths ; into another a lion's head has been let in, apparently to serve as a spout. Some yards to the south is a large quadrangular cistern, hewn out of the rock. Originally small, it seems to have been greatly enlarged and deepened in Roman times. In this large cistern the great subterranean aqueduct, of which some account has been given (vol. 2. p. 114), comes to an end. The aqueduct has now been traced along the southern side of the Acropolis as far east as the Dionysiac theatre. It consists of a tunnel hewn in the rock and measuring about 1.40 metres in height by .65 metre in width, though in some places the dimensions are greater. A remarkable feature is that above it is a second similar tunnel, which communicates at certain places with the lower tunnel. The object of this upper tunnel is unknown.[1] At intervals of 30 to 40 metres both tunnels are connected with the surface of the ground by perpendicular shafts; one of these shafts is no less than 12 metres (nearly 40 feet) deep. Dr. Dörpfeld's theory is that this aqueduct was constructed by Pisistratus for the purpose of reinforcing the supply of water of the spring Callirrhoe when that proved insufficient for the growing wants of Athens.

Reasons for refusing to accept this theory have already been given in the text. Further consideration and more evidence appear to me greatly to strengthen these reasons, which have now been stated with much force by Mr. Ch. Belger (*Berliner philolog. Wochenschrift*, 14 (1894), pp. 91-94; *ib.* 15 (1895), pp. 829-832, 859-864; *ib.* 16 (1896), pp. 157-160, 188 *sq.*, 508-510, 540-544; *Archäologischer Anzeiger*, 1895, pp. 110-116; *ib.* 1896, pp. 22 *sq.*, 40-45), Prof. J. M. Stahl (*Rheinisches Museum*, N. F. 50 (1895), pp. 566-575; *ib.* 51 (1896), pp. 306-311), Prof. Milchhöfer (*Philologus*, 55 (1896), pp. 170-179), and Prof. C. Wachsmuth ('Neue Beiträge zur Topographie von Athen,' *Abhandlungen d. philolog. histor. Cl. d. k. sächs. Gesell. d. Wissenschaften*, 18 (1897), No. 1. pp. 1-32). Dr. Dörpfeld has attempted to reply to the two first of these scholars, but his replies are ineffective (*Berliner philolog. Wochenschrift*, 16 (1896), pp. 123-128; *Archäologischer Anzeiger*, 1896, pp. 19-21; *Rheinisches Museum*, N. F. 51 (1896), pp. 127-137). His theory has however been accepted by Mr. E. Bodensteiner ('Enneakrunos und Lenaion,' *Blätter für das Gymnasial-Schulwesen*, 31 (1895), pp. 209-226) and Prof. J. B. Bury (*Athenaeum*, 22nd February 1896, p. 257). Apart from the chain of testimony of other ancient writers which seems to link the Enneacrunus or Callirrhoe indissolubly to the Ilissus and the south-eastern quarter of Athens, the considerations that tell conclusively against Dr. Dörpfeld are two, namely, first the evidence of Thucydides, and second the nature of the remains themselves.

(1) In describing the extent of Athens as it was before the time of Theseus, Thucydides says (ii. 15) that the city in those days comprised only the Acropolis and the part below it mainly to the south (τὸ ὑπ᾿ αὐτὴν πρὸς νότον μάλιστα τετραμμένον). To prove that the ancient city included the Acropolis, Thucydides points to the sanctuaries of the gods on the Acropolis and to the fact that in his own time the Acropolis was still known specially as 'the city.' To prove that the ancient city, so far as it exceeded the limits of the Acropolis, lay chiefly to the south of it, Thucydides points to the sanctuaries in that quarter of the city, namely the sanctuary of Olympian Zeus, the

---

[1] On the analogy of the ancient drainage-works of the Copaic Lake in which remains of two tunnels, one above the other, have also been observed (see above, p. 117), I would suggest that the upper tunnel was constructed first and that at a later time, when this tunnel did not answer its purpose, either from not being deep enough or not having a sufficient slope, the lower tunnel was constructed to replace it.

Pythium, the sanctuary of Earth, the sanctuary of Dionysus in the Marshes, and further to the fountain of Enneacrunus. He explains that in his time the fountain was called Enneacrunus ('with nine jets'), because the tyrants (Pisistratus or his sons) had converted it into that form, but that of old, when the springs were open, the fountain was named Callirrhoe ('fair-flowing'). His reason for referring to it as evidence of the extent of the ancient city was that down to his own day the water of that spring was still used at marriages and other sacred ceremonies, from which he infers that it must have been similarly used for the most important purposes by the Athenians in days of old.

The passage, thus interpreted in its simple and natural sense, is clear and logical. Thucydides first makes two statements as to the extent of the ancient city, and then supports these two statements by two separate sets of proofs. If the Enneacrunus and the sanctuaries mentioned by him as outside of the Acropolis were not situated to the south of it, then Thucydides's statement that the ancient city, so far as it exceeded the limits of the Acropolis, extended chiefly to the south, is left unsupported by any evidence, and the reference to the Enneacrunus and the sanctuaries outside of the Acropolis has no bearing whatever on the matter in hand. Yet Dr. Dörpfeld holds that the Enneacrunus and the sanctuaries in question lay, without a single exception, either to the west or the north of the Acropolis. If he is right, we must conclude that in order to prove that ancient Athens extended to the *south* of the Acropolis, the historian appealed to structures all of which were situated to the *west* or *north* of it. If this is not to stultify Thucydides I cannot imagine what would suffice to do so.

(2) The remains of ancient water-works brought to light by Dr. Dörpfeld at the northern foot of the Pnyx hill are appealed to by him as conclusive evidence that he has found the Enneacrunus. To me they seem to prove precisely the reverse. What has he found ? A perennial spring sufficient to form a fountain with nine jets such as we know the Enneacrunus to have been ? Not at all. He has found, according to his own account (*Archäologischer Anzeiger*, 1896, p. 41), a cistern hewn in the rock from the back wall of which water occasionally issues in winter. And this was the town-well (*Stadt-brunnen*) from which, according to his own account, all the Athenians in the early days of Athens drew their water ! How could they have drawn it in summer when there was none to draw ? Even in winter the flow would seem to be exceedingly rare and scanty. I have visited the scene of Dr. Dörpfeld's excavations repeatedly in winter without ever, to the best of my recollection, observing a driblet of flowing water. Mr. Ch. Belger, who enjoyed the advantage of Dr. Dörpfeld's own guidance, saw some water standing down below in a round basin, but none flowing. All that Dr. Dörpfeld himself claims to have discovered are "several natural veins of water," every one of them, apparently, subterranean. But a natural vein of water which oozes scantily and intermittently in winter can never have formed the 'fair-flowing' spring Callirrhoe and the nine-mouthed fountain of Enneacrunus. Such a spring in fact does not exist anywhere at the present day in the hollow

between the Pnyx and the Areopagus, and that no such spring existed there in antiquity is abundantly demonstrated by the deep wells, over 100 in number, with which the ground is studded, as well as by the great aqueduct which brought water to this dry and rocky district. Where there is a good spring on the surface, men do not honeycomb the rock with deep wells to find water, nor do they laboriously bring it in aqueducts from distant sources. The existence here of an aqueduct, to which Dr. Dörpfeld ventures to appeal as evidence in his favour, tells in fact most strongly against him. Even if we grant, what has not been made out, that the aqueduct was constructed by Pisistratus, this would not prove that it had any connexion with the Enneacrunus. For in describing the change made by Pisistratus at the spring neither Thucydides nor Pausanias says a word about an aqueduct ; all they give us to understand is that the springs, which before were open, were enclosed with masonry by the tyrant and that the water thenceforth issued through nine spouts. Finally, the square rock-cut chamber which Dr. Dörpfeld identifies with Callirrhoe would seem to have been only one of many similar rock-cut cisterns of which a whole series, connected with each other by passages, has recently been laid bare by the German excavations a little further to the south (*Mittheil. d. arch. Inst. in Athen,* 21 (1896), p. 104). In them we see a system of water-works which Dr. Dörpfeld is probably right in referring to an earlier age than that of Pisistratus. Had they only come to light sooner, it would hardly have occurred to anybody to identify the neighbouring cistern as the Enneacrunus, and thus the study of Athenian topography would have been spared another weary and barren controversy.

Some excavations were made in the bed of the Ilissus, on the traditional site of the Enneacrunus, by the Greek Archaeological Society in 1893. At the foot of the ledge of rock which here extends across the bed of the stream were discovered two large artificial basins or reservoirs hewn out of the rock but choked with masses of heavy stones. When these stones were removed water gurgled up from the ground in such volume that the workmen had great difficulty in diverting it. The more northerly of the basins is 21 metres long by 11 metres wide and from 4.80 to 5.80 metres deep ; the southern is 18.60 metres long and 6.10 metres deep. In Byzantine times the northern basin was roofed over with a barrel vault, of which traces remain. Besides these reservoirs there were found several channels cut in the bed of the river for the purpose, apparently, of conveying the water of the springs, first, to a large aqueduct a little lower down, and, next, by means of the aqueduct, to the Piraeus. A long wall, badly built, was also discovered stretching partially across the bed of the river a few yards below the northern reservoir. It may have been a weir or dam, but whether it is ancient or not seems doubtful. Mr. Ch. Belger suggests that what Pisistratus did was to build a wall across the bed of the stream in front of the springs so as to dam up the water and then to let it issue from the wall in nine spouts (*Archäologischer Anzeiger,* 1895, p. 113 ; *id.,* 1896, p. 43). On the right bank of the stream, not many yards from the northern basin, the same excavations laid bare a piece of the city wall, evidently of the Roman period, for it is built in a very solid style of all sorts of stones bonded with mortar. It appears to have been faced with large stones, which have, however, been removed. The sides of a square tower projecting from the wall are also preserved. Just within this fragment of the city wall the excavations revealed the remains of a small temple of Roman date, which had afterwards been converted into a church. The foundations of the temple are built of small stones and mortar ; the upper part is constructed of stones taken from older buildings. The careless style of the masonry marks the period of the decline. As to the plan of the temple, it apparently comprised a *cella* with a portico at each end, the whole being surrounded by a colonnade. To judge from some small fragments of a Doric *geison*, the temple seems to have been built in the Doric style. The deity to whom it was dedicated is unknown. See A. N. Skias, in Πρακτικὰ τῆς Ἀρχαιολογικῆς Ἑταιρίας, 1893, pp. 111-136 ; *id.*, in Ἐφημερὶς ἀρχαιολογική, 1893, p. 103 *sq.*

P. 116 line 8 from top, **the spring forms a pool** etc. When I revisited the Callirrhoe spring in the bed of the Ilissus, 23rd November 1895, there was only a little water trickling from the foot of the rocks, not nearly enough to supply drinking-water or to wash clothes. In the bed of the stream there lay some large marble blocks, including two pieces of fluted columns about 2 feet in diameter.

P. 118, note on i. 14. 2. **the Egyptians ―― dispute the claims of the Phrygians.** This is a reminiscence of Herodotus (ii. 2), who tells how an experiment made by Psammetichus, king of Egypt; to determine which was the most ancient nation resulted in favour of the Phrygians.

P. 121 line 4 from top, **he entered a cave and slept** etc. Many more examples of the Epimenides or Rip van Winkle type of story are collected by Mr. E. S. Hartland (*The Science of Fairy Tales*, p. 166 *sqq.*). One of the most striking comes from China (N. B. Dennys, *The Folk-lore of China*, p. 98). It relates how a certain Wang Chih, wandering on the mountains in search of firewood, entered a cave in which some old men were seated intent on a game of chess. He laid down his axe and watched them playing. Presently one of them handed him something like a date-stone, telling him to put it into his mouth. No sooner had he tasted it than he became oblivious of hunger and thirst. After some time one of the players said, "It is long since you came here, you should go home now," whereupon Wang Chih attempted to pick up his axe, but found that its handle had mouldered into dust. On reaching his home he learned that hundreds of years had rolled away since he left it to go to the mountains, and that no vestige or memory of his kinsfolk remained. A similar tale is told in Japan of a woodman who going into the mountains to cut wood followed a fox into a bamboo thicket. Here on a green lawn, where the sunbeams fell dimly through the matted leaves of the bamboos, he beheld two damsels of wondrous beauty playing chess. Absorbed in watching them he did not mark the flight of time. At last he turned to go, but lo and behold a long white beard covered his breast, his knees were stiff and weak with age, and the handle of his axe, with which he would fain have supported his tottering steps, crumbled into dust under his hand. Slowly and painfully he crept back to his native village. But there he knew no one, and no one knew him ; for since he went out to hew wood on the mountains seven generations of men had come and gone. This Japanese version of the tale is reported by D. Brauns (*Japanische Märchen und Sagen*, pp. 366-368). The Indians of the north-west coast of America tell a story in which an incident of the same sort occurs. A fisherman who has harpooned a seal is drawn by it far away out to sea and goes through many adventures. Amongst other things he marries a wife and stays with his father-in-law, as it seems to him, for four days, but in truth for four years. On his return home he is surprised to find the house very dirty and no one in front of the door, where he had left his father. Entering he perceives his father, now grown very old, sitting by the fire, and the old man at first fails to recognise his son, who, he says, had gone away long ago to hunt a seal and had never returned. This tale is reported by Fr. Boas (*Indianische Sagen von der Nord-Pacifischen Küste Amerikas*, Berlin, 1895, pp. 191-193).

P. 132 line 20 *sq.* from foot, **The Painted Colonnade** etc. A conjectural reconstruction of the picture of the battle of Marathon in the Painted Colonnade has been made by Prof. C. Robert with the help of an artist, Mr. H. Schenck (*Die Marathonschlacht in der Poikile, und weiteres über Polygnot*, Halle a. S., 1895). In this work Professor Robert touches also upon the other pictures in the Painted Colonnade and upon the paintings of Polygnotus in general. He supposes that the Painted Colonnade comprised a central hall with two wings projecting from it at right angles, and that the pictures of the battles of Oenoe and Marathon occupied the back walls of the two wings, while the pictures of the battle with the Amazons and the capture of Troy occupied the back wall of the central hall, the battle with the Amazons being to the right and the capture of Troy to the left, viewed from the standpoint of the spectator. He accepts the view, advocated by O. Jahn and H. Brunn, that the picture of the battle of Marathon was painted by Micon and Panaenus conjointly, though he holds that Micon had probably the greater share in it. All the pictures in the Colonnade, according to Prof. Robert, were painted between 460 and 457 B.C. Mr. P. Girard is of opinion that the picture of the battle of Marathon in the Painted Colonnade is imitated in one of the sculptured friezes at Gjölbaschi in Lycia which represents the battle between the Greeks and Trojans in the plain. See O. Benndorf und G. Niemann, *Das Heroon von Gjölbaschi-Trysa* (Vienna, 1889), pp. 115-123 ; P. Girard, *La Peinture antique*, p. 185 *sq.*

P. 137 line 2 from foot, **The battle of Oenoe.** The date of the battle of Oenoe has recently been discussed by Prof. Busolt (*Griechische Geschichte*, 3. p. 323 *sqq.*). He seems inclined to accept the earlier date assigned to it by Prof. C. Robert.

P. 139 line 6 from top, **Theseus —— fighting the Amazons.** This picture by Micon appears to have been reproduced more or less freely by the vase-painters of his time. For on the black-figured vases of an earlier period which represent battles with the Amazons the adversaries of the Amazons are Hercules and Achilles, not Theseus, and the women are generally depicted fighting on foot ; a combat between a mounted Amazon and a Greek hero on one of these earlier vases is rare. Whereas on red-figured vases which from their style may be contemporary with or later than Micon, the fighting Amazons are generally portrayed on horseback, as they were in Micon's picture, and it is on vases of this sort that Theseus first appears as their adversary. See A. Klügmann, *Die Amazonen in der attischen Literatur und Kunst* (Stuttgart, 1875), p. 46 *sqq.* ; C. Robert, *Die Marathonschlacht in der Poikile,* p. 13. Micon's picture would seem even to have influenced the sculpture of a later time, if not indeed to have been freely translated into stone ; for one of the friezes at Gjölbaschi in Lycia which represents a battle with the Amazons "appears as if pieced together, like a mosaic, out of red-figured vase-paintings of the severe and beautiful style which depict single combats of Theseus and other Attic heroes with mounted Amazons and which, as Klügmann has shown, are derived from Micon's wall-painting in the Painted Colonnade" (O. Benndorf und G. Niemann, *Das Heroon von Gjölbaschi-Trysa,* Vienna, 1889, p. 138). Cp. P. Girard, *La Peinture antique,* p. 186.

P. 141 line 22 from foot, **Echetlus.** In the picture Echetlus was no doubt represented wielding a ploughshare, since it was with a ploughshare that according to tradition he had slaughtered the Persians. Now on a series of Etruscan urns a combatant appears armed with a ploughshare. Winckelmann interpreted him as Echetlus, and this interpretation is accepted by Prof. C. Robert (*Die Marathonschlacht in der Poikile,* p. 32 *sqq.*), who further agrees with the late J. Töpffer in thinking that the hero Echetlus with his plough was akin to another Attic hero, Buzyges (J. Töpffer, *Attische Genealogie,* p. 140, note 1). The names of both point to a close connexion with agriculture, Buzyges meaning 'yoker of oxen' and Echetlus 'he of the plough-handle.'

P. 141 line 24 from foot, **Butes.** Prof. C. Robert would assign the figure of Butes to the picture of the battle with the Amazons rather than to the picture of the battle of Marathon (*Die Marathonschlacht in der Poikile,* p. 13 *sq.*).

P. 150 line 23 *sq.* from foot, **The intercolumniation** etc. According to my measurements the intercolumniation is 4 ft. 9 in. between the corner columns at the sides, and 5 ft. 4 in. between the other columns at the sides.

P. 151 line 4 from foot, **The sculptures of the gables** etc. The traces left by the sculptures in the gables of the so-called Theseum have been examined by Prof. B. Sauer. According to him, the traces are so many and so clear that the composition of the groups in both gables can be determined. The subject represented in the eastern gable was the birth of Erichthonius. Athena, surrounded by the serpent-bodied Cecrops and his three daughters Pandrosus, Herse, and Aglaurus, seems to have been portrayed in the act of receiving the infant Erichthonius from the giantess Earth. In the middle of the western gable Hephaestus appeared kneeling before Thetis and Eurynome in the sea-cave (Homer,

Il. xviii. 393 *sqq.*), while in the corners the chariots of the Sun and Moon were represented, the one rising from, the other sinking into the sea. If Prof. Sauer is right in thus interpreting the marks in the gables, his investigations strongly confirm the view taken in the text (vol. 2. p. 155) that the temple was dedicated to Hephaestus, the father of Erichthonius. Or the temple may, as Prof. Sauer suggests, have been dedicated to Hephaestus and Athena jointly, though in common speech it passed as the temple of Hephaestus only. See B. Sauer, in *Archäologischer Anzeiger*, 1897, p. 84.

P. 156 line 23 from foot, **the pictures in the Theseum.** Prof. C. Robert thinks that both the battle-pieces in the Theseum were painted by Polygnotus, not by Micon (*Die Marathonschlacht in der Poikile*, p. 46 *sq.*). He holds (p. 50 *sqq.*) that the picture of the battle of the Centaurs and Lapiths, particularly the group representing Theseus and the dead Centaur, is partly reproduced both in an existing vase-painting now at Berlin (E. Curtius, *Gesammelte Abhandlungen*, 2. pl. vii.) and in the sculptures of the western gable of the temple of Zeus at Olympia. Prof. O. Benndorf considers that the same picture influenced the sculptor who carved the same subject on one of the friezes at Gjölbaschi in Lycia (O. Benndorf und G. Niemann, *Das Heroon von Gjölbaschi-Trysa*, p. 186).

P. 157 line 18, **When Minos brought Theseus** etc. The vase-paintings which represent Theseus's visit to Amphitrite at the bottom of the sea have been again discussed by Mr. G. Ghirardini (*Rendiconti della Reale Accademia dei Lincei*, Serie Quinta, vol. 4 (1895), pp. 86-100). On the vase found at *Truvo* Theseus holds some object in his left hand. What the object is, does not appear; it is certainly not a ring. Mr. Petersen suggested that it may be a little jewel-box or casket containing the ring which Minos had thrown into the sea; but that Theseus should have found such a little box in the depths of the sea and brought the ring back in it, as from a jeweller's shop, is an idea which is hardly likely to have occurred to the artist. The notion, though it has found favour with Prof. C. Robert (*Die Marathonschlacht in der Poikile*, p. 51), is justly scouted by Mr. Ghirardini, who also, very properly, rejects as baseless the theory of Prof. Robert, that the picture on the vase found at *Girgenti* is a copy of the one in the Theseum. We have absolutely no description of the painting in the Theseum; Pausanias only tells the legend without describing the picture, and he expressly informs us that even in his time the picture was so obscure, partly from the effects of time, partly because the artist had not painted the whole story, that it was not easy to understand it. Yet Prof. Robert professes not only to recognise a copy of this lost picture but even to trace its artistic antecedents (*Die Marathonschlacht in der Poikile*, pp. 50-52).

The story of Theseus's quarrel with Minos and his plunge into the sea to fetch up the king's ring is told at some length by Bacchylides in a recently-discovered poem, which through the kindness of Dr. J. E. Sandys I have been permitted to see in proof. So closely does the poet's version of the legend agree with the prose version of

Hyginus (*Astronomica*, ii. 5) that it can hardly but have been known to Hyginus either directly or indirectly. But whereas Hyginus apparently lays the scene of the story in Crete, Bacchylides lays it on board the ship that was bearing Theseus and his youthful comrades to their doom. Minos himself, according to the poet, was on board the vessel and ordered it to proceed at full speed as soon as Theseus had disappeared beneath the brine. No doubt the wicked king thought he had thus rid himself of the troublesome stripling who dared to oppose his lawless wishes. But fate, says the poet, ordained it otherwise.

P. 166 line 9 *sq.*, **the marriage of the Dioscuri to the daughters of Leucippus.** The rape of the daughters of Leucippus by the Dioscuri is represented in great detail and in a lively style on one of the sculptured friezes at Gjölbaschi in Lycia ; and some archaeologists, such as Professors O. Benndorf, C. Robert, and M. Collignon, are of opinion that the scene on the frieze is a copy, more or less close, of the picture by Polygnotus here mentioned by Pausanias. In the centre of the scene is a temple, from the door of which two men are rushing. To the right of the temple, in the upper band of the frieze, men are preparing to skin a ram and an ox which have just been slaughtered. A great kettle and other vessels for cooking show that a feast is being made ready. In the lower band of the frieze an old man, no doubt Leucippus, is praying, women are talking, and two of them make gestures of dismay and sorrow. On the other side of the temple the Dioscuri are carrying off the two brides, each in a chariot drawn by four horses, while the two sons of Aphareus pursue them on horseback accompanied by a number of armed retainers on foot. The relation of this last scene to the two former seems plain. Friends and relations have assembled to celebrate the wedding of the sons of Aphareus to the daughters of Leucippus ; the usual sacrifices have been offered in the temple and the preparations for the banquet are in full swing, when word comes that the brides have just been carried off by Castor and Pollux ; hence the despair of the old father and the dismay of the women. Thus the sculptor's rendering of the legend agrees with the tradition that the Dioscuri had been invited to the wedding and had there and then ravished away the brides (Schol. on Homer, *Il.* iii. 243 ed. Bekker ; Schol. on Pindar, *Nem.* x. 112). If the conjecture is well founded that in these reliefs of Gjölbaschi we possess a copy or imitation of the picture of Polygnotus, it will follow that Pausanias was wrong in describing the subject of the picture as the marriage of the Dioscuri to the daughters of Leucippus ; the subject was really the marriage of the sons of Aphareus to these damsels and its sudden interruption in consequence of the abduction of the brides. In none of the vase-paintings which illustrate the rape of the maidens is any indication given of the preparations for their marriage to the sons of Aphareus. See O. Benndorf und G. Niemann, *Das Heroon von Gjölbaschi-Trysa*, pp. 159-168 ; J. Overbeck, *Geschichte des griech. Plastik,*[4] 2. p. 207 *sq.* ; M. Collignon, *Hist. de la Sculpture grecque*, 2. p. 210 ; C. Robert, *Die Marathonschlacht in der Poikile*, p. 53 *sqq.*

P. 166 line 18 *sq.* from foot, **a painting by Micon of those who**

sailed with Jason etc. Prof. Benndorf accepts the view, to which in the text I have given the preference, that the subject of the picture was the funeral games held by Acastus in honour of his father Pelias (*Das Heroon von Gjölbaschi-Trysa,* p. 166 *sq.*). On the other hand Prof. Robert still defends his theory that in the picture the Argonauts were represented before, instead of after, their voyage to Colchis (*Die Marathonschlacht in der Poikile,* pp. 61-63).

P. 168 line 23 from foot, **Athena put Erichthonius in a chest** etc. An interesting illustration of this story was procured for the Louvre in 1880. It is a statue of Athena standing and carrying on her left arm a box or basket, from which a serpent has protruded his head. The serpent is no doubt the youthful Erichthonius. See P. Jamot, 'Minerve à la Ciste,' *Monuments Grecs,* vol. 2. Nos. 21-22 (1893-1894), pp. 17-39, with pl. 12.

P. 175 line 10 from top, **The Serapeum —— at Alexandria.** Some remains of this great sanctuary have recently been excavated by Dr. Botti, Director of the Alexandrian Museum (*American Journal of Archaeology,* 11 (1896), p. 67 *sq.*).

P. 180 line 8 *sq.* from top, **buttresses on the south side.** The platform of the Olympieum is strengthened with buttresses on the east as well as on the south side.

P. 185 line 19 from foot, **a vast structure of Roman date** etc. On the eastern side of the great quadrangle which formed the gymnasium or library of Hadrian there remain in position four bases of columns at the southern end of the colonnade. The bases are of white marble. Each is quadrangular, but supports a round base on which the column rested directly. On the most southerly of the bases a piece of the shaft of the column is still standing; it is of green and white marble and is unfluted. A portion of the back wall of this eastern colonnade, forming the outer wall of the whole building on the east, is still standing in Aeolus Street. It is about 30 paces long and is well built of ashlar masonry. Five buttresses project on its outer side.

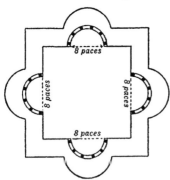

Of the building which occupied the centre of the spacious quadrangle enough remains (contrary to what I have said in the text) to enable us to make out the general plan in a rough way. It appears to have comprised a square open court measuring about 19 or 20 paces on the sides and enclosed on each side by a semicircular colonnade (see the annexed cut). The cloisters surrounding this central court seem to have been paved throughout with mosaics arranged in an ornamental pattern. Of the semicircular colonnades on the north and south sides of the court, the foundations, stylobates, and portions of the mosaic pavement remain, and in the north colonnade there is further a base of a column in position on the stylobate. Stylobates and base are of white marble. Of the semicircular colonnade on the west side the foundations and parts of the mosaic pavement are left, but the stylobate is gone. On the east side, where the fourth semicircular colonnade should be, there is the apse of a Christian church, which may have absorbed part of the colonnade. The diameter of each semicircular colonnade, on the inner side, is about 8 paces. Further, at the north-east corner of this small cloistered court there are standing two short pieces of walls meeting at a right angle ; one of them faces south, the other east. Both are built of well-cut and well-jointed rectangular blocks of white marble laid in regular horizontal courses. The foundations, built of common stone in the same style as the marble walls, are exposed to a depth of several courses. Walls and foundations together are standing to a height of ten courses. In the piece of wall which faces south there is an arched doorway, which seems to have led from the eastern side of the northern semicircular colonnade into the central court. On the south side of the court, in front of the semicircular colonnade, there is a marble stylobate and on it stand three columns and an *anta* of white marble, all supporting their architraves. These columns and *anta* appear to have belonged to the Christian church.

P. 186 line 19 from top, **Facing this anta, a little to the north of it, is a jamb of the door.** This is not exact. The jamb does not face the *anta*, being a little to the east as well as to the north of it. The inscription referred to in the text is on the south face of the jamb and high up.

P. 186 line 20 *sq.* from foot, a **market-place of Roman date.** Only the south-eastern corner of the Roman market-place had been excavated when I was in Athens last (December 1895). The gateway is at a lower level than the neighbouring Tower of the Winds ; steps lead down to it, and from the gateway again four or five more steps lead down into the court of the market-place, which is at a still lower level. The width of the gateway is 10 paces. Portions of all the columns both outer and inner of the gateway are standing ; the pieces of the two columns on the inner side of the gateway are about 4 metres (13 feet) high. The two *antae* of the outer colonnade of the gateway, together with large pieces of the side walls, are also standing.

P. 193 line 1, **Cynosarges.** The view that Cynosarges lay on the south-eastern side of Lycabettus, on or near the site now occupied by the Monastery of the Angels, has been disputed by Dr. Dörpfeld, who would look for it to the south of the Ilissus, near the Church of *H. Marina.* Accordingly excavations have been made by the British School under the direction of Mr. Cecil Smith at a place on the south bank of the river, due south of the Olympieum, where the ground falls away perpendicularly from a small plateau. The excavations on the plateau have revealed the foundations, built of small stones, of a large building which seems to date from the sixth century B.C. and which from its plan may possibly have been a gymnasium. But no inscriptions have yet been found which identify it as Cynosarges. Both within and without the building many tombs were discovered; but it was observed by the excavators that the tombs inside of the building were all either earlier than the sixth or later than the fourth century B.C. Mr. Cecil Smith draws from this observation an argument in favour of the view that the edifice was the gymnasium of Cynosarges, since that gymnasium appears from the law of Solon touching theft to have been in existence at the beginning of the sixth century B.C. and was destroyed by Philip V., king of Macedonia, in 200 B.C. (see vol. 2. p. 194). But if any of the tombs within the building date from the third century B.C., the edifice can hardly be Cynosarges. Amongst the objects found in the necropolis is a series of vases decorated in the geometrical style. In an adjoining field the English archaeologists discovered remains of a large Roman building, apparently a colonnade enclosing an oblong space and measuring no less than 230 feet on the side. Mr. Cecil Smith conjectures that it may have been built by Hadrian to replace the old gymnasium of Cynosarges which had been destroyed. See *American Journal of Archaeology*, 11 (1896), p. 227 ; *Classical Review*, 10 (1896), p. 222 ; *Archäologischer Anzeiger*, 11 (1896), p. 73 ; *Berliner philolog. Wochenschrift*, 20th February 1897, p. 255 *sq.* ; *Mittheil. d. arch. Inst. in Athen*, 21 (1896), p. 463 *sq.* ; Cecil Smith, in *Journal of Hellenic Studies*, 16 (1896), p. 337 *sq.* ; *id.*, in *Annual of the British School at Athens*, No. 2, Session 1895-96, pp. 23-25.

P. 203 line 24 *sq.* from foot, **a temple of Huntress Artemis.** Dr. Dörpfeld would identify with this temple the remains of a small but elegant temple of the Ionic order which, converted into a church of the Virgin of the Rock (*Panagia eis ten Petran*), existed down to the middle of the eighteenth century. It stood on the southern bank of the Ilissus, about a hundred yards above Callirrhoe. The temple, built entirely of white marble, rested on three steps and measured about 42 feet long by 17 feet wide. A portico, supported by four Ionic columns, adorned either end of the building. Some shattered remains of the foundations were excavated by Mr. Skias for the Greek Archaeological Society in 1897. See Stuart and Revett, *The Antiquities of Athens*, vol. 1 (London, 1762), pp. 7-11, with plates i.-viii. ; W. Dörpfeld, in *Mittheilungen d. arch. Inst. in Athen*, 22 (1897), p. 227 *sq.*

P. 205 line 21 from foot, **a stadium.** Excavations made in the stadium in 1895 proved that the long sides of the stadium were not straight but curved. A part of the passage (*diazoma*) which divided the seats horizontally into an upper and a lower block was found well preserved. See *Mittheilungen d. arch. Inst. in Athen*, 20 (1895), p. 374 ; *Journal of Hellenic Studies*, 16 (1896), p. 338.

P. 206 line 6 *sq.* from foot, **the hills which bound the stadium** etc. On the hill which bounds the stadium on the north-east I found (23rd November 1895) only some foundations built of small stones and mortar, together with a single block of white marble. On the higher hill which bounds the stadium on the south-west I observed some large ancient squared blocks, also remains of a wall or foundations built of small stones and mortar.

P. 207 line 6 from foot, **curved marble panels.** At the top of each of these panels a pair of small tripods is sculptured in low relief.

P. 209 line 23 from top, **statues thus placed under tripods.** It is possible that some of the images which Pausanias mentions as being placed under or enclosed by tripods were not separate works of art but served as supporters to the basin or kettle, which was the essential part of a tripod. Prof. Percy Gardner has collected instances of basins thus supported by sculptured figures (*Journal of Hellenic Studies*, 16 (1896), pp. 275-280). Amongst them is a limestone tripod at Oxford, the three legs of which are carved in the likeness of three women standing on lions. A fragment of a similar tripod was found by the Germans at Olympia (G. Treu, in *Olympia : Ergebnisse*, Textband 3. pp. 26-29). At Delphi more recently the French have found three graceful figures of girls dancing round a trunk of a tree which may have supported a tripod (*Bulletin de Corresp. hellénique*, 18 (1894), p. 180; *Gazette des Beaux Arts*, December 1894, p. 450, with illustration facing p. 452). In the Louvre there is a terra-cotta bowl of Etruscan style supported by four figures of women (E. Pottier, *Catalogue des Vases Antiques de terre cuite du Louvre*, 1. p. 168, No. 396). And Herodotus describes (iv. 152) a great bronze bowl resting on three kneeling giants which the Samians dedicated to Hera.

P. 210 line 9 *sq.* from foot, **the statue of a boy Satyr holding out a cup.** The Dresden Museum possesses the cast of a statue of a youthful satyr, bequeathed to the Museum by Raphael Mengs, which Mr. P. Bienkowski holds to be a copy of the statue here mentioned by Pausanias; the original, he considers, was by one of the sons of Praxiteles (*Revue archéologique*, 3me Série, 26 (1895), pp. 281-285). The theory appears to me arbitrary and unproved.

P. 215 line 14 from top, **the sanctuary of Dionysus in the Marshes.** Dr. Dörpfeld has now fully described the enclosure excavated by him which he believes to have been the sanctuary of Dionysus in the Marshes (*Mittheilungen d. arch. Inst. in Athen*, 20 (1895), pp. 161-206, 368-370). It lies in the trough between the Pnyx, the Areopagus, and the Acropolis, on the eastern side of the ancient road which led from the market-place to the Acropolis. The modern carriage-road runs a little to the west of it. The enclosure formed a triangle, bounded on all three sides by ancient streets. Its greatest length was about 45 metres, its greatest breadth about 25 metres, and its area comprised about 560 square metres. The boundary-wall was almost everywhere a supporting-wall as well, because the interior of the enclosure lay for the most part below the level of the surrounding streets. The difference in level was originally as much as 2 metres (6 ft. 7 in.), and later it increased, as the streets gradually rose. The wall is built throughout of polygonal blocks of blue limestone, but the style of masonry varies in different places. In some places the lower part is built of large blocks well fitted together, and the upper part of small stones; in another place the lowest course consists of nearly rectangular blocks; while in the rest of the wall large and small stones, cut in polygons, occur side by side, giving the masonry an air of great antiquity. These differences in style seem to show that the wall was repaired at various periods. No gateway has been found; probably the entrance was at the south end of the east side, where there is now a gap in the wall.

About the middle of the precinct are the remains of a platform of masonry which seems to have been originally 3.10 metres square, and to have supported an altar or sacrificial table resting on four legs. The holes for three of the legs are preserved. A quadrangular groove .49 metre long, .13 metre wide, and .08 metre deep is sunk in the platform near its western edge; and a similar groove, which is only partially preserved, seems to have extended in a line with it to the south.

In the north-western part of the precinct is a wine-press of the sort which may still be seen in many parts of Greece. It forms an irregular quadrangle about 4.70 metres long and 2.80 metres wide. The floor, constructed of pebbles and lime-mortar, slopes towards the south-east corner, where a hole in the bottom of the wall allowed the juice of the grapes, as they were trodden on the floor, to pour into a round earthen-ware vessel sunk in the ground immediately in front of the hole. This wine-receiver is still in its place; it is .50 metre wide and holds about 55 litres. Adjoining the wine-press on the east is another but more ruinous apartment with a similar floor and a vessel sunk in it. Probably it too was used in making the wine, but whether it was a wine-press is uncertain. With regard to the date of the wine-press, Dr. Dörpfeld would assign it to the fourth century B.C. on the strength of a boundary inscription found in a Club-room (*Lesche*) on the opposite side of the ancient street; for the front wall of the Club-room is built in the same style as the walls of the wine-press. But some remains of another floor below the existing one seem to show that there had been a still older wine-press on the same site. And at a later time yet another wine-press was constructed above the two older ones. It occupied only about a third of the area of its predecessor and had a floor made of lime and pebbles with a slope to the east.

In the southern part of the precinct were found the remains of a small temple, which seems to have consisted of a square chamber with a fore-temple (*pronaos*) or portico facing southward. The length of the building is only 5.40 metres and its breadth 3.96 metres. The walls, so far as they exist, are built of polygonal blocks of limestone in a very archaic style. Dr. Dörpfeld regards the building as more ancient than the older temple of Eleutherian Dionysus near the Dionysiac theatre; he would assign it to the sixth or seventh century B.C. It is remarkable that the little temple appears to have been cut off from the northern and larger part of the precinct by a wall extending across the precinct from east to west. However in this partition-wall, immediately to the west of the temple, is a doorway which gave access from the southern to the northern part of the enclosure.

Many potsherds decorated in the early geometrical style, together with many of the later black-figured and red-figured sorts, were found within the precinct. On the strength of the former and of the style of the enclosing wall Dr. Dörpfeld believes that the precinct is older, perhaps by several centuries, than the sixth century B.C.

At some time, which cannot be precisely determined, the precinct was abandoned and left to utter decay, for by the end of the Greek or the beginning of the Roman period it was already buried deep under the soil. This is proved by the remains of later buildings which were found at a height of about 2 metres or more above the ancient precinct. These buildings belong to two different periods, first, the late Greek or early Roman, and, second, the late Roman. Of the former the remains are scanty; they consist only of foundations built of small stones bonded with clay, not mortar. So far as can be made out from these foundations the new building seems to have consisted of a hall extending east and west with a series of rooms attached to it on the north and perhaps also on the south. It occupied the eastern part of the ancient precinct; when it was built the old temple, altar, and wine-press had already disappeared under the soil. At a still later time another building was erected on the same site. A long and well-preserved inscription, which seems to date from about the middle of the third century A.D. (_Mittheil. d. arch. Inst. in Athen_, 19 (1894), pp. 248-282 ; E. Maass, _Orpheus_, p. 16 _sqq._) proves that this latest building was called the Baccheum and was the club-house of a religious society called the Iobacchians. The building itself, however, is older than the inscription; Dr. Dörpfeld considers that it is probably earlier than the third century A.D. It was larger than its predecessor and extended across the ancient street which had formerly bounded the precinct on the east. The main part of the edifice consisted of a great hall 18.80 metres long and 11.25 metres wide, with a quadrangular apse at the east end. Two rows of columns divided the hall into a broad central nave and two narrow side-aisles. There were four columns in each row. The foundations and bases of most of the columns are preserved. Further, in the eastern part of the hall two curved rows of smaller columns, making together the shape of a horseshoe, led up to the door of the apse. In the middle of the apse was found standing a round altar adorned with ox-heads and garlands carved in relief; and behind it, lying on the ground, was a quadrangular altar, on three sides of which are carved scenes relating to the worship of Dionysus, including the sacrifice of a goat and of another animal which looks like a boar. On the fourth side of this latter altar is an inscription which shows that the altar was dedicated to "the Child-rearing Goddess beside Artemis." This inscription seems to be older than the sculptured scenes and to have been hastily scratched out when they were carved. Artemis appears to have been worshipped in a small chamber which opened off the apse on the north, for in this chamber were found a statue and a statuette of Artemis and a small square altar bearing the inscription ΑΡΤΕΜΙΔΟΣ ΕΡΕΙΘΟΥ ('of Artemis the Day-labourer').

Dr. Dörpfeld is of opinion that the old precinct with its altar, temple, and wine-press was the sanctuary of Dionysus in the Marshes. His grounds for thinking so are mainly the existence, first, of the wine-press in a corner of the precinct and, second, of the club-house of the Iobacchic society built over the ancient precinct. These facts seem to him to prove that the precinct had been sacred to Dionysus; and from a passage of Thucydides (ii. 15), to which reference has already been made, he concludes that the precinct must have been the sanctuary of Dionysus in the Marshes. For Thucydides plainly implies that that sanctuary was in the same quarter of the city as the spring called Enneacrunus or Callirrhoe, and as Dr. Dörpfeld identifies Callirrhoe with a vein of water which in winter occasionally issues from the rock not far from the precinct, he concludes that the precinct in question must have been the sanctuary of Dionysus in the Marshes. He believes that in one of the grooves beside the altar may have been set the inscribed tablet which Demosthenes, or a writer who passes under his name, tells us stood beside the altar in the sanctuary of Dionysus in the Marshes ([Demosthenes,] *Or.* lix. pp. 1370, 1371). Further, he till lately identified the precinct in question with the Lenaeum, which he held to be the same as the sanctuary of Dionysus in the Marshes, and he laid great weight on the wine-press discovered by him as evidence that the precinct in which it was found could be no other than the Lenaeum, since the very name Lenaeum means 'place of the wine-press.' The attempt to identify the precinct in question with the Lenaeum he has now given up, and to the reasons he gives for abandoning it (*Mittheil. d. arch. Inst.* 20 (1895), pp. 368-370) might be added a still better one, which he omits to mention. That reason is that the Lenaean festival is known from an inscription of 192/3 A.D. (*C. I. A.* iii. No. 1160) to have been held at a time when the club-house of the Iobacchians, discovered by Dr. Dörpfeld, was already in existence and when, therefore, the precinct which Dr. Dörpfeld formerly identified with the Lenaeum was buried deep under ground. But the Lenaean festival can only have been held in the Lenaeum, and if it continued to be held after the precinct in question was not only deserted but hidden out of sight under the soil, that is a conclusive proof that the buried precinct cannot have been the Lenaeum. However, though he can no longer maintain that the precinct is the Lenaeum, Dr. Dörpfeld clings to the belief that it is the sanctuary of Dionysus in the Marshes. On this theory I would make the following observations :

(1) It directly contradicts the evidence of Thucydides (ii. 15), who places the sanctuary of Dionysus in the Marshes, along with the Olympieum, the Pythium, the sanctuary of Earth, and the Enneacrunus, to the south of the Acropolis. I have already pointed out (p. 484 *sq.*) that Dr. Dörpfeld's interpretation of this much-contested but really clear and straightforward passage of Thucydides stultifies the argument of the historian and must therefore be rejected.

(2) It is in the highest degree improbable that by the beginning of the Roman period the sanctuary of Dionysus in the Marshes, one of the oldest and most famous shrines in Athens, should have been so long abandoned that it already lay buried about 6 feet or more under the earth.

(3) A more inappropriate designation than 'the Marshes' for this

high, arid, and rocky district it would be hard to find. It is certainly anything but a marsh at the present day, and if proof be wanted that there was no marsh here in antiquity we have it to hand in the great rock-hewn aqueduct and the deep wells, over a hundred in number, with which the rocky ground has here been honeycombed in the search for water. Do men dig wells in a marsh or bring water in an aqueduct to a swamp?

(4) In so ancient and celebrated a sanctuary as that of Dionysus in the Marshes inscriptions relating to the god and his worship probably abounded. But none such has come to light in the enclosure which Dr. Dörpfeld so confidently identifies with that renowned shrine.

(5) The existence of the wine-press in the enclosure does not prove, though it raises a presumption, that the sanctuary was dedicated to Dionysus. Still less does it prove or even raise a presumption that the sanctuary is the particular one of Dionysus in the Marshes. It is at least worth remembering that ancient houses, thickly packed together, have been revealed by Dr. Dörpfeld's excavations close to the sacred enclosure in question. It is just possible, I do not say probable, that the wine-press may have belonged to one of them. At the present day the Greek peasant sometimes presses the grapes at home, not in the vineyard. At *H. Georgios*, near Phlius, the centre of a great wine-growing district, I saw my host treading the purple clusters in a tub under his own roof.

On these grounds I agree with Mr. Ch. Belger (*Archäologischer Anzeiger*, 1896, p. 44 *sq.*), Prof. J. M. Stahl (*Rheinisches Museum*, N. F. 50 (1895), p. 572), Prof. A. Milchhöfer (*Philologus*, 55 (1896), p. 170 *sqq.*), and Prof. C. Wachsmuth ('Neue Beiträge zur Topographie von Athen,' *Abhandlungen d. philolog. histor. Cl. d. k. sächs. Gesell. d. Wissenschaften*, 18 (1897), No. 1. pp. 33-56) in rejecting Dr. Dörpfeld's proposed identification and in continuing to look for the sanctuary of Dionysus in the Marshes where Thucydides placed it, namely to the south of the Acropolis.

This is perhaps the most convenient place to mention that some 35 yards or so to the south of the precinct which has been under discussion, beside the ancient street that leads in the direction of the Acropolis, Dr. Dörpfeld has excavated another precinct which from inscriptions found in it appears to have been originally dedicated to a divinity of healing named Amynus. The precinct is in the shape of an irregular quadrangle, about 19 metres long by 13 metres wide. Its enclosing walls are built of polygonal blocks of blue limestone, well cut and carefully fitted together. Within the enclosure the excavations revealed a well, with a great stone which had once covered its mouth, the bases of votive offerings, and some scanty foundations of a very small building, perhaps a chapel of Amynus. Inscriptions found in the precinct, and dating apparently from the fourth century B.C., prove that Aesculapius was here worshipped along with Amynus, and that associated with these two divinities was a third, to wit Dexion. This Dexion was no other than the deified poet Sophocles (*Etymolog. Magnum*, p. 256, *s.v.* Δεξίων). One of the inscriptions, however, mentions a sanctuary of Dexion distinct from the common sanctuary of Amynus and Aesculapius. Some pieces of sculpture were also found in the sanctuary. They appear to have been offerings presented by patients who had been healed of their ailments, and who commemorated their cure by dedicating in the sanctuary sculptured likenesses of their diseased parts or scenes representing the adoration of the deity by his grateful worshippers. Amongst these pieces of sculpture are representations of fingers, a pair of ears, the male organs of generation, and a woman's breast with a dedication to Aesculapius, all carved in marble. Another curious relief represents a bearded man in a long robe standing behind a colossal leg, which he grasps with both arms. The leg is cut off sharply at the knee and a swollen vein is indicated extending down to the ankle. The patient who dedicated this piece probably suffered from a varicose vein ; the man who is represented grasping the leg may be the patient himself or his physician in the act of presenting his thank-offering to the god. On two plates of marble a serpent is seen rearing itself in coils ; it is doubtless the sacred snake of the healing god, whether Aesculapius or Amynus. Another relief represents a goddess, probably Health, standing beside a wreathed altar and receiving the adoration of a train of two men, two women, and a child, all of whom are, as usual, portrayed as diminutive in comparison with the divinity. Another relief of small size and careless workmanship represents the healing god or hero in an attitude which is characteristic of Aesculapius ; he stands with crossed legs leaning on his staff which is planted under his left armpit ; his right hand rests on his hip, his breast is bare. Approaching him are a man and a woman with raised right hands in an attitude of prayer. Amongst the potsherds found in the sanctuary were some decorated in the geometrical style, one of the early kind called Proto-Corinthian, and two of the Attic black-figured sort. All the later styles of Attic pottery are also represented among the fragments. See A. Körte, in *Mittheil. d. arch. Inst. in Athen*, 18 (1893), pp. 231-256, and *ib.* 21 (1896), pp. 287-332.

P. 215 line 17 from foot, **two temples**, etc. The remains of these two temples are fully described and illustrated with plans by Dr. Dörpfeld in his recent work on the Greek theatre (W. Dörpfeld und E. Reisch, *Das griechische Theater*, p. 11 *sqq.*), from which I extract the following particulars.

Of the older and smaller temple nothing is standing but the foundations and socle of a part of the north wall, very short pieces of two other walls projecting southward from it, and a piece of a step extending round the north-west angle. The length of the north wall, so far as it is preserved, is about 9 metres (30 feet). The two walls which project southward from it enclosed between them a chamber about 6.50 metres long from east to west, which was probably the cella of the temple. In front of the temple were found some architectural fragments (fluted drums of columns, pieces of triglyphs, half the capital of an *anta*, and a piece of a pediment) which seem to have belonged to it. From their dimensions and other indications Dr. Dörpfeld conjectures that the temple was about 13 metres long from east to west by 8 metres broad from north to south, and that it had on the east a portico (*pronaos*) 4 metres deep, the gable of which was supported on two columns between *antae*. With regard to materials, the foundations are built of the hard bluish limestone of the Acropolis, while the socle of the wall is built of another lighter coloured limestone, also very hard, which is quarried at *Kara* at the foot of Hymettus. The upper part of the temple, to judge by the architectural fragments which have been found, was constructed of Piraeic limestone. These three materials appear to have been employed together at Athens only in buildings which date from before the Persian sack; hence Dr. Dörpfeld infers that the temple is not later than the sixth century B.C. This date, he thinks, is confirmed by the style of masonry and by the shapes of the clamps employed (⌐╌┘ and └╌┘).

The existing north wall of this small temple abuts at an angle upon the foundations of what seems to have been a colonnade opening to the south and about 32 metres long from east to west. Besides the foundations of the colonnade, there remain a few stones belonging to the front steps and some tall slabs which formed part of the walls. The materials of which these remains consist are breccia, the bluish Hymettian marble, and Piraeic limestone. The simultaneous employment of these three sorts of stones characterises Athenian buildings which date from the fourth to the second century B.C. From this and from the shape of the clamps employed (┣━┥) Dr. Dörpfeld concludes that the colonnade was built in the fourth century B.C. At the western end of its south front the foundations have been cut away at an angle in order to spare the old temple of Dionysus.

The later temple is believed by Dr. Dörpfeld to have had at its eastern end a portico (*pronaos*) with four columns in front and two on the sides, the corner columns being counted twice. But as nothing of the temple remains but the foundations this conjectural restoration is, he admits, uncertain. He would assign the temple to the beginning of the fourth century B.C. rather than to the end of the fifth, but thinks it possible that, as Prof. Reisch formerly conjectured (*Griechische Weihgeschenke*, p. 100), it may be "the temple surmounted by choregic tripods" which Nicias dedicated in the sanctuary of Dionysus (Plutarch, *Nicias*, 3). In that case the temple could not be more recent than 415 B.C., the date of Nicias's death.

A few yards to the south-east of this temple are foundations of what was probably an altar. They form a rectangle 11.50 metres long by 3.30 metres wide, and are built of breccia, like the foundations of the later temple with which they may be contemporary.

P. 216 line 5 from foot, **Dionysus bringing Hephaestus up to heaven.** This subject is depicted on a black-figured Corinthian vase of the sixth century B.C. See G. Loeschcke, 'Korinthische Vase mit der Rückführung des Hephaistos,' *Mittheil. d. arch. Inst. in Athen*, 19 (1894), pp. 510-525.

P. 222, line 8 from top, **the theatre at Athens.** The remains of the Dionysiac theatre at Athens are now fully described and the history of the building set forth by Dr. Dörpfeld (*Das griechische Theater:*

Beiträge zur Geschichte des Dionysos-Theaters in Athen und anderer griechischer Theater, von W. Dörpfeld und E. Reisch, Athens and Leipsic, 1896, p. 24 *sqq.*). His views on the history of the building remain, with a few unimportant modifications, substantially as they are stated in the text. For a full and clear statement of the detailed architectural evidence on which these views are based the reader must consult the book itself; all that I can do here is, following Dr. Dörpfeld, to correct and supplement on a few points the account given in the second volume of this work.

The supporting-walls of the auditorium are, as we have seen (vol. 2. p. 224), two in number, an outer and an inner, which are connected with each other by short cross-walls. These walls are well preserved on the west side of the theatre. The inner wall is built of squared blocks of pebble-conglomerate (breccia) and is about 1.60 metres (5 ft. 3 in.) thick. The cross-walls, which are also built of breccia, are placed at equal intervals of about 7 metres (23 feet), and have a thickness of 1.35 metres (4 ft. 5 in.). The outer wall, about 1.35 metres thick, is cased with quadrangular blocks of Piraeic limestone of uniform size, while its core is composed of quadrangular blocks of breccia. The hollow spaces between the cross-walls were filled with earth.

The auditorium was probably divided horizontally by two passages (*diazomata*), not merely by one, as is stated in the text. It is true that traces of only one passage (the upper) are left, but the space between it and the orchestra is so great that we are driven, in Dr. Dörpfeld's opinion, to assume the former existence of a lower passage. The upper passage was made very wide because it had to serve at the same time as a public road leading to the Acropolis from the eastern part of the city. On the slope above this upper passage there seem to have been fourteen tiers of seats. The cuttings in the rock which may still be seen at the top of the theatre were not the seats themselves, but merely the beds on which the seats made of Piraeic limestone were placed. Different opinions have been expressed as to the date of the marble chairs which form the lowest tier of seats. Vischer assigned them to the age of Lycurgus in the fourth century B.C.; Messrs. Ziller and Julius would place them at the beginning of the imperial age. On technical and artistic grounds Dr. Dörpfeld confirms decidedly the opinion of the judicious Vischer. The masonry is so perfect and the style of the reliefs so excellent that he has no hesitation in referring both to the fourth century B.C. Of the number of persons who could be seated in the theatre Dr. Dörpfeld forms a much lower estimate than the one given in the text (vol. 2. p. 224). He thinks that there may have been seventy-eight tiers of seats, and that the total number of spectators whom the theatre could contain may have been about 14,000, or at most 17,000.

The dimensions of the orchestra, as it was constructed by Lycurgus in the fourth century B.C., have been wrongly stated in modern books, because the diameter has been measured from the marble parapet which now runs round the inner side of the broad water-channel or gutter. But this parapet was made in the Roman age at a time when the gutter was paved over and when accordingly the size of the orchestra was increased by the breadth of the gutter. In the time of Lycurgus, on the other hand, the gutter was open and therefore formed no part of the orchestra, since we cannot suppose that the chorus danced in the gutter. Deducting, therefore, the breadth of the gutter, we find that the diameter of the orchestra was 19.61 metres, and hence that its radius was 9.805 metres or exactly 30 Greek feet, if that foot be reckoned at .327 metre (see vol. 3. p. 497 *sq.*). Many dimensions of the Dionysiac theatre, when reckoned in feet of this sort, can be stated in round numbers ; from which Dr. Dörpfeld concludes that this foot was the standard used in building the theatre. The existing marble pavement of the orchestra is believed by Dr. Dörpfeld to have been laid down when the theatre was partially remodelled in the reign of Nero. To the same date he now assigns the covering of the gutter with marble slabs and the erection of the marble parapet or balustrade which divides the front row of seats from the orchestra. Excavations made in the winter of 1894-95 revealed the existence of a circular well and of several passages hewn out of the rock below the level of the orchestra, but there is nothing to show that they had any connexion with the theatre. The well must have been filled up long before the theatre was built, for amongst the rubbish with which it was choked were found potsherds of the Mycenaean style and several vases with geometrical decorations, not to mention some pieces of the antlers of deer. The passages, the directions of which are not symmetrical with the axis of the theatre or with each other, must have been made at a later date than the well, for all the potsherds discovered in them belong to the fifth or fourth century B.C.

Of the labyrinth of ruined walls which make up the existing remains of the stage-buildings, Dr. Dörpfeld assigns the earliest to the age of Lycurgus. In doing so he relies for evidence on the style of the workmanship and on the nature of the materials of which the oldest walls are built. For the foundations are of breccia ; above them is laid a course of Piraeic limestone ; and the upper part of the edifice, so far as it remains, is built of blue Hymettian and white Pentelic marble. Now since, as we have seen (p. 501), the simultaneous use of breccia, Piraeic limestone, and blue Hymettian marble is characteristic of Athenian buildings which date from the fourth to the second century B.C., and since further the excellence of the masonry points to the best period of Greek architecture, we can hardly doubt that the stage-buildings in question formed part of the new theatre which Lycurgus built or at least completed in the fourth century B.C. Of any older stage-building there remains no trace. If any such building existed in the fifth century B.C., it has wholly disappeared. The general plan of the stage-buildings erected by Lycurgus has already been described (vol. 2. p. 226). From various technical indications Dr. Dörpfeld infers that the front both of the central body of the stage-building and of its two projecting wings was adorned with a row of Doric columns. In fact remains of columns and an architrave which seem to have originally decorated the front of one of the wings were discovered in the excavations of 1895. The height of this row of columns, with their architrave, triglyph frieze, and cornice, is calculated by Dr. Dörpfeld to have been about 4 metres (13 feet). This, then, may be taken to be approximately the height of the stage-buildings erected by Lycurgus. The depth from front to back of the long hall which formed the central and main part of the stage-buildings is 6.45 metres, measured on the inside. The roof of this hall would therefore furnish a stage of ample width, and its height would but slightly exceed the maximum height (12 feet) allowed by Vitruvius (v. 7. 2) for the height of a Greek stage. Dr. Dörpfeld, however, holds that down to the time of Nero the players acted not on but in front of the stage-building, the columned front of which, in his view, formed a background representing the exterior of a palace, a house, a temple or what not. An argument in favour of the traditional view that the actors appeared on rather than in front of the stage-building may perhaps be drawn from an explanation which Dr. Dörpfeld himself has given of a certain arrangement in the interior of the stage-building. The back wall of the long hall is strengthened on the inner side by a low wall of breccia, in the top of which at regular intervals of about 2.60 metres large square holes measuring .35 to .40 metre are sunk. These holes, it is to be observed, do not occur along the whole of the back wall, but only along that portion of it which faces the orchestra. Dr. Dörpfeld considers it indubitable that strong wooden posts were fixed upright in these holes, and he conjectures that they supported a wooden upper storey which in some plays may have represented the upper storey of a house, in others the home of the gods in Olympus, and so on, while in other plays it need not have been used at all. This is quite possible; but it is also possible that the framework which rested on these posts and which rose above the roof of the stage-buildings formed the regular, not the occasional, background of every play, that in short it always supported the scenery, and that the actors regularly appeared in front of it on the roof of the hall or, in other words, on the stage.

The first important modification of the stage-buildings of Lycurgus is now conjecturally assigned by Dr. Dörpfeld to the first century B.C. He suggests that when Athens was captured by Sulla in the year 86 B.C. the theatre may have suffered as the adjoining Music Hall certainly did (Paus. i. 20. 4), and that the remodelling of the stage-buildings may have been carried out when the theatre was repaired after the sack. The change consisted in cutting off the front part of both wings and erecting a line of columns in the central space between the wings. The stylobate which supported this line of columns still exists; it is parallel to the line of the stage-building of Lycurgus and at a distance of about 1.25 metres from it. The foundations are built of rubble and squared blocks, bonded together with lime-mortar. Slabs of bluish marble laid on the top of the foundations formed the stylobate proper; circular marks on the marble still show where the columns stood. The style of masonry is indifferent; the foundations are carelessly built: the upper surface of the slabs is not smoothed, and their edges do not fit closely. Altogether the workmanship is far inferior to that of the walls which may be ascribed to the age of Lycurgus. Of the columns themselves nothing remains, but from their diameter (.51 metre), as shown by the marks on the stylobate and from other indications, Dr. Dörpfeld concludes that their height was the same as that of the columns which adorned the front of the older stage-building. The space between the two central columns was wider than the space between any other pair of columns, and was closed with a double folding door, as appears from the holes in the threshold for the bolts and sockets; and there are some traces of a smaller side door in the intercolumniation immediately to the west of the central one. All the other spaces between the columns were probably closed with moveable painted panels, whether of wood or stone, as in the theatre at Oropus (vol. 2. p. 469); the absence of any marks of walls on the stylobate proves that the intervals between the columns were not filled up with masonry. This line of columns formed, on the traditional view, the front of the new stage, which was thus advanced somewhat nearer to the audience than the old stage (if stage it was) in the theatre of Lycurgus. The depth of the new stage or, in other words, of the platform supported by the new line of columns in front of the old stage-building, is estimated by Dr. Dörpfeld at 2.80 metres (9 ft. 2¼ in.); but since it was continuous with, and at the same level as, the old stage, there seems no reason why it should not have included as much of the latter as might seem desirable.

In the reign of Nero both the stage-buildings and the orchestra were thoroughly remodelled. Abundant evidence of this reconstruction is furnished by existing walls, marble pavement, architectural members, and sculptures, and its date is fixed by an inscription, found in the theatre, which records a dedication to Eleutherian Dionysus and Nero by some person whose name is lost (*C. I. A.* iii. No. 158). The inscription is carved on an architrave which, supported on Corinthian pillars, seems to have been placed against the back wall of the stage. A whole shaft of one of these pillars, together with several fragments of other shafts, bases, and capitals, came to light in the course of the excavations. The chief changes made at this time were the construction of a low broad Roman stage advancing far into the orchestra, the laying down of a marble pavement in the orchestra, and the separation of the auditorium from the orchestra by a marble parapet or balustrade. The front line of the new stage is now believed by Dr. Dörpfeld to have coincided with the front line of the still later stage of Phaedrus, except that it was not prolonged on either side till it met the seats of the spectators. Thus the communication between the *parodoi* and the auditorium was maintained. The reliefs which still adorn the front of the later stage of Phaedrus were probably made for Nero's stage. Judging from what would seem to have been their original height (for the slabs have been barbarously cut down to fit them into the later stage), Dr. Dörpfeld infers that Nero's stage was 1.46 metres high. Probably it was connected with the orchestra by one or more short staircases.

The still later stage of Phaedrus appears to date from the third or perhaps even the fourth century A.D. What the reasons for rebuilding the stage at this time may have been we do not know; but Dr. Dörpfeld inclines to think that the change may have been due partly to the disrepair into which the front of Nero's stage had fallen and partly to a desire to convert the orchestra into a water-basin in which naval combats might be exhibited for the amusement of the populace. Evidence of this latter motive he finds in the strong back walls with which at this time the front of the stage and the marble parapet of the orchestra were strengthened, for the effect of this must have been to render both these structures water-tight. Moreover, pieces of earthenware pipes which seem to have led the water into and out of the orchestra have been found in the theatre.

P. 227 line 8 from foot, **statues of tragic and comic poets.** Inscriptions of the Roman period prove that statues of the poets Philemon, Thespis, Timostratus, and Dionysius stood in the theatre at Athens (*C. I. A.* iii. 1. Nos. 948, 949, 950, 951).

P. 227 line 7 from foot, **Astydamas, a writer of voluminous tragedies** etc. A block of Hymettian marble which appears to have formed part of the pedestal of Astydamas's statue has been found in the theatre of Dionysus. It is inscribed with the first four letters of his name (ΑΣΤΥ) and seems to have stood on the edge of the orchestra, at the lower end of the wall which supports the western wing of the auditorium. Here it has now been set up again. See *C. I. A.* ii. No. 1363; Dörpfeld und Reisch, *Das griechische Theater*, p. 71 *sq.* Other inscriptions attest the popularity of this prolific playwright (*C. I. A.* ii. Nos. 973, 977). Cp. U. Köhler, in *Mittheilungen d. arch. Inst. in Athen*, 3 (1878), p. 112 *sqq.*

P. 228 line 18 *sq.* from foot, **a fine seated statue of Menander in the Vatican.** Some archaeologists, however, deny that this statue (as to which see W. Helbig, *Führer durch die öffentlichen Sammlungen klassischer Alterthümer in Rom*, No. 199) represents Menander. Amongst those who doubt or deny its connexion with Menander are G. Scharf (*Transactions of the Royal Society of Literature*, Second Series, 4 (1853), p. 388), Prof. Furtwängler (*Meisterwerke d. griech. Plastik*, p. 532 note 2), and Prof. Studniczka (in *Berliner philolog. Wochenschrift*, 14th December 1895, p. 1627). The last-mentioned scholar considers that we possess the poet's portrait in a series of heads which have been enumerated by Prof. Bernoulli and regarded by him, with considerable hesitation, as perhaps portraits of Pompey (*Römische Ikonographie*, 1. p. 123 *sq.*, with pl. viii.). The most beautiful replicas, according to Prof. Studniczka, are in the Museum at Corneto and the Gymnasium at Corfu.

P. 236 line 12 from top, **constructed of polygonal masonry.** The masonry is partly quadrangular, and the four bases which stand round about the mouth of the shaft are round, not square, as stated in the text.

P. 237 line 8 *sq.* from foot, **the bringing of the god from Peloponnese to Athens.** The date when the worship of Aesculapius was introduced into Athens has been examined by Mr. A. Körte (*Mittheilungen d. arch. Inst. in Athen*, 18 (1893), pp. 240-250, 19 (1896), pp. 313-332). If he is right in restoring Astyphilus as the name of the archon in the inscription (*C. I. A.* ii. No. 1649) which records the introduction of the worship, Aesculapius first came to Athens, or at all events his sanctuary was founded, in 420 B.C. This date is accepted by Prof. Usener (*Götternamen*, p. 148).

P. 237 line 9 *sq.* from top, **the square shaft of an ancient well.** According to my measurements this shaft is 8 ft. 9 in. wide by 8 ft. 2 in. deep. The western side of the shaft has been built up again.

P. 241 line 28 from foot, **The Music Hall of Herodes Atticus.** In the Music Hall of Herodes Atticus the number of staircases dividing the seats is six, of which two are at the ends. The two wings of the stage-buildings are standing to a height of four stories, as is shown by the arched windows in the walls. At the west end of the western *parodos* is a niche in which the statue of a man in Roman costume is still standing.

P. 251 at top, **the two side gateways.** The clear width of these gateways, according to my measurement, is 4 ft. 1½ in., without the stone door-jambs. The lower courses of the walls which flank the gateways are of black Eleusinian stone, not of white Pentelic marble like the rest of the Propylaea.

P. 252 line 21 *sq.*, **the ruts in which the wheels ran can still be seen in the rock.** I was not able to verify this statement. But on some of the slabs which pave the central part of the passage, as well as on the rocks inside of the Propylaea, there are rows of parallel cross grooves, which may have been meant to keep the wheels of the chariots and the feet of the horses from slipping.

P. 253 line 9 from top, **the third column, with which it is joined by an architrave.** This column, the westernmost of the three, is now wanting and with it the architrave. But the circle which marks the place of the column can still be clearly seen on the stylobate.

P. 254 line 26 *sqq.*, **The remains consist of a wall about 20 feet long and a few feet high, with a short wall joining it at right angles and terminated by a marble anta.** The longer of these two walls is about 5 ft. 10 in. high. The short wall, including the *anta*, is 7 feet long, measured on the south-west front, and is about 11 ft. 5 in. high.

P. 257 line 21 *sq.* from foot, **a temple of Wingless Victory.** Some light has now been thrown on the question of the date of this temple by an inscription which Mr. Cavvadias found in 1897 while excavating the north slope of the Acropolis, below the cave of Apollo. The inscription, which contains the three-stroke *sigma* ($\leq$), seems to date from the middle of the fifth century B.C. It refers to a sanctuary which was to be provided with a new door and to a stone temple and altar which were to be built in the sanctuary by Callicrates, one of the architects of the Parthenon (Plutarch, *Pericles*, 13). Mr. Cavvadias and Dr. Dörpfeld agree in thinking that the temple referred to can be no other than that of the Wingless Victory or rather of Victory Athena. If they are right, the inscription finally disposes of Prof. Furtwängler's theory as to the date of the temple, against which I have already argued on other grounds (vol. 2. p. 260). See *Mittheilungen d. arch. Inst. in Athen*, 22 (1897), p. 226 *sq.*

P. 262 line 2 *sq.* from foot, **how many of the pictures —— were by Polygnotus.** Amongst those who deny that any of the pictures in this gallery were by Polygnotus are G. Hermann (*Opuscula*, 5. p. 227), Prof.

C. Robert (*Bild und Lied*, p. 182 note 31 ; *Die Iliupersis des Polygnot*, p. 25 *sq.* ; *Die Marathonschlacht in der Poikile*, p. 66 note 27), and apparently Prof. Milchhöfer (*Jahrbuch d. arch. Inst.* 9 (1894), p. 72 note 36). They hold that the pictures which Pausanias in this passage ascribes to Polygnotus were not in the gallery at the Propylaea but elsewhere. The other and more probable view that two at least and perhaps more of the pictures in the gallery at the Propylaea were by Polygnotus is accepted by Mr. P. Girard (*La Peinture antique*, p. 167 *sqq.*).

P. 266 line 3 *sq.* from top, Achilles —— in the company of the maidens at Scyros. Prof. C. Robert professes to recognise a copy of Polygnotus's painting of this subject (*Archäologischer Anzeiger*, 1889, p. 151 ; *Die Nekyia des Polygnot*, p. 37 *sq.* ; *Die Marathonschlacht in der Poikile*, p. 66 *sq.*). The supposed copy is a relief, executed in fine Greek style, on a gold plate which was found in a grave near Nicopol, in the south of Russia. Stephani explained the reliefs differently as illustrating the Attic version of the story of Alope. See *Compte Rendu* (St. Petersburg) for 1864, pp. 142-171, with the Atlas, pl. iv. The subject of Polygnotus's picture (Achilles in the company of the maidens at Scyros) is represented in relief in very fair style on a sarcophagus at San Fruttuoso to which Prof. von Duhn has called attention (*Archäologischer Anzeiger*, 1895, p. 159 *sq.*).

P. 270 line 9 from foot, a sixth relief —— representing the Graces. There are remains of colour on this relief, as I was able to observe for myself in the museum on the Acropolis. The hair of Hermes and two of the Graces is red ; the hair of the first of the Graces is yellow ; the dress of the second Grace is yellow ; the background is green. Cp. P. Kastriotes, Κατάλογος τοῦ Μουσείου τῆς 'Ακροπολέως (Athens, 1895), No. 702.

P. 271 line 21 from top, the figure of Hermes etc. In the Acropolis Museum at Athens there is preserved a fine relief representing the legs of a man, life-size, striding to the spectator's right. This relief, of which the upper part is lost, was found in the Propylaea, and is by some regarded as a fragment of the figure of Hermes of the Portal mentioned by Pausanias. See P. Kastriotes, Κατάλογος τοῦ Μουσείου τῆς 'Ακροπολέως, No. 1334.

P. 280 line 20 *sq.* from foot, Four holes on the top of the block. I could not perceive more than one or at the most two holes. The corners of the upper surface of the block are all broken away.

P. 285 line 15 *sqq.*, wooden statues etc. Wooden statues were also made by Damophon (Paus. viii. 31. 6).

P. 289 line 12 from foot, Athena —— striking Marsyas. Prof. C. Sittl has essayed to show (*Parerga zur alten Kunstgeschichte*, pp. 25-29) that the existing monuments representing the group of Athena and Marsyas belong to two different types and may be traced back to two distinct originals. In one type, represented by the vase-painting, Marsyas is portrayed as having dropped the flutes on which he has been playing and as recoiling in alarm at the sudden appearance of Athena. This is the earlier type, and its original was the group here described by Pausanias, which Prof. Sittl conjectures to have been dedicated in the early part of the fifth century B.C. by the tragic poet Pratinas as a memorial of a poetical victory and a mark of his contempt for flutes and flute-players (cp. Athenaeus, xiv. p. 617 b-e). In the other type, represented by the coins and the relief, Athena is portrayed as throwing away the flutes and Marsyas as stealing up to them with an air of surprise. This was the later type, and its original was the work of Myron mentioned by Pliny (*Nat. hist.* xxxiv. 57). With regard to the marble statue in the Lateran and the bronze statuette in the British Museum, Prof. Sittl denies that either of them is a copy of Myron's work or has anything to do with any group of Athena and Marsyas; the Lateran statue, according to him, is nothing but a dancing Satyr, the London statuette is merely a Satyr scratching his head in a thoughtful attitude. But the distinctions drawn by Prof. Sittl appear to me unfounded, and I prefer to believe that all the monuments he discusses may be traced back to one original work of Myron, namely the group here described by Pausanias.

P. 298 line 19 from top, **The temple was surrounded by a colonnade** etc. A well-preserved piece of what seems to have been the floor of the colonnade is to be seen at the south-east corner; the blocks are polygonal and fairly well fitted together.

P. 298 line 17 from foot, **Built into the northern wall of the Acropolis** etc. These architectural fragments are built into the Acropolis wall to the east of the Erechtheum. Into the wall to the north of the Erechtheum there are built some large marble drums and capitals.

P. 299 line 10 from top, **an inscription** etc. Beside the inscription is a cutting in the rock, 19 inches by 17 inches, to receive the image.

P. 303 line 14 *sqq.* from top, **They set barley** etc. The sacrifice of the *bouphonia* has recently been discussed by Mr. H. von Prott, who would explain it as a substitute for human sacrifice (*Rheinisches Museum*, N. F. 52 (1897), pp. 187-204). Mr. P. Stengel disputes his conclusion and maintains that the sacrifice was originally bloodless (*ib.* pp. 399-411). Both writers confess themselves unable to conceive of a remote age in which the slaughter of a beast was regarded as a capital offence. They seem to be quite unaware that down to the present day pastoral tribes in Africa regard their cattle as sacred, and that among the Caffres even to defile the cattle-pen is an offence which is punished with death (H. Lichtenstein, *Reisen im südlichen Africa*, 1. p. 479). Some of the facts illustrative of the sanctity of cattle among pastoral tribes in ancient and modern times have been put together by W. Robertson Smith (*Religion of the Semites*,[2] p. 296 *sqq.*). To discuss the traces of savagery in ancient Greece without some knowledge of savage life and modes of thought is perfectly futile.

P. 304 line 15 from top, **the Parthenon.** The technical construction of the Parthenon has been studied by a French architect, Mr. L. Magne (*Le Parthenon: Études faites au cours de deux missions en Grèce*, Paris, 1895). The temple suffered considerably from the earthquake of April 1894, but the necessary repairs have been carried out in accordance with the advice of the distinguished German architect, Mr. Joseph

Durm.   See *Mittheilungen d. arch. Inst. in Athen*, 19 (1894), pp. 529-
531 ; Ἐφημερὶς ἀρχαιολογική, 1895, pp. 1-50 ; Πρακτικὰ τῆς Ἀρχαιολογικῆς Ἑταιρίας, 1895, pp. 12-15, 194-200 ; *Archäologischer Anzeiger*,
1895, pp. 100-102 ; *American Journal of Archaeology*, 10 (1895), pp.
532-537.   An interesting discovery has been made by Mr. E. Andrews
of the American School at Athens.   He has proved that an inscription
was fastened by nails to the eastern architrave of the temple, and by
carefully examining the prints of the nails he has been able to decipher
the inscription.   As read by him, it records that the Council of the
Areopagus, the Council of the Six Hundred, and the Athenian people
conferred some honour, not specified, on the most high and mighty
emperor Nero, in the eighth generalship of Titus Claudius Novius, son
of Philinus.   The reference to the eighth generalship of Novius proves
that the date of the inscription is 61 A.D.   The honour conferred on
the emperor may perhaps have consisted in the erection of a statue of
him in front of the temple.   See *Berliner philologische Wochenschrift*,
28th March 1896, p. 414 *sq.* ; *Classical Review*, 10 (1896), p. 222;
Journal of Hellenic Studies, 16 (1896), p. 339.

The discussion of the sculptured decoration of the Parthenon
shows no sign of abating.   The metopes are the subject of papers
by Mr. W. Malmberg (Ἐφημερὶς ἀρχαιολογική, 1894, pp. 213-226)
and Mr. E. Pernice ('Über die mittleren Metopen der Südseite des
Parthenon,' *Jahrbuch d. arch. Inst.* 10 (1895), pp. 93-103), who argues
that the subjects of the nine central metopes on the south side are all
drawn from the legendary history of Erichthonius.   The head of a
Lapith belonging to one of the metopes, but now in the Louvre, is the
subject of an article by Mr. A. Heron de Villefosse which should have
been mentioned in the text (*Monuments Grecs*, vol. 2. Nos. 11-13 (1882-
1884), pp. 1-12) ; the head of a Centaur, now at Wurzburg, which
seems to have belonged to another of the metopes, has been identified
and discussed by Prof. Michaelis (*Jahrbuch d. arch. Inst.* 11 (1896),
pp. 300-304) and Prof. G. Treu (*ib.* 12 (1897), p. 101 *sq.*).   Overbeck
maintained that the figure commonly called the Victory of the Parthenon
is really Iris and belongs to the eastern gable (*Berichte über die Verhandlungen d. k. sächs. Gesell. d. Wissen. zu Leipzig*, Philolog. histor. Classe,
44 (1892), pp. 24-30).   Professor Furtwängler and Miss Harrison have
discussed the interpretation of certain figures in the gables together with
the much-debated question whether the cloth which a boy in the middle
of the eastern frieze holds in his hands is the robe of Athena or a carpet.
Prof. Furtwängler defends the older view that it is the robe ; Miss
Harrison advocates the theory, first proposed by E. Curtius, that it is a
carpet.   See *Classical Review*, 9 (1895), pp. 85-92, 272-276, 427 *sq.* ;
Berliner philolog. Wochenschrift, 15 (1895), pp. 1277-1280, 1308-
1312.   Mr. A. H. Smith has shown (*Journal of Hellenic Studies*, 14
(1894), pp. 264-266) that certain reduced copies in terra-cotta of the
Parthenon frieze which Prof. Furtwängler (*Meisterwerke d. griech.
Plastik*, p. 743 *sq.*) had assigned to the age of Augustus are most prob-
ably modern forgeries.   Still more recently Prof. Furtwängler announced
(*Intermezzi* (Leipsic and Berlin, 1896), pp. 15-32) that he had dis-

covered in Paris the original statue of Athena by Phidias which occupied the centre of the eastern gable of the Parthenon. The statue had hitherto been known among archaeologists as the Torso Medici, and had been by Prof. Furtwängler himself formerly regarded as a copy of the great bronze Athena of the Acropolis. The joy of archaeologists at the professor's discovery appears to be seasoned with a due proportion of salt (Miss E. Sellers, in *Classical Review*, 10 (1896), p. 444 *sq.*; Fr. Hauser, in *Berliner philolog. Wochenschrift*, 17 (1897), p. 49; B. Sauer, in *Wochenschrift für klassische Philologie*, 21st April 1897, pp. 455-457). Mr. Kalkmann has pointed out that we have no ancient authority for assigning any part of the sculptured decoration of the Parthenon — frieze, metopes, or pediments — to the hand of Phidias (*Archäologischer Anzeiger*, 1896, pp. 98-100). A restoration of the figures of the western gable has been attempted by Mr. K. Schwerzek (*Erläuterungen zu der Reconstruction des Westgiebels des Parthenon*, Wien, 1896); but his restoration has been severely criticised by Prof. Furtwängler (*Berliner philolog. Wochenschrift*, 12th December 1896, pp. 1592-1595). A less unfavourable opinion of it has been expressed by Prof. B. Sauer (*Wochenschrift für klassische Philologie*, 20th January 1897, pp. 89-94). The restoration and interpretation of the sculptures of both gables have been discussed at some length by Prof. Wizemann (*Die Giebelgruppen des Parthenon*, Stuttgart, 1895). A fragment which perhaps belonged to the western gable is discussed by Mr. W. Malmberg ('Zum Westgiebel des Parthenon,' *Jahrbuch des Archäolog. Instituts*, 12 (1897), pp. 92-96). A brief notice of some pieces of the Parthenon sculptures which are now in the Louvre is given by Mr. Ph. E. Legrand (*Revue archéologique*, 3me Série, 26 (1895), pp. 237-239).

P. 304 line 23 *sq.* from top, **the entablature.** Very large portions of the entablature both on the north and the south side of the Parthenon are preserved in their places, but the central parts of it on both these sides are gone.

P. 304 line 25 *sq.* from top, **the western wall of the cella.** More strictly speaking, it is the back wall of the western portico (*opisthodomos*) of which considerable portions are preserved.

P. 304 line 28 from top, **a vast substruction.** Parts of the outer walls of this great substruction are exposed to view in two deep pits near the south-western corner of the Parthenon. In the more easterly of the pits a narrow winding staircase leads down through the wall, which is built partly of polygonal and partly of ashlar masonry. In the other pit the wall, so far as it is exposed, is built of ashlar masonry only.

P. 305 line 14 *sq.* from top, **metopes, of which forty-one still remain** etc. The westernmost metope on the south side of the Parthenon is in its place and well preserved. It represents a Centaur with his left arm round the neck of a Lapith and his right arm raised to strike.

P. 312 line 11 *sqq.* from top, **the image itself** etc. To the copies of Phidias's statue of Virgin Athena enumerated in the text should perhaps be added a mutilated marble head of a helmeted goddess which was found at Cologne in 1882. See G. Loeschcke, ' *Kopf der Athena Parthenos des Pheidias*,' *Festschrift zum fünfzigjährigen Jubiläum des Vereins von Alterthumsfreunden im Rheinlande* (Bonn, 1891), pp. 1-16. A small copy of the statue, wanting the head and arms, has been discovered in the course of the German excavations between the Pnyx and Areopagus ; it agrees with the Varvakion statuette (*Mittheilungen d. arch. Inst. in Athen,* 21 (1896), p. 284). Another copy, superior in style to the Varvakion statuette, has lately come to light at *Patras* : the head and arms are missing, and so is part of the shield, the remains of which, nevertheless, the battle of the Greeks and Amazons can be distinguished (*Chronique des Arts*, 1896, p. 358 ; *Archäologischer Anzeiger*, 1896, p. 212 ; *ib.* 1897, p. 63). The dimensions of the original statue have been discussed by Miss A. L. Perry (*American Journal of Archaeology*, 11 (1896), pp. 335-346, with note by Mr. A. Emerson, pp. 346-349).

P. 320 line 10 *sqq.* from foot, **a temple of Rome and Augustus** etc. The remains of the columns and architrave of this temple are still to be seen lying in front of the Parthenon. The columns measure 2 feet in diameter at the base.

P. 321 line 3 from top, **Locust Apollo.** In South Mirzapur, in India, when a flight of locusts comes, the people catch one, decorate his head with a spot of red lead, salaam to him, and let him go, when he is supposed immediately to depart with his fellows (W. Crooke, *Introduction to the Popular Religion and Folklore of Northern India,* p. 380). In this worship of an individual locust for the purpose of propitiating and averting the rest we may have in germ the worship of a deity like Locust Apollo. See the note on v. 14. 1 (vol. 3. p. 558 *sq.*). In Japan a man who is supposed to be possessed by the ruler of crows hops about like a crow and goes through various odd evolutions for the purpose of averting crows from the fields. The ceremony takes place once a year on a mountain called Futagani San in the province of Mimasaka. See W. Weston, *Mountaineering and Exploration in the Japanese Alps* (London, 1896), pp. 304-306. Here we have something like an approach to a propitiation of a Crow God.

P. 322 line 25 from foot, **Dinomenes.** Tatian, a contemporary of Pausanias, mentions that he saw at Rome a statue by a sculptor Dinomenes representing the Paeonian queen Besantis who had given birth to a black child (*Oratio ad Graecos*, 33, p. 132 ed. Otto). The statue may have stood in the theatre of Pompey, where another of the statues referred to by Tatian, that of Eutychis by Periclymenus, is known to have stood (Tatian, *op. cit.* 34, p. 134 ed. Otto ; Pliny, *Nat. hist.* vii. 34). But the statue of Besantis by Dinomenes at Rome cannot have been identical with the statue of Io by Dinomenes at Athens, as Prof. G. Loeschcke has suggested (*Observationes Archaeologicae,* p. 10 *sq.*). The sculptor, however, who made the one statue may very well have made the other, and he may have been identical with the sculptor of the first century B.C. (*C. I. A.* ii. No. 1648) rather than with the sculptor of the same name who flourished at the beginning of the third century B.C. (Pliny, *Nat. hist.* xxxiv. 50). See E. Loewy, *Unter-*

suchungen zur griech. Künstlergeschichte, pp. 34-36 ; W. Gurlitt, *Ueber Pausanias*, p. 267 *sq.*

P. 322 line 18 from foot, figures —— dedicated by Attalus. Of these figures the group which represented the battle of the Athenians with the Amazons is the subject of a recent monograph by Mr. G. Habich (*Die Amazonengruppe des attalischen Weihgeschenks*, Berlin, 1896).

P. 325 line 2 from foot, Panactum. The identification of Panactum suggested by the French surveyors is accepted by Prof. Milchhöfer. The ruined fort is situated above the south-west edge of the plain of *Skourta*, about 500 feet higher up than the villages of *Kako-Nistiri* and *Kavasala*. Portions of the circuit-wall and of a tower together with some other foundations are still to be seen. One piece of wall, better preserved than the rest, is constructed partly of large squared blocks, partly of polygonal blocks with small stones in the interstices. See A. Milchhöfer, in *Karten von Attika, Erläuternder Text*, Heft vii.-viii., p. 15. An inscription, found at Eleusis and dating apparently from the end of the fourth or the beginning of the third century B.C., mentions Panactum along with Eleusis and Phyle as places which were garrisoned and the walls of which had been recently repaired ('Εφημερὶς ἀρχαιολογική, 1884, p. 135 *sqq.*). Another inscription of about the same date mentions the garrisons of these three places (*C. I. A.* ii. No. 1217).

P. 329 line 13 from foot, a seated image of Athena by Endoeus. The date of the sculptor Endoeus has been examined by Mr. H. Lechat (*Revue des Études grecques*, 5 (1892), pp. 385-402 ; *id.*, 6 (1893), pp. 22-32). He argues that the statue by this sculptor which Pausanias saw on the Acropolis must have been made after the Persian invasion of 480-479 B.C., since if it had been set up earlier it must have perished in the sack of Athens. Hence, while admitting that the inscriptions prove Endoeus to have been at work in the last quarter of the sixth century B.C., Mr. Lechat holds that the sculptor must have survived and exercised his profession till about 475 B.C. He rejects the statement of Pausanias that Endoeus was a pupil of Daedalus. With regard to the seated image of Athena which has been conjecturally identified with the one mentioned by Pausanias, Mr. Lechat considers that it is not earlier than the last quarter of the sixth century B.C. and that it may belong to the fifth century B.C. Whether it is by Endoeus or not, he would leave an open question.

P. 329 line 6 from foot, the sculptor's name is carved etc. This inscription is now published in *C. I. A.* iv. p. 179, No. 373[7].

P. 332 line 5 from top, a ground of dark Eleusinian marble. Three blocks of this dark marble are still above the epistyle at the eastern end of the temple.

P. 332 line 7 from top, six Ionic columns. Three of these columns are adorned with patterns in relief both on the base and on the neck below the capital : on the base the pattern is composed of interlaced lines ; on the neck it is composed of the 'egg and dart' above and palmettes below. This richness of decoration is very unusual, if not unique, in Greek architecture.

P. 332 line 14 *sq.* from top, **four engaged Ionic columns.** The bases of three of these columns and a small part of the fourth column, with its base, are still standing on the top of the wall.

P. 332 line 23, **a flight of steps led up to the door.** Rather the staircase led *down* to the door. For while the Caryatid portico is at the higher, the door is at the lower level of the temple. Hence inside of the portico a staircase, of which a few steps only remain, led down to the door. A great part of the coffered ceiling of the Caryatid porch is preserved in its place, and so is about a third of the coffered ceiling of the north-western porch of the Erechtheum. In the Caryatid porch the dark colour of the terra-cotta Caryatid easily distinguishes her from her marble sisters.

P. 346 line 15, **The statues are life-size** etc. This is true only of three or four of them. The statues in fact vary greatly in size; some are much less than life. Only three or four of them, if any, can possibly have been Caryatids.

P. 348 line 18 from foot, **a bronze image of Athena** etc. Mr. S. Reinach believes that we possess an exact copy of this colossal statue (the Athena *Promachos*) in a bronze statuette which was found at Coblenz and is now in the Boston Museum. He further holds that a bronze statuette recently found at Tchan, near the Dardanelles, reproduces the type of the colossal bronze statue which is described by Nicetas and which was preserved at Constantinople down to the beginning of the thirteenth century A.D. See *Comptes Rendus de l'Académie des Inscriptions et des Belles-Lettres*, 4me Série, 23 (1895), p. 313; *American Journal of Archaeology*, 11 (1896), p. 133. As to the statue described by Nicetas, see vol. 2. p. 350.

P. 352 line 22 from foot, **a bronze chariot.** The position of the bronze chariot on the Acropolis has been discussed by Mr. Hauvette (*Hérodote*, p. 47 *sqq.*). He thinks that the restoration of the chariot, after its overthrow or destruction by the Persians, may have taken place on the occasion of the Athenian victory at Oenophyta in 456 B.C., and that the chariot was then set up in front of the old entrance to the Acropolis, where Herodotus saw it; but that afterwards, when the grand portal of Mnesicles was built, the chariot was removed and placed inside the Acropolis, where Pausanias saw it.

P. 354 line 15 *sq.* from top, **copies of the Lemnian Athena** etc. Prof. Furtwängler's identification of the two Dresden torsoes and the Bologna head as copies of the Lemnian Athena of Phidias has been rejected by Mr. P. Jamot on weighty grounds, of which the following are the chief:—

(1) The Bologna head is too small for the body on which Prof. Furtwängler has set it.

(2) The style and technique of the head are entirely different from those of the body, the crisp, sharp, delicate chiselling of the head contrasting strongly with the broad, solid, grandiose treatment of the body; the head is most probably, as Prof. Furtwängler holds, a copy of a bronze original, the treatment of the body is entirely appropriate to marble.

(3) There is nothing in the Bologna head to recall the style of Phidias; on the contrary, with its high skull, its narrow face tapering downwards to a point, its delicate features, thin nose, thin tightly-shut lips, and dainty chin it is the direct antithesis of the square massive heads with broad cheeks, thick noses, thick parted lips, strong jowls, and heavy chins, which on the strength of the Parthenon sculptures and the copies of the Virgin Athena we are justified in regarding as characteristic of the art of Phidias.

(4) The Lemnian Athena is mentioned by only two ancient authors, Pausanias and Lucian, neither of whom says anything about the pose of the statue; hence any attempt to identify existing statues as copies of it are necessary futile.

Mr. Jamot concludes that the Bologna head does not belong to either of the Dresden bodies; that it has nothing to do with Phidias or his school; and that we cannot possibly identify copies of a statue of which we possess no description. In all these conclusions I agree with Mr. Jamot. Prof. Furtwängler, while he attempts to defend the hybrid which he calls the Lemnian Athena, admits the apparent disproportion and the discrepancy of style between the head and the body, but boldly asserts that these are intentional and characteristic of the goddess and of the art of the period. With Mr. Jamot I fail to understand how a glaring discord between the head and body of a statue can be thought a characteristic beauty, above all in a statue which ancient critics regarded as the most beautiful work of their greatest master. See P. Jamot, in *Monuments Grecs*, vol. 2. Nos. 21-22 (1893-1894), pp. 23-35 ; *id.*, 'L'Athéna Lemnia de Phidias,' *Revue archéologique*, 3me Série, 27 (1895), pp. 1-5 ; A. Furtwängler, in *Classical Review*, 9 (1895), pp. 269-272 ; H. Lechat, in *Revue des Études grecques*, 9 (1896), pp. 260-262. Prof. Furtwängler has pointed to some engraved gems which he considers as copies of the Lemnian Athena (*Revue archéologique*, 3me Série, 28 (1896), pp. 1-6). One of them, now become a corner-stone of his theory, he formerly damned as a forgery. He would further identify as a copy of the Lemnian Athena a figure of the goddess carved in relief on a tablet of Pentelic marble, which was found in the sanctuary of Aesculapius at Epidaurus. Athena is here represented standing with her helmet in her raised right hand. Facing her is a man leaning on a staff and apparently touching Athena's helmet with his right hand. Prof. Furtwängler would interpret him as Hephaestus giving the helmet to Athena. See A. Furtwängler, 'Zur Athena Lemnia,' *Sitzungsberichte d. philosoph. philolog. und d. histor. Classe d. k. bayer. Akad. d. Wissenschaften zu München*, 1897, pp. 289-292.

P. 355 line 24 *sqq.* from foot, **a much older fortification-wall** etc. A well-preserved piece of the Pelasgic wall is to be seen at the east end of the Acropolis, on the north side of the building called the Small Museum. It is built of the native red and blue limestone of the Acropolis and is from 12 to 13 feet thick. In the piece of the Pelasgic wall at the southwest corner of the Acropolis there is a block 6 feet long.

P. 356 line 1 *sqq.*, **Two groups of these foundations** etc. The western of the two groups of Pelasgic remains referred to in the text is

18 paces long from east to west by 5 paces broad from north to south. The outer walls, which in one place are standing to a height of 7 feet, are built of large rough blocks in the Cyclopean style ; the inner walls are constructed of smaller stones. Enclosed by walls of large rough stones about 3 feet thick is a small apartment or cell measuring about 6 feet square on the inside.

P. 359 line 6 *sqq.* from foot, **the staircase is arched** etc. Only part of the staircase leading down to the Clepsydra spring is arched over ; the greater part of it is open.

P. 360 line 15 from foot, **a sanctuary of Apollo in a cave.** The Greek Archaeological Society proposes to excavate completely the whole of the northern and western sides of the Acropolis. Excavations, directed by Mr. Cavvadias, were begun towards the close of 1896 at the north-west corner of the Acropolis, and have been continued during the spring and summer of 1897. Amongst other results attained they have proved once for all that the cave of Apollo was, as I have maintained in the text, the shallow high-arched cave, situated a little to the east of the Clepsydra spring, of which the walls are studded with niches for votive offerings. For in front of this cave Mr. Cavvadias found no less than twenty-five marble tablets or fragments of tablets carved with wreaths of myrtle or laurel and inscribed with dedications to 'Apollo under the High Rocks' ('Ἀπόλλωνι ὑπὸ Μακραῖς) or to 'Apollo under the Heights' ('Ἀπόλλωνι ὑπ' Ἄκραις). The inscriptions belong to the Roman age. From them and from three similar inscriptions which had been found before (*C. I. A.* iii. 1. Nos. 91, 92 ; *Mittheilungen d. arch. Instituts in Athen*, 3 (1878), p. 144) we gather that the nine archons and their secretary stood in some special relation to the Apollo who was worshipped in the cave, for eleven at least out of the twenty-eight tablets seem to have been dedicated by one or more of the archons or by their secretary. Mr. Cavvadias may be right in supposing that at the end of their term of office the archons regularly dedicated tablets to Apollo at the cave in token that they had kept the oath which they swore when they entered on office (see vol. 2. p. 57 *sq.*). He thinks that the oath which they took on the Acropolis (Aristotle, *Constitution of Athens*, 55) may have been taken at an altar in front of the cave of Apollo, for here, immediately in front of the cave, Mr. Cavvadias discovered a quadrangular sinking in the rock (2.45 metres long by 2 metres wide), in which an altar probably stood. It may have been one of the altars mentioned by Euripides (*Ion*, 937). These discoveries prove that the cave of Apollo was not, as has been sometimes supposed, the shallow cave a little further to the west, close to the Clepsydra spring. In this latter cave there are no niches for votive offerings, so far as I could perceive (and herein my observation is confirmed by that of Mr. Cavvadias); there are only some natural rifts in the rocky sides of the cave. The statement in the text (vol. 2. p. 361) must accordingly be corrected ; it was made at second hand before I had visited the cave.

Three or four yards to the east of the cave of Apollo, in front of the companion cave mentioned in the text (vol. 2. p. 361), Mr. Cavvadias found a round hole in the rock of somewhat irregular shape, about

2 metres wide and from 2 to 2½ metres deep. He conjectures that it may be the cleft, said to have been made by Poseidon's trident, down which Erechtheus vanished (Euripides, *Ion*, 281 *sq*.). Just beside this hole, on the east, the excavations revealed the low entrance to another cave which runs into the rock in two different branches, each about 10 metres long. This cave, which has three separate mouths, all of them low, is identified by Mr. Cavvadias with the cave of Pan. In favour of this view it may be said that the dark recesses of such a cave would be a more suitable place for a secret meeting like that of Cinesias and Myrrhina (Aristophanes, *Lysistrata*, 911 *sqq*.) than any of the other three caves further to the west, all of which are too shallow and open to afford concealment. I am, therefore, disposed to accept Mr. Cavvadias's identification and to withdraw the view adopted in the text that the cave of Apollo was also the cave of Pan. Mr. Cavvadias further conjectures that, according to the original legend at least, the meeting of Apollo and Creusa also took place in the newly-discovered cave, that the worship of Apollo thence extended over the neighbouring caves, and that it was not until the time of the Persian wars that the dark winding cave was transferred from Apollo to the new-comer Pan.

A little to the east of the cave of Pan, as we may now call it, the recent excavations laid bare a staircase hewn in the rock and ascending in an easterly direction to the wall of the Acropolis. Seventeen steps are preserved ; the rest have been destroyed at some period to make room for a building. The staircase leads to a postern (now built up) in the wall of the Acropolis. Inside the postern a staircase of twenty-two steps, discovered in 1885, leads up to the plateau of the Acropolis some 50 metres to the west of the Erechtheum. This entrance to the Acropolis was either kept secret or had fallen into disuse before the time of Pausanias, who knew of no entrance except the regular one by the grand portal (i. 22. 4). Probably the postern was "the hole at the cave of Pan," through which Lysistrata caught one of the women endeavouring to steal out of the Acropolis (Aristophanes, *Lysistrata*, 270 *sq*.).

Still further to the east Mr. Cavvadias has found a narrow underground passage, about 33 metres long, running eastward to the cavern or hollow in the rock which has sometimes been identified with the sanctuary of Aglaurus (see vol. 2. p. 167). The cavern is about 4 metres high and has an opening of about 8½ metres across. A short branch of the underground passage, near the cavern, communicates by means of a staircase with a fissure in the rock, through which you can pass under the fortification-wall into the Acropolis. Entering by this fissure and ascending by a short staircase to the plateau of the Acropolis you find yourself to the north-west of the Erechtheum, within the precinct of the Arrephoroi (Paus. i. 27. 3). Thus the underground passage discovered by Mr. Cavvadias may perhaps have been the one by which the Arrephoroi descended on their secret mission. The existing staircase in the passage is of Frankish or Turkish origin, the steps being constructed of marble slabs, bricks, and mortar. Between the upper nine and the lower five steps there is an empty space of

6½ metres enclosed on either side by the sheer rock. This gap in the staircase was probably bridged over by means of a hanging ladder. In antiquity all the steps of the staircase seem to have been of wood ; the holes in which the ends of the steps were inserted can still be seen in the rock.

In the cavern to which the underground passage leads and which, as we have seen, has sometimes been identified as the sanctuary of Aglaurus, Mr. Cavvadias found undoubted traces of religious worship. A niche for the reception of a votive offering is cut in the wall of the cavern, and among the rubbish which littered the floor was discovered a quadrangular marble pedestal, which to judge from the hollow on its upper surface may have supported a statue half the size of life. Relics of earlier ages came to light lower down. They include pieces of black-figured vases, fragments of a bronze kettle, and a headless clay statuette of a seated woman of archaic style.

See P. Cavvadias, in *Comptes Rendus de l'Académie des Inscriptions*, 25 (1897), pp. 116-118 ; *id.*, in Πρακτικὰ τῆς Ἀρχαιολογικῆς Ἑταιρίας, 1896 (published 1897), pp. 17-19 ; *id.*, in Ἐφημερὶς ἀρχαιολογική, 1897, pp. 1-32, 87-92, with plates 1-4. Compare Ch. Belger, in *Berliner philologische Wochenschrift*, 11th September 1897, pp. 1147-1151 ; *ib.* 25th September 1897, pp. 1212-1214 ; *ib.* 2nd October 1897, pp. 1244-1246.

P. 362 line 2 from foot, **the other sides slope gently to the plain.** This is misleading. The upper part of the Areopagus is composed of a mass of bare rock which on the south and south-west, as well as on the north-east, ends in a line of low precipices. Below this line of precipices the hill slopes gently down into the hollow which divides it from the Museum and Pnyx hills.

P. 363 line 2 *sq.* from top, **remains of rock-hewn seats.** These are correctly described by Wordsworth (*Athens and Attica*,[4] p. 62):— "Immediately above the steps, on the level of the hill, is a bench of stone excavated in the limestone rock, forming three sides of a quadrangle, like a triclinium : it faces south."

P. 363 line 14 *sqq.* from top, **Curtius supposes that the writer of the Acts of the Apostles** etc. Curtius's interpretation of *Acts* xvii. 19 is rejected on good grounds by the Rev. A. F. Findlay, who maintains the traditional and more probable view that St. Paul preached on the Areopagus Hill, not before the Council of the Areopagus in the market-place (*Annual of the British School at Athens*, No. 1 (Session 1894-5), pp. 78-89).

P. 366 line 20 from foot, **a talisman which secured the safety of the state.** With the motives which led the Athenians to keep the grave of Oedipus a state secret, we may compare the motives which induce the negroes of Calabar to preserve in secret places the heads of deceased chiefs. "The heads of important chiefs in the Calabar districts are usually cut off from the body on burial and kept secretly for fear the head, and thereby the spirit, of the dead chief, should be stolen from the town. If it were stolen it would be not only a great advantage to its new possessor, but a great danger to the chief's old town, because he would know all the peculiar ju-ju [charms, talismans] relating to it. For each town has a peculiar one, kept exceedingly secret, in addition to the general ju-jus, and this secret one would then be in the hands of the new owners of the spirit. It is for similar reasons that brave General MacCarthy's head was treasured by the Ashantees, and so on " (Mary H. Kingsley, *Travels in West Africa*, London 1897, p. 449 *sq*.).

P. 373 line 7 *sqq*. **Prof. Milchhöfer has plausibly identified Phreattys** etc. Prof. Milchhöfer's grounds for placing Phreattys on the shore at the eastern side of the entrance to Zea rather than, with H. N. Ulrichs, on the shore a little to the south-west of the entrance to Zea, scarcely hold good. The oval holes which he describes certainly exist in the rock just where he says ; but similar holes are to be seen in much greater numbers at the spot which Ulrichs identified as Phreattys. At the latter place I counted about thirty of these rock-hewn basins on the shore between the entrance to Zea and the spring *Tzirloneri*. Most of them are oval in shape, but some are circular. The women wash clothes in them. One of the oval basins which I measured was 1 metre long, .46 metre wide, and about .60 metre deep. A circular basin, measured by me, was more than a metre in diameter and about half a metre deep. Just at the place in the shore where these basins occur the rock has been hewn away to form two roughly quad-rangular compartments opening off each other with a rude bench or step running nearly all round them. This reminds us of the somewhat similar rock-hewn bench on the summit of the Areopagus (see above, p. 518). Was this bench beside the sea the place where the court of Phreattys sat in judgment ? At the place which Prof. Milchhöfer would identify as Phreattys I saw only nine or ten of the little oval basins in the rock beside the sea.

P. 374 line 1, **the Pythium** etc. Dr. Dörpfeld still maintains his proposed identification of the Pythium mentioned by Thucydides (ii. 15) with the cave of Apollo on the north side of the Acropolis (*Mittheil. d. arch. Inst. in Athen*, 20 (1895), p. 198 *sq*.). The reasons for rejecting this identification appear to me to be conclusive.

(1) The passage of Thucydides in question (ii. 15) suffices by itself to prove that the Pythium, along with the Olympieum, the sanctuary of Earth, and the sanctuary of Dionysus in the Marshes, lay to the south of the Acropolis. But on this head I have already said enough (p. 484 *sq*.).

(2) This is not the only reference to the Pythium in Thucydides. Elsewhere (vi. 54) he mentions an altar dedicated by Pisistratus, son of Hippias, in the Pythium. The situation of the Pythium referred to in this latter passage is known and is not disputed by Dr. Dörpfeld. It was to the south-east of the Acropolis, on the right bank of the Ilissus, near the Olympieum and the spring Callirrhoe (see vol. 2. p. 189). Now if Dr. Dörpfeld is right, Thucydides in two different passages refers to two different Pythiums without giving a hint that they were distinct and lay in opposite quarters of Athens, and that too though in one of the passages (ii. 15) the gist of the argument turns entirely on a knowledge of the exact situation of the sanctuaries referred to. Can we suppose Thucydides to have been guilty of such gross and culpable ambiguity? The supposition is incredible.

(3) The cave of Apollo on the north side of the Acropolis was merely a cave, not a building. It is hardly likely, therefore, that its existence should have been pointed to by Thucydides as evidence of the extent of the ancient city. Does the cave of Pan on Hymettus or the Corycian cave on Parnassus prove the existence of an ancient city in these places?

(4) Strabo mentions (ix. p. 404) that there was a sacrificial hearth of Lightning Zeus on the city-wall (ἐν τῷ τείχει) between the Pythium and the Olympieum. This reference creates a double difficulty for Dr. Dörpfeld; for, first, there is no city-wall and, second, there is no Olympieum in the neighbourhood where, if he is right, they should both be, that is, near the cave of Apollo on the north side of the Acropolis. These difficulties, however, which might have given pause to any one else, are met by Dr. Dörpfeld very simply by assuming both the desired edifices in the desired situations. In the first place the city-wall referred to by Strabo was, he thinks, the city-wall not of Strabo's but of Cecrops's time, in other words the Pelargicum. This far-fetched explanation might perhaps have been allowed to pass if the Pelargicum had existed as a fortress in Strabo's time. But that it had ceased to exist as a fortress at least 400 years before Strabo's time has been conclusively demonstrated by Prof. J. Williams White (Ἐφημερὶς ἀρχαιολογική, 1894, p. 25 *sqq.*; see above, vol. 2. p. 357). That demonstration, though it demolishes a theory of his own, is not mentioned by Dr. Dörpfeld. On the other hand the real city-wall of Strabo's time ran, just where we should expect to find it from his description, between the real Pythium and the real Olympieum to the south-east of the Acropolis. A piece of it, belonging to the Roman age, was excavated a few years ago by the Greek Archaeological Society some 60 or 70 yards to the south of the Olympieum (Πρακτικὰ τῆς Ἀρχαιολογικῆς Ἑταιρίας, 1893, p. 133; see above, p. 486 *sq.*). In the second place, the Olympieum to which Strabo refers and which Dr. Dörpfeld places on the northern slope of the Acropolis can be no other than the famous Olympieum to the south-east of the Acropolis, since Strabo says (ix. p. 396) that the king who dedicated it left it half finished—a remark which can only apply to the great temple of Olympian Zeus begun by Pisistratus, continued by king Antiochus Epiphanes, and not finished till the time of Hadrian, long after Strabo's death. Strabo clearly knew of only one Olympieum, and that lay to the south-east of the Acropolis. As to the supposed Olympieum on the north side of the Acropolis, it will be time enough to consider it when it emerges from the soil under which, according to Dr. Dörpfeld, it still lies buried.

(5) Finally, the recent excavations made at the cave by Mr. Cavvadias for the Greek Archaeological Society have brought to light a number of inscribed marble tablets which prove that Apollo was here worshipped under the title of 'Under the Heights' or 'Under the High Rocks,' but none which mentions him under the name of Pythian (see above, p. 516). This tells very strongly against Dr. Dörpfeld's theory that the cave was the Pythium.

Both the Dörpfeldian Pythium and the Dörpfeldian Olympieum are rejected by Prof. C. Wachsmuth ('Neue Beiträge zur Topographie

von Athen,' *Abhandlungen d. philolog. histor. Cl. d. k. sächs. Gesell. d. Wissenschaften*, 18 (1897), No. 1. pp. 49-51).
  P. 376 line 15 *sqq.* from foot, **Two of the blocks of this wall** etc. One of these two enormous stones is no less than 18 feet long, 8 feet high, and 4 feet thick. In the upper terrace, on which these two great blocks stand, there are several rows of seats cut in the rock, one above the other, on either side of the speaker's platform (*bema*). Can these rock-hewn seats, facing north over the area of the Pnyx, have been the seats of the Presidents (*prutaneis*)? From the upper terrace a short flight of three steps leads up through the scarped rock to the top of the Pnyx hill. On the southern brow of the hill, towards its western end, a piece of the ancient city-wall is preserved for a length of 16 paces. From one to three courses of masonry are standing. The thickness of the wall seems to have been 11 feet. It is built of squared blocks of conglomerate (breccia) laid in horizontal courses.
  P. 379 line 26 from foot, **an enclosure sacred to Artemis.** In 1896 excavations were made by the Greek Archaeological Society in the hope of discovering the ancient road which led from the Dipylum to the Academy. About 200 yards north-west of the Dipylum a broad paved street running northward was laid bare, and beside it were found the remains of a Greek building which may perhaps have been the sanctuary of Fairest Artemis mentioned by Pausanias, since that sanctuary is mentioned in an inscription found on the spot (*Mittheil. d. arch. Inst. in Athen*, 21 (1896), p. 463; *Athenaeum*, 9th January 1897, p. 55; Πρακτικὰ τῆς Ἀρχαιολ. Ἑταιρίας, 1896 (pub. 1897), pp. 20-22).
  P. 393 line 6 from top, **a new and holy fire was fetched from the altar at Delphi** etc. Two inscriptions engraved on the walls of the Treasury of the Athenians at Delphi seem to show that on stated occasions a holy new fire was brought, along with a sacred tripod, on a waggon from Delphi to Athens. Perhaps, as E. Curtius conjectured, the occasion of fetching the new fire was the expiatory festival of the Thargelia. See *Bulletin de Corresp. hellénique*, 18 (1894), pp. 87-93; E. Curtius, in *Archäologischer Anzeiger*, 1895, p. 109 *sq.*
  P. 396 line 10 from foot, **The small townships of Attica.** Mr. Gurlitt suggests that in this passage (i. 31) Pausanias describes the small townships of Attica in the order in which they lay on the main roads that radiated from Athens. Thus Alimus, Zoster, Prospalta, Anagyrus, and Cephale, according to Mr. Gurlitt, lay on the west coast of Attica and were reached by the road that started from the Itonian gate (see vol. 2. p. 37) or from a gate in the south wall of Athens : Prasiae, Lamptrae, and Potami were reached by a road that started from the gate of Diochares, near the Lyceum (Strabo, ix. p. 397); and Acharnae was reached by the road that led from the Acharnian gate (Hesychius, *s.v.* Ἀχαρνικαὶ πύλαι). See W. Gurlitt, *Ueber Pausanias*, pp. 285-287, 336-338. The theory is ingenious and accords well with Pausanias's method elsewhere of describing the roads that radiate from a capital city, as for example Mantinea, Megalopolis, and Thebes. Yet, as Mr. R. Heberdey has pointed out (*Die Reisen des Pausanias in Griechenland*, p. 98), there are difficulties in the way of accepting it. For why

should Lamptrae be interpolated between Prasiae and Potami? Prospalta between Zoster and Anagyrus? Myrrhinus between Phlya and Athmonia? It is to be remembered, however, that the sites of some of these townships have not been identified with certainty, and that the apparent want of topographical order in Pausanias's description may be due merely to our ignorance. Mr. Heberdey thinks that the townships in question are grouped together according to the deities worshipped in them or the objects of interest they contained. Thus he holds that the link between Prasiae, Lamptrae, and Potami was their famous graves; that the link between Phlya, Myrrhinus, and Athmonia was the worship of Artemis; and that the link between the townships mentioned in § 1 was their worship of Demeter, the Mother of the Gods etc.

P. 402 line 12 from top, **Cephale.** Another sepulchral inscription recording the name of a woman of Cephale has lately been found at *Keratea;* on the same stone is carved the name of a woman of Lamptrae (*Mittheil. d. arch. Inst. in Athen*, 21 (1896), p. 465).

P. 404 line 5 from foot, **The prehistoric necropolis of Prasiae** etc. A few more details as to the excavation of this necropolis are given by Mr. B. Staes (Πρακτικὰ τῆς Ἀρχαιολογικῆς Ἑταιρίας, 1894, p. 21). The tombs excavated, twenty-two in number, resemble those at Mycenae, Nauplia, and Epidaurus, being chambers cut in the rock and approached by sloping passages (*dromoi*) or, in some cases, by staircases. The largest of the sepulchral chambers is 4 metres square by 2½ metres high. In almost all of the tombs several persons were interred; in one of them the number of bodies was ten. Of the vases found, numbering about two hundred, two-thirds are perfect and in good preservation. Amongst the other objects discovered are five bronze razors or knives, one gold ring, and one silver ring. Another prehistoric necropolis of the Mycenaean period has been discovered and partially excavated by Mr. Staes at a place called *Ligori*, about half-way between the bay of Prasiae (*Porto Raphti*) and the village of *Markopoulo.* Here, owing to the nature of the ground, which is nearly level, the tombs are sunk beneath the surface and approached by staircases. Ten were excavated by Mr. Staes; the largest measures about 3 metres square by 1.80 metres high. All contained more than one body. Amongst the objects found in them, besides Mycenaean pottery, were a bronze razor, a bronze brooch for the hair, a piece of a ring made of silver but alloyed with another metal, perhaps iron, and a number of leaden wires which, from the place in which one of them was found, seem to have been attached to the ears and passed round the chin of the dead, in order to prevent the lower jaw from falling. Near the necropolis Mr. Staes observed some traces of a later settlement which he conjectures may have been Cytherus, one of the twelve ancient towns of Attica (Strabo, ix. p. 397; Stephanus Byzantius, *s.v.* Κύθηρος). See B. Staes, in Ἐφημερὶς ἀρχαιολογική, 1895, pp. 202-210.

P. 408 line 3 *sqq.* from top, **Thoricus** etc. I visited Thoricus 27th November 1895, and can supplement the description in the text on some points. The two fortification-walls which cross the peninsula of St. Nicholas are about a quarter of a mile apart. The more easterly of

the two is distant about half a mile from the foot of Mt. *Velatouri.*
A small chapel of St. Stephen (not St. Nicholas) stands on the summit
of the promontory at the point where the easterly wall crosses it. This
east wall, which is much better preserved on the northern than on the
southern side of the promontory, is built of large rough unhewn blocks
not fitted together, or rather its two outer faces are so built; the core
was probably filled with smaller stones. The thickness of the wall is
about 8 feet; one and two courses are preserved to a height of 5 feet.
On the north side of the isthmus, below the chapel, a square tower
projects eastward (not westward, as stated in the text) from the wall.
It is over 17 feet broad, projects 10 ft. 6 in. from the curtain, and is
standing to a height of from 3 ft. 9 in. to 5 ft. 6 in. There are
doubtful traces of two other towers projecting eastward from this wall.
The westerly wall seems to have been built in the same style and to
the same thickness as the eastern wall, but though its line is clearly
traceable, very little of the wall is left. Vestiges of one or perhaps
two square towers projecting westward from it may be seen on the
northern side of the promontory.

The tower at the south-western foot of Mt. *Velatouri* measures 21
feet square and is built of ashlar, but not very regular masonry. Six to
nine courses are preserved; where nine courses are standing the height
is about 12 feet. Adjoining the tower on the east is a piece of wall 13
paces long, built of large blocks, of which, however, only one course is
standing.

With regard to the theatre of Thoricus, the distance between the
outer back-wall of the auditorium and the inner wall, built of thin slabs,
is only 10 paces or about half the distance stated in the text (p. 409).
The back-wall of the auditorium is preserved in places to a height of
from 7 to 9 feet. At its eastern end the auditorium rests partly on the
rock which has been hewn perpendicularly so as to present the appearance of a supporting wall. In the upper part of the theatre I saw no
remains of seats anywhere. The walls of the little temple of Dionysus,
which seems to have comprised a *cella* and fore-temple (*pronaos*) but
no back-chamber (*opisthodomos*) or peristyle, are now not more than
2 ft. 4 in., and 1 ft. 8 in. high on the north and west sides respectively.
The inner cross-wall, dividing the *cella* from the fore-temple, is about
3 feet high. Dr. Dörpfeld's brief description of the theatre (*Das
griechische Theater*, pp. 109-111) adds little or nothing to our knowledge of it.

As to the two beehive tombs discovered at Thoricus within recent
years (see vol. 3. p. 138) a few more particulars, taken from my journal,
may be given here. Of the tomb on the saddle between Mt. *Velatouri*
and its sister hill to the north the *dromos* or horizontal approach is
about 11 paces long and 7 feet wide, but its sides are only partially
cleared. At a distance of 3 or 4 paces from its outer end the passage
was closed by a cross-wall, which is still about 3 feet high. The
doorway leading from the passage (*dromos*) into the beehive chamber,
so far as it is cleared, is 4 ft. 4 in. wide, 6 feet high, and 10 feet
long (deep). One of the stones of the lintel is about 6 ft. 7 in. long

by 3 feet broad.   My measurements of the elliptical beehive chamber
agree fairly with those in the text.   The masonry of the tomb throughout is wretched, the walls being built of small irregular stones bonded
with mortar.

The other beehive tomb is on the eastern slope of Mt. *Velatouri*,
exactly opposite the promontory of St. Nicholas, about a third of the
way down the slope.   It opens to the north.   The *dromos* or horizontal
approach is about 26 feet long and 9 ft. 6 in. wide.   Its side-walls are
well preserved ; the outer end of the passage is walled up.   The doorway of the tomb, which is also well preserved, is 5 ft. 8 in. wide at the
bottom, between 10 and 11 feet high, and about 11 feet long ; it
narrows upward.   The lintel, formed of three large slabs, is in its place.
The beehive chamber is as usual circular ; its diameter is 29 ft. 7 in. ;
the walls are standing to a height of about 16 feet, but the upper part
of the dome is gone.   As has been mentioned in the text, three graves
are dug in the floor of the tomb, and two small quadrangular walled
compartments are constructed on opposite sides of the beehive chamber
in such a way that the wall of the chamber forms one side of each of
these little compartments.   One of the compartments partly covers one
of the graves ; it is 8 ft. 4 in. long on the front by 3 ft. 6 in. on the
sides ; its wall is standing to a height of 4 ft. 5 in.   The masonry of
this beehive tomb with its *dromos* resembles that of the other beehive
tomb at Thoricus ; the walls are built of small stones and mortar, but
the general effect is more imposing.   Although the tomb had been
rifled before its discovery by Messrs. Staes and Mayer, enough remained
to prove that it had been the burial-place of a wealthy and probably
princely house.   For among the objects found by the excavators were
a few terra-cotta vases of good Mycenaean style, the lid of a gold box,
the disc of a bronze mirror, the half of a round box containing a spiral
ornament of ivory, a rosette of glass-paste, and some stone arrow-heads
(B. Staes, in Ἐφημερὶς ἀρχαιολογική, 1895, p. 225).

P. 410 line 10 *sqq.*, "**an entire city has been found at Thoricus**"
etc.   The discovery announced in these grandiloquent terms by the
American reporter reduces itself, on examination, to very moderate proportions.   On the conical summit of the hill of Thoricus (*Velatouri*)
excavations conducted in 1893 for the Greek Archaeological Society by
Mr. B. Staes revealed the existence of a very small Mycenaean settlement, and beneath it the vestiges of a still earlier and smaller settlement.   Owing to the nature of the ground, which slopes away steeply
on all sides from the conical summit, the construction of even a palace
of the ordinary Mycenaean type was here impracticable.   In point of
fact the length of the settlement is just 20 metres, and its breadth 12
metres, while the breadth of the older settlement is only 8 metres.   The
remains consist of a number of underground chambers enclosed by a
triple wall which had been rebuilt or repaired at various times.   That
the rooms were subterranean, or at all events were not used as dwellings,
seems proved by the absence of doors and windows in the walls.   Some
of them are paved with stones and may have been used as store-rooms ;
others can only have served as foundations on which to raise an upper

storey, for in the middle of some of them, occupying a great part of the space, were found lying huge stones, which must certainly have been removed if the rooms had ever been occupied as dwellings or store-houses. The stone floors of the other rooms would seem to date from the later or Mycenaean settlement, for beneath them are the graves of the older inhabitants. These graves consist for the most part of round holes excavated in the rock to a depth of .50–.80 metre and containing each a single large jar in which were deposited the bones of the dead and some rude hand-made pottery. Only two of the graves are oblong, and in these nothing at all was found. The practice of burying the dead in large jars prevailed, as we shall see (below, p. 560), amongst the early inhabitants of Aphidna, but there is this difference between the modes of burial at the two places, that whereas at Aphidna the graves were away from the dwellings and were covered over with a barrow, at Thoricus they were dug in the floors of the houses. Again, the custom of raising the dwelling-rooms to a considerable height above the ground and leaving the ground-floor either unused or occupied only as store-rooms is known to have been practised at Mycenae (see vol. 3. pp. 121 *sq.*, 159 *sq.*). At Thoricus the walls of the Mycenaean period, built of small rough stones bonded with clay, are easily distinguished by their style from the earlier walls, which are carelessly built of larger stones. The objects found within the houses consist almost wholly of pottery; nothing of metal was discovered. The pottery of the older settlement, found in the lowest strata of the excavations, is of various sorts. First, a great deal of it is rude hand-made ware of a coarse gritty clay, like the pottery placed with the dead in the jars. Second, much of it consists of black potsherds decorated with incised lines which have been filled with white paint. Third, some of the potsherds exhibit white lines painted, not incised, on a black or reddish ground. The pottery of the Mycenaean period which was found in the upper strata of the excavations is of the common lustrous sort. Fragments of black-figured vases also came to light, proving that the summit of the hill continued to be occupied in the historical Greek period. Both the older settlements appear, from traces of conflagration and wilful destruction, to have come to a violent end at the hand of enemies. See B. Staes, in Πρακτικὰ τῆς 'Αρχαιολογικῆς 'Εταιρίας, 1893, p. 15 *sq.*; *id.*, in 'Εφημερὶς ἀρχαιολογική, 1895, pp. 221-234.

P. 410 line 16 *sq.* from top, **the remains of a colonnade** etc. This building was re-excavated by Mr. Staes in 1893. His account of it confirms the one given in the text, but goes to show that the building was a temple or sanctuary and not a mere colonnade. For, first, at the eastern entrance there stand two pedestals, one on either hand, of which one bears a mutilated dedicatory inscription; second, the fragment of an archaic female statue, like those found on the Acropolis of Athens, was discovered near one of the pedestals, on which it seems originally to have stood; and, third, there came to light in this neighbourhood some time ago an inscription (ΗΟΡΟΣ ΤΕΜΕΝΟΥΣ ΤΟΙΝ ΘΕΟΙΝ, 'boundary of the precinct of the two deities') which makes it probable that the edifice was a sanctuary of Demeter and

Proserpine. Yet the arrangement of the building is not like that of an ordinary Greek temple, for its greatest length lies north and south or, more strictly, north-east and south-west, and it has an entrance in the middle of the long east side. Whether it had also a door or doors at one or both the narrow ends, does not appear. The edifice seems to date from the beginning of the fifth century B.C. See B. Staes, in Πρακτικὰ τῆς Ἀρχαιολογικῆς Ἐταιρίας, 1893, p. 16 *sq.*, with pl. B.

P. 414 line 4 from foot, **Amarynthus in Euboea.** The site of the great sanctuary of Amarysian Artemis in Euboea has not yet been determined, but from a number of inscriptions found near the village of *Vathia* to the east of Eretria it seems probable that, as I have indicated in the text, the sanctuary was in that neighbourhood. The exact spot may be marked by the ancient ruins now called *Palaeochora*, situated beside the sea at the eastern end of the plain of *Vathia*. It is true that the distance of the place from Eretria is much more than the seven furlongs mentioned by Strabo, but the geographer or one of his copyists may easily have made a slip in the number. See D. S. Stauro-poullos, in Ἐφημερὶς ἀρχαιολογική, 1895, pp. 155-162. Following the indication of Strabo the Americans made some excavations at *Kotroni*, distant a little more than seven furlongs to the east of Eretria ; but they discovered no trace of the sanctuary (*American Journal of Archaeology*, 10 (1895), pp. 335-337).

P. 417 line 3 *sqq.*, **the ancient township Paeonidae** etc. The exact situation of Paeonidae or Paeonia is still uncertain, but a consider-able step towards determining it has been made by Prof. Milchhöfer's identification of Lipsydrium, the place which the Alcmaeonids fortified "above Paeonia" (Herodotus, v. 62 ; cp. Aristotle, *Constitution of Athens*, 19). On the summit of one of the spurs of Mount Parnes named *Karagoufolesa*, which rises four kilometres (2½ miles) to the north of the village of *Menidi*, is an ancient fort some 126 paces long from east to west by 65 paces broad. The walls, from 3 to 4 paces thick, are somewhat roughly built, but every advantage has been taken of the nature of the ground to strengthen them. Fragments of glazed tiles, both flat and curved, litter the ground. The hill or rather moun-tain is about 2000 feet high and commands a wide view not only over the Athenian plain but also through the gap between Pentelicus and Hymettus into the country to the east. This ancient fortress, dis-covered by Prof. Milchhöfer, is probably Lipsydrium. It may very well, as its modern discoverer supposes, be much older than the time of the Alcmaeonids. The site of Lipsydrium being determined, we must look for Paeonidae somewhere in the plain at the foot of the mountain. Now at the south-eastern foot of the mountain near a chapel of the Panagia there are some ancient remains consisting of large hewn blocks and foundations. These, Prof. Milchhöfer thinks, may mark the site of Paeonidae. The district is now called *Gaitana*. Much more extensive remains of an ancient settlement, consisting of walls and pottery, are to be seen at the foot of the mountains about a mile to the north-east, near a church of St. George. The district is now called *Bilesa.* See A. Milchhöfer, in *Karten von Attika, Erläuternder Text,* Heft vii.-viii. p. 7.

P. 421 line 9 from top, **the fortress of Phyle.** As to Phyle and its neighbourhood see Kaupert, in *Archäologischer Anzeiger,* 1892, p. 10 *sq.*; A. Milchhöfer, in *Karten von Attika, Erläuternder Text,* Heft vii.-viii. p. 8 *sq.* The walls of the fortress are 3 metres (about 10 feet) thick and are preserved on three sides, though in a more or less ruinous state, for a total length of 150 metres. On the west, where the crag falls away very precipitously, the wall has disappeared. On the south side an ancient gateway or rather doorway is flanked by a square tower which projects from the curtain 5 metres further to the west. Two other square towers project from the wall, one on the northern and the other on the southern side of the fortress. The interior of the stronghold forms an oval about 100 metres long from north-west to south-east, with a mean breadth of 30 metres. An Attic inscription of the end of the fourth or beginning of the third century B.C. proves that at that time Phyle was garrisoned and that its walls had recently been repaired ('Ἐφημερὶς ἀρχαιολογική, 1884, p. 135 *sqq.*). From the same inscription we learn that sacrifices were offered to Artemis at Phyle. Another inscription, found like the preceding at Eleusis and dating apparently from the end of the fourth century B.C., records a dedication to Demeter and the Maid by the garrisons of Eleusis, Panactum, and Phyle (*C. I. A.* ii. No. 1217; Dittenberger, *Sylloge Inscr. Graec.* No. 121; Loewy, *Inschriften griech. Bildhauer,* No. 104).

P. 431 line 16 from top, **Marathon.** The battle of Marathon continues to be fought over again by scholars with as much vigour as ever. See A. Hauvette, *Hérodote* (Paris, 1894), pp. 236-265; G. Busolt, *Griechische Geschichte,* 2.² pp. 578-593; R. W. Macan, *Herodotus, the Fourth, Fifth, and Sixth Books,* vol. 2. pp. 149-248; W. Schilling, 'Die Schlacht bei Marathon,' *Philologus,* 54 (1895), pp. 253-273; J. B. Bury, 'The battle of Marathon,' *Classical Review,* 10 (1896), pp. 95-98. Of these writers Messrs. Macan and Schilling have independently propounded theories which to a certain extent coincide with each other and offer a reasonable solution of some of the difficulties connected with Herodotus's narrative. Both of them conjecture that the delay of several days between the landing of the Persians and the battle was due to the unwillingness of the Persians to attack the Greeks in their strong position and the resolve of the Greeks not to abandon that position and meet their adversaries in the plain. Both of them suppose that the Persians, despairing at last of luring the Greeks into the open, resolved to give them the go-by and move on Athens, and that it was while they were engaged in making this movement that the Greeks saw their opportunity and delivered their attack. But while Mr. Macan thinks that the Persians resolved to march on Athens by the highroad to the south of Pentelicus and that their column was attacked on the march as it was defiling southward past the Greek position, Mr. Schilling supposes that they had resolved to go by sea, that the greater part of their army, including the cavalry, had already embarked, and that there remained on shore only a strong corps of picked troops, which had faced the Greeks and held them in check till the rest of the troops were on board. It was when this rear-guard of say 20,000 men had begun to follow their comrades to the shore that, on Mr. Schilling's theory, the Greeks charged them, running across the intervening mile of ground to overtake the retreating enemy before he could reach his ships. There is much in this theory to commend it. It explains the long delay of the battle, the hurriedness of the Greek attack when it came at last, the absence of the Persian cavalry in the action, the comparatively small losses of the Persians, and the escape of a great part of the army and nearly the whole of the fleet. On the other hand, Mr. Macan's theory, so far as it differs from that of Mr. Schilling, labours under two serious difficulties. Where was the Persian cavalry? and how did the vast army, fleeing in confusion from the Greek swords, contrive to embark and escape? To get over the former difficulty, Mr. Macan supposes that the cavalry was to be sent round by sea and had already embarked. But if the infantry was to march on Athens, why not the cavalry? The country between Marathon and Athens on the route assumed by Mr. Macan presents no obstacle to the movement of cavalry, whose services would have been invaluable in reconnoitring, foraging, and repelling light bands of the enemy which might otherwise have harassed the huge unwieldy column of infantry on the march. Why Prof. Bury should say that on the march to Athens the cavalry would have been a useless encumbrance, I am quite unable to understand. The second difficulty—the embarkation of nearly the whole of the defeated army and the escape of the whole armada except seven ships—is not met by Mr. Macan at all. On the whole, Mr. Schilling's theory may perhaps be regarded as the most plausible that has yet been suggested.

Here I wish to put on record a conjecture of my late lamented friend, W. Robertson Smith, which, if it were accepted, would solve two of the problems connected with the battle. He suggested in conversation that the weather may never have allowed the Persians to land their cavalry at all. This would explain not only the absence of the cavalry from the battle, but the long delay which preceded the action—the Persians were waiting for the sea to moderate and allow them to land the horses. My friend thought that the disembarkation of cavalry is a difficult operation and can only be effected in calm weather. This opinion, however, was not confirmed by an officer of experience whom I consulted through a friend. According to him, it is easy to land cavalry even in rough weather, for the horses have merely to be driven into the water and allowed to swim ashore ; all that is needed is a good beach where the animals can take the ground. Such a beach there is at Marathon.

Here, too, I desire to correct a mistake of my own. In the text (vol. 2. p. 442) I have spoken of Athens as if it were an unwalled town at the time of the battle of Marathon. I did this, not in reliance on the opinion of Professor von Wilamowitz-Moellendorff (*Aus Kydathen*, p. 97 *sqq.*) and Dr Dörpfeld (in Miss Harrison's *Ancient Athens*, p. 21) that it was so, but merely because I overlooked the testimony of Herodotus

(ix. 13) and Thucydides (i. 89) that it was not. On a question of the state of Athens in the fifth century B.C. I decidedly prefer the evidence of Herodotus and Thucydides to that of Dr. Dörpfeld and Professor von Wilamowitz-Moellendorff.

P. 434 line 13 *sqq.* from foot, **a large slab of Pentelic marble** etc. This inscribed slab lies beside a well, close to a church of St. Constantine on the east side of the highroad. The place may be about a mile and a half to the south of the plain of Marathon.

P. 436 line 10 *sqq.* from foot, **the church of St. George** etc. The situation of the church and monastery at *Vrana*, on the side of a mountain and the edge of a glen, appeared to me too small and confined to allow us to suppose, with Bursian, that here was the precinct of Hercules within which the Greek army encamped before the battle of Marathon.

P. 437 line 10 *sqq.* from foot, **The remains of two life-size statues** etc. On visiting the ruined gateway, 23rd November 1895, I found the remains of the statues referred to in the text. One of the fragments, lying on its side, is the lower half of a marble statue of a man or woman seated in a chair and wearing a garment which reaches almost to the feet: carved in relief on the side of the chair which is uppermost is a griffin; the wings and leg of the creature are still distinct. Near it I found a piece of another, or perhaps of the same, statue; from the breast it would seem to have represented a woman. Close to it, lastly, I observed what appeared to be a piece of yet another statue, not made of marble; it apparently represented the head and bust of a woman clad in a garment of which the folds could be traced.

P. 445 line 25 from foot, **Brauron.** Some prehistoric tombs of the Mycenaean period have been discovered and excavated by Mr. B. Staes in recent years at the Bay of *Vraona* (Brauron). They are cut in the slope of the hill which faces westward towards the isolated rocky hillock at the foot of which stands the ruined chapel of St. George. Owing to the crumbling nature of the rock most of the tombs are now ruinous; only three were found in tolerable preservation. They are small, measuring only about 2 metres square and 2½ metres high. The short narrow passages leading into them were blocked with unhewn stones. Each tomb seems to have contained more than one dead body. A few vases of the later Mycenaean period, including a stirrup-jar (see vol. 3. p. 112), were found entire in the graves, together with fragments of two other stirrup-jars and eight small perforated stones which Mr. Staes regards as buttons. See B. Staes, in Ἐφημερὶς ἀρχαιολογική, 1895, pp. 196-199.

P. 448 line 25 *sqq.* from foot, **Rhamnus** etc. I visited Rhamnus 18th December 1895, and found that the description of the hill and fortress of Rhamnus given in the text needs to be corrected in a few points. The most accessible side of the hill is the south-eastern, not the south-western. It is on the south-eastern side that the gradual slope connects the hill with the glen. On the south-western side, on the other hand, the hill ends in high and precipitous rocks which would seem to have rendered fortification superfluous. Here, too, at its south-west (not north-west) corner the hill attains its greatest height. Further, it is on the south and the east (not south-west) sides that the fortification walls are standing to a considerable height. The masonry of the eastern wall is not nearly so careful and good as that of the southern wall; the courses are irregular, some of the blocks are polygonal instead of squared, and there are small stones in the interstices. However, a square tower which projects from the eastern wall is built of regular ashlar masonry, like the southern wall; four and five courses are preserved, giving a height of 3 metres (about 10 feet). The number of towers in the circuit-wall is five, of which three are in the south wall, one at the south-east angle, and one in the eastern wall. The material of walls and towers is marble, but outwardly at least it is grey rather than white. The gateway described in the text is about 3.45 metres wide. With regard to the outwork mentioned in the text (vol. 2. p. 450, near top), it consists of a broad and massive but now ruined wall which descends from the top of the hill to within a few feet of the water's edge, where it rests upon rocks. It is at the north-western, not the north-eastern corner of the hill, and was clearly designed to prevent an enemy from making his way from the west along the sea-side of the fortress.

Of the keep which occupied the highest part of the hill, at its south-west corner, the walls may be traced on two sides, the east and north. The eastern wall, irregularly built of polygonal blocks of various sizes, is about 2 metres (6 ft. 6 in.) high at the most. As it does not rise above the surface of the soil on its inner side, where the ground is higher, the wall has more the appearance of a terrace-wall than a fortification-wall. However, at its northern end there are remains of a square tower. On the north side of the keep the wall is traceable for a short distance, but there is little of it above ground. On the south and west sides the steep slopes and precipitous rocks appear to have been deemed a sufficient defence. At least I looked in vain for any certain indications of walls on these sides. Within the keep I observed the lower parts of the walls of a quadrangular building constructed of small stones; a few large stones are also lying about. Amongst the ruins outside of the keep and lower down the hill may be mentioned a round building 4 paces in diameter on the inside; the walls, built of small irregular stones, are about 1.60 metres high. A doorway in this round building opens towards the gate of the fortress. The four chairs of white marble mentioned in the text (vol. 2. p. 450) are still to be seen at Rhamnus, on the side of the hill some 20 yards or so below the wall of the keep. Three of them stand in a row on a long low base of white marble; the fourth is lying on the ground near them.

P. 451 line 11 from top, **vestiges of the ancient buildings, which Pausanias mentions.** In the little stretch of level ground at the eastern foot of the fortress, between the sea and the hills I found the remains of a building of white marble, which seems to have comprised a quadrangular chamber about three and a half paces square on the inside, an antechamber, and a porch. In the square chamber there are remains of a plain mosaic pavement. The walls, so far as they exist, are well built and tolerably thick.

P. 451 line 14 from top, **the terrace.** The terrace on which the temples of Nemesis and Themis stand is supported by walls on the north and east sides. The terrace-wall on the north is from six courses (2.50 metres) to nine courses (3.30 metres) high. It is built of marble; about half of it is of a grey colour, while the other half is of a yellowish hue; yet the marble is apparently the same. Both colours may be due to weathering. The wall is well and carefully built in horizontal courses, but the joints are not vertical. With regard to the temple of Nemesis, the white marble pavement of most of the south colonnade, and large parts of the pavement of the east colonnade and of the fore-temple (*pronaos*) are preserved. Remains of only six (not seven) columns of the south colonnade are now standing in their places; they consist in each case of a single drum which is unfluted except for an inch or so at the bottom. The small temple of Themis is raised, like the temple of Nemesis, on three steps. It was not surrounded by a colonnade or peristyle. The walls are not now standing to quite the height mentioned in the text. The north wall is 1.90 metres high and the south wall 1.40 metres at most; the west wall is not quite so high as either. Of all three walls the outer face is constructed of fine well-jointed polygonal masonry; the inner face is built of much smaller stones and in an inferior style. The wall dividing the portico or *pronaos* from the *cella* is also standing to a height of some feet. Further, the stylobate of the *pronaos* is preserved; but the inner foundations and pavement are gone, or at least do not appear. The marble of which the temple of Themis is built is grey rather than white on the outside; but this may perhaps be an effect of weathering.

P. 455 line 10 *sqq.*, **the sanctuary is on a lofty and very steep height** etc. I ascended the steep, rocky, bushy height which bounds on the west the little glen through which the path leads down from the temple of Nemesis to the fortress of Rhamnus. Here I expected to find the sanctuary of Amphiaraus; but though I traversed the crest of the rocky ridge from its northern end, opposite the fortress, to its southern end at the temple, I found no trace of a sanctuary; the whole crest seemed to be in a state of nature.

P. 460 line 15 from top, **the sources of the Nile** etc. The opinion that the Nile had its source in Mount Atlas, not far from the Atlantic, was held by Juba, king of Libya (Pliny, *Nat. hist.* v. 51), Vitruvius (viii. 2. 6 *sq.*), and Dio Cassius (lxxv. 13). Vitruvius mentions the existence of crocodiles in the rivers of Western Africa as a confirmation of this view.

P. 469 line 15 from top, **a small theatre.** As to the theatre at Oropus see W. Dörpfeld, in *Das griechische Theater* (Athens and Leipsic, 1896), pp. 100-109. He thinks that the ordinary seats for spectators must have been of wood, since no traces of stone seats, except the five marble chairs, have been found. There is neither a gutter round the orchestra nor a semicircular passage dividing it from the auditorium. The columns which adorned the front of the stage and which were still standing when I visited Oropus in 1890 have since been barbarously thrown down and broken. The entablature which they supported, consisting of an architrave, a triglyph frieze, and a cornice (*geison*), has been found. Like the columns, it is of white marble. At the back of the triglyphs and cornice are holes and cuttings intended to receive the ends of the wooden floor of the stage. The height of the stage is estimated by Dr. Dörpfeld (who consistently with his theory denies that it was a stage at all) at 2.51 metres. Its depth seems to have been about 2 metres. No vestige of a staircase connecting the stage with the orchestra has come to light, but on the other hand both the *parodoi* slope upward from the orchestra to a level with the stage. This slope is artificial, the ground having been banked up and supported by walls at the back and sides of the stage-buildings. At the back of the stage, there seems to have been a wall surmounted by a Doric entablature on which is carved the inscription (*C. I. G. G. S.* 1. No. 423) recording the dedication of "the scene and doorways" to Amphiaraus. At least this is the position which Dr. Dörpfeld believes the inscription to have occupied, and a better it would be hard to find. From various technical indications Dr. Dörpfeld infers that there was a wide opening in the back wall of the stage, and he conjectures that machinery may have been placed in it whereby deities and other supernatural beings were swung forward, as if flying, into the view of the spectators. Both of the inscriptions which relate to the reconstruction of the stage-buildings (*C. I. G. G. S.* 1. Nos. 423, 423 a, pp. 147, 745) seem to belong to the second or first century B.C., which may accordingly be taken to be the date when the changes recorded by them were effected.

P. 477 line 16 *sqq.* from foot, **Salamis.** On the topography and ancient remains of Salamis, see A. Milchhöfer, in *Karten von Attika, Erläuternder Text*, Heft vii. viii. pp. 26-37. He inclines to think that the site of the older city of Salamis, to which Strabo refers (ix. p. 393), may be marked, as I have conjectured in the text (vol. 2. p. 478), by the ancient remains which Dodwell observed in the south-western part of the island. The same conjecture had been made independently by J. Töpffer (*Quaestiones Pisistrateae* (Dorpat, 1886), p. 11 ; *Beiträge zur griech. Altertumswissenschaft* (Berlin, 1897), p. 9). The place is on the shore of the Bay of *Kanakia*, so called from an island *Kanakiani* which lies off the bay and renders it very snug. From the head of the bay a valley stretches inland. A stream flows down the valley, and near the shore there is a spring of good water. Some vestiges of antiquity, including the ruts of chariot-wheels in the rock and an inscription (*C. I. A.* iii. No. 728) in honour of a man who had set up images of the emperors at his own expense and had been their first high-priest, were observed here in 1871 by K. B. Stark and E. Curtius. See K. B. Stark, *Nach dem griechischen Orient* [2] pp. 350 sq., 406 ; F. Curtius, *Alterthum und Gegenwart*, 2. p. 95. If the older city of Salamis lay here, the stream which flows into the head of the bay may be, as Prof. Milchhöfer conjectures, the ancient Bocarus or Bocalia.

Lolling's identification of the Cychrean Hill with the hill of *Magoula* (vol. 2. p. 479) is rejected by Prof. Milchhöfer, who prefers to regard the remarkable tumulus on the hill, not as prehistoric, but as identical with the 'tomb of many men' which appears from an inscription ('Εφημερὶς ἀρχαιολογική, 1884, p. 179 line 33) to have existed in Salamis near the trophy set up for the victory over the Persians. If Prof. Milchhöfer is right, we may conjecture that the men buried in the tumulus were the Greeks who fell in the great sea-fight. Excavations might decide the question whether the tumulus is prehistoric or not. From the southern side of the hill of *Magoula* a wall ascends the back of the promontory, then turns westward and runs along the ridge to near the village of *Ambelaki*. The purpose of this wall, as Prof. Milchhöfer conjectures, was probably to protect the town and harbour of Salamis on the south.

Further, Lolling's identification of Cape Sciradium (vol. 2. p. 479) is rejected by Prof. Milchhöfer, who thinks that Sciradium may have been either the southern extremity of the island, now called Cape *Kolonnaes*, or the headland now called *Prikonia*, at the south-west extremity of the island, to the south of the island of *Kanakiani*.

P. 483 line 10 *sq.* from foot, **The battle of Salamis** etc. The problems connected with the battle continue to excite discussion. See, besides the writers cited in the text, J. Töpffer, *Quaestiones Pisistrateae* (Dorpat, 1886), p. 15 *sqq.* (*Beiträge zur griech. Altertumswissenschaft*, p. 11 *sqq.*); A. Hauvette, *Hérodote* (Paris, 1894), pp. 400-424; A. Milchhöfer, in *Karten von Attika, Erläuternder Text*, Heft vii. viii. p. 29 *sqq.* An interesting memorial of the great battle has lately come to light at *Ambelaki*, the site of the historical city of Salamis. It consists of an inscription containing two lines of the metrical epitaph on the Corinthians who fell in the battle; the inscription is in the Doric dialect and alphabet, and seems to date from the first half of the fifth century B.C. The slab of white marble on which it is engraved was found in digging the foundations of a house beside the large church of the Panagia, on the north side of the public square. Many ancient tombstones have been found and are still being found almost daily by the inhabitants in this neighbourhood, proving that here was the graveyard of Salamis. This tallies with the statement of Plutarch (*De Herodoti malignitate*, 39) that the Athenians allowed the Corinthians, for their bravery, to be buried beside the city of Salamis. In the same passage Plutarch quotes the epitaph in full, but without mentioning the author. The pseudo-Dio Chrysostom also quotes the epitaph in full and ascribes it to Simonides (*Or.* xxxvii. *Corinthiaca*, vol. 2. p. 298 ed. Dindorf). The attribution of the epitaph to Simonides has recently been questioned by Prof. Hauvette (*De l'authenticité des épigrammes de Simonide* (Paris, 1896), p. 77 *sq.*), but it is confirmed by the discovery of the original inscription, which seems to have been at least contemporary with the poet. For the inscription see S. N. Dragoumes, in *Mittheilungen des arch. Inst. in Athen*, 22 (1897), pp. 52-58.

P. 486 line 1, **monastery of Daphni.** The Byzantine church of *Daphni* has suffered severely from earthquakes since the description in the text was printed. I found it much dilapidated on my last visit (Christmas Eve, 1895).

P. 486 line 8 from top, **left bank of a dry water-course.** The ancient road is on the right, not the left, bank of the water-course.

P. 487 line 16 *sq.*, **where the road to Eleutherae branches off across the plain.** It is the road to the village of *Kalyvia* that branches off here, not the road to Eleutherae. The point where the roads fork seemed to me more than half a mile from the salt pools of the Rhiti.

P. 498 line 17 from top, **These foundation-walls, nearly 30 feet thick** etc. This is quite a mistake. To judge by the eye, the walls are only 6 or 8 feet thick ; indeed the east wall is only about 5 feet thick.

P. 502 line 6 from top, **a place which they call Erineus.** About a mile and a half to the north of Eleusis an isolated hill rises from the plain to a height of some 250 feet. It extends in the form of a ridge for three-quarters of a mile or so from south-west to north-east. The Eleusinian Cephisus skirts the foot of the hill closely on the north and west. The present name of this isolated hill is *Zoumakaziki* or *Magoulesa;* at the beginning of the century it seems to have been known as *Magoula,* a name now transferred to a large modern village at the foot of the hills about a mile to the north-west. *Magoula* is an Albanian word signifying 'a hill in a plain.' Prof. Milchhöfer conjectures that the hill of *Zoumakaziki* or *Magoulesa* may be the ancient Erineus. On its south-western summit are the ruins of an ancient tower, and at the south-eastern foot of this summit some traces of ancient foundations may be seen. Leake, who overestimated the distance of these remains from Eleusis, thought that they might mark the site of Thria, which gave its name to the Thriasian Plain (Stephanus Byzantius, *s.v.* Θρία ; Leake, *Topography of Athens,*[2] 2. p. 150). But Thria seems to have occupied the site of *Kalyvia,* a large village in the plain three miles to the north-east of Eleusis, for this is the only place outside of Athens where inscriptions relating to Thria and the Thriasians have been found (*Mittheil. d. arch. Inst. in Athen,* 12 (1887), p. 326, Nos. 467, 478). See A. Milchhöfer, in *Karten von Attika, Erläuternder Text,* Heft vii. viii. pp. 22 *sq.*, 24.

P. 503 line 1, **Eleusis.** The exploration of the sacred precinct at Eleusis was continued in 1895 and 1896 under the direction of Messrs. Philios and A. N. Skias, but since the discovery of the Callichorum well nothing of importance has come to light. Most of the excavations have been made in the southern part of the precinct ; in particular the remains of the building commonly held to be the Council House have been carefully examined and described in detail. See Πρακτικὰ τῆς ᾿Αρχαιολογικῆς ῾Εταιρίας, 1893, p. 11 *sq.* ; *ib.* 1894, pp. 14-17 ; *ib.* 1895, pp. 159-193 (where the results of the excavations of 1896 are also embodied) ; *ib.* 1896, pp. 26-28. A popular account of Eleusis and its remains has been written by the most competent authority on the subject, Mr. D. Philios (*Éleusis, ses mystères, ses ruines et son Musée,* Athens, 1896). The inscriptions discovered have been published by Mr. D. Philios (*Bulletin de Corresp. hellénique,* 19 (1895), pp. 113-136, 265-267) and Mr. A. N. Skias (᾿Εφημερὶς ἀρχαιολογική, 1894, pp. 189-212 ; *ib.* 1895, pp. 83-124 ; *ib.* 1896, pp. 23-56 ; *ib.* 1897, pp. 33-66). Perhaps the most interesting of these is a mutilated metrical inscription on a cylindrical base of Pentelic marble which was found on the Processional Road between the grand portal and the Hall of Initiation. From this inscription we learn that the pedestal supported the statue of a priest of the mysteries who had " saved the mysteries for his country by repelling the lawless Sarmatians " and had initiated Antoninus. It is a plausible conjecture that the Sarmatians here mentioned were the tribe of Costobocs who invaded Greece in the reign of Marcus Antoninus, and who may have penetrated as far as Eleusis. See Pausanias, x. 34. 5 with the note. Mr. D. Philios suggests that these barbarians may have sacked and partially destroyed the sacred precinct and that this may be the reason why, as the existing remains prove, the great Hall of Initiation was entirely rebuilt in the Roman period. The rhetorician Aristides, a contemporary of Pausanias, refers in vague and extravagant terms to certain impious people who had seemingly in his own lifetime, profaned the mysteries and fired the precinct (*Or.* xix. vol. I. p. 421 *sqq.*, ed. Dindorf). These impious people may have been no other than the Costobocs. See D. Philios, in *Bulletin de Corresp. hellénique*, 19 (1895), pp. 119-128 ; *id.,* in *Mittheil. d. arch. Inst. in Athen*, 21 (1896), pp. 242-245. Amongst the sculptures found at Eleusis in recent years are two votive reliefs, probably copies of images of Demeter, Proserpine, and Triptolemus which stood in the sacred precinct. One of these reliefs, executed in a rude archaic style, is described below (p. 536 *sq.*). The other, carved in the graceful but dignified style of the fourth century B.C., represents Triptolemus seated between the standing figures of Demeter and Proserpine, while a group of four small figures, doubtless portraits of the persons who dedicated the relief, are approaching the deities. A winged dragon is rearing its head beside Triptolemus, who seems to be sitting on a throne rather than in a car. See D. Philios, in *Mittheil. d. arch. Inst. in Athen*, 20 (1895), pp. 245-266 ; O. Rubensohn, in *Archäologischer Anzeiger*, 1896, pp. 100-102. Two statuettes found at Eleusis are described by Prof. Furtwängler (*Mittheil. d. arch. Inst. in Athen*, 20 (1895), pp. 357-359) ; one of them represents Proserpine seated on the lap of Demeter. Lastly, Mr. Skias has discovered at Eleusis a number of graves containing many early vases decorated in the geometrical style ; some of the vases are very large. One grave, in which a woman was found buried in a sitting posture, contained no less than sixty-eight vases of various sorts and a quantity of feminine ornaments, including finely-made earrings of gold with amber beads, bronze and iron brooches, bronze armlets, rings of silver, bronze, and iron, besides three Egyptian scarabs and a statuette of Isis (*Mittheil. d. arch. Inst. in Athen*, 20 (1895), p. 374 ; *Classical Review*, 9 (1895), p. 428 ; *American Journal of Archaeology*, 10 (1895), p. 551). The woman may have been a priestess, and if so the discovery of the Egyptian objects in her grave lends some countenance to the theory, in itself improbable, of Mr. P. Foucart that the Eleusinian mysteries were derived from Egypt (*Recherches sur l'origine et la nature des mystères d'Éleusis*, Paris, 1895).

P. 503 line 12 *sqq.*, **the square Frankish tower which occupies** the most westerly and the highest point of the ridge. In point of fact the ridge extends some way to the west of the tower and rises to a greater height in that direction, but there is a dip in it immediately to the west of the tower. Excavations at the tower have revealed the remains of a good many meanly-built walls, apparently mediaeval.

P. 503 line 25 *sqq.* from foot, The town of Eleusis etc. The traces of the lower town of Eleusis in the plain beside the sea have now almost wholly vanished (A. Milchhöfer, in *Karten von Attika, Erläuternder Text,* Heft vii. viii. p. 25).

P. 504 line 3 *sqq.* from foot, the middle of the three towers. Of this tower no less than twenty-three courses of masonry are preserved, but most of them are below the present level of the ground. The fortification-wall on the south side of the sacred precinct is standing to a height of thirteen courses of masonry above ground.

P. 505 line 19 *sqq.* from foot, there are a number of holes through which the water poured into a corresponding number of small basins. Rather, there is a hole in each little basin through which the water drained into a channel or gutter which runs in front of all the basins.

P. 505 line 15 *sqq.* from foot, an ancient well etc. The Callichorum well is at the eastern foot of the steps leading up to the Great Propylaea. Its mouth is circular and is enclosed by masonry.

P. 506 line 1, a colossal medallion of white marble. Mr. Philios thinks that this medallion, which is much mutilated, may perhaps represent the emperor Antoninus Pius, and that hence the Great Propylaea may have been built by him (*Eleusis,* p. 59).

P. 507 line 8 from foot, the marble head of a beardless young man etc. Mr. D. Philios holds that this head neither represents Eubuleus nor is by the hand of Praxiteles ; it is more probably, he thinks, a portrait of one of the successors of Alexander, perhaps of Demetrius Poliorcetes (*Mittheil. d. arch. Inst. in Athen,* 20 (1895), p. 263 *sqq.*). I agree with Mr. Philios and Prof. E. A. Gardner (*Handbook of Greek Sculpture,* p. 487 note 1) in seeing no resemblance whatever between this head and that of the Hermes of Praxiteles, and in regarding as little more than an arbitrary conjecture the opinion that it represents Eubuleus.

P. 508 line 21 *sq.* from top, the bases of all these columns except one are still to be seen in their places. The bases of several columns of the most southerly row but one are now missing or covered up.

P. 508 line 8 *sqq.* from foot, a spacious portico etc. The pavement of the portico of Philo, constructed of square blocks of black Eleusinian stone, is preserved almost entire.

P. 511 line 3 from top, a building. Mr. D. Philios conjectures that this may have been the second of the two treasuries, rebuilt in Roman times (*Eleusis,* p. 63).

P. 513 line 22 from top, the images of Demeter and Proserpine etc. Another votive tablet has recently been found at Eleusis which represents Demeter and Proserpine very nearly in the attitudes described in the text. Demeter, portrayed as a matron in flowing robes, is seated to the spectator's left on a chair without back or arms, her feet resting on a stool ; she wears a crown from beneath which her long hair falls loosely down her back ; in her raised left hand she grasps a long sceptre and in her extended right hand she holds three ears of corn. Before her stands the maiden Proserpine, a more youthful but still squat and dumpy figure, wearing her hair bound up in a turban and holding a torch in either hand. The relief is executed in an archaic style which points to the early part of the fifth century B.C. It may very well be, as Mr. Philios thinks, a copy of the images set up immediately after the Persian sack of Eleusis. The chief difference between it and the other votive reliefs, in which Mr. O. Kern with great probability recognises copies of the images, is that in this particular relief Demeter is seated on a chair, whereas in the others she is seated on the cylindrical *cista* or sacred basket. The latter was probably, as Mr. Kern supposes, the way in which the goddess was represented in the original statue. The discovery of this tablet confirms beyond the reach of question the view taken in the text (vol. 2. p. 118) that in the great Eleusinian relief the goddess to the spectator's left with the long flowing hair and the sceptre in the left hand is Demeter, while the goddess to the spectator's right with her hair bound up in a knot and a torch in her hand is Proserpine. Prof. Furtwängler had confidently asserted (*Meisterwerke d. griech. Plastik*, p. 39 note 4) that the goddess with the flowing hair must be Proserpine ; but this view is abundantly refuted by Mr. Philios in his discussion of the recently-found relief. See D. Philios, in *Mittheil. d. arch. Inst. in Athen*, 20 (1895), pp. 245-255, with pl. v.

P. 516 line 8 *sq.*, a police-barrack etc. The police-barrack is beyond, that is, nearer to the ruins of Eleutherae than, the khan of *Kasa*.

P. 516 line 14 from top, **The ruins of Eleutherae.** In November 1895 I revisited the ruins of Eleutherae and was able to make more accurate measurements of the fortifications than on my former visit. In the north wall, which is by far the best preserved, there are remains of eight square towers. The two towers which stand on lower ground at the eastern and western ends of the wall are ruinous, but the intermediate six are preserved to heights varying from twelve to fourteen courses on the outer (northern) side and from six to ten courses on the inner (south) side. The ground falls away here from south to north, so that on the inner side of the wall it is considerably higher than on the outer. I was able to measure three of the towers to their full height on the inner side of the wall. Their heights were 15 ft. 5 in. (with nine courses of masonry), 15 ft. 1 in. (with ten courses of smaller stones), and 14 ft. 6 in. (with eight courses). The heights of the other three towers on the inner side of the wall I estimated at from 13 to 15 feet. On the outer side of the wall I was unable to measure the full heights of the towers but I estimated them at from 22 to 25 feet, the number of courses preserved varying from twelve to fourteen. Contrary to the general usage of Greek fortifications the towers project inward from the wall as well as outward. On the outside the projection varies from 8 ft. 6 in. to 9 ft. 6 in. ; on the inside it is uniformly 3 ft. 6 in. Five of the towers are entered from the ramparts by a pair of doors, one on each side of the tower; and two towers have besides a third door on their inner (southern) face at the level of the ground. Another tower (the second from the west) has only a door at the level of the ground, but none opening off the ramparts. These doorways in the towers are mostly 3 feet wide and 6 feet high. With regard to the north wall itself, between the towers, it is standing in general to a height of from 9 to 15 feet on the outside, with from five to ten courses of masonry preserved. On the inner side the number of courses varies from four to seven. Where six courses are standing the height is about 10 feet. The thickness of the wall varies from 6 ft. 4 in. to 7 ft. 2 in. Three staircases, more or less ruinous, lead down from the wall on its inner side. Further it should be noted that the north wall is pierced with two doorways. One of these doorways is 4 ft. 5 in. wide; the other is 4 feet wide and 9 feet high and has its lintel preserved.

About 8 paces south of this fine fortification-wall, but wholly unconnected with it, are the remains of the "oblong rectangular edifice" mentioned in the text (vol. 2. p. 516). It seems to have been a sort of inner fort or keep. The wall, 4 feet thick, is built of massive well-jointed polygonal masonry and may be traced all round the building which is 19 paces long from north to south by 12 paces broad from east to west. At the north-west angle the wall is about 6 feet high.

P. 517 line 8 *sqq.* from foot, **the ruins —— may be those of Oenoe** etc. The identification of the ruins at *Myoupoli* as those of the ancient Oenoe is regarded by Prof. Milchhöfer as certain. The ground here, bounded by beds of streams on the east and south, but opener to the west, rises to a moderate elevation. A fortification-wall, carried in a series of straight lines, surrounds what seems to have been the citadel. Seven minutes suffice to walk round it. The towers on the north side are best preserved, especially one towards the north-east corner which has eleven or twelve courses of large blocks of conglomerate standing. In this north wall there are two gates. Traces of houses and other remains of foundations may be seen especially in the south and south-west. Many potsherds lie strewn about. That the communications of the place were protected by outlying forts is proved by the isolated remains of towers and foundations in the neighbourhood, notably to the north and north-east. See A. Milchhöfer, in *Karten von Attika, Erläuternder Text*, Heft vii. viii. p. 16 *sq.* One of these outposts of Oenoe stands in the little plain to the south of Eleutherae, about twenty minutes' drive (between 2 and 3 miles) south-east of the khan of *Kasa*. Here some 50 yards or so to the east of the highroad which connects Athens with Thebes are considerable remains of an ancient tower built of regular ashlar masonry. Originally the tower must have been about 30 feet square, but only the north-eastern angle of it is well preserved. In the north wall no less than thirty-one courses of masonry, with a block of the thirty-second, are standing. As the courses average from 17 to 21 inches high, the height of the tower at present is probably about 50 feet. There are five loop-holes in the northern and one in the eastern wall.

P. 525 line 24 from foot, **Solon stirred them up by his verses** etc. The difficulties raised by the traditional accounts of the Athenian conquest of Salamis have been discussed by J. Töpffer (*Quaestiones Pisistrateae*, p. 1 *sqq.* ; *Beiträge zur Altertumswissenschaft*, p. 1 *sqq.*). See also G. Busolt, *Griechische Geschichte*, 2.² p. 217 *sqq.*

P. 532 line 22 from top, **like the Egyptian wooden images.** On the strength of certain Egyptian and Phoenician statuettes Mr. E. Pottier argues that Greek sculpture was influenced by Egyptian models at some period not earlier than the second half of the seventh century B.C. He supposes that Greek artists residing in Egypt produced small models of Egyptian statues, and that these copies found their way to Greece in the way of commerce. The influence, in his opinion, is betrayed chiefly in the advance of the left leg of archaic male statues like the so-called Apollos of Tenea, Orchomenus, etc., and with this he would connect the tradition that Daedalus was the first to make statues with their feet apart. See E. Pottier, 'Note sur le style égyptisant dans la plastique grecque,' *Bulletin de Corresp. hellénique*, 18 (1894), pp. 408-415.

P. 533 line 9 from top, **graves in the city.** To the examples of burial in the market-place which are cited in the text a few more may be added. The tomb of the herald Talthybius was shown in the market-place of Aegium (Paus. iii. 12. 7, vii. 24. 1). Oxylus was buried in the market-place at Elis (Paus. vi. 24. 9). And the bones of Hesiod are said to have been laid, long after his death, in the middle of the market-place of Orchomenus (Proclus, *Vita Hesiodi*, 4, in *Biographi Graeci*, ed. Westermann, p. 49).

P. 543 line 1 *sq.*, **Aegosthena.** A few years ago Aegosthena was visited by some members of the British School at Athens. The results of their researches have recently been reported by Mr. E. F. Benson (*Journal of Hellenic Studies*, 15 (1895), pp. 314-324). From his description and plans I gather the following particulars.

The walls seem to have formed a rough quadrangle about 600 yards long from east to west by 200 yards wide from north to south. Beginning on high ground at the east they extended westward and downward to the sea. The most easterly and highest part of the site, naturally defended on three sides by steep and in some places almost precipitous slopes, was cut off from the rest of the town by an inner cross-wall to form an acropolis. The walls are well preserved on the east and north, but the south wall has almost wholly disappeared. On this southern side a river, descending from the hills in a steep bed enclosed by high rocks, flows along the whole length of the town, and on its southern bank some traces of a fortification-wall have been observed, consisting of a long line of stones and hewn blocks now overgrown with bushes and resembling the "long lines of fallen walls which mark ruined Norman or mediaeval castles in England." This line of stones, therefore, which may be traced down to the sea, is probably a remnant of the south wall, which would seem to have crossed over from the north to the south bank of the river at a point some 170 yards or so west of the great tower which occupies the south-eastern angle of the fortified enclosure. Whether there was ever a west wall along the shore of the gulf has been doubted. Mr. Benson thinks that there was not ; but many hewn blocks lie along the shore, and it seems highly improbable that one whole side of the town would have been left open and undefended. The examples of Piraeus and Larymna would be enough to prove, if proof were needed, that the Greeks are not likely to have overlooked the necessity of defending their cities on the side of the sea as well as of the land. With regard to Aegosthena in particular, did this obscure little town ever possess a command of the sea so complete that it could afford to neglect the chance of an attack from the side of the sea by such naval powers as Athens and Corinth ? If Athens, the mistress of the sea, defended her shore line with massive walls, must not Aegosthena have done so too ?

Walls and towers of the acropolis and of the lower town are built in the same style. The towers are constructed of strictly ashlar masonry ; the blocks, which average a metre in length by half a metre in height and breadth, are squared and laid in horizontal courses. On the other hand, the lower courses of the curtain are constructed in great part of well-jointed polygonal masonry. The materials employed are a hard limestone of the district and a less durable conglomerate rock.

Best preserved and most imposing of all is the eastern wall of the acropolis. This fine wall stands almost complete and unbroken, crowning a steep rocky slope which descends into the valley. Four square towers project from it at intervals of about 50 metres. The only means of egress on this side is a small postern between the two central towers. The tower at the south-eastern angle is probably, as Mr. Benson says, the finest existing specimen of a Greek fortification. It rises, according to him, $11\frac{1}{2}$ metres (37 ft. 9 in.) above the top of the adjoining wall, and is complete on three sides from top to bottom ; on the south side it is finished on the top by a flat gable, but the corresponding gable on the north side is gone. Internally the tower is built solid from the ground up to a height of 10 feet above the top of the wall. At this level a narrow doorway gives access to the interior which consists of a chamber 8 metres square and lighted by two very narrow oblong windows. The height of the door above the wall suggests that it was reached by a ladder which could be drawn up in case of necessity. Thus even if the acropolis were carried by an enemy, a few of the garrison could still defend themselves in this tower. At present there is but one room in the tower, but if we may judge from the analogy of the tower at the north-east angle, this south-eastern tower probably contained originally two chambers, one above the other.

The tower at the north-eastern angle of the acropolis, to which reference has just been made, is built up solid with rubble to a level with the top of the wall, from which it was entered by a door. The upper part of the tower has fallen, but eight courses up a complete row of holes for roof beams may be seen on one side, and on the adjacent sides there are larger holes for the main rafters. Though the tower now rises only a few courses above these holes, it is clear that originally it contained two stories. The tower at the north-west angle of the acropolis is also built up solid to a level with the top of the wall, and there is some slight evidence to show that the tower at the south-west angle, which has almost disappeared, was built similarly. On the other hand all the intermediate towers seem to have been hollow down to the ground; at least this is the case with the two intermediate towers on the eastern and one intermediate tower on the southern side of the acropolis. The motive for building the towers at the angles in a more solid style than the intermediate towers was doubtless to compensate them for their greater liability to suffer from the siege operations of an enemy. It is to be observed that contrary to the usual rule the towers of Aegosthena project inwards as well as outwards from the wall. In this they resemble the towers of Eleutherae (vol. 2. p. 516 and above, p. 537).

The eastern wall of the acropolis is 8 feet high on the inside at its southern end; outside and inside it is faced with large hewn blocks, the interior being filled up solid with rubble. Between the great tower at the south-east angle and the next tower to the north the wall is preserved almost entire on its outer face, but the inner facing of masonry and the core of rubble have mostly disappeared. The original north wall of the acropolis extends unbroken throughout its whole length, rising in some places to a height of 7 metres (23 feet); nowhere is it less than 4 metres (13 feet) high. The west wall, on the other hand, has been almost entirely rebuilt, probably at a late date, for the purpose of banking up the ground.

The north wall of the lower city, starting from the north-west angle of the acropolis, extends down to the sea. It is defended throughout its whole length by square towers built like those of the acropolis and placed at intervals of about 60 metres. Only three of these towers are now complete up to or above the first storey. In this north wall there were at least two gates. One of them is placed in a retreating angle and defended on the left, as you approach it, by a projecting tower. Mr. Benson conjectures that there was a third gate just below the north-west angle of the acropolis.

On the south side of the acropolis, but outside the line of its existing fortifications, there is a cave in the rock, the entrance to which is faced with large blocks of masonry. The peasants say that it is the entrance to a subterranean passage which leads up into the acropolis, ending at the great south-eastern tower. This passage, if it exists, is now filled up with earth. The English archaeologists dug into it for a considerable distance without coming to an end of the cave. They found that it sloped upwards, which confirms the statement of the peasants. It has been suggested that the cave was sacred and connected with the worship of Melampus. But of this there is no evidence, and the existence of a similar cave on the eastern side of the acropolis, just outside of the great tower, favours the view that they were secret sally-ports for the garrison. Close to the southern cave is an isolated piece of wall built of large polygonal stones in a style which can hardly be more recent than the early part of the sixth century B.C. It runs along the edge of a steep rock for 9 metres, and probably formed part of a circuit-wall much more ancient than the existing fortifications, which may belong to the fifth or fourth century B.C.

Some excavations were made by the English archaeologists in four cemeteries which lie just outside the town, two on the north side and two on the south. They found a few small clay idols of the rudest sort and a whole series of little seated figures made of terra-cotta, which serves to illustrate the development of the Greek type of the seated goddess. Mixed up with these were potsherds of all styles from the early Dipylum (see vol. 3. p. 230) down to the red-figured style. Amongst the later remains found by the English at Aegosthena were a few unimportant inscriptions of imperial date and the base of a bust of Hadrian who in the inscription is called 'founder.' A statue of the same emperor was set up by the people of Aegosthena, as we learn from an inscription recently published by Mr. de Ridder, who has edited along with it a few other small inscriptions found on the spot (*Bulletin de Corresp. hellénique*, 18 (1894), pp. 497-499).

P. 549 line 19 from top, **funeral games.** In Futuna or Horne Island the funerals were followed by a grand feast, to which succeeded dances and pugilistic encounters (*Journal of the Polynesian Society*, vol. I. No. 1 (April, 1892), p. 39).

P. 553. **The Pre-Persian temple.** Dr. Dörpfeld has recently reiterated his opinion that this temple was rebuilt after the Persian war and continued to exist down to the time of Pausanias at least. He now accepts Miss Harrison's theory that the temple of Athena Polias described by Pausanias (i. 26. 6-i. 27. 1) was not, as he had hitherto believed, the Erechtheum but the Pre-Persian temple, and he holds that the ancient image of Athena Polias always stood in the Pre-Persian temple and never in the Erechtheum. This latter opinion seems to contradict the well-known official inscription (*C. I. A.* i. No. 322) in which the Erechtheum is described as "the temple on the Acropolis in which is the ancient image" (τοῦ νεὼ τοῦ ἐν πόλει, ἐν ᾧ τὸ ἀρχαῖον ἄγαλμα). Dr. Dörpfeld would interpret this phrase to mean "the temple in which the ancient image is to be placed hereafter." He admits that the Erechtheum was built to receive the ancient image of Athena Polias as well as to house the cult of Erechtheus, but he does not attempt to explain why the intention of placing the image in it was never carried out. See his paper 'Der alte Athena-tempel auf der Akropolis,' *Mittheilungen des arch. Inst. in Athen*, 22 (1897), pp. 159-178.

In my paper on this question I maintained, in opposition to Dr. Dörpfeld, that Athena Polias was always the goddess of the Erechtheum alone (vol. 2. pp. 570-580). But my friend Mr. W. Wyse points out to me that in *C. I. A.* i. No. 273 Athena Polias is almost certainly the goddess to whom the great bulk of the sacred moneys belongs, and that presumably therefore she is the goddess of the Parthenon. Further, from a comparison of this and other inscriptions (as *C. I. A.* i. Nos. 188, 189, *C. I. A.* ii. Nos. 661, 699) Mr. Wyse infers that in inscriptions the goddess of the Parthenon was generally spoken of simply as Athena or 'the goddess,' and that the title Polias was only added when it was desirable to distinguish her from another Athena, especially from Victory Athena. No distinction, in Mr. Wyse's opinion, was drawn between the Athena of the Erechtheum and the Athena of the Parthenon : the goddess of the two temples was one and the same, who might be spoken of either as Athena simply or as Athena Polias. If Mr. Wyse is right—and without feeling sure I incline to agree with him—it will follow almost necessarily that not only the Parthenon but its predecessor the Pre-Persian temple could be properly described as the temple of Athena Polias, and consequently there is nothing in the language of Pausanias and Strabo (ix. p. 396) to preclude the supposition that, as Dr. Dörpfeld now holds, the temple of Athena Polias described by both of them was the Pre-Persian temple. But even if this were certain, I should continue to believe, on the strength of the other arguments, that the Pre-Persian temple was never rebuilt after its destruction in 480 B.C., and that the temple described by Pausanias and Strabo was the Erechtheüm. At the same time, I should then, as always, hold myself ready to abandon this belief and accept Dr. Dörpfeld's theory unreservedly if he could produce fresh and convincing evidence in support of it. This, so far as I can judge, he has not done in his last paper on the subject.

P. 554 note 2, **one of the gables of the temple was adorned with sculptures** etc. The fragments of the sculptures which occupied one of the gables of the Pre-Persian temple have now been carefully put together by Mr. H. Schrader. As Prof. Studnizcka was the first to perceive (*Mittheilungen d. arch. Inst. in Athen*, 11 (1886), pp. 185-199), the composition represented Athena in the battle of the gods and giants. In the centre appeared Athena bending over a fallen giant. On either side of this central group a male human figure, probably a god, seems to have been represented striding against a foe ; and in each of the corners of the gable was a giant creeping on the ground. Two figures appear to have been lost. All three giants are portrayed in full human form and naked. The material of which the sculptures are made is a coarse-grained marble. Numerous traces of colours, especially blue and red, may be detected on the figures, the nude parts of which seem, however, to have been left unpainted with the exception of the lips and eyes. The robes of Athena are arranged and coloured in a manner closely resembling that of the drapery of the well-known archaic figures of women which were found on the Acropolis some years ago. See H. Schrader, ' Die Gigantomachie aus dem Giebel des alten Athenatempels auf der Akropolis,' *Mittheilungen d. arch. Inst. in Athen*, 22 (1897), pp. 59-112.

P. 573 note 3, **Athena Polias.** An Athena Polias was worshipped also at Daulis (*C. I. G. G. S.* 3. No. 65).

P. 576 note 11. The priestess of Athena Polias is also mentioned in an inscription recently found at Eleusis ('Εφημερὶς ἀρχαιολογική, 1895, p. 109, Inscr. No. 23).

VOL. III

P. 5 line 21 *sqq.* from foot, an **ancient fortification-wall** etc. In December 1895 I traced for some hundreds of yards to the west of the sanctuary of Poseidon the ancient fortification-wall which here crosses the Isthmus of Corinth, but I did not observe any of the square projecting towers mentioned in the text. The wall is here standing in places to a height of one and two courses, but in general its line is marked chiefly by a mass of blocks which have tumbled down the slope. Where the wall exists, the style of masonry is ashlar, the blocks being squared and laid in horizontal courses. From the regularity of the masonry I judged the wall, at the place where I first traced it, to be of the good Greek period, though with signs of Byzantine or mediaeval repairs. Thus about 120 yards or so to the west of the sanctuary the wall makes a bend to the south in order to cross a small ravine or shallow glen, and here in the ravine there is a fragment of the ashlar wall with a piece of brick wall on the top of it, this upper bit of wall being built of flat bricks and mortar in the usual late Roman or Byzantine style of which there are many remains in Greece. In the same little ravine, a short way further to the west, the ashlar wall is preserved to a height of about ten courses; but some of the blocks of which it is composed have apparently been taken from older buildings; the lowest block in the wall, for example, has a moulding, and in the two blocks of the course above it there are holes as if for the attachment of some objects. Again, to the east of the sanctuary of Poseidon the fortification-wall is standing in the hollow bed of a torrent to a height of nine courses. Here it is built of squared blocks laid in horizontal courses; but the blocks are not closely fitted together, and the small stones, bricks, and mortar which occur in the joints both perpendicular and horizontal even of the lowest courses prove that in its present form at least the wall was built in late Roman or Byzantine times.

P. 9 line 19 *sqq.* from foot, **the Isthmian sanctuary** etc. The three gates of the Isthmian sanctuary, excavated by Mr. Monceaux, are still plainly to be seen. The gate towards the eastern end of the north wall is well preserved. On its outer side it is flanked on either hand by the remains of a round tower resting on a square basement of masonry two courses high. The foot of the round tower on the west is adorned with a projecting moulding which runs all round it. From between these towers a passage about 6 paces long leads up to the gate proper. The walls of the passage are still standing to a height of six and seven courses; like the towers, they are built of perfectly regular ashlar masonry, the blocks being exactly squared and laid in horizontal courses. Towards its outer end each of the side-walls of the passage is adorned with two pilasters; and there are considerable remains of a pavement of white marble. Two great square holes are visible on each side of the gateway; perhaps the bolts were shot into them, though they seem almost too large to have served that purpose. On the whole the gateway, fortified though it is, has all the appearance of having been built rather for show than for strength, and I am disposed to agree with Mr. Monceaux in referring it to the age of Augustus. The southern gateway, which has been blocked up by a later wall, is a simple opening flanked on the east by a ruined round tower. The wall at this point is about 3.70 metres thick and is standing to a height of four courses. The style of the masonry here and wherever the wall exists is of the regular ashlar sort, resembling that of the north-east gateway. Hence Mr. Monceaux is probably right in assigning the whole existing fortifications of the sanctuary to the Augustan age. On the eastern side of the sanctuary three square towers project from the curtain. The western wall would seem to have been also strengthened with towers, the positions of which, however, are at present marked only by projecting mounds.

P. 14 line 23 from foot, **many drums of Ionic columns.** I found these drums still lying at the north-east gate of the Isthmian sanctuary, 12th December 1895. I measured the diameter of several and found it to be .83 metre. At least two bases of Ionic (or Corinthian) columns are lying in the same place. The diameter of the column which rested on one of these bases is .81 metre.

P. 20 line 9 from top, **Corinth.** In 1896 excavations made at Corinth by the American School under the direction of Prof. Richardson led to the discovery of the theatre. Its remains, consisting of foundations of seats and portions of flights of steps worn by feet, are situated on the edge of the plateau about a hundred rods to the west of the old temple. The theatre seems to have been rebuilt in Roman times. At the top of the auditorium were found a number of archaic statuettes of terra-cotta representing men, women, and many animals, especially horses. The statuettes of women are more numerous than those of men, and some of them are said to exhibit a type of Aphrodite. All these figurines are probably votive-offerings from some temple in the neighbourhood. Thirty-five fragments of Ionic columns, from 5 to 8 feet long, came to light not very far from the theatre. Further the Americans excavated the remains of what is supposed to have been a colonnade of the Greek period, about 100 feet long, several houses, and a short piece of a well-paved street. See *Athenaeum*, 27th June 1896, p. 850; *id.*, 2nd January 1897, p. 24; *American Journal of Archaeology*, 11 (1896), p. 371 *sq.*; *Journal of Hellenic Studies*, 16 (1896), p. 340; *Berliner philolog. Wochenschrift*, 13th February 1897, p. 222.

P. 24 line 23 *sqq.* from top, **a marble staircase** etc. The staircase which now leads from "the bath of Aphrodite" to the top of the rocky terrace is of common stone, not marble. The reddish-brown, ochrelike deposit left by the water on the rocks and on the ground under the overhanging ledge is conspicuous.

P. 29 line 9 *sqq.* from foot, **On this side the Acro-Corinth is connected by a saddle with a lower, but still rugged and rocky, height** etc. This is a mistake. The lower height referred to in the text is included within the fortifications of the Acro-Corinth, of which it forms in fact the western and lower summit. The ascent is not between it and the higher eastern summit, but to the west of the western and lower summit. The Acro-Corinth is practically an isolated mountain of rock.

In the third and highest of the triple line of fortifications which guards the approach to the Acro-Corinth on the west there are considerable remains of ancient Greek masonry. This third wall extends in the form of a great crescent on either side of the gate, and the ancient masonry is visible in three places, namely at the extremities of the crescent and in the tower which flanks the gateway on the right or south side. At the extremities, especially the southern extremity, of the crescent the Greek walls are standing to a height of many courses; and the front of the tower which flanks the gateway consists chiefly of ancient masonry, eighteen or nineteen courses of it being preserved. In all these places the style of masonry is ashlar; the blocks are squared and laid in horizontal courses. The difference between it and the Venetian masonry above it is obvious to the least practised eye.

P. 44 line 15 *sqq.* from top, **The ancient walls ran all round the tableland** etc. On the western edge of the acropolis of Sicyon, above the glen of the Helisson, I found (15th October 1895) here and there remains of the fortification-wall sufficient to prove that it originally ran all along this western face of the acropolis. The remains are slight, generally consisting of a single course of blocks extending for a few feet or yards, but in several places the wall is standing to a height of two or three courses for a short distance. The blocks are squared and laid in horizontal courses. In one place two parallel rows of blocks, being probably parts of the outer and inner faces of the wall, are preserved. To judge from the distance of these rows from each other the wall was about 9 feet thick. At the south-west end of the plateau which formed the acropolis, above the glen of the Helisson, there seems to have been a gate. At least there is here a hollow leading down southward to the narrow ridge which connects the plateau with the hills; and on its west side this passage is lined with an ancient wall two courses high. Here it may be observed that the ridge which connects the plateau with the hills on the south is a mere knife-edge; a footpath occupies its whole width, and on each side of it the ground slopes away steeply to end in precipices on the eastern side. Moreover the ridge is far below the level of the plateau, so that on the whole its existence hardly, if at all, impaired the strategical strength of Sicyon's position. On the eastern edge of the acropolis, above the glen of the Asopus, I found no vestige of a wall and no sign that a wall had ever existed. The reason is obvious. The tremendous white precipices on this side rendered fortification needless; whereas on the western edge of the plateau the slope to the glen of the Helisson, though long and steep, is not precipitous and might have been scaled by an enemy.

The northern and lower plateau on which stood the city, as distinguished from the acropolis, of Sicyon, appears to have been surrounded on its outer edge by a fortification-wall, for I found some remains of it, mostly insignificant, on the western, northern, and eastern edges of the plateau. Of these remains the most considerable are to be seen in a deep natural cleft or fissure in the edge of the plateau immediately to the west of the village of *Vasiliko.* This fissure may be about 300 yards long. In the bottom of it are some small gardens with trees, and a road leads up it to the village. At the upper end of the fissure may be seen some massive pieces of ancient Greek masonry, perhaps the ruins of a gate. First there is a wall, some 20 feet or so long, running across the upper end of the fissure and abutting on the native rock at each end. It is built of large squared blocks laid in regular horizontal courses, of which seven are preserved. A few yards lower down the fissure is a piece of a similar wall about 11 paces long, extending at right angles to the former wall and standing in part to a height of seven courses. Still lower down the fissure I observed a few other remains of antiquity, such as squared blocks, a couple of drums of columns, fragments of houses built of thin flat bricks and mortar, two Roman graves cut out of the rock and lined with brickwork, and so on. Further to the north, in the line of the fissure, is an ancient burying-ground where, as I was informed, human bones have been found together with pottery and jewellery.

At the house of Constantine Barilos, in the village of *Vasiliko,* I copied the following inscription. It is carved on a block of marble 30 inches long and about 6 or 7 inches high, which is built into a wall outside of the house. The letters are well cut and rather more than an inch high.

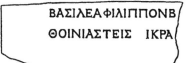

ΒΑΣΙΛΕΑΦΙΛΙΠΠΟΝΒ
ΘΟΙΝΙΑΣΤΕΙΣ   ΙΚΡΑ

The block is broken off on two sides, namely below and to the right. Apparently it formed part of a pedestal of Philip, one of the Macedonian kings of that name.

P. 44 line 3 *sqq.* from foot, **the remains of a large building** of **Roman date** etc. These remains, situated 200 paces north of the theatre, cover a considerable area. One piece measures about 41 paces from north to south, terminating in the latter direction in a semicircular apse. The walls, built of thin bricks laid flat with mortar between them, are 3 ft. 2 in. thick and are standing to a height of from 8 to 12 feet at least. The bricks are not a mere facing but go right through the wall, as may be seen where the walls are broken. In the interior of the building is a doorway with a brick arch over it.

P. 49 line 14 from top, **the theatre.** As to the theatre at Sicyon, see W. Dörpfeld, in *Das griechische Theater* (Athens and Leipsic, 1896), pp. 117-120. From that work and from my own notes made on the spot (15th and 16th October 1895) I may here briefly supplement and correct the description given in the text. The number of staircases dividing the lower part of the auditorium is sixteen, not fourteen, as I have stated. The front row of seats consists of a series of stone benches with backs, and with arms at the ends of each bench. There are not separate armchairs, nor are the seats in each bench divided from each other by arms. Six such benches exist, though one of them is broken. They are made of a common stone, not of marble.

The lower parts of most of the existing walls of the stage-buildings are hewn out of the rock, and therefore may be presumed to have remained unaltered since the time they were first made. Two ramps or inclined planes lead up to the stage, one at each end; they are also hewn out of the rock, and from the height to which they lead up (from 3 to 3.50 metres) we may safely infer the height of the stage. Thus the height of the stage must have conformed to the rule laid down by Vitruvius (v. 7. 2) for the height of Greek stages in general. The existing front wall of the stage is built of *opus incertum* (small stones mixed with brick and mortar) and is therefore of Roman date. But along its front extends a step formed of a row of marble blocks each about 1 foot high and 1 ft. 10 in. thick. This marble step probably supported the columned front of a stage which was taken down when the Roman stage was built. The depth of the stage, from the front of the marble step to the back wall, was about 10 ft. 6 in., according to my measurement. Immediately at the back of the marble step and under the wall of *opus incertum* is a row of blocks of common stone, which from the square cuttings in them seem to have supported a wooden framework consisting of strong posts connected with each other by planks. This wooden framework was perhaps the front of the oldest stage. Behind the stage lie the foundations of a long quadrangular structure divided by walls into several apartments, which probably served as green-rooms, store-rooms, etc. Two ramps cut out of the rock led up to the roof of this quadrangular structure, one from each end; they are side by side with, but behind, the two ramps which, as we have seen, led up to the stage.

In the middle of the stage a staircase, five steps of which are preserved, leads down into an underground passage which extends into the middle of the orchestra at right angles to the stage. The passage is about 2 ft. 3 in. wide and 5 ft. 5 in. high. Its sides are lined with ashlar masonry. At the middle of the orchestra it was apparently met by a branch of the drain which runs round the orchestra. This branch of the drain is in a straight line with the underground passage, of which it forms in fact a continuation. At its other end the passage is prolonged under the stage and the apartments at the back of the stage to a point outside of the theatre altogether. In this prolongation beyond the staircase which leads down to it from the stage, the sides of the passage are merely hewn out of the rock, not lined with masonry, so far as I observed. This difference of construction points to the conclusion that, while the whole passage served as a drain, the part of it between the stage and the middle of the orchestra was also used to allow actors to make their way unseen from the stage to the middle of the orchestra.

The exact date of the theatre is unknown, but from the number of times it has obviously been rebuilt Dr. Dörpfeld inclines to attribute the oldest part of it, including the wooden stage, to the fourth or third century B.C. The stone stage of which the front rested on the marble step may, he thinks, have belonged to the second or first century B.C. It is hardly necessary to add that here as elsewhere he denies the existence of a raised stage before the Roman period. What I have called the stage he regards as the ornamental background in front of which the players acted. As to this theory see vol. 3. p. 254 and below, p. 582 *sqq.*

P. 56 line 15 from foot, **Two vaulted passages** etc. I observed only one of these passages, that on the eastern side of the auditorium, at a considerable height above the level of the orchestra. It is a vaulted tunnel, about 18 paces long; the roof, built on the true principle of the arch, is formed of massive squared blocks placed in straight rows.

P. 77 line 23 *sqq.* from foot, **the acropolis of Phlius** etc. The hill of Phlius projects boldly and abruptly, like a great tongue, westwards into the flat ground from the chain of hills that bounds the plain on the east. Its height may be from 300 to 400 feet, and its length from east to west half a mile. The slopes both to the north and south are steep, but towards the west the hill descends in three great steps or terraces, of which the uppermost is much the longest and broadest. The rock of which the hill is composed is a rough conglomerate of pebbles (breccia). At the western end of the hill the rock crops up in great masses which at a distance may easily be mistaken for fortifications. The surface of the broad uppermost terrace, now overgrown with the brown, prickly, dried-up plants so common in Greece, is separated by a hollow from the higher hills on the east. Along the western crest of this hollow a fragment of the ancient walls of Phlius may be traced; it consists merely of one or two courses of masonry half-buried in the ground and extending in a line for a dozen paces. On the second terrace stands a modern white-washed building which is constructed to a considerable extent of large ancient squared stones. Other ancient blocks are also lying about the terrace. On the third or lowest terrace there are some ruins of a quadrangular building which may be ancient. But the most considerable of the scanty remains of antiquity at Phlius are to be seen at the south-western foot of the hill, a few paces to the east of the road from *H. Georgios.* Here are preserved three walls of solid masonry supporting a sort of quadrangular platform on which no doubt some ancient building, perhaps a temple, was erected. The eastern supporting-wall is 27 paces long, the southern 31, and the western 17. The west wall consists of two courses of massive blocks of the native breccia, each block being about 4 ft. 6 in. long by 1 ft. 6 in. high. The east wall is standing to a greater height, but of the south wall only the extremities are visible, the rest being buried under the soil.

Here I may print two inscriptions which I copied on my way from Phlius to Stymphalus, 29th September 1895; so far as I am aware they have not been published before. They are engraved on two square marble columns about 5 feet high, terminating in busts, which I found, one standing and the other lying, a few hundred yards east of the hamlet of *Petre*, at the point where a stream, fringed with reeds and poplars, crosses the path. The head of the fallen bust is lost, but part of the folded vesture on the breast is preserved, and under it, all in one line, is the inscription

ΜΟΡΦΗΝΣΕΚΟΥΝΔΙΛΛΕΣΜΕΜΗΤΡΟΣΕΙΣΟΡΑΣ

"In me you behold the form of mother Secundilla." The head of the standing bust is preserved; the face indeed is much mutilated, but the curly locks at the back of the head remain. On the front of the square column are traces of the male genital organs. The inscription, carved in a single line under the bust, is nonsensical, as taken down by me; but I give my copy, such as it is, on the chance that some one may be able to correct it either by conjecture or by comparison with the stone :

Κ(?)ΟΠΣΜΟΣΕΤ(or Γ?)ΤΑΡΤΟΣΗΓΟΥΜΑΓ(or Η?)ΕΝΟΥ ꓿ (?)

The two columnar busts are of the same size, material, and style.

P. 90 line 27 *sqq.*, a temple of Nemean Zeus etc. The *echinus* of the columns of the temple at Nemea is very flat, which points to a late rather than an early date for the temple. Of the walls of the *cella* the lowest course is partly preserved for a length of about 18 paces. It consisted originally of two rows of immense slabs set on their narrow edges and placed back to back, so that two such slabs formed the thickness of the wall. The lowest courses of the north and west walls of the *cella* were similarly constructed, as may be seen by the scanty remains. One of the two existing slabs of the west wall is about 9 feet long, 4 ft. 9 in. high, and 1 ft. 6 in. thick. The floor of the temple, of which a considerable part is preserved, is constructed of massive squared blocks of stone (not marble). At the east end of the temple may be seen remains of the three steps on which the building was raised. The foundations are well preserved at the northeast corner. Opposite the temple, at its eastern end, is a square platform of stone at a lower level than the steps on which the temple stood. It may perhaps have supported an altar. About 150 yards or so to the south of the temple considerable remains of an ancient building exist. I was told that it had been a tomb which was converted into a Byzantine church. Among the remains are small drums of columns with flatedged flutes. The modern village of *Herakleia*, with its houses built of sun-dried brick or mud, stands only a few hundred yards to the southwest of the ruined temple.

P. 94 line 11 *sqq.* from top, The spring —— Adrastea etc. Water was again flowing from the Turkish fountain identified as Adrastea when I saw it, 28th September 1895. The water issues from a wall of the usual sort and falls into a trough. Beside the fountain is a pond, and beside the pond grow fig-trees and poplars. The spot is a pleasant one. The three solitary columns of the temple of Zeus are conspicuous in the valley not far to the west.

P. 96 line 18 *sqq.* from top, **the Inachus** etc. I crossed the Inachus at different points on the 10th and 12th December 1895, and on both occasions its bed was quite dry.

P. 98 line 14 from foot, **Mycenae.** Excavations continue to be made year by year at Mycenae by Mr. Tsountas for the Greek Archaeo-logical Society. In 1895 the whole eastern half of the acropolis was excavated, with the result that considerable remains of houses of the Mycenaean period were here brought to light. (For some particulars as to these houses, see below, p. 557.) On the western slope of the acropolis in the same year pieces of two ancient roads leading up to the palace were discovered ; one of them—the principal road—is preserved for a length of many yards and rests on a high supporting-wall built of large stones. Three fragments of sculptured reliefs were found within the acropolis ; they are believed to have belonged to the metopes of the temple which was built on the ruins of the palace in the sixth century B.C. One of the fragments exhibits the head and breast of a woman in fine archaic style and good preservation. Further, in a room of an ancient house on the acropolis there was found a hoard of 3786 ancient silver coins, mostly of Corinth, Phlius, and Argos ; they seem to have been deposited in their hiding-place in the third century B.C. Outside the acropolis the excavations of the same year revealed fifteen more tombs hewn in the rock. Amongst the objects found in these tombs were eight bronze swords, two axes, a spear-head, two alabaster vessels, a narrow fillet of twisted gold, golden plates making a belt, fifty-nine small golden ornaments which seem to have been attached to a head-dress, many other small golden ornaments of various shapes, gold beads of necklaces, fourteen engraved gems, two mock gems of glass - paste, six gold rings finely engraved, a silver cup with gilt handle and gilt brim, two bronze vessels, and four stone vessels of which one is prettily adorned with sculptured reliefs. Most of the devices engraved on the gems represent animals. See Chr. Tsountas, in Πρακτικὰ τῆς Ἀρχαιολογικῆς Ἑταιρίας, 1895, pp. 23-25 ; A. Lampropoulos, *ib.* pp. 25-27 ; *id.*, in Ἐφημερὶς ἀρχαιολογική, 1896, pp. 137-200. Amongst the objects discovered outside of the acropolis special mention may be made of a tombstone which was found, not in its original position, serving with other stones to wall up a grave which was hewn in the side of a circular sepulchral chamber. The material is sandstone, on which are painted in a variety of colours three horizontal bands of figures set in ornamental borders. In the lowest band is a procession of four deer and a hedgehog ; in the middle band five warriors march in single file, each carrying a shield and brandishing a spear in his raised right hand ; of the highest band only a fragment remains, but it seems to have contained one or perhaps two figures clad in long robes and seated on chairs. It is remarkable that the five warriors resemble almost exactly in attitude, equipment, and style the fighting warriors depicted on the well-known vase found by Schliemann at Mycenae (see C. Schuchhardt, *Schliemann's Ausgrabungen,*[2] p. 326 *sq.*, with fig. 301 ; Perrot et Chipiez, *Histoire de l'art dans l'antiquité,* 6. p. 935, fig. 497). The discovery of this tombstone accordingly refutes the theory lately broached by Mr. E. Pottier that the vase in question, to which archaeologists have appealed as furnishing evidence of the equipment of warriors in the Mycenaean age, has nothing to do with the Mycenaean age or style but belongs to the class of Attic vases of the seventh century B.C. (E. Pottier, 'Observations sur la céramique mycénienne,' *Revue archéologique*, 3me Série, 28 (1896), pp. 17-23). See Chr. Tsountas, in Ἐφημερὶς ἀρχαιολογική, 1896, pp. 1-22, with pl. 1 ; S. Reinach, 'Une peinture mycénienne,' *Revue archéologique*, 8 (1897), pp. 19-26. The excavations of 1896 at Mycenae revealed the existence of seven more tombs hewn out of the rock in the shape of chambers. Further, another beehive tomb, built of hewn blocks of stone and well preserved, was excavated. In the floor of the beehive chamber, which measures about 8 metres in diameter, there are three quadrangular graves, which were covered with large slabs of stone. These graves had been plundered long ago, perhaps, as Mr. Tsountas thinks, by decayed and poverty-stricken members of the old family to whom the tomb belonged. However, on the floor of the beehive chamber were found some tablets of glass-paste adorned with reliefs which represent animal-headed figures standing on either side of a tripod or altar and carrying vessels in their hands. This is the first time that figures of this sort, so common on gems, have been found on ornaments made of glass-paste. Further, on the western side of the acropolis, beside the so-called polygonal tower, where the depth of soil is greater than in any other part of the citadel, there were laid bare many remains of houses. In one of them was found a woman's head, made of limestone, about .17 metre high. The hair, eyes, ears, and mouth of the head are coloured, and on the neck is painted a necklace of red and blue beads. Moreover, the face is adorned with four painted rosettes, one on the brow, one on the chin, and one on each cheek. This seems to show that in the Mycenaean age the faces of the women were tattooed. See Chr. Tsountas, in Πρακτικὰ τῆς Ἀρχαιολογικῆς Ἑταιρίας, 1896 (pub. 1897), pp. 29-31.

From other parts of the Greek world evidence of the wide diffusion of the Mycenaean civilisation continues to pour in. Many more remains of Mycenaean settlements and art have been discovered by Messrs. L. Mariani, A. J. Evans, J. L. Myres, and others in Crete. See L. Mariani, 'Archaeological Researches in Crete,' *Academy*, No. 1191, 2nd March 1895, p. 198 ; A. J. Evans and J. L. Myres, 'A Mycenaean military road in Crete,' *Açademy*, No. 1204, 1st June 1895, p. 469 *sq.* (reprinted in *American Journal of Archaeology*, 10 (1896), pp. 399-403); *Athenaeum*, 22nd June 1895, p. 812 *sq.* ; *Revue archéologique*, 3me Série, 27 (1895), pp. 353-359 ; A. J. Evans, 'Explorations in Eastern Crete,' *Academy*, Nos. 1258, 1259, 1261, 1262, 1264 (June 13, 21, July 4, 18, 1896) (reprinted in *American Journal of Archaeology*, 11 (1896), pp. 449-467). Excavations made for the Trustees of the British Museum in 1895 and 1896 have led to the discovery of two burying-grounds of the Mycenaean period at Curium and Salamis in Cyprus (*American Journal of Archaeology*, 11 (1896), pp. 139-141, 422-424 ; *Athenaeum*, No. 3585, 11th July 1896, p. 74 ; *Journal of Hellenic Studies*, 16 (1896),

p. 341). On the north-eastern coast of Melos excavations made by the British School in May 1896 revealed the remains of a prehistoric fortress or palace, the plan of which in some respects resembles that of the palace at Tiryns. The walls are standing in places to a height of several yards, and in the soil vast quantities of Mycenaean pottery of all stages were found; in the lower strata are traces of prehistoric pottery and a complete layer of flint implements. See *Journal of Hellenic Studies*, 16 (1896), p. 356. In northern Greece three more beehive tombs have been discovered, two in Thessaly at the village of *Marmargiane*, northeast of Larisa, and one near the village of *Goura* in Phthiotis. All three are built of stone, not hewn out of the rock. The one near *Goura*, which by the exertions of the peasants has now been converted into a lime-kiln, contained bones, painted vases, various ornaments of gold and silver, and rings. In the two Thessalian tombs the ornaments found were insignificant, but much pottery came to light of a sort which apparently cannot be classed with Mycenaean ware. The shapes of some of the vases resemble those of the early pottery found in the Cyclades. Most are unpainted, but some exhibit elaborate geometrical patterns painted with lustrous colours. See *Mittheilungen d. arch. Inst. in Athen*, 21 (1896), p. 247. In the island of Salamis, near the modern arsenal, excavations directed by Mr. P. Cavvadias in 1893 laid bare more than a hundred prehistoric graves arranged in seven parallel lines. Each grave consisted of an oblong hole so small that the corpse must have been doubled up in it. In the graves were found some common pottery together with rings, brooches, and spindles of bronze. The only objects of gold discovered were three small spirals of gold wire, which had clearly been used to curl the hair of the dead, since two of them were found on either side of a skull. Two of the graves consisted of round holes in which were deposited urns containing ashes and bones. This fact seems to indicate that the necropolis was constructed at a time when the custom of burying the dead, which prevailed in the Mycenaean age, was giving way to a custom of burning them. See P. Cavvadias, *Catalogue des Musées d'Athènes* (Athens, 1895), p. 25 *sq.* In Caria the researches of Messrs. W. R. Paton and J. L. Myres go to prove that that country, far from being, as Prof. Köhler supposed, the centre from which the Mycenaean civilisation spread over the coasts of the Aegean, felt the influence of that civilisation only towards the close of the Mycenaean age (*Journal of Hellenic Studies*, 16 (1896), p. 265).

The problems suggested by the Mycenaean remains in Greece and elsewhere continue to exercise archaeologists. Some of them have been discussed afresh by Prof. U. Köhler ('Ueber Probleme der griechischen Vorzeit,' *Sitzungsberichte d. k. preuss. Akad. d. Wissen. zu Berlin*, 11. März 1897, pp. 258-274). An attempt has been made by Mr. H. Kluge to decipher the inscriptions; he essays to show that their language is Greek (H. Kluge, *Die Schrift der Mykenier*, Cöthen, 1897). His reading of the inscriptions is not accepted by Mr. Fr. Koepp (*Wochenschrift für classische Philologie*, 16 June 1897, pp. 675-678). Mr. Ch. Belger has discussed the construction of the double circle of slabs which encloses the royal graves on the acropolis of Mycenae, rejecting the theory of Mr. Chr. Tsountas that the circle served to support a barrow heaped over the graves (Ch. Belger, 'Mykenische Studien I., Erbauung und Zerstörung des mykenischen Plattenringes,' *Jahrbuch d. archäolog. Instituts*, 10 (1895), pp. 114-127). Mr. Tsountas has defended his theory and has further adduced evidence to show that at some time after its foundation the citadel of Mycenae was extended both to the east and to the west, the western extension comprising within it the royal graves which down to that time had been outside of the acropolis ('Zu einigen mykenischen Streitfragen,' *Jahrbuch d. arch. Inst.* 10 (1895), pp. 145-147). Controversy still rages round the question of the people who created the Mycenaean civilisation. In an essay read before the French Academy of Inscriptions Mr. W. Helbig has argued that the so-called Mycenaean art is nothing but Phoenician art of the second millennium B.C. Following in the footsteps of Mr. E. Pottier he points out that the monuments of Mycenaean art which must have been executed on the spot where they were found, such as the Gate of the Lions, the sculptured tombstones, and the fresco of the palace at Tiryns, are far inferior in style and execution to the portable objects, such as the inlaid daggers, the ivory handles, the golden seals, the golden vases found at *Vaphio*, etc. ; and from this difference in workmanship he infers that the two sets of objects were made by two different peoples, the former by the native workmen on the spot, the latter by Phoenician craftsmen working either in Phoenicia or in Greece. Amongst the products of Phoenician industry he apparently includes the pottery. See W. Helbig, 'Sur la question mycénienne,' *Mémoires de l'Académie des Inscriptions et Belles-lettres*, vol. 35. pp. 291-373. An abstract of the paper and of the discussion to which it gave rise is printed in the *Comptes Rendus de l'Acad. des Inscriptions et Belles-lettres*, 4me Série, 23 (1895), pp. 237-240, 242 *sq.*, 244-250, in *L'Ami des Monuments*, 9 (1895), pp. 174, 176, 189-196, and in the *American Journal of Archaeology*, 10 (1895), pp. 554-557. Mr. Helbig's theory has been adversely criticised by Mr. J. L. Myres (*Classical Review*, 10 (1896), pp. 350-357). On the other hand it has been on the whole accepted by Mr. H. v. Fritze (*Berliner philolog. Wochenschrift*, 27th March 1897, pp. 399-404). A theory very like that of Mr. Helbig is maintained by Mr. E. Pottier. The only difference of moment between their views would seem to be that Mr. Pottier admits that the characteristic Mycenaean pottery was made by the natives of the Aegean coasts, while Mr. Helbig maintains that it was made and imported by the Phoenicians. See E. Pottier, 'L'orfèvrerie mycénienne,' *Revue des Études grecques*, 7 (1894), pp. 117-132 ; *id., Catalogue des Vases antiques de terre cuite du Musée du Louvre*, Première Partie (Paris, 1896), pp. 181-210. Mr. Helbig finds a confirmation, as he thinks, of his theory in a painting which was discovered a few years ago in a tomb at Thebes in Egypt. It represents a fleet putting in to shore and the mariners landing and trafficking with the natives. According to Mr. Helbig the natives are Egyptians, the foreign mariners are Phoenicians, and among the wares which they are unlading is pottery of the so-called Mycenaean type. See G. Daressy, 'Une flotille

phénicienne,' *Revue archéologique*, 3me Série, 27 (1895), pp. 286-292 ;
W. Helbig, ' Ein ägyptisches Grabmal und die mykenische Frage,'
*Sitzungsberichte d. philosoph. philolog. und d. histor. Classe d. k. b.
Akad. d. Wissen. zu München*, 1896, pp. 539-582.   More recently
the claims of the long-discredited Pelasgians to have been the creators
of the Mycenaean civilisation have been strongly urged by Professor
W. Ridgeway (*Journal of Hellenic Studies*, 16 (1896), pp. 77-119) and
Prof. O. Montelius (*Journal of the Anthropological Institute of Great
Britain and Ireland*, 26 (1897), pp. 254-266).   Under a nominal
agreement, however, the views of these two scholars conceal a fundamental difference, Prof. Montelius maintaining that the Pelasgians,
whom he identifies with the Tyrrhenians and Etruscans, were a foreign
people who migrated from Asia Minor to Greece and thence to Italy,
while Prof. Ridgeway argues that the Pelasgians were a Greek stock and
spoke a Greek language.   The arguments adduced by Prof. Ridgeway
against the view that Mycenaean art was a creation of the Achaeans
are powerful, and his own theory is perhaps the one which best
explains all the facts.   It has been accepted on the whole by Mr. S.
Reinach (*L'Anthropologie*, 8 (1897), p. 25 *sq.*), but more evidence is
required before the theory can be regarded as established, and I understand from my friend that such evidence is forthcoming.

On the strength of an examination of Egyptian chronology Mr. C.
Torr (*Memphis and Mycenae*, Cambridge, 1896) concludes that there is
no sufficient evidence for the early date (from about 1600 B.C. to about
1100 B.C.) now generally assigned to the golden age of Mycenae.   But
his views have not met with acceptance.   See Ed. Meyer, in *Literar-
isches Centralblatt*, 5th December 1896, p. 1756 *sq.* ; J. L. Myres, in
Classical Review, 10 (1896), pp. 447-452.   On the other hand the
generally-received date of the Mycenaean civilisation has been confirmed
by objects of Egyptian manufacture found in the Mycenaean necropolis
at *Enkomi*, near Salamis in Cyprus.   For in the opinion of an expert
these objects belong to the fourteenth and thirteenth centuries B.C.   See
Mr. Flinders Petrie, ' Fresh Mycenaean dating,' *Athenaeum*, No. 3626,
24th April 1897, p. 550 *sq.*

A zoologist, Mr. Fr. Houssay, believes that on the pottery of Mycenae
he has found the birth or at all events the infancy of the famous myth
of the barnacle goose ; but his belief is apparently not shared by
others.   See Fr. Houssay, ' Les théories de la genèse à Mycéne et le
sens zoologiques de certains symboles du culte d'Aphrodite,' *Revue
archéologique*, 3me Série, 26 (1895), pp. 1-27 ; E. Pottier, ' Observations
sur la céramique mycénienne, *ib.* 28, (1896), pp. 23-32.   As to the
mediaeval and modern myth of the barnacle goose, see F. Max Müller,
Lectures on the Science of Language,[6] 2. pp. 585-604.   Still more
recently Mr. Houssay has published further researches into the mythical
conceptions which the Mycenaean people may possibly have entertained
of plants and animals (' Nouvelles recherches sur la faune et la flore des
vases peints de l'époque mycénienne,' *Revue archéologique*, 3me Série,
30 (1897), pp. 81-105).   A Greek scholar has essayed to prove that the
beehive tombs at Mycenae are often alluded to by the Greek tragedians

(S. N. Dragoumes, ' οἱ ἐν Μυκηναῖς Θησαυροί,' *Mittheilungen d. arch. Inst. in Athen*, 20 (1895), pp. 127-160, 371 *sq.*).

The general results of recent researches in Mycenaean art and civilisation have been summarised by Mr. J. L. Myres ('Prehistoric man in the eastern Mediterranean,' *Science Progress*, 5 (1896), pp. 335-359); and Mr. Tsountas's valuable work on this subject, to which many references are made in the text, has been translated, adapted, and enriched with additional matter and fresh illustrations by Prof. J. I. Manatt (Chr. Tsountas and J. Irving Manatt, *The Mycenaean Age*, London, 1897).

So much for recent publications.

I revisited Mycenae 11th and 12th December 1895, and made some notes which may serve to supplement and occasionally correct the description in the text.

In regard to the walls and gates of the citadel it seems not to have been sufficiently observed that the differences in the styles of masonry generally coincide with differences of material; for while the Cyclopean walls are for the most part built of dark limestone, the two gateways and the walls lining the approaches to them are constructed, not only in a totally different style (namely in the ashlar or quadrangular instead of the Cyclopean style), but also of a totally different material, namely of breccia instead of limestone. These differences of style and material seem to point to the conclusion that the existing gateways were built at a later time than the walls and possibly by a different people. In this connexion it is to be observed that the two great beehive tombs known as the Treasury of Atreus and the Tomb of Clytaemnestra are built in the same style and of the same material as the gates of the citadel. This confirms the view that the beehive tombs belong to the later rather than to the earlier period of Mycenaean history. In regard to the pieces of well-jointed polygonal masonry which occur in the walls of the citadel, Dr. Adler is probably right in considering that they are much later repairs and have nothing to do with the true Cyclopean constructions. The so-called tower on the south-west is entirely built of closely-jointed polygonal blocks of breccia; the faces of the blocks are partially smoothed. It is not really a tower, but merely a part of the wall, above the level of which it does not rise, though its height may be about 30 feet. The piece of polygonal wall at the north-east corner of the citadel, referred to in the text (vol. 3. p. 100), is very small; it is interposed in the midst of the true Cyclopean wall. A little to the east of it are a few blocks of regular quadrangular masonry resting on the top of the Cyclopean wall. It should be observed that the builders of the Cyclopean walls, though as a rule they employed the dark limestone, seem not to have wholly rejected the use of breccia; at least on the north-east side of the citadel I observed a large block of breccia in the lowest part of the wall, which is here high and built of the dark limestone.

At the extreme east end of the citadel, facing across a ridge of rocks which runs eastward into the glen, there is a small Cyclopean doorway through the wall, which is here about 7 paces thick. The doorway, which is about 10 feet or so below the top of the wall, is about 1 metre wide and 2 metres high up to the spring of the pointed vault. It seemed, when I saw it in December 1895, to have been only recently excavated.

P. 103 line 18 *sqq.* from foot, **The postern gate** etc.   The postern gate opens to the east.   In both the great blocks of breccia which form the doorposts there are square holes for the reception of the bolts, and in the third great block of breccia which forms the lintel there are two round holes for the sockets or pivots of the door.   Inside of the gate, in the wall on the left-hand side as you enter, there is a small chamber or rather hole for the porter, as at the Lions' Gate.

P. 104 line 12 *sqq.*, **an opening in the circle** etc.   This opening is a regular passage about 4 paces long, paved with three great slabs and flanked on each side by a wall which is composed of three tall upright slabs like those of which the circle itself is built.   Each of these upright slabs is 1.40 metre high.   The existence of this carefully-built passage into the circle seems a strong argument against Mr. Tsountas's view that the space within the circle was filled with a tumulus.   All the graves within the circle are now exposed to view in pits at a considerable depth below the level of the ground.   They are all quadrangular and are lined to a height of some feet with walls built of small unhewn stones.

P. 120 line 19 *sqq.* from top, **the great circular hearth** etc.   The piece of this hearth is now covered up.   Of the women's apartments in the palace hardly any remains exist.

P. 121 line 23 *sqq.* from top, **a complex of buildings** etc.   All the south-west part of the acropolis of Mycenae is crowded with the walls of rooms and passages built of smallish unhewn stones bonded with clay or mortar (I think clay).   In one of these rooms, a little to the south-east of the so-called tower, I found a large block of breccia nearly square, with raised edges and a round basin-like hole at one end ; it is clearly the floor of a bath.

Recent excavations have shown that the whole of the eastern and north-eastern part of the acropolis was similarly closely packed with a labyrinth of rooms all connected with each other and all built of small irregular stones bonded with mortar or clay.   No account of this multitude of apartments has yet, so far as I know, been published (see above, p. 551).   Some of the rooms have stone thresholds and there is stucco on many of the walls.   In some rooms near the glen the walls are very thick.   These buildings have been constructed, in part at least, on an earlier edifice ; for in them at one place, running in an oblique line, is a row of not less than four round bases of columns standing at short intervals of 5 feet or so.   Two of the bases are in one room and two more in an adjoining room.

P. 123 line 20 from top, **was carried along the western slope of the ridge** etc.   Here on the western brow, a good deal south of the conspicuous white-washed chapel of the Panagia which stands on the crest of the ridge, I found a well-preserved piece of the Cyclopean wall of the lower city.   It is about 39 paces long, 1.70 metres high at the highest, and is built of rough, not very large stones which are not fitted together. North of the Panagia chapel is another small piece of the city-wall on the western brow of the ridge ; one course of stones is standing here for a few yards.

P. 124 line 12 *sqq.* from foot, **The passage or dromos** etc. Some of the stones in the walls of the passage or *dromos* are immense. One that I measured was 3.34 metres long. Another is 4 paces long ; another (the custodian told me) is 6.30 metres long. The material of which the walls of the *dromos*, like the walls of the beehive chamber, are constructed is a hard conglomerate or breccia.

P. 127 line 8 *sqq.* from top, **the Tomb of Clytaemnestra** etc. The so-called Tomb of Clytaemnestra, like the Treasury of Atreus, is built of squared blocks of breccia laid in horizontal courses. But the blocks both of the *dromos* and of the beehive chamber are much smaller than those in the Treasury of Atreus. The two bases of half-columns referred to in the text are still standing, one on either side of the doorway of the tomb. Both bases are made of a hard blue stone thickly veined with red. The one on the left-hand side of the doorway still supports the half-column mentioned in the text. This half-column is semicircular, and the flutes are slightly indicated ; the stone seemed to me a greenish-white marble. The triangular space over the doorway is not completely blocked up, as stated in the text ; on the contrary it is quite open.

P. 128 line 16 *sqq.* from top, **six other smaller tombs** etc. On my last visit to Mycenae (11th and 12th December 1895) I visited all the beehive tombs, eight in number, which had then been excavated. A few notes on the six smaller tombs, which have as yet been described in print either slightly or not at all, may not be out of place.

(1) The beehive tomb between the so-called Tomb of Clytaemnestra and the wall of the acropolis had not yet been fully excavated at the time of my visit. The lintel of the doorway is formed of three large blocks. The tomb faces south.

(2) The beehive tomb situated a little to the north of the Lions' Gate has been briefly described in the text (vol. 3. p. 128). The sides of the doorway, which is 5 paces long, are built of breccia ; but the façade of the doorway and the walls of the *dromos* and beehive chamber are built of quite a different stone, perhaps a limestone, which on the outside at least is of a light brown or yellowish colour. This tomb faces north.

(3) Some little way, perhaps 200 yards, to the west of and below the chapel of the Panagia is a beehive tomb facing south. The *dromos,* which is not lined with masonry, is about 14 paces long, and 6 paces wide. The doorway, built of rough masonry, is about 5 paces deep and is closed at its inner end by the remains of a wall of large rough stones. Five large blocks form the lintel, which is in its place. The beehive chamber is of the usual shape. It is large, but is built of small irregular stones.

(4) At a considerable distance, perhaps half or three-quarters of a mile, to the north-west of the chapel of the Panagia is a beehive tomb facing west. The *dromos* is 2 paces wide, but has not yet been fully

excavated. It is hewn out of the rock; the sides are not lined with masonry. The doorway, 3 paces deep, is built of rough stones bonded with clay. Three large slabs form the lintel, which is in its place. The beehive chamber is circular and measures 8 paces in diameter. Its walls are standing to a height of about 10 feet or so, but the upper part of the vault is gone. The masonry of the chamber resembles that of the doorway.

(5) A short way to the north of the preceding tomb is another beehive tomb facing west. The *dromos* is 11 paces long by 3 paces wide; its walls are built of squared blocks laid in regular courses, with mortar in the joints. The material is a brownish limestone (?), the same stone of which beehive tomb No. 2 is mostly built. The doorway is 2 paces wide, 3½ paces deep, and perhaps 13 feet high. It is built in the same style as the walls of the *dromos*. The lintel is formed of three large slabs. The beehive chamber measures 11 paces in diameter. Its walls are built of small squared blocks of the brownish stone but in a style inferior to that of the *dromos*. The lowest course is formed of larger blocks than the others. A grave is cut in the rocky floor.

(6) On the west side of the ridge, just below the chapel of the Panagia, is a beehive tomb facing west; it is near, but a little to the east of, beehive tomb No. 3. The *dromos* is 14 paces long by 3 paces wide; its walls are roughly built of small, rather irregular blocks laid in approximately horizontal courses. The doorway, including both the façade and the passage, is built of good ashlar masonry, the material being the same brownish stone which is employed in tombs Nos. 2 and 5. The passage of the doorway is 2 paces wide, 3 paces long, and perhaps about 12 feet high. Two large slabs form the lintel. The beehive chamber is 8 paces in diameter and is built, like the walls of the *dromos*, in rather poor style. There is clay or mortar in the joints of all the walls. The upper part of the dome is gone.

Of the nine beehive tombs at Mycenae three, including the Tomb of Clytaemnestra, face south; three face west; one faces north; and one (the Treasury of Atreus) faces east. The direction in which the ninth faces (above, p. 552) is not stated. Seemingly there was no fixed rule as to the direction in which the tombs should face.

P. 129 line 7 *sqq.* from foot, **The seventy and odd tombs** etc. I examined between twenty and thirty of these rock-cut tombs, and found that the length of the *dromos* or passage leading through the rock to the tomb varied from 6 to 29 paces, and its width from 1½ to 2½ paces. The estimate of the size of the sepulchral chambers given in the text appears to me, judging from the tombs I visited, to be under the mark. I found the chambers to measure variously from 3 to 8 paces across. A number of them are circular. The general disposition of these rock-cut tombs, in spite of the fact that the chambers are sometimes quadrangular with gable-like roofs, resembles that of the built beehive tombs very closely. We can hardly doubt but that both sets of tombs are the works of the same people and the same period.

P. 138 line 15 *sqq.* from foot, **a beehive tomb —— at Thoricus** etc. For some more particulars as to the two beehive tombs found at Thoricus, see above, p. 523 *sq.*

P. 141 line 2 *sq.* from foot, **some prehistoric tombs** etc. These tombs are to be seen in rows on a hill-side, now occupied by an olive-grove, a little to the east of *Pronia*, which is a suburb of Nauplia. The hill is an eastern continuation of the lofty *Palamidi*, the fortifications of which are seen rising a little to the south-west. I visited a number of these tombs, 9th December 1895. They are roughly and carelessly constructed. The largest of the sepulchral chambers, so far as I observed, measures 6 paces by 5 paces ; the *dromos* or descending passage to it is 22 paces long.

P. 144 line 15 *sq.* from foot, **a barrow at Aphidna** etc. Prof. Wide's discoveries at Aphidna have now been fully described by himself. In August 1894 he found some potsherds of Mycenaean style on the eastern slope of the hill of Aphidna. In October and November of the same year he and his countryman Mr. Kjellberg excavated a large tumulus situated on the south side of the *Charadra* river, about 25 minutes' walk distant from the top of the hill of Aphidna. Within the tumulus they found thirteen ancient graves, of which some had been already plundered. The graves were of various sorts. Some were pit-graves, others were built of great stones or slabs, and others, six in number, consisted of great jars of coarse brownish-red clay. One of these jars contained, besides the bones of the dead, six gold rings, one silver ring, and a number of earthenware pots, most of them made of grey clay. The contents of the graves seem to show that the people buried here were in the bronze period ; for gold, silver, and bronze were found in the graves, together with knives and arrow-heads of flint and beads of transparent stone, but no iron nor any weapons of metal. The pottery discovered is of four sorts :—

(1) Large bowls of coarse, brownish-red clay decorated with geometrical patterns painted in dull colours on a yellowish-white ground : some of these bowls are wheel-made, others hand-made.

(2) Undecorated vases of various sizes made of a coarse brownish-red clay.

(3) Vessels of grey clay decorated occasionally with shallow horizontal grooves. This is the type of which most specimens were found.

(4) Vessels of a reddish-grey clay imperfectly fired, painted black and polished before they were fired. The few specimens of this sort are covered with incised geometrical patterns.

The pottery resembles certain primitive wares found in the Greek islands. The large vessels decorated with geometrical patterns painted in dull colours on a pale ground resemble vessels found in Aegina and other islands, as well as on the mainland at Thoricus and on the Acropolis of Athens. Vases of grey clay like those of Aphidna have been found in the prehistoric settlements at Troy, in the islands (especially Cyprus), and at Thoricus. The incised geometrical patterns have also their analogues in the pottery found in the prehistoric settlements of Troy and the older burying-grounds of the islands, especially Cyprus. Prof. Wide inclines to hold that in the pottery of Aphidna we see an intermediate stage between the oldest pottery with geometrical patterns and the later fully-developed pottery with geometrical patterns which is known as Dipylum ware ; and he conjectures that the custom of adorning pottery with geometrical patterns was not, as is commonly supposed, introduced into Greece by the Dorian conquerors at the close of the Mycenaean period, but had been practised by the aboriginal inhabitants of Greece before the beginning of the Mycenaean era and was only temporarily thrown into the shade by the new-fashioned Mycenaean ware which he supposes to have been imported from the east.   He points out that the finest type of geometrically-decorated pottery—the Dipylum ware—is found in Attica, where the Dorians never were.   As no fragments of Mycenaean pottery were found in the tumulus at Aphidna, Prof. Wide supposes that the people buried in it lived either before, or at latest in the early part of, the Mycenaean period.   See S. Wide, 'Aphidna in Nordattika,' *Mittheil. d. arch. Inst. in Athen*, 21 (1896), pp. 385-409.

P. 161 line 9.   For **north-west** read **north-east.**   The passage leading from the acropolis to the cistern passes under the wall a little to the east of the postern gate but a little to the west of the Cyclopean doorway already described (p. 556 *sq.*).

P. 165 line 6 from top, **the Heraeum.**   Brief reports of the last excavations made by the Americans at the Heraeum are now published (*American Journal of Archaeology*, 10 (1895), pp. 238 *sq.*, 413 *sq.*, 543-547 ; *Fourteenth Annual Report of the American School of Classical Studies at Athens*, 1894-95, pp. 37-48), but the substance of these reports has already, thanks to the kindness of Prof. Waldstein, been embodied in the third volume of this work.   More of the inscriptions have also been edited (*American Journal of Archaeology*, 11 (1896), pp. 42-61) ; one of them (No. 12), which seems to date from a time not later than 500 B.C., contains the earliest known mention of the four Doric tribes.   I visited the Heraeum 10th December 1895, and made a few notes, some of which are given below.

P. 167 line 4 from top, **a piece of an ancient wall** etc.   This piece of wall, 17 paces long, runs east and west parallel to the southern face of the terrace, from the edge of which it is distant 13 paces.   It is .45 metre high.

P. 167 line 7 from top, **portions of a pavement** etc.   The pavement is preserved almost entire on the south side of the terrace, and large portions of it exist both at the eastern and western ends of the terrace.

P. 174.   Above the eastern portion of the North Colonnade I observed three quadrangular chambers with walls built of fine ashlar masonry ; they are in a line with the dwellings of the priestesses, but farther to the east and a little lower down.   In the easternmost and largest of the chambers there are three square bases of columns, made of white limestone, in a row ; a drum of a column stands on one of them.   In the middle of the central chamber there is also a base of a column.

P. 174 line 23 from top, **another Cyclopean wall.**   A good many yards to the east of this small piece of Cyclopean wall there is another piece of wall, forming a right angle, which served to support, at a slightly lower level, an extension of the upper terrace to the east.   On its eastern face the wall, which is constructed almost entirely of large squared blocks laid in horizontal courses, is 12 paces long and about 2.50 metres high.

P. 174 line 14 from foot, **supported on the east and south by strong walls.**   These walls are built of great squared blocks of conglomerate laid in horizontal courses.   At the south-east angle eight courses of masonry are preserved, giving a height of about 5 metres (16 ft. 5 in.).

P. 175 line 10 *sq.* from top, **remains of what seem to have been tables or couches extending along the walls.**   I found these remains in the central chamber only.   They consist of blocks of stone .70 metre high fitted into the wall and projecting .42 metre from it.   The interval between the blocks is 1.24 metres.   On the top of each block are four square holes, for the purpose perhaps of attaching a seat or table. Further, in the most westerly of the three chambers there are square cuttings in the wall in which similar blocks were probably inserted.

P. 175 line 11 *sqq.* from top, **The entrance to the building was in the north wall of the most westerly of the three chambers.**   Rather it was in the north wall at the end of a passage between the central and the western chamber.

P. 175 line 13 *sq.* from top, **with some drums of columns** etc.   I saw only one such drum in its place, namely at the north-east corner of the colonnade ; and there is only one place, so far as I could see, in which the wall of the West Building is standing to a height of several courses.

P. 175 line 22 *sq.* from top, **the ruins of an early structure.**   The edifice is composed of two long rows of quadrangular halls and chambers side by side ; its greatest length is from east to west.   The walls are roughly built.

P. 175 line 12 *sq.* from foot, **on four or five there are still standing drums of fluted Doric columns.**   The number of bases on which drums are standing is four, not five.   The diameter of the drums is .83 metre.   The number of fallen drums of the easternmost column is four, not three, as stated in the text, and they lie behind, not in front of, the base of the column.

P. 176 line 18 *sq.*, **another colonnade which extended eastwards for a considerable distance.**   The square bases of the eight columns (there were no more) of this colonnade have been found in a row.   Each base is about .90 metre square.   The interval between them is about 4 paces.

P. 183 line 14 from top, **the marriage of Zeus and Hera**   A fragment of the early Greek prose writer Pherecydes on this subject has recently been discovered in a papyrus.   The passage had been already known in part from Clement of Alexandria (*Strom.* vi. pp. 741, 767 ed. Potter).   See Grenfell and Hunt, *New classical fragments and other Greek and Latin papyri* (Oxford, 1897), p. 23 ; H. Weil, ' Un nouveau fragment de Phérécyde de Syros,' *Revue des Études grecques*, 10 (1897), pp. 1-9; H. Diels, 'Zur Pentemychos des Pherekydes,' *Sitzungsberichte der k. preuss. Akad. d. Wissen. zu Berlin*, 25th February 1897, pp. 144-156. I hope to discuss the fragment elsewhere. Meantime I will merely point out that the clue to explain the "winged oak" which has so much exercised scholars is probably furnished by the images of oak-wood dressed as brides at the Boeotian festival of the Daedala (Pausanias, ix. 3).

P. 193 line 19 from top, **Cleobis and Biton.** We know from Herodotus (i. 31) that statues of these two robust and pious youths were dedicated at Delphi; and there, between the Treasury of the Athenians and the Treasury of the Siphnians, the recent French excavations have brought to light a pair of twin statues which Mr. Homolle, who at first took them for images of Apollo, would now identify as the portraits of Cleobis and Biton. They represent two square-built, broad-shouldered muscular men with great heads, bull necks, and brawny arms glued to their sides. The faces, with their great goggle staring eyes, are dull, heavy, and expressionless, relieved, however, by a touch of good humour. The hair is bound by a ribbon, below which it escapes in six or seven curls that hang down on the shoulders. From the stiff archaic style of the figures Mr. Homolle would date them about 580 B.C. They belong to the Argive school of sculpture. A few letters (. . . μέδης) of the name of the Argive sculptor may still be read on one of them. See Th. Homolle, in *Bulletin de Corresp. hellénique*, 18 (1894), p. 184 *sq.*; *id.*, in *Gazette des Beaux-Arts*, Décembre 1894, pp. 444-446, and *ib.* Avril 1895, pp. 321-324.

P. 195 line 22 *sq.* from top, a **wall built of great polygonal blocks.** The ancient polygonal masonry of this wall is preserved at the two ends, but the intermediate portion is to a great extent modern or at least much later; some very large blocks, however, of the original wall remain under these later repairs. In the places where the ancient wall is well preserved it is built of large, well-cut, and well-jointed polygonal blocks. The height of the wall is about 3.40 metres. At the north and south ends it makes a short return westward to support the terrace in these directions. On the last block at the north end of the front wall are carved a relief and an inscription, both much defaced. A few yards to the south is another inscription cut on the face of the wall. I was able to distinguish the following letters

ΔΩΝΤΑ

ΥΣ[Ι]Ο

but the letters in the second line are doubtful. The semicircular niche or seat cut in the rock at the back of the terrace is 2.17 metres wide. It occupies the innermost point of a quadrangular recess, some 12 paces deep and 8 paces wide at the narrowest, which has been cut out of the rock at the back of the terrace. On the top of the rock-walls both at the sides and back of the recess stand walls built of small stones and mortar, and faced on the outside with thin bricks laid flat. This terrace with the rock-hewn recess and semicircular niche at its back is distant some 150 yards or so to the north of the theatre.

P. 195 line 6 from foot, **a theatre** etc. On revisiting the theatre of Argos, 10th December 1895, I found that a trench dug from the middle of the auditorium across the orchestra had revealed short portions of other rows of seats, also cut out of the rock, below the tiers of seats which were visible before. The excavations have also laid bare pieces of several lines of stage-buildings, the foundations being constructed of small stones and the upper walls (so far as they exist) of squared blocks of white limestone. Three steps, also made of white limestone, lead down from the back of one of the lines of stage-buildings. But of a subterranean passage leading from the stage to the orchestra I saw nothing. At the south-eastern corner of the theatre are the remains of a quadrangular building with an apse at the west end. As it stands, the building is about 20 yards long from east to west by 13 yards broad from north to south. The walls are faced with thin bricks laid flat, but the core is of small stones and mortar. The north wall is standing to a height of many feet, perhaps 40 or 50; in its upper part it shows the spring of a vault, proving that the building had a vaulted roof.

P. 210 line 13 *sqq.* from foot, **the water of the Erasinus** etc. I visited the springs of the Erasinus, 8th December 1895, and found that the description of the spot given in the text, though in general accurate enough, needs to be corrected on some points. The modern highroad from Argos to Lerna does not go near the springs, but passes at a considerable distance, perhaps a mile and a half, to the east of them. To reach the springs we turn off from the highroad and proceed westward through a beautiful avenue of fine silver poplars, plane-trees, and oleanders. The spring, issuing from under rocks at the foot of the high rugged mountain, forms at once a large and clear but shallow pool in which water-plants of a vivid green grow thickly. The pool is dammed up by a wall pierced by a number of arches through which the water issues to form two streams flowing in different directions. A fine plane-tree grows beside the pool, and the streams lower down are shaded by trees. Just above the spring there are two caves, a large one and a small one, side by side. A staircase leads up to them. The small cave to the right has been converted into a little chapel of the Panagia. The large cave to the left has two mouths. One of them is beside the mouth of the small cave; indeed the two mouths are closed by one and the same wall, and the entrances to the caves are through two doors side by side in the wall. The other mouth of the large cave opens a few feet further to the left. This large cave has several branches. The main cave runs straight into the mountain; it is long, and with its high-arched roof, encrusted with stalactites, resembles the nave of a Gothic cathedral. A few feet inward from the mouth of the cave a branch strikes off to the left at right angles to the main cave. It is shorter than the main cave, but has, like it, a high-arched roof. Near its end, on the left side, there is a low, narrow, pitch-dark opening. With a light I crept into it and saw that at its further extremity there was a crevice some 18 inches or so high descending apparently into the bowels of the mountain. Further, on the right-hand side of this branch-cave there opens another and longer branch which runs parallel to the main cave and communicates with it at its inner end. At this inner end there is a window-like opening to the upper air through which a little daylight penetrates into the dark cave, spreading a dim twilight around. Outside of the cave, in front of its mouth, is built a sort of summer-house or covered shed, with white-washed walls and pillars and seats round it. The spot, I was told, is a favourite one for holiday-makers from Argos in summer.

P. 213 line 1 *sqq.*, the **Pyramid of Cenchreae** etc. I visited the Pyramid of Cenchreae 8th December 1895; and as my notes partly supplement the descriptions given of this interesting and mysterious building by previous writers, I will venture to reproduce them in full. A bridle-path leads westward from the springs of the Erasinus to the pyramid in about half an hour. The building occupies a knoll to the left (south) of the bridle-path; but another bridle-path runs on the other side of it, still further to the south. The two paths probably meet in the valley higher up. The pyramid is square, and its sides face north, west, south, and east. It rests in part on the native rock of the knoll, which thus forms a basement a few feet high, especially on the south side. Where this natural basement is wanting, its place is supplied by a base of masonry from .60 metre to 1.65 metres high, according to the inequalities of the ground. The sides of this base of masonry are perpendicular, whereas the sides of the pyramid, of course, slope inward. As it stands, the north face of the pyramid is exactly 12 metres long, but some blocks have fallen at the western corner; perhaps the original length of the north face was 12.50 metres. The east face of the pyramid, at the level of the ground, is about 14 metres long. At its south-east corner the pyramid is standing to a height of about 3.20 metres. On the southern face the wall is about 4 metres high, and on the east and north sides the walls are standing to about the same absolute height, though, as the soil is here higher, the height of the walls above the ground is not so great. On the west face the wall is more ruinous. All these outer walls are built of large well-cut blocks of a dark hard stone. On the east and south sides the blocks are mostly quadrangular; but on the west and north sides there are many polygonal blocks. In many of the joints there is mortar, which seemed to me original. Probably there was mortar in all the joints at first, though it has now disappeared from many. At the south-east corner of the pyramid a right angle is, as it were, cut out, and in this right angle, facing east, is a doorway 1.20 metres wide surmounted by a pointed arch, which is formed by the convergence of the stones on both sides. On the right-hand side of the doorway there are visible in the wall the two square holes in which the bolts of the door were shot. From this doorway a passage of the same breadth leads to the opposite (west) wall of the pyramid. At the end of this passage is a doorway on the right leading into a chamber. In this inner doorway the large lower blocks of the stone doorposts are preserved on both sides; in the right-hand doorpost are two square holes in which the bolts were shot. The stone threshold of the doorway is also preserved, but the lintel is gone.   The chamber into which this doorway opens is 7 metres square.   In it there are remains of partition-walls dividing the chamber into four apartments, one large apartment occupying all the southern part of the chamber, and three small apartments in a row occupying the smaller northern portion of it.   But these partition-walls are perhaps modern.   The inner walls of the chamber seemed to me to show traces of much later, if not modern repairs; in particular the mortar looks fresh and brown, quite different from the grey old mortar of the outer walls.   The small apartment in the north-east corner appears to have been used in Roman or mediaeval times as a cistern; for its walls up to a height of .70 metre are lined with a casing of small stones, bricks, and mortar, the whole being coated with stucco, of which there are remains in one of the angles.   Moreover, just above this casing there is a square hole cut through the north wall of the pyramid; a water-pipe may have been passed through this hole to feed the cistern.   In the large apartment I found lying some remains of an object which may serve to throw some light on the purpose of the pyramid.   The remains consist, first, of two semicircular blocks of breccia which together formed a sort of shallow basin 1 metre in diameter.   In the centre of the basin is a circular elevation which is at present only about 5 centimetres high.   But its top is rough and uneven as if a piece had been broken off; and beside the broken basin I found, secondly, a small circular slab or disc of breccia of the same diameter (.35 metre) as the circular elevation in the basin.   It may be conjectured that this circular elevation in the basin was a pedestal and supported a votive offering; for in shape the basin resembles some inscribed stands for votive offerings which have been found in the sanctuary of Aesculapius at Epidaurus (below, p. 571 *sq.*).   If this conjecture should prove right, it would go to show that the pyramid served a religious purpose, that in fact it was consecrated to the worship of some divinity or deceased person or persons.   In the latter case the pyramid may very well have been, as Ross and Clark suggested, one of the common tombs (*poluandria*) mentioned by Pausanias.

P. 219 line 7 *sq.* from top, **Around the lower citadel** etc.   I estimated the height of the wall of the lower citadel at 30 feet on the west, 18 to 20 feet on the north, and 23 feet at the northern end of the east side.   On the east side the wall is ruinous in some places.

P. 221 line 9, **a long narrow staircase.**   This staircase is 7 feet wide, so it is hardly fair to call it narrow.

P. 224 line 3 from top, **the round stone bases still remain in their places.**   Only three of them were visible when I revisited Tiryns, 7th December 1895; and the circular hearth itself, enclosed by the pillars, had also disappeared or been covered up.

P. 224 line 15 from foot, **its foundation shows a rectangle** etc.   These foundations, or rather lower parts of walls, are built in a very poor style exactly resembling that of the walls of the palace; the stones are small, rough, and irregular.   It is difficult to believe that they are the walls of a temple.

P. 231 line 11 *sqq.* from top, **Midea** etc.   I visited the ruins of

Midea 7th December 1895, and my notes of them may supplement and perhaps correct the description in the text. The ruins are situated on a high pointed rocky hill which rises abruptly from the eastern side of the plain of Argos, about a mile to the south-east of the village of *Dendra*. The hill, which may be about 800 feet high, is rocky and precipitous on the west and south, but descends to the north in a long gradual slope or series of terraces. At its northern foot, about half a mile from *Dendra*, is the little chapel of St. Thomas perched upon some rocks. The summit of the mountain is a narrow rocky ridge, highest on the west, from which it gradually descends eastwards, expanding as it descends. At first, on the west, it is only about 12 paces broad and is so covered with rugged rocks that clearly no building ever occupied it. Further to the east there are some small level platforms where the rock seems to have been cleared away and smoothed to make room for buildings. Still further to the east the ridge ends in a terrace about 60 paces long from north to south by 11 paces wide from east to west. This terrace, probably in part artificial, is supported on the east by a wall of Cyclopean masonry 22 feet thick, built of huge polygonal almost unhewn stones which are roughly dressed on their outer surface and have small stones inserted in their interstices. The height of the wall, so far as I could estimate it, varies from 9 to 18 feet. Beyond and below the terrace to the north the Cyclopean wall continues to run as a fortification-wall in a north-west-northerly direction. It is here preserved on both faces. The thickness is the same as before (22 feet). On its inner face the wall is from 5 to 7 feet high; on its outer face it is from 13 to 18 and 20 feet high in places. After running northward in this direction for 100 yards or so the wall turns to the west, and is carried in this direction across the northern slope of the hill. Here it again serves as a support to a terrace; its height varies from 5 to 12 feet. In some places the old wall has tumbled down hill and been replaced by a low wall of small stones. This wall of small stones is clearly a modern terrace-wall built to support the soil, which at present grows corn. Towards its western end the wall is quite ruinous—a mere mass of tumbled stones. On the western face of the hill a piece of the Cyclopean wall may be seen which is 11 paces long and about 12 feet high. Like the wall on the eastern side of the hill it is built of great stones which are roughly hewn on their outer face and have small stones inserted in their interstices. From this point the line of wall is again traceable running up hill in a south-easterly direction for 100 yards or so till it ends at the rocks which on the western face of the hill, at its southern and highest point, render fortification needless. On its inner face this wall, towards its termination at the rocks, is from 3 to 5 feet high; on its outer face it is merely a heap of fallen stones. Thus the fortifications of Midea, so far as I observed them, formed three sides of a quadrangle on the northern slope of the hill, the fourth side of the quadrangle being occupied by the crest of rocks on the southern summit of the hill. My observations, in short, entirely confirm the sketch-plan of the fortress published by Messrs. Conze and Michaelis (*Annali dell'*

Instituto, 33 (1861), Tav. d' agg. F. 1). If there were, as has been asserted, four separate lines of defence, one above the other, I certainly did not see them. I did indeed observe, lower down the northern slope, a line of wall encircling the hill about two-thirds of the way up it. But this wall was clearly modern, being nothing but a heap of rough stones piled one on the top of the other without any attempt at fitting them together. Within the ancient fortification-walls and again lower down on the northern slope of the hill there is a considerable quantity of potsherds strewed about, some of which are painted in the Mycenaean style.

P. 232 line 18 *sqq.* from foot, **one of the best-preserved fortresses** etc. I visited the two ancient fortresses now called *Kasarmi* and *Kastraki*, 6th December 1896, and will describe them from my notes.

The small fortress of *Kasarmi* is situated about ten minutes' walk north, but in full view of, the road which leads from Nauplia to *Ligourio* and the Epidaurian sanctuary of Aesculapius. Its distance from Nauplia by road is 13 kilometres ($8\frac{1}{2}$ miles). The place is a small hill, defended by high rocky precipices on the west and by lower precipitous rocks on the north ; its top measures only about 70 yards from north to south by 50 yards from east to west. Round this little top run the remains of the ancient walls, built of massive and well-jointed polygonal masonry. On the eastern side of the hill the wall is preserved unbroken to a height varying from 6 to 18 feet, but most of it is nearer 18 than 6 feet high. The height of the southern wall is from 6 to 12 feet, but there are two gaps in it. On the north and west the wall, being built on the top of precipitous rocks, is low ; indeed it seems to have been discontinued above the highest precipices on the west. The thickness of the wall, at least at the north-east corner where I measured it, is 6 feet. Three round towers project from the south-western, the south-eastern, and the north-eastern angles of the fortress. The tower at the south-east angle is about 18 feet high, but only the first three or four courses of it are built of the ancient polygonal masonry ; all the upper part is mediaeval, being constructed of small stones, bricks, and mortar. The tower at the north-east angle is standing in part to a height of 12 feet, but it is partially ruinous and a square mediaeval tower has been built on the top of it. From this tower a staircase, of which eight steps are preserved, descended northward along the top of the wall (the tower stands a few feet south of the north-east angle of the fortress). The tower at the south-west angle, built of massive polygonal masonry, is standing in part to a height of 8 feet. In the eastern wall, near its northern end, there is a doorway roofed over by the wall and at present blocked up at its inner end. The top of the doorway is now only 4 feet above the ground, its lower part having been filled up by the soil. The "structure somewhat in the style of the covered galleries at Tiryns," of which mention is made in the text, may be seen inside of the fortress and close to its eastern wall. It is obviously neither more nor less than a cistern, and the comparison of it to the covered galleries at Tiryns is absurd. It is 8 paces long and 9 feet wide ; its present depth is 4 ft. 6 in., but it is partly filled up with earth so that its full depth does not appear. The sides, coated with stucco of which some pieces still adhere to the stones, converge as if to meet overhead.   No doubt the cistern was originally vaulted over.

Here may be mentioned an ancient bridge, apparently of the Mycenaean age, which spans the bed of a small stream about a quarter of a mile to the west of *Kasarmi*. The bridge, distant only some 20 or 30 yards from the carriage-road, is built of huge rough almost unhewn blocks.   Three courses of these great stones on each side constitute the arch ; they project inwards one above the other and are united at the top by roughly triangular blocks which formed the keystone, thus : The clear height of the bridge is about 6 feet.   The width of the bridge, measured along the bed of the stream, is 6 paces. This gives the breadth of the ancient road which the bridge supported.

The small quadrangular fortress of *Kastraki* in size and disposition closely resembles that of *Kasarmi*.   Its situation is correctly described in the text (vol. 3. p. 233).   It occupies the summit of a small rocky hill some three-quarters of a mile or so to the north of the carriage-road from Nauplia to *Ligourio*.   Just below the hill on the north, in the hollow between it and the towering rocky pinnacle of Mount Arachnaeus, runs the road from *Ligourio* to Argos.   The summit of the hill, now overgrown with lentisk bushes, is but small, measuring only some 60 or 70 yards square.   High precipitous rocks on a great part of the north and west faces of the hill rendered fortification in these directions almost needless, and accordingly the traces of walls here are comparatively few. But on the south and east the walls are well preserved.   They are somewhat rudely built of blocks of various shapes and sizes which are only roughly fitted together, the crevices being filled with small stones.   The south wall is 7 feet thick and, though partly ruinous, is standing to a height of 18 or 20 feet for a distance of about 20 yards.   The east wall is also partly ruinous, but a considerable piece of it is preserved to a height of 16 feet.   Four towers project from the four angles of the fortress.   The two towers at the north-western and south-western angles are round ; the two at the north-eastern and south-eastern angles are square. The height of the tower at the south-west angle, like that of the wall which adjoins it on the east, is about 20 feet.   This tower is built of polygonal masonry in a better and more careful style than the wall.   The tower at the north-western angle, perched on the top of high precipitous rocks, is built of massive blocks.   In the southern wall of the fortress, facing south-west, is the principal gate.   Great pains have obviously been taken to render it impregnable.   It is placed in a sort of recess, the sides of which are flanked on the right by a round tower and on the left by the wall of the fortress.   The gateway, about 7 ft. 8 in. wide, leads into a quadrangular court about 7 paces long, and at the inner end of this court there is a second gateway facing the first and of the same width.   The stone doorposts of this inner gateway are preserved ; there is a square hole on the inner face of each, as a picturesque and obliging shepherd was good enough to point out to me.   The tower which flanks the outer gateway is built of large rough stones : the outer faces of the stones are rudely cut into polygons, smoothed, and fitted together.   In

the west wall of the fortress there is a small postern with remains of
steps leading down from it through the rocks.

P. 233 line 21 *sq.* from top, **a chapel of St. Marina** etc. The
chapel, which seems to be Byzantine, stands about a quarter of a mile
to the north of the carriage-road, just at the foot of the rocky slope
of Mount Arachnaeus, which here attains its highest point. Faded
paintings adorn the walls. The dome is supported by four columns, all
of which contain remains of ancient Ionic columns. In one of the
columns there is a complete shaft of an Ionic column measuring about
18 inches in diameter. In the other three columns there are three
Ionic capitals, and one of the columns has besides the drum of an
Ionic column. Some 200 or 300 yards to the east of the church, in a
bare stony field at the foot of the rocky slope of Mount Arachnaeus, I
found the remains of the ancient pyramid mentioned in the text. It is
square and measures 14 paces on each side. Only the lower part
remains to a height of about 6 feet at most. It is built of large massive
blocks of a dark hard limestone—the native rock which crops up all
over the adjoining slope of Mount Arachnaeus. The blocks, which are
mostly polygonal, are well fitted together and their faces are smoothed.
In several places, especially at the angles, the inward slope of the sides
is clearly seen. At one angle the wall, slanting inward, measures 6 feet
from the ground to the top, though it is composed of two blocks only.
One of these blocks is 5 feet long. Another, on a different side of the
pyramid, is about 5 feet long and 3 feet high. I did not observe any
trace of a door or window in the pyramid.

P. 234 line 9 from foot, **one of the goats** etc. A bronze coin of
Epidaurus now in the Cabinet des Medailles at Paris exhibits the
suckling of the infant Aesculapius by the goat and the discovery of goat
and infant by the goatherd. It is figured in the work of Messrs. A.
Defrasse and H. Lechat, *Épidaure : Restauration et description des
principaux monuments du Sanctuaire d'Asclépios,* p. 25.

P. 235 line 13 from foot, **Lebene in Crete.** A number of inscriptions
from the sanctuary of Aesculapius at Lebene have been found in recent
years, almost all of them at the village of *Miamou* in Crete. Some of
them record cures, others dedications, while others again relate to the
administration of the sanctuary and other subjects. See J. Baunack,
in *Philologus,* 48 (1889), pp. 401-404 ; F. Halbherr, in *Museo Italiano
di antichità classica,* 3 (1890), pp. 719-734, Inscriptions 170-182 ;
J. Zingerle, ' Heilinschrift von Lebena,' *Mittheilungen d. arch. Inst. in
Athen,* 21 (1896), pp. 67-92. The fame of the sanctuary of Aesculapius
at Lebene is attested by Philostratus who says that people flocked to it
from all quarters of Crete just as people flocked from all parts of Asia
to the sanctuary of Aesculapius at Pergamus ; and he adds that many
Libyans crossed over to it from Africa (*Vit. Apollon.* iv. 34).

P. 236 line 3 from top, **The sacred grove of Aesculapius** etc.
Some of the principal buildings in the Epidaurian sanctuary of Aesculapius have been conjecturally restored by Mr. A. Defrasse in a hand-
somely-illustrated work to which Mr. H. Lechat has contributed an
explanatory text (*Épidaure : Restauration et description des principaux*

SANCTUARY OF AESCULAPIUS
AT EPIDAURUS

GROUND PLAN

Showing the Excavations to December 1895

BY J. G. FRAZER

Scale of Yards

0 10 20 30 40 50 60 70 80 90 100

Metres

0 10 20 30 40 50 60 70 80 90 100

GRAND PORTAL

Road to Epidaurus

Well

NORTH CLOISTERS

SOUTH CLOISTERS

EAST
BATHS

Subterranean
Aqueduct

TEMPLE OF
APHRODITE

BATHS OF
ANTONINUS

GREAT CISTERN

ROMAN HOUSE

TEMPLE OF AESCULAPIUS

TEMPLE OF ARTEMIS

ROTUNDA

Great Colonnade

West Colonnade

PORTAL OF GYMNASIUM

MUSIC HALL

ORCHESTRA

STAGE

75½ Yards

GYMNASIUM

83 Yards

STARTING LINE

S T A D I U M

GOAL

Stanford's Geographical Estab! London.

London : Macmillan & C.º L.ᵈ

monuments du Sanctuaire d'Asclépios, Paris, 1895). The book has been criticised by Mr. Ch. Chipiez (*Revue archéologique*, 3me Série, 28 (1896), pp. 38-59, 380-382), to whom Mr. Lechat has replied (*ib.* pp. 369-379). To the inscriptions found in the sacred precinct and published by Mr. Cavvadias in his work *Fouilles d'Épidaure*, vol. 1 (Athens, 1893), thirty-two additional inscriptions have been added by Mr. Chr. Blinkenberg, who has also corrected and added to the copies of the inscriptions already published by Mr. Cavvadias. See Chr. Blinkenberg, 'Les Inscriptions d'Épidaure,' *Nordisk Tidsskrift for Filologi*, Tredie Raekke, 3 (1895), pp. 153-178.

I revisited the sanctuary of Aesculapius near Epidaurus, 4th-6th December 1895, and found that the continued excavations of the Greek Archaeological Society had laid bare many buildings which at the time of my former visit (1890) were still buried under the soil and which on the plan published by Mr. Cavvadias and reproduced in the third volume of this work are represented either in outline merely or not at all. That plan, indeed, and the descriptions hitherto given convey no idea of the extent of the sanctuary, which, if we reckon it from the theatre to the great northern portal in the one direction and to the western extremity of the stadium in the other, far exceeds in size both the Olympic and the Delphic sanctuaries. In default of an authoritative plan and description I venture to supplement the account given in my third volume by reproducing the substance of my notes and illustrating them by a sketch-plan (pl. viii.) in which I have embodied the results of my own rough measurements and of some information courteously communicated to me by Mr. Koromantsos, the superintendent of the works. Mr. Koromantsos was good enough to accompany me over the scene of the excavations and to correct some misapprehensions into which, before entrusting myself to his guidance, I had fallen. I gladly avail myself of this opportunity of thanking him for his kindness and patience.

Opposite the theatre and distant from it some 150 yards or so to the north-west, there has been excavated a very large building of which mention has already been made (vol. 3. p. 255). The edifice, which does not appear on the sketch-plan, is of a square shape and measures 88 paces on each side. It is enclosed by walls of polygonal masonry 3 ft. 4 in. thick and at present 2 feet high. There are two entrances in the north wall and two in the south ; the latter, each about 12 feet wide, would seem to have been the principal entrances. Internally the building is divided into four quadrangular sections each consisting of a central court surrounded by a colonnade with eighteen chambers opening off the colonnade, namely five chambers on each of two sides and four chambers on each of the two others. The total number of chambers was thus seventy-two. A great many of the stone thresholds of the rooms are preserved. On the walls of one chamber I observed a thick coat of stucco. In the building may be seen some architectural fragments, including *geisa* with their mutules and *guttae*, and pieces of small fluted Doric columns ; one drum which I measured was 19 inches in diameter. Other objects of interest lying about in the building are some stands for votive offerings in the shape of shallow stone basins resting on cylindrical, pillar-like pedestals. Pedestal and basin together are hewn out of a single block of stone and are about 2 ft. 6 in. high ; the diameter of the basin is also about 2 ft. 6 in. At first I took these stands to be wash-basins, but afterwards in the sanctuary proper of Aesculapius I found similar stands with inscriptions of which one at least is dedicatory. The large build-ing which has just been described is believed to be a gymnasium ; for it is known from an inscription that there were two gymnasiums, and one of them has been found near the stadium. Accordingly we may provisionally call this large building opposite the theatre the East Gymnasium.

The other gymnasium, which for the sake of distinction we may call the West Gymnasium, lies about 100 yards south of the temple of Aescula-pius and about the same distance to the east of the stadium. It has been already briefly described (vol. 3. p. 238), but a few more particulars, extracted from my journal, may here be given. The building is in the form of a great quadrangle, measuring 83 paces from north to south by 75 or 76 paces from east to west. Its walls, both outer and inner, are beautifully built of solid masonry without any core of rubble. They are 2 ft. 3 in. thick, and are standing to a uniform height of 2 ft. 6 in. ; the top of the wall is accurately levelled. Only one course is standing. The blocks are from 3 to over 6 feet long ; on the outer side they bulge and are only roughly hewn. One block is 6 ft. 10 in. long. On the east side of the building is an entrance about $12\frac{1}{2}$ feet wide. Internally the gymnasium seems to have consisted of a great open central court enclosed on each side by a single row of quadrangular apartments ; but at the time of my visit (December 1895) the south side of the gymnasium, with the exception of the outer wall, had not yet been excavated. In some of the rooms the stone thresholds of the doorways are preserved. The chambers on the north side are much shallower than those on the east and west sides, because a deep colonnade ran on the inner side of them from east to west. In this colonnade the athletes may have taken exercise in rainy weather.

The greater part of the central court of the gymnasium is now occupied by the ruins of an Odeum or Music Hall, of which a brief notice has already been given (vol. 3. p. 238). The auditorium, the stage, and the walls of the stage-buildings to a certain height are pre-served. They are built of thin flat bricks. The auditorium, which faces west, is 21 paces broad. I counted eight or nine tiers of seats, but as they are ruinous it is not easy to be sure of their number. A single passage leads up through the auditorium. The stage is nearly 18 feet deep from front to back. Three staircases lead up to it, one at the middle and two at the sides. In the front of the stage are also two semicircular niches, one on each side of the central staircase. The front wall of the stage is standing to a height of 25 inches, which must have been very nearly its full height, as is proved by the level of the two doorways which open on the stage, one at each end. The back-wall of the stage is standing in part to a height of 6 feet ; it is pierced with three doorways giving access to a long hall or series of rooms at the back of the stage. Thus the number of doors opening on the stage was five. The two at the ends lead into two quadrangular rooms, which communicate with the long hall at the back of the stage. Both *parodoi* are preserved. At the back of the auditorium there is a set of six chambers arranged in a row from north to south ; in three of them there are doors at the back (east side) leading out of the Music Hall. These chambers give access to a curved passage at the back of, and parallel to, the seats of the auditorium. At either end of the passage are remains of a staircase leading up to the seats.

Of the grand portal or propylaeum which leads into the gymnasium from the north a great part of the pavement is preserved ; it is constructed of great slabs of stone 4 ft. 8 in. square. A ramp, which is also well preserved, leads up to it from the north.

The large building marked G on the plan in the third volume (p. 237) has now been fully excavated. It lies immediately to the north-east of the great portal of the West Gymnasium and to the south-east of the temple of Artemis. In form the edifice is a quadrangle measuring 37 paces from north to south by 31 paces from east to west. The outer face of its west wall is built of large slabs of stone 2 ft. 7 in. high in a style which at first sight resembles that of the finely-built walls of the West Gymnasium. But a closer inspection of them seemed to me to show that the blocks had been brought from elsewhere, many of them perhaps from the West Gymnasium at the time when it was partly demolished to make room for the Music Hall. The inner face of this west wall is mostly built of small stones and mortar, and so are all the inner walls of the building. The outer walls on the north and east, as well as the west wall, are well preserved to the height of a few feet, but they are evidently constructed for the most part out of materials taken from older and better buildings. In the west wall is the chief entrance, which leads into a square central court with four square bases arranged at the angles. The northern part of the building, opening off this central court, was perhaps a covered colonnade ; many pieces of columns, 21 inches in diameter, are standing in it. The other three sides of the central court—west, east, and south—are lined with a series of small chambers ; on the south side this row of small chambers is two deep, and one of the rooms is circular. In the southern wall there is a small entrance, from which a passage leads between the little chambers to the central court. This building is believed to be the Colonnade of Cotys mentioned by Pausanias. See vol. 3. p. 257.

The quadrangular building marked E on the plan, immediately to the north of the temple of Artemis (vol. 3. p. 237), has now been fully excavated. Its arrangement, so far as revealed by the foundations, is indicated on the accompanying plan. All its walls, both inner and outer, are well built of ashlar masonry ; the building seems to belong to the good Greek period. Its west front appears to have been a portico or colonnade. A small room about 10 feet square, opening off the north end of the portico, contains a pavement of stone with a gutter running all round it. This gutter is supposed, as we have seen (vol. 3. p. 236), to have been meant to receive the blood of victims sacrificed in the chamber. At the entrance of the chamber on the west is a stone step or small basement on which the sacrificing priest may have stood.

About 100 yards to the north-east of this building some Roman baths have been excavated in recent years. To distinguish them from the Baths of Antoninus which face them on the west we may call them the East Baths. The remains, which are extensive, prove these East Baths to have been constructed in a style of considerable magnificence, therein presenting a contrast to the Baths of Antoninus which are meanly built. They measure about 41 paces from north to south by 30 paces from east to west. But it is possible they may have extended further to the south and east, as the ground in these directions has not been excavated; at least it was not excavated at the time of my last visit. The inner walls are mostly built of flat bricks, small stones, and mortar. One long hall is elaborately paved with marbles of various colours and a mosaic of pebbles. In it lie two small columns of a green stone speckled with pieces of quartz; it seemed to me to be *verde antico*, the ancient *lapis Lacedaemonius* (as to which see vol. 3. p. 374). Two more columns of the same sort lie in a small room adjoining the hall on the south-west. Some of the rooms had hypocaust floors supported on little pillars made of flat circular bricks. In one of the rooms part of the floor still stands supported on these little pillars, which are about 18 inches high and contain seven or eight flat bricks apiece. The floor of this room is of concrete, and in it at one side, next to the wall, is a row of square holes to let the hot air rise into the chamber from the fire below. One room, projecting outward at the east side of the building, seems to have been a swimming bath; there are neither doors nor windows in the walls, so far as they are standing, but on the other hand there are remains of a staircase leading down into the bath. A small room in another part of the building contains two little semicircular baths, each with a step or seat on which the bather probably sat. The front wall, that is the west wall, of the East Baths is continued southwards for a distance of 77 paces, mostly in a very poor style of masonry. Whether this continuation formed part of the baths or not I could not determine, but probably it did not. About 27 paces southward along this wall and on the east side of it is a large vaulted cistern. Further, not many yards to the south-west of the East Baths a staircase of some twenty steps leads down to a subterranean aqueduct, about 3 ft. 6 in. high, hewn out of the rock. Mr. Koromantsos informed me that the aqueduct is carried further to the west than to the east.

Abutting upon the west side of the East Baths are the remains of a great cloistered court, which, to distinguish it from a similar court immediately to the north, I have called the South Cloisters. It seems to have comprised a great open court surrounded by colonnades or cloisters. At present the remains of the court with its cloisters extend east and west for a length of about 74 paces, but at its eastern end a small piece has been cut off by the East Baths, which proves that the East Baths are of later date than the South Cloisters. The eastern side of the South Cloisters is preserved for a length of 28 paces from north to south, but here it is broken off by the wall of a later building. Thus all that is left is the northern colonnade and part of the eastern. The northern colonnade is 7 paces deep to the back or north wall. The lowest drums of all the inner row of columns, ten in number, are standing in their places. They are fluted and of the Doric order and measure about 3 feet high by 22 inches in diameter. On the front or south side of this north colonnade the stylobate is preserved, but no remains of columns are standing on it. Along the front of the stylobate, in the open court, are large remains of a pavement of cobbles. The pavement is 3 ft. 6 in. wide, and beyond it, parallel to the front of the colonnade, is a stone gutter or water-channel 16 inches wide, with elliptical expansions at regular intervals of 9 paces. In the eastern colonnade of the South Cloisters only one drum of the inner row of columns is standing; it resembles the drums in the north colonnade.

Immediately to the north of the South Cloisters is another great cloistered court which may be called the North Cloisters. One and the same wall served as the south wall of the North Cloisters and the north wall of the South Cloisters. The North Cloisters seems to have measured 62 paces from east to west by 25 paces from north to south and to have comprised a series of chambers surrounding a cloistered court. Remains of the chambers can be seen on several sides, and on the north and south sides are foundation-walls that supported the colonnades in front. On its south side the building is traversed by a water-channel which comes from the East Baths and runs westward to a cistern. It would seem that the North Cloisters was built later than, and occupies part of the ground originally covered by, the South Cloisters; for the west wall of the South Cloisters is continued northward for 34 paces past the end of the North Cloisters.

A little to the north of the North Cloisters are the remains of a wall which seems to have bounded the sacred precinct on this side. The chief approach to the sanctuary was from the north, for here the road from Epidaurus entered it. A piece of the road, enclosed by walls, may be seen about 100 yards north of the boundary wall. The breadth of the road is 17 paces. Here, on the road, exactly 100 paces north of the boundary wall, are the foundations and pavement of a grand portal measuring 20 paces long from north to south by 15 paces broad from east to west. The pavement, composed of blocks of limestone each 3 ft. 8 in. square, is preserved almost entire. Two ramps lead up to it, one from the north, the other from the south. The southern ramp, like the pavement of the portal, remains almost entire. At and near the portal, especially on its north side, I saw lying remains of Ionic columns, including many drums, two bases, and one capital. I measured two of the drums; one was 26 and the other 29 inches in diameter. The diameter of the column at the neck, under the capital, was 2 feet. On the east side of the road, just on the inner or south side of the great portal, are three stone basins, each about 1 ft. 9 in. deep, built into the ground. They may have contained holy water with which persons entering or departing from the sacred precinct were expected to sprinkle themselves.

Further, on the west side of the road and about 20 paces south of the portal, is a deep circular well, the sides and mouth of which are enclosed by ancient masonry. On the other or outer side of the portal the ancient road is traceable running northwards in the direction of Epidaurus; pieces of the walls which enclosed it may be seen on both sides. Many large squared blocks of ancient buildings stand on a knoll about 120 yards north of the portal, but they seem to have been brought thither from the sanctuary in mediaeval or modern times.

If we now retrace our steps southward and re-enter the sacred precinct we perceive on the right, some 30 yards or so to the south-west of the entrance, the foundations of a temple, which is believed to have been the temple of Aphrodite mentioned by Pausanias (see vol. 3. p. 256). These foundations, distant about 91 paces north of the temple of Aesculapius, are built of a friable red stone and measure 14 paces east and west by 8 paces north and south. Though nothing is left but the foundations the temple appears to have consisted simply of a *cella* and fore-temple (*pronaos*), without a back-chamber (*opisthodomos*). About 50 yards or so to the west of the temple of Aphrodite, if such it was, is a very large cistern, 50 metres long from east to west by 15 metres broad from north to south. The walls are of masonry and are preserved to some height. A stone water-channel leads into it from the east. This great cistern is of the Greek, not the Roman, period.

To the south of the temple of Aphrodite, abutting on the eastern end of the East Colonnade, is a large building supposed to be the Baths of Antoninus (see vol. 3. pp. 238, 257). It seems to extend for about 55 paces from north to south by 26 paces from east to west, and contains a great many small quadrangular rooms and at least one round chamber, which is 4 paces in diameter. In one of the rooms there are two baths with steps leading down into them. Another room contains a mosaic pavement of common white stones, not arranged in a pattern.

Some 100 yards or so to the west of the portal of the West Gymnasium is the stadium, which was being excavated during my last visit. Considerable portions, including a number of tiers of seats both on the north and the south sides, and the two ends of the race-course proper, had already been laid bare (compare vol. 3. p. 257). The course extends east and west or, to be more accurate, east-north-east and west-south-west; the semicircular end was at the east. The seats are made some of white, and others of reddish limestone. On the south side remains of about ten tiers of seats, rising above each other on the slope of the embankment, have been exposed to view; but of these only the three or four lowest tiers are well preserved. On the north side the seats are more ruinous, but remains of about twenty tiers have been laid bare. Some of the seats on the south side of the stadium bear inscriptions, of which some are dedicatory while others record only the name of the person to whom the seat belonged. On one of the seats of the front row I read the following fragmentary inscription :—

O   ΑΣΣΩΣΑΑΣΚΛΑΠΙΩΙ.

On the north side of the stadium, about 57 paces west of the eastern end of the course, there is a vaulted passage leading through the embankment. The passage is 45 paces long, 5 ft. 9 in. wide, and was roofed with a semicircular vault which is preserved for a length of about 15 paces. Walls and vault of the passage are built of squared blocks of stone laid in horizontal courses; the material is a stone of a light brown colour. The seats at the semicircular end of the stadium had not yet been excavated at the time of my visit, or rather trial trenches seemed to show that the seats had disappeared.

The race-course proper, enclosed by embankments on three sides—the north, east, and south—has the form of a long rectangle. Round the race-course, at a distance of 2 ft. 10 in. from the seats, runs a stone border 11 inches wide with a gutter or water-channel in the middle of it. At intervals of 30 paces the channel opens into oblong basins placed on the inner side of the stone border; these basins are 3 ft. 8 in. long. This channel with its basins perhaps held drinking-water for the use of the athletes. At the semicircular end of the stadium the stone border forms a rectangle, not a semicircle, and at a distance of 15 paces from the eastern extremity of the course there is what I took to be the Apheteria or starting-point, though Mr. Koromantsos regarded it as the goal. It consists of a stone sill or row of slabs, each 19 inches wide, running across the course from side to side at right angles to the length of the course. In these slabs are cut pairs of lines parallel to each other and to the line of slabs. Each line is 4 ft. 2 in. long and is distant 4 inches from its companion parallel line. These pairs of parallel lines are separated by intervals of 14 inches; in each interval there is a square hole, in which no doubt a post was fixed. There are eleven of these pairs of parallel lines in the breadth of the stadium, thus:—

At each end of the starting-point, as I shall call it for the sake of convenience, next to the stone border there is standing a piece of an unfluted column on a square base. Thus the arrangement of the starting-point resembles almost exactly that of the starting-point in the stadium at Olympia (vol. 4. p. 80). We may suppose that each runner, before the start, stood on the stone sill with his toes or heels at the pairs of parallel lines, perhaps with the heel of one foot at the front line and the toes of the other foot at the back line.

This would seem to have been the simple original arrangement of the starting-point. But the existing remains suggest that at some later time this original manner of starting the races was modified, if not abandoned. For immediately in front of the stone sill, with its pairs of parallel lines, are foundations of seven half-columns with remains of the half-columns standing on all the bases. One of the half-columns, about 5 feet high, comprises a base, a fluted section or half-drum, and an Ionic capital. But an examination of the other half-columns proves that this particular one, though surmounted by its capital, is not complete. Each of the half-columns would seem to have originally comprised a base about 7 inches high, a lower unfluted section or half-drum 3 ft. 9 in. high, an upper fluted section or half-drum 3 feet high, and an Ionic capital about 8 inches high. Thus if each half-column had only one unfluted and one fluted section (though it may quite well have had more), its original height was 8 feet. What the use of these half-columns may have been, it is difficult to see. They are placed at intervals against, that is abutting upon, the stone sill in front, but they are not arranged symmetrically with reference to the pairs of parallel lines cut in the sill. Thus one half-column will be found standing opposite one of the intervals between the pairs of parallel lines, while another stands opposite a pair of the lines themselves, and so on ; from which we seem forced to conclude that when these half-columns were set up the pairs of parallel lines in the stone sill had ceased to be used in starting the runners. Nor are these half-columns the only complication introduced at a later time. In front of the stone sill and abutting upon it, at a distance of 5 feet from the northern edge of the race-course, is set a block of stone which projects 2 feet from the sill into the race-course. The stone is 6 inches high and, I think, 3 ft. 8 in. wide; at least this is the width of a corresponding stone at the west end of the race-course (see below). The centre of the block is hollowed out in a line parallel with the axis of the race-course ; the width of this hollow is 20 inches. On the other or south side of the stadium, at a distance of about 6 feet from the edge of the race-course, a similar block of stone, hollowed out in the middle, is set against the front of the stone sill. It has been suggested that there was formerly a row of these blocks placed in front of the stone sill right across the race-course, and that each runner before starting took his stand on one of them with his feet in the hollow of the stone. If this was so, it would seem that this manner of placing the runners was substituted at some later time for the earlier practice of placing them on the stone sill with their toes and heels to the parallel lines.

To complete the description of the east end of the stadium it is necessary to mention that on the outer or eastern side of the stone sill and at its two ends are two pedestals, one on the north and one on the south side of the race-course. Each pedestal abuts on the base of the column which terminates the stone sill. The southern pedestal is square and is uninscribed. The northern pedestal is cylindrical and bears an inscription which has been published (Πρακτικὰ τῆς Ἀρχαιολογικῆς Ἐταιρίας, 1894, p. 13). It runs as follows :—

ΧΑΡΜΑΝΤΙΔΑ_   ΑΔΑ
ΕΠΙΔΑΥΡΙΟΣΑΙ   \ΛΩΝΙ
ΛΥΚΛΑΠΙΟΙΑΝΕΘΗΚΕΝ
ΘΡΑΣΥΜΗΔΗΣΕΠΟΙΗΣΕΝ.

From this inscription we learn that the pedestal supported a statue made by Thrasymedes and dedicated to Apollo and Aesculapius by Charmantidas, an Epidaurian. From the style of the letters the inscription is believed to date from the beginning of the fourth century B.C.

This helps us to date the sculptor Thrasymedes, who is most probably the artist mentioned by Pausanias (ii. 27. 2, note) as having made the image of Aesculapius.

Lastly, we must notice that on the south side of the race-course, 16 inches west of the base of the column which terminates the stone sill on this side, there begins a row of four blocks which stand together abutting on the stone border of the race-course throughout their whole united length, which is 15 feet. The height of the blocks is 17 inches and their breadth 16 inches. Mr. Koromantsos regards these blocks as the seats of the umpires. If he is right, then what I have called the starting-point was more probably the goal.

From what I have called the starting-point westward to the extremity of the stone border which ran along the whole length of the race-course I measured 199 paces. Three paces short of the western end of the stone border is a square base at each side of the stadium ; and on the base on the north side stands a piece of an unfluted column, like the columns at the two ends of the starting-point. The line between these two bases at the western end of the stadium was, if I am right, the goal. According to Mr. Koromantsos it was the starting-point. On the eastern or inner side of the base on the north side of the race-course there is a hole or horizontal slit 4 inches long. Into this hole something was doubtless fastened, but what it was is not known. There is no stone sill with pairs of parallel lines at the western end of the stadium ; but on the other hand there is a block of stone hollowed out in the middle, like the two which stand against the stone sill at the eastern end of the race-course. This block stands on the line which I regard as the goal and it is distant 5 ft. 4 in. from the northern edge of the race-course, that is from the stone water-channel which bounds the course.

At intervals of 100 Greek feet along both sides of the race-course were set small quadrangular stones to mark the distance. As the race-course was 600 Greek feet long, there were originally five of these stones on each side of the course. The five on the north side are still standing in their places, but on the south side only three remain. They all stand just inside the stone border which runs round the course. Each stone measures 11 inches by 8½ inches on the sides, and stands 14 inches above the ground. I paced all the intervals between these stones. In four cases (namely, one on the north side and all three on the south side) I estimated the interval at 33 paces ; in one case at 32 paces 8 inches ; in another at 32 paces ; in another at a trifle over 32 paces ; in another at 31 paces 4 inches ; and in another at between 32 and 33 paces. Beyond the third of these stone posts, counting from the east, the water-channel which forms the border of the race-course is not preserved on the south side.

An inscription found in 1896 at a distance of about a quarter of an hour from the stadium proves that there was also a hippodrome attached to the sanctuary (Πρακτικὰ τῆς Ἀρχαιολογικῆς Ἑταιρίας, 1896 (pub. 1897), p. 32).

P. 236 line 13 *sq.* from top, **The surrounding mountains, though** grey and barren, with undulating uniform outlines etc. This description of the mountains which enclose the sacred valley is hardly correct. Mount Arachnaeus in the north-west is indeed grey and barren, but its outline is hard and it rises into sharp points. The hills on the eastern and southern sides of the valley are of softer outline and green with bushes, thus contrasting with the naked rock of Mount Arachnaeus.

P. 242 line 4 *sqq.* from foot, **Thrasymedes** etc. As to the base inscribed with the name of the sculptor Thrasymedes see above, p. 578 *sq.*

P. 244 line 4 *sq.* from top, **A staircase of nineteen steps** etc. The number of steps in this staircase is fourteen, as stated in my notes of 1890, not nineteen, as Mr. Cavvadias has, by an oversight, twice stated in print. I was able to verify my original note on this point in 1895.

P. 244 line 22 *sq.* from top, **One of these benches is still to be seen** etc. This bench, which is lying, not standing, is 20 inches high and 19 inches broad.

P. 244 line 23 *sqq.* from top, **The upper storey of the western colonnade** etc. This account of the upper storey of the western colonnade must be based on a conjectural restoration, since only remains of the lower storey are now standing.

P. 244 line 34 *sq.*, **the stones in which these tablets were fastened can still be seen against the northern half of the east wall.** Two blocks of stone with holes for the insertion of tablets were also observed by me in the southern half of the colonnade and at its eastern end, in fact close to the blocks described in the text.

P. 245 line 9 from top, **the Rotunda.** It has been suggested by Mr. H. Lechat that the Rotunda in the sanctuary of Aesculapius was built to enclose a sacred well, the water of which flowed through the concentric passages of the subterranean vault till it reached the circular shaft in the middle, where alone it could be drawn up. He supposes that the mouth of this central shaft or well was open at the level of the floor, and in confirmation of this view he observes that no circular flag, such as would have been required to close it, has been found among the remains of the pavement (P. Cavvadias, *Fouilles d'Épidaure*, p. 14). Mr. Lechat has further conjectured, with all due reserve, that the Rotunda and the " water-basin worth seeing for its roof and decorations " which Pausanias speaks of (ii. 27. 5) may have been one and the same building, the mention of them as two different edifices being a blunder of Pausanias's. This explanation of the Rotunda as a sacred well-house is rejected by Mr. Chipiez. See A. Defrasse et H. Lechat, in *Bulletin de Corresp. hellénique*, 14 (1890), pp. 631-638 ; *id.*, *Épidaure : Restauration et description des principaux monuments du Sanctuaire d'Asclépios*, pp. 100-105 ; H. Lechat, in *Revue archéologique*, 3me Série, 28 (1896), pp. 261-278 ; Ch. Chipiez, in *Revue archéologique*, 3me Serie, 28 (1896), pp. 44-53, 380-382. Excavations made in 1896 to the west of the long double colonnade brought to light the foundations of a quadrangular edifice ; and still further to the west a portion of a curious oblong and very narrow structure, resembling a well, was excavated. Possibly, as has been suggested, the latter was the water-basin mentioned by Pausanias. Further researches, however, are needed to settle the question. See Πρακτικὰ τῆς Ἀρχαιολογικῆς Ἑταιρίας, 1896 (pub. 1897), p. 32.

P. 247 line 17, a long inscription etc. This inscription has been discussed at great length by Prof. B. Keil ('Die Rechnungen über den epidaurischen Tholosbau,' *Mittheilungen d. arch. Inst. in Athen*, 20 (1895), pp. 21-115, 405-450). I have not read his lucubrations ; but from a reference to them by Dr. Dörpfeld (*Das griechische Theater*, p. 130) I gather that Prof. Keil believes the Rotunda to have been begun in the early part of the fourth century B.C. and to have been still unfinished by about the year 330 B.C. Dr. Dörpfeld apparently accepts this conclusion, and holds that the parts of the building not mentioned in the inscription, especially the beautiful Corinthian columns of the interior with their architrave, the fine pavement of black and white stones, the rich marble ceiling, and the floral cornice with its gargoyles in the shape of lions' heads, were executed after 330 B.C. (*Das griechische Theater*, p. 130 *sq.*).

P. 251 line 5 from foot, a theatre etc. As to the theatre of Epidaurus see W. Dörpfeld, in *Das griechische Theater* (Athens and Leipsic, 1896), pp. 120-133. The diameter of the orchestra within the stone circle is not 24.32 metres, as stated in the text, but 19.54 (2 × 9.77) metres, according to Dr. Dörpfeld ; if the stone circle be included, the diameter is 20.30 (2 × 10.15) metres. The ring enclosing the orchestra is .38 metre wide and is formed of slabs of hard white limestone. The paved passage or gutter which runs half round the orchestra, dividing it from the seats of the spectators, is 6 ft. 10 in. wide, according to my measurement. The other passage (*diazoma*), which divides the seats of the spectators horizontally into an upper and a lower block, is 6 ft. 3 in. wide, according to my measurement ; the wall at the back, that is on the upper side, of this passage is 3 ft. 9 in. high.

The length of the stage, exclusive of the wings, was 22.60 metres. Its front was adorned with twelve half-columns and two quarter-columns, all of the Ionic order. At each end of the stage a wing, 2.57 metres broad, projects for a length of 1 metre. The front of each wing was adorned with two three-quarter columns, also of the Ionic order. None of the columns is now standing, but remains of them and of the entablature which they supported were found in sufficient number to enable us to reconstruct on paper the front of the stage with its wings. The entablature consisted of, first, an architrave divided, as is usual with Ionic architraves, into three horizontal sections, second, a plain frieze, and, third, a row of dentils. The height of the stage, according to Dr. Dörpfeld's calculations, was 3.53 metres, and its depth from front to back 3.20 metres. Some holes in the upper surface of the blocks which formed its outer edge seem to indicate that a metal railing extended along the front of the stage to prevent the actors from falling into the orchestra. A steep ramp gave access to the stage at either end. The entrance to each ramp, at its lower end, was through a stately doorway flanked with Corinthian columns on which rested a triple architrave and a graceful frieze, surmounted by dentils. A single door in the front wall of the stage, between the two central half-columns, gave access to the rooms under and behind the stage. Besides this central door there was in the front wall of each of the wings a door in which perhaps one of the theatrical machines called *periaktoi* (Pollux, iv. 126) may have been placed.

Side by side with each of the doorways leading to the ramps was a larger doorway which gave access to the *parodos* and was flanked, like the smaller doorways, by Corinthian columns supporting an elegant entablature. Few stones of these doorways were found in their original places when the theatre was excavated, but almost all the missing architectural members came to light not far off, so that a reconstruction of the doorways was possible.

With regard to the date of the theatre, Dr. Dörpfeld believes that the key is furnished by a comparison of the Corinthian architecture of the doorways with the Corinthian architecture of the Rotunda in the adjoining sanctuary of Aesculapius. Pausanias tells us that Rotunda and theatre were built by the same architect, Polyclitus, and this statement is confirmed by the resemblance between the Corinthian architecture of the two buildings. But on various grounds Dr. Dörpfeld is of opinion that the beautiful Corinthian columns and the delicately-moulded cornice, with its projecting lion-heads, of the Rotunda cannot be earlier and may be several decades later than the end of the fourth century B.C. ; and that therefore the theatre also was built either at the end of the fourth or in the early part of the third century B.C. Hence he concludes that the Polyclitus who built both theatre and Rotunda can have been neither the elder nor the younger sculptor of that name, but a third Polyclitus later than them both, the same to whom on epigraphical grounds Prof. Dittenberger would assign a statue of which the inscribed base is preserved in the church of St. George at Thebes (*C. I. G. G. S.* 1. No. 2532). With regard to the stage, Dr. Dörpfeld adduces some grounds for holding that the columned front described above was not contemporary with the theatre but was added at a later period. His grounds, which seem very slight, are, first, that the stylobate of the stage-front is .12 metre higher than the stone circle enclosing the orchestra, which seems, in Dr. Dörpfeld's opinion, to show that when the existing stage-front was built the original surface of the orchestra was already underground ; and, second, that the two narrow rooms, one at each end of the long hall behind the stage, are only explicable on the hypothesis that they originally extended further towards the orchestra in the form of wings (*paraskenia*) broader than the existing wings, which again, if the hypothesis is correct, would prove that the original stage-front had been at some time modified so as to give it the form which at present it exhibits. This modification, if it was such, must have been the last change made ; for of a reconstruction of the theatre or stage-buildings in Roman times there is, according to Dr. Dörpfeld, no trace.

P. 254 line 16 from top, **Dr. Dörpfeld has propounded a theory** etc. Dr. Dörpfeld has now stated fully his grounds for holding that in theatres of the Greek, as distinguished from the Roman, type there never was a raised stage at all and that down to the latest times the players regularly acted on the level of the orchestra. But in the elaborate work which he has published in conjunction with Prof. Reisch and which is mainly devoted to establishing this thesis (*Das griechische Theater: Beiträge zur Geschichte des Dionysos-theaters in Athen*, Athens and Leipzig, 1896) I cannot perceive that he has adduced any fresh arguments of weight in favour of his theory or that he has invalidated a single one of the many arguments which tell against it. On the contrary I gather from his book new reasons for adhering to the traditional view. Amongst these reasons are the following :—

(1) In several existing Greek theatres, as in those of Epidaurus, Sicyon, and Oropus, the raised platform (*proskenion*) which Dr. Dörpfeld refuses to recognise as a stage communicates with the level of the ground at either end by means of a ramp or inclined plane. If these ramps were not meant to afford the players access to the raised platform, in other words, to the stage, what were they there for ? Dr. Dörpfeld suggests that in the theatre at Epidaurus the ramps may have served "for hauling up machines and other similar objects." But, as he himself points out, the entrance to each of these ramps from the level of the ground was through a stately doorway flanked with Corinthian columns and surmounted by an elegant entablature. Is it likely that the Greeks would thus have graced a passage which served for nothing but hauling " machinery and other similar objects " up and down ?

(2) Dr. Dörpfeld holds that the front wall of what I call the stage and he calls the *proskenion* was the background before which the players acted. But he admits that in this wall, as we find it in extant Greek theatres, there was usually but one door ; and that in certain Greek theatres, as those of Megalopolis and Piraeus, there is no trace of a door at all in the wall. How then can this wall have been the background of the play when we know that in the background of Greek theatres there were regularly three doors at least (Pollux, iv. 125 *sq.*) ?

(3) The fundamental ground on which Dr. Dörpfeld refuses to recognise the *proskenion* as a stage is that it was too high and narrow to allow the players to act on it freely and safely. Falls from such a stage, he would say, must have been frequent and painful. And so in fact they were. Lucian tells us (*Gallus*, 26) that tragic actors, while playing for example the part of Cecrops or Sisyphus or Telephus, often took a step in empty air (κενεμβατήσας) on the middle of the stage and fell down, to the amusement of the audience, smashing their masks and kingly crowns, breaking their real heads, and displaying their bare legs and the sorry clouts which they wore under their gorgeous robes. The expression "taking a step on emptiness " clearly implies that the players in such cases stepped over the edge of the stage, and the description of the disastrous consequences of their fall proves that they fell from a height. The passage furnishes conclusive evidence that down to Lucian's time the players in Greek theatres regularly acted on a high stage.

(4) Dr. Dörpfeld asserts (p. 351) that no single notice of an ancient author tells against his theory that actors and chorus performed together in the orchestra. He is mistaken. Pollux says (iv. 123) that the stage (*skene*) was reserved for the actors and the orchestra for the chorus.

Phrynichus says (*Ecl.* p. 163 ed. Lobeck) that the place where the comedians and tragedians performed was called the stage (*logeion*), and that the place where the flute-players and choruses performed was called the orchestra. Opinions may differ as to the nature and position of the structure which Pollux and Phrynichus here designate respectively as *skene* and *logeion;* but if these two passages do not imply that actors and chorus acted in different places, words have no meaning. It is curious that the passage of Pollux should have been here overlooked by Dr. Dörpfeld, since he had actually quoted it only a few pages before.

The special arguments against Dr. Dörpfeld's theory which are furnished by the theatre at Epidaurus have been stated very cogently by Mr. H. Lechat (*Épidaure : Restauration et description des principaux Monuments du Sanctuaire d'Asclépios*, pp. 214-228).

Fresh and powerful arguments, based chiefly on the remains of the theatre at Delos and of similar theatres in Asia, have recently been urged against Dr. Dörpfeld's views by Mr. J. Chamonard (*Bulletin de Corresp. hellénique*, 20 (1896), pp. 291-312). He justly emphasises the extreme improbability of Dr. Dörpfeld's hypothesis that the Roman theatre was not so much developed as created at a single blow out of the Greek theatre by the excavation of one-half of the orchestra, the other half being left as a stage for the actors to perform upon. It is difficult to imagine that anybody in real life should have conceived the idea of obtaining a stage by such a round-about, awkward, and expensive proceeding ; for it is to be remembered that the floor of the orchestra was often the natural rock, which would have to be laboriously cut away in order to create a stage in this fashion. An hypothesis so far-fetched would need the support of the strongest and most indubitable historical evidence if it were to win acceptance. Yet Dr. Dörpfeld has no historical evidence at all to adduce in its favour ; he expects it to carry conviction simply by the strength of its own intrinsic probability ! And it is on this hypothesis, grossly improbable in itself and unsupported by any evidence whatever, that he relies as a conclusive proof of his general theory of the absence of a stage in Greek theatres (*Das griechische Theater*, p. 362). But the hypothesis of the sudden creation of the Roman out of the Greek theatre is more than improbable ; it is, as Mr. Chamonard has well shown, irreconcileable with the existence of theatres of a type inter-mediate between the Greek and the Roman type. Such theatres are to be found in Asia, notably at Termessus, and their existence raises a strong presumption that the low broad stage of the Roman theatres was developed gradually and naturally, through a series of intermediate stages, out of the high narrow stage of the Greek theatre.

P. 277 line 7 sq. from foot, Cynortium —— Maleatian Apollo etc. In December 1895 I visited the scanty remains which have been identified as those of the sanctuary of Maleatian Apollo. Accompanied by a guide I started from the sanctuary of Aesculapius and ascended the hill which rises to the north-east of the theatre. The path lay through-out among olive-groves over brown earth which had been in corn. In thirteen minutes from leaving the theatre we reached a terrace or platform on the hillside facing northward, on which I found, besides remains of ancient Greek walls, a large well-preserved cistern of Roman date, probably the cistern which, as we learn from Pausanias (ii. 27. 7), was constructed by Antoninus. The structure is 27½ paces long and 7 paces broad. It had a roof consisting of two arched vaults supported down the middle by a row of pillars, of which four are standing, together with a large part of the roof. Of these pillars the lower part of two is composed of a drum of an ancient fluted column. The better preserved drum is about 21 inches in diameter; its flutes are worn, and the column is partly covered with a thick layer of stucco. The sides of the cistern are also coated with stucco. Of ruins which seemed to belong to the good Greek period I noted five blocks forming an angle of a wall quite close to the cistern. The blocks are squared and laid in a horizontal course. Here, too, are a number of squared ancient blocks lying together under a fig-tree. Further off on the terrace, to the north-west, an edge of a wall is visible for some yards running east and west, and a little further to the west are some slight vestiges of walls. To the north-east of these vestiges there are remains of a wall running along the northern edge of the terrace for a distance of 14 paces. Beside it are some large hewn blocks, which have formed part of a circular or semicircular pedestal. Just below this point, on the steep northern slope of the terrace, lie some squared blocks that probably have been brought or have rolled down from the terrace above. The terrace itself, distant from the theatre about a mile or rather less to the north-east, is now stony cornland ; some olive-trees grow on it. It commands a fine view over the whole of the sacred valley.

Descending from the terrace westward we came in a few minutes to another large cistern, about 35 paces long by 12 paces broad. The walls, built of solid ashlar masonry and coated with stucco, are standing to a height of 20 feet and more. Four short cross-walls, built in the same style, project into the cistern on each side ; they obviously supported an arched roof, for the spring of the arch is visible on most of them. This cistern probably belongs to the Greek, not to the Roman, period ; no bricks are visible in it. Immediately above the cistern, to the east, are remains of an aqueduct or water-channel built of stone. It is 5 feet wide and is preserved for about 38 paces through the olive-grove. To judge by its direction it probably served to unite the upper with the lower cistern.

In 1896 some excavations made by the Greek Archaeological Society at the sanctuary of Maleatian Apollo brought to light remains of buildings, sculptures, and inscriptions recording dedications to Apollo. See Πρακτικὰ τῆς Ἀρχαιολογικῆς Ἑταιρίας, 1896 (pub. 1897), p. 32.

P. 259 line 4 from foot, **the city of Epidaurus.** I visited the ruins of the city of Epidaurus 3rd and 4th December 1895, and the notes I made on the spot may supplement and correct the account given in the text. As the route by which I reached the ancient city, namely by following the mountainous coast from Troezen, is seldom taken by travellers, and I observed by the way some small remains of antiquity, I will begin by describing it.

We left the ruins of Troezen at half-past twelve in the afternoon, and rode northward across the broad flat neck of land which connects the mountainous peninsula of Methana with the mainland. At 1.20 we reached the shore of the lagoon which is formed at the head of the Bay of Methana by the *Potami* river, the Golden Stream of Pausanias (ii. 31. 10). After making a detour round the lagoon we came, at 1.30, to the beach at the point where the stream flows out of the lagoon into the sea. Thence we rode for some way along the beach, then over a rocky point, after which the path kept inland a little from the sea. But all through our journey from Troezen to *Kato-Phanari* the mountains rose at no great distance from us on the left. By half-past two we were opposite *Lesia*, a hamlet at the foot of a high rocky mountain, with a glen on its eastern side, down which comes a stream. But the bed of the stream, when we crossed it, was dry. Below the hamlet in the plain are olives. At 3.53 we came to a ruined mediaeval or modern tower perched on an eminence to our right, between us and the sea. Near it stands a small chapel beside a fine carob-tree. The mountains now advanced to the water's edge, and our path led along their bushy and rocky slopes, winding round bays and headlands at a considerable height above the sea. Here we enjoyed fine views across the spacious bay to the high, mountainous, and rugged peninsula of Methana, which wears a sombre aspect due perhaps to the dark colour of its volcanic rocks. Further on the path, though never far from the sea, trended inland and we passed over a great deal of stony ground mostly planted with olives. At many places along our route in the course of the day the peasants were at work gathering the olives from the trees. Another feature in the day's ride was the great number of carob-trees we passed, some of them very fine trees, with dark smooth glossy leaves. Finally the path ascended a steep rocky slope and brought us at half-past four to the village of *Kato-Phanari*, very picturesquely situated high on the side of a mountain, which a short way above the village rises up in rugged precipices of grey rock. Twilight was coming on, but enough of daylight remained to allow me to appreciate the beauty of the prospect from the loftily situated village across the sea to the islands, the high conspicuous peninsula of Methana, and the long line of headlands stretching away towards Epidaurus, all bathed in the warm though fast fading light of a winter evening.

Next morning we left *Kato-Phanari* soon after eight o'clock. The path rose steeply up the mountain-side in view of the sea. In a little less than an hour we reached *Ano-Phanari*, a village overlooking the sea, situated far up the side of a lofty rocky mountain which faces southward to the still higher precipitous mountain on whose seaward face, below the precipices, stands the lower village of *Kato-Phanari*. On this latter mountain, or rather on the summit of the range to which it belongs, called Mount *Ortholithion*, certain ceremonies are said to have been performed, time out of mind, by the peasants in seasons of drought and pestilence (A. Meliarakes, Γεωγραφία τοῦ νομοῦ ᾿Αργολίδος, p. 211). At *Ano-Phanari* I heard of remains of an ancient fortress in the neighbourhood, and set off with a guide to visit them.

A walk of a few minutes in a north-easterly direction brought us to the top of the mountain, where the remains are to be seen. The situation is a remarkably fine one. Precipices descending towards the sea encircle the summit on the north and north-east, and the views across the Saronic Gulf to Aegina, Salamis, and Megara are magnificent. Some mediaeval remains, comprising walls and two or more ruined chapels, are to be seen on the summit, and on its southern side, towards the village, there is a ruined fortification-wall built of large irregular blocks. This wall seemed to me to be ancient. At its western end, nearest to the village, there are remains of a square tower projecting from the wall and built in a similar style. At the other or eastern end of the wall there is an entrance to the summit between the rocks, and here may be seen the ruins of an ancient gateway, 12 feet wide, with steps made of large blocks. On the right side of the gateway as you enter there is a small piece of ancient wall built of tolerably large stones laid in horizontal courses, but with slanting joints. Three courses are standing. At the back of this fragment of ancient wall there are remains of a small square mediaeval tower with thin walls. Thus the ancient fortress which occupied this commanding situation appears to have been repaired and inhabited in the Middle Ages. What the name of the place was in antiquity we do not know.

The villagers called my attention to several holes in the rocks between the fortress and the village from which streams of warm air issue. The air from one of the holes was hot enough to warm me, though the morning was cold. In this particular hole, too, I could hear a rumbling sound as of water boiling or wind blowing underground.

We left *Ano-Phanari* about ten o'clock and descended westward, out of sight of the sea, into a small trough-like plain or valley surrounded on all sides by rocky and barren mountains. Here I was overtaken by a schoolmaster from *Kato-Phanari*, an elderly but active priest who kept us company for some way. He guided me to a piece of an unfluted column 3 feet high and 19 inches in diameter, standing apparently in its original position on flat open ground in the valley. Many broken stones, as of some ruined building, lie near the column, and some 50 yards or so to the south-west of it is a well lined with masonry, which seemed to me ancient. A few yards west of the well is a small ruined chapel which the schoolmaster thought was dedicated to St. Nicholas. From the little plain we now ascended the mountains northward by a steep rocky path. In an hour and a half from quitting the village my companion showed me the remains of a small round structure a few paces to the right of the path. Two large blocks, apparently ancient, are hewn in the curves of a circle ; one of them formed part of a pavement with a raised border on the outer edge. Within the circle, though not in its centre, is a stone basin sunk in the ground and half covered with a large stone.

Thence we continued to ascend the mountains by a rough path that led into a narrow upland valley running north and south and enclosed by hills, the sides of which were shaggy with bushes of various sorts. This dale we traversed from end to end. Through a narrow opening or gorge in the mountains on its eastern side we obtained a striking glimpse of part of the promontory of Methana, mostly in shadow, but with gleams of sunshine resting on it here and there. At the northern end of the valley, ascending a ridge, we saw stretched out below us at some depth a wide open valley of roughly circular shape. Our path, which was again very rugged, did not descend into the valley, but skirted its eastern side, keeping up on the mountain, till it turned eastward through a gap in the hills. On passing through the gap a view of the sea with all its coasts and islands shining in the sun (for after a dull morning the day had brightened) suddenly burst upon us. Salamis was conspicuous to the north, and to the east of it appeared Mount Pentelicus with the marble quarries visible even at that distance as white patches on its side. Far below us lay Epidaurus, its little peninsula stretching out into the blue bay. We were at a great height above the sea, but now gradually descended to it in the direction of Epidaurus by a steep rugged path running obliquely down the bushy side of the mountain. Thus we came at last into a little maritime plain, traversed it from south to north, and passing some lemon-groves reached the modern village of *Palaea Epidauros* or Old Epidaurus about half-past two. The village stands on the shore at the head of a deep narrow sheltered inlet formed by the peninsula of ancient Epidaurus on the south and a higher promontory, wooded with low green pines, on the north. Beside the village a little headland runs out into the water; it is crowned with a white-washed chapel of St. Nicholas, which stands in a large walled enclosure with two cypress-trees growing in front of it. The church seems to occupy the site of the sanctuary of Hera mentioned by Pausanias.

From the village I was rowed across to the peninsula where are the ruins of Epidaurus. The site of the ancient city is remarkably beautiful. The peninsula, now mostly overgrown with brushwood and shrubs, commands fine views both seaward and landward. Aegina and the high rugged mountain-mass of Methana are seen to especial advantage. The coast, too, southward in the direction of Troezen is very bold and grand, the mountains rising here abruptly to a great height from the sea. At the head of the bay, on the other hand, the hills, clothed with pines, are lower, and between them appears the mouth of the valley up which the path leads through thickly wooded glens to the sacred grove of Aesculapius.

The ancient fortification-wall is best preserved on the southern side of the peninsula. Beginning at the south-western corner above a line of perpendicular cliffs of no great height, the wall may be traced eastward for several hundreds of yards, keeping above and at some distance from the sea even after the cliffs have come to an end, which they very soon do. The wall, though ruinous in places, is preserved in others to a height varying from 5 to 11 feet. The style of masonry is somewhat rough; the stones, which are large, are cut in polygons and fitted together but not very closely. The thickness of the wall seems to have been about 5 ft. 6 in. Remains of a single square tower, about 5 feet high, project from it. Towards the eastern end of the peninsula the line of wall is traceable in great part only by scattered blocks. A ruined mediaeval wall, built of small stones, bricks, and mortar, also exists above the precipices at the south-west corner of the peninsula, and is continued for some distance along its western face, overlooking the flat isthmus which joins the peninsula to the mainland.

The northern shore of the peninsula is in a manner the converse of the southern, for while, towards the west, it is flat, towards the east it descends to the sea in cliffs, which, however, are not very high. Just above the level stretch of ground which skirts the western part of the shore I found a small piece of fortification-wall, about 4 feet high, built in the polygonal style ; and further east, at the point where the low sea-cliffs begin, I came upon a ruinous piece of a similar wall extending down the slope to the brink of the precipices, but not running along their edge. On the level part of the northern shore there are some remains of a building constructed of flat bricks and mortar ; and broken stones and pottery are here scattered about.

The peninsula rises into two summits, an eastern and a western, of which the eastern is the higher. Both summits would seem to have been enclosed by separate fortification-walls. On the southern side of the western peak a piece of this inner fortification-wall is preserved for a length of about 65 paces. It is built of squared blocks of dark stone laid in horizontal courses, of which from two to six are standing. But flat bricks and small stones interposed between the courses seem to show that the wall was repaired, if not built, in the Middle Ages. Westward, towards the isthmus, this wall is continued for a little way by another wall which is undoubtedly mediaeval or modern, being constructed of small stones, bricks, and mortar. The traces of fortification-walls enclosing the eastern summit are slight and doubtful. The rocks a little to the east of its top have been cut and smoothed into a sort of platform where a temple may have stood. Beside this platform I found two or three pieces of what at first I took to be columns, but which more probably were pieces of basin-like stands for offerings such as I afterwards observed in the sanctuary of Aesculapius. A ruined church occupies the top of the western summit. Lower down, at the western foot of the peninsula, where the isthmus begins, there are remains of a building faced with bricks, but with small stones and mortar forming the core of the walls. Beside it I found the lower half of a white marble statue representing a man in Roman costume. Further, on the southern side of the western peak, not far from the top, but a little lower down than the repaired fortification-wall, there lies a block bearing the following inscription in letters which are widely spaced out :

```
            Γ    O    P    Δ
N (or M)   O    Λ (?)  Θ    E    N    H    Σ
H    Λ    E    Φ    A    N    H    Σ    Λ.
```

Outside of a peasant's house on the isthmus I was shown some remains of antiquity, including a torso of a statue over life-size clad

apparently in a cuirass; a drum of a fluted Doric column 2 feet in
diameter; another drum of a fluted Doric column about 2 ft. 10 in. in
diameter; and a number of squared blocks of stone. Here, too, I
copied a couple of inscriptions. One, which from the forms of the
letters I thought might be of the fifth or fourth century B.C., is carved
on a round pedestal. It runs thus:

ΠΥΘΕΑΣΤΙΜΑΙΝΕΤΟΣ
ΤΟΙΦΡΟΥΡΟΙΛΥΚΕΙΩΙ

The other inscription is carved on a slab of stone measuring 30
inches by 26 inches and 10 inches thick, which lay on the top of the
round pedestal. Only the last part of the original inscription remains,
the upper part of the stone having been broken away. Engraved in
well-cut letters it runs as follows:

ΟΙΕΠΙΔΑΥΡΙΟΙΑΝΑΘΕΝ
ΙΣΤΟΥΣΤΩΝΣΕΒΑΣΤΩΝΑΓΩ
ΝΑΣΔΗΝΑΡΙΑΜΥΡΙΑΚΑΙΤΗΠΟΛΕΙΔΡΑΧΜΑΣ
ΠΕΝΤΑΚΙΣΧΕΙΛΙΑΣ ΑΡΕΤΗΣΕΝΕΚΑ

This inscription seems to show that games were celebrated at
Epidaurus in honour of the Roman emperors.

Further, on the isthmus, but at some little distance from the
peasant's 'cottage, I was shown a life-size torso of a woman in Roman
costume reclining on a couch; it seemed to be the top of a sarcophagus.
Near it lay a large slab, the whole of which, below the gable-shaped top,
was covered with a long inscription, a good deal defaced. Apparently
the inscription records the names of the men who perished in a certain war.
I copied a few fragments of it as follows. It begins with the words
ΟΙΔΕΑΠΕΘΑΝΟΝ (then defaced or obscure letters) ΠΟΥΙΣ. Then
many lines lower down I read ΚΙΦΡΩΝΑΣ, and then, after an interval
of a line

ΑΡΙΣΤΟΚΡΑΤΗΣΘΕΟ
ΣΘΕΝΕΙΔΑΣΑΙΣΤΑ
ΦΙΛΙΣΤΙΔΑΣΕΥΚΡΑΤ

then some lines lower down

ΣΩΣΙΚΡΑΤΗΣΑ

A few sculptured tombstones of no particular merit are preserved in
a shed in the village of *Palaea Epidauros*. On one of them is carved in
relief the figure of a soldier standing and holding his horse, with a boy
attendant beside him. Above these figures is cut the inscription:

ΤΙΜΟΚΛΗ   ΧΑΙΡΕ

The style of the relief proves it to be of Roman date. Another
tombstone exhibits within an arch the figure of a woman holding up a
torch in each hand. Above her is the inscription

ΕΥΑΡΕΤΑ   ΧΑΙΡΕ

The prehistoric tombs mentioned in the text (vol. 3. p. 261) are situated on the mainland just opposite the isthmus of the peninsula. A narrow descending passage, like the *dromos* of a beehive tomb, leads down to one of them ; it ends in a low narrow doorway ; the whole is hewn out of the rock.

P. 263 line 24 from foot, a **temple of Aphrodite.** In 1894 some remains of very early buildings were excavated by Mr. Staes beside the temple of Aphrodite in Aegina. Trenches dug to the west and south of the temple revealed the existence of ancient walls extending under the foundations of the temple. To the east of the temple, at a distance of a few yards, Mr. Staes laid bare the remains of a dwelling which he would refer to the seventh century B.C. It consists of three quadrangular rooms communicating with each other by small doors. The walls, up to a height of about 3 feet, are built of wrought polygonal stones, while the upper part was of unburnt bricks, of which there are many remains. Many potsherds decorated in the geometrical style known as proto-Corinthian were found in the dwelling, and serve to date it. Near this building, and perhaps contemporary with it, Mr. Staes discovered a pit about 6 feet long and 3 feet wide, in which were deposited a number of objects, apparently old votive offerings which had been thrown away as worthless. Amongst these objects may be mentioned fragments of many vases of various shapes, eleven Egyptian scarabs, fragments of idols and of vessels made of Egyptian porcelain, two clay tablets of peculiar shape adorned with geometrical patterns in the so-called Dipylum style, and lastly a terra-cotta tablet bearing in relief the figure of a goddess who stands clad in a striped petticoat and holding her hands to her breasts. The style of the relief is very rude and archaic. That the pit in which these votive offerings were found is older than the neighbouring temple and hence than the fifth century B.C. is proved by its position under the bed of cement or concrete above which the temple and sacred precinct were constructed. At a still lower depth, Mr. Staes discovered the remains of a large and complex building which he at first assigned to the Mycenaean period, but which he now dates still earlier. It is composed of a number of small quadrangular rooms, apparently dwelling - houses, built in the same style as the houses on the acropolis of Mycenae. The walls, constructed of small stones and clay, are thinly coated with cement ; the floors are paved with small polygonal stones. The doors are low and narrow with sides that converge upward. Bones of animals and birds were found in the rooms. Graves of three different sorts exist in these dwellings : some are oblong and sunk beneath the floor ; others are round and built upon the floor ; while others are niches let into the walls. In the round graves, of which the diameter seems to have been only about 18 inches, the bones of the dead may have been deposited in jars, as at Thoricus and Aphidna (see above, pp. 525, 560). The niches in the walls seem to have been properly graves of infants, though bones of adults were also found in them. The practice of burying the dead in the house prevailed, as we have seen (above, p. 525), at Thoricus ; it is said to have been the regular custom in early Greece (Plato, *Minos*, p. 315 d).

Another proof of the great age of the building discovered by Mr. Staes is furnished by the shape and style of the pottery found in it, which closely resembles the so-called 'Island' pottery found in Cyprus, Rhodes, Thera, and Amorgus, as well as on the Acropolis of Athens, in the lowest strata at Thoricus, and in the tumulus at Aphidna. On the other hand no certain trace of Mycenaean art came to light in the course of the excavations. See B. Staes, in Πρακτικὰ τῆς Ἀρχαιολογικῆς Ἑταιρίας, 1894, pp. 17-19; Ἐφημερὶς ἀρχαιολογική, 1895, pp. 235-264.

P. 265 line 8 from top, a **sanctuary of Aphaea.** Some excavations were made here by Mr. Staes in 1894, but without result. The walls of the sacred enclosure, which alone remain, are built of massive polygonal blocks on the west, but of square blocks on the south, where the ancient wall has clearly been repaired. See B. Staes, in Πρακτικὰ τῆς Ἀρχαιολογικῆς Ἑταιρίας, 1894, p. 20.

P. 266 line 10 from top, **Auxesia and Damia.** An Epidaurian inscription, copied by Mr. Chr. Blinkenberg at the sanctuary of Aesculapius, records a dedication by Lucius, priest of Aesculapius, to Mnia and Ausesia ; and in another inscription, copied by Mr. Blinkenberg at the same place but unfortunately mutilated, mention is made of Mnia and Azosia. Both inscriptions are of Roman date. We can hardly doubt that Mnia and Ausesia or Azosia are only altered forms of Damia and Auxesia. See Chr. Blinkenberg, in *Nordisk Tidsskrift for Filologi*, Tredie Raekke, 3 (1895), p. 166 *sq.*, Inscriptions 18 and 19. The etymologies of the two names have been discussed by Mr. O. A. Danielssohn. He argues that the form Mnia is derived from Damia through an intermediate Dmia (comparing Hesychius, *s.v.* Δμία), and that the root is *dam* in the sense of 'build.' The name Auxesia, Azesia, or Azosia is derived by him from a root *aiz* in the sense of 'grow,' 'thrive.' See O. A. Danielssohn, 'Damia-Amaia und Azesia-Auxesia,' in *Eranos : Acta philologica Suecana*, 1 (Upsala, 1896), pp. 76-85. Prof. B. Keil would derive the name Azosia or Azesia from a root *zes,* 'boil,' 'seethe' (*Mittheilungen d. arch. Inst. in Athen*, 20 (1895), p. 422 *sq.*).

P. 272 line 15 from foot, **Sphettus.** Mr. B. Staes is of opinion that the Attic township of Sphettus occupied the eminence on which the modern village of *Markopoulo* now stands. There are many traces of ancient dwellings here, especially near the railway-station, but that these are the remains of Sphettus has not been proved. About a mile and a quarter to the south-east of *Markopoulo*, at a place now called *Kopreza*, Mr. Staes discovered and partially excavated a prehistoric necropolis of the Mycenaean period. The tombs, which closely resemble those of Mycenae and Nauplia, are cut out of the rock and reached either by very narrow descending passages or, in most cases, by staircases. The passages are relatively long, sometimes as long as 10 metres, but not more than 3 metres deep ; the staircases are shorter but deeper, often as much as 5 metres deep. In two of the passages a niche is cut in the right-hand side of the passage, just outside the entrance to the sepulchral chamber. Each of these niches was walled up and contained a single

body. The entrances to the sepulchral chambers were carefully built up
from top to bottom. The chambers are mostly square. The largest,
which contained ten bodies, is 4 metres square and $2\frac{1}{2}$ metres high ; the
smallest, which contained three bodies, is about 2 metres square and
2 metres high. In the two-and-twenty tombs here excavated by Mr.
Staes about 200 vases were discovered. They belong to the later
Mycenaean period, exhibiting the characteristic lustrous glaze and a
decoration composed chiefly of lines and spirals but sometimes of plants
and shells. Among them are many specimens of the stirrup-jar (see vol
3. p. 112) and the wine-pourer (*oinochoe*). Other objects found were five
bronze razors, a bronze chisel, a gold ring, a silver ring, and a quantity
of stone buttons (whorls). See B. Staes, in Ἐφημερὶς ἀρχαιολογική,
1895, pp. 210-221.

P. 273 line 2 from top, **Troezen.** I visited the ruins of Troezen
1st and 2nd December 1895, and will here supplement from my
notes the description given in the text.

The scattered and insignificant ruins lie at and near the foot of the
mountains that bound the plain on the west. Amongst them the most
conspicuous is a high quadrangular tower standing at the eastern
foot of the steep and rugged hill which seems to have formed the
acropolis. This tower is about 13 paces square. Its lower part,
to a height of over 20 feet, is ancient, being built of squared stones
laid in horizontal courses, of which seventeen are preserved. Its
upper part, which may be from 12 to 20 feet high, is mediaeval, being
constructed of small stones and mortar. The tower stands close to the
mouth of the deep ravine which, bounding the acropolis hill on the north,
winds away into the heart of the mountains and is spanned a little way
up by the Devil's Bridge (see below). Some blocks of the ancient
fortification-wall abut on the north side of the tower, and another small
piece of the wall, built of large roughly squared blocks in two courses,
may be seen a few yards to the south of it. Further, some 30 yards
or so to the south of the tower, nearer to the village of *Damala*, are the
ruins of another square tower, built in a wholly different style, its walls
consisting of a core of small stones faced outside and inside with bricks.

The hill which is believed to have been the acropolis of Troezen is
not isolated, but forms part of the range which bounds the plain on the
west. On the north it descends abruptly in high rocky precipices into
the ravine in which is the Devil's Bridge. Olive-groves extend up a
great part of the steep southern slope, but beyond them the hill rises
in the form of a crag or pinnacle of rock, some 200 feet or so high,
the small top of which is bounded by precipices on three sides. The
view from this airy summit is extensive and fine ; it comprises a great
part of the Attic coast, but Sunium seemed to me to be hidden by the
island of Calauria ; and as for Parnassus, which is said to be visible in
clear weather far to the north-west, I saw nothing of it, the clouds
hanging low over the mountains in that direction. Of ancient remains
on the acropolis I did not discover a single stone ; but on the eastern
side of the rocky pinnacle into which the hill runs up, I found, near the
top, considerable remains of a vaulted mediaeval cistern, and lower down

on a small level space, which but for the crag above it might be regarded as the top of the hill, there are some pieces of mediaeval fortifications built of small stones, bricks, and mortar, also ruins of rudely-constructed dwellings. Still lower down on the eastern slope of the hill are two small ruined chapels which may perhaps occupy the sites of ancient temples.

The Devil's Bridge in the ravine on the northern side of the acropolis hill has been already described (vol. 3. p. 273). A walk of ten minutes up the glen takes us to it from the high tower at the foot of the acropolis. We follow a path which leads along the southern side of the glen, high above the stream. At the narrowest point of the ravine, where its sides are formed of lofty and perpendicular walls of rock, the path crosses the abyss by a bridge consisting of a single small arch. This is the Devil's Bridge. High beetling crags rise above it ; one of the rocky sides of the lyn beneath it is mantled thick with ferns and ivy ; and trees droop over the stream which murmurs in the depths below. A small aqueduct, formed of a groove cut in a long single block of stone crosses the bridge side by side with the path. A good deal of water flowed in the ravine at the bridge when I saw it, but some of it was diverted to turn two mills lower down, and lower still, in the plain, I found the bed of the stream quite dry. Most of its water was probably used to feed the luxuriant lemon-groves which line the banks of the stream at the point where it issues from the glen. This brook or mountain torrent, now called the *Potami* or *Kremastos*, is probably the Golden Stream of Pausanias.

About a quarter of a mile east of the mouth of the ravine, in the direction of the sea, are some ruins of brick buildings which may be Roman. They form two blocks side by side. One block is composed of thick walls built entirely of flat bricks ; the walls are standing to a considerable height, and there are arched recesses in them. The walls of the other block are not so thick and their core is made of small stones.

Another and much more considerable group of ruins, some of which were excavated by Mr. Legrand, a French archaeologist, a few years ago, is to be seen some ten minutes' walk to the north of the point at which the *Potami* issues from the glen. The most conspicuous of them is the ruined mediaeval building known as *Palaeo-Episkopi* (vol. 3. p. 273). It stands on a mound ; the walls, built of small stones, flat bricks, and mortar, contain some fragments of antiquity, comprising a few inscriptions which have been already published.

About 100 yards or so to the south of *Palaeo-Episkopi* are the remains of the large building excavated by Mr. Legrand, of which some account has been given in the text (vol. 3. p. 274). The well-built walls, which are 2 ft. 10 in. thick and nowhere more than 2 ft. 6 in. high, are faced outside and inside with squared slabs of blue limestone set up on their narrow edges. So far as it is excavated the building consists of a long hall extending north and south, with two wings projecting eastward from its two ends. The great hall, 31 paces long by 10 paces wide, is entered from the east by two doorways, each 6 feet wide, the thresholds of which are preserved. All round the hall there are arranged, in a somewhat peculiar way, a number of blocks, each with a quadrangular groove cut in its upper surface. Many of these blocks are

preserved entire in their places.   Each of them measures 31 inches long,
11 inches broad, and 12 inches high.   The grooves are each 4 inches
wide and 3 inches deep; they are open at one end of the stone, but
closed at the other.   The disposition of the blocks round the sides of the
hall seems to have been this :—

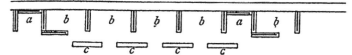

The intervals marked *b b b* are larger than those marked *a a*.   Of the
blocks marked *c c c* only fragments remain, not enough to show with
certainty whether they were grooved like the others or not; but I think
that they were not so grooved.   Lying about within the building are some
thin broken slabs of white marble, which seem to have measured 3 feet
long by 14½ inches wide.   They may have rested on the grooved blocks
and so served as seats.   Further, there runs down the whole length of
the hall a row of square hearths (?) equidistant from each other.   There
are four of these hearths.   Each is about 4 feet square, and is built of
four blocks enclosing an empty space.   This row of hearths, if hearths
they be, is nearer the west than the east wall of the hall.   Corresponding
to them are two hearths nearer the east than the west wall, one at each
end of the hall.   The floor of the hall seems to have been covered with
a mosaic pavement, of which a small piece is left.   In the projecting
wings at each end there were a number of chambers, which appear to
have been similarly fitted up with grooved blocks arranged all round the
walls; at least this was the case with the chambers of the south wing, in
which remains of similar grooved blocks are to be seen.   The two doors
in the east wall of the hall open into a quadrangular court which was
enclosed on three sides by the hall and its wings.   Excavations in the
court have laid bare the remains of four broad stone gutters or water-
channels forming a large rectangle.   Each channel is about 4 ft. 6 in.

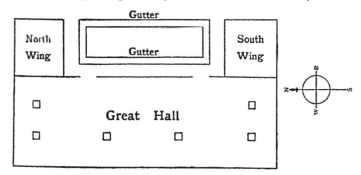

wide, and consists of a shallow depression in the stone.   It is possible
that the building was originally a quadrangle enclosing this court, though

only three sides of the quadrangle have at present been excavated ; for at a distance of 8½ paces to the east of the eastern water-channel a small excavation has revealed some remains of what seems to have been an outer wall built in the same style as the other walls. Perhaps the edifice was a bathing establishment with the baths in a central court, while all round the court were halls and rooms in which the bathers dressed and lounged. The plan of the building, so far as it has been excavated, is illustrated by the annexed cut (p. 595).

The remains of the temple discovered by Mr. Legrand (see vol. 3. p. 274) are situated 36 paces south-west of the large building just described. Only the foundations are now standing, but they are well built and well preserved. They are constructed of squared blocks laid in horizontal courses and measure 22 paces in length by 11 paces in breadth. At a corner where their full height has been exposed by an excavation three courses of masonry are preserved. I was told that a large drum of a fluted Doric column which I saw near the stadium had been transported thither from the site of the temple. The drum is 3 ft. 9 in. in diameter ; the number of its flutes is twenty. At present no architectural fragments are to be seen at the temple.

The stadium occupied a hollow between *Palaeo-Episkopi* and the *Potami* river, but much nearer to the former than to the latter. About 70 yards or so to the south of it stands a house, the property of a retired naval officer who was good enough to show me over the group of ruins which I have been describing. They are all on his land and within a few minutes' walk of his house. The race-course is now occupied by a lemon-grove, where the yellow fruit hung ripe at the time of my visit. At the hollow semicircular end, which opens eastward, there are remains of a curved wall built of large polygonal stones. This wall probably divided the seats of the spectators from the racecourse. A few yards to the west of it a spring rises among rocks. Its water flows into a modern cistern in front of the polygonal wall. Can this spring be the Hippocrene mentioned by Pausanias (ii. 31. 9) ? More probably it was the spring of Hercules which rose in front of the house of Hippolytus (Paus. ii. 32. 4) ; for the house of Hippolytus may be supposed to have been near his stadium.

Lastly, I observed in its original position one of the three remarkable columns which Gell describes and which he conjectured might have belonged to the very ancient sanctuary of Thearian Apollo mentioned by Pausanias. The column stands by itself at a spot between the *Potami* river and the stadium, some 150 yards or so to the north-east of the mouth of the ravine. We came to it in twenty minutes after passing the village of *Damala.* It is a monolith of rather dark brownish colour, eight-sided, and 9 feet high. The ground at the foot of it has been excavated

P. 285 line 24 *sqq.* from foot, **a holy sanctuary of Poseidon** etc. Since the description in the text was printed I have visited the sanctuary of Poseidon in Calauria (30th November 1895) and the Swedish archaeologists who excavated it have published their report (*Mittheil. d. arch. Inst. in Athen,* 20 (1895), pp. 267-326), accompanying it with plans of which one is here reproduced (pl. ix.). The following description is based partly on their report and partly on my own notes.

The sanctuary is situated very picturesquely on a saddle between the two highest peaks of the island, both of which are covered with pine-woods. A walk of about an hour takes us to it from *Poros*, the modern capital of the island. The path at first skirts the southern shore of the island for a short way, then turns and ascends in a north-westerly direction through the pine-forest. From the sanctuary, which stands at a height of about 600 feet above the sea, beautiful and wide prospects open between the wooded hills both to the north and the south. We look down on the sea with its multitudinous bays, creeks, promontories, and islands stretched out before us and framed as in a picture between the pine-clad hills on either hand. A fitter home could hardly have been found for the sea-god whose favourite tree—the pine—still mantles the greater part of the island.

The temple of Poseidon stood within a separate precinct at the north-eastern end of the sanctuary, away from the other buildings. The precinct forms a rectangle 55.5 metres long by 27.6 metres wide, and is enclosed by walls of hard blue limestone, about 3 ft. 6 in. thick, which are preserved all round to an average height of about 2 feet. These walls are meanly built of small irregular stones, like Scotch dykes. The north wall and part of the east wall rest on a four-stepped base. There are two openings in the walls of the precinct, one on the east and the other on the south. The eastern gateway, situated in the axis of the temple, was the principal entrance. Of the temple itself the remains are exceedingly scanty, consisting almost entirely of a few small pieces of pavement or foundations built of small stones in a very indifferent style. From the remains, however, such as they are, Prof. Wide judges that the temple was surrounded by a Doric colonnade with six columns at each of the narrow ends and twelve columns on each of the long sides. A small Doric capital, 2 ft. 3 in. in diameter, lies on the ground on the site of the temple, and near it is a fragment of a similar capital. According to Prof. Wide, the foundations of the colonnade were built of soft limestone, and the walls of the temple of hard blue limestone. The cornice (*sima*) was of marble with palmettes painted on it. The clamps, which were of iron, had a Z shape and were run with lead. From the shape of the clamps and other small indications Prof. Wide concludes that the temple was built in the sixth century B.C.

To the south-west of the temple there lies a group of buildings forming three sides of a large quadrangle. It comprises three colonnades, a large irregularly-shaped building with a portico or colonnade in front and four rooms behind, and lastly a smaller building on the south-west side, in which was probably the portal leading into the quadrangle. Of this group of buildings the colonnade at the north-eastern corner (marked East Colonnade on the plan) is the best preserved. It is about 22 paces distant from the sacred enclosure of the temple. This colonnade faced south or, to be more exact, south-east, and measured 30.15 metres in length by 11 metres in depth. Preserved almost in their entire length are the stylobate in front and the lower parts of the three outer walls on the east, north, and west. The stylobate is beautifully constructed of large square slabs of trachyte measuring uniformly 6 ft. 6 in. long, about 3 feet wide, and about 10 inches high. It rests upon a lower course similarly constructed of large squared slabs, and that again rests on a foundation-course built in a commoner style. Some of the blocks of the stylobate are wanting at the west end. The outer walls of the colonnade on the east, north, and west are 2 feet thick and are standing throughout to a height of from 2 to 3 feet. Each wall consists of a core of small stones faced on the outside and inside with polygonal blocks of blue limestone which are well cut and well fitted together. The faces of the blocks are smoothed. The masonry is excellent. Two rows of columns ran along the entire length of the colonnade, an outer row on the south front, and an inner row parallel to it down the middle of the building. The outer row consisted of sixteen Doric columns, the inner row of four Ionic columns. A drum of one of the Doric columns made of tufa and measuring about 28 inches in diameter is still in position, and a Doric capital also made of tufa and measuring about 33 inches in diameter lies not far off. The four Ionic columns of the inner row rested on four separate foundations, which are still preserved. A base of one of the columns, made of tufa and about 2 ft. 10 in. in diameter, is standing on one of the foundations. To judge from the fine style of its masonry this colonnade must belong to the best period of Greek architecture, probably to the fifth or fourth century B.C. Prof. Wide assigns it to the fifth century.

In a line with this colonnade to the west and divided from it only by a passage about 11 feet wide, are the remains, far less complete, of another colonnade which is marked as the Middle Colonnade on the plan. It was about 33 paces long, and apparently of the same depth (11 paces) as the East Colonnade. Like the East Colonnade, too, it was enclosed on the east, north, and west by walls faced outside and inside with polygonal blocks of blue limestone. These walls are partly preserved on the north and west; on the east side foundations alone remain. Of the colonnade proper nothing is left but two square foundations of columns of the inner row.

Opposite to the East Colonnade and distant from it about 33 paces to the south, or rather south-east, is another colonnade which on the plan I have called the South Colonnade. Its length from east to west is 34.30 metres and its depth 11.80 metres; the north foundation-wall, built of squared blocks, is preserved throughout. The colonnade opens to the north or rather north-west.[1] It had two rows of columns, an outer and an inner. The square foundations of the five columns which composed the inner row are preserved. On one of them is standing the base of an Ionic column made of tufa and measuring about 3 feet in diameter. A fine Ionic capital belonging to this row of columns is also preserved, and some pieces of a *geison*, with mutules and *guttae*, made of tufa, are lying in the colonnade. The style of masonry of this

---

[1] I make this statement on the authority of Prof. Wide's plan. According to my notes, the colonnade opens to the south.

THE SANCTUARY OF POSEIDON IN, CALAURIA.

TEMPLE

EAST COLONNADE

A

MIDDLE COLONNADE

B

SOUTH COLONNADE

C

D

E

WEST COLONNADE

F

G

Scale of Feet

Metres

colonnade is fair, but not so fine as that of the East Colonnade. On a
large block which lies in it I observed the mason's marks ΠV. A few
feet to the north of the Ionic base there is a slab of white marble
measuring 34 inches by 32 inches and about 11 inches high, which
from its mouldings and the marks of attachment on its upper surface
evidently formed the top of the pedestal of a statue.

Immediately to the west of the South Colonnade is a building of
some size (marked D on the plan) which has the form of a rectangle
with a large corner cut off. Its northern front is 31.35 metres and
its eastern (or rather north-eastern) wall 31.7 metres long, while the
length of its short western (or rather south-western) wall is only 13.25
metres. The back wall, which was perhaps at the same time the
boundary-wall of the sanctuary, is preserved to a considerable extent
on the south and south-west. It is built of quadrangular blocks of blue
limestone laid in horizontal courses of which from two to four are
standing. The building comprised a portico or colonnade on the north,
four inner rooms, and apparently an open court of irregular shape
between these rooms and the outer wall. The back walls of the rooms
are built of rough polygonal stones.

The western or rather south-western side of the great quadrangle
round which the edifices just described were grouped was closed by a
building (marked E on the plan) which seems to have included a portal
leading into the quadrangle, a colonnade opening in the same direction,
and two or three rooms lying at the back of the colonnade.

To the south-west of this group of buildings, and at a short distance
from them, are the foundations of what seems to have been a long
colonnade with projecting wings. On the plan the building is marked
as the West Colonnade. It faced south-east, and its total length,
including the wings, is 48.4 metres. Of the back wall almost nothing is
left, but the foundations of an inner row of columns are preserved, and
from the thickness of the front wall we may infer that it supported an
outer row of columns. Best preserved are the foundations and stylobate
of the north-eastern wing. In front of this wing stand three foundations
which probably supported statues. Close to it lies also a quadrangular
pedestal of dark marble [1] which from an inscription carved on it appears
to have borne the statue of a certain Agasicles, son of Sosiphanes. From
the style of letters of the inscription I judged it might belong to the
second or first century B.C. Following a suggestion of Dr. Dörpfeld's,
Prof. Wide conjectures that this colonnade with the projecting wings
was a Council House. The grounds for thinking that it was so are, first,
that it resembles a building at Mantinea which on independent grounds
is conjectured to have been a Council House (see vol. 4. p. 216); and,
second, that an inscription found by the Swedish archaeologists at the
sanctuary of Poseidon makes mention of "the statues at the Council
House." This inscription proves that there was a Council House at the
sanctuary and that statues stood at or near it, which accords very well
with the presence of foundations for statues in front of the colonnade in
question.

[1] Prof. Wide says white limestone. I follow my notes.

About 29 paces to the south-west of the West Colonnade are foundations and walls of a quadrangular edifice (marked G on the plan) which I
conjecture to have been the dwellings of priests and officials. It appears
to have consisted of an open court about 12 metres square surrounded by
rooms. The building, whatever it was, stands on higher ground than the
rest of the sanctuary, just at the beginning of the slope of the pine-clad
hill which bounds the sanctuary on the west. Indeed the rooms abut
on the rocks on the top of which the pine-wood begins, and from them
charming views are to be had over the forest to the sea, which with its
capes and islands is visible both on the north and the south. The entrance
to the building is from the east. To the left of the entrance is a square
chamber with a well-preserved floor of concrete ; a great part of the first
course of the walls of this room is also standing. On the opposite or
western side of the court are two rooms, the walls of which are standing
to a height of several feet. The foundations are built of squared blocks
of limestone, but in the upper part of the walls bricks occur, which
seems to show that the building was repaired in late, perhaps Roman
times ; but from the style of some ante-fixes of terra-cotta found on the
spot Prof. Wide seems inclined to date the original building in the third
century B.C. The door of the larger of the western rooms opened between two Ionic half-columns ; the base of one of these half-columns still
exists. Stone benches seem to have run round the walls of this larger
room, and a statuette of Aesculapius, with a dedicatory inscription of
Roman date, was found in it. Hence Prof. Wide conjectures that the
room may have been the meeting-place of a religious society ; he compares a similar room in the sanctuary of Zeus the Hurler near Megara
(see vol. 2. p. 550). Rooms with stone benches running round the
walls have been found also at the Heraeum (vol. 3. p. 175) and Olympia
(vol. 4. p. 88). Stone benches also lined the walls of the long colonnade
in the sanctuary of Amphiaraus (vol. 2. p. 468). In the building which
I conjecture to have been the priests' dwelling I observed some fragments of thick red pottery, a piece of a small fluted column of tufa, and
two small quadrangular bases.

The objects found in the sanctuary by Messrs. Wide and Kjellberg
were few and on the whole unimportant. Most of them were discovered
in the earth which had been heaped up in order to obtain a level
area for the precinct enclosing the temple of Poseidon. Amongst
the objects here brought to light were sherds of the various early
kinds of pottery known as Mycenaean, geometrical, proto-Corinthian,
and Corinthian. As nothing more recent than Corinthian pottery was
found in this rubbish-heap, Prof. Wide infers that the precinct may
have been constructed in the sixth century B.C. But the discovery of
Mycenaean potsherds on the spot goes to show, as he rightly observes,
that a sanctuary of some sort existed here at a much remoter era.
Amongst the inscriptions found is one which mentions Amphictyones
and Sacred Secretaries (*hieromnamones*). The significance of this
inscription, which is overlooked by the editors, has been pointed out
by Professor von Wilamowitz-Moellendorff ('Die Amphiktionie von
Kalaurea,' *Nachrichten von der königl. sächs. Gesell. der Wissenschaften*,

Philolog. historische Klasse, 1896, Heft 2. pp. 158-170). It proves that at the time when the inscription was carved, perhaps in the third century B.C., the league of which Strabo speaks (viii. p. 374) still existed. See vol. 3. p. 286.

A walk of about half an hour down from the sanctuary in a north-easterly direction brings us to the Bay of *Vajonia*, where some remains of ancient docks or ship-sheds may still be seen. This, therefore, was the port of the ancient sanctuary. A road led from it by a gentle ascent up the northern declivity of the mountain to the shrine, ending between the West Colonnade and the edifice which I conjecture to have been the abode of the priests. The harbour may have sheltered the vessels of the seven cities which made up the league of Calauria.

P. 299 line 3 *sqq.* from top, **Asine** etc. I visited Asine from Nauplia 9th December 1895, and will describe the ancient remains from my notes.

The ruins of Asine occupy a peninsula or headland which rises into a rocky pinnacle on its northern or landward side, just above the isthmus which unites it to the land. The bay into which the headland projects is spacious and possesses a fine shelving beach of sand and pebbles. A level maritime plain, occupied by cornfields and olives, borders on the bay to the east and north-east of the peninsula. On the other hand the peninsula itself is for the most part a mass of rugged rocks which on the east and west descend in precipices into the sea. But at the north-western foot of the cape, below a line of high precipitous rocks, there is a stretch of comparatively level ground ; and again on the eastern side of the peninsula, above the rocks, there are some terraces of earth. On these more level parts the ancient town probably stood, but it can never have been a large one. In regard to its defences, the peninsula is protected on the east and west by sea-cliffs which might seem to render fortifications unnecessary ; and on the west side there appears in fact to have been no wall except in a narrow opening between the cliffs through which a steep slope leads down to the water's edge. At its southern extremity, on the other hand, towards the open sea the promontory slopes more gradually and a rugged path here leads down through the rocks to the water. On this side, accordingly, a fortification-wall, of which there are remains, crossed the peninsula from west to east at the head of the slope, and it was continued round the angle on the east side, where there are also remains of it. It may very well have been continued all along the eastern face of the peninsula, above the sea-cliffs, though beyond a certain point it has now disappeared. On the landward or northern side of the headland there is also a line of high rocks which contributes to the natural strength of the place, and this natural defence was further strengthened by a fortification-wall running along the top of the rocks. The points at which Asine was most easily accessible and therefore weakest were at the north-eastern and north-western foot of the rocky peninsula, above the shore of the bay. Both these places were accordingly protected by fortifications, of which remains exist.

The fortifications of Asine seem clearly to belong to three different periods, the Mycenaean, the Greek, and the Venetian. (1) Of the

Mycenaean walls the remains are but scanty. To affirm, as Schliemann did, that they are better preserved than the walls of Tiryns is a most monstrous exaggeration. Such as they are, they are best seen in the wall which crosses the peninsula from east to west on its southern or seaward side. Parts of this wall are built in true Cyclopean or Mycenaean fashion of great blocks of stone hardly fitted together; one block is 2 metres long and 1 metre high, another is 2 metres long and 1.85 metres high. Further, at the eastern end of the wall, where it has turned the angle and begun to follow the eastern face of the peninsula, there is a square projecting tower built of true Cyclopean masonry. It measures 13 paces on the front and 10 paces on the sides and supports a terrace of earth, above the surface of which the walls of the tower do not rise. The front wall of the tower, supporting the terrace, is about 3 metres high; it is built of large rough blocks scarcely hewn on the outside and only rudely fitted together. Within the tower, that is on the small terrace supported by it, there are remains of Cyclopean walls and a cavity in the ground which seems to have been a cistern. But even the southern wall of Asine, though in part Mycenaean or Cyclopean in style, is by no means exclusively so. Beginning on the western edge of the peninsula with a small square tower built of large roughly-hewn quadrangular blocks, it is preserved unbroken for about 30 paces eastward. Both faces of the wall are standing. It is 1.80 metres thick, and is standing to a height varying from 1 metre to about 2.70 metres. The stones of which it is composed are of various sizes, roughly cut in polygons and fitted together; but the masonry, though rough, seems too regular to be called Cyclopean or Mycenaean except for a few yards at the west end. The same rough polygonal, but not Cyclopean, masonry appears again in a projecting angle of the wall on the south-eastern face of the peninsula, close to the Cyclopean tower already described. The wall, where it makes this projecting angle, is 3.50 metres high. The other two places where remains of Mycenaean or Cyclopean masonry may be seen are in the gap between the cliffs on the western side of the peninsula and again in the fortification-wall at the north-western foot of the peninsula. In the former place—the gap between the cliffs—there are remains of a roughly-built wall of ill-fitting blocks some few yards long and 6 or 7 feet high. In the latter place— the fortification-wall at the north-western foot of the peninsula—there is a piece of a similar rough wall under a wall of a totally different kind, namely a wall of well-jointed polygonal masonry which certainly belongs to the good Greek period. Both these pieces of rough walls are probably, though not certainly, Mycenaean. That there was a Mycenaean settlement at Asine is proved by the abundant remains of painted Mycenaean pottery on the peninsula, especially on its south-western side. I picked up and brought away a good many small sherds which seemed to me Mycenaean.

(2) Of the fortifications belonging to the Greek or classical age there are massive remains at the north-eastern foot of the peninsula, facing eastward across the sandy beach of the bay. The remains consist of a wall built of well-cut and well-jointed polygonal blocks and strengthened

with two square projecting towers, which are built to some extent in the same style though with a strong tendency to quadrangular blocks and horizontal courses. The wall is standing to a height of from 4.50 metres to 5 metres. The more easterly of the towers is 9 metres broad and projects 7 metres from the wall. Its height may be about 8.50 metres ; fourteen courses of masonry, each apparently averaging about 60 or .70 metre, are preserved. Though the tower is square, its corners are rounded. The other tower of the Greek period, further west, is partly ruinous, but its northern face is standing to a height of about 4 metres. Its style of masonry is intermediate between the polygonal and rectangular. Still further to the west are more remains of the historical Greek period. One is a piece of a square tower well built in horizontal courses, of which four are preserved, giving a height of 2.30 metres. This tower stands on flat ground at the northern foot of the rocky peninsula. Beside it are some mediaeval ruins and a little to the west of it is a chapel of the Panagia. Another remnant of the historical Greek period is a square tower of polygonal masonry built tolerably high up on the rocky northern face of the peninsula, immediately above the battlemented Venetian wall which is a conspicuous feature of Asine on this side. The tower in question is about 5 metres square and several metres high. On the west it abuts on high precipitous rocks. The last piece of fortification belonging to the classical Greek age which we have to notice is a wall at the northwestern foot of the peninsula, just above the beach and facing west across the bay. This wall, about 30 paces long, consists at its southern end of well-jointed polygonal masonry built on the top of a rough wall which is probably Mycenaean (see above). Here the wall is between 2 and 3 metres high. At its northern end only one course of the polygonal wall is visible above ground.

(3) A mediaeval wall, battlemented in part and built of small stones, bricks, and mortar, runs along the crest of some of the high rocks on the northern and north-eastern face of the peninsula. To some extent it stands on the top of portions of the ancient Greek wall built of polygonal masonry which has been already described. This battlemented wall is no doubt a work of the Venetians.

Within the fortification-wall at the north-eastern foot of the peninsula there is a short piece of wall built of good ashlar masonry which may have formed part of the inner side of a gateway. The place would be appropriate for a gateway, as the peninsula is easily accessible on this side.

P. 300 line 22 *sqq.* from top, a mountain which they call Pontinus etc. I visited Lerna 8th December 1895, and the notes I made on the spot may help to give the reader a clearer idea of the situation of the marsh and of the Pontinus and Amymone streams.

At the southern end of the great Argolic plain Mount Pontinus advances abruptly eastward to within a few hundred yards of the sea. South of it the hills again retire, leaving another small maritime plain between their base and the beach. The pass between the foot of Mount Pontinus and the sea may be about half a mile long from north to south by 300 yards wide. Within this narrow space are comprised the two ancient streams the Pontinus and the Amymone, the Lernaean marsh, and the modern village of Lerna. The two streams rise at the foot of the mountain but at opposite ends of the pass, the Pontinus at the northern and the Amymone at the southern end. Most of the Lernaean marsh lies between them, but much nearer to the Amymone. Indeed the Amymone, in its short course, flows through the marsh, which it partly feeds; whereas the Pontinus is clear away from it to the north. The modern village of Lerna, a station on the railway line from Argos to *Tripolitsa*, lies a quarter of a mile or so to the south of the Pontinus, immediately to the north and east of the marsh.

Mount Pontinus which rises above the village is a hill of no great height, but of broad massive outline. On its crest are seen from below against the sky the walls and towers of a mediaeval castle crowning the summit. The slope of the hill towards Lerna is on the whole even and uniform and tufted with low plants, but toward the south-east it is broken by some high lines of rocks. The carriage-road from Argos skirts the foot of the hill and traverses the village. Beside the road rise the springs both of the Pontinus brook and the Amymone; and between the road and the sea is the Lernaean marsh. In approaching Lerna from Argos and entering the pass between Mount Pontinus and the sea we first come to the rush-fringed spring of the Pontinus on the left side of the road. The stream is a mere brook of clear water bordered by rushes and tall grasses and almost choked with green water-plants. A great part of the water is diverted at the spring to turn a mill which stands on the shore some 30 or 40 yards north of the mouth of the stream. The whole course of the brook from its source to the sea is probably not more than 200 or 300 yards.

After passing the source of the Pontinus and traversing in a few minutes the village of Lerna we come to the springs of the Amymone, which rise beside the road at the southern end of the village, a few yards to the north of a white-washed chapel of St. John. The springs are copious and issue from under rocks, forming at once a shallow pool of beautifully clear water, from which the stream flows towards the sea in a bed fringed with reeds. Great beds of reeds, marking the site of the Lernaean marsh, grow also beside the pool and in the narrow stretch of flat swampy ground between it and the sea. A fig-tree has rooted itself among the rocks from which the springs flow, and a few yards further off to the south are a mulberry-tree and a silver poplar. Some eighty yards or so to the north-east of the springs but completely hidden by a screen of trees is the Alcyonian Lake described by Pausanias. It is a pool of still, dark, glassy water surrounded by great reeds and grasses and tall white poplars with silvery stems. Though distant only about thirty yards from the highroad and the village the spot is as wild and lonely as if it lay in the depths of some pathless forest of the New World. I sought it for some time in vain, and when at last I came upon it, in the waning light of a winter afternoon, everything seemed to enhance the natural horror of the scene. The sky was dark save for one gleam of sunlit cloud which was reflected in the black water of the pool. The wind sighed among the reeds and rustled the thin leaves of the poplars. Altogether I could well imagine that superstitions might gather about this lonely pool in the marsh. Of such a spot in England tales of unhappy love, of murder and suicide would be told. To the Greeks of old it seemed one of the ways to hell. The man who drove me from Argos said, like Pausanias, that the pool had never been fathomed and was bottomless.

In its short course to the sea the Amymone assumes the proportions of a broad full stream, in fact of a small river not unlike the Cam at Granchester. But the greater part of its water comes, I think, not from the springs beside the road, but from the Alcyonian Lake, in which there seem to be deep subterranean springs. Close to the sea the stream, after flowing through the reedy marsh, expands into a millpond, fringed with grass, white poplars and other trees, which is divided from the beach only by an embankment and a stone dyke. Part of the water of the pond turns a mill beside the shore; the rest is diverted into a canal, shaded by trees and bordered by rushes and water-grasses, which skirts the beach for a short way southward and then allows the pent-up water to escape with an impetuous flow into the sea. The narrow beach is of fine sand, firm under the tread. Beyond the outflow of the canal the stone dyke is continued for a little way further south along the shore and is then joined by a wall which strikes down eastward from near the highroad to the sea. About 20 yards further south there is a parallel wall which, however, stops short a few yards before it reaches the shore. The object of these parallel walls was doubtless to confine the Lernaean marsh on the south and to prevent it from inundating the cornfields and olive-groves of the neighbouring plain.

P. 305 line 11 from foot, **what is called Anigraea** etc. On the difficult question of the topography of Thyreatis see R. Heberdey, *Die Reisen des Pausanias in Griechenland*, p. 51 *sqq.* In agreement with Lolling he would identify the ruins called *Helleniko* as those of Thyrea, the capital of the district. He observes that Thyrea is not mentioned and hence was probably not visited by Pausanias, who seems on entering the Thyrean plain from the north by the Anigraean pass to have immediately turned inland up the valley of the Tanus and ascended it till he reached the Laconian frontier on the crest of Mount Parnon, about 3 miles or so beyond the modern village of *H. Petros.* Mr. Heberdey supposes that all the three villages mentioned by Pausanias, namely Athene, Neris, and Eva, were on this route. Athene he would place at *Loukou*, Neris at *Oraeo-Kastro*, and Eva at *H. Petros.*

P. 308 line 17 from top, **the monastery of Loukou.** Four large marble columns have lately been found at the spring near the monastery (*Mittheilungen d. arch. Inst. in Athen*, 21 (1896), p. 466).

P. 315 line 5 from top, **took sanctuary** etc. Sanctuaries for criminals existed also among the Californian Indians (Boscana, 'Chinigchinich,' appended to [A. Robinson's] *Life in California* (New York, 1846), p. 262); and sanctuaries taking the form of cities of refuge are found among the Kafirs of the Hindu Kush (Sir George S. Robertson, *The Kafirs of the Hindu Kush* (London, 1896), p. 441) and in some parts of West Africa (Miss Mary H. Kingsley, *Travels in West Africa*, (London, 1897), p. 466). In regard to the West African towns of this class Miss Kingsley was good enough to give me in conversation some details which do not appear in her book. The Jews also had their cities of refuge (Numbers xxxv. 6, Deuteronomy iv. 41-43, xix. 1-10, Joshua xx.). In the light of these instances it becomes probable that the tradition as to the origin of Rome was well founded. To this subject I hope to return elsewhere.

P. 317 line 11 *sqq.*, **Decelea** etc. The township of Decelea seems, according to Prof. Milchhöfer, to have had its centre in the hollow between the King's park at *Tatoi* and the hill which bounds the hollow on the south. Traces of walls and large single blocks of limestone may be seen extending from the new inn to the royal stables. The inscription referred to in the text was found near the stables. On the hill which closes the hollow towards the south is a ruined fortress which Prof. Milchhöfer believes to be the one erected by the Lacedaemonians in 413 B.C. The wall still encircles the hill about half-way up except on the south-east side, where it seems to have approached the summit. It forms an ellipse about 800 metres in circumference. Only the lower courses remain, and of them nothing but the outer surface is visible, the wall serving as a support to the soil above. The blocks are of moderate size and not all of them are squared. See A. Milchhöfer, in *Karten von Attika, Erläuternder Text*, Heft vii. viii. p. 2 *sq.*

P. 330 line 13 from foot, **those who sail to India.** To the literature dealing with the subject of Greek intercourse with India may be added an article by Mr. S. Lévi, 'La Grèce et l'Inde d'après les documents indiens,' published in the *Revue des Études grecques*, 4 (1891), pp. 24-45.

P. 340 line 2 from top, **Lycurgus.** The historical existence of the Spartan legislator Lycurgus is defended with characteristic good sense and insight by J. Töpffer (*Beiträge zur griechischen Altertumswissenschaft* (Berlin, 1897), pp. 347-362). It should never have been called in question.

P. 340 line 8 from foot, **Artemis Anaeitis.** Mention is made of Artemis Anaeitis (or Anaitis) in Lydian inscriptions. See Μουσεῖον καὶ βιβλιοθήκη τῆς Εὐαγγελικῆς Σχολῆς (Smyrna, 1880), pp. 127, 164 ; *Revue archéologique*, 3me Série, 6 (1885), p. 105.

P. 348 line 3 from top, **Death.** The Greek conception of death as embodied in literature and art is the subject of a recent monograph by Mr. A. de Ridder (*De l'idée de la mort en Grèce à l'époque classique*, Paris, 1897).

P. 359 line 14 *sq* from foot, **little leaden figures** etc. On these votive offerings see P. Perdrizet, 'Offrandes archaïques du Menelaion et de l'Amyclaion,' *Revue archéologique*, 3me Série, 30 (1897), pp. 8-19, where many of them are figured. Among the tiny statuettes are several of winged goddesses, and one of a goddess (probably Artemis) shooting an arrow from a bow. Two represent lions. Some of the figures are now at Munich, others at Athens. A few objects of the same sort were found by Mr. Tsountas in the sanctuary of Apollo at Amyclae.

P. 365 line 19 from foot, **Hellenes —— Hellas.** The history of the names Hellas and Hellenes has been examined by Prof. J. B. Bury (*Journal of Hellenic Studies*, 15 (1895), pp. 217-238). He attempts to show how the name Hellas, from designating originally a small territory in the south of Thessaly, came in time to stand for the whole of Greece. According to him, there was an intermediate stage when the name was applied to the district in the north of Peloponnese afterwards known as Achaia. This, he holds, is the application which the name has in *Odyssey*, xv. 80, where Menelaus proposes to conduct Telemachus "through Hellas and mid Argos." The name Hellenes, on Prof. Bury's theory, did not come into use as a general name for all the Greeks until the seventh century B.C.

P. 389 line 15 from top, **a wide-spread custom of throwing offerings into volcanoes** etc. The Indians of Nicaragua used to throw maidens into the volcano of Masaya, "thinking by their lives to appease the fire, that it might not destroy the country" (Herrera, *General History of America*, translated by Capt. John Stevens, vol. 3. p. 341).

P. 398 line 24 from foot, **the dolphin at Poroselene.** In the reign of Augustus there is said to have been a dolphin which carried a boy on its back daily to and from school between Baiae and Puteoli (Pliny, *Nat. hist.* ix. 25 ; Solinus, xii. 7 *sq.* ed. Th. Mommsen). Poroselene, or Pordoselene as it seems to have been more properly called, was an island between Lesbos and the mainland (Strabo, xiii. p. 618 *sq.* ; Scylax, *Periplus*, 97). On the question of the credibility of the story here told by Pausanias see the Introduction.

P. 420. The statement of Pausanias (iv. 27. 11) as to the persistence of the Doric dialect in Messenia down to a late time is confirmed by inscriptions (Dittenberger und Purgold, *Die Inschriften von Olympia*, p. 502, note on No. 399).

P. 429 line 12 from foot, **Messene.** Excavations made by the Greek Archaeological Society in 1895 laid bare a great part of the ancient market-place, including a stately building with colonnades and portals. A fountain, supposed to be the ancient Arsinoe mentioned by Pausanias (iv. 31. 6), was also found. One of the marble walls with a spout is preserved, and in the interior is a piece of a marble conduit or aqueduct. Amongst the inscriptions discovered is one that describes the boundaries of Messene. Another mentions a certain Marcus who had built the four colonnades of the sanctuary of Aesculapius ; and another speaks of a man Aristeus who had been sent as an ambassador of Greece to Nero. See *Mittheilungen d. arch. Inst. in Athen*, 20 (1895), p. 375 ; *Athenaeum*, 21st December 1895, p. 879 ; *Berliner philolog. Wochenschrift*, 6th January 1896, p. 735 *sq.* ; *American Journal of Archaeology*, 11 (1896), p. 244 ; *Classical Review*, 10 (1896), p. 76.

P. 435 line 15 *sqq.* from top, **the victims —— black bulls** etc. A wealthy man of Elatea provided in his will, which is partially preserved in an inscription, that a bull should be periodically sacrificed and games held at his tomb (*C. I. G. G. S.* 3. No. 128).

P. 456 line 17 from top, **Coryphasium** —— **Pylus.** Fresh light has been thrown on the topography of Pylus or Coryphasium and the neighbouring island of Sphacteria, as well as on Thucydides's narrative of the military operations there in 425 B.C., by the researches of Messrs. G. B. Grundy and R. M. Burrows, who in 1895 by a somewhat curious coincidence examined both sites independently at an interval of a week or two. Mr. Grundy made a survey of the ground which he has published along with a paper in which he propounds certain novel theories as to the battles and Thucydides's account of them (*Journal of Hellenic Studies*, 16 (1896), pp. 1-54, with plates ii. and iii.). The results of Mr. Burrows's researches are set forth in the same journal (vol. 16 (1896), pp. 55-76) in an able article, which may be regarded as the most important contribution yet made towards the elucidation of Thucydides's narrative. Both writers confirm in the most positive manner two of the conclusions which, without having visited the site, I had adopted in the text. The first of these conclusions is, that Arnold's well-known proposal to identify *Palaeo-Kastro* with Sphacteria and the hill of *Hagio Nikolo* with Pylus is absolutely refuted by a study of the ground, which proves beyond question or cavil that the island still called Sphagia is the ancient Sphacteria and that *Palaeo-Kastro* is the Pylus or Coryphasium of Thucydides and Pausanias. The second conclusion in which Mr. Grundy and Mr. Burrows agree unhesitatingly is that the lagoon of *Osman Aga* at the eastern foot of *Palaeo-Kastro* is not, as Leake and others have supposed, a modern encroachment of the sea upon what in antiquity was a level stretch of sand, but that on the contrary it is an old arm of the sea which has been converted into a lagoon by the gradual growth of sandbars both on the north and the south, and which is now in process of being silted up. Both writers are of opinion that the lagoon existed as a navigable sheet of water in the time of Thucydides and communicated with the bay of *Navarino* on the south by a channel which was also navigable for ancient ships. They only differ as to the probable width of the channel, Mr. Grundy assuming that it was narrow and Mr. Burrows that it was wide. The latter view is made the more probable by Thucydides's silence as to the existence of the lagoon. For if the passage was wide, the lagoon would be practically a part of the bay of *Navarino* and so would not call for any special mention; whereas if the passage was narrow the lagoon would have formed a separate harbour, and thus there would have been two harbours instead of one, whereas Thucydides speaks throughout of one only. Mr. Grundy is indeed driven by his theory to suppose that there were two harbours and that Thucydides confused them; but there is no need to impute any mistake of this sort to the historian if we only assume with Mr. Burrows that the opening was a wide one.

Making use of the papers of Messrs. Grundy and Burrows I propose now to correct on certain points and to supplement the account of Pylus and Sphacteria given in the text. The summit of Pylus is 450 feet high, not 720 feet, as I have stated. Almost the whole of its eastern side, towards the lagoon, is a sheer and inaccessible precipice; only at the northern and southern ends, above the bay of *Voidokoilia* and the *Sikia* channel respectively, does the line of cliffs descend and merge into a more or less steep slope. These two places therefore are the points on the landward side which would need to be fortified by any force holding Pylus. Mr. Burrows has made it highly probable that the Athenian wall which the Spartans purposed to batter down with siege engines (Thucydides, iv. 13) ran along the top of the low slope at the southern end of the line of cliffs. For the terms in which Thucydides mentions this purpose seem to show that the point of assault was not accessible to the Spartans from the land but could only be reached by disembarking both engines and men from the fleet. Now if, as seems probable, at the time of the siege the lagoon communicated with the Bay of *Navarino* by a broad channel and its waters washed the foot of the eastern cliffs of Pylus for the greater part of their length, the sandy slope at the southern end of the cliffs could only have been reached by the Spartans from their ships. It was probably on this sandy slope that Demosthenes beached his ships under the fortification which he had erected on the top of the slope (Thucydides, iv. 9), and it was here that the Spartans intended to plant their battering-rams. If they had intended to batter the Athenian fortifications at the northern end of the cliffs they could have done so without landing men from the fleet, since that end of the cliffs was connected, as at present, with the mainland by a level stretch of sand of which the Spartans were in undisputed possession.

With regard to the Athenian fortifications at the northern end of Pylus, Mr. Burrows has shown good grounds for believing that they did not include the northern extremity of the promontory as far as the Bay of *Voidokoilia* but followed a steep and nearly continuous line of cliffs which crosses the northern slope of the hill from east to west. The cave of Nestor is below the eastern end of this line of cliffs. At their other or western end, about 100 yards or so from the sea, these cliffs fall away and there is a level space by which an enemy could pass through to the south. Here accordingly was probably the Athenian fortification which the Spartan army vainly assaulted (Thucydides, iv. 9, 11-13), and here Mr. Burrows found extensive remains of a wall which in its style answers well to Thucydides's description (iv. 4) of the fortifications hastily run up by the Athenians, being built of unhewn stones of no great size piled together without mortar. The advantages to the small Athenian garrison of choosing this line of defence instead of embracing the northern end of the promontory within their fortifications were great. It saved them from building several hundred yards of wall, which in the short time at their disposal they could hardly have accomplished; and they had now to defend the base instead of two sides of a triangle, while even of this base half, at least, would require no wall at all, and a quarter more would require only a slight one.

The place where the Spartans, led by Brasidas, attempted to land and to carry the Athenian fortifications by storm is quite unmistakeable and answers to Thucydides's description (iv. 9, 11) exactly. It is at the south-west end of the promontory, facing towards the open sea.

Here the shore is studded for several hundreds of yards with masses of detached and jagged rocks, on which it is no wonder that the Spartan pilots feared to break their ships in the attempt to effect a landing. Yet bad as the landing-place is, it was the best to be had, for further to the north the sea-coast of Pylus consists of a line of inaccessible cliffs where no ship could put in. At the point where Brasidas and the Spartans essayed to force a landing, the Athenian fortification-wall must have run inland from the rugged rocks which here stud the shore ; for over these rocks no wall could have been built. And inland from these rocks in fact Mr. Burrows came across foundations of an ancient Greek fortification-wall which, however, from the regular style of its masonry cannot have formed part of the works so hastily thrown up by the Athenians, though it probably follows the same line. Indeed there are a few rough pieces in it which may possibly date from the Athenian occupation. It was on the rocky shore outside of this wall that Demosthenes, the Athenian commander, drew up his men to repel the Spartan landing (Thucydides, iv. 9).

On the north-east side of Pylus, near the spit of sand which divides the lagoon from the Bay of *Voidokoilia*, Mr. Burrows found traces of massive Cyclopean walls and what appeared to him to be a gateway of the same age as Tiryns and Mycenae. The existence of these remains, if Mr. Burrows's opinion as to their date is correct, confirms the view that the Homeric Pylus was at *Palaeo-Kastro*.

The *Sikia* channel, which divides Pylus (*Palaeo-Kastro*) on the north from Sphacteria on the south, is only 132 yards wide at the narrowest point. Towards the sea it is deep, but at its eastern end, where the channel widens a little, it is so shallow as to be easily fordable, there being only about 2 feet of water. This ford is perhaps 250 yards across from shore to shore, with a breadth of about 40 or 50 yards. On each side of it the water deepens very rapidly. There is a tradition that the ford was created by the Turks who, after the battle of Lepanto, blocked up the channel with stones and sunken ships in order to protect their ships which had taken refuge in the bay. Mr. Grundy, however, is of opinion that a bar is gradually forming across the channel like those which now enclose the lagoon on the north and south.

The island of Sphacteria would seem to have scarcely changed since antiquity. The depth of water close to the shore on all sides forbids us to suppose that its outline can have been much altered by the action of the sea. Its length is 2¾ miles ; its breadth varies from one-third to half a mile. The northern end of the island consists of a short ridge running east and west with a dip in the middle and reaching its highest point at the eastern extremity. This summit, now known as Mount *Elias*, is also the highest point of the whole island. Its height is about 500 feet. From the summit the ground falls away in steep but climbable slopes on the north, west, and south. On the east the peak descends in a cliff some 80 feet high into a small hollow, on the further edge of which the ground rises again into a jagged but lower peak, then drops sheer into the sea in a perpendicular cliff several hundreds of feet high. The hollow between the upper and lower peak is about 50 yards

wide by 100 yards long from north to south. It is accessible from the
north by an easy slope, and from the south by a steep and difficult
gully, like an Alpine 'chimney,' between perpendicular sea-cliffs on
either hand. Mr. Burrows is probably right in supposing that by this
steep gully the Messenians clambered up into the hollow and took the
Spartans in the rear (Thucydides, iv. 36). The northern and lower
end of the hollow must certainly have been defended by the Spartans.
Here indeed Mr. Burrows discovered, almost hidden under a thick
growth of brushwood, a line of fortification stretching right across the
hollow from the edge of the cliffs. It was, we may well suppose, while
the Athenians were attacking and the Spartans defending this wall that
the Messenians, emerging from the gully, suddenly appeared on the
sky-line—in mid-air, as Thucydides puts it—above and behind the
Spartans, the sight of them at once infusing fresh courage into the
assailants and striking with dismay the defenders who, thus taken
simultaneously in front and rear, soon laid down their arms. There are,
it is true, distinct traces of another wall running across the south end of
the hollow, a few feet from the top of the gully; but this wall the
Spartans, trusting to the natural strength of the position, may very well
have left undefended. As the gully descends steeply to the water's
edge between cliffs which apparently afford no foothold to a climber, we
must suppose that the Messenians reached the foot of it by boat, though
this is not mentioned by Thucydides.

On the other sides of the summit, namely on the north-west, west,
and south-west, Mr. Burrows found the remains of the "ancient fort
made of rough stones" which Thucydides mentions (iv. 31). It
begins both on the south-west and north-west in a curved line, following
the shape of the hill some yards below the top, but on the long western
side its line is broken by four projecting rectangular bastions. The
stones of which it is built are large and rough and are not bonded
together with bricks or mortar. Two and three courses of these stones
are preserved at various points, but some of the best preserved pieces
are hidden under a thick undergrowth of wild olive, wild strawberry, and
other trees. In one place the wall is still 3 ft. 6 in. high. Part of it
was observed and described by Schliemann (*Mittheilungen d. arch. Inst.
in Athen*, 14 (1889), p. 133). But he overlooked the wall in the hollow
on the north-eastern side of the peak which formed a necessary part of
the fort.

The southern end of Sphacteria is, roughly speaking, a plateau
about 150 feet above sea-level with a coast-line which consists for the
most part of perpendicular cliffs from 100 to 150 feet high. On the
northern edge of the plateau the ground rises into two hills each about
300 feet high. Between these hills on the south and Mount *Elias* on
the north there intervenes about a mile of comparatively level but still
very rugged and difficult ground. Along its eastern edge runs a ridge
which connects the two higher extremities of the island. On the east
this ridge falls down into the sea in precipices from 100 to 300 feet
high; on the west it slopes steeply to the stretch of low-lying ground
beside the open sea. The coast of this low ground is itself low but

rocky; in calm weather landing is possible on it.   On the eastern side of the island, towards the Bay of *Navarino*, the long line of lofty precipices forbids a landing except at three or four points, the best of which is at the chapel of the Panagia, near the middle of the island. A gap in the cliffs here gives access to the rest of the island. But owing to the height of the cliffs this and all the other landings on the eastern side of Sphacteria are out of sight of any one stationed either on the central plain or even on the northern peak.   Hence it was easy enough for the Athenians to land, a little before dawn, without attracting the attention of the Spartan sentries (Thucydides, iv. 31).   The island is uninhabited and almost wholly uncultivated.   Its rocky surface is overgrown with low scrub, and trees are scattered about it singly or in clumps, especially on the flat ground.   The only spring is just where Thucydides says (iv. 31) it was, in the middle and level part of the island.   It was here that the main body of the Spartans was posted, and it was from here that, fighting hard, they were driven slowly over the rugged ground northward to Mount *Elias*, beset by the enemy both from the ridge and from the shore and| blinded by the dust which rose in clouds under their feet as they trampled over the recently-burnt scrub (Thucydides, iv. 31-35).

We have seen (vol. 3. p. 460) that Thucydides greatly underestimated the width of the two entrances to the Bay of *Navarino*.   Of this mistake Mr. Burrows has suggested an explanation which has the merit of being simple and on the face of it not improbable.   He supposes that when the Athenian fleet sailed into the bay by both entrances simultaneously (Thucydides, iv. 14), one squadron passed through the narrow northern channel in a column of two ships abreast, while the other squadron entered by the broad southern channel in a column of eight ships abreast ; and that these numbers were afterwards communicated by one of the admirals or captains in command to Thucydides, who consequently fell into the not unnatural mistake of estimating the width of the two channels by the number of the ships that entered them abreast.   The intention which Thucydides attributes to the Spartans of blocking up the two entrances with their ships may be, as Mr. Burrows surmises, nothing more than a lame excuse afterwards offered by the Spartans for the fatal blunder they made in garrisoning Sphacteria.   It is indeed almost incredible that the Spartans, with the ships at their command, should ever have seriously contemplated the possibility of blocking the southern channel (about three-quarters of a mile wide) against the Athenian fleet.   Finally, the mistake as to the length of Sphacteria which occurs in our texts of Thucydides may perhaps be explained most simply, as Mr. Burrows conjectures, by the mistake of a copyist who by omitting the first Δ (10) of ΔΔΠ (25) converted 25 furlongs into 15.   In point of fact the island is about 24 Greek furlongs long, and if we allow for the ups and downs of its surface 25 furlongs will be a fair estimate.

Mr. Burrows's views have been criticised, on the whole adversely, by Mr. Grundy (*Classical Review*, 10 (1896), pp. 371-374; *id.*, 11 (1897), pp. 155-159), but I cannot see that his objections carry weight.

The reply made by Mr. Burrows to the first set of these objections is powerful and on the whole convincing (*Classical Review*, 11 (1897), pp. 1-10). Mr. Grundy's own theories as to the operations at Pylus it is hardly necessary to discuss : the most original of them has already been retracted by its author.

P. 458 line 24, **a cave.** In June 1896 Mr. Laurent of the French School of Archaeology dug up a number of painted potsherds in the cave of Nestor at Pylus. These sherds form a series dating from the earliest period down to Roman times. Many of them are fragments of large vases (*crateres*) of late Mycenaean style ; the decoration, laid on with lustrous paint, consists of broad black horizontal bands on a pale yellow ground ; the inside is coated with a black glaze. A handle of a large vase, adorned with broad black-brown stripes and pierced with a hole for suspension, is assigned by Mr. Tsountas to an age earlier than the Mycenaean. Some fragments exhibit patterns of the geometrical sort. See *Bulletin de Corresp. hellénique*, 20 (1896), pp. 388-390. The discovery of Mycenaean pottery here furnishes another ground for holding that the Homeric Pylus was at Coryphasium (*Palaeo-Kastro*).

P. 523 line 1, **the labours of Hercules.** The reliefs representing the labours of Hercules in the metopes of the temple of Zeus are now published in *Olympia: Ergebnisse*, Tafelband 3. plates xxxv.-xlv., and discussed by Prof. G. Treu, *ib.*, Textband 3. pp. 138-181.

P. 536 line 24 from foot, **paintings by Panaenus.** Prof. E. A. Gardner's proposed arrangement of the paintings of Panaenus on the barriers of the throne of Zeus has been accepted by Prof. C. Robert (*Die Marathonschlacht in der Poikile* (Halle a. S., 1895), p. 83). On the other hand Mr. Murray's arrangement has been accepted by Mr. Trendelenberg, who bases on it a somewhat fanciful and improbable theory of the meaning of the pictures, in ignorance, apparently, of the better arrangement advocated by Prof. E. A. Gardner. See *Archäo logischer Anzeiger*, 1897, pp. 25-29. Dr. Dörpfeld still adheres to Mr. Murray's view, and proposes to defend it by translating the words of Pausanias, ὑπελθεῖν ὑπὸ τὸν θρόνον, 'to go close up to the throne,' a translation which is simply impossible. The words can mean nothing but 'to go under the throne.' See *Mittheilungen d. arch. Inst. in Athen*, 22 (1897), p. 231 *sq.*

P. 543 line 9 from top, **The footstool** etc. It has been suggested by Mr. Klügmann (*Die Amazonen in der attischen Literatur und Kunst*, p. 62) that the remark which Pausanias makes as to the battle of Theseus with the Amazons ("This battle was the first deed of valour done by the Athenians against foreign foes") may have been taken from an Attic metrical inscription carved on the front of the footstool. One of the words here employed by Pausanias (ἀνδραγάθημα) seems to occur nowhere else in his work, and another (ὁμόφυλοι) only once (iv. 3. 2). Both words are Attic.

P. 545 line 17 from foot, **the things which project from an elephant's mouth.** The question whether an elephant's tusks are teeth or horns seems to have exercised the ancients a good deal. It is discussed at some length by Oppian (*Cyneget.* ii. 489-514) and Philostratus (*Vit. Apollon.* ii. 13), Oppian arguing in favour of horns and Philostratus of teeth. Juba, the learned king of Libya, held that they were horns (Pliny, *Nat. hist.* viii. 7 ; Philostratus, *l.c.*), but his opinion was rejected by Pliny (*l.c.*) as well as by Philostratus. The controversy is alluded to by Aelian (*Nat. anim.* iv. 31). Cp. A. Kalkmann, *Pausanias der Perieget*, p. 32.

P. 556 line 7 from top, **the altar of Olympian Zeus.** The only remains of this altar found by the German excavators were ninety-eight rough stones of the foundation, distributed in seven groups half-way between the north-eastern angle of the temple of Zeus and the south-western angle of the Metroum. Thus for our knowledge of the plan of the altar we are still dependent almost entirely on Pausanias's description. Dr. Adler believes that the altar of ashes was conical in shape and rested on a circular platform built of stone, the *prothusis*, to which two ramps also built of stone led up from opposite sides. From the platform (*prothusis*) he supposes that two winding ramps led up from opposite sides to the summit of the altar, on which the thighs of the victims were burned. The dimensions of the two stages of the altar, as given in our texts of Pausanias, must, Dr. Adler thinks, be wrong ; the circumference of the first stage or *prothusis* was probably 225 feet (not 125 feet) and the circumference of the second stage 132 feet (not 32 feet) ; and the text of Pausanias should be altered accordingly. The second of these changes, as he points out, can be easily made by altering the superfluous and meaningless ἑκάστου into ἑκατόν. See Fr. Adler, in *Olympia : Ergebnisse*, Textband 2. pp. 210-214.

P. 561 line 8 from foot, **Thunderbolt Zeus.** Dedications to Thundering Zeus have lately been found at Nacolea in Phrygia (*Bulletin de Corresp. hellénique*, 20 (1896), p. 107 *sq.*).

P. 565 line 6 from top, **Zeus the Descender.** Another inscription which marked the site of a sanctuary of Zeus the Descender (Διὸ[ς Καται]βάτο(υ) ἄβ[ατον] ἱερόν) has been found near the sanctuary of Aesculapius at Athens (*Revue de Philologie*, N. S. 19 (1895), p. 129 ; *Revue archéologique*, 3me Série, 27 (1895), p. 234). The sanctuary no doubt enclosed a spot which had been struck by lightning. Two conspicuous rocks in Melos are inscribed with the name of Zeus the Descender (*Journal of Hellenic Studies*, 17 (1897), p. 8 *sq.*, Nos. 21, 22).

P. 593 line 15 from foot, **purified themselves with a pig.** In an inscription found at Eleusis mention is made of two pigs which were used to purify the sanctuary ('Εφημερὶς ἀρχαιολογική, 1883, p. 119 *sq.*, line 49 *sq.*).

P. 595 line 24 from foot, **Hermes bearing the infant Dionysus.** The statue of Hermes by Praxiteles has now been described and discussed by Prof. G. Treu (*Olympia : Ergebnisse*, Textband 3. pp. 194-206). With regard to the objects which Hermes held in his hands, Prof. Treu comes to the conclusion, in which archaeologists seem disposed to acquiesce, that he grasped a herald's staff in his left hand and a bunch of grapes in his right. Miss E. Sellers thinks that the statue was not by Praxiteles, but by Cephisodotus who is said by Pliny (*Nat. hist.* xxxiv. 87) to have made a statue of Hermes nursing the infant Dionysus (' L'Hermes d'Olympie,' *Gazette des Beaux-Arts*, August 1897, pp. 119-139).

P. 621 line 18 from top, **Metroum.** An inscription on an architrave of the Metroum proves that the temple was dedicated by the Eleans to the worship of Augustus, "the saviour of the Greeks and of the whole world" (*Die Inschriften von Olympia*, No. 366). The colossal torso of a statue which was found lying on the southern edge of the stylobate of the Metroum is now interpreted by Prof. G. Treu as a portrait of Augustus represented in the character of Zeus, and from its dimensions compared with those of the temple he judges that the statue was made on purpose to be set up in the temple as the image to which the homage of worshippers was to be addressed. The torso is of Pentelic marble and is the largest in scale of all the sculptures found at Olympia. See G. Treu, in *Olympia: Ergebnisse*, Textband 3. pp. 232-235 ; *id.*, in *Archäologischer Anzeiger*, 1896, p. 97. Prof. Treu has also described and discussed the three other statues of Roman emperors which seem to have stood in the Metroum (*Olympia: Ergebnisse*, Textband 3. pp. 243-248, with Tafelband 3. plate lx. 1-3 and plate lxi. 1. 2). All three are of Pentelic marble and in standing postures. The one which portrays Claudius in the garb and attitude of Zeus bears an inscription which proves that it was made by two Athenian sculptors, Philathenaeus and Hegias (*Die Inschriften von Olympia*, No. 642). The statue of Titus represents the emperor clad in a cuirass on which are carved in high relief two Nereids seated on sea-horses with a dolphin under each horse. The statue of the third emperor is headless, but the evidence goes to show that it represents Domitian. He wears a cuirass adorned with the figures of two goddesses of Victory arranging a trophy. Prof. Treu is further of opinion that three statues of women found at Olympia represent three ladies of the Roman imperial families and that they stood on one side of the *cella* of the Metroum facing the statues of Claudius, Titus, and Domitian, with which they agree closely in size, material, style, and technique. He supposes that one of them represents the empress Domitia, another the younger Agrippina, and the third Julia, daughter of Titus. Only one of the three—that which Prof. Treu takes to represent the younger Agrippina—retains its head ; an inscription on this statue proves that it was made by an Athenian sculptor Dionysius, son of Apollonius (*Die Inschriften von Olympia*, No. 646). See *Olympia: Ergebnisse*, Textband 3. pp. 255-258, with Tafelband 3. pl. lxiii. 1-3.

P. 643 line 13, **the image of Victory** etc. The statue of Victory by Paeonius has now been described and discussed by Prof. G. Treu (*Olympia: Ergebnisse*, Textband 3. pp. 182-194). His view of the date and historical events which led to the erection of the statue agrees with the conclusions which I have adopted in the text.

VOL. IV

P. 17 line 8 *sq.* from foot, **represented on the pedestal of his statue.** The reliefs on the pedestal of the statue of Pulydamas have now been described and discussed by Prof. G. Treu (*Olympia: Ergebnisse*, Textband 3. pp. 209-212). In the second of the scenes described in the text it would seem that Pulydamas is seated rather than standing on the carcase of the lion : his left hand rests on one of the lion's fore-paws, and his right hand is placed on one of the beast's hind-legs. The third scene, where Pulydamas appears in presence of King Darius Ochus, is believed by Prof. Treu to represent the combat of the athlete with one of the 'Immortals.' The monument seems to have stood in front of the north-east corner of the temple of Zeus at the point where the East Terrace wall bends in a north-westerly direction round the pedestal of the Eretrian bull. As the statue of Pulydamas was by Lysippus it must have been made long after the athlete's Olympian victory, which was won in 408 B.C.

P. 39 line 9 from foot, **a bronze statue.** This statue has now been fully described and discussed by Mr. Th. Homolle (*Comptes Rendus de l'Académie des Inscriptions*, 4me Série, 24 (1896), pp. 362-384). The inscription on the base shows that it was dedicated by a certain Polyzalus, who was most probably the brother of the Syracusan tyrants Gelo and Hiero. But the mutilated state of the inscription leaves it uncertain whom the statue represents. Mr. Homolle now inclines to believe that it represents Gelo, and was set up to commemorate a Pythian victory won by him. Mr. Croiset, while admitting that the statue was dedicated by Polyzalus, brother of Gelo and Hiero, maintains that the name neither of Gelo nor of Hiero occurs in the inscription, and that the person commemorated is more probably Polyzalus himself (*Comptes Rendus de l'Académie des Inscriptions*, 4me Série, 24 (1896), pp. 214-216).

P. 48. "The boys' race in the horse-course" mentioned by Pausanias (vi. 16. 4) was a race run on foot, not on horseback. See Plato, *Laws*, viii. p. 833 b; Pollux, iii. 147; A. Boeckh, *Kleine Schriften*, 6. p. 393 *sq.*; *id.*, on *C. I. G.* No. 1515; J. H. Krause, *Die Gymnastik und Agonistik der Hellenen*, 1. p. 348 *sq.* note 13.

P. 56 line 23 from foot, **the treasuries.** The Olympic treasuries are the subject of an essay by E. Curtius ('Die Schatzhäuser von Olympia,' *Sitzungsberichte* of the Berlin Academy, 5th March 1896, pp. 239-251).

P. 72 line 11 from foot, **the marble statues.** The remains of the statues which adorned the Exedra of Herodes Atticus at Olympia are now described and their arrangement examined by Prof. G. Treu (*Olympia: Ergebnisse*, Textband 3. pp. 260-278). Amongst the remains found in the lower tank is a piece of a large male statue, naked, supposed by Prof. Treu to have belonged to a statue of a deity which may have stood in one of the two rotundas at either end of the lower tank. He conjectures that an image of Zeus occupied the eastern, and an image of Hera the western, rotunda (p. 270).

P. 82 line 24 from foot, **The Olympic hippodrome** etc. Some details as to the dimensions of the Olympic hippodrome are given in a Greek parchment manuscript (No. 1), which is preserved in the Old Seraglio at Constantinople. The whole length of the course, from the starting-point to the turning-post and back again, was 8 Olympic furlongs (*stades*). Of the two sides of the hippodrome, which are known from Pausanias to have been of unequal length, one, probably the shorter, was 3 furlongs and 1 *plethron* long. The breadth of the hippodrome at the starting-point was 1 furlong and 4 *plethra*. Further, we learn from the manuscript that not the whole of the course but only a portion of it 6 furlongs long was traversed in the races. Chariots drawn by pairs of foals had to make three rounds : chariots drawn by pairs of full-grown horses had to make eight rounds, and so had chariots drawn by four foals : chariots drawn by four full-grown horses had to make twelve rounds. See R. Schöne, in *Archäologischer Anzeiger*, 1897, p. 77 *sq.* ; *id.*, ' Neue Angaben über den Hippodrom zu Olympia,' *Jahrbuch des archäolog. Instituts*, 12 (1897), pp. 150-160. Pindar clearly indicates that the chariots had to round the turning-post twelve times (*Olymp.* iii. 59 *sq.* ; cp. *Olymp.* ii. 92, vi. 126, *Pyth.* v. 45). The scholiasts on Pindar (*Olymp.* iii. 59 and *Pyth.* v. 39) state that chariots drawn by (four) full-grown horses had to traverse the course twelve times, and that chariots drawn by (four) foals had to traverse it eight times. These statements, therefore, agree so far with the statements in the Constantinople manuscript. Cp. E. Pollack, *Hippodromica*, p. 103 *sq.* On the Olympic hippodrome and the mode of starting the chariots in it see the article by A. Martin, in Daremberg and Saglio's *Dictionnaire des Antiquités*, *s.v.* ' Hippodromos,' vol. 3. p. 196 *sqq.*

P. 96 line 21 from foot, **the Argive Phidon.** The date of Phidon has been further discussed by Mr. Evelyn Abbott (Excursus VI. to his edition of the fifth and sixth books of Herodotus, pp. 319-325) and Mr. R. Macan (note on Herodotus, vi. 127). The former inclines to accept the eighth Olympiad (748 B.C.) on the authority of Pausanias; the latter would prefer the twenty-eighth Olympiad (666 B.C.), altering the text of Pausanias accordingly.

P. 119 line 2 from top, **the oracle of Clarus.** Some verses purporting to be oracular responses of the Clarian Apollo are preserved (*Anthologia Palatina*, Appendix Nova, ch. vi. Nos. 134-139, p. 490 ed. Cougny).

P. 125 line 12 from foot, **one at Branchidae.** The ruins of the temple of Apollo at Branchidae are now being completely excavated by the French. Inscriptions found on the spot show that the temple was rebuilt in the second century B.C. : the work was going actively forward about the middle of the century, but to judge by the existing remains was never finished. The temple, unlike most Greek temples, rested on seven high steps, which, opposite the five central intercolumniations on the long sides, were divided each into two, thus forming a stately staircase of thirteen steps. The most remarkable feature of the architectural remains, however, is that the great Ionic capitals of the columns are each adorned with two colossal heads of deities and a head of a bull. See B. Haussoullier, in *Comptes Rendus de l'Académie des Inscriptions*, 25 (1897), p. 32 *sq.*; *Archäologischer Anzeiger*, 1897, pp. 63-65.

P. 128 line 3 from top, **Hercules —— on his raft.** This subject is represented on two engraved gems which are now in the Berlin Museum. On one of them Hercules is seated on an upturned jar; on the other he is kneeling and seems to be setting a sail. See A. Furtwängler, *Königliche Museen zu Berlin: Beschreibung der geschnittenen Steine*, Nos. 231, 232, p. 25.

P. 140 line 13 from foot, **Pirus —— Olenus.** The old view that the ruins at *Kato-Achaia* are those of Olenus, not of Dyme, is maintained by Mr. R. Heberdey (*Die Reisen des Pausanias*, p. 77, note 74), chiefly on the strength of a passage of Herodotus (i. 145), who says that Olenus was beside the Pirus, which he describes as a "great river." This description, Mr. Heberdey holds, can only apply to the *Kamnitsa* river beside *Kato-Achaia*, and hence the ruins at *Kato-Achaia* must be those of Olenus. The argument is a strong one, and if we identify the *Kamnitsa* with the Pirus we must inevitably, it would seem, accept the view that *Kato-Achaia* is on the site of Olenus. But on the other hand the concordant evidence of Pausanias, Strabo, and the Tabula Peutingeria as to the distance of Dyme from Patrae goes to show that the ruins at *Kato-Achaia* are those of Dyme, and this conclusion is confirmed, as we have seen (vol. 4. p. 136) by an inscription. Where the evidence is so conflicting it is best perhaps to leave the question open.

P. 146 line 19 from top, **the people bring the edible kinds of birds** etc. With Pausanias's description of the holocaust offered to Artemis at Patrae we may compare Herrera's description of a sacrifice offered by the Tlascallans to a hunter god. He says: "One of those goddesses they worshipped, had a son, who was a great sportsman, whom the Tlascallans took for their god, and because that province is very full of game, they kept a solemn festival in honour of him, sounding an horn at the dawn of the day, when they all assembled, with their bows, arrows, nets, and other implements for hunting. They carried their idol in procession, a multitude of people followed to an high mountain, on the top whereof was an arbour, and in the midst of it an altar well adorned, on which they placed the idol, attended all the way with much noise of horns, cornets, pipes, and drums. When come to the place, they encompassed all the side of that mountain, and setting fire to it on every side, abundance of deer, hares, and other creatures came out, flying from the fire towards the top; the hunters pursued them with great cries, sounding their instruments, till they had drove them before the idol, where they hemmed them in so close, that leaping to make their escape, some tumbled down, others fell upon the people, and others upon the altar, which rendered the sport very agreeable" (*General History of America*, translated by Capt. John Stevens, vol. 3. p. 206 *sq.*). The wild animals in this Tlascallan sacrifice, however, were slain, not burnt, and their flesh was consumed by the people.

P. 151 line 13 from top, **an infallible mode of divination** etc.

The practice of this mode of divination at the sanctuary of Demeter indicates that in one of her aspects Demeter was regarded as a goddess of healing. There is some more, though scanty, evidence to the same effect. See O. Rubensohn, 'Demeter als Heilgottheit,' *Mittheil. d. arch. Inst. in Athen,* 20 (1895), pp. 360-367.

P. 180 line 8 *sq.*, **Pisistratus collected the scattered verses of Homer.** The tradition that Pisistratus collected and edited the Homeric poems has recently been examined and rejected by Mr. M. Valeton ('De carminum Homericorum recensione Pisistratea,' *Mnemosyne,* N. S. 24 (1896), pp. 405-426).

P. 201 line 20 from foot, **the ruins of Mantinea.** The inscriptions found by the French excavators at Mantinea have now been published, after a long delay, by Mr. G. Fougères (*Bulletin de Corresp. hellénique,* 20 (1896), pp. 119-166). In several of them (Nos. 1, 2, 17) the city is called Antigonea or the city of the Antigonians, as to which title see Paus. viii. 8. 11 with the note. One inscription (No. 9) is from the base of a statue of King Antigonus after whom the city took the name of Antigonea. The inscription referring to the reconstructions carried out in the market-place by Euphrosynus and his wife Epigone (No. 2 ; see vol. 4. p. 214 *sq.*) seems to date from the last years of the first century A.D. The inscription recording the name of Zeus Eubuleus, which I have published from a copy of my own (vol. 4. p. 209), is now published as No. 8 (p. 138) by Mr. Fougères. It is engraved in large letters on a cube of limestone. Mr. Fougères regards Zeus Eubuleus as identical with Pluto. One inscription (No. 12) is dated by the year in which Philopoemen was general of the Achaeans for the fourth time. Another (No. 13) appears to be a fragment of the inscription engraved on the very portrait of Polybius which Pausanias mentions (viii. 9. 2). The name of Podares occurs in another inscription (No. 17) ; Pausanias knew of two Mantineans of that name (viii. 9. 9 *sq.*). The inscription recording the construction of a colonnade and halls "for the city of Mantinea and for the native god Antinous" (vol. 4. p. 213) is published by Mr. Fougères as No. 18 (p. 152). It is engraved on a marble architrave 3 metres long, .30 metre high, and .72 metre thick. The last words of the inscription (διὰ τὸν κληρονόμον "on account of the heir") are understood by Mr. Fougères to mean that Eurycles died before the colonnade was built, and that the work of building it was carried out by his heir. The name of the "god Antinous" occurs also in a metrical epigraph published by Mr. Fougères (No. 31, p. 163). Lastly may be mentioned two small pyramids engraved with the name of Artemis (Nos. 15, 26, pp. 149, 158) and apparently representing the goddess. One of them (No. 26), made of terra-cotta, was dedicated by a certain woman Phoebe ; the other, found not at Mantinea but in a small sanctuary of Artemis at the foot of Mount Parthenius (see vol. 4. p. 446), was dedicated by a man named Cnimas. With these pyramidal images we may compare the pyramidal images of Apollo and Zeus mentioned by Pausanias (i. 44. 2 ; ii. 9. 6).

P. 206 line 18 *sq.* from top, **the Muses and Marsyas** etc. The arrangement of the reliefs which were found by the French at Mantinea has been discussed by Prof. P. Gardner ('The Mantinean basis,' *Journal of Hellenic Studies*, 16 (1896), pp. 280-284). He at first argued that there never was a fourth slab, and that the three existing slabs were arranged in a row on the front of the pedestal, the slab with Apollo and Marsyas occupying the middle place. But he has since withdrawn this opinion and accepted Dr. Amelung's view that there were originally four slabs, of which two were placed on the front of the pedestal and one on each of the two sides, the slab with Marsyas and Apollo occupying the right-hand half of the front of the pedestal, while the missing slab with the three remaining Muses occupied the other or left-hand half of the front (*Journal of Hellenic Studies*, 17 (1897), p. 120 *sq.*). On this view the back of the pedestal was unadorned with sculpture. Dr. Amelung's arrangement is to be preferred to the one adopted by me in the text, according to which the four slabs were placed one on each of the four sides of the pedestal. It has the great advantage of giving a pedestal of sufficient dimensions (2.70 metres by 1.43 metres) to support a group of three life-size figures.

P. 219 line 2 from foot, **this Sicily is a small hill not far from Athens.** The identification of this Sicily with the little rocky hill which lies to the south of the Museum hill, on the opposite side of the Ilissus, seems to have been first proposed by H. G. Lolling in a paper published in 1874 and recently reprinted (*Mittheilungen d. arch. Inst. in Athen*, 21 (1896), pp. 339-346). The road to the ancient Phalerum (the modern *St. George*) runs on the south-eastern side of the hill, following approximately the line of the ancient Long Wall which connected Phalerum with Athens. Seen from this road, according to Lolling, the hill appears to be divided into three parts, each of which reaches its highest point on the side next to the road. These three elevations give to the hill, as seen from the Acropolis, the triangular shape of the island of Sicily. On the side next to the sea, which is partially cultivated, the hill slopes gradually to the plain. Lolling conjectured that the oracle which bade the Athenians occupy Sicily may have been given at the time when the wall to Phalerum had fallen into decay, and when accordingly it became desirable to strengthen the fortifications of Athens on this side. The hill of Sicily and the ambiguous oracle relating to it are mentioned by Dio Chrysostom (*Or.* xvii. vol. i. p. 277 ed. Dindorf).

P. 219 line 5 *sq.* from foot, **the grave of Hannibal was at Libyssa.** The recent researches of Mr. O. Schwab have made it probable that Libyssa was at or near the modern *Dil*, a place beside the sea on the railway which runs from *Ismid* (Nicomedia) to *Kadikoi* (Chalcedon). Here a river, the *Dil Dere*, breaks through a chain of hills and flows into the sea, traversing an alluvial and in part marshy delta with a sandy shore, which may be the " sandy place beside the sea " described by Plutarch (*Flamininus*, 20). On either side of the little delta the rocks and cliffs advance to the water's edge, leaving no room for a settlement. The distance of *Dil* from *Ismid* is about 36 kilometres (23 miles), which agrees very well with the distance of Libyssa from Nicomedia, namely 22 Roman miles according to one ancient itinerary or 25 Roman miles according to another. If this identification of *Dil* with Libyssa is right, the river *Dil Dere* is the ancient Libyssus mentioned by Appian (*Syr.* 11), who also speaks of the plain formed by the river. In fact there is a stretch of fertile and well-cultivated cornland in the valley of the *Dil Dere* a little way inland from the sea, and here on the right bank of the stream, where the western chain of hills descends in terraces into the valley, there is a rocky plateau covered with a thin layer of soil and strewed with potsherds. Mr. Schwab conjectures that this may be the site of Libyssa, which Plutarch (*l.c.*) describes as a large village. Libyssa cannot, as some have supposed, have occupied the site of *Gebize*, a place 47 kilometres (30 miles) from *Ismid* (Nicomedia) and standing on high ground about 5 miles from the sea ; for the situation of *Gebize* does not at all answer to that of Libyssa, as described by the ancients. There are, however, some fragments of Greek architecture and inscriptions at *Gebize*, and about twenty minutes' walk to the south-east of the village is a barrow which legend designates as the grave of Hannibal. The barrow is of elliptical form, and is shaded by two tall cypresses which are conspicuous near and far. The commanding situation of this tumulus, from which there are wide views over the whole plateau and the Gulf of *Ismid*, seems certainly to mark it out as the tomb òf some distinguished man. See O. Schwab, in *Berliner philolog. Wochenschrift*, 26th December 1896, pp. 1661-1663.

P. 223 line 18 from foot, **Essenes.** To the examples given in the text of priests or other religious functionaries who bore the names of animals as an official title, a few more may be added. The priestesses of Demeter in Laconia were called 'fillies' (πῶλοι, *C. I. G.* No. 1449). The officials whose duty it was to eject unruly members from the club-house of an Iobacchic society at Athens went by the name of Horses (ἵπποι, see the inscription in *Mittheilungen d. arch. Inst. in Athen*, 19 (1894), p. 260 *sq.*, line 140 *sqq.*) ; they were appointed by the priests. The men who were initiated in the mysteries of Mithras were called Lions, the women Lionesses, and the attendants Crows (Porphyry, *De abstinentia*, iv. 16).

P. 228 line 25 *sq.* from foot, **to draw down curses** etc. The modern Greek custom of cursing an enemy by throwing stones has been described also by Pouqueville (*Voyage de la Grèce*, 2me Edition, 4. p. 386). He says : "To accomplish the imprecation, the name of curse [*anathema*] is given to some spot of ground which the person curses by throwing at it the stone of reprobation. All the bystanders do the same, and afterwards passers-by never fail to add their mite, so that a heap of stones soon rises on the accursed spot. The consequence of this excommunication is that the enemy of the people becomes a *vricolacas* or wandering ghost after his death ; his body cannot decay in the grave, and his children are afflicted with ailments."

P. 237 line 17 from top, **Rhoecus.** In the precinct of Aphrodite at Naucratis there was found a vase inscribed with a dedication to the goddess by a certain Rhoecus, who is supposed to be no other than the early Greek sculptor of that name. The inscription is in Ionic letters of the sixth century B.C. See E. A. Gardner, *Naukratis*, Part ii.

pp. 41, 59, 65, with pl. xxi. No. 778 ; *id.*, *Handbook of Greek Sculpture*, p. 101 ; M. Collignon, *Histoire de la Sculpture grecque*, 1. p. 158 *sq.* If this identification is right, it would seem that Rhoecus studied in Egypt, as his son or colleague Theodorus is expressly said to have done (Diodorus, i. 98). The discovery in Egypt of this vase inscribed with the sculptor's name countenances the view that Rhoecus and Theodorus did not invent, but merely borrowed from Egypt, the art of casting bronze statues, an art in which the Egyptians attained a high degree of skill. See M. Collignon, *l.c.*; A. S. Murray, *History of Greek Sculpture*, 1. p. 76 *sq.*

P. 330 line 15 from foot, **a theatre** etc. As to the theatre at Megalopolis, see W. Dörpfeld, in *Das griechische Theater*, pp. 133-143. Amongst the reasons which he gives for dating the Thersilium before the theatre are the difference in the materials and the difference in the form of clamps used in the two buildings. For whereas the Thersilium is built of hard limestone and tufa, the theatre is built of hard limestone and breccia, and these two last materials, according to Dr. Dörpfeld, occur in the later buildings at Megalopolis, for example in the colonnade of Philip and in the columns which were added in the Thersilium at a later time. Again, while in the Thersilium the iron clamps are of the older ⊢⊣ pattern, those of the theatre have the later swallow-tailed shape. The existence of the long low foundation-wall in the *skanotheka* is explained by Dr. Dörpfeld in the same way as by Mr. Schultz (see above, vol. 4. p. 337 *sq.*), and on this explanation of it he justly lays weight as a strong argument in favour of his view that when the theatre was built there was no raised stage. For it is to be observed that the foundation-wall is on a level with the lowest step of the portico of the Thersilium, in other words on a level with the floor of the orchestra. Hence if the wall in question supported, as seems possible, the move-able scenery which could be run in front of the portico when it was wanted, it follows that the scenery also, when it was in position in front of the portico, rested on the floor of the orchestra, and that accordingly the players, appearing in front of it, must have been in the orchestra, not on a raised stage. It would of course be no answer to this to say that the orchestra was not originally at this level, but was reduced to it at a later period ; for that would only go to show that the theatre continued to lack a raised stage for some time after it was built. In saying (vol. 4. p. 346) that after a permanent stone stage was built in front of the portico the moveable scenery may have been run on to it from the *skanotheka*, I overlooked the difference of level between the stage and the *skanotheka*. For this difference seems to preclude the view sug-gested in the text.

P. 367 line 13 from foot, **the sanctuary of the Mistress.** A full account of the excavation of the sanctuary, so far as it was carried down to the end of 1895, has now been published by Mr B. Leonardos, the archaeologist who directed the work (Πρακτικὰ τῆς Ἀρχαιολογικῆς Ἑταιρίας, 1896 (pub. 1897), pp. 93-126). His plan of the sanctuary is here reproduced (pl. x.). One of the results of the excavation is to confirm Pausanias's description. He says (viii. 37. 1 *sq.*) that

SANCTUARY OF THE MISTRESS AT LYCOSURA (GROUND PLAN)

Vol. V.

Starford's GeogᶦEstabᵗLondon.

London: Macmillan & Cᵒ Lᵗᵈ.

COLONNADE

TEMPLE OF THE MISTRESS

ALTAR OF DEMETER

ALTAR OF THE MISTRESS

ALTAR OF THE GREAT MOTHER

Scale of Feet

10 5 0 10 20 30 40 50 60 70 80 90 100

Metres

5 0 5 10 15 20 25 30

on entering the sacred precinct you had on the right a colonnade, and that in front of the temple stood three altars. Remains of all these have been found in the situations described by Pausanias. The sacred precinct, which occupied a terrace on the northern slope of the hillock called *Terze*, was enclosed on the north by a boundary-wall strengthened by buttresses. The only entrance to the precinct was from the east, to the south of the ruined chapel of St. Athanasius, which does not stand on the top of the hill, as stated in the text (vol. 4. p. 367). The colonnade mentioned by Pausanias is situated on the north side of the precinct, hence on the right as you entered. Measured on the inside, its length from east to west is 64 metres, its depth from north to south 5.82 metres. At the back it was connected by short cross-walls with the boundary-wall of the precinct. It opened to the south, and here the façade was supported by Doric columns made of the native stone. Some of these columns have been found. They are unfluted, but fluted half-columns of the Doric order have also come to light. At the west end of the colonnade is a chamber about 3.80 metres square, measured on the inside. The walls of the chamber, so far as they exist, are built of squared blocks set upright, two of these blocks making the thickness of the wall. In this chamber an archaic bronze statuette was found: it represents a woman, perhaps Athena, wearing a sort of helmet and clad in a tunic which reaches to her feet. A little to the south of the colonnade are the remains of the three altars mentioned by Pausanias. They stand in a row from east to west. The most easterly is faced on the outside with marble fragments brought from some other structure. The middle one is built more regularly of large blocks of the native limestone; two courses are preserved. Of the western altar only three stones remain. From the order in which Pausanias mentions the altars we may infer that the eastern was the altar of Demeter, the middle one the altar of the Mistress, and the western the altar of the Great Mother.

The temple of the Mistress stood towards the western end of the precinct, immediately to the south of the west end of the colonnade. Its remains have now been accurately described by Mr. Leonardos. The length of the edifice from east to west, including the three steps at the east end, was 21.35 metres; the breadth at the east end, including the steps, was 12.31 metres; the breadth at the west end, where there are no steps, was 11.15 metres. The foundations, the lower part of the walls, the pavement of the fore-temple (*pronaos*), and the great pedestal which supported the images are all made of the native limestone, which is of a grey colour streaked with red. The upper part of the walls, above a socle of squared stones, is composed of large, thick, imperfectly fired bricks bonded together, apparently, with mortar. The eastern façade, including the six Doric columns which supported it, was of white marble from *Doliana*. The western gable was of the same material. Only the eastern façade was adorned with columns. The lower drums [1] of the two most southerly of the columns are still standing in their places.

---

[1] In the text (vol. 4. p. 368) it is said that the bases of these columns are standing. This is, of course, a mistake. Being of the Doric order the columns had no bases.

They have twenty flutes. One block of the architrave and five fragments of the frieze of triglyphs and metopes have been found. The style of these architectural members and of the lions' heads which served as water-spouts is not of the best. In the interior of the *cella* the walls were coated with stucco, some of which at least was painted. The eastern part of the *cella*, paved with a design in mosaic (see vol. 4. p. 368), was divided from the western and smaller part, in which stood the images, by a barrier running across the floor from side to side. Remains of this barrier, consisting of narrow quadrangular stones with sockets for the attachment of a railing or balustrade, may still be seen. Almost the whole of the floor to the west of this barrier is occupied by the great pedestal that supported the four images mentioned by Pausanias of which so many fragments have been found (vol. 4. p. 372 *sqq.*). The shape of the pedestal is well adapted to its purpose, for in the middle there is a quadrangular projection, on which the two seated figures of the Mistress and Demeter were doubtless placed, while the two standing figures of Artemis and Anytus may be supposed to have occupied the two retiring wings of the pedestal. The sides of the pedestal are constructed of four courses of quadrangular blocks. The lowest course is plain; the second and fourth are adorned with mouldings: the third is composed of plain blocks set upright. A remarkable and very unusual feature of the *cella* remains to be noticed. About the middle of the south wall there is a doorway which leads by three descending steps to an open passage 1.65 metre wide which runs round the temple. This doorway, which seems to be contemporary with the wall, is probably the one referred to by Pausanias when he says: "On the right as you leave the temple there is a mirror fitted into the wall."

From an inscription carved on the southern *anta* of the temple we learn that in the Imperial age the building was repaired by a certain Xenarchus, son of Onasicrates, and that in gratitude for his services the people of Megalopolis and the Roman merchants resident there resolved to set up statues and portraits of Xenarchus, his wife Nicippa, and their children in the sanctuary of the Mistress. The same inscription refers to a temple of the Roman Emperors (*Sebastoi*) which Xenarchus built, and to a temple of the Maid (*Kore*) which he repaired. See Ἐφημερὶς ἀρχαιολογική, 1896 (pub. 1897), p. 217 *sqq.*, No. 17. A pedestal inscribed with a dedication by the same Xenarchus was found in the *cella* of the temple (Ἐφημερὶς ἀρχαιολογική, 1896, p. 235, No. 26). Another inscription, found higher up the hill, refers to a repair of "the temple" and "the fore-temple" by a certain woman Democratea (?), daughter of Agias or Agiadas; but whether the temple in question is that of the Mistress or not, we cannot say (Ἐφημερὶς ἀρχαιολογική, 1896, p. 236, No. 27). The dedication by Epagathus mentioned in the text (vol. 4. p. 370) appears to have been to the Mistresses, not to the Mistress (Ἐφημερὶς ἀρχαιολογική, 1896, p. 238, No. 28). Pausanias elsewhere (v. 15. 4 and 10) speaks of the Mistresses, meaning thereby Demeter and Proserpine.

On the ridge of the hillock above the temple, towards the western end, there is a well-built ancient cistern and beside it a piece of wall of polygonal masonry. Lower down than the cistern are some remains of walls built of large carefully-hewn stones. Some excavations made here in 1895 brought to light three archaic statuettes made of thin sheets of bronze, a piece of a small clay idol wearing a helmet, another piece of a clay idol with a ram's head, and broken tiles of terra-cotta inscribed with the name of the Mistress. The bronze statuettes represent men stretching out their hands in supplication. Lower down the hill than the cistern, moreover, was discovered a building (11 metres by 8 metres), the walls of which, preserved to a height of about 1.50 metres, are built of large squared blocks of limestone. Two fallen columns were found lying within the edifice. See Πρακτικὰ τῆς Ἀρχαιολογικῆς Ἑταιρίας, 1896 (pub. 1897), pp. 121-124.

P. 378 line 5 *sq.* from top, **the date of these sculptures and of the artist Damophon.** On the vexed question of the date of Damophon and of the Lycosura sculptures, Prof. E. A. Gardner adheres to the old view that Damophon belonged to the fourth century B.C. "He may best be understood if we regard him as a man who lived in the fourth century, but apart from the general stream of its artistic tendencies, feeling deeply the influence of the high ideals of the age of Phidias, but of sufficient originality to introduce into his art some innovations as yet unknown to his contemporaries, though they anticipate the custom of the Hellenistic age" (E. A. Gardner, *Handbook of Greek Sculpture*, p. 403). Prof. Percy Gardner takes the same view, rightly observing that "the historical probabilities that Damophon worked in the time of the foundation of Megalopolis and the restoration of Messene by Epaminondas are so overpowering, that we must very closely scrutinize any archaeological evidence on the other side" (*Classical Review*, 11 (1897), p. 71). On the other hand Prof. Collignon, arguing from the style of the Lycosura sculptures and especially from that of the drapery with its elaborate reliefs, holds that Damophon cannot have belonged to the fourth century B.C. but may have been at work about the beginning of the second century B.C. (*Histoire de la Sculpture grecque*, 2. pp. 627-630).

P. 402 line 16 from top, **The twelve fragments of the metopes** etc. The remains of the triglyphs and metopes at Phigalia (Bassae) have lately been examined afresh by Mr. H. Dragendorff, and his examination of them has made it quite certain that only the metopes of the fore-temple and back-chamber were sculptured, while all the outer metopes of the temple were plain. This correction of Prof. B. Sauer's view that the outer metopes of the temple were sculptured is published by Prof. Sauer himself with commendable candour. See his article 'Nachträgliches zu den Metopen von Phigalia,' *Mittheilungen d. arch. Inst. in Athen*, 21 (1896), pp. 333-338.

P. 437 line 26 *sqq.* from foot, **a series of reliefs** etc. The Pergamene relief representing the suckling of Telephus by the lioness (?) is figured in Overbeck's *Geschichte des griech. Plastik* [4] (2. p. 284, Fig. 201 b) and Collignon's *Histoire de la Sculpture grecque* (2. p. 529, Fig. 275).

P. 439 line 22 *sq.* from top, **the base of a statue bearing the name of Ageladas.** This inscription is now published as No. 631 of *Die Inschriften von Olympia,* edited by W. Dittenberger and K. Purgold. Commenting on the inscription Prof. Dittenberger expresses his opinion that two sculptors are mentioned in it, namely Atotus and Argeiadas, son of Hagelaidas, and that the epithet τἀργείου attached to the name of Hagelaidas is a personal name (Argius), not a national designation (Argive). A sculptor of the name of Argius is mentioned by Pliny (*Nat. hist.* xxxiv. 50), but as he was a pupil of Polyclitus he cannot be the same with the Hagelaidas Argius of the inscription, who to judge from the character of the letters would seem to have flourished at the beginning of the fifth, if not at the end of the sixth century B.C. Prof. Dittenberger rejects the view that Argeiadas was the slave of Hagelaidas.

VOL. V

P. 21 line 4 from top, **a sanctuary of Athena.** The painting by Polygnotus in this temple represented, as Pausanias tells us, the slaying of the wooers by Ulysses. The same subject is carved in relief on one of the friezes at Gjölbaschi in Lycia, and archaeologists incline to believe that the sculptor of the frieze was influenced in his treatment of the theme by the picture of Polygnotus. The sculptor has represented a long pillared hall in which the suitors, fourteen in number, are seen reclining, as at a banquet, on eight couches. At one end of the hall stands Ulysses with his bow bent, drawing an arrow to the head ; at his side Telemachus is advancing with drawn sword. Some of the suitors are already struck ; others hold up tables, a bed, or their garments to ward off the fatal arrows. A youthful cupbearer is escaping by the door behind Ulysses. In another scene the sculptor shows Penelope in her chamber. Euryclea is presenting to her the faithful handmaids ; while at the other end of the room Ulysses, with a torch in his left hand and a sword in his right, strides away grimly to take vengeance on the faithless abigails. The scene of the slaughter of the suitors is also depicted on a vase of the fifth century B.C. found at Corneto and now in the Berlin Museum (*Monumenti Inediti,* 10 (1878), pl. 53 ; H. Heydemann, in *Annali dell' Instituto,* 50 (1878), pp. 222-225 ; P. Girard, *La Peinture antique,* figs. 87, 88, pp. 164, 165). On one side of the vase Ulysses appears bending his bow ; behind him stand two women watching. On the other side of the vase are painted three of the suitors, one of them kneeling on a couch and hit by an arrow in the back, another sitting up on the same couch and vainly trying to screen himself with his uplifted mantle, while the third crouches on the ground behind a table which he is holding up as a shield. The resemblance between the vase-painting and the frieze is so close that both are probably copies of a common original. That original may very well have been the picture by Polygnotus in the temple of Athena at Plataea. See O. Benndorf und G. Niemann, *Das Heroon von Gjölbaschi-Trysa* (Vienna, 1889), pp. 96-105 ; J. Overbeck, *Geschichte d. griech. Plastik*,[4] 2. p. 203 *sq.* ; M. Collignon, *Histoire de la Sculpture grecque*, 2. pp. 206-208 ; P. Girard, *La Peinture antique*, p. 165 *sq.* ; C. Robert, *Die Marathonschlacht in der Poikile*, pp. 63-65.

P. 21 line 16 *sq.* from top, **the other, by Onasias, depicts the former expedition of the Argives** etc. The same subject, namely the attack on Thebes by the Seven Champions, is sculptured in relief on one of the friezes at Gjölbaschi in Lycia, and archaeologists think that the sculptor may have imitated to some extent the picture of Onasias in the temple of Athena at Plataea. This conjecture is all the more probable since, as we have just seen, there are independent grounds for believing that a picture by Polygnotus in the same temple was copied more or less closely on another of the friezes in the same building at Gjölbaschi. The sculptor has placed the combat between Eteocles and Polynices, or rather the preparation for it, in the centre of the scene. At either side is a chariot drawn by four horses : the one to the left is that of Adrastus, who is fleeing ; the one to the right, sinking into the ground, is that of Amphiaraus. The city of Thebes is represented by a tower at the foot of which a trumpeter is blowing his trumpet, while Capaneus is tumbling from a ladder which he has planted against the wall. See O. Benndorf und G. Niemann, *Das Heroon von Gjölbaschi-Trysa*, pp. 187-200 ; J. Overbeck, *Gesch. d. griech. Plastik*,[4] 2. p. 201 *sqq.* ; M. Collignon, *Histoire de la Sculpture grecque*, 2. p. 209 ; C. Robert, *Die Marathonschlacht in der Poikile*, pp. 30 *sq.*, 65.

P. 138 line 13 from foot, **the Sphinx.** The Sphinx as she appears in Greek art and legend is the subject of a monograph by Mr. J. Ilberg (*Die Sphinx in der griechischen Kunst und Sage*, Leipzig, 1896).

P. 160 line 9 from top, **Creusis.** Fragments of a bronze statue of Poseidon, somewhat less than life-size, were lately fished up from the sea near the village of *H. Vasilios*, which corresponds to the ancient Creusis. The god is represented naked and bearded, standing with the right foot in advance : in his left hand, which is raised, he seems to have grasped the trident. On the bronze socle is an inscription in the Boeotian dialect, 'Sacred to Poseidon' (τῶ Ποτειδάονος ἱαρός). See *Comptes Rendus de l'Académie des Inscriptions*, 25 (1897), pp. 173-175 ; *Mittheilungen d. arch. Inst. in Athen*, 22 (1897), p. 229.

P. 199 line 19 from top, **a temple of King Zeus.** Another long fragment of the inscription relating to the building of this temple was found in 1891. See *Bulletin de Corresp. héllénique*, 20 (1896), pp. 318-335. Another small fragment has been published by Mr. A. Wilhelm (*Mittheilungen d. arch. Inst. in Athen*, 22 (1897), pp. 179-182).

P. 202 line 3 from top, **the Water of Forgetfulness —— the Water of Memory.** A few years ago there was found in a tomb at Eleutherna in Crete a thin gold plate on which is inscribed an abridgment in three lines of the Orphic poem mentioned in the text (A. Joubin, 'Inscription crétoise relative à l'Orphisme,' *Bulletin de Corresp. hellénique*, 17 (1896), pp. 121-124). Hence Mr. Foucart conjectures with some probability that in the Petilia and Eleutherna inscriptions we have extracts from or abridgments of a ritual poem, which contained full directions for the guidance of the soul on its arrival in the other world, and of which copies or extracts were commonly deposited with the dead in the grave, just as for a similar purpose the Egyptians placed copies of the Book of the Dead in the tombs (P. Foucart, *Recherches sur l'origine et la nature des mystères d'Éleusis* (Paris, 1895), p. 66 *sqq.*).

P. 205 line 1, **the handiwork of Daedalus.** Prof. Waldstein has suggested that the archaic image of a goddess discovered by Mr. Homolle at Delos and now in the National Museum at Athens (Th. Homolle, *De antiquissimis Dianae simulacris Deliacis*, pl. I.; P. Cavvadias, Γλυπτὰ τοῦ Ἐθνικοῦ Μουσείου, No. 1; M. Collignon, *Histoire de la Sculpture grecque*, I. p. 120 *sq.*; J. Overbeck, *Geschichte der griech. Plastik*,[4] I. p. 95 *sq.*) is a close imitation or copy of the wooden image of Aphrodite which, as we learn from the present passage of Pausanias (ix. 40. 3 *sq.*), was preserved in Delos and passed for a work of Daedalus. At all events archaeologists seem to agree that this very archaic marble image is a copy of a wooden image. Prof. Waldstein further contends for the historical existence of a very early Greek sculptor named Daedalus. See his article 'Dédale et l'Artemis de Délos,' in *Revue archéologique*, Nouvelle Série, 42 (1881), pp. 321-330.

P. 268 line 11 from foot, **other statues dedicated by the Argives.** In a number of the *Bulletin de Correspondance hellénique* for 1896, which has been delayed in the press and of which through the courtesy of Mr. Homolle I have just received (December 1897) an extract (pp. 581-732), Mr. Homolle describes and discusses in detail several of the buildings and sculptures discovered by him at Delphi of which some account has already been given in this volume. I propose here to supplement and correct that account on some points by the help of Mr. Homolle's latest papers on the subject.

I. **The Argive offerings** (*Bull. de Corresp. hellénique*, 20 (1896), pp. 605-608). The Argive kings and heroes whose statues graced the semicircular monument on the north side of the Sacred Way were, according to Mr. Homolle's reading of the inscriptions, as follows: Lynceus, Abas, Acrisius, Danae, Perseus, Alectryon, Alcmena, and Hercules. The inscriptions are all carved in fine letters of the fourth century B.C., although by an affectation of antiquity they read from right to left.

II. **The Sicyonian treasury** (*Bull. de Corresp. hellénique*, 20 (1896), pp. 657-675). The building measures 8.43 metres by 6.35 metres. The style of architecture is early Doric of the sixth century B.C., as shown by the breadth of the capitals with their shallow rounded *echinus*. The columns have only sixteen flutes. Mr. Homolle now inclines to hold that the sculptured metopes belonged to the original structure of which the architectural fragments compose in large measure the foundations of the later treasury. From a comparison of them with the sculptured metopes of the temples at Selinus, he infers that they date from the decade 570-560 B.C., being a little later in style than the metopes of temple C and much earlier than those of temple F at Selinus.

This, therefore, in Mr. Homolle's judgment, is the date of the foundation of the Sicyonian treasury.

III. The Siphnian or Cnidian treasury (*Bull. de Corresp. hellénique*, 20 (1896), pp. 581-602). The dimensions of this building, as given by Mr. Homolle, are 8.90 metres by 6.28 metres. A broken drum of bluish marble found at the west front of the treasury seems to have belonged to the façade. It is of the Ionic order, but the number of flutes is only sixteen and they have sharp edges. Part of the dedicatory inscription has been found carved on four fragments of slabs, which perhaps formed part of a step. The letters are archaic. The inscription runs thus :

$$\text{τὸν θησαυρὸν τόνδε καὶ τἀγ[άλ]ματα}$$

"The treasury and the images." Mr. Homolle has now adduced further evidence to show that the treasury was dedicated by the Cnidians, not by the Siphnians, as archaeologists have generally assumed. The facts on which he relies as evidence are :—(1) the occurrence in the dedicatory inscription of symbols for the long and short o (O and C = ω and o), which are found only at Melos and Cnidus ; (2) five decrees in honour of Cnidians which are carved on one of the *antae* of the portico. Further, he points out that Pausanias, immediately after speaking of the Sicyonian treasury, which adjoins the building in question on the east, mentions images dedicated by the Cnidians which stood (according to our texts of Pausanias) "beside the treasury of the Sicyonians" (παρὰ τὸν Σικυωνίων θησαυρόν). Mr. Homolle suggests that our texts of Pausanias are here corrupt, and that we should either omit the words "of the Sicyonians" or alter "Sicyonians" into "Cnidians" (Κνιδίων). In the former case Pausanias would say that the images dedicated by the Cnidians "stand beside the treasury" (namely, of the Cnidians). From the allusion which Pausanias afterwards makes to the Cnidian treasury (x. 11. 5), we gather that it was richly ornamented, and the sculptured decoration of the treasury hitherto commonly known as the Siphnian would justify such an allusion. Moreover, the dedicatory inscription makes mention of images as well as of a treasury, and this would answer perfectly to Pausanias's description of the images set up by the Cnidians "beside the treasury." These grounds are strong, and on the whole the balance of evidence inclines decidedly in favour of Mr. Homolle's conclusion that the treasury in question belonged to the Cnidians, not to the Siphnians.

Mr. Homolle has now modified on several points his interpretation of the sculptured friezes of the treasury. The frieze on the southern wall, he thinks, represents the rape of the daughters of Leucippus by the Dioscuri rather than the chariot-race between Pelops and Oenomaus. Three chariots appear at least in the scene ; one of them may be supposed to convey the father of the damsels or one of the bridegrooms hastening after the ravishers. The horsemen may belong to the parties both of the pursuers and the pursued. The subject of the eastern frieze, Mr. Homolle now believes, is taken from the seventeenth book of the *Iliad*, which has for its theme the doughty deeds of Menelaus.

In the frieze Menelaus occupies the chief place; opposite him are Hector and Aeneas (*Iliad*, xvii. 72 *sqq.*, 322 *sqq.*) and behind him is Meriones (*Iliad*, xvii. 259, 669), whose name is just legible. The dead man on the ground over whom the combat rages is probably Euphorbus (*Iliad*, xvii. 59 *sq.*), not Sarpedon. The name of Achilles cannot, Mr. Homolle tells us, be detected on the shield of one of the combatants, as he formerly fancied that it might. Arguing from the style of the architecture, of the sculptures, and of the dedicatory inscription Mr. Homolle concludes that the treasury was built between 540 or 530 B.C. and 500 B.C. The subjects of the sculptures confirm, in Mr. Homolle's opinion, the view that the treasury was dedicated by the Cnidians; for Cnidus was a colony of Lacedaemon (Herodotus, i. 174), and the subjects of the sculptures are, with a small admixture of Oriental elements, mainly taken from Dorian and especially Lacedaemonian legends. Hercules was the great Dorian hero; the Dioscuri belong especially to Lacedaemon; and it was at Lacedaemon that Menelaus reigned. In the battle of the gods and giants, which forms the subject of the frieze on the north wall, two figures are unusual and therefore perhaps specially significant. One of them is the Asiatic goddess Cybele; the other is Aeolus in the act of letting loose the winds. Of these two, Cybele would not be out of place in an offering of an Asiatic city; Aeolus would be peculiarly appropriate in an offering of Cnidus, since Lipara, the isle of Aeolus, was a Cnidian colony (Thucydides, iii. 88; Pausanias, x. 11. 3 note), and according to one legend Aeolus, son of Hellen, was through his daughter Canace the grandfather of the Cnidian hero Triopas (Apollodorus, i. 7. 3, 4).

IV. **The Athenian treasury** (*Bull. de Corresp. hellénique*, 20 (1896), pp. 608-617). A dedicatory inscription has been found in fragments, most of them lying among the ruins of the treasury. As restored by Mr. Homolle the inscription runs thus :

'Aθεναῖοι τ[δ]ι 'Απόλλον[ι ἀπὸ Μέδ]ον ἀκ[ροθ]ίνια τῆς Μαραθ[δ]νι μ[άχες].

"The Athenians (dedicated) to Apollo first-fruits of the battle at Marathon (taken) from the Medes." The letters, though they feign to be archaic, are really of the fourth century B.C., which seems to prove that the inscription is not the original one but only a copy of it made a century or so afterwards. The stones on which it is carved appear to have belonged to a socle or base which stood on the terrace immediately adjoining the treasury on the south. The upper surface of the base is studded with holes, apparently for the attachment of bronze objects. Doubtless these objects were the offerings referred to as first-fruits in the inscription. From the position which the base occupied, parallel to but distinct from the treasury, Mr. Homolle infers that it was set up after the treasury was finished.

V. **The Athenian colonnade** (*Bull. de Corresp. hellénique*, 20 (1896), p. 615 *sq.*). Mr. Homolle holds that the dedicatory inscription of this colonnade (see above, p. 283) clearly dates from the sixth century B.C.   He conjectures that the colonnade may have been built to commemorate the victories of 506 B.C., when the Athenians drove Cleomenes from the plain of Eleusis, defeated the Boeotians, and captured Chalcis in Euboea (Herodotus, v. 74-77).

VI. **The great altar** (*Bull. de Corresp. hellénique*, 20 (1896), pp. 617-633).   The rectangular base on which the altar rested measures 8.50 metres by 2.20 metres.   It is built on the top of the polygonal terrace-wall and faces both towards the Sacred Way and towards the esplanade in front of the eastern façade of the temple.   At this point the ground slopes so steeply that the altar, which is 3 metres (9 ft. 10 in.) above the Sacred Way, is just on a level with the esplanade. The dedicatory inscription (see above, p. 309) is carved in fine letters of the fifth century B.C. on a long cornice of white marble which was found, broken in two pieces, lying on the pavement of the Sacred Way not far from the altar.   The other inscription, recording the privilege granted to the Chians by the Delphians (see above, p. 309), is carved in large carefully-cut letters on the third step of the base.   It seems not to be earlier than the third century B.C.   Other inscriptions allow us to trace the history of the altar down to the middle of the second century B.C.   One of them records a decree of the Amphictyons in honour of Leochides a Chian who had been sent from Chios in an official capacity and had seen to the altar and other offerings of the Chians at Delphi.   Another inscription proves that a statue of King Eumenes was set up by the Delphians beside the altar.   The ground in the neighbourhood between the Sacred Way and the eastern wall of the sanctuary has proved to be crowded with and almost composed of ashes and the remains of votive offerings in bronze and terra-cotta. The fragments belonging to the sixth century B.C. and those of the still earlier styles known to archaeologists as Corinthian, proto-Corinthian, geometric, and Mycenaean, occur here in regular layers, one below the other, the most ancient of all resting on the virgin soil.   This proves that the great altar, built probably in the early part of the fifth century B.C., occupied a place which had been the scene of worship and sacrifice from a remote age.

VII. **The temple of Apollo** (*Bull. de Corresp. hellénique*, 20 (1896), pp. 641-654, 677-701, 702-732).   Remains of the temple built by the Alcmaeonids in the sixth century B.C. have been found by Mr. Homolle and his colleagues, some in the substructions of the later temple, some employed as building materials in other parts of the sanctuary, and others again in embankments which seem to have been thrown up in the fourth century B.C.   Amongst them are drums of Doric columns made of tufa and coated with a fine white stucco.   A single tolerably preserved capital has come to light.   It is made of tufa in the style of the sixth century, with high abacus and broad rounded *echinus*, like the capitals of the old temple at Corinth.   Other fragments found are pieces of architraves, some of white Parian marble, some of tufa; a triglyph and fragments of a cornice, all of white Parian marble; two gargoyles in the shape of lions' heads; and a single fragment of the tympanum.   The temple was roofed with large marble tiles of the usual two kinds, namely flat tiles with raised edges, and gable-shaped tiles which were placed so as to cover the juxtaposed edges of each pair of flat tiles. From the dimensions of the architectural fragments Mr. Homolle calculates that the temple was about 58 metres long by 23 metres broad, which is nearly the size of the later temple.

Further, the French archaeologists have discovered a number of archaic sculptures which appear almost certainly to have occupied the gables of the temple of the sixth century B.C. They were found in front of the eastern façade of the temple on and under the pavement of the Sacred Way, most of them to the north-east, near the pedestal of the offerings of Gelo. Along with them were dug up vast quantities of broken bronzes and pottery, mostly archaic, much of the pottery being decorated in the geometrical style ; and sometimes these remains were embedded in a thick layer of ashes. Apparently the sculptures had been used with other worn-out old materials to form embankments for the support of terraces, probably about the middle of the fourth century B.C. The figures, which are larger than life, fall into two sets, one made of marble, the other of tufa. Some are in the round, others in high relief. Those in the round are only roughly worked at the back, showing that they were meant to be seen only in front. Tenons and mortises at the back of some of the figures indicate still more clearly that they were destined to be set up against a wall. Both sets of figures are executed in the artistic style characteristic of the end of the sixth century B.C., in which severity is tempered by an effort after elegance. The women are draped in ample finely-folded Ionian garments ; the nude bodies of the men are rendered in a dry hard conventional manner. There is a leanness combined with precision about the heads of the horses ; the manes are indicated by zigzags or undulations.

The unity of style which pervades these sculptures, the place where they were found, and the similarity of the purpose to which they were obviously meant to be applied combine to make it highly probable that they occupied the two gables of the temple of Apollo which was built by the Alcmaeonids in the sixth century B.C. and destroyed, apparently by an earthquake, in the fourth century B.C. It is to be observed that, while all are badly broken, their surfaces with the colours are well preserved. They seem to have been smashed by a fall and afterwards to have lain underground, where they have been protected from the action of the atmosphere and weather.

The marble figures comprise three women standing erect and motionless in the attitude and wearing the costume of the archaic female statues of the Acropolis ; a man also standing erect and motionless ; the front parts of three horses (one of them with the head preserved), all facing the spectator and bending the neck to the right or left ; and lastly the head of a bearded man. The tufa figures comprise a draped woman walking swiftly to the left ; a draped man also walking to the left ; a man supporting himself with hands and knees on the ground ; the torso of a naked man turning his back to the spectator ; and the head, breast, and front legs of a horse. To these must be added fragments of limbs of men and animals and pieces of drapery. Traces of colours (red, blue, green, yellow) abound on the drapery, flesh, and hair of the tufa figures; they are much fewer and fainter on the marble figures.

While they resemble each other in artistic style, the two sets of sculptures present an absolute contrast in respect of composition, the marble figures being simply set beside each other in all the motionless rigidity of soldiers standing "eyes front" on parade, while the tufa figures are in violent action, some turning their faces, others their backs, others their profile to the spectator, all seemingly combined by unity of action into an artistic group. A similar contrast between immobility and isolation on the one hand and a fierce tustle on the other is presented by the figures of the two gables of the great temple at Olympia (vol. 3. p. 504 *sqq.*). What were the scenes represented by these sculptures of the old Delphic temple we cannot say. One thing is clear. They are not the sculptures described by Pausanias (x. 19. 4), since the latter were executed or rather begun by a pupil of Calamis, a master who, as we have seen (p. 338), was at work as late as 427 B.C., whereas the sculptures in question are manifestly works of the sixth century B.C. The discovery of these archaic sculptures may therefore be regarded as establishing the view which on other grounds I have adopted above (p. 336 *sqq.*, and vol. 1. p. xciii. *sq.*), namely that the temple built by Spintharus and described by Pausanias was the temple not of the sixth but of the fourth century B.C.

The inscription which has hitherto been held to mention the destruction of the temple in the fourth century B.C. (*Rheinisches Museum*, N. F. 51 (1896), p. 351 *sqq.*; above, p. 329) is now interpreted otherwise by Mr. Homolle. Arguing from the style of the letters and from the names of the persons mentioned he would date the inscription about 325 B.C., and he proposes to restore the mutilated word so as to make the reference be to the completion instead of to the destruction of the temple (κατ[ην]ύθη instead of κατ[ελ]ύθη). If he is right, the inscription proves that the temple, after its destruction at the end of the fifth or beginning of the fourth century B.C., was completely rebuilt by about 325 B.C. But I cannot feel that his restoration of the mutilated word is satisfactory. This use of the verb κατανύειν in the sense of "to complete a material object" such as a building appears to be unexampled in Greek of the fourth century B.C., and until Mr. Homolle can adduce instances of its employment in this sense by writers or in inscriptions of the best period I shall prefer to restore κατ[ελ]ύθη and to regard the inscription as containing a mention of the destruction of the temple. With regard to the cause of the destruction Mr. Homolle has made it clear that this can only have been an earthquake, not a conflagration. The ashes lie nowhere in such thick and extensive layers as to suggest a total destruction of the temple by fire. Moreover the remains of the old temple, far from being scorched and blackened, are not even smirched by smoke or flames; smashed as they are they preserve their colours in comparative freshness; the delicate surface of the marble is intact.

All the existing foundations are now referred by Mr. Homolle to the temple of the fourth century B.C. The differences of construction and material between the eastern and western foundations—the regu-

larity and homogeneity of the eastern and the irregularity and hetero-
geneity of the western — are explained by him on the supposition
that while the new temple was building a fresh shock of earthquake
occurred which threw down the western part of the edifice to its foundation, and that the damage thus done was hastily repaired with the first
materials to hand. As to the date of the destruction of the old temple
Mr. Homolle points out that it must have happened between the year
415 B.C. (when Euripides in the *Ion* describes the temple as if it were
intact) and the year 371 B.C. (when the congress took place at Sparta
in which it was proposed to invite contributions towards the restoration
of the temple ; see above, p. 329). He conjectures that the earthquake
may have been the same which destroyed Helice and Bura in the winter
of 373-2 B.C. (see vol. 4. p. 165, note on vii. 24. 6), but he admits it to be
strange that ancient writers, in speaking of that earthquake and the havoc
it wrought, should have said nothing about the destruction of the temple
at Delphi if that event had really been brought about by the same cause.

From the dated accounts of the commission charged with the restoration of the temple (see above, p. 330 *sq.*) it appears that the work was
begun in the spring of 361 B.C. ; at least the commission seems to have
met then for the first time. The interval between the destruction of
the building, whenever that took place, and the beginning of the
restoration may have been employed in collecting funds. Inscriptions
found by the French at Delphi record the contributions made by states
and individuals towards the pious work. These contributions seem
to have been made in two different forms or on two different scales.
Individuals and some states, such as Apollonia, Megalopolis, Messene,
Naxos, and Naucratis in Egypt, offered first-fruits. The offering of
Apollonia consisted of a tithe of the harvest, to wit, 3000 *medimnoi* of
barley. An Athenian actor Theodorus and a physician Xenotimus sent
a tithe of their earnings. States that offered on a different scale,
which Mr. Homolle thinks may have been a twelfth, were Megara,
Troezen, Epidaurus, Lacedaemon, Corinth, the Thessalians of Matro-
polis, the Magnesians, the Hesperian Locrians, and the Phocians of
Tithronium. Of the private persons whose names appear in the lists of
subscribers most are natives of Peloponnese ; but some stray subscriptions dribbled in from Attica, Boeotia, Northern Greece, the islands,
Africa, and Sicily. The total receipts for the year 355 B.C. amounted
to about 19,000 Delphic drachms. One inscription shows that col-
lectors went about from house to house to stimulate the liberality of the
faithful, and the fruit of their labours in the mission field appears in
a list of persons who had, in the popular phrase, " come forward,"
most of them with the modest sum of one Attic drachm or eightpence-
halfpenny. The work seems, if Mr. Homolle interprets the inscriptions
aright, to have been completed by 330 or 329 B.C.

The vicissitudes of the temple in the first century B.C. and the first
century A.D., as to which some rather vague and uncertain information
has reached us (see above, p. 331 *sq.*), are believed by Mr. Homolle
not to have affected the main structure of the temple, which appears, so
far as the existing remains allow us to judge, to have remained sub-

stantially in the time of Pausanias as it had been built in the fourth century B.C. We have, therefore, every reason to believe that Pausanias, in describing the temple of the fourth century B.C., described it from personal observation exactly as it existed in his own time. It is true that the sculptures which he saw and described in the gables have not been found by the French; but their disappearance after his visit to Delphi is a circumstance for which he can hardly be held responsible.

An inscription of the early part of the third century A.D. speaks of some repairs executed by the governor Cn. Claudius Leonticus. This is the last mention of the Delphic temple in the inscriptions which have hitherto come to light. Apparently the temple, unlike so many other ancient shrines, was never converted into a Christian church. The final destruction of the building seems to have been caused by a terrible shock of earthquake, which dislocated the foundations in a way which must necessarily have brought the whole upper building to the ground. Christian fanaticism may also have contributed to the dilapidation of what might be regarded by the adherents of the new faith as the chief stronghold of paganism in Greece.

VIII. **The Cnidian Lesche** (*Bulletin de Corresp. hellénique*, 20 (1896), pp. 633-639). The terrace on which the Lesche stood is supported on the south by a high retaining-wall built of blue limestone in the regular ashlar style. No doubt this is the wall referred to in the inscription of the third century B.C. (above, p. 357). The edifice itself formed a rectangle 18.70 metres long by 9.53 metres broad. Nothing of it now remains above the foundations except some blocks of the first course on the north side. At the south-west corner even the foundations have partly disappeared. An earthquake or more probably a great flood of the torrent *Rodini* seems to have destroyed the building and swept away the stones, some of which were found lower down the hill at the level of the great altar or even as low as the eastern entrance to the sanctuary.

The two long walls of the building were on the north and south sides respectively. All along the north wall ran another wall built of polygonal masonry which protected the edifice from the thrust of the ground above and served at the same time as the boundary of the sacred precinct. This boundary wall was supported at its two ends by short walls at right angles to it, one at each end, which skirted the eastern and western ends of the Lesche so closely as to render the building inaccessible on these sides. Hence there can have been no doors in the two short sides of the Lesche. The terrace on which the Lesche rests is hardly longer than the building itself, but it is deeper by 3.28 metres. Thus there was room for a passage along the southern side of the Lesche, and as this was its only accessible side the building must have opened to the south. The passage or walk is continued westward to a point where two roads seem to have met, one coming from the east along the foot of the terrace, the other from the theatre which lies to the west. In the interior of the Lesche four cubes of marble have been found occupying their original positions in the eastern half of the building. They are disposed so as to form a square of 4.50 metres, the sides of which are symmetrical to the walls. In the

upper surface of each there is a deep narrow socket, into which the foot
of a wooden pillar was probably fixed. A similar arrangement existed
in the western half of the building. Mr. Homolle concludes that we
have to conceive of the Lesche as a quadrangular building closed on all
sides except that the southern wall was broken by a doorway and
perhaps by windows. There was, he thinks, no colonnade on any side,
and no large opening in the walls. In the interior eight pillars,
arranged in two parallel rows, supported the roof, in which there may
have been an opening to light the building. Round the walls benches
may have run where idlers could lounge and talk. The paintings of
Polygnotus, in Mr. Homolle's opinion, began on each side of the door,
to the right and left as Pausanias says (x. 25. 2, x. 28. 1); they were
continued round the short walls and met at the middle of the long north
wall just opposite to the door. Thus each of the two great pictures (*Troy
after its capture* and *Ulysses in hell*) was distributed in three different
sections over three separate walls. Traces of this triple division may, Mr.
Homolle thinks, be detected in Pausanias's description of the paintings.

Lastly, at the moment of going to press (January 1898), I have
received from Mr. Homolle a number of the *Bulletin de Correspondance
hellénique* (vol. 21. September-October 1897) which contains the first
of a series of articles by him on the topography of the Delphic precinct
(pp. 256-320, wrongly numbered 420). I will make a few extracts from it.

I. **Statue of Phaylus the Crotonian** (*Paus.* x. 9. 2). Fragments
of the pedestal which supported this statue have been found. The
inscription is mutilated, but may be restored thus :

[Κ]ροτω[ν]ιᾶται [Φαύ]λλον [τοῦ δεῖνος Ἀπόλλωνι ἀνέθηκ]αν

"The people of Crotona dedicated (this statue of) Phayllus son of so-
and-so to Apollo." The pedestal was circular and of grey limestone.
See *Bull. de Corresp. hellénique*, 21 (1897), p. 274.

II. **The Corcyraean bull** (*Paus.* x. 9. 3). The rectangular pedestal
of reddish limestone on which the figure of the bull is believed to have
rested bears the following inscription :

[Κορκυραῖοι] τὠπόλλωνι ἄνεθεν
[Θ]εόπροπος ἐποίε(ι) Αἰγινάτας

"The Corcyraeans dedicated (this statue) to Apollo. Theopropus an
Aeginetan made (it)." As the inscription is not in the Corinthian alphabet, Mr. Homolle thinks that it cannot be earlier than the middle of the
fifth century B.C. *See Bull. de Corresp. hellénique*, 21 (1897), p. 275 *sq.*

III. **The Tegean (or rather Arcadian) offering** (*Paus.* x. 9. 5 *sq.*).
The pedestals of the statues of Callisto, Azan, and Aphidas have been
found inscribed with the signatures of the three sculptors mentioned by
Pausanias. The inscriptions run thus :

Καλλιστώ
Παυσανίας ἐποίησε
Ἀπολλωνιάτας

"Callisto. Pausanias of Apollonia made (the statues)."

Ἀζάν
[Σαμ]όλας ἐποίησε Ἀρκάς

"Azan.   Samolas an Arcadian made (the statues)."

Ἀφείδ[ας]
Ἀντιφάνης ἐπο[ίη]σε Ἀργεῖος

"Aphidas.   Antiphanes an Argive made (the statues)."
Further, the bases of the statues of Arcas and Triphylus have been found. The former bears the name of Arcas and a mutilated couplet in his honour ; the latter bears the name of Triphylus (Τρ[ίφ]υλος) alone. See *Bull. de Corresp. hellénique*, 21 (1897), pp. 276-283.

IV. **The Lacedaemonian trophy** (*Paus.* x. 9. 7-11). The quadrangular chamber which contained this trophy is about 26 metres long by 6 metres deep. It is built of the local breccia and grey limestone. Within this chamber the statues seem to have been arranged in two tiers. Of the statues which stood in the upper tier seven pedestals have been found inscribed with the names of (1) Cimmerius, an Ephesian, son of Pelasgus ; (2) Aeantides, a Milesian, son of Parthenius ; (3) Theopompus, a Melian (not a Myndian, as Pausanias says), son of Lapompus ; (4) Autonomus, an Eretrian, son of Samius ; (5) Apollodorus, a Troezenian, son of Calliphon ; (6) Comon, a Megarian ; and (7) a Corinthian, whose personal name is lost. Pausanias mentions the statues of the first six of these as well as the statues of two Corinthians, namely Aristophantus and Pythodotus. Further, inscriptions on the bases of the statues of Aeantides and Theopompus prove that these statues were respectively made, as Pausanias says, by the sculptors Tisander and Alypus. See *Bull. de Corresp. hellénique*, 21 (1897), pp. 284-288.

V. **An Arcadian offering and a statue of Philopoemen** (*not mentioned by Pausanias*). At the foot of the great Lacedaemonian monument is a long narrow socle (12 metres long) covered with inscriptions recording Delphic decrees in honour of various Arcadians, citizens of Mantinea, Megalopolis, Tegea, etc. Hence we may infer that the pedestal which rested on this socle supported offerings of the Arcadians. Opposite this socle, on the left side of the Sacred Way, was found the pedestal of a statue of Philopoemen dedicated by the Achaean League. The pedestal is of grey limestone. Only the front part of it has been found. The inscription records that the statue of Philopoemen the Megalopolitan, son of Craugis, was dedicated by the confederacy of the Achaeans in recognition of his virtue and good-will towards themselves. See *Bull. de Corresp. hellénique*, 21 (1897), pp. 289-294.

VI. **The Wooden Horse** (*Paus.* x. 9. 12). A few letters of an inscription which Mr. Homolle thinks may have recorded the dedication of this statue have been found not far from the spot which the statue probably occupied. From the character of the letters Mr. Homolle believes the inscription to be considerably earlier than 456 B.C. If he is right in dating the inscription and referring it to the statue of the Wooden Horse, it will follow that that statue cannot have been made, as Pausanias affirms, by Antiphanes of Argos (as to whom see above, p. 262 *sq.*). But even if the inscription refers to the Wooden Horse, the archaic form of the letters, of which barely five are preserved, may have been feigned. See *Bull. de Corresp. hellénique*, 21 (1897), pp. 294-297 (numbered 397).

VII. **The statues of the Epigoni** (*Paus.* x. 10. 4). The diameter of the semicircular monument on which these statues probably stood is 14 metres, not 9 metres as stated above (p. 268). See *Bull. de Corresp. hellénique*, 21 (1897), p. 299 (numbered 399).

VIII. **Offerings of the Tarentines** (*Paus.* x. 10. 6). On the south side of the Sacred Way, between the semicircular monument of the Epigoni and the Sicyonian treasury, two slabs of black limestone, of very fine workmanship, have been found which from the marks of attachment on their upper surfaces appear to have supported bronze statues and perhaps horses. The fragmentary inscription on the slabs (ΣΔΕΚΑΤΑΝ), in letters of the fifth century B.C., proves that the statues were a tithe-offering. Probably, as Mr. Homolle now thinks, they were no other than the statues dedicated by the Tarentines and described by Pausanias. See *Bull. de Corresp. hellénique*, 21 (1897), p. 301 (numbered 401) *sq.* Cp. above, p. 269.

IX. **Statue of Hiero** (*not mentioned by Pausanias*). Below the Sacred Way, between the semicircular monument of the Epigoni and the Sicyonian treasury, a block of limestone has been found bearing in archaic letters the name of Hiero. Mr. Homolle conjectures that it may have belonged to the pedestal of the statue of the tyrant Hiero which Plutarch mentions (*De Pythiae oraculis*, 8) after the statues of the Lacedaemonian admirals. See *Bull. de Corresp. hellénique*, 21 (1897), p. 303 (numbered 403) *sq.*

X. **A Megarian offering** (*not mentioned by Pausanias*). A considerable number of inscriptions recording Delphic decrees in honour of Megarian citizens have been found between the Sicyonian treasury and the angle which the Sacred Way makes in ascending the slope towards the Athenian treasury. These come no doubt from some monument dedicated by the Megarians. Mr. Homolle conjectures that the monument may have rested on the long foundation which may be seen on the north side of the Sacred Way, immediately opposite the Siphnian or Cnidian treasury. See *Bull. de Corresp. hellénique*, 21 (1897), pp. 309-320 (numbered 409-420).

END OF VOL. V

Printed by R. & R. CLARK, LIMITED, *Edinburgh*

MACMILLAN AND CO.'S BOOKS FOR

CLASSICAL STUDENTS.

THE HISTORY OF GREECE FROM ITS COMMENCEMENT TO THE CLOSE OF THE INDEPENDENCE OF THE GREEK NATION. By ADOLF HOLM. Authorised Translation from the German. Revised by F. CLARKE, M.A. In four volumes, 8vo. Vol. I. Up to the end of the Sixth Century B.C. 6s. net. Vol. II. The Fifth Century B.C. 6s. net. Vol. III. The Fourth Century B.C. up to the Death of Alexander. 6s. net. Vol. IV. The Graeco-Macedonian Age, the Period of the Kings and the Leagues, from the Death of Alexander down to the Incorporation of the last Macedonian Monarchy in the Roman Empire. 7s. 6d. net.

CAMBRIDGE REVIEW.—"The 'History of Greece' of the day."
CLASSICAL REVIEW.—"Wonderfully successful."
SPEAKER.—"The best short history of Greece in existence."
ACADEMY.—"A new Greek history of moderate size was badly wanted in England, and this translation is likely to fill the place very successfully."
TIMES.—"The translation is careful and readable."

A HISTORY OF GREEK ART. WITH AN INTRODUCTORY CHAPTER ON ART IN EGYPT AND MESOPOTAMIA. By F. B. TARBELL, Professor of Archaeology in the University of Chicago. Extra Crown 8vo. Price 6s.

A HANDBOOK OF GREEK SCULPTURE. By ERNEST ARTHUR GARDNER, M.A., late Fellow of Gonville and Caius College, Cambridge; and formerly Director of the British School of Archaeology at Athens. With Illustrations. Extra Crown 8vo. Part I., 5s. Part II., 5s. Complete, 10s.

GREEK SCULPTURED TOMBS. By PERCY GARDNER, Professor of Archaeology in the University of Oxford. With Thirty Collotypes and Numerous Illustrations in the Text. Super Royal 8vo. 25s. net.

A HANDBOOK OF GREEK CONSTITUTIONAL HISTORY. By A. H. J. GREENIDGE, M.A., Lecturer and late Fellow of Hertford College, and Lecturer in Ancient History at Brasenose College, Oxford. With Map. Extra Crown 8vo. 5s.

THE MYCENAEAN AGE. A STUDY OF THE MONUMENTS AND CULTURE OF PRE-HOMERIC GREECE. By Dr. CHRESTOS TSOUNTAS, Ephor of Antiquities and Director of Excavations at Mycenae, and Professor J. IRVING MANATT, Ph.D., LL.D., Professor of Greek Literature and History in Brown University. With an Introduction by Dr. DÖRPFELD. 4to. 24s.

MACMILLAN AND CO., LTD., LONDON.

Printed in Great Britain
by Amazon